Let's Go Publications

Let's Go: Alaska & the Pacific Northwest 2000
Let's Go: Australia 2000
Let's Go: Austria & Switzerland 2000
Let's Go: Britain & Ireland 2000
Let's Go: California 2000
Let's Go: Central America 2000
Let's Go: China 2000 **New Title!**
Let's Go: Eastern Europe 2000
Let's Go: Europe 2000
Let's Go: France 2000
Let's Go: Germany 2000
Let's Go: Greece 2000
Let's Go: India & Nepal 2000
Let's Go: Ireland 2000
Let's Go: Israel 2000 **New Title!**
Let's Go: Italy 2000
Let's Go: Mexico 2000
Let's Go: Middle East 2000 **New Title!**
Let's Go: New York City 2000
Let's Go: New Zealand 2000
Let's Go: Paris 2000
Let's Go: Perú & Ecuador 2000 **New Title!**
Let's Go: Rome 2000
Let's Go: South Africa 2000
Let's Go: Southeast Asia 2000
Let's Go: Spain & Portugal 2000
Let's Go: Turkey 2000
Let's Go: USA 2000
Let's Go: Washington, D.C. 2000

Let's Go *Map Guides*

Amsterdam	New Orleans
Berlin	New York City
Boston	Paris
Chicago	Prague
Florence	Rome
London	San Francisco
Los Angeles	Seattle
Madrid	Washington, D.C.

Coming Soon: *Sydney* and *Hong Kong*

Let's Go

2000

AUSTRIA &
SWITZERLAND

Julie K. Allen
Editor

Sarah P. Rotman
Associate Editor

Researcher-Writers
Joshua Derman
Nathaniel Popper
Christoper M. Sahm
Rebecca Tinio

St. Martin's Press ✖ New York

Maps by David Lindroth copyright © 2000, 1999, 1998, 1997, 1996, 1995, 1994, 1993, 1992, 1991, 1990, 1989, 1988 by St. Martin's Press.

Distributed outside the USA and Canada by Macmillan.

ISBN: 0-312-24451-7

First edition
10 9 8 7 6 5 4 3 2 1

Let's Go: Austria & Switzerland is written by Let's Go Publications, 67 Mount Auburn Street, Cambridge, MA 02138, USA.

Let's Go® and the thumb logo are trademarks of Let's Go, Inc.
Printed in the USA on recycled paper with biodegradable soy ink.

HOW TO EAT THIS BOOK

This book is a full-fledged smorgasbord of tasty travel offerings. We assembled the buffet, but it's up to you to create the perfect vacation sandwich. We've tried to arrange the fixings as clearly as possible to make sure you can find the spicy mustard and sweet, low-fat mayo and Dijonnaise. The **Index** will be your menu throughout the course of your munchings; all of the ingredients you need to get cookin' are at your fingertips. Whet your appetite with the **Discover** chapter, then dive right into the hearty meal.

The key to a well-made sandwich is balance. To help you get your bearings, we've provided a few utensils. The **Essentials** section will be the plate that supports everything, made up of practical details to prepare you for a meal without unpleasant surprises—no one likes to find *Kümmel* in their *Brot* when they specifically asked for none. When you've consumed your essential first course, you're ready for the entrees: **Austria** and **Switzerland,** roasted until tender to melt in your mouth, but not in your hand. In an attempt to be absolutely faithful to the geography of Austria and Switzerland, this year's guide has undergone extensive reorganization, in addition to its flashy face-lift. The Austrian *Bundesländer* are wrapped clockwise from the capital, Vienna, to Upper Austria. In Switzerland, the meal begins with the capital city of Bern and the Bernese Oberland, spiraling out in clockwise fashion (picture a steaming hot cinnamon roll) to encompass the surrounding cantons, in appropriate geographical groupings. The **black tabs** on the edge of each page and the **headers** on top are the toothpicks that secure everything in place (they come in minty varieties too).

We hunted high and low to find the best quality meats and cheeses, and the results of this strenuous research appear as ▧**Let's Go picks.** We shop for quality, value, and something a little extraordinary, like flecks of jalapeño peppers in your Gruyère. We know you all have healthy appetites, but to keep your rear end in callipygious form, we have added more and better **hiking coverage** than ever before. We also covered opportunities for death-defying **adventure sports** all over Austria and Switzerland, but we recommend waiting at least 1 hour after eating before attempting tandem flight or bungee jumping, or you might lose your lunch. For snacks and munchies, smaller towns that make good **daytrips** from larger cities are listed following the relevant town, with all of the transportation information first. After you eat, you may be too tired to read fine print, so we've made planning your next meal easier with appetizing **icons** and a svelte new format. Best of all, you can impress your friends with your captivating table conversation and obscure tidbits of Austrian and Swiss trivia, provided by our nifty **grayboxes.** If you discover something you just can't wait to call home about, we've got it under control: just check the new **phone code boxes** in each town to find city-specific codes.

So what's for dessert, you ask? Besides scrumptious Swiss chocolate, the sweetest rewards you'll get are the recipes you discover yourself. So venture out and try new spicy foods. Sure, you may get indigestion sometimes, but for every case of heartburn, there's always Pepto Bismol. Besides, you may just find that fondue pot at the end of the *Regenbogen* (see Lucerne, p. 355) that changes your life forever.

A NOTE TO OUR READERS The information for this book was gathered by *Let's Go*'s researchers from May through August. Each listing is derived from the assigned researcher's opinion based upon his or her visit at a particular time. The opinions are expressed in a candid and forthright manner. Those traveling at a different time may have different experiences since prices, dates, hours, and conditions are always subject to change. You are urged to check beforehand to avoid inconvenience and surprises. Travel always involves a certain degree of risk, especially in low-cost areas. When traveling, especially on a budget, always take particular care to ensure your safety.

CONTENTS

MAPS

ACKNOWLEDGMENTS

THE AUSTRIA AND SWITZERLAND BOOKTEAM THANK: First and foremost we want to thank Kathy Lu and Lime for their meticulous edits, cheerfulness, confidence, and all-night companionship; Anne Chisholm for providing us with stress dots and anti-RSI desks, and especially for battling dragons on our behalf. We want to thank Adam Stein, even though he is the one who got us into this mess in the first place, for his schedules, spreadsheets, and inspiring staff meetings; Ben Harder and Ben Wilkinson for their support; and the receptionists. We can't thank the map guys (especially Kurt) enough, nor Production for keeping things running smoothly. Endless thanks to the Romance pod, especially Olivia for her savory snacks, CDs, and dating tips; Ben and Aarup for their wisdom and relative sanity; and Jonathan for his great GI-boxes, sarcastic comments, strange ideas of pronounciation, and limitless faith in researcher-writers.

JULIE K. ALLEN THANKS: This book would never have happened without Sarah, my gorgeous night-owl associate editor who boasts the ability to catch anything that perches, lurches, towers, leans, offers, provides, etc. I'm also grateful to Brent for answering all of my travel, geography, and linguistic questions, and for putting up with an empty apartment and late late nights; and to my supportive family. Thanks to Anna for her smiles and Jen for bailing me out. Thanks to everyone at Let's Go for an absolutely unforgettable experience.

SARAH P. ROTMAN THANKS: Many thanks and much love to Julie K. Allen, my erudite editor, for keeping me sane, tempering my cynicism but allowing my alliteration urges, and just being generally fahb-ulous; Nathalie and Hans-Peter for insider opinions; the Romance pod for late nights and sing-a-longs; my better half, Valerie de Charette de la Contrie, for shopping and girlie stuff; my family for supporting me even though I didn't come home much; and K, for constant moral support, fragrant flowers, and other good stuff.

Editor
Julie Kalani Smith Allen
Associate Editor
Sarah Pollak Rotman
Managing Editor
Kathy Lu

Publishing Director
Benjamin Wilkinson
Editor-in-Chief
Bentsion Harder
Production Manager
Christian Lorentzen
Cartography Manager
Daniel J. Luskin
Design Managers
Matthew Daniels, Melissa Rudolph
Editorial Managers
Brendan Gibbon, Benjamin Paloff, Kaya Stone, Taya Weiss
Financial Manager
Kathy Lu
Personnel Manager
Adam Stein
Publicity & Marketing Managers
Sonesh Chainani, Alexandra Leichtman
New Media Manager
Maryanthe Malliaris
Map Editors
Kurt Mueller, Jon Stein
Production Associates
Steven Aponte, John Fiore
Office Coordinators
Elena Schneider, Vanessa Bertozzi, Monica Henderson

Director of Advertising Sales
Marta Szabo
Associate Sales Executives
Tamas Eisenberger, Li Ran

President
Noble M. Hansen III
General Managers
Blair Brown, Robert B. Rombauer
Assistant General Manager
Anne E. Chisholm

RESEARCHER-WRITERS

Joshua Derman   *Vorarlberg, Tyrol, Carinthia, Styria*

Forging paths where no researcher had gone before, Josh wrote up new town and hiking coverage with zeal and eloquence. He tramped down lonely roads, far from the madding backpacker crowd, coping well with adverse weather conditions and complicated transportation issues. A *Let's Go* veteran and published journalist, Josh covered the Austrian backcountry with finely honed researching and writing skills, while polishing his German in preparation for entering the international work force in Berlin.

Nathaniel Popper   *Zurich, Schaffhausen, St. Gallen, Appenzell, Liechtenstein,*
                         Graubünden, Bernese Oberland, Central Switzerland

Sexy suspenderman extraordinaire, Nathaniel grappled glaciers to expand hiking coverage in the Engadine Valley and Bernese Oberland, adding copious detail and uneditable insight. Armed with his Mach 3 razor and dog-eared Proust, Nathaniel overcame less-than-hospitable conditions (natural and otherwise) to unearth the Swiss gems truly worth seeking out (like Swiss chocolate, of which he sent back frequent provisions—a fine young man, he is indeed). Fortunately, Nathaniel kept a journal of his hair-raising hiking exploits, so future generations of researcher-writers can benefit from his hard-won expertise.

Christopher M. Sahm   *Vienna, Burgenland, Lower Austria, Upper Austria, Salzburg*

One part sketch-resistant, two parts deliciously fabulous, Chris delved into Vienna and its sweaty nightlife with gusto, leaving a trail of broken hearts behind him. His insatiable appetite guided his exhaustive restaurant research, while his sixth sense—"the fabulous sense"—sent him to sniff out the new backpacker hotspot in Grünau. Chris was always in tune to what travelers *really* need to know (like how to get your caffeine fix when you can't order a latté, and other essential cultural codes). Now that he has conquered Austria, Chris is ready to show his stuff in Amsterdam, his residence as of this fall.

Rebecca Tinio   *Geneva, Neuchâtel, Basel, Solothurn, Bern, Valais, Ticino*

Tireless in her quest against flakiness and in her pursuit of budget-travel truths, Becky put every briefcase-toting, well-paid professional travel writer to shame. In the course of her travels, Becky scouted out remote cheese factories, developed a discerning wine palate, and explored the extreme with a paragliding exploit. Becky made her work her first priority, remaining charming and genuine, no matter how long the line or steep the hill. Conscientious and clever to the end, Becky repeatedly went the extra mile (literally) to get the inside scoop on out-of-the-way hostels and out-of-this-world *gelato*.

Noah Bloom	*Freelance contributor*
Claudia Grégoire	*Bodensee*
Brady Gunderson	*The French Alps*
Michelle Aitken	*Bratislava*
Dana Scardigli	*Český Krumlov*
Marc Wallenstein	*Como*
Alicia DeSantis	*Fertőd*

LET'S GO PICKS

BEST OUT-OF-THE-WAY HOSTELS: The **Treehouse** in Grünau (p. 266), **Chalet St. Martin** in Gryon (p. 475), and the **Hiking Sheep Guesthouse** in Leysin (p. 473).

BEST DOWNTOWN HOSTELS: **Believe It or Not** in Vienna (p. 96), **Backpackers** in Lucerne (p. 355), **Backpacker's Villa Sonnenhof** and **Funny Farm** in Interlaken (p. 320), and the **Riviera Lodge** in Vevey (p. 469).

BEST PLACES TO MEET THE MOUNTAINS UP CLOSE AND PERSONAL: **Munt la Schera** in the Swiss National Park (p. 389), anywhere around **Zermatt** (p. 424), **Kandersteg** (p. 337), and the **Ötztal Arena** (p. 182).

BEST SKIING: **Upper Engadine Valley** (p. 393), **Zermatt** (p. 424), and the **Ötztal Arena** (p. 182).

BEST APRÈS SKI: **Le Crock Bar** in Verbier (p. 437).

MOST ROMANTIC OLD TOWNS: **Schaffhausen** (p. 364), **Steyr** (p. 259), **Solothurn** (p. 498), **Lucerne** (p. 355), and **Feldkirch** (p. 218).

WHERE TO TAKE THE PLUNGE: The **Aare River** in Bern (p. 307) and the **Wörthersee** (p. 165) in Carinthia.

AND WHERE TO TAKE A BOAT: The **Vierwaldstättersee** near Lucerne (p. 355), and a DDSG cruise on the **Danube River** (p. 281).

MOST FABULOUS MUSEUMS: The **Austrian Gallery** and **Kunsthistoriches** in Vienna (p. 124), **Kunsthaus Zurich** (p. 350), the **Rheinhart collection** in Winterthur (p. 353), **Ars Electronica** in Linz (p. 252), and the **Swiss Open-Air Museum** in Brienz (p. 318).

BEST PLACES TO PRETEND YOU'RE A PRINCE(SS): **Burg Hochosterwitz** (p. 170), all of Thun especially **Schloß Oberhof** (p. 315), **Riegersburg** (p. 156), and **Schönbrunn** in Vienna (p. 108).

BEST PLACE TO GO OUT OF YOUR WAY FOR A GREAT MEAL: **Hotel Schweizerhof** (p. 337), Kandersteg.

THE BEST CAFÉS: are in Vienna (p. 99). Trust us.

FUNKIEST, FANCY-FREE FESTIVALS: **Montreux Jazz** (p. 464), **Basler Fasnacht** (p. 490), and the **Open-Air** music festivals all over Switzerland (p. 303).

BEST PLACE TO GET TIPSY AND CALL IT "CULTURE": Wine tasting in **Cressier** (p. 479), **Grape Cure Week** in Baden (p. 278), and the **Gauderfest beer festival** in Zell am Ziller (p. 204).

BEST PLACE TO BUY HAND-EMBROIDERED SUSPENDERS: **Appenzell** (p. 376).

BEST PLACE TO LIVE *LA DOLCE VITA*: **Ascona** (p. 410), in Ticino canton (Italian Switzerland). It hasn't been mistaken for Utopia for nothin.'

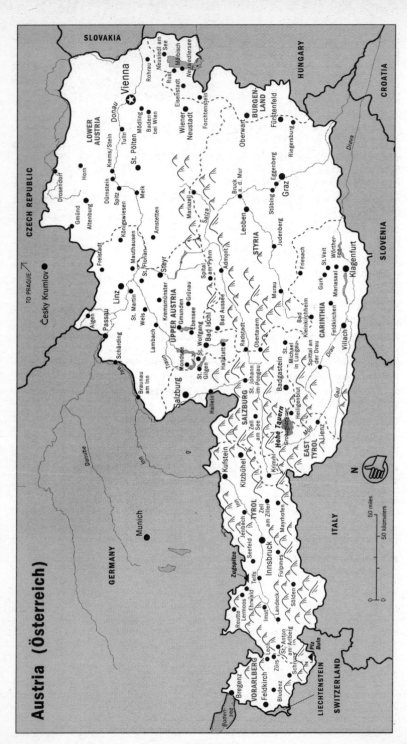

Austria (Österreich)

SLOVAKIA

CZECH REPUBLIC

HUNGARY

CROATIA

SLOVENIA

GERMANY

ITALY

LIECHTENSTEIN

SWITZERLAND

TO PRAGUE

Český Krumlov

Vienna

LOWER AUSTRIA

UPPER AUSTRIA

BURGENLAND

STYRIA

SALZBURG

CARINTHIA

TYROL

EAST TYROL

VORARLBERG

Hohe Tauern

Drosendorf
Gmünd
Altenburg
Horn
Rohrau
Neusiedl am See
Rust
Mörbisch
Neusiedlersee
Eisenstadt
Wiener Neustadt
Baden bei Wien
Mödling
St. Pölten
Tulln
Krems/Stein
Dünstein
Spitz
Melk
Amstetten
Forchtenstein
Oberwart
Fürstenfeld
Riegersburg
Königswiesen
Freistadt
Mauthausen
St. Florian
Steyr
Spital am Pyhrn
Mariazell
Bruck a. d. Mur
Stübing
Eggenberg
Graz
Aigen
Passau
Linz
Wels
St. Martin
Lambach
Kremsmünster
Gmunden
Grünau
Admont
Leoben
Judenberg
St. Veit
Wörthersee
Klagenfurt
Schärding
Ebensee
Bad Ischl
Bad Aussee
Radstadt
Murau
Friesach
Gurk
Mariasaal
Feldkirchen
Villach
Braunau am Inn
Mondsee
St. Wolfgang
St. Gilgen
Hallstatt
Obertauern
Bad Kleinkirchheim
Salzburg
Hallein
St. Johann im Pongau
Badgastein
Michael in Lungau
Spittal an der Drau
Lienz
Zell am See
Krimml
Heiligenblut
Grossglockner
Kufstein
Kitzbühel
Zell am Ziller
Mayrhofen
Jenbach
Seefeld
Innsbruck
Fulpmes
Telfs
Imst
Landeck
Sölden
Munich
Zugspitze
Reutte
Lermoos
Ehrwald
St. Anton am Arlberg
Piz Buin
Stuben
Lech
Zürs
Bregenz
Feldkirch
Bludenz
Schruns

Donau
Danube
Inn
Traun
Salza
Mur
Enns
Drau
Drava
Gail
Moll
Bodensee

N

50 miles
50 kilometers

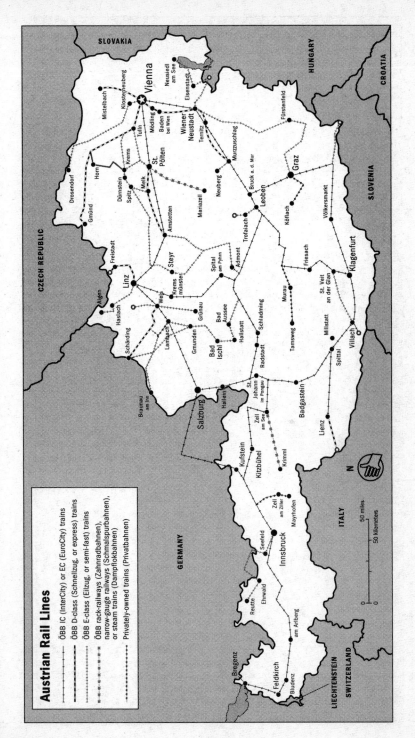

Austrian Rail Lines

—⊥—⊥—	ÖBB IC (InterCity) or EC (EuroCity) trains
———————	ÖBB D-class (Schnellzug, or express) trains
—+—+—+—	ÖBB E-class (Eilzug, or semi-fast) trains
—✳—✳—✳—	ÖBB rack-railways (Zahnradbahnen), narrow-gauge railways (Schmalspurbahnen), or steam trains (Dampflokbahnen)
—·—·—·—	Privately-owned trains (Privatbahnen)

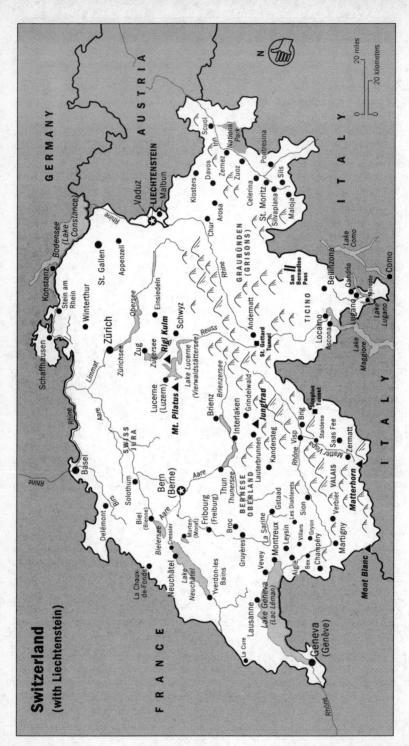

Switzerland
(with Liechtenstein)

Swiss Rail Lines

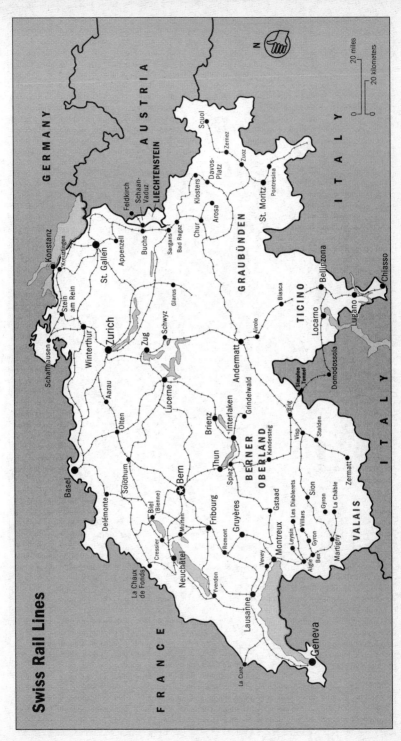

Austria and Switzerland: Map of Chapter Divisions

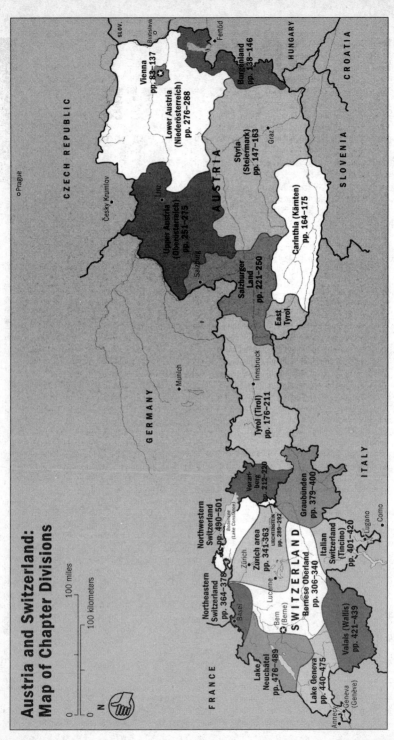

Vienna pp. 83–137

Lower Austria (Niederösterreich) pp. 276–288

Burgenland pp. 138–146

Upper Austria (Oberösterreich) pp. 251–275

Styria (Steiermark) pp. 147–163

Carinthia (Kärnten) pp. 164–175

Salzburger Land pp. 221–250

East Tyrol

Tyrol (Tirol) pp. 176–211

Vorarlberg pp. 212–220

Northwestern Switzerland pp. 490–501

Northeastern Switzerland pp. 364–378

Zürich area pp. 341–363

LIECHTENSTEIN pp. 289–292

Graubünden pp. 379–400

Lake Neuchâtel pp. 476–489

Bernese Oberland pp. 306–340

Italian Switzerland (Ticino) pp. 401–420

Lake Geneva pp. 440–475

Valais (Wallis) pp. 421–439

CZECH REPUBLIC
HUNGARY
CROATIA
SLOVENIA
AUSTRIA
GERMANY
ITALY
FRANCE
SWITZERLAND
SLOV.

Prague
Bratislava
Fertőd
Graz
Český Krumlov
Linz
Salzburg
Munich
Innsbruck
Bodensee (Lake Constance)
Zürich
Basel
Lucerne
Bern (Berne)
Lugano
Como
Geneva (Genève)
Annecy

N
100 miles
100 kilometers

DISCOVER AUSTRIA AND SWITZERLAND

Behind the sleepy rural facade of cowbells and chocolate, Austria and Switzerland teem with exciting opportunities for city slickers and nature lovers alike—all you have to do is partake. World-class cities Vienna, Zurich, and Geneva showcase many of Europe's most prized artistic, musical, and architectural treasures. Stratospheric peaks overlooking temperate crystal lakes and lush valleys provide immediate access to unparalleled natural adventures, ranging from time-tested mountain-climbing and glacier skiing to cutting-edge adventure sports like paragliding and river rafting. The incredible array of man-made and natural attractions in Austria and Switzerland is complemented by a dense network of welcoming budget accommodations that counter the prevailing high-altitude prices, making the region ideal for budget travelers of all ages and constellations. Add centuries of complex history and prolific artistic production, and there is even more to Austria and Switzerland than meets the eye.

FACTS AND FIGURES

- **Capital of Austria:** Vienna
- **Population:** 8,120,000
- **Land Area:** 83,858km² (32,378mi.²)
- **Language:** German
- **Religion:** 85% Catholic, 6% Protestant
- **Major Exports:** machinery, equipment, iron, steel, lumber, textiles, chemicals, and paper products

- **Capital of Switzerland:** Bern
- **Population:** 7,444,000
- **Land Area:** 41,290km² (15,938mi.²)
- **Languages:** German, French, Italian, and Romansch
- **Religion:** 48% Catholic, 44% Protestant
- **Major Exports:** machinery, chemicals, metals, and agricultural products

---

THE GREAT OUTDOORS

It's not for nothing that Austria and Switzerland are internationally famous for their natural splendor. Yet the diversity of earthly wonders is nearly matched by the number of ways to enjoy them. Every valley provides spectacular hikes, hundreds of glaciers invite skiers and hikers to cool off in summer, and nothing can compare to alpine skiing in the Alpine states (see p. 6). Both downhill and slalom skiing were invented here, and a vast array of ski towns keeps the tradition alive. Rather than resting on their laurels, however, Austria and Switzerland have developed a thriving adventure sport scene in recent years: **Interlaken** (p. 320) is a major center for adventure sports of every stripe, including paragliding, canyoning, sea kayaking, river rafting, skydiving, hang-gliding, bungee jumping, and glacier trekking. Other areas that cater to the adventure sport rush are **Leysin** (p. 473), **Gstaad** (p. 338), **Les Diablerets** (p. 471), **Thun** (p. 315), **Ehrwald** (p. 198), **Mayrhofen** (p. 206), **Zell am See** (p. 240), and **Zell am Ziller** (p. 204).

GOT CULTURE?

From gilded drones to porcelain thrones, the museums in Austria and Switzerland cover it all. **Vienna** reigns supreme on the two-dimensional front: haunting Caravaggios, fleshy Rubens, and busy Brueghels collected by the Habsburgs await at the

Kunsthistorisches Museum (p. 124), while the Austrian Gallery assembles an unparalleled Secessionist army, including Klimt's "The Kiss" (p. 124). You can simulate flight in the Ars Electronica in Linz (p. 252), peek at traditional Austrian peasant life in the Österreichisches Freilichtmuseum in Stübing (p. 156), or admire eccentric toilets at the Klo und So Museum in Gmunden (p. 265). Switzerland has more than its fair share of excellent exhibition halls as well. Be sure not to miss radical Kunsthaus Zürich (p. 350), which juxtaposes unusual works by well-known masters with cutting-edge new art; the comprehensive Oskar Reinhart collections in Winterthur (p. 354); 18th-century Jacquet-Droz automatons at the Musée d'Art et d'Histoire in Neuchâtel (p. 478); the painstakingly authentic Swiss Open-Air Museum in Brienz (p. 318); and the powerful International Red Cross Museum in Geneva (p. 451).

THE BACKPACKER SCENE. . .

You'll discover pretty quickly that the backpacker's world is a small one; large, centrally-located hostels in strategic locations throughout Austria and Switzerland serve as magnets for the footloose and fancy-free. If you want to follow the beaten path and go with the partying crowd, Switzerland's backpacker mecca is Interlaken (p. 320), which boasts a dizzying aggregation of hostels and young, high-on-life English-speaking travelers all year round. Other Swiss hotspots are Zermatt (p. 424), Zurich (p. 342), Montreux (p. 464), and Geneva (p. 440). In Austria, nothing can touch Vienna and its vast array of accommodations (p. 83) for backpacker-congregating, though Innsbruck (p. 183) and Salzburg (p. 222) put up a good fight.

. . . AND THE ROAD LESS TRAVELED

If you didn't come to Europe to hear American pop music pumped at ear-splitting volume through crowded hostels with the same sweaty backpackers every night, don't miss the handful of smaller, more personal backpacker getaways that are hidden in the hills of Austria and Switzerland. Not only are these out-of-the-way hostels generally more comfortable and service-oriented than mainstream ones, but they also give you the opportunity to get to know both the owners and the countryside well. Some of the best-kept secrets in Austria are the Treehouse hostel in Grünau (p. 266), gorgeous Schloß Röthelstein in Admont (p. 162), Jugendherberge im Cillitor inside the fortress in Riegersburg (p. 156), and just about any place in Hallstatt (p. 269). On the Swiss side of things, gravitate towards the tiny but home-like Baracca Backpacker in Aurigeno (p. 410), the backpacker's Nirvana a.k.a. Swiss Alp Retreat in Gryon (p. 475), the super-friendly Hiking Sheep Guesthouse in Leysin (p. 473), and the adrenaline-pumping Swiss Adventure Hostel in Boltigen (p. 317).

ONCE UPON A TIME

Centuries of serfdom, oppression, and feudalism have left their mark on the landscape of Austria and Switzerland, with crumbling castles dotting the hills and elaborate palaces adorning the cities. History and architecture buffs can wander in Austria through the ruins of Burg Dürnstein (p. 285), where Richard the Lionheart was held for ransom, hike up to the impressively restored Burg Hochosterwitz (p. 170), shiver in the Witches' Room of Burg Kronegg in Riegersburg (p. 156), or tour the Great Hall of Schloß Eggenberg (p. 156) near Graz. Vienna and Salzburg have dozens of magnificent palaces, most of which are now museums: among the most impressive are Schloß Hellbrunn (p. 240), Schloß Mirabell (p. 233), Schloß Schönbrunn (p. 119), Schloß Belvedere (p. 119), and the Hofburg (p. 112). In Switzerland, the Château de Chillon in Montreux (p. 467) is the subject of a famous poem by Lord Byron, but other equally fascinating though less-lauded châteaux (in various states of disrepair) can be found around Bellinzona (p. 402), Ascona (p. 410), Sion (p. 421), Gruyère (p. 487), and Thun (p. 315).

SUGGESTED ITINERARIES

There is no right or wrong way to go about traveling in Austria or Switzerland, but taking a little extra time to plan your trip before you go will enable you to maximize your time, money, and energy. The following itineraries are by no means the only ones possible; use them as a springboard for planning your perfect vacation.

THE AUSTRIAN ROMANTIC ROAD (MIN. 2 WEEKS) You can travel this route from Salzburg to Vienna or vice-versa. From the enchanted cobblestoned streets of **Salzburg,** where the spirit of Mozart wanders, move on through the *Salzkammergut* to **Mondsee,** a jewel of a town perched on a lake, where the von Trapp wedding in *The Sound of Music* was filmed. Meander down via **St. Wolfgang,** a hamlet made famous by the operetta *Zum weißen Rössl* (White Horse Inn), to **Bad Ischl,** once the summer of home of Franz Léhar and Empress Sisi. Dip down to **Hallstatt,** balanced between cliffs and a lake, for a glimpse of the cradle of European civilization as well as the stunning Dachstein ice caves. Backtrack up to **Gmunden** for a free tour of Archduke Salvator's lake fortress before admiring the Benedictine abbey and verdant landscape of **Kremsmünster.** Wander through the picturesque *Altstadt* of **Steyr,** then revel in the sonorous tones of Bruckner's organ in the abbey of **St. Florian.** Make your way over to **Melk,** with its unmistakable yellow abbey perched high on a hill, but don't forget to save an afternoon for the Renaissance courtyard, Romanesque fortress, and Gothic chapel at **Schloß Schallaburg,** only 5km away. The imposing ruins of **Schloß Dürnstein** loom over the valley as you make your way to **Krems/Stein,** where medieval buildings stand shoulder to shoulder with modern ones. Drop in on Karl IV's elaborate palace/monastery in sleepy **Klosterneuburg** before entering **Vienna** itself, the Imperial headquarters of romance. The magic of Strauss's waltzes and the thunder of Beethoven symphonies resonate through Vienna's magnificent Baroque buildings. From the stately **Staatsoper** to the glittering **Musikverein,** the majestic **Hofburg** to Otto Wagner's simple **Kirche am Steinhof,** Vienna's attractions will enchant your senses and blow your mind.

BEST OF SWITZERLAND (MIN. 2 WEEKS) Starting in Geneva and moving east is one option, but this route can be easily tweaked to your convenience. Spend at least 2 days in **Geneva,** where you can prowl the labyrinthine cobbled streets and quiet squares around John Calvin's Cathédrale de St-Pierre in the *vieille ville*, promenade past the Jet d'Eau on the shores of Lac Léman, then rest your tired feet in a garden of 40,000 roses. For a taste of the "Swiss Riviera," spend a day in elegant **Montreux** (if you time it right, you can catch the Montreux Jazz Fest in early July). From there, move up to the compact capital city of **Bern,** where in one day you can window-shop along arcaded streets, buy farm-grown produce at the open market outside the Parliament, feed the bears in the *Bärengraben,* and take a dip in the brisk Aare River. Next stop: the Bernese Oberland, in the heart of Switzerland. Using lively **Interlaken** as a base, take a few days to hike trails in the surrounding Alps. The more adventurous can try paragliding, bungee jumping, or various other death-defying "sports." Trains from Interlaken go directly to **Lucerne,** a postcard-perfect hamlet straight out of a fairy tale. A ferry ride on Lake Lucerne will introduce you to the mountains that inspired Goethe, Twain, and Wagner, while **Zurich,** an hour's train ride north, will satiate your thirst for high culture and thriving nightlife. If you only visit one museum in Switzerland, make it Zurich's innovative *Kunsthaus* (art museum). Spend 2 days in the city if you can, then move on to the hiker's paradise of **Appenzell** for a taste of the traditional rural Swiss lifestyle. Your last days can be spent skiing in eastern Switzerland (check out beautiful and budget-friendly ski haven **Arosa**), hiking around the Lower Engadine valley, or basking in the sun and eating gelato on the shores of Lago Maggiore in Italo-Swiss **Lugano** to the south.

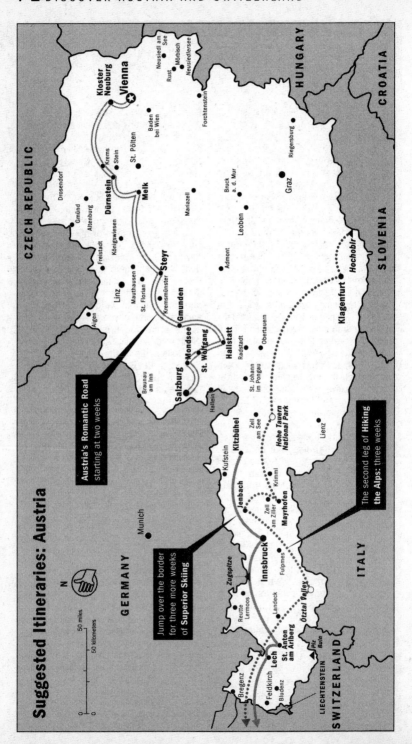

Suggested Itineraries: Austria

N

50 miles

50 kilometers

Austria's Romantic Road
starting at two weeks

The second leg of Hiking the Alps: three weeks

Jump over the border for three more weeks of **Superior Skiing**

CZECH REPUBLIC

HUNGARY

CROATIA

SLOVENIA

ITALY

SWITZERLAND

LIECHTENSTEIN

GERMANY

Kloster Neuburg

Vienna

Krems
Stein
St. Pölten

Neusiedl am See
Rust
Mörbisch
Neusiedlersee

Baden bei Wien

Forchtenstein

Drosendorf

Dürnstein

Melk

Gmünd
Altenburg

Königswiesen

Freistadt

Mariazell

Riegersburg

Graz

Bruck a. d. Mur

Leoben

Steyr

Linz
Mauthausen
St. Florian

Kremsmünster

Gmunden

Admont

Algen

Mondsee

St. Wolfgang

Hallstatt

Radstadt

Obertauern

Hochobir

Klagenfurt

Salzburg

Braunau am Inn

Hallein

St. Johann im Pongau

Zell am See

Hohe Tauern National Park

Lienz

Kitzbühel

Kufstein

Jenbach

Zell am Ziller

Mayrhofen

Krimml

Munich

Innsbruck

Fulpmes

Zugspitze

Ötztal Valley

Reutte
Lermoos

Landeck

St. Anton am Arlberg

Lech

Piz Buin

Bregenz

Feldkirch

Bludenz

Suggested Itineraries: Switzerland

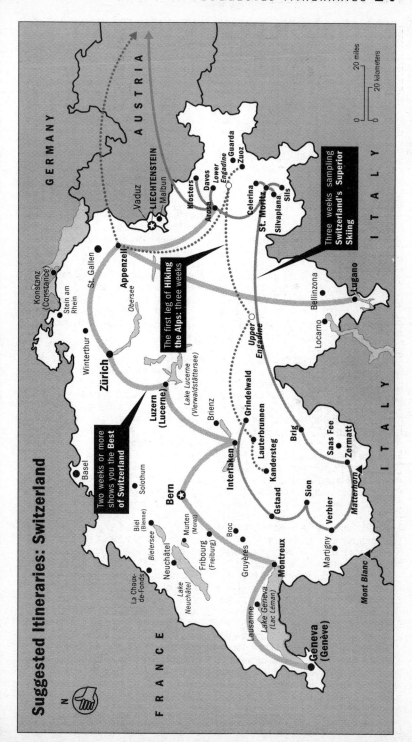

N

Two weeks or more shows you the **Best of Switzerland**

The first leg of **Hiking the Alps**: three weeks

Three weeks sampling Switzerland's **Superior Skiing**

20 miles
20 kilometers

GERMANY

AUSTRIA

LIECHTENSTEIN

Vaduz
Malbun

Konstanz (Constance)
Stein am Rhein
St. Gallen
Appenzell
Obersee
Klosters
Arosa
Davos
Lower Engadine
Guarda
Zuoz
Celerina
St. Moritz
Silvaplana
Sils

Winterthur

Zürich

Lake Lucerne (Vierwaldstättersee)
Luzern (Lucerne)
Brienz
Brig
Bellinzona
Locarno
Lugano

ITALY

Basel

Solothurn

La Chaux-de-Fonds
Biel (Bienne)
Bielersee
Neuchâtel
Murten (Morat)
Fribourg (Freiburg)
Broc
Gruyères
Bern
Interlaken
Grindelwald
Lauterbrunnen
Kandersteg
Gstaad
Sion
Verbier
Saas Fee
Zermatt
Matterhorn
Upper Engadine

Lake Neuchâtel

Lausanne
Lake Geneva (Lac Léman)
Martigny
Montreux

Mont Blanc

Geneva (Genève)

FRANCE

ITALY

SUPERIOR SKIING (MIN. 3 WEEKS)

You could land just about anywhere in Switzerland or western Austria in the winter and have a fabulous skiing experience, but this itinerary points out some snowbound hotspots that give you a great deal for your money and the chance of glimpsing some famous faces! One good place to start is medieval **Innsbruck,** home of the 1964 and 1976 Winter Olympics and surrounded by heavenly slopes piled high with fresh powder. If you haven't exhausted yourself there, highbrow resorts lie within reach on every hand, including **Kitzbühel,** where downhill skiing was born; **Zell am Ziller,** tucked into a narrow valley; and ritzy **Seefeld in Tirol,** one of Europe's major international ski resorts. You're most likely to see stars in **St. Anton am Arlberg,** but if you make the trek up to **Lech,** you can catch the ones who are hiding out, as well as excellent skiing. If you're looking for high-quality, low cost skiing, hightail it over to happening **Arosa** in eastern Switzerland, where hostel beds come complete with affordable ski passes. As Arosa is a newcomer to the ski circuit, students and families can enjoy the slopes without paying through the nose. Back on the road more travelled, **Klosters, Davos,** and **St. Moritz** are familiar names in any skiing household, particularly the royal families of Sweden, Britain, and Hollywood. St. Moritz is the hub of an extensive skiing network that encompasses such hidden treasures as **Sils, Celerina, Pontresina,** and **Silvaplana.** When you're ready for some serious skiing and celebrating, take the cog railway up to **Zermatt,** the hedonistic ski paradise in southwestern Switzerland. French Switzerland does its best to compete with its easterly neighbors, with elegant resorts in **Verbier** and **Sion,** lead competitor for the 2006 Winter Olympics. As you move north, back into German Switzerland, you'll run across thriving **Gstaad/Saanen,** an international jet-set magnet, **Mürren,** a tiny village perched high above the Lauterbrunnen valley, and **Grindelwald,** the gateway to some of the finest powder and the most breathtaking panoramas known to humankind. Whether you choose to follow the stars or hide out in the hills, this is where you want to be.

HIKING THE ALPS (MIN. 2 WEEKS)

Full of towering mountains, Switzerland and Austria are a hiker's paradise. Many of the places that offer great skiing have excellent hiking as well, but no travel guide could ever list every inviting peak or spectacular hike in the Alps. Here are just a few highlights. Starting in central Switzerland, **Kandersteg** has some of the best glacier hiking in the world. Just a bit north and east, the **Lauterbrunnen Valley,** in the shadow of the Jungfrau, offers easy access to countless varied, fantastic hikes in **Gimmelwald, Mürren,** and **Wengen.** Stay in Lauterbrunnen or Gimmelwald and just explore the valley. Moving east to Graubünden, beautiful short hikes await you in the **Upper Engadine** valley, but longer hikes in the **Lower Engadine** allow you to leave civilization far behind as you wander through the Swiss National Park, using **Zuoz** or **Guarda** as a base. Finishing up in eastern Switzerland, spend a couple of days in **Appenzell** to make your ascent up to Säntis, taking advantage of the many cozy mountain huts.

Over the border in Austria, the wild and impressive scenery of the **Ötztal** is easily accessible from **Sölden, Hochgurgl,** and **Obergurgl.** On the other side of Innsbruck, the **Zillertal** has more than just prime skiing—the same mountains offer countless hiking venues. Just take the reliable but antique Zillertalbahn from **Jenbach** to **Mayrhofen;** you can get off at any village that strikes your fancy or ride all the way to Mayrhofen to sample the smorgasbord of hikes the valley offers. As you move eastward, you'll run into the **Hohe Tauern National Park,** home to 246 glaciers and 304 mountains over 3000m. In the park, countless paths lead through meadows, along glaciers, and up to the roaring **Wasserfallwinkel** (2548m). The rugged **Karawanken Mountains** along the Slovenian border in southern Austria may look daunting, but nearly every peak has easily accessible trails all the way to the *Gipfelkreuz* (summit cross). Just southeast of **Klagenfurt,** for example, the **Hochobir** (2142m) provides a bird's-eye view of Carinthia, and a peek into Slovenia. Panoramas await you on every hand—pack sturdy shoes, a camera, and a good topographical map, then set out to conquer the mighty Alps.

ESSENTIALS

Budget travel can be challenging in expensive countries, but the key to success is preparation. The more legwork you do before your trip, the smoother things will run once you get there. Nasty surprises await the uninformed traveler: get as much information as you can to avoid them. Plan carefully, then relax and enjoy!

WHEN TO GO

The best time to visit the Alpine states of Austria and Switzerland depends on what you're looking for. November to March is peak season for skiing, with the result that prices in western Austria and eastern Switzerland double and travelers need reservations months in advance. The situation is reversed in the summer, when the flatter, eastern half of Austria and western Switzerland fill up with vacationers. Not only is the weather nice, but sights and accommodations are cheaper and less crowded in the shoulder season (May/June, September/October). If you're a music or theater fan, be aware that the Vienna State Opera, the Vienna Boy's Choir, and major theaters throughout Austria and Switzerland don't have any performances during July and August.

HOLIDAYS! Just about everything closes down on public holidays in Austria and Switzerland, so plan accordingly. Both countries observe the following national holidays: **New Year's Day** (Jan. 1-2), **Good Friday** (April 21), **Easter Monday** (April 25), **Labor Day** (May 1), **Ascension** (June 1), **Whit Monday** (June 12), and **Christmas** (Dec. 25-26). Austrians also celebrate **Epiphany** (Jan. 6), **Corpus Christi** (June 22), **Assumption of the Virgin** (Aug. 15), **Austrian National Day** (Oct. 26), **All Saints' Day** (Nov. 1), and **Immaculate Conception** (Dec. 8). The Swiss celebrate **Swiss National Day** on August 1.

CLIMATE. Although Austria and Switzerland are on about the same latitude as Newfoundland, their climates are considerably milder than one might expect. In general, winters are cold and snowy enough for skiing, while summers are warm enough for outdoor cafés. Though worldwide weather spasms in recent years make guaranteeing any particular kind of weather difficult, July is usually the hottest month and February the coldest, with temperatures down to -10°C (5°F). Summer temperatures can reach 38 C (100 F) for brief periods, although summer evenings are usually cool. Mountainous areas of Austria and Switzerland are, understandably, cooler and wetter the higher you get; as a rule, temperatures decrease about 1.7°C (3°F) with each additional 300m elevation. Snow cover lasts from late December to March in the valleys, from November to May at about 1800m, and stays year-round above 2500m. Warm sweaters are the rule September to May; add a thick coat, hat, and gloves in winter. Switzerland's lake areas, in the temperate swath of plain that extends across from Lake Constance in the northeast through Zurich and Bern down to Geneva, are very rainy all year. In the lake regions of both countries, it rains frequently, so don't forget your umbrella. For up-to-date weather and temperature information on a particular city, check www.wunderground.com/global/ or www.weatherlabs.com.

TIME ZONES. Switzerland and Austria both use Central European time (abbreviated MEZ in German), which is 6 hours later than Eastern Standard Time and 1 hour later than Greenwich Mean Time. Subtract 9 hours from Eastern Australia Time and 11 hours from New Zealand Time. Austria and Switzerland use the 24-hour clock for all official purposes, so 7:30pm is the same as 19.30.

GETTING STARTED

NATIONAL TOURIST OFFICES

Austria and Switzerland are old pros at tourism. Before visiting either country, contact the national tourist office, which can provide copious information for planning your trip, ranging from help with a specific itinerary to personalized information for travelers with specific concerns.

AUSTRIAN NATIONAL TOURIST OFFICES

Canada: Montreal, 1010 Ouest rue Sherbourne #1410, Montreal, P.Q. H3A 2R7 (tel. (514) 849 3709; fax 849 9577; email atcmtr@istar.ca); **Toronto,** 2 Bloor St. East #3330, Toronto, ON, M4W 1A8 (tel. (416) 967 3381; fax 967 4101; email antotor@sympatico.ca); **Vancouver,** Granville Sq. #1380, 200 Granville St., Vancouver, BC V6C 1S4 (tel. (604) 683 86 95; fax 662 85 28; email atradebc.uniserve.com).

U.S.: New York, 500 Fifth Ave., Suite 800, PO Box 1142, New York, NY 10108-1142 (tel. (212) 944 6880; fax 730 4568; email antonyc@ibm.net); **Los Angeles,** 11601 Wilshire Bd., Suite 2480, Los Angeles, CA 90025 (tel. (301) 477 2038; email antolax@ix.netcom.com).

SWISS NATIONAL TOURIST OFFICES

Canada: Toronto, 154 University Ave., Toronto, ON M5H 3Y9 (tel. (416) 971 9734); **Etobicoke,** 926 East Mall, Etobicoke, ON M9B 6K1 (tel. (416) 695 2090; fax 695 2774; email sttoronto@switzerlandtourism.com; www.switzerlandtourism.com).

United Kingdom: London, Swiss Centre, Swiss Court, London W1V 8EE (tel. (0171) 734 19 21; fax 437 45 77).

U.S.: New York, 608 Fifth Ave., New York, NY 10020 (tel. (212) 757 5944; fax 262 6116); **Chicago,** 150 N. Michigan Ave., Chicago, IL 60601 (tel. (312) 630 5840; fax 630 5848); **San Francisco,** 260 Stockton St., San Francisco, CA 94108 (tel. (415) 362 2260); **Los Angeles,** 222 N. Sepulveda Blvd., El Segundo, CA 90245 (tel. (310) 335 5980; fax 335 5982).

DOCUMENTS AND FORMALITIES

ENTRANCE REQUIREMENTS.

Passport (p. 10). Required for all foreign visitors.

Visa (p. 12). Required only for a continuous stay of more than 3 months.

Immunizations (p. 22). Standard immunizations should be up to date. If hiking and camping, check into getting a vaccine for tick-borne encephalitis abroad.

Work Permit (p. 12). Required for anyone planning to work in Austria or Switzerland.

Driving Permit (p. 47). Required for all those planning to drive.

EMBASSIES AND CONSULATES

The Austrian or Swiss Embassy/Consulate in your home country can supply you with legal information concerning your trip, arrange for visas (when necessary), and direct you to a wealth of other information about tourism, education, and employment in Austria and Switzerland.

AUSTRIAN EMBASSIES AND CONSULATES

Australia: Embassy, 12 Talbot St., Forrest, Canberra ACT 2603 (tel. (02) 6295 1533 or 6295 1376; fax 6239 6751; email austria@dynamite.com.au); **Consulates: Adelaide,** 12 Park Terrace, Bowden SA 5007 (tel. (08) 8269 0664; fax 8340 7152); **Brisbane,** 30, Argyle St., Breakfast Creek, Queensland 4010 (tel. (070) 3262 8955; fax 3262

8082); **Melbourne,** Suite 1, 107 Wellington St., Windsor Vic 3181 (tel. (03) 9533 6900; fax 9533 6500); **Sydney,** 2 Kingsland Rd., Bexley, Sydney, NSW 2207 (tel. (02) 9567 1008; fax 9567 2322).

Canada: Embassy, 445 Wilbrod St., Ottawa, ON KIN 6M7 (tel. (613) 789 1444); **Consulates: Montréal,** 1350 Rue Sherbrooke Quest, Suite 1030, Montréal, P.Q. H3G 1J1 (tel. (514) 845 8661); **Toronto,** 360 Bay St., Suite 1010, Toronto, ON M5H 2V6 (tel. (416) 683 0649); **Vancouver,** 1810 Alberni St., Suite 202, Vancouver, B. C. V6G 1B3 (tel. (604) 687 3338).

Ireland, 15 Ailesbury Court Apts., 93 Ailesbury Rd., Dublin 4 (tel. (01) 269 45 77 or 269 14 51; fax 283 08 60).

New Zealand, Consulate: Consular General, 22-4 Garrett St., Wellington (tel. (04) 801 9709). For visas or passports, contact Australian office.

South Africa: Embassy, 1109 Duncan St., Momentum Office Park, 0011 Brooklyn, Pretoria; Post: P.O. Box 95572, 0145 Waterkloof, Pretoria (tel. 012 462 483); **Consulates: Johannesburg,** JHI-House 7th fl., Craddock Ave. 11, Rosebank, Johannesburg; Post: P.O. Box 782 195, Sandton 2146 (tel. (011) 447 65 51; fax 447 61 91); **Capetown,** Standard Bank Centre, Main Tower, 1001 Hertzog Blvd., 8001 Capetown (tel. (021) 421 14 40, 421 14 41, or 421 62 15; fax 425 34 89).

U.K.: Embassy, 18 Belgrave Mews West, London SW1 X 8HU (tel. (0171) 235 37 31, 344 02 90, or 354 40 291; fax 344 02 92; email embassy@austria.org.uk or austria@co.uk); **Consulate: Edinburgh,** 18 South Groathill Ave., Edinburgh EH4 2LW (tel. (0131) 315 60 00; fax 315 61 10).

U.S.: Embassy, 3524 International Court NW, Washington DC 20008-3035 (tel. (202) 895 6775 or 895 6700; fax 895 6772); **Consulates: Chicago,** Wrigley Bldg, Suite 707, 400 North Michigan Ave., Chicago, IL 60611 (tel. (312) 222 1515); **Los Angeles,** 11859 Wilshire Blvd., Suite 501, Los Angeles, CA 90025 (tel. (310) 444 9310); **New York,** 31 East 69th St., New York, NY 10021 (tel. (212) 737 6400).

SWISS EMBASSIES AND CONSULATES

Australia: Embassy, 7 Melbourne Ave., Forrest, Canberra, ACT 2603 (tel. (02) 6273 3977; fax 6273 3428; email swiemcan@dynamite.com.au); **Consulates: Melbourne,** 420 St. Kilda Rd., 7th fl., P.O. Box 7026, Melbourne VIC 3004 (tel. (03) 9867 2266; fax 9866 5907; email swisscgmelb@ozemail.com.au); **Sydney,** Suite 2301, Plaza II, 500 Oxford St., Bondi Junction NSW 202/P.O. Box 282, Bondi Junction NSW 1355 (tel. (02) 9369 4244; fax 9369 1334; email swicgsyd@ozemail.com.au).

Canada: Embassy, 5 Marlborough Ave., Ottawa, Ontario KIN 8E6 (tel. (613) 235 1837; fax 563 1394); **Consulates: Montréal,** 1572 Av. Dr. Pensfield, Montréal, P. Q. H3G 1C4 (tel. (514) 932 7181/82; fax 932 9028; email swicgmtl@netrover.com); **Toronto,** 154 University Ave., Suite 601, Toronto, Ontario M5H 3Y9 (tel. (416) 593 5371/73; fax 593 5083); **Vancouver,** World Trade Centre, 790-999 Canada Place, Vancouver, B.C. V6C 3E1 (tel. (604) 684 2231; fax 684 2806; email simm@sciencelink.org).

Ireland, 6 Ailesbury Rd., Ballsbridge, Dublin 4 (tel. (01) 218 6382/83; fax 283 0344; email swiemdub@iol.ie).

New Zealand, 22 Panama St., Wellington (tel. (04) 472 1593; fax 499 6302).

South Africa: Embassy: Pretoria, 818 George Ave., Arcadia 0083, P.O. Box 2289, 0001 Pretoria (tel. (012) 43 67 07; fax 43 67 71; email swiempre@cis.co.za); during the sessions of Parliament (Jan.-June), the embassy is based in **Capetown,** P.O. Box 1546, Capetown 8000 (tel. (021) 426 12 01/02; fax 423 16 06); **Consulates: Capetown,** NBS Waldorf, 9th fl., 80 St. George's Mall, P.O. Box 563, Capetown 8000 (tel. (021) 426 10 40/41; fax 424 93 44; email swiem@cis.co.za); **Johannesburg,** Cradock Heights, 2nd fl., 21 Cradock Ave., Rosebank 2196/P.O. Box 724, Parklands 2121 (tel. (011) 442 75 00; fax 442 78 91; email swisscgjoh@icon.co.za).

U.K.: Embassy, 16-18 Montague Place, London W1H 2BQ (tel. (0171) 616 60 00; fax 724 70 01; email vertretung@lon.rep.admin.ch); **Consulate:** Portland Tower, 6th fl.,

Portland St., Manchester M1 3LF (tel. (0161) 236 29 33; fax 236 46 89; email swis@cgmanchester.freeserve.co.uk).

U.S.: Embassy, 2900 Cathedral Ave. NW, Washington D.C. 20008-3499 (tel. (202) 745 7900; fax 387 2564); **Consulates: Chicago,** P.O. Box 11561, Chicago, IL 60611-0561 (tel. (312) 915 0061; fax 915 0388; email vertretung@chi.rep.admin.ch); **New York,** 633 Third Ave., 30th fl., New York, NY 10017-6706 (tel. (212) 599 5700; fax 599 4266; email vertretung@nyc.rep.admin.ch); **San Francisco,** 456 Montgomery St., Suite 1500, San Francisco, CA 94104-1233 (tel. (415) 788 2272; fax 788 1402; email vertretung@sfr.rep.admin.ch).

EMBASSIES AND CONSULATES IN SWITZERLAND AND AUSTRIA

AUSTRIA

All foreign embassies in Austria are based in Vienna. For a complete listing, look in the Vienna telephone book under *Botschaften* (embassies) or *Konsulate* (consulates). The first number in each address tells you in which district of Vienna they can be found. Most consular offices have the same contact information as the embassies. Any consulates not in Vienna are listed in the cities where they are located.

Australia, IV, Mattiellistr. 2-4 (tel. 512 85 80).

Canada, I, Laurenzerbergg. 2 (tel. 533 36 92).

Ireland, III, Landstrasser Hauptstr. 2, Hilton Center (tel. 715 42 460).

New Zealand: Embassy, Friedrichstr. 60, Berlin, Germany 10117 is also responsible for Austria; **Consulate:** XIX, Springsiedelg. 28 (tel. 318 85 05).

South Africa, XIX, Sandg. 33 (tel. 326 49 30).

U.K.: Embassy, III, Jaurèsg. 12 (tel. 713 15 74); **Consulate,** III, Jaurèsg. 10 (tel. 714 61 17).

U.S.: Embassy, IX, Boltzmanng. 16 (tel. 31339); **Consulate,** I, Gartenbaupromenade 2 (tel. 31339).

SWITZERLAND

Nearly all foreign embassies in Switzerland are located in Bern, southeast of the Kirchenfeldbrücke. Most consulates are located in Zurich (p. 345).

Australia, Alpenstr. 29 (tel. 351 01 43)

Canada, Kirchenfeldstr. 88 (tel. 352 63 81; fax 352 73 15)

Ireland, Kirchenfeldstr. 68 (tel. 352 14 42)

South Africa, Jungfraustr. 1 (tel. 352 20 11)

U.K., Thunstr. 50 (tel. 352 50 21)

U.S., Jubiläumstr. 93 (tel. 351 70 11; fax 351 73 44)

PASSPORTS

REQUIREMENTS. Valid passports are required of all visitors to Austria and Switzerland. Citizens of most EU and English-speaking countries, except South Africa, can visit for up to 3 months without a visa. If you do need a visa, make sure your passport is valid longer than the visa or you could be fined upon returning home.

Remember to photocopy the page of your passport that contains your photograph, passport number, and other identifying information, along with other important documents such as visas, travel insurance policies, airplane tickets, and traveler's check serial numbers, in case you lose anything. Carry one set of copies in a safe place apart from the originals and leave another set at home. Consulates also recommend that you carry an expired passport or an official copy of your birth certificate separate from other documents, just in case.

LOST PASSPORTS. If you lose your passport, immediately notify the local police and the nearest embassy or consulate of your home government. To expedite its replacement, you will need to know all information previously recorded and show identification and proof of citizenship. In some cases, a replacement may take weeks to process, and it may be valid only for a limited time. Any visas stamped in your old passport will be irretrievably lost. In an emergency, ask for immediate temporary traveling papers that will permit you to re-enter your home country. Your passport is a public document belonging to your nation's government. You may have to surrender it to a foreign government official, but if you don't get it back in a reasonable amount of time, inform the nearest mission of your home country.

NEW PASSPORTS. All applications for new passports or renewals should be filed several weeks or months before your departure date—remember that you are relying on government agencies to complete these transactions. Most passport offices offer emergency passport services for an extra charge. Citizens residing abroad who need a passport or renewal should contact their nearest embassy or consulate.

Australia: Citizens must apply for a passport in person at a post office, a passport office, or an Australian diplomatic mission overseas. Passport offices are located in Adelaide, Brisbane, Canberra, Darwin, Hobart, Melbourne, Newcastle, Perth, and Sydney. New adult passports AUS$126 (for a 32-page passport) or AUS$188 (64-page); child AUS$63 (32-page) or AUS$94 (64-page). Adult passports valid 10 years, child passports 5 years. Call toll-free (in Australia) 13 12 32, or visit www.dfat.gov.au/passports.

Canada: Application forms are available at all passport offices, Canadian missions, many travel agencies, and Northern Stores in northern communities. Passports CDN$60, plus a CDN$25 consular fee, are valid for 5 years, non-renewable. For additional info, contact the Canadian Passport Office, Department of Foreign Affairs and International Trade, Ottawa, ON, K1A OG3 (tel. (613) 994 35 00; www.dfait-maeci.gc.ca/passport). Travelers may also call (800) 567 6868 (24hr.); in Toronto, (416) 973 3251; in Vancouver, (604) 586 2500; in Montreal, (514) 283 2152.

Ireland: Citizens can apply for a passport by mail to either the Department of Foreign Affairs, Passport Office, Setanta Centre, Molesworth St., Dublin 2 (tel. (01) 671 16 33; fax 671 1092; www.irlgov.ie/iveagh), or the Passport Office, Irish Life Building, 1A South Mall, Cork (tel. (021) 27 25 25). Obtain an application at a local Garda station or post office, or request one from a passport office. Passports IR£45, valid for 10 years. Citizens under 18 or over 65 can request a 3-year passport, IR£10.

New Zealand: Application forms for passports are available in New Zealand from most travel agents. Applications may be forwarded to the Passport Office, P.O. Box 10526, Wellington, New Zealand (tel. (0800) 22 50 50; www.govt.nz/agency_info/forms.shtml). Standard processing time in New Zealand is 10 working days. Adult passport NZ$80, child NZ$40. Children's names can no longer be endorsed on a parent's passport—they must apply for their own, which are valid for up to 5 years. An adult's passport is valid for up to 10 years.

South Africa: South African passports are issued only in Pretoria. However, all applications must still be submitted or forwarded to the applicable office of a South African consulate. Tourist passports SAR80, valid for 10 years; children under 16 SAR60, valid for 5 years. Time for the completion of an application is normally 3 months or more from the the time of submission. Contact the nearest Department of Home Affairs Office (www.southafrica-newyork.net/passport.htm).

U.K.: Full passports are valid for 10 years (5 years if under 16). Application forms are available at passport offices, main post offices, and many travel agents. Apply by mail or in person to one of the passport offices, located in London, Liverpool, Newport, Peterborough, Glasgow, or Belfast. Adult passport UK£31, children under 16 UK£11. The

ESSENTIALS

process takes about 4 weeks, but the London office offers a 5-day, walk-in rush service; arrive early. The U.K. Passport Agency can be reached by phone at (0870) 521 04 10, and more information is available at www.open.gov.uk/ukpass/ukpass.htm.

U.S.: Citizens may apply for a passport at any federal or state courthouse or post office authorized to accept passport applications, or at a U.S. Passport Agency, located in most major cities. Refer to the "U.S. Government, State Department" section of the telephone directory or the local post office for addresses. Adult passports US$60, valid for 10 years; children under 18 US$40, valid for 5 years. Passports may be renewed by mail or in person for US$40. Processing takes 3-4 weeks. For more info, contact the U.S. Passport Information Agency's 24-hour recorded message (tel. (202) 647 0518) or look on the web at travel.state.gov/passport_services.html.

THE EUROPEAN UNION AND THE TRAVELER. Traveling between the fifteen member states of the **European Union** (E.U.) has never been easier, especially for E.U. citizens. Citizens of E.U. member states need only a valid state-issued identity card to travel within the E.U., and have right of residence and employment throughout the Union, though some regulations do apply (see **Visas, Invitations, and Work permits,** p. 12). **Freedom of mobility** within the E.U. was established on May 1, 1999; henceforth, with the exception of the U.K., Ireland and Denmark, border checks will be abolished at internal E.U. borders. However travelers should always carry a passport or E.U.-member issued identity card as police controls may still be carried out. Over the next 5 years, immigration and visa policies will be made on a Union-wide basis.

There are **no customs** at internal E.U. borders (travelers arriving in one E.U. country from another by air should take the **blue channel** when exiting the baggage claim), and travelers are free to transport whatever legal substances they like across the Union provided they can demonstrate that it is for personal (i.e. non-commercial) use. In practice, personal use is limited to quantities of less than 800 cigarettes, 10L spirits, 90L wine (60Lsparkling wine), and 110L beer. Correspondingly, on June 30, 1999, **duty-free was abolished** for travel between E.U. member states. Those arriving in the E.U. from outside will still have a duty-free allowance. January 1, 1999 saw the launch of the **Euro,** a common currency for 11 of the E.U. nations. While it exists only in electronic form as yet, in the future it will mean far fewer money-changing headaches for travelers in Europe (see **Money,** p. 14). The fifteen member states of the E.U. are: Austria, Belgium, Denmark, Finland, France, Germany, Greece, Ireland, Italy, Luxembourg, the Netherlands, Portugal, Spain, Sweden, and the United Kingdom.

VISAS AND WORK PERMITS

Citizens of Australia, Canada, Ireland, New Zealand, U.K., and U.S. do not need visas to visit Austria or Switzerland. For more detailed information about which nationalities require visas, visit either the Austrian Embassy website (www.bmaa.gv.at/embassy/uk/index.html.en) or the Swiss Embassy website (www.swissemb.org.). U.S. citizens can take advantage of the **Center for International Business and Travel (CIBT)** (tel. (800) 925 2428), which will secure visas for travel to almost all countries for a service charge. Admission as a visitor does not include the right to work, which is authorized only by a work permit, and studying in Austria or Switzerland requires a special visa (see **Alternatives to Tourism,** p. 59).

IDENTIFICATION

When you travel, always carry two or more forms of identification on your person, including at least one photo ID. A passport and driver's license or birth certificate usually serve as adequate proof of identity, age, and citizenship. Many establishments, especially banks, require several IDs before cashing traveler's checks. Never carry all your forms of ID together, however. It is useful to carry extra passport-size photos to affix to the various IDs or railpasses you may acquire.

STUDENT AND TEACHER IDENTIFICATION. The **International Student Identity Card (ISIC)** is the most widely accepted form of student identification. Flashing your ISIC can procure you discounts for many sights, theaters, museums, accommodations, train, ferry, bus, and airplane transportation. Present the card wherever you go and ask about discounts even when none are advertised. The international identification cards are preferable to school-specific cards because the tourism personnel in Austria and Switzerland are taught to recognize the former, though they may occasionally want to see your school ID as well. For U.S. cardholders traveling abroad, the ISIC also provides insurance benefits, including US$100 per day of in-hospital sickness for a maximum of 60 days, and US$3000 accident-related medical reimbursement for each accident (see **Insurance,** p. 26). In addition, cardholders have access to a toll-free 24-hour ISIC helpline whose multilingual staff can provide assistance in medical, legal, and financial emergencies overseas (tel. (800) 626 2427 in the U.S. and Canada; elsewhere call collect 44 181 666 90 25).

Many student travel agencies around the world issue ISICs, including STA Travel in Australia and New Zealand; Travel CUTS in Canada; USIT in Ireland and Northern Ireland; SASTS in South Africa; Campus Travel and STA Travel in the U.K.; Council Travel (www.counciltravel.com/idcards/index.htm) and STA Travel is the U.S.; and any other travel agency with a student focus. When you apply for the card, request a copy of the International Student Identity Card Handbook, which lists some of the available discounts by country. You can also write to Council for a copy. The card is valid from September of one year to December of the following year and costs AUS$15, CDN$15, or US$20. Applicants must be at least 12 years old and degree-seeking students of a secondary or post-secondary school. The **International Teacher Identity Card (ITIC)** offers the same insurance coverage, and similar discounts. The fee is AUS$13, UK£5, or US$20. For more information on these cards, contact the **International Student Travel Confederation (ISTC),** Herengracht 479, 1017 BS Amsterdam, Netherlands (from abroad call 31 20 421 28 00; fax 421 28 10; email istcinfo@istc.org; www.istc.org).

YOUTH IDENTIFICATION. The International Student Travel Confederation also issues a discount card to travelers who are 25 years old or younger but not students. Known as the **International Youth Travel Card (IYTC)** (formerly the GO25 Card), this one-year card offers many of the same benefits as the ISIC, and most organizations that sell the ISIC also sell the IYTC. To apply, you will need either a passport, valid driver's license or copy of a birth certificate, and a passport-sized photo with your name printed on the back. The fee is US$20.

CUSTOMS

GETTING IN. Austria and Switzerland prohibit or restrict the importation of firearms, explosives, ammunition, fireworks, booby traps, controlled drugs, most plants, lottery tickets, most animals, and pornography. They don't look keenly on items manufactured from protected species, either. To avoid hassles about prescription drugs, ensure that your bottles are clearly marked and carry a copy of the prescription. Upon entering Austria or Switzerland, you'll have to declare certain items (such as cigarettes, wine, perfume, etc.) brought with you from abroad and pay a duty on the value of those articles that exceed the allowance established by Austria or Switzerland's customs service. Keeping receipts for purchases made abroad will help establish values when you return. It is wise to make a list, including serial numbers, of any valuables that you carry with you from home; if you register this list with customs before your departure and have an official stamp it, you will avoid import duty charges and ensure an easy passage upon your return.

GOING HOME. Upon returning home, you must declare all articles acquired abroad and pay a duty on the value of articles that exceed the allowance established by your country's customs service. Goods and gifts purchased at duty-free shops abroad are not exempt from duty or sales tax at your point of return; you must declare these items as well. "Duty-free" merely means that you are eligible to receive a refund a tax in the country of purchase (see **Taxes,** p. 19). For more specific information on customs requirements, contact the following information centers:

Australia: Australian Customs National Information, Line 1 (tel. 30 03 63; www.customs.gov.au).

Canada: Canadian Customs, 2265 St. Laurent Blvd., Ottawa, ON K1G 4K3 (tel. (613) 993 0534 or 24hr. automated service (800) 461 99 99; www.revcan.ca).

Ireland: The Collector of Customs and Excise, The Custom House, Dublin 1 (tel. (01) 679 27 77; fax 671 20 21; email taxes@revenue.iol.ie; www.revenue.ie/customs.htm).

New Zealand: New Zealand Customhouse, 17-21 Whitmore St., Box 2218, Wellington (tel. (04) 473 6099; fax 473 7370; www.customs.govt.nz).

South Africa: Commissioner for Customs and Excise, Private Bag X47, Pretoria 0001 (tel. (012) 314 99 11; fax 328 64 78).

U.K.: Her Majesty's Customs and Excise, Custom House, Nettleton Road, Heathrow Airport, Hounslow, Middlesex TW6 2LA (tel. (0181) 910 36 02 or 910 35 66; fax 910 37 65; www.hmce.gov.uk).

U.S.: U.S. Customs Service, Box 7407, Washington D.C. 20044 (tel. (202) 927 6724; www.customs.ustreas.gov).

MONEY

Though Austria and Switzerland are not the cheapest destinations, there are ways to experience them on a budget. If you stay in hostels and prepare most of your own food, expect to spend anywhere from $30 to $65 per person per day in Switzerland, slightly less in Austria. **Accommodations** start at about $18 per night for a single, while a basic sit-down meal usually costs around $12. Carrying cash with you, even in a money belt, is risky but necessary; traveler's checks, depending on the currency you buy them in, are a good idea, but personal checks from home will almost never be accepted (even at banks).

CURRENCY AND EXCHANGE

As a general rule, it's cheaper to convert money in Austria or Switzerland than at home. It's wise to bring enough foreign currency to last for the first 24-72 hours of a trip to avoid being penniless after banking hours or on a holiday. Better yet, bring an ATM card and find the machine quickly—you'll be able to zip through the airport and start your vacation without languishing in lines. Travelers living in the U.S. can get foreign currency from the comfort of their home; **Capital Foreign Exchange** (tel. (888) 842 0880) or **International Currency Express** (tel. (888) 278 6628) will deliver foreign currency (for over 120 countries) or traveler's checks overnight (US$15) or second-day (US$12) at competitive exchange rates.

Currency exchange kiosks and change machines should be your last resort when you need local funds, since their unfavorable rates and hefty commissions will cripple your resources. Banks, post offices, and small train stations often have better rates, but ATMs and credit cards are your best bet, since you'll profit from their low corporate rates (see **Credit Cards,** p. 16). If you need to change cash or traveler's checks, take the time to compare the rates offered by different banks and kiosks (*Wechselstube* in German, *bureau de change* in French, *cambio* in Italian). A good rule of thumb is only to go to banks or kiosks with at most a 5% margin between their buy and sell prices. Since you lose money with each transaction, convert in large sums (unless the rate is disadvantageous). The currency chart below is based on published exchange rates from August 1999.

THE AUSTRIAN SCHILLING (AS/ÖS/ATS)

US$1 = 13.023AS	10AS = US$0.768
CDN$1 = 8.791AS	10AS = CDN$1.137
UK£1 = 20.851AS	10AS = UK£0.479
IR£1 = 17.472AS	10AS= IR£0.572
AUS$1 = 8.454AS	10AS = AUS$1.183
NZ$1 = 6.859AS	10AS = NZ$1.457
SAR1= 3.215AS	10AS = SAR4.686
SFR1 = 8.589AS	10AS = SFR1.164
EURO€1 = 13.762AS	10AS = EURO€0.726

THE SWISS FRANC (SFR/CHF)

US$1 = 1.516SFR	1SFR = US$0.659
CDN$1 = 1.023SFR	1SFR = CDN$0.977
UK£1 = 2.428SFR	1SFR = UK£0.412
IR£1 = 2.034SFR	1SFR= IR£0.491
AUS$1 = 0.984SFR	1SFR = AUS$1.016
NZ$1 = 0.798SFR	1SFR = NZ$1.252
SAR1= 0.248SFR	1SFR = SAR4.025
AS1 = 0.116SFR	1SFR = AS8.589
EURO€1= 1.602SFR	1SFR= EURO€0.624

The unit of currency in Austria is the **Schilling,** abbreviated as **AS, ATS, ÖS,** or, within Austria, simply **S.** Each *Schilling* is subdivided into 100 **Groschen (g).** Coins come in 2, 5, 10, and 50g, and 1, 5, 10, and 20AS denominations. Bills come in 20, 50, 100, 500, 1000, and 5000AS amounts. Exchange rates are standard among banks and exchange counters, while stores, hotels, and restaurants that accept payment in foreign currency apply a slightly lower exchange rate. Every establishment that exchanges currency charges at least 14AS. There are AmEx service offices in Vienna, Salzburg, Linz, and Innsbruck.

The Swiss monetary unit is the **Swiss Franc (SFr),** which is divided into 100 *centimes* (called *Rappen* in German Switzerland). Coins are issued in 5, 10, 20, and 50 *centimes* and 1, 2, and 5SFr; bills in 10, 20, 50, 100, 500, and 1000SFr denominations. Currency exchange is easiest at ATMs, train stations, and post offices, where rates are the same as or close to bank rates but where commissions are smaller.

THE EURO. On January 1, 1999, 11 countries of the European Union, including Austria, officially adopted the **euro** as their common currency. Euro notes and coins will not be issued until January 1, 2002, and until that time the euro will exist only in electronic transactions and traveler's checks. On June 1, 2002, the Schilling will be entirely withdrawn from circulation and the euro will become the only legal currency in Austria. *Let's Go* lists all prices in Austrian Schillings, as these will still be most relevant in 2000. However, all Austrian businesses must by law quote prices both in Schillings and euros.

Travelers who will be passing through more than one nation in the euro-zone should note that exchange rates between the 11 national currencies were irrevocably fixed on Januray 1, 1999. Henceforth currency exchanges will be obliged to interchange euro-zone currencies at the official rate and with no commission, though they may still charge a nominal service fee. Euro-denominated travelers checks may also be used throughout the euro-zone, and can also be exchanged commission-free throughout the 11 euro nations: Austria, Belgium, Finland, France, Germany, Ireland, Italy, Luxembourg, the Netherlands, Portugal, and Spain. Get updated information at www.europa.eu.int/.

TRAVELER'S CHECKS

Traveler's checks are one of the safest and least troublesome means of carrying funds, since they can be refunded if stolen. Several agencies and banks sell them, usually for face value plus a small percentage commission. (Members of the American Automobile Association, and some banks and credit unions, can get American Express checks commission-free; see **AAA**, p. 48). **American Express** and **Visa** are the most widely recognized. If you're ordering checks, do so well in advance, especially if you are requesting large sums. You can get traveler's checks in most currencies, including Swiss Francs and euros.

Each agency provides refunds if your checks are lost or stolen, and many provide additional services, such as toll-free refund hotlines in the countries you're visiting, emergency message services, and stolen credit card assistance.

In order to collect a **refund for lost or stolen checks,** keep your check receipts separate from your checks and store them in a safe place or with a traveling companion. Record check numbers when you cash them, leave a list of check numbers with someone at home, and ask for a list of refund centers when you buy your checks. Never countersign your checks until you are ready to cash them, and always bring your passport with you when you plan to use the checks.

American Express: Call (800) 251 902 in Australia; in New Zealand (0800) 441 068; in the U.K. (0800) 52 13 13; in the U.S. and Canada (800) 221 7282. In Austria, call (0800) 20 68 40; in Switzerland, call (0800) 55 01 00. If all else fails, call the U.S. collect 1 801 964 6665; www.aexp.com. American Express traveler's checks are available in 10 currencies, including Swiss francs and euros (in Austria, which is nice since they don't offer Austrian Schillings). Checks can be purchased for a small fee (1-4%) at American Express Travel Service Offices, banks, and American Automobile Association (AAA) offices. AAA members (see p. 47) can buy the checks commission-free. American Express offices cash their checks commission-free (except where prohibited by national governments), but often at slightly worse rates than banks. *Cheques for Two* can be signed by either of two people traveling together. The booklet *Traveler's Companion* lists travel office addresses and stolen check hotlines for each European country.

Thomas Cook MasterCard: From the U.S., Canada, or Caribbean call (800) 223 7373; from the U.K. call (0800) 622 101; from elsewhere, call collect 44 1733 318 950. Checks available in 13 currencies, including Swiss francs and euros. 2% commission, but *Sparkasse* banks in Austria will cash Thomas Cook traveler's checks for free.

Visa: Call (800) 227 6811 in the U.S.; in the U.K. (0800) 895 078; from elsewhere, call 44 1733 318 949 and reverse charges. Any of the above numbers can tell you the location of their nearest office. Check out www.visa.com for info on Visa TravelMoney.

CREDIT CARDS

Credit cards and debit cards are generally accepted in all but the smallest businesses in Austria and Switzerland. Major credit cards—**MasterCard** and **Visa** are welcomed most often—can be used to obtain cash advances in Schillings or Swiss francs from associated banks and teller machines. Credit card companies get the wholesale exchange rate, which is generally 5% better than the retail rate used by banks and other currency exchange establishments. **American Express** cards also work in some ATMs, as well as at AmEx offices and major airports. All such machines require a **Personal Identification Number (PIN).** You must ask your credit card company for a PIN before you leave; without it, you will be unable to withdraw cash with your credit card outside your home country. If you already have a PIN, check with the company to make sure it will work in Austria and Switzerland. As an extra bonus, many credit cards offer an array of other services, from insurance to emergency assistance.

Visa (U.S. tel. (800) 336 8472) and **MasterCard** (tel. (800) 307 7309) are issued in cooperation with individual banks and some other organizations. **American Express**

(U.S. tel. (800) 843 2273) has an annual fee of up to US$55, depending on the card. Cardholder services include the option of cashing personal checks at AmEx offices, a 24-hour hotline with medical and legal assistance in emergencies (tel. (800) 554 2639 in U.S. and Canada; from abroad call U.S. collect 1 202 554 2639), and the American Express Travel Service. Benefits include assistance in changing airline, hotel, and car rental reservations, baggage loss and flight insurance, sending mailgrams and international cables, and holding your mail at one of the more than 1700 AmEx offices around the world. The **Discover Card** (U.S. tel. (800) 347 2683; outside U.S., call 1 801 902 3100) offers small cash-back bonuses on most purchases, but it may not be readily accepted in Austria and Switzerland.

CASH OR DEBIT CARDS

Cash or debit cards—often called ATM (Automated Teller Machine) cards—can be used throughout Austria and Switzerland (and you can usually get an better rate of exchange with them, for a nominal fee). ATMs get the same wholesale exchange rate as credit cards. Despite these perks, do some research before relying too heavily on automation. There is often a limit on the amount of money you can withdraw per day (usually about US$500, depending on the type of card and account), and computer networks sometimes fail. If you're traveling from the U.S. or Canada, memorize your PIN code in numeral form since machines elsewhere often don't have letters on their keys. Also, if your PIN is longer than 4 digits, ask your bank whether the first 4 digits will work, or whether you need a new number. The two major international money networks are **Cirrus** (U.S. tel. (800) 4-CIRRUS, or (800) 424 7787) and **PLUS** (U.S. tel. (800) 843 7587 for the "Voice Response Unit Locator"). Look for signs reading "Bankomat" with a green or blue "B," and compare the symbols on the back of your card with those above the machine to find out which machines your card will work in.

ATM ALERT. All automatic teller machines require a 4-digit **Personal Identification Number (PIN),** which credit cards in the United States do not always carry. You must ask your credit card company to assign you one before you leave. Without a PIN, you will be unable to withdraw cash with your credit card abroad. There are no letters on the keypads of European ATMs, so work out your PIN numerically: ABC correspond to 2; DEF to 3; GHI to 4; JKL to 5; MNO to 6; PRS to 7; TUV to 8; and WXY to 9. If you punch the wrong code into an ATM 3 times it will eat your card. If you lose your card, call for help at the following toll-free numbers, all of which have English-speaking operators: **MasterCard** (tel. (0800) 90 13 87); **Visa** (tel. (0800) 90 20 33); **American Express** (tel. (0147) 77 72 00).

GETTING MONEY FROM HOME

AMERICAN EXPRESS. Cardholders can withdraw cash from their checking accounts at any of AmEx's major offices and many representative offices, up to US$1000 every 21 days (no service charge, no interest). AmEx also offers Express Cash at any of their ATMs or offices in Austria and Switzerland. Express Cash withdrawals are automatically debited from the cardmember's checking account or line of credit. Green card holders may withdraw up to US$1000 in a 7-day period. There is a 3% transaction fee for each cash withdrawal. To enroll in Express Cash, Cardmembers may call (800) CASH-NOW (227 4669) in the U.S.; outside the U.S. call collect 1 336 333 3211.

WESTERN UNION. Travelers from the U.S., Canada, and the U.K. can wire money abroad through Western Union's international money transfer services. In the U.S., call (800) 325 6000; in the U.K., call (0800) 833 833; in Canada, call (800) 235 0000; in Austria, call 0660 8066, in Switzerland, call the office in Zurich at tel. (512)

ESSENTIALS

Money From Home In Minutes.

If you're stuck for cash on your travels, don't panic. Millions of people trust Western Union to transfer money in minutes to 165 countries and over 50,000 locations worldwide. Our record of safety and reliability is second to none. For more information, call Western Union: USA 1-800-325-6000, Canada 1-800-235-0000. Wherever you are, you're never far from home.

www.westernunion.com

The fastest way to send money worldwide:

223 358. To cable money within the U.S. using a credit card (Visa, MasterCard, Discover), call (800) CALL-CASH (225 5227). The rates for sending cash are generally better than with a credit card, and the money is usually available within an hour.

U.S. STATE DEPARTMENT (U.S. CITIZENS ONLY). In emergencies, U.S. citizens can have money sent via the State Department. For US$15, they will forward money within hours to the nearest consular office, which will disburse it according to instructions. The office serves only Americans in the direst of straits abroad; non-American travelers should contact their embassies for information on wiring cash. Check with the State Department or the nearest U.S. embassy or consulate for the quickest way to have the money sent. Contact the Overseas Citizens Service, American Citizens Services, Consular Affairs, Room 4811, U.S. Department of State, Washington, D.C. 20520 (tel. (202) 647 5225; nights, Sundays, and holidays tel. (202) 647 4000; fax (on demand only) tel. (202) 647 3000; travel.state.gov).

TIPPING AND BARGAINING

There is technically no need for tipping in Switzerland, as gratuities are already automatically factored into prices; in Austria, menus will say whether service is included (*Preise inklusive* or *Bedienung inklusiv*); if it is, you don't have to tip. If it's not, leave a tip up to about 10%. However, it is considered polite both Austria and Switzerland to round up your bill to the nearest 5 or 10 Schillings as a nod of approval for good service; tell the waiter/waitress how much you want back from the money you give him/her. If you just say "Danke," the waiter/waitress will most likely assume that you intend for him/her to keep the change. Austrian restaurants expect you to seat yourself, and servers will not bring the bill until you ask them to do so. Say *Zahlen bitte* (TSAHL-en BIT-uh) to settle your accounts. Don't leave tips on the table. Be aware that some restaurants charge for each piece of bread that you eat during your meal.

Don't expect to bargain in shops or markets in Austria and Switzerland, except at flea markets and the Naschmarkt in Vienna. Most prices are fixed. If you are concerned about getting ripped off by taxi drivers or shopkeepers, get a few price quotes for the route or purchase so you know what range is reasonable.

TAXES

 Make sure you have your unused purchases and the U-34 form ON YOUR PERSON at the airport or train station so you can get the form validated and your taxes back!

No taxes are added to purchases made in Switzerland. In Austria, there is a 20% to 34% value added tax (VAT) on all books, clothing, souvenir items, art items, jewelry, perfume, cigarettes, alcohol, etc. Tourists must pay this tax at the time of purchase, but may get the tax refunded later if the amount of purchase is 1000AS (US$95) or greater at a particular store. To get the refund, fill out the Form U-34, available at most stores, and an ÖAMTC quick refund form to get a check at the airport or train station. Make sure the store affixes their store identification stamp to the forms at the time of purchase. When you leave the country, go to the VAT or Customs office (often located in the airport or train station) to get your form validated. To get the form validated, you must have the (unused) items on your person! They will then issue you a check for the amount of the refund, which can be cashed at bank tellers in the airport or train station.

SAFETY AND SECURITY

GENERAL SAFETY TIPS. Austria and Switzerland are relatively safe countries, so most safety and security concerns can be resolved by using common sense. In general, safety means not looking like a target. Tourists are particularly vulnerable to crime because they often carry large amounts of cash and are not as street savvy as locals. The gawking camera-toter is a more obvious target than the low-profile traveler, so avoid unwanted attention by trying to blend in. Familiarize yourself with your surroundings before setting out; if you must check a map on the street, duck into a cafe or shop. Also, carry yourself with confidence, as an obviously bewildered bodybuilder is more likely to be harassed than a stern and confident 98-pound weakling. If you are traveling alone, be sure that someone at home knows your itinerary and never admit that you're traveling alone. When you arrive in a new city, find out what areas to avoid from tourist information or the manager of your hostel. Stick to busy, well-lit streets. Whenever possible, *Let's Go* warns of unsafe neighborhoods and areas, such as drug hangouts (near the Parliament or along the Aare River in Bern; "Needle Park" in Zurich). Use your best judgement; if an area feels unsafe, don't wait to find out if your instincts are correct!

For a back-up plan, **Travel Assistance International** by **Worldwide Assistance Services, Inc.** (www.worldwide-assistance.com) provides its members with a 24-hour hotline for travel emergencies and referrals in over 200 countries. Their Per-Trip (starting at US$21) and Frequent Traveler (starting at US$88) plans include medical, travel, and communication services. Call (800) 821 2828 or (202) 828 5894, fax (202) 828 5896, email wassist@aol.com, or write them at 1133 15th St. NW, Ste. 400, Washington, D.C. 20005-2710. The **American Society of Travel Agents** provides extensive informational resources both at their website (www.astanet.com) and in their free brochure, *Travel Safety*. Get a copy by sending a request and self-addressed, stamped envelope to 1101 King St., Suite 200, Alexandria, VA 22314.

EMERGENCY NUMBERS.
In Austria: **police 133; fire 122; ambulance 144.**
In Switzerland: **police 117; fire 118; ambulance 144.**

SELF-DEFENSE. There is no sure-fire set of precautions that will protect you from all of the situations you might encounter when you travel. A good self-defense course will give you more concrete ways to react to different types of aggression. **Impact, Prepare, and Model Mugging** can refer you to local self-defense courses in the United States (tel. (800) 345 5425) and Vancouver, Canada (tel. (604) 878 3838). Workshop (2-3 hours) start at US$50 and full courses run US$350-500. Both women and men are welcome.

DRIVING SAFELY. Driving in Austria and Switzerland is a pleasant but expensive proposition. The roads are well maintained with the money drivers pay for the right to drive here (they won't even let you on the Autobahn in Switzerland without a permit sticker). Be sure to observe the speed limit and don't drive drunk—the Austrian and Swiss police will not hesitate to take away your license and your car if you have any alcohol in your blood. If you decide to drive a car, learn local driving signals and wear a seatbelt. Children under 40lbs. should ride only in a specially-designed carseat, available for a small fee from most car rental agencies. Study route maps before you hit the road; depending on the region, some roads have poor (or nonexistent) shoulders, few gas stations, and roaming animals. Twisty mountains roads may be closed in winter but, when open, require particular caution. Learn the **Alpine honk:** when going blind around an abrupt turn, stop and give the horn a toot before proceeding. Shift to low gear, drive slowly, brake occasionally, and *never ever* pass anyone, no matter how slow they're going.

If you plan on spending a lot of time on the road, you may want to bring spare parts. For long drives in desolate areas invest in a cellular phone and a roadside assistance program (see p. 47). Be sure to park your vehicle in a garage or well-traveled area, and use a steering wheel locking device in larger cities. Try not to leave valuable possessions—such as radios or luggage—in it while you are away. If your tape deck or radio is removable, hide it in the trunk or take it with you. If it isn't, at least conceal it under something else. Similarly, hide baggage in the trunk—although savvy thieves can tell if a car is heavily loaded by the way it sits on its tires. **Sleeping in your car** is one of the most dangerous (and often illegal) ways to get your rest, second only to sleeping in the open. If your car breaks down, wait for the police to assist you.

Let's Go does not recommend **hitchhiking** under any circumstances, particularly for women—see **Getting Around,** p. 43, for more information.

PROTECTING YOUR VALUABLES. Although Austria and Switzerland have generally low crime rates, thieves are happy to relieve ignorant tourists of their money. Be on the alert, particularly in crowds and city traffic. Beware of classic scams: sob stories that require money, distractions that allow enough time to steal your bag, and little kids with big newspapers. To prevent easy theft, don't keep all your valuables (money, important documents) in one place. **Photocopies** of important documents allow you to recover them in case they are lost or filched. Carry 1 copy separate from the documents and leave another copy at home. Label every piece of luggage both inside and out. **Don't carry your wallet or money in your back pocket.** Never count your money in public and carry as little as possible. If you carry a purse, buy a sturdy one with a secure clasp, and carry it crosswise on the side, away from the street with the clasp against you. Secure packs with small combination padlocks which slip through the 2 zippers. A **money belt** is the best way to carry cash; you can buy one at most camping supply stores. A nylon, zippered pouch with a belt that sits inside the waist of your pants or skirt combines convenience and security. A **neck pouch** is equally safe, though less accessible. Refrain from pulling it out in public; if you must, be very discreet. Avoid keeping anything precious in a waist-pack: your valuables will be highly visible and easy to steal. Keep some money separate from the rest to use for emergencies or in case of theft.

In public, watch your belongings at all times. Beware of con artists and **pickpockets** on the street and on public transportation (although neither Austria nor Switzerland has a big problem with street crime). On buses and trains, keep your bag close to you: don't check your baggage on trains, don't trust anyone to "watch your bag for a second," and don't ever put it under your seat in train compartments. If you take a **night train,** either lock your bag to the luggage rack or use it as a pillow. In your hostel, if you can't lock your room, lock your bag in lockers or at the train station (you'll need your own **padlock**).

DRUGS AND ALCOHOL. Drugs could easily ruin a trip. Every year thousands of travelers are arrested for trafficking or possession of drugs or for simply being in the company of a suspected user. Marijuana, hashish, cocaine, and narcotics are illegal in Austria and Switzerland, and the penalties for illegal possession of drugs, especially for foreigners, range from stern to severe. You may be imprisoned or deported, and a meek "I didn't know it was illegal" will not suffice. It is not unknown for a dealer to increase profits by first selling drugs to tourists and then turning them in to the authorities for a reward. Even such reputedly liberal cities as Vienna, Salzburg, and Zurich take an officially dim view of mussed-up tourists. The worst thing you can possibly do is carry drugs across an international border—you could not only end up in prison but also be hounded by a "Drug Trafficker" stamp on your passport for the rest of your life. If you are arrested, all your home country's consulate can do is visit, provide a list of attorneys, and inform family and friends. Remember that you are subject to the laws of the country in which you travel, not to those of your home country, and it is your responsibility to familiarize yourself with these laws before leaving.

Police officers, members of the *Polizei* or *Gendarmerie,* typically speak little English and tend to be very businesslike. Treat the police with the utmost respect at all times. Imbibing **alcohol** in Austria and Switzerland is generally trouble-free—beer is more common than soda, and a lunch without wine or beer would be unusual. In Switzerland, you must be 16 to drink legally. Each Austrian province sets a legal minimum drinking age; typically, anyone over 18 can drink whatever he or she wishes, and drinking beer is often legal at younger ages .

FURTHER INFORMATION. The following government offices provide travel information and advisories by telephone or on their websites:

Australian Department of Foreign Affairs and Trade, tel. (02) 6261 1111; www.dfat.gov.au.

Canadian Department of Foreign Affairs and International Trade (DFAIT), tel. (800) 267 8376 or (613) 944 4000 from Ottawa; www.dfait-maeci.gc.ca. Call for their free booklet, *Bon Voyage...But.*

United Kingdom Foreign and Commonwealth Office, tel. (0171) 238 45 03; www.fco.gov.uk.

United States Department of State, tel. (202) 647 5225. On the web, travel.state.gov. For their publication *A Safe Trip Abroad,* call (202) 512 1800.

HEALTH

Common sense is the simplest prescription for good health while you travel. Travelers complain most often about their feet and their gut, so take precautionary measures: drink lots of fluids to prevent dehydration and constipation, wear sturdy, broken-in shoes and clean socks, and use talcum powder to keep your feet dry. To minimize the effects of jet lag, "reset" your body's clock by adopting the time of your destination as soon as you board the plane.

BEFORE YOU GO

Preparation can help minimize the likelihood of contracting a disease and maximize the chances of receiving effective health care in the event of an emergency. Make sure you get a statement and prescription from your doctor if you'll be carrying insulin, syringes, or prescription medicine. Leave all medication in original, labeled containers. What is legal at home may not be legal abroad; check with your doctor or the appropriate foreign consulate to avoid nasty surprises. For minor health problems, bring a compact **first-aid kit,** including bandages, aspirin or other pain killer, antibiotic cream, a thermometer, a Swiss army knife with tweezers, moleskin, decongestant for colds, motion sickness remedy, medicine for diarrhea or stomach problems (Pepto Bismol tablets or liquid and Immodium), sunscreen, insect repellent, and burn ointment.

In your **passport,** write the names of any people you wish to be contacted in case of a medical emergency, and also list any **allergies** or medical conditions you would want doctors to be aware of. Allergy sufferers might want to obtain a full supply of any necessary medication before the trip. Matching a prescription to a foreign equivalent is not always easy, safe, or possible. Carry up-to-date, legible prescriptions or a statement from your doctor stating the medication's trade name, manufacturer, chemical name, and dosage. While traveling, be sure to keep all medication with you in your carry-on luggage.

IMMUNIZATIONS. Take a look at your immunization records before you go. Travelers over two years old should be sure that the following vaccines are up to date: MMR (for measles, mumps, and rubella); DTaP or Td (for diphtheria, tetanus, and pertussis); OPV (for polio); HbCV (for haemophilus influenza B); and HBV (for hepatitis B). Check with a doctor for guidance through this maze of injections.

USEFUL ORGANIZATIONS. The U.S. **Centers for Disease Control and Prevention (CDC)** (tel. (888) 232 3299; www.cdc.gov) is an excellent source of information with an international fax information service for travelers. The CDC also publishes the booklet *Health Information for International Travelers* (US$20), an annual global rundown of disease, immunization, and general health advice, including risks in particular countries. This book may be purchased by sending a check or money order to the Superintendent of Documents, U.S. Government Printing

Office, P.O. Box 371954, Pittsburgh, PA, 15250-7954. Orders can be made by phone (tel. (202) 512 1800) with a major credit card (Visa, MasterCard, or Discover).

The **United States State Department** (travel.state.gov) compiles Consular Information Sheets on health, entry requirements, and other issues for all countries of the world. For quick information on travel warnings, call the **Overseas Citizens' Services** (tel. (202) 647 5225; after-hours 647 4000). To receive the same Consular Information Sheets by fax, dial (202) 647 3000 directly from a fax machine and follow the recorded instructions. The State Department's regional passport agencies in the U.S., field offices of the U.S. Chamber of Commerce, and U.S. embassies and consulates abroad provide the same data, or send a self-addressed, stamped envelope to the Overseas Citizens' Services, Bureau of Consular Affairs, #4811, U.S. Department of State, Washington, D.C. 20520.

FURTHER READING. For detailed information and tips on travel health, including a country-by-country overview of diseases, check out the *International Travel Health Guide*, Stuart Rose, MD (Travel Medicine, $20). Information is also available at Travel Medicine's website (www.travmed.com).

For general health information, contact the **American Red Cross.** The ARC publishes *First-Aid and Safety Handbook* (US$5) available for purchase by calling or writing to the American Red Cross, 285 Columbus Ave., Boston, MA 02116-5114 (tel. (800) 564 1234; M-F 8:30am-4:30pm).

MEDICAL ASSISTANCE ON THE ROAD. Medical care in Austria and Switzerland is generally excellent. Most doctors and pharmacists speak at least some English. If you are concerned about being able to access medical support while traveling, contact one of these two services: **Global Emergency Medical Services (GEMS)** markets a *MedPass* that provide 24-hour international medical assistance and support coordinated through registered nurses who have online access to your medical information, your primary physician, and a worldwide network of screened, accredited English-speaking doctors and hospitals. Subscribers also receive a personal medical record that contains vital information in case of emergencies, and GEMS will pay for medical evacuation if necessary. Prices start at about US$35 for a 30-day trip and run up to about $100 for annual services. For more information contact them at 2001 Westside Dr. #120, Alpharetta, GA 30004 (tel. (800) 860 1111; fax (770) 475 0058; www.globalems.com). The **International Association for Medical Assistance to Travelers (IAMAT)** has free membership and offers a directory of English-speaking doctors around the world who treat members for a set fee schedule, and detailed charts on immunization requirements, various tropical diseases, climate, and sanitation. Chapters include: **U.S.,** 417 Center St., Lewiston, NY 14092 (tel. (716) 754 4883, 8am-4pm; fax (519) 836 3412; email iamat@sentex.net; www.sentex.net/~iamat); **Canada,** 40 Regal Road, Guelph, ON, N1K 1B5 (tel. (519) 836 0102) or 1287 St. Clair Ave. West, Toronto, ON M6E 1B8 (tel. (416) 652 0137; fax (519) 836 3412); **New Zealand,** P.O. Box 5049, Christchurch 5 (fax (03) 352 4630; email iamat@chch.planet.org.nz).

If your regular **insurance** policy does not cover travel abroad, you may wish to purchase additional coverage. With the exception of Medicare, most health insurance plans cover members' medical emergencies during trips abroad; check with your insurance carrier to be sure. For more information, see **Insurance,** p. 26.

SPECIAL MEDICAL CONDITIONS. Those with medical conditions (e.g., diabetes, allergies to antibiotics, epilepsy, heart conditions) may want to obtain a stainless steel **Medic Alert** identification tag (US$35 the first year, and $15 annually thereafter), which identifies the condition and gives a 24-hour collect-call information number. Contact the Medic Alert Foundation, 2323 Colorado Ave., Turlock, CA 95382 (tel. (800) 825 3785; www.medicalert.org). Diabetics can contact the **American Diabetes Association,** 1660 Duke St., Alexandria, VA 22314 (tel. (800) 232 3472), to receive copies of the article "Travel and Diabetes" and a diabetic ID card, which carries messages in 18 languages explaining the carrier's diabetic status.

ESSENTIALS

PREVENTING ILLNESS

HEAT EXHAUSTION, DEHYDRATION, AND SUNBURN. Heat exhaustion can lead to fatigue, headaches, and wooziness. Avoid **heat exhaustion** by drinking plenty of clear fluids (enough to keep your urine clear). Alcoholic beverages are dehydrating, as are coffee, strong tea, and caffeinated sodas. Wear a hat, sunglasses, and a lightweight longsleeve shirt in hot sun, and take time to acclimate to a hot destination before seriously exerting yourself. Continuous heat stress can eventually lead to **heatstroke,** characterized by rising body temperature, severe headache, and cessation of sweating. Heatstroke is rare but serious, and victims must be cooled off with wet towels and taken to a doctor as soon as possible. If you're prone to **sunburn,** apply sunscreen liberally and often. If you are planning on spending time near water or in the snow, you are at risk of getting burned, even through clouds. Protect your eyes with good sunglasses, since ultraviolet rays can damage the retina of the eye after too much exposure. If you get sunburned, drink more fluids than usual and apply Calamine or an aloe-based lotion.

HYPOTHERMIA, FROSTBITE, AND HIGH ALTITUDE. A rapid drop in body temperature is the clearest warning sign of overexposure to cold. Victims may also shiver, feel exhausted, have poor coordination or slurred speech, hallucinate, or suffer amnesia. Seek medical help, and *do not let hypothermia victims fall asleep*—their body temperature will continue to drop and they may die. To avoid **hypothermia,** keep dry, wear layers, and stay out of the wind. In wet weather, wool and synthetics such as pile retain heat. Most other fabric, especially cotton, will make you colder. When the temperature is below freezing, watch for **frostbite.** If skin turns white, waxy, and cold, do not rub the area. Drink warm beverages, get dry, and slowly warm the area with dry fabric or steady body contact, until a doctor can be found. Travelers to **high altitudes** must allow their bodies a couple of days to adjust to lower oxygen levels in the air before exerting themselves. Alcohol is more potent at high elevations. High altitudes mean that ultraviolet rays are stronger and the risk of sunburn is increased, even in cold weather.

INSECT-BORNE DISEASES. Many diseases are transmitted by insects—mainly mosquitoes, fleas, ticks, and lice. Be aware of insects in wet or forested areas, while hiking, and especially while camping. **Mosquitoes** are most active from dusk to dawn. Use insect repellents, such as DEET. Wear long pants and long sleeves (fabric need not be thick or warm; tropic-weight cottons can keep you comfortable in the heat) and buy a mosquito net. Wear shoes and socks, and tuck long pants into socks. Soak or spray your gear with permethrin, which is licensed in the U.S. for use on clothing. Natural repellents can be useful supplements: taking vitamin B-12 pills regularly can eventually make you smelly to insects, as can garlic pills. Calamine lotion or topical cortisones (like Cortaid) may stop insect bites from itching, as can a bath with a half-cup of baking soda or oatmeal. **Ticks**—responsible for Lyme and other diseases—can be particularly dangerous in rural and forested regions. Pause periodically while walking to brush off ticks using a fine-toothed comb on your neck and scalp. Do not try to remove ticks by burning them or coating them with nail polish remover or petroleum jelly.

Tick-borne encephalitis, a viral infection of the central nervous system, is transmitted during the summer by tick bites, and also by consumption of unpasteurized dairy products. The disease occurs most often in wooded areas. Symptoms can range from nothing to headaches and flu-like symptoms to swelling of the brain (encephalitis). A vaccine is available in Europe, but the immunization schedule is impractical for most tourists, and the risk of contracting the disease is relatively low, especially if you take precautions against tick bites. **Lyme disease,** also carried by ticks, is a bacterial infection marked by a circular bull's-eye rash of 2 in. or more that appears around the bite. Other symptoms include fever, headache, tiredness, and aches and pains. Antibiotics are effective if administered early. Left untreated, Lyme can cause problems in joints, the heart, and the nervous system. If you find a tick attached to your skin, grasp the tick's head parts with tweezers as close to your skin as possible and apply slow, steady traction. If you remove a tick within 24 hours, you greatly reduce your risk of infection.

OTHER INFECTIOUS DISEASES. Rabies is transmitted through the saliva of infected animals. It is fatal if untreated. Avoid contact with animals, especially strays. If you are bitten, wash the wound thoroughly and seek immediate medical care. **Hepatitis B** is a viral infection of the liver transmitted through the transfer of bodily fluids, by sharing needles, or by having unprotected sex. Its incubation period varies and can be much longer than the 30-day incubation period of Hepatitis A. Individuals may not begin to show symptoms until many years after infection. The CDC recommends the Hepatitis B vaccination for health-care workers, sexually active travelers, and anyone planning to seek medical treatment abroad. Vaccination consists of a 3-shot series given over a period of time, and should begin 6 months before traveling. **Hepatitis C** is like Hepatitis B, but the modes of transmission are different. Intravenous drug users, those with occupational exposure to blood, hemodialysis patients, or recipients of blood transfusions are at the highest risk, but the disease can also be spread through sexual contact and sharing of items like razors and toothbrushes, which may have traces of blood on them.

AIDS, HIV, STDS

Your risk of getting HIV, AIDS, and other STDs depends entirely upon you. The easiest mode of HIV transmission is through direct blood-to-blood contact with an HIV-positive person; *never* share intravenous drug, tattooing, or other needles. The most common mode of transmission is sexual intercourse. Health professionals recommend abstinence or the use of latex condoms. *Let's Go* lists AIDS-hotlines and testing centers where available. For more information on AIDS, call the **U.S. Centers for Disease Control's** 24-hour hotline at tel. (800) 342 2437. In Europe, contact the **World Health Organization,** Attn: Global Program on AIDS, Avenue Appia 20, 1211 Geneva 27, Switzerland (tel. 44 22 791 21 11, fax 791 31 11), for statistical material on AIDS internationally. Council's brochure, *Travel Safe: AIDS and International Travel*, is available at all Council Travel offices and at their website (www.ciee.org/study/safety/travelsafe.htm).

Sexually transmitted diseases (STDs) such as gonorrhea, chlamydia, genital warts, syphilis, and herpes are easier to catch than HIV, and some can be just as deadly. **Hepatitis B** and **C** are also serious sexually-transmitted diseases (see **Other Infectious Diseases,** above). Warning signs for STDs include: swelling, sores, bumps, or blisters on sex organs, rectum, or mouth; burning and pain during urination and bowel movements; itching around sex organs; swelling or redness in the throat; and flu-like symptoms with fever, chills, and aches. If these symptoms develop, see a doctor immediately. During intercourse, condoms may protect you from certain STDs, but oral or even tactile contact can lead to transmission.

WOMEN'S HEALTH

Women traveling in unsanitary conditions are vulnerable to **urinary tract** and **bladder infections,** common bacterial diseases that cause a burning sensation and painful and sometimes frequent urination. To try to avoid these infections, drink plenty of vitamin-C-rich juice and plenty of clean water, and urinate frequently, especially right after intercourse. Untreated, these infections can lead to kidney infections, sterility, and even death. If symptoms persist, see a doctor.

Women are also susceptible to **vaginal yeast infections,** a treatable but uncomfortable illness likely to flare up in hot and humid climates. Wearing loosely fitting trousers or a skirt and cotton underwear will help. Yeast infections can be treated with an over-the-counter remedy like Monostat or Gynelotrimin. Bring supplies from home if you are prone to infection, as they may be difficult to find on the road. Some travelers opt for a natural alternative such as plain yogurt and lemon juice douche if other remedies are unavailable.

Your preferred brands of **tampons** and **pads** may not be available, so consider taking supplies along. **Reliable contraceptive devices** may also be difficult to find. Women on the pill should bring enough to allow for possible loss or extended stays. Bring a prescription, since forms of the pill vary a good deal. Women who use a diaphragm should bring enough contraceptive jelly. Though condoms are widely available, you might want to bring your favorite brand before you go, as availability and quality vary. Women who choose to have an **abortion** while abroad should contact the **International Planned Parenthood Federation,** European Regional Office, Regent's College Inner Circle, Regent's Park, London NW1 4NS (tel. 44 171 487 7900; fax 487 7950), for more information.

FURTHER READING: WOMEN'S HEALTH.
Handbook for Women Travellers, Maggie and Gemma Moss. Piatkus Books (US$15).
Adventures in Good Company: The Complete Guide to Women's Tours and Out-door Trips, Thalia Zepatos. The Eighth Mountain Press (US$17).

INSURANCE

Travel insurance generally covers four basic areas: medical/health problems, property loss, trip cancellation/interruption, and emergency evacuation. Although your regular insurance policies may well extend to travel-related accidents, you may consider purchasing travel insurance if the cost of potential trip cancellation/interruption is greater than you can absorb.

ISIC and **ITIC** provide basic insurance benefits, including US$100 per day of in-hospital sickness for a maximum of 60 days, US$3000 of accident-related medical reimbursement, and US$25,000 for emergency medical transport (see **Identification,** p. 12). Cardholders have access to a toll-free 24-hour helpline whose multilingual staff can provide assistance in medical, legal, and financial emergencies overseas (tel. (800) 626 2427 in the U.S. and Canada; elsewhere call the U.S. collect (713) 267 2525. **American Express** (tel. (800) 528 4800) grants most cardholders automatic car rental insurance (collision and theft, but not liability) and ground travel accident coverage of US$100,000 on flight purchases made with the card.

Prices for travel insurance purchased separately generally run about US$50 per week for full coverage, while trip cancellation/interruption may be purchased separately at a rate of about US$5.50 per US$100 of coverage.

INSURANCE PROVIDERS. Council and **STA Travel** (see p. 40 for complete listings) offer a range of plans that can supplement your basic insurance coverage. Other private insurance providers in the **U.S. and Canada** include: **Access America** (tel. (800) 284 8300; fax (804) 673 1491); **Berkely Group/Carefree Travel Insurance** (tel. (800) 323 3149 or (516) 294 0220; fax 294 1095; info@berkely.com; www.berkely.com); **Globalcare Travel Insurance** (tel. (800) 821 2488; fax (781) 592 7720; www.globalcare-cocco.com); and **Travel Assistance International** (tel. (800) 821 2828 or (202) 828 5894; fax 828 5896; email wassist@aol.com; www.worldwide-assistance.com). Providers in the **U.K.** include **Campus Travel** (tel. (01865) 25 80 00; fax 79 23 78) and **Columbus Travel Insurance** (tel. (0171) 375 00 11; fax 375 00 22). In **Australia,** try **CIC Insurance** (tel. (02) 9202 8000; fax 9202 8220).

PACKING

Pack according to the extremes of climate you may experience and the type of travel you'll be doing. **Pack light:** a good rule is to lay out only what you absolutely need, then take half the clothes and twice the money. The less you have, the less you have to lose (or store or carry on your back). Don't forget the obvious things:

PACKING LIGHT, THE AUSTRIAN WAY In the summer of 1870, when the air was clean and all snow came from clouds, Austrian climbing legend Hermann von Barth took to the hills of the Karwendel Range in Tyrol and climbed no fewer than 88 peaks, 12 of which were first-ever ascents. His luggage consisted simply of a drinking cup, binoculars, smelling salts, a lighter, a can of paint and a paintbrush to paint his name on each peak, and a bottle of poison in case he fell and wasn't able to rescue himself. He never fell.

no matter when you're traveling, it's always a good idea to bring a rain jacket (Gore-Tex® is a miracle fabric that's both waterproof and breathable), a warm jacket or wool sweater, and sturdy shoes and thick socks. If you plan to be doing a lot of hiking, see **Camping and the Outdoors,** p. 31. Even casual hikers should bring water-proof **hiking boots;** pavement-pounding city-types should wear well-cushioned **sneakers.** Break in your shoes before you leave. A double pair of socks—light silk or polypropylene inside and thick wool outside—will cushion feet, keep them dry, and help prevent blisters. Remember that wool will keep you warm even when soaked through, whereas wet cotton is colder than wearing nothing at all. You may also want to add one dressier outfit beyond the jeans and t-shirt uniform, and a nicer pair of shoes if you have room. Be prepared for sudden weather shifts.

LUGGAGE. If you plan to cover a lot of ground on your travels, a sturdy **frame backpack** will be your best investment. **Internal-frame packs** mold better to your back, keep a lower center of gravity, and can flex adequately on difficult hikes that require a lot of bending and maneuvering. **External-frame packs** are more comfortable for long hikes over even terrain—like city streets—since they keep the weight higher and distribute it more evenly, but they make moving around trains very awkward. Look for a pack with a strong, padded hip belt to transfer weight from your shoulders to your hips. Good packs cost anywhere from US$150 to US$500. Before you leave, pack your bag, strap it on, and imagine yourself walking uphill on hot asphalt for three hours; this should give you a sense of how important it is to pack lightly. Organizations that sell packs through mail-order are listed on p. 32.

Toting a **suitcase** is fine if you plan to live in one or two cities and explore from there, but a very bad idea if you're going to be moving around a lot. Make sure suitcases have a handle and wheels that roll easily and consider how much they weigh even when empty. Hard-sided luggage is more durable but more weighty and cumbersome. Soft-sided luggage should have a PVC frame, a strong lining to resist bad weather and rough handling, and its seams should be triple-stitched for durability. In addition, you'll need a small backpack, rucksack, or courier bag will be very useful as a **daypack** for sight-seeing expeditions; it doubles as an airplane **carry-on.** An empty, lightweight **duffel bag** packed inside your luggage may also be useful.

SLEEPSACKS. Some youth hostels require that you have your own sleepsack or rent one of theirs. If you plan to stay in hostels often you can avoid linen charges

USEFUL THINGS TO BRING:
First-aid kit: moleskin (for blisters), medications, vitamins (see **Health,** p. 22).
Laundry supplies, such as a travel clothesline and small carton of detergent.
Shower supplies: towel, shampoo, slippers for the shower, soap.
Personal hygiene supplies: deodorant, tampons, razors, tweezers, condoms.
Sealable plastic bags (for damp clothes, food, shampoo, and other spillables).
Money belt for carrying valuables; small calculator for currency conversion.
Useful items: travel alarm clock, pocketknife, water bottle, needle and thread, safety pins, umbrella, sunscreen, sunglasses, sun hat, insect repellent, padlock, earplugs, flashlight, compass, string, electrical tape (for repairing tears).

by making the requisite sleepsack yourself: fold a full size sheet in half the long way, then sew it closed along the open long side and one of the short sides. Sleepsacks can also be bought at any Hostelling International outlet store.

ELECTRIC CURRENT. In Austria and Switzerland, electricity is 220V AC, enough to fry any 110V North American appliance. You can get an adapter (which changes the shape of the plug) and a converter (which changes the voltage) at a hardware store. Don't make the mistake of using only an adapter (unless appliance instructions explicitly state otherwise).

CONTACT LENSES. Machines which heat-disinfect contact lenses will require a small converter (about US$20) to 220V. Consider switching temporarily to a chemical disinfection system, but check with your lens dispenser to see if it's safe to switch; some lenses may be damaged by a chemical system. Contact lens supplies may be expensive and difficult to find; bring enough for your entire vacation.

FILM. Film in Austria and Switzerland costs about the same as anywhere else, generally around US$7 for a roll of 24 color exposures. If you're not a serious photographer, you might consider bringing a **disposable camera** rather than an expensive permanent one. Always pack film and cameras in your carry-on luggage.

FURTHER READING: PACKING.
The Packing Book, by Judith Gilford. Ten Speed Press (US$9).
Backpacking One Step at a Time, Harvey Manning. Vintage (US$15).

ACCOMMODATIONS

Like most things Austrian and Swiss, accommodations in these countries are usually clean, orderly, and expensive. Wherever you stay, be sure to ask for a **guest card.** Normally, the "card" is merely a copy of your receipt for the night's lodging, sometimes available only after staying 3 nights or more. Guest cards generally grant discounts to local sports facilities, hiking excursions, town museums, and public transportation. In Austria, the 10AS tax that most accommodations slap on bills funds these discounts—take advantage of them to get your money's worth.

Let's Go is not an exhaustive guide to budget accommodations. Most local tourist offices distribute extensive listings (the *Gastgeberverzeichnis*), and many will reserve a room for a small fee. National tourist offices can also supply more complete lists of campsites and hotels. Be aware that *Privatzimmer* and *Pensionen* may close their doors without notice; it's best to call ahead.

HOSTELS

Hostels (*Jugendherbergen* in German, *Auberges de Jeunesse* in French, *Ostelli* in Italian) are the hubs of the gigantic backpacker subculture that rumbles through Europe every summer, providing innumerable opportunities to meet travelers from all over the world. Hostels generally offer dorm-style accommodations, often in single-sex large rooms with bunk beds, although some hostels do offer private rooms for families and couples. They sometimes have kitchens and utensils for your use, bike or moped rentals, storage areas, and laundry facilities. There can be drawbacks: some hostels close during certain daytime "lock-out" hours, have a curfew, don't accept reservations, impose a maximum stay, or, less frequently, require that you do chores. In Austria and Switzerland, a dorm bed in a hostel averages around US$12-$18. Check out the **Internet Guide to Hostelling** (www.hostels.com), which provides a directory of hostels from around the world in addition to oodles of information about hosteling and backpacking worldwide.

A HOSTELER'S BILL OF RIGHTS. There are certain standard features that we do not include in our hostel listings. Unless we state otherwise, you can expect that every hostel has: no lockout, no curfew, a kitchen, free hot showers, secure luggage storage, and no key deposit.

Eurotrip (www.eurotrip.com/accommodation/accommodation.html) has information and reviews on budget hostels and several international hostel associations.

For their various services and lower rates at member hostels, hostelling associations, especially **Hostelling International (HI),** are worth joining. HI hostels are scattered throughout Austria and Switzerland and many accept reservations via the International Booking Network (tel. (02) 9261 11 11 from Australia, (800) 663 5777 from Canada, (01629) 58 14 18 from the U.K., (01) 301 766 from Ireland, (09) 379 4224 from New Zealand, (800) 909 4776 from U.S.; www.hiayh.org/ushostel/reserva/ibn3.htm) for a nominal fee. HI's umbrella organization's web page lists the web addresses and phone numbers of all national associations and can be a great place to begin researching hostelling in a specific region (www.iyhf.org). Other comprehensive hostelling websites include www.hostels.com and www.eurotrip.com/accommodation. To join HI, contact one of the following organizations:

Australian Youth Hostels Association (AYHA), 422 Kent St., Sydney NSW 2000 (tel. (02) 9261 1111; fax 9261 1969; email yha@yhansw.org.au; www.yha.org.au). 1yr. membership AUS$44, under 18 AUS$13.50.

Hostelling International-Canada (HI-C), 400-205 Catherine St., Ottawa, ON K2P 1C3 (tel. (800) 663 5777 or (613) 237 7884; fax 237 7868; email info@hostellingintl.ca; www.hostellingintl.ca). 1yr. membership CDN$25, under 18 CDN$12; 2-yr. CDN$35.

An Óige (Irish Youth Hostel Association), 61 Mountjoy St., Dublin 7 (tel. (01) 830 4555; fax 830 5808; email anoige@iol.ie; www.irelandyha.org). 1yr. membership IR£10, under 18 IR£4, families IR£20.

Youth Hostels Association of New Zealand (YHANZ), P.O. Box 436, 173 Cashel St., Christchurch 1 (tel. (03) 379 9970; fax 365 4476; email info@yha.org.nz; www.yha.org.nz). 1yr. membership NZ$24, ages 15-17 NZ$12, under 15 free.

Hostelling International South Africa, P.O. Box 4402, Cape Town 8000 (tel. (021) 24 2511; fax 24 4119; email info@hisa.org.za; www.hisa.org.za). 1yr. membership SAR50, under 18 SAR25, lifetime SAR250.

Scottish Youth Hostels Association (SYHA), 7 Glebe Crescent, Stirling FK8 2JA (tel. (01786) 891 400; fax 891 333; email info@syha.org.uk; www.syha.org.uk). Membership UK£6, under 18 UK£2.50.

Youth Hostels Association of England and Wales (YHA), 8 St. Stephen's Hill, St. Albans, Hertfordshire AL1 2DY, England (tel. (01727) 855 215 or 845 047; fax 844 126; email yhacustomerservices@compuserve.com; www.yha.org.uk). 1yr. membership UK£11, under 18 UK£5.50, families UK£22.

Hostelling International Northern Ireland (HINI), 22-32 Donegall Rd., Belfast BT12 5JN, Northern Ireland (tel. (01232) 324 733 or 315 435; fax 439 699; email info@hini.org.uk; www.hini.org.uk). 1yr.membership UK£7, under 18 UK£3, families UK£14.

Hostelling International-American Youth Hostels (HI-AYH), 733 15th St. NW, Suite 840, Washington, D.C. 20005 (tel. (202) 783 6161, ext. 136; fax 783 6171; email hiayhserv@hiayh.org; www.hiayh.org). 1yr. membership US$25, over 54 US$15, under 18 free.

DORMS

Many **colleges and universities,** (see **Vienna: University Dormitories,** p. 98), open their residence halls to travelers when school is not in session—some do so even during term-time. These dorms are often close to student areas—good sources for information on things to do, places to stay, and possible rides out of town—and are usually very clean. Rates tend to be low, and many offer free local calls. *Let's Go* lists colleges that rent dorm rooms among the accommodations for appropriate cities. College dorms are popular with many travelers, especially those looking for long-term lodging, so reserve ahead.

HOTELS

Hotels are expensive in Austria (singles 200-350AS; doubles 400-800AS) and exorbitant in Switzerland (singles 50-75SFr; doubles 80-150SFr). Switzerland has set the international standard for hotels; even 1-, 2-, and 3-star accommodations may be much nicer than their counterparts in other countries. The cheapest hotel-style accommodations have **Gasthof** or **Gästehaus** ("inn") in the name; **Hotel-Garni** also means cheap. Continental breakfast *(Frühstück)* is almost always included.

PRIVATE ROOMS AND PENSIONS

Renting a **private room** *(Privatzimmer)* in a family home is an inexpensive and friendly way to house yourself. Such rooms generally include a sink with hot and cold running water and use of a toilet and shower. Many places rent private rooms only for longer stays, or they may levy a surcharge (10-20%) for stays of less than 3 nights. *Privatzimmern* start at 25 to 60SFr per person in Switzerland. In Austria, rooms range from 250 to 400AS a night. Slightly more expensive, pensions *(Pensionen)* are similar to the American and British notion of a bed-and-breakfast. Generally, finding rooms for only one person might be difficult, especially for 1-night stays. Most places have room with double beds *(Doppelzimmer)*; if the rooms have 2 beds, single travelers will usually have to pay more. Continental breakfast is *de rigueur;* in classier places, meat, cheese, and an egg will grace your plate and palate. Since pensions are people's homes, be sure to treat them kindly. These popular lodgings fill quickly, so reserve ahead.

YMCA AND YWCAS

Not all **Young Men's Christian Association (YMCA)** locations offer lodging; those that do are often located in urban downtowns, which can be convenient but a little gritty. YMCA rates are usually lower than a hotel's but higher than a hostel's and may include the use of TV, air conditioning, pools, gyms, access to public transportation, tourist information, safe deposit boxes, luggage storage, daily housekeeping, multilingual staff, and 24-hour security. Many YMCAs accept women and families (group rates often available), and some will not lodge people under 18 without parental permission. There are several ways to make a reservation, all of which must be made at least two weeks in advance and paid for in advance with a traveler's check, U.S. money order, certified check, Visa, or Mastercard in US dollars. Visit www.ymca.org/otherymca.html.

Y's Way International, 224 E. 47th St., New York, NY 10017 (tel. (212) 308 2899; fax 308 3161). For a small fee (US$3 U.S. and Canada, US$5 elsewhere), this "booking service" makes reservations for the YMCAs in Vienna (tel. (1) 523 13 04), Linz (tel. (0732) 23 99 09), Zurich (tel. (01) 211 56 50), Wengen (tel. (033) 655 27 55), and St. Gallen (tel. (071) 127 89 24).

HOME EXCHANGE AND RENTALS

Home exchange offers the traveler the opportunity to live like a native in various types of homes (houses, apartments, condominiums, villas, even castles in some cases), and to cut down dramatically on accommodation fees—usually only an administration fee is paid to the matching service. Once you join or contact one of the exchange services listed below, it is then up to you to decide with whom you would like to exchange homes (remember—they will be living in your house while you live in theirs). Most companies have pictures of members' homes and information about the owners (some will even ask for your photo!). A great site listing many exchange companies can be found at www.aitec.edu.au/~bwechner/ Documents/Travel/Lists/HomeExchangeClubs.html. In order to assist you with exchanging your home with another person or family that suits your living habits, most companies offer personalized matching services. Home rentals, as opposed to exchanges, are much more expensive, and most likely not an option for the budget traveler. However, they can be cheaper than comparably-serviced hotels, and thus may be suitable for business travelers. Both home exchanges and rentals are ideal for families with children, or travelers with special dietary needs, as you often get access to your own kitchen, maid service, TV, and telephones.

Intervac International Home Exchange, www.intervac.com. For **Austria,** contact Hans and Ingeborg Winkler, Pestalozzistr. 5, A-9100 Völkermarkt (tel. and fax (0423) 23838; email hwinkler@asn-klu.ac.at); **Intervac Switzerland,** Oberdorfstr. 7, CH-9524 Zuzwil (tel./fax (071) 944 27 79; email farewell@blackpoint.ch). You must pay for each catalogue you receive and for listing your home in a catalogue.

The Invented City: International Home Exchange, 41 Sutter St., Suite 1090, San Francisco, CA 94104 (tel. (800) 788 2489 in the U.S. or (415) 252 1141 elsewhere; fax 252 1171; email invented@aol.com; www.invented-city.com). For US$75, you get your offer listed in 1 catalog and unlimited access to the club's database containing thousands of homes for exchange.

fair tours, Postbox 615, CH-9001 St. Gallen, Switzerland (email fairtours@gn.apc.org; www.gn.apc.org/fairtours). is a home exchange program that specializes in offering "personal" service—they take pride in matching home-owners with suitable exchange partners and in providing multi-lingual service for French, Italian and German speakers. After paying a small administration fee (US$40), you pay an additional fee (US$130-$180, depending on your destination) after you have confirmed an exchange arrangement. Contact them via mail or email to receive an application form (which entails a personal cover letter, pictures of yourself and your home, some general tourist info on the city you live in, and the administration fee). Services home-owners in Austria and Switzerland.

CAMPING AND THE OUTDOORS

With over 1200 campgrounds in Switzerland and more than 400 in Austria, camping can be one of the most inexpensive and enjoyable ways of touring Austria and Switzerland. In Switzerland, prices average 6-9SFr per person, 4-10SFr per tent—a joy to behold in such an expensive country. In Austria, prices run 50-70AS per person and 25-60AS per tent (plus 8-9.50AS tax if you're over 15), seldom making camping substantially cheaper than hosteling. You must obtain permission from landowners to camp on private property. Most sites are open in the summer only, but some 80 sites are specifically set aside for winter camping. Camping along roads and in public areas is forbidden. In Switzerland, there are fountains and water-spouts in nearly every town and campsite. The water is clean, so fill your canteens often to prevent dehydration.

USEFUL PUBLICATIONS

Several publishing companies offer hiking guidebooks to meet the educational needs of novice or expert. For information about camping, hiking, and biking, contact the publishers listed below for a free catalogue. You might also consider buying an **International Camping Carnet.** Similar to a hostel membership card, it's required at some campgrounds and provides discounts at others.

ENVIRONMENTALLY RESPONSIBLE TOURISM. The idea behind responsible tourism is to leave no trace of human presence behind. A campstove is the safer (and more efficient) way to cook than using vegetation, but if you must make a fire, keep it small and use only dead branches or brush rather than cutting vegetation. Make sure your campsite is at least 150 ft. (50m) from water supplies or bodies of water. If there are no toilet facilities, bury human waste (but not paper) at least four inches (10cm) deep and above the high-water line, and 150 feet or more from any water supplies and campsites. Always pack your trash in a plastic bag and carry it with you until you reach the next trash can. If you would like more information on these issues, contact one of the organizations listed below.

Earthwatch, 680 Mt. Auburn St., Box 403, Watertown, MA 02272 (tel. (617) 776 0188; fax 926 8532; email info@earthwatch.org; www.earthwatch.org).

Ecotourism Society, P.O. Box 755, North Bennington, VT 05257-0755 (tel. (802) 447 2121; email ecomail@ecotourism.org; www.ecotourism.org/tesinfo.html).

EcoTravel Center: www.ecotour.com.

National Audobon Society, Nature Odysseys, 700 Broadway, New York, NY 10003 (tel. (212) 979 3066; email travel@audobon.org; www.audobon.org).

Tourism Concern, Stapleton House, 277-281 Holloway Rd., London N7 8HN, England (tel. (0170) 753 33 30; www.gn.apc.org/tourismconcern).

Automobile Association, A.A. Publishing. Orders and enquiries to TBS Frating Distribution Centre, Colchester, Essex, CO7 7DW, U.K. (tel. (01206) 25 56 78; www.theaa.co.uk). Publishes *Camping and Caravanning: Europe* (UK£9) and big road atlases for Europe.

Family Campers and RVers/National Campers and Hikers Association, Inc., 4804 Transit Rd., Bldg. #2, Depew, NY 14043 (tel./fax (716) 668 6242). Membership fee (US$25) includes their publication *Camping Today.* For US$35, you can also get the International Camping Carnet, which is required by some European campgrounds, but can usually be bought on the spot.

The Caravan Club, East Grinstead House, East Grinstead, West Sussex, RH19 1UA, U.K. (tel. (01342) 32 69 44; fax 41 02 58; www.caravanclub.co.uk). Produces one of the most detailed English-language guides to campsites in Europe.

The Mountaineers Books, 1001 SW Klickitat Way, #201, Seattle, WA 98134 (tel. (800) 553 4453 or (206) 223 6303; fax 223 6306; email mbooks@mountaineers.org; www.mountaineers.org). Many titles on hiking (the *100 Hikes* series), biking, mountaineering, natural history, and conservation.

CAMPING AND HIKING EQUIPMENT

Purchase equipment before you leave. This way you'll know exactly what you have and how much it weighs. Spend some time examining catalogues and talking to knowledgeable salespeople. Whether buying or renting, finding sturdy, light, and inexpensive equipment is a must. Camping equipment is generally more expensive in Australia, New Zealand, and the U.K. than in North America.

Sleeping Bag: Most good sleeping bags are rated by "season," or the lowest outdoor temperature at which they will keep you warm ("summer" means 30-40°F at night and "four-season" or "winter" often means below 0°F). Sleeping bags are made either of down (warmer and lighter, but more expensive, and miserable when wet) or of synthetic material (heavier, more durable, and warmer when wet). Prices vary, but might range from US$80-210 for a summer synthetic to US$250-300 for a good down winter bag. **Sleeping bag pads,** including foam pads (US$10-20) and air mattresses (US$15-50) cushion your back and neck and insulate you from the ground. **Therm-A-Rest** brand self-inflating sleeping pads are part foam and part air-mattress that partially inflate upon unrolling, US$45-80. Bring a **"stuff sack"** or plastic bag to store your sleeping bag and keep it dry.

Tent: The best tents are free-standing, with their own frames and suspension systems; they set up quickly and only require staking in high winds. Low-profile dome tents are the best all-around. When pitched their internal space is almost entirely usable, which means little unnecessary bulk. Tent sizes can be somewhat misleading: two people *can* fit in a 2-person tent, but will find life more pleasant in a 4-person. If you're traveling by car, go for the bigger tent, but if you're hiking, stick with a smaller tent that weighs no more than 5-6 lbs (2-3kg). Good 2-person tents start at US$90, 4-person tents at US$300. Seal the seams of your tent with waterproofer, and make sure it has a rain fly. Don't forget a **battery-operated lantern,** a **plastic groundcloth,** and a **nylon tarp.**

Backpack: If you intend to do a lot of hiking, you should have a frame backpack. **Internal-frame packs** mold better to your back, keep a lower center of gravity, and can flex adequately to allow you to hike difficult trails that require a lot of bending and maneuvering. **External-frame packs** are more comfortable for long hikes over even terrain since they keep the weight higher and distribute it more evenly. Whichever you choose, make sure your pack has a strong, padded hip belt, which transfers the weight from the shoulders to the legs. Any serious backpacking requires a pack of at least 4000 cubic inches (16,000cc). Allow an additional 500 cubic inches for your sleeping bag in internal-frame packs. Sturdy backpacks cost anywhere from US$125-420. This is one area where it doesn't pay to economize—cheaper packs may be less comfortable, and the straps are more likely to fray or rip. Before you buy any pack, try it on and imagine carrying it, full, a few miles up a rocky incline. Better yet, insist on filling it with something heavy and walking around the store to get a sense of how it distributes weight before committing to buy it. A **waterproof backpack cover** will prove invaluable. Otherwise, plan to store all of your belongings in plastic bags inside your backpack.

Boots: Be sure to wear hiking boots with good **ankle support** which are appropriate for the terrain you plan to hike. Your boots should fit snugly and comfortably over one or two wool socks and a thin liner sock. Breaking in boots properly before setting out requires wearing them for several weeks; doing so will spare you from painful and debilitating blisters.

Other Necessities: Raingear in two pieces, a top and pants, is far superior to a poncho. **Synthetics,** like polypropylene tops, socks, and long underwear, along with a pile jacket, will keep you warm even when wet. When camping in autumn, winter, or spring, bring along a **"space blanket,"** which helps you to retain your body heat and doubles as a groundcloth (US$5-15). Plastic **canteens** or water bottles keep water cooler than metal ones do, and are virtually shatter- and leak-proof. Large, collapsible **water sacks** will significantly improve your lot in primitive campgrounds and weigh practically nothing when empty, though they are bulky and heavy when full. Bring **water-purification tablets** for when you can't boil water, unless you are willing to shell out money for a portable water-purification system. Though most campgrounds provide campfire sites, you may want to bring a small **metal grate** or **grill** of your own. For those places that forbid fires or the gathering of firewood (virtually every organized campground in Europe), you'll need a **camp stove.** The classic Coleman stove starts at about US$40. Purchase a **fuel bottle** and fill it with propane to operate it. A **first aid kit, Swiss Army knife, insect repellent, calamine lotion,** and **waterproof matches** or a **lighter** are other essential camping items.

The mail-order/online companies listed below offer lower prices than many retail stores, but a visit to a local camping or outdoors store will give you a good sense of items' look and weight.

Campmor, P.O. Box 700, Upper Saddle River, NJ 07458-0700 (U.S. tel. (888) 226 7667, outside U.S. call (201) 825 8300; email customer-service@campmor.com; www.campmor.com).

Discount Camping, 880 Main North Rd., Pooraka, South Australia 5095, Australia (tel. (08) 8262 3399; fax 8260 6240; www.discountcamping.com.au).

Eastern Mountain Sports (EMS), 327 Jaffrey Rd., Peterborough, NH 03458 (tel. (888) 463 6367 or (603) 924 7231; email emsmail@emsonline.com; www.emsonline.com). Call for the branch nearest you.

L.L. Bean, Freeport, ME 04033-0001 (U.S./Canada tel. (800) 441 5713; U.K. (tel. (0800) 962 954; elsewhere, call U.S. (207) 552 6878; www.llbean.com). If your purchase doesn't meet your expectations, they'll replace or refund it.

YHA Adventure Shop, 14 Southampton St., London, WC2E 7HA, UK (tel. (01718) 36 85 41).

Mountain Safety Research Inc., P.O. Box 24547, Seattle, WA 98124 (tel. (800) 877 9677; email info@msrcorp.com; www.msrcorp.com). Stores in North America, South America, Europe, the Middle East, Asia, South Africa, and Australia. High-quality maintenance kits, emergency kits, stoves, water filters, and climbing gear.

WILDERNESS SAFETY

Stay warm, stay dry, and stay hydrated. The vast majority of life-threatening wilderness situations result from a breach of this simple dictum. On any hike, however brief, you should pack enough equipment to keep you alive should disaster befall. This includes **raingear, hat** and **mittens, a first-aid kit, a reflector, a whistle, high energy food,** and extra **water.** Dress in warm layers of **synthetic materials** designed for the outdoors, or **wool.** Pile fleece jackets and Gore-Tex raingear are excellent choices. Never rely on **cotton** for warmth. This "death cloth" will be absolutely useless should it get wet. Make sure to check all equipment for any defects before setting out, and see **Camping and Hiking Equipment,** above, for more information.

Check **weather forecasts** and pay attention to the skies when hiking. Weather patterns can change suddenly. Don't hike when visibility is low. Whenever possible, let someone know when and where you are going hiking, either a friend, your hostel, a park ranger, or a local hiking organization. Do not attempt a hike beyond your ability—you may be endangering your life. See **Health,** p. 22 for information about outdoor ailments such as heatstroke, hypothermia, giardia, rabies, and insects, as well as basic medical concerns and first-aid.

For more information, consult *How to Stay Alive in the Woods,* by Bradford Angier (Macmillan, US$8).

CAMPERS AND RVS

Many North American campers harbor a suspicion that traveling with a **camper** or **recreational vehicle** (RV) is not "real camping." The stigma is not as prevalent in Europe, where RV camping, or "caravanning," is both popular and common. European RVs are smaller and more economical than the 40-foot Winnebagos of the American road. Renting an RV will always be more expensive than tenting or hosteling, but the costs compare favorably with the price of staying in hotels and renting a car (see **Rentals,** p. 49) and the convenience of bringing along your own bedroom, bathroom, and kitchen makes it an attractive option for some, especially older travelers and families with small children.

It is not difficult to arrange an RV rental from overseas, although you will want to begin gathering information several months before your departure. Rates vary widely by region, season (July and August are the most expensive months), and type of RV. It always pays to contact several different companies to compare vehi-

FURTHER READING: CAMPING AND RVS.

Camping Your Way through Europe, Carol Mickelsen. Affordable Press (US$15).
Exploring Europe by RV, Dennis and Tina Jaffe. Globe Pequot (US$15).
Great Outdoor Recreation Pages, www.gorp.com.

cles and prices. **Avis** (tel. (800) 331 1084) and **Hertz** (tel. (800) 654 3001) are U.S. firms that can arrange RV rentals overseas; **Auto Europe** (U.S. tel. (800) 223 5555, U.K. tel. (0800) 899 893) and **National Car Rentals** (tel. (800) 227 3876, (800) 227 7368 in Canada) are European firms with branches in North America.

HIKING

Austria and Switzerland are renowned for their hiking, with paths ranging from simple hikes in the foothills of the Swiss Jura to ice-axe-wielding expeditions through the glaciers of the Berner Oberland. Free **hiking** maps are available from even the most rinky-dink of tourist offices. Hiking trails are marked by signs indicating the time to nearby destinations, which may not bear any relation to your own expertise and endurance. ("Std." is short for *Stunden*, or hours.) Paths marked *"Für Geübte"* require special mountain-climbing equipment and are for experienced climbers only. For lengthy hikes, consider taking a detailed map of the region you will be hiking. The best maps are the **Freytag-Berndt** or **Kümmerly-Frey** maps (around US$10), available in bookstores all over Austria and Switzerland and from **Pacific Travellers Supply,** 12 W. Anapamu St., Santa Barbara, CA 93101 (tel. (805) 963 4438). Check these books out, too:

100 Hikes in the Alps. Details various trails in Austria and Switzerland (US$15). Write to The Mountaineers Books, 1001 Klickitat Way, Ste. 201, Seattle, WA 98134 (tel. (800) 553 4453; fax 223 6306).

Walking Austria's Alps, by Jonathan Hurdle. The Mountaineers Books (US$11).

Walking Switzerland the Swiss Way, by Marcia and Philip Lieberman. The "Swiss Way" refers to hiking hut-to-hut. The Mountaineers Books (US$13).

Downhill Walking in Switzerland, (US$12). Old World Travel Books, Inc., P.O. Box 700863, Tulsa, OK 74170 (tel. (918) 493 2642).

Swiss-Bernese Oberland, by Philip and Loretta Alspach. (US$17, handling US$2.50). Intercon Publishing, P.O. Box 18500-L, Irvine, CA 92623 (tel. (714) 955 2344; fax 833 3156).

Walking Easy in the Austrian Alps and **Walking Easy in the Swiss Alps,** by Chet and Carolee Lipton (US$11). Gateway Books, 2023 Clemens Rd., Oakland, CA 94602 (tel. (510) 530 0299, orders only (800) 669 0773; fax 530 0497).

AUSTRIA

Membership in the **Österreichischer Alpenverein (ÖAV)** provides in-depth exposure to the Tyrolean Alps. The group maintains a series of **mountain huts** across Tyrol and throughout Austria, all located a day's hike from each other. This hut-to-hut option is provided to members at half-price and a place in any of the huts is always assured. Third-party insurance, accident provision, travel discounts, and a wealth of maps and mountain information are also included with membership. For information, contact the Österreichischer Alpenverein, Willhelm-Greil-Str. 15, A-6010 Innsbruck (tel. (0512) 58 78 28; fax 58 88 42). Membership (US$55, students under 25 US$40; one-time fee US$10) also includes use of some of the huts operated by the **Deutscher Alpenverein** (German Alpine Club). Sleeping in one of Austria's refuges is safer for the environment and generally safer for you—when you leave, you are expected to list your next destination in the hut book, thus alerting search-and-rescue teams if a problem should occur. Prices for an overnight stay without membership are 50-150AS (no reservations necessary).

 HIKING MAPS. For hiking, you will want a *Wanderkarte* of at least 1:50,000 scale. Kümmerly and Frey make good color maps that are easy to read (available at most tourist offices and bookstores in Austria and Switzerland).

The Austrian National Tourist Office publishes the pamphlet *Hiking and Backpacking in Austria*, with a complete list of Freytag-Berndt maps and additional tips. The **Touristenverein "Die Naturfreunde,"** Viktoriag. 6, A-1150 Vienna (tel. (01) 892 35 34), also operates a network of cottages in rural and mountain areas.

SWITZERLAND

"A pocket knife with a corkscrew, a leathern drinking cup, a spirit flask, stout gloves, and a piece of green crepe or coloured spectacles to protect the eyes from the glare of the snow, should not be forgotten," wrote Karl Baedeker in his 1907 guide to Switzerland. The Swiss National Tourist Office still suggests ski glasses to avoid **snow blindness,** but somehow the spirit flask has dropped out of the picture.

It's a good place for walkin': 9000km of **hiking trails** lace the country; yellow signs give directions and traveling times to nearby destinations. Bands of white-red-white mark trails; if there are no markings, you're on an "unofficial" trail, which is not always a problem—most trails are well maintained. Blue-white-blue markings indicate that the trail requires special equipment, either for difficult rock climbs or glacier climbing. Lowland **meandering** at its best awaits in the Engadin valley near St. Moritz; for steeper climbs, head to Zermatt or Interlaken. **Swiss Alpine Club (SAC) huts** are modest and extremely practical for those interested in trekking in higher, more remote areas of the Alps. Bunk rooms sleep 10 to 20 weary hikers side by side, with blankets (no electricity or running water) provided. SAC huts are open to all, but SAC members get discounts. The average rate for one night's stay without food is 30SFr, members 20-25SFr. Membership costs 126SFr, but as a bonus you'll receive the titillating publication *Die Alpen*. Contact the SAC, Sektion Zermatt, Haus Dolomite, CH-3920 Zermatt, Switzerland (tel. (028) 67 26 10).

SKIING

Western **Austria** is one of the world's best skiing regions. The areas around Innsbruck and Kitzbühel in Tyrol are saturated with lifts and runs. Skiers swoosh year-round down some glaciers, including the Stubaital near Innsbruck and the Dachstein in the Salzkammergut. High season normally runs from mid-December to mid-January and from February to March. Tourist offices provide information on regional skiing and can suggest budget travel agencies that offer ski packages.

Contrary to popular belief, **skiing in Switzerland** is often less expensive than in the U.S. if you avoid the pricey resorts. Ski passes (valid for transportation to, from, and on lifts) run 30-50SFr per day and 100-300SFr per week. A week of lift tickets, equipment rental, lessons, lodging, and *demi-pension* (half-pension—breakfast plus one other meal, usually dinner) averages 475SFr. Summer skiing in both countries is no longer as prevalent as it once was, but it's still available in Zermatt, Les Diablerets, and in Mayrhofen, Zell am See, and Zell am Ziller.

With peaks between 3000 and 30,000m, the Alpine vertical drop is ample—1000 to 2000m at all major resorts. For mountain country, winter **weather** in the Austrian Alps is moderate, thanks to lower elevation and distance from the ocean. Daytime temperatures in the coldest months (Jan. and Feb.) measure around -7 C (20 F). Humidity is low, so snow on the ground stays powdery longer.

KEEPING IN TOUCH

MAIL

SENDING MAIL TO AND RECEIVING MAIL IN AUSTRIA/SWITZERLAND.

Austria and Switzerland have rapid, efficient postal systems. Letters take 1 to 3 days within Switzerland and 1 to 2 days within Austria. **Airmail** from North America takes 4 to 5 days from either country. Mark all letters and packages "Mit Flugpost" or "Par Avion." In all cases, include the postal code if you know it; those of Swiss cities begin with "CH," Austrian with "A". There are several ways to arrange pick-up of letters sent to you by friends and relatives while you are abroad.

General Delivery: Mail can be sent to Austria and Switzerland through **Poste Restante** (the international phrase for General Delivery; *Postlagernde Briefe*) to almost any city or town with a post office. Address *Poste Restante* letters to: Anne CHISHOLM, *Postlagernde Briefe,* A-1010 Vienna, Austria. The mail will go to a special desk in the central post office, unless you specify a post office by street address or postal code. As a rule, it is best to use the largest post office in the area, and mail may be sent there regardless of what is written on the envelope. It is usually safer and quicker to send mail express or registered. When picking up your mail, bring a form of photo ID, preferably a passport. There is generally no surcharge; if there is a charge, it generally does not exceed the cost of domestic postage. If the clerks insist that there is nothing for you, have them check under your first name as well. *Let's Go* lists post offices in the **Practical Information** section for each city and most towns.

American Express: AmEx's travel offices throughout the world will act as a mail service for cardholders if you contact them in advance. Under this free **Client Letter Service,** they will hold mail for up to 30 days and forward upon request. Address the letter in the same way shown above. Some offices will offer these services to non-cardholders (especially those who have purchased AmEx Travelers Cheques), but call ahead to make sure. Check the **Practical Information** section of the countries you plan to visit; *Let's Go* lists AmEx office locations for most large cities. A complete list is available free from AmEx (tel. (800) 528 4800).

If regular airmail is too slow, **Federal Express** (U.S. tel. for international operator (800) 247 4747) can get a letter from New York to Vienna in 2 days for a whopping US $25; rates among non-U.S. locations are prohibitively expensive (London toVienna, for example, costs upwards of US $56). By **U.S. Express Mail,** a letter from New York would arrive within four days and would cost US$1.

Surface mail is by far the cheapest and slowest way to send mail. It takes 1 to 3 months to cross the Atlantic and 2 to 4 to cross the Pacific—appropriate for sending large quantities of items you won't need to see for a while. When ordering books and materials from abroad, always include 1 or 2 **International Reply Coupons (IRCs)**—a way of providing the postage to cover delivery. IRCs should be available from your local post office and those abroad (US$1.05).

SENDING MAIL HOME FROM AUSTRIA AND SWITZERLAND. The cheapest option is to send **aerorammes,** printed sheets that fold into envelopes and travel via airmail (available at post offices). Most post offices will charge exorbitant fees or simply refuse to send aerogrammes with enclosures. Mark all letters "airmail," "mit Luftpost," or "par avion," or get a sticker from the post office. For letters, have them weighed at the post office for correct postage. Airmail from Austria or Switzerland averages 7 to 20 days, although times are more unpredictable from smaller towns.

TELEPHONES

CALLING AUSTRIA OR SWITZERLAND FROM HOME. To call Austria or Switzerland direct from home, dial:

1. The international access code of your home country. **International access codes** include: Australia 0011; Ireland 00; New Zealand 00; South Africa 09; U.K. 00; U.S. 011. Country codes and city codes are sometimes listed with a zero in front (e.g., 033), but after dialing the international access code, drop successive zeros (with an access code of 011, e.g., 011 33).

2. 43 (for Austria) or 41 (for Switzerland).

3. The city code minus the 0 (see the city's **Phone Code** box) and local number.

CALLING HOME FROM AUSTRIA OR SWITZERLAND. A **calling card** is probably your best and cheapest bet. Calls are billed either collect or to your account. **MCI WorldPhone** also provides access to MCI's Traveler's Assist, which gives legal and medical advice, exchange rate information, and translation services. Other phone companies provide similar services to travelers. **To obtain a calling card** from your national telecommunications service before you leave home, contact the appropriate company below. Ask your calling card provider for directions on calling home with their calling card.

U.S.: AT&T (tel. (888) 288 4685); **Sprint** (tel. (800) 877 4646); or **MCI** (tel. (800) 444 4141; from abroad dial the country's MCI access number).

Canada: Bell Canada **Canada Direct** (tel. (800) 565 4708).

U.K.: British Telecom **BT Direct** (tel. (0800) 34 51 44).

Ireland: Telecom Éireann **Ireland Direct** (tel. (0800) 250 250).

Australia: Telstra **Australia Direct** (tel. 13 22 00).

New Zealand: Telecom New Zealand (tel. (0800) 000 000).

South Africa: Telkom South Africa (tel. 09 03).

Wherever possible, use a calling card for international phone calls, as the long-distance rates for national phone services are often exorbitant. You can usually make direct international calls from pay phones, but if you aren't using a calling card you may need to drop your coins as quickly as your words. Where available, prepaid phone cards and occasionally major credit cards can be used for direct international calls, but they are still less cost-efficient. Although incredibly convenient, in-room hotel calls invariably include an arbitrary surcharge (as much as US$10).

If you dial direct, first insert the appropriate amount of money or a prepaid card, then dial the country code and number you want to call. **Country codes** include: Australia 61; Ireland 353; New Zealand 64; South Africa 27; U.K. 44; U.S. and Canada 001. The expensive alternative to dialing direct or using a calling card is using an international operator to place a **collect call.** An English-speaking operator from your home nation can be reached by dialing the appropriate service provider listed above, and they will typically place a collect call even if you don't possess one of their phone cards.

CALLING WITHIN AUSTRIA AND SWITZERLAND. The simplest way to call within the country is to use a coin-operated phone. You can also buy **prepaid phone cards,** available at kiosks, post offices, or train stations. Phone rates are highest in the morning, lower in the evening, and lowest on Sunday and late at night. Dial the city code (refer to the phone code box in each city's Practical Information) before each number when calling from outside the city; within the city, dial only the actual number.

EMAIL AND INTERNET

Internet access is widespread in Austria and Switzerland. You can check your email from cybercafés, which *Let's Go* lists in the practical information for each city, or sometimes from universities, libraries, or hostels. Though limited free access is often available in bookstores or libraries, regular Internet access isn't cheap, and will generally run about US$8 per hour. For a complete listing of cybercafés in Austria and Switzerland, visit cybercaptive.com or netcafeguide.com.

Free, web-based email providers include Hotmail (www.hotmail.com), Rocket-Mail (www.rocketmail.com), and Yahoo! Mail (www.yahoo.com). Many free email providers are funded by advertising and some may require subscribers to fill out a questionnaire. Almost every Internet search engine has an affiliated free email service.

GETTING THERE

BY PLANE

When it comes to airfare, a little effort can save you a bundle. If your plans are flexible enough to deal with the restrictions, courier fares are the cheapest. Tickets bought from consolidators and standby seating are also good deals, but last-minute specials, airfare wars, and charter flights often beat these fares. The key is to hunt around, to be flexible, and to persistently ask about discounts. Students, seniors, and those under 26 should never pay full price for a ticket.

DETAILS AND TIPS

Timing: Airfares to Austria and Switzerland peak between July and August, and holidays are also expensive periods in which to travel. During ski season, it may be cheaper to fly to a non-skiing destination, like Paris or Frankfurt, and then take the train. Midweek (M-Th morning) round-trip flights run US$40-50 cheaper than weekend flights, but the latter are generally less crowded and more likely to permit frequent-flier upgrades. Return-date flexibility is usually not an option for the budget traveler; traveling with an "open return" ticket can be pricier than fixing a return date when buying the ticket and paying later to change it.

Route: Round-trip flights are by far the cheapest; "open-jaw" (arriving in and departing from different cities) and round-the-world (RTW) flights are pricier but reasonable alternatives. Patching one-way flights together is the least economical way to travel. Flights between capital cities or regional hubs will offer the most competitive fares.

Boarding: Whenever flying internationally, pick up tickets for international flights well in advance of the departure date, and confirm by phone within 72hr. of departure. Most airlines require that passengers arrive at the airport at least two hours before departure. One carry-on item and two pieces of checked baggage is the norm for non-courier flights. Consult the airline for weight allowances.

Fares: Fares from the U.S. to Austria and Switzerland vary tremendously depending on air-fare wars and special deals. For a round-trip ticket during peak season, expect to spend anywhere from US$400-$1000; $200-400 during off-season. It's worth extra effort to find bargain fares!

BUDGET AND STUDENT TRAVEL AGENCIES

A knowledgeable agent specializing in flights to Austria and Switzerland can make your life easy and help you save, too, but agents may not spend the time to find you the lowest possible fare—they get paid on commission. Students and under-26ers holding **ISIC and IYTC cards** (see **Identification**, p. 12), respectively, qualify for big discounts from student travel agencies. Most flights from budget agencies are on major airlines, but in peak season some may sell seats on chartered aircraft.

Campus/Usit Youth and Student Travel, 52 Grosvenor Gardens, **London** SW1W OAG (in U.K. call (0870) 240 1010, in North America call 44 171 730 21 01, worldwide call 44 171 730 81 11; www.usitcampus.co.uk). Other offices include: 19-21 Aston Quay, O'Connell Bridge, **Dublin** 2 (tel. (01) 677 8117; fax 679 8833); New York Student Center, 895 Amsterdam Ave., **New York,** NY, 10025 (tel. (212) 663 5435; email usitny@aol.com). Additional offices in Cork, Galway, Limerick, Waterford, Coleraine, Derry, Belfast, and Greece.

Council Travel (www.counciltravel.com). U.S. offices include: Emory Village, 1561 N. Decatur Rd., **Atlanta,** GA 30307 (tel. (404) 377 9997); 273 Newbury St., **Boston,** MA 02116 (tel. (617) 266 1926); 1160 N. State St., **Chicago,** IL 60610 (tel. (312) 951 0585); 10904 Lindbrook Dr., **Los Angeles,** CA 90024 (tel. (310) 208 3551); 205 E. 42nd St., **New York,** NY 10017 (tel. (212) 822 2700); 530 Bush St., **San Francisco,** CA 94108 (tel. (415) 421 3473); 1314 NE 43rd St. #210, **Seattle,** WA 98105 (tel. (206) 632 2448); 3300 M St. NW, **Washington, D.C.** 20007 (tel. (202) 337 6464). **For U.S. cities not listed,** call (800) 2-COUNCIL (226 8624). Also 28A Poland St. (Oxford Circus), **London,** W1V 3DB (tel. (0171) 287 33 37), **Paris** (tel. 01 44 41 89 89), and **Munich** (tel. (089) 39 50 22).

CTS Travel, 44 Goodge St., **London** W1 (tel. (0171) 636 00 31; fax 637 53 28; email ctsinfo@ctstravel.com.uk).

STA Travel, 6560 Scottsdale Rd. #F100, Scottsdale, AZ 85253 (tel. (800) 777 0112; fax (602) 922 0793; www.sta-travel.com). A student and youth travel organization with over 150 offices worldwide. Ticket booking, travel insurance, railpasses, and more. U.S. offices include: 297 Newbury Street, **Boston,** MA 02115 (tel. (617) 266 6014); 429 S. Dearborn St., **Chicago,** IL 60605 (tel. (312) 786 9050); 7202 Melrose Ave., **Los Angeles,** CA 90046 (tel. (323) 934 8722); 10 Downing St., **New York,** NY 10014 (tel. (212) 627 3111); 4341 University Way NE, **Seattle,** WA 98105 (tel. (206) 633 5000); 2401 Pennsylvania Ave., Ste. G, **Washington, D.C.** 20037 (tel. (202) 887 0912); 51 Grant Ave., **San Francisco,** CA 94108 (tel. (415) 391 8407). U.K. offices: 6 Wrights Ln., **London** W8 6TA (tel. (0171) 938 47 11 for North American travel). In New Zealand, 10 High St., **Auckland** (tel. (09) 309 04 58). In Australia, 222 Faraday St., **Melbourne** VIC 3053 (tel. (03) 9349 2411).

Travel CUTS (Canadian Universities Travel Services Limited), 187 College St., Toronto, Ont. M5T 1P7 (tel. (416) 979 2406; fax 979 8167; www.travelcuts.com). 40 offices across Canada. Also in the U.K., 295-A Regent St., **London** W1R 7YA (tel. (0171) 255 19 44).

Wasteels, Victoria Station, London, U.K. SW1V 1JT (tel. (0171) 834 70 66; fax 630 76 28; www.wasteels.dk/uk). A huge chain in Europe, with 203 locations. Sells the

Wasteels BIJ tickets, which are discounted (30-45% off regular fare) 2nd class international point-to-point train tickets with unlimited stopovers (must be under 26); sold only in Europe.

Other organizations that specialize in finding cheap fares include:

Cheap Tickets (tel. (800) 377 1000) flies worldwide to and from the U.S.

Travel Avenue (tel. (800) 333 3335) rebates commercial fares to or from the U.S. and offers low fares for flights anywhere in the world. They also offer package deals, which include car rental and hotel reservations, to many destinations.

COMMERCIAL AIRLINES

The commercial airlines' lowest regular offer is the **APEX** (Advance Purchase Excursion) fare, which provides confirmed reservations and allows "open-jaw" tickets. Generally, reservations must be made 7 to 21 days in advance, with 7- to 14-day minimum and up to 90-day maximum-stay limits, and hefty cancellation and change penalties (fees rise in summer). Book peak-season APEX fares early, since by May you will have a hard time getting the departure date you want.

   Although APEX fares are probably not the cheapest possible fares, they will give you a sense of the average commercial price, from which to measure other bargains. Specials advertised in newspapers may be cheaper but have more restrictions and fewer available seats. Popular carriers to Austria and Switzerland include:

Austrian Air (tel. (800) 843 0002; www.austrianair.com).

Swiss Air (tel. (800) 221 4750; www.swissair.com).

Icelandair (tel. (800) 223 5500; www.centrum.is/icelandair) has last-minute offers to Hamburg, Frankfurt, Milan and Paris. Flying to one of these cities on a cheap flight and then taking the train to Vienna, Geneva, Bern, or Zurich might be worth your while.

OTHER CHEAP ALTERNATIVES

AIR COURIER FLIGHTS

Couriers help transport cargo on international flights by guaranteeing delivery of the baggage claim slips from the company to a representative overseas. Generally, couriers must travel light (carry-ons only) and deal with complex restrictions on their flight. Most flights are round-trip only with short fixed-length stays (usually one week) and a limit of a single ticket per issue. Most of these flights also operate only out of the biggest cities, like New York. Generally, you must be over 21 (in some cases 18), have a valid passport, and procure your own visa, if necessary. Groups such as the **Air Courier Association** (tel. (800) 282 1202; www.aircourier.org) and the **International Association of Air Travel Couriers,** 220 South Dixie Hwy., P.O. Box 1349, Lake Worth, FL 33460 (tel. (561) 582 8320; email iaatc@courier.org; www.courier.org) provide members with lists of opportunities and courier brokers worldwide for an annual fee. For more information, consult *Air Courier Bargains* by Kelly Monaghan (The Intrepid Traveler, US$15) or the *Courier Air Travel Handbook* by Mark Field (Perpetual Press, US$10).

CHARTER FLIGHTS

Charters are flights a tour operator contracts with an airline to fly extra loads of passengers during peak season. Charters can sometimes be cheaper than flights on scheduled airlines, some operate nonstop, and restrictions on minimum advance-purchase and minimum stay are more lenient. However, charter flights fly less frequently than major airlines, make refunds particularly difficult, and are almost always fully booked. Schedules and itineraries may also change or be cancelled at the last moment (as late as 48 hours before the trip, and without a full refund), and check-in, boarding, and baggage claim are often much slower. As always, pay with a credit card if you can, and consider traveler's insurance against trip interruption.

Discount clubs and **fare brokers** offer members savings on last-minute charter and tour deals. Study their contracts closely; you don't want to end up with an unwanted overnight layover. **Travelers Advantage,** Stamford, CT (tel. (800) 548 1116; www.travelersadvantage.com; US$60 annual fee includes discounts, newsletters, and cheap flight directories) specializes in European travel and tour packages.

STANDBY FLIGHTS

To travel standby, you will need considerable flexibility in the dates and cities of your arrival and departure. Companies that specialize in standby flights don't sell tickets but rather the promise that you will get to your destination (or near your destination) within a certain window of time (anywhere from 1-5 days). You may only receive a monetary refund if all available flights which depart within your date-range from the specified region are full, but future travel credit is always available.

Carefully read agreements with any company offering standby flights, as tricky fine print can leave you in the lurch. To check on a company's service record, call the Better Business Bureau of New York City (tel. (212) 533 6200). It is difficult to receive refunds, and clients' vouchers will not be honored when an airline fails to receive payment in time.

Airhitch, 2641 Broadway, 3rd Fl., New York, NY 10025 (tel. (800) 326 2009 or (212) 864 2000; fax 864 5489; www.airhitch.org) and Los Angeles, CA (tel. (310) 726 5000). In Europe, the flagship office is in Paris (tel. (0147) 00 16 30) and the other one is in Amsterdam (tel. (020) 626 32 20). Flights to major cities in Western Europe (such as Amsterdam and Paris) cost US$159 each way when departing from the Northeast, US$239 from the West Coast or Northwest, US$209 from the Midwest, and US$189 from the Southeast. Once you get to Europe, catch a train to Austria or Switzerland.

TICKET CONSOLIDATORS

Ticket consolidators, popularly known as **"bucket shops,"** buy unsold tickets in bulk from commercial airlines and sell them at discounted rates. The best place to look is in the Sunday travel section of any major newspaper, where many bucket shops place tiny ads. Call quickly, as availability is typically extremely limited. Not all bucket shops are reliable establishments, so insist on a receipt that gives full details of restrictions, refunds, and tickets, and pay by credit card. For more information, check the website Consolidators FAQ (www.travel-library.com/air-travel/consolidators.html) or the book *Consolidators: Air Travel's Bargain Basement,* by Kelly Monaghan (Intrepid Traveler, US$8).

ONCE THERE

TOURIST INFORMATION AND TOWN LAYOUTS

The **Swiss National Tourist Office** and the **Austrian National Tourist Office** publish a wealth of information about tours and vacations; every single town has a tourist office. To simplify things, all offices are marked by a standard "i" sign (green in Austria, blue in Switzerland). *Let's Go* lists tourist offices in the Practical Information section of each city. The staff may or may not speak English—the skill is not a requirement in smaller towns, and we'll try and let you know whether they do or don't. Tourist offices are good for free maps. In Swiss cities, look for the excellent **Union Bank of Switzerland maps,** which have very detailed streets and sites.

One thing to keep in mind is that the Austrian and Swiss creative palette for small-town names is pretty meager. Many towns, even within the same state or province, have the same names (Gmünd or Stein, for instance). Most Austrian and Swiss train stations have luggage storage, currency exchange, and bike rentals (at a discount if you have a train ticket for that day or a valid railpass). The **post office** is often next door to the train station, even in larger cities. Most towns are small enough that all sights are within walking distance. Public transportation is usually pretty good, too. Buy local public transport tickets from *Tabak* stands, which sell them for reduced rates. Most ticket validation is based on the honor system, and many tourists interpret that as a free ride. Though certainly a tempting budget option, **Schwarzfahren** (i.e., riding without a ticket) can result in big anti-budget fines, and playing "dumb tourist" probably won't work.

GETTING AROUND

Fares on all modes of transportation are either one-way ("single") or round-trip ("return"). "Period returns" require you to return within a specific number of days; "day return" means you must return on the same day. Unless stated otherwise, *Let's Go* always lists one-way fares.

BY TRAIN

Given that trains are likely to be your preferred mode of transportation in Austria and Switzerland, it is fortunate that European trains are generally comfortable, convenient, and reasonably swift. In fact, the train can get you places throughout Austria and Switzerland where a car cannot. European trains retain the charm and romance that their North American counterparts lost generations ago. Second-class travel is pleasant, and compartments, which seat 2 to 6, are excellent places to meet fellow travelers. Trains, however, are not always safe; lock your compartment door (if possible) and keep your valuables on your person at all times. Nonsmokers probably won't be comfortable in smoking compartments, which tend to be very, very smoky. Train trips tend to be short since both Austria and Switzerland are relatively small. Get your stuff together a few stops early since trains pause only two to three minutes before zipping off. For longer trips, make sure that you are on the correct car, as trains sometimes split at crossroads. Towns in parentheses on schedules require a train switch at the town listed immediately before the parenthesis. "Salzburg-Attnang-Puchheim-(Bad Ischl-Hallstatt)" means that in order to get to Bad Ischl or Hallstatt, you have to disembark at Puchheim and pick up a different train. You might want to ask if your route requires a change of trains, as the schedules are sometimes about as decipherable as dolphin noises.

The **Österreichische Bundesbahn** (ÖBB), Austria's federal railroad, is one of Europe's most thorough and efficient. The ÖBB prints the yearly *Fahrpläne Kursbuch Bahn-Inland*, a compilation of all rail, ferry, and cable-car transportation schedules in Austria. The massive compendium is available at any large train station, along with its companion tomes, the *Kursbuch Bahn-Ausland* for international trains, and the *Internationales Schlafwagenkursbuch* for sleeping cars. Getting around Switzerland is also a snap. Federal **(SBB, CFF)** and private railways connect most towns and villages, with trains running in each direction on an hourly basis. **Schnellzüge** (express trains) speed between metropoli, while **Regionalzüge** chug into podunk cowtowns. The national telephone number for rail information is tel. 157 22 22 or tel. 01717 and has English-speaking operators. Be aware that sometimes only private train lines go to remote tourist spots, and therefore Eurail and Swisspasses might not be valid. Yellow signs announce departure times *(Ausfahrt, départ, partenze)* and platforms *(Gleis, quai, binario)*. White signs are for arrivals *(Ankunft, arrivé, arrivo)*. On major Austrian lines, make reservations at least a few hours in advance.

Even with a railpass, you are not guaranteed a seat unless you make a reservation (US$3-10); they are advisable during the busier holiday seasons, and often required on major lines. Also, while many high-speed or quality trains (e.g., EuroCity and InterCity) are included in a railpass, a supplement (US$10-25) is required to ride certain international trains, such as the German ICE. For overnight travel, a tight, open bunk called a **couchette** is an affordable luxury (about US$20). Both seat and couchette reservations can be made by your local travel agent or in person at the train station (reserve at least a few hours in advance for seats; at least a few days for couchettes).

DISCOUNTED RAIL TICKETS

You can purchase **individual tickets** at every train station in Austria and Switzerland, at Bahn-Total service stations, at the occasional automat, or from the conductor for a small surcharge. Over 130 stations accept the major credit cards as well as American Express Traveler's Cheques and Eurocheques. British and Irish citizens **over the age of 60** can buy their national senior pass and receive a 30% discount on first- and second-class travel in Austria and Switzerland. Restrictions on travel time may apply.

For travelers under 26, **BIJ** tickets (Billets Internationals de Jeunesse) are a great alternative to railpasses. Available for international trips within Europe as well as most ferry services, they knock 20-40% off regular second-class fares. Tickets are good for 60 days after purchase and allow a number of stopovers along the normal direct route of the train journey. Issued for a specific international route between two points, they must be used in the direction and order of the designated route (side- or back-tracking must be done at your expense) and must be bought in Europe. Tickets are sold under the names British Rail, Eurotrain, and Wasteels. They are available from European travel agents, at Wasteels or Eurotrain offices (usually in or near train stations), or directly at the ticket counter. Contact Wasteels in Victoria Station, adjacent to Platform 2, London SW1V 1JT (tel. (0171) 834 70 66; fax 630 76 28), or look for an office near you in Austria or Switzerland.

RAILPASSES

Ideally, a railpass allows you to jump on any train in the specified zone, go wherever you want whenever you want, and change your plans at will for a set length of time. In practice, it's not so simple; you must still wait to pay for supplements, seat reservations, and couchette reservations, as well as to have your pass validated when you first use it. More importantly, railpasses don't always pay off. For ballpark estimates, consult the **DERTravel** or **RailEurope** railpass brochure for prices of point-to-point tickets. Add them up and compare with railpass prices.

NATIONAL RAILPASSES. In Austria, children under 4 travel free and fares are 50% off for children ages 5 to 14. In Switzerland, children under 16 travel free with a parent in Switzerland with the Swiss Family Card (see p. 45). For adults, **Swiss regional passes** are available in major tourist offices for holders of Eurailpasses (50-175SFr). However, national railpasses are the way to go if you're going to be covering long distances within Austria or Switzerland. Nearly all are sold either through RailEurope or at local train stations. Consider the following options:

Austrian Railpass: Sold worldwide, this pass is valid for 3 days unlimited train travel in a 15-day period on all Austrian Federal Railway lines, state and private rail lines in Austria, as well as granting a 50% discount on bicycle rental in over 160 railway stations and on DDSG steamers between Passau, Linz and Vienna. You can purchase up to 5 additional rail days. 1 adult, 2nd class $102, each additional day $22. **Austrian Rail Pass Junior,** for travelers under 12, provides the same discounts as its parent, but for less (2nd class US$51, additional days US$7.50). The card itself has no photo, so you must carry a valid ID in case of inspections. The Rail Pass Junior is cheaper than many round-trip fares, so it may be an economical option even for short stays.

European East Pass: This pass is good for 5 days of 1st class, unlimited travel in a 1 month period, as well as various discounts on steamers and private railways, within Austria, the Czech Republic, Hungary, Poland, and the Slovak Republic. You can purchase up to 5 days additional travel. Adult $250, each additional day $23; child $102.50, $11.50.

Bundesnetzkarte (National Network Pass): Allows unlimited train travel in all of Austria, including Wolfgangsee ferries and private lines, as well as half-price tickets for Bodensee and Danube ferries. No surcharge on EC and SC first-class trains. 1 month of 2nd class 4000AS, 1st class 6000AS. Picture required. Sold only in Austria at train stations.

Kilometer Bank: Also sold only in Austria, this card is good for a pre-purchased allotment of kilometers to be used by 1-6 persons traveling together on trips of over 70km one-way in 1st or 2nd class. The conductor deducts the distance of the trip for each passenger age 16 or older, but only half the distance for children 6-15.

Seniorenausweis: Senior citizens get 50% off bus and train fares in Austria for 1 yr. 350AS (see **Older Travelers,** p. 54 for more details).

Swiss Card: Good for a one-day trip from any entry point (airport or border crossing) to any single destination in Switzerland and a one-day trip from any place in Switzerland to any departure point, as well as 50% off unlimited rail and bus tickets. You have 1 month to complete your travel. 1 person, second class costs $128.

SwissPass: Sold worldwide, this pass offers unlimited rail travel for 5 consecutive-day periods: choose between 4 days, 8 days, 15 days, 21 days, or 1 month, 1st or 2nd class. In addition to rail travel, it entitles you to unlimited urban transportation in 30 cities, unlimited travel on certain private railways and lake steamers, and discounts on other private railways. 2 people traveling together qualify for a 40% companion discount on the second Swiss Pass. 1 adult, second class 4 day-passes start at US$188, 8 days at $238, 15 days at $288, 21 days at $320, and 1 month at $400.

Swiss Flexipass: This pass entitles you to 3 days unlimited rail travel in a 1-month period, 1st or 2nd class, with the same benefits as the Swiss Pass. You can purchase up to 6 days additional travel. 1 adult, second class costs $176, $24 for each additional day.

Swiss Rail 'n Drive Pass: Works like a Flexipass but adds 3 days of car rental with unlimited mileage and unlimited travel on some of the private railways, such as the Glacier Express near Zermatt and the Panoramic Express. If you're traveling with 3 or 4 people, only 2 will have to buy the Rail 'n' Drive pass and the others need only buy the Swiss Flexipass. The pass includes car rental with manual transmission only, and rates vary depending on the car category you choose (2nd class runs US$340-415).

Swiss Family Card: This card allows children under 16 to travel free if accompanied by at least one parent and holder of a rail ticket, Swiss Pass, Swiss Flexipass, or Swiss Card. If purchased in Switzerland, the Swiss Family Card costs 20SFr, but it is free from Rail Europe with the purchase of a Swiss train ticket or rail pass.

INTERNATIONAL RAILPASSES. A **Eurailpass** remains perhaps the best option for non-EU travelers who plan on hitting major cities in several countries. Eurailpasses are valid in Austria, Belgium, Denmark, Finland, France, Germany, Greece, Hungary, Italy, Luxembourg, Netherlands, Norway, Portugal, Republic of Ireland, Spain, Sweden, and Switzerland. These passes must be sold at uniform prices determined by the EU, so no particular travel agent is better than another as far as the pass itself is concerned. However, some agents tack on a $10 handling fee. First class passes are also available.

EURAIL PASSES	15 days	21 days	1 month	2 months	3 months
Eurail Saverpass	US$470	US$610	US$756	US$1072	US$1324
Eurail Youthpass: ages 12-25	US$388	US$499	US$623	US$882	US$1089

Eurail Saverpass: Unlimited first-class travel for those traveling in a group of 2-5.

Youth Flexipasses: Second-class travel for those under 26: 10 days (US$458), 15 days (US$599). Children 4-11 pay half price, and children under 4 travel free.

Europasses: Combines France, Germany, Italy, Spain, and Switzerland in one plan. With a Europass you can travel in any of these 5 countries from 5-15 days within a window of 2 months. Second-class youth tickets begin at US$233 and increase incrementally by about $29 for each extra day of travel. For a fee, you can add associate countries; call for details. Be sure to plan your itineraries in advance before buying a Europass; if you cut through a country you haven't purchased you will receive a fine. It will save you money if your travels are confined to between 3 and 5 adjacent Western European countries, or if you know that you want to go only to large cities. Europasses are not appropriate if you like to take lots of side trips—you'll waste rail days. If you're tempted to add lots of rail days and associate countries, consider the Eurailpass.

It is best to buy your Eurailpass/Europass before leaving; they are hard to find in Europe. Contact Council Travel, Travel CUTS (see **Budget Travel Agencies,** p. 40), or almost any travel agent handling European travel. Eurailpasses must be used within 6 months of purchase and are not refundable once validated; if your pass is completely unused and unvalidated and you have the original purchase documents, you can get an 85% refund from the place of purchase within 6 months. You can get a replacement for a lost pass only if you have purchased insurance on it under the Pass Protection Plan (US$10). All Eurailpasses can be purchased from a travel agent, or from **Rail Europe Group,** 500 Mamaroneck Ave., Harrison, NY 10528 (in the U.S. tel. (800) 438 7245; fax (800) 432 1329; in Canada tel. (800) 361 7245; fax (905) 602 4198; www.raileurope.com), which also sells point-to-point tickets. They offer special rates for groups of 10 or more travelling together.

Euro-Domino passes are available to anyone who has been resident at least 6 months in Europe. You cannot buy a Euro-Domino pass for the country you are in. These single-country passes include most supplements for high-speed trains, but reservations must still be purchased separately. You also get a 25% discount on rail travel from the country of residence to the destination country. They are available for 1st and 2nd class travel, with a special rate for travelers under 26, and offer 3-8 days of unlimited travel in a 1-month period. Tickets should be bought in your country of residence, and can be found at travel agents and major train stations.

EURO-DOMINO PASS (AUSTRIA)	3 days	5 days	8 days
2nd class	165SFr	200SFr	253SFr
2nd class youth (under 26)	128SFr	154SFr	192SFr
EURO-DOMINO PASS (SWITZ.)	3 days	5 days	8 days
2nd class	1322AS	1575AS	1955AS
2nd class youth (under 26)	998AS	1125AS	1477AS

European residents planning to cover more than 1 country should consider **InterRail Passes;** the same eligibility terms apply as for Euro-Domino. For information and ticket sales in Europe, contact Student Travel Center, 1st fl., 24 Rupert St., London, W1V 7FN (tel. (020) 743 70 121, 743 76 370, or 743 78 101; fax 773 43 836; www.student-travel-centre.com). Tickets are also available from travel agents or major train stations; they should be purchased in your country of residence.

Under 26 InterRail Card: 14 days or 1 month of unlimited travel within 1, 2, 3 or all 7 zones into which InterRail divides Europe; the cost is determined by the number of zones the pass covers. If you are from a European country and you buy a ticket including your zone, you only have to pay 50% fare for the tickets inside your own country. Prices range UK£159-259.

Over 26 InterRail Card: unlimited second-class travel in 20 European countries (Austria, Bulgaria, Croatia, Czech Republic, Denmark, Finland, Germany, Greece, Hungary, Republic of Ireland, Luxembourg, Netherlands, Norway, Poland, Romania, Slovakia, Slovenia, Sweden, Turkey, and Yugoslavia) for 15 days (UK£215) or 1 month (UK£275).

In addition to simple railpasses, many countries (and Europass and Eurailpass) offer rail-and-drive passes, which combine car rental with rail travel—a good option for travelers who want to visit cities accessible by rail and make side trips.

 MORE INFO: GETTING AROUND EUROPE BY TRAIN.

European Railway Server: mercurio.iet.unipi.it/home.html
Thomas Cook European Timetable (US$28; US$39 including a map of Europe with all train and ferry routes; postage US$5).
On the Rails Around Europe, Melissa Shales. Passport Books (US$19).
Traveling Europe's Trains, Jay Brunhouse. Pelican Publishing (US$16).
Europe By Eurail 1999, Laverne Ferguson. Globe Pequot (US$16).
Eurail and Train Travel Guide to Europe. Houghton Mifflin (US$15).

BY BUS

Just like the railroads, the bus networks of Austria and Switzerland are very extensive, efficient, or comfortable; it may be difficult to negotiate the route you need, but short-haul buses can reach rural areas inaccessible by train. Bus stations are usually adjacent to the train station. The efficient Austrian system consists mainly of orange **BundesBuses** that generally complement the train system, serving mountain areas inaccessible by train rather than duplicating long-distance, inter-city routes already covered by rail. They cost about the same as trains, but no railpasses are valid. Always purchase round-trip tickets if you plan to return to your starting point. Buy tickets at a ticket office at the station or from the driver. For buses in heavily touristed areas during high season (such as the Großglockner-straße in summer), you should probably make reservations. All public buses are non-smoking. Anyone can buy discounted tickets, valid for one week, for any particular route. A **Mehrfahrtenkarte** gives you 6 tickets for the price of 5. The **Seniorenausweis** (see p. 54) is valid on buses. Trips can be interrupted under certain conditions, depending on your ticket—be sure to ask. Small, regional bus schedules are available for free at most post offices. For more **bus information,** call (0222) 71101 within Austria (from outside Austria dial 1 instead of 0222).

In Switzerland, PTT **postal buses,** a barrage of banana-colored coaches delivered to you expressly by the Swiss government, connect rural villages and towns, picking up the slack where trains fail to go. SwissPasses are valid on many buses, Eurailpasses are not. Even with the SwissPass, you might have to pay a bit extra (5-10SFr) if you're riding one of the direct, faster buses. In cities, public buses transport commuters and shoppers alike to outlying areas. Buy tickets in advance at automatic machines, found at most bus stops. The system works on an honor code and inspections are infrequent, but expect to be hit for 30-50SFr if you're caught riding without a valid ticket. *Tageskarten,* valid for 24 hours of free travel, run 2-7.50SFr, but most Swiss cities are small enough to cover on foot.

BY CAR

Cars offer speed, freedom, access to the countryside, and an escape from the town-to-town mentality of trains. Unfortunately, they also insulate you from the *esprit de corps* of rail traveling. Although a single traveler won't save by renting or leasing a car, 3 or 4 usually will. As a rule, it is cheaper to rent in Germany than in Austria or Switzerland. Before setting off, know the laws of the countries in which you'll be driving (z.B., no right turn on red allowed anywhere in Austria or Switzerland). The **Association for Safe International Road Travel (ASIRT)** can provide more specific information about road conditions. It is located at 5413 West Cedar Lane 103C, Bethesda, MD 20814 (tel. (301) 983 5252; fax 983 3663; email asirt@erols.com; www.asirt.org). ASIRT considers road travel (by car or bus) to be relatively safe in both Austria and Switzerland. Austrian and Swiss highways are excellent. With armies of mechanized road crews ready to remove snow at moment's notice, roads at altitudes of up to 1500m generally remain open throughout winter. (Mountain driving does present special challenges, however; see p. 20.) The **speed limit** is 50km per hour (31mph) within cities unless otherwise indicated; outside towns, the limit is 130km per hour (81mph) on highways and 100km per hour (62mph) on all other roads. Driving under the influence of alcohol is a serious offense—fines begin at 700SFr (5000AS) and rise rapidly from there. Violators may also lose their licenses. The legal blood-alcohol limit is *very low.*

Many small Austrian and Swiss towns forbid cars to enter; some forbid only visitors' cars, require special permits, or restrict driving hours. EU citizens driving in Austria and Switzerland don't need any special documentation—registration and license will suffice. All cars must carry a first-aid kit and a red emergency triangle. All passengers in both countries must wear seatbelts, and children under 12 may not sit in the front passenger seat unless a child's seatbelt or a special seat is installed. Emergency phones are located along all major highways. The **Austrian Automobile, Motorcycle, and Touring Club** (ÖAMTC; tel. (1) 71 19 97, in emergencies 120) provides an English-language service and sells a set of 8 detailed road maps, far superior to the tourist office's map (open daily 6am-8pm). The **Swiss Touring Club,** rue Pierre-Fatio 9, CH-1211 Geneva 3 (tel. (022) 737 12 12) operates road patrols that assist motorists in need; dial 140 for help.

DRIVING PERMITS: INTERNATIONAL DRIVING PERMIT (IDP). If you plan to drive a car while in Austria, you must have an International Driving Permit (IDP), in addition to your driver's license. Most car rental agencies in Switzerland don't require the permit, but it may be a good idea to get one anyway, in case you're in a situation (e.g. an accident or being stranded in a smaller town) where the police do not know English. Information on the IDP is available from local automobile clubs, printed in ten languages, including French, Italian, and German.

Your IDP is valid for one year, and it must be issued in your own country before you depart; AAA affiliates cannot issue IDPs valid in their own country. You must be 18 years old to receive the IDP. A valid driver's license from your home country must always accompany the IDP. The IDP application needs to include one or two photos, a current local license, an additional form of identification, and a fee.

Australia: Contact your local Royal Automobile Club (RAC) or the National Royal Motorist Association (NRMA) if in NSW or the ACT (tel. (08) 9421 4298; www.rac.com.au/travel). Permits AUS$15.

Canada: Contact any Canadian Automobile Association (CAA) branch office in Canada, or write to CAA, 1145 Hunt Club Rd., Suite 200, K1V 0Y3 Canada. (tel. (613) 247 0117; fax 247 0118; www.caa.ca/CAAInternet/travelservices/internationaldocumentation/idptravel.htm). Permits CDN$10.

Ireland: The Irish AA (tel. (01) 677 9481) is on 23 Suffolk St., Rockhill, Blackrock Co., Dublin. They honor most foreign AA memberships as well. You can also write to the U.K. address (see p. 48). Permits IR£4.

New Zealand: Contact your local Automobile Association (AA) or the main office at Auckland Central, 99 Albert St. (tel. (9) 377 4660; fax 302 2037; www.nzaa.co.nz.). Permits NZ$8.

South Africa: Contact your local Automobile Association of South Africa office or the head office at P.O. Box 596, 2000 Johannesburg (tel. (11) 799 1000; fax 799 1010). Permits SAR28.50.

U.K.: Visit your local AA Shop, contact the Automobile Association headquarters at tel. (990) 500 600; www.theaa.co.uk/motoring/idp.asp, or write to: International Documents, Fanum House, Erskine, Renfrewshire PA8 6BW. Permits UK£4.

U.S.: Visit any American Automobile Association (AAA) office or write to AAA Florida, Travel Related Services, 1000 AAA Drive (mail stop 100), Heathrow, FL 32746 (tel. (407) 444 7000; fax 444 7380). Sells the International Driving Permit (IDP). You do not have to be a member of AAA. Permits US$10.

American Automobile Association (AAA) Travel Related Services, 1000 AAA Dr. (mail stop 100), Heathrow, FL 32746 (tel. (800) 222 4357). Provides road maps and many travel guides free to members. Offers emergency road services (for members), travel services, and auto insurance. The is available for purchase from local AAA offices. To obtain an IDP in the U.K., contact the **Automobile Association Headquarters** (tel. (0990) 44 88 66).

CAR INSURANCE. Most credit cards cover only supplemental insurance, though gold and platinum cards usually cover standard insurance. If you have car insurance on your own car, check with your insurer to have your insurance applied to your rental car. If you rent, lease, or borrow a car, you will need a **International Insurance Certificate (green card),** to prove that you have liability insurance. Obtain it through the car rental agency; most include coverage in their prices. If you lease a car, you can obtain a green card from the dealer. Some travel agents offer the card; it may also be available at border crossings. Verify whether your auto insurance applies abroad; even if it does, you will still need a green card to certify this to foreign officials. If you have a collision abroad, the accident will show up on your domestic records if you report it to your insurance company.

RENTALS. To rent a car in **Austria,** you must be over 21 (older in some cases) and must carry an International Driver's Permit and a valid driver's license that you have had for at least 1 year (see p. 47). Most Austrian companies restrict travel into Eastern Europe. Rental taxes are high (21%). In **Switzerland,** the minimum rental age varies by company but is rarely below 21. You must possess a valid driver's license that you have had for at least one year (foreign licenses are valid). In both countries, drivers under 25 must pay a daily fee. Rates for all cars rented in Switzerland include an obligatory 40SFr **road toll,** called a *vignette.* In Austria, drivers must purchase a highway permit at the border (70AS per week).

You can **rent** a car from a U.S.-based firm (Alamo, Avis, Budget, or Hertz) with European offices, from a European-based company with local representatives (Europcar), or from a tour operator (Auto Europe, Europe By Car, and Kemwel Holiday Autos) which will arrange a rental for you from a European company at its own rates. Multinationals offer greater flexibility, but tour operators often strike better deals. Rentals vary by company, season, and pick-up point; picking up your car in Germany is usually cheaper than renting in Austria or Switzerland. Expect to pay around US$300-400 per week for a teensy car. Reserve well before leaving for Austria or Switzerland and pay in advance if at all possible. It is always significantly less expensive to reserve a car from, for example, the U.S. than from Austria or Switzerland. Always check if prices quoted include tax, unlimited mileage, and collision insurance; some credit card companies will cover this automatically. Ask about discounts and check the terms of insurance, particularly the size of the deductible. Non-Europeans should check with their national motoring organization (like AAA or CAA) for international coverage. Ask your airline about special fly-and-drive packages; you may get up to a week of free or discounted rental. You can rent cars in Europe from the following rental agencies:

Auto Europe, 39 Commercial St., P.O. Box 7006, Portland, ME 04101 (tel. 888 223 5555; fax 800 235 6321; www.autoeurope.com).

Avis (in U.S. and Canada, tel. (800) 331 1084; in U.K., tel. (0990) 90 05 00; in Australia tel. (800) 22 55 33; www.avis.com).

Budget (in U.S., tel. (800) 472 3325; in Canada, tel. (800) 527 0700; in U.K., tel. (0800) 18 11 81; in Australia, tel. 13 27 27; www.budgetrentacar.com).

Europe by Car, One Rockefeller Plaza, New York, NY 10020 (tel. (800) 223 1516, (212) 581 3040; www.europebycar.com).

Europcar, 145 Avenue Malekoff, 75016 Paris (tel. (800) 227 3876; (800) 227 7368 in Canada; (1) 45 00 08 06 in France; www.europcar.com).

Hertz (tel. (800) 654 3001; in Canada, (800) 263 0600; in U.K. (0990) 99 66 99; in Australia, 13 30 39; www.hertz.com).

Kemwel Holiday Autos (tel. (800) 678 0678; www.kemwel.com).

Payless Car Rental (tel. (800) 729 5377).

LEASING AND BUYING. For longer than 17 days, **leasing** can be cheaper than renting; it is often the only option for those ages 18-21. The cheapest leases are agreements to buy the car and then sell it back to the manufacturer at a prearranged price. As far as you're concerned, though, it's a lease and doesn't entail enormous financial transactions. Leases generally include insurance coverage and are not taxed, though they may include a VAT. The most affordable ones originate in Belgium, France, or Germany. Expect to pay at least US$1200 for 60 days.

Unless you're staying for a long time in Austria or Switzerland, **buying** a car is too much hassle to be cost-efficient, involving lots of paperwork, intricate regulations, and taxes. If you're still interested, check with the appropriate consulate about import-export laws concerning used vehicles, registration, and safety and emission standards. David Shore and Patty Campbell's **Europe by Van and Motorhome** (US$14 plus postage) guides you through the entire process of renting, leasing, buying, and selling vehicles in Europe including buy-back options, registration, insurance, and dealer listings. Contact Shore/Campbell Publications, 1842 Santa Margarita Dr., Fallbrook, CA 92028 (tel./fax (800) 659 5222 or (760) 723 6184; email shorecam@aol.com; www.members.aol.com/europevan). Eric Bredesen's **Moto-Europa** (US$16 plus postage), available from Seren Publishing, 2935 Saint Anne Dr., Dubuque, IA 52001 (tel. (800) 387 6728; fax (319) 583 7853), is another thorough guide to all these options including itinerary suggestions, a motorists' phrasebook, and chapters on leasing and buying vehicles.

BY AIR

No air deals can compare with railpass bargains in Austria and Switzerland, so flying across Europe on regularly scheduled flights can devour your budget. **Alitalia** (tel. (800) 223 5730; www.alitalia.it) sells "Europlus": in conjunction with a transatlantic flight on Alitalia, for US$299 you may purchase a package of 3 flight coupons good for anywhere Alitalia flies within Europe. Unlimited additional tickets cost $100. To non-Europe residents, **Lufthansa** (tel. (800) 399-LUFT (5838); www.lufthansa.com) offers "Discover Europe," a package of 3 flight coupons which vary in cost, depending on country of origin, destination and season (US$105-200 each). Student travel agencies sell cheap tickets, and budget fares are frequently available in the spring and summer on high-traffic routes between northern Europe and resort areas in Italy, Greece, and Spain. Consult budget travel agents and local newspapers. The **Air Travel Advisory Bureau** in London (tel. (0171) 636 5000; www.atab.co.uk) can also point the way to discount flights.

BY BICYCLE

Today, biking is one of the key elements of the classic budget Eurovoyage. With the proliferation of mountain bikes, you can do some serious natural sight-seeing. May, June, and September are prime biking months in Austria and Switzerland, for leisurely or hard-core bicycling. Take some reasonably challenging day-long rides at home to prepare yourself before you leave, and have your bike tuned up by a reputable shop. Wear visible clothing, drink plenty of water (even if you're not thirsty), and use the international signals for turns. Know how to fix a modern derailer-equipped mount and change a tire, and practice on your own bike. A few simple tools and a good bike manual will be invaluable. For info about touring routes, consult national tourist offices or any of the numerous books available. The **Touring Club Suisse,** Cyclo Tourisme, chemin Riantbosson 11-13, CH-1217 Meyrin (tel. (022) 785 12 22; fax 785 12 62), will send you information, maps, brochures, route descriptions, and mileage charts. If you are nervous about striking out on your own, **Blue Marble Travel** (in Canada tel. (519) 624 2494; in U.S. tel. (800) 258 8689 or (973) 326 9533; www.bluemarble.org) offers bike tours designed for adults aged 20 to 50. Pedal with or without your 10 to 15 companions through the Alps and Austria. Full-time graduate and professional students may get discounts, and "stand-by" fares may be obtained in Europe through the Paris office. **CBT Tours,** 415 W. Fullerton, #1003, Chicago, IL 60614 (tel. (800) 736-BIKE (2453) or (773) 404 1710; www.cbttours.com), offers full-package 1- to 7-week biking, mountain biking, and hiking tours, priced around US$150 per day. Tours run between June and September, with departures every 7 to 10 days.

Riding a bike with a frame pack strapped on it or your back is about as safe as pedaling blindfolded over a sheet of ice; panniers are essential. The first thing to buy, however, is a suitable **bike helmet** (US$25-50). U-shaped **Citadel** or **Kryptonite locks** are expensive (starting at US$30), but the companies insure their locks against theft of your bike for 1 to 2 years. For mail order equipment, **Bike Nashbar,** 4111 Simon Rd., Youngstown, OH 44512 (tel. (800) 627 4227; www.nashbar.com), beats competitors' offers and ships anywhere in the U.S. or Canada.

Renting a bike beats bringing your own if your touring will be confined to 1 or 2 regions. *Let's Go* lists bike rental shops for most cities and towns. Some youth hostels rent bicycles for low prices. In Switzerland, train stations rent bikes and often allow you to drop them off elsewhere; check at bike rental offices at train stations throughout Europe for similar deals. If you prefer your own bike, many airlines will count your bike as your second piece of luggage, while others charge extra (US$60-110 each way). Bikes must be packed in a cardboard box with the pedals and front wheel detached; many airlines sell bike boxes at the airport (US$10). Most ferries let you take your bike for free or for a nominal fee. You can always ship your bike on trains as well, for a fee.

MORE INFORMATION.
Mountaineers Books, 1001 S.W. Klickitat Way #201, Seattle, WA 98134 (tel. (800) 553 4453 or (206) 223 6303; www.mountaineers.org) published *Europe By Bike,* by Karen and Terry Whitehill (US$15).

BY MOPED AND MOTORCYCLE

Motorized bikes don't use much gas, can be put on trains and ferries, and are a good compromise between the high cost of car travel and the limited range of bicycles. However, they're uncomfortable for long distances, dangerous in the rain, and unpredictable on rough roads and gravel. Always wear a helmet, and never ride with a backpack. If you've never been on a moped before, a twisting alpine road is not the place to start. Expect to pay about US$20-35 per day; try auto repair shops, and remember to bargain. Motorcycles are more expensive and normally require a license, but are better for long distances. **Bosenberg Motorcycle Excursions**, Mainzer Str. 54, 55545 Bad Kreuznach, Germany (tel. (49) 671 67 312; www.bosenberg.com) arranges tours in Austria and Switzerland; they also rent motorcycles (Apr.-Oct.). Before renting, ask if the quoted price includes tax and insurance, or you may be hit with an unexpected additional fee. Avoid handing your passport over as a deposit; if you have an accident or mechanical failure you may not get it back until you cover all repairs. Pay ahead of time instead. *Europe by Motorcycle*, by Gregory Frazier (Arrowstar Publishing; US$20) is helpful for planning your itinerary and making arrangements.

BY THUMB

No one should hitch without careful consideration of the risks involved. Not everyone can be an airplane pilot, but any bozo can drive a car. Hitching means entrusting your life to a random person who happens to stop beside you on the road and risking theft, assault, sexual harassment, and unsafe driving. The choice, however, remains yours. In Austria and Switzerland, men and women traveling in groups and men traveling alone might consider hitching (called "autostop") beyond the range of bus or train routes. If you're a woman traveling alone, don't hitch. It's just too dangerous. A man and a woman are probably the safest viable combination, while 2 men will have a harder time, and 3 will go nowhere. If you do decide to hitch, consider where you are. Where one stands is vital. Experienced hitchers pick a spot outside of built-up areas, where drivers can stop, return to the road without causing an accident, and have time to look over potential passengers as they approach. Hitching (or even standing) on super-highways is usually illegal: one may only thumb at rest stops or at the entrance ramps to highways. In the **Practical Information** section of many cities, we list tram or bus lines that take travelers to strategic points for hitching out.

Finally, success will depend on what one looks like. Successful hitchers travel light and stack their belongings in a compact but visible cluster. Most Europeans signal with an open hand, rather than a thumb; many write their destination on a sign in large, bold letters and draw a smiley-face under it. Drivers prefer hitchers who are neat and wholesome. No one stops for anyone wearing sunglasses. Safety issues are always imperative, even for those who are not hitching alone. Safety-minded hitchers avoid getting in the back of a 2-door car and never let go of their backpacks. They will not get into a car that they can't get out of again in a hurry. If they ever feel threatened, they insist on being let off, regardless of where they are. Acting as if they are going to open the car door or vomit on the upholstery will usually get a driver to stop. Hitchhiking at night can be particularly dangerous; experienced hitchers stand in well-lit places, and expect drivers to be leery of nocturnal thumbers (or open-handers).

Most large cities in Austria and Switzerland offer a ride service (listed as **Mitfahrzentrale** in the **Practical Information**), a cross between hitchhiking and the ride boards common at many universities, which pairs drivers with riders; the fee varies according to destination. Riders and drivers can enter their names on the Internet through the **Taxistop** website (www.taxistop.be), but be aware that not all of these organizations screen drivers and riders; ask in advance.

 HITCHHIKERS BEWARE. *Let's Go* strongly urges you to consider seriously the risks before hitching. We do not recommend it as a safe means of transportation, and none of the information presented here is intended to do so.

SPECIFIC CONCERNS

WOMEN TRAVELERS

Women travelers will likely feel safer in Austria and Switzerland than just about anywhere in the world—violent crime is generally rare. Unlike in some parts of southern Europe, catcalls and whistling are not acceptable behavior in Austria and Switzerland. Still, women exploring on their own inevitably face some additional safety concerns, but it's easy to be adventurous without taking undue risks. If you are concerned, you might consider staying in hostels which offer single rooms that lock from the inside or in religious organizations that offer rooms for women only. Communal showers in some hostels are safer than others; check them before settling in. Stick to centrally located accommodations and avoid solitary late-night treks or metro rides. Generally, the less you look like a tourist, the better off you'll be. Dress conservatively, especially in rural areas. Wearing a conspicuous **wedding band** may help prevent unwanted overtures. Some travelers report that carrying pictures of a "husband" or "children" is extremely useful to help document marriage status. Even a mention of a husband waiting back at the hotel may be enough in some places to discount your potentially vulnerable, unattached appearance.

In cities, you may be harassed no matter how you're dressed. Your best answer to verbal harassment is no answer at all; feigned deafness, sitting motionless and staring straight ahead at nothing in particular will do a world of good that reactions usually don't achieve. The extremely persistent can sometimes be dissuaded by a firm, loud, and very public "Go away!" (in German: *"Lass mich in Ruhe"* (lass mish in roo-uh), French: *"Laissez-moi tranquille"* (lay-say mwa trrah-keel), and Italian: *"Vai via!"* (viy vee-uh)).

When traveling, always carry extra money for a phone call, bus, or taxi. **Hitching** is never safe for lone women, or even for 2 women traveling together. Choose train compartments occupied by other women or couples. Look as if you know where you're going (even when you don't) and consider approaching older women or couples for directions if you're lost or feel uncomfortable. Don't hesitate to seek out a police officer or a passerby if you are being harassed. *Let's Go: Austria & Switzerland* lists emergency numbers (including rape crisis lines) in the Practical Information listings of most cities. Memorize the emergency numbers in the places you visit. Carry a **whistle** or an airhorn on your keychain, and don't hesitate to use it in an emergency. An **IMPACT Model Mugging** self-defense course will not only prepare you for a potential attack, but will also raise your level of awareness of your surroundings as well as your confidence (see **Self Defense,** p. 20). Women also face some specific health concerns when traveling (see **Women's Health,** p. 25).

 FURTHER READING: WOMEN TRAVELERS.

A Journey of One's Own: Uncommon Advice for the Independent Woman Traveler, Thalia Zepatos. Eighth Mountain Press (US$17).

Adventures in Good Company: The Complete Guide to Women's Tours and Outdoor Trips, Thalia Zepatos. Eighth Mountain Press (US$17).

Active Women Vacation Guide, Evelyn Kaye. Blue Panda Publications (US$18).

Travelers' Tales: Gutsy Women, Travel Tips and Wisdom for the Road, Marybeth Bond. Traveler's Tales (US$8).

A Foxy Old Woman's Guide to Traveling Alone, Jay Ben-Lesser. Crossing Press. (US$11).

More Women Travel: Adventures, Advice & Experience. Miranda Davies and Natania Jansz. Penguin Books (US$16.95).

TRAVELING ALONE

There are many benefits to traveling alone, among them greater independence and challenge. As a lone traveler, you have greater opportunity to interact with the residents of the region you're visiting. Without distraction, you can write a great travel log in the grand tradition of Mark Twain, John Steinbeck, and Charles Kuralt. On the other hand, any solo traveler is a more vulnerable target of harassment and street theft. Lone travelers need to be well-organized and look confident at all times. Try not to stand out as a tourist, and be especially careful in deserted or very crowded areas. If questioned, never admit that you are traveling alone. Maintain regular contact with someone at home who knows your itinerary. A number of organizations supply information for solo travelers, and others find travel companions. Here are a few to get started:

American International Homestays, P.O. Box 1754, Nederland, CO 80466 (tel. (303) 642 3088 or (800) 876 2048; email ash@igc.apc.org; www.commerce.com/ homestays). Arranges lodgings with English-speaking host families in Austria.

Connecting: Solo Traveler Network, P.O. Box 29088, 1996 W. Broadway, Vancouver, BC V6J 5C2, Canada (tel. (604) 737 7791; email info@cstn.org; www.cstn.org). Bi-monthly newsletter features going solo tips, single-friendly tips and travel companion ads. Annual directory lists holiday suppliers that avoid single supplement charges. Advice and lodging exchanges facilitated between members. Membership US$25-35.

Travel Companion Exchange, P.O. Box 833, Amityville, NY 11701 (tel. (516) 454 0880 or (800) 392 1256; www.travelalone.com). Publishes the pamphlet *Foiling Pickpockets & Bag Snatchers* (US$4) and *Travel Companions*, a bi-monthly newsletter for single travelers seeking a travel partner (subscription US$48).

FURTHER READING; TRAVELING ALONE.
Traveling Solo, Eleanor Berman. Globe Pequot (US$17).
The Single Traveler Newsletter, P.O. Box 682, Ross, CA 94957 (tel. (415) 389 0227). 6 issues US$29.

OLDER TRAVELERS

Austria and Switzerland have among the highest mean life spans in the world, so senior citizen travelers are in good company. Seniors often qualify for hotel and restaurant discounts as well as discounted admission to many tourist attractions. If you don't see a senior citizen price listed, ask and you may be delightfully surprised. In **Switzerland,** women over 62 and men over 65 qualify as seniors, and women over 60 and men over 65 get senior status in **Austria.** A **Seniorenausweis** (Senior Citizen Identification Card) entitles holders to a 50% discount on all Austrian federal trains, Postbuses, and BundesBuses, and the card works as an ID for discounted museum admissions. The card costs about 350AS, requires a passport photo and proof of age, and is valid for one calendar year. It is available in Austria at railroad stations and major post offices, as well as the main train station in Zurich. Both National Tourist Offices offer guides for senior citizens. Many discounts require proof of status, so prepare to be carded. Agencies for senior group travel are growing in enrollment and popularity. Here are a few of them:

ElderTreks, 597 Markham St., Toronto, ON, Canada, M6G 2L7 (tel. (800) 741 7956 or (416) 588 5000; fax 588 9839; email passages@inforamp.net; www.eldertreks.com).

Elderhostel, 75 Federal St., Boston, MA 02110-1941 (tel. (617) 426 7788 or (877) 426 8056; email registration@elderhostel.org; www.elderhostel.org). Offers culture, history, and nature courses in Austria and Switzerland of varying lengths throughout the spring, summer, and fall. Must be 55 or over (spouse can be of any age).

The Mature Traveler, P.O. Box 50400, Reno, NV 89513 (tel. (775) 786 7419 or (800) 460 6676; www.maturetraveler.com). Subscription US$30.

Walking the World, P.O. Box 1186, Fort Collins, CO 80522 (tel. (970) 498 0500; fax 498 9100; email walktworld@aol.com; www.walkingtheworld.com), arranges walking tours in Switzerland.

FURTHER READING: OLDER TRAVELERS.
No Problem! Worldwise Tips for Mature Adventurers, Janice Kenyon. Orca Book Publishers (US$16).
A Senior's Guide to Healthy Travel, Donald L. Sullivan. Career Press. (US$15).
Unbelievably Good Deals and Great Adventures That You Absolutely Can't Get Unless You're Over 50, Joan Rattner Heilman. Contemporary Books (US$13).
Have Grandchildren, Will Travel. Pilot Books (US$10).
Doctor's Guide to Protecting Your Health Before, During, and After International Travel. Pilot Books (US$10).
Europe the European Way: A Traveler's Guide to Living Affordably in the World's Great Cities. Globe Piquot Press (US$14).

GAY AND LESBIAN TRAVELERS

As Austria and Switzerland are conservative countries with limited tolerance for homosexuality, public displays of affection can attract unfriendly attention. On the other hand, Geneva, Zurich, and Vienna have a wide variety of homosexual organizations and establishments, from biker and Christian groups to bars and barber shops, though these services can be difficult to find; tourist offices sometimes have info, otherwise check the local listings. The German word for gay is *schwul;* for lesbian, *lesben* (LEZ-ben) or *lesbisch* (LEZ-bisch). Bisexual is *bisexual* or simply *bi* (bee). In French, *homosexuelle* can be used for both men and women, but the preferred terms are *gai* (GEH) and *lesbienne* (les-bee-YENN).

The age of consent in **Austria** is 18 for gay men, 14 for lesbians. **Homosexuelle Initiative** (HOSI) is a nation-wide organization with offices in most cities which provides information on gay and lesbian establishments, resources, and supports and publishes warnings about aggressively intolerant areas and establishments. HOSI Wien, II, Novarag. 40, Vienna (tel. 216 66 04), publishes Austria's leading gay and lesbian magazine, the *Lambda-Nachrichten*, quarterly. A number of smaller and alternative organizations operate throughout the country. The age of consent in **Switzerland** is 16. There are several gay working groups in the larger cities, such as **Homosexuelle Arbeitsgruppe. Dialogai,** headquartered in Geneva, av. Wendt 57, mailing address: Case Postale 27, CH-1211, Geneva 7 (tel. (022) 340 00 00; fax 340 03 98), formed a partnership with **l'Aide Suisse contre le Sida** (ASS), an organization that works against AIDS. Several gay publications are available in centers and bookshops; *Dialogai Info* provides information on French Switzerland, articles, interviews, and more. For information about organizations, centers, and other resources in specific cities, consult the city's **Practical Information** section; for information on bars and nightclubs, see the individual **Sights and Entertainment** sections. Listed below are contact organizations, mail-order bookstores and publishers which offer materials addressing some specific concerns.

Gay's the Word, 66 Marchmont St., London WC1N 1AB (tel. (0171) 278 7654; email gays.theword@virgin.net; www.gaystheword.co.uk). The largest gay and lesbian bookshop in the U.K. Mail-order service available. No catalogue of listings, but they will provide a list of titles on a given subject.

Giovanni's Room, 345 S. 12th St., Philadelphia, PA 19107 (tel. (215) 923 2960; fax 923 0813; email giophilp@netaxs.com). An international feminist, lesbian, and gay bookstore with mail-order service which carries the publications listed here.

International Gay and Lesbian Travel Association, 4331 N. Federal Hwy., Suite 304, Fort Lauderdale, FL 33308 (tel. (954) 776 2626 or (800) 448 8550; fax (954) 776 3303; email IGLTA@aol.com; www.iglta.com). Organization of 1350 companies serving gay and lesbian travelers. Call for lists of travel agents, accommodations, and events.

International Lesbian and Gay Association (ILGA), 81 rue Marché-au-Charbon, B-1000 Brussels, Belgium (tel./fax (322) 502 24 71; email ilga@ilga.org; www.ilga.org). Provides political information, such as homosexuality laws of individual countries.

RESOURCES FOR GAY AND LESBIAN TRAVELERS.
Spartacus International Gay Guide. Bruno Gmunder Verlag. (US$33).
Damron Men's Guide, Damron's Accommodations, and *Damron's Women's Traveller.* Damron Travel Guides (US$14-19). For more information, call (415) 255 0404 or (800) 462 6654 or check their website (www.damron.com).
Ferrari Guides' Gay Travel A to Z, Ferrari Guides' Men's Travel in Your Pocket, Ferrari Guides' Women's Travel in Your Pocket, and *Ferrari Guides' Inn Places.* Ferrari Guides (US$14-16). For more information, call (602) 863 2408 or (800) 962 2912 or check their website (www.q-net.com).
The Gay Vacation Guide: The Best Trips and How to Plan Them, Mark Chesnut. Citadel Press (US$15).

TRAVELERS WITH DISABILITIES

Austria and Switzerland are relatively accessible to travelers with disabilities *(behinderte Reisende)*. Tourist offices can usually offer info about which sights, services, etc. are accessible. Disabled visitors to **Austria** may want to contact the

FURTHER READING: DISABLED TRAVELERS.

Resource Directory for the Disabled, Richard Neil Shrout. Facts on file (US$45).
Wheelchair Through Europe, Annie Mackin. Graphic Language Press (tel. (760)
     944 9594; email niteowl@cts.com; US$13).
The Diabetic Traveler, P.O. Box 8223 RW, Stamford, CT (tel. (203) 327 5832). A
     short quarterly offering advice on flying, eating abroad, and visiting extreme cli-
     mates. A subscription (US$18.95) includes a list of organizations worldwide.
Global Access (www.geocities.com/Paris/1502/disabilitylinks.html) has specific
     links for disabled travelers in Switzerland, as well as general links.

Vienna Tourist Board, Obere Augartenstr. 40, A-1025 Vienna (tel. (1) 21114; fax 216
84 92), which offers booklets on accessible Vienna hotels and a general guide to
the city for the disabled. The Austrian National Tourist Office in New York and
Vienna offers many pages of listings for wheelchair-accessible sights, museums,
and lodgings in Vienna—ask for the booklet *Wien für Gäste mit Handicaps
(Vienna for Guests with Handicaps)*. With 3 days' notice, the Austrian railways
will provide a wheelchair for the train. The international wheelchair icon or a large
letter "B" indicates access. In **Switzerland,** disabled travelers can contact **Mobility
International Schweiz,** Hard 4, CH-8408 Winterthur (tel. (052) 222 68 25; fax 222 68
38). Most Swiss buildings and restrooms have ramps. The Swiss Federal Railways
have adapted most of their train cars for wheelchair access, and InterCity and
long-distance express trains have wheelchair compartments. The Swiss National
Tourist Office publishes a fact sheet of *Travel Tips for the Disabled.*

Cities, especially Vienna, Zurich, and Geneva, publish mounds of information
for handicapped visitors. *Let's Go* tries to indicate which budget acommodations
have wheelchair access. In general, those with disabilities should inform airlines
and hotels of their disabilities when making arrangements for travel; some time
may be needed to prepare special accommodations. Call ahead to restaurants,
hotels, parks, and other facilities to find out about the existence of ramps, the
widths of doors, the dimensions of elevators, etc.

Rail is probably the most convenient form of travel for disabled travelers in Austria and Switzerland, but you have to be willing to ask for assistance. Many trains
have a special compartment reserved for disabled travelers. Guide-dog owners
should inquire as to the specific quarantine policies of each destination country.
At the very least, they will need to provide a certificate of immunization against
rabies. Hertz, Avis, and National car rental agencies have hand-controlled vehicles
at some locations. The following organizations provide information or publications that might be of assistance:

Mobility International USA (MIUSA), P.O. Box 10767, Eugene, OR 97440 (tel. (541)
     343 1284 voice and TDD; fax 343 6812; email info@miusa.org; www.miusa.org). Sells
     *A World of Options: A Guide to International Educational Exchange, Community Ser-
     vice, and Travel for Persons with Disabilities* (US$35).

Moss Rehab Hospital Travel Information Service (tel. (215) 456 9600;
     www.mossresourcenet.org). A telephone and Internet resource center on international
     travel accessibility and other travel-related concerns for those with disabilities.

Society for the Advancement of Travel for the Handicapped (SATH), 347 Fifth Ave.,
     #610, New York, NY 10016 (tel. (212) 447 1928; fax 725 8253; email
     sathtravel@aol.com; www.sath.org). Advocacy group publishing a quarterly color travel
     magazine *OPEN WORLD* (free for members or US$13 for nonmembers). Also publishes
     a wide range of information sheets on disability travel facilitation and accessible desti-
     nations. Annual membership US$45, students and seniors US$30.

The following organizations arrange tours or trips for disabled travelers:

Directions Unlimited, 720 N. Bedford Rd., Bedford Hills, NY 10507 (tel. (800) 533
     5343; in NY tel. (914) 241 1700; fax 241 043; email cruisesusa@aol.com). Special-

izes in arranging individual and group vacations, tours, and cruises for the physically disabled. Group tours for blind travelers.

Flying Wheels Travel Service, 143 W. Bridge St., Owatonne, MN 55060 (tel. (800) 535 6790; fax 451 1685). Arranges trips for groups and individuals in wheelchairs or with other sorts of limited mobility.

TRAVELERS WITH CHILDREN

Family vacations often require that you slow your pace and always require that you plan ahead, but that doesn't mean they can't be done cheaply. Austria and Switzerland are decidedly family-friendly, offering transportation discounts and a plethora of attractions. Children under 4 travel free on Austrian trains, and children 4-12 for half-price. The **Kilometer Bank** (see **National Railpasses,** p. 44) is a great deal for families traveling by train in Austria. The **Swiss Family Card** (see **National Railpasses,** p. 44) lets children under 16 travel free with at least 1 parent holding a valid ticket. Make sure car rental companies provide a car seat for younger children.

When deciding where to stay, the special needs of young children can limit your choice of accommodations; once you decide on a *Pension* or *Privatzimmer*, call ahead and make sure it's child-friendly. *Let's Go* notes which accommodations are particularly family-oriented. Look for hostels with kitchens where you can prepare your own food. When you tire of grocery-store fare, look for restaurants which offer children's menus, half-portions, and discounts. Virtually all museums and tourist attractions also have a children's rate. Children under 2 generally fly for 10% of the adult airfare on international flights (this does not necessarily include a seat). International fares are usually discounted 25% for children from 2 to 11.

As always, good preparation will lessen the difficulty of travel. Make sure each child, no matter how young, has a valid passport. Underschedule yourself with free days for unexpected emergencies. Check with your family doctor to be sure your child's immunizations are up to date; schedule a well-child checkup if it's been a while since the last one. Take along useful equipment, such as a baby carrier (if your baby is small enough), not only for walking trips and hikes, but also to free your hands to juggle luggage, particularly when boarding or disembarking trains; a wrist-to-wrist leash might be helpful for keeping track of an active toddler. Be sure that your child carries some sort of ID in case of an emergency or if he/she gets lost, and arrange a reunion spot in case of separation when sight-seeing. Avoid unnecessary changes in your child's routines before a trip and maintain them as much as possible while on the trip.

FURTHER READING: TRAVELERS WITH CHILDREN.

Backpacking with Babies and Small Children, Goldie Silverman. Wilderness Press (US$10).

Take Your Kids to Europe, Cynthia W. Harriman. Globe Pequot (US$17).

How to Take Great Trips with Your Kids, Sanford and Jane Portnoy. Harvard Common Press (US $10).

Have Kid, Will Travel: 101 Survival Strategies for Vacationing With Babies and Young Children, Claire and Lucille Tristram. Andrews and McMeel (US$9).

Adventuring with Children: An Inspirational Guide to World Travel and the Outdoors, Nan Jeffrey. Avalon House Publishing ($15).

Trouble Free Travel with Children, Vicki Lansky. Book Peddlers (US$9).

MINORITY TRAVELERS

Although Austria and Switzerland are predominantly Caucasian, they are quite tolerant of minority travelers, particularly in larger cities. The majority of minority travelers will likely never encounter any difficulty, though the further you venture out into the countryside, the more likely it is that you will encounter the occasional odd stare. Villagers are notoriously curious, so don't be surprised or offended if old women linger in their windows to catch a glimpse of you. In recent years, a growing population of foreign workers (particularly Turks) has felt the sting of Swiss anxiety about economic recession, but physical confrontations are rare—Austrians and Swiss tend to be much too mild-mannered to provoke violence or hurl insults.

For further reading, consult *Go Girl! The Black Woman's Book of Travel and Adventure*, by Elaine Lee (Eighth Mountain Press, US$18).

RELIGIOUS CONCERNS

Despite the overwhelmingly Christian population of Austria and Switzerland, serious religious intolerance is uncommon and unauthorized. While the predominance of Catholics and Protestant churches make it simple for anyone of those faiths to find a place to worship or attend services, however, the same task can be challenging for those of other religions and faiths. Locating religous communities outside the mainstream is easiest in large cities, as is attending services in English. As usual, the Internet can be an invaluable resource, since most religious organizations maintain some kind of webpage or email list. For example, **Muslims** can turn to www.islam.ch (available in German, French, or Italian) for information and addresses throughout Switzerland. The largest Muslim congregation is located in Zurich. For Austria, www.angelfire.com/nm/nourmedia offers Islamic news specific to Austria, and most Muslims are concentrated in Vienna.

Though the Dalai Lama visited Switzerland, it is Austria that hosts an array of **Buddhist** organizations, with centers in Vienna (Fleischmarkt 16, 1st fl., A-1010 Vienna; tel. (01) 513 38 80; email bodhidharma.zendo@blackbox.at), Innsbruck (An der Furt 18, II., A-6020 Innsbruck; tel./fax (0512) 36 71 13; email aldo.deutsch@uibk.ac.at), and Salzburg (Schlossstr. 38, A-5020 Salzburg; tel./fax (62) 74 75 16; email sunyata@magnet.at). Switzerland, on the other hand, has several **Hindu** temples, including a Swami temple in Bern (Verein Murugan Temple, Looslistr. 21A, 3027 Bern; tel. (031) 992 20 98) and a Shiva temple in Zurich (Sivan Temple, Wehntalerstr. 293, 8046 Zurich; tel. (01) 371 02 42).

Switzerland is particularly attractive to members of the Church of Jesus Christ of Latter-day Saints (commonly called LDS or **Mormons**), who can attend one of their temples in Zollikofen, near Bern (Tempelstr., Ch-3052 Zollikofen; tel. (031) 911 09 12). In addition, the Chur congregation of the LDS Church maintains a website at www.spin.ch/~hlt-chur/schweiz.html, which provides a link to the contact information and meeting schedules of each LDS congregation in Switzerland. For information on the LDS Church in Austria, contact numbers, and meeting schedules, go to www.ettl.co.at/mormon/english/. Similar websites exist for **Jehovah's Witnesses**; check out www.watchtower.org for more information.

Jewish communities in Austria and Switzerland are small but vigorous. The majority of Austrian Jews live in Vienna, where the Stadttempel is the only synagogue in operation. The Jewish Welcome Service (tel. (01) 533 88 91) helps Jewish visitors to Vienna, including those who plan to remain in the city for an extended period of time. In addition, the Federation of Austrian Jewish Communities (Seitenstetteng. 4, Postfach 145, A-1010 Vienna; tel. (01) 53 10 40; fax 53 15 77) is a good resource for information on Jewish congregations elsewhere in Austria. Switzerland has its own version of the same organization, the Federation of Swiss Jewish Communities (SIG) (Gotthardstr. 65, 8002 Zurich; tel. (01) 201 55 83; fax 202 16 72). The largest Jewish communities in Switzerland are in Zurich, Basel, and Geneva, where the World Jewish Congress has headquarters.

If you're looking for services in **English,** you'll have the most luck in larger cities like Vienna and Zurich. Ask at the tourist office for contact information or look on the Internet for details on the meetings of specific religious groups.

DIETARY CONCERNS

The dairy-based cuisine in Austria and Switzerland is not particularly vegan-friendly, but the growing health and environmentally-conscious movements in both countries mean more options for vegetable-eaters. Vegans will likely have difficulty outside of large cities, but ovo-lacto vegetarians can enjoy many traditional meatless dishes. *Let's Go* lists vegetarian and vegetarian-friendly restaurants under Food listings in each city or town. Tourist offices list hotels and retaurants that serve vegetarian, organically grown, or whole food. In addition, locating vegetarian restaurants in major cities can be done on the Internet. Visit www.vrg.org/travel/ for suggestions, reviews, and links to specific vegetarian restaurants. The European Vegetarian Union maintains the webpage www.ivu.org/evu/. Contact the **North American Vegetarian Society,** P.O. Box 72, Dolgeville, NY 13329 (tel. (518) 568 7970; email navs@telenet.com; www.cyberveg.org/navs/).

Travelers who keep kosher should contact synagogues in larger cities for information on kosher restaurants. The Swiss National Tourist Office distributes the pamphlet *The Jewish City Guide of Switzerland* (published by Spectrumpress International, Spectrum-House, Tanegg., 8055 Zurich), which lists synagogues, rabbis, butchers, kosher hotels and restaurants, along with other useful information and phone numbers for kosher and Jewish travelers. Kosher food may not be available outside of large cities. When preparing your trip, it might be helpful to consult the **Jewish Travel Guide,** which lists synagogues, kosher restaurants, and Jewish institutions in Austria and Switzerland (available from Vallentine-Mitchell Publishers, Newbury House 890-900, Eastern Ave., Newbury Park, Ilford, Essex, U.K. IG2 7HH (tel. (0181) 599 88 66; fax 599 09 84); in the U.S. ($16) from ISBS, 5804 NE Hassallo St., Portland, OR 97213-3644 (tel. (800) 944 6190)).

FURTHER READING: DIETARY CONCERNS.
The Vegetarian Traveler: Where to Stay if You're Vegetarian, Jed Civic. Larson Pub. (US$16).
Europe on 10 Salads a Day, Greg and Mary Jane Edwards. Mustang Publishing. (US$10, UK£9).

ALTERNATIVES TO TOURISM

STUDY

There are a plethora of study abroad programs in both Austria and Switzerland. In Austria, there are summer or year-long academic programs associated with American Universities in Vienna, Salzburg, Innsbruck, and Bregenz. You can study anything from architecture to social work to Vienna's psychologists. German language programs are available for study abroad in both Austria and Switzerland. In Switzerland, there are summer and winter sessions for universities in Geneva and Zurich. The University of Delaware organizes a summer-long Swiss Hospitality Program. In addition, there are walking, bicycling, and hiking programs that can be arranged for students visiting both countries.

If you plan to study abroad Switzerland for more than 3 months, you need to fill out a residency permit and receive authorization from Swiss authorities. To study in Austria, citizens of non-EU countries must have visas. All foreigners must have valid study permits. Most U.S. universities will arrange permits for students.

UNIVERSITIES

Most American undergraduates enroll in programs sponsored by U.S. universities. However, if your German is already good local universities can be much cheaper than an American university program, though it can be hard to receive academic credit. Schools that offer study abroad programs to foreigners are listed below.

Webster University in Geneva and Vienna, contact: Study Abroad Office, Webster University, 470 E. Lockwood, St. Louis, MO, USA 63119 (tel. (317) 968 6988 or (800) 984 6857; fax (314) 968 7119; email brunote@websteruniv.edu; webster2.websteruniv.edu). More than 400 students from 65 countries come here to pursue full degree programs or summer and semester sessions in a range of concentrations and electives. All courses are taught in English and are fully accredited.

American Institute for Foreign Study, College Division, 102 Greenwich Ave., Greenwich, CT 06830 (tel. (800) 727 2437, ext. 6084; www.aifs.com). Organizes programs for high school and college study in universities in Austria. Summer, fall, spring, and year-long programs. Scholarships available. Contact Dana Maggio at dmaggio@aifs.com.

Beaver College Center for Education Abroad, 450 S. Easton Rd., Glenside, PA 19038-3295 (tel. (800) 755 5607 or (888) BEAVER9; fax (215) 572 2174; email cea@beaver.edu; www.beaver.edu/cea). Operates summer-, semester- and year-long programs in Austria and Switzerland. Applicants preferably should have completed 3 full semesters at an accredited university. Programs run anywhere from US$1900 for a summer program to $20,000 for a full year abroad.

Central College Abroad, Office of International Education, 812 University, Pella, IA 50219 (tel. (800) 831 3629 or (515) 628 5284; fax 628 5316; email StudyAbroad @Central.edu; studyabroad.com/central/). Offers semester- and year-long study abroad programs in Austria and Switzerland. US$25 application fee. Scholarships available. Applicants must be at least 18, have completed freshman year of college, and have a minimum 2.5 GPA.

LANGUAGE SCHOOLS

Programs are run by foreign universities, independent international or local organizations, and divisions of the local universities. Programs vary in cost tremendously, and may or may not include lodging, daytrips, and cultural activities.

University of Geneva Summer Courses, contact: Mr. Gerard Benz, University of Geneva, summer courses, rue de Candolle 3, CH-1211 Geneva 4, Switzerland (tel. (22) 750 74 34; fax 750 74 39; bisatti@uni2a.unige.ch). Teaches French language and civilization at all levels and offers excursions to Geneva and its surroundings. Tuition for a 3-week summer couse SF470. Minimum age 17.

Wiener Internationale Hochschulkurse, contact: Magister Sigrun Anmann-Trojer, Wiener Internationale Hochschulkurse, Universität, Dr. Karl Lueger-Ring 1, A1010 Wien, Austria (tel. 405 12 54; fax 405 125 410). Offers German courses for beginners and advanced students, as well as lectures on German and Austrian literature, music, linguisics, and Austrian culture, including exposure to the Vienna waltz and choir singing. Tuition for a 4-week summer course 4300AS, accommodations 6000AS.

FURTHER READING: STUDY.

Academic Year Abroad. Institute of International Education Books (US$45).
Vacation Study Abroad. Institute of International Education Books (US$40).
Peterson's Study Abroad Guide. Peterson's (US$30).

WORK

AUSTRIA

Austria has strict work restrictions. If you are a citizen of an EU country, you do not need a work permit for employment in Austria. Otherwise, you need to obtain a work permit before leaving your country of origin. Of course, as a stroke of bureaucratic genius, this is virtually impossible for casual and seasonal work. Expect to pay 16% of your salary to mandatory health and Social Security programs (except for au pairs). To find employment in Austria, German-speakers can contact the state-run employment office *Arbeitmarktservice*. There are no private employment offices in Austria. The easiest jobs for foreigners to find are in the hotel and agriculture industries. Also, English teachers and au pairs are always in demand.

SWITZERLAND

Switzerland's equally strict immigration policies can make it very difficult for foreigners to find work. A free booklet entitled *Living and Working in Switzerland* can be obtained from the Swiss Embassy for full information on their policies. A residence permit covers both the right to live and work in Switzerland. Do not attempt to find employment there without a permit, as ski resorts have been known to hire police solely for the purpose of checking visas. Employers may be fined 3000SFr for hiring illegal workers. One job you don't (usually) need a permit for is busking—street musicians in Bern can do quite well by the end of the day—but check with the local police for a list of authorized areas and times.

Swiss hotels hire foreign workers for their summer and winter tourist seasons. It's worth it to start looking for a job early: April/May for the summer season and September/October for the winter season. Writing ahead to places can save you grief later. Fluency in German will be helpful, sometimes necessary, in finding a job. To find employment in the ski resort industry, try the **Jobs in the Alps Agency** (17 High Street, Greton, Northants, NN17 3DE). Tourist offices may also be of help.

If you are interested more in a rural experience than in making money, a job in the agriculture industry might be suited to you. One-third of summer farm hands are foreign workers. The hours are long but room and board is generally included. In general, expect to work very hard, long hours. The Swiss hold very high standards for cleanliness and productivity but are willing to pay high wages in return.

AU PAIR

Accord Cultural Exchange, 750 La Playa, San Francisco, CA 94121 (tel. (415) 386 6203; fax 386 0240; email leftbank@hotmail.com; www.cognitext.com/accord), offers au pair jobs to people aged 18-29 in Austria. au pairs work 5-6 hours a day, 30 hours a week, plus 2 evenings of babysitting. Light housekeeping and childcare in exchange for room and board plus US$250-400 per month salary. Program fees US$750 for the summer, US$1200 for the academic year. US$40 application fee.

interExchange, 161 Sixth Ave., New York, NY 10013 (tel. (212) 924 0446; fax 924 0575; email interex@earthlink.net) provides information on international work, au pair programs, and au pair positions in Austria and Switzerland.

Childcare International, Ltd., Trafalgar House, Grenville Place, London NW7 3SA (tel. (0181) 906 31 16; fax 906 34 61; email office@childint.demon.co.uk; www.childint.demon.co.uk) offers au pair positions in Austria and Switzerland. Provides information on qualifications required and local language schools. The organization prefers a long placement but does arrange summer work. UK£80 application fee.

TEACHING ENGLISH

International Schools Services, Educational Staffing Program, P.O. Box 5910, Princeton, NJ 08543 (tel. (609) 452 0990; fax 452 2690; email edustaffing@iss.edu; www.iss.edu). Recruits teachers and administrators for American and English schools in Austria and Switzerland. All instruction in English. Applicants must have a bachelor's degree and two years of relevant experience. Nonrefundable US$100 application fee. Publishes *The ISS Directory of Overseas Schools* (US$35).

Office of Overseas Schools, A/OS Room 245, SA-29, Dept. of State, Washington, D.C. 20522-2902 (tel. (703) 875 7800; fax 875 7979; email overseas.school@state.gov; state.gov/www/about_state/schools/). Keeps a list of schools abroad and agencies that arrange placement for Americans to teach abroad.

AGRICULTURE

Willing Workers on Organic Farms (WWOOF), PO Box 2675, Lewes, U.K. BN7 1RB (email fairtours@gn.apc.org or wwoof@dataway.ch; www.phdcc.com/sites/wwoof or www.dataway.ch/~reini/wwoof/). Membership (US$10) in WWOOF allows you to receive room and board at a variety of organic farms in Austria and Switzerland in exchange for your help on the farm.

VOLUNTEER

Volunteer jobs are readily available almost everywhere. You may receive room and board in exchange for your labor. You can sometimes avoid the high application fees charged by the organizations that arrange placement by contacting the individual workcamps directly; check with the organizations.

Service Civil International Voluntary Service (SCI-VS), 814 NE 40th St., Seattle, WA 98105 (tel./fax (206) 545 6585; email sciivsusa@igc.apc.org). Arranges placement in workcamps in Europe for those age 18 and over. Local organizations sponsor groups for physical or social work. Registration fees US$50-250, depending on the camp location.

Volunteers for Peace, 1034 Tiffany Rd., Belmont, VT 05730 (tel. (802) 259 2759; fax 259 2922; email vfp@vfp.org; www.vfp.org). A nonprofit organization that arranges speedy placement in 2-3 week workcamps in Austria or Switzerland comprising 10-15 people. Most complete and up-to-date listings provided in the annual *International Workcamp Directory* (US$15). Registration fee US$195. Free newsletter.

FURTHER READING: VOLUNTEER.
International Jobs: Where they Are, How to Get Them, Eric Kocher and Nina Segal. Perseus Books (US$16).
How to Get a Job in Europe, Robert Sanborn. Surrey Books (US$22).
The Alternative Travel Directory, Clayton Hubbs. Transitions Abroad (US$20).
Work Abroad, Clayton Hubbs. Transitions Abroad (US$16).
International Directory of Voluntary Work, Victoria Pybus. Vacation Work Publications (US$16).
Teaching English Abroad, Susan Griffin. Vacation Work (US$17).
Overseas Summer Jobs 1999, Work Your Way Around the World, and *Directory of Jobs and Careers Abroad.* Peterson's (US$17-18 each).

OTHER RESOURCES

THE WORLD WIDE WEB

Switzerland has a comprehensive web network. Even in the smallest towns, everything is online. Business, tourist offices, hostels, and individuals in the smallest villages have great user-friendly websites. Austria is a bit behind Switzerland, but is still fairly up-to-date. It is definitely worth your time to search the Internet for Austrian and Swiss websites before you go; they can be helpful both in planning your vacation and learning more about Austrian and Swiss culture in general.

Swiss Search Engines: Try www.search.ch or www.sear.ch.

Austrian Search Engines: These have been under construction, but try www.search.at or www.suchmaschine.at.

Youth Hostel Listings: The official hostel webpages for Austria (www.jgh.at) and Switzerland (www.jugendherberge.ch) can be useful to get an overview of all hostels at a glance.

Budget Airfare: Check out www.travelocity.com, www.lowestfare.com, www.bestfares.com, or www.cheaptickets.com.

WWW TIP. The domain for most Swiss webpages is **ch**; Austria's is **at**.

Rail Passes: The Eurail website is www.raileurope.com; the SwissPass site is www.raileurope.com/us/rail/passes/switzerland_index.htm.

The CIA World Factbook: (www.odci.gov/cia/publications/factbook/index.html) has tons of vital statistics on Austria and Switzerland. Check it out for an overview of either country's economy and government.

Foreign Language for Travelers: (www.travlang.com) can help you brush up on your German, French, and Italian for travel in Austria and Switzerland.

Let's Go: (www.letsgo.com) is where you can find our newsletter, information about our books, up-to-the-minute links, and more.

FURTHER READING: THE WORLD WIDE WEB.
How to Plan Your Dream Vacation Using the Web. Elizabeth Dempsey. Coriolis Group (US$25).
Nettravel: How Travelers Use the Internet, Michael Shapiro. O'Reilly & Associates. (US$25).
Travel Planning Online for Dummies, Noah Vadnai. IDG Books. (US$25).

AUSTRIA

US$1 = 13.023 SCHILLINGS (AS)	10AS = US$0.768
CDN$1 = 8.791AS	10AS = CDN$1.137
UK£1 = 20.851AS	10AS = UK£0.479
IR£1 = 17.472AS	10AS = IR£0.572
AUS$1 = 8.454AS	10AS = AUS$1.183
NZ$1 = 6.859AS	10AS = NZ$1.457
SAR1 = 3.215AS	10AS = SAR4.686
1SFR = 8.589AS	10AS = 1.164SFR
1DM = 7.035AS	10AS = 1.421DM
1Kč = 0.379AS	10AS = 26.328Kč
1FT = 0.054AS	10AS = 184.06FT
EURO€1 = 13.762AS	1AS = EURO €0.624

PHONE CODES	The **country code** for Austria is 43. International calls from Austria require the prefix 900 (from Vienna) or 00.

Although the mighty Austro-Hungarian Empire crumbled after World War I, Austria today remains a complex, multiethnic country with a fascinating political and cultural history. At the peak of Habsburg megalomania, the Austrian empire encompassed Bohemia, Moravia, Galicia, Transylvania, Hungary, Bosnia-Herzegovina, Dalmatia, Croatia, and substantial portions of Italy. The nine semi-autonomous provinces, or *Bundesländer*, of present-day Austria reflect the diversity engendered by that cultural constellation. Clockwise from the northeast, Austria's provinces are: Vienna *(Wien)*, Burgenland, Styria *(Steiermark)*, Carinthia *(Kärnten)*, Tyrol *(Tirol)*, Vorarlberg, Salzburg, Upper Austria *(Oberösterreich)*, and Lower Austria *(Niederösterreich)*. Each of these provinces was once an independent region that became part of the Habsburg lands by marriage, treaty, or trade, and each retains deep-rooted regional identities and unique dialects. Ethnic diversity made it difficult for any sort of unified Austrian identity to form, and the push and pull of various forces in the region meant constantly changing authority. As a result, Austria has changed governments like some people go through clothes, moving from centuries of imperial rule via the First Republic and Hitler's mad barbarism to the 20th century's sedate and sanguine Second Republic.

Austria owes much of its contemporary fame and fortune to its overpowering physical beauty. The mention of Austria evokes images of onion-domed churches set against snow-capped Alpine peaks, lush meadows blanketed with mustard flowers, pristine mountain lakes, dark cool forests, and mighty castles towering over the Danube. Forests and meadows cover two-thirds of Austria's total land area, while more than half of the country is studded with mountains. Western Austria is almost entirely taken over by them. The *Großglockner*, Austria's highest peak, towers at 3797m (12,457 ft.). The mountains generate year-round tourism: Alpine sports dominate the winter scene, while lakeside frolicking draws visitors in the warmer months. The (no longer so blue) Danube, Europe's longest river, has been central to Austrian industry and aristocracy since the country's beginning: both the Babenbergs and the Habsburgs set up residences on its shores. Now, river cruises showcase their ruined castles as well as the thriving vineyards whose magic potion made the Middle Ages bearable. Vienna, once the imperial headquarters and now the country's capital, majestically straddles the river. Vienna's stately Baroque architecture mixes with the modern urban landscape, housing artistic treasures, historical landmarks, and an increasingly dynamic and cosmopolitan population, not to mention unearthly beautiful music and *really* delicious pastry.

A BRIEF HISTORY OF AUSTRIA

IN THE BEGINNING

Beginning in Paleolithic times, nomadic hunter-gatherers roamed through what is now Austria for thousands of years, gradually becoming more settled as they began to farm, domesticate stock animals, and mine Austria's rich salt deposits. The 25,000 year old carved stone fertility goddess Venus of Willendorf (which is so valuable that the National Museum displays only a copy) bears witness to their level of civilization, as do 4000 year old pottery shards found near Mondsee. By 6000 BC, even the remotest areas of Austria were part of a vigorous commercial network that linked mining centers and agricultural communities, as the recent discovery of the hunter-trader Ötzi has proved.

As economic opportunities in the area diversified, more aggressive peoples wanted a share of the wealth. Around 500 BC, the **Celts** took control of the salt mines and established the kingdom of **Noricum**, which developed a relatively affluent economy (for the time) based on a thriving salt and iron trade. In turn, the **Romans** conquered their Austrian neighbors to secure the Danube frontier against marauding Germanic tribes. Christianity came to Austria via the Roman soldiers, while legions, traders, and missionaries came via Roman roads along the Danube and through the Alps.

Germanic raids finally forced Romans to retreat from Noricum in the 5th century. Over the next three centuries, during the *Völkerwanderung*, (tribal migration) various peoples, including the Huns, Ostrogoths, and Langobards romped through the Austrian territories, but none established any lasting settlement. Eventually, three groups divided the region: the **Alemanni** in the south, the **Slavs** in the southwest, and the **Bavarians** in the north. The dukes of Bavaria concentrated on converting the population to Christianity in an attempt to establish law and order and create a power-base. The result of their efforts was the creation of the Archbishopric of Salzburg, which remained Austria's ecclesiastical center for centuries.

FROZEN IN TIME On September 19, 1991, hikers accidentally discovered the deep-frozen corpse of a middle-aged man in a glacier, 10,000 feet above sea level, along the Austro-Italian border. The dead man, nicknamed Ötzi the Iceman after the Ötztal valley where he was found, lived approximately 5,300 years ago, but his body was perfectly preserved in the ice. Ötzi's appearance has been a boon to prehistoric research, but the question of who owned his body was hotly debated for several years. Although he was found by Austrians, his resting place was just within the Italian border. In 1998, Ötzi was put on display in Bolzano, Italy, where he lies behind bulletproof glass at -6° Celsius and 98% humidity. The Italians appreciate their oldest resident, not least because of brisk trade in chocolate Ötzis, Ötzi ice cream, Ötzi pizza, Ötzi wine, and Ötzi sausage throughout Bolzano.

80,000 BC The first *Homo Sapiens* venture into the Danube river valley.

23,000 BC The statuette now known as Venus of Willendorf is carved.

500 BC Celts establish the kingdom of Noricum in present-day Austria, and mine "white gold" (salt).

15 BC-AD 488 Roman troops under Caesar Augustus conquer and occupy Noricum, establishing settlements at Carnuntum and Vindobona (present-day Vienna).

AD 375-800 The Romans abandon Noricum. Various Germanic tribes, followed by Huns, Slavs, Avars, and Magyars sweep through the area during the great Tribal Migration.

Mid-7th century Bavarian dukes fight the Slavs and Magyars for religious and political control of the Danube Valley and its mines.

798 The Archbishopric of Salzburg is established as Austria's ecclesiastical headquarters.

803 Charlemagne establishes Austria as the eastern frontier (Ostmark) of the Holy Roman Empire German Nation.

955 Emperor Otto I defeats the Magyars, winning back the Austrian territories in the Battle of Lechfeld.

976 Marchio Liutpoldus, the first Babenberg, receives control of Austria.

996 The name Austria (Ostarrichi) appears for the first time in an official document.

1156 Emperor Friedrich Barbarossa raises Austria to the status of a duchy.

1246 After the death of the last Babenberg duke, Ottokar II of Bohemia rules Austria for 26 years.

DYNASTIC AUSTRIA: FAMILY FEUD

Austria had its first taste of imperialism in the mid-9th century when **Charlemagne,** founder of the Holy Roman Empire, turned his eyes east in hopes of heading off invaders on the frontiers of his empire. When he died, Charlemagne's kingdom collapsed and the eastern regions were overrun by marauding tribes. After his father drove Magyar invaders out of the area, Holy Roman Emperor Otto II entrusted Margrave Liutpoldus (a.k.a. Leopold of Babenberg, see **A rose by another name?** p. 68) with the defense of the Empire's eastern territories, the "Ottonian Mark" or *Ostarrichi* (Old High German for *Österreich*). The Babenberg dynasty concentrated on stabilizing the frontiers but also on extending its protectorate by shrewdness and strategic marriages. By founding monasteries and abbeys, as well as importing German-speaking settlers, the Babenbergs built up a core of loyal subjects that supported them in their political maneuvering between the Holy Roman Emperor and the Pope. Pragmatically, they supported whichever side benefitted them the most. For example, when the Emperor put a price on the head of **Richard the Lionheart,** Leopold V (whom Richard had offended while crusading) was happy to detain him on his way home from the Third Crusade, in return for a share of the enormous ransom England paid for her king.

Unfortunately for the dynasty, the last Babenberg died childless, leaving the country fragmented during a 19-year *Interregnum.* The major contestants for the Austrian lands were the Bohemian King Ottokar II and the new Holy Roman Emperor, the Swiss nobleman **Rudolf of Habsburg.** Although Ottokar had married the widowed Babenberg queen and was already in power, Rudolf beat him out in the battle of Marchfeld, laying the foundation for 6 centuries of Habsburg dynastic rule in Austria.

Like their Babenberg predecessors, the Habsburgs made every effort to increase their property by means of treaties and marriages, with memorable success (though they lost their original Swiss holdings after a farmer's revolution). Gradually, the Habsburgs accumulated the various regions that make up modern Austria and then some. Duke Albrecht acquired the duchies of Carinthia, South Tyrol, and Slovenia, while **Rudolf the Founder**'s short rule (1358-1365) was marked by his acquisition of the Earldom of Tirol, as well as the founding of the University of Vienna. Between 1375 and 1523, the Habsburgs purchased Vorarlberg. Friedrich III strategically arranged the marriage of his son, **Maximilian I,** to the heiress of the powerful Burgundian kingdom, giving the Habsburgs control over the Low Countries.

Maximilian is credited with the adaptation of Ovid's couplet: *"Bella gerant alii, tu felix Austria nube."* (Let other nations go to war; you, lucky Austria, marry—an early riff on "Make love, not war.") Maximilian's son Philipp married into the Spanish royal house, endowing his son, Charles V, with a vast empire that encompassed Austria, the Netherlands, Castile, Spanish America, Aragon, and its Italian and Mediterranean possessions. As if this weren't enough, Charles was elected Holy Roman Emperor in 1519, gaining nominal control of Germany as well. At this point, the Habsburg Empire was really quite large, which explains why Charles gave Austria to his brother **Ferdinand,** who, despite not knowing German, Czech, or Hungarian, managed to get himself crowned in Bohemia and Hungary as well.

Despite their massive possessions and imperial veneer, the Habsburg ship hit rough waters in the 16th and 17th centuries. For one thing, the **Reformation** fomented social unrest throughout the empire and threatened stability to the point that Austrian nobles hired mercenaries to crush the rebels in the Peasants' Wars of 1525-1526. The Catholic Church made Austria the first battleground of the **Counter-Reformation,** a daring choice since the population was overwhelmingly Protestant at the time. Early victories over Protestant forces during the Thirty Years War (1618-1648) restored Habsburg control of Bohemia, where they promptly (and forcibly) converted most of the peasants back to Catholicism. With the end of the war and the Treaty of Westphalia, however, the Habsburgs forfeited vast tracts of territory. To make matters worse, the Black Plague decimated the population. Finally, adding insult to injury, the Ottoman Turks kept besieging Vienna, until **Prince Eugene of Savoy** drove them out (not only of Austria, but of Hungary, Transylvania, and Croatia as well!). After the death of the last Spanish Habsburg, the plucky prince then led the Habsburg troops to victory over the French in the **War of Spanish Succession,** which ended with a treaty giving Spain to France, while the Habsburgs gained Belgium, Sardinia, and parts of Italy. By 1718, the Habsburgs had control of Bohemia, Moravia, Silesia, Hungary, Croatia, Transylvania, Belgium, Lombardy, Naples, Sicily, and, of course, Austria.

WAR GAMES & POWER STRUGGLES

Like a house of cards, the Habsburg empire teetered as it grew. When, thanks to the **Pragmatic Sanction** passed by her father (which allowed Habsburg succession through the female line), Maria Theresia ascended the throne in 1740, her European neighbors were eager to see Habsburg power diminished. King **Friedrich the Great** of Prussia snatched Silesia (now southwest Poland), one of the Habsburg's most prosperous provinces; Maria Theresa spent the rest of her life unsuccessfully maneuvering to reclaim it. In the **War of Austrian Succession** between 1740 and 1748, Maria Theresa maintained her rule with help from the Hungarians, but at the cost of Lombardy. The marriage of Maria Theresa's daughter Marie Antoinette to the future Louis XVI was a tragic attempt to forge an alliance with France, which was quickly negated by the **French Revolution.** The French Revolutionary National Assembly declared war on Austria in 1792, showcasing the military genius of young commander General **Napoleon Bonaparte,** who secured French possession of Belgium and most of Austria's remaining Italian territories. Napoleon's troops even invaded Vienna, where Napoleon took up residence in Maria Theresa's favorite palace, Schönbrunn, and married her granddaughter.

Oddly enough, Napoleon's success led to the official establishment of the Austrian empire. In 1804, Franz II renounced his claim to the now-defunct Holy Roman crown and pro-

AUSTRIA

1278 Holy Roman Emperor Rudolf von Habsburg defeats Ottokar, beginning more than 600 years of Habsburg rule in Austria.

1452 Friedrich III is crowned Holy Roman Emperor by the Pope in Rome, subsequently claiming the imperial throne as the hereditary right of the Habsburgs.

1496 Philipp the Handsome, Friedrich III's grandson, marries Juana of Aragon (daughter of Ferdinand and Isabella of Spain). Their sons Karl and Ferdinand become, respectively, Holy Roman Emperor Charles V and King Ferdinand of Austria.

1527 Ferdinand is crowned King of Bohemia and Hungary, founding the Danube Monarchy.

1529 The Ottoman Turks under Sultan Suleiman unsuccessfully lay siege to Vienna.

Mid-16th century The Protestant Reformation reaches Austria, followed by the

Catholic Counter-Reformation.

1618-1648 Austria is involved in the Thirty Years War between Catholics and Protestants.

1679 The plague wreaks havoc throughout Austria.

1683 The Ottoman Turks surround and besiege Vienna. The Austrians drive the Turks out of Hungary.

1701-1714 Austria fights France in the War of Spanish Succession.

1740 Thanks to the Pragmatic Sanction, Maria Theresa is crowned Empress of Austria, Queen of Hungary and Bohemia. During her reign, Austria loses several territories to Prussia.

1780 Josef II abolishes serfdom and grants freedom of religion.

1804 Napoleon's troops occupy Vienna. The Holy Roman Empire of the German Nation

A ROSE BY ANOTHER NAME?

Medieval history celebrates Austria's two major ruling families: the Babenbergs (976-1246) and the Hapsburgs (1278-1918). Unfortunately for the history books, the Babenbergs were not actually named Babenberg, but rather Poppon; furthermore, their family seat was not the Castle Babenberch in Bamberg, Germany, but a nameless castle somewhere in German Swabia. The name Babenberg was an invention of the 12th-century historian Otto von Freising, himself a Poppon, who found the name of his ancestor Poppo von Grabfeld unsuitable for his patriotic purposes. He casually renamed the dynasty "Babenberg," which later historians adopted and embellished with individual heroic epithets, such as Ernst the Brave and Leopold the Glorious. This relatively harmless deception quickly became an integral part of Austrian history, with the result that historians today still refer to the "Babenbergs" without a second thought.

claimed himself Franz I, Emperor of Austria. During the Congress of Vienna, which redrew the map of Europe after Napoleon's defeat, Austrian Chancellor **Clemens Wenzel Lothar von Metternich** tried to restore the old order while masterfully orchestrating the re-consolidation of Austrian power. Metternich preached the gospel of legitimacy and stability—in other words, the perpetuation of conservative government—to achieve a European balance of power. His machinations ushered in a long peace of flourishing commerce and industry.

In Austria, as elsewhere in Europe, the first half of the 19th century was marked by immense technological progress and social change. The French philosophy of middle-class revolution reached Austria in the spring of 1848. Working together, students and workers built barricades, took control of the imperial palace, and demanded a constitution and freedom of the press. Metternich was so stunned he fled to England. Ethnic rivalries and political differences divided the revolutionary forces, however, and the government was able to suppress the worker's revolution and a Hungarian rebellion. The epileptic emperor **Ferdinand I** paid the price for the renewed stability; he was pressured to abdicate in favor of his nephew, **Franz Josef I,** whose 68-year reign was one of the longest in history.

Austria's position in Europe continued to shift throughout Franz Josef's life. Prussia under **Otto von Bismarck** dominated European politics, defeating Austria in 1866 and prompting the **Ausgleich** (compromise) of 1867, which established the dual Austro-Hungarian monarchy. Still, non-German speakers were marginalized within the **Austro-Hungarian Empire,** until 1907, when the government ceded basic civil rights to all peoples in the Empire and accepted universal male suffrage. Austria was divided about **Pan-Germanism,** which sought a united German nation, and ultimately did not join the alliance of German states that make up Germany. Nevertheless, by the turn of the century, Vienna was in political turmoil; the anti-Semitic **Christian Socialists** under **Karl Lueger** were on the rise. Meanwhile, burgeoning nationalist sentiments, especially among the Serbia-inspired South Slavs, led to severe divisions within the multinational Austro-Hungarian Empire. Tired and disheartened after half a century on the throne, the suicide of his only son, and the murder of his wife, Franz Josef wanted to maintain *Ruhe und Ordnung* (peace and order), but he could not stop the tide of modernity.

CURRENTS OF MODERNITY

Brimming with ethnic tension and locked into the rigid system of alliances that resulted from the 19th century wars, the Austro-Hungarian Empire was a disaster waiting to happen. The spark that set off the explosion was the ill-fated journey **Franz Ferdinand,** the heir to the imperial throne, and his wife Sophie took to Sarajevo in June 1914, where they were assassinated by a young Serbian nationalist named Gavrilo Prinzip, a member of the terrorist organization The Black Hand. Austria's declaration of war against Serbia set off a chain reaction that pulled most of Europe into the conflict: Russia hurried to support Serbia, Germany to support Austria, and France to support its Entente partner, Russia. Franz Josef died in 1916, leaving the throne to his reluctant grandnephew **Karl I** (see **Charlie's Last Stand,** p. 69) who struggled in vain to preserve the Habsburg inheritance (going so far as to initiate secret negotiations with the French). Despite his valiant efforts and those of the army, declarations of independence by the Empire's non-German peoples and the desperate maneuvering of Viennese intellectuals ensured the demise of the monarchy. On November 11, 1918, Karl finally got the peace he had striven for, but only after liberals declared the first **Republic of Austria,** ending the 640-year-old Habsburg dynasty.

Between 1918 and 1938, Austria had its first, bitter taste of parliamentary democracy. After the Entente forbade a unified *Deutsch-Österreich*, the shrunken Austrian state became the **First Republic,** consisting of the German-speaking lands of the former Habsburg empire minus those granted to Italy, Czechoslovakia, and Hungary. The Republic suffered massive inflation, unemployment, and near economic collapse, but by the mid-1920s, the Austrian government had stabilized the currency and established economic relations with neighboring states. Still, violent internal strife between political parties weakened the Republic's already shaky democratic foundation. In 1933, the weak coalition government gave way to **Engelbert Dollfuss**'s declaration of martial law. In order to protect Austria from Hitler, Dollfuss entered an ill-fated alliance

is officially dissolved and the former Holy Roman Emperor becomes Emperor Franz I of Austria.

1814 The Congress of Vienna, made up of representatives from 200 states, duchies, and independent cities, tries for nine months to solve Europe's political problems while costing the Emperor 80,000 guilders a day for entertainment.

1848 The so-called "Storm Year" witnesses workers' revolutions throughout the Europe and the Danube-Monarchy. Disheartened, Emperor Ferdinand abdicates in favor his nephew Franz Josef.

1867 To resist Prussian aggression, Emperor Franz Josef agrees to the dual monarchy of Austria-Hungary.

1914 The heir to the Austrian throne, Franz Ferdinand is murdered in Sarajevo by a Serbian nationalist on June 28. One month later, Austria-Hungary declares war on Serbia, which triggers World War I.

CHARLIE'S LAST STAND Contrary to popular history, Karl I, the last emperor of the Austro-Hungarian empire, did not abdicate. Leaders of the Republic were willing to let him remain Emperor as long as he signed an agreement renouncing all political involvement. Karl signed (in pencil), but in Feldkirch, on the Swiss border, he composed the "Feldkircher Manifest," which nullified all agreements he had signed since October 1918. The Austrians banned him from the country, so Karl mounted a campaign to reclaim the Hungarian throne, but, alas, the Hungarians arrested and deported him to England. Within a year, Karl died of tuberculosis on the island of Madeira.

AUSTRIA

1916 Emperor Franz Joseph dies and is succeeded by his grand-nephew Karl I.

1918 The Austro-Hungarian empire collapses; the first Republic of Austria is established and the Habsburgs lose the Austrian throne.

1920s Social Democrats and Christian Socialists struggle for domination of the new parliamentary democracy.

1933 Chancellor Dollfuss dissolves Parliament and declares martial law.

1935 Dollfuss is murdered by Nazis.

1938 Chancellor Schuschnigg calls for a plebiscite against annexation by Nazi Germany. Hitler forces Schuschnigg to resign. German troops invade Austria and the country is absorbed into the Nazi German empire as the "Ostmark" (Eastern Province).

with fascist Italy. Two years later, just as Mussolini and Hitler made peace, Austrian Nazis assassinated Dollfuss. His successor, **Kurt Schuschnigg,** was also ultimately unable to maintain Austrian independence in the face of Nazi pressure.

The well-known conclusion to the tale of the First Republic is the Nazi annexation of Austria. On March 9, 1938, hoping to stave off a Nazi invasion, Schuschnigg called for a referendum against unity with Germany, but Hitler demanded Schuschnigg's resignation. On March 12, the new Nazi chancellor invited German troops into Austria where they met no resistance. Although Goebbels' propaganda wildly exaggerated the enthusiasm of Austrians for Hitler (as did a phony referendum in April, in which 99% of Austrians approved of annexation), many Austrians wanted to believe the **Anschluß** (union with Germany) would make their future brighter. When the Nazis marched into Vienna on March 14, thousands turned out to cheer them on. Disillusionment quickly set in, as Austria lost both its name (it became the "Ostmark," then merely the "Alpine district") and its self-respect. Aside from individual resistance fighters, cooperation with the Nazis and anti-Semitism became the rule in Austria, though disillusionment about empty Nazi promises of peace and prosperity soon set in. While WWII raged, tens of thousands of Jews, among them many of Austria's leading intellectuals, artists, and writers, were forced to emigrate or sent to concentration camps, along with political and religious dissidents, handicapped persons, Gypsies, and homosexuals. Only a few thousand came home alive.

After Soviet troops brutally "liberated" Vienna in 1945, Austria was divided into 4 zones of occupation by Allied troops. As a Nazi victim, however, Austria enjoyed some political rights. Already in April 1945, a provisional government was established with 75-year old **Karl Renner** as president. In November, the National Assembly declared Austria's independence from Germany (*Wir sind kein zweiter deutscher Staat; wir sind nichts anders als Österreicher,* 'We are not a second German state; we are nothing but Austrians'). During the Allied occupation of Austria, the Soviets tried to make Austria Communist, but finally settled for stripping their sector of anything that could be moved. The immediate post-war period was a time of general political, economic, and psychological chaos throughout Austria, but most Austrians rejoiced in their new-found independence and eagerly grasped their second chance at creating a democracy. Despite Russian plundering and severe famines in the late 1940s, the Marshall Plan helped to jump-start the Austrian economy, laying the foundation for Austria's present prosperity. In 1955, a 10-year diplomatic stalemate ended in a favorable constellation of Cold War negotiations after Stalin's death, which made the restoration of Austria's full sovereignty possible through the signing of the **State Treaty.** In return, Austria declared its complete neutrality.

CONTEMPORARY POLITICS

Since then, Austria has cultivated a new identity—one that is internationally neutral, democratic, and Western-oriented. The period from 1945 to the present, commonly referred to as the **Second Republic,** has emerged as a progressive social democratic welfare state as stable as any other in the hemisphere. It has faced significant challenges, particularly the question of denazification, institutionalized political corruption, and international outrage at the election of Kurt Waldheim, a former Nazi sympathizer, but has also made significant progress toward the Austrian ideal of a united, democratic state. The Austrian constitution was established in 1920, amended in 1929, suspended in 1938, restored in 1945, and is still in effect today. It provides for a president (head of state), a chancellor (head of government), a bicameral legislature, three supreme courts, and provincial governments. All citizens 18 years of age and older are eligible to vote.

Elected in May 1992 and re-elected in 1998, the current president of Austria is **Thomas Klestil,** a member of the Austrian People's Party. In January 1997, **Viktor Klima** was appointed Chancellor and became the leader of the Social Democratic Party of Austria. In his previous role as finance minister, Klima helped bring about Austria's membership in the European Union (EU) and oversaw Austria's participation in the Economic and Monetary Union (EMU), which inaugurated the **euro,** a common European currency, on January 1, 1999. (All prices in Austria should be listed in both *Schillinge* and euros, though the euro will not circulate until 2002.)

Since the end of World War II, Austrian politics have been dominated on the federal level by Klima's party, the Social Democrats *(Österreichische Sozialdemokratische Partei*—SPÖ). For decades, the SPÖ has led coalition governments formed with either the second-largest party, the People's Party of Austria *(Österreichische Volkspartei*—ÖVP) or with the right-wing Freedom Party *(Freiheitliche Partei Österreichs*—FPÖ). Under these governments, Austria has built up one of the world's most successful industrial economies, with enviably low unemployment and inflation rates, as well as a generous, comprehensive welfare state. Since the mid-1970s, alternative political groups have striven to combat the negative side-effects of this prosperity. The Green Alternative List (GAL), for instance, which is made up of several environmental parties and independents, such as the Green Alternative *(die grüne Alternative)* and the United Green Party of Austria *(Vereinte Grüne Österreichs)*, promotes environmental concerns, peace, and social justice. The challenges of large-scale immigration from the former Eastern Block and war-torn Yugoslavian countries have led to divisions among the parties. Charismatic xenophobe **Jörg Haider** has used the FPÖ in recent years to exploit Austrian anxiety about immigration, though other leaders in the party protested by splitting off and forming the Liberal Forum.

All in all, modern Austria has done much to promote Emperor Franz Josef's goal of *Ruhe und Ordnung* (peace and order). Dealing with Cold War tensions made Austria one of the major players on the European diplomatic stage and a gateway to much of Eastern Europe. In addition to participating in the EU and the Council of Europe, Austria has closely affiliated itself with the United Nations, as demonstrated by

1941 Deportations of Austrian Jews begins.

1943 Allied powers publish the Moscow Declaration stating that Austria was a victim of Nazi aggression.

1945 Vienna is liberated by Soviet troops and a provisional Austrian government is formed under Karl Renner.

1955 The State Treaty is signed and Allied troops withdraw, restoring Austria's independence. Austria declares absolute neutrality.

1995 Austria joins the European Union.

1998 Austria assumes the 6-month presidency of the EU.

AUSTRIA

the UN-City in Vienna. After forty years on the eastern edge of Europe, the events associated with the disintegration of the Iron Curtain and Soviet hegemony have placed Austria back in the heart of Europe.

CULTURE AND CUSTOMS

Due no doubt in part to *The Sound of Music*, the prevailing stereotype of Austrians among English-speakers is of a homogenous white population with essentially the same culture as Germany. First impressions may support this illusion, but those who look beyond appearances discover the ethnic, religious, and linguistic diversity that gives Austria a unique cultural flavor.

PEOPLE

Austrians are a hardy people who are fiercely proud of their culture, history, and principles. Following the pattern established by their beloved Emperor Franz Joseph, Austrians live on average about 77 years. They are hard-working and frugal, though more laid-back than their German neighbors. They place great emphasis on education, which is responsible for over 99% literacy throughout the country. Comprehensive welfare ensures few homeless people, though street musicians congregate in heavily touristed areas. Unemployment hovers at around 7%. Ethnically, the Austrian people embody the idea of the "melting pot," for although 99% of Austria's 8 million people call themselves German, nearly every Austrian has genealogical ties to at least one of the countless ethnic groups once encompassed by the Habsburg empire. As befits the erstwhile stronghold of the Counter-Reformation, 78% of Austrians are Roman Catholic. 5% are Protestant, while 17% belong to Muslim, Jewish, Baptist, Mormon, and other religious denominations.

Austrians are as impressed as any tourist by the beauty of their country and they actively appreciate it by making extensive *Wanderungen* (hikes) and climbing mountains. They often spend summer vacations near the lakes of Carinthia and the Salzkammergut, and ski the winters away in Tirol and Vorarlberg. It was a Moravian Austrian, Matthias Zdarsky, who invented skiing around the

GRASS-ROOTS DEMONSTRATION A vocal group of women concerned over women's status in Austrian society have joined forces to form the U.F.F. *(Unabhängiges Frauen Forum)*. This non-radical, non-separatist women's group, comprised of an equal number of journalists, single mothers living in poverty, and middle-class women, formed in response to recent budget cuts they found especially detrimental to women. The U.F.F. developed a manifesto that focuses on economic equality between women and men. Their demands, relayed through media, demonstrations, and sit-ins, include: salary increases in badly paid jobs almost exclusively held by women, an end to glass ceilings, all-day, all-year child care facilities throughout the country, and the right to part-time work for both men and women with children with the right to return to full-time. The U.F.F. received such support that a national plebiscite was held—the *Frauenvolkbegehrens*. The U.F.F.'s mandate received enough votes to force discussion of the issue in Parliament. Their demands were debated by the Austrian government, which consisted of 20% female members and a conservative Minister of Women's Affairs. However, to the deep dissatisfaction of the U.F.F. and many Austrians, only the most minor reforms on the list were actually implemented. The U.F.F., now with branches in Salzburg, Tirol, and Vorarlberg, and a platform that has evolved to include issues of violence and discrimination, continues to lobby, and holds demonstrations in Stephanspl. on the first Saturday of each month. The U.F.F. is currently considering forming an independent political party. You can check their web page for updates at www.uff.at.

turn of the century; his contemporaries mocked him for sliding pointlessly down hills with boards strapped to his feet, but Austrians today claim him proudly as the father of their most lucrative tourist industry. In addition to their obsession with winter sports and lakes, most Austrians are passionately supportive of their soccer teams.

LANGUAGE

Although German is the official language of Austria, common borders with the Czech Republic, Slovakia, Hungary, Italy, Slovenia, Liechtenstein, and Switzerland make speaking more than one language imperative for most Austrians. In addition to foreign languages, however, the German spoken in Austria differentiates itself by accent and vocabulary from other German-speaking countries—interestingly, Austrian German is a Bavarian dialect. German-speakers don't need to be too worried about being understood: all Austrians speak High German, but as the inhabitants of each region speak a particular dialect, it is helpful to know some general peculiarities of Austrian German. As a result of the international connections of the Habsburg Empire, there are lots of French, Italian, Czech, Hebrew, and Hungarian words mixed in to the German, for example *Babuschka* for old woman. One easy way to recognize familiar words in Austrian German is to remember that Austrians add a diminutive '*erl*' (like the High German '*chen*' or '*lein*') to a lot of words; store clerks may ask if you want a *Sackerl (*a small bag), waiters might inquire if you would like a *bisserl* (a little bit) more of this or that, and a young girl is called a *Mäderl*. Something else to watch out for is that many vegetables have unique names in Austrian German: the German *Kartoffel* (potato) becomes *Erdapfel*, tomatoes are *Paradeiser*, corn is not *Mais* but *Kukuruz*, and green beans are *Fisoln*. Austrians mean "this year" when they say *heuer* and January when they say *Jänner*. If you get to know an Austrian well, chances are they'll say *Baba!* for goodbye.

FOOD AND DRINK

Just as the Austrians and their language are ethnically jumbled, many of the most famous Austrian dishes are foreign in origin: *Gulasch* is Hungarian, *Knödel* (dumplings) are Bohemian, and the archetypal Austrian dish, *Wienerschnitzel*, probably originated in Milan. Immigrants continue to influence Austrian cooking, and Turkish dishes like *Dönerkebab* are on their way to becoming an integral part of Austrian cuisine. In addition, each region of Austria contributes traditional dishes to the national cuisine, such as Carinthian *Kasnudeln* (large cheese- or meat-filled pasta squares) or Salzburger *Nockerl* (a mountain of sweetened, baked egg whites). Most of Austria's culinary inventions appear on the dessert cart. *Tortes* commonly contain *Erdbeeren* (strawberries) and *Himbeeren* (raspberries). Don't miss *Marillen Palatschinken*, a crepe with apricot jam, or *Kaiserschmarrn*, the *Kaiser's* favorite (pancake bits with a plum compote). Austrians adore the sweet dessert *Knödeln*, especially *Marillenknödel* (sweet dumplings with a whole apricot in the middle), though the typical street-stand dessert is the *Krapfn*, a hole-less doughnut usually filled with jam. The pinnacle of Austrian baking, however, are the twin delights of *Sacher Torte* (a rich chocolate cake layered with marmalade) and *Linzer Torte* (a light yellow cake with currant jam embedded in it).

Loaded with fat, salt, and cholesterol, traditional Austrian cuisine is a cardiologist's nightmare but a delight to the palate. Staple foods are simple and hearty, centering around *Schweinefleisch* (pork), *Kalbsfleisch* (veal), *Wurst* (sausage), *Ei* (egg), *Käse* (cheese), *Brot* (bread), and *Kartoffeln* (potatoes). Austria's most renowned dish, *Wienerschnitzel*, is a meat cutlet (usually veal or pork) fried in butter with bread crumbs. Although *Schnitzel* is Austria's most famous, its most scrumptious meat dish is *Tafelspitz*, beautifully cooked boiled beef. Soups are also an Austrian speciality; try *Gulaschsuppe* (gulasch soup) and *Frittatensuppe*

SACHER SCANDAL Austria takes its desserts very seriously. *Linzer Torte* is extremely important to the residents of Linz, and the whole country has a love affair with *Apfelstrudel*, but things work a little differently in Vienna, where *Sacher Torte* reigns supreme. It is one of the country's most famous cakes, but it is not clear who deserves credit for this celebrated dessert. While legend praises Franz Sacher as the originator of the confection Prince von Metternich loved, Café Demel doesn't agree—its proprietors claim the original recipe. Demel sued the Hotel Sacher, and the suit has resulted in bankruptcy, the sale of Demel to a corporation, and the suicide of Sacher's general manager. It's probably safest to stick to *Strudel*.

(pancake strips in broth). Recently, vegetarianism has gained popularity in Vienna, and even meaty dishes are showing the influence of a lighter, vegetable-reliant style. Vegetarians should look for *Spätzle* (a homemade noodle often served with melted cheese), *Steinpilze* (enormous mushrooms native to the area), *Eierschwammerln* (tiny yellow mushrooms), or anything with the word "Vegi" in it. Supermarket connoisseurs should have a blast with Austrian staples: yogurt (rich, almost dessert-like); the cult favorite Nutella (a chocolate-hazelnut spread); *Almdudler* (a lemonade-like soft drink); *Semmeln* (very cheap, very fresh rolls); the original *Müesli* (granola of the gods); and all kinds of chocolate, including Milka (you can't miss the purple cow) and Ritter Sport.

In the afternoon, Austrians flock to *Café-Konditoreien* (café-confectioners) to nurse the national sweet tooth with *Kaffee und Kuchen* (coffee and cake). You will discover pastries to suit every taste in Austria. While drinking a *Mélange*, the classic Viennese coffee with frothed cream and a hint of cinnamon, nibble on a heavenly *Mohr im Hemd*, a chocolate sponge cake topped with hot whipped chocolate, or just about anything with *Mohn* (poppyseed) in it. If you get the chance, try some steam-cooked *Buchteln* with vanilla sauce or poppy seeds.

Of course, you've got to have something to wash all that down. The most famous Austrian wine is probably *Gumpoldskirchen* from Lower Austria, the largest wine-producing province. *Klosterneuburger*, produced in the eponymous district near Vienna, is both reasonably priced and dry. Austrian beers are outstanding. *Ottakringer* and *Gold Fassl* flow from Vienna breweries, *Stiegl Bier* and *Augustiner Bräu* from Salzburg, *Zipfer Bier* from upper Austria, and *Gösser Bier* from Styria. Austria imports a great deal of Budweiser beer, but theirs is *Budvar*—the original Bohemian variety, not the chintzy American imitation..

THE ARTS

The most difficult question in any discussion of Austrian art history is where to stop. Austrian history is illuminated by so many stellar artists, musicians, and writers that any chronicle of them is necessarily insufficient, but it is impossible to appreciate the majesty and magnificence of Austrian culture without being familiar with at least a few of the brightest stars.

MOVEMENTS AND MUSICIANS

Austrian music occupies a central position in the Western Classical tradition, primarily due to the unique constellation of composers who created the **Viennese Classic.** These Austrian greats, including Haydn, Mozart, Schubert, and Beethoven, invented "Classical music" as we know it today. The rules they made up govern and constrain Western music still. Yet Austria is in many ways also the birthplace of modern music, having sheltered many of those who challenged these rules, including luminaries like Gustav Mahler and Arnold Schönberg. Austria is where Western Classical music was done and undone.

THE CLASSICAL ERA. Toward the end of the 18th century, Vienna was a musical madhouse. Composers hung out in salons, made fun of each other, and listened to themselves play music they wrote or music their friends wrote. The whole thing fed on itself: the more music was written, the more people wanted to write music.

One of the early stalwarts amidst this musical melee was **Christoph Willibald Gluck,** who composed many of his best-known operas in Vienna, including "Alceste" and early versions of "Orfeo," while at the same time acting as *Kapellmeister* for the court of Empress Maria Theresa. A staunch opponent of Italian opera factions, Gluck defended the use of German in song and promoted German operas by such illustrious contemporaries as Carl von Weber and Wolfgang Amadeus Mozart. Through his friendships with younger musicians and his own pioneering approach to music, Gluck influenced later Romantic composers.

The first master musician of Viennese Classicism is **Josef Haydn**. Born into the family of a poor wheelwright in Rohrau (Lower Austria) in 1732, Haydn began his career as a chorister in the cathedral of St. Stephen in Vienna before working for the princes of Esterházy (see **Eisenstadt,** p. 138). He soon became the conductor of the court orchestra and one of the most celebrated composers in Europe. Haydn created a variety of new musical forms that led to the shaping of the sonata and the symphony, structures that dominated musical doctrines throughout the 19th century. Fifty-two piano sonatas, 24 piano and organ concertos, 104 symphonies, and 83 string quartets provide rich and abundant proof of his pioneering productivity. He wrote the imperial anthem, *Gott erhalte Franz den Kaiser*, in order to rouse patriotic feeling during the Napoleonic wars. After WWI, Germany adopted the melody of *Gott erhalte* for its new anthem *Deutschland über Alles*.

The work of **Wolfgang Amadeus Mozart** represents the pinnacle of Viennese Classicism. Born in Salzburg in 1756, Mozart was the ideal child prodigy, playing violin and piano by age four, composing simple pieces by five, and touring Europe's imperial courts at age six. At 13, Mozart became *Konzertmeister* of the Salzburg court, but he disliked the town's narrow bourgeois atmosphere. In 1781 the Wunderkind finally fled Salzburg for Vienna, where he produced his first mature concerti, his best-known Italian operas, including *Don Giovanni* and *La Nozze di Figaro*, and the beloved and shamefully overwhistled string showpiece, *Eine kleine Nachtmusik*. Mozart wrote with unprecedented speed, creating 626 works of all kinds during his 35 years, always jotting down music without preliminary sketches or revisions. Mozart's overwhelming emotional power found full expression in his (unfinished) *Requiem*, which he continued composing until the last hours before his death, fulfilling his bitter aside to favorite student Franz Süssmayr: "You see, I *have* been writing this Requiem for myself." Although many people have postulated mysterious reasons for the genius' demise, most historians agree that Mozart died of kidney failure. Within a few decades of his death, Mozart was recognized once more as a master, who in Tchaikovsky's words was "the culmination of all beauty in music."

Only **Ludwig van Beethoven** could compete with Mozart for the devotion of the Viennese. Born into a family of Flemish musicians in Bonn in 1770, he lived in Vienna all his adult life and died there too. Beethoven was an innovator in a music scene steeped in tradition. His gifts were manifest in his 32 piano sonatas, string quartets, overtures, and concertos, but shone most intensely in his nine epoch-shattering symphonies. His *Ninth Symphony* had an enormous cultural impact, in part because of his introduction of a human voice to the symphonic form—the chorus sings the text to Friedrich Schiller's *Ode to Joy*. Beethoven's *Fidelio*, which premiered May 23, 1814 at the Kärntnertortheater in Vienna, is regarded as one of the greatest, if weightiest, German operas. Due to increasing deafness, the composer could maintain contact with the world only through a series of conversational notebooks, which provide an extremely thorough, though one-sided, record of his conversations (including his famous emotional outpouring, the *Heiligenstadt Testament*, written in Vienna's 19th district). Music historians locate Beethoven somewhere between Viennese Classicism and Romanticism.

AUSTRIA

Like Beethoven, **Johannes Brahms** straddled musical traditions. In his home near the Karlskirche in Vienna, Brahms composed his Hungarian Dances, piano concertos, and numerous symphonies, all of which were first performed by Hans Richter and the Vienna Philharmonic. Despite his own Romantic compositions, Brahms is often regarded as a classicist who used his position in the Viennese *Musikverein* and his status as a major composer to oppose Romanticism and the musical experiments of his arch-rival, Wagner. In the process, Brahms became the grand old man of the Viennese music scene. Although he was rigorously formalistic in his music, Brahms demonstrated the delight of the Viennese in the lighter things in life. When a well-wisher approached him in the opera house and asked the great composer for a momento of their meeting, he penned the opening bars of the Blue Danube Waltz on her fan and wrote underneath: "Unfortunately not by your Johannes Brahms."

THE ROMANTIC ERA. Franz Schubert's music is the soul of Romanticism. Born in the Viennese suburb of Lichtenthal in 1797, Schubert began his career as a chorister in the royal imperial Hofkapelle and later made his living teaching music. Mainly self-taught, he composed the *Unfinished Symphony* and the *Symphony in C Major*, which are now considered masterpieces but were virtually unknown during his lifetime. His lyrical genius was more readily recognized in his *Lieder*, musical setting of poems by Goethe, Schiller, and Heine. Through his compositions, the *Lied* became a serious work in the tradition of Viennese Classicism. The great song cycles made famous during Schubert's musical soirées—*Die schöne Müllerin* and the quietly despairing *Winterreise*—frame Schubert's greatest and most mature creative period. This burst of creativity was cut short by his early death in 1828 at the age of 32. Despite the brevity of Schubert's career, his genius for pure melody was a catalyst for later musical innovations by (among others) Schumann, the Strausses, and Gustav Mahler.

THE NINETEENTH CENTURY. Anton Bruckner is famous for his massively orchestrated symphonies. Born and bred in the Danube valley, Bruckner sang as a choirboy and became organist at the monastery of St. Florian before moving to Vienna in 1868 at age 44 to write his most renowned compositions, including the Third, Fourth, and Seventh Symphonies. Bruckner was derided as a bumpkin during his life, but posthumously recognized as a virtuoso organist and one of the greatest symphonic masters of the 19th century.

Beginning with **Johann Strauss the Elder** (1804-1849), the Strauss family kept Vienna on its toes for much of the 19th century. Johann Sr. composed mostly waltzes and showy pieces, including the famous *Radetzkymarsch*, which is still played every New Year by the Vienna Philharmonic. Largely responsible for the "Viennese Waltz," **Johann Strauss the Younger** (1825-1899) shone in his youth as a brilliant violinist and savvy cultural entrepreneur. The waltz became popular during the Congress of Vienna, offering a new exhilaration that broke free from older, more stiffly formal dances. The quick step allowed for more intimate physical contact as partners whirled about the room, arm in arm, constantly on the verge of falling down or getting intoxicatingly dizzy. Richard Wagner, of all people, noted admiringly on a visit to the city that Viennese waltzing was "more potent than alcohol." Sensing the trend, Johann became its master, eventually writing the *Blue Danube* and *Tales from the Vienna Woods*, two of the most recognized waltzes of all time, thereby earning the title, "King of the Waltz." In his spare time he managed to knock off some popular operas as well, *Die Fledermaus* being his most celebrated. His brothers, Josef (1827-1870) and Eduard (1835-1916) also worked as conductors and composers.

Hugo Wolf is little-known in the English-speaking world, due mainly to the fact that his chosen form, the *Lied*, is not an established genre in the average concert repertoire. Wolf perfected the *Lied* as a dramatic symphonic miniature, in which music and words are indissolubly linked. He frequently set poems by Goethe,

FALCO! Somewhere between the 12-tone system of Schönberg and the sweeping harmonics of Brahms, Falco bursts into Austrian musical history. Attempting to reconcile an artistic quest for the self with the nationalistic and naturalistic intellectual bent of the era, his rockin' *Amadeus* permeated the subconscious of radio listeners across the globe in the 80s. The song took as its subject Wolfgang Amadeus Mozart, and attempted, in the infamous "historical breakdown," to reconcile the classical past with the rock'n'roll present. History goes something like: Mozart, then Falco, nothing in between. Sadly, Falco died in a car crash in the Dominican Republic in February 1998 while allegedly planning a comeback. For a nostalgic reexamination of Falco's talent, seek out *The Remix Collection*, a compendium of his greatest hits.

AUSTRIA

Eichendorff, and Mayreder to music, creating such masterful collections as the *Mörike Lieder* (1888) and the *Italienisches Liederbuch* (1890). A key figure in the development of Austrian classical music, Wolf's *Lieder* rank among some of the loveliest and most evocative music ever composed in Vienna.

As a direct precursor to the Second Viennese experiments of Arnold Schönberg, **Gustav Mahler**'s music incorporates fragments and deliberately inconclusive segments which read like nostalgic remnants of a once certain and orderly world. During his lifetime Mahler was mainly known as a conductor—he revolutionized the opera houses of Prague, Vienna, and New York, although his most interesting work took place at the Viennese *Staatsoper*. As a composer, Mahler employed unusual instrumentation and startling harmonic juxtapositions. His Eighth Symphony, often called *Symphony of Thousand*, requires an orchestra and two full choruses. Mahler's music hides formalist experimentation beneath a deeply moving emotional beauty. His works form an integral part of the *fin de siècle* Viennese avant-garde.

THE MODERN ERA. While Mahler destabilized the traditional forms of composition, **Arnold Schönberg** broke away from traditional tonality altogether. Originally a devotee of Richard Wagner, Schönberg rejected tonal keys in favor of what is generally called atonality but which Schönberg himself preferred to think of as pantonality, or the disappearance of any dominant tone. His system of whole tones uses all 12 notes before any is repeated. His music, no longer confined to linear relationships of centered sounds, becomes an unlimited medium of abstractions based on a 12-tone scale that is symmetrically rearranged in a kind of serialism. Some of his most famous works are *Pierre Lunaire* and the string piece *Verklärte Nacht*. Strangely, the 12-tone system became a fad around the same time psychoanalysis did. Schönberg moved to Hollywood after the rise of Nazism.

Anton von Webern studied under Schönberg, eventually adopting and expanding the latter's 12-tone system. Webern's music is incredibly sparse, a sharp contrast to the lush, opulent, often overwritten music of his contemporaries. His music is also concerned with reinterpretation of traditional forms: he wrote *Lieder* and was obsessed with words and poetry in relation to music. His highly formal style was at once the height of tradition and its reversal, its overturning. Webern drifted into obscurity and depression as the Nazis took over. While fleeing the Nazis, Webern was accidentally shot by U.S. troops in Salzburg.

Alban Berg, another student of Schönberg's, was a perfectionist who completed very few works because of his obsession with ideal expression. His music started a riot in March 1913 when both the audience and performers, upset with his disruption of all recognizable structure or melody, got violent. Berg wrote using the 12-tone system, but also using complex chromaticism—technically within the traditional tonal system but obscuring it. His work achieved a strange effect through combination: it employed classical styles and motifs but always set with and against atonality. Like Schönberg and Webern, he suffered under the Nazis as a creator of "degenerate art" and died young after a short illness in 1935.

VISUAL ART AND ARCHITECTURE

Landlocked in the middle of Europe and rolling with cash, the Habsburgs married into power and bought into art. In keeping with the cosmopolitan nature of their empire and outlook, the imperial family pursued a cultural policy that decidedly favored foreign artists over their own native sons and daughters. With the popularity of Baroque palaces and churches in the 17th- and 18th-centuries, however, the empire's artists began to develop a distinct, graceful architectural style that still dominates the old centers of former Habsburg towns across Central and Eastern Europe. Around the turn of the 20th century, Austrian artists finally got fed up with traditionalism and foreign decadence and decided to stir up the coals a bit. (See **Vienna: Sights,** p. 108 for more discussion of art and architecture.)

BAROQUE EXTRAVAGANCE. By emphasizing grandiosity, Baroque architecture embodies Imperialism: its gaudiness stems from the desire to inspire awe and opulence, the desire to be rich and to look it. With fluidly ornate forms orchestrated into a succession of grand entrances, dreamy vistas, and overwrought, cupid-covered facades, the Baroque invokes what was then the most popular art form in Europe, music. The turbulent swell of Haydn or Beethoven is incarnated in stone and mortar. Austria's preeminent Baroque architects were Johann Bernhard Fischer von Erlach, Lukas von Hildebrandt, and Johann Prandtauer. **Johann Bernard Fischer von Erlach,** born in Graz to a sculptor father, drew up the plans for Vienna's Schönbrunn and Hofburg palaces. His best works, however, were ecclesiastical in nature, including the **Trinity** and **Collegienkirche** in Salzburg and the ornate **Karlskirche** in Vienna. **Prandtauer** was a favorite of the Church. His yellow Benedictine abbey at **Melk** perches on rocky cliffs over the Danube. **Lukas von Hildebrandt** shaped Austria's more secular side. After battering the Turks, Prince Eugène of Savoy got him to revamp his newest acquisition, the Belvedere palace. Hildebrandt's penchant for theatricality shows up in the palace's succession of pavilions and grand views of Vienna; stone sphinxes dotting his ornamental gardens allude to Eugene's victory over the Ottomans.

THE RINGSTRAßE. Austria's 19th-century conservative modernism is showcased by the **Ringstraße,** the broad circular boulevard that demarcates Vienna and that was authorized in 1857 by Emperor Franz Josef to replace fortified medieval walls. Although the Ringstraße was the pet project of Viennese bourgeois liberals, the street has distinctly authoritarian roots. During the Revolution of 1848, rebels barricaded themselves inside the old city wall. After quashing the rebellion, unnerved generals of the Habsburg military insisted the wall be razed and the grand boulevard built in its place. The leafy, tree-lined *Ringstraße* was built exceptionally wide not merely for beauty's sake, but also with the covert intention of preventing barricades and giving the imperial army ready access to subversive behavior in any part of the city. Emperor Franz Josef lined the boulevard with centers of bourgeois constitution and culture: a *Universität*, a *Rathaus*, a *Parlament*, and a *Burgtheater*. Architects designed each building in a different historical style deemed symbolic of its function. The neo-gothic *Rathaus* celebrates the civic strength of the *Bürgermeister* and their medieval town halls; the early baroque style of the *Burgtheater* recalls the 17th-century golden era of the theatrical arts, while the stately Renaissance design of the university highlights the cult of rationalism and science. This historicist taste was identified with Vienna and came to be known as the **Ringstraße Style** (see p. 115).

BIEDERMEIER. Between Napoleon and the foundation of the republic, Austria developed a large, dissatisfied middle class. Since political expression and social critique were virtually impossible during this era, artistic expression was funneled into a narrow channel of naturalistic and applied art centered around the family circle and domestic ideals, dominated by genre, landscape, and portrait painting.

The *Biedermeier* period is remembered today primarily as a furniture style, but it was also an artistic movement with limited crossover into literature, characterized by a predilection for symmetries, technique, naturalism, and harmonious detail.

JUGENDSTIL (A.K.A. ART NOUVEAU). In the early years of the 20th century, Vienna's artistic community was racked by disagreement. In 1897, the "young" artists split from the "old," as proponents of *Jugendstil* modernism took issue with the Viennese Academy's rigid conservatism and traditional symbolism. The idea was to leave behind prevailing artistic conventions and formulate a new way of seeing the world. **Gustav Klimt** and his followers founded the **Secession** movement. They aimed to provide the nascent Viennese avant-garde with an independent forum in which to show their work and to encourage contact with foreign artists. In their revolt against the calcified artistic climate of the old-guard Künstlerhaus, Secessionists sought to create space and appreciation for symbolist, naturalist, impressionist, and other new artistic styles. Their trademark style was Art Nouveau. Josef Maria Olbrich's **Secession building** was a reaction to the self-aggrandizing kitsch of the Ringstraße. The composer Richard Wagner's idealization of the *Gesamtkunstwerk* (total work of art) was an important subtext of Secessionist aesthetic ambitions. Their fourteenth exhibition was their crowning glory, an attempted synthesis of all major artistic media, featuring **Max Klinger's** Beethoven statue, Klimt's allegorical tribute to the composer, Josef Hoffmann's interior, and Mahler's music.

Once the *Jugendstil* fever broke, ornamentation was firmly streamlined, and a new ethic of function over form gripped Vienna's artistic elite. Vienna's guru of architectural modernism, **Otto Wagner,** cured the city of its "artistic hangover." His Steinhof church and Postal Savings Bank enclose fluid *Jugendstil* interiors within stark, delineated structures. Wagner frequently collaborated with his student **Josef Maria Olbrich**, notably on the Majolicahaus (on the Linke Wienzeile, VII) and the Karlsplatz Stadtbahn. Wagner's admirer **Josef Hoffmann** founded the **Wiener Werkstätte** in 1903, drawing on Ruskin's English art and crafts movement and Vienna's new brand of streamlined simplicity. The *Werkstätte* appropriated objects from daily life and reinterpreted them, using basic geometry and pricey materials (marble, silk, gold). Its influence later resonated in the **Bauhaus** of Weimar Germany.

Adolf Loos, Hoffmann's principal antagonist, strongly opposed such attention to luxury. Loos once said, "Ornamentation is criminal," setting himself against the Baroque grandeur that Imperial Vienna supported. Thanks to this opposition, few examples of his work reside in his native city. His indictment of the Ringstraße, entitled *Potemkin City*, affiliated him with the early Secessionist movement, but his notorious **Goldman and Salatsch building** (1909-1911) in the Michaelerplatz went a step beyond their aesthetic toward a more starkly functional architecture.

EXPRESSIONISM. Oskar Kokoschka and **Egon Schiele** revolted against "art *qua* art," seeking to present the frailty, neuroses, and sexual energy formerly concealed behind the Secession's aesthetic surface. Kokoschka is often considered (though never by himself) the founder of Viennese **Expressionism.** Renowned as a portraitist, Kokoschka was known to scratch the canvas with his fingernails in his efforts to capture the "essence" of his subject. Kokoschka's work is profoundly humanist and unafraid to be emotionally and psychologically involved with its subject. Schiele, like the young Kokoschka, paints with a feverish intensity in line and color. His paintings are controversial even today, for their depictions of tortured figures seemingly destroyed by their own bodies or by debilitating sexuality. His figures are twisted, gnarled, and yet oddly erotic. **František Kupka** studied at the Vienna academies at the same time as Kokoschka and Schiele, but soon left for France to study Pointillism, developing a strongly musical expressionism in his style. Kupka became one of the early pioneers of abstract art.

URBAN SOCIALISM. In the 1920s and early 1930s, the **Social Democratic** administration built thousands of apartments in large **municipal projects,** their style reflecting the newfound assertiveness of the workers' movement. The most outstanding

FROTHY FACTS The first historical documentation of beer is over 6,000 years old, as a staple food of the Sumerian people. In the Babylonian epic *Gilgamesh*, soldiers of the realm were paid in beer. More than 20 recipes for the fermentation of beer appear in ancient Egyptian scrolls, but the Teutonic tribes will go down in history for creating the celebrated mix of hops, barley, malt, yeast, and water that greases the wheels of the Western world today. There are few, if any, places in the world that provide a better opportunity to sample traditional brews than Austria. If you saunter up to a bar in Austria and simply order "ein Bier," you're likely to get a **Shankbeir**, a fairly mild, frothy beverage with a sharp hops aftertaste, served in a standard bar mug (*Schankglas*). If, however, an Austrian joins you at the bar, he/she will probably request "ein Pils," which is a native staple slightly stronger than Shankbier, served in a tulip glass. The ultra-dark beer in a tall tumbler is simply called **Dunkel**—it can stand on its own feet. For a more carbonated beer, try a **Weizenbier,** either "Kristall" or "Hefetrüb," or venture into the unknown with a **Bockbier,** a strong, full-bodied, dark amber beer consumed mostly at Christmas and Easter. This heavy brew was originally called "liquid bread," so that drinking it would not violate religious fasts. An Austrian custom, imported from Bavaria centuries ago, dictates that a rather special ritual be performed on the earliest brew of the season in order to ensure its quality: when the first keg is filled, old wives from the town must dance around the barrel and spit into its frothy content to bless the remainder of the brewing year. If you decide to sample some of a brewery's first yield, be sure to ask for your **Stein ohne Schleim** (without slime).

project of the era is the **Karl-Marx-Hof** (Heiligenstädter Str. 82-92, XIX). The huge structure, completed in 1930, extends over 1km and consists of 1600 apartments clustered around several courtyards. The Austrian Socialist party fought a pitched battle with rightist rioters in this apartment complex just before the outbreak of World War II. Another impressive socialist edifice is the Art Nouveau public baths of **Amalienbad** in Vienna (X, Reumannpl. 9). **Friedensreich Hundertwasser** (translation: Peaceful Hundredwaters; given name: Friedrich Stowasser) began with big brush strokes and bright colored canvas and moved on to more plastic material. A builder of buildings, he designed KunstHaus Wien and the Hundertwasser House, which attempt to make architecture organic and to bring natural life back into the "desert" that the city had become.

The structures created by American-trained architect **Hans Hollein** recall the sprawling abandon of his training ground while maintaining the Secessionists' attention to craftsmanship and elegant detail. His exemplary contribution to Viennese **postmodern** architecture is the **Haas House** (I, Stock-im-Eisen-Pl.), completed in 1990. Controversy has surrounded the building ever since sketches were published in the mid-80s, mainly because it stands opposite Vienna's landmark, St. Stephen's Cathedral. Over the past 20 years, Vienna's architects have focused their attention on designing interiors for boutiques and bistros. Examples of these designs are the **Restaurant Salzamt** (I, Ruprechtspl. 1) and **Kleines Café** (III, Franziskanerpl. 3), both by **Hermann Czech.**

LITERATURE

EARLY EXAMPLES. In the Roman settlement Vindobona, **Marcus Aurelius** wrote his *Meditations*, starting a long tradition of Viennese immigré (and emigré) artists. A collection of poetry dating from around 1150 and preserved in the abbey of Vorau in Styria marks the earliest known Austrian literature in German. Apart from sacred poetry, the courtly style known as *Minnesang* developed in the 12th and 13th centuries culminated in the lyrical works of minstrel **Walther von der Vogelweide.** On a more epic scale, the **Nibelungenlied,** which dates from around 1200, is one of the most impressive heroic epics in German (it is also the primary source for Richard Wagner's *Ring of the Nibelungen* operas). **Emperor Maximilian I** (1459-1519), nicknamed "The Last Knight," provided special support for theater and the dramatic arts during his reign. Splendid operas and pageants frequently involved the whole of the imperial court and led to a flurry of popular religious drama that has survived in the form of rural **passion plays.**

THE CLASSICAL WRITERS. Born in Vienna in 1801, **Johann Nestroy** wrote biting comedies and satires lampooning social follies. Although his name is not readily recognized by Anglophones, Nestroy is one of the canonical figures of German drama, famous for such plays as *Der Talisman* and *Liebesgeschichten und Heiratssachen*, as well as the *Tannhäuser* on which Wagner based his famous opera. Karl Kraus was one of his great fans; across the ocean Thornton Wilder busily adapted Nestroy's *The Matchmaker* into what eventually became the hit American musical *Hello Dolly*. Often called Austria's greatest novelist, **Adalbert Stifter** wrote around the same time period as Nestroy but concerned himself much more with classical *Bildungs-roman* themes and strongly metaphysical descriptions of nature. Stifter was a poetic realist who falls into the same school as Theodor Fontane. Many of his short stories and novels, such as *Der Condor* (1840), *Die Mappe meines Urgroßvaters* (1841), and *Der Nachsommer* (1857), belong to the canon of German literature.

A classicist with a more lyrical style, **Franz Grillparzer** penned plays about the conflict between a life of thought and a life of action. Although his work often looks back to the great classical achievements of writers such as Goethe and Schiller, it chronicles the disillusionment of idealism as it encounters painful compromise with reality. Grillparzer worked as a clerk in the Austrian bureaucracy and wrote some of his most critically acclaimed plays, such as *The Waves of the Sea and Love* (1831) in his spare time. Most of Grillparzer's fame came posthumously, when interest grew in his published work and the beautifully composed semi-autobiography *Der arme Spielmann* was discovered among his papers.

FIN DE SIÈCLE. Around 1890, Austrian literature rapidly transformed in the heat of the "merry apocalypse" atmosphere that permeated society at the turn of the century. The literature dating from this second heyday of Austrian culture is legendary. **Sigmund Freud** diagnosed the crisis, **Karl Kraus** implacably unmasked it, **Arthur Schnitzler** dramatized it, **Hugo von Hofmannsthal** ventured a cautious eulogy, and **Georg Trakl** commented on the collapse in feverish verse. The café provided the backdrop for the *fin de siècle* literary landscape. Like many popular institutions of its time, the relaxed elegance of the Viennese café was part fantasy, part imaginative camouflage of an ugly and best ignored reality. Vienna faced severe shortages of both housing and firewood, and the café was the only place where many people could relax in relative comfort and warmth. Some even had their mail addressed to them at their habitual cafe. At the Café Griensteidl, **Hermann Bahr**—lyric poet, critic, and one-time director of the *Burgtheater*—loosely presided over a pioneer group known as **Jung Wien** (Young Vienna), which rejected the **Naturalism** of Emile Zola in favor of a psychological realism aimed at capturing the subtlest nuances of the Viennese atmosphere. Hofmannsthal walked a tightrope between Impressionism and verbal decadence, creating such exquisite pieces of drama as *Yesterday* (1891) and *Everyman* (1911) while at the same time collaborating with Richard Strauss to write librettos for, among other things, *Der Rosenkavalier*. Schnitzler, a playwright and colleague of Freud, was the first German to write stream-of-consciousness prose. He skewered Viennese aristocratic decadence in dramas and essays, exposing the moral bankruptcy of their code of honor in such works as *Leutnant Gustl* (translated as *None but the Brave*). He also shocked contemporaries by portraying the complexities of erotic relationships in many of his plays, including his famous *Merry-Go-Round* (1897).

Many of Austria's literary titans, such as **Marie von Ebner-Eschenbach** and **Franz Kafka**, lived within the Habsburg protectorate of Bohemia. Ebner-Eschenbach is often called the greatest female Austrian writer, known for her vivid individual portraits and her defense of women's rights. Like her contemporaries in Prague, Ebner-Eschenbach deals in her works with the language crisis of German-speakers living outside the language community. Prague was a major literary center around the turn of the century, in dialogue with the literary scene in Vienna. Kafka often traveled to Vienna to drink coffee at the Herrenhof café and swap story ideas with other writers. No one else could master the surrealism of Kafka's writing, however, as demonstrated in *The Metamorphosis*, a bizarre and disorienting tale which presents the idea of waking up one day and *really* not feeling like yourself (if you usually feel like a giant cockroach, which Kafka might have, it isn't such a strange sensation). In *The Trial*, Kafka pries into the dehumanizing power of the bureaucratized modern world.

The collapse of the Austro-Hungarian monarchy marked a major turning point in the intellectual and literary life of Austria. Novelists **Robert Musil** and **Joseph Roth** concerned themselves with the consequences of the empire's breakdown. Roth's novels, *Radetzkymarsch* and *Die Kapuzinergruft*, romanticize the former empire. Musil invented the term *Parallelaktion* (parallel action) to describe his symbolic use of the moribund monarchy. His writing is fiercely subversive and anti-hierarchical, and shows the potential for narrative to be used as a tool of resistance. He is most famous for his unfinished work in 3 volumes *Der Mann Ohne Eigenschaften (The Man Without Qualities)*.

THE 20TH CENTURY. By WWI, the cult of despair had replaced the cult of art. **Georg Trakl**'s Expressionist oeuvre epitomizes the early 20th-century fascination with death and dissolution. "All roads empty into black putrefaction" is his most frequently quoted line, and his *Helian* remains one of the most important Germanic lyrical works. At the outbreak of WWI, Trakl served on the front; he eventually ended his life with a large dose of cocaine in an army hospital.

Other Prague-born greats such as **Franz Werfel** *(The Forty Days of Musa Dagh)* and **Rainer Maria Rilke** shaped Austrian literature between the wars. Werfel's works investigate the dark side of the human psyche. In addition to his essays and stories, Rilke is most famous for his lyric poetry cycles the *Duino Elegies* and *Sonnets to Orpheus*. Rilke pushed his language to such extremes of subtlety, purity, and nuance that he came close to creating his own language within the poems. After WWII, Rilke's poetry and Kafka's oppressive parables of a cold world became the models for a new generation of writers. These artistic movements owe their fascination with the unconscious to the new science of psychoanalysis and its most famous proponent, **Sigmund Freud.** Freud is best known for his theories of sexual repression, which he considered particularly applicable for bourgeois society, and his theories of the unconscious, which recast the literary world forever.

Austrian literature today is still affected and informed by its literary tradition, but there is plenty of innovation as well. **Ingeborg Bachman**'s stories and novels left an important legacy for Austrian feminism which **Elfriede Jelinek** has taken even further in her explicit novels, such as *The Piano Teacher* and *Lust*, which shocked Catholic church-goers with its audacity. One of the stalwarts of modern Austrian writing, **Thomas Bernhard** wrote *Holzfäller* (Woodcutters) and *Wittgenstein's Nephew.* His work is in many ways a cogent and mature critique of Austrian society. In short, literature in Austria still thrives, and will continue to as long as people are still upset enough to write.

VIENNA (WIEN)

From its humble origins as a Roman camp along the Danube, Vienna became the cultural heart of Europe for centuries, prodding fledgling musicians, writers, artists, philosophers, and politicians to greatness or, at least, infamy. It was not without reason that home-grown satirist Karl Kraus once dubbed Vienna—birthplace of psychoanalysis, atonal music, functionalist architecture, Zionism, and Nazism—a "laboratory for world destruction." From the glory days of the Habsburg dynasty under Maximilian I and Maria Theresia to *fin de siècle* Vienna's feverish brilliance, Vienna has rivaled Paris, London, and Berlin in significance, thanks to its inspired musicians (including Mozart, Beethoven, Schubert, Strauss, Brahms), vast imperial wealth, and impeccable taste in Baroque art, architecture, and decor. At the height of its artistic ferment, during the smoky and caffeine-permeated days of the great café culture, the Viennese were already self-mockingly referring to their city as the "merry apocalypse." That nervous atmosphere of disruption and disintegration was the reaction of a civilization staring down its own dissolution. Vienna's smooth veneer of waltz music and *Gemütlichkeit* concealed a darker reality expressed by Freud's theories, Kafka and Musil's dark fantasies, and Mahler's deathly beautiful music.

Streets overflow with Baroque flourishes, stucco onion-domed churches, sinuous art nouveau facades, and cafés with pooling light and worn, nicotine-stained velvet sofas. Vienna has long had the air of living absent-mindedly in the past, but that mood is rapidly fading as the city picks up speed with the second half of the 20th-century. Postmodern architecture and ecological fantasies by Friedensreich Hundertwasser share space with *Biedermeier* apartment buildings. Post-war diplomatic debates positioned Vienna on the threshold between East and West. Now that the Cold War is over and the Iron Curtain has mostly crumbled, Vienna has been trying to renew business connections in the former Communist bloc and reestablish itself as the political, cultural, and economic gateway to Eastern Europe. The city has also made concerted efforts to broaden its international status by attempting to match Geneva as a European center for the United Nations.

Despite stereotypes of a white, Catholic, conservative Vienna, the city's remarkable social, cultural, and ethnic diversity is immediately recognizable in support for activist causes such as women's rights, gay rights, and environmentalism. From July to December 1998, Austria held the European Union's (E.U.) presidency. Vienna threw a "celebration between E and U" festival, referring not only to Vienna's role as a truly central-European city easily accessible to the former Communist Bloc, but also to the city's fusion of "E" (a term for classical, traditional music) and "U" (popular and modern). Vienna is once more reconnecting with its turn-of-the-century identity as a place where experimentalism thrives, where rules of genre, style, and structure are made and unmade in everything from music to contemporary film and art.

HIGHLIGHTS OF VIENNA

■ Drink in Vienna's rich culture, history, and coffee at one of countless **cafés** (p. 103).
■ Venture into the **Wienerwald** (Vienna Woods) for a vineyard visit and taste new wine in the *Heurigen* (wine gardens) dotting the suburbs of Vienna (p. 107).
■ Wander along the **Ringstraße,** which circles Vienna's medieval first district and showcases such architectural triumphs as the Classical *Parlament,* the Renaissance *Universität,* the Gothic *Rathaus,* Otto Wagner's Jugendstil *Postsparkasse,* the Staatsoper, the Hofburg, and elaborate public gardens (p. 115).
■ Discover how art was "made and unmade" in Vienna's world-class art **museums,** especially the *Kunsthistorisches Museum,* Vienna's "Louvre" (p. 124).
■ Climb the tower of **St. Stephan's cathedral** in the heart of Vienna (p. 109).

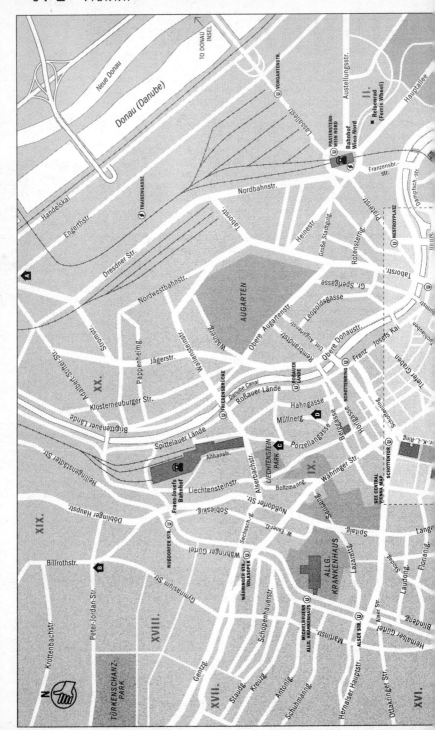

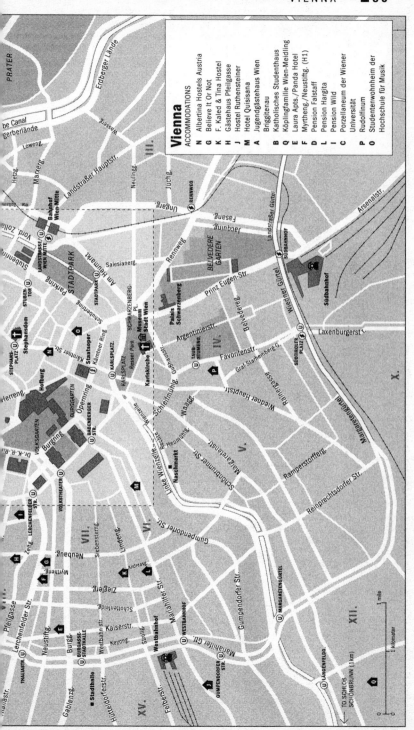

Vienna
ACCOMMODATIONS
N Albertina Hostels Austria
G Believe It Or Not
K F. Kaled & Tina Hostel
H Gästehaus Pfeilgasse
J Hostel Ruthensteiner
M Hotel Quisisana
A Jugendgästehaus Wien
  Brigittenau
B Katholisches Studenthaus
Q Köplingfamilie Wien-Meidling
E Laura Apts./Panda Hotel
F Myrtheng./Neustiftg. (H1)
D Pension Falstaff
L Pension Hargita
I Pension Wild
C Porzellaneum der Wiener
  Universität
P Rudolfinum
O Studentenwohnheim der
  Hochschule für Musik

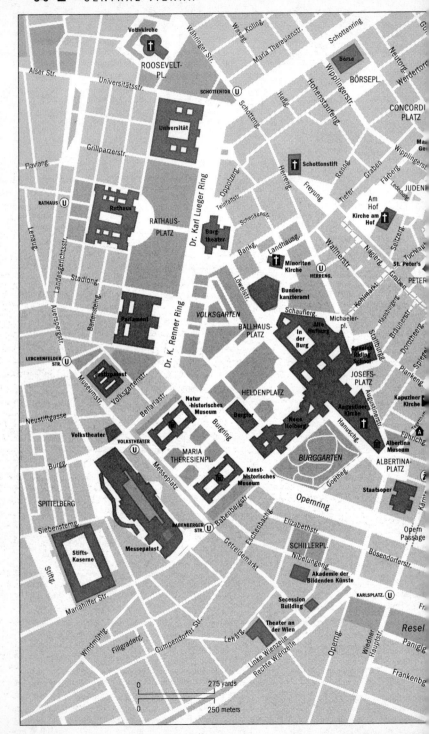

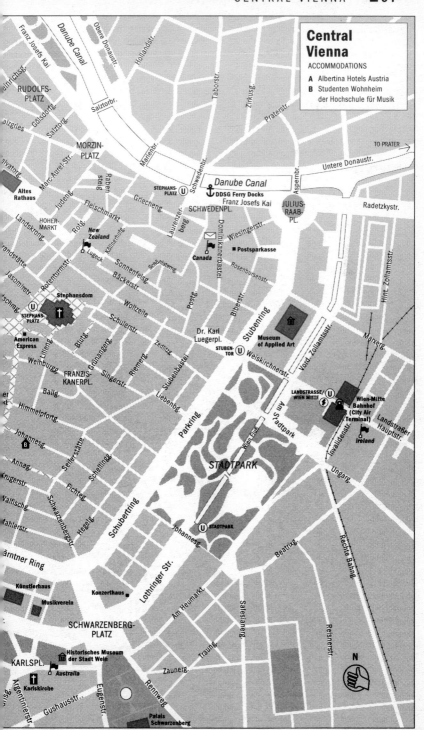

Central Vienna

ACCOMMODATIONS

A Albertina Hotels Austria
B Studenten Wohnheim
der Hochschule für Musik

Vienna Public Transport

■ ■ ■ S15 ■ ■ ■	S-Bahn lines
U1	U-Bahn lines
R 50	Commuter train
⟷	Local train to Baden

Tulln, Krems

Kahlenbergerdorf

Nußdorf

R40,42 · S40 · S45

Heiligenstadt

U4

Spittelau

Oberdöbling

Krottenbachstr.

Nußdorfer Str.

S40
R 40 · R 42
Franz-Josefs-Bahnhof

Gersthof

Währinger Str.-
Volksoper

Michelbeuern
AKH

Hernals

Alser Str.

S45

Ottakring

Josefstädter Str.

Thaliastr.

Johnstr. · Schweglestr.

Burgg.-
Stadthalle

Zielerg.

Neubaug.

U3

Breitensee

Purkersdorf-Sanatorium · Weidlingau-Wurzbachtal · Hardersdorf-Weidlingau

Hütteldorf

S15 · S45

Penzing

R 50 · S50 · S15

Westbahnhof · i

S50
R50

To St. Pölten,
Linz, Salzburg

U4

S15

Gumpendorfer Str.

Ober St. Veit

Unter St. Veit

Braunschweigg. · Hietzing · Schönbrunn · Meidling Hauptstr.

Längenfeldg.

Margaretengürtel

Pilgramg.

Niederhofstr.

Speising

S15

Wolfgangg.
Lokalbahn

Eichenstr.

Meidling
Philadelphiabrücke

S3

Matzleinsdorfer Pl.

Hetzendorf

S1,2

R10

Schöpfwerk · Gutheil-Schoder-G.

Inzersdorf Ort.

Inzersdo
Metzger-
weke

R11

Atzgersdorf-Mauer

Tshertteg.

Am Schöpfwerk

Alterlaa

Inzersdorf
Personenbhf.

Erlaaer Str.

Neuerlaa

Perfektastr.

Laxenburger Allee

Siebenhirten

U6

Vösendorf
Siebenhirten

Baden
⟷

Wiener, Neustadt,
Graz, Villach

Wiener Neusta

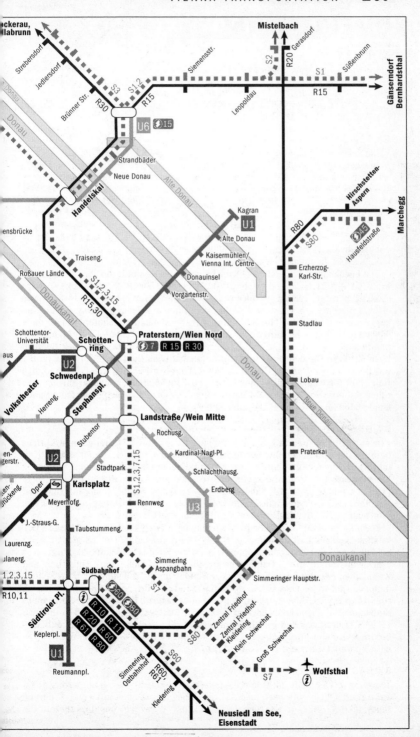

🄴 GETTING THERE

BY PLANE

Vienna's airport is the **Wien-Schwechat Flughafen,** home of **Austrian Airlines** (tel. 1789; open M-F 8am-7pm, Sa-Su 8am-5pm). There is a daily flight to and from **New York** and frequent flights to **London, Rome,** and **Berlin,** among other places. Travelers under 25 qualify for discounts if tickets are bought 2 weeks in advance. Student travelers ages 25 and 26 also qualify.

BY TRAIN

Vienna's 3 main train stations—Westbahnhof, Südbahnhof, and Franz-Josefs Bahnhof—send trains in all different directions and serve various European cities. For train information, call 1717 (24hr.) or check www.bahn.at. From the **Westbahnhof,** XV, Mariahilferstr. 132, trains run primarily west to destinations including **Salzburg** (3hr., every hr., 410AS), **Linz** (2hr., every hr., 280AS), **Innsbruck** (6hr., every 2hr., 660AS), **Bregenz** (8hr., 5 per day, 820AS), **Zurich** (9hr., 3 per day, 1160AS), **Amsterdam** (14hr., 1 per day, 2170AS), **Paris** (14hr., 2 per day, 2198AS), **Hamburg** (9½hr., 2 per day, 2100AS), **Munich** (4½hr., 5 per day, 788AS), but also east to **Budapest** (3-4hr., 9 per day, 436AS) and north to **Krakow** (6½hr., 2 per day, 492AS). The Westbahnhof train **information counter** is open daily 7:30am-8:40pm.

The **Südbahnhof,** X, Wiedner Gürtel 1a, sends trains south to **Graz** (2¾hr., every hr., 310AS), **Villach** (5hr., every hr., 470AS), **Prague** (5hr., 3 per day, 524AS), **Rome** (14hr., 2 per day, 1230AS), **Venice** (8hr., 5 per day, 760AS), and east to **Bratislava** (1hr., 4 per day, 136AS), as well as to other cities in **Poland, Germany, Russia, Turkey, Greece,** and **Spain.** The Südbahnhof train **information counter** is open daily 6:30am to 9:20pm. The third major station, **Franz-Josefs Bahnhof,** IX, Althamstr. 10, handles mostly commuter trains. There are also two smaller stations: **Bahnhof Wien Mitte,** in the center of town, and **Bahnhof Wien Nord,** by the Prater on the north side of the Danube Canal. Bahnhof Wien Nord is the main S-Bahn and U-Bahn link for trains heading north, but most Bundesbahn trains go through the other stations. Some regional trains (Krems, for example) also leave from **Spittelau,** located on the U-4 and U-6 subway lines.

BY BUS AND BOAT

Travel by bus in Austria is seldom cheaper than travel by train; compare prices before you buy a ticket. **City Bus Terminals** are located at Wien Mitte/Landstr., Hütteldorf, Heiligenstadt, Floridsdorf, Kagran, Erdberg, and Reumannpl. Domestic **BundesBuses** run from these stations to local and international destinations. (Ticket counter open M-F 6am-5:50pm, Sa-Su 6am-3:50pm.) Many international bus lines also have agencies in the stations, each with different hours. For bus information, call BundesBus at tel. 71101 (7am-7pm).

For a more exotic trip to or from Vienna, try a **ferry.** The famous **Donaudampffschiffahrtsgesellschaft Donaureisen** (DDSG), I, Friedrichstr. 7 (tel. 58 88 00; fax 588 80 440; email info@ddsg-blue-danube.at; www.ddsg-blue-danube.at), organizes cruises up and down the Danube, hitting the cities of Melk, Spitz, Dürnstein, and Krems/Stein. **Ferries** leave Vienna every Sunday during the summer from Schwedenplatz (get there with U-1, U-4, tram #1, and #2). Prices hover around 190AS, round-trip 260AS. Bike transport is free, but call ahead. **Hydrofoils** will take you to **Bratislava** (1¾hr., 240AS, round-trip 360AS) or **Budapest** (5-6hr., 780AS, round-trip 1100AS). Eurailpass and ISIC holders get 20% off travel within Austria, and families travel for half-price (min. one parent and one child age 6-17; under 6 travel free with a parent (see p. 281 for more info).

BY CAR

Traveling to Vienna by car is fairly simple; the capital city lies on numerous *Autobahn* routes. From the **west,** take A1, which begins and ends in Vienna. From the **south,** take A2, A21, or A3 (the latter two cross A2, which runs directly into the city). From the **east,** take A4. From the **north,** take A22, which runs along the Danube. There are also a number of much smaller highways that access Vienna, including Routes 7 and 8 from the north and Route 10 from the south.

Ride-sharing is another option. **Mitfahrzentrale Wien,** VIII, Daung. 1a (tel. 408 22 10), off Laudong., pairs drivers and riders. From Schottentor, take tram #43 to "Skodag." and walk down Skodag. to Damag. where you'll meet your ride. Call first to see which rides are available. (Open M-F 8am-noon and 2-7pm, Sa-Su 1-3pm.) A ride to **Salzburg** costs 210AS, to **Prague** 450AS. Two days advance reservation is recommended. **Hitchhikers** headed for Salzburg have been seen taking U-4 to "Hütteldorf"; the highway leading to the *Autobahn* is 10km farther. Hitchers traveling south often ride tram #67 to the last stop and wait at the rotary near Laaerberg.

▣ GETTING AROUND

FROM THE AIRPORT AND TRAIN STATIONS

The **airport** is far from the city center (18km), but it's easily accessible by public transportation. The cheapest way to get to and from the airport is to take the U- and S-Bahn. U-3 and U-4 both reach "Wien Mitte/Landstr." where you can catch the S-7 "Flughafen/Wolfsthal" which stops at the airport (on the hour; 38AS; Eurailpass not valid). There is also a daily train service between Wien Nord or Wien Mitte and the airport (30min., every 30min, 38AS). The heart of the city, Stephansplatz, is an easy ride from **Wien Mitte** or the **Westbahnhof** on the orange U-3 line. From the **Südbahnhof,** take tram D (dir.: Nußdorf) to "Opera/Karlspl." From **Franz-Josefs Bahnhof,** take tram D (dir.: Südbahnhof).

A more convenient option is taking the **Vienna Airport Lines Shuttle Bus** (70AS). Buses leave the airport for the City Air Terminal downtown (at the Hilton opposite "Wien Mitte" station) every 20 minutes from 6am to 11pm and every 30 minutes from 11pm to 6am. Buses leave from the airport for Südbahnhof and Westbahnhof every 30 minutes from 8:10am to 7:10pm and on into the night with less frequent service. Similarly, buses travel to the airport from the city stations. By far the easiest but also the most expensive way to and from the airport is by **private airport shuttle** services, such as **JetBus** (tel. (7007) 38779), located just outside the baggage claim, which deliver passengers to any address in the city for 160AS per person. Call 1 day in advance to arrange pick-up for a return trip. Parties of 3 or more get discounts when booking a return trip.

WITHIN THE CITY

Public transportation in Vienna is extensive and dependable; call 58000 for general info. The **subway** (U-Bahn), **tram** (Straßenbahn), **elevated train** (S-Bahn), and **bus** systems operate under one ticket system. A single fare is 22AS if purchased from a machine on a bus, 19AS if purchased in advance from a machine in a station, ticket office, or tobacco shop *(Tabak* or *Trafik)*. This ticket permits you to travel to any single destination in the city and switch from bus to U-Bahn to tram to S-Bahn, as long as your travel is uninterrupted. This bit's tricky: to validate a ticket, punch it in the machine immediately upon entering the first vehicle of your journey. This action records the time and date of your trip, and you should not stamp the ticket again when you switch trains. A ticket stamped twice or not stamped at all is invalid, and plain clothes inspectors may fine you 565AS plus the ticket price for freeloading *(Schwarzfahren).* Other ticket options (available at the same places as pre-purchased single tickets) are a **24-hour pass** (60AS), a **3-day "rover" ticket** (150AS), a **7-day pass** (142AS; valid from M 9am to the following M 9am), or an **8-day pass** (300AS; valid any 8 days, not necessarily consecutive; valid also for several people traveling together). The **Vienna Card** (210AS) offers free travel on the public transportation system for 72 hours, as well as substantial discounts at museums, sights, and events, and is especially useful for non-students.

If you are traveling with a child over 6 years old, a bicycle, or a dog, you must buy a half-price ticket (11AS) for your companion. Children under 5 always ride free, and, on Sundays and school holidays, anyone under 15 rides free. (The pocket map available at the tourist offices lists official holidays.) You can take bicycles on all underground trains, but the U-6 line only allows bikes on the middle car, which is marked with a bicycle symbol.

All regular trams and subway cars stop running between 12:30am and 5am. **Nightbuses** run all night (every 30min.) along most tram, subway, and major bus routes. In major hubs like Schottentor, some of the buses leave from slightly different areas than their daytime counterparts. "N" signs with yellow cat eyes designate night bus stops (25AS; day transport passes not valid). A complete night bus schedule is available at bus info counters in U-Bahn stations.

The **public transportation information line** (tel. 790 91 05) gives public transportation directions to any point in the city (open M-F 6:30am-6:30pm, Sa-Su 8:30am-4pm). **Information stands** (marked with in "i") in many stations also provide detailed instructions. The staff can explain how to purchase tickets and can provide an indispensable free pocket map of the U-Bahn and S-Bahn systems. A comprehensive map of Vienna's public transportation is 15AS. Stands in the U-Bahn at Karlspl., Stephanspl., and the Westbahnhof are the most likely to have information not in German (open M-F 6:30am-6:30pm, Sa-Su and holidays 8:30am-4pm). Other stands are located at Praterstern, Philadelphiabrücke, Landstr., Floridsdorf, Spittelau, and Volkstheater (open M-F 6:30am-6:30pm). Website www.wiennet.at/efa calculates the shortest route between two points (commonly known as a "line").

✦ ORIENTATION

Vienna's layout reflects its history. The city is divided into 23 **districts** *(Bezirke)*. The first district is the *innere Stadt*, or *Innenstadt* (city center), and the rest of the districts radiate out from it like the spokes of a wheel. The *Innenstadt* is defined by the **Ringstraße**, once the site of the old city fortifications and now a massive automobile artery, on three sides, with the Danube Canal on the fourth. The Ringstraße (or "Ring") consists of many different segments: Opernring, Kärntner Ring, Dr.-Karl-Lueger-Ring, etc. This fragmentation occurs because of the tendency of Austrian streets to change names after a few blocks.

Many of Vienna's major attractions are in the first district and around the Ringstraße, including the **Kunsthistorisches Museum**, the **Rathaus**, and the **Burggarten**. At the intersection of the **Opernring, Kärntner Ring**, and **Kärntnerstraße** stands the **Staatsoper** (Opera House), with the **tourist office** and the **Karlsplatz** U-Bahn stop. Districts two through nine spread out from the city center following the clockwise, one-way traffic of the Ring. The remaining districts expand from yet another ring, the **Gürtel** ("belt"). Like the Ring, this major two-way thoroughfare has numerous segments, including Margaretengürtel, Währinger Gürtel, Neubaugürtel, etc. Street signs indicate the district number in Roman or Arabic numerals, and postal codes correspond to the district number: 1010 for the first district, 1020 for the second, 1110 for the eleventh, etc. *Let's Go* includes district numbers for establishments before the street address.

DISTRICT NAMES AND NUMBERS: Moving in a roughly clockwise direction, Vienna's 23 districts are: I, **Innere Stadt**; II, **Leopoldstadt**; III, **Landstraße**; IV, **Wieden**; V, **Margareten**; VI, **Mariahilf**; VII, **Neubau**; VIII, **Josefstadt**; IX, **Alsergrund**; X, **Favoriten**; XI, **Simmering**; XII, **Meidling**; XIII, **Hietzing**; XIV, **Penzing**; XV, **Rudolfsheim Fünfhaus**; XVI, **Ottakring**; XVII, **Hernals**; XVIII, **Währing**; XIX, **Döbling**; XX, **Brigittenau**; XXI, **Floridsdorf**; XXII, **Donaustadt**; XXIII, **Liesing**.

---

⑦ PRACTICAL INFORMATION

TOURIST OFFICES

Main Tourist Office: I, Kärntnerstr. 38, behind the Opera House, serve hordes of people. If possible, call Wiener Tourismusverband (see below) instead. The tourist office has an assortment of brochures, including a free, city map (which unfortunately lacks an index). The brochure *Youth Scene* provides vital information for travelers of all ages. The office books 300-400AS rooms for a 40AS fee plus a 1-night deposit. Open 9am-7pm.

Branch Offices: Westbahnhof, open Apr.-Oct. 7am-10pm, Nov.-Mar. 7am-9pm. **Airport,** open 8:30am-9pm. **Highway exit "Wien Auhof,"** off A1. Open Easter Week to Oct. 8am-10pm, Nov. 9am-7pm, Dec.-Mar. 10am-6pm. **Highway exit "Zentrum,"** off A2, XI, Trierstr. 149. Open July-Sept. 8am-10pm; Easter Week to June and Oct. 9am-7pm. **North Danube Island,** open May-Sept. 10am-7pm. **Vienna International Center,** open Tu and F 9am-2pm, Th noon-5pm.

Wiener Tourismusverband: II, Obere Augartenstr. 40 (tel. 21 11 40; fax 216 84 92). No walk-in hours, but the knowledgeable staff responds to telephone inquiries and sends faxes and brochures. Open M-F 8am-4pm.

Jugend-Info Wien (Vienna Youth Information Service): Bellaria-Passage (tel. 1799; email jiw@blackbox.at), in the underground passage at the Bellaria intersection. Enter at the "Dr.-Karl-Renner-Ring/Bellaria" stop (trams #1, 2, 46, 49, D, or J) or at the "Volkstheater" U-Bahn station. Hip staff has information on cultural events, housing, and employment opportunities and sells discount youth concert and theater tickets. Get the indispensable *Jugend in Wien* brochure here. Open M-Sa noon-7pm.

Österreichisches Verkehrsbüro (Austrian National Travel Office): I, Operng. 3-5 (tel. 58800), opposite the Opera House. Open M-F 9am-6pm, Sa 9am-noon.

Ökista, IX, Türkenstr. 8 (tel. 40 14 80) specializes in student travel, such as tickets, passes, and discounts. Open M-F 9am-7:30pm.

EMBASSIES AND CONSULATES

Generally, each country's embassy and consulate are located in the same building, listed under *"Botschaften"* or *"Konsulate"* in the phone book. Contact consulates for assistance with visas and passports and in emergencies.

Australia, IV, Mattiellistr. 2-4 (tel. 512 85 800), behind the *Karlskirche.* Open M-Th 8:30am-1pm and 2-5:30pm, F 8:30am-1:15pm.

Canada, I, Laurenzerburg 2, 3rd fl. (tel. 53138, ext. 3000). Open M-F 8:30am-12:30pm and 1:30-3:30pm. Leave a message in an emergency.

Ireland, III, Hilton Center, Landstraßer Hauptstr. 21, 6th fl. (tel. 715 42 460; fax 713 60 04). Open M-F 9:30-11:30am and 2-4pm.

New Zealand, XIX, Springsiedleg. 28 (tel. 318 85 05; fax 318 67 17). No regular office hours; call in advance. If no answer, contact consulate in Bonn at 0049 228 228 070.

South Africa, XIX, Sandg. 33 (tel. 320 64 93). Open M-F 8:30am-noon.

U.K., III, Jauresg. 10 (tel. 71 61 30; fax 716 132 999), near *Schloß Belvedere.* Open M-F 9:15am-noon.

U.S. Embassy, IX, Boltzmanng. 16, off Währingerstr. and **Consulate** at I, Gartenbaupromenade 2 (tel. 31339 for both), off Parkring. Phone hours M-F 8:30am-noon and 1-5pm. Open M-F 8:30am-noon. Some services for American citizens are open at different or variable times; call ahead.

TRANSPORTATION SERVICES

Taxis: (tel. 31300, 40100, 60160, 81400, or 91011). Stands at Westbahnhof, Südbahnhof, and Karlspl. in the city center. Accredited taxis have yellow and black signs on the roof. Rates generally 27AS plus 14AS per km. 26AS surcharge for taxis called by radio-phone; 27AS surcharge Sundays, holidays, and nights (11pm-6am); 13AS surcharge for luggage over 20kg, 26AS for over 50kg.

Car Rental: Avis, I, Opernring 3-5 (tel. 587 62 41). Open M-F 7am-6pm, Sa 8am-2pm, Su 8am-1pm. **Hertz,** (tel. 700 72 661), at the airport. Open M-F 7:15am-11pm, Sa 8am-8pm, Su 8am-11pm.

Auto Repairs: If your car needs fixing, call **ÖAMTC** (tel. 120) or **ARBÖ** (tel. 123).

Parking: In the 1st district, parking is allowed M-F 9am-7pm for 1½hr. Buy a voucher (6AS per 30min.) at a *Tabak* and display it, with the time, on the dashboard. It's easiest to park cars outside the *Ring* and walk into the city center. Garages line the Ringstr., including 2 by the Opera House, 1 at Franz-Josef Kai, and 1 at the Marek-Garage at Messepalast. In districts VI through IX, parking is permitted M-F 9am-8pm for 2hr. **Parking cards** (50AS) enable all-day parking there and can be purchased either from a *Tabak* or the machine on the street.

Bike Rental: At Wien Nord and the Westbahnhof. 150AS per day, 90AS with a train ticket from the day of arrival. Elsewhere in the city, including Donauinsel, rentals average 50AS per hr. **Pedal Power,** II, Ausstellungsstr. 3 (tel. 729 72 34; fax 729 72 35; email office@pedalpower.co.at; www.pedalpower.co.at) rents bikes for 60AS per hr., 300AS per half day, 395AS for 24hr. with delivery. They also offer bike tours of the city (180-280AS). Discounts available for students and Vienna Card holders. Open May-Oct. 8am-8pm. Pick up *Vienna By Bike* at the tourist office for details on the bicycle scene.

Luggage Storage: Lockers (30-40AS per 24hr.) at all train stations. Adequate for sizable backpacks. **Luggage watch** 30AS. Open 4am-1:15am.

Lost Property: Fundbüro, IX, Wasag. 22 (tel. 313 44 92 11 or 9217). For items lost on public transportation, call 79090. Open M-F 8am-3pm. For items lost on trains, call 580 03 29 96 (Westbahnhof) or 580 03 56 56 (Südbahnhof).

FINANCIAL SERVICES

Currency Exchange: ATMs are your best bet. Nearly all accept Cirrus, Eurocard, MC, and Visa (see p. 17). **Banks** and **airport exchanges** use the same official rates. Minimum commission 65AS for traveler's checks, 10AS for cash. Most are open M-W and F 8am-12:30pm and 1:30-3pm, Th 8am-12:30pm and 1:30-5:30pm. **Train station** exchanges offer long hours and a 50AS charge for changing up to US$700 of traveler's checks. The 24hr. exchange at the **main post office** has excellent rates and an 80AS fee to change up to $1100 in traveler's checks. The **24hr. bill exchange** machines in the *Innenstadt* have horrible rates. The **casino** (open late on weekends) has slightly better rates.

American Express: I, Kärntnerstr. 21-23, P.O. Box 28, A-1015 (tel. 51540), down the street from Stephanspl. Cashes AmEx and Thomas Cook (3% commission) checks, sells theater, concert, and other tickets, and holds mail for 4 weeks for AmEx customers. Open M-F 9am-5:30pm, Sa 9am-noon. For 24hr. refund service, call (0800) 206 840.

LOCAL SERVICES

Bookstores: Shakespeare & Company, I, Sterng. 2 (tel. 535 50 53; fax 535 505 316; email bookseller@shakespeare.co.at; www.ping.at/members/shbook). Eclectic and intelligent. Great British magazine selection. Open M-F 9am-7pm, Sa 9am-5pm. **Frauenzimmer,** Langeg. 11 (tel. 406 86 78; fax 407 16 20). Women's bookstore with some English language books and travel literature. Open M-F 10am-6:30pm, Sa 10am-1pm (10am-5pm the first Sa of each month). The **British Bookshop,** I, Weihburgg. 24 (tel. 512 19 45; fax 512 10 26) has an extensive collection of books, many travel-oriented. Open M-F 9am-6:30pm, Sa 10am-5pm. **Big Ben's Bookstore,** IX, Serviteg. 4a (tel. 319 64 120; fax 319 64 123) sells English books and a bigger selection of ESL books. Open M-F 9am-6:30pm, Sa 9:30-12:30am.

Bisexual, Gay, and Lesbian Organizations: The bisexual, gay, and lesbian community in Vienna, though small, is more integrated than in other cities. The lovely **Rosa Lila Villa,** VI, Linke Wienzeile 102 (tel. 586 81 50), is a favored resource and social center for Viennese homosexuals and visitors to the city. Friendly staff provides counseling, information, a library, and nightclub listings (see **Nightlife,** p. 130). Open M-F 5-8pm. **Homosexuelle Initiative Wien (HOSI),** II, Novarag. 40 (tel. 216 66 04; fax 585 41 59). Lesbian group and phone network W at 7pm. Youth group Th at 8pm. Prints a political newspaper, *Lambda Nachrichten.* Open Su 6-8pm (includes phone counseling), Th 7-9pm (for youth). Café open Su 5-10pm. **Lesbischwul und Transgender Referat** (tel. 588 015 890; email efisher@mail.zserve.tuwien.ac.at). Gay student counseling group. Open F 4-6pm. For the gay goings on around town, pick up either the monthly Viennese magazine (in German) called **Connect,** the free monthly publication **Bussi** at any gay bar, café, or club, or consult the straight but hip **Falter** newspaper, which lists gay events under a special heading.

Laundromat: Schnell und Sauber, VII, Westbahnhofstr. 60 (tel. 524 64 60); U-6: "Burgg. Stadthalle." 6kg wash 60AS. Detergent included. Spin-dry 10AS. Open 24hr. **Münz-wäscherei Karlberger & Co.,** III, Schlachthausg. 19 (tel. 798 81 91). Wash 90AS per 7kg, dry 10AS. Soap 10AS. Open M-F 7:30am-6:30pm. Many hostels offer laundry facilities (50-60AS).

Public Showers and Toilets: At Westbahnhof, in Friseursalon Navratil downstairs from subway passage. Well-maintained. 30min. shower 48AS, with soap and towel 60AS (10AS extra for either on Sunday). Showers are also available at **Jörgerbad,** XVII, Jörgerstr. 42-44, and at the airport. There are toilets in most underground stations (1-5AS), and a special *Jugendstil* toilet in Kärtnerstr.

Snow Reports: In German for Vienna, Lower Austria, and Styria (tel. 1583); for Salzburg, Upper Austria, and Carinthia (tel. 1584); for Tyrol and the Voralberg (tel. 1585).

 CRIME IN THE CITY. Vienna is a metropolis with crime like any other; use common sense, especially after dark. Karlsplatz is home to many pushers and junkies. Avoid areas in the 5th, 10th, and 14th districts, as well as Landstraßer Hauptstr. and **Prater Park,** after dark. Vienna's skin trade operates in sections of the Gürtel, and beware of the city's small skinhead population.

EMERGENCIES

Emergencies: Police, tel. 133. **Ambulance,** tel. 144. **Fire,** tel. 122. Alert your consulate of any emergencies or legal problems.

Poison Control: tel. 406 43 43. Open 24hr.

Medical Assistance: Allgemeines Krankenhaus, IX, Währinger Gürtel 18-20 (tel. 404 00). **Emergency care,** tel. 141. **24hr. pharmacy,** tel. 15 50. A consulate can provide a list of English-speaking physicians.

Crisis Hotlines: All hotlines can find English speakers.

House for Threatened and Battered Women: tel. 545 48 00, 202 55 00, or 408 38 80. 24hr. emergency hotline.

Rape Crisis Hotline: tel. 523 22 22. Open M 10am-6pm, Tu 2-6pm, W 10am-2pm, Th 5-9pm. **24hr. immediate help:** tel. 71719.

Psychological Counseling Hotline: tel. 319 35 66 or 402 78 38. Open M-F 8pm-8am, Sa-Su 24hr.

English-language "Befrienders" Suicide Hotline: tel. 713 33 74. Open M-F 9:30am-1pm and 6:30-10pm, Sa-Su 6:30-10pm. They have message machines.

COMMUNICATION

Internet Access: Free access at the back of the **Amadeus Media Café,** I, Kärtnerstr. 19, on the fifth floor of the **Steffl** department store (www.amadeusbuch.co.at). M-F 9:30am-7pm, Sa 9:30am-5pm. **Café Stein,** IX, Währingerstr. 6 (tel. 319 72 41) offers Net access for 65AS per 30min. Open daily 5-11 pm. Present ID at the bar. The **National Library,** I, Neue Burg 1 (tel. 53 41 00), in Heldenpl. at the Hofburg, has 2 terminals and long lines. 50AS per 30min. Open M-Sa 10am-4pm, Su 10am-1pm. **Libro,** XXII, Donauzentrum (tel. 202 52 55), provides free access at 6 terminals. Open Su-F 7am-7pm, Sa 9am-5pm. **Jugend-Info des Bundesministeriums,** I, Franz-Josefs-Kai 51 (tel. 533 70 30). Free access at 2 PCs. Open M-F 11am-6pm.

English Language Radio: Blue Danube radio, 103.8FM. Mixes classical, oldies, and mainstream music with news updates every 30min. until 7pm in English, French and German, including the BBC World Service. "What's on in Vienna" airs at 1pm.

Post Offices: Hauptpostamt, I, Fleischmarkt 19. Vast structure containing exchange windows, phones, faxes, and mail services. Open 24hr. Address *Poste Restante* to "MAAS, Oedipa; Postlagernde Briefe; Hauptpostamt; Fleischmarkt 19; A-1010 Wien." Branches throughout the city and at the train stations; look for the yellow signs with the (un)muted trumpet logo. **Postal Codes:** In the 1st district A-1010, in the 2nd A-1020, in the 3rd A-1030, and so on, to the 23rd A-1230.

PHONE CODES	The **city code** for Vienna is 0222 for calls placed from within Austria, 1 for calls from abroad.

▊ ACCOMMODATIONS AND CAMPING

One of the few unpleasant aspects of Vienna is the hunt for cheap rooms during peak tourist season (June-Sept.). Write or call for reservations at least 5 days in advance. Otherwise, plan on calling from the train station between 6 and 9am during the summer to put your name down for a reservation. If your choice is full, ask to be put on a waiting list, or ask for suggestions—don't waste time tramping around. A list of budget accommodations in Vienna is available at almost every tourist office. Those unable to find a hostel bed should consider a *Pension*. One-star establishments are generally adequate and are most common in the 7th, 8th, and 9th districts. Singles start around 350AS, doubles around 500AS. The summer crunch for budget rooms is slightly alleviated in July, when university dorms are converted into makeshift hostels. Bear in mind that these "dorms" are singles and doubles, not dormitories, and are priced accordingly.

If you're staying for a longer period of time, try **Odyssee Reisen und Mitwohnzentrale,** VIII, Laudong. 7 (tel. 402 60 61). They find apartments for 225-350AS per person per night. A week costs about 1200AS, and a month starts at 2000AS. They charge 20% commission on each month's rent. Bring your passport to register. (Open M-F 10am-2pm and 3-6pm.) Otherwise, visit either *Österreichische Hochschülerschaft* at Rooseveltpl. 5 or the bulletin boards on the first floor of the *Neues Institut Gebäude* (NIG building) on Universitätstr. near the *Votivkirche*.

HOSTELS AND DORMITORIES

▧ **Believe It Or Not,** VII, Myrtheng. 10, Apt. #14 (tel. 526 46 58). From Westbahnhof, take U-6 (dir.: Heiligenstadt) to "Burgg./Stadthalle," then bus #48A (dir.: Ring) to "Neubaug." Walk back on Burgg. 1 block and take the first right on Myrtheng. (15min.). From Südbahnhof, take bus #13A (dir.: Skodag./Alerstr.) to "Kellermanng." Walk 2 blocks to your left on Neustiftg. and turn left on Myrtheng. Ring the bell. A converted apartment, this sociable hostel has a **kitchen** and 2 co-ed bedrooms full of bunks. After helping you plan your itinerary, the amazing caretaker kicks you out (10:30am-12:30pm) to clean. Her personal crash-course on Vienna is a must. 160AS; Nov.-Easter 110AS. Reception 8am until early afternoon—call early. Reservations recommended. No curfew.

▧ **Hostel Ruthensteiner (HI),** XV, Robert-Hamerlingg. 24 (tel. 893 42 02; fax 893 27 96; email hostel.ruthensteiner@telecom.at; www.hostelruthensteiner.com), is 5min. from the Westbahnhof and about a 10min. ride from the city center. Exit Westbahnhof at the main entrance, turn right and head to Mariahilferstr. Turn right again and continue until Haidmannsg. Turn left, then take the first right on Robert-Hammerlingg., and continue to the middle of the block. This top-notch hostel not only offers exceptional value and extremely knowledgeable, English-speaking staff, but also spotless rooms and a beautiful sun-filled oasis of ivy for a courtyard, complete with a barbecue and oversized chess set. "The Outback" summer dorm 125AS; 10-bed dorms 145AS; 3- to 5-bed dorms 169AS; singles 245AS; doubles 470AS. Breakfast 28AS. Showers and sheets (except for 10-bed rooms) included. Snack bar open all day. Lockers and kitchen available. Net access from 20AS. Reception 24hr. 4-night max. stay. Phone or email reservations recommended, but empathetic owners often hold beds for spontaneous travelers.

Hostel Panda, VII, Kaiserstr. 77, 3rd Fl. (tel. 522 53 53). From Westbahnhof, take tram #5 to "Burgg." From Sudbahnhof, take tram #18 to "Westbahnhof," then tram #5 to "Burgg." Housed in an old-fashioned, semi-*Jugendstil* Austrian apartment building, this fun and eclectic hostel has 18 mattresses packed into 2 co-ed dorms with huge ceilings and Chinese lanterns. Dorms 160AS; Nov.-Easter 110AS. 50AS surcharge for 1-night stays. **Kitchen** and TV. Bring lock for lockers.

Myrthengasse (HI), VII, Myrtheng. 7, across the street from Believe it or Not, and **Neustiftgasse (HI),** VII, Neustiftg. 85 (tel. 523 63 16; fax 523 58 49; email oejhv-wien-jgh-neustiftg@oejhv.or.at). These simple, Swedish-modern hostels, under the same management, are a 20min. walk from the *Innenstadt.* From Jan. 1-Mar.18 and Oct. 29-Dec. 23 4- to 6-bed dorms with shower 170AS; 2-bed dorms 200AS. Rest of the year 4- to 6-bed dorms with shower 185AS; 2-bed dorms with shower 215AS. Non-member surcharge 40AS. Breakfast and sheets included. Lockers and keys provided. Lunch or dinner 65AS. **Laundry** 50AS. Reception at Myrtheng. 7am-11:30pm. Curfew 1am. Lockout 9am-2pm. Reservations recommended; accepted only by fax or email.

Turmherberge Don Bosco, III, Lechnerstr. 12 (tel. 713 14 94), near the U-3 "Kardinal-Nagl-Pl." stop. The cheapest beds in town are here in a barren former bell tower, which gets hot in summer, though separate quarters for guys and girls help keep things cool. 80AS per person. Curfew 11:45pm. Open Mar.-Nov.

Kolpingfamilie Wien-Meidling (HI), XIII, Bendlg. 10-12 (tel. 813 54 87; fax 812 21 30). Take U-4 or U-6 to "Niederhofstr." Head right on Niederhofstr. and take the 4th right onto Bendlg. This well-lit, modern hostel has 202 beds and stores valuables at the reception. It's kind of boring, but you didn't come to sit in the youth hostel, did you? 8- and 10-bed dorms 130AS; 4- and 6- bed dorms 180AS. Breakfast 45AS. Sheets included. Showers in all rooms, baths in some. Non-members add 40AS. Reception 6am-midnight. Check-out 9am. Lockout midnight-4am.

Schloßherberge am Wilhelminenberg (HI), XVI, Savoyenstr. 2 (tel. 485 85 03, ext. 700; fax 485 85 03, ext. 702; email SHB@wigast.com). Take U-6 to "Thaliastr.," then tram #46 (dir.: Joachimsthalerpl.) to "Maroltingerg." Or take tram #44 from Schottentor to "Wilhelminenstr." then bus #146B or #46B to "Schloß Wilhelminenberg." Unfortunately, the hostel is not in the palace, but to the left of it. Near the *Wienerwald* (Vienna woods), the hostel has a great view of the city. 164 impeccable 4-bed dorms with bathrooms 220AS. Keycard 25AS. Breakfast and sheets included. **Laundry** 65AS. Reception 7am-11pm. Lockout 9am-2pm. Curfew 11pm. Reserve at least 2 days in advance.

Jugendgästehaus Wien Brigittenau (HI), XX, Friedrich-Engels-Pl. 24 (tel. 332 82 94 or 330 05 98; fax 330 83 79; email oejhv-wien-jgh-brigiltneu@oejhv.or.at), 25min. from city center. Take U-1 or U-4 to "Schwedenpl.," then tram N to "Floridsdorferbrücke/ Friedrich-Engels-Pl." Or take U-6 to "Handelskai" and bus #5a or 11a to the tram stop. Either way, follow the signs. It's the large green building behind the tram stop across the street and to the left of the tracks. This roomy, above-average hostel with exceptional facilities for the disabled is unfortunately distant from the city center. 5-night max. stay. 24-bed dorms 145AS; 4-bed dorms 180AS; 2-bed dorms with bath 210AS per person. Breakfast, lockers, and sheets included. Lunch and dinner 65AS. Non-member surcharge 40AS. Reduction of 15AS Jan. 1-Mar. 13 and Nov. 1-Dec. 23. Reception 24hr. Lockout 9am-1pm. Reservations by fax or phone.

Jugendgästehaus Hütteldorf-Hacking (HI), XIII, Schloßbergg. 8 (tel. 877 15 01; fax 877 02 632; email JGH@wigast.com). From Karlspl., take U-4 to "Hütteldorf," take the Hadikg. exit, cross the footbridge, and follow signs to the hostel (10min.). Weary backpackers take bus #53B from the side of the footbridge opposite the station to the hostel. From Westbahnhof, take S-50 to "Hütteldorf." 35min. from the city center, this secluded hostel with sprawling sunny green grounds sits in one of Vienna's most affluent districts and has great views of the city. Often packed with high school groups. 271 beds in 2-, 4-, 6-, and 8-bed rooms, one room with 22 beds; some doubles with showers. 170AS (200AS with "American Breakfast.") Add 30AS for rooms with showers or for one of the few singles. Keycard 25AS. Discounts for groups of 18 or more. Free luggage storage. Lunch and dinner 65-72AS. Reception 7am-11:45pm. Lockout 9:30am-3:30pm. Curfew 11:45pm. Bring your own lock. Reservations by phone or fax. MC, Visa.

UNIVERSITY DORMITORIES

From July through September, many university dorms become hotels, usually with singles, doubles, and a few triples and quads. These rooms don't have much in the way of character, but showers and sheets are standard, and their cleanliness and relatively low cost suffice for most budget travelers, particularly for longer stays.

Porzellaneum der Wiener Universität, IX, Porzellang. 30 (tel. 317 72 820; fax 317 72 830). From Südbahnhof, take tram D (dir.: Nußdorf) to "Fürsteng." From Westbahnhof, take tram #5 to "Franz-Josefs Bahnhof," then tram D (dir.: Südbahnhof) to "Fürsteng." 10min. from the Ring. 177 beds. Singles 190AS; doubles 380AS; quads 760AS. Sheets included. Reception 24hr. Reservations recommended.

Rudolfinum, IV, Mayerhofg. 3 (tel. 505 53 84; fax 5055 385 450). Take U-1 to "Taubstummeng." for rock 'n' roll and MTV. More serious guests watch CNN. Large rooms. Great location. Singles 270AS; doubles 480AS; triples 600AS. Breakfast included. **Laundry** facilities 65AS. **Kitchen** available by prior arrangement. Reception 24hr.

Gästehaus Pfeilgasse, VIII, Pfeilg. 6 (tel. 40174; fax 401 76 20; email acahot @academia-hotels.co.at). Take U-2 to "Lerchenfelderstr.," go right, then right again on Lange Gasse, and left on Pfeilg. Singles 270AS; doubles 480AS; triples 600AS. Breakfast included. Reception 24hr. Reservations recommended. Credit cards accepted.

Katholisches Studentenhaus, XIX, Peter-Jordanstr. 29 (tel./fax 347 47 312). From Westbahnhof, take U-6 (dir.: Heiligenstadt) to "Nußdorferstr.," then bus #35A or tram #38 to "Hardtg." and turn left. From Südbahnhof, take tram D to "Schottentor" then tram #38 to "Hardtg." Enjoy the laid-back atmosphere in the 19th district. Singles 250AS; doubles 400AS. Showers and sheets included. Reception closes at 10pm. Call ahead.

Studentenwohnheim der Hochschule für Musik, I, Johannesg. 8 (tel. 514 84 48; fax 514 84 49). Walk 3 blocks down Kärnterstr. away from the Stephansdom and turn left onto Johannesg. Fabulous location, inexpensive meals. Singles 430AS, with bath 490AS; doubles 760AS, 940AS; triples 840AS; quads 1000AS; quints 1250AS. Breakfast and showers included. Reduction for groups larger than 20. Apartment also available (includes 2 double rooms, bathroom, kitchen, living room). 350AS per person, 500AS per person for single occupancy, 1200 AS for entire apartment. Reception 24hr.

HOTELS AND PENSIONS

Check the hostels section for good singles deals as well. The prices are higher here, but you pay for convenient reception hours, no curfews, and no lockouts.

Lauria Apartments, VII, Kaiserstr. 77, Apt. #8 (tel. 522 25 55). From Westbahnhof, take tram #5 to "Burgg." From Sudbahnhof, take tram #18 to "Westbahnhof" then tram #5 to "Burgg." Close to city center and Westbahnhof. Fully equipped **kitchens.** Dorms 160AS; singles and student-bunk twins 480AS; doubles 530AS, with shower 700AS; student-bunk triples 600AS; triples 700AS, 800AS; quads 850AS, 940AS. Sheets and TV included. 2 night min. for reservations. Credit cards accepted except for dorm beds.

Pension Hargita, VII, Andreasg. (tel. 526 19 28; fax 526 04 92). Take U-3 to "Zieglerg." then head down Mariahilferstr., away from the city center to Andreasg. This *Pension* offers comfort and a prime location. Singles 400AS, with shower 450AS; doubles 600AS, 700AS, with bath 800AS. Breakfast 40AS. Reception 8am-10pm.

Pension Wild, VIII, Langeg. 10 (tel. 406 51 74; fax 402 21 68; email info@Pension-wild.com; www.pension-wild.com). Take U-3 to "Volkstheater," U-2 to "Lerchenfelderstr.," and take the 1st right. From Südbahnhof, take bus #13A (dir.: Alserstr./Skodag.) to "Piaristeng." Turn left onto Lerchenfelderstr., and left again onto Langeg. 15min. walk from the city center. 35 beds. Friendly, English-speaking staff. Singles 490-690AS; doubles 590-990AS; triples 1030-1230AS. Breakfast and shower included. **Kitchen** access. Reception 7am-10pm. Reservations by fax recommended.

Pension Kraml, VI, Brauerg. 5 (tel. 587 85 88; fax 586 75 73). Take U-3 to "Zierierg." exit onto Otto-Bauerg. Take 1st left, then 1st right. From Südbahnhof, take bus #13A to Esterhazyg. and walk up Brauerg. Situated near the *Innenstadt* and the Naschmarkt. Large rooms and a lounge with cable TV. 38 beds. Singles 310AS; doubles 560AS, with shower 640AS, with bath 760AS; triples 720AS, with shower 930AS. Apartment with bath 1120-1250AS for 3-5 people. Breakfast buffet 60AS.

Pension Falstaff, IX, Müllnerg. 5 (tel. 317 91 27; fax 317 91 864). Take U-4 to "Roßauer Lände." Cross Roßauer Lände, head down Grünentorg., and take the 3rd left onto Müllnerg. to find this slightly campy establishment. Singles 390AS, with shower 500AS; doubles 660AS, 760AS, with bath 860AS. Extra bed 250AS. Breakfast included. 10% reduced rate for stays of 1 week or more in off-season; 15% for 2 weeks, 30% for more than 1 month. 100AS reduction Nov. 1-March 30 (excluding Christmas and Jan.) Reception 7:30am-9pm. Reservations by phone or fax. Credit cards accepted.

Pension Reimer, IV, Kircheng. 18 (tel. 523 61 62; fax 524 37 82), is centrally located and has huge orange-hued rooms. Singles 500AS, in winter 470AS. Doubles 740AS, with bath 860AS; in winter 680AS, 810AS. Breakfast included. Credit cards accepted.

Pension Amon, VII, Daung. 1 (tel./fax 405 01 94). Take tram #5 from Westbahnhof or #13 from Südbahnhof to Alserstr. and Skodag. Walk down Skodag. and turn left onto Daung. Colorful and pleasant. Singles with shower 450AS; doubles with shower 700AS. Reception 24hr. **Kitchen.** Reservations by fax or phone. Credit cards accepted.

F. Kaled and Tina, VII, Lindeng. 42 (tel. 523 90 13; fax 526 25 13). Take U-3 to "Ziederg." Follow Ziederg. 2 blocks to Lindeng. This *Pension* has private rooms with cable TV. Singles with bath 450AS; doubles 550AS, with bath 650AS; triples 700AS, 800AS. Breakfast 75AS. 2-night min. stay. Reservations by phone or fax.

CAMPING

Wien-West, Hüttelbergstr. 80 (tel. 914 23 14; fax 911 35 94). Take U-4 to "Hütteldorf," then bus #14B or 152 (dir.: Campingpl.) to "Wien West." This convenient campground, 8km from the city center, is crowded but grassy and pleasant. 73AS per person in July-Aug, 67AS rest of the year, children 38AS, tent 37-42AS, camper 62-69AS. Electricity 40AS. In July and Aug. 2- and 4-person cabins available for 250AS and 400-440AS. **Laundry** machines, grocery stores, handicapped access, and **cooking facilities.** Reception 7:30am-9:30pm. Closed Feb.

Aktiv Camping Neue Donau, XXII, Am Kleehäufel 119 (tel./fax 202 40 10), is 4km from the city center and adjacent to Neue Donau beaches. Take U-1 to "Kaisermühlen" then bus 91a to "Kleehäufel." July-Aug. 73AS, children 38AS, camper 69AS, tent 42AS, electricity 40AS. May, June, and Sept. 67AS, children 38AS, camper 62AS, tent 37AS, electricity 40AS. Showers included. **Laundry,** supermarket, **kitchen.** Handicapped access. Open May 17-Sept. 12.

Campingplatz Schloß Laxenburg (tel. (02236)71333; fax 71 33 44), at Münchendorfer Str., Laxenburg, is 15km from Vienna, but extremely popular and beautifully situated near the Gumpoldskirchen vineyards. Facilities include a restaurant, **boat rental,** heated **pool,** children's pool, and supermarket. July-Aug. 73AS per person, children 38AS; caravans 69AS; tents 42AS; electricity 40AS. Rest of season 67AS, children 38; caravans 69AS; tents 37AS; electricity 40AS. Open April 1-Oct. 31.

◖ FOOD AND DRINK

"Here the people think only of sensual gratifications."

—Washington Irving, 1822

In a world full of uncertainty, the Viennese believe that the least you can do is face things with a full stomach. Food is not mere fuel for the body; it is an aesthetic, even philosophical experience that begins when you wish someone *"Mahlzeit"* (enjoy). Food and drink are in harmony here, and the city consumes both in great quantities. Cafés, *Beisln* (pubs), and *Heurigen* (wine gardens) all maintain their own particular balances between consumption and entertainment.

Viennese culinary offerings reflect the crazy patchwork empire of the Habsburgs. *Serbische Bohnensuppe* (Serbian bean soup) and *Ungarische Gulaschsuppe* (Hungarian spicy beef stew) reflect Eastern European influences. *Knödel*, bread dumplings found in most side dishes, come from the former Czechoslovakia. Even the famed *Wienerschnitzel* (fried and breaded veal cutlets) probably first appeared in Milan. Boiled beef *(Tafelspitz)* is one of the few original national treasures. Vienna is renowned for sublime desserts and chocolates—unbelievably rich, and priced for patrons who are likewise blessed. Most residents, however, maintain that the sumptuous treats are worth every *Groschen*. Unless you buy your sin wholesale at a local bakery, *Sacher Torte*, *Imperial Torte*, and even *Apfelstrudel* can cost up to 50AS.

Vienna's restaurants are as varied as its cuisine. *Gästehäuser*, *Imbiße* (food stands), and *Beisln* serve inexpensive meals that stick to your ribs and are best washed down with copious amounts of beer. *Würstelstände*, found on almost every corner, provide a quick, cheap lunch (a sausage runs 27AS or so). The restaurants near **Kärntnerstraße** are generally expensive—a better bet is the neighborhood north of the university and near the Votivkirche (take U-2 to "Schottentor"), where **Universitätsstraße** and **Währingerstraße** meet. Cafés with cheap meals also line **Florianig** in the 8th district. The area radiating from the **Rechte** and **Linke Wienzeile** near Naschmarkt (take U-4 to "Kettenbrückeng.") houses a range of cheap restaurants, and the **Naschmarkt** itself contains open-air stands where you can purchase aromatic delicacies (bread and a variety of ethnic food) to sample while shopping at Vienna's premier flea market (weekends only; see p. 118). Come before 11am and walk to the far end of the square to find the cheapest prices from local farmers (open M-F 7am-6pm, Sa 7am-1pm). Almost all year long, **Rathausplatz** hosts food stands tied into whatever the current festival happens to be. At Christmas-time, **Christkindlmarkt** offers hot food and spiked punch amid vendors of Christmas charms, ornaments, and candles. From the end of June through July, the **Festwochen** celebration brings international foodstuffs to the stands behind the seats of the various films (stands open 11am-11pm.) The open-air **Brunnenmarkt** (take U-6 to "Josefstädterstr." then walk up Veronikag. 1 block and turn right) is colorful and tends to be cheap. The **Wienerwald** chain has branches for chicken-lovers in most districts (Annag. 3, Freyung 6, Bellariastr. 12, and Schotteng; open 7am-midnight). *Bäckereien* (bakeries) permeate the city.

As always, supermarkets provide building blocks for cheap, solid meals. The lowest prices can be found on the shelves of **Billa, Hofer,** and **Spar. Julius Meinl** is mid-range and everywhere. Other chains include **Ledi, Mondo, Renner,** and **Zielpunkt.** Travelers can buy kosher groceries at the **Kosher Supermarket,** Hollandstr. 10 (tel. 216 96 75). Most places close Saturday afternoons and all of Sunday (on the first Sa of every month, most shops close at 5 or 6pm). In general, restaurants stop serving after 11pm. To join the legions of Viennese conquering the summer heat, seek out the **Italeis** or **Tichy** ice cream vendors or visit the delicious **Gelateria Hoher Markt,** I, Hoher Markt, just off Rotenturmstr. Expatriate Italians flock here to sample all 23 mouth-watering *gelato* flavors (open daily Mar.-Oct. 9am-11pm).

EAT THE MENÜ, BABY! if you're trying to pinch pennies but not starve in the process, eating the *Menü* is the way to go. In Austria, a *Menü*, much like a *prix-fixe* meal, is a three-course meal served only for lunch. Most *Menüs* cost between 55-85AS for soup, an entree, and dessert (drinks not included). The same meal would cost double for dinner, so get into the habit of eating a large *Menü* lunch to save money and still savor Austrian cuisine.

RESTAURANTS

INSIDE THE RING

Bizi Pizza, I, Rotenturmstr. 4 (tel. 513 37 05), on the corner of Stephanspl. The best deal in the city center, Bizi will whip up a fresh pizza or pasta that rivals Italy's best for a pittance (pasta 65-75AS, whole pizza 60-75AS, slices 28AS, salad bar 39-69AS). Open daily 11am-11:30pm. **Branches** with same hours at Franz-Josefs-Kai (tel. 535 79 13), Mariahilferstr. 22-24 (tel. 523 16 58), and X, Favoritenstr. 105 (tel. 600 50 10).

Café Ball, I, Ballg. 5 (tel. 513 17 54), near Stephanspl. off Weihburgg. This charming café has candlelit tables, friendly staff, and terrific food. Listen to opera music as you enjoy your lunch. *Menüs* 75AS. Open M-Sa 11am-1am, Su noon-midnight.

La Crêperie, I, Grünangerg. 10 (tel. 512 56 87), off Singerstr. near Stephanspl. The sensual decor of this little restaurant complements the scrumptious crepes, both sweet and savory (60-250AS). Try the exotically garnished *Himbeer* (raspberry) soda. Open 11:30am-midnight.

Rosenberger Markt, I, Mayscderg. 2 (tel. 512 34 58), behind the Sacher Hotel. This large and chaotic subterranean buffet offers a gargantuan selection of decent food at reasonable prices. Food stations include salad, fruit salad, waffle, antipasto, potato, and pasta bars. You pay by the size of your plate, not by weight, so pile high. Salads 29-64AS, waffles 55AS, vegetable dishes 24-64AS. Open 10:30am-11pm.

Levante, I, Wallnerstr. 2 (tel. 533 23 26; fax 535 54 85). Walk down the Graben away from the Stephansdom, turn left on Kohlmarkt, and right on Wallnerstr. This Greek-Turkish restaurant features street-side dining and heaps of delicious dishes, including vegetarian delights. Entrees 80-150AS. **Branches** at I, Wollzeile 19 (off Rotenturm, take U-3 or U-1 to "Stephanspl."); Mariahilferstr. 88a; and VIII, Josefstädterstr. 14 (take U-2 to "Rathaus"). All open 11am-11:30pm.

Margaritaville, I, Bartensteing. 3 (tel. 405 47 86). Take U-2 to "Lerchenfelderstr." and walk across the triangular green to Bartensteing. Get creative Mexican food, most notably the *Fajita Lupita,* at this sizzling joint with a tiny outdoor garden. Entrees 90-250AS. Open M-Sa 6pm-2am (heated food until 1am), Su 6pm-midnight.

Brezelg'wölb, I, Lederhof 9 (tel./fax 533 88 11), near Am Hof. Excellent hearty cuisine even the Viennese call *"Altwiener"* (old Viennese). Cobblestones and classical music enhance the atmosphere of this old-fashioned *Backstube*. Don't leave without glancing at the rare piece of the intact medieval city wall in the courtyard—the rest was torn down to build the Ringstraße. Reservations recommended in the evening, but lunch is a sure bet (around 100AS). Open daily 11am-1am, hot food until midnight.

Maschu Maschu, I, Rabensteig 8 (tel. 533 29 04). This hole-in-the-wall joint serves filling and super-cheap Israeli *falafel* (38AS) and *schwarma,* outdoors in summer. Open M 11am-midnight, Tu 11am-1am, W 11am-2am, Th 11am-3am, F-Su 11am-4am.

Inigo, I, Bäckerstr. 18 (tel. 512 74 51). This contemporary diner, across from Vienna's Jesuit church, was founded by a Jesuit priest as part of a socio-economic reintegration program. It provides transit employment, training, and social work for 17 people who are long-term unemployed or have no job qualifications. Menu includes eclectic international dishes, many whole wheat and vegetarian options, and a salad bar. Try the delicious, original *Schweinekotlett Gorgonzola* (108AS). Entrees 60-110AS, salad 22-58AS. Open M-Sa 8:30am-11pm, Su 10am-2pm.

Trzesniewski, I, Dorotheerg. 1 (tel. 512 32 91; fax 513 95 65), 3 blocks down the Graben from the Stephansdom. A famous stand-up restaurant, this unpronounceable establishment has been serving petite open-faced sandwiches for over 80 years. Favorite toppings include salmon, onion, paprika, and egg. This was Franz Kafka's favorite place to eat, but it is more atmospheric than affordable at 10AS per dainty slice—you'll want 5-6 of them for a solid lunch. Open M-F 9am-7pm, Sa 9am-1pm. **Branches** at VI, Mariahiferstr. 95 (tel. 596 4291); III, Hauptstr. 97 (tel. 712 99 64) in Galleria.

OUTSIDE THE RING

■ **Blue Box,** VII, Richterg. 8 (tel. 523 26 82). Take U-3 to "Neubaug.," turn onto Neubaug., and take your 1st right onto Richterg. Although the interior looks more like a nightclub than a restaurant—an orange chandelier, blue leather couches, and not much light—the emphasis is on the food. Dishes are fresh, flamboyant, and very original, often centering around themes. DJs pick music to match the meals. A great place to come for a late (or really late) breakfast (until 5pm). Choose from Viennese, French, or vegetarian cuisine. Entrees from 53-116As. Open Tu-Su 10am-2am, M 6pm-2am.

■ **Tunnel,** VIII, Florianig. 39 (tel. 42 34 65). Take U-2 to "Rathaus," then, with your back to the *Rathaus,* head right on Landesgerichtstr. and left on Florianig. Pronounced "Too-nehl," this is a student crowd paradise, dark and smoky with funky paintings, heavy tables, and the occasional divan. Tunnel is a popular place prized for its dilapidated hipness, live nightly music, and affordable food. Daily lunch *Menüs* 45AS. Choose between Italian, Austrian, and Middle Eastern dishes, with many vegetarian options (45-125AS). Some of the cheapest beer in Vienna (0.50L *Gösser* 27AS), good pizza (55-85AS), and a breakfast menu (28AS) until 11:30am. Open 10am-2am.

■ **Café Willendorf,** VI, Linke Wienzeile 102 (tel. 587 17 89). Take U-4 to "Pilgramg." and look for the big pink building which also houses the the Rosa Lila Villa, Vienna's gay and lesbian center. This café, bar, and restaurant with a leafy outdoor terrace serves excellent, creative vegetarian fare for under 100AS. Mixed crowd and a warm community atmosphere. Open 7pm-2am; meals until midnight.

■ **OH Pot, OH Pot,** IX, Währingerstr. 22 (tel. 319 42 59). Take U-2 to "Schottentor." This adorable joint serves amazingly good Spanish food at rock-bottom prices. Try one of their filling name-sake "pots" (70-85AS), which are stew-like concoctions in veggie and meat varieties. Terrific *Empanadas* (60AS). Open M-F 10:30am-2:30pm and 6-11pm.

Elsäßer Bistro, IX, Währingerstr. 30 (tel. 319 76 89). U-2: "Schottentor." Within the palace that houses the French Cultural Institute—walk in the garden and follow your nose. Wonderful food and beautiful French wines. Most dishes hover around 120AS. Open M-F 11am-3pm and 6-11pm. Kitchen closes 1hr. earlier.

Schnitzelwirt Schmidt, VII, Neubaug. 52 (tel. 523 37 71). Take U-2 or U-3 to "Volkstheater," then bus #49 to "Neubaug." You'll find every kind of *Schnitzel* (65-115AS) imaginable here. It's not gourmet, but servings are guaranteed to be so big they go over the edge of the plate. If you can't finish it, ask for paper to wrap it up in (you won't be the first to do so). Open M-Sa 11am-11pm.

Fischerbräu, XIX, Billrothstr. 17 (tel. 319 62 64). Take U-6 to "Nußdorfer Str." then walk up Währinger Gürtel, left on Döblinger Hauptstr., and left on Billrothstr. Popular spot for young locals. The leafy courtyard and jazz music make this restaurant ideal for consuming home-brewed beer (large 40AS) and delicious veal sausage (60AS) and chicken salad (87AS). Open M-Sa 4pm-1am, Su 11am-1am. Jazz brunch Su noon-3pm.

Amerlingbeisl, VII, Stiftg. 8 (tel. 526 16 60). Take U-2 to "Babenbergerstr." or U-3 to "Neubaug." Halfway between the stops on Mariahilferstr., turn onto Stiftg. After a couple of blocks you'll hit a cluster of outdoor restaurants. Walk past the first to reach Amerlingbeisl, a bamboo courtyard roofed with grape vines. Eat vegetarian food in this unofficial alternative community center while listening to sprays of water falling on leaves. Occasional live music. Entrees 58-113AS, late breakfast 58-130AS. Open daily 9am-2am (hot food served until 1am).

Lecker, III, Ungarg. 57, on the #O tram line. A vegetarian nirvana, this cozy Taiwanese vegetarian restaurant offers tofu, *seitan,* and soy-delights artfully disguised as beef, chicken, and fishies. Open 11:30am-2:30pm and 5:30-11:45pm.

Restaurant am Radetzkyplatz, III, Radetzkypl. 1 (tel. 712 57 50), is a mellowed old Austrian pub wih 150 years of beer (0.50L 30AS) to its credit. Well-worn bar railings testify to its popularity. Sit outside under an awning and enjoy some of the cheapest food (70-175AS) in Vienna. Robust servings and veggie options. Open 8am-11pm.

Nells, XVII, Alseggerstr. 26 (tel. 479 13 77). Take U-2 to "Schottentor" then tram #40 to "Alseggerstr." The inviting wooden interior and funky versions of traditional Viennese dishes draw a hip twenty-something crowd. Lots of different beers and *Heuriger* wines. Open M-Sa 4pm-2am, Su 11am-2am.

Café Nil, VII, Siebensterng. 39 (tel. 526 61 65). Take tram #49 from the *Volksgarten* three stops away from the inner city to reach this serene and low-key incense-scented Middle Eastern café. Enjoy tasty dishes, all pork-free and many vegetarian (54-105AS). Open M-Th 10am-midnight, F-Sa 10am-1am, Su 10am-midnight. Breakfast until noon, Sa until 3pm.

Stomach, IX, Seeg. 26 (tel. 310 20 99). Take tram D to "Fürsteng." then walk down Porzellang. to Seeg. and turn right. This sophisticated establishment serves 1st-class Austrian cooking with a Styrian kick (130-230AS). Eat your beautifully cooked food inside or outside in a lovely courtyard. Twenty-something crowd. Open W-Sa 4pm-midnight, Su 10am-10pm. Reservations recommended.

Hatam, IX, Währingerstr. 64 (tel. 310 94 50). Take tram #38, 40, or 41 to "Spitalg." for Persian food at good prices. Try their unbeatable *gorme sabse* (spiced eggplant dish with rice) or grab a *Döner* to go (40-60AS). Entrees 75-165AS. Open daily 11am-11pm.

University Mensa, IX, Universitätsstr. 7, on the 7th Fl. of the university building, between U-2 stops "Rathaus" and "Schottentor." Visitors can ride the old-fashioned *Pater Noster* elevator (no doors and it never stops; you have to jump in and out, so say your prayers) to the 6th floor and take the stairs up. There isn't much atmosphere but the food is cheap. Typical caféteria meals 40-60AS. Open M-F 8am-6pm.

Other inexpensive student caféterias serve their constituencies at:

Music Academy, I, Johannesg. 8 (tel. 512 94 70). Open M-F 7:30am-3pm. Food served 11am-2pm; in July and Aug. and weekends 7:30-10am.

Academy of Applied Art, I, Oskar-Kokoschka-Pl. 2 (tel. 718 66 95). Open M-Th 8:30am-6pm, F 8:30am-3pm.

Academy of Fine Arts, I, Schillerpl. 3 (tel. 58 81 61 38). Open M-F 9am-5pm. Closed June to early Sept.

Afro-Asiatisches Institut, IX, Türkenstr. 3, near Schottentor. Open M-F 11:30am-2pm.

Vienna Technical University, IV, Wiedner Hauptstr. 8-10 (tel. 586 65 02). Open M-F 11am-3pm.

Catholic University Student's Community, I, Ebendorferstr. 8 (tel. 408 35 87 39). *Menü* 33-40AS. Open M-F 11am-2pm.

Economics University, IX, Aug. 2-6 (tel. 310 57 18). Open M-F 8am-7pm, holidays until 3pm.

COFFEEHOUSES AND KONDITOREIEN

"Who's going to start a revolution? Herr Trotsky from Café Central?"

—Austrian general quoted on the eve of the Russian Revolution

There is an unwritten rule for the Vienna coffeehouse—the drink matters, but the atmosphere *really* matters. The 19th-century coffeehouse was a haven for artists, writers, and thinkers who flocked to soft, brooding interiors to flee badly heated, telephone-less apartments. In the coffeehouses, they surrounded themselves with dark wood and dusty velvet, ordered a cup of coffee, and stayed long into the night composing operettas, writing books, and cutting into each other's work. The bourgeoisie followed suit, and the coffeehouse became the living room of the city. At its tables gathered the intellectual world of Vienna and, in many cases, Europe. A grand coffeehouse culture arose. Peter Altenberg, "the café writer," scribbled lines, Oskar Kokoschka grumbled alone, and exiles Vladimir Lenin and Leon Trotsky played chess. Theodor Herzl made plans here for a Zionist Israel, and Kafka came from Prague to visit the Herrenhof. Karl Kraus and a circle of minor writers baited Hugo von Hofmannsthal and Arthur Schnitzler. The original literary café, right on the cusp of the "merry apocalypse" *fin de siècle* culture, was Café Griensteidl. After it was demolished in 1897, the torch passed first to Café Central and then to Café Herrenhof. Cafés still exist under all these names, but only Café Central looks like it used to. Adolf Loos, pioneer of 20th-century Minimalist architecture, designed the interior of the Museum Café in smooth, spacious lines. Coffeehouses now rest partway in the past. The best places resist massive overhauls, succumbing to a noble, comfortable decrepitude.

VIENNESE COFFEE CULTURE Vienna's time-honored coffeehouse culture is arguably more famous than the Vienna Philharmonic or the Ring-straße. In venues ranging from wood-paneled elegance to new-age swank, Vienna's café culture encourages philosophical discussions, people watching, and the writing of deeply psychological novels. There is, however, considerably more to mastering the finer points of Viennese coffee-drinking than simply ordering a *café latte*, as many an ignorant visitor has discovered with chagrin. Here is a quick reference guide to some of the most common and delectable Viennese coffees:

Melange: espresso-like coffee with hot milk, optional whipped cream and cinnamon
Mokka: strong black coffee, much like espresso
Piccolo: black coffee served in a tiny cup with or without whipped cream
Verlängerter: weak coffee with cream
Kapuziner: small *Mokka* with cream, sprinkled with cocoa, chocolate, or cinnamon
Fiaker: black coffee with rum
Pharisäer: black coffee with rum, sugar, and whipped cream
Kaffee Verkehrt: more milk than coffee
Philosoph: black coffee with brandy, vanilla, sugar, and whipped cream
Kaisermelange: a regular *Melange* with an egg yolk mixed in
Türkischer: strong black coffee brewed in a copper pot, with sugar
Mazagran: cold coffee with rum or maraschino liqueur, served over ice cubes
Wiener Eiskaffee: chilled black coffee and vanilla ice cream, with whipped cream
Maria Thesesia: coffee with orange liqueur and whipped cream
Einspänner: coffee and a glass filled with whipped cream

Viennese coffee is distinct, not quite as strong as an espresso, but with more kick than your average Dripmaster. The quintessential Viennese coffee is the *Melange*, and you can order every kind of coffee as a *Kleiner* (small) or *Grosser* (large), *Brauner* (brown, with a little milk), or *Schwarzer* (black—enough said). Whipped cream is *Schlag* (short for *Schlagobers*); if you don't like it, say *"ohne Schlag, bitte."* Choosing your coffee is an art form in Vienna (see **Viennese Coffee Culture,** above). Opulent pastries complete the picture: *Apfelstrudel*, cheesecakes, tortes, *Buchteln* (warm cake with jam in the middle—diabolical), *Palatschinken*, *Krapfen*, and *Mohr im Hemd* have all helped place Vienna on the culinary map. The *Konditoreien* are no less traditional, but they focus their attention onto delectables rather than coffee. These pastries are something of a national institution—Switzerland may have its gold reserves, but Austria could back its currency with its world-renowned *Sacher Torte*. To see a menu, ask for a *Karte*.

Most cafés also serve hot food, but don't order food and coffee together (except pastries), unless you want to be really gauche. Coffee may seem expensive (30-40AS) if you only consider the drink you're buying, but when you realize that you're actually paying to linger for hours and read newspapers, the price suddenly seems much more reasonable. The most serious dictate of coffeehouse etiquette is the requirement to linger. The waiter (often outfitted with black bow tie and always committed to his work) will serve you as soon as you sit down, and then leave you to sip, read, and brood. He's known as *Herr Ober* in Austria, not as a *Kellner*. Daily newspapers and magazines, many in English, are neatly racked for patrons. When you are ready to leave, just ask to pay: *"Zahlen bitte!"*

INSIDE THE RING

■ **Café Hawelka,** I, Dorotheerg. 6 (tel. 512 82 30), 3 blocks down Graben from the *Stephansdom*. With its dusty wallpaper, dark wood, and old red-striped velvet sofas, the Hawelka is shabby and glorious. Josephine and Leopold Hawelka put this legendary café on the map when they opened it in 1937—Leopold received an award from the Austrian government and Josephine a visit from Falco. *Buchteln* (served fresh from the oven at 10pm) 35AS. Coffee 30-50AS. Open M and W-Sa 8am-2am, Su 4pm-2am.

▓ **Demel,** I, Kohlmarkt 14 (tel. 535 17 17), 5min. from the Stephansdom down Graben. The most luxurious Viennese *Konditorei,* Demel's was confectioner to the imperial court until the empire dissolved. All of the chocolate is made fresh every morning. A fantasy of mirrored rooms, cream walls, and a display case of legendary desserts. Waitresses in convent-black serve the divine confections (40-50AS). Don't miss the *crème-du-jour.* Open 10am-6pm.

▓ **Café Central,** I (tel. 533 37 63), at the corner of Herreng. and Strauchg. inside Palais Ferstel. Café Central has unfortunately surrendered to tourists because of its fame, but this mecca of the café world is definitely worth a visit. Theodor Herzl, Sigmund Freud, Karl Kraus, and Vladimir Ilych Ulianov (better known by his pen name, Lenin) hung out here, as well as Leon Trotsky, who played chess. Alfred Polgar published an essay titled *Theorie de Café Central,* where he wrote: "It is a place for people who know how to abandon and be abandoned for the sake of their fate, but do not have the nerve to live up to this fate. It is a true asylum for people who have to kill time so as not to be killed by it...a first-aid station for the confused...all their lives in search of themselves and all their lives in flight from themselves..." Oh, they serve coffee, too, at elegant tables in an arcade court. Open M-Sa 9am-8pm. Live piano 4-7pm.

Hotel Sacher, I, Philharmonikerstr. 4 (tel. 512 14 87), around the corner from the main tourist information office. This historic sight has served world-famous **Sachertorte** (50AS) in red velvet opulence for years. During the reign of Franz Josef, elites invited to the Hofburg would make late reservations at the Sacher (the emperor ate quickly, Elisabeth was always dieting, and as nobody dared eat after the imperial family had finished, all the guests left hungry and had a real dinner later at Sacher). Exceedingly elegant; most of the clientele is bejeweled, but casual is fine. Open 7am-11:30pm.

Café MAK, I, Stubenring 3-5 (tel. 714 01 21), inside the Museum für Angewandte Kunst. Take tram #1 or 2 to "Stubenring." Light, bright, white, and very tight at night, this café feels like a display case in the museum, but the people are stunning and the furniture is *Bauhaus* but funkier. Peek through glass walls into the museum, or dine outside among sunflowers. The café gets rowdy with students after 10pm and hosts techno-rave parties on Saturdays in July. Open Tu-Su 10am-2am (hot food until midnight).

Café Alt Wien, I, Bäckerg. 9 (tel. 512 52 22) is a bohemian, nicotine-stained place behind the Stephansdom. Smoky red sofas and layers of avant-garde posters set the mood. Open M-Th 10am-2am, F-Su 10am-4am.

Café Museum, I, Friedrichstr. 6 (tel. 56 52 01), near the Opera. Head away from the *Innenstadt* to the corner of Operng. and Friedrichstr. Built in 1899 by Adolf Loos, in a plain, spacious style with striking curves, this café once attracted a crowd of cabaret artists, painters, and famous musicians including Lehár, Berg, Musil, Kokoschka, and Schiele. Once known as "Café Nihilism," the place lost much of its importance (and a number of its clientele) after the bloody 1918 revolution. It now attracts a mixed bag of artists, lawyers, students, and chess players. Open 8am-midnight.

Kleines Café, I, Franziskanerpl. 3. Turn off Kärtnerstr. onto Weihburg. and follow it to the *Franziskanerkirche.* This tiny, cozy café, designed by architect Hermann Czech, features green paneling, a low-vaulted ceiling, art exhibits, nightclub posters, and tables spilling out into the courtyard. The salads here are minor works of art, costing on average 65AS. Open M-Sa 10am-2am, Su 1pm-2am.

Café Opera Zum Peter, I, Riemberg. 9 (tel. 512 89 81). A low-key, opera-mad crowd lingers here among walls plastered with a hodgepodge of autographed photos, posters, and pictures of opera performers and performances. Open M-F 8am-2am, Sa 5pm-2am.

Bräunerhof, I, Stallburgg. 2 (tel. 512 38 93). This delightfully shabby café's location—on a small alley near the Hofburg—has left it virtually untouched by tourists. Hosts many readings and piano concerts. You can order bread, *Käse* and *Schinken,* or Austrian salad from a menu lined with Peter Altenberg prose (35-65AS). Open M-F 7:30am-8:30pm, Sa 7:30am-6pm, Su 10am-6pm.

Café Prückel, I, Stubenring 24 (tel. 512 61 15). High-ceilinged and spacious, this artsy café, has developed a noble slouch over time. Prückel hosts numerous readings and performances, patronized by art students from the MAK (Museum of Applied Arts) down the street. Open 9am-10pm. Kitchen open noon-8pm.

Hotel Imperial, I, Kärnter Ring 16 (tel. 50 11 03 63; fax 50 11 03 55). From the opera, turn left onto the Ring and walk 5min. This elegant, chandeliered café, with a lovely flower-hung courtyard, serves its own insignia-stamped, marzipan-filled *Imperial Torte* (50AS), which some prefer to the rival *Sachertorte.* Karl Kraus became a regular here after deciding Café Central was too noisy, and brought Hugo von Hofmannsthal, Rainer Maria Rilke, Peter Altenberg, and Franz Werfel with him. Freud occasionally came here and was not above having an informal psychoanalytic consultation at his table. Trotsky played chess here, too. Open 7am-11:30pm.

Waldland, I, Peterspl. 11 (tel. 533 41 56). This tiny *Konditorei* bakes everything imaginable topped with poppyseed *(Mohn)* and honey and serves it in a charming setting. Decadent cookies, cakes, rolls, pastries (30-50AS). Open M-F 9am-6pm, Sa 9am-1pm.

OUTSIDE THE RING

🖼 **Café Sperl,** VI, Gumpendorferstr. 11 (tel. 586 41 58), 15min. from the Westbahnhof. Take U-2 to "Babenbergstr.," walk one block on Getreidemarkt, and turn right on Gumpendorferstr. Built in 1880, Sperl is one of Vienna's oldest and most beautiful cafés. Though some of the original trappings were removed during renovations, the *fin de siècle* atmosphere remains. Franz Lehár was a regular here; he composed operettas at a table by the entrance. This luxurious café is also the former home for Vienna's *Hagenbund,* an Art Nouveau group excluded from the Secession. Coffee 30-50AS; cake 35-45AS. Open M-Sa 7am-11pm, Su 3-9pm; July-Aug. closed Su.

🖼 **Café Savoy,** VI, Linke Wienzeile 36, is a scruffy *fin de siècle* café with dark wood and decrepit gold trim. Check yourself out in the gigantic mirror as you step inside. A large gay and lesbian crowd moves in to make this a lively nightspot on weekends. Open Tu-F 5pm-2am, Sa 9am-6pm and 9pm-2am.

🖼 **Berg das Café,** IX, Bergg. 8 (tel. 319 57 20). Take U-2 to "Schottentor" and take a right off Währingerstr. onto Bergg. A super-swank gay café/bar by night and casual hang-out by day, this place is always crowded. Wonderful food, desserts, and music in a relaxed atmosphere make this a delightful place for anyone. It recently merged with nearby gay and lesbian bookstore **Das Löwenherz,** so you can browse during the day while you drink your *Melange.* Plenty of English titles. Open 10am-1am.

Alte Backstube, VIII, Langeg. 34 (tel. 406 11 01). Around the corner from Theater in der Josefstadt, this popular after-theater café/restaurant functioned as a bakery from 1701 until 1963. The café serves Austrian dishes, coffees and pastries, but more interestingly, it is also a **museum of bakery art.** On display are the original baking ovens, 300-year-old bakers' equipment, articles, photos, and all sorts of baked-goods devotionalia. Open Sept. to mid-July Tu-Sa 10am-midnight, Su 4pm-midnight.

Kunsthaus Wien Café, III, Untere Weißgerberstr. 13 (tel. 712 04 97). Situated in a overgrown courtyard in the undulating Kunsthaus museum (see p. 125 for directions), this café serves typical drinks in a Hundertwasserian atmosphere. Open daily 10am-midnight.

Café Stein, IX, Währingerstr. 6 (tel. 319 72 41; fax 319 72 412), near Schottentor, has chrome seats outside to see and be seen, and clustered tables indoors in the smoky red-brown and metallic interior. Intimate and lively, it slides into the night as "Stein's Diner," when DJs appear. Billiards and **internet access** (65As per 30min. 5-11pm; present ID at the bar). Breakfast until 8pm. Open M-Sa 7am-1am, Su 9am-1am. **Stein's Diner** in the basement open M-Sa 7pm-2am.

Café Drechsler, VI, Linke Wienzeile 22 (tel. 587 85 80), near Karlspl. Head down Operng. and continue on Linke Wienzeile. This is *the* place to be the morning after the night before. Early birds and night owls roost in this less-than-fresh café over pungent cups of *Mokka.* Great lunch menu (60-90AS). Open M-F 4am-8pm, Sa 4am-6pm.

Café Rüdigerhof, V, Hamburgerstr. 20 (tel. 586 31 38). In a 1902 building designed by students of Otto Wagner, this *Jugendstil* café is adorned with floral patterns and leather couches, with a large outside garden. Soups (35-45AS), omelettes, and meat and fish dishes (30-100AS). Open daily noon-10:30pm; garden open for drinks until midnight.

Das Frauencafé, VIII, Lange Gasse 11, near the U-6 station "Lerchenfelderstr." Vienna's sole permanent women's café has a relaxed, inviting atmosphere. Open M-Sa 8pm-1am.

HEURIGEN (WINE GARDENS)

Created by imperial edict in the early 18th century, *Heurigen* are one of Vienna's most beloved institutions. Citizens have met to discuss and celebrate life in these pastoral settings for generations. To this day, *Heurigen*, marked by a hanging branch of evergreen at the door, sell new wine and snacks. The wine also called *Heuriger* is young wine from the most recent harvest and has typically been grown and pressed by the *Heuriger* owner himself. Good *Heuriger* wine is generally white, fruity, and full of body (try *Grüner Veltliner* or *Riesling*). *Heuriger* is ordered by the *Achtel* or the *Viertel* (eighth or quarter liter respectively). In local parlance, one doesn't drink the wine, one "bites" it, mixing it with air inside the mouth to better taste its youth and freshness. *G'spritzer* (wine and soda water) is a popular drink; patrons often order a bottle of wine and water to mix themselves.

Half of the pleasure of visiting a *Heuriger*, however, comes not from the wine but from the atmosphere. The worn picnic benches and old shade trees provide an ideal spot to contemplate, converse, or listen to *Schrammelmusik (*sentimental, wine-lubricated folk songs played by elderly musicians who inhabit the *Heuriger*). Drunken patrons often take the matter into their own hands and begin belting out verses praising the *Bäckchen* (cheeks) of girls in the Wachau. A *Heuriger* generally serves simple buffets (grilled chicken, salads, pickles) that make for enjoyable and inexpensive meals. Those looking for some traditional fare should order *Brattfett* or *Liptauer*, a spicy soft paprika-flavored cheese for your bread.

At the end of the summer, *Sturm* (sweet, cloudy, unpasteurized wine) is available at the *Heurigen*. At the end of August or the beginning of September in **Neustift am Walde,** now part of Vienna's 19th district, the *Neustifter Kirchtag mit Winzerumzug* rampages through the wine gardens: local vintners march in a 500m-long procession through town, carrying a large crown adorned with gilt nuts. After the **Feast of the Martins** on November 11, the wine from last year's crop becomes "old wine," no longer proper to serve in the *Heurigen*. The Viennese do their best to spare it this fate by consuming the beverage in Herculean quantities before the time's up. Grab a *Viertel* to help them in their monumental task.

Heurigen cluster together in the northern, western, and southern Viennese suburbs, where the grapes grow. They are each open for only a couple of months during the year—stroll along the street and look for the evergreen branches. The most famous region, **Grinzing,** produces strong wine, perhaps to distract the touristy clientele from the high prices. *Heurigen* in Grinzing (incidentally Beethoven's favorite district) are unfortunately well known to tour bus operators. You'll find better atmosphere and prices among the hills of **Sievering, Neustift am Walde, Stammersdorf,** and **Neuwaldegg.** Authentic, charming, and jolly *Heurigen* abound on Hochstr. in **Perchtoldsdorf.** To reach Perchtoldsdorf, take U-Bahn #4 to "Hietzing" and tram #6 to "Rodaun." Walk down Ketzerg. until Hochstr. and continue for a few minutes to reach the *Heurigen* area. True *Heuriger* devotees should make the trip to **Gumpoldskirchen,** a celebrated vineyard village with bus and train connections to Vienna and Mödling, and on the S-bahn line from Südbahnhof. Most vineyard taverns are open 4pm to midnight. *Heuriger* costs about 25AS per *Viertel*.

🍷 **Heuriger Josef Lier,** XIX, Wildgrubeng. 44 (tel. 320 23 19). Take tram #38 from Schottentor to the end of the line; walk up the Grinzigerstiege to the *Heiligenstädter Friedhof* (cemetery), and follow the road uphill to the left (5min. from the cemetery). Set right into the vineyards, this *Ur-Heuriger* recalls the times before electric-powered grape presses and mass commercialism. The place boasts clambering roses and a panoramic view of Vienna from the natural beauty of the Vienna Woods. Only one white and one red wine are sold here—Josef Lier's own, from the vineyards you're sitting in. The dishes are equally *Alt-Wiener* and equally excellent—boiled eggs, pickles, *Liptauer*, and *Wurst*. *G'spritzer* 18AS. Quarter liter 24AS. Open W-F from 3pm, Sa-Su from noon.

Buschenschank Heinrich Niersche, XIX, Strehlg. 21 (tel. 440 21 46). Take U-1 to "Währingerstr./Volksoper" then tram #40 to "Pötzleing." or bus #41A to "Pötzleindorfer Höhe." Walk uphill 1 block and turn right on Strehlg. On a small side-street hidden from tourists, the beautiful garden overlooks the fields of Grinzing—an oasis of green grass, cheerful voices, and relaxation in a neighborly atmosphere. *Weiße G'spritzter* (white wine with soda water) 18AS. Open Su-M and W-Sa 3pm-midnight.

Weingut Heuriger Reinprecht, XIX, Cobenzlg. 22 (tel. 32 01 47 10). Take U-4 to "Heiligenstadt" then bus #38A to "Grinzing." This *Heuriger* embodies the stereotype, with endless picnic tables under an ivy-laden trellis, and *Schrammel* musicians strolling from table to table. Despite the many tourists here, don't be surprised to hear whole tables of nostalgic Austrians break into song on their own. There's quite a bottle opener collection near the entryway. *Viertel* 30AS. Open Mar.-Nov. daily 3:30pm-midnight.

Zum Krottenbach'l, XIX, Krottenbachstr. 148 (tel. 440 12 40). Take U-6 to "Nußdorferstr." then bus #35A (dir.: Salmannsdorf) to "Kleingartenverein/Hackenberg." With a terraced garden on the fertile slope of Untersievering, this *Heuriger* offers a comfortable spot for savoring the fruit of the vine. Hot and cold buffet. *Viertel* about 30AS. Open daily 3pm-midnight.

Weingut Helm, XXI, Stammersdorferstr. 121 (tel. 292 12 44). Take tram #31 to the last stop, turn right by the *Würstelstand,* then turn left. The family who owns and staffs this establishment keeps it low-key and friendly. Their garden tables are shaded by enormous old trees. Open Tu-Sa 3pm-midnight.

Franz Mayer am Pfarrplatz Beethovenhaus, XIX, Pfarrpl. 2 (tel. 37 12 87). Take U-4 to "Heiligenstadt" then bus #38A to "Fernsprechamt/Heiligenstadt." Walk up the hill and head right onto Nestelbachg. Beethoven used to stay in the *Heuriger* when it offered guest quarters. Festive patios. Somewhat pricey at 38AS per *Viertel.* Open M-F 4pm-midnight, Su and holidays 11am-midnight. Live music 7pm-midnight.

▣ SIGHTS

Viennese streets are by turns startling, *gemütlich,* scuzzy, and grandiose. The best way to get to know the city streets is simply to get lost in them. The city is filled with monuments, palaces, parks, and historical sites. To wander on your own in a more organized manner, grab the brochure *Vienna from A to Z* (with Vienna Card discount 50AS; available at the tourist office). Whatever you do, don't miss the **Hofburg, Schloß Schönbrunn, Schloß Belvedere,** or any of the buildings along the **Ringstraße.** The range of available **tours** is equally overwhelming—walking tours, ship tours, bike tours and tram tours, bus tours, tours in a cup, tours over easy. For a quick do-it-yourself tour, take #1 or 2 around the Ring. The tourist office provides a brochure *Walks in Vienna,* which lists all 57 theme tours. Tours are 130AS; some require admission fees to sites. All are worthwhile, but "Vienna in the Footsteps of *The Third Man,*" which takes you into the sewers and the graffiti-covered catacomb world of the Wien River's underground canals, is one of the best. (Bring your own flashlight.) Tours on turn-of-the-century "old-timer" **trams** run May to October (tel. 790 944 026; 1½hr., 200AS; departs from Karlspl. near the Otto Wagner Pavilion Sa-Su 9:30, 11:30am, and 1:30pm). The legendary drivers of **Fiaker,** or horse-drawn carriages, are happy to taxi you wherever your heart desires, but be sure to agree on the price before you set out (usually around 400AS for 20min.). For **cycling tours,** contact Vienna-Bike, IX, Wasag. (tel. 319 12 58), for bike rental (60AS) or a 2- to 3-hour tour. (280AS.) **Bus tours** operate through Vienna Sight-seeing Tours, III, Stelzhamerg. 4/11 (tel. 712 46 83) and Cityrama, I, Börgeg. 1 (tel. 53413). Tours start at 200AS.

INSIDE THE RING

The **First District** (*die Innere Stadt* or "inner city"), Vienna's social and geographical epicenter, is enclosed on 3 sides by the massive **Ringstraße** and on the northern end by the **Danube Canal.** With the mark of master architects on everything from palaces and theaters to tenements and toilet bowls, the *Innere Stadt* is a gallery of the history of aesthetics, from Baroque to *Jugendstil.*

FROM THE STAATSOPER TO STEPHANSPLATZ. During the construction of the Ringstraße (see p. 115), the **Staatsoper** had first priority and was completed in 1869. *(Take U-1, U-2, U-4, or tram #1, 2, J, D, etc. to "Karlsplatz." Follow signs for the Staatsoper exit.)* Due to a mistake in laying the foundation, however, the builders had to cut a full story from the building's height. When Franz Josef saw the building, he agreed with the consensus that it was "a little low." The two architects wanted so badly to impress that the lukewarm reactions drove one to suicide and caused the other to die two months later "of a broken heart." The emperor was so shocked that for the rest of his life, whenever he was presented with something he responded, *"Es ist sehr schön, es hat mich sehr erfreut"* (It's very beautiful, it pleases me very much). Over the years, the Viennese became very attached to their flagship building and their collective heart broke when Allied bombs destroyed the Staatsoper in 1945. Vienna meticulously restored the exterior and re-opened the building in 1955. Today, the Staatsoper is still at the heart of Viennese culture. The list of the Opera's former directors is formidable, including Gustav Mahler, Richard Strauss, and Lorin Maazel. If you can't make it to a performance, at least **tour** the gold, crystal, and red velvet interior. *(Tours July-Aug.: 10, 11am, 1, 2, and 3pm; Sept.-Oct. and May-June: 1, 2, and 3pm; Nov.-Apr.: 2 and 3pm. 40AS, students 25AS.)* Seeing an opera is cheaper, though—ground-floor standing room tickets with an excellent view are only 30AS (balcony 20AS; see p. 127 for more details).

Across from the back of the Opera, at the end of Kärntnerstr., stands another memorial to silk hats and white gloves—the flag-bedecked **Hotel Sacher** (see **Sacher Scandal,** p. 74 and **Hotel Sacher,** p. 105). This legendary institution (founded by the cigar-smoking Anna Sacher) once served magnificent dinners over which the elite discussed affairs of state. The hotel's *chambres separées* provided discreet locations where the elite conducted affairs of another sort. In stark contrast to such lightheartedness, Alfred Hrdlicka's 1988 sculpture **Monument Gegen Krieg und Faschismus** (Memorial Against War and Fascism), located behind Hotel Sacher on Albertinapl., graphically commemorates the suffering caused by WWII.

From the Staatsoper, cross Philharmonikerstr. and head down Tegetthoffstr., which leads to the spectacular **Neuer Markt.** In the middle stands George Raphael Donner's **Donnerbrunnen,** a graceful embodiment of the Danube surrounded by 4 gods, who represent her tributaries. The pale orange, 17th-century **Kapuzinerkirche** stands modestly in one corner of the square. Inside, its **Imperial Vault** *(Gruft)*, a series of subterranean rooms filled with coffins, includes the remains (minus heart and entrails) of all the Habsburg rulers since 1633. Empress Maria Theresia rests next to beloved hubby Franz Stephan of Lorraine in an ornate Rococo sepulcher surrounded by cherubim and a dome. Maria Theresia was crushed by the death of her husband and visited his tomb frequently. When she got old, the Empress had an elevator installed. On her last trip, the elevator stalled 3 times, prompting the empress to exclaim that the dead did not want her to leave. She was entombed a week later. *(Open 9:30am-4pm. 30AS, children 20AS.)*

Just a quick step down Donnerg. or up from the Staatsoper lies **Kärntnerstraße**, Vienna's grand boulevard, lined with chic cafés and boutiques. Street musicians play everything from Peruvian folk to Neil Diamond. Kärntnerstr. brings you into the heart of the city, the **Stephansdom,** reflected in the glass and aluminum of the **Haas Haus.** The view is even better from inside the *Haus*, which has a restaurant on the top floor. Primarily a shopping center, the *Haus*, which opened in 1990 amid rumors of bureaucratic bribery, is considered something of an eyesore by most Viennese (much to the dismay of postmodern architect Hans Hollein).

ECCLESIASTICAL VIENNA: THE STEPHANSDOM. Vienna's most treasured symbol, the **Stephansdom** (known affectionately as *"Der Steffl"*), fascinates viewers with its Gothic intensity and smoothly tapered **South Tower.** WWII fighting almost leveled the place (along with the rest of Vienna); a series of photographs inside chronicles the painstaking process of reconstruction. The exterior bears some remarkable sculptures; circle around the building before you enter it. The oldest

V I E N N A

A BAD PACT WITH THE DEVIL Years ago, during the construction of the North Tower of the Stephansdom, a young builder named Hans Puchsbaum wished to marry his master's daughter. The master, rather jealous of Hans's skill, agreed on one condition: Hans had to finish the entire North Tower on his own within a year. Faced with this impossible task, Hans despaired until a stranger offered to help him. The good Samaritan required only that Hans abstain from saying the name of God or any other holy name. Hans agreed, and the tower grew by leaps and bounds. One day during construction the young mason spotted his love in the midst of his labor, and, wishing to call attention to his progress, he called out her name: "Maria." With this invocation of the Blessed Virgin, the scaffolding collapsed, and Hans plummeted to his death. Rumors of a satanic pact spread, and work on the tower ceased, leaving it in its present condition.

sections of the cathedral, the Romanesque **Riesentor** (Giant Gate) and **Heidentürme** (Towers of the Heathens), were built during the reign of King Ottokar II when Vienna was a Bohemian protectorate. Habsburg Duke Rudolf IV later ordered a complete Gothic retooling and thus earned the sobriquet "the Founder." Inside, some of the important pieces include the early 14th-century Albertine Choir and the Gothic organ loft by Anton Pilgram, so delicate that Pilgram's contemporaries warned him that it would never bear the organ's weight. Pilgram replied that he would hold it up himself and carved a self-portrait at the bottom, bearing the entire burden on his back. The high altar piece of the **Stoning of St. Stephen** is just as stunning. *(Take U-1 or U-3 to "Stephansplatz." Tours of the cathedral in English M-Sa at 10:30am and 3pm; Su and holidays 3pm; 40AS. Spectacular evening tour July-Sept. Sa 7pm; 100AS.)* The **North Tower** was originally intended to be equally high and graceful as the South Tower, but construction ceased after a spooky tragedy (see **A Bad Pact with the Devil,** p. 110). Take the elevator up the North Tower *(open Apr.-Sept. 9am-6pm; Oct.-Mar. 8am-5pm; elevator ride 40AS)* for a view of the Viennese sprawl, or climb the 343 steps of the South Tower for a 360-degree view, as well as a close-up view of the gargoyles. *(Open 9am-5:30pm; 30AS.)* Downstairs in the **Catacombs,** the skeletons of thousands of plague-victims line the walls. The lovely **Gruft** (vault) stores all of the Habsburg innards. *(Tours M-Sa 10, 11, 11:30am, 2, 2:30, 3:30, 4, and 4:30pm, Su and holidays 2, 2:30, 3:30, 4, and 4:30pm. 50AS.)* Everyone wanted a piece of the rulers—the Stephansdom got the entrails, the Augustinerkirche got the hearts, and the **Kapuzinergruft** (on Neuer Markt) got the remainder. High above it all hangs the **bell** of the Stephansdom, the world's heaviest free-ringing bell (the whole bell and not just the clapper moves). It is hardly ever rung because the stress of the vibrations might crack the church foundations.

FROM STEPHANSPLATZ TO HOHER MARKT. From Stephanspl., walk down Rotenturmstr., cross Fleischmarkt to Rabensteig, and turn left onto Seitenstetteng. to reach Ruprechtspl., home to a slew of street cafés known as the Bermuda Triangle (see p. 130) and the Romanesque **Ruprechtskirche,** the oldest church in Vienna. The present church, dating from the 13th century, was built on the site of a Carolingian church from AD 740 and one of the gates of the Roman settlement Vindobona. Maria Theresia donated the well-clad skeleton of an early Christian martyr that lives in a glass case in the corner.

Walk back down Ruprechtsstiege onto Seitenstetteng. to find the Jewish **Stadttempel,** the only synagogue of Vienna's 94 temples to escape Nazi destruction during **Kristallnacht** (Night of Broken Glass) on November 9-10, 1938. The *Stadttempel* was spared because it stood on a residential block, concealed from the street. The torching of neighboring buildings damaged the synagogue, but it has been restored to its original *Biedermeier* elegance. Today, an armed guard patrols the synagogue as a precaution against repeats of the 1983 terrorist attack, which killed 3 people. *(Seitenstetteng. 2-4. Take your passport. Open Su-F. Free.)*

Back at the top of Seitenstetteng. runs **Judengasse** (Lane of the Jew), a remnant of Vienna's old Jewish ghetto. *Biedermeier*-era apartments line the streets leading up to **Hoher Markt,** the center of town during the Middle Ages and the heart of the Roman encampment **Vindobona.** *(Roman ruins beneath the shopping arcade on the south side of the square open Sa-Su 11am-1pm. 25AS.)* The oldest square in town, it was once both market and execution site; Fischer von Erlach's **Vermählungsbrunnen** (Marriage Fountain), depicting the union of Mary and Joseph, is the square's centerpiece. The square's biggest draw, however, is the corporate-sponsored *Jugendstil* **Ankeruhr** (clock). Built in 1914 by Franz Matsch, the magnificent mechanical timepiece has 12 3m-tall historical figures, ranging from Emperor Marcus Aurelius to Maria Theresia to Joseph Haydn, which rotate past the old Viennese coat of arms, accompanied by music of their time period. *(One figure per hr. At noon, all the figures appear in succession.)* Take a peek under the bridge to see depictions of Adam, Eve, an angel, and the Devil.

FROM HOHER MARKT TO AM HOF. From Hoher Markt, follow Wipplingerstr. west (right) past the impressive Baroque facade of the **Böhmische Hofkanzlei** (Bohemian Court Chancellory), designed by Fischer von Erlach and now the seat of Austria's Constitutional Court. The **Altes Rathaus** stands directly across the street. Occupied from 1316 until 1885, when the government moved to the Ringstr., the building is graced by another Donner fountain depicting the myth of Andromeda and Perseus. The *Altes Rathaus* is also home to the **Austrian Resistance Museum** and various temporary exhibits. *(Friedrich-Schmidt-Pl. Tel. 52550. Open M, W, Th 9am-5pm. Free. Tours M, W, and F 1pm.)* A quick right off of Wipplingstr. after the *Altes Rathaus* down Stoß-im-Himmel brings you to **Maria am Gestade,** a gem of a Gothic church with an extraordinarily graceful spire of delicately carved stone, which depicts the Virgin's heavenly crown. The church's cramped position on the very edge of the old medieval town accounts for the nave's crookedness, while the sharp drop from the west door leading to **Tiefergraben,** a former tributary of the Danube explains the name "Am Gestade," meaning "by the riverbank."

Judenplatz, the pretty square on the opposite side of the Hofkanzlei is the site of the city's first Jewish ghetto. It contains a statue of Jewish playwright Gotthold Ephraim Lessing (1729-81). Originally erected in 1935, the statue was torn down by Nazis and a new model was returned to the spot in 1982. The square has an outdoor exhibit about the Stadttempel and viewable excavations of a synagogue built in 1294 and burned down in a 1421 pogrom. House #2, *Zum grossen Jordan,* bears a 16th-century relief and Latin inscription commemorating the early medieval purge of Vienna's Jews. On the other side of Judenpl., Drahtg. opens into the grand courtyard **Am Hof,** which hosts a weekend market *(open Sa-Su 11am-1pm).* The Babenbergs used this square as the ducal seat when they moved the palace in 1155 from atop Leopoldsberg (in the *Wienerwald*) to the present site. The medieval jousting square now houses the **Kirche am Hof** (Church of the Nine Choirs of Angels; built 1386-1662). Pope Pius VI gave the papal blessing here at the request of Baron von Hirsch on Easter in 1782, and Emperor Franz II proclaimed his abdication as Holy Roman Emperor in 1806 from the terrace. Am Hof was in use long before the Babenbergs, as evidenced by more Roman ruins. In the middle of the square looms the black **Mariensäule** (Column to Mary), erected by Emperor Ferdinand III to thank the Virgin Mary for her protection when the Protestant Swedes threatened Vienna during the Thirty Years War.

FROM AM HOF TO GRABEN. Head right from Am Hof to **Freyung,** an uneven square with the **Austriabrunnen** (fountain) in the center. Freyung was used for public executions in the Middle Ages, but now, the annual **Christkindl markt** held here each year before Christmas blots out such unpleasant memories. Three major art galleries flank Freyung: the **Museum in Schottenstift,** the **Kunstforum,** and **Palais Harrach.** Freyung (sanctuary) got its name from the **Schottenstift** (Monastery of the Scots), where fugitives could claim asylum in medieval times. Freyung is linked to Herreng. by the **Freyung-Passage,** a shopping arcade that leads through

VIENNA

the Italianate **Palais Ferstel,** past a statue of the Donau Mermaid. Palais Ferstel is now home to **Café Central** (see p. 105), but it was originally the National Bank of Austria and the Stock Exchange. **Herrengasse** was the home of Vienna's nobility during the Habsburg era.

Go down Landhausg. or Regierungsg. off Herreng. to reach peaceful **Minoriten-platz,** which shelters the 14th-century **Minoritenkirche.** The church's tower was destroyed during the Turkish siege of Vienna in 1529. A mosaic copy of da Vinci's *Last Supper,* commissioned by Napoleon and purchased by Franz I, adorns the north wall of the church. On the south side of the square stands the **Bundeskanzler-amt** (Federal Chancery), where the Congress of Vienna met in 1815 and where Chancellor Engelbert Dollfuss was assassinated in 1934.

Follow Schauflerg. to the left and you'll run into **Michaelerplatz,** named for the unassuming **Michaelerkirche** on its eastern side. Leopold "the Glorious" Babenberg purportedly founded the church in gratitude for his safe return from the Crusades. The church's Romanesque foundation dates back to the early 13th century, but construction continued until 1792, as the Baroque embellishment over the Neo-classical doorway reveals. *(Open May-Oct. M-Sa 10:30am-4:30pm, Su 1-5pm. 25AS.)* In the middle of Michaelerpl. lie the excavated foundations of Roman Vienna—the Roman military camp called **Vindobona** where Marcus Aurelius penned his *Medita-tions.* The square is otherwise dominated by the neo-Baroque, half-moon-shaped **Michaelertor,** the main gate of the Hofburg (see p. 112). On the corner of Kohlmarkt and Herreng. stands the **Looshaus,** constructed by Adolf Loos in 1910-11. Emperor Franz-Josef branded it "the house without eyebrows," as a result of the shocking lack of window pediments customary on Viennese buildings. On the opposite corner, a reconstructed **Café Griensteidl** invites nostalgic visitors to imagine them-selves drinking coffee alongside *Jung Wien* writers Arthur Schnitzler, Hermann Bahr, and Hugo von Hofmannsthal. The original café was demolished in 1897 and the authors moved down the street to Café Central, but it was reconstructed and reopened in 1990 (though no starving artist could afford the coffee there now).

Kohlmarkt, the site of the old charcoal market, extends away from Michaelerpl. towards **Graben,** one of Vienna's main pedestrian streets, passing **Demel Café** (see p. 105) which, in turn, leads back to the Stephansdom. Turn right at the Julius Meinl supermarket onto Graben (ditch), once a moat surrounding the Roman camp. The landscape of Graben shows the debris of Baroque, *Biedermeier,* *Jugendstil,* and postmodern trends, including the **Ankerhaus** (#10) and the red-marble **Grabenhof** by Otto Wagner. One of the most interesting (and interactive) sights is the underground *Jugendstil* public toilet complex, designed by Adolf Loos. The **Pestsäule** (Plague Column) in the square's center was built in 1693, in gratitude for the passing of the Black Death. According to the inscription, the mon-ument is "a reminder of the divine chastisement of plagues richly deserved by this city." The Viennese had ways of dealing with guilt complexes (and phallic sym-bols) long before Freud. To the left off Graben is tiny Peterspl., home of the **Peter-skirche.** Charlemagne founded the first version in the 8th century. Town architects just couldn't resist tinkering with the structure throughout the ages. The Baroque ornamentation was completed in 1733, with Rottmayer on fresco duty.

IMPERIAL VIENNA: THE HOFBURG. A tangible reminder of their 700-year reign, the sprawling, grandiose **Hofburg** was the Habsburgs' winter residence. Construc-tion on the original fortress began in 1279, but it didn't become the official dynastic seat until the mid-16th century. Over the centuries, the Hofburg experienced peri-ods of neglect when various emperors chose to live in other palaces, such as Schönbrunn and Klosterneuburg, but it remained the symbol of the family's power. As few Habsburgs were willing to live in their predecessors' quarters, hodge-podge additions and renovations continued until the end of the family's reign in 1918, by which time the palace had become a mini-city. Today, the complex houses several museums, the **Österreichische Nationalbibliothek** (Austrian National Library), the performance halls of the Lipizzaner stallions and the Vienna Boys' Choir, a conven-tion center, and the offices of the Austrian President. The Hofburg is divided into

SISI, THE AUSTRIAN SENSATION

An anarchist murdered the Empress of Austria In Switzerland in 1898. Today, Austria remembers Empress Elisabeth (better known as Sisi) not for her untimely death, her accomplishments, or even her life—instead, she has been immortalized for her beauty. When she married Franz Josef in 1854, the 16-year-old Bavarian princess was considered by some to be the most gorgeous woman in Europe. Love, however, did not flourish—even in the hundreds of rooms of the Hofburg and Schönbrunn palaces, the imperial couple could not get far enough away from each other. Franz Josef built the Hermes Villa in the Vienna Woods for his wife's private residence. There, she unhappily wrote: "Love is not for me. Wine is not for me. The first makes me ill. The second makes me sick." In other poems, she complained about her duties as Empress, disparaged her husband, and labeled her children bristle-haired pigs. Yet Austrians have never forgotten Sisi. Over a century later, this melancholy, tight-lipped, beautiful woman is plastered on postcards and in guide books, and immortalized in various musicals and plays.

VIENNA

several sections, including the **Kaiserappartements, In der Burg,** the **Alte Burg,** the **Neue Burg, Heldenplatz, Josefsplatz,** the **Burggarten,** and the **Volksgarten.** *(Take tram #1 or 2 from anywhere on the Ring to Heldenplatz, or enter through the Michaelertor.)*

Once you navigate your way past the costumed concert-solicitors outside Michaelertor, you'll be standing directly under the intricately carved ceiling of the **Michaelerküppel.** The solid wooden door on the right leads to the **Kaiserappartements** (Imperial Apartments), once the private quarters of Emperor Franz Josef (1848-1916) and Empress Elisabeth (1838-1898). Neither of them spent much time in the Hofburg (or with each other, for that matter), so the rooms are disappointingly lifeless. Amid all the Baroque trappings, the two most personal items seem painfully out of place: Emperor Franz Josef's military field bed and Empress Elisabeth's personal wooden gym bear mute testimony to lonely lives. Franz Josef's rooms are unelectrified—he didn't approve of most of the advances of the Industrial Age, although Sisi did manage to convince him to install running water for her bathtub. The **Hofsilber und Tafelkammer** (Court Silver and Porcelain Collection), on the ground floor opposite the ticket office, displays examples of the outrageously ornate cutlery that once adorned the Imperial table. *(Imperial apartments 80AS; combined admission to Silver and Porcelain Collection 95AS. Open daily 9am-4:30pm.)*

As you continue through the Michaelertor, you'll enter the courtyard called **In der Burg** (within the fortress). The central monument to Emperor Franz II isn't too exciting, but on your left you'll find the more visually stimulating red and black striped **Schweizertor** (Swiss Gate), erected in 1552 and named for the Swiss mercenaries who guarded it under Empress Maria Theresia. Behind the gate lies the **Schweizerhof,** the inner courtyard of the **Alte Burg** (Old Fortress), which stands on the same site as the original 13th-century palace. The stairs on the right lead up to the Gothic **Burgkapelle,** where the heavenly voices of the **Wiener Sängerknaben** (Vienna Boys' Choir) grace Mass-goers on Sundays (except in July-Aug.; see p. 127). Just below the Burgkapelle is the entrance to the **Schatzkammer** (Treasury), where the Habsburg jewels, the crowns of the Holy Roman and Austrian Empires, Imperial christening robes, and an elaborate cradle presented by the city of Paris in 1811 to the infant son of Napoleon and his Habsburg wife are stashed. The **Holy Lance** is reportedly the one that pierced Christ's side during his Crucifixion. *(Open daily except Tu 10am-6pm. 80AS, senior and students 50AS. English tours, one per day, 30AS.)*

The arched passageway at the rear of In der Burg leads past the line of **Fiaker** (horse-drawn carriages) into **Heldenplatz** (Heroes' Square), an enormous park-cum-parking lot. During WWII, the entire square was planted with potatoes to feed the starving populace. The equestrian statues (both done by Anton Fernkorn) depict two of Austria's greatest military commanders: Prince Eugene of Savoy and Archduke Karl, whose charger rears triumphantly on its hind legs with no other support, a feat of sculpting never again duplicated. Poor Fernkorn went insane, supposedly due to his inability to recreate the effect.

On the left is the vast **Neue Burg** (New Fortress), built between 1881 and 1926, the youngest wing of the palace and the only part which no Habsburg ever inhabited. The double-headed golden eagle crowning the roof symbolizes the double empire of Austria-Hungary. Planned in 1869, the Neue Burg's design called for a twin palace across Heldenplatz, both connected to the Kunsthistorisches and Naturhistorisches Museums by arches spanning the Ringstraße. WWI put an end to the Empire and its grand designs. Today, the Neue Burg houses Austria's largest working library, the **Österreichische Nationalbibliothek** (Austrian National Library), which contains millions of books and an outstanding little museum of papyrus, scriptures, and musical manuscripts. The main reading room is open to the public; anyone can request books for in-library use with a picture ID. *(Tel. 534 10 397. Open May 7-Oct. 26 M-Sa 10am-4pm, Th until 7pm, Su and holidays 10am-1pm; Nov.-April M-Sa 10am-1pm. Museum admission May-Nov. 60AS, students 40AS; Nov.-April 40AS.)*

The Neue Burg also contains an array of museums, including 2 minor branches of the **Kunsthistorisches Museum** that exhibit an extensive weapons collection and an assortment of antique instruments, including a shepherd's bagpipes. Among the harps and violins are Beethoven's harpsichord and Mozart's piano with a double keyboard. Downstairs, the **Ephesus Museum** contains the massive findings of an Austrian excavation of Roman ruins in Turkey. On the far side of the Neue Burg, the **Völkerkunde Museum** houses artifacts from non-European places collected by Austro-Hungarian colonists in 18th- and 19th-century expeditions (see p. 124). Despite the demise of the Habsburg dynasty, the Hofburg continues an association with the Austrian government; the building attached to the Neue Burg is the **Reichskanzleitrakt** (State Chancellery Wing), most notable for the labors of Hercules, a group of buff statues said to have inspired the 11-year-old Arnold Schwarzenegger, then on his first visit to Vienna, to pump up.

The best way to get an overview of the entire Imperial complex is to stroll along the perimeter. Back at Michaelerpl., with the palace behind you, follow the street on the right to the **Stallburg** (Palace Stables) inside the passage. The Stallburg is home to the Royal Lipizzaner stallions of the **Spanische Reitschule** (Spanish Riding School). This renowned equine breed is a relic of the Habsburg's connections to the Spanish royal house (see **Hot to Trot,** p. 115). The cheapest way to get a glimpse of the famous steeds is to watch them train. *(Mid-Feb. to June and Nov. to mid-Dec. Tu-F 10am-noon; Feb. M-Sa 10am-noon, except when the horses tour. Tickets sold at the door at Josefspl., Gate 2, from about 8:30am. 100AS, children 30AS. No reservations.)* For a more impressive (and more expensive) display, you can try to attend a **Reitschule performance,** but sold-out performances require you to reserve tickets months in advance. *(Tel. 533 90 32; fax 53 50 186. Apr.-June and Sept. Su 10:45am, W 7pm; Mar. Su 10:45am; 1½hr. Write to: Spanische Reitschule, Hofburg, A-1010 Wien. If you reserve through a travel agency, expect at least a 22% surcharge. Reservations only; no money accepted by mail. Tickets 250-900AS, standing room 200AS.)* You can also learn about the Lipizzaner's history and training at the **Lipizzaner Museum.** *(I, Reitschulg. 2. Tel. 526 41 84 30; fax 526 41 86. Open daily 9am-6pm. 50AS, students 35AS, tour 20AS. See p. 126.)*

From the Stallburg, Augustinerstr. leads to the Baroque **Josefsplatz,** so named because of the large statue of Emperor Josef II in the center. The modest emperor would no doubt be appalled at his statue's bare-chested Roman garb, but the sculptor probably couldn't bring himself to depict the decrepit hat and patched-up frock coat the emperor favored. Glorious High Masses are held each Sunday at the 14th-century Gothic **Augustinerkirche** on the left side of the square. *(Mass 11am. Free to the public.)* Eighteenth-century renovations (and some Napoleonic flourishes) have altered the interior. The Augustinerkirche witnessed the wedding of Maria Theresia and Franz Stephan and is now the final resting place of the hearts of the Habsburgs, which are stored in the **Herzgrüftel** (Little Heart Crypt). *(Church open M-Sa 10am-6pm, Su 1-6pm.)* In the back of the square, the entrance to the **Prunksaal** (Grand Hall) of the Österreichische Nationalbibliothek; see p. 115) is marked by a small plaque next to very modest doors. All architectural restraint stops at the doors, however, as the imposing staircase suggests, and the immense Baroque Prunksaal, glittering with gilded wood, frescoes, and marble pillars, confirms. The

HOT TO TROT What's white, royal, dancing, and one of the biggest tourist attractions in Vienna? No, it is not the Royal Ballet's performance of Swan Lake. In Vienna, these 3 traits classify horses—more specifically, the Lipizzaner stallions of the Spanische Reitschule (Spanish Riding School). The Royal Stables, some of the best original Renaissance buildings in Vienna, were built as a residence for the Archduke Maximilian in the mid-16th century and were later converted to the stables of the royal stud. Lipizzaner horses, known for their snowy-white coats and immense physical strength and grace, descend from a "celebration" equine breed ordered by the Austrian Emperor in Lipizza, near Trieste, upon the Habsburg's annexation of Spanish lands in the late 16th century. Breeders mixed Arab and Berber genes, and once the stud line had been established, the Lipizzaners were imported to Austria proper to dance in the spotlight of the Renaissance heyday of haute école horsemanship. Despite their fame, the Lipizzaners have held on tenuously to their survival over the centuries. The horses ran from the French in the Napoleonic wars, and they barely survived the poverty that ensued after WWI and the breakup of the Empire. During WWII, they escaped destruction in a safe haven in Czechoslovakia. In 1945, U.S. General Patton flagrantly violated his own orders to stay put by leading a madcap Eastern push to prevent the plundering Russians, who confiscated just about everything in their path, from reaching the four-legged treasures first. In the early 1980s, an epidemic of virus in the stud killed upwards of thirty of the brood mares; today, stud farmers worry that the decreasing number of Lipizzaners may lead to health problems resulting from inbreeding. Recently, UN peace keepers ran across starving Lipizzaners near Banja Luca in Bosnia, prompting the Lipizzaner Society to start a fund-raiser to save the beasts from an ugly death.

Prunksaal, begun in 1723, is the secular counterpart to Fischer von Erlach's magnificent Karlskirche (see p. 117). Though just a part of the National Library, this impressive room is the largest Baroque library in Europe. Multi-media exhibits in the free, functional part of the library on Heldenpl. give three-dimensional tours of the hall (see p. 114). Wander through the floor-to-ceiling bookcases that house more than 200,000 leather-bound books, marvel at the *trompe l'oeil* balconies, and pay your respects to the 16 marble statues of various Habsburg rulers, including one of library founder Karl VI. *(Tel. 53 41 00. Prunksaal open June-Oct. M-Sa 10am-4pm, Su 10am-1pm; Nov.-May M-Sa 10am-noon. Closed first 3 weeks of Sept. 50AS.)*

Heading towards Augustinerpl., Augustinerstr. passes the **Albertina,** the southern wing of the Hofburg. Once inhabited by Maria Christina (Maria Theresia's favorite daughter) and her hubby Albert, is part original Augustinian monastery, and part 18th-century palace. Today, the Albertina houses a film museum and the celebrated **Collection of Graphic Arts** with its array of old political cartoons and drawings by Dürer, Michelangelo, da Vinci, Raphael, Cezanne, and Schiele. *(Tel. 53483. Open Tu-Sa 10am-5pm. 70AS.)*

Upon rounding the tip of the Albertina, cut to your right around the monument to Erzherzog Albrecht and enter the peaceful **Burggarten** (Palace Gardens; see p. 122), laid out in the style of an English garden and reserved for Habsburg use until 1918. A large **Mozart-Denkmal** (monument) stands in the far corner of the park, and an elegant, though neglected, glass **Palmenhaus** lines one side of the park. The opposite end of the garden opens onto the Ring and then the main entrance into the Hofburg, just a few meters to the right. Enter through the enormous stone gate into Heldenpl. On the other side of Heldenpl. stretches the triangular **Volksgarten,** a formal French garden built on the site of a fortifications blown up by Napoleon's troops in 1809. The **Theseus-Tempel** sits in the center of the park, with statues of Empress Elisabeth and author Franz Grillparzer at either end. *(Park open April-Oct. daily 8am-10pm; Nov.-March 8am-8pm. Free.)*

MONUMENTAL VIENNA: THE RINGSTRAßE. The **Ringstraße** defines the boundaries of the inner city. In 1857, Emperor Franz Josef commissioned this 57m-wide, 4km-long boulevard to replace the city fortifications that had encircled Vienna's medieval center since the last siege by the Ottoman Turks in 1683, separating the old town from the suburban districts. The military, still uneasy in the wake of the revolution attempted 9 years earlier, demanded that the first district be surrounded by fortifications; the erupting bureaucratic bourgeoisie, however, argued for the removal of all formal barriers and for open space within the city. Imperial designers reached a compromise: the walls would be razed to make way for the Ringstraße, a peace-loving, tree-studded spread of boulevard and, at the same time, a sweeping circle designed for the efficient transport of troops. This massive architectural commitment attracted participants from all over Europe. Urban planners put together a grand scheme of monuments dedicated to staples of Western culture: scholarship, theater, politics, and art. In total, 12 giant public buildings were erected along the Ring; counter-clockwise from Schottenring, they are the Börse, the Votivkirche, the Universität, the Rathaus, the Burgtheater, the Parlament, the Kunsthistorisches and Naturhistorisches Museen, the Staatsoper, the Museum für angewandte Kunst, and the Postsparkasse, each built in the appropriate Historicist style. The overall result became known as the **Ringstraße Style.** Freud used to walk the circuit of the Ring every day during his lunch break. It took him a brisk 2 hours.

The first stretch of the Ring extending south from the Danube Canal, called **Schottenring,** leads past the Italianate **Börse** (stock exchange) to **Schottentor,** which is surrounded by university cafés, bookstores, and bars. Across Universitätsstr. rise the twin spires of the **Votivkirche,** a neo-Gothic wonder surrounded by rose gardens and home to a number of expatriate religious communities. Franz Josef's brother Maximilian commissioned the church as a gesture of gratitude after the Emperor survived an assassination attempt near the spot in 1853 (see **Starch or no Starch?** p. 117). Immediately to the south of Schottentor, where Schottenring meets **Karl-Lueger-Ring,** is the **Universität Wien,** founded in 1365. An 1848 student revolt against the government failed, but when the University was rebuilt during construction of the Ring, the architects sought to dispel the ghosts of dissatisfaction and rebellion through the building's design, using Renaissance Italy—the cradle of state-sponsored liberal learning—as their model. Inside the university is a tranquil courtyard lined with busts of famous departed professors.

Further down, on **Dr.-Karl-Renner-Ring,** the neo-Gothic **Rathaus** (town hall) faces the Baroque **Burgtheater.** The *Rathaus*, with fluted arches and red geraniums in the windows, is meant to honor the Flemish burghers who pioneered the idea of town halls and civic government in Europe. The Viennese, just emerging from imperial constraints through the strength of the growing bureaucratic middle class, sought to imbue their city hall with the same sense of budding freedom and prosperity. There are art exhibits inside, and the city holds outdoor festivals out front on the **Rathausplatz,** which is the inner city's largest square. *(Free tours W at 1pm; meet at the blue Information booth outside.)* Smaller but no less impressive, the Burgtheater was once the Imperial Court Theater. It has seen the premieres of some of the most famous German operas and plays, including Mozart's *La Nozze di Figaro.* Inside, frescoes by Gustav Klimt, his brother, and his partner Matsch depict the interaction between drama and history through the ages. Klimt used contemporary faces as models for the audience members; notables of the day sent him baskets of fruit and tasteful presents in hopes of being covertly included in one of the murals. *(Performance season runs from Sept.-June. Tours July-Aug. M, W, and F 1, 2, and 3pm; Sept.-June on request. 50AS.)*

Continuing along the Ring, the Neoclassical **Parlament,** built between 1873 and 1883, overlooks the rosebeds of the **Volksgarten** (see p. 115 and p. 121). Now the seat of the Austrian National and Federal Councils, it was once the meeting place for elected representatives of the Austro-Hungarian Empire. Its Historicist style was intended to evoke the great democracies of ancient Greece. *(Tours mid-Sept. to mid-July M-F at 11am and 3pm; mid-July to mid-Sept. M-F 9, 10, 11am, 1, 2, and 3pm; Easter holidays 11am and 3pm.)*

On **Burgring,** opposite the Hofburg, the nexus of Vienna's imperial glory, stand two of Vienna's largest and most comprehensive museums, the **Kunsthistorisches Museum** (Museum of Art History) and the **Naturhistorisches Museum** (Museum of

STARCH OR NO STARCH? The Habsburgs habitually strolled around Vienna with a full retinue of bodyguards. These casual jaunts were supposedly incognito—the emperor demanded that his subjects pretend not to recognize the imperial family. On one of these constitutional walks in 1853, a Hungarian insurrectionist leapt from nearby bushes and attempted to stab the emperor. Franz Josef's collar was so heavily starched, however, that the knife drew no blue blood, and the crew of bodyguards dispatched the would-be assasin before he could strike again. Saved by his starch, but still afraid of open spaces, Franz Josef began the building of the Ringstraße.

Natural History) on either side **Maria-Theresien-Platz** (see p. 124 and p. 126). When construction was complete, the builders realized with horror that Apollo, patron deity of art, stood atop the Naturhistorisches Museum, and Athena, goddess of science, atop the Kunsthistorisches. Tour guides claim that each muse is situated intentionally to look down on the appropriate museum. In the center of the square, a huge statue immortalizes the throned Empress Maria Theresia, surrounded by her key statesmen and advisers. The statue purportedly faces the Ring so that the Empress may extend her hand to the people. She holds a copy of the Pragmatic Sanction, which granted women the right to succeed to the Austrian throne.

Between **Opernring** and **Kärntnerring** stands the **Staatsoper**, the heart of Vienna's musical life (see p. 109). The **Stadtpark** follows **Parkring** (see p. 121), and near the end of **Stubenring**, down a small side street, hides Otto Wagner's greatest triumph of function over form, the **Postsparkasse** (Post Office Savings Bank). A bulwark of modernist architecture, the building raises formerly concealed elements of the building, like the thousands of symmetrically placed metallic bolts on the rear wall, to a position of exaggerated significance. The distinctly Art Nouveau interior is open during banking hours free of charge. (George-Coch-Pl. 2. Open M-W and F 8am-3pm, Th 8am-5:30pm.)

OUTSIDE THE RING

KARLSPLATZ, RESSELPARK, AND LINKE WIENZEILE. As impressive as the *Innenstadt* is, many of Vienna's most interesting sights lie outside the Ring, clustered around Karlsplatz. (Take the U-1, U-2. U-4, or any number of trams to "Karlsplatz." Exit towards Resselpark.) Once a central gathering place for the Viennese, Karlsplatz is now isolated behind a major traffic artery, but it is home to Vienna's most impressive Baroque church, the **Karlskirche**, and is surrounded by the ornate **Musikverein** and several major museums, including the **Secession,** the **Künstlerhaus,** and the garish **Kunsthalle.** Situated in the center of the gardens where the Naschmarkt (see p. 118) was held until the 1890s, the Karlskirche is an eclectic masterpiece, combining a Neoclassical portico with a Baroque dome and towers on either side. Two massive columns, covered with spiraling reliefs depicting the life of St. Carlo Borromeo, to whom the church is dedicated, frame the central portion of the church. The interior of the church is overwhelmingly beautiful, with colorful ceiling frescoes and a sunburst altar. Designed by Fischer von Erlach and completed by his son, Johann Michael, this imposing edifice was constructed in 1793 to fulfil a vow Emperor Karl VI made during a plague epidemic in 1713. In front of the church, a reflecting pool and modern sculpture designed by **Henry Moore** connect it to the 20th century. (Church open M-Sa 9-11:30am and 1-5pm, Su 1-5pm. Free.)

The rest of the park, named for Josef Ressel (the Czech gentleman who invented the propeller), is peaceful and shady, ringed by museums. The **Historisches Museum der Stadt Wien**, whose unassuming appearance gives stands to the left of the Karlskirche (see p. 126). The blocky yellow and blue **Kunsthalle**, however, stands out at the opposite end of the park (see p. 125). Above one side of the park, a terrace links the *Jugendstil* **Karlsplatz Stadtbahn Pavilions,** designed in 1899 by **Otto Wagner,** who, even more than Adolf Loos, is the architect responsible for Vienna's *Jugendstil* face. These graceful, gold-edged pavilions are part of a series Wagner produced for the city's rail system when the system was redesigned at the turn of the century. All of the U-6 stations between Längenfeldg. and Heiligenstadt are also Wagner's work. His attention to the most minute details on station buildings, bridges, and even lampposts give the city's public transportation an elegant coherence. Wagner's two arcades in Karlspl. are still in use: one functions as a café, and the other as an exhibition hall.

The physical representations of two of Vienna's most traditional establishments are visible from the pavilions, across Lothringerstr.: the **Künstlerhaus,** the home of Vienna's artistic community, from which the Secession artists seceded in 1897 (see p. 125); and the acoustically miraculous **Musikverein,** home of the **Vienna Philharmonic Orchestra.** The modest exterior of the Musikverein conceals the brilliance of the **Grosser Saal,** where the *crème de la crème* of the international music world performs, but standing room concert tickets offer an inexpensive way to admire the golden caryatids that line the hall (see p. 127).

Northwest of the Resselpark, across Friedrichstr., stands the nemesis of the Künstlerhaus, the **Secession Building,** whose white walls, restrained decoration, and gilded dome (hence the nickname the "Golden Cabbage") are meant to clash with the Historicist Ringstraße. Otto Wagner's pupil Josef Olbrich built this *fin de siècle* monument to accommodate artists who broke with the rigid, state-sponsored Künstlerhaus. The inscription above the door reads: *"Der Zeit, ihre Kunst; der Kunst, ihre Freiheit"* (To the age, its art; to art, its freedom). The Secession exhibits of 1898-1903, which attracted cutting-edge European artists, were led by Gustav Klimt. His painting, *Nuda Veritas* (Naked Truth), became the icon of a new aesthetic ideal. Wilde's *Salomé* and paintings by Gauguin, Vuillard, van Gogh, and others created an island of modernity amid an ocean of Habsburgs and Historicism. The exhibition hall remains firmly dedicated to the displaying the cutting-edge (see p. 125). Those ensnared by the flowing tendrils of *Jugendstil* architecture can find plenty of other turn-of-the-century examples of it in Vienna—ask the tourist office for the *Art Nouveau in Vienna* pamphlet, which contains photos and addresses of *Jugendstil* treasures throughout town. Diehards should also visit the acclaimed **Majolicahaus,** at Linke Wienzeile 40, a collaborative effort by Wagner and Olbrich. The wrought-iron spiral staircase is by Josef Hoffmann, founder of the **Wiener Werkstätte,** a communal arts-and-crafts workshop and key factor in the momentum of *Jugendstil.* The Majolicahaus's golden neighbor, the **Goldammer** building, is another Wagnerian mecca.

Diagonally opposite the Secession building, along Linke Wienzeile, is the beginning of the **Naschmarkt,** a colorful, multi-ethnic food bazaar that moved from the Karlspl. to its present location in the 1890s. During the week, the Naschmarkt, which derives its name from the German verb *naschen* (to nibble), presents a dazzling array of fresh fruits and vegetables laid out in front of bakeries, cafés, *Wurst* vendors, and cheese and spice shops. On weekends, the Naschmarkt becomes a massive flea market, where shrewd bargainers can acquire anything from loose junk to traditional Austrian clothing. Further down Linke Wienzeile, opposite the Naschmarkt, stands **Theater an der Wien,** which hosted the premiere of Mozart's *Die Zauberflöte* once upon a time (see p. 128). The name of the street and the theater commemorate the Wien river, which used to flow freely through Vienna, but is now almost completely buried under city streets.

SOCIALIST VIENNA: ARCHITECTURE FOR THE PEOPLE. From constructing opulent palaces and public edifices before the war, post-WWI Vienna turned its architectural attention to the socialist (and desperately necessary) task of building public housing. Throughout the 1920s and 30s, the Austrian Social Democratic Republic set about constructing "palaces for the people." Whatever your political opinions, the sheer scale of these apartment complexes impresses. The most famous is the **Karl-Marx-Hof,** XIX, Heiligenstadterstr. 82-92 (take U-4 or 6 to "Heiligenstadt"). This single building stretches out for a full kilometer and encompasses over 1600 identical orange-and-pink apartments, with common space and interior courtyards to garnish the urban-commune atmosphere. The Social Democrats used this structure as their stronghold during the civil war of 1934, until army artillery shelled the place and broke down the resistance.

Breaking with the ideology and aesthetic of *"Rot Wien"* (Red Vienna, the socialist republic from 1918 until the *Anschluß*) that resulted in housing complexes like Karl-Marx-Hof, Fantastic Realist and environmental activist **Friedensreich Hundertwasser** (translation: Peace-filled Hundredwaters; given name: Friedrich Stowasser) designed **Hundertwasser Haus**, III, a 50-apartment building at the corner of Löweng. and Kegelg. (take tram N from Schwedenpl. to "Hetzg."). Completed in 1985, the multi-colored building makes both an artistic and a political statement. Hundertwasser included trees and grass in the undulating balconies as a means of bringing life back to the urban "desert" that the city had become; trees sticking out of windows, oblique tile columns, and free-form color patterns all contribute to the eccentricity of this blunt rejection of architectural orthodoxy. Hundertwasser created what he called a "Window Bill of Rights," which guaranteed everyone living within a building he designed the ability to decorate the area around their window for as long a space as their arm could reach. Architectural politics aside, this place is fun, bordering on the insane—Hundertwasser's design team must have included droves of finger-painting toddlers. The Viennese have nicknamed it the "Bowling Pin House." Despite the droves of visitors, Hundertwasserhaus remains a private residence, where tenants decorate their window spaces as they see fit.

Kunst Haus Wien, another Hundertwasser project, is just 3 blocks away at Untere Weißgerberstr. 13. The house is a museum devoted to the architect's graphic art (see p. 125) on the lower floors and controversial contemporary artists above (Robert Mapplethorpe and Annie Lennox have both been exhibited here). A café built along the lines of a Hundertwasser blueprint is inside the museum (see p. 106). Hundertwasser devotees may also want to check out the **Müllbrennerei** (garbage incinerator), behind the "Spittelau" U-Bahn station. This huge jack-in-the-box of a trash dump has a high smokestack topped by a golden disco ball. He also designed a ferry that cruises the Danube under the auspices of the DDSG.

High on a hill in northwest Vienna, Wagner's **Kirche am Steinhof** embodies another approach to architecture for the people. Commissioned for the inmates of the state mental hospital in 1907, this light, cheerful church combines streamlined symmetry and Wagner's signature functionalism with a Byzantine influence. The white walls are tiled for easy cleaning, the holy water in the basins by the door runs continuously for maximum hygiene, all corners are rounded to avoid injuries, and the pews are widely spaced to give nurses easy access to unruly patients. The church faces north-south, in order to allow patients to enjoy the maximum amount of daylight through the stained-glass windows, designed by Koloman Moser, a vanguard member of the Secession. Above the altar, bright gold mosaics of holy figures seem to levitate. *Jugendstil* sculptor Lukasch fashioned the statues of Leopold and Severin poised upon each of the building's twin towers. The people of Vienna were shocked by Wagner's breaks with tradition and declared, "That crazy church belongs out there with the crazy people." *(Take U-2 or U-3 to "Volkstheater" then bus #48A. XIV, Baumgartner Höhe 1. Tel. 91 06 02 00 31. Open M-F 8am-3pm, Sa 3-4pm. 40AS, students 20AS. Guided tours (in German only) 40AS. Call ahead.)*

PALATIAL VIENNA: SCHWARZENBERG, BELVEDERE, AND SCHÖNBRUNN. As if the Hofburg weren't enough palace for any city, there are several smaller, very elegant aristocratic residences scattered throughout Vienna. The 3 most prominent of these are Palais Schwarzenberg, Schloß Belvedere, and Maria Theresia's favorite, Schönbrunn. Its present location on a traffic island makes it hard to believe that **Palais Schwarzenberg,** designed in 1697 by Fischer von Erlach's rival architect, Lukas von Hildebrandt, was once the center of a neighborhood preferred by Vienna's nobility. The palace is now a swank hotel, where, rumor has it, daughters of the super-rich gather annually to meet young Austrian noblemen at the grand debutante ball. If you're not a hotel guest, the palace is off limits. The palace sits behind an illuminated fountain on **Schwarzenbergplatz,** down from Karlspl. along Friedrichstr. (which becomes Lothringerstr.), an elongated square with an unsavory military history. During the Nazi era, the occupied city renamed the square "Hitlerplatz," and when the Russians brutally "liberated" Vienna, they renamed it "Stalinplatz" and erected an enormous **Russen Heldendenkmal** (Russian Heroes' Monument), a concrete colonnade behind a column bearing the figure of a Russian soldier, with a quotation from Stalin inscribed in the base. The Viennese have attempted to destroy the monstrosity three times, but the product of sturdy Soviet engineering refuses to be demolished. Vienna's disgust with their Soviet occupiers is further evident in their nickname for an anonymous Soviet soldier's grave: "Tomb of the Unknown Plunderer." Across the street from Schwarzenbergpl., on the Ring, **Café Schwarzenberg** is one of the poshest meeting-places in the city.

Schwarzenberg, along most other palaces in the world, can't hold a candle to the striking Baroque complex that makes up **Schloß Belvedere,** IV, whose landscaped gardens begin just behind the Schwarzenberg. *(Take tram #D to "Schwarzenberg," tram #71 one stop past Schwarzenbergpl., or walk up from Südbahnhof.)* Also designed by Hildebrandt, Belvedere was originally the summer residence of **Prince Eugène of Savoy,** Austria's greatest military hero. His distinguished career began when he routed the Ottomans in the late 17th century. Though publicly lionized, his appearance was most unpopular at Court—Eugene was a short, ugly, impetuous man. The Belvedere summer palace (originally only the **Untere** (Lower) **Belvedere**), ostensibly a gift from the emperor in recognition of Eugene's military prowess, was more likely intended to get Eugene out of the imperial hair. Eugene's military exploits, however, had left him with a larger bank account than his Habsburg neighbors (a fact that didn't improve their relationship), and he decided to improve upon his new home. The result is the **Obere** (Upper) **Belvedere,** designed as a place to throw bacchanalian parties. The building has one of the best views of Vienna. Eugene's *pièce de resistance* was a rooftop facsimile of an Ottoman tent, which called undue attention to Eugene's martial glory. After Eugene's death without heirs in 1736, his cousin sold off his possessions and Empress Maria Theresia snatched up the palace as a showroom for the Habsburgs art collection and opened the extensive formal gardens to the public. Though the imperial art moved to the Kunsthistorisches Museum in the 1890s, Archduke Franz Ferdinand lived in the Belvedere until his 1914 assassination. The grounds of the Belvedere, stretching from the Schwarzenberg Palace to the Südbahnhof, now contain 3 spectacular sphinx-filled gardens (see p. 121) and an equal number of excellent museums (see p. 124).

In fact, the Habsburgs need not have fretted over being outshone by Prince Eugene; Belvedere pales in comparison to **Schloß Schönbrunn,** XIII, the former Imperial summer residence. From its humble beginnings as a hunting lodge, Schönbrunn, named after a "beautiful brook" on the property, was destroyed twice before Fischer von Erlach conceived a plan for a palace to make Versailles look like a gilded outhouse. Construction began in 1696, but the cost was so prohibitive that the project was slowed down considerably until, 3 emperors later in 1740, Maria Theresia inherited the project and created the Rococo palace that became her favorite residence. Its cheery yellow color has been named *"Maria Theresien gelb"* after her. When Napoleon conquered Vienna, he shared Maria Theresia's fondness for the place and promptly moved in. Tours of some of the palace's 1500 rooms reveal the elaborate taste of her era. The frescoes lining the **Great Gallery** once observed the dancing Congress of Vienna, which loved a good party after a long day of divvying up the continent. The 6-year-old Mozart played in the **Hall of Mirrors.** The **Million Gulden Room** wins the prize for excess: Oriental miniatures cover the chamber's walls. *(Take U-4 to "Schönbrunn." Apartments open daily Apr.-Oct. 8:30am-5pm; Nov.-Mar. 8:30am-4:30pm. 100AS. Headphone tour 90AS, students 80AS. More worthwhile grand tour 120AS, students 105AS. English tour 145AS, students 130AS.)*

Even more impressive than the palace itself are the classical gardens behind it that extend nearly 4 times the length of the palace, designed by Emperor Josef II. The gardens include an encyclopedic orchestration of various elements, ranging from a sprawling **zoo** to the massive stone **Neptunbrunnen** (Neptune fountain) and bogus **Roman ruins.** Edging the geometric flower beds, the trees have been carefully pruned to create the effect of a vaulted arch. Walk past the **flower sculptures** to reach Schönbrunn's labyrinths, rose gardens, and nature preserves. At one end of the garden is the **Palmenhaus,** an enormous greenhouse of tropical plants and the **Schmetterlinghaus** (Butterfly House), an enclosure where soft-winged beauties fly free in the tropical environment. The compendium is crowned by the **Gloriette,** an ornamental temple serenely perched upon a hill with a beautiful view. If you're feeling indulgent, drink a somewhat pricey *Melange* in the temple's new café. In summer, open-air opera is performed in the park. *(Park open 6am-dusk. Free.)* Built to amuse Maria Theresia's husband in 1752, the **Schönbrunn Tiergarten** (Zoo) is the world's oldest menagerie. *(Zoo open daily May-Sept. 9am-6:30pm; Feb. and Oct. 9am-5pm; Nov.-Jan. 9am-4:30pm; Mar. and Oct. 9am-5:30pm; Apr. 9am-6pm. 95AS, students 45AS.)*

VIENNA SIX FEET UNDER: THE ZENTRALFRIEDHOF. The Viennese like to describe the **Zentralfriedhof** (Central Cemetery), XI, Simmeringer Hauptstr. 234 (tel. 76041), as half the size of Geneva but twice as lively. The phrase is meant not only to poke fun at Vienna's rival but also to illustrate Vienna's healthy attitude toward death. In bygone days, the phrase "a beautiful corpse" was a common way of describing a dignified funeral in Vienna, and the event of one's death was treated as, well, an event. Death doesn't get any better than at the Zentralfriedhof. The **Dr. Karl-Lueger-Kirche** marks the center of the cemetery, with the graves of the famous, infamous, and unknown spreading out from it in a grid. The tombs in this massive park (2km² with its own bus service) memorialize the truly great along with the ones who want to be so considered. The cemetery is the place to pay respects to your favorite Viennese decomposer: the 2nd gate **(Tor II)** leads to Beethoven, Wolf, Strauss, Schönberg, Moser, and an honorary monument to Mozart, whose true resting place is an unmarked paupers' grave in the **Cemetery of St. Mark,** III, Leberstr. 6-8. St. Mark's deserves a visit not just for sheltering Mozart's dust, but also for its *Biedermeier* tombstones and the wild inundation of lilac blossoms that flower everywhere for 2 weeks in spring.

Tor I leads to the **Jewish Cemetery** and Arthur Schnitzler's burial plot. The state of the Jewish Cemetery mirrors the fate of Vienna's Jewish population—many of the headstones are cracked, broken, lying prone, or neglected because the families of most of the dead are no longer in Austria. Various structures throughout this portion of the burial grounds memorialize the millions slaughtered in Nazi death camps. **Tor III** leads to the Protestant section and the new Jewish cemetery. To the east of the Zentralfriedhof is the melancholy **Friedhof der Namenlosen** on Alberner Hafen, where the nameless corpses of people fished out of the Danube are buried. This little cemetery is accessible by bus #6A from the terminus of tram #71. *(Take tram #71 from Schwarzenbergpl., or tram #72 from Schlachthausg. The tram stops 3 times, at each of the main gates. Tor II is the main entrance. Bus #6A also services the other gates. You can also take S-7 to "Zentralfriedhof," which stops along the south-west wall of the cemetery. 38AS. Open May-Aug. 7am-7pm; Mar.-Apr. and Sept.-Oct. 7am-6pm; Nov.-Feb. 8am-5pm.)*

▲ GARDENS AND PARKS

The Viennese have gone to great lengths to brighten the urban landscape with patches of green. The Habsburgs opened and maintained the city's primary public gardens throughout the last 4 centuries; the areas became public property after WWII. There are several parks along the Ring, including the Stadtpark, Resselpark, Burggarten, and Volksgarten, and in nearly every suburb of the city. The gardens of Schloß Schönbrunn and Palais Belvedere (see p. 119) are particularly beautiful. During food shortages after WWII, the city distributed plots of land in sections of the 14th, 16th, and 19th districts to citizens to let them grow their own vegetables. These community *Gärten* still exist, full of roses and garden gnomes.

ALONG THE RING. Vienna's *Innere Stadt* is demarcated on 3 sides by the Ringstraße and on the fourth by the Danube Canal. Just south of the Ring, the canal branches into the tiny **Wien River,** which flows to the southwest, passing through *Innenstadt* along the Linke Wienzeile, where it hides beneath the city streets, and, eventually reappears near Schloß Schönbrunn. On its merry way, the Wien, replete with ducks and lilies, bisects the **Stadtpark** (City Park; take U-4 to "Stadtpark"), which snuggles up to Parkring. Established in 1862, this area was the first municipal park outside the former city walls. The sculpted vegetation, with one of Vienna's most photogenic monuments, the gilded **Johann-Strauss-Denkmal,** in the center, provides a soothing counterpoint to the central bus station and nearby Bahnhof Wien-Mitte/Landstr.

Clockwise up the Ring, past the Staatsoper, lies the **Burggarten** (Palace Gardens; see p. 115), a quiet park with monuments to such Austrian notables as Mozart, Emperor Franz Josef, and Emperor Franz I, Maria Theresia's husband. The **Babenberger Passage** leads from the Ring to the marble **Mozart Denkmal** (1896), which depicts the composer standing on a pedestal surrounded by instrument-toting cherubim, with reliefs from his operas and portraits of his father and sister on the sides. Reserved for the imperial family and members of the court until 1918, the Burggarten is now a favorite for lounging students, young lovers, and hyperactive dogs. The Burggarten borders Heldenplatz, across from the Kunsthistorisches Museum and behind the Hofburg, which abuts the **Volksgarten,** once the site of a defensive bastion destroyed by Napoleon's troops. The focal point of the park is the **Temple of Theseus,** the monument to Austrian playwright Franz Grillparzer, which outshines the monument to Empress Elisabeth designed by Hans Bitterlich. The throned empress casts a stony glance upon Friedrich Ohmann's goldfish pond. The most striking feature of the park is the riotous **Rose Garden,** which showcases several thousand different varieties.

AUGARTEN. The Augarten, on Obere Augartenstr., northeast of downtown Vienna in Leopoldstadt, is Vienna's oldest public park. To reach the park, take tram #31 up from Schottenring or tram N to "Obere Augartenstr." and head left down Taborstr. Originally a formal French garden, the Augarten was given a Baroque face-lift and opened to the public by Kaiser Josef II in 1775. Today, the Augarten is no longer as fashionable as it was in the days of Mozart and Strauss, due primarily to the daunting WWII **Flaktürme** (concrete anti-aircraft towers) that dominate the central portion of the park. The sturdy construction of these and other *Flaktürme* in parks around the city has thwarted repeated demolition attempts (the walls of reinforced concrete are up to 5m thick). Despite the dampening influence of the towers, children play soccer between the flowers. Buildings located within the Augarten include the headquarters for the **Wiener Porzellanmanufaktur** (Vienna China Factory), founded in 1718, and the **Augartenpalais,** now a boarding school for the Vienna Boys' Choir.

PRATER. For many nostalgic Viennese, the symbol of their city is the **Prater,** an old-school amusement park extending southeast from the Wien Nord Bahnhof/Praterstern, with its stately wooden 65m-tall **Riesenrad** (Giant Ferris Wheel; 50AS; ride lasts 20min.). The wheel, which provides one of the best views of Vienna, is best known for its cameo role in Orson Welles' *The Third Man.* Locals cherish this wheel of fortune, and when it was destroyed in WWII, the city built an exact replica, which has been turning since 1947. The park was a private game reserve for the Imperial Family until 1766, and the site of the World Expo in 1873. Squeezed into a riverside woodland between the Donaukanal and the river proper, the park is surrounded by ponds, meadows, and stretches of forest. The area near the U-1 stop "Praterstern" is the actual amusement park, which contains various rides, arcades, restaurants, and casinos. Entry to the complex is free, but each attraction charges admission (generally 40AS). The garish thrill machines and wonderfully campy spook-house rides are packed with children during the day, but the Prater becomes less wholesome after sundown, due to the proliferation of seedy peep shows. (Open May-Sept. 9am-midnight; Oct.-Nov. 3 10am-10pm; Nov. 4-Dec. 1 10am-6pm.)

ON THE DANUBE. Once the Viennese were able to tame it, the **Danube** became a favorite recreation spot for tired city-dwellers. The river's spring floods became problematic once settlers moved outside the city walls, so the Viennese stretch of the Danube was diverted into canals (and the sewer-like structures documented in *The Third Man*) from 1870 to 1875 and again from 1972 to 1987. One of the side benefits of this restructuring was the creation of new recreational areas, ranging from new tributaries (including the **Alte Donau** and the **Donaukanal**) to the **Donauinsel,** a narrow island stretching for kilometers. The Donauinsel is devoted to bike paths, soccer fields, swimming areas, barbecue plots, boats, discos, and summer restaurants. The northern shore of the island, along the Alte Donau, is lined with beaches and bathing areas. (Take U-1 (dir.: Kagran) to "Donauinsel" or "Alte Donau." Open May-Sept. M-F 9am-8pm, Sa-Su 8am-8pm. Beach admission is roughly 50AS.) You can get one of the most spectacular views of Vienna from the **Donaupark:** take the elevator up to the revolving restaurant in the **Donauturm** (Danube Tower), near the UN complex. (Take the U-1 to "Kaisermühlen/Vienna International Center" and follow signs to the park. Tower open daily April-Sept. 9:30am-midnight; Oct.-March 10am-10pm. 60AS.) The whole area celebrates during the annual open-air **Donauinsel Fest,** which stages jazz and rock concerts and fireworks displays, in late June (see **Festivals,** p. 129).

IN THE SUBURBS. Vienna's outlying suburbs shelter somewhat wilder parks than the tame enclaves in the center of the city. Nearly every district has public gardens tucked away somewhere, like the **Türkenschanz Park,** in the 18th district, which attracts a plethora of leashed dachshunds. The garden is famous for its Turkish fountain, pools, and peacocks. In summer, feed ducks or gaze in rapture at the water lilies. In winter, come for sledding or ice-skating. (Take bus #40A or #10A, and enter the park anywhere along Gregor-Mendel-Str., Hasenauerstr., or Max-Emmanuelstr.)

West of the 13th district is the **Lainzer Tiergarten** (Lainz Game Preserve). Once an exclusive hunting preserve for the royals, this enclosed space has been a nature park and reserve since 1941. Along with paths, restaurants, and spectacular vistas, the park encloses the **Hermes Villa.** This erstwhile retreat for Empress Elisabeth houses exhibitions by the Historical Museum of Vienna, most recently one about the unhappy empress herself. (Take U-4 (dir.: Hütteldorf) to "Hietzing," change to streetcar #60 to "Hermesstr.," then take bus #60B to "Lainzer Tor." Open Tu-Su and holidays 10am-6pm, Oct.-Mar. 9am-4:30pm. Villa admission 50AS, students and seniors 20AS; family card 75AS.)

The 14th, 17th, 19th, and 20th districts peter off into well-tended forests that invite *Spaziergänger* (people out for a stroll) and hikers alike. The **Pötzleindorfer Park,** at the end of tram line #41 (dir.: Pötzleindorfer Höhe) from Schottentor, overlaps the lower end of the *Wienerwald* (Vienna Woods). Wild deer roam through overgrown Alpine meadows and woodland.

THE VIENNA WOODS. Far to the north and west of Vienna sprawls the forested hills of the **Wienerwald,** made famous by Strauss's catchy waltz, "Tales from the Vienna Woods," which extend all the way past Baden bei Wien to the first foothills of the Alps. The woods are known for their excellent *Heuriger* and divine new wines (see p. 107). There are countless ways to enter the *Wienerwald,* by tram #38 to "Grinzing," tram D to "Nußdorf," tram #43 to "Neuwaldegg," etc. One of the most famous and most easily accessible routes is via **Kahlenberg** and **Leopoldsberg,** 2 hills north of Vienna which provide a great view of the city and direct entrance to the woods. **Kahlenberg** (484m) is the highest point of the rolling *Wienerwald,* and affords spectacular views of Vienna, the Danube, and distant Alps. The Turks besieged Vienna from here in 1683, and Polish king Jan Sobieski celebrated his liberation of the city from Saracen infidels in the small **Church of St. Joseph.** (Open May-Oct. Sa noon-6pm, Su and holidays 9am-6pm.) Just off the central square of Kahlenberg stands the trusty **Stefania Warte** tower; catch the views from part of the river valley's old fortifications. (Take U-4 to "Heiligenstadt" then bus #38A to "Kahlenberg," or hike up the steep 1km-long Nasen Weg from the Kahlenbergdorf S-Bahn station.)

The area around Kahlenberg, Cobenzl, and Leopoldstadt is criss-crossed with hiking paths *(Wanderwege)* marked by colored bars blazed on tree trunks. Kahlenberg and its country cemetery are within easy walking distance of the wine-growing districts of **Nußdorf** and **Grinzing.** You can follow in an early Pope's footsteps and hike over to the **Leopoldskirche,** a renowned pilgrimage site. It's 1km east of Kahlenberg on **Leopoldsberg** (425m), site of a Babenberg fortress destroyed by the Turks in 1529. Leopoldsberg is named for St. Leopold III of the royal Babenberg family, and offers all-encompassing views of the surrounding city and river valleys. (You can also take bus #38A from Kahlenberg to Leopoldsberg; 20min.) **Klosterneuburg,** a decadently Baroque monastery town founded by Leopold, (see p. 133) is only a 1½-hour hike from Leopoldsberg.

🏛 MUSEUMS

Vienna owes its vast selection of masterpieces to the acquisitive Habsburgs as well as the city's own crop of art schools and world-class artists (see p. 78). Though painting and architecture dominate most museums, Vienna's treasures are as diverse as the former imperial Habsburg possessions. The vast array of venues can boggle the mind, so take it one step at a time and plan your attack strategy well. An exhaustive list is impossible to include here, but the tourist office's free *Museums* brochure lists all opening hours and admission prices. All museums run by the city of Vienna are free on Friday morning before noon; they are marked in the brochure with a coat of arms. Individual museum tickets usually cost 20-80AS, discounted with the **Vienna Card** (though student or senior citizen discounts are usually comparable; see p. 91). If you're going to be in town for a long time, investing in the **Museum Card** (issued through the *Verein der Museumsfreunde*) will save you a bundle on museum entrance fees (ask at a museum ticket window).

ART MUSEUMS

🎨 **Kunsthistorisches Museum** (Museum of Fine Arts; tel. 52 52 40), across from the Burgring and Heldenpl. on Maria Theresia's right, houses the world's 4th-largest art collection, including vast amounts of 15th- to 18th-century Venetian and Flemish paintings. The works by Brueghel are unrivaled, and the museum possesses entire rooms of Rembrandt, Rubens, Titian, Holbein, and Velàzquez. Ancient and classical art, including an Egyptian burial chamber, are also well represented. The lobby is pre-Secession Klimt—a mural depicting artistic progress from the classical era to the 19th century—painted in the Historicist style he would later attack. Open Tu-Su 10am-6pm. Picture gallery also open Th until 9pm. During the summer, Easter, and Christmas, English guided tours are offered at 11am and 3pm (30AS). 100AS, students and seniors 70AS. Small **branches** of the museum reside in the Neue Burg (see p. 114): the **Ephesus Museum,** which has an ancient Greek temple and statues transported from Ephesus; the **Arms and Armor Collection** (the 2nd-largest collection in the world); and the **Ancient Musical Instruments Collections.** Same hours as picture gallery. 40AS, students and seniors 30AS.

🎨 **Austrian Gallery,** III, Prinz-Eugen-Str. 27 (tel. 79 55 70), in the Belvedere Palace behind Schwarzenbergpl. (see p. 120). Walk up from the Südbahnhof or take tram D, #566, 567, 666, 668, or 766 to "Prinz-Eugen-Str." The collection is split into 2 parts. The **Upper Belvedere** (built in 1721-22 by Hildebrandt) houses Austrian Art of the 19th and 20th centuries. Most of the famous Secessionist works reside here. Especially well-represented are Schiele, Kokoschka, and Klimt, whose gilded masterpiece, *The Kiss,* has enthralled visitors for nearly a century. Use the same ticket to enter the **Lower Belvedere,** which contains the **Baroque Museum's** extensive collection of sculptures by Donner, Maulbertsch, and Messerschmidt, as well as David's famous coronation of Napoleon; and the **Museum of Medieval Austrian Art,** with its Romanesque and Gothic sculptures and altarpieces. Both Belvederes open Tu-Su 10am-5pm. Admission until 4:30pm. English guided tours at 2:30pm. 60AS, students 30AS.

Akademie der Bildende Kunst (Academy of Fine Arts), I, Schillerpl. 3 (tel. 588 16 225 or 588 16 228), near Karlspl., was designed in 1876 by Hansen of *Parlament, Musikverein,* and *Börse* fame. The excellent, manageable collection includes Hieronymus Bosch's *Last Judgment* and impressive works by Peter Paul Rubens. Open Tu-Su 10am-4pm. 50AS, students 20AS.

Secession Building, I, Friedrichstr. 12 (tel. 587 53 07), on the western side of Karlspl. (see p. 118). Originally built to house artwork that didn't conform to the *Künstlerhaus's* standards, the Secession building gave the pioneers of modern art space to hang their work. Klimt, Kokoschka, and the "barbarian" Gauguin were featured early on in the building that the Viennese nicknamed "The Golden Cabbage." Rather than canonize early *Jugendstil* pioneers, the museum continually seeks to exhibit the new and fresh. Substantial contemporary works are exhibited here, whereas most major Secessionist works are housed in the Belvedere. Klimt's *Beethoven Frieze* is the exception—this 30m-long work is his visual interpretation of Beethoven's *Ninth Symphony.* Open Tu-Sa 10am-6pm, Su and holidays 10am-4pm. 60AS, students 40AS.

Museum Moderner Kunst (Museum of Modern Art; tel. 317 69 00; email museum@MMKSLW.or.at; www.MMKSLW.or.at/) is split between 2 locations. The 1st is in **Palais Liechtenstein,** IX, Fürsteng. 1. Take tram D (dir.: Nußdorf) to "Fürsteng." The *Schloß,* surrounded by a manicured garden, holds a collection of 20th-century masters including Magritte, Motherwell, Picasso, Miró, Kandinsky, Pollock, Warhol, and Klee. The 2nd location is the **20er Haus** (tel. 799 69 00), III, Arsenalstr. 1, opposite the Süd-bahnhof. Its large, open *Bauhaus* interior provides the perfect setting for the substantial collection of ground-breaking 60s and 70s work—Keith Arnatt and Larry Poons among them—alongside contemporary artists. It sits in a large sculpture garden stocked with pieces by Giacometti, Moore, and others. Open Tu-Su 10am-6pm. 45AS, students 25AS for each exhibit; 60AS, children 30AS for both exhibits. Wheelchair accessible.

Österreichisches Museum für Angewandte Kunst (aka the MAK; Austrian Museum of Applied Art), I, Stubenring 5 (tel. 71 13 60). Take U-3 to "Stubentor." The oldest museum of applied arts in Europe, each room is designed by a different artist and dis-plays an international collection of furniture, textiles, and relics. The collection includes Oriental carpets, Art Deco goblets, Biedermeier coffee-pots, Renaissance linens, a Baroque palace room, a 20th-century fire table, and the designs and archives of the Wiener Werkstätte arts and crafts workshop. The basement displays jewelry, textiles, and divans from the 17th century to the present. Open Tu-W and F-Su 10am-6pm, Th 10am-9pm. 90AS, students 45AS.

Kunst Haus Wien, III, Untere Weißgerberstr. 13 (tel. 712 04 91; see p. 119). Take U-1 or 4 to "Schwedenpl.," then bus N to "Radetzkypl." Built by Hundertwasser, this museum displays many of his paintings, graphic drawings, architectural models, and environ-mental machines (the "plant water purification plant," for instance). The building itself is one of Hundertwasser's greatest achievements. The floor bends and swells, creating (in Hundertwasser's words) "a melody for the feet." The Kunst Haus also hosts exhibits of contemporary art from around the world. Open 10am-7pm. 95AS, students 50AS for each exhibit; 150AS, students 110AS for both exhibits. M ½-price.

Kunsthalle Wien, IV, Treitlstr. 2 (tel. 521 890; see p. 117), in Karlspl. International exhibits of contemporary painting, sculpture, photography, film, music, and more. Open daily 10am-6pm, Th 10am-10pm. 80AS, students 60AS.

Künstlerhaus, Karlspl. 5 (tel. 587 96 63; see p. 118). Once the home of the Viennese artistic establishment, this museum invites temporary exhibits, usually of contemporary and non-European art. The theater hosts numerous **film festivals.** Open M-W and F-Su 10am-6pm, Th 10am-9pm. 90AS, students 60AS. M students 40AS.

Palais Surreal, Josefspl. 5 (tel. 512 25 49). Take U-3 to "Herreng." The Baroque palace of the Pallavicini family now houses a small but renowned collection of Surrealist sculp-tures by Dalí, including a wobbly work called "Space Elephant," and ethereal sculptures done in glass. Open 10am-6pm. 90AS, students and elderly 50AS.

ASSORTED MUSEUMS

Museum für Völkerkunde, I, (tel. 53 43 00; see p. 114), in the Neue Burg on Heldenpl. Take U-2 or U-3 to "Volkstheater." Habsburg agents brought back a fabulous collection of African and South American art from their travels. Admire Benin bronzes, West Afri-can Dan heads, and Montezuma's feathered headdress. The museum also displays art and artifacts from North America, the Middle East, and the Far East, in addition to special exhibits. Open Apr.-Dec. Su-M and W-Sa 10am-4pm; Jan.-Mar. Su-M and W-Sa 10am-6pm. Tours Su 11am. 80AS, students 40AS, children under 10 free.

Historisches Museum der Stadt Wien (Historical Museum of the City of Vienna), IV, Karlspl. 5 (tel. 505 87 47), to the left of the Karlskirche (see p. 117). This amazing collection of historical artifacts and paintings documents Vienna's evolution from the Roman encampment through the Turkish siege of Vienna, and the subsequent 640 years of Habsburg rule. Don't miss the memorial rooms to Loos and Grillparzer, the *fin de siècle* art, or the temporary exhibitions on all things Viennese. Open Tu-Su 9am-6pm. Free on Fridays 9am-noon. 50AS, students 20AS, seniors 25AS.

Naturhistorisches Museum (Natural History Museum; tel. 52 17 70), opposite the Kunsthistorisches Museum. This vast museums displays the usual animalia plus giant South American beetles and dinosaur skeletons. Two of its star attractions are manmade: a spectacular floral bouquet comprised of gemstones and a copy of the fascinating Stone-Age beauty *Venus of Willendorf* (the original is locked in a vault). Open W 9am-9pm, Th-M 9am-6:30pm, admission until 5:30pm; in winter, 1st floor only 9am-3pm. 45AS, students 30AS.

Sigmund Freud Haus, IX, Bergg. 19 (tel. 319 15 96), near the Votivkirche. Take U-2 to "Schottentor," then walk up Währingerstr. to Bergg. This disappointing (no cigars) museum was Freud's home from 1891 until the *Anschluß*. Freud moved almost all original belongings with him out of the country, including the leather divan. Lots of photos and documents, including the young Freud's report cards and circumcision certificate. Open July-Sept. 9am-6pm; Oct.-June 9am-4pm. 60AS, students 40AS. Tours 75AS.

Lippizaner Museum, I, Reitschulg. 2 (tel. 526 41 84). If you ever liked horses, this is the place for you. What used to be the imperial pharmacy now serves as a museum dedicated to the imperial horses, featuring paintings, harnesses, video clips, and a small viewing window through which you can glimpse the stables. Open daily 9am-6pm. 50AS, students 35AS, tour 20AS. Call ahead to arrange an English tour.

Jewish Museum, I, Dorotheerg. 11 (tel. 535 04 31). Focuses on the history and contributions of Austria's Jewish community, with a permanent display telling Viennese Jewish history through holographs. Temporary exhibits focus on prominent Jewish figures and contemporary Jewish art. Open M-F 10am-6pm, Su 10am-8pm. 70AS, students 40AS.

Bestattungsmuseum (Undertaker's Museum), IV, Goldeg. 19 (tel. 501 954 227). The Viennese take their funerals seriously, giving rise to a morbidly fascinating exhibit that is, in its own way, as typically Viennese as *Heurigen* (wine taverns) and waltzes. Contains coffins with alarms (should the body decide to rejoin the living) and Josef II's proposed reusable coffin. Open M-F noon-3pm by prior arrangement only.

🎵 ENTERTAINMENT

MUSIC

The heart of Vienna beats to musical rhythms. Vienna's musical history is full of big names: Mozart, Beethoven, and Haydn wrote their greatest masterpieces in Vienna, creating the First Viennese School; a century later, Schönberg, Webern, and Berg teamed up to form the Second Viennese School. Every Austrian child must learn to play an instrument during schooling, and the Vienna **Konservatorium** and **Hochschule** are world-renowned conservatories. All year, Vienna presents performances ranging from the above-average to the sublime, with many surprisingly accessible to the budget traveler.

INSTITUTIONS

Patronage was the name of the game in 18th-century music-making, so when the Habsburg emperors wanted an Austrian operatic tradition to rival Italy's, they could make it happen, commissioning such masterpieces as Mozart's *Le nozze di Figaro* and *Die Entführung aus dem Serail* (The Abduction from the Seraglio). In 1869, Emperor Franz Josef inaugurated the **Vienna Court Opera**, today's **Staat-**

TO EVERYTHING THERE IS A SEASON. The State Opera and the Philharmonic Orchestra are closed in July and August. The Vienna Boys' Choir is off in July and on tour in August. The Lipizzaner Stallions do not dance in July and August. Many an unsuspecting tourist has carefully planned a trip, only to be disappointed by these most inconvenient facts of Viennese life.

soper (State Opera). It was conceived as an alternate performance space to the famous **Theater an der Wien,** which sheltered the first performance of *Die Zauberflöte (The Magic Flute)*. The State Opera soon dominated the opera scene, hosting the newest Wagner to an occasionally turbulent audience. Mahler became Director of the Opera in 1897, transforming the Staatsoper from a place of elegant, palatable entertainment into a serious music place. In 1919, composer **Richard Strauss** and director Franz Schalk took control. Since then, the Vienna Staatsoper has become one of the three great opera houses of the world, along with Milan's *La Scala* and the New York Metropolitan Opera. The opera house was destroyed during WWII, but artistic standards remain in full force. The new opera house, constructed by August Siccard von Siccardsburg and Eduard van der Null, is one of the most magnificent edifices on the Ringstraße, and holds special sentimental value for the Viennese. When reconstructing the bombed-out center of the city after WWII, the opera was the first public building to be reconstructed, outranking even St. Stephen's cathedral. It reopened on November 5, 1955, with a phenomenal production of Beethoven's *Fidelio*.

Operated by the *Gesellschaft der Musikfreunde* (Society of Music Lovers) since its founding in 1812, the **Musikverein** is Austria's—perhaps the world's—premier concert hall. Danish architect Theophil Hansen constructed the building in 1867, creating a concert hall of unparalleled acoustic perfection. The building is now a National Trust, and the Vienna Philharmonic shares its stage with the world's finest orchestras. The Musikverein's program is essentially conservative, although it occasionally includes contemporary classical music. It leaves experimental and ultra-modern programs to the **Konzerthaus** across the river Wien.

The 500-year-old **Wiener Sängerknaben** (Vienna Boys' Choir) functions as Austria's "ambassador of song" on their extensive international tours. Dressed in sailor suits, they export great works of music to the entire world. Emperor Maximilian I founded the group in 1498, and Franz Schubert was a chorister, Wolfgang Amadeus Mozart was appointed court composer, and Anton Bruckner held the post of organist and music teacher. Today, the choir provides a forum where Mozart, Hadyn, Schubert, and Bruckner, not to mention Beethoven's gorgeous Mass in C Op 86, can be heard as they were originally meant to be performed—sung by the clear sweet voices of a boy's choir. Besides going on world tour, members of the *Sängerknaben* are always on hand to sing Mass in the Hofburg chapel at 9:25am Sunday mornings (open to all; Sept. 15-June 30).

PERFORMANCES

"Too many notes, dear Mozart," observed Josef II after the premiere of *Abduction from the Seraglio*. "Only as many as are necessary, Your Majesty," was the genius's reply. The Habsburgs may be forgiven this critical slip, for they have provided invaluable support of opera: the **Staatsoper** remains one of the top 5 companies in the world and performs about 300 times from September through June. There are 3 budget options for seeing an opera there: the cheapest option is **standing-room tickets,** which give you a glimpse of world-class opera for a pittance. *(Balcony 20AS, orchestra 30AS. Formal dress not necessary, but no shorts.)* Those with the desire (and the stamina) should start lining up at least 1½ hours before curtain (2-3hr. in tourist season and for more popular productions) in order to get orchestra tickets—the side views from the balconies are limited, though cooler. The earlier you get there, the better your view will be. The standing room line forms inside the side door on the western side of the Opera (by Operng.). Once you get your precious ticket, hurry to secure yourself a space on the rail and tie a scarf around it to

VIENNA

reserve your spot. The second option is **last-minute student tickets** that go on sale at the box office a half-hour before curtain; unclaimed tickets go for 100-150AS (ISIC *not* valid—bring a university ID). Line up to the left inside the main entrance at least an hour before curtain. The third option is advance tickets (ranging from 100 to 850AS) that go on sale a week before the performance at the **Bundestheaterkasse**, I, Hanuschg. 3 (tel. 514 442 960; www.oebthv.gv.at), around the corner from the opera. *(Open M-F 8am-6pm, Sa-Su 9am-noon. ISIC not valid for student discounts, university ID required.)* Get there at 6-7am of the first day for a good seat; some Viennese camp overnight for major performances. The Bundestheaterkasse also sells tickets for the 3 other public theaters: the **Volksoper, Burgtheater,** and **Akademietheater.** The Volksoper shows operas and operettas in German, sometimes translated; the other 2 venues feature classic dramas in German. Discount tickets go on sale half an hour before curtain at the individual box offices (50-400AS).

The world-famous **Wiener Philharmoniker** (Vienna Philharmonic Orchestra) has been directed by the world's finest conductors, including Gustav Mahler and Leonard Bernstein. Regular Philharmonic performances as well as other guest performances take place in the **Musikverein**, I, Dumbastr. 3 (tel. 505 81 90), on the northeast side of Karlspl. Tickets to Philharmoniker concerts are mostly on a subscription basis, but you can occasionally get a good deal at the box office. *(Box office open Sept.-June M-F 9am-7:30pm, Sa 9am-5pm. Standing-room tickets available at the box office; price varies by concert. Write Gesellschaft der Musikfreunde, Bösendorferstr. 12, A-1010 Wien for more information.)* Vienna's second fiddle, the **Vienna Symphony Orchestra,** is frequently on tour but plays some concerts at the Konzerthaus, III, Lothringerstr. 20 (tel. 712 12 11).

The **Vienna Boys' Choir** is another famous attraction. The pre-pubescent prodigies perform Sundays at 9:15am (mid-Sept. to June only) in the **Burgkapelle** (Royal Chapel), the oldest section of the Hofburg. Reserve tickets (60-310AS) at least 2 months in advance; write to Hofmusikkapelle, Hofburg, A-1010 Wien, but do not enclose money. Pick up tickets at the Burgkapelle on the Friday before mass from 11am to noon or on the Sunday of the mass by 9am. Unreserved seats go on sale from 5pm on the preceding Friday, maximum 2 per person. Standing room is free, despite rumors to the contrary, but you have to arrive before 8am to make it into the Burgkapelle. The lads also perform every Friday at 3:30pm at the Konzerthaus during May, June, September, and October. For tickets (390-430AS), contact *Reisebüro Mondial*, Faulmanng. 4, A-1040 Wien (tel. 588 04 141; fax 587 12 68; email ticket@mondial.at). If you miss the boys, don't miss the glorious—and free—musical experiences at the **Sunday High Masses** at 10 or 11am in the major churches (Augustinerkirche, Michaelerkirche, Stephansdom) all year round.

THEATER AND CINEMA

In the past few years, Vienna has made a name for itself as a city of musicals, with productions of such Broadway and West End favorites as *Phantom of the Opera* and *Les Misérables*, or the long-running home-grown favorite *Elisabeth*, a creative interpretation of the late empress's life. Take U-1, U-2, or U-4 to "Karlspl." and just off the Ring you'll find the **Theater an der Wien**, VI, Linke Wienzeile 6 (tel. 58830), which once produced musicals of a different sort, hosting in its 18th-century edifice the premieres of Beethoven's *Fidelio* and Mozart's *Die Zauberflöte* (The Magic Flute). The nobility felt that Mozart had crossed the line of good taste by composing an opera in German, so they blocked the scheduled premiere at the Staatsoper. The masterpiece was finally performed, thrilling the regular citizens, who could, at long last, understand the plot. For the sake of tradition, the Staatsoper still occasionally sends productions of Mozart opera to be performed here.

Vienna's English Theatre, VIII, Josefsg. 12 (tel. 402 12 60), presents English-language drama. (Box office open M-F 10am-6pm, Sa-Su 10am-4pm. Tickets 150-420AS, student rush 100AS.) The **International Theater**, IX, Porzellang. 8 (tel. 319 62 72; tickets 260-280AS, under 26 140AS), is another English-language venue. **WUK**, IX, Währingerstr. 59 (tel. 401 21 10), is a workshop and cultural center that puts on dance, concerts, and readings. **Films** in English usually play at **Burg Kino**, I, Opernring 19 (tel. 587 84 06; last show usually around 8:30pm, Sa around 11pm); **Top Kino,** VI, Rahlgassel 1 (tel. 587 55 57; open 3pm-10:30pm), at the intersection of Gumpendorferstr.; and **Haydnkino** (last show usually around 9:30pm), on Mariahilferstr. near the U-3 stop "Neubaug." More and more theaters show movies in English or with subtitles—look in the newspaper for films with OF, OV, EOV, or OmU after the title. **Votivkino,** Währingerstr. 12 (tel. 317 35 71), near Bergg. and Schottentor, is an art-house popular with the university crowd and shows all films with German subtitles. **Artis Kino, Filmcasino,** and **Stöberkino** also show subtitled art and foreign films. **Künstlerhauskino,** I, Karlspl. 5 (tel. 505 43 28), hosts art house film festivals. Prices for shows range from 70-120AS; be warned—you pay for the row you sit in. On Monday, all seats are discounted to 70AS. In summer, there are several **open-air cinemas** in the *Augarten* park (all shows at 9:30pm; 70AS). From Schottenring, take tram #31 to "Gaußpl." Ask at the tourist office for details on occasional free movies in the *Volksgarten*. While Vienna hosts a full-sized film festival in August (see **Festivals,** p. 129), the rest of the year the Austrian **Filmmuseum,** Augustinerstr. 1 (tel. 533 70 540), shows a rotating program of classic and avant-garde films.

FESTIVALS

Vienna hosts an array of important annual festivals, mostly musical. The **Vienna Festival** (mid-May to mid-June) has a diverse program of exhibitions, plays, and concerts. (For info, tel. 58 92 22; fax 589 22 49; email festwochen@festwochen.at; www.festwochen.or.at/wf.) Of particular interest are the celebrated orchestras and conductors joining the party. The Staatsoper and Volkstheater host the annual **Jazzfest Wien** during the first weeks of July, featuring many famous acts. For information, contact Jazzfest Wien (tel. 503 56 47; www.viennajazz.at.) While other big guns take summer siesta, Vienna has held the **Klangbogen** every summer since 1952, featuring excellent concerts across Vienna, including **Wiener Kammeroper** (Chamber Opera; tel. 513 60 72), performances of Mozart's operas in an open-air theater set among the ruins of Schönbrunner Schloßpark. Pick up a brochure at the tourist office. From the end of July to the beginning of August, the **Im-Puls Dance Festival** (tel. 523 55 58; www.impuls-tanz.wien.at) attracts some of the world's great dance troupes and offers seminars to enthusiasts. Some of Vienna's best parties are thrown by the parties (political, that is). The Social Democrats host a late-June **Danube Island Festival,** which draws millions of party goers annually, while the Communist Party holds a **Volkstimme Festival** in mid-August. Both cater to impressionable youngsters with free rock, jazz, and folk concerts. In mid-October, the annual city-wide film festival, the **Viennale,** kicks off. In past years, the program has featured over 150 movies from 25 countries. One final free treat not to be missed is the **nightly film festival** in July and August, in the Rathauspl. at dusk. Taped operas, ballets, operettas, and concerts enrapture the audience.

WINTER FESTIVITIES

The Viennese don't let long winter nights go to waste. Christmas festivities begin in December with **Krampus** parties. *Krampus* (Black Peter) is a hairy devil that accompanies St. Nicholas on his rounds and gives bad children coal and sticks. On December 5th, people in *Krampus* suits lurk everywhere, rattling their chains and chasing passersby, while small children nibble marzipan *Krampus* effigies.

As the weather gets sharper, huts of professional *Maroni-* (chestnut) roasters and *Bratkartoffeln-* (potato pancake) toasters pop up everywhere. Cider, punch, red noses, and *Glühwein* (a hot, spicy mulled wine) become ubiquitous on sidewalks. **Christmas markets** *(Christkindlmärkte)* open around the city. The somewhat tacky **Rathausplatz Christkindlmarkt** is probably the best known of the yule marketplaces, offering, among other things, excellent *Lebkuchen* (a spicy, very strong gingerbread-like cake), *Langos* (a Hungarian round bread soaked in hot oil, garlic, and onions), and beeswax candles (open 9am-9pm). **Schloß Schönbrunn's** *Weihnachtsmarkt* offers old-fashioned Christmas decorations (open M-F noon-8pm, Sa-Su 10am-8pm). Visit the happy **Spittelberg** market, where artists and university kids hawk offbeat creations (open M-F 2-8pm, Sa-Su and holidays 10am-

8pm). The **Trachtenmarkt** shop in Schotteng. near Schottentor offers atmospheric Christmas shopping. Most theaters, opera houses, and concert halls have Christmas programs (see **Musical Performances,** p. 127 or **Theater and Cinema,** p. 128). The city also turns the Rathauspl. into an enormous outdoor skating rink in January and February.

Before Christmas festivities have even died down, the Viennese gear up for New Year's Day. The climax of the New Year's season is the **Neujahrskonzert** (New Year's concert) by the Viennese Philharmonic, broadcast worldwide. The refrain of the *Radetzkymarsch* by Strauss signals that the new year has truly begun. New Year's also brings a famously flashy **Imperial Ball** in the Hofburg (for tickets, contact Kongresszentrum Hofburg, A-1014 Wien; tel. 587 55 71, ext. 249; fax 535 64 26). For those lacking 7-digit incomes, the City of Vienna organizes a huge chain of *Silvester* (New Year's) parties in the Inner City. Follow the **Silvesterpfad,** marked by lights hung over the street, for outdoor karaoke, street waltzing, firecrackers, and hundreds of people drinking champagne in the streets. At midnight, the giant bell of St. Stephen's rings across the country, broadcast by public radio stations.

New Year's is barely over before **Fasching** (Carnival season) arrives in February and spins the city into a bubbly daze of bedlam. These are the weeks of the Viennese waltzing balls. The most famous is the **Wiener Opernball** (Viennese Opera Ball), which draws Princess Stephanies and Donald Trumps the world over, which takes place on a Thursday evening in the beginning of February. Tickets must be reserved years in advance (international celebrities, contact *Opernballbüro,* A-1010 Wien, Goetheg. 1; tel. 514 442 606). You don't have to sit out if you can't make the *Opernball*—there's something for everyone. Even the kindergartners in public pre-schools have *Fasching Krapfen* parties, and McDonald's puts up carnival crepe banners. For a free *Fasching* celebration, join the **carnival parade** that winds its way around the Ring, stopping traffic the day before Lent.

◪ NIGHTLIFE

With one of the highest bar to cobblestone ratios in the world, Vienna is a great place to party, whether you're looking for a quiet evening with a glass of wine or a wild night in a disco full of black-clad Euro muscle men and drag queens. The *Heurigen* on the outskirts of Vienna provide a culturally immersive way to spend an evening (see p. 107), but if you're looking for a more urban type of night-wandering, head downtown. Take the subway (U-1 or U-4) to "Schwedenplatz," which will drop you within blocks of the **Bermuda Dreieck** (Triangle), so-called both for the 3 block triangle it covers and for the tipsy revelers who never make it home. The area is packed with lively, crowded clubs. If your vision isn't foggy yet, head down **Rotenturmstrasse** towards St. Stephen's cathedral or walk around the areas bounded by the Jewish synagogue and Ruprecht's church. Another good zone to search for nightlife in the inner city is the smooth, dark **Bäckerstraße** and its cellar bars. Slightly outside the Ring, the streets off Burgg. and Stiftg. in the 7th district and the university quarter (8th and 9th districts) have tables in outdoor courtyards and loud, hip bars. They can be a good place to seek refuge when the summer crowd in the Bermuda Triangle feels too pubescent or touristy.

Vienna's kinetic club scene rages every night of the week, later than most bars. DJs spin wax until 4 or even 6am, and some clubs will keep it going after hours until 11am the next morning. One fact of Viennese nightlife: it starts late. If you arrive at some place at 11pm, it will be a scene from a high school dance, full of adolescents toting cell phones and smoking cigarettes. As usual, the best nights are Friday and Saturday, beginning around 1am or so. Cover charges are reasonable, and the theme nights are varied and frenetic enough to please anyone. While techno still rears its digitalized head, house, jungle, and trip-hop have a strong following as well. For the scoop on raves, concerts, and parties, grab the fliers at swanky cafés like MAK or Berg das Café, or pick up a copy of the indispensable **Falter** (28AS)—besides some excellent articles in German, it prints listings of everything from opera and theater to punk concerts and updates on the gay/les-

THE REGENBOGENPARADE At the end of June or beginning of July every year, Austrians gather for an afternoon and evening of gay pride in Vienna at the Rainbow Parade, which consists of over 40 floats sponsored by social, political, and commercial organizations from around Austria, as well as the Czech Republic and Slovakia. Everyone from Dykes on Bikes and the Rosa Lila Villa to Jewish Homosexuals and AIDS awareness organizations takes part. The effervescent parade parties its way along the Ringstraße down to Karlspl., where the public celebration concluded—to be continued privately in bars the rest of the night. The Viennese gay community also hosts the annual "Life Ball," the only charity event held in Vienna's *Rathaus*, which raises money for people with AIDS and HIV.

bian scene, and will list places that have sprung up too recently for *Let's Go* to review. (Vienna's club turnover is too rapid to keep up with in a guide updated only once a year.) Also, be sure to grab a schedule for the **Nightbus** system, which runs across Vienna all night after the regular public transportation shuts down at midnight (look for a Nightbus marker at your daytime stop to see if it stops there).

BARS

The term "bar" has a loose definition in Vienna. Many restaurants (see **Restaurants,** p. 101) live a Dr. Jekyll-Mr. Hyde dual existence as a place both to eat and to party.

INSIDE THE RING

Cato, I, Tiefer Graben 19 (tel. 533 47 90). Take U-3 to "Herreng.," walk down to Strauchg., turn right, and continue on to Tiefer Graben; this tiny place will be on your left. This laid-back bar is super comfortable and you'll be singing songs with the friendly clientele before the end of the evening. Enjoy the music, art-deco decor, and delicious champagne cocktails. Open Su-Th 6pm-2am, F-Sa 6pm-4am.

Club Berlin, I, Gonzag. 12 (tel. 533 04 79). Go downstairs in this house of swank to see Vienna's bold and beautiful wind their way around the partitions in this former wine cellar with great music. Open Su-Tu 6pm-2am, F-Sa 6pm-4am.

Santo Spirito, I, Kampfg. 7 (tel. 512 99 98). From Stephanspl., walk down Singerstr. and turn left onto Kampfg. (5min.). The stereo pumps out Rachmaninoff's second piano concerto while excited patrons co-conduct. Busts on the wall pay homage to famous baton-wavers. Owner vacations in July, otherwise open from 6pm until people leave.

Centro, I, Bäckerstr. 1. Behind the Stephansdom, turn right off Rotenturmstr. onto Lugeck, which leads to Bäckerstr. Come and chill among colorful posters in this mellow joint. Open M-F 4pm-2am, Sa 4pm-4am.

Benjamin, I, Salzgries 11-13 (tel. 533 33 49). Just outside of the Triangle area. Go down the steps from *Ruprechtskirche*, left onto Josefs Kai, and left again on Salzgries. Dark and rickety, this is a punk-rocker's heaven. Candles tilt in wax-covered wine bottles while a slightly hard-core but perfectly nice student crowd parties on. Great beer—*Budvar* (37AS) and *Kapsreiter* (43AS). Open Su-Th 7pm-2am, F-Sa 7pm-4am.

Café MAK, I, Stubenring 3-5 (tel. 714 01 21), inside the Museum für Angewandte Kunst (see p. 105). This bright café is a happening, rowdy bar by night with techno-rave parties on Saturdays in July. Open Tu-Su 10am-2am.

Zwölf Apostellenkeller, I, Sonnenfelsg. 3 (tel. 512 67 77), behind the Stephansdom. To reach this underground tavern, walk into the archway, take a right, go down the long staircase, and discover grottoes that date back to 1561. One of the best *Weinkeller* (wine cellars) in Vienna and a definite must for catacomb fans. Beer 37AS. *Viertel* of wine from 25AS. Open Aug.-June 4:30pm-midnight.

Esterházykeller, I, Haarhof 1 (tel. 533 34 82), off Naglerg. One of Vienna's least expensive *Weinkeller*. Relaxed cellar bar, popular with local twenty- and thirty-somethings. Try the Burgenlander *Grüner Veltliner* wine (26AS). Open in summer M-F 11am-11pm; in winter M-F 11am-11pm and Sa-Su 4-11pm.

Jazzland, I, Franz-Josefs-Kai 29 (tel. 533 25 75). near "Schwedenpl." Excellent live jazz of all styles and regions filters through the soothing brick environs, pleasing its clientele of older jazz fans. 50AS cover. Open Tu-Sa 7pm-2am. Music 9pm-1am.

Kaktus, I, Seitenstetteng. 5 (tel. 533 19 38), in the heart of the Triangle. Packed with the bombed and the beautiful, this candle-lit bar caters to the more sophisticated revelers. Open Su-Th 6pm-2am, F-Sa 6pm-4am.

OUTSIDE THE RING

🏴 **Alsergrunder Kulturpark,** IX, Alserstr. 4 (tel. 407 82 14). On the old grounds of a turn-of-the-18th-century hospital, Kulturpark is not one bar but many. A young Viennese crowd flocks to the beautifully landscaped grounds for the beer garden, *Heurigen,* champagne bar—the list goes on. All sorts of people and all sorts of nightlife—just about anything you might want for a happening night out. Open Apr.-Oct. daily 4pm-2am.

🏴 **Chelsea,** VIII, (tel. 407 93 09), Lerchenfeldergürtel under the U-Bahn between Thaliastr. and Josefstädterstr. The best place in Vienna for underground music: live bands from across Europe play here (except in summer). Cover 50-200AS. Open daily 4pm-4am.

Objektiv, VII, Kirchbergg. 26 (tel. 522 70 42). Take U-2 or U-3 to "Volkstheater," walk down Burgg. 2 blocks, and turn right on Kirchbergg. to find one of the most eclectic bars in Vienna, with old stoves and sewing machines as tables and cowboy boots as decorations. A mellow atmosphere, lively local crowd, and cheap drinks top things off. Happy hour daily 11pm-1am. Open M-Sa 6pm-2am, Su 6pm-1am.

Europa, VII, Zollerg. 8 (tel. 526 33 83). Buy a drink and strike a pose. Surrounded by concert posters and funky light fixtures, the hip twenty-something crowd hangs out late *en route* to further intoxication. Open 9am-4am.

Eagle Bar, VI, Blümelg. 1 (tel. 587 26 61). Come to scope the scene and be scoped by it at this bar for gay men only. The diverse, young clientele is derived from the leather and/or denim set. Open 9pm-4am.

Miles Smiles, VIII, Langeg. 51 (tel. 405 95 17). Take U-2 to "Lerchenfelderstr." Head down Lerchenfelderstr. and take the 1st right. This place has a cool, if somewhat touristy, atmosphere. The music is post-1955 jazz. Open Su-Th 8pm-2am, F-Sa 8pm-4am.

Das Möbel, VII, Burgg. 10 (tel. 524 94 97). This high-ceilinged café also functions as a showcase for furniture designers. At night, the metal couches, car seat chairs, Swiss-army-tables, and other pieces —which rotate every 6 weeks if not bought—are in full use by a hip crowd. Open M-F noon-midnight, Sa-Su breakfast buffet 10am.

Kunsthalle Café, IV, Treitlstr. 2 (tel. 586 98 64). Inside the bright yellow contemporary art museum, as well as outside on its large rocky terrace, this chill café-by-day is filled nightly with students and the bright sounds of funk/jazz/blues. Open 10am-3am or whenever the last person leaves.

Flieger, IV, Schleifmühlg. 19 (tel. 586 73 09). One of Vienna's 1st New Wave bars, Flieger's alternative scene is usually crowded and lively. The Katu drink, made with cactus juice, is rumored to be "mind-moving." Open M-Th 6pm-2am, F-Su 6pm-4am.

Nightshift, VI, Corneliusg. 8 (tel. 586 23 37). This hard-core joint caters to gay men only, preferably in black leather. This is not a place for the faint of heart (or the straight), as lots of bare chests cruise by. Su-Th 10pm-4am, F-Sa 10pm-5am.

DISCOS AND DANCE CLUBS

🏴 **U-4,** XII, Schönbrunnerstr. 222 (tel. 85 83 18). Take U-4 to "Meidling Hauptstr." Packed with all types, this place keeps the music fresh and the party going. U-4 has all the trappings, including 2 dance areas, multiple bars, and rotating theme nights to please a varied clientele. Th Gay Heaven Night. Cover 70-120AS. Open daily 11pm-5am.

Why Not, I, Tiefer Graben 22 (tel. 535 11 58). The neon interior of this relaxed gay and lesbian bar/disco holds both a chill chatting venue and a hip-hop-happening subterranean black-box dance floor. Saturday is the night to be here, with drink specials for 43AS. Cover 70AS. Open F-Sa 10pm-4am, Su 9pm-2am. Women-only 1 Th per month.

Flex Halle, I, Donaulände/Augartenbrücke (tel. 533 75 29), near the Schottenring U-Bahn station, seems more forbidding than it actually is. Head towards the river and down a narrow staircase. This small, dark, on-the-water club with neon lights and a slummy feel has live bands and chemically-enhanced excitement. Good dancing. Cover 70-150AS. Open 10pm-whenever.

DAYTRIPS FROM VIENNA

For other possible daytrips, see **Eisenstadt** (p. 138), **Baden bei Wien** (p. 278), **Melk** (p. 285), and **Krems** (p. 281).

NEAR VIENNA: STIFT KLOSTERNEUBURG

Easily accessible via bus or S-bahn #40 from Heiligenstadt (15min., every 30min., 19AS).

Founded by Margrave Leopold III in 1114, the **Chorherrenstift (monastery)** put the small town of Klosterneuburg on the map as the center of medieval Austrian art and culture. In 1133, Leopold elevated the institute to its present monastic status as **Stift Klosterneuburg.** In 1730, Emperor Karl IV, Maria Theresia's father, moved into Klosterneuburg and began expanding the complex with a **palace** intended to match the grand scale of the monastery and thus symbolize the importance of the *Kaiserreich* (Emperor's kingdom) to the *Gottesreich* (God's kingdom). Only two of the nine projected domes were completed, but it's still damn impressive. Today, the monastery-cum-palace is still functional, but most parts are open to the public. The ornate church contains the renowned high Gothic Verduner Altar, with its elaborate wood and gold detail. *(*Stiftsplatz 1. Open year-round M-Su 9am-5pm.*)* To quench your thirst for knowledge, visit the **museum** (open May-Nov. Tu-Su 10am-5pm). Call ahead for a guided tour of the complex. (Tel. (02243) 411212. Tours every 30min. 9am-noon and 1:30. 60AS, students 30AS.)

NEAR VIENNA: MÖDLING AND HEILIGENKREUZ

Trains and S-bahn #1 and 2 make the short journey from Vienna Südbahnhof to Mödling all day long (20min., 30AS; Eurailpass valid). Buses leave every hour from Südtiroler-Pl. in Vienna. In Mödling, bus #365 connects to Heiligenkreuz (dir.: Hinterbrühl; every 3hr., 19AS).

"Poor I am, and miserable," Beethoven wrote before his arrival in **Mödling.** Seeking physical and psychological rehabilitation, he schlepped all this way for that *je ne sais quoi* only a mineral spring could offer. He wrote *Missa Solemnis* within Mödling's embrace, and his spirits thoroughly improved. A recovering victim of industrialization, Mödling is slowly but surely regaining the charm that drew the likes of Schubert, Wagner, Strauss, Hugo Wolf, Schönberg, and Gustav Klimt here. From the train station, walk up the hill and left down Hauptstr. all the way to the end at the *Rathaus* (open M-F 8am-noon and 1-4pm). Hauptstr. provides delightful meandering, cafés, and shops. Head to Mödling's **tourist office** *(Gästedienst)*, Elisabethstr. 2 (tel. (02236) 26727), next to the *Rathaus*, for the lowdown on the city and *Privatzimmer*. When you're through wandering, pick up some picnic supplies and catch a bus into the countryside near **Heiligenkreuz**.

Heiligenkreuz itself is a both a peaceful village and a harmonious Cistercian monastery that seems to have grown whole from the grassy hills in this remote corner of Austrian countryside. The bus stops twice in Heiligenkreuz; get off at the second stop to visit the 700-year-old monastic retreat that bears the same name as the village. Founded by Leopold V, notorious for holding Richard the Lionheart for ransom, the monastery was originally intended as a "school of love" and a refor-mation of the pre-existing Benedictine order. Life at Heiligenkreuz has never been particularly austere, however—visit the *Weinkeller* where the monks still press their own grapes, enjoy beer and bratwurst in the shade of the *Stiftsgasthaus Heiligenkreuz*, or simply stand in the Zen-like quiet of the monastery's blooming central courtyard to experience the serene continuity of centuries. The vaulted chapel houses magnificent stained-glass windows, still intact despite threats from

VIENNA

stern church elders of putting the abbot, prior, and cellarers on a fast of bread and water until they were removed. Visitors can enter the abbey itself only by taking a tour. (Open 9am-6pm. 65AS, senior citizens 55AS, students 30AS, children 25AS.)

NEAR VIENNA: CARNUNTUM

Carnuntum is accessible by S-bahn S7 from Wien Mitte or Wien Nord (1hr., every 30min., 76AS). The park is a well-marked 10-minute walk from the station. You'll pass a little tourist office booth on the way to the park on Hauptstr. By car from Vienna, take highway A4, exit at Fischamend, and follow road B9 to Petronell-Carnuntum.

By 15 BC, the Romans had conquered the Alps, Dolomites, and Danube river valleys, using the river route to transport soldiers, slaves, and goods through the empire. Of their many outposts, which included Vindobona (Vienna), Iuavum (Salzburg), and Brigantium (Bregenz), Carnuntum was by far the largest and most impressive until conquered by the Germanic Alemanni tribe in the AD 3rd century. Archaeological digs have uncovered houses, public baths, canals, and a temple to the goddess Diana all dating from the first to 3rd centuries. Today, the site is a work-in-progress to discover and preserve that history. Most artifacts are on display in the **Archäologischer Park Carnuntum,** where you can sign up to tour the place or to take part in the digging. (Hauptstr. 465. Tel. (02163) 33770; fax 33775; email info@carnuntum.co.at; www.carnuntum.co.at. Open Apr.-Nov. M-F 9am-5pm, Sa-Su 9am-6pm. 48AS, students 38AS; guided tours 38AS.)

Twenty kilometers of bike paths lead from the train station through the Heidentor ruins (from 300 BC), an amphitheater, an ancient military camp, and (in nearby Bad Deutsch-Altenburg) the **Archäologisches Museum Carnuntum,** the largest Roman museum in Austria. (Open Jan. 15-Dec. 15 Tu-Su 10am-5pm. 60AS, students 40AS; guided tours 35AS. Combo museum/park ticket 85AS, students 60AS.) Carnuntum hosts annual Roman festivals including the **Roman Athletic Competition** in April, the **Art Carnuntum** fest from July to August with open-air cinema, theater, and concerts (tel. (02163) 3400 for information; email pb@artcarnuntum.co.at), and a **Roman Christmas market** in December.

NEAR VIENNA: STIFT ALTENBURG

Stift Altenburg can be reached by bus from Wien-Mitte directly (7am) or with a change in Horn (5 per day, 160AS). A pleasant option in good weather is to walk along the picturesque 6km path from Horn to the Stift (follow green signs).

The Benedictine abbey **Stift Altenburg,** founded in 1144 by Countess Hildburg von Poigen-Rebgau in memory of her deceased husband, swells with Baroque paintings and sculpture. The abbey was frequently attacked by Hussites and Swedes during the Thirty Years War, and most of what is visible now dates from after the sacking of the monastery by Swedish soldiers in 1645. Altenburg was subsequently rebuilt under the architect and pupil of Prandtauer, Joseph Munggenast, who replaced most of the Gothic cloister, although remnants of it have been excavated and are visible today. Stift Altenburg is famous not only for its magnificent church buildings, but also for the **library** housed within the abbey, conceived in the Baroque mind as a temple to human wisdom, in playful contrast to the neighboring temple to Divine Wisdom. Much of the art in the church and library, as well as the ceremonial staircase and intriguing **crypt,** was done by Paul Troger. His sculptures, paintings, and frescoes depict Biblical scenes along with benevolent mythological divinities. The abbey underwent extensive restoration after being badly damaged in both world wars. It hosts annual art exhibits and summer concerts given by the **Stift Altenburger Music Akademie.** (Open May-Nov. Tu-Su 9am-noon and 1-5pm. To see the crypt and library, you must take a guided tour 11am, 2, and 4pm. 60AS, students 30AS. Guided tours of the art exhibit 9:30am, 1, and 3pm. 80AS, students 40AS. Combination ticket for both tours 130AS, students 65AS. For more info contact the Stift (tel. (02982) 34 51 21; fax 34 51 13; email stift.altenburg@wvnet.at). For concert tickets, call (02982) 53080, in winter (011) 586 19 00.

NEAR VIENNA:BRATISLAVA, SLOVAKIA

Get to Bratislava by train from Vienna Südbahnhof (1-1½hr., 3-4 per day, 164AS).

Squeezed between Vienna and Budapest, Bratislava is experienced most often as a passing blip—a blur of Soviet-style apartment blocks, polluted roadways, and crumbling buildings—on the way to bigger, more cosmopolitan cities. Prague continues to loom over Bratislava, reminding Slovaks of the relative disappointment of post-Czechoslovak independence. However, Bratislava's cobblestoned Old Town hosts relaxing cafés, talented street musicians, and several stunning Baroque buildings, while vineyards and castle ruins lace the outskirts of town. If nothing else, Bratislava offers visitors the thrill of an "undiscovered" city, and a glimpse into the psyche of a nation struggling to redefine itself.

◪ ORIENTATION AND PRACTICAL INFORMATION. When you arrive in Bratislava, avoid getting off at the **Nové Mesto** train station; it's much farther from the center than **Hlavná stanica** (Main Station). To get downtown from Hlavná stanica, head straight past the waiting buses, turn right on [ancová and left on [tefánikova; or take tram 1 to "Poštová" at **nám. SNP** (the city center lies between nám. SNP and the river). From there, Uršulínska leads to the tourist office. From the bus station, take trolleybus 215 to the center; or turn right on Mlynské nivy, walk 10-minutes to Dunajska, then follow it to Kamenné nám (a block from the tourist office). The **tourist office,** called the **Bratislavská Informa⁻ná Slu°ba (BIS),** Klobu⁻nicka 2 (tel. 54 43 37 15 and 54 43 43 70; fax 54 43 27 08; email bis®isnet.sk; www.isnet.sk/bis). Sells maps (28Sk), gives city tours, and books rooms (singles July-Aug. 300Sk, Sept.-June 900Sk) for a 50Sk fee (open M-F 8am-7pm, Sa-Su 8:30am-1:30pm). **Trams** and **buses** run through the city throughout the day (4am-11pm; 10Sk per ride; buy tickets at kiosks or the orange *automats* in most bus stations). **Night buses** marked with black and orange numbers in the 500s require 2 10Sk tickets; they run at midnight and 3am. Most trams pass by nám. SNP, while most buses stop at the north base of Nový Most. The fine for joyriding is 1000Sk. **Tourist passes** are sold at some kiosks (24-hour 45Sk, 48-hour 80Sk, 3-day 100Sk, 7-day 150Sk). For **currency exchange, VÚB,** Gorkého 9 (tel. 59 55 79 76; fax 59 55 80 90), charges a 1% commission on traveler's checks (open M-W and F 8am-5pm, Th 8am-noon). A **24-hour currency exchange machine** outside Bank Austria, Mostová 6, changes US$, DM, and UK£ into Sk for no commission but at exorbitant rates. **ATMs** are everywhere.

▊▊ ACCOMMODATIONS AND FOOD. In July and August, several dorms open up as hostels; until then, good deals are hard to come by. Most cheap beds are near the station on the north side of town, a 20-minute walk or 5-minute tram ride from the center. Pensions or **private rooms** provide a cheap and comfortable alternative. Try **Pension Gremium,** Gorkého 11 (tel. 54 13 10 26; fax 54 43 06 53), centrally located off Hviezdoslavovo nám., which has fluffy beds, sparkling private showers, fans, and a popular café downstairs. (Singles 890Sk; doubles 1290Sk. Breakfast included. English spoken. Only 5 rooms, so call ahead. Check-out 9am. V, MC.) While the city is bursting with red-canopied cafés, virtually none serve food. A few restaurants serve the region's spicy meat mixtures with west Slovakia's celebrated **Modra** wine. If all else fails, you can always chow at one of Bratislava's ubiquitous burger or chicken stands. For **groceries,** try **Tesco Potraviny,** Kamenné nám. 1 (open M-W 8am-7pm, Th 8am-8pm, F 8am-9pm, Sa 8am-5pm, Su 9am-5pm). Dark alcoves with funky sculptures and a leafy terrace set **Prašná Bašta,** Zámo⁻nícka 11 (tel. 54 43 49 57) apart, as does their excellent traditional Slovak dishes (88-175Sk). Ask for the English menu. (Open daily 11am-11pm.) For dessert, head to **Antica Gelateria del Corso,** Michalská 14-16 (tel. 54 4193 38), which provides a large selection of Italian gelato (open daily 10am-midnight).

▣ ▥ SIGHTS AND MUSEUMS. Almost everything worth seeing in Bratislava is located in **Old Bratislava** (Stará Bratislava), centered around **nám. SNP.** From nám. SNP, which commemorates the bloody Slovak National Uprising against the fascist regime, walk down Uršulínska to **Primaciálné nám.** and the square's Neoclassi-

YOU WANT FRIES WITH THAT? The only thing less comprehensible to Westerners than a Slovakian menu is a menu at one of Bratislava's many burger stands. A *syrový burger* (cheeseburger) costs less than a *hamburger so syrom* (hamburger with cheese) because, as the stand owner will explain with humiliatingly clear logic, a cheeseburger is made of cheese—*only* cheese. A *pressburger,* named after Bratislava's former moniker Pressburg, consists of bologna on a bun, and hamburgers are actually ham. Everything comes boiled, except, of course, the cheese.

cal **Primate's Palace** (Primaciálny Palác), Primaciálne nám. 1, which dates from 1781. Napoleon and Austrian Emperor Franz I signed the Peace of Pressburg here in the Hall of Mirrors (Zrkadlová Sie) in 1805. (Open Tu-Su 10am-5pm. 20Sk.) A walk to the left (as you exit the palace) down Klobu⁻nícka leads to **Hlavné nám.;** from there, a quick right up Zámo⁻nicka will bring you to the 13th-century **St. Michael's Tower** (Michalská Brána), the only preserved gateway from the town's medieval fortifications (open M and W-F 10am-5pm, Sa-Su 11am-6pm; 20Sk to climb up and view the city). Retrace your steps to to Hlavné nám. and set foot in the square's Old Town Hall (Stará Radnica), Hlavné nám. 1, to view the **Town History Museum** (Muzeum Histórie Mesta). You don't need a ticket to see the wonderful 1:500 model of 1945-55 Bratislava just inside. (Open Tu-F 10am-5pm, Sa-Su 11am-6pm. 25Sk, students 10Sk.)

From Hlavné nám., walk left down Rybárska Brána until you reach the eastern end **Hviezdoslavovo nám,** dominated by the 1886 **Slovak National Theater** (Slovenské Národné Divadlo) to your left. Continue straight ahead down Mostová (the continuation of Rybárska Brána on the other side of the square) and turn left at the Dunaj river to reach the **Slovak National Museum** (Slovenské Národné Múzeum), Vajanského nábr. 2, which houses local archaeological finds including casts of Neanderthal skeletons (open Tu-Su 9am-5pm; 20Sk, students 10Sk). Backtrack along the Dunaj past nám. Štúra to the **Slovak National Gallery**, Rázusovo nábr. 2, which displays sculpture, frescoes, and paintings from the Gothic and Baroque periods, as well as some modern works (open Tu-Su 10am-6pm; 25Sk, students 5Sk). Continue with the Dunaj on your left to **New Bridge** (Nový Most), whose reins are held by a giant flying saucer (10Sk to climb to the top). Turn right on Staromestská and follow it away from the river to get to **St. Martin's Cathedral** (Dóm sv. Martina), a fairly typical Gothic church where the kings of Hungary were crowned for 3 centuries (now undergoing renovations). Cross the highway on the far side of St. Martin's using the pedestrian overpass to view articles of a vanished population at the **Museum of Jewish Culture** (Múzeum Zidovskej Kultúry) at Zidovská 17 (open M-F and Su 11am-5pm; last entry 4:30pm) 50Sk). **Schlossberg**, the old Jewish quarter, was bulldozed in the name of "progress."

Perched on a hill to the west of the city center, and just uphill from the Museum of Jewish Culture, the 4-towered **Bratislava Castle** (Bratislavský hrad) is Bratislava's defining landmark. Of strategic importance for more than a millennium, the castle's heyday came in the 18th century, when Austrian Empress Maria Theresa held court there. The castle was destroyed by fire in 1811 and by bombs during WWII; what's left today is largely communist-era restoration. The view of the Danube is more impressive than the castle itself. The **Historical Museum** (Historické Muzeum) inside displays temporary exhibits from the Slovak National Museum (open Tu-Su 9am-5pm; 30Sk, students 15Sk).

🎭 **ENTERTAINMENT AND NIGHTLIFE.** For film, concert, and theater schedules, get a copy of *Kám v Bratislave* at the tourist office; although it's entirely in Slovak, the info is easy to decipher. **Slovenská Filharmonia** plays regularly at Palackého ul. 2; the box office is around the corner on Medená (tel. 54 43 33 51; open M-Tu and Th-F 1-7pm, W 8am-2pm). The Filharmonia as well as most theaters vacation in July and August. Tickets to the **National Theater** (Národné Divadlo) are sold at the box office at Laurinská 20 (open M-F noon-6pm; tickets from 50Sk). A dozen **cinemas** are scattered across the city; unfortunately, most films are dubbed into Slovak. Bratislava's sleekest twenty-somethings gather at the **Alligator Club,** Laurinská 7, to hear live rock and blues bands (daily at 7pm) and sip mixed drinks (80-120Sk; open M-F 10am-midnight, Sa 11am-midnight, Su 11am-10pm). **Dubliner,** Sedlarská 6, Bratislava's *ersatz* Irish pub, has pricey Guinness (75Sk) and local brands (45Sk; open M-Sa 10am-1am, Su 11am-midnight).

BURGENLAND

Just southeast of Vienna, Burgenland is Austria's most scarcely populated province (pop. 70,000) and one of Austria's last territorial acquisitions. Until Burgenland was ceded to Austria in 1921, it was part of Hungary; in fact, it owes its name to 3 castles that now lie beyond its borders. Given its history, it is not surprising that Burgenland has a Hungarian-influenced cuisine and pockets of Hungarian speakers in the more rural parts of the province. However, Burgenland's Hungarians are now outnumbered by the region's Croatian minority, which accounts for 10% of the population. Local Hungarian landowners invited Croation settlers into the region in the 16th century, to restore the area after widespread devastation byt the Ottoman Turks. Geographically, Burgenland is quite diverse, stretching from a region of rolling hills and dense woodlands in the west to the Neusiedlersee in the north-east, with the Leitha River running along its northern border and the peaks of the Rosaliengebirge marking the present Hungarian border. Burgenland's gentle hills and lush river valleys make it world-famous for its rich wines and Heurigen (cozy, vine-hung taverns).

EISENSTADT

Where I wish to live and die.
    —Josef Haydn

Haydn, *Heurigen,* and Huns are the three pillars of Eisenstadt's cultural significance, the tiny provincial capital of Burgenland (pop. 11,000). As court composer for the **Eszterházy** princes, powerful Hungarian landholders claiming descent from Attila the Hun, **Josef Haydn** composed the melodies here that inspired Mozart. The town is still basking in his glory. To this day one of the wealthiest families in Europe, the Eszterházys first settled in Eisenstadt when it was part of Hungary and decided to remain there even after the change in borders. Today they own many of the region's famed vineyards, whose new wines rival those produced in Bordeaux.

⊿ ORIENTATION AND PRACTICAL INFORMATION. Trains leave for Eisenstadt from **Wien Meidling** in Vienna (1hr., 2-3 per hr., 76AS). Another option is to take the S-bahn from the Südbahnhof (1½hr., every hr., 95AS) and switch trains in **Neusiedl am See,** or you may find it more convenient to take a direct **bus** from **Wien Mitte** to Eisenstadt (1½hr., every hr. 6am-8:45pm, 70AS). Buses run from Eisenstadt to **Rust, Mörbisch,** and **Wiener Neustadt.** The **bus station** (tel. 2350) is on Dompl. next to the cathedral. To get to Eisenstadt by **car,** take Bundesstr. 16 or Autobahn A2 or A3 south from Vienna (50km). From Wiener Neustadt, take Bundesstr. 153 or Autobahn S4 east. There is an underground parking garage (25AS per hr.) outside the Eszterházy Palace.

Eisenstadt is centered around Hauptstr., the city's *Fußgängerzone.* From the train station, follow Bahnstr. (which becomes St. Martinstr. then Fanny Eißlerg.) to the middle of this central area (20min.). From the bus stop, walk half a block to the church. With your back to the church, cross Pfarrg. and walk down tiny Marck-ingstr. to Hauptstr. Turn left and walk to the end, where Schloß Eszterházy is on your right. The **tourist office** (tel. 67390; fax 67391; email tve.info@bnet.at) is in the right wing of the castle. The staff has information on accommodations, musical events, guided tours, and *Heurigen* in Eisenstadt and surroundings. For a rural living experience, ask about *Beim Bauern Zur Gast,* which lists winegrowers who rent rooms in their houses. The station (tel. 62637) **rents bikes** (150AS per day, 120AS per half-day; with train ticket 100AS, 80AS; mountain bikes 175-200AS; reservations advised). **Exchange currency** at the post office or at **Creditanstalt Bankverein** on the corner of St. Martin and Dompl. (open M-Th 8am-1pm and 2-4pm, F 8am-3pm). **Public bathrooms** are at Dompl., Eszterházy Palace, and the parking lot behind Colmanpl. near the tourist office. The **post office** (tel. 62271), on the corner of Pfarrg. and Semmelweise, has good rates for traveler's checks (open M-F 7am-6pm, Sa 7am-1pm). The **postal code** is A-7000.

PHONE CODE	The **city code** for Eisenstadt is 02682.

▌▛ ACCOMMODATIONS AND FOOD. Consider Eisenstadt as a daytrip—with no youth hostel in the vicinity, *Privatzimmer* are the only budget option. Most are on the outer city limits and rent only during July and August. The youth hostels in **Vienna** (see p. 96), **Neusiedl am See** (see p. 143), and **Wiener Neustadt** are cheaper and only an hour away. During July and August, migrant hordes descend and reservations are a must. At **Gasthaus Kutsenits,** Mattersburgerstr. 30 (tel. 63511), a clean, quiet room can be yours at a reasonable price if you're willing to walk a kilometer. From Schloß Eszterházy, head down Rusterstr. to Mattersburgerstr. (Singles 250 AS, with shower 350AS; doubles 400AS, with shower 500AS; 50AS supplement for 1-night stays. Breakfast included.) At **Wirtshaus zum Eder,** Hauptstr. 25 (tel. 62645), in Hauptpl., you can engage in deep conversation over wine in an airy courtyard before retiring for the night (singles 440-590AS; doubles 590AS; triples 790AS; breakfast included).

When looking for food in Eisenstadt, your best bet is to wander along Hauptstr., following your nose. **Café Central,** Hauptstr. 40 (tel. 75 22 34), is a pleasant, unassuming little café (named after the famous Viennese haunt) in a shady courtyard off the main street, where a quiet crowd consumes scrumptious baguettes (40AS) and ice cream specialties (open M-Th 7am-midnight, F-Sa 7am-2am, Su 9am-midnight). Near the palace and opposite the hospital, **Stüberl zum "alten Gewölbe,"** Eszterházystr. 21 (tel. 73813), features a daily *Menü* of homemade soup, entree, and dessert for 58AS. Quench your thirst with fresh-pressed carrot or apple juice for 15AS. (Open M-F 6:30am-6pm.) Another option is to grab some big, cheap *Schnit-*

BURGENLAND

zelsemmeln (a mere 29AS) and other meaty sandwiches at **Fischhandlung Golosetti** (tel. 62437), in the middle of Joseph-Stanislaus-Albachg. off Hauptpl. The many **Heurigen** offer modest, generally affordable meals with their wines. Grocery stores are always the cheapest option; try **Spar Markt**, Eszterházystr. 38 and Bahnstr. 16-18 (both open M-F 7am-12:30pm and 2:30-6pm, Sa 7am-noon), or **Julius Meinl**, Hauptstr. 13 (open M-F 8am-6pm, Sa 7:30am-noon).

📷 🎏 **SIGHTS AND FESTIVALS.** As one might expect, most of the sights in Eisenstadt are directly connected to Haydn or the Eszterházy family, but they're authentic and sincere enough to interest all comers, Haydn fans or no.

THE ESZTERHÁZY PALACE. Built on the footings of the Kanizsai family's 14th-century fortress, the castle-turned-palace now known as **Schloß Eszterházy** acquired its cheerful hue when the Hungarian Eszterházy family showed allegiance to the great Austrian Empress in the 18th century by painting the building *Maria Theresien gelb* (Maria Theresian yellow). More recently, the fabulously wealthy Eszterházys, who still own the building, leased the family home to the Austrian provincial government, allowing the bureaucrats to occupy 40% of the castle while the family retrenched itself in the remaining 60%. When it bought its portion for 125,000AS, the government apparently overlooked the Eszterházys's clause that made it responsible for renovation and maintenance costs. Rumor has it the government has spent more than 40 million *Schilling*s on the upkeep of the Red Salon's silk tapestry alone. In the magnificent **Haydnsaal** (Haydn Hall), the hard-working composer conducted the court orchestra almost every night from 1761 to 1790. Classical musicians consider the Haydnsaal an acoustic mecca. When the government took over the room, they removed the marble floor and replaced it with a wooden one. Now the room is so acoustically perfect that seats for concerts in the room are not numbered—supposedly every seat provides the same magnificent sound. Guest artists are invited to sing, but more often than not Haydn fills the hall. During tours of the *Schloß*, tourists are encouraged to lift their voices in song in order to test out the hall's sound properties. Even when the music stops, the room is an aristocratic symphony of red velvet, gold, monumental oil paintings, and woodwork. *(At the end of Hauptstr. Tel. 71930. 50min. tours Easter-Oct. daily every hr. on the hour 9am-4pm; Oct.-Easter M-F. 50AS, students and seniors 30AS.)*

HAYDN EVENTS. Catering to the town's Haydn obsession, **Haydnmatinees** (tel. 71930; fax 719 32 23), held from May to October feature four fine fellows, bewigged and bejeweled in Baroque costumes of imperial splendor, playing a half-hour of impeccable Haydn. *(Tu and F 11am in the palace. 80AS.)* The palace also hosts **Haydnkonzerte.** *(July-Aug. Th at 8pm; May-June and Sept.-Oct. Sa at 7:30pm. 160-320AS.)* True Haydn enthusiasts can wait for The Big One: the **Internationale Haydntage**, featuring concerts, operas, and large free video screenings of the best of past festival concerts outdoors near the *Schloß*. The festival runs from September 7 to 17. *(Festival office tel. 61866; fax 61805; email office@hadynfestival.at. Tickets 200-1400AS.)*

THE OLD TOWN. The *Kapellmeister* had a short commute to the concert hall each day: he lived just around the corner. His modest residence is now the **Haydn-Haus,** Haydng. 21 (tel. 62652), where original manuscripts and other memorabilia are exhibited. *(Open Easter-Oct. daily 9am-noon and 1-5pm. Guided tours by appointment.*

EISENSTADT'S JEWISH COMMUNITY The history of Jews in Eisenstadt is an extraordinary tale of growth and tragic downfall. As early as 1675, Prince Paul Eszterházy was moved by the plight of the persecuted Jews and decided to shelter them as "Schutzjuden" (protected Jews) on his estates. From 1732 on, the Jewish quarter of Eisenstadt formed the prosperous independent community of "Unterberg-Eisenstadt," which remained unique in Europe until 1938. In that year, the Jews of the Burgenland were among the first to be affected by the deportation orders of the Nazis. Today, only a few Jewish families remain in Eisenstadt.

30AS, students 15AS. Combination ticket for Haydn-Haus and Landesmuseum 50AS, students 25AS.) After composing in Eisenstadt, Haydn now decomposes here. The *maestro* lies buried in the **Bergkirche** (tel. 62638). From the palace, make a right on to Eszterházystr. and walk two blocks. Haydn's remains were placed there in 1932 after phrenologists removed his head to search for signs of musical genius on the skull's surface. After being displayed at the Vienna Music Museum for years, Haydn's head was reunited with his body in 1954. Entrance to the *Bergkirche* includes admission to the **Kalvarienberg,** a pilgrimage annex to the church, which illustrates the 14 Stations of the Cross with hand-carved Biblical figures. Stand in the central nave and try to distinguish the real Doric columns from the *trompe l'oeil* paintings. The church's rooftop stations provide a great view of surrounding Burgenland. *(Open Easter-Oct. daily 9am-noon and 1-5pm. 30AS, students 15AS.)*

JEWISH MUSEUM. On a different note, Eisenstadt's **Jüdisches Museum** presents a history of Jewish life in Eisenstadt and the Burgenland region. The Eszterházys were known for their hospitality toward Jews, who played a major part in their rise to power. By settling Jews in Eisenstadt, they circumvented the law preventing Christians from lending money with interest. The museum's display is organized according to Jewish holidays and contains religious items dating from the 17th century. The building contains an original private synagogue with a beautiful ark in the style of Empress Josephine as well as Gothic and Oriental murals from the early 1800s. *(From the palace, make a right and then another right onto Glorietteallee, then your first left to Unterbergstr. 6. Tel. 65145; email info@oejudmus.or.at; www.oejudmus.or.at/ oejudmus. Open May-Oct. T-Su 10am-5pm. 50AS; students 40AS.)* Around the corner on Wertheimer-Str., near the hospital, is a small **Jewish cemetery** dating back several centuries.

FESTIVALS. Leaving Eisenstadt without sampling the wine would be like leaving Vienna without tasting *Sachertorte*. In early July the Winzerkirtag Kleinhöflein floods Hauptpl. with kegs, flasks, and bottles as local wineries attempt to sell their goods. Mid-August brings the Festival of 1000 Wines, when wineries from all over Burgenland crowd the palace's *Orangerie* with their Dionysian delicacies. If you like music with your wine, visit at the end of May when the free, outdoor Eisenstadt Fest provides all kinds of sounds, from classical music to rock. At any other time of the year, fresh wine is available straight from the source in the wineries themselves. Most are small and aren't allowed to open for more than three weeks per year to sell their wine. Fear not—the wineries stagger their opening times so that wine is always available. To find out which *Buschenschenken*, or *Schenkhäuser*, are open, ask the tourist office for the schedule or look in the local newspaper. Most of the *Buschenschenken* are clustered in Kleinhöfler-Hauptstr.

NEAR EISENSTADT: FERTŐD, HUNGARY

Buses leave hourly for Fertőd from platform #11 in Sopron's station on Lackner Kristóf (45min., 265Ft). There is a hotel inside the mansion; after a period of renovation, it should reopen in 2000. For reservations, especially during the Haydn Festival in early fall, book with Ciklámen Tourist in Sopron, Ógabona tér 8 (tel. (99) 31 20 40), on the way to city center from the bus station.

If you haven't had enough of the Eszterhazys after Eisenstadt, you can wander over the Hungarian border to **Fertőd** (FER-tewd), 27km east of Sopron, where you'll find an even more magnificent, Baroque **Eszterházy Palace,** Bartók Béla u. 2 (tel. (99) 37 09 71), nicknamed the "Hungarian Versailles." Miklós Eszterházy, known as **Miklós the Sumptuous** before he squandered his family's vast fortune, ordered the palace built in 1766 to host his extended bacchanal feasts, claiming boldly, "What the emperor can afford, I can afford as well." The mansion grounds alone, which encompass an opera house, a Chinese pavilion, and a puppet theatre, make a visit worthwhile. Though the uninhabited palace interior is now somewhat bare, the tour (1hr.) explains everything from the marble floors to the painted ceilings, including the cleverly concealed door in the prince's bedroom. Used as a stable and then a hospital during WWII, the mansion was restored with much-needed

BURGENLAND

government funds directly after the 1957 revolution; the investment is now protected by the felt slippers visitors are forced to don upon entrance. Another celebrated Eisenstadt resident has close ties to both the Eszterházys and Fertőd—**Josef Haydn** spent 30 years composing here; **concerts** held during the annual fall **Haydn Festival** recreate the premier performances of many of his most famous works. (Check at Tourinform in Sopron for a schedule. Előkapu u. 11. Tel. 33 88 92. Open M-F 9am-5pm, Sa 9am-noon.) The mansion itself hides behind an area of tall greenery, across from the parking lot with souvenir stands. (Open Apr. 16-Dec. 15 Tu-Su 9am-5pm; Dec. 16-Apr. 15 Tu-Su 9am-4pm. 600Ft, students 250Ft.)

THE NEUSIEDLERSEE REGION

Burgenland's major lake, the Neusiedlersee, is a mere vestige (320 sq. km) of the water that once blanketed the entire Pannenian Plain. It is so large that you cannot see the opposite shore, but, with no outlets or inlets save underground springs, Austria's only steppe lake never gets deeper than 2m. The water line recedes periodically, exposing thousands of square meters of dry land, and from 1868-1872, the lake dried up entirely. Warm and salty, the lake is a haven for more than 250 species of waterfowl. The marsh reeds (sometimes almost 2m high) that surround the lake shelter many rare animals and plants, including bugs, which can make it unpleasant to swim anywhere other than at designated areas. **Storks,** however, thrive on this vegetation—see if you can spot their chimney-nests, believed to bring good luck. In 1992, the lake and surrounding area was incorporated into the national park **Neusiedlersee-Seewinkel,** in order to preserve this natural wonder for generations of birds.

Humans enjoy the lake as well, with thousands of sun-hungry vacationers visiting its resorts each summer for swimming, sailing, fishing, and cycling. **Cruises** on the Neusiedlersee allow you to travel between Rust, Illmitz, and Mörbisch with your bike for 60AS one-way and 100AS round-trip. **Gangl** (tel. (02175) 2158 or 2794) runs boats every hour from Illmitz to Mörbisch (May-Sept. 9am-6pm). In Mörbisch, **Schifffahrt Weiss** (tel. (02685) 8324) cruises to Illmitz (May-Sept. every 30 min. 8:30am-9pm). For more information about the region, contact the **Neusiedlersee Regionalbüro** at Hauptpl. 1, A-7100 Neusiedl am See (tel. (02167) 8717; fax (02167) 2637; email info@neusiedl-tourism.or.at; www.neusiedl-tourism.or.at/info-ns/).

NEUSIEDL AM SEE

Less than an hour from Vienna by express train, Neusiedl am See is the gateway to the Neusiedlersee region. The principal attraction is the lake, not the town, so consider Neusiedl a day at the beach. Proximity to the lake, the array of water sports, and affordable accommodations make Neusiedl a popular destination for families with children.

⊠ ORIENTATION AND PRACTICAL INFORMATION. Neusiedl am See's **Hauptbahnhof,** 15 minutes by foot from the town center, is the destination of trains from Vienna and Eisenstadt. (Information and ticket window open 5am-9pm. Eisenstadt 19AS; Vienna 76AS.) By **car** from Vienna, take A4 or route 10 east. From Eisenstadt, take route 50 north and route 51 east. To get to town, take a right on Bahnstr. and follow the road right onto Eisenstädterstr. (which becomes Obere Hauptstr.) and into Hauptpl. The **bus station,** centrally located on Seestr. 15a, at the end of Untere Hauptstr. (tel. 24 06), offers a **Fahrradbus** (#1813) that carries bikers and bikes to and from Mörbisch, Neusiedl, and Illmitz. There's frequent service to **Vienna** (95AS) and **Bruck an der Leitha** (38AS).

The **tourist office** (tel. 2229; fax 2637), in the *Rathaus* on Hauptpl., helps with accommodations and offers advice on boat and bike rentals (open July-Aug. M-F 8am-7pm, Sa 10am-noon and 2-6pm, Su 4-7pm; May-June and Sept. M-F 8am-4:30pm; Oct.-Apr. M-Th 8am-noon and 1-4:30pm, F 8am-1pm). **Raiffeisbank,** Untere Hauptstr. 3 (tel. 25 64), has the best **currency exchange** rates (open M-F 8am-

12:30pm and 1:30-4pm). Given the sprawling town layout, it may make your day easier to **rent a bike** at the train station (70AS per half-day, 90AS per day with train ticket, otherwise for 120AS and 150AS). **Store luggage** at the train station as well (30AS). Dial 133 in an **emergency.** The **post office,** Untere Hauptstr. 53, is on the corner of Untere Hauptstr. and Lisztg. (open M-F 8am-noon and 2-6pm, Sa 8-10am). The **postal code** is A-7100.

PHONE CODE	The **city code** for Neusiedl am See is 02167.

■░▓ ACCOMMODATIONS, FOOD, AND ACTIVITIES. Heavy tourist activity, partly generated by Neusiedl's proximity to Vienna, makes finding accommodations tough. To reach the newly renovated **Jugendherberge Neusiedl am See (HI)**, Herbergg. 1 (tel./fax 2252), follow Wienerstr. and turn left onto Goldbergg. The hostel is on the corner at Herbergg. It's an uphill walk, but don't get discouraged—renovations have equipped the hostel with a sauna and winter greenhouse. The hostel sports 86 beds in 21 quads and one double. There are showers in every room, but bathrooms are in the hall. (170AS, under 19 150AS. Breakfast included. Sheets 20AS. Key deposit 100AS. Reception 8am-2pm and 5-8pm. Open Mar.-Oct. Reservations recommended.) **Gasthof zur Traube,** Hauptpl. 9 (tel. 2423), with its cordial staff and pretty pink rooms is family-friendly (singles 410AS; doubles 650AS; breakfast included). **Rathausstüberl** (tel. 2883; fax 288307), around the corner from the *Rathaus* on Kircheng., has a lovely shaded courtyard, great wine, and plenty of fresh fish and vegetarian dishes (entrees 70-150AS; open Mar.-Dec. daily 10am-midnight). **Rathausstüberl** doubles as a sunny 15-room *Pension* with 2 singles and 13 doubles (270-490AS per person with breakfast buffet; reservations recommended). On your way to the beach grab a picnic at the **Billa** grocery store on Seestr. (open M-Th 7:30am-6:30pm, F 7:30am-8pm, Sa 7am-5pm). **Rauchkuchl,** Obere Hauptstr. 57 (tel. 2585), offers *Blaufränker* red wine or other homemade specialties as well as the opportunity to hear local dialect (open Tu-Sa 5-11pm).

You're here, you've got your bathing suit and towel, now where's the **beach?** Head to the end of Seestr. (1km), or catch the bus from the *Hauptbahnhof* or Hauptpl. (every hr. until 6pm). The beach is a bit rocky, but pleasant (25AS, children 20AS). The **Segelschule Neusiedl am See** (tel. 340044) at the docks on the far right will rent you a sailboard (1hr. 148-160AS, half- or full-day 450-800AS), dinghy (3- to 4-person boat 160AS per hr.), or standard surfboard (400AS for the weekend; open daily 8:30am-6pm). Close by on Seestr., you'll find **paddleboats** (80AS per hr.) and **rowboats** (40AS per hr.) at **Bootsvermietung Leban.**

In August, Neusiedl hosts a **Stadtfest,** during which the *Fußgängerzone* comes to life with countless food booths and modern music bands. Admission is free; call the festival information office for more information (open daily 1-3pm; tel. 3293).

RUST

During the summer, tourists inundate the tiny wine capital of Austria to partake of the fruit of the vine. Ever since 1524, when the Emperor granted the wine-growers of Rust the exclusive right to mark the letter "R" on wine barrels, Rust has been synonymous with good—really good—wine. The town is particularly known for sweet dessert wines, called *Ausbruch* (literally "outbreak"). They come from grapes allowed to dry toward raisinhood and sweeten up before the farmer "breaks out" the center and presses the juice. The quantity of desiccated grapes needed for a bottle is astounding, and consequently, so is the price. Income from the wine enabled the town to purchase its independence from Kaiser Leopold I in 1861. The price? 60,000 gold guilders and 36,000 liters of priceless *Ausbruch*. Wine isn't Rust's only attraction, however. The unspoiled town center with medieval houses and nesting storks and Rust's location on the Neusiedlersee make this town one of the most addictively beautiful places of the Austrian countryside.

🚪 ORIENTATION AND PRACTICAL INFORMATION. Rust lies 17km east of Eisenstadt on the Neusiedlersee. Rust does not have a train station, but **postal buses** run between **Eisenstadt** and Rust several times per day (38AS), and between Rust and **Vienna** (Wien Mitte/Landstr.) four times a day (114AS). The **bus station** is a glorified bus stop located just behind the post office at Franz-Josef-Pl. 14. By **car** from Vienna, take Autobahn A3 to Eisenstadt and then from Eisenstadt take Bundesstr. 52 straight into Rust. To reach the *Fußgängerzone* (whose *Fußgänger* status is sometimes disrupted by the gentle roar of tractors rumbling down village streets), leave the post office and turn left. You will almost immediately come to the intersection of four streets, with Conradpl. diagonally across the intersection. Walk straight across Conradpl. to the triangular plaza where the *Rathaus* stands. Inside, the **tourist office** (tel. 4502 or 6574; fax 50210) hands out maps, plans bicycle tours, and gives information on wine tastings, the beach, and *Privatzimmer* (open M-F 9am-noon and 2-6pm, Sa 9am-noon, Su 10am-noon; Oct.-Apr. M-F 9am-noon and 1-4pm). The **Raiffeisenkasse Rust,** Rathauspl. 5 (tel. 607 05), is the best place to **exchange money** (open M-F 8am-noon and 1:30-4pm). The Raiffeisenkasse has a 24-hour **ATM. Reisebüro Blaguss** in the *Rathaus* and **Ruster Freizeitcenter** (tel. 595) by the beach are open late and provide emergency currency exchange. Call **taxis** at tel. 6576. The **post office,** Franz-Josefs-Pl., exchanges money but not traveler's checks (open M-F 8am-noon and 2-6pm). The **postal code** is A-7071.

PHONE CODE	The **city code** for Rust is 02685.

📫🍴 ACCOMMODATIONS AND FOOD. If you want to stay in Rust, getting a *Privatzimmer* is the way to go. Reservations are strongly recommended for all *Privatzimmer* during festival times (July and August). Some will not accept telephone reservations for a one-night stay, but most won't turn you away at the door if there's a free room. Be warned: prices may rise in the high season. You'll receive a warm welcome at **Gästehaus Ruth,** Dr. Alfred-Ratzg. 1 (tel. 4277 or 6828; fax 6828), where rooms range from 210-250AS. Rust's new **Jugendgästehaus,** administered from Conradpl. 1, but located half a mile away at Ruster Bucht 2 (tel. 591; fax 5914) sits on the beachfront near tennis courts and bike paths. Dorms cost 150-180AS per night. From April through October, there's always room for tent-dwellers at **Ruster Freizeitcenter** (tel. 595), which offers showers, washing machines, a game room, a playground, and a grocery store. (Reception 7:30am-10pm. 44-55AS, children 16-27AS; tent 38-44AS. Showers included.) The grounds are only five minutes from the beach, to which guests receive free entrance.

You'll find plenty of good eating options along Rathausstr., though the ravenous should seek out **Zum Alten Haus** (tel. 230), on the corner of Raiffenstr. and Franz Josefpl., which serves up enormous portions of *Schnitzel* and salad for only 80AS (open Tu-Su 9am-10pm). Ubiquitous vineyard-restaurants called *Buschenschenken* offer cheap snacks and superb wine; the tourist office has a complete list. Though a bit far from town, **Alte Schmiede** (tel. 467), Seezeile 24, roofed with grape vines, serves traditional Austrian food with a Hungarian twist. **A & O Markt Dreyseitel** (tel. 238) on Weinbergg. between Mitterg. and Schubertg. sells the raw materials for a meal (open M-F 7am-noon and 3-6pm).

📷🎭 SIGHTS AND ENTERTAINMENT. Wine and storks are the primary reasons to come to Rust, though its *Altstadt* is one of the three in Austria named a "model city" by the Council of Europe (the others are Salzburg and Krems). The award praises Rust's architectural and natural preservation. Rust's dusty stucco lanes are quiet and slow, lined with shady elms.

WINE ACADEMY. Rust is home to Austria's only **Weinakademie.** The institution offers courses ranging from wine cultivation to basic bartending, and holds wine tours and tastings. *(Hauptstr. 31. Tel. 6451 or 453; fax 6431. Open for wine tastings F-Su 2-6pm. 150AS for 10 tastes.)* Many vintners *(Weinbauern)* offer wine tastings and

It's a **big world.**

And we've got the **network** to cover it.

Use **AT&T Direct**® Service
when you're out exploring the world.

Global
connection
with the AT&T
Network

AT&T
direct
service

Exploring the corners of the earth? We're with you. With the world's most powerful network, **AT&T Direct® Service** gives you fast, clear connections from more countries than anyone,* and the option of an English-speaking operator. All it takes is your AT&T Calling Card. And the planet is yours.

For a list of AT&T Access Numbers, take the attached wallet guide.

AT&T

*Comparison to major U.S.-based carriers.

AT&T

AT&T Direct® Service

AT&T Access Numbers

Austria ●	0800-200-288	Egypt ● (Cairo)	510-0200
Albania ●	00-800-0010	(Outside Cairo)	02-510-0200
Armenia ● ▲	8◆10111	Estonia	800-800-1001
Bahrain	800-000	Finland ●	9800-100-10
Belgium ●	0-800-100-10	France	0-800-99-0011
Bulgaria ▲	00-800-0010	Germany	0800-2255-288
Croatia	0800-220111	Greece ●	00-800-1311
Czech Rep. ▲	00-42-000-101	Hungary ●	00-800-01111
Cyprus ●	080-90010	Ireland ✓	1-800-550-000
Denmark	8001-0010	Israel	1-800-94-94-949

Italy ●	172-1011	Russia ● ▲	
Luxembourg †	0-800-0111	(Moscow) ▶	755-5042
Macedonia, F.Y.R. of ○		(St. Petersburg) ▶	325-5042
	99-800-4288	Saudi Arabia ◇	1-800-10
Malta	0800-890-110	South Africa	0-800-99-0123
Monaco ●	800-90-288	Spain	900-99-00-11
Morocco	002-11-0011	Sweden	020-799-111
Netherlands ●	0800-022-9111	Switzerland ●	0-800-89-0011
Norway	800-190-11	Turkey ●	00-800-12277
Poland ● ▲	00-800-111-1111	U.K. ▲ ❖	0800-89-0011
Portugal ▲	0800-800-128	U.K. ▲ ❖	0500-89-0011
Romania ●	01-800-4288	U.A. Emirates ●	800-121

FOR EASY CALLING WORLDWIDE
1. Just dial the AT&T Access Number for the country you are calling from.
2. Dial the phone number you're calling. *3.* Dial your card number.

For access numbers not listed ask any operator for **AT&T Direct®** Service. In the U.S. call 1-800-331-1140 for a wallet guide listing all worldwide AT&T Access Numbers.
Visit our Web site at: www.att.com/traveler
Bold-faced countries permit country-to-country calling outside the U.S.
  ● Public phones require coin or card deposit.
  ▲ May not be available from every phone/payphone.
  ▶ Additional charges apply outside the city.
  ◇ Calling available to most countries.
  ◆ Await second dial tone.
  ✓ Use U.K. access number in N. Ireland.
  ❖ If call does not complete, use 0800-013-0011.
  † Collect calling from public phones.
  ○ Public phones require local coin payment through the call duration.

When placing an international call *from* the U.S., dial 1 800 CALL ATT.
©1999 AT&T

LOOK WHAT THE STORK BROUGHT Since 1910,

Rust's storks have been attracted to the high chimneys of the *Bürger* houses, and by 1960 nearly 40 pairs were nesting in the old city. Soon, however, locals noticed a decline and began to voice their concern over the dwindling number of these endangered birds. In 1987, Rust and the World Wildlife Federation initiated a special program to protect and reestablish the birds. The storks eat mainly frogs, fish, snakes, and beetles—critters found among Neusiedlersee's reedy marshes. When the reeds grew too tall, the storks had difficulty finding food. Rust borrowed cattle from another part of Austria and set them in the marshes as natural lawnmowers. Blue placards mark the houses with chimneys that the storks habitually return to nest in. The storks come to Rust at the end of March, and from the end of May you can see the (stork) babies in the nests. The chicks stay home for 2 months before flying away and beginning their adult lives. The storks have also hatched a post office, the **Storks' Post Office,** A-7071 Rust, at the *Rathaus*. Its stork postmark provides funds to support the birds.

tours of their cellars and vineyards. **Rudolf Beilschmidt,** Weinbergg. 1 (tel. 326) has tours May through September on Fridays at 5pm. **Weingut Marienhof,** Weinbergg. 16 (tel. 251), conducts tours on Tuesdays from April to September at 6pm (60AS).

FISHERMAN'S CHURCH. Rust's **Fischerkirche,** around the corner from the tourist office, was built between the 12th and 16th centuries and is the oldest church in Burgenland. In the 13th century, Queen Mary of Hungary, after being rescued from the Mongols by fishermen, donated the Marienkapelle, an interior chapel containing lovely 15th-century sculptures of Madonna. Fortunately, the Romanesque and Gothic sections have survived the ravages of Baroque remodeling fervor. *(Open May-Sept. M-Sa 10am-noon and 2:30-6pm, Su 11am-noon and 2-4pm. Tours by appointment. Call Frau Kummer at tel. 550. 10AS, students 5AS.)*

LAKE ACCESS AND ACTIVITIES. Sun worshippers can sit and splash on the south shore of the **Neusiedlersee.** There is a **public beach** complete with showers, lockers, restrooms, phones, water slide, and snack bar. Though the murky waters of the lake daunt some swimmers, the water is actually of drinking quality. The muddy color comes from the shallow, easily disturbed clay bottom (2m at its deepest). For wimps who remain unconvinced, the beach also has a chlorine pool. Be sure to keep the entrance card—you'll need it to exit the park again. *(Tel. 501. 40AS per person, after 4pm 30AS.)* To reach the beach, walk down Hauptstr., take a left onto Am Seekanal, then a right onto Seepromenade, which cuts through all of the marsh lands (about 7km) surrounding the perimeter of the lake.

If lounging at the beach isn't active enough for you, rent a **boat** from **Family Gmeiner** (tel. 493 or (62683) 5538), next to the beach on the water's edge. **Sailboats** are 60AS per hour or 270AS for 5 hours. **Paddleboats** are 80AS per hour, 325AS for five hours. **Electric boats** are 130AS per hour, 380AS for five hours. The same company runs **Schiffrundfahrten** (boat tours) that can transport you to Illmitz on the opposite shore. *(Boats leave Rust Apr.-Oct. Th-Su and holidays at 10am and 4pm and return from Illmitz at 11am and 5pm.)* Besides swimming, boating, and bird-watching, tourists flock to the Neusiedlersee area to **bike.** The lake area is criss-crossed with bicycle routes, many along the lake shore or winding in and out of the little towns along the Austro-Hungarian border. The route covers 170km, but those out for less intense biking can do a section and then take the bus back, or take the Illmitz boat to the opposite shore and then bicycle back.

NEAR RUST: MÖRBISCH

Buses from Eisenstadt to Mörbisch leave every two hours (38AS). The #1820 bus makes the trip from Rust to Mörbisch in 5 minutes (19AS), or you can walk or bike from Rust along the 6km country lane to Mörbisch (about 90min. by foot).

The tiny village of Mörbisch lies 5km south of Rust along the *Neusiedlersee,* the last settlement on the western shore before the Hungarian border. The road from

Eisenstadt and Rust is lined with *Hüterhütten*, stone huts where young men would spend weeks in solitude, guarding grapes from human and winged trespassers. Mörbisch centers around Hauptstr., where the **tourist office** lies at #23 (tel. (02685) 8856; fax 84309). Pick up brochures on Mörbisch and the surrounding Burgenland, as well as a list of accommodations. (Open 9am-noon and 1-6pm; Nov.-Feb. M-Th 9am-3pm.) The town has its own beach, which includes a floating theater that hosts an operetta festival each summer—the **Mörbisch Seefestspiele.** Performances float atop the lake most Thursdays and every Friday, Saturday, and Sunday from mid-July to the end of August. Tickets are 200AS to 800AS and can be purchased at the theater ticket office. **Blaguss Reisen** (tel. (01) 50 18 00) in Vienna arranges a shuttle bus to Mörbisch at 6pm from Wiener Hauptstr. 15 in Vienna (round-trip 180AS).

There are many *Pensionen* and *Privatzimmer* in Mörbisch. For a sunny room and cheerful surroundings less than 5 minutes from downtown, stay at **Winzerhof Schindler,** Kinog. 9 (tel./fax 8318). Taste their homegrown wine and grape juice on a seaside terrace. (300-350AS per person. 15AS surcharge for 1-night stays. Breakfast included. Open Apr.-Nov.)

Mörbisch is truly a wine town, which is never more evident than during the **Weinfesttage** just before the opening of the *Seefestspiele*. The main street becomes one large *Heurige* filled with thirsty Austrians. During the **Weinblutenfest** in mid-June, visitors can ride a horse-drawn carriage from one vineyard to the other, stopping at each to sample the wine (100AS per person).

STYRIA (STEIERMARK)

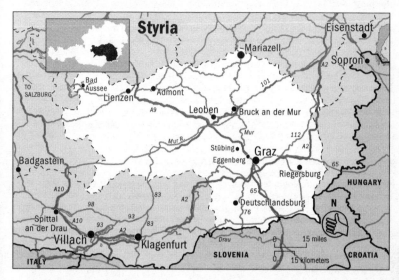

Styria, promoted by tourist offices as "the Green Heart of Austria," is Austria's second largest province (in terms of geography, not population). The province is made up primarily of mountains, which range from craggy, bare peaks in the northwest to gentle, thickly forested slopes in the southeast. Though the region provides striking views and excellent skiing, Styria has been spared the brunt of the tourist incursions, which allows it to preserve many of Austria's folk traditions and ancient forests. Styrians are stubbornly individualistic, with a dialect that few outsiders can understand, gamey local cuisine, and a gruff sense of humor. The province is home to many pilgrimage shrines, a strong rural economy, and the stud farm for Austria's breed of Lipizzaner horses.

HIGHLIGHTS OF STYRIA

- ■ Storm the Old Arsenal by day, then kick back a few at a *Biergarten* in **Graz** (p. 147).
- ■ Besiege the invincible medieval fortress in **Riegersburg** (p. 156).
- ■ Pilgrimage to the alpine village of **Mariazell,** home to some of Austria's finest *Lebkuchen* (gingerbread) bakeries (p. 160).

GRAZ

Sequestered in the southeastern corner of Styria, Graz seems to be trying (successfully) to escape the attention of most tourists. With 240,000 inhabitants, Graz is Austria's second largest city, but it remains under-touristed, even during the exciting festival season in late July and August. Once you've seen the city itself, it's even harder to understand why: Graz is blessed with striking architecture (both old and modern), idyllic scenery, and its very own mini-mountain, the **Schloßberg.** Much of the city's energy comes from the 45,000 students studying at the famous Karl-Franzens-Universität, founded in 1585, where Johannes Kepler hit the books. The thriving modern art community has adapted comfortably to the traditional architecture and plazas of the city center. The university supports the only jazz department in all of Europe—concerts and performances are held in churches, arcades, and squares throughout the beautiful *Altstadt*.

Since Charlemagne claimed this strategic gateway to Hungary and Slovenia for his empire in the 9th century, Graz has been fought over by Slavs, Frenchmen, and Russians. The ruins of the fortress crumbling on the Schloßberg commemorate the turmoil—the stronghold withstood battering at the hands of the Ottoman Turks in the 17th century, Napoleon's armies (3 times) in the 19th, and the Soviet Union during WWII. Down below, the city, with its red-tiled roofs, enticing parks, and diverse museums, shows no evidence of the centuries of conflict. Graz is known to the world primarily for the exploits of hometown hero **Arnold Schwarzenegger,** who lived in Graz before he left his family and athletic trainer (who still live here) to become Conan, the Terminator, and, in the biggest leap of Hollywood imagination, pregnant. The small pond where Arnold proposed to Maria Shriver is now a pilgrimage site for determined fans, despite the bemused protestations of tourist officials that it's "nothing special."

▐ GETTING TO AND FROM GRAZ

Flights arrive at the **Flughafen Graz,** Flughafenstr. 51, 9km from the city center. Take bus #631 from the *Hauptbahnhof* into town (30min., 6 per day 5:35am-6:20pm, 20AS). All trans-continental flights are routed through Vienna. **Train lines** converge at the **Hauptbahnhof,** on Europapl., west of the city center. (The *Ostbahnhof* on Conrad-von-Hötzendorf-Str. is mainly a freight station; don't get off there unless you came in a crate.) The **Graz-Köflach Bus** (GKB) departs from Griespl. for West Styria. For the rest of Austria, the **BundesBus** departs from Europapl. 6 (next to the train station) and from Andreas-Hofer-Pl.

▐ ORIENTATION AND PRACTICAL INFORMATION

Graz spreads across the Mur River in the southeast corner of Austria, on the northern edge of the Graz plain. The city is a gateway to Slovenia (50km south) and Hungary (70km east). Two-thirds of Graz's 5km² area consists of beautiful parks, earning it pithy nicknames like "Garden City" and "Green City." **Hauptplatz,** on the corner of Murg. and Sackstr., directly in front of the *Rathaus*, forms the social and commercial center of the city. **Jakominiplatz,** near the Eisernes Tor and 5 minutes from Hauptpl., is the hub of the city's bus and streetcar system. **Herrengasse,** a pedestrian street lined with cafes, boutiques, and ice cream shops, runs from the Hauptpl. to Jakominipl., forming the heart of the *Fußgängerzone*. The **Universität** is tucked away in the northeast part of Graz, near the posh residential district of St. Leonhard. The **Hauptbahnhof** lies on the other side of the river, a short ride from Hauptpl. on tram #3, 6, or 14. To get to the city center by foot from the train station, follow Annenstr. up and over Hauptbrücke (15min.).

TRANSPORTATION

Flights: Flughafen Graz (tel. 2902). Six shuttles (20AS) run daily between the airport and Graz (last bus at 6:20pm), stopping at the train station, Hotel Weitzer, and Griespl. before returning to the airport. The information office at the airport is open 6am-8pm.

Trains: Hauptbahnhof, Europapl. (tel. 7848, info 1717; lines open 7am-9pm). To: **Salzburg** (4¼hr., 10 per day 6:22am-10pm, 410AS); **Linz** (3¾hr., 7 per day 6:22am-6:22pm, 350AS); **Innsbruck** (6¼hr., 8 per day 6:22am-10pm, 550AS); **Vienna** (3¾hr., 17 per day 6:22am-6:22pm, 310AS); **Zurich** (10hr., 4 per day 6:22am-10pm, 1022AS); and **Munich** (6¼ hr., 9 per day 6:22am-6:22pm, 708AS).

Buses: Graz-Köflach Bus (GKB), Köflneherg. 35-41 (tel. 5987), is open M-F 8am-5pm. The Post Bus office, Andreas-Hofer-Pl. 17, is open M-F 7am-6pm. The **branch** at the *Hauptbahnhof* is open M-F 9am-noon.

STYRIA

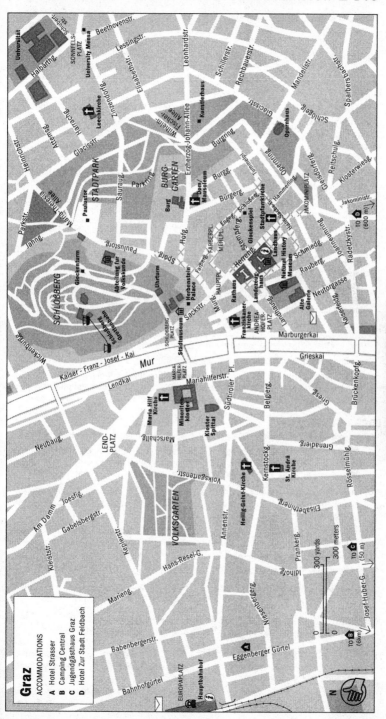

STYRIA

Public Transportation: For information on all buses, trams, and trains, call **Mobil Zentrale,** Schönaug. 6, (tel. 82 06 06). Open M-F 8am-5pm. Purchase single tickets (20AS) and 24hr. tickets (42AS) from the driver, booklets of 10 tickets (160AS) or week-tickets (100AS) from any *Tabak.* Tickets are valid for all trams, buses, and the **cable car** that ascends the Schloßberg. Children half-price. 500AS penalty for riding without a ticket. Most tram lines run until 11pm, most bus lines until 9pm. Check the schedules posted at every *Haltestelle* for details.

Taxi: Funktaxi, Griespl. 28 (tel. 983). **City-Funk,** Glockenspielpl. 6 (tel. 878).

Car Rental: Avis, at the airport and Schlögelg. 10 (tel. 81 29 20; fax 84 11 78). **Budget,** Europapl. 12 (tel. 71 69 66; fax 72 20 74), and at the airport (tel. 2902, ext. 342). **Hertz,** Andreas-Hofer-Pl. 1 (tel. 82 50 07; fax 81 02 88). **Europcar,** at the airport (tel. 29 67 57; fax 24 25 47).

Automobile Clubs: ÖAMTC, Conrad-von-Hötzendorf-str. 127 (tel. 504). **ARBÖ,** Kappellenstr. 45 (tel. 271 60 00).

Bike Rental: At the train station. 150-200AS per day, 90-160AS with Eurailpass or valid ticket. Open M-F 6:30am-6pm, Sa 6:30am-4pm, Su 7am-3:30pm. **Bicycle Graz,** Korüsistr. 5 (tel. 825 71 316), citybikes 80AS per day, 150AS per weekend; mountain bikes 150AS, 250AS. Open M-F 7am-1pm and 2-6pm.

TOURIST AND FINANCIAL SERVICES

Tourist Office: Main office, Herreng. 16 (tel. 80750; fax 807 55 15; email info @graztourismus.at; www.graztourismus.at), has free city maps and a walking guide of the city (10AS). Free room reservations. **Tours** of the *Altstadt* in English and German start out front (2½hr., June-Sept. daily 2:30pm; Oct.-May Sa only; 75AS). Open in summer M-F 9am-7pm, Sa 9am-6pm, Su and holidays 10am-3pm; in winter M-F 9am-6pm, Sa 9am-3pm, Su and holidays 10am-3pm. **Branch,** Europapl. 6 (tel. 71 68 37), at the *Hauptbahnhof.* Open M-Sa 9am-1pm and 2-6pm.

Consulates: South Africa, Villefortg. 13 (tel. 32 25 48). **U.K.,** Schmiedg. 10 (tel. 82 61 05).

Currency Exchange: Best rates at the main **post office** (cashier open M-F 7am-5pm, Sa 7am-2pm). Most banks open M-F 8am-noon and 2-4pm. The train station has the longest hours (M 5am-10pm, Tu-Su 5:45pm-10pm).

LOCAL SERVICES

Luggage Storage: At station, 30AS per day. Open daily 6am-midnight. Lockers 30-50AS.

English-Language Bookstores: English Bookshop, Tummelpl. 7 (tel. 82 62 66; email english.books@aon.net; members.aon.net/english.books), has 2 vast floors of fiction, non-fiction, you name it. Open M-F 9am-6pm, Sa 9am-noon.

Bi-Gay-Lesbian Organizations: Verein Frauenservice Graz (Women's Information Center), Idlhofg. 20 (tel. 71 60 22). Office open M, W, F 9am-1pm, Tu 5-7pm. Medical help available W 5-7pm.

Laundromat: Putzerei Rupp, Jakominstr. 34 (tel. 82 11 83), has do-it-yourself (5kg load 75AS, soap 10AS) and professional handling. Open M-F 8am-5pm, Sa 8am-noon.

AIDS Hotline: Steirische AIDS-Hilfe, Schmiedg. 38 (tel. 81 50 50). Counseling available W 11am-1pm, F 4-7pm. Blood tests Tu and Th 4:30-7:30pm.

Pharmacy: Bärenapotheke, Herreng. 11 (tel. 83 02 67), opposite the tourist office. Open M-F 8am-12:30pm and 2:30-6pm, Sa 8am-noon. AmEx, MC, Visa.

EMERGENCY AND COMMUNICATION

Hospital: Krankenhaus der Elisabethinen, Elisabethinerg. 14 (tel. 7063).

Emergencies: Police, tel. 133. **Ambulance,** tel. 144.

Police Office: Europapl. 7 (tel. 888 27 75), outside of the main train station. From 8pm-5am, enter from train platform 1.

Internet Access: A 15min. walk from the center of town, **Jugendgästehaus Graz,** Idlhofg. 74 (see p. 151), has nifty coin-operated machines that cost 5AS for 10min. **Café Zen-**

tral, Andreas-Hofer-Pl. 9 (tel. 83 24 68), charges 60AS for 1hr. minimum, divided among as many visits as you want. Open M-Sa 6:30-10pm.

Post Office: Main office, Neutorg. 46. Open M-F 7am-9pm, Sa 8am-2pm. Cashier closes M-F at 5pm. A **branch office,** Europapl. 10, is next to the main train station. Open 24hr. **Postal Code:** A-8010; branch office A-8020.

PHONE CODE	The **city code** for Graz is 0316.

ACCOMMODATIONS

Sniffing out a cheap bed in Graz may require a bit of detective work, as most budget hotels, guest houses, and pensions run 300-450AS per person, and many are in the boondocks. Luckily, the web of local transport provides a reliable and easy commute to and from the city center. Ask the tourist office about *Privatzimmer* (150-300AS per night), especially in the crowded summer months.

Jugendgästehaus Graz (HI), Idlhofg. 74 (tel. 71 48 76; fax 714 87 688), 15min. from the train station. Exit the station and cross the street, head right on Eggenberger Gürtel, left on Josef-Huber-G. (after the car dealership), then take the 1st right at Idlhofg. The hostel is behind a parking lot on your right. Buses #31, 32, and 33 run here from Jako-minipl. (last bus around midnight). This spiffy renovated hostel has its own café and restaurant, as well as cheap **Internet access** (5AS for 10min.). 4- to 6-bed dorms 220AS, singles 320AS, doubles 540AS. Mattress on the floor 155AS. Small breakfast included. **Laundry** 40AS, soap 5AS. Reception 7am-11pm. No real curfew; security guard opens the doors every 30min. from 10pm-2am. Key available (300AS deposit).

Hotel Strasser, Eggenberger Gürtel 11 (tel. 71 39 77; fax 71 68 56; email hotel.strasser@noten.com), 5min. from the train station. Exit the station, cross the street, and head right on Bahnhofgürtel; the hotel is on the left, across from the Midas station. Big, breezy rooms with big windows and attractive rugs. Top-rate restaurant serves the best budget cocoa in Austria. Singles 360AS, with shower 440AS; doubles 580AS, 660AS; triples 840AS; quads 1000AS. Breakfast included. Free parking.

Hotel Zur Stadt Feldbach, Conrad-von-Hötzendorf-Str. 58 (tel. 82 94 68; fax 84 73 71), 20min. walk south of Jakominipl. From Hauptpl. or Jakominipl., take tram #4 (dir.: Liebnau) or #5 (dir.: Puntigam) to "Jakominigürtel." The hotel is on the right. Linoleum-floored rooms with patterned blankets. Singles 350AS; doubles 500AS, with shower stall, 650AS; triples with shower 800AS. Breakfast 50AS. 24hr. reception on 2nd floor.

Camping Central, Martinhofstr. 3 (tel. (0676) 378 51 02, fax (0316) 69 78 24). Take bus #32 from Jakominipl. to "Badstraßgang" (20 min.), turn right at the Billa supermarket and walk up the road. This clean campground has a **swimming pool** and miniature golf (25AS, children 20AS). 155AS per person, includes tent site, shower, and use of the swimming pool; additional adults 80AS, children 4-14 50AS. Camper 205AS for 2 people. Tax 5AS; laundry 70AS. Reception 8am-10pm. Open Apr.-Oct.

FOOD

Graz's student community sustains a bonanza of cheap eateries. Inexpensive meals await at Hauptpl. and Lendpl., off Keplerstr. and Lendkai, where concession stands sell *Wurst*, ice cream, beer, and other fast food until late. There are markets along Rösselmühlgasse, an extension of Josef-Huber-G., and on Jakoministr. directly off Jakominipl. Low-priced student hangouts line Zinzendorfg. near the university. Note that most salads come dressed in the local dark pumpkin-seed oil.

RESTAURANTS

University Mensa, Sonnenfelspl. 1 (tel. 32 33 62), just east of the Stadtpark at the intersection of Zinzendorfg. and Leechg. Take bus #39 to "Uni/Mensa" for the best deal in town. Simple and satisfying *Menüs*, vegetarian *(Vollwert)* or with meat, for 47-53AS.

Large à la carte selection includes diverse salads (16AS) and pizza (25AS). Continental breakfast 29AS. Open M-F 8:30am-2:30pm.

Kebap Haus, Jakoministr. 16 (tel. 81 10 06), just south of Jakominipl., is a superior Turkish restaurant with inexpensive sandwiches on homemade pitas (38-52AS) and delicious Mediterranean pizzas (72-89AS). Try the *Etli Pidde*, a fresh pizza with lamb, tomatoes, garlic, peppers, and oregano. Lunch specials include soup, entree, and salad (85AS). High-quality falafel (76AS). Open M-Sa 11am-midnight.

Mangolds, Griesgasse 11 (tel. 71 80 02), serves vegetarian entrees, desserts, and a varied salad bar in a huge restaurant that's an appealing mixture of Scandinavian design and rustic arts-and-crafts. Styrian potato soup (25AS), spaghetti (44AS), yoghurt desserts (29AS). Open M-F 11am-8pm, Sa 11am-4pm.

Gastwirtschaft Wartburgasse, Halbärthg. 4 (tel. 38 87 50). Antique posters and loud music make this indoor/outdoor café/bar Graz's premier student hangout. Well-made standard dishes make up for the wait. Choose between lunch specials (68-110AS) and pasta, vegetarian, or meat entrees (42-120AS). Open 9am-2am.

Calafati, Lissag. 2 (tel. 91 68 89), a 3min. walk from the hostel away from the train station. Lunch combos (main course, soup or spring roll, dessert 42-75AS) make this slightly out-of-the-way Chinese restaurant a bargain. Several vegetarian and take-out options (65-89AS). Lunch specials 11:30am-3pm; dinner 5:30-11:30pm.

Interspar Restaurant, Lazarett-Gürtel 55, at the supermarket in the City Park mall. Nice salad bar and an extensive warm buffet. *Schwammerlgulasch mit Knödel* (69AS) and fruit tarts (17AS) are among the many options. Open M-F 7am-7:30pm, Sa 8am-5pm.

MARKETS

There are **outdoor markets** at Kaiser-Josef-Pl. and Lendpl. (M-Sa 8am-1pm), as well as on Hauptpl. and Jakominipl. (M-F 7am-6pm, Sa 7am-12:30pm) where vendors hawk their fruits and vegetables amid a happy splash of colors.

Merkur, Europapl., left as you leave the *Bahnhof*. In the basement of Hotel Ibis. Free underground parking. Open M-Th 8am-7pm, F 7:30am-7:30pm, Sa 7am-5pm.

Interspar, Lazarett-Gürtel 55 (tel. 71 04 36), in the enormous City Park shopping mall. Open M-F 9am-7:30pm, Sa 8am-5pm. Another branch next door to the *Mensa*. Open M-F 8am-1pm and 4-6:30pm, Sa 7:30am-12:30pm.

👁 🏛 SIGHTS AND MUSEUMS

The **Landesmuseum Joanneum** is Austria's oldest public museum. The assembled holdings are so vast that officials have been forced to categorize the legacy and to house portions in separate museums scattered throughout the city. One ticket, purchased at any of the locations, is valid for the arsenal, the natural history museum, and most of the art museums in the city. *(60AS, students and seniors 40AS.)*

THE OLD TOWN. An entertaining way to explore Graz is to use the tourist office's guide, *Old Town Walk* (10AS). The tourist office is in the **Landhaus,** the seat of the provincial government, and a sight in itself. The building was remodeled by architect Domenico dell'Allio in 1557 in Lombard style. Through the arch to the right is an arcaded stone courtyard, where *Classics in the City* is held (see p. 154).

PROVINCIAL ARSENAL. On the other side of the tourist office is the fascinating **Landeszeughaus,** built between 1642 and 1644 by Anton Solar. The 1st floor details the history of the arsenal and the Ottoman Turk attacks in a series of placards and displays, with English translations. In 1749, after the Turks had packed their cannon and gone home, the armory was marked for dismantling, but an eloquent protest by the Styrian nobles convinced Empress Maria Theresia to preserve the arsenal as a symbolic gesture. The building, with its massive collection of arms and armor intact, served as a firehouse until 1882, when it first opened as a museum. Today, the 4-story collection includes enough spears, muskets, and armor to outfit 28,000 burly mercenaries. The full experience is an extravagant spectacle, with thousands of metal barrels and blades spread out (on the ceiling and walls) in abstract geometrical patterns. Windows from the poorly lit halls look out over the *Landhaus* arcade. Allow at least 2 hours to learn the history and peruse the collection. *(Herreng. 16. Tel. 801 79 810. Open Apr.-Oct. M-F 9am-5pm, Sa-Su 9am-1pm. Tours 11am and 3pm, call ahead for English ones. Admission with a Joanneum ticket.)*

ART MUSEUMS. The Joanneum includes the **Neue Galerie,** housed in the elegant Palais Herberstein at the foot of the Schloßberg, which showcases off-beat, avantgarde works and a collection of 19th- and 20th-century paintings. *(Sackstr. 16. Tel. 82 91 55; fax 81 54 01; email neue-galerie-graz@sime.com; www.sime.com/neue_galerie. Open M-F 10am-6pm, Sa 10am-1pm. Admission with Joanneum ticket.)* Its older counterpart, the **Alte Galerie,** presents a mid-sized collection of Medieval and Baroque art, mostly by Styrian artists. Notable holdings include **Lucas Cranach's** *Judgment of Paris* and Jan Brueghel's copy of his father's gruesome *Triumph of Death. (Neutorg. 45. Tel. 801 74 770. Open Tu-Su 10am-5pm. Tours Su at 11am. Admission with Joanneum ticket. English descriptions available.)* The Alte Galerie shares space with the **Kunstgewerbe,** an exhibition space for late 19th- and 20th-century art and design. *(Tel. 801 74 780. Hours vary by exhibition. Admission with Joanneum ticket.)* The **Künstlerhaus,** an independent museum in the Stadtpark, hosts exhibitions ranging from Tibetan artifacts to Secessionist paintings by Klimt. *(Open M-Sa 9am-6pm, Su 9am-noon. 15AS, students free.)*

HISTORY AND SCIENCE MUSEUMS. Next door to the Neue Galerie at the western foot of the Schloßberg is the **Stadtmuseum.** On the third floor, a series of 19th-century drawings of the city are presented alongside modern photographs and a large-scale model circa 1800. *(Sackstr. 18. Tel. 82 25 80. Open Tu 10am-9pm, W-Sa 10am-6pm, Su 10am-1pm. 50AS, students and children 30AS.)* Up on the Schloßberg, the **Garnisonsmuseum** exhibits its modest collection of military uniforms and feathered helmets. *(Open Tu-Su 10am-5pm. 20AS, students and children 10AS. Combo ticket including Schloßberg tour 40AS, 20AS.)* The Joanneum's scientific component is the **Natural History Museum,** which encompasses geology, paleontology, mineralogy, zoology, and other -ologies. The museum has a specimen of the largest beetle in the world and a truly splendid collection of minerals and semi-precious stones. Ask in the Geology gallery to leave the museum through the secret coal mine. *(Rauberg. 10. Tel. 301 74 760, -50, -40, or -30. Open Tu-Su 9am-4pm. Admission with Joanneum ticket.)*

CHURCHES. Graz has 7 churches, each with its own charms. The 13th-century Gothic **Leechkirche,** Zinzendorfg. 5, between the Stadtpark and the university, is the city's oldest structure. The lemon yellow **Stadtpfarrkirche,** diagonally across Herreng. from the Landeszeughaus, was the Abbey Church of the Dominicans in the 16th century. The late-Gothic church suffered severe damage in WWII air raids. When Salzburger artist Albert Birkle designed new stained-glass windows for the church in 1953, one made worldwide news: the left panel behind the high altar portrays the scourging of Christ, silently watched over by two figures bearing a marked resemblance to Hitler and Mussolini. The church holds **organ concerts** July 22 to August 26 on Thursdays at 8pm. *(60AS, students 40AS.)*

On Hofg., opposite the Burggarten and the Burgtor stands Graz's **Dom** (cathedral), built in 15th-century Gothic style by Emperor Friedrich III. In 1485, the church mounted a picture of the "Scourges of God" on the south side of the building to remind Christians of the most palpable trinity of the time: the plague, Ottoman invasions, and the locusts—a combination that had wiped out 80% of the population 5 years earlier. The Dom also holds **free organ concerts** every Sunday at 8pm in August and September.

OTHER SIGHTS. Around the corner, on Burgg., the solemn 17th-century Habsburg **Mausoleum** is one of the finest examples of Austrian Mannerism. The domed tomb holds the remains of Ferdinand II in the underground chamber. Somewhat cryptic English placards are pasted to the stone walls. Master architect Fischer von Erlach (responsible for much of Vienna's Ringstraße) designed the beautiful frescoes upstairs. *(Open M-Sa 10am-12:30pm and 2-4pm. 10AS, children 5AS.)* Down the street, the magnificent **Opernhaus** (opera house), at Opernring and Burgg., was built in less than 2 years by Viennese theater architects Fellner and Helmer. The **Glockenspiel**, located just off Engeg. in Glockenspielpl., opens its wooden doors every day at 11am, 3, and 6pm to reveal life-size wooden figures spinning to a slightly out-of-tune folk song. The black and gold ball underneath turns to show the phases of the moon.

CASTLE MOUNTAIN. North of Herreng. and Hauptpl., the wooded **Schloßberg** rises 123m above Graz. The hill is named for a castle which stood on it from 1125 until 1809, when it was destroyed by Napoleon's troops. Though the castle is almost completely gone, the Schloßberg remains a beautiful city park. From Schloßbergpl., visitors can climb the zigzagging stone steps of the **Schloßberg-stiege,** built by Russian prisoners during WWI and traditionally known as the *Russenstiege* (Russian steps) or the *Kriegstiege* (war steps). The path continues through the terraced **Herberstein Gardens** to the top of the hill. The top of the Schloßberg is a carefully tended park, with sweeping views out over the vast Carinthian plain surrounding Graz. Napoleon didn't manage to capture the Schloßberg until *after* he conquered the rest of Austria—he then razed the fortress in an infantile rage. The **Glockenturm** (bell tower), built in 1588, is one of the few castle structures still standing, which the little Emperor spared in return for a sizeable ransom from the citizens of Graz. *(Tower open 9am-5pm, except during guided tours; 15AS, students and children 10AS.)* Its enormous bell ("Liesl") draws a crowd with its 101 clangings daily at 7am, noon, and 7pm. The nearby **Uhrturm** (clocktower) dates from 1265. A guided tour of the Schloßberg includes viewing the Uhrturm clockworks of 1712. *(Tours in German or English Apr.-Oct. every 2hr., meet at Glockenturm, Tu-Su 9am-5pm on the hour; 30AS, students and children 15AS.)*

From Schloßbergpl., the **Schloßberg Passage** penetrates the *Berg.* A network of tunnels was blasted into the hill during WWII to serve as a mass bomb shelter for up to 50,000 civilians. Visitors may walk through the cool, dark main passage and peer down spooky side tunnels. (Open daily 8am-8pm; free.) The **Grazer Schloßberg Grottenbahn** travels for 30 minutes through the mountain past illuminated scenes from fairy tales, history, and literature, including a stuffed dummy Gulliver restrained by dozens of dusty Lilliputian Ken dolls. *(Open daily 10am-6pm; last train at 5:30pm, tickets up to 35AS.)*

PARKS AND GARDENS. Down the hill on the eastern side near the Uhrturm and through the Paulustor arch is the lovely **Stadtpark.** Separating the old city from the university quarter, the gardens attract walkers, sun-bathers, and frisbee players. Graz acquired the ornate central fountain, which has 8 figures holding huge spitting fish, at the 1873 Vienna World's Fair. Paris snatched up the 2 complementary side pieces, now in Pl. de la Concorde. South of the fish fountain, the Stadtpark blends into the **Burggarten,** a bit of carefully pruned greenery complementing what remains of Emperor Friedrich III's 15th-century **Burg.** His cryptic wall inscription "A.E.I.O.U." remains a mystery, varyingly interpreted as *"Austria Est Imperare Orbi Universo," "Austria Erit In Orbe Ultima,"* or *"Alles Erdreich Ist Österreich Untertan."* A vague desire for Austria to rule the universe can be intuited. Or a love of vowels. Friedrich's son, Maximilian I, enlarged the building and in 1499 commissioned the Gothic double spiral staircase, predating Watson and Crick by almost 500 years. He also inserted the **Burgtor** (Castle Gate) into the city wall. *(Garden open 7:30am-7pm.)*

🎵 ENTERTAINMENT

Students can check the **student administration office** of the university, which has billboards papered with concert notices, student activity flyers, and carpool advertisements for all of Austria. For professional music and dance performances, Graz's neo-Baroque **Opernhaus,** at Opernring and Burgg. (tel. 8008), sells standing-room tickets an hour before curtain call. The program includes operas and ballets of worldwide repute; for many young hopefuls, Graz is considered a stepping stone to an international career. One big show comes each July while the regular companies are on vacation—1998 brought the Kirov, 1999 "Stomp," and in 2000 a production of "Porgy and Bess" will grace the stage. Tickets cost a pretty penny (360-1490AS), but standing-room slots start at 50AS, and student rush tickets cost 150AS. The **Schauspielhaus** (tel. 8005), the theater on Freiheitspl. off Hofg., sells bargain seats just before showtime. All tickets and performance schedules are available at the **Theaterkasse**, Kaiser-Josef-Pl. 10 (tel. 8000; open M-F 8am-6:30pm, Sa 8am-1pm), and the **Zentralkartenbüro**, Herreng. 7 (tel. 83 02 55).

In late September and October, the **Steierischer Herbst** (Styrian Autumn) festival celebrates avant-garde art with a month of films, performances, art installations, and parties. Contact the director of the festival, Sackstr. 17 (tel. 823 00 70; email stherbst@ping.at; www.ping.at/members/stherbst), for details. Since 1985, the city has hosted its own summer festival, **Styriarte,** as well. Mostly classical concerts are held daily from late June to early July in the gardens of the Schloß Eggenberg, the large halls of Graz Convention Center, and the squares of the old city. The renowned Graz conductor, Nikolaus Harnoncourt, sets the tone. Tickets are available at Palais Attems (Sackstr. 17; tel. 82 50 00; email styriarte@mail.styria.co.at; www.styriarte.com; open M-F 8:30am-12:30pm and 2-6pm, Sa 9am-1pm). The award-winning movie theater **Rechbauerkino,** Rechbauerstr. 6 (tel. 83 05 08), occasionally screens un-dubbed arthouse films in English (85AS, children 70AS). The **Royal Kino,** Conrad-von-Hötzendorfstr. 10, a few blocks south of Jakominipl., shows new releases in English, without subtitles (70AS before 6:45pm, 85AS after). In summer, the **Classics in the City Festival** shows free films of great opera performances in the *Landhaus* courtyard next to the tourist office (July-Aug. daily at 8:30pm). Every summer the **American Institute of Musical Studies** transfers to Graz. Vocal and instrumental students perform works ranging from Broadway to Schönberg on the streets and in concert halls—ask for a schedule at the tourist office. From July to mid-August, organ concerts are held every Thursday at the Stadtpfarrkirche and every Sunday at the *Dom* (8pm; 70AS, students 40AS). July and August also bring **Jazz-Sommer Graz** (tel. 60 53 11), a festival of free concerts by international jazz legends like Art Farmer, Toots Thielemans, and Tommy Flanagan (Th-Sa, 8:30pm at Maria Hilferpl.). The cultural magazine *Graz Derzeit,* free at the tourist office, prints a complete daily listing of events with details on prices and locations (www.iic.wifi.at/graz/veranstaltungen/derzeit).

◤ NIGHTLIFE

The hub of after-hours activity in Graz can be found in the so-called **"Bermuda Triangle,"** an area of the old city behind Hauptpl. and bordered by Mehlpl., Färberg., and Prokopiag., and Puerto Rico. The Triangle's dozens of beer gardens and bars are packed with people all night, every night; sitting in an outdoor café is *de rigueur,* at least until 11pm, when local ordinance requires that festivities move indoors. Most of the university students prefer to down their beers in the pubs lining Zinzendorfg. and Halbärthg. on the other side of the Stadtpark.

Café Harrach, Harrachg. 26 (tel. 32 26 71). At this grad-student hangout, a half-liter of *Gösser* goes for 29AS, but almost everyone's throwing back white wine spritzers (26AS). Open July-Sept. M-F 5pm-midnight, Sa-Su 7pm-midnight; Oct.-May M-F 9am-midnight, Sa-Su 7pm-midnight.

Tom's Bierklinik, Färberg. 1 (tel. 84 51 74), has the largest stock of international beers in Austria. Go ahead and try prescriptions from Hawaii, Trinidad, or India (all 75AS), or just get a local fix with a glass of *Murauer Pils* (32AS). Walk-in hours M-Sa 8pm-4am.

Kulturhauskeller, Elisabethstr. 30 (tel. 38 10 58), underneath the Kulturhaus. Young crowd and cool locale dictate the overwhelming dance music. The partying doesn't get started until 11pm on weekends. *Weißbier* 34AS. No shorts or military duds. 19 and up. Obligatory coat check and security fee 20AS. Open Tu-Sa 10pm-3:30am.

Triangel, Burgg. 15, below the Kommod bar/restaurant. Vaulted brick ceilings, mirrored arches, and a low-key, well-dressed clientele of trendy twenty-somethings. Open 8pm-4am. Occasional bands, no cover.

NEAR GRAZ: SCHLOß EGGENBERG

Take tram #1 (dir.: Eggenberg) to "Schloß Eggenberg" (5am-midnight).

To the west of Graz, the grandiose **Schloß Eggenberg** (closed until 2000 for construction) contrasts sharply with the surrounding shabby suburban neighborhood. Built for Prince Ulrich of Eggenberg, this 5-towered palace now holds an extensive coin museum, an exhibition of artifacts from antiquity, and a prehistoric museum, all under the auspices of the Landesmuseum Joanneum. The guided tour of the elegant **Prunkräume**—filled with 17th-century frescoes, tile ovens, and ornate chandeliers—reveals the convoluted cosmological design of the palace. (Eggenberger Allee 90. Tel. (0316) 58 32 64. Antiquities and coin collection open Tu-Su 9am-noon and 12:30-5pm; prehistoric museum open Tu-Su 9am-1pm and 1:30-5pm. Museum entrance 120AS including the *Prunkräume*, otherwise 100AS; groups, children, and students 70AS. Tours in German and English; every hr., 10am-noon and 2-4pm. Tour 20AS, plus entrance to the museums.) Royal blue peacocks wander freely in the game preserve surrounding the palace. (Free with castle entrance; 2AS for gardens only; open daily 8am-7pm.) Classical concerts are held in the castle's **Planetensaal** (Planet Hall; tel. 82 50 00; Aug.-Sept. M at 8pm; tickets from 130AS).

NEAR GRAZ: ÖSTERREICHISCHES FREILICHTMUSEUM

The museum is an easy day-trip from Graz, particularly if you have a car. Drivers should take the road to Salzburg and turn off at Gratwein. Trains run to Stübing from Graz every hour (74AS return); from the Stübing train station, turn left onto the main road and walk 25-30min. to the museum. Buses run irregularly between Stübing and the museum (4 per day, 15AS), so you're best off walking unless you're lucky enough to catch one. The most convenient transport is by bus that runs from Lendplatz in Graz (M-Sa at 9am and 12:30pm) straight to the museum, returning at 1:23pm and 4:40pm (74AS return).

The **Österreichisches Freilichtmuseum (Austrian Open-air Museum),** in the nearby town of **Stübing,** showcases Austrian farm life as it existed in the not-so-distant past. The museum consists of 80 farmhouses, barns, mills, and storehouses from all over Austria, transported plank-by-plank and lovingly restored, surrounded by woods and grain fields. Plan on spending at least 2½ hours there if you want to see everything. If you're accustomed to your food arriving in neat supermarket packaging, the museum will enlighten you as to how grain is farmed, cheese made, and bees kept. There are also reconstructions of blacksmithies, water mills, stables, and elaborate birdhouses. A snack bar at the mid-point of the tour serves slices of bread with *Schweineschmalz* (lard), or pastries for the less adventurous (free, but you ought to give a reasonable donation). An exhibit house near the far-end of the museum displays pictures and charts of agricultural techniques through the ages. You might even see people reaping grain in the museum's fields or doing traditional crafts. (Tel. (03124) 53700. Open Apr.-Oct., Tu-Su, 9am-5pm. 75AS, students 40AS, children 30AS. Exhibits in German. English guidebook 30AS.)

RIEGERSBURG

Not to be confused with Riegersburg in Lower Austria, the hillside town of Riegersburg in Styria is home to one of the finest castles in Austria, never conquered by any enemy. In the 13th century, the castle consisted of 2 separate fortresses on the plateau: the older Burg Kronegg to the north, and Burg Lichtenegg to the south. In the 17th century, Elisabeth von Wechsler had the lower castle torn down and Burg Kronegg fortified against the Turks, making it one of the largest and most impregnable strongholds in Austria—108 rooms surrounded by 3km of walls with 5 gates and 2 trenches. The fearsome castle withstood the 1664 Ottoman onslaught, driving back the Turks in the great Battle of Mogersdorf. In 1822, the Princes of Liechtenstein acquired the castle, restored it, and moved in. Today, the *Schloß* balances on the edge of a steep cliff, looking out across vast panoramas of rolling farmland and distant, misty hills. It's a magical, well-preserved spot worth exploring and enjoying at your leisure.

⊉ ORIENTATION AND PRACTICAL INFORMATION. If you've got a **car,** Riegersburg is an easy, 55km trip from Graz. Take A-2 and exit at Ilz. Otherwise, poor train-bus connections necessitate precise planning. Ride the **bus** directly from **Graz** (from Andreas-Hofer-Pl.; 2hr., M-Sa 12:35pm, M-F 5:30pm, Su 10:45am, round-trip 202AS), or take the **train** from Graz to **Feldbach** (1hr., every hr. 6:18am-10:43pm, 90AS) and switch to the bus into Riegersburg (M-F 7 per day, Sa usually 1 per day, 20min., 20AS). Buses from Riegersburg to Graz generally leave at pre-dawn hours (2hr., M-Sa 5:40 and 6:05am, Su 5:35pm). Still, a 100AS ticket purchased on the bus back to Feldbach (M-F, 7 per day 6:50am-5:50pm) is valid for train connections back to Graz (every hr. 4:20am-8:22pm). If necessary, you can always call a **taxi** (tel. 381) to take you back to Feldbach (170-210AS). Otherwise, the **tourist office** (tel. 8670), just up the street toward the castle from the bus stops, can help you find a room (open M-Sa 11am-6pm, Su 10am-6pm). **Exchange currency** at the **post office,** Riegersburgstr. 26 (open M-F 8am-noon and 2-6pm, Sa 8am-noon; exchange until 5pm) or at **Raiffeisen Bank,** across the street at Riegersburgstr. 30 (open M-Th 8am-noon and 2-4:30pm, F 8am-noon and 2-5pm). The **postal code** is A-8333.

PHONE CODE	The **city code** for Riegersburg is 03153.

⌐⌐ ACCOMMODATIONS AND FOOD. One of the compelling reasons to come to Riegersburg is the **⊠Jugendherberge im Cillitor (HI),** Riegersburg 3 (tel. 8217; fax 82174; mobile phone tel. (0664) 551 39 22; email oejhu-stmk@oejhv.or.at), which is actually incorporated into the fortress walls. Walk toward the castle, and up the very steep stone path. The hostel entrance is in the archway you pass through as you veer left. 14-bed dorms have arrow-slits from which to fight off advancing school groups. Friendly proprietors are always willing to dispense advice on local sights. (Dorms 135AS. Breakfast included; other meals 55-65AS. Hall showers and toilets. Curfew 10pm. Open May-Oct.) At the bottom of Riegersburg's hill, **Lasslhof** (tel. 8201 or 8202), is a yellow hotel with a popular bar/restaurant and a ghastly art collection in the halls between the 2-, 3-, and 4-bed rooms. (Doubles 360AS, with shower 480AS; triples 540AS, 720AS; quads 720AS, 960AS. Breakfast included. Reception 8am-10pm.) At the restaurant downstairs, wolf down *Wienerschnitzel* with potatoes and salad (77AS), or snack on *Frankfurter mit Gulaschsaft* (38AS). Stock up on groceries at **SPAR Market,** across from the start of the stone path (open M-F 7am-noon and 2:45-6:15pm, Sa 7am-12:30pm).

◙ ⌐ SIGHTS AND ENTERTAINMENT. Naturally, Riegersburg relies heavily on the revenue from tourists who gawk at the well-preserved remains of Burg Kronegg, the huge medieval fortress, the town's only man-made attraction. But like the foreign invaders of the past, sightseers must also tackle the steep, stone-paved path leading up to the castle. Bring sturdy shoes and bottled water, lest you share the fate of many a young 17th-century Turk. The path itself is arguably the best part of the castle: the castle's slopes are blanketed by thick vineyards, sweeping views reward visitors at every turn, and benches, stone arches, and monuments provide good excuses to catch your breath. Ask a local to point out the Prince and Princess of Liechtenstein's current residence—note the swimming pool instead of a moat. You might circle the castle and climb up the *Eselstiege* (donkey stairs) instead. Legend claims that this back entrance was built in the 17th century when 2 feuding brothers owned the place, and one closed off the top entrance. Actually, the stairs were laid in the 15th century as a food transportation route before the quarrelsome brothers were even a glint in their aristocratic father's eye. On your

STYRIA

way up, look for an inconspicuous crescent moon carved into the stone wall to mark the highest point reached by invading Turks.

The castle itself houses several well-maintained exhibits and museums. The **Burgmuseum** showcases 16 of the castle's 108 rooms, packed with art and self-congratulatory historical notes on the Liechtenstein family (yes, like the country), who bought the castle in 1822 and still own it. The **Weiße Saal** (White Hall), with its wedding-cake ceiling flourishes and crystal chandeliers, lacks only couples in decolleté gowns waltzing around the floor. The **Witches' Room** contains an eerie collection of portraits of alleged witches (including Katharina "Green Thumb" Pardauff, executed in 1675 for causing flowers to bloom in the middle of winter) and a real iron maiden. There's also Prince Friedrich's (the current owner of the castle) gallery of derivative amateur photography. The **Hexenmuseum** (Witch Museum) spreads over 12 more rooms, with an exhibit on the most expansive witch trial in Styrian history (held between 1673 and 1675). Filled with torture devices, funeral pyres, and other gruesome exhibits, the museum investigates, with historical rigor, the accusation that 95 women and men had caused hail and thunderstorms. (Tel. 82131. Open Apr.-Oct. daily 9am-5pm. Admission to each museum 90AS, students 60AS; combination ticket 130AS, 90AS. 1hr. tours in German throughout the day. 10AS. Exhibits in German, English brochure available.)

You can best appreciate the castle's beauty from the surrounding network of gravel paths and stone staircases. Take a good look at the elaborate iron pattern covering the well in the castle's second courtyard—it's said that any woman who can spot a horseshoe within the complex design will find her knight in shining armor within a year. In the shadow of the castle chirps the rather meager **Greifvogelwarte Riegersburg,** showcasing caged birds of prey (open Apr.-Oct. 60AS, students 30AS; shows with trainers dressed in castle finery M-Sa 11am and 3pm, Su 11am, 2, and 4pm). At one of the many *Buschenschenken* on the hills surrounding the castle, you can sample Schilcher wine, a rosé grown from hearty native grapes. After a long, hot day of castle conquering and hiking, you might want to plunge into the **Seebad Riegersburg** below the town, a small swimming lake created by nature and nurture together (30AS, under 16 15AS).

THE MURTAL

Eons ago, the **Mur River** in central and southern Styria carved a valley among the Gleinalpen to the west, Seetaler Alpen to the south, and Seckauer and Niedere Tauern to the north. The Mur begins in Salzburger Land and eventually joins the Drau in Slovenia. Low, rolling hills make the region ideal for cyclists and hikers. Half of the region is covered by forests, and another quarter by grasslands and vineyards that produce some of Austria's finest wines. Sprinkled among the ups and downs are small towns, old fortresses, and farms. The countryside retains the charm of an earlier age. The Murtal has long been a valued source of iron ore, and the old iron trade route, the **Steirische Eisenstraße** (Styrian Iron Road), winds through valleys and waterfalls from Leoben to Styria's pride and joy, the Erzberg (Iron Mountain), and on through the Enns Valley.

LEOBEN

The buckle of Austria's "Iron Belt," Leoben (pop. 27,000) lies between a ring of mountains and the Mur River. Although 1000-year-old Leoben is the largest city in Styria after Graz, it retains a pastoral feeling. At the southernmost point on the *Steirische Eisenstraße*, Leoben is the proud home of a **Mining University,** as well as 7 other research institutions. Happily, the world of heavy labor and industry doesn't mar the natural beauty of Leoben. Three-quarters of the town's area is woodland, crowned by the idyllic city park "Am Glacis," visited by, among other notables, Emperor Napoleon Bonaparte. Its floral splendors have won Leoben the title of "most beautiful town in Styria" in the **Provincial Flower Competition,** and many residents cultivate kaleidoscopic backyard gardens brimming with tiger lilies and marigolds. Leoben makes a nice change of pace from the more hectic tourist-oriented sites in Austria. Take the time to enjoy the local specialties, including mushroom goulash, unappetizingly called **Shepherd's Spit,** and the excellent (and cheap) local *Gösser* beer.

▊ ORIENTATION AND PRACTICAL INFORMATION. The Mur River surrounds Leoben; from the train station, you must cross it to reach the center of town. **Franz-Josef-Strasse** (the main traffic artery) and **Peter-Tunner-Strasse** run parallel for the length of the town, leading to Hauptpl. and beyond. Leoben is just minutes from Autobahn A9, which runs south to Graz and northwest to Steyr and Linz. The **information counter** (tel. 42545, ext. 390) at the train station in Leoben can help decipher the snarl of rail lines (open M-F 8am-6pm). From there, direct trains run to **Graz** (every 2hr., 114AS), **Vienna Westbahnhof** (every 2hr., 260AS), **Salzburg** (3hr., every 2hr., 370AS), and **Klagenfurt** (every hr., 240AS). For smaller destinations such as **Mariazell,** take the train to **Bruck an der Mur** (15min., 1-2 per hr., 38AS) and catch a bus. The train station also has **lockers** (20AS) and **luggage storage** (30AS; open 6:30am-9pm). For local connections, the main **bus station** in Leoben is a 10-minute walk from the train station at the corner of Franz-Josef-Str. and Parkstr.

Leoben's **tourist office,** Hauptpl. 12 (tel. 440 18; fax 482 18), dispenses a hotel list and a complimentary map. Walk straight out of the train station, cross the river, and take your second right onto Franz-Josef-Str. Follow the road past the bus terminal to the main square. The tourist office is on the right. (Open M-Th 7am-noon and 1:30-5pm, F 7am-1pm.) A new underground **parking garage** is under Hauptpl.; the old one stands on Kärtnerstr. (5AS per 30min.). **Taxi stands** are at Hauptpl. and the train station. Mail a postcard at the **post office,** Erzherzog-Johann-Str. 17 (open M-F 8am-7:30pm, Sa 8-10am). The **postal code** is A-8700.

PHONE CODE	The **city code** for Leoben is 03842.

▛ ACCOMMODATIONS. Leoben has few budget accommodations and only 9 establishments total. During July and August, the **Schulverein der Berg-und-Hüttens-chule Leoben,** Max-Tendlerstr. 3 (tel. 44888; fax 44 88 83), rents out 80 dorm beds. From the train station walk straight and cross the river. Turn right on Stadtkai until Peter-Tunner-Str., and follow it until Max-Tendlerstr. Turn right and walk to the end. (10min.) Rooms are large and plain. (207AS per person, breakfast included for 2-bed dorms. Hall showers.) **Gasthof Altman,** Südbahnhofstr. 32 (tel. 42216), has 22 beds and a small bowling alley in a convenient, albeit busy, location. Walk alongside the rail tracks for 10 minutes; the hotel is on the right. Private TV sets, showers, and hardwood floors make Altman more luxurious than most hotels in this price range. The 3-lane bowling alley fills with locals joyfully and copiously partaking of fermented beverages. To reach the hotel, walk out of the train station and immediately turn left on Südbahnhofstr. (Singles 350AS; doubles 580AS. Breakfast included. Other meals 55-155AS. Bowling alley open Tu-Sa 10am-midnight, Su 10am-3pm; 10AS for 10min. English spoken. Free parking. MC, Visa.)

▙ FOOD. Fans of Italian or typical Austrian cooking will have no trouble feeding their faces in Leoben. Kirchgasse is home to a number of cheap restaurants. **Gasthof Familie Hölzl,** Homanng. 8 (tel. 42107), across from the Stadttheater, cooks up tasty traditional dishes as well as lighter, health-conscious meals. (Pasta 60-76AS, salads tossed in olive oil 42-54AS, and fish 95-98AS.) Try the *Eierschwammerln with Semmelknödeln,* a mushroom soup topped with a big doughy ball for 98AS. (Open M-F 8am-8pm, Sa 8am-2pm, Su 9am-3pm.) Another alternative is **La Pizza,** Langg. 1 (tel. 45347), which has large pizzas for 2 (59-94AS) but nowhere to sit—take out a pie to enjoy by the river (open M-F 11am-2pm and 5-10pm, Sa-Su 11am-10pm). Or, get some edibles at the **markets** along Franz-Josef-Str., **Billa,** Langg. 5 (open M-W 8am-7pm, Th 7:30am-7pm, F 7:30am-7:30pm, Sa 7:30am-5pm), or the **farmer's market** on Kirchpl. (Tu and F 7am-1pm).

◎ 🎵 SIGHTS AND ENTERTAINMENT. Most of Leoben's attractions center around **Hauptplatz**, 10 minutes from the train station (cross the bridge and bear right onto Franz-Josef-Str.). Sights are designated by a square sign with an ostrich eating iron horseshoes, one held daintily between its toes and the other protruding from its beak. This city symbol alludes to Leoben's dependence on the iron trade—in the Middle Ages, ostriches were thought capable of eating and digesting iron. That's a goose, you say? Well, when it was designed, no one in Leoben knew what an ostrich looked like.

Most of the buildings on Hauptpl. are former homes of the **Hammerherren** (Hammer men). The most ornate of the bunch is the 1680 **Hacklhaus**, bearing a dozen statues on its pink facade. Justice holds a sword and a balance, Hope brandishes an anchor, and Wisdom views the world through the mirror in his hand. Now that's wise. Standing guard at the entrance to Hauptpl. are the **Denkmäler und Monumente** (memorial statues and monuments), beautifully crafted works erected to ward off the fires and plague that devastated much of Styria in the early 18th century. Look for St. Florian the fire-proof and St. Rosalia the plague-resistant. Just outside Hauptpl. is the **Pfarrkirche Franz Xaver**, a rust-colored church with twin towers built from 1660 to 1665 by the Jesuits. The plain exterior conceals an elaborate interior. The **Schwammerlturm** (Mushroom Tower) guards the bridge over the Mur.

Leoben is full of meticulously manicured gardens. Stroll through the **Stadtpark "Am Glacis"** one block past Hauptpl. There, you can visit the **Friedensgedenkstätte** (Peace Memorial), which commemorates the 1791 treaty with Napoleon. (Open May-Sept. daily 9am-1pm and 2-5pm. Free.) The small museum showcases an exhibit detailing the political and military events surrounding the treaty—see the very feather pen that Napoleon used to inscribe his signature.

A scenic 30-minute walk along the Mur rewards you with the chance to inspect the **Gösser brewery** (tel. 20 90 58 02). Examine antique brewing machinery, wander around inside the **Göss Abbey** (the oldest abbey in Styria), and swill down a free stein of fresh brew. You can only tour if you arrange ahead of time (it's worth it). The **Stadttheater**, Homanng. 224 (tel. 406 23 02), is the oldest functioning theater in all of Austria (box office open M-Sa 9:30am-12:30pm and Th-F 4-6:30pm; theater closed June-Sept.). The city fills the summer void with the **Leobener Kultursommer**, a program of theater, classical and pop concerts, literary readings, and treasure hunts (June-Sept.). Pick up a free program from the tourist office.

MARIAZELL

Tilting precariously on the side of the Alps, the little town of Mariazell, somewhat extravagantly subtitled *Gnadenzentrum Europas* (Europe's Center of Mercy), is both unabashed resort and important pilgrimage site. It's also beautiful. The faithful come here to pay homage to a miraculous Madonna made of linden wood, once owned by Magnus, the traveling monk who founded the town by establishing a shrine to the Virgin here in 1157. Travelers not so spiritually inclined come to Mariazell to ski in the **Bürgeralpe** or bathe in the waters of the **Erlaufsee.**

⬛ ORIENTATION AND PRACTICAL INFORMATION. Mariazell is accessible from St. Pölten by a zippy little mountain train called the **Mariazellerbahn** (2½hr., 7 per day, 140AS). **Buses** connect Mariazell to **Bruck an der Mur** (1¾ hr., 5:45am-6:10pm, 94AS), **Graz** (5:45am-3:30pm), and **Vienna** (3hr., 5:25am-4:10pm, 170AS). The **bus station** is directly behind the post office near Hauptpl. (open M-F 8am-noon and 2-4pm, Sa 8-11am; information desk open M-F 9:30-11:30am and 2:30-4:30pm, Sa-Su 9:40-10:10am and 3:15-3:55pm). To reach Mariazell **by car** from **Vienna,** take Autobahn A-1 west to St. Pölten, and exit onto Rte. 20 south (1hr.). From **Graz,** take Rte. S-35 north to Bruck an der Mur then Rte. S-6 to Rte. 20 north.

The **tourist office,** Hauptpl. 13 (tel. 2366; fax 3945), has information on local skiing, boating, fishing, hiking, transportation, and accommodations. They make free room reservations. From the train station, turn right on St. Sebastian and walk

MARY, MARY, QUITE CONTRARY In 1157, monk Magnus the Good set out on a mission in the mountains. Ever prepared, he brought a servant, a horse, and his precious hand-carved statue of the Holy Virgin Mary. One night, Magnus and his companion encountered a robber who, seeing how fiercely Magnus defended the statue, drew his dagger and demanded that Magnus hand it over. Magnus rose and held the statue at arm's length in front of him. The mesmerized robber dropped his dagger and muttered "Maria," giving the monk and his companion time to flee. They set up camp a safe distance away and went to bed. Shortly after midnight, Magnus heard a woman's voice pleading with him to wake up. The monk opened his eyes to a shimmering vision of Mary, insisting that he take the statue and run. The monk woke his companion, and they took off into the night. Turns out a pack of robbers was in hot pursuit. Thanks to Mary, the two had a head start, and they were getting away just fine until they came to a huge, impassable sheer cliff. Without hesitation, Magnus held the statue aloft and said a heartfelt prayer. With a great rumble and creak, a passage opened in the stone, just wide enough for the two travelers. They walked into a lush green valley, where slightly bewildered lumberjacks said something like, "Make yourselves at home." At Magnus's request the locals built a little wooded chapel, or "Zell," for the miraculous Mary statue, which became "Mariazell."

until the fork, then left up the hill to Wienerstr. Follow it to Hauptpl.; the office is straight ahead. (Open May-Sept. M-F 9am-12:30pm and 2-5:30pm, Sa 9am-noon and 2-4pm, Su 10am-noon; Oct.-Apr. M-F 9am-noon and 2-5pm, Sa 9am-noon.) The **train station,** Erlaufseestr. 19 (tel. 2230), **rents bikes** (100AS per day with train ticket) and **stores luggage** (30AS per day; open daily in summer 5am-7:10pm; in winter 5am-6:30pm). For **currency exchange** or a 24-hour **ATM,** stop by **Sparkasse,** Grazerstr. 6 (tel. 2303), just behind the post office (open M-F 8am-noon and 2-4pm, Sa 8-11am). In **emergencies,** call the St. Sebastian Hospital, Spitalg. 4 (tel. 2222). Head to **Zur Gnadenmutter,** Hauptpl. 4 (tel. 2102), for pharmaceutical needs (open M-F 8am-noon and 2-6pm, Sa 8am-noon, Su 9:30am-12:30pm). The **post office** is upstairs (open M-F 8am-noon and 2-6pm, Sa 8-10am). The **postal code** is A-8630.

| PHONE CODE | The **city code** for Mariazell is 03882. |

▍▐ ACCOMMODATIONS AND FOOD. Mariazell's **Jugendherberge (HI),** Erlaufseestr. 49 (tel. 2669; fax 26 69 88), has a new building near the train station (270AS per person, extra 50AS for single room). Enjoy the comforts of home at **Haus Wechselberger,** Bilderiweg 8 (tel. 2315). The Wechselberger family rents out a few rooms in their house, complete with antique beds. Several rooms have balconies and views of the surrounding hills. (180AS; 10AS surcharge in winter. Breakfast and hall showers included.) For a quiet stay on the mountainside, try the lovely **Alpenhaus Ganser,** Brünnerweg 4 (tel. 4685). On the way to town from the train station, turn left from Wienerstr. at the tennis courts. Around the bend, stairs built into the mountain provide a shortcut. Uphill and indoors you'll find homemade furniture, hand-carved wood, and fantastic views. Other amenities include a parking garage and sleds that you can ride (in winter) directly to the cable car. A ski trail leads straight to the front door. (180AS per person. Breakfast and showers included. 2-night min. stay.) Though crowded and far (5km) from town, **Camping Erlaufsee** (tel. 2148 or 2116), behind Hotel Herrenhaus near the west dock, is beautifully located by the lake on Erlaufseestr., with showers, toilets, and an activity room. (50AS, children under 15 25AS; tents 40AS. Open May to mid-Sept.)

Cheap food and occasional live music can be found at **Stüberl Goldener Stiefel** (tel. 2731) at the corner of Wiener-Neustadt-Str. and Dr.-Karl-Lueger-Str. (pizza 45-80AS; open daily 8:30am-midnight). For some history with your supper, stop by the **Wirtshaus Brauerei,** Wiener Str. 5 (tel. 2523). Made with a warmer fermentation process than industrial lagers, the unfiltered *Altbier* is best when fresh (27AS). Grab a handful of sweet malt or a homemade pretzel (17AS) to accompany the beer. The restaurant proudly displays 4 generations of family portraits and a photo of Kaiser Franz Josef's 1910 visit to Mariazell. (Open M-W 10am-11pm, F-Sa 10am-midnight, Su 10am-7pm.) There is a **Julius Meinl** supermarket on Wienerstr. (open M-F 5am-6pm, Sa 8am-5pm), and many wonderful *Lebkuchen* (gingerbread) stands operate outside the town church. Specializing in bee products, **Hotel Goldener Löwe**, Hauptpl. 1a, across from the church, lets you sit on the terrace overlooking Hauptpl. while sipping homemade mead (drink of the gods). The hotel also lets the craft-happy try candle-making (Sa-Su 3pm) or gingerbread-baking (by appointment; 35AS, plus a fee for materials). But the real reason to visit is the **1st-floor men's bathroom**—as you enter, the pissoir lights up by itself. A waterfall runs on the wall, and a map of constellations in the stall helps you ponder your fate. Each stall is also equipped with a 15-minute hourglass. Says a vendor across the street: "I have been to Paris; I have been in the grand hotels of New York City. But never have I seen such a bathroom."

🎦 🏔 **SIGHTS AND OUTDOOR ACTIVITIES.** This pilgrimage town—Mariazell means "Mary's chapel"—has welcomed millions of devout Christians over the centuries, all journeying to visit the **Madonna** within the **Basilika,** with its black spires visible from any point in town. International crowds file into the church to admire the miraculous Madonna, resting on the **Gnadenaltar** (Mercy Altar). Empress Maria Theresia, who had her first holy communion in Mariazell, donated the silver and gold grille that encloses the Gnadenaltar. (Tel. 2595. Church open daily 6am-7pm. Free guided tours by appointment through the Superiorat, Kardinal-Tisserant-Pl. 1.) The church's amazing **Schatzkammer** (treasure chamber) contains gifts from former pilgrims (open Tu-Sa 10am-3pm, Su 11am-3pm. 40AS, students 20AS).

Mariazell caters to throngs of bronzed, ultra-healthy outdoor types. Located just under the Bürgeralpe and a short jaunt from the Gemeindealpe, the area is ideal for **skiing.** A **cable car** at Wienerstr. 28 (tel. 2555) zips to the top of the Bürgeralpe. (Every 20min. July-Aug. 8:30am-5:30pm; Apr.-June and Oct.-Nov. 9am-5pm; Sept. 8:30am-5pm. Ascent 75AS, descent 50AS, round-trip 105AS; with guest card or student ID 70AS, 55AS, 95AS.) Ski lifts and trails line the top. (1-day pass 260AS, 2-day 470AS.) For ski information on the Bürgeralpe, Gemeindealpe, Gußwerk, Tribein, and Köcken-Sattel Mountains (no lifts), call the Mariazell tourist office. In the summer, you can hike until you shout on Mariazell's **hiking trails.**

All of Mariazell's water sports revolve around the **Erlaufsee**, a wondrous alpine oasis 6km outside city limits. Bunches of lakeside beaches allow for some of the best sunbathing in central Austria. **Buses** (tel. 2166) run from Mariazell to the lake (summer only, 9:10am, 1:30, and 3:45pm; 20AS). **Steam train engines** (tel. 3014), proclaimed by the tourist office to be "the oldest in the world," also whiz around the lake (July-Sept. weekends and holidays; 50AS, round-trip 80AS). Once at the water's edge, try renting an **electric boat** (90-120AS for 30min.) or a **paddle** or **row boat** (50-60AS for 30min.) from Restaurant Herrenhaus (tel. 3138). For **scuba diving** in the Erlaufsee, contact **Harry's Tauchschule,** Traismauer 5 (tel. (02783) 7747).

ADMONT

Tiny Admont, the gateway to the Gesäuse Alpine region, lies on the border between Styria and Upper Austria, along the Enns River. Benedictine monks built an abbey here in the 11th century, and, although fire has repeatedly ravaged the complex, the stubborn friars have refused to let the church go up in smoke.

🛈 **ORIENTATION AND PRACTICAL INFORMATION.** Trains run to **Selzthal**, the regional hub (6-7 per day, 40AS). Get to Selzthal from Linz (2hr., 168AS; see **Linz**, p. 252) or via Bruck an der Mur (1¼hr., 6-7 per day, 170AS). **Buses** to Linz depart from the front of the post office and marketplace. The Admont **tourist office** (*Fremdenverkehrsbüro;* tel. 2164; fax 3648) tracks down rooms for free. To get there from the train station, turn left down Bahnhofstr. and take the second right at the conspicuous post office; the tourist office is 5 minutes away on the left. (Open M-F 8am-noon and 2-6pm, Sa 9am-noon; Sept.-May M 8am-noon, Tu-F 8am-noon and 2-5pm.) The **postal code** is A-8911.

PHONE CODE	The **city code** for Admont is 03613.

⌐⌐ ACCOMMODATIONS AND FOOD. The most convincing reason to come to Admont is—honestly—the youth hostel, **◪Schloß Röthelstein (HI)** (tel. 2432; fax 27 95 83), reputedly the most beautiful in Europe. Housed in a restored 330-year-old castle, the hostel offers winter ice skating, a sauna (costs extra), a tennis court, a soccer field, even a small track. Indoors, the main dining area is a huge hall draped with ivy and chandeliers, and an exquisite *Rittersaal* (knights' hall) functions as a concert venue. The rooms contain bay windows, brass fixtures, wood furniture, private telephones, and elegant lamps. The only challenge is getting here—yes, it *is* that lone castle sitting very high on the very big hill. From the train station, turn left down Bahnhofstr. and left again at the post office. Cross the tracks and continue straight down that road for 25 minutes (don't turn right at the "Fußweg" sign pointing to the castle, unless you feel mountain-goatish), past the lumberyard. Turn right at the "Schloßherberge Röthelstein" sign and follow the paved road as it curves up and up. **Taxis** (tel. 2801 or 2323) from the station run about 80AS. (6- to 8-bed dorms 235AS, singles and doubles 340AS per person. Breakfast included. Nonmembers add 40AS. Open Jan.-Oct. Parking. Reception 7am-midnight.)

If the trek is too intimidating, try a *Privatzimmer*. Several line Paradiesstr. along the route to the hostel and generally run about 180-250AS. Closer to the town center, **Frühstückspension Mafalda,** Bachpromenade 75 (tel. 2188), awaits. At the post office, turn left and cross the rail tracks, then make the next 2 rights and cross the tracks again. Mafalda is right under the tracks—a fact all too evident come sleepy-time. (220-240AS per person. Hall showers and breakfast included. 50AS surcharge for 1-night stays.) The **ADEG supermarket** is on the way to the tourist office (open M-F 7:30am-noon and 3-6pm, Sa 7:30-noon).

◨ ▥ SIGHTS AND MUSEUMS. Aside from its hostel, Admont is best known for its **Benediktinerstift** (Benedictine abbey), founded in 1074 and currently staffed by 29 monks who, in addition to their clerical duties, run a high school and a profitable door-making factory. The abbey was almost completely rebuilt after the great fire of 1865; only the **library**, built in 1776, was unharmed. It is, incidentally, the largest monastic library in the world (in floor space, not the size of its collection). With its frescoed ceilings and snow-white walls, the library is a Baroque masterpiece. The walls and bookshelves are adorned with bronzed wood statues by Joseph Stammel—in the center of the library are representations of heaven, hell, death, and the final judgment. The bespectacled devil at the foot of the latter statue is said to resemble the abbey accountant of Stammel's time, who was notoriously late with his payments. Hidden stairways lead to the upper balconies—the guides happily direct wayward wanderers. The **Natural History Museum,** full of bottled snakes and insects and the world's largest collection of flies, is housed in the same building. Next door, a special collection of manuscripts, some as old as the 11th century, are displayed in aesthetically-pleasing lucite boxes. (Library and museums open Apr.-Oct. 10am-1pm and 2-5pm daily; Nov.-Mar. by group appointment. Combined admission 60AS, students 30AS. English info sheets 5AS.)

STYRIA

CARINTHIA
(KÄRNTEN)

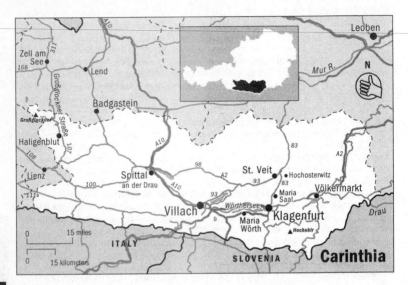

The province of Carinthia (Kärnten) cradles the southern half of Austria. In the west, it juts in between East Tirol and Salzburger Land, reaching into the Hohe Tauern National Park and the Glockner mountain range. The peaks that guard the Italian and Slovenian borders in Carinthia may look severe, but their mass shields the region from cold northern winds. The sunny climate, Italian architecture, and laid-back atmosphere give Carinthia a Mediterranean feel not unlike Switzerland's Ticino region. Though non-Austrians take little notice of this part of the country, natives consider Carinthia a vacation paradise, thanks to its scenic vistas and relaxing lakesides. There are nearly 200 lakes in Carinthia, including the **Wörthersee, Ossiachersee, Faakersee,** and **Millstättersee.** In summer, the warm water attracts families to the countless lake resorts, which offer an array of recreational activities. If your land-legs are surer than your sea-legs, there are rock faces to tackle on every side. Abbeys and castles dot the mountainsides, mute witnesses to Carinthia's distant past. If you'll be in Carinthia for an extended period of time, consider investing in a **Kärnten Card,** good for up to 3 weeks of unlimited local transportation, free admission to most area sights and museums, and discounts on many cable cars, boat cruises, toll roads, stores, and restaurants. The card, available at area tourist offices, is a great deal at 385AS (ages 5-16 160AS).

HIGHLIGHTS OF CARINTHIA

■ Escape to the warm and seductive **Wörthersee**, home base to many vacationers as well as one Austrian soap opera (p. 170).

■ Travel the (mini-)world in Klagenfurt's **Minimundus** amusement park (p. 169).

■ Admire the view from the impressive medieval castle in **Hochosterwitz** (p. 170).

KLAGENFURT

Situated at the crossroads of north-south and east-west trade routes and on the edge of the idyllic Wörthersee, Klagenfurt (pop. 90,000) is a major summertime destination for Austrians, though it is overlooked by most foreigners. Klagenfurt means "ford of laments," harking back to harsher times when travel across the lake and the surrounding marshes was a matter of life and death. Celts and Romans settled here, and in 1518, Klagenfurt became the administrative and cultural capital of Carinthia. Playfully dubbed "the Austrian Riviera," this easygoing, southernmost provincial capital now attracts thousands of work-weary Austrians who unwind in its beachfront suburbs. Klagenfurt's Wörthersee is the warmest alpine lake in Europe and serves as Europe's largest skating arena in winter. Only 60km north of Italy, the Carinthian capital lives life like its Italian counterparts: locals enjoy casual strolls around a palette of outdoor cafés, Italian Renaissance courtyards, and tree-lined avenues framed by Alpine peaks.

GETTING TO KLAGENFURT

Planes arrive at the **Klagenfurt-Wörthersee Airport** (tel. 41 50 00). Flights from Vienna are budget-hostile (every 3hr., round-trip 4080AS; ask travel agents about weekend and youth discounts). To get to the airport from the train station, take bus #40, 41, or 42 to "Heiligengeistpl.," then switch to bus #45 to "Flughafen." **Trains** chug to the **Hauptbahnhof** at the intersection of Südbahngürtel and Bahnhofstr. To reach the town center from the station, follow Bahnhofstr. to Paradeiserg. and turn left. Neuer Platz is two blocks down on the right. The **Ostbahnhof**, at the intersection of Meißtalerstr. and Rudolfsbahngürtel, is for shipping only. **Buses** depart from opposite the main train station. **By car,** Klagenfurt lies on Autobahn A2 from the west, Rte. 91 from the south, Rte. 70 from the east, and Rte. 83 from the north. From **Vienna** or **Graz,** take Autobahn A2 south to Rte. 70 west.

ORIENTATION AND PRACTICAL INFORMATION

Alterplatz, Neuer Platz, and **Heiligengeistplatz,** the town's bus centers, comprise the 3-ring circus of the city's center. They lie within the **Ring,** the inner district of Klagenfurt, which is also the center of social and commercial activity, bordered by St. Veiter Ring, Völkermarkter Ring, Viktringer Ring, and Villacher Ring. Streets within the Ring generally run in a north-south/east-west grid. The **Lendkanal,** a narrow waterway, and **Villacherstr.** go from the city's center 3km to the Wörthersee.

Trains: Hauptbahnhof (tel. 1717). To: **Lienz** (2½hr., 12 per day, 200AS), **Salzburg** (3hr., 9 per day, 330AS), the **Vienna Südbahnhof** (4¼hr., 12 per day, 430AS), **Villach** (30min., 72AS), and **Graz** (3hr., 12 per day, 330AS). Make other connections in Salzburg or Vienna. Open 24hr.

Buses: BundesBuses reach most destinations in Carinthia. To: **Villach** (74AS), **Pörtschach** (54AS), **St. Veit** (45AS), **Friesach** (86AS), and **Graz** (201AS). Ticket window open M-F 7-11am and 11:30am-3pm. Info line (tel. 581 13 50) open M-F 7am-4:30pm. For info on weekends call 06 60 51 88. Buy tickets either at the train station ticket window or aboard the bus.

Public Transportation: Klagenfurt's bus system is punctual and comprehensive. The tourist office can provide a *Fahrplan* (bus schedule). The central bus station is at Heiligengeistpl. Single-fare rides 22AS. Buy individual tickets or a 24hr. pass (40AS) from the driver. *Tabak* kiosks sell cut-rate blocks of tickets. Illegal riders risk a 400AS fine.

Car Rental: Hertz, St. Ruprechterstr. (tel. 56147); **Avis,** Villacherstr. 1c (tel. 55938).

Bike Rental: At the *Hauptbahnhof.* 150AS, with that day's train ticket 90AS. **Impulse** (tel. 51 63 10) has 9 stations all over town, including the tourist office, across from the train station, and the campground. 30AS for 1hr., 50AS for 3hr., 90AS for 1 day (students 50AS), 300AS for 1 week. The tourist office distributes the pamphlet *Radwandern*, detailing local bike paths.

Tourist Office: Gäste Information (tel. 53 72 23; fax 53 72 95; email tourismus @klagenfurt.at; www.info.klagenfurt.at) is on the 1st floor of the *Rathaus* in Neuer Pl. From the station, go down Bahnhofstr. and left on Paradeiserg., which opens into Neuer Pl. The English-speaking staff supplies colorful brochures and helps find rooms for free. Daily tours of the *Altstadt* July-Aug. 10am (call 2 weeks in advance to arrange a tour in English). Open May-Sept. M-F 8am-8pm, Sa-Su 10am-5pm; Oct.-Apr. M-F 8am-5pm. The **Jugend Info** youth information office, Fleischbankg. 4 (tel. 1799), focuses on academic, social, and legal issues and has a knowledgeable staff that can recommend entertainment and restaurants as well. Open M-Th 7:30am-4pm, F 7am-12:30pm.

Currency Exchange: Best rates in town are at the main post office (exchange machine 24hr.) and its train station branch.

Luggage Storage: At the train station. 30AS per piece. Lockers 20AS. Open M-Sa 6:30am-10:30pm, Su 7am-10:30pm.

Bi-Gay-Lesbian Organizations: Gay Hot-Line Klagenfurt, Postfach 193 (tel. 50 46 90). Hotline open W 7-9pm. **Bella Donna Frauenzentrum** (Women's Center), Villacherring 21/2 (tel. 51 12 48). Open M-F 9am-midnight.

Pharmacy: Landschafts-Apotheke, Alterpl. 32, and **Obir-Apotheke,** Baumbachpl. 21, are 2 of many. Check local newspaper to find out which are open on a given night and on weekends.

Hospital: Klagenfurt Krankenhaus, St.-Veiter-Str. 47 (tel. 538).

Emergencies: Ambulance, tel. 144. **Medical Assistance,** tel. 141. **Police,** tel. 133 or tel. 5333.

Post Office: Main post office, Pernhartg. 7, off Neuer Pl. (tel. 55655). Open M-F 7:30am-6pm, Sa 7:30-11am. **Train station branch,** Bahnhofpl. 5. (tel. 5810). Open M-F 7am-10:30am, Sa-Su 8am-9pm. **Postal Code:** A-9020.

PHONE CODE	The **city code** for Klagenfurt is 0463.

▶ ACCOMMODATIONS AND CAMPING

Though the summer heat dries up the pool of available rooms, Klagenfurt does find ways to compensate: 2 student dorms convert to youth hostels during July and August. Be aware, however, that only Jugendherberge Klagenfurt offers dorm accommodations; for the others, you'll pay considerably more for converted student single or double rooms. The tourist office helps locate rooms for free and distributes the helpful *Hotel Information* (with a city map) and *You are Welcome* pamphlets, in English, as well as the German pamphlets *Ferienwohnungen, Ferienhäuser,* and *Privatquartiere,* which list private rooms.

Jugendherberge Klagenfurt, Neckheimg. 6 (tel. 23 00 20; fax 23 00 20 20), at Universitätstr., is close to the university, a 20min. walk from the Wörthersee, and a 30min. walk from the center of the city. From the train station, take bus #40, 41, or 42 to "Heiligengeistpl." then bus #10 or 11 to "Neckheimg." from stand #2. Buses run about every hour in the evenings (last bus to Neckheimg. 11:30pm). Most rooms have 6 bunkbeds, a shower, and a toilet. 190AS, non-members 230AS. For singles add 100AS; doubles add 50AS. Breakfast (7-8am) and sheets included. Dinner 80AS. Key deposit 200AS, passport, or student ID. Reception 7-9am and 5-10pm. Curfew 10pm. Reservations recommended.

Jugendgästehaus Kolping, Enzenbergstr. 26 (tel. 56965; fax 569 65 32). From the station, head right down Bahnhofstr., right on Viktringer Ring, left on Völkermarkter Ring, right at Feldmarschall-Conrad-Pl. (which becomes Völkermarkterstr.), and right on Enzenbergstr. (20min.). A student dormitory during the year, Kolping opens its doors to travelers during the summer, offering huge rooms with gleaming bathrooms. Students never had it so good. HI members 260AS per person, 80AS extra for single, 40AS for

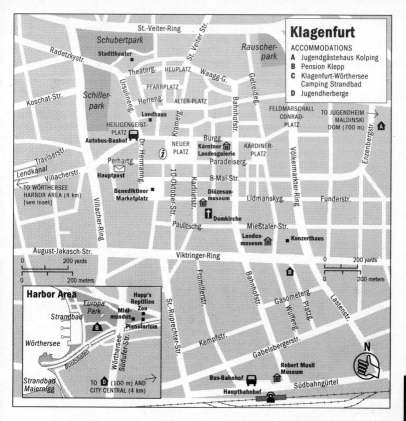

Klagenfurt

ACCOMMODATIONS
A Jugendgästehaus Kolping
B Pension Klepp
C Klagenfurt-Wörthersee
  Camping Strandbad
D Jugendherberge

TO JUGENDHEIM MALDINSKI DOM (700 m)

TO WÖRTHERSEE HARBOR AREA (4 km) [see inset]

Harbor Area

TO ⌂ (100 m) AND CITY CENTRAL (4 km)

CARINTHIA

single-night stay; non-HI members 300AS per person, 80AS for single, 40AS for single-night stay. Breakfast included. 24hr. reception. Open early July to early Sept.

Pension Klepp, Platzg. 4 (tel. 32278). Klepp is a 10min. walk from both the station and the city center. From the station, follow Bahnhofstr., take the 3rd right onto Viktringer Ring, then the 2nd right onto Platzg. The comfortable rooms have large windows. Singles 250AS; doubles 415AS; triples 600AS. Hall showers and toilets.

Jugendheim Mladinski Dom, Mikschallee 4 (tel. 35651; fax 356 51 11). From the train station, turn right on Südbahngürtel, right on St.-Peter-Str., cross Ebentalerstr., follow the road that curves to the left, and take the 1st left. Or take bus #40, 41, or 42 to "Heiligengeistpl.," then bus #70 or 71 (dir.: Ebental) to "Windischkaserne" from stand 13, and continue in the same direction (bus runs M-Sa until 6:50pm). Mladinski Dom, which serves as a dorm for Slovenian students during the school year, converts into a bed-and-breakfast in summer. Singles 280AS; doubles 460AS; triples 510AS. Children under 12 130AS, under 6 90AS. 20AS discount after 3 nights. Breakfast included. Parking available. Reception M-F 6am-midnight, Sa-Su 24hr. Curfew 10pm; key available. Open July 12-Aug. 31.

Klagenfurt-Wörthersee Camping-Strandbad (tel. 21169; fax 211 69 93), on Metnitzstrand off Universitätsstr. From the train station, take bus #40, 41, or 42 to "Heiligengeistpl." then bus #12 to "Strandbad Klagenfurter See." Turn left immediately upon disembarking and walk 2min. The crowded campsite is on the left, on the edge of the Wörthersee. On-site grocery store, miniature golf, and beach. Mid-June to mid-Aug. 80AS per person, ages 3-14 40AS; large site 100AS; small site 20AS. May to mid-June and late Aug. to Sept. 50AS, ages 3-14 25AS. 12AS tax for persons over 18. Showers and beach entry included. Open May-Sept.

FOOD

You don't have to walk far or look hard to find a cheap place to eat in Klagenfurt, especially in Neuer Pl., Kardinalpl. and along Burgg. The tourist office prints *Sonntagsbraten*, a pamphlet listing the addresses and operating hours of cafés, restaurants, clubs, and bars.

Landhaus Restaurant (tel. 50633), inside the courtyard of the Landhaus on Ursulineng. Savor inexpensive, tastefully presented meals in the shadow of one of Klagenfurt's most distinctive buildings. Tagliatelle 98AS, mouth-watering *Marillenknödel* 68AS. *Tagesmenü* 75 or 105AS. Open 10am-midnight daily except Su.

Café Musil, 10-Oktoberstr. 14, is the city's most famous cake and coffee connection. Open 7am-7:30pm, with a larger bistro version at 10-Oktoberstr. 14, open until 10pm.

Anni's Café-Konditorei-Imbiße, Feldmarschall-Conrad-Pl. 6 (tel. 51 18 35). This everything-in-one café is a quick and cheap haven for any meal. Chow down on *Salatschüssel* (a salad concoction; 35-50AS) and *Schinken-Käse Toast* (ham and cheese on toast; 30AS) in the sun-drenched, ivy-enclosed *Gastgarten* out back. Also serves ice cream (7AS), candy, and fresh baked goods (12-28AS). Open M-F 7am-7pm, Sa 7am-1pm.

Rathausstüberl, Pfarrpl. 35 (tel. 57947), on a cobblestone street right by the Pfarrkirche, serves fresh Carinthian specialties at low prices. *Käsenudel mit grünem Salat* (cheese and potato dumplings with green salad) and other daily specials 75AS. Italian entrees 65-78AS. People-watch on the outdoor terrace on balmy summer evenings. English menus available. Open M-F 8:30am-midnight, Sa 8:30am-2pm and 7pm-2am.

Arcobaleno, Wienerg. 11, at the corner of Heupl., serves up an unimaginably large variety of authentic Italian gelato for 10AS a scoop. Open 10:30am-midnight.

Seerestaurant-Strandbad, Strandbad Klagenfurt See (tel. 26 13 96), has a large salad buffet, snacks, and, from 4:30pm in summer, scrumptious grilled fish, flesh, or fowl. Try the *Grillhendl* (grilled chicken) and enjoy the open air. Open 8am-midnight.

La Crêperie, 8-Mai Str. 19 (tel. 50 35 98). This small, jazzy restaurant serves small, jazzy crepes (20-45AS). Open M-F 10:30am-9:30pm, Sa 10:30am-6pm.

MARKETS

Every Thursday and Saturday from 8am to noon, the compact **Benediktinerplatz** on the lower west side of the *Altstadt* welcomes a barrage of rickety, wooden stands showcasing fresh fruits and vegetables.

SPAR Markt, Hermang. just off Heiligengeistpl. Open M-F 8am-6:30pm, Sa 8am-1pm. Another on Bahnhofstr. with a small, cheap restaurant inside. After 3pm, breads and sweets in the *Konditorei* are half-price. Open M-F 7:30am-6:30pm, Sa 7:30am-5pm. There is also a **SPAR** on Villacherstr., 5min. from the youth hostel.

◉ 🏛 SIGHTS AND MUSEUMS

THE OLD TOWN. Get the pamphlet, *A Walk Round Klagenfurt's Old Town*, from the tourist office to explore on your own, or participate in one of several **free guided tours.** *(Tours leave from the front of the Rathaus. July-Aug. M-Sa 10am; usually in German.)* Buildings in this part of town display a strange amalgam of architectural styles: Biedermeier, Italian Renaissance, Mannerist, Baroque, and *Jugendstil* facades all attempt to upstage each other. At the edge of Alterpl. stands the 16th-century **Landhaus,** originally an arsenal and later the seat of the provincial diet. The symmetrical towers, staircases, and flanking projections create an elegant courtyard sprinkled with the banana umbrellas of numerous outdoor cafés. The flourishes of the interior truly deserve accolades—665 brilliant coats of arms blanket the walls. Artist Johann Ferdinand Fromiller took nearly 20 years to complete these pieces. Don't let the ceiling's "rounded" edges fool you—the room is perfectly rectangular. *(Open Apr.-Sept. M-F 9am-noon and 12:30-5pm. 10AS, students 5AS.)*

A stroll down Kramerg., one of the oldest streets in Klagenfurt, leads directly to **Neuer Platz.** Here, merry-go-rounds for the young, cafés for the caffeine-addicted, and soapboxes for the cantankerous are all readily available amid a torrent of motion and activity. Standing proudly over the eastern end, a statue of Empress Maria Theresia glares regally at the skateboarders launching themselves off her pedestal. Compounding the indignity, a 60-ton half-lizard/half-serpent copper creature spits water in her direction. This fountain depicts the **Lindwurm,** Klagenfurt's heraldic beast. This virgin-consuming monster once terrorized the area, preventing settlers from draining the marshes. Enter Hercules, monster-slayer, and all-around *Übermensch,* who quickly dispatched the beast—and saved the village. Today, the *Lindwurm* still terrorizes Klagenfurt, albeit more subtly—stuffed animals reminiscent of Puff the Magic Dragon are for sale *everywhere.*

CATHEDRAL. Two blocks south of Neuer Pl., off Karfreitstr., is Klagenfurt's **Domplatz** and **Kathedrale.** Rebuilt after Allied bombing in 1944, the modern exterior of the church and the surrounding square render the church almost indistinguishable from the surroundings. The cathedral's interior, however, is awash in high arches, crystal chandeliers, pink and white floral stucco, and a brilliant gold altar. Other ecclesiastical paraphernalia are on display in the tiny **Diözesanmuseum** next door, including the oldest extant stained-glass window in all Austria—a humble, 800-year-old sliver portraying Mary Magdalene. *(Lidmanskyg. 10. Tel. 57 70 84. Open mid-June to mid-Sept. M-Sa 10am-noon and 3-5pm; mid-Sept. to mid-Oct. and May to early June 10am-noon. 30AS, students 15AS, children 15AS.)*

HISTORICAL MUSEUM. One of Klagenfurt's largest museums is the **Landesmuseum,** which was Emperor Franz Josef's favorite. It houses the *Lindwurmschädel,* a fossilized rhinoceros skull discovered in AD 1335 that, 3 centuries later, inspired the Lindwurm statue at Neuer Pl. Other pieces include 18th-century musical instruments, a giant Großglocknerstr. relief map, and ancient Celtic and Roman artifacts. The Medusas at the corners of the miraculously intact 3rd-century Dionysus mosaics could take on a *Lindwurm* any day. *(Museumg. 2. Tel. 536 30 552. Open Tu-Sa 9am-4pm, Su 10am-1pm. 30AS, children 15AS.)*

ART MUSEUM AND MUSIL MUSEUM. The **Kärntner Landesgalerie,** 2 blocks east of Neuer Pl., is home to an eccentric collection of 19th- and 20th-century artwork, with a focus on Carinthian Expressionism and well-endowed papier-mâché turkeys. *(Burgg. 8. Tel. 536 30 542. Open M-F 9am-6pm, Sa-Su 10am-noon. 20AS, students 5AS.)* The **Robert Musil Museum,** across the street from the train station, honors the work of its namesake, perhaps Austria's most famous modern writer, with an archive of his writings, but not much else. *(Bahnhofstr. 50. Tel. 50 14 29. Open M-F 10am-5pm, Sa 10am-2pm. 40AS, students 20AS.)*

CASTLES AND MANSIONS. Klagenfurt and its suburbs are home to no fewer than 23 castles and mansions; the tourist office's English brochure *From Castle to Castle* gives a suggested path and details on architecture and operating hours. Another tourist office brochure, the German *Museumswandern,* gives addresses and opening hours for the city's 15 museums and 22 art galleries.

AMUSEMENT PARK. Eager to see more of the world? Don't miss Klagenfurt's most shameless concession to tourist kitsch, the **Minimundus** park, only minutes from the Wörthersee. From the train station, take bus #40, 41, or 42 to "Heiligengeistpl." then switch to bus #10, 11, 20, 21, or 22 (dir.: Strandbad) to "Minimundus." Artists have created intricately detailed models of over 170 world-famous buildings and sights—all on a 1:25 scale. You'll be on eye level with the Parthenon, Big Ben, the Taj Mahal, and many more. Unfortunately, they are unlabeled, so you'll need a guidebook or an architectural encyclopedia. For a taste of home, depending on where home is, check out the Sydney Opera House, a Maori Communal House, Buckingham Palace, or the Statue of Liberty. This must be what Godzilla feels like. At night, an outstanding lighting system illuminates the models. All profits go to the Austrian "Save the Child" society, a fact you can use to soothe your stinging wallet. *(Villacherstr. 241. Tel. 21 19 40. Open July-Aug. Su-Tu and Th-F 9am-7pm, W and Sa 9am-9pm; May-June and Sept. 9am-6pm; Apr. and Oct. 9am-5pm. 120AS, children 6-15 40AS, seniors 90AS, groups of 10 or more 90AS per person. English guidebook 35AS.)*

ZOO. Next door to Minimundus is **Happ's Reptilien Zoo.** To prevent the persecution of the Lindwurm's descendents, the zoo presents exhibits on snakes' environments and histories. Evidently Herr Happ has a rather loose definition of "reptile"—along with puff adders, tortoises, and iguanas, the reptile zoo features spiders, scorpions, rabbits, guinea pigs, and fish. The accident-prone should avoid Saturday's piranha and crocodile feeding. *(Tel. 23425. Open May-Sept. 8am-6pm; Oct.-Apr. 9am-5pm. 75AS, students 65AS, children 35AS.)* Behind the zoo, see a shooting star at the **planetarium** (tel. 21700), as Elton John croons beneath the German narration. *(May-Sept. daily; Oct.-Apr. Sa-Su only. 85AS, under 18 45AS.)*

🏔 OUTDOOR ACTIVITIES

On hot spring and summer days, crowds bask in the sun and loll in the clear water of the nearby Wörthersee. This water-sport haven is Carinthia's warmest, largest, and most popular lake. The two closest **beaches** to Klagenfurt are **Strandbad Klagenfurter See** and **Strandbad Maiernigg.** The former is crowded but near the hostel and easily accessible by public transportation. From the train station, take bus #40, 41, or 42 to "Heiligengeistpl." then bus #10, 11, or 12 to "Strandbad Klagenfurter See." (Both open 8am-8pm. 35AS, children 15AS; after 3pm 20AS, children 7AS. Family card with 1 adult and up to 5 children 50AS, with 2 adults 80AS. Locker key deposit 50AS.)

To enjoy the water without getting (too) wet, rent a **rowboat** (30min., 24AS), **paddle boat** (42AS), or **electric boat** (66AS). Strandbad Maiernigg is far from the noise and fuss of its busier counterpart, but you'll need a car or a bicycle to get there. From downtown, ride along Villacherstr. until it intersects Wörthersee Südüferstr., and then follow signs to "Wörthersee Süd." **Stadtwerke Klagenfurt Wörthersee-und-Lendkanal-Schiffahrt** (tel. 21155; fax 211 55 15) offers scenic cruises on the lake and short rides down the canal. The 2-hour **cruise** goes as far as **Velden,** on the opposite shore, and stops at designated docks along the way. (Round-trip 190AS, advance purchase 170AS.) The Stadtwerke Klagenfurt information center in Heiligengeistpl. sells advance tickets. A *Radwandern* brochure, free at the tourist office, suggests bike tours, including one covering a castle-church circuit. The Karawanken mountains south of Klagenfurt, such as the **Hochobir** (2139m) provide good hiking, but many are accessible only by car. Ask at the tourist office about details and fees.

🎭 NIGHTLIFE

The best of Klagenfurt's nightlife rages in the pubs of **Pfarrplatz** and **Herrengasse.** To maximize your entertainment *Schilling*, read the tourist office's *Veranstaltung-Kalender* (calendar of events), available in English. The tourist office distributes brochures listing concerts, gallery shows, museum exhibits, and plays. Get tickets from **Reisebüro Springer** (tel. 387 00 55). The **Stadttheater,** built in 1910, is Klagenfurt's main venue for major operas and plays. *(Box office tel. 55 26 60. 40-520AS, students and seniors half-price. Open mid-Sept. to mid-June Tu-Sa 9am-noon and 4-6pm.)*

DAYTRIPS FROM KLAGENFURT

NEAR KLAGENFURT: BURG HOCHOSTERWITZ

Hochosterwitz is located just outside the town of Launsdorf, northeast of Klagenfurt and 10km east of St. Veit. Trains run to Launsdorf from Klagenfurt (30min., 10 per day, fewer on weekends, round-trip 112AS), although they tend to be unevenly spaced and run less frequently on weekends. Drivers can take route 83 from Klagenfurt to St. Veit and switch to the district road to Hochosterwitz. From Launsdorf, walk 2km to the base of Hochosterwitz (you really can't miss it), and 10min. more to the main parking lot and entrance kiosk.

Dominating the countryside from the top of a steep hill that seems to rise out of nowhere, **Burg Hochosterwitz** is a striking testament to the erstwhile wealth and power of Carinthia's nobility. This is the stuff that medieval dreams were made of—a long, fortified wall winds around the hillside, culminating in a stocky castle with turrets and towers. The sight is made even more impressive by the castle's high elevation above pasturelands and fields of corn and wheat. It's hard to believe that the well-preserved fortress is not a recent creation, but it has, in fact, been around (at least in its present form) since 1571, when German nobleman and governor of Carinthia Georg von Khevenhüller bought the property and made an extensive and costly renovation of the castle. Irked by marauding Ottoman Turks, Georg constructed the 14 massive gates that guard the road up to the castle, each with its own nickname and strategically designed shooting apertures. The gates alone took 13 years to build; the church was finished in 1586, although later generations of Khevenhüllers tinkered with the walls and fortifications. The path to the top commands postcard-worthy views at each and every turn, taking in all the neighboring countryside and some of the towns and mountains beyond. (Castle open Apr. and Nov. 9am-5pm; May-Sept. 8am-6pm. 70AS, children 6-15 35AS. English brochure 33AS.) A steep, 30-minute walk along the outer wall takes you up to the top of the hill; a **funicular** also ferries visitors up a nearly vertical track to the top (round-trip 40AS). There's a **restaurant** at the top as well as a small **museum** (same hours as the castle; free with castle admission), filled with old paintings of various Khevenhüllers and a collection of medieval arms. Look for the portrait of the castle's current owner, 80-year-old Max Khevenhüller-Metsch, a descendant of the castle's founder.

NEAR KLAGENFURT: MARIA SAAL

Numerous buses and trains (every hr., 40AS) from Klagenfurt stop in Maria Saal daily.

The original church at Maria Saal, called "Sancta Maria in Solio," was located atop a rocky hill 8km north of Klagenfurt. It dated from the 8th century, when it was used as headquarters for monks who came to Germanize the local Slavs. The present church was rebuilt upon the original foundation in the 15th century. Its brooding Gothic exterior contains reliefs and inscriptions from the Roman era as well as a heap of medieval tombstones. A fortress wall encircles the compound; it was erected as protection from Turkish invasions. The church's twin towers are made from local volcanic rock, and its 6600kg bell was fabricated out of 11 Turkish cannonballs. To get to the church from the train station, exit the station and turn left, following the road across the railway tracks and beyond (1km).

The church also houses the **Landschaftsmuseum Schloß Trautenfels** (tel. (03682) 25130), which displays temporary art exhibits and a collection of Carinthian furniture dating from the 17th century (open Easter-Oct. 9am-5pm; 60AS, students 40AS). Signs from the church point to the **Kärntner Freilichtmuseum** (tel. (04223) 2182) a small village of Carinthian farmhouses (open May-Oct. Tu-Su 10am-6pm; 60AS, students 30AS). The **tourist office** (tel. (04223) 22140) is located in a small shack up the main road from the bottom of the church (open daily 8:30am-2pm).

NEAR KLAGENFURT: MARIA WÖRTH

Get to Maria Wörth from Klagenfurt by boat (45min., boats leave at 10am, noon, 2pm, and 4pm; mid-June to Sept. 9 also at 1pm and 5pm; 55AS; free with Kärnten Card) or by bus (40AS, 4-5 per day except Sunday). Boats leave Klagenfurt from the long wooden dock flanked by white banners, past the Strandbad bathing area; purchase tickets at the boat.

Recognizable from afar by its distinctive church steeples, the village of Maria Wörth sits on the shores of the Wörthersee, a large, alluring turquoise lake that attracts boatloads of ritzy Austrian and German tourists in the summer months. Water sports like windsurfing, waterskiing, and parasailing flourish here, as do less rigorous pursuits, such as swimming or the casual cultivation of a beach chair. Unfortunately, there is no public beach in Maria Wörth; the nearest is in neighboring Reifnitz. To paddle in the Wörthersee's waters, you'll need to either stay at a pension with access to a private beach (not necessarily a pension on the waterfront), or else use the beach at the **Strandrestaurant Ebner,** next to the Hotel Astoria (open 8am-midnight; 50AS, children 25AS; beach chairs 20AS; sun umbrellas 20AS). Boats dock at the shore just beneath the 12th-century **church,** which contains a magnificent 17th-century Baroque altar. To reach the **tourist office** (tel. (04273) 2557), follow the main road away from the shore. The office, on the second floor of the building, offers advice on accommodations and recreation in the area. (Open daily 9:30am-12:30pm and 1-5pm.) For a **taxi,** dial 1712.

Housing in Maria Wörth doesn't come cheap, but the splurge may be worth it if you're traveling with a family and want the Wörthersee resort experience. A waterfront pension will set you back at least 450AS per person; the tourist office has a vast list of accommodations. Some of the better bargains can be found in neighboring Reifnitz, but you'll need a car or motorcycle to get there. In Maria Wörth itself, **Pension Watzenig,** St. Anna-Weg 2 (tel. (04273) 2010), is located on a hill above the center of town; walk up the main road inland and turn left at the intersection. This pension provides access to a private beach, shared with a few other guesthouses, 5 minutes away. (Rooms with balcony and TV 250AS per person; apartments with kitchen 750AS per day.) If you can't stand to be more than a stone's throw from the water, **Pension Beatrice** (tel. (04273) 3606), right on the waterfront in Dellach, 2km from Maria Wörth, has its own stable of paddle and electric boats (360-400AS per person, breakfast included). When you get hungry, **Café Primushaus** (tel. (04273) 2500), beneath the tourist office in Maria Wörth, serves up a large variety of dishes on its outdoor patio (pizzas 89-105AS; *Schnitzel* with salad 125AS; open daily 9am-10pm).

Aside from swimming and sunbathing, there are plenty of activities going on in this tiny town. The tourist office can give you a brochure that details who you should contact for **boat rental, bike rental, fishing,** shopping, aerobics, private art galleries, **golf,** indoor pools, bowling, massage, mini-golf, horseback riding, **sailing,** diving, **wind-surfing,** dancing, and tennis. The **Pyramidenkogel** observation tower looms on the hillside above Maria Wörth. You can climb to its top (905m, 1½hr. from town) and survey the Wörthersee and the Karawanken Alps.

THE DRAUTAL

Thanks to its moderate climate and proximity to southern Europe, central Carinthia's **Drautal** (Drau Valley) feels decidedly un-Teutonic, but it provides access to the traditional Alpine activities and then some. The region offers **skiing, hiking,** and **water sports** in highlands and lowlands carved by the **Drau river,** between the Hohe Tauern range and the Villacher Alps. In addition to the transportation hub of **Villach** and an electronic components industry, the Drautal features a variety of lakeside resorts, including the **Millstättersee, Ossiachersee,** and **Faakersee.** In winter, ice skaters pirouette on the ponds while skiers swoosh down nearby slopes. At a paltry 2000m (a baby-step above the timberline), the mountains are favored not just with lumber and the white stuff but also with valuable minerals: iron ore, lead, tungsten, zinc, and manganese. Between and below the peaks are numerous lakes, streams, and curative warm-water springs.

VILLACH

Villach (pop. 55,000) is an attractive city with a divided cultural personality; even the street musicians reveal the influence of neighbors with their traditional Slavic, German, and Italian tunes. An important transportation hub to Italy and Slovenia, Villach is a pleasant place to spend the day, exploring the nearby **Mt. Gerlitzen,** the castle **Schloß Landskron,** or the **Ossiachersee** and **Faakersee.**

🛈 ORIENTATION AND PRACTICAL INFORMATION

Villach sprawls on both sides of the Drau River. The train and bus stations are both on Bahnhofspl., just north of the center of town. Bahnhofstr. leads from the station and over a 9th-century bridge to **Hauptplatz,** the modern commercial and social heart of the city. Narrow cobblestone paths weave through this central area, revealing hidden restaurants and cafés on every new corner. Two sweeping arcs of stores flank Hauptpl., closed off at one end by a towering church and by the Drau at another.

Trains go to **Vienna Südbahnhof** (5hr., 12 per day, 1:21am-7:55pm, 450AS); **Innsbruck** (4½hr., 12 per day, 6:03am-10:55pm, 410AS); **Klagenfurt** (35min., 43 per day, 1:21am-11:40pm, 68AS); **Salzburg** (2¾hr., 12 per day, 4:55am-8:30pm, 280AS); and **Graz** (3½hr., 13 per day, 4:14am-8:12pm, 370AS). A **free city bus** travels a circuit every 20 minutes (M-F 8:40am-6:20pm, Sa 8:40am-12:20pm). **Ferries** cruise up and down the Drau, from Villach in the east to Weinberg-Bad in the west and back again. Boats depart from the dock beneath the north end of the main bridge (1½hr. round-trip; seasonal schedules are complex, but boats usually leave around 10am, 11:50am, 2:30pm, and 4:20pm; 120AS, children ages 6-15 60AS). A **taxi** stand is located at the *Bahnhof*, or dial 28888 or 23333. **Hertz,** inside the **Springer Reisebüro** at Hans-Gasser-Pl. 1 (tel. 26970), rents cars (open M-F 8am-noon and 2-5pm). You can **rent bikes** at the train station (150-200AS per day, with train ticket or Eurailpass 90-160AS) or at **Das Radl,** Italienstr. 22b (tel. 26954), in the alley next to the large pink building (120-140AS per day).

Villach's **tourist office,** Rathauspl. (tel. 24 44 40; fax 244 44 17), gives advice on attractions and skiing and helps find accommodations for free. From the train station, walk out to Bahnhofstr. over the bridge and through Hauptpl. to Rathauspl. The office is at the far end, on the left. (Open in summer M-F 9am-6pm, Sa 9am-noon; in winter M-F 9am-12:30pm and 1:30-5pm.) The **regional tourist office** in St. Ruprecht (tel. 42000; fax 42777) offers up-to-date ski information. There are **ATMs** throughout the city, including locations on Hauptpl. and in the *Hauptbahnhof*. The station also has 24-hour electronic **lockers** (20-40AS), as well as a **luggage check** (tel. 202 03 161; open 6:30am-8:30pm; 30AS). The local **hospital** is on Dreschnidstr. (tel. 2080). Dial 20330 to reach the **police** headquarters at Tralteng. 34. **Internet access** is available at **Ken-i-di,** Ledererg. 16 (tel. 21322) for 60AS per hour (open M-F 10am-10pm, Sa-Su 10am-2am). The main **post office,** 8-Mai-Platz 2 (tel. 25510), also **exchanges currency** (open daily 8am-noon and 2-5pm). The **postal code** is A-9500.

PHONE CODE	The **city code** for Villach is 04242.

⛰ ACCOMMODATIONS

Budget accommodations accessible by foot in Villach are rare. You might consider spending the night in nearby **Klagenfurt** (20min. by train; see p. 166) or **Warmbad Villach,** a neighboring resort accessible by bus #1. Travelers with cars should check out the tourist office's Pension list, which details many outlying bargains accessible only by car. The most reasonably priced establishment in town is **Jugendgästehaus Villach (HI),** Dinzlweg 34 (tel. 56368). From the train station, walk up Bahnhofstr. and go over the bridge and through Hauptpl. Turn right on Postg., walk through Hans-Gasser-Pl., which merges into Tirolerstr., and bear right at St. Martinstr. Dinzlweg is the first street on the left (30min.). The hostel is tucked away past all of the tennis courts. This facility, plastered with neon yellow and orange à la 1976, houses 150 in spacious 5-bed dorms, each with its own shower. (Dorms 190AS. Breakfast and sheets included. Lunch or dinner 80AS each. Free sauna. **Bike rental** 120AS per day. Keys available with passport or ID. Reception 7-10am and 5-10pm. Curfew 10pm.)

FOOD

There's plenty of affordable food in Villach, so take the opportunity to sample Carinthian cuisine, such as *Kasnudeln* (pasta pockets filled with cheese). **Lederergasse** overflows with small, cheap eateries, while **Hauptplatz** and the sprawling **Kaiser-Josef-Platz** seat swankier patrons. **Pizzeria Trieste**, Weißbriachg. 14 (tel. 25 00 58), bakes its great-smelling pies for 65-120AS (open 10am-11pm). Overlooking the Drau at Nikolaipl. 2, **Konditorei Bernhold** (tel. 25442) tempts with warm pastries (12-29AS), devilish ice cream concoctions, and a river view worthy of a slowly sipped cappuccino (open M-F 7:30am-8pm, Sa 8am-8pm, Su 9:30am-8pm). Picnic supplies wait at **SPAR Markt**, on Hans-Grasser-Pl. and at 10-Oktoberstr. 6 (open M-F 7:30am-6:30pm), or at the **farmer's market** in Burgpl. on Wednesday and Sunday mornings.

◉♫ SIGHTS AND ENTERTAINMENT

Villach lies off the beaten tourist path for foreigners, but Austrians congregate throughout the lake district in the summer, escaping the city heat of Vienna, Graz, and Salzburg. The attractions here are subtle, but the welcoming atmosphere invites exploration and relaxation.

DOWNTOWN. Any tour of Villach traverses **Hauptplatz,** the 800-year-old commercial heart of the city. The southern end of the square lives in the shadow of the mighty Gothic **St. Jakob-Kirche,** one of Villach's 12 lovely churches. Slightly raised on a stone terrace, this 12th-century church was converted during the Reformation in 1526 and thereby became Austria's first Protestant chapel. Today, one Counter-Reformation later, the dazzling Catholic altar's gilt canopy almost obscures the Gothic crucifix suspended in front. An ascent up the church's **Stadtpfarrturm,** the tallest steeple in Carinthia (94m), provides your daily exercise and a view of Villach and its environs. *(Church open July-Aug. M-Th and Sa 10am-6pm, F 10am-9pm, Su noon-6pm; June-Sept. M-Sa 10am-6pm; Oct. and May M-Sa 10am-4pm. Free admission. Steeple 20AS, children 10AS. Free organ concerts June-Aug. Th at 8pm.)*

CITY MUSEUM. Villach's **Stadtmuseum,** founded in 1873, exhibits archaeological and mineral displays from six millennia, clocks, hats, 18th-century portraits, and the original gold-on-black Villach coat of arms from 1240. The 90kg, soldered statue of Eisner Leonhard, patron saint of prisoners, formerly stood in St. Leonhardskirche. A local tradition required that anyone who wanted to marry must first be able to carry the statue around the church. Many honeymoons were ruined by hernias. *(Widmanng. 38. Tel. 20 53 49. Open May-Oct. daily 10am-4:30pm; Nov.-Apr. M-F 10am-6pm, Sa 10am-noon and 2-5pm. 30AS, students 20AS, children under 15 free.)*

SCHILLER PARK. A short walk from the congested streets of Hauptpl. lies the small **Schillerpark,** home of the Relief von Kärnten, an enormous topographic model of Carinthia. The park has made molehills out of mountains—all the better to see them, my dear. Walk up Hauptpl. until it turns into 10-Oktoberstr. and turn left on Peraustr. The park is 1 block down on your right. *(Open May-Oct. M-Sa 10am-4:30pm. 20AS, students 10AS, under 15 free.)*

OTHER SIGHTS AND FESTIVALS. Two blocks farther down Peraustr. looms the Baroque **Heilig-Kreuz-Kirche,** the dual-towered pink edifice visible from the city bridge. On the other side of the Drau, the **Villacher Fahrzeugmuseum** is parked at Draupromenade 12. Hundreds of antique automobiles present a rubber-burning ride into the history of transportation. *(Tel. 25530 or 22440; fax 255 30 78. Open M-Sa 10am-noon and 2-4pm; mid-June to mid-Sept. M-Sa 9am-5pm, Su 10am-5pm; 60AS, ages 6-14 30AS.)* In summertime, the **Villach Kirchtag** (Church Day), held since AD 1225 on the first Saturday of August, helps the town celebrate its "birthday" with raucous revelry. *(Entrance to the Altstadt 80AS, 60AS with advance tickets.)*

OUTDOOR ACTIVITIES. Villach lies in a valley between the small but lovely **Ossiachersee** (8km from Villach) and the placid **Faakersee** (10km), so there is plenty of ideal terrain for **swimming, boating,** and **cycling** in easy reach. Trains on the Villach-Ljubljana line stop at Faak am See on the Faakersee, while settlements on the northern shore of the Ossiachersee (i.e., Annenheim, Bodensdorf) lie along the Villach-St. Veit line. Buses service the pleasant southern shore, stopping in the villages of St. Andrä and Ossiach. A well-marked bicycle path leads from Villach to the Ossiachersee and encircles it, while ferries crisscross between the northern and southern shores of the lake. The sleek peaks around Villach make for excellent summer **hiking** and winter **skiing,** with a plethora of resorts to woo the winter traveler. A 1-day regional lift ticket valid for 4 areas costs 330AS (children 190AS), with other combinations available.

TYROL (TIROL)

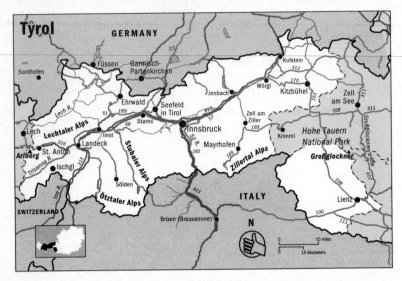

Tyrol's mountains overwhelm the average mortal with their superhuman scale and beauty. Stern contours in the Kaisergebirge above St. Johann and Kufstein in the northwest soften slightly into the rounded shapes of the Kitzbühel Alps to the south, but the peaks rise again above the blue-green Zeller See, just over the border into Salzburger Land. East Tyrol (*Osttirol*) is the geopolitical oddity of the region, technically a semi-autonomous, wholly owned subsidiary of the province of Tyrol, though the 2 provinces share no common border. Although East Tyrol resembles its mother province culturally and topographically, Easterners retain a powerful independent streak. To complicate matters, Italy signed the secret Treaty of London during WWI and was awarded part of Austria—South Tyrol (*Südtirol*)—in exchange for switching sides to join England, France, and Russia. South Tyrol today is a bilingual Italo-German province that slices into East Tyrol.

HIGHLIGHTS OF TYROL AND EAST TYROL

■ Beat the heat **summer skiing** in the Hintertux glacier near Mayrhofen (p. 207).
■ Pet porcupines at Innsbruck's **Alpenzoo,** the highest-altitude zoo in Europe (p. 192).
■ Hike the razor-sharp, snow-streaked **Ötztal Arena,** Austria's largest skiing and snow-boarding playground, using **Sölden** as a base (p. 182).

THE ARLBERG

Half-way between the Bodensee and Innsbruck, the jagged peaks of the Arlberg mountains provide the setting for some of the world's swankiest ski resorts. This is, after all, where modern Alpine skiing was invented. In summer, streams pouring down steep mountainsides create countless waterfalls, providing spectacular **hiking** prospects. Most lifts operate in summer for high-altitude hikes, but **skiing** remains the area's main draw. With hundreds of miles of ski runs ranging in altitude from 1000 to 3000m, the Arlberg offers unparalleled terrain from December through April. Dauntingly long cross-country trails (up to 42km) link various villages throughout the valleys. All resorts have ski schools in German and English for children, beginners, and proficient skiers. In fact, the world's first ski instructor still lives in Oberlech. The comprehensive **Arlberg Ski Pass** gives access to some of Austria's most lusted-after slopes, including the famed **Valluga** summit. The pass is valid for over 88 mountain railways and ski lifts in St. Anton, St. Jakob, St. Christoph, Lech, Zürs, Klösterle, and Stuben, amounting to more than 192km of prime snow-draped terrain. Locally, the Galzigbahn lift tends to attract the longest morning lines because of its central location just outside St. Anton's *Fußgängerzone*, while the Rendl ski area remains largely pristine.

On the eastern side of the Arlberg tunnel, in the province of Tyrol, you'll find the hub of the region, **St. Anton,** and its distinctly less cosmopolitan cousin, **St. Jakob.** The western Arlberg is home to the classy resorts **Lech, Zürs,** and **St. Christoph.** In winter, book rooms 6-8 weeks in advance; in the off season, 2 weeks is sufficient. Buses link the Arlberg towns together, and trains connect St. Anton to the rest of Austria. Bus #4235 runs from Landeck to St. Anton every hour; #4248 runs from St. Anton to St. Christoph, Zürs, and Lech 5 times per day and returns 4 times per day. For more info on the region, contact the **Arlberg Tourist Office** (tel. (05583) 21610; fax 3155; email info-lech@lechtourismus.vol.at; www.lech.at).

ST. ANTON AM ARLBERG

Don't be fooled by the pious name, the bucolic hillside farms, or the cherubic schoolchildren. As soon as the first winter snowflake arrives, St. Anton (non-tourist pop. 2500) awakens with a vengeance as an international playground brimming with playboys, partygoers, and plenty of physical activity (including skiing, skating, and snow-shoeing). To escape the tabloid reporters in St. Moritz, many members of the European jet-set (including Prince Edward of England) winter here. St. Anton loves its flock of traveling socialites; establishments accept all major credit cards, and salespeople have solid command of English. The occasional *Lederhosen*-clad marching band, colorful festival, or early evening cattle drive through the *Fußgängerzone* round out the Tyrolean experience. St. Anton isn't just for the fabulously wealthy. Prices plummet during the summer into the bargain range; during the winter, the neighboring town of **St. Jakob** (10min. by bus) offers many reasonable accommodations. The summer season runs from the beginning of July until the end of September, while the winter season begins in December and ends on May 1. Despite the lack of skiing, summer in St. Anton offers beautiful, isolated hiking trails and quiet, affordable accommodations.

> ⚠ Be warned that this posh ski town doesn't emerge from spring hibernation until mid-July. If you visit in May or June, you may feel as if you've entered a ghost town—the majority of the hotels and restaurants will be closed or running on reduced hours.

 ORIENTATION AND PRACTICAL INFORMATION

St. Anton lies at the bottom of a steep, narrow valley, with the neighboring towns of **St. Jakob** and **St. Christoph** a few minutes east and west along the valley, respectively. Several major train and bus routes connect St. Anton with major destinations. Even the **Orient Express** stops here. More than 40 **trains** come and go daily, with destinations including **Innsbruck** (1½hr., 14 per day 6:14am-6:05pm, 153AS), **Munich** (4hr., 6:14am-6pm, 478AS), and **Zurich** (2½hr., 5 per day 3:36am-3:57pm, 460AS). The St. Anton **train station** (tel. 240 23 85) will **store luggage** for 30AS. During the high seasons (late June to Sept. and Dec.-Apr.) **buses** run 2-5 times per day between St. Anton and the neighboring Arlberg villages, including **Lech** (46AS), **St.**

Christoph (10AS), and **St. Jakob** (5 min., free from 6:30am-9pm, 30AS from 9pm-3am). Year-round buses run frequently to **Landeck** (6am-7pm, 46AS). A *Tageskarte* allows unlimited bus travel between the towns (80AS). The bus station is opposite the tourist office, under Sport Pangratz.

St. Anton has only one main road, which runs the length of the *Fußgängerzone*. From the train station, walk down the hill to the right (or straight ahead if you're coming from the tunnel beneath the platform). Within seconds you'll find yourself on the main drag, the *Fußgängerzone* to the left. To reach the **tourist office** (tel. 22690; fax 2532; email st.anton@netway.at; www.stantonamarlberg.com), turn right on the main road as you exit the station. The tourist office is off a small square on the left just before the railroad crossing. The office is as chic as the town—leather chairs, polished wood reception stands, free maps, and brochures in multiple languages. (Open July to mid-Sept. M-F 8am-noon and 2-6pm, Sa-Su 10am-noon; May to early June and mid-Sept. to Dec. M-F 8am-noon and 2-6pm; Dec.-Apr. M-F 8am-6pm, Sa 9am-noon and 1-7pm, Su 10am-noon and 3-6pm.) **Exchange currency** (at exorbitant rates) at any of the 24-hour ATM machines around town or at the 3 local banks, all in the *Fußgängerzone* (banking hours M-F 8am-noon and 2-4:30pm). **Biking** in the Arlberg is arduous but rewarding. The folks at **Intersport Alber** (tel. 3400; fax 3106) in the pedestrian zone will happily rent you a bike and dispense maps and trail advice. (Full day rental 280AS, morning 150AS, afternoon 180AS, evening 150AS. Prices 20-30AS lower with guest card. Open M-F 9am-noon and 2-6pm, Sa 9am-noon.) **Taxis** await at tel. 2315, 2806, and 2275, or at the late-night taxi stand left of the railroad crossing (10pm-7am). Dial 2565 for 24-hour **ski conditions;** for **weather reports,** dial 22690. To **report accidents,** dial 2352. For the **police,** dial 2237. In an **emergency,** dial 144. To find the **post office** (tel. 3380; fax 3530), take a left from the station and walk to the end of the *Fußgängerzone*, then turn right opposite Hotel Schwarzer Adler (open in summer M-F 8:30am-noon and 2-6pm; in winter M-F 8:30am-7pm, Sa 9-11am). The **postal code** is A-6580.

PHONE CODE	The **city code** for St. Anton is 05446.

■ ACCOMMODATIONS AND FOOD

In the summer, affordable accommodations are relatively easy to find. During the ski season, however, prices generally double. If you book far enough in advance (about 2 months), you *may* find relatively cheap housing. During the ski season, accommodations are usually booked around week-long (Sa-Sa) stays. It can be very difficult to get a room for less than one week, except in December and April. One useful resource is the **24-hour electronic accommodation board** outside the tourist office, which lists all *Pensionen*, hotels, and prices, and has a free telephone to call for reservations. **Pension Pepi Eiter** (tel. 2550) sits to the right on the hill behind the train station. Cross the railroad tracks behind the train station and follow the main road uphill. Look carefully for a green sign about 200m up the road, on the left—turn right at the sign, follow the path up the side of Haus Schollberg and up the hill. Pepi Eiter provides luscious beds, light pine rooms, and a chocolate on your pillow. (In summer, singles 200-230AS; doubles 400-500AS. In winter, singles 400-500AS; doubles 800-1000AS. Add 20AS in summer and 50AS in winter for stays shorter than 3 nights. 2 apartments available for 850AS in summer, 1700-2300AS in winter. All rooms with TV. Breakfast and parking included.) **Pension Elisabeth** (tel. 2496; fax 29254) is one of the town's least expensive 3-star B&Bs. Follow the directions to Pension Pepi Eiter; Pension Elizabeth is up the stairs to the right before you make the sharp turn uphill. The friendly young owner speaks fluent English. (300AS per person. In winter, 560AS. Bath, TV, radio, breakfast, and parking included.)

Your best bet for an affordable winter accommodation is in nearby **St. Jakob** (5min. from St. Anton by free bus). Ask the tourist office for suggestions, or try **Haus Bergwelt** (tel. (05446) 2995), which has spacious, quiet rooms, some with balconies that look out on peaceful, grazing cows. (In summer, 130-180 per person; in winter, 260-420AS per person. All rooms come with shower, bathroom, and TV. Breakfast included.)

The *Fußgängerzone* is riddled with pricey, mediocre restaurants. **SportCafé Schneider** (tel. 2548), opposite the hulking Sport Hotel, serves up a fine selection of soups and sandwiches (35-55AS), spaghetti bolognese (85AS), and ice cream desserts (35-65AS; open 9am-midnight). **Dixie's**, near the end of the *Fußgängerzone*, offers pizzas (100-120AS), salads (40-80AS), and *Käsespätzle* (homemade cheese noodles; 119AS). To combat St. Anton's generally high prices, the local supermarkets may be your best bet. The **Nah und Frisch Supermarket** (tel. 3581) beckons from the *Fußgängerzone* (open summer M-F 7:30-noon and 3-6pm, Sa 7:30am-noon; winter M-Sa 7am-noon and 2-6:30pm). The local **Spar Markt** is farther down the main road, just past the *Fußgängerzone* (open M-F 7am-noon and 2-6pm, Sa 7am-12:30pm).

▲ OUTDOOR ACTIVITIES

HIKING. St. Anton in the summer is a quiet haven for mountain hikers and sport-lovers. On summer Sundays, the local **hikers** hit the **Wanderwege** with walking sticks and full Tyrolean hiking costume—join them for some spectacular mountain views and beautiful hikes along rushing streams. The tourist office dispenses maps and detailed directions for the myriad trails around St. Anton. Once a week in July, the tourist office sponsors wildflower hikes. The office has lists of hikes and a trail map. Crack cyclists might try for the **Arlberg Mountainbike Trophy**, bestowed every August upon the winner of a treacherous 20.5km race with steep climbs and dangerously rapid downhill sections. Entry in the tourney is 400AS, 100AS for kids (tel. 22690). Otherwise, 60km of marked mountain bike paths await you, including the popular Ferwall Valley and Moostal trails.

SKIING MUSEUM. To reach the **Ski-Heimat Museum** (tel. 2475), go uphill on the main road behind the train station, and turn right at the red Museum Café sign. Ski bums will get a kick out of the old boots, bindings, and skis worn by St. Anton's alpine pioneers. Exhibits also detail the building of the massive Arlberg tunnel, as well as the history of the Brotherhood of St. Christoph, a medieval order of do-gooders who rescued travelers in danger. (Open Th-M 10am-6pm.)

SWIMMING POOL. The wooden footbridge to the left of the museum leads to the heated, outdoor **Waldbad** swimming pool. There is a striking view of the snow covered peaks from poolside, plus a 36m twisty red slide. Dry off in the café. (Tel. 2856. 60AS for day pass, 45AS with St. Anton guest card, 15AS children. 40AS for ½ day pass starting at 1 pm, 30AS with St. Anton guest card. Lockers 50AS, 40AS with St. Anton guest card. Open 9am-7pm daily June 18-mid-Sept.)

SKIING. St. Anton's main draw has traditionally been, and always will be, its exceptional **ski** slopes and **skiing** conditions. Ski passes for the Arlberg region are normally sold at the larger hotels, but can also be purchased at the ski lift stations (Galzigbahn, Rendlbahn, St. Christophbahn, and Nasserein-Lift), or at the ticket

T Y R O L

THE ARLBERG CHANNEL St. Anton's economy (like its full name) depends on that pretty old hunk of rock, the Arlberg. Understandably, the town really likes its pet peak. How much? The town has set up a TV channel (29) that provides nothing but live footage of the mountain—hour after hour of trees, rocks, more rocks, and snow. All Arlberg, all the time. Showing up-to-the-minute weather, the channel is ostensibly a service for skiers, but anyone in town can tell you the real reason for it: St. Anton is simply paying high-tech homage to its provider. Twenty-four-hour surveillance replaces burnt offerings—and, anyway, you never know when the mountain might pack up and leave if no one kept an eye on it.

window behind the train station in the *Fußgängerzone*. (½ day pass 355AS, children 215AS; 1-day pass 430-475AS, 260-285AS; 6-day pass 1960-2180AS, 1180-1320AS. Discounts available on passes of 6 days or longer for guests staying in St. Anton, St. Jakob, St. Christoph, Stuben, Zürs, or Lech.)

In January, the **Kandahar Ski Race** on the World Cup circuit attracts the sport's best. (It fluctuates between men's and women's skiing on alternate years; 2000 brings the men's competition.) Or watch the **Synchro Ski World Cup,** where two skiers tackle the mountain simultaneously and are judged not only on speed but also on how closely they mirror each other's form with Germanic precision. Most exciting of all, St. Anton is gearing up for the **Alpine Ski World Championships** (Jan. 28-Feb. 10, 2001). In preparation for the championships, St. Anton is shifting the railway line to the other side of town—skiers will be able to come all the way down the slopes into the town center. All races will finish at a single newly built stadium. Non-champion skiers are discouraged to visit St. Anton during these weeks if they want time on the slopes.

TENNIS. In December, St. Anton hosts the professional **Isospeed tennis tournament,** which features well-known European players, like Thomas Muster, Tommy Haas, and Goran Ivanisevic.

NEAR ST. ANTON: LECH

During the off season (May-July and Oct.-Dec.), Lech is almost inaccessible by public transportation, with only a few buses each day from nearby Langen. In the high skiing and hiking seasons (Dec.-Apr. and June-Sept.), several buses run daily to St. Anton, Zürs, Langen, and Bludenz. (44AS one-way, day pass 80AS; from St. Anton, the beautifully scenic ride takes 30min., and buses run from 8:12am-6pm. Last bus returns at 6:37pm.)

In 1300 the call went out: "There's gold in them thar hills," and the settlers came, leading their cattle from the Valais region of western Switzerland to Lech. As others found, however, the real gold here is powdery and white. The ski resort industry saw a seminal event here when some lost Tyrolean daredevil skiers happened upon the Swiss dairymen in their little valley between the **Rüfikopf** (2362m), **Karhorn** (2416m), and **Braunarlspitze** (2648m) peaks. Smiling contentedly at the mountain slopes, they took a quick swig of schnaps, checked their bindings, and immediately shooshed to the nearest bank. They mortgaged all they had to bring the sport of skiing (and its wealthy practitioners) to the valley. The skiing was so good that people couldn't head up the hill quickly enough; 1939 saw the first T-bar lift. Lech is farther up the mountain than its equally ritzy neighbor St. Anton—above the tree line, in fact. The snow-streaked mountains in all directions are an immediate temptation to start some serious **skiing** or **hiking** (depending on the season), while 1200 sq. meters of outdoor, heated swimming pool waters called the **Waldbad** invite you to take a dip. Get free access to all cable cars, local buses, child care, and swimming facilities with a Lech guest card.

◪ **ORIENTATION AND PRACTICAL INFORMATION.** The **tourist office** (tel. 21610; fax 3155; email lech-info@lech.at; www.lech.at), is just down the road from the bus stop on the right. Hiking maps and English guidebooks are 60AS together. Guided hikes are available. The **24-hour electronic accommodations board** in the foyer has a free phone to make reservations, and there's a **travel agency** in the office. **Lockers** downstairs cost 10AS. (Open late June to mid-Sept. M-Sa 8am-1pm and 2-6pm, Su 9am-noon and 3-5pm; mid-Sept. to Nov. M-F 9am-noon and 2-5pm,

THREE MEN PLUS BABY During the first week of the new year on Three Kings' Day, troupes of devout Austrian school children go door to door singing the story of Casper, Melchior, and Balthasar in exchange for charity. Donors receive a chalk inscription on their doors worth a year of good luck. The inscriptions read "wx–C+M+B–yz" where w, x, y, and z stand for the digits of that given year in order. So good luck for 2000 is 20–C+M+B–00. Write that on some doors for luck!

Sa 9am-noon; Dec.-Apr. M-Sa 9am-6pm, Su 9am-noon and 3-5pm; May to late June M-F 9am-noon and 2-5pm.) Nearby banks are generally open 8:30am to noon and 2 to 4pm. **Raiffeisenbank,** opposite the church and next to the post office, has a **24-hour ATM. Free parking** is available in the Esso garage under the church during the summer season. For **weather reports,** dial 18 in Lech. To **report accidents,** dial 144. For the **police,** dial 2203; for the **Red Cross,** dial 2032. Walk past the church and down the hill to the **post office** (tel. 2240; fax 2250; open M-F 8am-noon and 2-6pm; exchange closes at 5pm). The **postal code** is A-6764.

PHONE CODE	The **city code** for Lech is 05583.

▐▗▌ ACCOMMODATIONS AND FOOD. Guest beds outnumber permanent Lech residents five to one, but when the snowflakes fall the beds fill up and the prices rise. Luckily, there is a **youth hostel** in Lech, kept discreetly at a distance. From the bus stop, head down the main road into town, and continue along this road. Take the last fork downhill before leaving Lech, and cross back over the river. Continue for about 15 minutes, curving toward Lech at the tiny white chapel, and then head uphill around *Haus Tristeller.* **Jugendheim Stubenbach (HI)** (tel. 2419; fax 24194) is at the top of that hill, decorated by a large mural of a prophet right in the middle of a revelation. Lovely mountain views come for a bargain price. (180AS per person, 160AS for 2 nights or more. In winter, 300AS, 280AS. Breakfast included. Closed Oct., May, and June.) To get to **Haus Brunelle** (tel. 2976), follow the main road downhill past the church and over the river. Haus Brunelle is on your right at #220. (Singles 190-220AS. In winter, 330-350AS. Open late June-early Sept. and Dec.-Apr. Breakfast included.)

If you're hungry, **Pizza Charly** (tel. 2339) will serve you right. Down the main road past the church and just after the bridge, it's underneath the cables of the *Schloßkopfbahn* (where they hang tablecloths in the summer). Pizza (90-205AS) and pasta (90-175AS) are served by the river. (Open July to late Apr. daily 11am-2pm and 4pm-midnight. Take-out available.) **S'Caserol Bistro** (tel. 37 41) lies past the church on the right beneath the Volksbank sign and serves crispy baguettes and pasta with vegetarian options for 95-150AS (high season only, 11am-1pm).

TRANSPORTATION HUB: LANDECK

Encircled by mountains and pine forests, the small transit hub of Landeck lacks the magnificent peaks or pristine wilderness of some of its neighbors, but the local tourist office bills the town as "the ideal excursion center in Tyrol." Most tourists are just passing through, but the town's proximity to the Arlberg, the Ötztal, and the Lechtaler mountains make it a decent—if low-key—base for exploring those regions. But then again, you might be best off just heading for the higher ranges. If you do stay in Landeck, the unusual number of bars and restaurants makes for a relatively lively atmosphere.

The **train station** is 2km from the center of town. **Buses** leave for the center every 30 minutes (18AS). Trains run to **St. Anton** (30min., 15 per day, 54AS), **Bahnhof Ötztal** (30min., 25 per day, 46AS), and **Innsbruck** (1¼hr., 30 per day, 46AS). To reach the **tourist office** (tel. (05442) 62344; fax 67830) from the bus stop, follow Malserstr. into town, past the second bridge. The office can help with private accommodations. (Open M-F 9am-noon and 2-6pm, Sa 9am-noon and, in summer, 4-7pm). The **post office** is just up the street from the tourist office towards the central bus stop (open M-F 8am-8pm, Sa 8-11am).

Your best bet for budget accommodations are the *Pensions* in Perfuchs, a hilly suburb across the river from the town center. To get to **Pension Thialblick** (tel. 62261), cross the bridge near the tourist office, follow the road right, and climb the stairs. Follow the path up the hill and turn left at the end of the street (10min.). This pension has quiet, flower-themed rooms on a hill overlooking town. (240-300AS per person. Breakfast included.) **Prima**, up the street from the tourist office, serves fast food Austrian-style: big slabs of *Wienerschnitzel* (85AS), plus a salad bar that seems to contain everything but lettuce. After a tough day of activities, you might want to repair to **KLA4** (pronounced "Klavier"), on the first floor of the mall opposite the tourist office, a pub/restaurant with views of the roaring river below (*Tagesmenü* 70-84AS; beer 39AS; open 9am-2pm and 6pm-2am).

THE ÖTZTAL

Wending its way between hundreds of sharp 3000m peaks on the Italian border, the Ötztal (Ötz valley) offers some of the wildest and most impressive scenery in the Tyrolean Alps. Tiny farms cling impossibly to the mountainside, as rivulets carve their way through rocks to feed into silt-gray rivers. The 1991 discovery of a frozen man who lived 5000 years ago, nicknamed Ötzi (see **Frozen in Time**, p. 65), proves that visitors have been enjoying the breathtaking views here for millennia. There's no reason to stay *that* long if you want to appreciate the hiking and skiing attractions of the Ötztal region. The area, known as the Ötztal Arena, is Austria's largest skiing and snowboarding center, thanks to the perfect balance it strikes between skiing comfort and winter idyll. The four main resorts in the Arena are **Sölden, Hochsölden, Vent,** and **Zwieselstein;** each one has a very distinct character. Two major glaciers, the **Rettenbach** and the **Tiefenbach,** form the largest interconnected year-round skiing area in the Eastern Alps. At the mouth of the valley **Bahnhof Ötztal** sends trains to **Innsbruck** (40min., 24 per day, 86AS) and **Landeck** (30min., 20 per day, 56AS). **Buses** ply the 67km route up the Ötztal valley, passing through the main town of Sölden before forking into the narrow Gurgler and Venter ranges. The region is fairly accessible by public transportation, although buses to the more remote towns run on reduced hours in the summer and fall.

SÖLDEN

Sitting pretty in a neck of the Ötztal valley 40km south of Bahnhof Ötztal, Sölden's prime location makes it an ideal base for exploring the surrounding villages. Although the town is a major ski resort in winter with slopes for all levels of skiing difficulty, Sölden keeps up a modest appearance; it's the razor-sharp, snow-streaked mountains on either side that really steal the show.

⊉ ORIENTATION AND PRACTICAL INFORMATION. Buses arrive in the center of town from **Bahnhof Ötztal** (1hr., 18 per day, 78AS) and **Innsbruck** (2hr., 4 per day, 142AS) before departing for the higher villages of **Vent** (30min., 3-5 per day, 46AS) and **Obergurgl** (25min., 15 per day, 33AS). Sölden is stretched out along the glacially-fed Ötztaler Ache river; to reach the **tourist office** (tel. 22120; fax 3131; email oetztalarena@netway.at; www.tis.co.at/tirol/oetztalarena) from the bus stop, turn left (facing the river) and walk about 100m down the main street. The tourist office eagerly dispenses advice on skiing, hiking, activities, and accommodations. (Open M-Sa 8am-6pm, Su 9am-noon and, in summer, 1-5pm.) **Rent bikes** at any one of the 5 sports shops in town (1 hr. 60-80AS, half-day 100-200AS, full day 225-250AS, weekend 350-720AS). The **post office** sits next to the bus stop (open M-F 8am-noon and 2-6pm. Cashier closes at 5pm). The **postal code** is A-6450.

PHONE CODE	The **city code** for Sölden is 05254.

⊞⊞ ACCOMMODATIONS AND FOOD. Summer accommodations can be quite affordable in Sölden, but be warned that prices rise steeply in winter as skiers hit the slopes. Check with the tourist office for a list of private accommodations or try **Pension Mina,** Rettenbach 90 (tel. 2146), a few meters up the hill across the brook from the post office. The friendly proprietor offers comfortable rooms with TV, shower, and bathroom. (In summer, 220-300AS per person, in winter 360-450AS. Credit cards not accepted.) Located above a shoe store about 100m past the post office, **Haus Glanzer** (tel. 2223; fax 24264; www.glanzer.at), has rooms with gleaming bathrooms and big wooden bedsteads. (In summer, 200-300AS per person, in winter 350-650AS; rates depend on the month.)

There are several restaurants in town, though many close down during the summer season. One of the few budget establishments open year-round is **Café Corso**, by the river across the bridge from the tourist office. (Pizza 88-138AS, pasta 98-148AS. Open noon-midnight daily except W.)

◪ OUTDOOR ACTIVITIES. The high altitude of Sölden's **skiing** areas (1377-3058m) guarantees snow in the winter time, as locals are proud to note. Even in summer, you can ski happily on the glaciers above Sölden. Slopes of all difficulty levels are spread out over Hochsölden, Gaislachkogl, and the Rettenbach and Tiefenbach glaciers. The **Gaislachkoglbahn** whisks passengers up to the top of the 3058m Gaislachkogl in a twin-cable gondola, and is the largest of its type in the world (open mid-June to mid-Sept., Dec.-May, round-trip 220AS). **Lift tickets** for the 32 cable cars and lifts that serve Sölden's slopes are sold at the Gaislachkoglbahn booth at the southern end of town. (Apr.-May and Oct., 1-day pass 420AS; Dec. 12-Jan. 8 and Jan. 25-Apr. 4, 460AS; Jan. 9-Jan. 24, 410AS; June-Sept., 350AS. Discounts available for children, teenagers, and senior citizens.) There are several ski and snowboard schools in and around Sölden, including **Total Vacancia Sölden** (tel. 3100; fax 2939) and **Ötztal 2000** (tel. 2203, ext. 500; fax 225951). Ask at the tourist office about toboggan parties on the 5.5km long toboggan run, which is illuminated along its length in the evening.

In summer, opportunities for **hiking** abound in the surrounding mountains and hills. You can use the network of cable cars to gain and lose altitude. The tourist office runs two free guided tours every week and sells a book of detailed hiking maps and itineraries (25AS). There are various summer glacier hikes, including one up to the site where Ötzi was discovered, as well as outings to mountain lakes. A newly created High Alpine Panorama Trail offers a wealth of hiking routes that provide unique views of the Ötztal and Stubai Alps. **Cyclists** will enjoy the mountain trails around Sölden, ranging from easy 30-minute outings to the strenuous 70km "Mountain Riders Trail" that runs from Bahnhof Ötztal to the Karlsruher Refuge.

NEAR SÖLDEN: OBERGURGL

Buses run from Sölden to Obergurgl (25min., 15 per day, 33AS).

The road from Sölden winds past hairpin turns on the way to Obergurgl, Austria's highest village and home to both top-notch winter skiing and summer hiking. The town consists of little more than an outcrop of hotels and guesthouses at the base of the mountains, but there's enough here to sustain the hardy sportsman or woman. The **tourist office** (tel. (05256) 6466; fax 6353) is around the corner, in the same building as the bus stop. The staff will help you with accommodations, travel tips, and suggestions for what to do in the magnificent mountains. (Open M-F 8am-12:30pm and 2-6pm, Sa 8am-12:30pm and 1:30-4:30pm, Su 10am-12:30pm.) Weather permitting, a ski-lift can carry you, white-knuckled, to the top of **Hohe Mut** (2670m), where the stunning view encompasses icy glaciers and the far-off peaks of Italian Tyrol. (Round-trip 120AS. Open 8:30am-4pm in summer, 9am-4pm in winter.) The **restaurant** at the top serves filling *Gulasch* with *Würstl* (95AS) and beer (47AS). A network of hiking paths covers the mountainsides and woodlands—ask at the tourist office for a map and more information. When the flakes start falling, **skiing** claims Gurgl's heart and soul. You can purchase **lift tickets** at the 2 lift stations (in peak season, 1-day adult pass 440AS; in off-season, 400AS).

INNSBRUCK

Although the 1964 and 1976 Winter Olympics were held in Innsbruck, bringing international recognition to the beautiful mountain city, the unpretentious city has resisted the glamour of its ski-resort status. Instead, Innsbruck offers more substantive temptations to justify its status as one of the most touristed cities in Austria. Massive, snow-capped peaks are so close they seem to advance down the cobblestoned streets of the *Altstadt* at every turn. The city's rich history seems tangible as one strolls past the intricate facades of Baroque buildings or examines the imperial artifacts of the Habsburg legacy. If the natural beauty, the history, and the skiing don't tempt you enough, the university district near the center of town and several quiet mountain suburbs offer a low-key allure all their own.

▣ GETTING TO INNSBRUCK

Flights arrive and depart from **Flughafen Innsbruck,** Fürstenweg 180 (tel. 22525). The airport is 4km from town. Bus F shuttles to and from the main train station every 15 minutes (21AS). **Austrian Airlines** and **Swissair,** Fürstenweg 176 (tel. 1789), have offices in Innsbruck. **Tyrolean Airways** (tel. 2222) offers regional flights. (See **Essentials: Getting There,** p. 39.) **Trains** arrive at the **Hauptbahnhof** on Südtirolerpl., on bus lines A, D, E, F, J, K, R, S, and #3; **Westbahnhof** and **Bahnhof Hötting** are cargo stops. **Cars** from the east or west take Autobahn A12. From Vienna take A1 west to Salzburg then A8 west to A12. From the south, take A13 north to A12 west. From Germany and the north, take A95 to Bundesstr. 2 east.

✳ ORIENTATION

Most of Innsbruck lies on the eastern bank of the **Inn River. Maria-Theresien-Straße,** the main thoroughfare, runs north to south and south to north. The street, open only to taxis, buses, and trams, is crowded with tourists and open-air cafés. To reach the *Altstadt* from the main train station, take tram #3 or 6 or bus A, F, or K to "Maria-Theresien-Str.," or turn right and walk to Museumstr. then left and walk for about 10 minutes. Small maps of the city are available at the train station information booth, the *Jugendwarteraum,* or any tourist office. Continue down Museumstr. and toward the river (curving left onto Burggraben, across Maria-Theresien-Str., and onto Marktgraben) to reach the **university district,** near Innrain. The university itself is to the left down Innrain. Most sights are clustered between the **Innbrücke** and the **Hofgarten,** a relatively short walk from the train station.

▨ PRACTICAL INFORMATION

TRANSPORTATION

Trains: Hauptbahnhof, Südtirolerpl. (tel. 1717). Open 24hr. Information open 7:30am-7:30pm. To: **Salzburg** (2hr., 10 per day, 4:39am-11:33pm, 350AS); **Vienna** (5¼hr., 13 per day, 12:39am-11:33pm, 660AS); **Zurich** (4hr., 8 per day, 6:31am-2:39pm, 592AS); **Munich** (2hr., 9per day, 4:36am-8:37pm, 350AS); **Berlin** (10hr., 12 per day, 4:37am-9:30pm, 1692AS); and **Venice** (5hr., 5 per day, 402AS).

Buses: BundesBuses (tel. 58 51 55 or 35 11 93) leave from the station on Sterzinger-str., next to the *Hauptbahnhof* and left of the main entrance.

Public Transportation: The main bus station is in front of the main entrance to the train station. You can purchase single-ride, 1-zone tickets (21AS), 24hr. tickets (35AS), 4-ride tickets (61AS), and week-long bus passes (123AS) from any driver or *Tabak.* Punch your ticket when you board the bus or pay a 400AS fine. Most buses stop running 10:30-11:30pm. Check each line for specifics. A free *Nachtbus* runs every night, heading east from Marktpl. at 1 and 2am, and heading west from Maria-Theresien-Str. at 1:30 and 2:30am.

Taxis: Innsbruck Funktaxi (tel. 5311, 1718, or 33500). Approx. 120AS from the airport to the *Altstadt.*

Car Rental: Avis, Salurnerstr. 15 (tel. 57 17 54). **Budget,** Leopoldstr. 54 (tel. 58 84 68; fax 58 45 80).

Auto Repairs: ARBÖ (tel. 123). **ÖAMTC** (tel. 120).

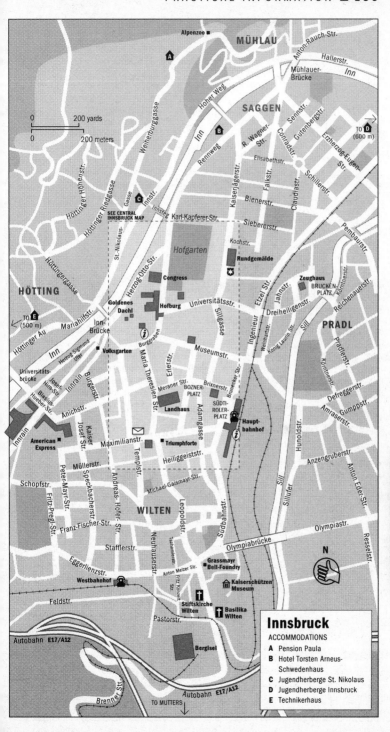

Innsbruck

ACCOMMODATIONS

A Pension Paula
B Hotel Torsten Arneus-
  Schwedenhaus
C Jugendherberge St. Nikolaus
D Jugendherberge Innsbruck
E Technikerhaus

Central Innsbruck

0   100 yards
0   100 meters

N

Innstr.

Walther-park

Hofgarten

Inn

Herzog-Otto-Str.

Congress Innsbruck

Rennweg

Herreng.

Kaiserjägerstr.

Kapuzinerkirche

Dom St. Jakob

Bade.

Pfarrg.

Landes-Theater

Universitätsstr.

Heblinghaus

Goldenes Dachl

Hofburg

Hofg.

Tiroler Volkskunstmuseum

Herzog-Friedrich-str.

Stadtturm

Goldener Adler Inn

Rieseng.

Hof-kirche

Angerzellg.

Prof.-Franz-Mayr-G.

Sillg.

Klebachgasse

Stiftg.

Burggraben

Tiroler Landesmuseum Ferdinandeum

Klara-Pölt-Weg

Seiler.

Schlosserg.

Marktgraben

Museumstr.

Stainerstr.

SPARKASSEN-PLATZ

Erlerstr.

Gilmstr.

Wilhelm Greil-str.

Meinhardstr.

ADOLF-PICHLER-PLATZ

Maria Theresien Str.

Annasäule

BOZNERPL.

Brixnerstr.

Anichstr.

Meranerstr.

Landhaus

American Express

Adamg.

Wilhelm Greil-str.

LANDHAUS PLATZ

SÜDTIROLER PLATZ

Hauptbahnhof

Salurnerstr.

Weserg.

Südbahnstr.

Maximilianstr.

Triumphpforte

Templstr.

Leopoldstr.

Heiliggeiststr.

Müllerstr.

TYROL

Hitchhiking: Hitchers usually take bus K to "Geyrstr." and go to the Shell gas station by the DEZ store off Geyrstr.

Bike Rental: At the train station (tel. 503 53 95). Open Apr. to early Nov. 150-200AS per day, with Eurailpass or that day's train ticket 90-160AS. **Sport Neuner,** Salurnerstr. 5 (tel. 56 15 01), near the station, rents mountain bikes. 200AS per day.

TOURIST AND FINANCIAL SERVICES

Although Innsbruck's myriad tourist offices offer comparable services, the two central offices at Burggraben 3 will probably give the most straightforward information. All offices hawk the **Innsbruck Card,** which gives free access to dozens of local attractions and all public transportation for 24, 48, or 72 hours (230AS, 300AS, 370AS; children 115AS, 150AS, 185AS). A 2-hour **bus tour,** including the *Altstadt* and a visit to the ski jump, leaves from the train station (in summer at noon and 2pm, in winter at noon; 160AS, children 70AS).

Innsbruck Information Office, Burggraben 3 (tel. 59850; fax 59807; email info @innsbruck.tvb.co.at; www.discover.com/innsbruck/), on the 3rd floor. Official and not-for-profit, this office has tons of brochures and a helpful staff. Open M-F 8am-6pm, Sa 8am-noon. It's in the same building as **Innsbruck-Information,** Burggraben 3 (tel. 5356; fax 53 56 14), on the edge of the *Altstadt* just off the end of Museumstr. Huge and high-tech with hundreds of brochures. This private, profit-maximizing consortium of local hotels oversees the offices, so arrange tours and concert tickets but don't expect to reserve budget accommodations. Exchange closes 20min. before office. Open M-Sa 8am-7pm, Su and holidays 9am-6pm. **Branches** at the train station and major motor exits. **Jugendwarteraum** (tel. 58 63 62), in the *Hauptbahnhof* near the lockers, gives directions, suggests hostels, and hands out free maps and skiing information. English spoken. Open M-F 11am-7pm, Sa 10am-1pm. Closed July to mid-Sept.

Österreichischer Alpenverein (ÖAV), Wilhelm-Greil-Str. 15 (tel. 59547; fax 57 55 28). The Austrian Alpine Club's main office provides mountains of hiking information and discounts on Alpine huts and hiking insurance. Members only. Membership 530AS, ages 18-25 and over 60 390AS, under 18 180AS. Open M-F 9am-1pm and 2-5pm.

Budget Travel: Tiroler Landesreisebüro (tel. 59885) on Wilhelm-Greil-Str. at Boznerpl. Open M-F 9am-6pm. AmEx, MC, Visa.

Currency Exchange: Innsbruck Information tourist office, on Burggraben. Open M-Sa 8am-6:40pm, Su 9am-5:40pm. **Banks** are open M-F 8am-noon and 2:30-4pm.

American Express: Brixnerstr. 3, A-6020 Innsbruck (tel. 58 24 91; fax 57 33 85). From the station, take a right then the 1st left. Holds mail. No commission on its checks; small fee for cash. Open M-F 9am-5:30pm, Sa 9am-noon.

Consulate: U.K., Matthias-Schmidtstr. 12 (tel. 58 83 20). Open M-F 9am-noon.

LOCAL SERVICES

Luggage Storage: Luggage watch for 30AS at the train station. Open July-Aug. 6:30am-midnight; Sept.-June 6:30am-10:30pm.

Bookstores: Wagner'she, Museumstr. 4 (tel. 59 50 50; fax 595 05 38). Open M-F 9am-6pm, Sa 9am-5pm. **Buchhandlung Tirolia,** Maria-Theresien-Str. 15 (tel. 59611; fax 58 20 50). Open M-F 9am-6pm, Sa 9am-5pm.

Library: Innsbruck Universität Bibliothek, Innrain 50, where it crosses Blasius-Heuber-Str. Take bus O, R, or F to "Klinik." Copy machine 1AS per page. Open July-Aug. M-F 8am-8pm, Sa 8am-noon; Sept.-June M-F 8am-10pm, Sa 8am-6pm.

Bi-Gay-Lesbian Organizations: Homosexuelle Initiative Tirol, Innrain 100, A-6020 Innsbruck (tel. 56 24 03; 57 45 06; email hose.tirol@tirol.com). All meetings at 8:30pm: mixed younger crowd M, lesbian night T, gay night Th, trans-gender night every other F. **Frauenzentrum Innsbruck** (Women's Center), Liebeneggstr. 15, A-6020 Innsbruck (tel. 58 08 39), runs a women's-only café for lesbians and straights 3 times per week, as well as discotheques and poetry readings. Call for schedules and information.

Laundromat: Bubble Point, Andreas-Hofer-Str. 37 (tel. 336 97 28), at the corner of Franz-Fischer-Str. It really tries, but it's just a laundromat (with a pinball machine and a lot of graphics). 5.5kg washer 45AS, 7kg 55AS, 5min. in the dryer 5AS. Soap included. Open M-F 7am-10pm, Sa-Su 7am-8pm.

Public Showers: At the train station, near the rest rooms. 30AS.

Mountain Guide Information Office: tel. 532 01 75. Open M-F 9am-noon.

Weather Report: tel. (04501) 991 55 608. **Snow report:** tel. (04501) 990 00 011.

Ski Rental: Skischule Innsbruck, Leopoldstr. 4 (tel. 58 17 42). Skis, boots, poles, and insurance 270AS.

EMERGENCY AND COMMUNICATIONS

Emergencies: Police, tel. 133. Headquarters at Kaiserjägerstr. 8 (tel. 59000). **Ambulance,** tel. 144 or 142. **Fire,** tel. 122. **Mountain Rescue,** tel. 140.

Medical Assistance: University Hospital, Anichstr. 35 (tel. 5040).

Post Office: Maximilianstr. 2 (tel. 500), down from the *Triumphpforte* and straight ahead from the station. Open M-F 7am-11pm, Sa 7am-9pm. Address *Poste Restante:* Postlagernde Briefe, Hauptpostamt, Maximilianstr. 2, A-6020 Innsbruck. **Branch** next to the station (tel. 500 74 09). Open M-F 7am-8pm, Sa 8am-6pm. **Postal Code:** A-6020.

PHONE CODE	The **city code** for Innsbruck is 0512.

◤ ACCOMMODATIONS AND CAMPING

Although 9000 beds are available in Innsbruck and suburban Igls, inexpensive accommodations are scarce in June when only two hostels are open: Jugendherberge Innsbruck and Jugendherberge St. Niklaus. The opening of student dorms to backpackers in July and August alleviates the crush somewhat. Book in advance if possible. Visitors should join the free **Club Innsbruck** by registering at any Innsbruck accommodation (see p. 192). Membership gives discounts on skiing and ski buses (Dec. 21-Apr. 5), bike tours, and the club's fine hiking program (June-Sept.).

▨ **Haus Wolf,** Dorfstr. 48 (tel. 54 86 73), in Mutters. Take the Stubaitalbahn tram to "Birchfeld" then walk down Dorfstr. in the same direction (30min.) The Stubaitalbahn leaves from the 3rd traffic island in front of the train station's main entrance. (26AS, week-long ticket 94AS. Last train 10:30pm. Buy tickets from machines on the platform.) An appealingly nutty and very social atmosphere prevails here on the mountainside. Proprietor Titti Wolf spoils her guests with big breakfasts and fond attention; the views across the pastureland are equally exceptional. Singles 190AS; doubles 380AS; triples 570AS. Breakfast and shower included.

Hostel Torsten Arneus-Schwedenhaus (HI), Rennweg 17b (tel. 58 58 14; fax 585 81 44; email youth.hostel@tirol.com; www.tirol.com/youth-hostel). From the station, take bus C to "Handelsakademie," continue to the end and straight across Rennweg to the river. Or walk right from the station, left on Museumstr., right at the end of the street onto Burggraben, and follow it under the arch and onto Rennweg (20min.). This 95-bed hostel offers a convenient location and a front-yard view of the Inn River, complete with stained-glass windows and fishtanks. On summer weekdays, you can store your luggage at the front desk any time. 3- to 4-bed dorms 120AS. Private shower and bathroom included. Breakfast 7:30-8:30am, 45AS. Sheets 20AS. Reception 6-9am and 5-10:30pm. Lockout 9am-5pm. Curfew 10:30pm; keys on request. Open July 1-Aug. 31 and Dec. 27-Jan. 9. Reservations honored until 7pm.

Jugendherberge Innsbruck (HI), Reichenauer Str. 147 (tel. 34 61 79 or 34 61 80; fax 34 61 79 12; email yhibk@tirol.com). Take bus R to "König-Laurin Str." from the train station then bus O to "Jugendherberge" (5min.). With tinted octagonal windows and sliding doors, this 178-bed hostel resembles a high-powered corporation. 3 large lounges with hot plates, TV, and a small library. Large turquoise lockers in the rooms offset flowered 70s quilts. Quiet time from 10pm. 6-bed dorms 146AS 1st night, then 116AS; 4-bed dorms 176AS, 146AS. Showers and sheets included. July-Aug. singles and doubles in an adjacent building with private showers and no lockout 350AS, 500AS. Non-members add 40AS. Breakfast 7-8:30am; dinner 6-8pm, 85AS. Notify the desk by 5pm if you intend to do **laundry** (45AS). Reception 7am-12:30pm and 5-10pm. Lockout 10am-5pm. Curfew 11pm; key available. Phone reservations honored until 5pm.

Haus Kaltenberger, Schulg. 15 (tel. 54 85 76), near Haus Wolf. Take the Stubaitalbahn to "Mutters," then walk towards the church, turn right on Dorfstr., and take the 1st left. You'll find well-kept rooms with attractive balconies and mountain views in this comfy house. Singles 180AS, doubles 360-400AS. Breakfast and shower included.

Technikerhaus, Fischnalerstr. 26 (tel. 28 21 10; fax 282 11 017). Take bus R to "Unterbergerstr./Technikerhaus," or walk from the train station onto Salurnerstr. Take the 1st right onto Maria-Theresien-Str. then left onto Anichstr. Cross the bridge on Blasius-Hueber-Str., go left on Fürstenweg, and left on Fischnalerstr. Though far from the station, this student-housing complex is near the university and the *Altstadt.* **Restaurant** and 2 TV rooms. Singles 225AS, with student ID 190AS, without breakfast 150AS; doubles 215AS per person; triples 205AS per person. Breakfast and showers included. 24hr. reception. Open mid-July through Aug. Make reservations for groups of 3 or more.

Pension Paula, Weiherburgg. 15 (tel. 29 22 62; fax 29 30 17). Take bus K to "St. Nikolaus" then walk uphill. Satisfied guests frequently return to this inn-like home downhill from the Alpenzoo. Views of the river and city center in rooms filled with antique furniture; many rooms with balcony. You can swap books in the multilingual exchange library. Singles 330AS, with shower 420AS; doubles 550AS, 680AS; triples 740, 900AS. Breakfast included. Reservations recommended in summer.

Youth Hostel St. Niklaus (HI), Innstr. 95 (tel. 28 65 15; fax 286 51 514; email yhniklaus@tirol.com; www.tirol.com/yhniklaus). From the train station take bus K to "Schmelzerg." and cross the street. If you're in a good mood, the crowded rooms and gruff management of this sociable bar/restaurant/hostel with wooden bunkbeds and a sleepover-camp feel aren't too bothersome. Dorms 160AS 1st night, then 145AS; 4-bunk rooms 175AS per person. Doubles 390AS; triples 555AS; quads 700AS. Breakfast included. 7min. showers 10AS. **Internet access** 10AS per 10min. Reception 8-10am and 5-8pm. Wake-up at 8:30am. Breakfast 8-9am. **Restaurant** serves filling portions of Austrian cuisine (*Wienerschnitzel* 89AS). Lockout 10am-5pm. Curfew 11pm; key available with 220AS or passport deposit.

Camping Innsbruck Kranebitten, Kranebitter Allee 214 (tel. 28 41 80; www.cda.at/tourismus/campibk/html). During the day, take bus LK from Bozner Platz (near the Bahnhof) to "Klammstr." (20min.); at night, take bus O to "Lohbachsiedlung" and switch to the LK. Walk downhill to the right, and follow the road. These pleasant grounds in the shadow of a snow-capped mountain include a playground for the kiddos. 68AS, children under 15 45AS; tents 40AS; cars 40AS. Tax 7AS. Showers included. Tent rental 75-110AS per person. **Restaurant** open 8am-noon and 4pm-midnight. **Laundry** 50AS. Reception 8am-noon. If reception is closed, find a site and check in the next morning.

☐ FOOD

Most tourists first glimpse cosmopolitan Innsbruck from the glamour of Maria-Theresien-Str. Gawking at the overpriced delis and *Konditoreien* won't fill your stomach, so escape the *Altstadt* and its profiteers by crossing the river to Innstr. in the university district where you'll uncover ethnic restaurants, *Schnitzel Stuben,* and grocers.

■ **Philippine Vegetarische Küche,** Templstr. 2 (tel. 58 91 57), in the grey building at the corner of Müllerstr. A vegetarian rest stop on a highway of meat, this whimsically decorated restaurant serves some of the best food in carnivorous Innsbruck. Everything is tasty and expertly prepared, from carrot-orange soup (44AS) to potato cannelloni with smoked tofu (112AS). Salad bar 48-88AS. Daily specials. Cheaper, smaller portions available. *Menü* with soup and entree 75AS. Open M-F 10am-11pm. DC, MC, Visa.

TYROL

Gasthof Weißes Lamm, Mariahilfstr. 12, on the 2nd floor (tel. 28 31 56). This home-style, Tyrolean restaurant is deservedly popular with the locals, serving up Alp-sized portions for under 100AS. Window tables with lavender tablecloths offer a pleasant view of the river. Check out the daily *Menüs* (soup, entree, and salad 85-115AS). Other entrees 100-200AS. Open daily except Th 11:30am-2pm and 6-10pm.

Salute Pizzeria, Innrain 35 (tel. 58 58 18), on the side of the street farthest from the river. This pizzeria is a popular student hangout near the university. Pizza 40-100AS; pasta 60-95AS. Open 11am-midnight.

Churrasco la Mamma, Innrain 2 (tel. 58 63 98), next to the bridge. Watch the moon rise from the shady outdoor seating next to the river, and fall in love over a plate of spaghetti. Pasta 78-112AS. Brick-oven pizza 68-118AS. Open 9am-midnight. DC, MC, Visa.

Al Dente, Meranestr. 7 (tel. 58 49 47), is a snug candle-lit place with lots of those hand-colored photographs of little children in adult clothing kissing each other on the lips. After finishing your entree (82-142AS), try the delicious *tiramisu* (46AS). Plenty of vegetarian options. English menu. Open M-Sa 7am-midnight, Su and holidays 11am-11pm. AmEx, DC, MC, Visa.

Crocodiles, Maria-Theresien-Str. 49 (tel. 58 88 56). This tiny restaurant on the right of Intersport Okay serves 33 different brick-oven pizzas, including 8 vegetarian options. English menus and a "croco-crew" of waiters are available to help you decide. Large pizzas 60-90AS. Open M-F 11am-10:30pm, Sa 11am-3pm.

Rosenkavalier, Südtirolerpl. 5 (tel. 58 20 24), in the train station. 4 dining rooms serve fine *Wienerschnitzel* for a pittance, which makes this restaurant popular with locals and tourists alike. *Schnitzel* with fries 78AS, spaghetti with meat sauce 74AS. Open M-F 7am-10:30pm, Sa-Su 7am-8:30pm.

University Mensa, in the basement of the white building marked "Leopoldino-Francisca." Cheaper eats in Innsbruck would be hard to come by. This student cafeteria is open to the public. 3 daily menus (soup, entree, and salad 43-55AS). Open M-F 11am-2pm and 5-7pm.

MARKETS

M-Preis Supermarket has the lowest prices around. Branches on the corner of Reichenauerstr. and Andechstr.; on Maximilianstr. by the arch; at Innrain 15; and on the corner of Salurnerstr. and Sterzingerstr. Open M-Th 7:30am-6:30pm, F 7:30am-7:30pm, Sa 7:30am-5pm.

Indoor Farmer's Market, in the Markthalle near the river at Innrain and Marktgraben. Food, flowers, and other stuff. Open M-F 7am-6:30pm, Sa 7am-1pm.

Farmer's Markets on Thursdays from 9am-1:30pm at Franziskanerpl., on Fridays from 9am-2pm at Sparkassenpl., on Saturdays from 8-11:30am at Viktor-Franz-Hess-Str. and 8-11:30am at St. Nikolaus-Brunnenpl.

◧ 🏛 SIGHTS AND MUSEUMS

If you plan on visiting many museums in Innsbruck, invest in the **Innsbruck Card,** which is available at museums, cable cars, and the tourist office, which allows free entry into all museums, cable cars, buses, and trains. *(230AS for 24hr., 300AS for 48 hr., 370AS for 72hr.)*

THE OLD TOWN. Tourists of all races, colors, and creeds flood the *Altstadt*, a tiny aggregation of old buildings, churches, and museums bordered by the river Inn. Its centerpiece is the **Goldenes Dachl** (Little Golden Roof) on Herzog Friedrichstr., a shiny, shingled balcony built to commemorate the marriage of the Habsburg couple Maximilian I and Bianca. They were great-great-great-great-great-great grandparents of Empress Maria Theresia. Beneath the 2,657 shimmering gold squares, Maximilian and his wife kept watch over a crew of jousters and dancers in the square below. Inside the building, the **Maximilianeum Museum** commemorates Innsbruck's favorite emperor. Maximilian, who ruled Austria from 1490 to 1519, used his smarts (and well-timed marriages) to create an empire whose size was exceeded perhaps only by the emperor's nose. The small room of exhibits is short on actual artifacts and doesn't really hang together without the recorded commentary. *(Open May-Sept. 10am-6pm; Oct.-Apr. Tu-Su 10am-12:30pm and 2-5pm. 60AS, students 30AS, seniors 50AS, family pass 120AS.)*

Many splendid old buildings surround the *Goldenes Dachl*. To the left, the flush salmon facade of the 15th-century **Helblinghaus** is blanketed with a pale green, 18th-century Baroque floral detail. A modest climb up the graffiti-lined staircase of the 15th-century **Stadtturm** (city tower), across from Helbinghaus, yields a modest view of the city, perhaps worth exactly the modest cost of admission. *(Open daily July-Aug. 10am-6pm; Sept.-Oct. and Apr.-June 10am-5pm; Nov.-Mar. 10am-4pm. 27AS, students and children 15AS.)* The 15th-century **Goldener Adler Inn** (Golden Eagle Inn) is a few buildings to the left. Goethe, Heine, Sartre, Mozart, Wagner, Camus, and even Maximilian I ate, drank, and made merry here. Innsbruck's most distinctive street is **Maria-Theresien-Straße,** which begins at the edge of the *Altstadt* and runs due south. The street, lined by pastel-colored Baroque buildings, gives a clear view of the snow-capped *Nordkette* mountains that dwarf the city. At the beginning of the street stands the **Triumphpforte** (Triumphal Arch) built in 1765 to commemorate the betrothal of Emperor Leopold II. Down the street, the **Annasäule** (Anna Column), erected between 1704 and 1706 by the provincial legislature, commemorates the Tyroleans' victory on St. Anne's Day (July 26, 1703) after a bloody and unsuccessful Bavarian invasion during the War of Spanish Succession.

CATHEDRAL. One block behind the *Goldenes Dachl* rise the twin towers of the **Dom St. Jakob** (remodeled 1717-1724). The unassuming grey façade conceals a riot of pink and white ornamentation within. *Trompe l'oeil* ceiling murals by C.D. Asam depict the life of St. James. The cathedral's prized possession is the altar painting of "Our Lady of Succour" by Lucas Cranach the Elder. A 1944 air raid destroyed much of the church, but renovations have restored it to its former grandeur. *(Open daily Apr.-Sept. 8am-7:30pm; Oct.-Mar. 8am-6:30pm. Free.)*

HABSBURG PALACE. Behind the *Dom St. Jakob* and to the right is the entrance to the grand **Hofburg** (Imperial Palace), built in 1460 and completely remodeled in 1754-70 under the direction of Empress Maria Theresia. Imposing furniture and large portraits fill more than 20 sumptuously decorated rooms. Highlights include a set of fine mesh reliquaries, the dubious "Chinese Room," and a portrait of Maria's youngest daughter, Marie Antoinette (with head). *(Tel. 58 71 86, ext. 12. Open daily 9am-5pm. Last entrance 4:30pm. 55AS, students 35AS, children 10AS. German tours at 11am and 2pm. English guidebook 25AS. Call ahead for English tour.)* Around the corner, the cavernous **Gothic Cellar,** a kitchen in Maxmillian's time, is sometimes open for special exhibits.

HANDICRAFTS MUSEUM AND IMPERIAL CHURCH. Across Rennweg sits the **Tiroler Volkskunstmuseum** (Tyrolean Handicrafts Museum) and the **Hofkirche** (Imperial Church), which are housed in the same building. Built between 1553 and 1563 as the "New Abbey," the building was converted into a school in 1785 and a museum in 1929. The exhaustive collection of odd implements, peasant costumes, and period rooms provides a dusty introduction to Tyrolean culture. The most interesting exhibit is a collection of incredibly-detailed *Krippen* (nativity scenes) that depict Jesus and the Wise Men. *(Open M-Sa 9am-5pm. Museum alone 60AS, students 35AS, children 20AS. Combined ticket 75AS, 55AS, 35AS.)*

The *Hofkirche* houses an intricate sarcophagus decorated with alabaster scenes from Maximilian I's life and the *Schwarze Mander*, 28 larger-than-life bronze statues of Habsburg saints and Roman emperors that line the nave. Dürer designed the statues of King Arthur, Theodoric the Ostrogoth, and Count Albrecht of Habsburg who pay their last respects to the emperor. Ironically, Maximilian's final resting place is not in the Hofkirche, but in Wiener Neustadt, near Vienna. The elegant Silver Chapel holds instead the corpse of Archduke Ferdinand II

TYROL

amidst wallpaper with faded cherubim resembling hard-boiled eggs. *(Open daily July-Aug. 9am-5:30pm; Sept.-June 9am-5pm. Church alone 30AS, students 20AS, children 15AS. For combination ticket, see above.)*

IMPERIAL GARDEN. Up Rennweg past the *Dom*, the **Hofgarten** (Imperial Garden) is a beautifully manicured park, complete with ponds, flower beds, a concert pavilion, and an outdoor chess set with 3ft. tall pieces. It's a lovely spot to escape the crowds of the *Altstadt*.

REGIONAL MUSEUM. The **Tiroler Landesmuseum Ferdinandeum**, Museumstr. 15 (tel. 59489), showcases the history of Tyrolean art, from medieval altars to modern abstractions. A small collection of non-local art includes a Schiele, a Klimt, and a pint-sized Rembrandt. The **Zeughaus extension** (across town) collects local art and funky traveling exhibits. *(Open May-Sept. M-W and F-Su 10am-5pm, Th 10am–9pm; Oct.-Apr. Tu-Sa 10am-noon and 2-5pm, Su 10am-1pm. 60AS, students 30AS, children 20AS.)*

ALPINE ZOO. Near the Schwedenhaus youth hostel, across the covered bridge, signs point to the **Alpenzoo**, the highest-altitude zoo in Europe, which houses every vertebrate species indigenous to the Alps. *(Tel. 29 23 23. Open daily summer 9am-6pm; in winter 9am-5pm. 70AS, students and children 35AS.)* When you've had your fill of baby ibex, descend the network of scenic trails that weave across the hillside. Tram #1 or 4 or bus C, D, or E to "Hungerbergbahn" drops you at the summit's cable car.

CRYSTAL MUSEUM. Outside the city but well worth seeing is the **Swarovski Kristallwelten**, a multimedia crystal theme-park with a veneer of New Age hokeyness and modern art pretension. Take bus #4125 from the *Busbahnhof* to "Waltens" *(35min., every 30min. 7:45am-8:22pm, 82AS round-trip.)* Above the underground entrance, the fabulous **Giant,** a mossy face on a hillside, spits water and peers through glowing eyes. Inside, purple walls, moving sculptures, and a stele by Keith Haring are augmented by unusual smells and a heavily synthesized soundtrack. The creator of the Kristallwelten, André Heller, has filled it with homages to Viennese artist Gustav Klimt. *(Open daily 9am-6pm. 75AS, students 65AS, children free.)*

◪ HIKING AND SKIING

A **Club Innsbruck** membership lets you in on one of the best deals in Austria. The club's excellent mountain **hiking** program provides guides, transportation, and equipment (including boots) absolutely free to hikers of all ages. Participants assemble in front of the Congress Center (June-Sept. daily at 8:15am), board a bus, and return from the mountain ranges by 4-5pm. The hike isn't strenuous, the views are phenomenal, and the guides are qualified and friendly. Register for Club Innsbruck at any central accommodation. Free night-time lantern hikes leave every Tuesday at 7:45pm for Gasthof Heiligwasser, just above Igls; enjoy an Alpine hut party once there. The **Patscherkofelbahn** in Igls takes hikers up beautiful trails to the **Alpine Garden,** the highest botanical garden in Europe. (Open daily 9am-4:30pm, round-trip 180AS, kids 90AS; one-way 110AS, kids 55AS. Garden open June-Sept. 9:30am-4pm; free; guided tours Friday 2 and 3pm for 20AS). If you want to hike on your own, you're better off taking on the gentler mountains in Innsbruck's suburbs (Mutters and Natters), rather than the enormous Nordkette mountains overlooking the city. Ask at the tourist office for maps and information.

The Club Innsbruck membership also significantly simplifies winter **ski** excursions; just hop the complimentary club ski shuttle (schedules at the tourist office) to any suburban cable car (Dec. 18-Apr. 24). Membership provides discounts on ski passes. **Innsbruck Gletscher Ski Pass** (available at all cable cars and at Innsbruck-Information offices) is a comprehensive ticket valid for all 62 lifts in the region (3 days 1260AS, 6 days 2270AS; with Club Innsbruck card 1020AS, 1830AS). The tourist office also **rents equipment** on the mountain (Alpine approximately 270AS per day; cross-country 160AS; bobsled 250AS per person per ride). The summer bus to **Stubaier Gletscherbahn** (for glacier skiing) leaves at 7:20 and 8:30am. Take the earlier bus—summer snow is often slushy by noon. In winter, buses also leave at 9:45, 11am, and 5pm (1½hr., last bus back at 4:30pm, round-trip 150AS). One day of winter glacier skiing costs 420AS; summer passes cost 280AS after 8am, 235AS after 11am, and 170AS after 1pm. You can rent skis for about 270AS at the glacier. Both branches of **Innsbruck-Information** offer glacier ski packages (599AS including bus, lift, and rental).

For a one-minute thrill, summer and winter **bobsled** rides are available at the Olympic bobsled run in Igls (tel. 33 83 80; fax 33 83 89), 5km from Innsbruck. Summer rides, however, are akin to spruced-up *Cool Runnings* carts with wheels. Professionals pilot the four-person sleds. Reservations are necessary. (Tel./fax (512) 37 71 60 or 37 75 25. Summer W, Th, F at 4 and 6pm; winter Tu at 10am, and Th at 7pm; 360AS.) For a calmer ride, try the **Hafelekar Cable Car** (daily; 260AS, 230AS with Club Innsbruck card).

⬛ ENTERTAINMENT

At a corner of the *Hofgarten*, the **Congress Center** and **Tiroler Landestheater** (tel. 52 07 44) host a number of festivals and concert series in Innsbruck. In August, the **Festival of Early Music** features concerts by some of the world's leading soloists on period instruments at the Schloß Ambras, Congress Center, and *Hofkirche*. (For tickets, call 56 15 61; fax 53 56 14.) The Landestheater also presents top-notch plays, operas, and dance most nights of the year. (Concerts 85-590AS, standing room 50AS; plays 70-500AS, standing room 40AS; rush tickets 90AS, available 30min. before the show to anyone under 21 and students under 27.)

The **Tyroler Symphony Orchestra of Innsbruck** (tel. 58 00 23) plays in the Congress Center, across from the *Landestheater*, between October and May (tickets 280-440AS; 30% discount for children and students). **Chamber music concerts** cost 160 to 260AS; the same discounts apply. The Spanish Hall at Schloß Ambras holds **classical music concerts** most Tuesday nights in summer (140-600AS, 30% discount for students and children). Late June and mid-July bring renowned dancers from Paris, New York, and Moscow to the **International Dance Summer** to the Congress Center to perform in a range of styles (modern dance 315-650AS, classical 540-1000AS; no student or rush tickets).

⬛ NIGHTLIFE

Most visitors collapse into bed after a full day of alpine adventure, but there is enough action to keep party-goers from pillows. Nightlife revolves around students, making the **university quarter** a mecca for late-night revelry. The **Viaduktbogen,** a stretch of theme bars huddled beneath the arches of the railway along Ingenieur-Etzel-Str., contains animated and un-touristy nightlife.

Krah Vogel, Anichstr. 12 (tel. 58 01 49), off Maria-Theresien-Str. Green and orange lanterns illuminate the darkness in this stylish bar/restaurant. A student-age crowd fills up the tables and small garden patio in the back. Ice cream 38-56AS; beer 29-37AS. Open M-Sa 9:30am-1am, Su 4pm-1am.

Hofgarten Café (tel. 58 88 71), inside the *Hofgarten* park. Follow Burggrabenstr. around under the archway and past Universitätstr., enter the park after passing the Landestheater through the small gateway, and follow the path—you'll hear the crowd. During the day, casual diners sip their beers beneath the big white tent; at night it is a sprawling outdoor affair with networking twenty- and thirty-somethings. Note: the park closes at 10pm—use the back entrance to get to the café. Snack food 50-100AS, beer 28-48AS, wine spritzers 31AS. Open daily 10-2am, F until 4am.

Treibhaus, Angerzellg. 8 (tel. 58 68 74; www.treibhaus.at). Turn left on Museumstr. one block past the *Altstadt*, then turn right into the alley next to China Restaurant. Innsbruck's favorite alterna-teen club has both a well-lit indoor café and an outdoor tent. Jazz-oriented. Food 50-95AS. Open M-F 9am-1am, Sa-Su 10am-1am.

Die Alte Piccolo Bar, Seilerg. 2 (tel. 58 21 63). Take the second left after entering the *Altstadt* from Maria-Theresien-Str. This cozy cellar bar attracts a primarily gay male crowd, though women are welcome. Friday and Saturday nights are most popular. Open daily 9pm-4am, except W.

Jimmy's, Wilhelm-Greilstr. 17 (tel. 57 04 73), by Landhauspl. East meets West beneath the all-seeing eyes of the fluorescent Buddha. Chic students and snowboarders strike a pose and contemplate the zebra-striped surfboard. Burgers 76-104AS. Pasta 76AS. Open M-F 11am-1am, Sa-Su 7pm-1am. AmEx, MC, Visa.

DAYTRIPS FROM INNSBRUCK

NEAR INNSBRUCK: SCHLOß AMBRAS

The castle stands in a park to the far southeast of Innsbruck and is accessible by tram #6 (dir.: Igls) to "Schloß Ambras." Follow the signs from the stop. Or, take the shuttle bus that leaves every hour from Maria-Theresien-Str. just opposite McDonalds. Walk from the city only if you have a hiking map since the trail is poorly marked.

One of Innsbruck's most impressive edifices and museums is **Schloß Ambras**, a Renaissance castle built by Archduke Ferdinand of Tyrol in the late 16th century. The medieval castle was a royal hunting lodge, but Ferdinand transformed it into one of the most beautiful Renaissance castles and gardens in Austria. The museum contains an impressive exhibit of good-as-new casts of armor, swords, and lances, paintings by Velazquez and Titian, as well as Archduke Ferdinand's personal *Wunderkammer* (cabinet of curiosities; see **Ferdinand's Curio Cabinet**, p. 195). The walls of the Spanish Hall, Ambras's most famous room, are covered with mythological scenes and portraits of Tyrol's princes. The castle's gardens, stocked with medicinal plants, are also pleasant for a stroll. (Schloßstr. 20. Open Su-M and W-Sa 10am-5pm. 60AS, children and students 30AS; with tour 85AS, 55AS.)

NEAR INNSBRUCK: WILTEN

From the Innsbruck train station, take tram #1 or 6 to "Bergisel."

Wilten, the southernmost district of Innsbruck, is perhaps the city's oldest corner, having once served as the site of the Roman camp of Veldidena. It's primarily a residential district with few traces of its distant past, but it has a few churches and museums that draw tourists.

BASILICA AND STIFTSKIRCHE WILTEN. Pilgrims traveled to the **Basilika Wilten** on foot in the Middle Ages, but now they arrive in tour buses to inspect its rococo interior. The church was built in 1751-56 under the watchful eyes of Maria Theresia, although the sandstone sculpture of Mary and the infant Jesus above the altar dates back to the 14th century. The sides and ceiling of the church bristle with ornate stone and gold details, but nevertheless manages to keep up an airy demeanor. *(Open 8:30am-5pm.)*

Just south of the *Basilika* and across the street stands the **Stiftskirche Wilten**, a church said to have been built upon the site where the giant Haymon fought and killed the giant Thyrsus. The church and adjoining abbey hold a treasure trove of decorated rooms, frescoes, a library, and an altar. *(Tel. 58 30 48. Admission only with free guided tours, which include the Basilika and meet outside the Stiftskirche. Tours meet July-Sept., M at 4pm, W at 10am, and F at 4pm. English tours by request. Call ahead.)*

MILITARY MUSEUMS. The **Kaiserschützen Museum,** across the street from the *Basilika*, celebrates the Tyrolean militiamen who fought on the mountainous Italian front during WWI. The museum features a small collection of uniforms and a much larger collection of oil paintings and sketches documenting life in the snow-bound trenches. *(Open M-Sa 10am-4pm, Su 10am-1pm. Free.)* For a snazzier presentation of the same material, follow the path up the hillside to the **Bergisel-Museum.** This time, the oil paintings and photos commemorate the men who fought under Andreas Hofer in the Tyrolean War of Independence against Bavaria

FERDINAND'S CURIO CABINET

Once upon a time, wealthy princes sent their messengers all over the world to collect the freakiest objects they could find. These bizarre creatures and artifacts filled the royal *Wunderkammer* (cabinets of curiosities), which might encompass anything from two-headed sheep to the daintiest of miniature Chinese paintings. These *Wunderkammer* sought to convey both the resplendence of God's creation and their owners' intimate acquaintance with foreign lands and fabulous riches. During the Renaissance, collecting-mania reached such a frenzy that many princes spent more effort on their *Wunderkammer* than governing their kingdoms.

The *Wunderkammer* of Archduke Ferdinand II, a particularly avid collector, is housed in Schloß Ambras. Ranged on the gallery's walls are portraits of Gosalvus "The Hairy Man" of Tenerife and his daughter, both of whose faces are entirely covered with shaggy hair; a nearby painting displays the unlikely victim of a hunting accident, who has a wooden lance sticking straight through his head (he apparently lived for a year after this misfortune). Beside these hangs a portrait of Vlad Tepesch, the brutal Romanian nobleman later immortalized by Bram Stoker as "Dracula." One of the collection's most bizarre items is a thick tree trunk that appears to have two deer antler growing out of its sides. Glass cabinets hold objects that are perhaps more familiar to 20th-century visitors, but would have amazed Ferdinand and his friends: stuffed sharks and pufferfish, wooden birdcages, coral jewelry, and a primitive version of a Swiss Army knife. Ferdinand's collection tempted even the imagination of later generations—the German poet Goethe and Queen Christine of Sweden both visited his assemblage of oddities.

in 1809. More guns, maps, and mannequins; the paintings, however, can sometimes be quite moving in their own right, particularly Egger-Lienz's depiction of a bayonet charge in "Die Namenlosen." *(Open April-Oct. 9am-5pm. 25AS, children 15AS.)*

BELL FOUNDRY. The **Grassmayr Bell-Foundry,** one block from the *Basilika* towards the city, has been crafting bells for 14 generations, since 1599. In the museum and exhibition rooms, you can watch how these dainty—or behemoth— bells are hand-cast on the premises. *(Leopoldstr. 53. Tel. 594 16 37. Open M-F 9am-6pm, Sa 9am-noon. Castings take place every Friday at 1, 2, and 4pm. Entrance 40AS, children 25AS.)*

OLYMPIC SKI JUMP. From the base of the hill Bergisel, paths also lead up to the **Olympische Sprungschanze** (Olympic Ski Jump), used in the 1964 and 1976 Winter Olympic games. For fear that you'll end up with all the other unfortunate Olympic failures in the graveyard at the bottom of the hill, visitors are not allowed to actually take the plunge—the best you can do is fantasize about weightless flight while taking in the view of the city and outlying mountains.

NEAR INNSBRUCK: STAMS

Regional trains from Innsbruck heading west towards Landeck stop in Stams (60AS). By car, take autobahn A12/E60 or highway 171 directly to the abbey.

When you're going for Baroque, you might as well go all out and head for **Stift Stams,** a magnificent monastery 40km west of Innsbruck. Founded by the Tyrolean Duke Meinhard II in 1273, the cloisters were completely restyled in the 18th century. The 26 Cistercian monks who reside there allow several guided tours per day through the ornate and majestic **Basilika** and the heavily frescoed **Fürstensaal.** The basilica, restored for its 700th anniversary in 1974, features the Baroque masterwork of local artist Andrä Thamasch. Twelve of his gilded wooden statues line the walls of the **crypt** where Meinhard and his wife, among many others, are buried. A little farther down the nave, Thamasch's modest *Madonna* hangs on the wall—its striking asymmetrical composition makes it unique in its genre. Thamasch died while making it, leaving an empty space for St. John. At the far end of the church, the 14km **tree of life** towers over the altar. Designed by Bartholomäus

Steinle in 1613, the tree features 84 golden figures suspended against a blue plaster background, which was added for structural support in the early 1700s. The **Rose Screen**, completed in 1716, is comprised of almost 100 flower bulbs, each laboriously carved from a single piece of iron. Entrance to the cloisters only with the tour. (Oct.-Apr. daily every hr. from 9-11am and 2-4pm; May also at 5pm; June and Sept. also at 1 and 5pm.)

NEAR INNSBRUCK: KUFSTEIN

Regular trains connect Kufstein to Innsbruck (45min., 127AS.) The train station is located on the west bank of the Inn river (ticket office open M 5:25am-8pm, Tu-Sa 5:35am-8pm, Su 7:30am-8:30pm).

In a region dotted with seemingly identical ski-burrows, the town of Kufstein stands out by virtue of its turbulent history. The Habsburgs and the Bavarians quarrelled over Kufstein for centuries, until finally, in 1504, Maximilian I bombarded the Bavarians with cannonballs from a nearby hill until they gave up and went home. Today, though the Habsburgs and the feisty Bavarian nobles are long gone, Kufstein is still a desirable destination for nature lovers. The **tourist office,** Unterer Stadtpl. 8 (tel. (05372) 62207; fax 61455), just across the river from the train station, distributes free hiking, biking, and skiing maps, as well as a complete list of accommodations and restaurants (open M-F 8:30am-12:30pm and 2-5pm, Sa 9am-noon). You can **rent bikes** at the train station (150AS, 90AS with ticket). **Exchange currency** at the **post office,** Oberer Stadtpl. 5 (tel. 62551; open M-F 7am-7pm, Sa 8-11am). **ATMs** are located next to **Spar Market** on Unterer Stadtpl. and in the **Sparkasse** on Oberer Stadtpl. Nights are cheap and cozy at **Haus Reheis,** Hugo-Petler-Str. 1 (tel. (05372) 68322; 360AS for doubles without bath). Otherwise, try **Camping Kufstein,** Salurnerstr. 36 (tel. 622 29 55; fax 63 68 94). Shady spots along the river will cost you a mere 50AS (33AS for children; cars 40AS, guest tax 7AS; reception daily 8-11am and 6-11pm).

Aside from the incredible surroundings, Kufstein's main attraction is the 13th-century **Festung** (fortress), which raises its crenellated fist high above the river Inn. Climb to the fortress grounds via a medieval *Gangsteig* (covered staircase) designed by Balthasar Laumianello, or take the elevator (open end of March to mid-Nov. and mid-Dec. to Feb. daily 9am-5pm; one-way 30AS, students 15AS; round-trip 30AS, 20AS). Once you're within the walls of the *Festung*, you're free to wander about the quiet grassy knolls and stone ramparts. Poorly lit archways make you feel like a spelunker. The drafty, drippy *Rockpassage* cuts from one side of the fortress to the other and was used as a refuge during both World Wars. At the top of the fortress, the **Heimatmuseum** (tel. 60 25 30; fax 71060) features a motley crew of pre-historic and early modern artifacts, as well as a room of sacred art with crushed red velvet wallpaper and a pickled two-headed chicken. (Open daily 9am-5pm; guided tours Apr.-Oct. Combined entrance to fortress and museum 130AS, students 70AS.) The *Festung* also houses the 4037 pipes of the **Heldenorgel** (Heroes' Organ), the world's largest open-air organ, which was constructed in 1931 in honor of Austrian soldiers who died in WWI. The organ is played, on the keyboard at the base of the fortress, for all to hear every day at noon and, during the summer season, again at 6pm (10AS for auditorium seat). To reach some non-man-made heights, take the **Wilder Kaiser Chairlift** high into the mountains (open M-F 8:30am-4:30pm, Sa-Su 8am-4:30pm; round-trip 130AS; children 55AS; ascent only 100AS, 40AS).

SEEFELD IN TIROL

After Innsbruck borrowed its smaller neighbor's terrain for nordic skiing events during the 1964 and 1976 Winter Olympic games and made it internationally famous, Seefeld in Tirol found itself in a position to lay serious claim to winter-sports-mecca status. As in most alpine towns, skiing is the cash cow in Seefeld, but the same mountains provide summer hiking for a fraction of the price.

❼ ORIENTATION AND PRACTICAL INFORMATION. Trains connect Seefeld to **Innsbruck,** 26km away (40min., 17 per day 6:32am-8:12pm, 46AS). **Buses** leave from in front of the train station. To get to the *Fußgängerzone* and the center of town, head down Bahnhofstr. Seefeld's main square, Dorfpl., is on your left at the first major intersection. After Dorfpl., Bahnhofstr. becomes Klosterstr.; the cross-street (the other main arm of the *Fußgängerzone*) is Münchenstr. to the right of the Dorfpl. and Innsbruckstr. to the left.

From the station, walk up Bahnhofstr. and past Dorfpl. to the **tourist office,** Klosterstr. 43 (tel. 2313; fax 3355; email info@seefeld.tirol.at; www.tiscover.com/ seefeld) to get a list of accommodations (open mid-June to mid-Sept. and mid-Dec. through Feb. M-Sa 8:30am-6:30pm; mid-Sept. to mid-Dec. and Mar. to mid-June M-Sa 8:30am-12:15pm and 3-6pm). **Exchange money** at banks (open M-F 8am-12:30pm and 2-4pm) or the post office until 5pm. **Taxis** (tel. 2630, 2221, 2700) wait in front of the train station. You can **store luggage** (30AS) and **rent bikes** (150-200AS per day, 100-175AS with train ticket) at the station as well. If all the station bikes are rented, try **Sport Sailer** (tel. 2530) in Dorfpl. (mountain bike 220AS for a full day, 350AS for weekend; open during high seasons M-F 9am-6pm, Sa 9am-4:30pm, Su 10:30am-noon and 3:30-5pm; off season M-F 10am-noon and 3-6pm). The **Tip-Top Laundromat,** Andreas-Hofer-Str. 292 (tel. 2044), is behind and to the right of the station. Leave a load to be washed-and-dried for 150AS (open M-F 8am-12:30pm and 2:30-6:30pm, Sa 9am-noon). For a **snow report,** dial 3790. The **post office,** Klosterstr. 367 (tel. 2348), is down the road from the tourist office (open M-F 8am-noon and 2-6pm, cashier closes at 5pm; Dec. 16-Apr. 15 and June-July also Sa 9am-noon). The **postal code** is A-6100.

| PHONE CODE | The **city code** for Seefeld in Tirol is 05212. |

❏❏ ACCOMMODATIONS AND FOOD. Seefeld boasts 7 five-star hotels (that's *thirty-five* stars!), but no hostel. As the price of a hotel bed runs 540 to 4260AS (depending on the season), *Pensionen* or *Privatzimmer* are the best budget options. Prices for these rooms average 220AS to 320AS per night in the summer; slap on about 50AS more in winter. Make reservations in advance, particularly if you're traveling alone in high season, since singles are few and far between. The tourist office has a list of all accommodations: call ahead and the staff will help you find a room. Wherever you stay, inquire about a **guest card** *(Kurkarte)* for 10-20% discounts on skiing, swimming, concerts, and local attractions.

Several *Pensionen* cluster along Kirchwaldstr. To get there, walk from Dorfpl. down Klosterstr. past the sports center, then up the narrow, uphill road lined by a guard rail. **Haus Felseneck,** am Kirchwald 309 (tel. 2540), has luxurious rooms, each with balcony, TV, bathroom, and a view you'll wish you could write a quick message on the back of, stamp, and send home. The friendly owners like to practice their English. (In summer singles 270AS, doubles 540AS, 4-person apartment with kitchen 750AS; in winter singles 360AS, doubles 720AS. Breakfast and shower included.) **Boznerhof,** Hocheggstr. 355 (tel. 2941), offers guests the use of a **kitchen,** free parking, and a large breakfast (In summer singles 250AS, with WC 260AS; doubles 500AS, 520AS. In winter singles 300AS, 350AS; doubles 600, 660AS. Breakfast and shower included).

The entire *Fußgängerzone* is stocked with rows of pricey restaurants, outdoor cafés, and bars, but **Gasthof Batzen Hausl,** Klosterstr. 44 (tel. 2292), at the end of the *Fußgängerzone,* has some good deals. The *Tagesmenü* includes soup, entrée, and dessert for 108AS. (Open daily 10am-1:30am.) **Luigi and Lois,** Innsbruckstr. 12 (tel. 22 58 67), operates on a goofy gimmick—Italian fare on the Luigi side and Tyrolean fare *chez* Lois. The food is decent and the decor entertaining. Luigi's pasta costs 89-125AS; Lois' *Gröstl* is 98AS. (Kitchen open 10:30am-11pm, bar until 1am. AmEx, MC, Visa.) The **Albrecht Hat's supermarket,** Innsbruckstr. 24 (tel. 22 29), is located across from Sport Sailer just off Dorfpl. (open M-Th 8:30am-6:30pm, F 8am-7:30pm, Sa 8am-6pm).

TYROL

OUTDOOR ACTIVITIES. The tourist office distributes *Seefeld A-Z*, a detailed listing of the wide range of summer and winter activities offered in town, as well as season-specific activity calendars. The **Olympia Sport Center,** at the end of the *Fußgängerzone*, is a popular attraction year-round, featuring an **indoor pool** and a massive **sauna** complex. (Tel. 3220. Pool open summer and winter 9:30am-10pm; fall and spring 1-10pm. 88AS with guest card, children 44AS. Sauna open daily 2-10pm. Sauna and pool 165AS with guest card, children 125AS.) The Center also screens **movies** nightly during July and August (80AS).

Summer in Seefeld brings a multitude of outdoor activities. The tourist office and the **Tyrol Alpine School** run an excellent summer **hiking** program of 4- to 6-hour hikes that wind among the sky-scraping peaks surrounding Seefeld, including the 2569m **Pleisenspitze** and the 2367m **Gehrenspitze.** (Hikes leave mid-June to mid-Sept. Tu-F at 8am. Register by 5pm the day before the hike. 250AS with guest card.) The **Kneipp Hiking Society** invites visitors to join its free weekly 3- to 5-hour outings, which depart from the train station Thursdays at 12:30pm. To wander on your own, pick up hiking maps at the tourist office (55AS). If you prefer flatter terrain, **Strandbad Wildsee** (tel. 3387) is open for swimming from 9:30am to 7pm. (June-Sept., 30AS).

Seefeld offers 2 money-saving ski passes to winter tourists. The **Seefelder Card** is valid for Seefeld, Reith, Mösern, and Neuleutasch (1-day pass 350AS, ages 5-15 210AS, ages 16-17 315AS). The **Happy Ski Pass** is valid for skiing at Seefeld, Reith, Mösern, Neuleutasch, Mittenwald, Garmisch-Zugspitze, Ehrwald, Lermoos, Biberwier, Bichlbach, Berwang, and Heiterwang (pass available for 3-20 days and requires a photograph; 3 days 990AS, ages 5-15 620AS, ages 16-17 910AS). Twelve different **sports equipment rental shops** lease alpine and cross-country skis, snowboards, and toboggans at standardized rates. (Downhill skis with poles and boots 100-200AS, children 80-130AS; boots 50-100AS; snowboard 200-300AS.) A free **ski bus** runs every 20 minutes (daily 9am-4:40pm) between town and the **Rosshütte** and **Gschwandtkopf** ski areas. For those who prefer their skiing on the level, choose from the 100km of *Langlauf* (cross-country) trails (trail map available at the tourist office), or try skating, tobogganing, or snow hiking.

THE LECHTALER ALPS

The Lechtaler Alps offer some of the best skiing in the world. Hugging the German border in northwestern Tyrol, this region of 3000m peaks is four-fifths uninhabitable. The **Inn River,** the primary waterway of the valley, runs southwest to northeast from the Swiss frontier at Finstermünz to the German border by Kufstein. Parallel to and north of the Inn, the **Lech River** has eroded its own wide valley. Between the lowlands of the Inn and Lech, the mountains are virtually people-free. Unless you like crowds, the best time to visit the Lechtal is when the mountains are your only companions, e.g. off season (April-June or Oct.-Nov.).

EHRWALD

Of his hometown Ehrwald, poet Ludwig Ganghofer once prayed, "If You love me, please let me live here forever." His request went unheeded: he died abroad in 1920 and was buried near Munich. But some divine power has certainly smiled on the city. Other than a few damaged buildings, both World Wars spared the town, and to date nothing has blemished Ehrwald's prized attraction, the majestic **Zugspitze** (2962m, Germany's highest mountain). Of course, what could? It's a big, craggy, tooth-shaped mountain on the German-Austrian border that draws 400,000 tourists a year. Ehrwald is more pleasant than neighboring German resort towns in many ways: it's quieter, it has a fast cable car (the Tiroler Zugspitzbahn), and it's cheaper (rooms run 50-100AS less).

ORIENTATION AND PRACTICAL INFORMATION. Ehrwald lies in a cul-de-sac of the Austrian Alpine railroad: all trains to and from Ehrwald must pass through Garmisch-Partenkirchen in Germany, where Ehrwald-bound travelers must switch onto a 2-car train. **Trains** run to **Garmisch-Partenkirchen** (30min., 9 per day, 38AS), **Innsbruck** (1½hr., 8 per day, 123AS), **Munich** (2hr., 9 per day, 256AS), and **Salzburg** (4hr., 12 per day, 430AS). By **car**, Autobahn A12 follows the Inn from Innsbruck to Mötz, the old market town. Bundesstr. 314 runs north from Mötz to Ehrwald, close to Germany and Garmisch-Partenkirchen. Bundesstr. 198 runs along the Loesach river.

Ehrwald has few street signs. To reach the town center from the train station, bear left and cross the tracks onto Bahnhofstr., which then merges with Hauptstr. After about 20 minutes, Hauptstr. veers left and uphill as it becomes Kirchpl. The **tourist office,** Kirchpl. 1 (tel. 2395; fax 3314; email ehrwald@zugspitze.tirol.at; www.tiscover.com/ehrwald), is in the center of town, a few steps beyond the church (open M-F 8:30am-noon and 1:30-6pm; mid-June to Sept. and mid-Dec. to Feb. also open Sa 8:30-noon). **Currency exchange** is available at banks (open M-F 8am-noon and 2-4:30pm) and the post office. There is a **24-hour ATM** at the Bank für Tirol und Vorarlberg (BTV), Kirchpl. 21a. The little Ehrwald train station (tel. 22 01 34) offers **luggage storage** (30AS; open M-Sa 6am-9pm, Su 7am-9pm). For a **taxi,** dial 2268 or 2325. **Rent bikes** at Zweirad Zirknitzer, Zugspitzstr. 16 (tel. 3219), across the tracks and up the hill (70AS per half-day, 90AS per day; mountain bikes 50AS per hr., 100-150AS per half-day, 200AS per day, 350AS per weekend; children's bikes discounted). The **post office,** Hauptstr. 5 (tel. 3366), is on the right about 100m before the town center as you walk from the train station (open M-F 8am-noon and 2-5:30pm). Ehrwald's **postal code** is A-6632.

PHONE CODE	The **city code** for Ehrwald is 05673.

■■◪ **ACCOMMODATIONS AND FOOD.** Ehrwald is filled with fairly inexpensive guest houses. The tourist office has a complete listing of prices and locations. Wherever you stay, be sure to pick up a **guest card** for tourist discounts. **Gästehaus Konrad,** Kirweg 10 (tel. 2771), is only a few minutes down Hauptstr. from the station toward the town center. After you pass the post office and SPAR market, take the first right onto Kirweg. Konrad is on your right, down a private driveway. Each room has a painted Alpine scene. Step out onto the balcony for the real thing: a phenomenal view of green fields, small villages, and mountains in every direction. (In summer, singles with shower 220-250AS, doubles 440-500AS. In winter, 250AS per person. Breakfast included.) Camping is available—if you're willing to walk about 25 minutes uphill—at **Camping Dr. Lauth** (tel. 2666; fax 26664; www.camping-ehrwald.at). Head left out of the train station and immediately turn left up the hill. Take the right-hand fork past Zweirad Zirknitzer and continue uphill (ignore the "Leaving Ehrwald" sign). After the road curves left at the Thörleweg intersection, the well-marked campground is on the right. Pitch your tent in the shadow of the Zugspitze. Phones, **restaurant,** and **laundry** (70AS wash and dry) are on-site. (70AS per person; tent and car 70AS; tax 10.50AS. Reception open 8am-10pm.)

The **Metzgerei Restaurant,** Hauptstr. 15 (tel. 2341), serves traditional dishes and vegetarian entrees in its friendly dining room. The *Tiroler Knödel,* two balls of starch laced with succulent ham and served scalding hot over sauerkraut, are a bargain at 54AS. (Open 11:30am-8:30pm, limited menu from 2-5pm.) If you're planning a picnic on the summit of the Zugspitze, try the local **SPAR supermarket,** Hauptstr. 1 (tel. 2740), next to the post office (open M-Th 8am-7pm, F 8am-7:30pm, Sa 7:30am-1pm; July to mid-Sept. and mid-Dec. to Mar. Sa until 6pm).

■ ◪ **SIGHTS AND ENTERTAINMENT.** The **Tiroler Zugspitzbahn** (tel. 2309) is Ehrwald's leading tourist attraction and greatest feat of engineering. This cable car climbs 2950m to the summit of the Zugspitze in a hold-your-breath (for some, hold-your-lunch) 7 minutes and 12 seconds. The outdoor platforms of the observation station (open mid-May to mid-Oct.) at the ride's end have what some deem the most breathtaking view on the continent. Be sure to bring a sweater, since snow

TYROL

may still be on the ground. (Open late May to late Oct. and late Nov. to mid-Apr. daily 8:40am-4:40pm. Round-trip 420AS, children 250AS.) The **restaurant** at the summit gives you more food than you could possibly eat for unusually low prices (*Tagesmenü* 85AS). The **Ehrwalder Almbahn** (tel. 2468) doesn't climb quite so high ("only" 1510m), but the prices aren't so high either (May 21-Oct. 18, 8:30am-4:40pm; Dec.-Apr. 9am-4pm; 130AS, children 65AS). To reach either cable car, hop on any of the green buses that stop at green "H" signs (every hr., 46AS).

In summer, the Ehrwald tourist office organizes **mountain bike** and **hiking tours** daily. You can book a tour at Bergsport-Total, across the street from the tourist office (free on M, otherwise 180-250AS per person). The tourist office also provides information on hiking, fishing, swimming, billiards, boats, skating, climbing, **paragliding,** horseback riding, squash, tennis, **kayaking,** and river rafting in Ehrwald and neighboring areas. Visitors can **swim** outdoors at **Hotel Spielmann,** Wetterstr. 4 (tel. 2225), or indoors at the **Familienbad Ehrwald,** Hauptstr. 21 (tel. 2718), a short distance before the town center (look for Sport Center sign).

For winter guests, Ehrwald offers the **Happy Ski Pass.** The cheerful little card gives access to 143 lifts, 200km of alpine ski runs, 100km of cross-country trails, and several other winter sports arenas. (For more information and prices, see **Seefeld,** p. 196.) Shops in the main square and at lift stations **rent skis** and equipment (boots, skis, and poles around 410AS per day, 1300AS for 6 days).

KITZBÜHEL

When Franz Reischer arrived in Kitzbühel in 1892, his 2m snowshoes and wild ideas about sliding down mountains stirred up a fair amount of skepticism. Two years later the first ski-championship was held in town, and everyone wanted a piece of the big-shoe action. The 6 peaks surrounding Kitzbühel were named the "Ski-Circus," and life was never the same again. Now the annual **International Hahnenkamm Race** (see p. 203), considered the toughest course in the world, attracts amateurs, professionals, and spectators. Even with all this attention, Kitzbühel retains a small-town feel, welcoming wealthy vacationers and poor ski-bums alike.

▐ GETTING TO KITZBÜHEL

Kitzbühel has 2 **train stations.** Trains from Salzburg arrive at the **Hauptbahnhof;** those from Innsbruck or Wörgl at the **Hahnenkamm Bahnhof. Buses** stop next to both train stations. Kitzbühel lies on Bundesstr. 161 north/south and the east terminus of Bundesstr. 170. By **car** from Salzburg, take Bundesstr. 21 south to 312 west; at St. Johann in Tirol, switch to 161 south, which leads straight to Kitzbühel. From Innsbruck, take Autobahn A12 east to Wörgl and switch to either Bundesstr. 312 or Bundesstr. 170.

▐ ORIENTATION AND PRACTICAL INFORMATION

Kitzbühel sits pretty on the hilly banks of the Kitzbüheler Ache River. Nearby, the **Schwarzsee** proffers warm, mineral-rich waters and curative mud-baths. The town is in the shade of a number of impressive peaks, including the Kitzbüheler Horn (1996m) and the Steinbergkogel (1971m). To reach the *Fußgängerzone* from the main train station, head straight out the front door down Bahnhofstr. and turn left at the main road. At the traffic light, turn right and follow the road uphill. The city center is a maze of twisting streets; if you get confused, look for the *Zentrum* (center) signs to point you back to the middle.

Trains: Hauptbahnhof (tel. 640 551 385) and Hahnenkamm Bahnhof. To: **Innsbruck** (1hr., 12 per day 5:12am-11:30pm, 142AS); **Salzburg** (2½hr., 17 per day 12:39am-8:23pm, 250AS); **Vienna** (6hr., 13 per day 12:39am-8:23pm, 570AS); and **Zell am See** (45 min., 14 per day 12:39am-8:23pm, 106AS).

Taxis: In front of the Hauptbahnhof, or call 62617 or 62157.

Car Rental: Hertz, Josef-Pirchlstr. 24 (tel. 64800; fax 72144), at the traffic light on the way into town from the main station. Open M-F 8am-noon and 2-6pm, Sa 9am-noon. 20% discount with valid guest card. AmEx, MC, Visa.

Bike Rental: At the main train station. 150AS per day, with train ticket for that day 90AS. Mountain bikes 200AS, 160AS.

Parking: There are 4 lots in Kitzbühel: **Griesgasse, Pfarrau, Hahnenkamm,** and **Kitzbühlerhorn.** The latter 2 are next to the major ski lifts. In winter a free park-and-ride service operates between the lots and lifts. Free parking at the Fleckalmbahn for the cable car (open 8am-6pm). Winter parking at Hahnekamm is 40AS per day.

Tourist Office: Hinterstadt 18 (tel. 62 15 50; fax 62307; email info@kitzbuehel.com; www.kitzbuehel.com), near the *Rathaus* in the *Fußgängerzone*. Free room reservation service, free telephone at the **electronic accommodations board** (daily 6am-10pm). Maps and English brochures also available at the board. A **bank** in the office exchanges money in high season. Free **guided walks** in English start at the office M-F at 8:45am (May-Oct.). Guided hikes on weekends on demand. Open July-Sept. and mid-Dec. to late Apr. M-F 8:30am-6:30pm, Sa 8:30am-noon and 4-6pm, Su 10am-noon and 4-6pm; Oct. to mid-Dec. and late Apr. to June M-F 8:30am-12:30pm and 2:30-6pm.

Budget Travel: Reisebüro Eurotours, Rathauspl. 5 (tel. 71304; fax 71 30 44). Provides discounts on package tours. Exchanges currency at average rates. Open M-F 8:30am-noon and 3-6:30pm, Sa 8:30am-noon and 4:30-6:30pm, Su 9am-1pm.

Currency Exchange: At banks, travel agencies, and the post office. The post office and most banks have **ATMs** outside.

Luggage Storage: At both stations. Open 5am–1pm. 30AS.

Laundromat: Kleider-Fix, Wegscheidg. 5 (tel. 63520). Wash and dry 180AS; wash only 150AS. Open M-Th 7am-6pm, F 7am-5pm, Sa 9-11am.

Emergencies: Police, tel. 133. **Fire,** tel. 122. **Red Cross Ambulance Service,** tel. 64 01 10. **Medical,** tel. 144. **Auto Repair,** tel. 123.

Ski Conditions: tel. 181 (German) or tel. 182 (English).

Post Office: Josef-Pirchlstr. 11 (tel. 62712), between the stoplight and the *Fußgänger-zone*. Bus schedules, fax, and a self-serve copier inside. Open M-F 8am-noon and 2-6pm. **Currency exchange** open M-F 8am-noon and 4-5pm. **Postal Code:** A-6370.

PHONE CODE	The **city code** for Kitzbühel is 05356.

ACCOMMODATIONS AND CAMPING

Kitzbühel has almost as many guest beds (7445) as inhabitants (8000), but the only youth hostel is far from town and restricted to groups. Pricey hotels with fancy pastel facades dominate the town center. Austrians claim that in Kitzbühel, you pay German prices for German comfort (read: twice the price, half the comfort). Rooms during the summer generally run 200 to 300AS per person; expect to shell out an extra 100AS during the winter. The Hahnenkamm Ski Competition in January creates a bed shortage so great that many residents vacate their homes and rent to visitors. During the year, cheaper lodging is also available a short bus or train ride away in **Kirchberg**, only 6km away (Kirchberg tourist office tel. (05357) 2309). Wherever you stay, be sure to ask for your **guest card** upon registration—it entitles you to discounts on most local attractions.

■ **Hotel Kaiser,** Bahnhofstr. 2 (tel. 64709), 2min. down the street from the main station. The native English-speaking owner and staff, all former backpackers, are happy to greet road-weary travelers, and if the hotel's 150 beds are full, the owner Michael will always help you find somewhere else to stay at a similar price. School groups book the hotel during Christmas and February, and it is occasionally closed during slow seasons, so call ahead. The hotel has a terrace, billiard table, and an inexpensive bar. Rates are 200AS per person in doubles and 4-6 bed dorms, although there may be winter surcharges. Michael offers a special deal in Nov.-Dec. for backpackers looking for work in the area: 120AS per person for a 4-6 bed dorm. **Laundry** 70AS (washed and dried for you). Parking available. AmEx, DC, MC, Visa.

Pension Hörl, Josef-Pirchlstr. 60 (tel. 63144). From the main station, turn left after Hotel Kaiser; Pension Hörl will be on the left. Quiet and unassuming with old furnishings and drab balconies. Reasonable rates. If they don't have an available bed, they'll try to put you up at their nearby **Gästehaus Hörl** (Bahnhofstr. 8). 180-220AS per person, with private shower 190-260AS. Add 40AS in winter. Breakfast included.

Pension Neuhaus "Motorbike," Franz-Reischstr. 23 (tel. 62200). From the tourist office, turn right, walk through the archway, and follow Franz-Reischstr. to the right. The *Pension* is on the left, near the chairlift. The proprietors *really* like motorcycles—the dining-room ceiling is covered with biker t-shirts. Rooms house up to 6 people. 200-300AS per person. Winter 300-390AS. Prices vary depending on length of stay. Breakfast included.

Haus Holzastner, Reitherg. 86 in Kirchberg (tel. (05357) 2752, offers modest rooms at a good price, but only in winter. 200AS per person. Breakfast and hall shower included.

Camping Schwarzsee, Reitherstr. 24 (tel. 62 80 60; fax 644 79 30). Take the train to "Schwarzsee" and follow the train tracks past the bathing areas and around the back of the lake. The campground is behind the Bruggerhof Hotel. If you're up for a really long walk, turn right at the tourist office and pass under the archway. Bear right at the Wienerwald up Franz-Reischstr., which becomes Schwarzseestr. and leads to the lake, or follow the signs from Franz-Reichstr. to the *Waldweg zum See* (forest path to the lake). 90AS per person, ages 2-12 70AS, under 2 free; guest tax 7AS; tents 96AS; caravans 90-100AS; dogs 40AS. Aug. 16-June 83AS per person, all other prices the same.

◪ FOOD

Although many of Kitzbühel's restaurants prepare gourmet delights at astronomical prices, cheaper locales pepper the area surrounding the *Fußgängerzone*. Local specialties include *Tiroler Speckknödel* (bacon-fat dumplings), served either *zu Wasser* (in broth) or *zu Lande* (dry, with salad or sauerkraut); and *Gröstl* (meat and potato hash topped with a fried egg).

Huberbräu-Stüberl, Vorderstadt 18 (tel. 65677). In the center of town with a terrace that overlooks the street, Huberbräu offers high-quality traditional cuisine at relatively low prices. Besides their *Wienerschnitzel* (98AS) and pizza *margherita* (70AS), check out the filling *Menü*—soup, entree, potato, and dessert for 130AS. Open 8am-midnight.

Café-Restaurant Prima, Bichlstr. 22 (tel. 638 85), on the 2nd floor. From the tourist office, walk right and through the arch. Inexpensive meals on a sunny patio or inside at coffeeshop booths. This self-serve chain has a wide selection, including spaghetti (60AS), and *Wiener Schnitzel* with soup, salad, and dessert (85AS). Open 9am-10pm.

La Fonda, Hinterstadt 13 (tel. 73673). This eclectic eatery in the heart of Kitzbühel, down the street from the tourist office, serves cheap, snack-style meals like hamburgers, nachos, spare ribs, curry, and *tsatsiki*. The Tyrol-Mex tacos don't taste quite like the ones they make in Texas, but you can afford to try them anyway—nothing on the menu is over 80AS. Open noon-midnight.

MARKETS

SPAR, Bichlstr. 22 (tel. 7488), on the corner of Ehrenbachg. and Bichlstr. Open M-F 8am-6:30pm, Sa 7:30am-1pm.

Billa, Hammerschmiedstr. 3 (tel. 64254), next to Hotel Hummer. Open M-W 8am-7pm, Th 7:30am-7pm, F 7:30am-7:30pm, Sa 7:30am-5pm.

👁 🎵 SIGHTS AND ENTERTAINMENT

Kitzbühel's church steeples define the town's skyline. The **Pfarrkirche** (parish church) and the **Liebfrauenkirche** (Church of Our Lady) lie in an ivy-cloaked courtyard surrounded by an old cemetery. Between the churches stands the **Ölberg Chapel,** dating from 1450, with frescoes from the late 1500s. The town itself is even older, having celebrated its 700th anniversary in 1971. The local **Heimatmuseum** stocks its wares in Kitzbühel's oldest house, which dates from the 12th century. Rusty tools from days of yore are displayed, including prehistoric European mining equipment and the first metal bobsled. (Hinterstadt 34. Tel. 67274. Open M-Sa 10am-12:30pm; July 10-Sept. 10 10am-4:30pm. 30AS, with guest card 25% discount, children 10AS.)

At the free **music concerts** in the center of town in July and August, you might find anything from folk harpists to Sousa bands (F 8:30pm, weather permitting). **Casino Kitzbühel** is near the tourist office. Go on, raise the stakes—you've got to finance that lift ticket for tomorrow. (Tel. 62300. Open daily July-Sept. 7pm-late. M ladies' night: free glass of champagne; Tu men's night: free glass of beer. No cover. 18 or older. Semi-formal.) At the end of July, the **Austrian Open** Men's Tennis Championships come to town, drawing such athletes as Austrians Thomas Muster and Goran Ivanesevic to the Kitzbühel Tennis Club (tel. 63325; email ticket-tennis@kitzbuehel.netwing.at; www.atp-turnier-kitzbuehel.com). Nearby, the 18-hole Golfclub Kitzbühel Schwarzsee offers a 30% discount with guest card. From mid-September until June trips to the driving range are usually 100AS.

🏔 OUTDOOR ACTIVITIES

Few visitors to Kitzbühel remain at ground level for long. The Kitzbühel **ski area,** the "Ski Circus," is one of the finest in the world. Site of the first ski championships in 1894, these very mountains honed the childhood skills of Olympic great Toni Sailer. Every winter since 1931, Kitzbühel has hosted the **Hahnenkamm Ski Competition,** part of the annual World Cup and long considered one of the world's most difficult runs. The competition turns the town into a rollicking 7-day party. (Tel. 73555 for tickets. 50-200AS per day).

SKIING. The best deal is the **Kitzbüheler Alpen Ski Pass,** which gives access to 260 lifts in 22 villages. (2200AS, children 1100AS; good for any 6 days of the ski season. Full-season pass 6200AS, children 3100AS.) A 1-day ski pass (high season 390-420AS, children 210AS) grants free passage on 64 lifts and on shuttle buses that connect them. Lift ticket prices drop after the first day. Tickets for 2 to 14 days are also available, as are tickets for individual lifts, such as the **Gaisberglift** (60AS, with guest card 59AS, children 30AS) and **Fleckalmbahn** (170AS, with guest card 150AS, children 86AS). Purchase passes at any of the lifts or at the *Kurhaus* **Aquarena,** which offers a pool, sauna, and solarium (tel. 64385; open daily 9am-8pm; 80AS, with guest card 70AS, children 50AS, 45AS; free entry in winter with ski passes of 2 days or more, in summer with 3-day vacation pass).

You can **rent skis** at the Hahnenkamm lift or from virtually any sports shop in the area. Try **Kitzsport Schlechter,** at Jochbergerstr. 7 (tel. 22 04 11; open M-F 8:30am-noon and 2:30-6pm, Sa 8:30am-12:30pm). Downhill equipment rental runs 170-500AS per day; lessons cost 500AS, snowboards 180AS to 350AS. Ask at the tourist office about **ski packages:** special low-season deals on lodging, ski passes, and instruction. Week-long packages without instruction start at 3900AS.

HIKING. For summer visitors, more than 70 **hiking trails** snake up the mountains surrounding Kitzbühel. Some of the best views are from the **Kampenweg** and **Hochetzkogel** trails, accessible via the Bichlalm bus which leaves daily from various stops in town (every hr. 8am-5:10pm; 26AS, with guest card 20AS). You can also take the **Hahnenkammbahn** (8am-5:30pm, 160AS up or round-trip, with guest card 140AS, children 80AS). You might also consider climbing up (about 2hr. of varying terrain). At the top are 2 cafeteria-style restaurants and the **Bergbahn Museum Hahnenkamm** (tel. 6957; open daily 10am-4pm; free).

The **Kitzbüheler Hornbahn lift** ascends to the **Alpenblumengarten,** where more than 120 different types of flowers blossom each spring (open late-May to mid-Oct. 8:30am-5pm; cable car 85AS per section, children 43AS). The smaller **Gaisberg, Resterhöhe,** and **Streiteck** lifts also run in the summer. A 3-day **summer holiday pass** is valid for unlimited use of all cable cars, free Bichlalm bus service, and Aquarena pool entrance (420AS, children 205AS). Guest card holders can take advantage of the tourist office's **mountain-hiking program.** Daily 3- to 5-hour hikes cover over 100 routes and come in 2 flavors: easy and moderate. (Mid-May to mid-Oct. M-F at 8:45am from the tourist office; call ahead for weekend hikes (min. 5 people). 90AS, free with guest card, but you pay for cable car rides.) Former Olympic ski champion Ernst Hinterseer (tel. 62920) leads hikes down the Streif downhill course by request. **Mountain bike trails** abound; rent a bike from Stanger Radsport, Josef-Pirchlstr. 42 (tel. 2549), for 250AS per day (open M-F 8am-noon and 1-6pm, Sa 9am-noon). Get the booklet detailing bike paths through the Kitzbüheler and other Alps at the tourist office (54AS) or try their free guided cycle tours (June-Sept. Tu and Th at 8:45am (or at other times on request); call in advance).

SWIMMING. The **Schwarzsee** (Black Lake), 2.5km northwest of Kitzbühel, is famed for its healing mud baths. Float in the deep blue water and gaze at the snow-capped mountains high above (see directions to Camping Schwarzsee). (Tel. 62381. Open 7am-8pm. 40AS, children 30AS; ½day pass after noon 30AS, after 4pm 15AS. 11% discount with guest card. Electric boats 80AS for 30min., 150AS for 1hr.; rowboats 45AS, 85AS.)

THE ZILLERTAL ALPS

The Zillertal (Ziller Valley) Alps provide spectacular, affordable, and easily accessible hiking and skiing away from crowds. Transportation in the region is simple and convenient, thanks to the **Zillertalbahn** (better known by its nickname, the **Z-bahn**), an efficient network of private buses and trains connecting the remote villages (tel. (05224) 4606; railpasses not valid). The starting point is **Jenbach,** and the route's southern terminus is **Mayrhofen** (61AS). You can reach Jenbach from **Innsbruck** (30min., 60AS, Eurailpass valid). The Z-bahn has 2 types of trains, the **Dampfzug** and the **Triebwagen.** The Dampfzug is an old, red steam train targeted at tourists; it costs twice as much and moves half as fast. The Triebwagen and the Z-bahn Autobus have the same rates, and one or the other leaves daily every hour from 6am to 9pm.

In the Zillertal, **skiing** reigns supreme. As of December 1999, the Zell am Ziller ski area should have been connected to the Gerlos and Königsleiten ski areas, thereby creating the largest ski zone in the Tyrol. The **Zillertal Super Skipass** (tel. 71650), covering this mammoth region, is available at any valley lift station and valid on all of the area's 251 lifts (4 days 1270AS, 7 days 1950AS, 10 days 2570AS, discounts for children). The cost of the lift ticket includes unlimited use of the Z-bahn network. The Zillertal Alps also have some of the best **hiking** in western Austria, with more footpaths than roads and more trail guides than police officers. The popular **Z-Hiking Ticket** is valid on all summer lifts in the Zillertal, including Zell am Ziller, Fügen, Mayrhofen, Gerlos, and Hintertux (6 days for 480AS, 9 days for 660AS, 12 days for 820AS, children ride free with the purchase of 2 regular tickets). Passes are available at tourist offices, lifts, or railway stations in Zell am Ziller and Mayrhofen.

ZELL AM ZILLER

Zell am Ziller (TSELL am TSILLER), 20km south of Jenbach, embodies many of the picture-book images of an Austrian mountain village, with clusters of wooden-shuttered alpine houses surrounded by fields of tall grass and much taller mountains. Founded by monks in the late 8th century, Zell surrendered to materialism in the 1600s when it flourished as a gold-mining town. Today, this beautiful and unassuming locale stands out as one of the best (and least hyped) ski-towns in Austria.

▣ ORIENTATION AND PRACTICAL INFORMATION. Zell stands at the south end of the Zillertal, between Jenbach and Mayrhofen. Those traveling by ÖBB train should get off at Jenbach and switch to the private **Zillertalbahn** (Z-bahn; tel. 2211; Jenbach to Zell am Ziller 55AS; see p. 204 for more information), which leaves from the front of the train station. Z-bahn trains and buses leave every hour for Jenbach or Mayrhofen. Railpasses are not valid in this region.

The center of town is Dorfplatz, straight out of the train station down Bahnhofstr. In turn, Dorfpl. intercepts both of Zell's main streets, Gerlosstr. near the river, and Unterdorfstr. by the railroad tracks. The **tourist office** is at Dorfpl. 3a (tel. 2281; fax 22 81 80; email tourist.info.zell@netway.at; www.tiscover.com/zell). From the rail station, head right along Bahnhofstr., and turn right at the end—the office is on your left. Pick up a town map, skiing information, and a pension list if you want to track down a room on your own. The staff will make reservations for free. (Open M-F 8:30am-12:30pm and 2:30-6pm, Sa 9am-noon and 4-6pm; in July-Oct. also Sa 9am-noon and 4-6pm.) Christophorus Reisen, Bahnhofstr. 2 (tel. 2520), handles **budget travel** concerns. Banks offer the best rates for **currency exchange** (open M-F 8am-noon and 2-5pm), and most have 24-hour **ATMs. Luggage storage** (30AS) is at the train station. For a **taxi**, dial 2625, 2345, or 2255. **Rent bikes** at the train station (150AS per day) or SB-Markt Hofer, Gerlosstr. 30 (tel. 2220), opposite the campground (mountain bikes 170AS per day; open M-F 7am-noon and 2:30-6:15pm). In an **emergency**, dial 133; for an **ambulance**, dial 2345. For **police**, call 2212. The **post office** is at Unterdorf 2 (tel. 2333; open M-F 8am-noon and 2-6pm; in summer also Sa 9-11am). The **postal code** is A-6280.

PHONE CODE	The **city code** for Zell am Ziller is 05282.

▣▣ ACCOMMODATIONS AND FOOD. Zell am Ziller has no shortage of lodgings. To reach **Haus Huditz**, Karl-Platzer-Weg 1 (tel. 2228), cross the rail tracks by the tourist office and continue onto Gerlosstr.; bear left onto Gauderg. (at the Mode Journal building) and look for Karl-Platzer-Weg on the left (10min.). The owner provides beverages, conversation *(auf Deutsch)*, cable TV downstairs, down comforters, and balconies with mountain views. (Singles 200AS 1st night, then 180AS; winter 210AS, 180AS. Doubles 380AS, 340AS; winter 400AS, 350AS. Breakfast included. Shower 15AS.) **Camping Hofer**, Gerlosstr. 33 (tel. 2248; fax 22488), offers a space for your tent only a block or so from the town center. **Laundry** (80AS), showers, barbecues, free bike tours, weekly hikes, and even a house band round out the offerings. There's a grocery across the street. (High-season 60AS per person. Off season 50-55AS. 60-80AS per campsite. Guest tax 12AS.)

When you stop for a bite to eat, sample some local specialties. A traditional summer dish is the *Scheiterhaufen*, a monstrous mixture of rolls, apples, eggs, milk, lemon, cinnamon, sugar, butter, and raisins, drizzled with rum. *Zillertaler Krapfen* are sweet, heavy doughnuts, available in every bakery. The cheapest place around is **SB Restaurant Zeller Stuben**, Unterdorf 12 (tel. 2271), which serves big, buffet-style portions (*Knödeln mit Sauerkraut* 50AS, *Gulaschsuppe* 35AS). The less casual restaurant upstairs features 5 daily *Menüs* including soup, entree, and dessert for 90-170AS. (Children's and vegetarian menus available. Open 11am-9pm.) **Gasthof Kirchenwirt**, Dorfpl. 4 (tel. 2280), serves up *Zillertaler Kasrahm-spätzln*, doughy noodles cooked with onions and garnished with cheese, for 70AS (open 8am-midnight). Cap off dinner with a visit to **Café-Konditorei Gredler**, Unterdorf 10 (tel. 2489), where 1995 Confectioner of the Year Tobias Gredler whips up delicate desserts for patrons to enjoy on the riverside patio (hazelnut creamcake 34AS, intricate sundaes 50-100AS; open 10am-11pm). The local **SPAR** supermarket is around the corner from the tourist office, across from the brewery on Roherstr. (open M-F 7:30am-12:30pm and 2-6:30pm, Sa 7:30am-12:30pm and 2-5pm).

TYROL

⚠ OUTDOOR ACTIVITIES. Zeller **skiing** comes in 2 packages: **day passes** for shorter visits, valid on the Kreuzjoch-Rosenalm and Gerlosstein-Sonnalm slopes (1 day 370AS, children 220AS; 2 days 690AS, 420AS; 3 days 990AS, 590AS); and **Super Skipasses** for longer visits (see p. 204). Single tickets are available for non-skiers who tag along to watch. Obtain passes at the **Kreuzjoch** (tel. 71650), **Gerlosstein** (tel. 2275), or **Ramsberg** (tel. 2720) cable car stations (all 3 lifts open 8:30am-5pm). **Rent skis** at any of Zell's sporting goods stores. Try Pendl Sport at Gerlosstr. 3 (tel. 2287; open M-F 8am-noon and 2:30-6:30pm, Sa 8am-noon and 3-6pm, Su 9-11am and 4-6pm; MC, Visa). **Summer skiing** is possible at the **Hintertux Glacier**, 25km south of Zell am Ziller and accessible by Z-bahn and BundesBus (tel. (05287) 8506 for lift tickets; 1-day lift tickets 430AS, youth 550AS, children 260AS).

Register in any town hotel or pension to get a **guest card,** which snags you a free hike led by the tourist office (June-Sept.; register one day in advance at the office). Most hiking around Zell am Ziller is lift-assisted. Two of the 3 ski lifts in Zell's vicinity offer **alpine hiking:** the **Kreuzjochbahn** (tel. 71650; open 8:40am-12:15pm and 1-5:10pm; round-trip 160AS, to mid-station 105AS) and the **Gerlossteinbahn** (tel. 22 75; open 8:30am-12:20pm and 1-5pm; round-trip 100AS). You can try **paragliding** as well—tandem flights cost 700-1500AS for 5- to 25-minute rides. The term "take-out" will develop a whole new meaning when you trust your life to the gliding guides at the world's smallest airline, **Pizza-Air,** Zelbergeben 4 (tel. 22890).

For a down-to-earth look at Zell's history, take a tour of the nearby **gold mine.** The journey begins at a petting zoo and adjacent cheese factory before proceeding on a scenic 45-minute hike down to the mine entrance. (Tel. 23010; fax 23014. 2hr. tours leave daily on the hr. 9am-4pm. 130AS, children 65AS. Reserve in advance for English tours.)

◪ FESTIVALS. The residents of Zell am Ziller are particularly fond of liquid gold, which flows freely on the first weekend in May, when the whole town gets sauced in a 3-day celebration of cold, frothy beverages known as **Gauderfest.** The name is derived from the estate that owns the local private brewery. The Bräumeister's vats, Tyrol's oldest, concoct the beloved and potent Gauderbock especially for the occasion. The festival even has its own jingle: *Gauderwürst und G'selchts mit Kraut,/ hei, wia taut dösmunden,/ und 10 Halbe Bockbier drauf,/ mehr braucht's nit zum G'sundsein!* ("Gauder sausage and smoked pork with sauerkraut, / Hey, how good it tastes,/ and 10 pints of beer to go with it,/ what more could you need for your health!") The festival's highlight is the **Ranggeln,** traditional wrestling for the title of "Hogmoar." There are also animal fights (attended by a veterinary surgeon) and customary activities like the **Grasausläuten** (ringing bells in order to wake the grass up and make it grow). Revelry continues into the night with Tyrolean folk singing and dancing.

MAYRHOFEN

At the southernmost end of the Zillertal, Mayrhofen is well-positioned for intense outdoor recreation. Four valleys (the **Zillergrund, Stillupgrund, Zemgrund,** and **Tuxertal**) provide endless opportunities for **hikers** in summer and **skiers** in winter. Proud of their natural splendor but eager to prove their mettle, Mayrhofer residents walk the walk when they're not talking the talk: Mayrhofen native Peter Habeler and fellow Tyrolean Reinhold Messner completed the first oxygen-unaided ascent of Mt. Everest. Habeler now runs the town's alpine school. This isn't some rarefied mountaineer's base-camp, however. Mayrhofen receives a steady stream of package tourists and families who enjoy the sports facilities, cable cars, and less strenuous activities.

⁊ ORIENTATION AND PRACTICAL INFORMATION. Mayrhofen is easily accessible from **Jenbach** (50min., 26 per day, 61AS) and **Zell am Ziller** (15min., 26 per day, 23AS) by Z-bahn trains and buses. The **train station** (tel. 62362) lies slightly northeast of town; to reach the center, walk uphill on the main road and turn left at the intersection. The **tourist office,** Dursterstr. 225 (tel. 6760), is located inside the massive octagonal information center on a slight hill above the center of town. The office dispenses gobs of information on outdoor pursuits, tours, and accommodations (although it won't make the reservations for you), and leads free **guided tours.** (Tours May-Oct. M-F; call for times and meeting points. Open M-F 8am-6pm, Sa 9am-noon, Su 10am-noon; July-Aug. also Sa 2-6pm.) The **post office** (tel. 623 51 11) is located at the intersection of Einfahrt Mitte and Hauptstr. (open M-F 8am-noon and 2-6pm; cashier closes at 5pm). **Store luggage** at the train station for 30AS per piece (M-Sa 7am-6:30pm, Su 7:30am-1pm and 1:30-6:30pm). **Banks** line Hauptstr. in the center of town; they are generally open M-F 7:45am-12:15pm and 2-4pm. Christophorus Reisebüro, Kramerg. 346 (tel. 63200), behind the church, handles all your **budget travel** needs, as well as booking local accommodations (open M-Sa 8am-6pm, Su 8:30am-1pm and 4-6pm). Dial 133 for **police,** 122 for **fire,** and 144 for an **ambulance.** The **postal code** is A-6290.

PHONE CODE	The **city code** for Mayrhofen is 05285.

▉▉ ACCOMMODATIONS AND FOOD. Finding a budget accommodation in Mayrhofen can be quite difficult, since package groups tend to book up most of the available bed-and-breakfasts. Try your luck at **Pension Fischnaller,** Hauptstr. 410 (tel. 62347; fax 63773), which occupies a stately house in the center of town. The quiet rooms and elegant furnishings are an oasis of calm in Mayrhofen's busy tourist program. The pension has no sign—ring the bell for service. (In summer 170-240AS per person; in winter 190-260AS. Add 20AS for a single room. Breakfast included.) **Pension Woldrich,** Brandbergstr. 355 (tel. 62325), rents huge rooms, some with a balcony. From the train station, walk up Einfahrt Mitte past the intersection with the post office, then take the next right. (In summer 150-230 per person; in winter 180-250AS. Add 30AS for single room.)

Touristy eateries, most of which are priced better than one might expect, crowd the center of town. **Mo's** (tel. 63435), up the street from the post office, tries to bring a piece of Americana to the Austrian Alps. ("Pork of the Rising Sun" 99AS, pizzas 79-102AS, burgers 52-68AS. Open Tu-Sa noon-1am, Su-M 4pm-1am.) **Café Dengg,** Hauptstr. 412 (tel. 64866), serves light fare and desserts beneath a green awning. (Sandwiches 65-78AS, salads 35-75AS, pizzas 85-103AS. Open daily except Su 10am-11pm.)

▉ OUTDOOR ACTIVITIES. Mayrhofen caters to the year-round sportsperson—an endless variety of **hiking** and **skiing** trails in the nearby valleys satisfy mountaineers of all levels. If you plan on doing extensive hiking in the area, it's worth stopping by the tourist office to pick up a detailed map (80-110AS) of routes and mountain huts, which offer both refreshment and lodging. Buses and taxis run frequently up the valleys, and can deliver you to and from the higher alpine zone. The **Z-Hiking-ticket** simplifies hiking arrangements by giving you free portage on all Zillertal cable cars, buses, and trains, unlimited dips in public swimming pools, as well as reductions on many museums and alpine/paragliding schools (see p. 204).

The first sight that greets many visitors to Mayrhofen is the **Penkenbahn,** with its dangling gondolas passing directly above the town on their way up to the top of the 1850m Penkenberg (May 22-Oct. 10. 9am-5pm; round-trip 145AS, children 90AS). Mayrhofen runs a variety of guided hiking and climbing programs, ranging from leisurely walks to hard-core mountain ascents. A different hike is offered every day, for a fee that ranges from 30-145AS per person. Register at the tourist office. Everest climber and local boy Peter Habeler runs an **alpine school** that teaches rudimentary through advanced skills in mountain and ice climbing (tel. 62829). There is **summer skiing** on the Hintertux glacier, 70km from Mayrhofen (1-day ticket 350AS, youth ages 14-18 280AS, children 145AS). **Paragliders** can catch thermals in the surrounding valleys, or take a tandem flight with instructors at Flugtaxi Mayrhofen (tel. 63142; 10min. flight 1100AS, 20min. 1600AS); or Stocky-

TYROL

Air (tel. 3786; 5min. flight 750AS, 15-20min. 1100AS). Opportunities abound for **kayaking**, **rafting**, and **canyoning** in the white-water rivers (check with the tourist office). Come winter, **skiers** and **snowboarders** flock to the Ahorn, Penken, and Horberg ski areas above town, all of which are covered by the **Ski Mayrhofen pass.** (Valid Dec. 4-April 24. 1 day 360AS, youth 290AS, children 215AS. 3 days 940AS, 750AS, 565AS.) The skipass also entitles you to free transit on the local ski buses. Snow-bunnies can also avail themselves of the regional, all-inclusive **Zillertal Super Skipass** (see p. 204). You can **rent skis** at shops along Hauptstr. for 100-250AS per day, 80-130AS for children.

EAST TYROL (OSTTIROL)

LIENZ

Bordered on the south by the Dolomites, the mountain range shared with Italy and Slovenia, and cut off from the rest of Tyrol by the Alps, Lienz is distinctive for its hybrid Mediterranean personality. Although the Alpine vista and the low-slung houses betray an Austrian heritage, the dusty cobblestone roads, summer heat, and authentic trattorias suggest Northern Italy (just 40km away). Even the weather cooperates—the valley around Lienz registers about 2000 hours of sunshine each year. Nevertheless, the tropical atmosphere of the summer is forgotten when winter ski-maniacs hit the Hohe Tauern slopes to the north.

> **! GET YOUR CITIES STRAIGHT.** Lienz is distinct from Linz, an industrial city in northeast Austria. Lienz is pronounced "LEE-ints"; Linz is known as Linz an der Donau. Make the distinction before boarding any trains.

▐ GETTING TO LIENZ

Lienz lies at the conjunction of several highways: Bundesstr. 108 from the northwest, 106 and 107 from the northeast, 100 from the west, and E66 from the east. **Trains** arrive at the **Hauptbahnhof** and connect directly to points all over Austria (and indirectly to points elsewhere). **Buses** leave from in front of the *Hauptbahnhof* for destinations throughout the region. (Ticket window (tel. 67067) open M-F 7:45-10am and 4-6:30pm, Sa 7:45-10am.) By **car** from Salzburg, take Autobahn A-10 south to 311, and, just before Zell am See, switch to 107 south to Lienz. From Innsbruck, take Autobahn A-12 east to 169 south. At Zell am Ziller, switch to 165 east, and at Mittersill take 108 south to Lienz.

▐ ORIENTATION AND PRACTICAL INFORMATION

The **Isel River,** which feeds into the Drau, splits Lienz. From the train station, the centrally located Hauptpl. is across Tirolerstr. and to the left through Boznerpl.

Transportation: Trains leave from the **Hauptbahnhof,** Bahnhofpl. (tel. 66060; information booth open M-F 9am-4:50pm; ticket window open M-Sa 6:20am-6:35pm, Su 8:15am-6:35pm; train info tel. 01717). To: **Klagenfurt** (1½-2¼hr., 6-7 per day 5:20am-7:23pm, 176AS), **Innsbruck** (3hr., 4 per day 5:28am-6:38pm, 165AS), and the **Vienna Südbahnhof** (6½hr., 3 per day 6:30am-2:49pm, 570AS). **Buses** leave from just beside the train station in the direction of **Arnbach** (1hr., 8 per day), **Kitzbühel** (2hr., 3 per day), **Heiligenblut** (4 per day, 95AS) and **Franz-Josefs-Höhe** (3-4 per day, 105AS). Bus information booth open a scanty M-F 7:45-8:15am and 5-6:20pm, or call BundesBus Auskunft tel. (01) 71101. From July 7-Aug. 23, a **free Stadtbus** circles the city, making fourteen stops before returning to the train station parking lot. (1 per hr. 8am-7pm.)

Taxi: tel. 63863, 65450, or 65111.

Parking: Free parking at Tirolerstr.; at Europapl., 3hr. for 15AS.

Automobile Association: ÖAMTC, Tirolerstr. 19a (tel. 6322).

Car Rental: Pontiller Autohaus, Kärtnerstr. 70 (tel. 62705).

Bike Rental: At the train station. 150AS per day, with train ticket or Eurailpass 90AS. Mountain bike 200AS, 160AS.

Tourist Office: Tourismusverband, Europapl. 1 (tel. 65265; fax 65 26 52; email lienz@netway.at; www.tiscover.com/lienz). From the station, turn left onto Tirolerstr. and right onto Europapl. Courteous staff showers you with brochures (mostly in English), including a list of private accommodations. A 24hr. electronic accommodations board is outside. Free **city tours** leave the office M and F at 10am (in German; groups may arrange English tours in advance). **National park tours** are offered in summer several times per week from neighboring towns (70AS, children under 14 free; call the **Igelsberg-Stronach Information Center,** tel. 64117).

Currency Exchange: Best rates are in the **post office.** Exchange desk open M-F 8am-noon and 2-5pm. Also at the train station and banks. Try **Lienzer Sparkasse,** Johannespl. 6. Open M-F 8am-noon and 2-4pm.

Luggage Storage: At the train station. 30AS per piece per day. Small lockers 20AS, ski lockers 40AS.

English-Language Books: Two shelves of English best-sellers on the 2nd fl. of **Tyrolia Lienz,** Roseng. 3, open M-F 8am-noon and 2-6pm, Su 8am-noon.

Hospital: Emanuel-von-Hibler-Str. 5 (tel. 606).

Emergencies: Police, Hauptpl. 5 (tel. 63155; fax 61657). **Fire,** tel. 122. **Mountain Rescue,** tel. 140. **Ambulance,** tel. 144 (also for **water rescue**).

Internet Access: Free at the *Öffentliche Bücherei* (public library), inside the *Klosterkirche* at the corner of Mucharg. and Schulstr. Open Tu-F 9am-noon and 3-6pm, Sa 9am-noon.

Post Office: Boznerpl. 1 (tel. 66 88 80), on the corner of Hauptpl. across from the train station. Open M-F 7:30am-7pm, cashier until 5pm, Sa 8-11am. **Postal Code:** A-9900.

PHONE CODE	The **city code** for Lienz is 04852.

▚ ACCOMMODATIONS

Even without a youth hostel, Lienz still offers affordable accommodations, most just beyond Hauptpl. and the town center. Most *Pensionen* and *Privatzimmern* cost between 250 and 300AS per person.

Egger, Alleestr. 33 (tel. 72098). From the station, take Stadtbus to "Hochsteinbahn" and walk 2 blocks. Or walk through Hauptpl., left on Andrä Krazg. to Roseng., and right at the ice cream shop onto tree-lined Alleestr. (30min.) This family-run hotel has large, high-ceilinged rooms with new wooden furniture in an old-fashioned square building. Doubles 320AS, 340AS for stays under 3 nights. Showers and big breakfast included.

Bauernhof im Siechenhaus, Kärtnerstr. 39 (tel. 62188). From the station, turn right onto Tirolerstr., walk across the Isel, take the 1st left, and then an immediate right. Walk 1 block to Kärtnerstr. and turn left. The hotel, adorned with 17th-century frescoes of Lazarus, is on the right. This working farmhouse that served as a home for the sick in the Middle Ages has thick, dark wooden beams and painted doors. 200AS per person in doubles and triples, 30AS supplement for single occupancy.

Camping Falken, Eichholz 7 (tel. 64022; fax 64 02 26), across the Drau River near the foot of the Dolomites. From the station, turn left onto Tirolerstr. and left at the ÖAMTC garage, then pass through the tunnel and over the Drau. Follow the road as it cruves past the soccer and track facilities, then head left down the small paved footpath through the field. There are plenty of sites here, surrounded by wide fields and mountains, with a ping-pong table, soccer field, and mini-playground. 47-62AS, children 30-

45AS; site 60-80AS; guest tax for adults 8AS per night; electricity 30AS. Showers 10AS (7am-10pm only), **laundry** (70AS), and a small store. Lockout 1-3pm and 10pm-7am. Reception daily 8-10am and 4-8pm. Reservations strongly recommended July-Aug. Open Dec. 15-Oct. 20.

🍴 FOOD

Calorie-laden delis, bakeries, butcheries, and cafés lie in wait in **Hauptplatz** and along **Schweizergasse.**

Imbiße Köstl, Kreuzg. 4 (tel. 62012). A mother-daughter duo prepares the cheapest eats in town (entrees from 19AS) in this diner-style restaurant/bakery. Chow down on the *Wienerschnitzel* (59AS), curry *Würstl* (35AS), or pastries (8-17AS). Eat-in or takeout. Open M-Th 7:30am-8pm, F 7:30am-10pm, Sa 7:30am-12:30pm.

Pizzeria-Spaghetteria "Da Franco," Ägidius Peggerstr. (tel. 65051). Head through Hauptpl. to Johannespl., turn left at Zwergerg., and continue down the small alley. Captained by Franco, a native Italian who decided to try to make it big up north, this restaurant serves terrific potato *gnocchi* and garlicky fresh tomato sauce. Pizza and pasta 65-115AS; salad 40-110AS. Open in summer 11:30am-2:30pm and 6pm-midnight; in winter 11:30am-2pm and 5pm-midnight. AmEx, MC, Visa.

MARKETS
ADEG Aktiv Markt, Südtirolerpl; next to the tall pink Hotel Traube; and in Hauptpl. Open M-F 8am-6:15pm, Sa 8am-12:30pm.

Bauernmarkt (farmer's market), Marktpl. Local produce. Sa 9am-noon.

🏔 OUTDOOR ACTIVITIES

Above Lienz, **Schloß Bruck** houses the **East Tyrolean Regional Museum,** as well as several interesting frescoes and tapestries, but will be closed until May 13, 2000 in preparation for a huge exhibit on Tyrolean culture.

HIKING. The **Hochsteinbahnen** chairlifts, which run from the base station near the castle at the intersection of Iseltaler-Str. and Schloßg., rise 1500m in 2 segments up to the alpine wonderland of **Sternalm** (runs July-Sept.; segment 1 open daily 9am-noon and 1-5pm; segment 2 open 9:15am-12:15pm and 1:15-4:45pm; round-trip for both 95AS, children 50AS; segment 1 only 60AS, 30AS). At the top, the unforgiving Dolomites to the south and the gently rounded Hohe Tauern to the north appear in spectacular confrontation. A "Fairy Tale Hike" (1½hr.) leads past limestone peaks to the **Hochsteinhütte** (2023m; get details at the tourist office or chairlift station). Also at the summit of the chairlift is the **Moosalm Children's Zoo,** with a menagerie of rabbits, goats, and ducks available for your petting pleasure (open 10am-5:30pm; free). You can take a taxi (tel. 63360; round-trip 120AS, children 70AS) to another challenging hiking base, the **Lienzer Dolomitenhütte** (1620m). Over 40 trails of varying difficulty spiral off from this alpine hut, while 17 other huts dot the area—for more information, contact Lienz's chapter of the **Österreichischer Alpenverein,** Franz-von-Defreggerstr. 11 (tel. 72105; open F 8:30-11:30am and 3-6pm).

A 5km hike from Lienz leads to the **Tristachersee,** a sparkling blue lake at the base of the Rauchkofel mountain. Cross the bridge by the train station and follow Tristacherstr. (Tel. 63820. 40AS, children 20AS; open June-Sept.) Couch potatoes can enjoy the lake by riding the free **Bäder- und Freizeitbus** (Bath- and Leisure-Bus) from the *Dolomitenstadion* across the Drau to "Parkhotel Tristachersee" (runs July-Aug. every hr. 8:53am-6:46pm.)

SKIING. Lienz serves as an excellent base to attack the **ski** trails of the **Lienzer Dolomiten Complex.** (One-day ski pass 320AS, seniors and youths 270AS, under 15 160AS. ½-day tickets 230AS, 185AS, 115AS. Off-season: one-day 275AS, 220AS, 145AS. ½-day 250AS, 210AS, 125AS. Prices subject to change.) The **Skischule Lien-**

zer **Dolomiten** (tel. 65690) at the Zettersfeld lift offers hour-long private lessons at 450AS for one person, 150AS for each additional person. Lessons cost 460AS for 4 hours. Private snowboard lessons are also available for 450AS per hour. **Hans Moser und Sohn** (tel. 69180), at the apex of the Zettersfeld lift, supplies **ski or snowboard rental.** A complete set of downhill equipment, here or elsewhere, runs 210AS per day, children 110AS; a snowboard with boots costs 300AS, 210AS.

♫ NIGHTLIFE AND FESTIVALS

Disco-lovers get stoked at hotspot **Stadtkeller-disco,** Tirolerstr. 30, near Europapl. (two bars and dance floor open 9pm-3am; cover 40AS). Across from the Pizzeria Da Franco in the Gastogarden, live jazz and the occasional pianist entertain a youngish crowd at **Türml Nightcafe** (open Tu-Su 5pm-2am). At **Cafe Wha,** Schweizerg. 3, the body-pierced crowd rocks and rolls way past the midnight hour, smoking and playing pool (beer 24-35AS; wine 21-25AS; open Tu-Su 6pm-1am).

During the second weekend of August, the sounds of alcohol-induced merriment reverberate across the pastel facades of Lienz's town buildings in celebration of the **Stadtfest** (admission to town center 50AS). The summer months also witness the reaffirmation of Tyrolean culture and heritage in a series of **Platzkonzerte.** Watch as local men dust off their old *Lederhosen* and perform the acclaimed **shoe-slapping dance** (July-Aug. W and Sa at 8pm, June-Sept. Su at 8pm; free). On January 23, 2000, the world's greatest male cross-country skiers will gather in Lienz to compete in the annual 65km **Dolomitenlauf** (entrance fee 450AS before Dec. 15, 500AS after; for 25km race 300AS, 350AS).

VORARLBERG

At the intersection of 4 nations, the residents of the **Vorarlberg** (1004 sq. mi.; pop. 322,551), Austria's western-most province, speak like the Swiss, eat like the Germans, ski with Liecht-ensteiners, and vote Austrian. Visitors should carry a passport at all times; since foreign borders are never more than 2 hours away, a short daytrip can easily become an international excursion. **Feldkirch,** on the Ill River, lies just minutes from Liechtenstein's border. **Bregenz,** on the banks of the **Bodensee** (Lake Constance), would be German but for half a dozen kilometers. As a result of its international tendencies, Vorarlberg is well-equipped to welcome visitors from all over the world. Tourism is by far the leading industry, since the mountainous terrain isn't particularly hospitable to agriculture or manufacturing (except chocolate).

From the tranquil Bodensee in the west, Vorarlberg juts increasingly upward as you move south and east, climaxing in the massive Arlberg Alps (passable only through the 10km Arlberg Tunnel) at the boundary to Tyrol. Snow conditions are generally *wunderbar* from December to April, with trails as high as 2600m. Glaciers provide summer skiing in many areas. Over 1600km of marked hiking paths ranging in altitude from 400 to 3350m crisscross the region, and mountain railways carry hikers to the summit quickly and conveniently. Alpine associations maintain huts that provide hikers with accommodations and food from May to October; opening times depend on the altitude, so check with local tourist offices. Vorarlberg's 161km network of cycling paths range from leisurely tours through the Bodensee plain to challenging climbs in the Alps. Cycling maps are available at bookstores and tourist offices. For more info, contact the **Vorarlberg Information Office** in Bregenz (tel. (05574) 49590; fax 49 59 69; www.vorarlberg-tourism.at).

HIGHLIGHTS OF VORARLBERG

■ Venture into the **Bregenzerwald**, a region of rural villages and towns outside of Bregenz, for hiking, skiing, and scenic daytrips (p. 216).

■ Wander through **Feldkirch**, the former seat of the Prince of Liechtenstein, for the sake of its medieval cobblestone towers and frescoed town buildings (p. 219).

■ Sneak over the border to **Lindau im Bodensee** for an island vacation (p. 217).

BREGENZ

Bregenz, the capital city of Vorarlberg, spreads along the eastern coast of the Bodensee (Lake Constance). Separating 3 countries by only a few kilometers, the lake serves as an international conduit for Swiss, German, and Austrian tourists in search of Alpine and marine getaways. The Celts came here first, then the Romans, who established a camp called Brigantia on the present-day site of the city. Later, Gallus and Columban, Irish missionaries, came upon the vast shimmering lake ringed by mountains and dubbed the locale "Bregenz" (Golden Bowl). They set up camp on the hill above the lake, where modern tourists now hike to soak up some medieval culture along with the sun's rays. The gray-green waters of the Bodensee and the historic buildings in the **Oberstadt** make Bregenz a pleasant day's tour and a convenient base for exploring the surrounding Bregenzerwald.

⌕ ORIENTATION AND PRACTICAL INFORMATION

Trains: Bahnhofstr. (tel. 67550; call 1717 for information). **Trains** to **Bludenz** (40min., 5am-10:44pm, 150AS); **St. Gallen** (45min., 6:30am-10:11pm, 134AS); **Zurich** (1¾hr., 6:30am-10:11pm, 378AS); **Innsbruck** (3¾hr., 5am-9:43pm, 290AS); **Vienna** (8hr., 5am-10:44pm, 800AS); and **Munich** (2½hr., 9:20am-8:21pm, 424AS). The station has **lockers** (20AS), **luggage storage** (30AS), **bike rental** (with ticket 80-140AS per day; otherwise 150-200AS per day), an **ATM,** and **public showers** (5AS).

Regional Buses: BundesBuses leave from the train station for the surrounding region.

Public Transportation: 4 bus lines run throughout the city. 13AS single ride, day pass 25AS.

Taxis: Tel. 1718.

Car Rental: Hertz, AutoImmler Handels GmbH, Am Brand 2 (tel. 44995), at the intersection of Deuringstr. and Belruptstr.

Parking: You'll find **free parking** by the *Festspielhaus.* The **Hypobank parking garage** is in the city center (10AS per hour). Metered street parking spaces (5AS per 30min).

Tourist Office: Bregenz Tourismus und Stadtmarketing, Bahnhofstr. 14 (tel. 49590; fax 495969; email tourismus@bregenz.at). Facing the lake, head right along Bahnhofstr.; the tourist office is in the snazzy green glass building. This brand new office makes hotel reservations (30AS) and dispenses *Privatzimmer* lists, hiking and city maps, and concert info. Open during the year M-F 9am-noon, 1-5pm, Sa 9am-noon, during the *Festspiele* (festival performances) M-Sa 9am-7pm, Su 4-7pm. **Free accommodations board** with a courtesy phone in the train station.

Consulate: U.K., Bundesstr. 110 (tel. 78586), in neighboring **Lauterach**.

Internet Access: S'Logo, Kirchstr. 47 (tel. 44191; email Slogo@vol.at). 1AS per minute. Open M-F noon-3pm, 5pm-midnight, Sa-Su 5pm-midnight.

Post Office: Seestr. 5 (tel. 4900; fax 45757). Continue 6 blocks past the tourist office, heading away from the train station. Open M-F 8am-7pm (cashier closes at 5pm), Sa 8am-2pm. **Postal Code:** A-6900.

PHONE CODE	The **city code** for Bregenz is 05574.

⌕ ACCOMMODATIONS AND CAMPING

Bregenz caters primarily to affluent vacationers, but backpackers can usually find a comfortable corner. When the *Festspiele* come to town during the last week of July and the first 3 weeks of August, prices soar and reservations are painfully necessary. Consider staying just over the border in Lindau im Bodensee (see p. 217).

Jugendgästehaus (HI), Mehrerauerstr. 3-5 (tel. 42867; fax 428 67 88; email bregenz@jgh.at; www.jgh.at/bregenz/index.htm), offers spic-and-span bunk-bed accommodations in 2-6 person rooms, with built-in bathroom and shower. To reach the hostel, cross the bridge next to the train station, go past the skateboard half-pipe, and look for the big, yellow-brick building immediately on your left. Or take bus #2 from the train station. This multi-purpose hostel also features an **Internet** café. 200 AS, including sheets, towels, and breakfast.

Pension Sonne, Kaiserstr. 8 (tel./fax 42572; email g.diem@computer.haus.at; www.bbn.at/sonne), offers quiet, spacious rooms with wood floors in the heart of the *Fußgängerzone* (pedestrian zone). From the station, go right (facing the lake) up Bahnhofstr. into the city, then right on Kaiserstr. Singles 340AS, with shower 440AS; doubles 640AS, with shower 800AS; triples 840AS, with shower 1050AS. During the *Festspiele*, add 90AS. All rooms have a sink. Breakfast included. VISA, MC. Reception open 7:30am-10pm.

Pension Gunz, Anton-Schneider-Str. 38 (tel. 43657), located 2 blocks behind the post office. This homey pension-cum-restaurant serves up tidy rooms, each with shower. Singles 340AS, doubles 600AS. 30AS surcharge for 1-night stays. Breakfast included. The restaurant serves traditional fare (*Wienerschnitzel* 88AS) as well as vegetarian dishes (70-85AS). Restaurant and reception open 8am-9pm. Cash only.

Camping Lamm, Mehrerauerstr. 50-51 (tel. 71701; fax 71 74 54) is 5min. on foot past the youth hostel. The campground is chock full o' caravans, but there's plenty of room for tents (45AS per person). Next door, the family-run **Gasthof Lamm** offers quiet rooms in a refurbished 18th century building. 350AS per person, 50AS extra per person for in-room shower and bathroom. Breakfast included.

⬢ FOOD

Ikaros, Deuringstr. 5 (tel. 52954). Look for the blue and white-striped awning at the corner of Deuringstr. and Rathausstr. in the *Fußgängerzone*. This exceptional expat café serves up a little taste of the Mediterranean on the Bodensee. A wide variety of Greek dishes, including daily specials (75AS), salads, and warm entrees (55-95AS) are served indoors or on pleasant tables outside. Open M-Sa 10am-1am.

Zum Goldenen Hirschen, Kirchstr. 8 (tel. 42815). Look for the old wooden building with the small stained-glass windows and a flying gold reindeer over the door. Dark wooden furniture and a half-timbered interior. Delicious Austrian fare, including vegetarian *Krautspätzle* (85AS) and some non-native dishes like *chili con carne* (85AS). Open 10am-midnight. AmEx, MC, Visa.

SPAR Café Restaurant (tel. 42291, ext. 15) on the 1st floor of the big "GWL" mall building in the *Fußgängerzone*. If Austrian food makes you daydream about fresh vegetables, the self-serve salad and fruit/dessert bars (10AS per 100g) are a godsend. Cafeteria-style entrees 56-98AS. Open M-F 8:30am-5:30pm, Sa 8:30am-3pm.

Farmer's Markets fill up Kornmarktstr. every Tuesday and Friday from 7am-noon.

👁 ⬛ SIGHTS AND OUTDOOR ACTIVITIES

THE OLD TOWN. On the hill above Bregenz looms the **Oberstadt,** or "high city," a once-fortified settlement that contains many of the city's oldest and most attractive buildings. A short hike up Maurachg. from the *Fußgängerzone* brings you to the towering walls, beyond which lie rows of pastel-painted houses that appear just as they might have centuries ago. For lack of building supplies, some of these houses have incorporated fragments of the old city walls in their construction. The major landmark of the *Oberstadt* is the wooden **Martinsturm,** originally built in 1362, which supports Europe's largest onion dome. The 2nd and 3rd floors of the tower house the **Vorarlberg Militärmuseum.** (*Open May-Sept. M-Su 9am-8pm. In winter 1-5pm. 10AS, children 7AS.*) Although you can see all of the museum in 10 minutes (20 if you can read the German descriptions), you may want to spend more time on the third floor with its sweeping view of the Bodensee and beyond. Next to the tower is the **Martinskirche,** filled with frescoes dating back to the early 14th century. Particularly noteworthy are the depictions of St. Christopher, the Holy Symbol of Grief, and the 18th-century Stations of the Cross. Across Ehregutapl. (with the fountain) from the Martinsturm is **Deuring Schlößchen,** a 17th-century castle that now houses a non-budget hotel.

CHURCHES. Shaded by overhanging trees and vines, Meissnersteige leads down from the corner of the castle to the bottom of the *Oberstadt*. Cross Thalbachg. and hike up Schloßbergstr. to reach **St. Gallus Pfarrkirche,** reputedly founded by medieval Irish missionaries St. Gallus and St. Columban. The white-stucco sanctuary of the 11th-century church now glows under lavish gold ornamentation and a detailed painted ceiling that dates from 1738. The shepherdess in the altar-painting has the face of Empress Maria Theresia, who donated 1500 guilders to the church in 1740. On the opposite side of the *Oberstadt*, the imposing **Herz-Jesu Kirche,** at the corner of Am Brand and Bergmannstr., points its twin steeples to the heavens. Built in 1907 and recently renovated in neo-Gothic style, the huge sanctuary's brick and wood furnishings bring out the Expressionist stained-glass windows.

HISTORICAL MUSEUM. The **Vorarlberg Landesmuseum,** on the waterfront between the tourist office and the post office, examines pre-tourist Bregenz. The museum's collection spans thousands of years, with carefully explained exhibits on the city's inhabitants from the Stone Age to the 18th century. *(Kornmarktpl. 1. Open Tu-Su 9am-noon and 2-5pm. Ring the bell if the door's locked. 20AS, students 10AS.)*

OUTDOOR ACTIVITIES. *Spazierengehen*, a leisurely ramble along the water, is an Austrian institution. There's no better place to stretch one's legs and check out the locals than the **Strandweg** and **Seepromenade**, which follow the curve of the Bodensee from one end of town to the other. All along the waterfront, carefully groomed paths, rose gardens, and strategically placed ice-cream stands surround playgrounds and mini-golf courses. **Boat rental** is available near the train station from 10am to 10pm in summer. (Paddle- and rowboats 130AS.) Away from the city center and past the train station sprawls the **Strandbad,** a huge swimming pool, sauna, and sunbathing area. (Tel. 44242. Open in fair weather mid-May to mid-Sept. Tu-F 9am-noon, Sa 9am-7pm, Su 10am-6pm. 35AS, students 28AS, seniors 28AS, children 11AS.)

Several sightseeing cruises on the Bodensee depart from the **Hafen** (harbor), Seestr. 4 (tel. 42868), opposite the post office. Ferries run to the **Blumen Insel Mainau** (Mainau Flower Isle; see p. 371) on the German side of the lake, which features a Baroque castle, an indoor tropical palm house, butterfly house, and gardens rife with orchids, tulips, dahlias, and 1100 kinds of roses. (Admission to all sights 127AS. Ferries leave Bregenz May-Sept. at 9:20, 10:20, and 11:25am; return from Mainau at 2:50, 4:15, and 4:55pm. Round-trip 293AS; special family rates available.) The **Drei-Länder-Rundfahrt** traces the Swiss, German, and Austrian waterfronts. (Ferries depart Bregenz at 2:30pm, returning at 5pm. 184AS, special family rates available.)

The **Pfänderbahn** cable car leaves from the top of Schillerstr., uphill from the post office, and sways up the **Pfänder** mountain (the tallest peak around the Bodensee) for a panorama spanning from the Black Forest to Switzerland. (Tel. 42 16 00; fax 421604; email office@pfaenderbahn.at, www.pfaenderbahn.at. Daily 9am-7pm, every 30min. Ascent 88AS, descent 63AS, round-trip 125AS. Discounts for seniors and children under 19.) At the top of the cable car ride, wander with native animals in the free **Alpine Wildlife Park,** or watch **bird flight shows** from May to October. (Daily at 11am and 2:30pm. 45AS, children 24AS.)

◪ FESTIVALS AND NIGHTLIFE

The concrete monstrosity on the edge of the lake is not a ski ramp gone awry but rather the world's largest **floating stage** and the centerpiece for the annual **Bregenzer Festspiele.** Every year from mid-July to mid-August, the Vienna Symphony Orchestra and other opera, theater, and chamber music groups come to town, bringing some 180,000 tourists with them. The main event is a performance on the

VORARLBERG

floating stage, drawing capacity crowds of 6800. In 2000, the floating opera will be Verdi's *Masked Ball*, premiering on July 21st. The *Festspielhaus* opera will be Rimsky-Korsakov's *The Golden Rooster*, premiering on July 20th. (Tickets go on sale in October. 300-1800AS. Students under 26 get 25% off, with the exception of the premiere night. Weekday performances rarely sell out more than a few days before the show. Standing room tickets available. For more info, write to Postfach 311, A-6901 Bregenz, call (5574) 4076, or email ticket@bregenzerfestspiele.com.)

For late-night entertainment, there are many popular student hangouts on and around Kirchstr. Check out **Uwe's Bier-Bar,** Kirchstr. 25, a popular bar with a mixed crowd. (18 and older; open 7pm-1am. Beer 39AS.)

DAYTRIPS FROM BREGENZ

NEAR BREGENZ: SCHWARZENBERG IM BREGENZERWALD

Buses and trains run over a dozen times a day from Bregenz to Schwarzenberg (50min.). Trains stop at nearby Dornbirn, from where a bus takes you the rest of the way. Alternately, you can take a bus the whole way, depending on which timing you find more convenient.

Spreading out to the south and east of Bregenz, the **Bregenzerwald** is home to many small towns and villages that preserve the rustic flavor of Vorarlberg's past. Though it is not a forest (*Wald*) in any real sense of the word, the *Bregenzerwald* consists of wide open pastures and stands of pine trees, coddled by the steeply rising mountainsides. The region, spotted with such towns as Egg, Bezau, Au, and Schwarzenberg, lies no more than an hour from Bregenz and makes for appealing daytrips from the city. **Schwarzenberg** exemplifies the rural and cultural charms of the *Bregenzerwald*. The village sits on a rolling swath of pasture land, near the center of a ring of mountains. The majority of Schwarzenberg's houses are made entirely of wood; when they fall into disrepair, local builders restore them using centuries-old techniques. One can't go far without smelling the pungent scents of wood, fresh-cut grass, and flowers in the colorful window boxes of most houses.

◪ ORIENTATION AND PRACTICAL INFORMATION. The **tourist office** (tel. (05512) 3570; fax 2902), is located near the town square where the bus from Bregenz stops. Follow the main road downhill from the church and turn right at the *Bäckerei-Konditorei*. The tourist office dispenses maps detailing the many hiking opportunities available in and around Schwarzenberg. Street signs in the town are labeled with hiking destinations, including the average time required to get there. (Keep in mind that you might not be as fit as the average outdoors-crazed Austrian!) The **Raiffeisenbank**, uphill towards the Heimatsmuseum, has an **ATM** (open M-F 8am-noon, 1:30-4pm, Sa 8-11am). Transportation in the *Bregenzerwald* is based around a regional *Netz* (network) of trains and buses. A **Netzticket** allows you unlimited travel by bus and train throughout the *Bregenzerwald* for a given amount of time: one day 90AS, one week 190AS, one month 550AS. One-way tickets (*eine Richtung*) are also available, priced according to distance. For all but the shortest trips into the *Bregenzerwald*, a **Tagesticket** (one day ticket) is the most economical option—in fact, the ticket window at the station may just automatically sell you one.

◪◪ ACCOMMODATIONS AND FOOD. Dozens of wooden guest houses dot Schwarzenberg and the outlying regions. The tourist office can also arrange for fairly inexpensive private accommodations. **Café Angelikahöhe** (tel. (05512) 2985), offers four double rooms with sink and table for 500AS, though prices go down the longer you stay. Children stay for 50%. Breakfast is included. To reach the pension from the town square, turn left at the *Bäckerei-Konditorei*, go straight, then turn right at the **ADEG** supermarket. Café Angelikahöhe also serves meals (80-135AS). You can stock up on groceries at the ADEG supermarket (open M-Th 7am-noon,

2:30-6:30pm, Sa 7am-12:30pm), or try some of the local produce and tasty cheeses at **Maria Vögel** (open M-W 7:30am-noon, 2:30-6pm, Sa 7:30am-noon), just downhill from the town square.

SIGHTS AND OUTSIDE ACTIVITIES. Schwarzenberg's man-made attractions include the **Pfarrkirche,** an airy church that features an altar painting by the town's most famous resident, Angelika Kauffmann (1741-1807). Kauffmann was one of the few lauded female painters of her age. Goethe and Herder were among her friends, and her work received great acclaim in England and Italy. The **Heimatsmuseum,** housed in an old wooden lodge a few minutes walk up the main road, contains a small permanent collection of her paintings and memorabilia, as well as an interesting exhibit of agricultural and domestic implements from days of yore. *(Tel. (05512) 2967. Open May-Sept. T, Th, Sa 2-4pm. 35AS, children 10AS.)* Schwarzenberg also hosts an annual **Schubertiade,** a festival of the composer's works (May 1-19 and Aug. 26-Sept. 15, 2000). Purchase tickets at the *Gemeindeamt,* down the hall from the tourist office.

NEAR BREGENZ: LINDAU IM BODENSEE

Just over the border in Germany, the island resort of Lindau makes an excellent daytrip from Bregenz by train (10min., 14 per day).

When geological forces crunched their way through southern Germany during the last ice age, Mother Nature decided that Lindau should be a resort. Connected to the lakeshore by a narrow causeway, the island sits cupped in aquamarine waters, enjoying a view of the Alps that's almost the same as the one you see on good chocolates. Tourists started floating in by steamship in 1835, and now close to a million come every year to soak in the balmy climate and wander among 14th-century gabled houses on Maximilianstr., which forms the central part of town.

ORIENTATION AND PRACTICAL INFORMATION. Lindau itself is an island in the Bodensee. Lindau's **tourist office,** Ludwigstr. 68 (tel. 26 00 30; fax 26 00 26), across from the train station, finds **rooms** for a DM5 fee (open mid-June to early Sept. M-Sa 9am-1pm and 2-7pm; May to mid-June and Sept. M-F 9am-1pm and 2-6pm, Sa 9am-1pm; April and Oct. M-F 9am-1pm and 2-5pm, Sa 9am-1pm; Nov.-March M-F 9am-noon and 2-5pm). **Tours** leave from the office at 10am (Tu and F in German, M in English. DM6, students and overnight guests DM4).

SIGHTS AND ENTERTAINMENT. Halfway down Maximilianstr., the **Altes Rathaus** is a fruity blend of frescoes. The **Cavazzen-Haus** in the Marktplatz houses the **Stadtmuseum,** which displays a collection of musical instruments and art ranging from fine French porcelain to 17th-century portraits of ugly German bluebloods. (Tel. 94 40 73. Open April-Oct. Tu-Su 10am-noon and 2-5pm. DM5, students DM3.) A walk down **In der Grub**—the less touristed equivalent of Maximilianstr.— leads to the ivy-covered **Diebsturm** (robbers' tower), which looks more like Rapunzel's tower than the prison it once was. For properly-dressed adults, the **Spielbank** (casino) by the Seebrücke offers the regular spinning of roulette wheels and thinning of wallets. The bet ceiling is DM12,000, so don't worry about losing too much money. (Open 3pm-4am. Admission DM5 and a passport. No jeans. 21+)

ACCOMMODATIONS AND FOOD. Brush up your Greek with the *text*ured napkins at **Taverna Pita Gyros,** Paradiespl. 16 (tel. (08382) 23702) while eating a *gyro* (DM10; open daily 10am-9pm). For **groceries** try **Plus,** in the basement of the department store at the intersection of In der Grub and Cramerg. (open M-F 8:30am-6:30pm, Sa 8am-1pm). The spectacular **Jugendherberge,** Herbergsweg 11 (tel. (08382) 96710; fax 496 71 50), lies across the Seebrücke off Bregenzer Str. Walk (20min.) or take bus #1 or 2 from the train station to "Anheggerstr.", then transfer to bus #3 (dir.: "Zech") to "Jugendherberge." (DM28. Under 27 and families with small children only. Breakfast, sheets, and *Kurtax* included. Reception 7am-midnight.

Curfew midnight. Call ahead.) You could eat off the sparkling floor in the rooms at **Gästehaus Holdereggen**, Näherweg 4 (tel. (08382) 6574). Follow the railroad tracks across the causeway to the mainland; turn right onto Holdereggengasse and left onto Jungfernburgstr. Näherweg is on the left (20min.). (Singles DM38, doubles DM76. DM3 *Kurtaxe* per person for one-night stands. Showers DM2.) **Campingplatz Lindau-Zech**, Frauenhofer Str. 20 (tel. (08382) 72236; fax 26 00 26), is 3km south of the island on the mainland. It's within spitting distance of the Austrian border. Take bus #1 or 2 to "Anheggerstr.," then bus #3 (dir.: "Zech") to the end. (DM9.50 per person. DM4 per tent. *Kurtax* DM1.50. Showers included. Open May-Oct.).

■ **OUTDOOR ACTIVITIES.** Water-lovers rent **boats** 50m to the left of the casino, next to the bridge. (Tel. (08382) 5514; open mid.-March to mid.-Sept. daily 9am-9pm; rowboats DM10-18; paddleboats DM14-18 per hr.; motor boat DM45.) One-hour excursions (tel./fax 78194) leave from the dock behind the casino at 11:30am, 1, 2:30, and 6pm (DM12, children DM6). Rent **bikes** (tel. (08382) 21261) at the train station (tel. (08382) 23539); open March to late Dec. M-F 9am-1pm and 3:20-6pm, Sa 9:30am-1pm, Su 9am-noon; DM13 per day). Alternatively, **Fahrradies**, In der Grub 5 will rent you wheels (open M-F 9:30am-1pm and 2:30-6pm, Sa 9:30am-1pm; DM12 per day, mountain bikes DM20). Lindau has 3 beaches. **Römerbad** (tel. (08382) 6830) is the smallest and most familial, located left of the harbor on the island (open M-F 10:30am-7:30pm and Sa-Su 10am-8pm; DM4, students DM3). To reach the quieter **Lindenhofbad** (tel. 6637), take bus #1 or 2 to "Anheggerstr." and then bus #4 to "Alwind" (open M-F 10:30am-7:30pm, Sa-Su 10am-8pm; DM4, students DM3). Lindau's biggest beach is **Eichwald** (tel. 55 39), a 30-minute walk to the right facing the harbor along Uferweg. Or take bus #1 or 2 to "Anheggerstr.," then bus #3 to "Karmelbuckel" (open M-F 9:30am-7:30pm, Sa-Su 9am-8pm; DM5).

FELDKIRCH

Just minutes from the borders of Switzerland and Liechtenstein, Feldkirch is a small city that has served for centuries as a hub of trade and transportation. More than in any other city in Vorarlberg, Feldkirch's historic past remains vivid today—the triangular *Altstadt* is a maze of pastel-colored Baroque buildings, lined by arcades that shelter shops and fruit stands. The annual Schubert festival attracts musicians and fans from all over Europe, adding international flair to an already lively atmosphere.

■ **ORIENTATION AND PRACTICAL INFORMATION.** Feldkirch is easily accessible by **train** from major regional cities: **Bregenz** (40min., 5:29am-11:59pm, 58AS); **Innsbruck** (3hr., 5:26am-10:10pm, 250AS); and **Salzburg** (4hr., 5:26am-10:10pm, 410AS). **Swiss PTT buses** travel from the train station to Buchs and Sargans in Switzerland, with connections to Liechtenstein (20min., every 45min., 34AS. Bus info tel. 73974; open M-Th 8am-12:30pm and 2-4:30pm, F 8am-noon). **City buses** *(Stadt-busse)* connect Feldkirch's various subdivisions (13AS, day pass 25AS). Hop in a **taxi** outside the station, or call for one (tel. 1715 or 1712).

The primary locations of interest in Feldkirch are clustered in the old city on the Ill River, a confusing warren of streets that makes a map necessary (free at the tourist office). To reach the city center and the **tourist office**, Herreng. 12 (tel. 73467; fax 79867; email tourismus@wtg.feldkirch.com), walk from the train station to the end of the road, turn left onto Bahnhofstr., and cross via the pedestrian underpass at the first major intersection. Go into the *Bezirkhauptmannschaft* building, and the office is about 50m ahead on the right. The office helps with reservations and hands out historic walking-tour maps and info about cultural events. (Open M-F 9am-6pm, Sa 9am-noon; in winter M-F 8am-noon, 1-5pm, Sa 9am-noon.) **Lockers** (20-30AS) are available at the train station. Feldkirch's **post office** is on Bahnhofstr. across from the station (open M-F 7am-7pm, Sa 7am-noon). The **postal code** is A-6800.

| **PHONE CODE** | The **city code** for Feldkirch is 05522. |

◨◪ ACCOMMODATIONS AND FOOD. Feldkirch's youth hostel, **Jugendherberge "Altes Siechenhaus,"** Reichstr. 111 (tel. 73181; fax 79399), might well be the highlight of your visit. Buses #2 and 60 (dir.: "Jugendherberge") run to the hostel from the station (5min.). You can also walk straight out of the station onto the main road, Bahnhofstr. (which becomes Reichstr.), turn right and walk 15 to 20 minutes. Buses to and from the city center run twice per hour until 2pm and once an hour until 11pm (M-Sa). The hostel is an ancient white brick and wood building on the right of the street next to a small stone church. This 600-year-old structure served as an infirmary during several plague epidemics. Later it was a poor house and then a grammar school after a 1697 fire. Inside, you'll find modern conveniences, with only an exposed wooden beam or two to remind you of the building's antiquity. (Dorms 150AS. Breakfast 50AS. **Laundry** 40AS. Linen 20AS. Candy, soft drinks, wine, and beer sold at the desk. Wheelchair accessible. Oct.-Apr. heating 25AS. Guests who wish to leave the hostel after 10pm must take a keycard with them: 14AS, 200AS deposit. Reception M-Sa 7:30am-10pm, Su 7:30-10am and 5-10pm. Closed end of Nov.-first week of Dec.) If medieval hostelry is not to your taste, take bus #1 or 3 (dir.: Tosters) to "Burgweg" to **Gasthof Löwen** (tel. 72868; fax 37857), in a suburb of Feldkirch. From the stop, walk a half-block toward the tall pink and white building on Egelseestr. The hotel has simple rooms in a quiet neighborhood. (Singles 350AS; doubles 580-660AS. TV, shower, and breakfast included.)

The *Fußgängerzone* is packed with restaurants and snack bars. **Pizzeria-Trattoria La Taverna,** Vorstadtstr. 18 (tel. 79293), offers authentic Italian dining, with affordable pizzas (85-100AS) and pastas (70-100AS), plus a pretty terrace to eat them on (open 11:30am-2pm and 5pm-midnight). For a quick meal, head to vegetarian-friendly **Ali Baba Kebap,** Kreuzg. 9 (tel. 38042), down the street from the tourist office. (Veggie *Kebap* 30AS. *Döner Kebap* 35AS. Open M-Sa 9am-11pm, Su 11am-11pm.) The restaurant inside the huge iron doors of the **Schattenburg** (see **Sights**) serves enormous portions of *Wiener Schnitzel* for 135AS, *Apfelstrudel* for 35AS, and their specialty *Jägertöpfle*, smoked ham with noodles and cream for 135AS (open Tu-Su 10am-midnight). In the center of the *Altstadt*, get picnic supplies at **Interspar Café/Markt,** under Hervis Sport Mode at the top of Johanniterg. off Marktpl. (open M-F 9am-7:30pm, Sa 8am-5pm) or **Billa,** on Bahnhofstr. between the hostel and train station (open M-F 7:30am-7pm, Sa 7:30am-5pm). The Marktpl. houses an **outdoor market** (Tu and Sa 7am-noon).

◨◪ SIGHTS AND ENTERTAINMENT. Feldkirch's Gothic **Dom** (cathedral), the St. Nikolaus Kirche, forms one edge of the *Altstadt* (old town). Mentioned in a manuscript already in 1287, the cathedral received a face-lift in 1478 after a series of devastating fires and now flaunts beautiful stained-glass windows and an elaborately vaulted ceiling. A *pietà*, crafted in 1521 by Wolf Huber (a master of the Danube School), graces the altar on the right. Frescoes of Feldkirch history and the coats of arms of local potentates adorn the 15th-century **Rathaus,** a former granary, on Schmiedg. On nearby Schloßberg. stands the **Palais Liechtenstein,** completed in 1697. The palace once supported the royal seat of the Prince of Liechtenstein, but now houses the city archives and the town library. Its 3rd-floor **art gallery** hosts frequent exhibitions, often free.

At the edges of the *Altstadt*, 3 towers remain of the original city wall: the **Katzenturm,** the **Pulverturm,** and the **Wasserturm.** Just outside the *Altstadt*, one block towards the station on Bahnhofstr., lies the **Kapuzinerkloster** (Capuchin monastery), built in 1605. For a fantastic view of the *Altstadt*, hike up either the castle staircase or Burgg. to **Schattenburg,** Feldkirch's most impressive structure. (Castle and café open Tu-Su 10am-midnight.) From the early 1200s until 1390, the castle was the seat of the Count of Montfort. The town purchased the castle in 1825 to save it from demolition and converted it into the **Feldkirch Heimatmuseum,** where you can imagine yourself back in the Middle Ages. (Tel. 71982. Open Tu-Su 9am-noon and 1-5pm. 25AS, youth 15AS, children 5AS.)

Feldkirch's annual **Schubertiade** (June 15-25 in 2000) honors one of Austria's most beloved composers. World-class musicians, including Dietrich Fischer-Dieskau and members of the Vienna Philharmonic, perform works by and inspired by Schubert in Feldkirch's concert halls and manor houses, while painters, sculptors, and performance artists exhibit throughout the city. (Tickets go on sale 1 year in advance for 300-1400AS. Tel. (05576) 72091, fax 75450. Schubertiade GmbH, Villa Rosenthal, Schweizerstr. 1, A-6845 Hohenerns, Postfach 100; email info@schubertiade.at, www.schubertiade.at.) During the 2nd weekend of July, Feldkirch's annual **wine festival** intoxicates all those who venture to Marktpl. The circus comes to town toward the end of the month, when the annual **Festival of Traveling Entertainers** sweeps jugglers, mimes, and clowns into every cobblestone path. If that's not enough, you can go **hot-air ballooning** with G. Schabau (tel. 51121; fax 52425; 1½-2hr. flights 3800AS.) December brings the annual **Christmas bazaar**, with crafts, candy canes, and crèches for sale during Advent.

SALZBURGER LAND

Salzburger Land is often considered to be the most Austrian of all the Austrian provinces, though it wasn't even a part of the Austro-Hungarian Empire until 1815, when the Congress of Vienna, while divvying up Europe, stripped the Archbishopric of Salzburg of its autonomy and gave it to the Habsburgs. The area was first united under Roman emperor Claudius in the 1st century, who coveted the region's "white gold" (salt, not cocaine). Salzburg's name comes from the German word for salt, *Salz*, while Hallstatt, an important salt-mining locale for the past 3000 years, derives its name from the Celtic equivalent, *Hall*. Although tourism displaced the salt trade long ago, images of St. Barbara, the patron saint of miners, linger everywhere.

The province of Salzburger Land encompasses many of the rugged peaks of the **Hohe Tauern National Park,** as well as a slice of the shining lakes and rolling hills of the **Salzkammergut,** which lies primarily in Upper Austria. The provincial capital is, of course, Salzburg, which is famous for just about everything musical, from

221

Mozart to Julie Andrews. The **Salzburger Festspiele,** held every July and August, is regarded as one of the premier events of the classical music world (see p. 238). In addition, many smaller local festivals pop up all summer throughout the region. For instance, every 3 years on the last Sunday in July (next time in 2001), a mock **Pirates' Battle** is held on the Salzach River at **Oberndorf.** According to the ritual plot, brigands rob a saltboat and then fire on the town of **Laufen,** on the Bavarian side of the river. Eventually, the defeated pirates try to escape. They are arrested and condemned to death, but their sentence is quickly modified to "death by drowning in beer," which signifies the beginning of a lavish feast.

HIGHLIGHTS OF SALZBURGER LAND

■ Have a wet and wild time at the *Wasserspiele* of **Hellbrunn** (see p. 240).
■ Traverse the dizzying **Großglocknerstraße** through the Hohe Tauern National Park, beneath 3000m peaks, glaciers, and tumbling waterfalls (see p. 246).
■ Lord it over Salzburg from the ramparts of **Festung Hohensalzburg** (p. 235).

SALZBURG

Let's get one thing straight right now: at no point in your visit to Salzburg will you see a group of Aryan children clad in curtains running through the city singing about a "needle pulling thread." You may, however, see hordes of tourists doing just that (in a slightly less graceful manner). Fortunately, Salzburg is much more than simply the scenic backdrop of an American movie. Wedged between mountains and dotted with church spires, medieval turrets, and resplendent palaces, Salzburg offers both spectacular sights and a rich musical culture, both past and contemporary. The city's adulation for homegrown genius Wolfgang Amadeus Mozart in particular and classical music in general reaches a deafening roar every summer during the **Salzburger Festspiele** (summer music festivals), when financially endowed admirers the world over come to pay their respects to the musical elite. The *Festspiele* last for 5 weeks, during which time hundreds of operas, concerts, plays, and open-air performances bedazzle the fawning fans. Crowds wander the streets of Salzburg year-round, thanks more to the one-two combination of "Wolfie" and Julie Andrews than Salzburg's (incidentally gorgeous) castle and Baroque palaces. Never mind that both Mozart and the von Trapps eventually left, finding Salzburg a bit too stifling (the former fled from the oppressive bourgeois atmosphere and his over-managerial father, the latter from the tone-deaf Nazis)— this Little City That Could couldn't keep away its onslaught of visitors even if it wanted to.

⊏ GETTING TO AND FROM SALZBURG

Salzburg has its own airport—the **Flughafen Salzburg** (tel. 858 00), 4km west of the city center, with frequent connections to **Paris, Amsterdam, Vienna, Innsbruck,** and other major European cities. It is considerably cheaper, however, to fly into **Munich** and take the train from there. If you do fly into or out of Salzburg, bus #77 (dir.: Bahnhof from the airport, Walserfeld from the train station) circles between the train station and the airport (15min., every 15-30min. 5:32am-11pm, 19AS). A taxi from the airport to the train station should cost roughly 150AS. **Trains** link Salzburg to most major international and domestic cities. There are 2 train stations in Salzburg: the **Hauptbahnhof** on Südtirolerpl. is the first Salzburg stop for trains coming from Vienna, while the Rangier Bahnhof (the first stop when coming from Innsbruck) is primarily a cargo station, so don't get off there. A new regional bus depot is (still) under construction. In the meantime, **buses** leave from behind the construction site, across from the train station. BundesBuses chug throughout the Salzburger Land and Salzkammergut regions (see p. 263).

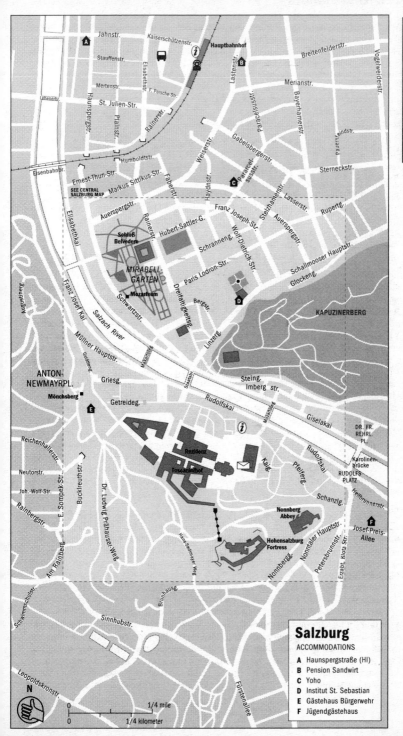

Salzburg

ACCOMMODATIONS

A Haunspergstraße (HI)
B Pension Sandwirt
C Yoho
D Institut St. Sebastian
E Gästehaus Bürgerwehr
F Jügendgästehaus

Motorists coming from Vienna can exit at any of the Salzburg-West exits off Autobahn A1. Among these, the Flughafen exit is near the airport, the Salzburg-Nord exit is near Itzling and Kasern, and the Salzburg-Süd exit lies south of the city near Schloß Hellbrunn and Untersberg. A8 and E52 lead from the west into Rosenheim and then branch off to Munich and Innsbruck. A10 heads north from Hallein to Salzburg. From the Salzkammergut area, take Grazer Bundesstr. #158. Since public transportation is efficient within the city limits, consider the **Park and Ride** parking lots—park for free when you get off the highway and take the bus into town. The most convenient lot is **Alpensiedlung Süd** on Alpenstr. (exit: Salzburg-Süd), but a bigger lot is open in July and August at the **Salzburger Ausstellungszentrum** (exit: Salzburg-Mitte).

▟ ORIENTATION

Salzburg, the capital of Salzburger Land, is surrounded by three thickly-forested hills. Just a few kilometers from the German border, the city covers both banks of the **Salzach River.** The *Hauptbahnhof* is on the northern edge of town, but buses #1, 5, 6, 51, and 55 connect it to downtown, or you can walk (15-20min.). From the bus, disembark at "Mirabellpl." or "Mozartsteg." On foot, turn left out of the station onto Rainerstr., and follow it all the way (under the tunnel) to **Mirabellplatz**, which is the center of the *Neustadt*, on the east bank of the river. The *Altstadt* lies on the west bank, in the shadow of the **Mönchsberg** (Monk's Mountain).

▟ PRACTICAL INFORMATION

TRANSPORTATION

Trains: Hauptbahnhof, (tel. 01717 for information) in Südtirolerpl. To: **Zell am See** (1¾hr., 24 per day 1:36am-9:24pm, 150AS); Badgastein in the **Hohe Tauern National Park** (1½hr., every 2hr. 7:14am-8:15pm, 170AS); **Innsbruck** (2hr., every 2hr. 12:39am-9:19pm, 350AS); **Graz** (4½hr., every 2hr. 3am-7:21pm, 410AS); **Vienna** (3½hr., every 30min. 1:15am-9:32pm, 410AS); **Munich** (2hr., every 30min. 4am-10pm, 298AS); **Zurich** (6hr., 8 per day 12:39am-4:30pm, 862AS); **Budapest** (6½hr., 10 per day 1:16am-8pm, 742AS); **Prague** (7hr., 4 per day, 852AS, connect in Linz); and **Venice** (6hr., 5 per day, last connection at 10:36pm, 540AS). For reservations dial 1700, M-F 7am-6:30pm, Sa 8am-12:30pm. Regular ticket office open 24hr.

Buses: Bus depot (tel. (0660) 51 88). BundesBuses zip to: **Mondsee** (1hr., every hr. 6:40am-7:20pm, 60AS); **St. Wolfgang** (1½hr., every hr. 6:40am-8:10pm, 90AS); **Bad Ischl** (1½hr., every hr. 6:40am-7:15pm, 100AS); and throughout Salzburger Land. For schedule information, dial 167.

Public Transportation: Get information at the **Lokalbahnhof** (tel. 87 21 45), next to the train station. 18 bus lines cut through the city, with central hubs at Hanuschpl. by Makartsteg, Äußerer Stein by Mozartsteg., Mirabellpl., and the *Hauptbahnhof*. Tickets are cheapest from *Tabaks* (one ride 19AS, day pass 40AS, week 105AS). You can also purchase packs of 5 single-ride tickets from vending machines at bus stops for 75AS or buy single tickets on the bus. Punch your ticket when you board in order to validate it, or suffer a 500AS fine. Buses usually make their last run from downtown to outer destinations at 10:30-11:30pm, earlier for less-frequented routes. Check the schedule posted at stops.

Parking: Consider the "Park and Ride" option (see p. 222). Otherwise, try **Altstadt-Garage** inside the Mönchsberg (open 24hr.); **Mirabell-Garage** in Mirabellpl. (open 7am-midnight; 28AS per hr.); or **Parkgarage Linzergasse** at Glockeng. off Linzerg. (open 7am-10pm; 20AS per hr. or 160AS for a full day). Other lots are at the airport, Hellbrunn, and Akademiestr. (15AS per hr.). Blue lines on the sidewalk indicate parking is available; buy a ticket for the space from one of the nearby automated machines.

Taxis: (tel. 8111 or 1716). Stands at Hanuschpl., Residenzpl., Makartpl., and the train station. **BusTaxi** fills in when the public buses stop running at night. Pick it up at the

Central Salzburg

stop at Hanuschpl. or Theaterg. and tell the driver where you need to go. Every 30min. nightly 11:30pm-1:30am. 35AS for any distance within the city limits.

Car Rental: Avis, Ferdinand-Porsche-Str. 7 (tel. 87 72 78; fax 88 02 35), and **Budget,** Innsbrucker Bundesstr. 95 (tel. 85 50 38; fax 85 49 87), are in the airport. All offices offer insurance and unlimited mileage.

Bike Rental: Climb every mountain and ford every stream with a bicycle from the train station counter #3 (tel. 888 73 163). 150AS per day, 90AS with that day's train ticket, half-day 70AS, 1 week 670AS. Bike paths wind throughout the city; maps at tourist office (84AS).

Hitchhiking: Hitchers headed to Innsbruck, Munich, or Italy (except Venice), have been seen on bus #77 to the German border. Thumbers bound for Vienna or Venice allegedly take bus #29 (dir.: Forellenwegsiedlung) to the *Autobahn* entrance at "Schmiedlinger-str." or bus #15 (dir.: Bergheim) to the *Autobahn* entrance at "Grüner Wald."

TOURIST AND FINANCIAL SERVICES

Tourist Office, Mozartpl. 5 (tel. 84 75 68 or 889 87 330; fax 889 87 342; email tourist @salzburginfo.or.at; www.salzburginfo.or.at), in the *Altstadt*. From the train station, take bus #5, 6, 51, or 55 to "Mozartsteg." then curve around the building into Mozartpl. On foot, turn left on Rainerstr., go to the end, cross Staatsbrücke, then continue along the river's west bank upstream to Mozartsteg. (20min.). The office has free hotel maps (exactly the same as the 1OAS city map), and the **Salzburg Card** (see p. 233). Reservation service 30AS, for 3 or more people 60AS, plus a 7.2% deposit deductible from the 1st night's stay. The overworked staff will tell you which hostels have available rooms. Open July-Aug. 9am-8pm; Sept.-June 9am-6pm. There are other **branches** at the train station platform #2a (tel. 889 87 340; open M-Sa 8:45am-8pm); and the Alpensiedlung Süd "Park and Ride" lot (tel. 889 87 360).

Budget Travel: ÖKISTA, Wolf-Dietrich-Str. 31 (tel. 88 32 52; fax 883 25 220; email info@oekista.co.at; www.oekista.co.at/oekista), near the International Youth Hotel. Open M-F 9am-5:30pm. **Albatros Travel Service,** Bergstr. 22 (tel. 881 67 10; fax 88 16 79), answers your travel questions in English. Open M-F 8:15am-6pm.

Consulates: South Africa, Buchenweg 14 (tel./fax 62 20 35). Open M-F 8am-1pm and 2-5pm. **U.K.,** Alter Markt 4 (tel. 84 81 33; fax 84 55 63). Open M-F 9am-noon. **U.S. Consulate Agency,** Alter Markt 1/3 (tel. 84 87 76; fax 84 97 77), in the *Altstadt*. Open M, W, and F 9am-noon.

Currency Exchange: Banks offer better rates for cash than AmEx offices but often charge higher commissions. Banking hours M-F 8am-12:30pm and 2-4:30pm. **Rieger Bank** at Alter Markt and Getreideg. has extended currency exchange hours. Open July-Aug. M-F 9am-7:30pm, Sa 9am-6pm, Su 10am-5pm; Sept.-June M-F 9am-6pm, Sa 9am-3pm, Su 10am-5pm. The train station's currency exchange is open 7am-9pm. **Panorama Tours** offers cash currency exchange at bank rates with no commission; available only to guests taking their tour (see p. 236).

American Express: Mozartpl. 5, A-5020 (tel. 8080; fax 808 01 78), near the tourist office. Provides all banking services and charges no commission on AmEx checks. Better rates than banks for cash and other checks. Holds mail for check- or card-holders, books tours, and reserves *Festspiele* tickets. Open M-F 9am-5:30pm, Sa 9am-noon.

LOCAL SERVICES

Luggage Storage: At the train station. Lockers 30-50AS (good for 2 calendar days). Luggage check 30AS per piece per calendar day. Open 6am-10pm.

English-Language Bookstores: American Discount, in a passage in Alter Markt 1 (tel. 75 75 41), sells American best-sellers and magazines. **Buchhandlung Motzko Reise,** Elisabethstr. 1 (tel. 88 33 11), near the train station, has travel guides and English-language books. Both open M-F 9am-6pm, Sa 9am-5pm.

Bi-Gay-Lesbian Organizations: Frauenkulturzentrum (Women's/Lesbians' Center), Elisabethstr. 11 (tel. 87 16 39). Office and hotlines open M 10am-12:30pm. Runs a **Woman's Café** on the 1st and 3rd F of every month, 8pm-midnight. **Homosexual Initiative of Salzburg** (HOSI), Müllner Hauptstr. 11 (tel. 43 59 27), hosts regular workshops and meetings, including a **Café-bar** open F from 9pm and Sa from 8pm.

Laundromat: Norge Exquisit Textil Reinigung, Paris-Lodronstr. 16 (tel. 87 63 81), on the corner of Wolf-Dietrich-Str. Self-serve wash and dry 82AS, soap 28AS. (You may not use your own soap.) Open M-F 7:30am-4pm, Sa 8-10am. Full-serve 185AS. Open M-F 7:30am-6pm, Sa 8am-noon. **Westinghaus,** Kaiserschützenstr. 10 (tel. 87 33 90), across from the train station. Self-serve 135AS. Open in summer M-F 7:30am-7pm, Sa 7:30am-1pm; in winter M-F 8am-6pm, Sa 8am-noon.

Public Toilets: In the *Altstadt* under the archway between Kapitelpl. and Dompl. (7AS). Cheaper ones in the Festungsbahn lobby (3AS) and at the fish market in Hanuschpl. (2AS.). McDonalds' sparkling free toilets are popular with tourists, including those who "forget" to purchase fries on their way out.

EMERGENCY AND COMMUNICATIONS

Emergencies: Police, tel. 133. Headquarters at Alpenstr. 90 (tel. 6383). **Ambulance,** tel. 144. **Fire,** tel. 122.

Rape Hotline: tel. 88 11 00.

AIDS Hotline: AIDS-Hilfe Salzburg, Gabelsburgerstr. 20 (tel. 88 14 88).

Pharmacies: Elisabeth-Apotheke, Elisabethstr. 1 (tel. 87 14 84), a few blocks left of the train station. **Alte f.e. Hofapotheke,** Alter Markt 6 (tel. 84 36 23), is the oldest pharmacy in Salzburg. Pharmacies in the city center are open M-F 8am-6pm, Sa 8am-noon; outside the center M-F 8am-12:30pm and 2:30-6pm, Sa 8am-noon. There are always 3 pharmacies open for emergencies; check the list on the door of any closed pharmacy.

Medical Assistance: When the dog bites, when the bee stings, when you're feeling sad, call the **Hospital,** Dr. Franz-Rebirl-Pl. 5 (tel. 658 00).

Internet Access: Cybercafé, Gstätteng. 29 (tel. 842 61 622). 80AS per hr. Open M-F 2-11pm, F-Su 2pm-1am.

Post Office: At the *Hauptbahnhof* (tel. 889 70). Mail your brown paper packages tied up with strings at the main office next to the train station. The office has self-serve **photocopiers** and **currency exchange.** Address *Poste Restante* to Postlagernde Briefe, Bahnhofspostamt, A-5020 Salzburg. Open 6am-11pm. Exchange open M-Th 6am-5pm, F 6am-6pm. **Branch** at Residenzpl. 9 (tel. 84 41 21). Open M-F 7am-7pm, Sa 8-10am. **Postal Code:** A-5020.

PHONE CODE   The **city code** for Salzburg is 0662.

■ ACCOMMODATIONS AND CAMPING

Salzburg has no shortage of hostels—but, then again, it has no shortage of tourists either. Housing in Salzburg is even more expensive than in Vienna. Most affordable accommodations are on the outskirts of town, easily accessible by local transportation. Ask for the tourist office's list of **private rooms** (separate from the hotel map) or the *Hotel Plan* for information on hostels. The tourist office charges 30AS plus a 7.2% fee to make reservations. From mid-May to mid-September, hostels fill by mid-afternoon—call ahead. During the festival, make reservations. Hotels fill months in advance, and most youth hostels and *Gästehäuser* are full days before. Be wary of hotel hustlers at the station, as they are up to no good.

HOSTELS AND DORMITORIES

Gästehaus Bürgerwehr, Mönchsberg 19c (tel. 84 17 29), towers over the old town from the top of the Mönchsberg. Take bus #1 (dir.: Maxglan) to "Mönchsberglift," then down the street a few steps and through the stone arch on the left to the Mönchsberglift (elevator), which takes you to the top of the mountain (runs 9am-11pm, round-trip 27AS). At its summit, turn right, climb the steps, and follow signs for "Gästehaus Naturfreundehaus." Get a princely view on a pauper's budget at the most scenic hostel in Salzburg. Only holds 26 in 2- to 6-bed rooms, so reserve ahead. Dorms 120AS. Fresh-baked breakfast on the terrace (with a magnificent view of Salzburg) 30AS. Showers 10AS per 4min. Sheets 20AS. Reception 8am-9pm. Curfew 1am—start hustling up those stairs at quarter till. Genial proprietors also run the terrific restaurant downstairs. Open May to mid-Oct.

International Youth Hotel (YoHo), Paracelsusstr. 9 (tel. 87 96 49 or 834 60; fax 87 88 10), off Franz-Josef-Str. Exit the train station to the left and turn left onto Gabelsbergerstr. through the tunnel. Take the 2nd right onto Paracelsusstr. (7min.). There are so many homesick Americans and Canadians here, you may forget you're in a German-speaking country. Filled with beer-sipping postcard writers in the afternoon and a frat-party atmosphere in the evening, this hostel is a bare-bones, clean place to crash. *The Sound of Music* screened daily at noon. 24hr. CNN in the bar (beer 25AS). Dorms 150AS; doubles 400AS; quads 680AS. Breakfast 30-55AS. Dinner entrees (including veggie options) 30-75AS. Showers 10AS per 6min. Lockers 10AS. Sleepsacks require 100AS deposit. The new YoHo membership card grants holders discounts at some of Salzburg's attractions. Reception 8am-noon. "Curfew" 1am (not very strict); theoretical quiet time starts at 10pm.

Institut St. Sebastian, Linzerg. 41 (tel. 87 13 86; fax 87 13 86 85). From the station, turn left on Rainerstr., go past Mirabellpl., turn left onto Bergstr., and left at the end onto Linzerg. The hostel is through the arch on the left just before the church (whose bell tolls early in the morning). Located smack-dab in the middle of the *Neustadt* on the St. Sebastian church grounds, this privately-owned institute is a women-only university dorm during the year but accepts travelers of either gender in summer. Rooftop terrace and piano practice room. Only 90 beds, so reserve ahead. Dorms only Oct.-June. Dorms 180AS, with sheets 210AS; singles 330-350AS, with private shower 390AS; doubles 500-580AS, 680AS; triples 870AS; quads 1000AS, 1080AS. Free lockers. Breakfast included. **Kitchen** facilities. **Laundry** 40AS. No curfew. Reception open daily in summer 7:30am-noon and 1-10pm, in winter 8am-noon and 4-9pm.

Eduard-Heinrich-Haus (HI), Eduard-Heinrich-Str. 2 (tel. 62 59 76; fax 62 79 80). Take bus #51 (dir.: Salzburg-Süd) to "Polizeidirektion." Cross the street, continue down Billrothstr., and turn left on the Robert-Stolz-Promenade footpath. Walk 200m and take the 1st right; the hostel is the large building up the driveway on the left. Enormous 6- and 7-bed rooms with lockers. Dorms 170AS, non-members add 40AS. Showers and breakfast included. Reception 7-9am and 5-11pm. Lockout 9am-5pm. Summer curfew midnight, winter 11pm; key with 300AS deposit.

Haunspergstraße (HI), Haunspergstr. 27 (tel. 87 50 30; fax 88 34 77), near the train station. Walk straight out Kaiserschützenstr. (past the Forum department store), which becomes Jahnstr. Take the 3rd left onto Haunspergstr. This student dorm becomes a hostel in summer. Houses 125 in spacious 2- to 4-bed rooms. Dorms 170AS. Nonmembers add 40AS 1st night. Breakfast, shower, and sheets included. **Laundry** 80AS. Reception 7am-2pm and 5pm-midnight. Curfew 11pm. Open July-Aug.

Jugendgästehaus Salzburg (HI), Josef-Preis-Allee 18 (tel. 842 67 00; fax 84 11 01), southeast of the *Altstadt*. Take bus #5, 51, or 55 to "Justizgebäude," or walk from the tourist office southeast (with traffic) along the river, bear right onto Hellbrunnerstr., turn right onto Nonntaler Hauptstr., then take the 1st left. Rule-oriented hostel with a Las Vegas lobby. School groups make frequent use of the on-site video game room, café, and disco. Boys lodged in the red sector of the hostel, girls in blue. 8-bed dorms 169AS; doubles with shower 269AS per person; quads with shower 219AS per person. Non-members add one-time fee 40AS for membership card. Breakfast, shower, and sheets included. Lunch or dinner 72AS. **Kitchen** facilities available. **Bike rental** halfday 65AS, full day 95AS. Handicapped access. Reception M-F 11am-midnight. Curfew midnight. Reservations recommended.

Aigen (HI), Aignerstr. 34 (tel. 62 32 48; fax 232 48 13). From the station, bus #6 or 51 to "Mozartsteg.," then bus #49 (dir.: Josef-Käut-Str.) to "Finanzamt" and walk 5min. in the same direction as the bus. It's the yellow building on your right. Large hostel with a nearby basketball net. Renovated in summer 1999, this hostel is eminently comfortable. 2-4 bed dorms 180-200AS, non-members add 40AS. Breakfast, showers, lockers, and sheets included. Reception 7-9am and 5pm-midnight. Curfew midnight.

HOTELS AND PENSIONS

Pensionen in the center of the city can be quite expensive, but better quality and lower prices await on the outskirts, and public transportation puts these establishments within minutes of downtown Salzburg. Rooms on **Kasern Berg** are officially out of Salzburg, which means the tourist office can't officially recommend them, but the personable hosts and bargain prices make these pensions a terrific housing option. All northbound regional trains run to Kasern Berg (generally 4min., every 30min. 6:17am-11:17pm, 20AS, Eurailpass valid). Get off at the first stop, "Salzburg-Maria Plain," and take the only road uphill. All the Kasern Berg pensions are along this road. If you call in advance, many proprietors will pick you up at the

Kasern station. Or, from Mirabellpl., take bus #15 (dir.: Bergheim) to "Kasern" then turn up Söllheimerstr. and hike up the mountain (15min.). By car, exit A1 on "Salzburg Nord." There are *Pensionen* in most suburbs of the city as well, some on outlying farms. Camping is a feasible option even for novices, as some of Salzburg's campsites have beds in pre-assembled tents.

■ **Haus Rosemarie Seigmann,** Kasern Berg 66 (tel. 45 00 01). English-speaking Rosemarie welcomes guests to bright rooms with fluffy comforters and mountain views. Doubles 380-400AS; triples 510-600AS. Breakfast included. 1-night stays welcome.

■ **Germana Kapeller,** Kasern Berg 64 (tel. 45 66 71), next to Haus Seigmann. Hostess Germana speaks perfect English and maintains traditional rooms. She also screens *The Sound of Music* upon group demand (houseguests only). Doubles 360-400AS; triples 510-600AS. Showers and breakfast included. Call ahead.

■ **Haus Christine,** Panoramaweg 3 (tel./fax 45 67 73). On a gravel road set back 16m back from the main Kasern Berg street at the top of the hill, Haus Christine has spacious rooms with a country motif. Breakfast (included) served on glass-enclosed patio overlooking the countryside. Christine will pick you up at the station if you call ahead. Families welcome. 170-200AS per person. Reservations recommended.

■ **Haus Matilda Lindner,** Panoramaweg 5 (tel./fax 45 66 81). Right next to Haus Christine, Matilda (Christine's sister) offers rooms with balconies for mountain views. Breakfast served in pleasant room which is available for guests' use during the day. Matilda will also pick you up from the station. Families welcome. 170-200AS per person.

Haus Moser, Turnebuhel 1 (tel. 45 66 76), above Haus Rosemarie Seigmann; climb up the hidden stairs on the right side of Kasern Berg road across from Germana Kapeller. The rooms in this dark-timbered home are filled with fur rugs and deer heads. Singles 170-200AS; doubles 340-400AS; triples 510-600AS; quads 700-800AS. "Welcome drink," all-you-can-eat breakfast, and shower included.

Haus Elisabeth, Rauchenbichlerstr. 18 (tel./fax 45 07 03). Take bus #51 to "Itzling-Pflanzmann" (last stop), walk up Rauchenbichlerstr. over the footbridge, and continue right along the gravel path. Plush rooms have TVs, balconies, and sweeping views of the city. Huge breakfast of corn flakes, yogurt, bread, and jam included. Singles with shower 300-330AS; doubles 500-550AS; one 4-person suite with kitchen 1000AS.

Pension Sandwirt, Lastenstr. 6a (tel./fax 87 43 51). Exit the main train station from the platform #13 staircase, turn right on the footbridge, turn right at the bottom onto Lastenstr., and go behind the building with the post sign (3min.). Rooms have aging furniture and chipped mirrors, but the convenience makes up for it. Triples and quads have TVs. **Free laundry.** Singles 300AS; doubles 460AS, with shower 550AS; triples 690AS, quads 880AS. Breakfast included.

Haus Ballwein, Moostr. 69 (tel./fax 82 40 29). Take bus #1 to "Hanuschpl." then bus #60—ask the driver to stop at Gsengerweg (guh-zang-ehr-veg). This country house has spotless rooms and wonderful farmland for a rural reprieve from city tourism. Breakfast includes eggs from the *Pension*'s own chickens. 200AS per person, with shower 240AS. Rooms with shower in new house 270AS. Breakfast included.

Haus Bankhammer, Moostr. 77 (tel./fax 83 00 67). This grand farmhouse in southern Salzburg has hotel-quality doubles with bath. Breakfast of homemade strawberry-rhubarb jam and fresh milk from the family dairy included. Helga speaks English fluently and will do laundry for guests. Rooms 440-500AS.

Haus Mayerhofer, Moosstr. 68c (tel. 82 24 79; fax 82 62 99; cmayerhofen@aon.at; www.members.aon.at/privatzimmer). Take bus #60 or 15 southbound to "Station Firmianstr." (2km from the *Altstadt*). Catering especially to students and young people, friendly hostess Elisabeth offers 3 comfortable, typical Austrian rooms. Shower, breakfast buffet, TV room, garden, and parking included. 220-240AS per person.

Haus Kernstock, Karolingerstr. 29 (tel. 82 74 69; fax 82 74 69). Take bus #77 (dir.: Flughafen) to "Karolingerstr." and follow signs for the street number as the road twists (25min. from rail station). Large bedrooms far away from the bustling *Altstadt,* but near the airport, a warehouse, and 2 bus lines. Friendly hostess screens *The Sound of Music* and has 2 bikes to lend. Singles 350AS; doubles 500-600AS; triples 750-1000AS; quads 1200-1300AS. Breakfast included. **Laundry** 80AS. MC, Visa.

CAMPING

Camping Stadtblick, Rauchenbichlerstr. 21 (tel. 45 06 52; fax 45 80 18), next to Haus Elisabeth, is run by Elisabeth's brother. By car, take exit "Salzburg-Nord" off A1. Behind a copse of trees with a sweeping view of the city. On-site store. 65AS, *Let's Go*-readers 60AS; tent 15AS; bed in a tent 80AS; car 25AS. 4-person mobile home with refrigerator and stovetop, 100AS per person. **Laundry** 70AS. Open March 20-Oct. 31.

Camping Nord-Sam, Samstr. 22-A (tel. 66 04 94). Take bus #33 (dir.: Obergnigl) to "Langmoosweg." Shady, flower-bedecked campground has a small swimming pool. May to mid-June and Sept. 50AS; mid-June to Aug. 79AS. **Laundry** 75AS.

🖸 FOOD AND DRINK

With countless beer gardens and pastry-shop patios, Salzburg is a great place to eat outdoors. The local specialty is *Salzburger Nockerl,* a large soufflé of egg-whites, sugar, and raspberry filling baked into three mounds that represent the three hills of Salzburg. Another regional favorite is *Knoblauchsuppe,* a rich cream soup loaded with croutons and pungent garlic—a potent weapon to be used wisely against pesky bunkmates. During the first 2 weeks of September, local cafés dispense *Stürm,* a delicious, cloudy cider (reminiscent, aptly enough, of a storm) that hasn't quite finished fermenting.

There are more of the world-famous **Mozartkugeln** (chocolate "Mozart balls") lining café windows than there are notes in all of Mozart's works combined. A Salzburg confectioner invented the treats in 1890, but mass production inevitably took over. Although mass-produced *Kugeln* wrapped in gold and red are technically *echt* (authentic), try to find the rarer, handmade ones wrapped in blue and silver, which are not available anywhere else. Reasonably priced samples are sold at the **Holzmayr** confectioners (5AS each, 7AS for the real McCoy) or whole balls at Konditorei **Fürst** (10AS), both on *Alter Markt.* Confectioners make *Mozartkugeln* by covering a hazelnut with marzipan and nougat then dipping it in chocolate; the blue and silver kind have more marzipan than the red and gold ones.

Bars, restaurants, and cafés in Salzburg are difficult to classify because, more often than not, they become each of those things at different times during the day, serving coffee in the morning, tea in the afternoon, and beer in the evenings.

RESTAURANTS

🖾 **Restaurant Zur Bürgerwehr-Einkehr,** Mönchsberg 19c (tel. 84 17 29). Follow the directions to the Bürgerwehr. The mom-and-pop owners of the Bürgerwehr (see p. 227) operate this restaurant at the top of the Mönchsberg. On sunny days, escape the tourist throng below as you recline beneath the terrace's red umbrellas and enjoy the best views in town. This restaurant has one of the most reasonably priced (and tastiest) *Menüs* around. Extraordinary *Gammerknödel* (bacon-filled dumplings with sauerkraut) for just 68AS. Open May-Oct. 10am-8:30pm.

🖾 **Shakespeare,** Hubert Sattlerg. 3 (tel. 87 91 06), off Mirabellpl. This culturally diverse restaurant serves everything from wonton soup to Greek salad to *Wienerschnitzel.* 36-136AS. Doubles as a bar(d) with hopping **live music,** from tango to *chansons.* Behind the bar is the **Electric Café,** a trip-hop and techno lounge. Restaurant open daily 9pm-2am, but the Chinese cook takes Sundays off. MC, Visa.

🖾 **Zum Fidelen Affen,** Priesterhausg. 8 (tel. 87 73 61), off Linzerg. Phenomenal food is served by a friendly staff in a dark-wood pub, pleasantly crowded with locals and tourists, but no apes. Sorry. Drinks 30AS. Full meal of salad and main course 87-110AS. Try the spinach *Spätzle* (doughy dumpling noodles, 88AS) or the beef with onion gravy (89AS). English menu available. Open M-Sa 5pm-midnight.

Spicy Spices, Wolf-Dietrichstr. 1, off of Linzerstr., near Zum Fidelen Affen, serves a wide range of vegetarian cuisine at reasonable prices. The friendly owners will even help you find other veggie joints throughout Austria. Open M-F 10am-6:30pm; Sa 10am-1pm.

Vegy, Schwarzstr. 21 (tel. 87 57 46). From Mirabellpl. walk through the park and turn left onto Schwarzstr. With an eat-in kitchen feeling, this place understands that vegetarian food doesn't have to mean cheese. Dozens of filling options to choose from, including a daily *Menü* with soup, coffee, and dessert for 87AS. Open M-F 11am-5pm.

University Mensa (tel. 844 96 09), across from Sigmund Haffnerg. 16 and through the iron fence. A good deal for penny-pinchers. 2 hot entrees, 1 carnivorous (52AS) and 1 herbivorous (41AS). Valid student ID required (ISIC accepted). Open M-Th 9am-4pm, F 9am-3pm. Get there early, before ravenous students deplete the food supply.

Pizza Casanova, Linzerg. 23 (tel. 87 50 31). Don't be put off by the burlesque joint with the same name next door—Pizza Casanova knows that the way to a man's heart is through his stomach. Large pies 68-115AS. Healthy selection of veggie and whole-grain pizza. Open 11am-3pm and 6-11pm.

Salad and Friends, Linzer Bundesstr. 44 (tel. 651 51 54), bus #27 (dir.: Obergnigl) to "Sterneckstr." This little *Beisl* is a cafeteria-style, vegetable-friendly restaurant, with an ample salad bar (all-you-can-eat 57AS), pasta with 4 kinds of sauce (51AS), and veggie burgers (38AS). Open M-Sa 11am-10pm.

Fischmarkt, at Hanuschpl. in the *Altstadt.* Mammoth trees poke through the roof of this Danish seafood restaurant. Very casual and very packed—the crowds may force you to eat outside. Fish sandwiches 50AS; glasses of beer 27AS. The restaurant sells fresh seafood and seafood salad by the kg. Open M-F 8:30am-6:30pm, Sa 8:30am-1pm.

Trzesniewski, Getreideg. 9 (tel. 84 07 69), behind the chocolate counter and butcher shop. Kafka's favorite hangout in Vienna has a franchise on the ground floor of Mozart's *Geburtshaus.* While indulging in their wonderful (but miniscule) open-faced sandwiches, you can ponder who would roll over in his grave first. Sandwiches 9AS, but you'll need about 4 to make a good lunch. Open M-F 8:30am-6pm, Sa 8:30am-1pm.

CAFÉS

▓ **Café im Künstlerhaus,** Hellbrunnerstr. 3 (tel 84 56 01). This low-key café is popular with students, artists, and their fans. Treat yourself to a café amaretto or a shot of tequila. Local bands play Tu and Th. Sa lesbian night. Open M-F 11am-11pm.

▓ **Café Tomaselli,** Alter Markt 9 (tel. 84 44 88), has been a favorite haunt for wealthier Salzburger clientele since 1705. In 1820, Mozart's widow and her second husband came here to write the dead man's bio. Today anyone can sit in its wood-paneled rooms with antique portraits, or find a chair on the balcony overlooking the *Alter Markt.* Coffee (27-37AS) and a mobile dessert counter. Open M-Sa 7am-9pm, Su 8am-9pm.

Café Bazar, Schwarzstr. 3 (tel 87 42 78). Enjoy affordable drinks and small meals in this tree-lined garden along the banks of the Salzach. Yogurt with raspberry juice 38AS. Come here for your Turkish coffee fix (38AS). Open mid-July to Aug. M 10am-6pm, Tu-Sa 7:30am-11pm; Sept. to mid-July M-Sa 9:30am-11pm.

Café Glockenspiel, Mozartpl. 1 (tel. 84 14 03). Near the tourist office, this place serves incredible ice cream concoctions and fantastic pastries (50-98AS). Sit under the awning or at the tables that spill onto the square to catch the occasional free concert that occurs there. Open M-F 8:30am-9pm, Sa-Su 9am-6pm.

Café Fürst, Brodg. 13 (tel. 84 37 59). Highly treaded upon by tourists, it faces off with the equally haughty Café Tomaselli across *Alter Markt.* Specializes in the original *Mozartkugeln* (10AS a pop—savor slowly). Fürst has a vast selection of candies, chocolates, pastries, *torte,* strudels, and cakes. Grab one of the sunny tables outside if you can. Branch in Mirabellpl. Open daily in summer 8am-9pm; in winter 8am-8pm.

Kaffeehäferl, Getreideg. 25 (tel. 84 32 49), in the passage across from McDonald's. Unpretentious courtyard café provides a needed respite from the tourist rush of Getreideg. The neighboring flower shop adds olfactory pleasure. Quiche Lorraine 48AS; strawberry milkshake 37AS. Open M-Sa 9am-7pm, Su noon-7pm.

MARKETS

In most cases, markets are open weekdays 8am to 6pm, Saturday 8am to noon. Salzburg has many supermarkets on the Mirabellpl. side of the river but very few in the *Altstadt*. **SPAR** is widespread, and a giant **EuroSpar** sprawls next to the train station bus terminal. **Open-air markets** are held on Universitätpl. (M-F 6am-7pm, Sa 6am-1pm) and Mirabellpl. down into Hubert-Sattlerg. (Th 5am-1pm). If you're in town on Saturday morning, you can pick up organic tomatoes and sausage lard at Max Rheinhardtpl. in the *Altstadt*.

BEER GARDENS AND BARS

Munich may be the beer capital of the world, but a good deal of that liquid gold flows south to Austria's beer gardens *(Biergärten)*. Alongside Mozart and *The Sound of Music*, beer gardens are an essential part of Salzburg's charm and an absolute must-visit for travelers. Many of the gardens also serve moderately priced meals, but like everything else in Salzburg, they tend to close early. These lager oases cluster in the center of the city by the Salzach River. Nightclubs in the *Altstadt* (especially along Gstätteng. and near Chiemseeg.) generally attract younger types and tourists. For a less juvenile atmosphere, hit the other side of the river— especially along Giselakai and Steing.

■ **2 Stein**, Giselakai 9 (tel. 88 02 01). Absolutely the funkiest bar in town, this place rocks at night. Previously a gay bar, 2 Stein is now a fave for a mixed clientele of all orientations. Zebra print barstools, inflatable animals, and occasional transvestite performances all add atmosphere (try the *Blue Devil*, one of many exotic drinks). Open M-W 6pm-4am, Th-F 6pm-5am, Sa 2pm-5am, Su 2pm-4am.

■ **Augustiner Bräu**, Augustinerg. 4 (tel. 43 12 46). From the *Altstadt*, follow the footpath from Hanuschpl. along the river, walking with the current. Go left up the flight of stairs past the Riverside Café, cross Müllner Hauptstr., and walk uphill. Augustinerg. is the 1st left. The brewery, inside the monastery with the big tower, is a Salzburg legend. The great beer brewed by the Müllner Kloster is poured into massive *Steins* from even more massive wooden kegs. The outdoor garden holds 1300 people, while the indoor salons seat an additional 1200, creating a rambunctious stadium atmosphere. Different halls attract different crowds, from hard-core Austrians shouting German drinking songs to the American collegiate scene. There are bratwurst stands for the hungry. 1 Liter 68AS (tip the tap-*meister* 4AS), ½liter 34AS. Open M-F 3-11pm, Sa-Su 2:30-11pm.

Pub Passage, Rudolfskai 22-26, under the Radisson Hotel by the Mozartsteg bridge. A shopping promenade for youthful bar-hopping. All these bars are located in the corridors of the "mall" and are open until 2-4am. Thouh remarkably similar, each bar has its own "unique" gimmick: **Tom's Bierklinik** brags beers from all over the world; **The Black Lemon** offers Latino night every Wednesday; **Bräu zum Frommen Hell** burns with 80s music; and **Hell** sells itself as a TV sports bar.

Vis à Vis, Rudolfskai 24 (tel. 84 16 10), is a lounge cut in the shape of an arched stone tunnel with paisley armchairs, smoking-room couches, and dark-wood coat-racks. A mixed crowd parties late into the night. Open Su-Th 8pm-4am, F-Sa 8pm-5am.

Shamrock, Rudolfskai 24 (tel. 480 12 90). Up the block from the Pub Passage, this Irish pub has a friendly tucked-in-shirt atmosphere and plenty of room for beer-guzzling groups to mingle. Open M 3pm-2am, Tu-W 3pm-3am, Th-Sa 3pm-4am, Su 2pm-2am.

Disco Seven, Gstätteng. 7 (tel. 84 41 81). Fun-loving bar with billiard tables and a dance floor upstairs. Drinks half-price W; Sa midnight-1am drinks 20AS. Open daily till 4am.

Schwarze Katze, Fruhdiele, Auerspergstr. 45 (tel 87 54 05). For those who miraculously found a late-night scene in Salzburg and/or got locked out of their hostels, the Black Cat magnanimously opens its doors. Dark, low-key bar/café atmosphere guaranteed not to grate on early morning nerves. Open Tu-Sa 4am-noon.

Frauencafé, Sittikusstr. 17 (tel. 87 16 39), is a relaxed venue where lesbians of all stripes come to hang out, drink, and chat. Open W-Sa 8pm-midnight.

⚙ SIGHTS

Salzburg is a relatively small town with a disproportionate number of *Sehenswür-digkeiten* (things worth seeing). Whether you're into decadent floral gardens or stoic fortresses, Salzburg's got it. To help bear the financial burden, the tourist office sells the **Salzburg Card,** which grants admission to all museums and sights, as well as unlimited use of public transportation, but is only really a good deal if you plan to cram a great deal of sight-seeing into a short period of time. *(24hr. card 200AS, 48hr. 270AS, 72hr. 360AS; children ages 7-15 half-price.)*

THE NEUSTADT

MIRABELL PALACE AND GARDENS. Whether you walk or take the bus from the train station, one of the places you should visit is **Mirabellplatz,** where the marvelous **Schloß Mirabell** stands. This rosy-hued wonder was built in 1606 by the supposedly vowed-to-celibacy Archbishop Wolf Dietrich for his mistress Salome Alt and their 10 children. He christened the palace "Altenau" in her honor, but when the new archbishop Markus Sittikus imprisoned Wolf Dietrich for arson, he seized the palace and changed its name to "Mirabell." The castle is now the seat of the city government, and some of the mayor's offices are open for public viewing. The palace hosts classical concerts in the evening, and fans swear that the *Marmorsaal* (Marble Hall) is one of the best concert halls in Europe. It is also a popular place to get married, especially among Japanese couples. *(Open M-F 8am-4pm. Free.)*

Behind the palace, the delicately manicured **Mirabellgarten** is a maze of extravagant seasonal flower beds and groomed shrubs. Students from the nearby Mozarteum often perform here, and Maria von Trapp and her over-worked children stopped here for a rousing rendition of "Do-Re-Mi." From the entrance off Mirabellplatz, walk up the tiny staircase to see the **Dwarf Garden,** a favorite play area for Salzburg toddlers named for the vertically challenged statues which are slightly more adorable than the von Trapp children. The statues' grotesque marble faces were supposedly modeled after Wolf Dietrich's court jesters.

From one of the hedge-enclosed clearings in the *Mirabellgarten,* you can see a tiny wooden, moss-covered shack called the **Zauberflötenhäuschen,** alleged to be where Wolfgang Amadeus composed *The Magic Flute* in just 5 months. It was transplanted from Vienna as a gift to Salzburg's conservatory for young musicians, the **Mozarteum,** which stands back to back with the gardens on Schwartzstr. 26-28. The Mozarteum was originally constructed for the Salzburg Academy of Music and the Performing Arts, but now holds regular performances in the concert hall (see p. 238). It is also known for its enormous **Mozart Archives** (entrance only by appointment, tel. 88940).

MOZART'S RESIDENCE. Just down the street from the Mozarteum stands **Mozarts Wohnhaus,** the composer's residence from 1773 to 1780, here Mozart moved with his family at age 17 from the house in the *Altstadt* where he was born. The house suffered major damage in WWII air raids, but subsequent renovations allowed the building to reopen on the composer's 240th birthday, January 27, 1996 with expanded displays about Mozart and his family and audio samples of his music. *(Makartpl. 8. Tel. 883 45 440. Open daily 10am-5:30pm. 65AS, kids 20AS.)*

MONASTERY AND CHURCH. Dreifaltigkeitsg. leads from a pretty Fischer von Erlach church down towards the river, and intersects **Linzergasse,** a shopping street similar to Getreidegasse (see below), at the base of the Kapuzinerberg. From under the stone arch on the right side of Linzerg. 14, a tiny stone staircase rises up the Kapuzinerberg. At its crest stands the simple **Kapuzinerkloster** (Capuchin Monastery) that Wolf Dietrich built in the late 16th century. Stages of the cross are represented by rubbery mannequins locked behind iron gates. Farther up Linzerg. at #41 is the 18th-century **Sebastianskirche.** Its graveyard contains the gaudy mausoleum of Wolf Dietrich and the tombs of Mozart's wife Constanze and father Leopold. *(Open Apr.-Oct. 9am-7pm, Nov.-Mar. 9am-4pm.)*

THE ALTSTADT

THE OLD TOWN. Rather than heading up Linzerg., crossing the Salzach on the Staatsbrücke will bring you into the *Altstadt*, where arcade passages open up into tiny courtyards filled with geraniums and creeping ivy that lead, in turn, to the tourist stampede along **Getreidegasse.** This labyrinth of winding pathways and 17th- and 18th-century facades is one of the best-preserved (and most-visited) streets in Salzburg. Many of Getreidegasse's shops have wrought-iron signs dating from the Middle Ages when the illiterate needed pictorial aids to understand which store sold what. Or so they claim. Some suspect a few of these signs are modern tourist revivals…golden arches, for example, don't objectively suggest hamburgers. Maybe Pavlov could explain.

MOZART'S BIRTHPLACE. The first place that most visitors rush to in the *Altstadt* is **Mozarts Geburtshaus** (birthplace), on the 2nd floor of Getreideg. 9. The long red and white flag suspended from the roof serves as a beacon for music pilgrims worldwide. Although he eventually settled in Vienna, his birthplace holds the most impressive collection of the child genius' belongings: his first viola and violin, a pair of keyboardish instruments, and a lock of hair purportedly from his noggin. A set of skillful dioramas chronicle previous *Festspiele* productions of Mozart's operas. *(Tel. 84 43 13. Open July-Aug. 9am-6:30pm; Sept.-June 9am-5:30pm. In summer show up before 11am to beat the crowds. 70AS, students and seniors 55AS, children 20AS.)*

UNIVERSITY CHURCH. Directly in Mozart's backyard stands the **Universitätskirche,** generally considered Fischer von Erlach's greatest masterpiece, which is one of the largest Baroque chapels on the continent. Its distinctive dome stands watch over Universitätspl. and its daily farmer's market, where *Mozartkugeln*, chocolate-covered pretzels, and fresh fruit mingle. Sculpted clouds coat the nave, with pudgy cherubim (lit by pale natural light from the dome) splattered all over the immense apse of the church.

OPERA HOUSE. Down Wiener-Philharmonikerg. from Universitätspl., the **Festspielhaus,** once the rock riding school for the archbishops' horses, now houses many of the big-name events of the annual *Festspiele*. It's actually composed of 3 separate performance spaces—the large Opera House, the small Opera House, and an open-air performance space (which appears in *The Sound of Music*). Tours of the opera house are given. *(June-Sept. daily at 9:30am, 2pm, and 3:30pm; Oct.-Dec. and Apr.-May daily at 2pm. 70AS, children 40AS.)*

MONASTERY, CHURCH, AND CEMETERY. Continuing down Hofstallg. from the *Festspielhaus* will bring you to Max-Reinhard-Platz and then into **Toscaninihof,** the courtyard of **St. Peter's Monastery,** from where steps lead up the Mönchsberg cliffs. Back at Max-Reinhard-Platz, Franziskanerg. brings you to **Stiftskirche St. Peter,** which began as a Romanesque basilica in the 1100s and still features a marble portal from 1244. In the 18th century, the building was remodeled in Rococo style, with green and pink moldings curling delicately across the graceful ceiling and gilded cherubim blowing golden trumpets. The church has the look and feel of a Fabergé egg turned inside-out. *(Open daily 9am-12:15pm and 2:30-6:30pm.)*

BOVINE BEFUDDLEMENT The only time the **Hohensalzburg** fortress was ever under any kind of siege was during the **Peasant Wars** (see **Dynastic Austria,** p. 66), when the peasants surrounded the fortress in an attempt to starve the archbishop out. When the stubborn archbishop had only one cow left, he painted the remaining beast with different spots on both sides and paraded him back and forth along the castle wall in distinct view of the peasants below. Since the peasants, as the saying goes, were simple-minded folk, they believed that the archbishop had a great reserve of food and promptly canceled their embargo.

By continuing through the arch to the right of the church, you'll enter **Petersfried-hof**, one of the most peaceful places in Salzburg—possibly because guided tours are denied entry. The tiny cemetery is filled with delicate flower-covered graves, some dating back to the 1600s. This secluded spot is a popular subject for romantic painters, and it served as a model for the cemetery where Rolf blew the whistle on the von Trapp family in *The Sound of Music*. *(Open Apr.-Sept. 6:30am-7pm; Oct.-Mar. 6:30am-6pm.)* Near the far end of the cemetery, against the mountains, is the entrance to the **Katakomben** (catacombs), relatively bare cave-like rooms where Christians allegedly worshipped in secret as early as AD 250. *(Tel. 844 57 80. Open in summer Tu-Su 10:30am-4pm; in winter W-Su 10:30am-3:30pm. 12AS, students 8AS.)*

CATHEDRAL. The exit at the opposite end of the cemetery from the Stiftskirche leads into **Kapitelplatz**, home of a giant chess grid, a fountain depicting Poseidon wielding his trident, and a bunch of tradespeople bartering their wares, which spreads out in front of one side of Salzburg's immense Baroque **Dom** (cathedral). Wolf Dietrich's successor, Markus Sittikus, commissioned the cathedral from Italian architect Santino Solari in 1628. Inside, the ceilings are resplendent with cartoonish paintings and ornate carvings. The dates above the archways list the years of the cathedral's renovations. The square to the left of the cathedral, **Domplatz**, features a statue of the Virgin Mary. Around her swarm four lead figures representing Wisdom, Faith, the Church, and the Devil. Mozart was christened here in 1756 and later worked at the cathedral as *Konzertmeister* and court organist.

ARCHBISHOP'S RESIDENCE. The square on the far side of the cathedral is **Residenzplatz**, named for the magnificent **Residenz** of Salzburg's powerful prince-archbishops. The ecclesiastical elite of Salzburger Land have resided here, in the heart of the *Altstadt*, since 1595. Tours lead through stunning Baroque **Prunkräume** (state rooms), which house an astonishing three-dimensional ceiling fresco by Rottmayr. *(Tel. 804 22 690. 40min. tours in German and English May-Oct., Dec. every 30min. 10am-4:30pm; Jan.-Apr. M-F every hr. 10am-4:30pm; 70AS, students and seniors 55AS, children 25AS.)* The *Residenz* also houses a gallery (see p. 237). Dead-center in Residenzpl. is an immense 15m **fountain**—the largest Baroque fountain in the world—which features amphibious horses charging through the water (note the webbed hooves). Appropriately, *Fiaker* (horse-drawn carriages) congregate near the fountain, which explains the barnyard odor. *(Carriage rides 380AS for 25min. Tel. 84 47 72.)*

Diagonally to the right of Residenzpl. begins yet another square, **Mozartpl.**, which is dominated by the **Neugebäude**, opposite the AmEx office, seat of the city government's bureaucracy. Atop the building, a 35-bell **Glockenspiel** (carillon) rings out a Mozart tune (specified on a notice posted on the corner of the *Residenz*) every day at 7am, 11, and 6pm, and the tremendous pipe organ atop the Hohensalzburg fortress bellows a response.

FORTRESS. The trail up to the fortress and the **Festungsbahn** (funicular) can be found at the far end of Kapitelpl. The road/stairs require about 20 minutes of uphill walking, while the Festungsbahn takes only a few minutes, but costs a bundle. Since the ride terminates inside the fortress walls, cable-car tickets include entrance. *(Tel. 84 26 82. Every 10min. 9am-9pm; Oct.-Apr. 9am-5pm. Ascent 59AS, children 32AS; round-trip 69AS, 37AS.)* Built between 1077 and 1681 by the ruling archbishops, **Festung Hohensalzburg**, looming over Salzburg from atop Mönchsberg, is the largest completely preserved castle in Europe, probably because it was never attacked. To view the splendid rooms inside, visitors must take one of the castle's tours, which wind through torture chambers, formidable Gothic state rooms, the fortress organ (nick-named the "Bull of Salzburg" for its off-key snorting), and an impregnable watchtower that affords an unmatched view of the city. They'll also show you the archbishop's medieval indoor toilet—a technological marvel of its day. The **Rainer Museum** inside the fortress displays medieval instruments of torture. *(Tel. 84 24 30. Open July-Sept. 8:30am-7pm; Nov.-Mar. 9am-5pm; Apr.-June 9am-6pm. 35AS, children 20AS. Admission only includes walking around the perimeter of the castle. To go inside,* *take the 1hr. castle tours in English and German. July-Aug. 9:30am-5:30pm, Apr.-June and Sept.-Oct. 9:30am-5pm, Nov.-Mar. 10am-4:30pm. Combo ticket includes castle tour, museum, and fortress 75AS, children 35AS.)*

The many footpaths atop the Mönchsberg give a bird's-eye view of the city; hikers meander down the leafy trails to the *Altstadt* below or descend via the **Mönchsberglift** (elevator) built into the mountain at Gstätteng. 13, near Café Winkler. *(Elevator operates daily 9am-11pm. 16AS, round-trip 27AS.)* Down the hill and to the right of the fortress, **Nonnberg Abbey** (where Maria von Trapp lived) is still a private monastic complex, but visitors can tour the church.

THE SOUND OF MUSIC

In 1964, Julie Andrews, Christopher Plummer, and a gaggle of 20th-Century Fox crewmembers arrived in Salzburg to film *The Sound of Music*, based on the true story of the von Trapp family. Salzburg has never been the same. The city encourages the increased tourism due to the film's popularity (although interestingly enough many Salzburgers have never seen the film, and most of those who have dislike it). Three official companies run **Sound of Music Tours** in Salzburg. These companies are remarkably similar; the best choice is often the one that stops closest to your accommodation—many hostels and pensions work exclusively with one of the firms and offer discounts to guests. **Salzburg Sightseeing Tours** (tel. 88 16 16; fax 87 87 76) and **Panorama Tours** (tel. 88 32 11; fax 87 16 18; email sightseeing@panoramatours.at) operate rival kiosks on Mirabellpl. *(400AS. Tours leave from Mirabellpl. daily 9:30am and 2pm.)* The renegade **Bob's Special Tours,** Kaig. 19 (tel. 84 95 11; fax 84 95 12), has no high-profile kiosk, but they do have a minibus. *(350AS; tours daily in summer 9am and 2pm; in winter 10am.)* The smaller vehicle enables them to tour more of the *Altstadt*, a location that the big tour buses can't reach. All 3 companies offer free pick-up from your hotel, and all tours last 4 hours. The tours are generally worth the money only if you're a big *Sound of Music* fan or if you have a short time in Salzburg and want an overview of the area—the tours venture into the Salzkammergut lake region as well.

If you have the time and enough interest, however, you could rent a bike and do the tour on your own. The film's writers and producers took a great deal of artistic license with the von Trapps' story—many of the events were fabricated for Tinseltown. Though Maria was a nun-apprentice in the film, in reality she merely taught at **Nonnberg Abbey,** high above the city near the Festung (see p. 236). In this abbey, the crew filmed the nuns singing "How Do You Solve A Problem Like Maria?" The little gazebo where Liesl and Rolf unleashed their youthful passion is on the grounds of **Schloß Hellbrunn** (see p. 240). The gazebo is disappointingly small but photogenic (no worries), and the walk back from Hellbrunn to Salzburg's *Altstadt* is lovely on summer afternoons. From the Hellbrun parking lot, head down Hellbrunner Allee. On the way, you'll pass the yellow castle used for the exterior of the von Trapp home (Maria sang "I Have Confidence" in front of the long yellow wall), which is now a dorm for music students at the Mozarteum. Continue along Hellbrunner Allee until it turns into Freisaalweg. At the end of Freisaalweg, turn right on Akadamiestr., which ends at Alpenstr. and the river. The river footpath leads all the way back to Mozartsteg. and Staatsbrücke (1hr.). The back of the von Trapp house (where Maria and the children fell into the water after romping around the city all day) was filmed at the **Schloß Leopoldskron** behind the Mönchberg, now a center for academic studies. Visitors are not welcomed, nor permitted to wander about the grounds, but if you're set on getting a glimpse of the house, take bus #55 to "Pensionistenheim Nonntal," turn left on Sunnhubstr., and left again up Leopoldskroner Allee to the castle. Other filming locations scattered throughout Salzburg include the **Mirabellgarten** (see p. 233) and the **Festspielhaus** (see p. 234).

The von Trapps were married in the church at Nonnberg Abbey, but Hollywood filmed the scene in **Mondsee** instead (see p. 274). The sightseeing tours allow guests to waddle around Mondsee for 45 minutes, but the town is really worth a whole daytrip for its beautiful lake and pastry shops. **Buses** leave the Salzburg train station from the main bus depot *(45min., every hr., 70AS).* The hills that are alive with the sound of music, inspiring Maria's rapturous twirling in the opening scene, are along the Salzburg-St. Gilgen route near Fusch, but any of the hills in the Salzkammergut region could fit the bill. For your own re-creational and recreational purposes, try the Untersberg, just south of Salzburg (see p. 240).

To squeeze the last *Groschen* out of starry-eyed tourists, the Stieglkeller hosts a **Sound of Music Live Dinner Show** (tel. 83 20 29; fax 83 20 29 13). Performers sing your favorite film songs while servers ply you with soup, *Schnitzel* with noodles, and crisp apple strudel. *(May-Oct. 8:30pm. 360AS. Dinner at 7:30pm plus the show 520AS. 30% student discount, children under 13 free.)*

🏛 MUSEUMS

Salzburg's small, specialized museums often get lost in the shadow of the *Festung*, *The Sound of Music*, and the *Festspiele*. The keywords in that sentence are "small" and "specialized." There are also small and specialized private galleries on Sigmund-Haffnerg. that allow budget art viewing.

ART MUSEUMS. The **Museum Carolino Augusteum,** named after Emperor Franz I's widow, Caroline Augusta, houses Roman and Celtic artifacts, including excellent mosaics and burial remains, preserved compliments of the region's salt, on its ground floor. The upper floors feature Gothic and Baroque art. *(Museumpl. 1. Tel. 84 11 34. Open W-Su 9am-5pm, Tu 9am-8pm. 40AS, students 15AS.)* Opposite the *Festspielhaus*, the **Rupertinum Gallery** hosts temporary exhibits of modern painting, sculpture, and photography in a graceful building remodeled by Friedensreich Hundertwasser. *(Wiener Philharmonikerg. 9. Tel. 80 42 23 36. Open mid-July to Sept. Su-Tu and Th-Sa 9am-5pm, W 10am-9pm; Oct. to mid-July Tu-Su 10am-5pm, W 10am-9pm. 40AS, students 20AS, under 16 free.)* The **Residenz Gallery**, in the Residenz, has rotating exhibits of 16th- to 19th-century art. *(Residenzpl. 1. Tel. 84 04 51. Open Apr.-Sept. 10am-5pm; Oct.-Mar. Su-Tu and Th-Sa 10am-5pm. 50AS, students 40AS, kids 15AS.)* Finally, the **Baroque Museum** in the Orangerie of the Mirabellgarten, pays elaborate tribute to the ornate aesthetic of 17th- and 18th-century Europe. *(Tel. 87 74 32. Open Tu-Sa 9am-noon and 2-5pm, Su 9am-noon. 40AS, students and seniors 20AS, ages 6-14 free.)*

CURIO MUSEUM AND EXCAVATIONS. Just inside the main entrance to the *Dom*, the **Dom Museum** houses an unusual collection called the **Kunst- und Wunderkammer** (Art and Curiosity Cabinet) that includes conch shells, mineral formations, and a 2ft whale's tooth. The archbishop accumulated these curiosities to impress distinguished visitors, as did many of his contemporaries. *(See p. 195; tel. 84 41 89. Open mid-May to mid-Oct. M-Sa 10am-5pm; Su 1pm-5pm. 50AS, students and ages 16-18 25AS, ages 6-15 20AS.)* On Residenzpl., the **Domgrabungsmuseum** displays excavations of the Roman ruins under the cathedral. You'll feel like an archaeologist clambering around in a dig. *(Tel. 84 52 95. Open May-Oct. W-Su 9am-5pm. 20AS, students 10AS.)*

BEER MUSEUM. Stiegl Brauwelt (Brew World) is Salzburg's own beer museum, attached to the Stiegl brewery just minutes from downtown, with 3 floors showcasing beer-making, the history of brewing, and modern beer culture—including "30 Ways to Open a Beer Bottle" and the wonder of the *Brauwelt*, a 2-story beer-bottle pyramid constructed of 300 Austrian beers. Hop on down to the final hands-on exhibit—the tour concludes with 2 complimentary glasses of Stiegl beer, a beer *Brezel* (pretzel), and a souvenir beer glass. *(Take bus #1 to "Brauhaus" and walk up the street to the giant yellow building. Brauhausstr. 9. Tel. 838 71 492; www.stiegl.co.at. Open W-Su 10am-4pm, 96AS, students 60AS, children 50AS.)*

NATURAL HISTORY MUSEUM. The **Haus der Natur,** opposite the Carolino Augusteum, is an enormous natural history museum with an eclectic collection—from live alligators to fossils to gems. Get up close and personal (through the glass, of course) with over a dozen giant snakes. *(Museumpl. 5. Tel. 84 26 53 or 84 23 22. Open 9am-5pm. 55AS, students 30AS.)*

TOY MUSEUM. The **Spielzeug Museum,** near the *Festspielhaus,* features 3 floors of puppets, wooden toys, dolls, electric trains, and nifty pre-Lego castle blocks from 1921. *(Bürgerspitalg. 2. Tel. 84 75 60. Open Tu-Su 9am-5pm. 30AS, students 10AS. Puppet show Tu-W 3pm.)*

🎵 MUSIC AND ENTERTAINMENT

FESTSPIELE

Max Reinhardt, Richard Strauss, and Hugo von Hofmannsthal founded the renowned **Salzburger Festspiele** (Festivals) in 1920. Every year since, Salzburg has become a musical mecca from late July to the end of August. A few weeks before the festival, visitors strolling along Getreideg. may bump into world-class stars taking a break from rehearsal. On the eve of the festival's opening, over 100 dancers don regional costumes, accessorize with torches, and perform a *Fackeltanz* (torch-dance) on Residenzpl. During the festivities themselves, operas, plays, films, concerts, and tourists overrun every available public space. Information and tickets for Festspiele events are available through the **Festspiele Kartenbüro** (ticket office) and **Tageskasse** (daily box office) in Karajanpl., against the mountain and next to the tunnel. (From July 1-21, ticket office open M-F 9:30am-noon and 3-5pm. From July 25-Aug, it's open daily at the same times. Box office open M-Sa 9:30am-5pm.) The festival prints a complete program of events that lists all concert locations and dates one year in advance. The booklet is available at any tourist office (10AS). Music fans snap up the best seats months before the festival begins. To order tickets, contact **Kartenbüro der Salzburger Festspiele,** Postfach 140, A-5010 Salzburg (tel. 804 55 79; fax 804 57 60; email info@salzburgfestival.at; www.salzburgfestival.at), no later than the beginning of January. After that, the office publishes a list of remaining seats, which generally include some cheap tickets to the operas (around 300AS), concerts (around 100AS), and plays (around 100AS), as well as standing room places (50-100AS). These tickets, however, are gobbled up quickly by subscribers or student groups, leaving very expensive tickets (upwards of 1000AS) and seats at avant-garde modern-music concerts (often as little as 200AS). Middle-man ticket distributors sell marked-up cheap tickets, a legal form of scalping—try American Express or Panorama Tours. Those 26 or younger can try for cheap subscription tickets (2-4 tickets for 200-300AS each) by writing about 8 months in advance to *Direktion der Salzburger Festspiele,* attn: Ulrich Hauschild, Hofstallg. 1, A-5020 Salzburg.

The powers that be have discontinued hawking last-minute tickets for dress rehearsals to the general public—nowadays, you've got to know somebody to get your hands on one of these tickets ("Oh, sure, Placido and I go *way* back!"). Those without the foresight to be hit by an international opera star while walking across the street should take advantage of the **Fest zur Eröffungsfest** (Opening Day Festival), when concerts, shows, and films are either very cheap or free. Folksingers perform in the evenings, and dancers perform the traditional *Fackeltanz* around the horse fountain, literally kicking off the festivities. Tickets for all these events are available on a first-come, first-served basis during the festival's opening week at the box office in the Großes Festspielhaus on Hofstallg. The only other event visitors can always attend without advance tickets is **Jedermann.** The city stages Hugo von Hofmannsthal's modern morality play about the life, love, and death of

> **MONK-Y BUSINESS** Legend has it that the robes of the Kapuzinerkloster's resident monks inspired the world's first cup of cappuccino. A café proprietor with an overactive imagination observed the pious gents on a noonday stroll and *voilà*—the world witnessed the birth of a drink with the rich coffee color of the monk's robes topped by white froth hoods. According to this theory, Italy's cappuccino is just a rip-off of the much older *Kapuziner,* still ordered in Austrian cafés today.

an immoral man, every year on a stage in front of the cathedral. At the end, people placed in strategic locations throughout the city cry out the eerie word "Jedermann," which then echoes all over town. Shouting contests determine which locals win the opportunity to be one of the ghostly criers. Standing-room places for shows are available at the Festspielhaus (60AS).

CONCERTS

Even when the *Festspiele* are not on, many other concerts and events occur around the city. The popular **Mozarteum** (Music School) performs a number of concerts on a rotating schedule, available at the tourist office. The school often dedicates one cycle of concerts to students and reduces the ticket price to 80AS. For tickets to any of the Mozarteum concerts, contact *Kartenbüro Mozarteum*, Postfach 156, Theaterg. 2, A-5024 Salzburg (tel. 87 31 54; fax 87 29 96; open M-Th 9am-2pm, F 9am-4pm). For a bit more money but a lot more kitsch, check out the evening **Mozart Serenaden** (Mozart's Serenades) in the Gothic Hall on Burgerstpitalg. 2. (daily 8:30pm in summer, otherwise 7:30pm; 200-420AS). Musicians in traditional garb (knickers, powdered hair, etc.) perform Mozart favorites. For information and tickets, contact *Konzertdirektion Nerat*, A-5020 Salzburg, Lieferinger Hauptstr. 136 (tel. 43 68 70; fax 43 69 70).

For a particularly enchanting (and expensive) evening, attend a **Festungskonzert** (Fortress Concert) in the fortress's ornate *Fürstenzimmer* (Prince's chamber) and *Goldener Saal* (Golden Hall). Concerts occur year-round and may include dinner at the fortress restaurant. Tickets are 360-450AS without dinner, 590-640AS with dinner. For more information, contact *Festungskonzerte*, Anton-Adlgasserweg 22, A-5020 Salzburg (tel. 82 58 58; fax 82 58 59; www.salzburg.co.at/festungskonzerte; open daily 9am-9pm). A less tourist-oriented activity is the year-round **Salzburger Schloßkonzerte** in Schloß Mirabell or the Residenz. Mozart is the most-performed composer, but he doesn't have a monopoly. In July and August, **outdoor opera** occasionally rings out from the historical hedge-theater of Mirabellgarten (330-560AS, students 190AS). Tickets for both series are available from the box office in Schloß Mirabell (tel. 84 85 86; fax 84 47 47; open M-F 9am-5:30pm).

The **Dom** also has a large concert program. In July and August, the church's organ has four separate pipe sections, creating a dramatic "surround sound" effect during its Thursday and Friday concerts at 11:15am. Tickets are available at the door (100AS, students 70AS, children free). The church has periodic evening concerts. Check the door for upcoming programs (280AS, students 180AS, standing room 100AS, children free). Other churches throughout Salzburg perform wonderful music during services and post information on other concerts, particularly near Easter and Christmas.

From May through August **outdoor performances,** including concerts, folk-singing, and dancing, dot the Mirabellgarten. The tourist office has a few leaflets on scheduled events, but an evening stroll through the park might prove just as enlightening. Listen to the word on the street. Mozartpl. and Kapitelpl. are also popular stops for talented street musicians and touring school bands, and the well-postered Aicher Passage next to Mirabellpl. is a great source of information for other upcoming musical events.

THEATER, MOVIES, AND GAMBLING

Right next to Mirabell gardens at the **Salzburger Marionettentheater** (tel. 87 24 06; fax 88 21 41; email info@marion.etten.at), handmade marionettes perform to recorded *Festspiele* opera. The theater is small in order to accommodate the diminutive size of the actors. For more information, contact Marionettentheater, Schwarzstr. 24, A-5020 Salzburg. (Box office open on performance days M-Sa 9am-1pm and 2hr. before curtain. 280-480AS, students 200AS. AmEx, MC, Visa.) Track down English-language **movies** with the film program in the **Das Kino** newspaper. Cinemas rotate a few films each month and often offer films in English with German subtitles. Win enough money to pay off your concert ticket loans at **Casino Salzburg** (tel. 85 46 20), located in Klessheim Palace. Slot machines, blackjack tables, and much more await you. Ask at the tourist office about the free shuttle service from the city center. (Open from 3pm onwards. 18 years or older, semi-formal attire required.)

⚠ OUTDOOR ACTIVITIES

If you're sick of all the sights and sounds of music that Salzburg offers its visitors, or you just want to get your blood pumping, try an adventure tour with **Crocodile Sports** (tel. 64 29 07), Gaisbergstr. 34a. Owner and operator Wolfgang will gleefully pick you up from your hotel and bring you for a day (or half a day) you'll never forget. Adventures are scheduled throughout the week (so call ahead) and include **canyoning** (590-2790AS), **canoeing** (590-2790AS), **paragliding** (1200AS), and **rafting** (550AS-840AS).

NEAR SALZBURG: HELLBRUNN AND UNTERSBERG

To reach Hellbrun, take bus #55 (dir.: Anif) to "Hellbrunn" from the train station, Mirabellpl., or Mozartsteg., or walk/bike 40min. down tree-lined Hellbrunner Allee (see p. 236).

Just south of Salzburg lies the unforgettable **Lustschloß Hellbrunn,** a one-time pleasure dome for Wolf Dietrich's nephew, the Archbishop Markus Sittikus. The sprawling estate includes a large palace, fish ponds, trimmed hedge gardens, the "I Am Sixteen, Going On Seventeen" gazebo, and tree-lined footpaths through open grassy fields. The **Steintheater** on the palace grounds is the oldest natural theater north of the Alps. To one side of the castle, the **Wasserspiele** (literally "water games") are perennial favorites—Archbishop Markus amused himself with elaborate water-powered figurines and a booby-trapped table that could spout water on his drunken guests. Prepare yourself for an afternoon of wet surprises, including the Neptune grotto and a water-powered doll-house. If you have to choose between the castle and the fountains, go for the *Wasserspiele.* (Tel. 820 00 30. Open July-Aug. 9am-10pm; May-June and Sept. 9am-5:30pm; Apr. and Oct. 9am-4:30pm. Admission only with tour. Castle tour 30AS, students 20AS. *Wasserspiele* tour 70AS, 35AS. Combined tour 90AS, 45AS.)

On the hill above the manicured grounds sits the tiny hunting lodge **Monats-schlößchen** (Little Month Castle), so named because someone bet the archbishop that he couldn't build a castle in a month. As one of the archbishop's many weaknesses was gambling, he accepted the challenge and began spending the church's money on architects, engineers, and laborers who toiled around the clock. He won. The castle now houses the **Folklore and Local History Museum,** which has 3 floors of surprising exhibits, including animals made out of bread, a papier-mâché-and-glitter diorama of St. George slaying the dragon, and several *Salzburger Schönperchten*—bizarre 2m hats worn in a traditional Austrian ceremony intended to scare away the demons of winter. (Tel. 820 37 221. Open mid-Apr. to mid-Oct. 9am-5pm. 20AS, students 10AS.) Near the castle lies the enormous **Hellbrunn Zoo.** The zoo is full of exotic animals and home to a gross-out masterpiece—the *Hansratte*—a domestic kitchen scene infested with slithery rats. (Tel. 82 01 76. Open 8:30am-4pm; extended summer hours. 80AS, students 60AS.)

Bus #55 continues south to the luscious **Untersberg peak,** where Charlemagne supposedly rests deep beneath the ground, prepared to return and reign over Europe once again when he is needed. Choose between dozens of hikes through color-soaked meadows, with mountains hovering in the distance. The **Eishöhlen** (ice caves) are only a 1½-hour climb from the peak. A **cable car** glides over Salzburg to the summit (tel. (06246) 87 12 17 or 724 77; July-Sept. Su-Tu and Th-Sa 8:30am-5:30pm, W 8:30am-8pm; Mar.-June and Oct. 9am-5pm; Dec.-Feb. 10am-4pm; ascent 130AS, descent 110AS, round-trip 215AS; children 75AS, 55AS, 105AS).

ZELL AM SEE

Surrounded by a ring of snow-capped mountains that slide into a broad turquoise lake, Zell am See (TSELL am ZAY) functions as a year-round resort spot for mountain-happy European tourists. Zell am See's horizon is dominated by 30 "3-thousanders," that is, 30 peaks over 3000m tall, which belong primarily to the Hohe Tauern range. For *Wanderlust*ing tourists, the mountainous terrain around Zell offers **hiking** and **skiing** challenges, while the cool blue lake calls to those who desire summer rest and relaxation. The center of town has bars and dance clubs to accommodate necessary après-ski debauchery.

⌐ GETTING TO ZELL AM SEE

Zell am See is accessible by **train** from most major Austrian cities, while **Bundes-Buses** service smaller towns. Zell am See lies at the intersection of Bundesstr. 311 from the north and Bundesstr. 168 from the west. It's also accessible by Bundesstr. 107 from the south, which runs into Bundesstr. 311 north. From Salzburg, take Bundesstr. 21 south to 312 south; at Lofer, switch to 311 south to Zell.

◪ ORIENTATION AND PRACTICAL INFORMATION

Zell am See's relative proximity to the German border, Salzburg, Innsbruck, and a wide range of natural attractions makes it a prime destination for international and Austrian tourists alike. Go to the right and up the hill from the train station to reach the *Fußgängerzone*.

Trains: The train station (tel. 732 14 357) is at the intersection of Bahnhofstr. and Salzmannstr. To: **Salzburg** (1¾hr., 24 per day 1:36am-9:24pm, 150AS); **Innsbruck** (2hr., 8 per day 5:06am-10:42pm, 250AS); **Vienna** (5¼hr., 5 per day 1:36am-4:19pm, 520AS); and **Kitzbühel** (45min., every hr. 8:42am-10:42pm, 105AS). Ticket office open M 5am-8pm, Tu-Sa 6am-8pm, Su 7am-8:50pm.

Buses: BundesBus station on Postpl., behind the post office and facing Gartenstr. Buy tickets from the driver.

Taxis: At the train station, or call 73171, 73359, or 57551.

Car Rental: ARAC Inter-Auto, Schmittenstr. 2 (tel. 74452).

Auto Repairs: ÖAMTC (Austrian Automobile and Touring Club), Loferer Bundesstr. (tel. 74132). In case of a breakdown, dial 120.

Parking: 24hr. parking garage at the *Kurcenter* sport center past the post office.

Bike Rental: At the train station. 150AS per day, with ticket 90AS. Mountain bike 200-270AS.

Tourist Office: Brucker Bundesstr. 3 (tel. 770; fax 72032; email zell@gold.at; zell.gold.at), within walking distance of the train station. From the station, turn right and follow the green "i" sign by the stairs on the left. A nifty computer prints information in German or English on accommodations, events, and services (printer open 8am-midnight). The staff can't make reservations, but they will ferret out vacancies and bury you under brochures. Open July to mid-Sept. and mid-Dec. to Mar. M-F 8am-6pm, Sa 8amnoon and 4-6pm, Su 10am-noon; Apr.-June and Sept. to mid-Dec. M-F 8am-noon and 2-6pm, Sa 9am-noon.

Currency Exchange: At banks or the post office. Almost every bank has an **ATM.**

Luggage Storage: At the train station. 30AS per piece, open M-Sa 6am-8:30pm. 24hr. electronic lockers with accommodations for both bags and skis 40AS.

Mountain Rescue: Bergrettung Zell am See (tel. 140).

Police: Bruckner Bundesstr. (tel. 73701).

Post Office: Postpl. 4 (tel. 73791). Open early July to mid-Sept. and late Dec. to Mar. M-F 7:30am-6:30pm, Sa 8-10am; mid-Sept. to late Dec. and Apr. to early July Sa 8-11am. Currency exchange closes at 5pm. **Postal Code:** A-5700.

| PHONE CODE | The **city code** for Zell am See is 06542. |

▲ ACCOMMODATIONS AND CAMPING

Zell am See has more than its share of 4-star hotels (priced accordingly), but it has not forgotten the budget traveler. Many affordable accommodations roll out the red carpet for the cost conscious. Ask for a **guest card,** which provides numerous discounts on activities throughout the city.

Pensione Sinilill (Andi's Inn), Thumersbacherstr. 65 (tel. 73523). Take the BundesBus (dir.: Thumersbach Ort) to "Krankenhaus" (19AS, last bus 7:14pm). Turn left upon exiting the bus, walk about 200m, and look for a *Zimmer Frei* sign on the left side of the street. If you call ahead, Andi will pick you up. On the north shore of the lake, this hostel features simple furniture and an easy-going atmosphere. Andi's swimming trophies and stories, Joy's culinary and karaoke prowess, and the friendliest hound this side of the Großglockner make for an eminently homey atmosphere. 200AS per person, though prices go down according to the number of people and duration of stay. Hall bathrooms and shower. Breakfast included.

Haus der Jugend (HI), Seespitzstr. 13 (tel. 57185; fax 57 18 54; email hostel-zell-se @salzburg.co.at). Exit the side of the train station facing the lake ("Zum See"), turn right, and walk along the footpath beside the lake; at the end of the footpath, take a left onto Seespitzstr. (15min.). As the footpath can feel quite deserted at night, you could also take the Stadtbus to "Alpenblick" (19AS). This clean, new hostel on the lakefront provides large rooms with bath and lakeside terraces. Other goodies include a TV room with VCR, a pinball machine, and a snack shop in the reception area. 106 beds divided into doubles, quads, and 6-bed rooms. Dorms 165AS 1st night, then 140AS. Breakfast included. Lunch and dinner each 65AS. 10AS deposit for lockers in some rooms. Key deposit 300AS or passport. Reception 7-9am and 4-10pm. Check-out 9am. Lockout noon-4pm. Curfew 10pm. Open Dec.-Oct. Reserve ahead.

Camping Seecamp, Thumersbacherstr. 34 (tel. 211; fax 72115), in Zell am See/Prielau, just down the road from Pension Sinilill. Situated on the lakefront, this massive campground has phones, a restaurant, a café with terrace, and even a small shopping market. 87AS per person, ages 2-15 45AS; tents 50AS; cars 30AS; trailers 100AS. Guest tax 9AS for adults. Showers included. Reception 7am-noon and 2-10pm. Check-out 11am. AmEx, MC, Visa.

◖ FOOD

In the Pinzgau region, food is prepared to sustain the strenuous labors of hearty farmers. Try the *Brezensuppe* (a clear soup with cheese cubes) as an appetizer and then *Pinzgauer Käsnocken* (homemade noodles and cheese, topped with fried onions and chives). Top it all off with *Lebkuchen Parfait* (spice cake parfait), *Blattlkrapfen* (deep-fried stuffed pancakes), or *Germknödeln* (a steamed sweet roll served with poppy seeds, butter, and sugar). Happy tummy times.

Ristorante Pizzeria Giuseppe, Kirchg. (tel. 72373), in the *Fußgängerzone*. From the station, walk past the church and continue straight. Plenty of vegetarian options. English menu. Pasta dishes 78-115AS; pizza 50-125AS; salads 55-89AS. Open Tu-Su 11:30am-11pm. AmEx, DC, MC, Visa.

Fischrestaurant "Moby Dick," Kreuzg. 16 (tel. 73320). The great white—with fries. Staggering double fishburger with potatoes and salad only 85AS. Single fishburger 25AS. A few entrees feature fish straight from the lake. Most dishes 85-160AS. English menu available. Open M-F 9am-6pm, Sa 8am-1pm.

Crazy Daisy Restaurant, Bruckner Bundesstr. 10-12 (tel. 725 16 58). Mexican and American food very popular with young, English-speaking types. Hamburgers 95AS; burritos 120AS; salads 40-60AS; "breath-killer garlic bread" 30AS. Children's portions available. Open daily 7pm-midnight.

Schloß Kammer, Maishofer 22 (tel. 78202), in the nearby village of Maishofer. Bike up the road past a hospital to a superb restaurant run by the local mayor. Vaulted ceilings, an authentic *Kachelofen* (tiled clay oven), and a large selection of regional dishes. *Fleischknochen* 95AS, *Kaiserschmarr'n* (scrambled pancakes with plum compote for 2) 75AS. Open daily 10am-10pm.

MARKETS

SPAR, Brucker Bundesstr. 4. Open M-Th 8am-7pm, F 8am-7:30pm, Sa 7:30am-1pm.

Billa, on Schulstr. near the Mozartstr. intersection. Open M-W 8am-7pm, Th 7:30am-7pm, F 7:30am-7:30pm, Sa 7:30am-5pm.

◣ RECREATIONAL ACTIVITIES

AROUND THE LAKE. Zell's buildings are clustered in the valley of the **Zellersee.** Stroll around the lake on the well-kept path or get wet at one of the **beaches: Strandbad Zell am See,** near the center of town (walk toward the lake down Franz-Josef-Str.), complete with platform diving and a waterslide; **Strandbad Seespitz,** by the Haus der Jugend; or **Thumersbacher Strandbad** on the eastern shore. (All open late May to early Sept. daily 9am-7pm; 30-60AS, generally half-price after 5pm and free after 6pm.) **Boat tours** around the lake depart from and return to the Zell Esplanade, off Salzmannstr. along the river (40min., 8 per day 10am-5:30pm, 80AS, ages 6-14 40AS). One-way trips across the lake leave every ½-hour (May to mid-Oct. 9am-6:45pm, 22AS, round-trip 38AS; purchase tickets on the boat).

REGIONAL MUSEUM. No visit to Zell am See would be complete without a glimpse of the toilet Franz Josef used when he visited the Schmittenhöhe. This artifact and 4 floors of equally random exhibits (the largest pike ever caught in the lake, old gingerbread-making utensils, and hundreds of minerals) join the erstwhile royal throne in the entertaining **Heimatmuseum** inside the *Vogtturm* (tower) on Kreuzg. 2. The tower itself is more than 1000 years old, and its walls have cracked from the vibrations caused by cannon fire through the roof hatches. The cannons were fired not at enemies of old but at oncoming thunderstorms, a practice believed to disperse the clouds. The process continued until the science of meteorology reached Zell sometime in the mid-19th century. (Tel. (06582) 72759. Open mid-Sept. to mid-June M-Tu and Th-F 10am-noon and 2-5pm, W, Sa, and Su 2-4pm; 20AS, ages 6-18 15AS. English guide available.)

MOUNTAIN LIFTS. From the lake, the landscape rises swiftly into rugged peaks crowned with snow. You can conquer these local mountains on one of the town's 5 **cable-cars.** The BundesBus (dir.: Schmittenhöhebahn/Sonnenalmbahn Talstation) goes to the **Schmittenhöhebahn,** about 2km north of town on Schmittenstr. (Mid-July to late-Oct. daily every 30min. 8:30am-5pm. 180AS, children 90AS; round-trip 235AS, with guest card 210AS, children 115AS.) The **Sonnenalmbahn,** which travels half the height, is adjacent to the Schmittenhöhebahn. (Early June to early Oct. daily 9am-5pm. 95AS, with guest card 85AS, children 50AS; round-trip 125AS, 110AS, 65AS.) It connects to the **Sonnkogelbahn,** which rises to 1834m. The **Zeller Bergbahn** (780-1411m) is right in the center of town at the intersection of Schmittenstr. and Gartenstr. (Mid-June to late Sept. daily 9am-5pm. Ascent 110AS, with guest card 100AS, children 55AS. Round-trip 145AS, 130AS, 70AS.)

HIKING AND ADVENTURE SPORTS. The Zell am See area provides many opportunities to work those calf muscles. The Schmittenhöhe lift provides several brochures (with English translations) detailing **hikes** ranging from leisurely strolls to cliff-hangers. In the former category, the **Erlebnisweg Höhenpromenade** connects the top stations of the Schmittenhöhe and Sonnkogel lifts. Displays on history, nature, and ecology along the way exercise your mind. The brochure *Three Panorama Trips of the Schmittenhöhe*, available at any cable-car station, suggests other light hikes. **Free guided hikes** leave from the lower stations (July-Oct. M-F, with a variety of themes including botanical hikes, forest walks, and children's hikes). Contact the **Schmittenhöhebahn Aktiengesellschaft** (tel. 7890) or the lower station for details. For longer hikes, grab a *Wanderplan* or consider the *Pinzgauer Spaziergang*, a leisurely 7-hour hike. The trail begins at the upper terminal of the Schmittenhöhebahn and is marked "Alpenvereinsweg" #19 or 719. For **rafting** (350-680AS), **canyoning** (550-790AS), **paragliding** (600-700AS), **climbing** (490AS), or **mountain bike** information, contact **Adventure Service,** Steinerg. 9 (tel. 73525; fax 74280).

SKIING. In keeping with regional tradition, winter turns Zell am See into a ski resort. The new **Zell/Kaprun Ski Pass** covers both Zell am See and nearby Kaprun; a free bus runs between the two every 15 minutes from December 20 to April 13. (2 days 710-780AS, students 640-700AS, children 435-470AS.) One-day passes are available for Zell's Schmittenhöhe lift (370-410AS, children 220-240AS). Get a report in German on ski conditions in the Schmittenhöhe area at tel. 73694; for the Kitzsteinhorn-Kaprun area dial (06547) 8444. The **Kitzsteinhorn** mountain (3203m) and its glacier in Kaprun offer **year-round skiing.** Get there early on summer days to avoid skiing in slush. A day pass for the mountain costs 255AS, children 140AS. Skis, boots, and poles run 255AS per day and snowboards are 180AS per day; all are available at **Intersport Bruendl** on the glacier (tel. (06547) 862 13 60; email office@bruendl.co.at; www.bruendl.co.at; open 8am-4:30pm).

◪ NIGHTLIFE

If all the mountain exercise hasn't worn you out, boogie down at night. Those who want to get really hammered should try the local drinking game **Nageln,** in which drinkers compete to see who can drive a nail into a tree stump first—with the sharp end of a hammer. Somehow, you end up drunk.

Bierstad'l, Kircheng. 1 (tel. 47090). 33 different brews in stock; you'll be on the floor by number 9. Creamy, dark *Hirtl* for 33AS. Open 8:30pm-4am.

Crazy Daisy's Bar, Brucker Bundesstr. 10-12 (tel. 725 16 59), is a fun (touristy) joint featuring their own wacky, irreverent t-shirts and the ever-popular aforementioned hammer-in-stump game. Open in summer 8pm-1am; in winter 4pm-1am. 2-for-1 happy hour in summer 8-10pm; in winter 4-6pm.

Wunderbar, Esplanade 4-6 (tel. 2388; fax 238 83 05), at the Grand Hotel, occupies the top floor of a classy waterfront hotel with glass walls and great views, making it quite a romantic spot. Open 7am-2am.

Pinzgauer Diele, Kircheng. 3 (tel. 2164), has 2 bars and a small dance area guaranteed to get you moving. Move. A mostly under-25 crowd. Mixed drinks 50-95AS, beer 60-75AS. Cover 85AS. Open Su-M and W-Sa 10pm-3am.

HOHE TAUERN NATIONAL PARK

The enormous **Hohe Tauern range,** part of the Austrian Central Alps, extends well into the provinces of Carinthia, Salzburg, Tyrol, and East Tyrol. All together, the range boasts 246 glaciers and 304 mountains over 3000m. Sheets of ice, grassy heaths, and forested bulwarks partition the Ice-Age valleys. The heart of this Alpine landscape remains largely unspoiled, a fact that prompted conservationists to lobby for the creation of a **national park.** Between 1958 and 1964, large tracts of mountain land in Salzburg and Carinthia were declared preserves. On October 21, 1971, the provincial government leaders of Carinthia, Salzburg, and Tyrol signed an agreement at Heiligenblut to "conserve for present and future generations the Hohe Tauern as a particularly impressive and varied region of the Austrian Alps."

Thus designated, the Hohe Tauern National Park became the largest national park in all of Europe, officially enclosing 29 towns and 60,000 residents, though most of the actual protected park territory is uninhabited.

Unlike national parks in other countries, the Hohe Tauern National Park is not owned by the government, but rather by a consortium of private farmers and members of the Österreichische Alpenverein (ÖAV; Austrian Alpine Society). With the exception of the park's mountainous core, many of the alpine meadows and valleys are used for agriculture and forestry. Farmers still herd their cattle over the same 2500m *Tauern* (ice-free mountain paths) once trod by Celts and Romans. The **Glocknergruppe,** in the heart of the park, contains Austria's highest peak, the **Großglockner** (3798m), as well as many alpine lakes and glaciers. Plant and animal life in the park contains rare ecosystems of trees and flowers, marmots, vultures, and lyre-horned ibex (reintroduced into the park in the 1950s and 60s after having been hunted to near extinction).

⚑ GETTING AROUND THE PARK

The park is accessible by car, bus, and, in certain parts, by train. By **car** from **Kitzbühel,** take Bundesstr. 161 south to 108, which leads through the park. From **Zell am See,** take Bundesstr. 311 south to 107. From **Lienz,** take Bundesstr. 107 or 108 north into the park. Two **train** lines service towns near the park: a rail line from **Zell am See** runs west along the northern border of the park, terminating in **Krimml** (1¾hr., 8 per day, 106AS); another runs south from **Salzburg** to **Badgastein** in the southwest corner of the park (1½hr., every 2hr. 7:14am-8:15pm, 170AS).

The park is criss-crossed by **bus** lines, which operate on an incredibly complicated timetable. Ask for specific connections at local tourist offices. Most buses don't have a number but are classified by their end station. Buses from all directions terminate in the center of the park at **Franz-Josefs-Höhe.** From **Zell am See** in the north, take bus #3064 (2hr.; June 19-Oct. 10 daily 10:15am; July 10-Sept. 12 M-F 9:15am and 12:15pm; 145AS). From **Lienz** in the south, take the bus to Heiligenstadt and connect to Franz-Josefs-Höhe (1½hr.; June 21-Sept. 26 M-Sa 8:04am and 10:05am, July 12-Sept. 12 daily 12:25pm; 105AS). **Return** trips run from Franz-Josefs-Höhe to **Zell am See** (2hr.; July-Sept. M-F 11:45am, 3, and 4pm, Sa-Su 3pm; Sept.-Oct. M-F 3 and 4pm, Sa-Su 3pm); **Heiligenblut** (30min.; June 20-July 11 M-F

3:40pm, Su 4:30pm; July 11-Sept. 9 M-F 11:50am, 2:40 and 3:40pm, Sa 11:50am, Su 11:50am and 4:30pm; Sept. 9-26 Su 4:30pm); and Lienz (1½hr., daily at 11:50am).

For anyone planning a lengthy stay in the area, BundesBus also offers a **National Park Ticket,** good for 10 days of unlimited travel between Lienz, Heiligenblut, *Hochtor,* and other stops in the region, as well as reduced fares on cable cars and other sights. The bus to the **Krimmler Wasserfälle** (see p. 248), the **Gletscherbahn** in Kaprun, and the **Schmittenhöhebahn** in Zell am See (see p. 243) are all fair game (mid-June to mid-Oct.; 590AS, children 295AS). For further details, check the brochure *Der BundesBus ist Wanderfreundlich* (available at the bus stations in Lienz and Zell am See and the tourist offices in Lienz and Heiligenblut), which contains a schedule of bus departure times, destinations, maps, hiking paths, and other general information. Travel to and from Lienz is cheaper with the new 24-hour **Verkehrs Verbund Kärnten** card (80AS), which provides for unlimited train travel in one region of Carinthia and discounts on buses. This card will save you a bundle on the Großglocknerstr., though you still have to pay the entrance fee. Get the red and yellow card at the Lienz train station. Look out for discounts on travel to the valley village of Heiligenblut, a great base for exploring the Hohe Tauern. The ride from Heiligenblut to Franz-Josefs-Höhe is on the Lienz line (47AS).

ORIENTATION

The center of the park, and BundesBus hub, is **Franz-Josefs-Höhe** and the **Pasterze glacier** (see p. 247), but despite its name, it is not a very high spot compared to the 3000m mountains that surround it. Aside from the skiing and hiking on those steep monsters, the main tourist attractions in the park are the **Krimml Waterfalls,** in the northwestern corner, and the **Großglocknerstraße** (Bundesstr. 107), a spectacular high mountain road that runs north/south through the center of the park, between Zell am See and Lienz. Several small towns are scattered throughout the park.

Due to the park's distribution over 3 different provinces, the network of tourist information is quite decentralized. Most of the park falls within Salzburger Land, but the Tyrolean branch is designated as the official headquarters for the entire national park. You're probably best off talking to the park service branch in whichever province of the park you are visiting. The **Carinthia (Kärnten) park tourist office** is located in Döllach (tel. (04825) 6161; email hohe.tauern@nationalpark-kaernten. or.at); the **Tyrol office** is located in Matrei (tel. (04875) 5161; email npht.tirol@net-way.at); and the **Salzburg office** is located in Neukirchen (tel. (06565) 6558; email nationalpark@salzburg.or.at). You can also find information on the park as a whole on the Internet at www.npht.sbg.ac.at/npht.

SIGHTS AND ACTIVITIES

THE GROßGLOCKNERSTRAßE

Each day more than 3000 visitors pack up their cars for a full-day sail among the Austrian Alps along the breath-taking **Großglocknerstraße,** one of the most beautiful highways in the world. Skirting the country's loftiest mountains, Bundesstr. 107 (its less catchy moniker) winds for 50km amid silent Alpine valleys, meadows of wildflowers, tumbling waterfalls, and huge glaciers. The road passes its highest point at **Hochtor,** 2505m above sea level. The slow, steady climb is choked with rubber-neckers and over-ambitious cyclists soaking up the stupefying views. Many of the high-mountains-sweeping-panorama-hairpin-turn-sports-car commercials (you thought German words were long) are filmed here. Switzerland and France used the Großglockner as a model when engineering their own mountain highways.

 DRIVING SAFETY TIPS. Many first-time drivers of the Großglocknerstraße are tempted to lean heavily on the brakes, which can lead to brake failure and overheating. Instead, shift to low gear, drive slowly, and never, ever pass anyone.

Consider the Austrian work ethic that made it possible: in only 5 years (1930-35), during a global economic crisis, over 3000 workers constructed the entire road.

Total transport time on the Großglockner (with scenic rest stops in between) is 5 hours. Many visitors find that they're much happier dividing these 5 hours over several days: that's how good-looking this stretch of road is. If you only have one day, resist the urge to disembark at any of the cutesy villages along the way; buses come so infrequently that you'll be stuck in Nowheresdorf for hours. Your time is better spent at the **Franz-Josefs-Höhe,** enjoying the magnificent views. Try to choose a clear day for your excursion—you don't want to pay the entrance fee when viewing conditions are poor. Many visitors traverse the Großglocknerstr. in a **tour bus** or **rental car,** neither of which is recommended for those with light pocketbooks or weak stomachs, but the public bus service is quite good (see p. 245). The hairpin curves along the narrow roads are dizzying, and you must pay a toll at Ferleiten (on the Zell am See side) or Roßbach (on the Heiligenblut side) of 350AS for cars and 230AS for motorcycles. Parking at Franz-Josefs-Höhe is free with your toll receipt. There are also parking and pull-off areas strategically situated at numerous lookout points along the road. The warmer weather from June to September creates the best driving conditions; be aware that the park forbids traffic from 10pm to 5am. Snowfalls, sometimes dumping up to 18m of heavy snow on the road, force the Großglockner to close entirely from October to April. For info on the road conditions call the information office in Heiligenblut (tel. (04824) 2212).

ALPINE NATURE EXHIBIT. The trip up to **Hochtor** takes you from the flora and fauna of Austria into Arctic-like environments (never exceeding 50°F even during the hottest summers). Although tours generally run from **Zell am See** or **Lienz** to the park, the highway is officially only the 6.4km stretch from **Bruck an der Großglockner** in Salzburg to **Heiligenblut** in Carinthia. Coming from Zell am See, you'll pass the **Alpine Nature Exhibit** (2300m). The small museum features well-designed nature exhibits, a 25-minute movie (in German), and frightening photos of hikers who forgot to wear sunblock. If you take the bus up here in the summer, you'll have half an hour to roam through the exhibits before the bus leaves for Franz-Josefs-Höhe. *(Open 9am-5pm. Free. English headphones 20AS.)*

FRANZ-JOSEFS-HÖHE. Großglocknerstraße buses from Zell am See, Lienz, and Heiligenblut finish their routes at **Franz-Josefs-Höhe,** a large observation and tourist center stationed above the **Pasterze glacier.** Naturally, Franz-Josefs-Höhe is packed with tour buses and camera-toting visitors, but even they can't detract from the sight of the glacier's icy tongue extending down the valley. If the weather's right, you can glimpse the summit of the **Großglockner** (3797m) peeking through the clouds on the left wall of the valley. Franz-Josefs-Höhe has its own **tourist office** (tel. (04824) 2727) at the beginning of the parking area, with its own free mini-museum and Hohe Tauern information center. The office organizes daily walks around the glacier—call ahead for prices and times. The staff can also answer questions about the availability and opening times of the mountain huts in the vicinity. (Open daily 10am-4pm.) There are several restaurants and snack-bars scattered around Franz-Josefs-Höhe, but be forewarned that the prices tend to be as high as the altitude.

GLACIER FUNICULAR AND OBSERVATION CENTER. The **Gletscherbahn funicular** ferries you down from Franz-Josefs-Höhe to the glacier itself, where you can walk about 100m across its hard-packed surface. Better catch it while you can—the glacier has shrunk 2m in depth in the last few years and will probably continue to shrink unless climate trends dramatically reverse. (Tel. (04824) 2502 or 2288. Funicular runs May 21 to Oct. 10, daily 9am-2pm. Round-trip 98AS, children 55AS.)

At the top of the hill at the end of the parking lot looms the **Swarovski Observation Center,** a crystal-shaped building that houses 3 floors of binoculars and telescopes for viewing the surrounding terrain. If you're lucky, you might spot some ibex chewing the grass on the mountain behind you. You won't need fancy specs to see the marmots, which are fat, furry, beaver-like rodents who beg crumbs from tourists. You're not supposed to feed them, but try saying no to those cute little noses. (Open daily 10am-4pm. Free.)

HIKING. More intrepid hikers can walk through the short tunnel in the side of the main restaurant and out along the path that snakes along the mountainside above the glacier. The path as far as **Hofmannshütte** (30min.) is fairly easy going; beyond that lies **Oberwalderhütte** (another 2hr.), which involves crossing an ice field and requires proper equipment and expertise. Proceed at your own risk. Between Hofmannshütte and the ice edge are several **waterfalls** that pour down from the glaciers above. The path to the huts isn't always open (due to rock slides), so ask at the tourist office before you head out. The tourist office also sells detailed hiking maps of the area (190AS; only in German).

You can also hire a **guide** for hiking, rock and ice climbing, or ski touring (call the park office in Heiligenblut, tel. (04824) 2700; fax 27004; daily 10am-5pm; prices vary—for Großglockner, 3100AS per day for 1 person, 3900AS for 2 people, 4500AS for 3, 5200AS for 4).

MUSEUM. The **Glocknerwiesen Museum** is inarguably the Großglocknerstraße's cutest attraction. Located in a small building off the road from Franz-Josefs-Höhe to Heiligenblut (1km before the Guttal intersection) next to the Schoeneck Café, this unmanned museum gives you the low-down on what the birds and the bees have been doing in these mountain pastures for millennia. Exhibits in English and German illustrate the variety of flora, local agricultural techniques, the scents of local flowers, and the erotic trickery employed by blossoms to woo bees. *(Open in "daylight hours," approx. 8am-9pm in summer. Free.)*

THE KRIMML WATERFALLS

From the small mountain town of Krimml, over 700,000 visitors per year charge up the sloping path to extraordinary **Wasserfälle**—a set of three roaring cascades totalling over 400m in height. Dropping a total of 380m, the highest waterfalls in Europe are pleasantly secluded amidst the spindly pines and mountain grasses of the Höhe Tauern National Park. Despite the large number of visitors, the falls retain an unspoiled atmosphere that gets increasingly wild the higher you walk. The path (built in 1900 by the ÖAV) that runs just alongside the falls allows for dozens of unusually close and pulse-quickening views of roaring water.

Krimml is accessible by bus and train. **Buses** are most convenient, since they drop you at the start of the path to the falls (bus stop: Maustelle Ort). Direct lines run from **Zell am See** (1½hr., 10 per day 6:28am-6:49pm, 110AS) and **Zell am Ziller** (1hr., 3 per day 9:21am-1:26pm, 58AS). The **Pinzgauer Lokalbahn** comes only from the east, through **Zell am See** (1½hr., 9 per day, 95AS, railpasses valid). The train station (tel. 7214) is 3km from the waterfall—either cross the street to catch the bus (19AS) to the falls, take a **taxi** (tel. 7281 or 7223; 50AS) or hike on the foot path. Don't forget a raincoat and camera bag; the mist is very wet. Entrance to the falls costs 15AS (children 5AS) between 8am and 6pm; at all other times entrance is free. The ÖAV Information stand, next to the ticket booth, offers a variety of English pamphlets and sells a number of German guides to the flowers, mushrooms, and rocks of the Höhe Tauern (50-180AS; tel. (06564) 7212; open May-Oct. M-Sa 11am-4pm. With a minimum of 10 people, the office offers free guided tours of the falls in English (call in advance).

WATERFALL HIKES. The source of the waterfalls is the Krimml "Kees" (glacier), 20km up the valley above the falls. The falls were almost dammed in the 1950s to provide hydroelectric power, but environmentalist pressure and the creation of the Hohe Tauern National Park helped save these marvels. The trail is called the **Wasserfallweg** (4km). The first and most spectacular cascade (150m) is visible past the entrance booth and to the left; it kicks up a huge skirt of spray that douses the rocks, plants, and tourists nearby.

FLOWER COWS Every spring, the local farmers around Krimml set their cattle free to graze on the mountainside. In the fall, they set out to round up the herd. At the end of September, farmers give thanks to the hardy cows who made it back by dressing them up in Carmen Miranda-style flower headdresses and parading them through town. The **Almatriebs-Fest** (Sept. 23, 2000) features live music, a crafts exhibition, and a farmer's market (entrance fee 20AS, children under 14 free).

A wide hiking path leads up to the second and third falls. Even though super-fit Austrian grandmothers appear to handle the climb with ease, the walk can be tough. It's about 30 minutes from the first falls to the second and an additional 30 minutes from the second to the third. Next to the second falls, which plunge a mere 100m, is a precipice called **Jägersprung** (hunter's leap). As legend will have it, a poacher once jumped from here to the other side of the falls to elude his pursuers—you can judge for yourself how likely this feat is. The third set of falls (140m) is perhaps the most scenic and least cluttered with gawking tourists. There is a jumble of boulders by the side of the river that provide unobstructed views of the falling water. It's a nice spot that's worth the walk and there's even a hotel up top that serves refreshing (but expensive) snacks. If you want to save some *Schillinge*, stock up at the **SPAR** down the main road in Krimml (open M-F 8am-6pm, Sa 8am-noon) and picnic at one of the many scenic benches overlooking the falls.

KRIMML TOWN. The town of Krimml provides a base for multiple waterfall trips and other hikes in summer, and skiing in winter. The full-service **tourist office** (tel. (06564) 7239 or 6564 (from outside Austria); fax 7550; email krimml.info@aon.at; www.salzburg.com/krimml-tourismus) is 2 minutes from the "Krimml Ort" bus stop, down the hill (open M-F 8am-noon and 2:30-5:30pm, Sa 8:30-10:30am; ski-passes run 200AS for a full day, and 1745AS per week; youth get 15% off, children 35%). Next door, the **post office** (tel. (06564) 7201) offers good **currency exchange** rates (open M-F 8am-noon and 2-5pm). There is a 24-hour **ATM** at the bank across the street from the church. **Bike rental** and cheap food can be had at **ADEG**, in front of the church (open M-F 7:30am-noon and 3-6pm, Sa 7:30am-noon; city and mountain bikes 200AS per day). **Ski and boot rental** at **Sport Lachmayer,** are next to ADEG (tel. (06564) 7247; open M-F 8am-noon and 2:30-6pm, Sa 8am-noon; full rental 195-275AS per day, 935-1490AS per week; DC, MC, Visa). Large doubles with waterfall views are only 220-240AS at **Bauernhof Mühleg,** Krimml 24 (tel. (06564) 7338). Follow the road past ADEG and the sport shop, and further downhill (5min.); the brown farmhouse is on the right, with flowers on every terrace.

NEAR HOHE TAUERN: HEILIGENBLUT

Heiligenblut can be reached by bus from Franz-Josefs-Höhe (30min., 4 per day, 47AS), Zell am See (2½hr., 3 per day, 145AS), and Lienz (1hr., 6 per day, 72AS). The bus stop is in the big parking lot in front of Hotel Glocknerhof.

The most convenient and inexpensive accommodations for those wishing to explore Franz-Josefs-Höhe and the Hohe Tauern region can be found in Heiligenblut, a tiny town on the Carinthian side of the Großglockner. The town's name, which means "holy blood," derives from a legend about a Byzantine general named Briccius who perished nearby in a snowstorm. He carried with him a precious vial supposedly containing a few drops of Christ's blood, which is now housed in a reliquary in the town church. (Church open daily 7am-7pm. Free.) The **tourist office** (tel. (04824) 20 01 21; fax 20 01 43), up the street from the bus stop and Hotel Glocknerhof, dispenses information about accommodations, sporting activities, and park transportation (open M-F 8:30am-noon and 2:30-6pm, Sa 9am-noon and 4-6pm; July-Aug. open M-F 8:30am-6pm). The **post office** is located below the center of town at the bottom of the hill. Follow the main road past the chair lift. (Open M-F 8am-noon and 1:30-5pm, Sa 8:30-10:30am.)

HOOKED ON PFONICS Ach, German—the musical language. A few German sounds are particularly charming to non-native speakers, such as the "pf" combination, found at the beginning of many German words and pronounced with two distinct consonants: "p-f." Try these few sentences to practice sounding like a native: *Ein Pfau in der Pfalz frißt einen pfirsichen Pfannkuchen. Ein pflaumenfarbiger Pferd fährt pfeilschnell durch eine Pforte und frißt den Pfau. Das Pferd war ein Pflanzenfresser, aber er hat gedacht, der Pfau sei eine Pflanze oder vielleicht eine Pfingstrose.* (A peacock in the Pfalz eats a peach pancake. Quick as an arrow a plum-colored horse bursts through a gate and eats the peacock. The horse was an herbivore, but he mistook the peacock for a plant, perhaps a peony.)

To reach the **Jugendherberge (HI),** Hof 36 (tel./fax (04824) 2259), take the steep path down from the wall behind the bus stop parking lot—the hostel is at the bottom. It offers institutional but pleasant rooms and clean toilets. (HI members only, though they might make exceptions, depending on space. Dorm bed with breakfast 180AS. Reception May-Sept. 7-11am and 5-9pm. Curfew 10pm, key available.) **Pension Bergkristall** (tel. (04824) 2005; fax 20 05 33), has rooms with balconies and is conveniently close to the main lift station (in summer, 300AS per person with breakfast; in winter, 280-420AS).

In winter, you can ski the slopes of the Hohe Tauern mountains. Ski passes are 340AS per day, children 170AS. You can purchase passes at the lift station past the tourist office. **Bike and ski rental** are available at Intersport Pichler, across from the tourist office. (Open M-Sa 9am-6pm, Su 10am-4pm; bikes 220AS per day; ski package 300AS per day.)

UPPER AUSTRIA

(OBERÖSTERREICH)

The province of Oberösterreich (Upper Austria) is comprised of 3 distinct regions: the northeastern corner is known as the **Mühlviertel;** the **Innviertel** covers the western half; and the southwestern corner encompasses the popular resort area, the **Salzkammergut.** The charming streets of the provincial capital **Linz** mask the city's industrial soul; it is a major center of iron, steel, and chemical production, and home to many Danube port installations. Despite extensive development, the gentle natural beauty of the Danube river valley remains unspoiled. While the mountains here are less rugged than in Tyrol, Salzburg, and Carinthia, the relatively flat terrain in Upper Austria makes for wonderful **bicycling** tours. Well-paved paths, suitable for cyclers of any ability, wind throughout the entire province.

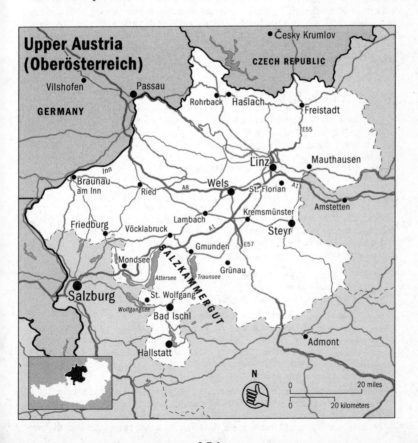

Upper Austria (Oberösterreich)

251

HIGHLIGHTS OF UPPER AUSTRIA

■ Munch melt-in-your-mouth, jam-saturated **Linzer Torten** while relaxing one of Linz's garden cafés (p. 255).
■ Cure what ails you in the warm salt baths of **Bad Ischl** (p. 266).
■ Sequester yourself in the mountains of **Grünau** for rest and relaxation at a backpacker's dream resort (p. 266).
■ Peruse potties, from *Biedermeier* boxes to turn-of-the-century tasseled toilets, at the Klo und So Museum in **Gmunden** (p. 265).

LINZ AN DER DONAU

Sandwiched between Vienna to the east and Salzburg to the west, Linz suffers from the typical middle-child syndrome—it is not as cosmopolitan as Vienna but not as small-town-charming as Salzburg either, so people generally ignore it. Nevertheless, Linz goes to great lengths to stand out from the pack, and the result is a sophisticated yet comfortable old-world town. The third largest city in the country, Linz was once home to Kepler, Mozart, Beethoven, Bruckner, and Hitler (not all at the same time). Technologically, Linz has won the sibling rivalry. The city, sitting on the banks of the blue(ish) Danube, rules magisterially over the industrial sector of Austria. Though the industrial city outskirts aren't particularly scenic, the wealth produced by factories has been used to modernize and gentrify the central city, with exclusive shops, modern art galleries, cyber-cafés, electronic bus stops, and a technology museum that will overload your mental circuits. Linz's citizens are quite friendly (unburdened by the tourist overload of Vienna and Salzburg), and its annual festivals—the classy **Brucknerfest** and the bedlam nuttiness of the **Pflasterspektakel** (street performer's fair)—draw artists and crowds from all over the world.

█ GETTING TO LINZ

Midway between Salzburg and Vienna, and on the rail line between Prague and Graz, Linz is a transportation hub for Austria and much of Eastern Europe. Frequent **trains** connect to major Austrian and European cities. All **buses** come and go from the **Hauptbahnhof,** where schedules are available (bus ticket window open M-F 7am-5:50pm, Sa 7am-1:20pm). **Motorists** arrive via Autobahn West (A1 or E16).

█ ORIENTATION AND PRACTICAL INFORMATION

Linz straddles the **Danube,** which weaves west to east through the city. Most of the *Altstadt* sights crowd along the southern bank, near the **Nibelungenbrücke.** This pedestrian area includes the huge **Hauptplatz,** just south of the bridge, and extends down **Landstraße,** which ends near the train station.

Trains: Hauptbahnhof, Bahnhofpl. (tel. 1717). **To: Vienna** (2hr., every 30min., 280AS); **Salzburg** (1½hr., every hr., 210AS); **Innsbruck** (3½hr., every 2hr., 490AS); **Munich** (3hr., every 1-2hr., 508AS); and **Prague** (4hr., 4 per day, 366AS).

Ferries: Wurm & Köck boats connects **Passau** (tel. (0851) 92 92 92; fax 35518), **Linz** (tel. (0732) 78 36 09), and **Krems.** To Passau (5-7hr., depending on current; daily 8am and 2:15pm; 242AS, round-trip 284AS) and Krems (Tu, Th, Su 9am). Boats dock in Linz at the **Donau Schiffstation,** on the south side of the river, and stop at a number of Austrian and Bavarian towns along the way. Discounts for seniors and children under 15. Ferries run late Apr. to Oct.

Public Transportation: Linz's public transport system runs to all corners of the city. Trams #1 and 3 start near the *Hauptbahnhof* and run north through the city along Landstr. and Hauptpl. and across Nibelungenbrücke. Several buses criss-cross Linz as well. Nearly all vehicles pass through **Blumauerplatz,** down the block and to the right from the train station. A hub closer to the city center is **Taubenmarkt,** south of Hauptpl. on Landstr. A ticket for 4 stops or less ("Mini") costs 9AS; more than 4 ("Midi") 18AS; and a day ticket ("Maxi") 36AS. Buy tickets from any machine at any bus or streetcar stop and stamp them before boarding; those caught riding without a ticket must fork over 400AS. The tourist office sells a 48AS combination ticket that includes a day ticket for tram #3 and a round-trip cable car ride to **Pöstlingberg.**

Taxis: At the *Hauptbahnhof*, Blumauerpl., and Hauptpl., or call 6969 or 1718.

Parking: Free parking at **Urfahrmarkt.**

Bike Rental: At the train station, 150AS per day, with train ticket 90AS. Or at **Oberösterreich Touristic Zentrale,** Kapuzinerstr. 3 (tel. 311 49 67), 15AS per hr., 80AS per day, 120AS for 2 days, 250AS for 5 days, 200AS per weekend. Book in advance.

Automobile Service: ARBÖ, Hatenstr. 6 (tel. 123), or **ÖAMTC,** Wankmüllerhofstr. 58 (tel. 120).

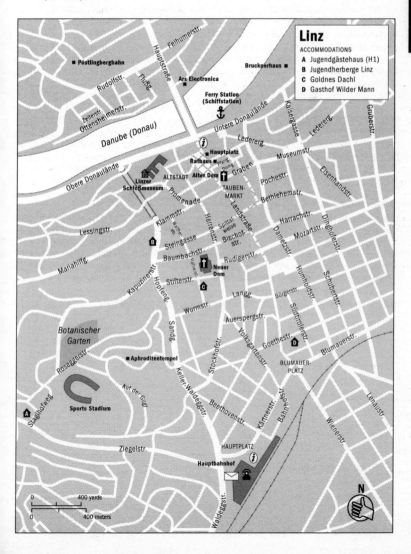

Tourist Office: Hauptpl. 1 (tel. 70 70 17, ext. 77; fax 77 28 73; email info.linz @upperaustria.or.at; www.tiscover.com/linz), in the *Rathaus*. The multilingual staff helps find rooms at no charge. Pick up *A Walk Through the Old Quarter* for a summary of the *Altstadt's* main attractions. The tourist office sells the **Linz City Ticket** (299AS) which provides discounts at various sights around the city. Open May-Sept. M-F 8am-7pm, Sa 9am-7pm, Su 10am-7pm; Oct.-Apr. M-F 8am-6pm, Sa 9am-6pm, Su 10am-6pm. There is a tourist info brochure counter in the train station.

Currency Exchange: Banks are open M-W 8am-4:30pm, Th 8am-5:30pm, F 8am-2pm. The **post office** offers better rates for cash. Exchange open M-F 7am-5pm, Sa 8am-1pm. 60AS commission. 24hr. currency exchange machine at the train station.

American Express: Bürgerstr. 14, A-4021 Linz (tel. 66 90 13). All traveler's checks cashed, but no currency exchanged. Open M-F 9am-5:30pm, Sa 9am-noon.

Luggage Storage: At the train station, 30AS. Lockers 30-50AS. At tourist office, 10AS.

Bi-Gay-Lesbian Organizations: Homosexuelle Initiative Linz (HOSI), Schubertstr. 36 (tel. 60 98 98). Discussion tables Th 8pm at Gasthaus Agathon, Kapuzinerstr. 46. **Frauenbüro,** Klosterstr. 7 (tel. 772 01 850).

Pharmacies: Downtown Linz has *Apotheken* everywhere. **Central Apotheke,** Mozartstr. 1 (tel. 77 17 83). Open M-F 8am-noon and 2-6pm, Sa 8am-noon.

Internet Access: At the **Ars Electronica Museum** (see p. 255).

Post Office: Bahnhofpl. 11, next to the train and bus stations. Open daily 6am-midnight. Information open M-F 8am-5pm, Sa 8am-4pm. **Postal Code:** A-4020.

PHONE CODE	The **city code** for Linz is 0732.

▐ ACCOMMODATIONS AND CAMPING

Linz suffers from a lack of cheap rooms. The city is just urban enough that locals aren't allowed to rent rooms privately, so it's usually best to stick to the youth hostels and budget hotels. It's a good idea to call ahead everywhere.

Jugendherberge Linz (HI), Kapuzinerstr. 14 (tel. 78 27 20 or 77 87 77), near Hauptpl., offers the cheapest beds in town in an excellent location. From the train station, take tram #3 to "Taubenmarkt," cross Landstr., walk down Promenade and Klammstr., then turn left on Kapuzinerstr. This no-frills hostel has 36 beds in 4- and 6-bed rooms. Dorms 160AS, under 19 130AS. Nonmembers add 40AS. Breakfast 30AS. Showers and sheets included. **Laundry** 45AS. Reception 8-10am and 5-8pm. No curfew; the key to your free locker opens the front door. Reservations recommended.

Jugendgästehaus (HI), Stanglhofweg 3 (tel. 66 44 34; fax 60 21 64). From the train station, take bus #27 (dir.: Schiffswerft) to "Froschberg." Walk straight on Ziegeleistr., turn right on Roseggerstr., and continue on to Stanglhofweg. Bland rooms are clean and spacious. Singles 335AS; doubles 235AS per person; triples 165AS per person. Guest tax 8AS. Breakfast and sheets included. Private showers and hall toilets. Parking. Reception 7:30am-4pm and 6-11pm. Curfew 11pm. Call ahead.

Goldenes Dachl, Hafnerstr. 27 (tel. 77 58 97). From the train station, take bus #21 to "Auerspergpl." Continue in the same direction along Herrenstr. for half a block, then turn left onto Wurmstr. Hafnerstr. is the 1st right. Large comfortable rooms. Singles 260AS; doubles 460AS, with shower 490AS. Only 17 beds—call ahead.

Gasthof Wilder Mann, Goethestr. 14 (tel. 65 60 78). From the station, go down Bahnhofstr., turn left on Landestr. at Blumauerpl., then turn right on Goethestr. (7min.). Just 2min. from Blumauerpl., the main transportation hub, this hotel has large, homey rooms, with embroidered drapes and chairs. Restaurant downstairs. Singles 300AS, with shower 370AS; doubles 540AS, 620AS. Breakfast 50AS. Reception 8am-10pm.

Camping Pleschinger See (tel. 24 78 70). Take tram #1 or 3 to Rudolfstr. and bus #22 to "Pleschinger See." On the Linz-Vienna biking path on Pleschinger Lake. You can take tram #1 or 3 to "Pleschinger See" and continue on foot, but you'll still have a long way to go. 45AS. Tents only. Open May to late Sept.

🍴 FOOD

Duck into the alleyway restaurants off Hauptpl. and Landstr. to avoid ridiculously inflated prices. Linz's namesake dessert, the **Linzer Torte,** is unique for its deceptively dry ingredients—lots of flour and absolutely no cream. The secret is in the red-currant jam filling, which slowly seeps through and moisturizes the dry, crumbly crust. Not all *Linzer Torten* are the same; the best *Torten* sit out for at least 2 days after baking for maximum jam saturation.

🍴 **Café Traxlmeyer,** Promenadestr. 16. From Hauptpl., head down Schmidttorstr., and turn right on Promenadestr. Giant orange awnings shade the garden tables of this Viennese-style café. For 55AS you can nibble on rolls and jam, sip coffee from your own little pot, flip through newspapers, and watch people play chess throughout the afternoon. *Torten* 24AS. Open M-Sa 8am-10pm.

🍴 **Gelbes Krokodil,** Dametzstr. 30 (tel. 78 40 90), in the Moviemento Theater, pleases a young student crowd. Varying menu includes soups (30AS), salads (60-80AS), and vegetarian entrees (80-90AS). Open 5-11pm. Theater shows international contemporary and classic films. Summer special is a double feature and a drink, for only 120AS.

Mangolds, Hauptpl. 3 (tel. 78 56 88), is Valhalla for vegetarians. This cafeteria-style restaurant offers only the fresh stuff. Nearly all the vegetables and eggs are 100% organic. Extravagant salad bar and freshly squeezed fruit and vegetable drinks. Pay by weight—100g for 16AS, 60AS per plate. Open M-F 11am-8pm, Sa 11am-5pm.

Levante, Hauptpl. 13 (tel. 79 34 30), has crowded outdoor seating on Hauptpl. and authentic Turkish and Greek food at low prices. 35AS sandwiches are a great deal. Open daily 11:30am-11:30pm.

Gasthaus Goldenes Schiff, Ottensheimerstr. 74 (tel. 23 98 79), sits on the scenic banks of the Danube. From Hauptpl., cross the bridge, turn left, go around the *Rathaus,* and walk upstream along the river for 7min. Local fishermen pound on wooden tables and drink beer in the *Gastgarten* while eating their 100AS dinners. Open W-Su 9am-10pm.

Pizzeria D'Alfredo and **Shalimar,** Bethlehemstr. 38 (tel. 77 80 55). In one room, enjoy Greek and Italian specialties under a fish-filled net and plant-hung ceiling. Huge selection of large pizzas (85-110AS), pasta dishes (80-95AS), and salads (40-80AS). If you're longing for more Eastern fare and tunes, move to the next room and taste a variety of Pakistani and Indian dishes (80-110AS). Open 11am-2:30pm and 5-11:30pm.

Jindrak Konditorei, Herrenstr. 22, with other branches throughout Linz. Rumored to serve the best *Linzer Torte* (19.50AS) in Linz. Other mouth-watering sweets and sandwiches line up beneath the glass counters. Open M-Sa 8am-6pm.

MARKETS

Julius Meinl, Landstr. 50. Open M-F 7:30am-6:30pm, Sa 7:30am-5pm.

SPAR Markt, Steing., near the hostels. Open M-F 7:30am-7pm.

👁️ 🎵 SIGHTS AND ENTERTAINMENT

THE OLD TOWN. Start your exploration of Linz at **Hauptplatz,** which hugs the Danube's south bank. The city constructed the enormous plaza in the 14th and 15th centuries when it grew wealthy from taxing all the salt and iron passing through town. The focus of the square is the marble **Trinity column,** commemorating the city's escape from the horrors of war, famine, the plague, and the 18th century. An octagonal tower and an astronomical clock crown the Baroque **Rathaus.** To date, only 2 people have ever addressed the public from its balcony: Adolf Hitler and Pope John Paul II. Free-spirited star-gazer Johannes Kepler (the fellow who formulated the elliptical geometry of planetary orbit) wrote his major work, *Harmonices Mundi,* while living around the corner at Rathausg. 5. In 1745, Linz's first print shop opened there; today, it houses Onkel Dagobert's Dart Kneipe—a few beers may inspire you to rethink the geometrical harmonies of the dartboard.

CATHEDRALS. On nearby Domg. stands Linz's twin-towered **Alter Dom** (Old Cathedral), where symphonic composer Anton Bruckner played during his stint as church organist. *(Open daily 7am-noon and 3-7pm.)* To the south, the neo-Gothic **Neuer Dom** (New Cathedral) impresses visitors with the 19th-century hubris necessary to create this Godzilla-scale edifice (the largest in Austria).

MUSEUMS. The **Ars Electronica,** just over the bridge from Hauptpl., bills itself as the "museum of the future." It's a bird, it's a plane, it's *you* strapped to the ceiling in a full-body flight simulator that sends you soaring over Upper Austria. After this not-so-natural high, head downstairs to the **CAVE,** an exciting interactive 3-D room. The museum café offers **email access** for visitors, included in the entrance fee. *(Hauptstr. 2. Tel. 7 27 20; email infoşaec.at; www.aec.at. Open W-Su 10am-6pm. 80AS, students and seniors 40AS.)* The **Neue Galerie,** Blütenstr. 15 (tel. 707 03 600), on the second floor of the Lentia 2000 shopping center on the north side of the river, has one of Austria's best contemporary art collections. Works by Klimt, Kokoschka, Lieberman, and others line the walls. *(Open June-Sept. M-W and F 10am-6pm, Th 10am-10pm, Sa 10am-1pm; Oct.-May M-W and F-Su 10am-6pm, Th 10am-10pm. 60AS, students 30AS.)* The **Linzer Schloßmuseum** presents the city's history as well as temporary exhibits. *(Tummelpl. 10. Tel. 77 44 19. Open Tu-F 9am-5pm, Sa-Su 10am-4pm. 50AS, students 30AS. English brochure available.)*

BOTANICAL GARDEN. For sheer olfactory ecstasy, visit the **Botanischer Garten's** world-famous cactus and orchid collections. The hill where the garden is located was saved from housing developments by grace of the fact that it is hollow—it is the site of an exploded ammunitions plant from WWII. *(Rosegerstr. 20. Tel. 707 01 880. Open daily May-Aug. 7:30am-7:30pm; Sept. and Apr. 8am-7pm; Oct. and Mar. 8am-6pm; Nov.-Feb. 8am-5pm. 10AS, under 18 free.)*

URFAHR AND PÖSTLINGBERG. Cross Nibelungenbrücke to reach the left bank of the Danube. This area, known as **Urfahr,** was a separate city until Linz swallowed it up in the early decades of the 20th century. It boasts some of the oldest buildings in the city and a captivating view of Linz from the apex of the **Pöstlingberg** (537m). To reach the summit, take tram #3 to "Bergbahnhof Urfahr," then either hike 0.5km up Hagenstr. (off Rudolphstr., which is off Hauptstr. near the bridge) or hop aboard the **Pöstlingbergbahn,** a trolley car that ascends the summit in a scenic 20 minutes. *(Tel. 780 17 545. Every 20min. M-Sa 5:20am-8pm, Su 11:40am-8pm. 25AS, round-trip 40AS, children half-price.)* The twin-towered **Pöstlingbergkirche,** symbol the city, stands guard from the crest of the hill. Indulge any nascent Romanticism by taking the **Grottenbahn** into the fairy-tale caves of Pöstlingberg. *(Open May-Sept. daily 10am-6pm; Apr. and Oct.-Nov. daily 10am-5pm. 50AS, under 15 25AS.)*

🎵 NIGHTLIFE AND FESTIVALS

Linzer nightlife is sleepy but does have a pulse, which beats at (yet another) **Bermuda Dreieck** (Bermuda Triangle), behind the west side of Hauptpl. (head down Hofg. or just follow the crowds of decked-out pub crawlers). Frequented by *Linzers* as well as tourists, this area has the highest bar/nightclub-to-square-meter ratio in the city. In Hauptpl. itself, try **Alte Welt Weinkeller,** Hauptpl. 4 (open M-Sa 5pm-2am; food served 6-11pm), an arcaded, Renaissance-era "wine and culture cellar" where you can soak up wine and spirits. **17er Keller,** Hauptpl. 17 (duck through the archway and enter the steel door on your right), will serve you an apple-juice-and-cinnamon tequila while you listen to a mix of jazz, funk, blues, and rock (open M-Sa 7pm-1am, Su 7pm-1am). **Coffee Corner Café,** Bethlehemstr. 30 (tel. 77 08 62), draws a sophisticated, mainly gay and lesbian crowd (open M-Sa 7pm to whenever people go home). Linzers also flock to the other side of the Danube for after-hours entertainment. **Cafe Ex-Blatt,** Waltherstr. 15 (tel. 77 93 19), covered in old Austrian advertisements and movie posters, attracts a hip retro crowd (open M-F 10pm-2am, Sa-Su 6pm-1am). Grab a bench at **Fischerhäusl,** Flußg. 3 (tel. 71 01 23), the beer garden on the left as you cross the bridge (open M-F 11am-2pm and

5pm-midnight, Sa-Su 5pm-midnight). Many busy night spots line Landstr.—look between shops for entrances to courtyard *Biergartens*. For dancing, try **My Way,** Goethestr. 51 (tel. 65 27 60; open M-Sa 7pm-2am, Su 7pm-midnight).

From mid-September to mid-October, the month-long **Brucknerfest** brings a rush of concerts paying homage to native son Anton Bruckner at the **Brucknerhaus** concert hall, an acoustically perfect venue (220-1100AS, standing room 40-50AS). For tickets, contact *Brucknerhauskasse*, Untere Donaulände 7, A-4010 Linz (tel. 77 52 30; fax 761 22 01; email kassaşliva.co.at; www.brucknerhaus.linz.at). The opening concerts (the end of the 2nd week in Sept.), billed as *Klangwolken* (sound-clouds), include spectacular outdoor lasers, a children's show, and a classical evening with Bruckner's Seventh Symphony broadcast live into the surrounding Donaupark to 50,000 fans. During the 3rd weekend of July, the city hosts **Pflaster-pektakel,** a free, 3-day, international street performers' festival. Every few steps down Landstr. and Hauptpl., different performers from as far away as New Zealand perform Houdini acts, fire-eating, outdoor theater, bongo concerts, punk rock, and other such feats before the young, funky, social crowd.

DAYTRIPS FROM LINZ

NEAR LINZ: MAUTHAUSEN

To reach the camp from Linz, take a train to Mauthausen (transfer at St. Valentin). A special Oberösterreichischer Verkehrsverbund day pass (102AS) covers the round-trip train ticket from Linz plus all city transportation in Linz and Mauthausen. Beware—the Mauthausen train station is 6km away from the camp, and a bus stops 2km from the camp only twice a day during the week and not at all on weekends. A better option is to store your pack (30AS) at the Mauthausen train station (tel. (67238) 22 07) and rent a bicycle (70AS with train ticket). You'll pass pastures, fields of hay, and orchards before reaching the bleak walls of the camp. Pick up a map from the train station. By car, exit Autobahn A1 (Vienna-Linz) at Enns.

About half an hour down the Danube from Linz, the remains of a Nazi *Konzentrationslager* (abbreviated KZ; concentration camp) keep their terrible vigil. Unlike other camps in south Germany and Austria, Mauthausen remains intact. Built by Dachau prisoners in 1938, Mauthausen was the central camp for all of Austria and administered 49 subcamps throughout the country. More than 200,000 prisoners passed through Mauthausen, mainly Russian and Polish POWs, along with Austrian homosexuals and political criminals, Italian POWs, Hungarian and Dutch Jews, Gypsies, and Communists. Mauthausen was infamous for its **Todesstiege** (Staircase of Death), which led to the stone quarry where inmates were forced to work until exhaustion. The steep, even steps currently in place were added for tourists' safety—when the inmates worked here, there was nothing but a stony drop dotted with boulders and jagged rocks. As the prisoners climbed up or down the path, the guards often shoved the last in line so that the entire group fell down the slope, along with the stones they were carrying on their shoulders. The inner part of the camp is now a museum (tel. (07238) 2269). The barracks, roll-call grounds, cremation ovens, and torture rooms are also accessible. A free brochure or audio-tape tour (in English) walks you though the central part of the camp. There is also an exhibit on the history of the camp and video documentaries in various languages. (Open Apr.-Sept. 8am-6pm; Oct. to mid-Dec. and Feb.-Mar. 8am-4pm. Last entrance 1hr. before closing. 25AS, students and seniors 10AS.)

NEAR LINZ: ST. FLORIAN'S ABBEY

To reach the abbey from Linz, take the bus (dir.: St. Florian Stift) to "Kotzmannstr." (30min., 24AS) in downtown St. Florian or "Lagerhaus." Both are a 15min. walk from the abbey.

The abbey of St. Florian, 17km from Linz, is Austria's oldest Augustinian monastery. According to legend, the martyr Florian was bound to a millstone and thrown in the Enns river. Although Florian perished, his stone miraculously floated (ouch—the irony) and serves as the abbey's cornerstone. The complex owes much of its fame to composer Anton Bruckner, who began his career here first as choir-boy, then as teacher, and finally as a virtuoso organist and composer. His body is interred beneath the organ, allowing him to vibrate in perpetuity to the sound of his dearly-beloved pipes. The abbey contains the **Altdorfer Gallery,** filled with altar-pieces by 15th-century artist Albrecht Altdorfer of Regensburg, an Old Master of the Danube school. The 14 **Kaiserzimmer** (imperial rooms), built in case of an impe-rial visit, virtually rumble with Baroque splendor. Inside the spectacular, recently renovated church (the only part of the abbey accessible without a tour) sits the enormous aforementioned **Bruckner Organ.** Concerts on the powerful instrument are held from May to October Sunday to Friday at 2:30pm (20min., 30AS, students 25AS). Tours of the abbey minus the *Kaiserzimmer* leave daily. (Tel. (07224) 89 02 10. Abbey open Apr.-Oct. 60AS, students 55AS, children 20AS. Tours 10, 11am, 2, 3, and 4pm.) The **tourist office,** Marktpl. 3 (tel./fax (07224) 56 90), has info about the abbey and accommodations (open M-F 9am-1pm).

NEAR LINZ: KREMSMÜNSTER

Trains go to Kremsmünster from Linz (45min., every hr. until 8:15pm, 72AS). From the sta-tion, follow Bahnhofstr. as it curves left, then right, then left again, and continue on to Marktpl. The path to the abbey starts at the tourist office, Rathauspl. 1 (tel. (07583) 72 12; open Tu-F 9am-noon and 3-6pm).

Fabulous **Kremsmünster Abbey,** 32km south of Linz, belongs to Austria's oldest order and dates from AD 777 (an auspicious year for an abbey). Some 75 monks still call the abbey home. The abbey owns most of the land in the area, including 3800 hectares of woods and a wine-producing vineyard. Their Borgesian **library,** which has 2 rows of books on every shelf and hidden doors in the bookcases, is Austria's third largest, full of medieval tomes. Visitors are not allowed to handle the books, but guides will take out any volume and page through it for you on request. The **Kaisersaal,** built to receive imperial visitors, is a rich Baroque gallery with marble columns and cartoonish ceiling frescoes that make the ceilings seem much higher than they actually are. The abbey's **Kunstsammlung** (art collection) tour covers the library, the *Kaisersaal,* several art galleries, and the **Schatzkam-mer** (treasury), which shelters a beautifully engraved golden chalice dating from the time of Charlemagne. The monks' collection of minerals and exotic animal specimens is on display in the 7-story **Sternwarte.** Also open to visitors is the **Fisch-kalter,** 5 fantastic fish fens for feeding fasting friars' friends fresh flounder. Actu-ally, the Fischkalter is a series of arcaded pools set with pagan and pastoral statues (including Falstaff look-alikes) spouting water. Wooden stag heads with real antlers adorn the room—see if you can find the two with radishes in their mouths. (Tel. (07583) 527 52 16. Open 9am-noon and 1-6pm. Central chapel free. Fischkalter 10AS—entrance through the ticket office. 1-hour Kunstsammlung tours Apr.-Oct. at 10, 11am, 2, 3, and 4pm; Nov.-Mar. at 11am and 2pm. 1hr. 55AS, students 30AS. Sternwarte tour May-Oct. 10am, 2, and 4pm. 60AS, students 30AS. Both 1½hr. tours include the Fischkalter. For the student rate, you have to buy tickets to both tours.)

The town of Kremsmünster itself is filled with twisty medieval streets and daunting, steep stairway paths overgrown with moss and wildflowers. Kremsmün-ster also claims to be the home of **Europe's first high-rise,** constructed in 1748-1758

BAAAHBY, IT'S COLD OUTSIDE! If you're planning a trip to Upper Austria in late spring or early summer, think about some warm clothes. The region receives two blasts of unseasonably cold weather in mid-May and mid-June. Three saints whose holy days fall during the first cold front are known as the *Eisheili-gen,* or "ice-saints." They are Pankratius (May 12th), Bonifatius (May 14th), and Sophie (May 15th). A little later, the *Schaffskälte* ("sheep's cold") hits, shortly after the poor animals have been taken up the mountain to higher ground. Only after the June chill ends is the wool shaved off their frisky pink bodies.

as a research center for the natural sciences. You'll find fresh fruit at the **open-air market** in Marktpl. (F 1-6pm). **Café Schlair** (tel. (07583) 7772), on Hauptstr. diagonally opposite from the tourist office, serves pastries and fresh fruit drinks for 30-50AS (open M-Tu and Th 8am-7pm, W 8am-noon, F 8am-8pm, Sa-Su 8am-6:30pm). If you decide to stay the night, try the **Bauernhof Gossenhub,** Schürzendorf 1 (tel. (07583) 7752), a lovely farmhouse with clean, simple rooms for 190AS (50AS surcharge for stays of less than 3 days). To get there, climb Gosenhuberstr. from the abbey until the cow pasture, then turn left at the "Föhrenleiten" sign.

NEAR LINZ: STEYR

Trains connect Steyr to Linz (45min., every hr. until 9:30pm, 90AS). To reach the city center from the station, exit the station, turn right and then left on Bahnhofstr. After crossing the river, turn left immediately down Engeg., which leads to Stadtpl.

Steyr is famous as a jewel of medieval city planning. Much of the city looks as it has for the past 500 years, with winding, narrow cobbled alleyways, carved arches, and high stone walls. Two mountain rivers, the **Steyr** and the **Enns,** intersect in the middle of the town, dicing Steyr into 3 parts. As in Linz, Steyr's comely surface hides the city's industrial identity. The city is well known for its iron trade and holds a unique position in the annals of modern technology—in 1884, Steyr was the first town in Europe to use electric street lighting. Who would have guessed?

The **Stadtplatz,** packed with 15th-century buildings, is the *Altstadt*'s focal point. The 16th-century **Leopoldibrunnen** (Leopold fountain) vies with the Rococo *Rathaus* across the square for the title of ornamental heavyweight champion. Gotthard Hayberger, Steyr's famous mayor, architect, and Renaissance man-about-town, designed the town hall. The former **Dominican Church** *(Marienkirche)*, also crammed onto Stadtpl., was born a Gothic building but grew a Baroque facade in the early 17th century. Most of Steyr's beautiful residences have been transformed into banks or shops with modern interiors hidden behind ornate facades. The major exception is the **Innerberger Stadel.** Now the local **Heimatmuseum,** it contains a plethora of puppets, an extensive stuffed bird collection, and the three Cs of medieval weaponry: crossbows, cannons, and cutlery. (Grünmarkt 26. Tel. 53248. Open Apr.-Oct. Tu-Su 10am-4pm. Free.) Berggasse, one of the numerous narrow lanes typical of Steyr, leads from Stadtpl. up to the pink **Lamberg Schloß,** where the **Schloß Galerie** showcases temporary exhibits (tel. 53222; open Tu-Su 10am-noon and 2-5pm; 25AS, students and children free). If you're not in the museum mood, wander in the palace's green courtyards.

The **tourist office,** Stadtpl. 27 (tel. 532 29; fax 532 29 15; email steyr-info@ris.at; www.upper.austria.org/regionen/steyr), in the *Rathaus,* offers **guided tours** (May-Oct. Sa 2pm) and **headset tours.** Both are 45AS. (Open Jan.-Nov. M-F 8:30am-6pm, Sa 9am-5pm, Su 10am-4pm; Dec. M-F 8:30am-6pm, Sa 9am-4pm, Su 10am-3pm.) Steyr hosts a **Musik Festival** from mid-August to mid-September featuring international classical, jazz, and folk. Contact the tourist office for more information.

THE MÜHLVIERTEL

Stretching north and west from Linz, the Mühlviertel's shaded woodland paths and pastures populated only by the occasional cow are becoming an increasingly popular hiking area for Austrians. Once upon a time, this region was the stomping grounds of pagan Celts. When the Christians stormed in during the Middle Ages, they constructed churches out of the supposedly Celt-proof local granite. This same granite filters the famed mineral-rich waters of the region, considered curative in homeopathic circles.

Although Mühlviertel is part of industrial Upper Austria, it's better known for its rich arts-and-crafts traditions than industrial sprawl. Along the old **Mühlviertel Weberstraße** (Weaver's Road), analogous on a country-lane scale to the Middle Eastern Silk Road, various textile-oriented towns display their unique methods of linen preparation. Other vacation trails include the **Gotischestraße,** which winds past multitudes of High Gothic architectural wonders, and the **Museumstraße,** which boasts more **Freilichtmuseen** (open-air museums) than you can shake a loom at. These museum villages typically recreate the 15th- and 16th-century peasant lifestyle of a functional hamlet. Poppies are another of the Mühlviertel's big selling points, with products ranging from poppy seed oil and lubricants to mouth-watering poppy seed strudels and poppy-seed-and-honey-filled tarts. Iron from Steiermark (Styria) once flowed through the Mühlviertel on its way to Bohemia along the **Pferdeeisenbahn,** an ancient trade route once traversed by horse-drawn caravans, now an excellent easy hike. Throughout this pastoral countryside, *Bauernhöfe* (farm houses) open their doors to world-weary travelers. For nifty tourist brochures about trails and *Bauernhöfe,* contact the **Mühlviertel Tourist Office,** Blütenstr. 8, A-4040 Linz, Postfach 57 (tel. (0732) 23 50 20 or 23 81 55).

FREISTADT

Freistadt, the largest town in the Mühlviertel, is a charming, compact village at the juncture of the **Jaunitz** and **Feldiast** rivers. Due to its strategic location on the *Pferdeeisenbahn* route that connected the Babenberg and Habsburg lands, Freistadt was a stronghold of the medieval salt and iron trade. In 1985, Freistadt received the International Europa Nostra Prize for the finest restoration of a medieval *Altstadt.* Freistadt's pride and joy is the **Freistädter Brauerei,** a community-owned brewery that is still in operation but, unfortunately, no longer open to the public.

⚑ ORIENTATION AND PRACTICAL INFORMATION. Freistadt is easily accessible from Linz. The most convenient option is the **post bus,** which leaves from Linz's main train station every 2 hours (6am-8pm, 78AS) and arrives at **Böhmertor** in Freistadt, just outside the old city walls, a 2-minute walk to Hauptpl. **Trains** also run from Linz (78AS), but they arrive at the *Hauptbahnhof,* 3km outside of town. The tiny **tourist office,** Hauptpl. 14 (tel./fax 757 00), has a free reservations service and provides info about the surrounding Mühlviertel villages (open May-Sept. M-F 9am-7pm, Sa 9am-12pm; Oct.-Apr. M-F 9am-5pm). The **post office,** Promenade 11 at St. Peterstr., **exchanges** only hard cash (open M-F 8am-noon and 2-5:30pm, Sa 8-10:30am). The **postal code** is A-4240.

PHONE CODE	The **city code** for Freistadt is 07942.

⚑⛯ ACCOMMODATIONS AND FOOD. Freistadt has a few reasonably priced accommodations. To get to the **Jugendherberge (HI),** Schlosshof 3 (tel. 743 65), from the tourist office, walk around the corner to the red building next to Café Lubinger. The hostel is fairly empty and the owner doesn't have reception hours, so you should call to let them know you're coming. Hand-painted stripes and silly cartoons decorate the walls, and the rooms are very comfortable and clean. The accommodating proprietress, Margarete Howel, will wait from 6 to 8pm to give you a key; if no one is there or you don't arrive in time, call her at home at tel. 3268. (Dorms 70AS, non-members 90AS. Hall showers and toilets. Breakfast 30AS. Sheets 30AS. **Kitchen** facilities in the youth center below.) For a list of pensions and **private rooms,** contact the tourist office.

There are a variety of cheap eats at cozy *Gästehäuser.* Enjoy a *tête-à-tête* at **Café Vis à Vis,** Salzg. 13 (tel. 74293). It offers the local *Mühlviertel Bauernsalat mit Suppe* (farmer's salad with soup; 60AS), *Freistädter* beer in a garden crowded with young people, and good pizzas (small 63AS, large 90AS; open M-F 9:30am-2am, Sa 5pm-1am). There's also plenty to eat around the Hauptpl. The best ice cream in all of Mühlviertel awaits at **Café Lubiner,** Hauptpl. 10 (soft-serve 12AS, scoops of the hard stuff 7AS each). Pastries (25AS) and a great breakfast selection round out the menu. (Open Su-M and W-F 8am-7pm, Sa 8am-6pm.) The most convenient grocery store is **Uni Markt,** Pragerstr. 2, at Froschau behind the Böhmertor side of the *Innere Stadt.* The market is a one-stop bargain shop for 6 varieties of *Freistädter* beer. (Open M-F 8am-7pm, Sa 7:30am-12:30pm.)

🎫 ⚡ **SIGHTS AND OUTDOORS ACTIVITIES.** Visitors can wander around Freistadt's well-preserved inner and outer wall fortifications, scan the horizon from its watch tower, feast inside its castle, and swim in the surrounding moat. The tower of Freistadt's remarkable 14th-century castle, the **Bergfried** (50m from the hostel), houses the **Mühlviertler Heimathaus,** a regional museum which displays traditional tools, clothing, and period pieces (tel. 72274; admission with tour only May-Oct. Tu-Sa 10am and 2pm, Su 10am; Nov.-Apr. Tu-F 2pm; 10AS).

Numerous **hiking trails** branch out to amazing Mühlviertel destinations; consider hiking out of town and catching a bus back. Freistadt lies on the Mühlviertel **Museumstraße,** a path linking many of the region's museums, and on the **Pferdeeisenbahn Wanderweg,** a 237km hiking trail along the former medieval trade route. A mildly strenuous 1-hour hike zigzags up Kreuzweg to **St. Peter's Church.** A large map on the Promenade illustrates other local hiking paths. Get hiking maps (10-35AS), free bus schedules, and biking maps (25AS) at the tourist office.

Each July and August, Freistadt holds a 2-month festival of food and international music, the **Wirthausmusi,** with daily events scattered throughout town. Multicultural meets medieval—or just another excuse to drink *Freistädter* beer?

NEAR FREISTADT: ČESKÝ KRUMLOV, CZECH REPUBLIC

Located just 20km north of the Austrian border and 16km southwest of České Budějovice, Česky Krumlov is acessible on public transportation by train from Freistadt to České Budějovice, then by bus from there (45min.; M-F 22 per day, Sa 8 per day, Su 12 per day; 22Kč). Trains from České Budějovice take longer than buses (1hr., 9 per day, 23Kč). The train station in Česky Krumlov is 2km outside of town, but a local bus connects the train station and the town center (5Kč).

The worst part about Česky Krumlov is leaving. Maybe it's the medieval cobblestone streets that poke about stone courtyards and Renaissance buildings, or maybe it's the Vltava, the winding river that darts in and around the town center and on into the South Bohemian countryside, or maybe it's the 13th-century castle that hovers over it all. Whatever it is, this UNESCO-protected town lures visitors in and doesn't let them go. Weeks could (and should) be spent hiking through the surrounding hills, kayaking down the Vltava, horse-back riding through the castle gardens, and exploring the meandering streets of the town. Come for a day, but you may be destined to stay for 40.

🏛 **ORIENTATION AND PRACTICAL INFORMATION.** If you get off at the small "Špičák" bus stop on the northern outskirts of town, it's an easy march downhill to the medieval center and the tourist office. From "Špičák," pass through **Budějovice gate** and follow **Latrán** past the castle and over the Vltava. The street becomes Radniční as it enters Staré Město and leads into the main **nám. Svornosti.** The **main bus terminal,** however, Kaplická 439 (tel. (0337) 3414), lies to the southeast. To get to nám. Svornosti from here, head to the upper street where stops #20-25 are located. With the station at your back, turn right and follow the small dirt path that veers to the left and heads uphill. At the path's intersection with Kaplická, turn right. At the light, cross the highway and head straight onto Horní, which brings you right into the square. The **tourist office,** nám. Svornosti 1 (tel. (0337) 71 11 83), in the town hall, books pensions (starting at 550Kč) and private rooms, which can be a bit cheaper (doubles 800Kč), and sells maps for planning bicycling trips (25-59Kč; open daily 9am-6pm). You can cash in your *Schillinge* at **Moravia Bank,** Soukenická 34 (tel. 71 13 77), or your traveler's checks for a 2% commission (min. 30Kč; open M-F 8am-4pm). A **24-hour ATM** is available on the left side of Horní just before it merges into nám. Svornosti.

📍 **ACCOMMODATIONS.** If you want to stick around town, Krumlov's many stellar hostels, however, undoubtedly offer the best beds in town. For **U vodníka,** Po vodě 55 (tel. 71 19 35; email vodnik@ck.bohem-net.cz), follow the directions from the main bus station, turn left onto Rooseveltova after the traffic light (the last street before the bridge), and follow the signs. This 13th-century hostel has a name that translates roughly to "the place of the river troll," but it is more like the place of the river god. American ex-pats Carolyn, Cal, and baby Aidan have lovingly turned their home into one of the best hostels in Europe. There's a forsythia garden out back where you can grill sausages on a spit or sit in a hand-carved stone seat overlooking the river. You can even borrow an innertube (free) to cruise down the Vltava. Best of all, beds are only 200Kč in the dorm and 250Kč in the two doubles. The staff will also do your laundry (100Kč for 5kg), rent you a mountain bike (200Kč per day), lend you books from their fine library, and arrange boat rentals. Another attractive option is **Krumlov House**, Rooseveltova 68 (same tel. as U vodníka), on your right before the highway with beautiful dragon doors. Do not think that, because it is listed second, Krumlov House is any less enticing than its sister hostel; both are unrankably divine. The same rates and services apply here as at U vodníka, but Krumlov House hosts a livelier crowd. Sleep in hand-carved birch-tree bunks, socialize with Australians in a huge kitchen (stereos and guitars included), and drink into the wee hours of the morning.

☐ FOOD. All of the hostels in Krumlov have kitchens, so get ready to cook. The most central supermarket in town is **SPAR** at Linecká 49 (open M-Sa 7am-6pm, Su 9am-6pm). For fresh fruits and veggies, head to the **Cerstvé Ovoce Zelenina**, Latrán 45; go through the hallway and the shop will be on your left. One great restaurant is **Na louži**, Kájovská 66 (tel. 71 12 80), where you'll find sizeable portions of great Czech cooking. Space is scarce, so be prepared to wait; it's well worth it. Huge chicken platters 112Kč, fried cheese dishes 69Kč. Skewered meat, the house specialty (108-130Kč), goes down well with 0.5L of beer (20Kč). (Open daily 10am-10pm.) For a more fiery experience, try **Cikánská jízba** (Gypsy Bar), Dlouhá 31 (tel. 55 85). Follow Radniční out of the main square and turn left down Dlouhá. Fire it up with "Devil's Pork" (*D'abelská arančka;* 80Kč) or spicy goulash (53Kč). Don't miss the *halušky,* a gnocchi-like pasta. (Open M-Th 2-11pm, F-Sa 3-11pm.)

☐☐ SIGHTS AND OUTDOOR ACTIVITIES. Perversely, pollution has been a boon to Český Krumlov. In the early 20th century, an upstream paper mill putrefied the river, and most citizens moved to the town's outskirts. Thanks to such benign neglect, the medieval inner city escaped "development." Originally a 13th-century fortress, the **castle** fell into the hands of wealthy families who had nothing better to do than fill it with fancy stuff. The main entrance to the castle is on Latrán. Take Radniční out of the town center, cross the river, and go up the stairs on your left. The castle gate is at the top of the stairs. The **stone courtyards** are open to the public for free. Don't miss the grizzly bears lurking in the moat (the skins of their forefathers are displayed in the castle's exquisite interior). Two tours cover the castle—the first visits the older wing, taking in the **Chapel of St. George,** passing through the Baroque Schwarzenberg chambers, and emerging in the **ballroom,** adorned by frescoes of characters from Dante's *Commedia Dell'Arte.* The second tour explores the older, Renaissance-style rooms before moving into the 19th-century areas of the castle and ending with the splendid Baroque **theater.** Czech tours are only 50Kč, but to understand anything more than "Blah, blah, Schwarzenberg, blah," take the hour-long **English tour.** (Open June-Aug. Tu-Su 9am-noon and 1-5pm; May and Sept. Tu-Su 9am-noon and 1-4pm; Apr. and Oct. Tu-Su 9am-noon and 1-3pm. Enter ticket office through the third stone courtyard. 110Kč, students 55Kč.) You can also visit the castle **tower** and ascend 162 steps for a fine view of the town. (Open May-Sept. daily 9am-6pm, last entrance 5:35pm; Oct. and Apr. daily 9am-5pm, last entrance 4:35pm. 25Kč, students 15Kč.) Wander the **galleries of the crypt** where local artists' sculptures and ceramics are displayed (open May-Oct. Tu-Su 10am-5pm; 30Kč, students 20Kč). Or, stroll in the castle **gardens,** which house a riding school and a summer palace (open May-Sept. daily 8am-7pm; Apr. and Oct. daily 8am-5pm).

The Austrian painter Egon Schiele (1890-1918) found Český Krumlov so enchanting that he decided to set up shop here in 1911. Sadly, the citizens ran him out after he started painting burghers' daughters in the nude. Decades later, the citizens realized how silly they'd been and founded the **Egon Schiele International Cultural Center,** Široká 70-72 (tel. 4232; fax 2820), with a wide variety of browsing material. Schiele's works, including his infamous nudes, share wall space with paintings by other 20th-century Central European artists, including Haher Fronius's excellent Kafka illustrations. The steep admission is well worth it. (Open daily 10am-6pm. 120Kč, students 80Kč.) The **city museum,** Horní 152 (tel. 71 16 74), covers Krumlov's history with bizarre folk instruments, bone sculptures, and log barges that once plied the river (open May-Sept. daily 10am-12:30pm and 1-5pm; Oct.-Apr. Tu-F 9am-noon and 1-5pm, Sa-Su 1-5pm; 30Kč, students 5Kč).

Hike into the hills for a pleasant afternoon of **horseback riding** at **Jezdecký klub Slupenec,** Slupenec 1 (tel. 71 10 53). Rides take you through trails high above Český Krumlov. From the town center, take Horní to its intersection with the highway. At the second light, turn left onto Křížová and follow the red trail to Slupenec. The horses are hungover after the weekend, so there are no rides on Mondays. (Open Tu-Sa 9am-noon and 1:30-5:30pm. 220Kč per hr. Call ahead.) Summer in Krumlov gets hot; if you're not up for a swim in the Vltava, check out the town's **indoor/outdoor pool and steambaths.** For only 18Kč per hour you can plunge into icy-cold waters with the Krumlov moms and sweat off your *pivos* in a steamy sauna. From the town square, take Radniční to Latrán. Walk past the castle and the post office, take a left on the highway *Chvalšinská,* then a right on Fialková. The pool is 2-minutes up on the left. (Pool open Tu-Th 2:30-4pm and 7-10pm, F 1:30-4:30pm and 6-9pm, Sa 1-10pm, Su 1-9pm. Steambaths open W and F 7-9pm, Sa 6-9pm. 20Kč lock deposit.) To fully enjoy the waters of the Vltava, ask at your hostel about innertubes and spend a day lazing down the river. Jump out next to **Pepo's Pub** (or you'll float to Budějovice) and repeat the circuit. You can also traipse the river on a canoe or kayak, which can be rented from **Maleček Boat Rental,** Rooseveltova 28 (tel./fax 71 25 08; 2-person canoe and round-trip transport 600Kč).

🎭 **ENTERTAINMENT.** The castle's **revolving theater** (Jihočeské divadlo) hosts productions of opera, Shakespeare, and classic comedies. Performances are in Czech, but watching the set revolve around the audience more than makes up for it (open June-Sept.; tickets 60Kč; check at the infocentrum for current showings and to purchase tickets). If you'd rather see something in English, **cinemas** abound in Český Krumlov, though most films usually have Czech subtitles. **Kino J&K,** Highway 159 next to the Špičák bus stop, is open year-round and shows all of the latest Hollywood blockbusters (M, W, and F 6:30pm; Sa 6pm; town film club Th 7pm. Tickets 30-40Kč). Or ask your hostel owner about the town's **open-air cinema** in the summer—it's like a drive-in, but without the cars. Check at the infocentrum for showings at both cinemas. The **Five-petal Rose Festival,** Krumlov's hip medieval gig the third weekend of June, is a great excuse to wear tights and joust with the locals. Krumlov also hosts 2 world-class music festivals—the **Early Music Festival** (the second week of July) with live appearances by basso di Gamba and other cool old instruments, and the **International Music Fest** (mid-August), which attracts hordes of major Czech acts.

THE SALZKAMMERGUT

Each year in early summer, tourists in the know, bands of Austrian school children, and tour groups of elderly Europeans come to the smooth lakes and furrowed mountains of the Salzkammergut. The wave of visitors breaks at the locally-flavored resort towns that speckle the countryside, beneath rolling hills and dark, furry evergreens. The region takes its name from the salt mines that, in their glory days, underwrote Salzburg's architectural treasures. Salzkammergut translates literally as "the property of the Imperial Salt Chamber," a reference to the times when salt was as valuable as gold, hence, of primary interest to the emperor. Today, the white gold of the Salzkammergut is no longer salt, but pure sunshine on sparkling water in summer and tons of fresh snow in winter.

UPPER AUSTRIA

⊡ GETTING AROUND THE SALZKAMMERGUT. The Salzkammergut is both peacefully remote and easily navigable, with 2000km of footpaths, 12 cable cars and chairlifts, and dozens of hostels to welcome visitors year-round. Within the region, there is a dense network of **buses** that are the most efficient and reliable method of travel into and through the lake region, since the mountainous area is barren of rail tracks. (Dial 167 from Salzburg for complete schedule information.) Traveling by **car** is also convenient in the Salzkammergut, thanks to well-paved roads and strategically located parking lots. **Hitchers** from Salzburg allegedly take bus #29 to Gnigl and come into the Salzkammergut at Bad Ischl. The lake district is one of the rare, refreshing Austrian regions in which hitchhikers can make good time. Two-wheeled transport is much more entertaining, but only with a good **bike**—some mountain passes top 1000m. Pedaling the narrow, winding roads on the lake banks is far less strenuous and equally scenic. Reasonably priced **ferries** (round-trips 15-85AS) service each of the larger lakes (railpass discounts on the **Wolfgangsee, Attersee,** and **Traunsee** lines).

⌐ ACCOMMODATIONS. Hostels are common throughout the area, but you can often find far superior rooms in private homes and *Pensionen* at just-above-hostel prices. *"Zimmer Frei"* signs peek out from virtually every house. **Campgrounds** dot the region, but many are trailer-oriented. Away from large towns, many travelers camp discreetly almost anywhere, generally without trouble. Hikers can capitalize on dozens of **cable cars** in the area to gain altitude before setting out on their own, and almost every community has a local trail map available. At higher elevations there are **alpine huts.** These huts are on trails for experienced hikers and are difficult to reach. Hiking, at all levels, is plentiful in this lush area, and is some of the best around because of the natural beauty of the region. Ask at any tourist office for hiking maps, or contact the **Österreichischer Alpenverein** (Austrian Alpine Club; tel. 512 594 47), for info and rental. Their central office is in Innsbruck, but locally experienced volunteers staff regional branches.

⚐ REGIONAL FESTIVALS. Every February brings **Carnival,** called *Fastnacht* in Western Austria and *Fasching* everywhere else. Carnival commences with the January ball season. In rural areas, traditional processions of masked figures are the season headliners, featuring *Schiache* (ugly evil masks). At the **Ausseer Fasching,** the carnival at Bad Aussee, *Trommelweiber* (men impersonating women in white nighties and night-caps while beating drums) march through town. The Carnival near *Ebensee* culminates in the **Fetzenfasching** (carnival of rags): the people sing in falsetto, imitate spooky voices, and wave old umbrellas.

On January 5, the **Glöcklerlaufen** (running of the figures with special caps) takes place after dark in the Salzkammergut. These *Glöckler* derive their name from the custom of knocking at the door (*glocken* means "to knock") and not from the bells attached to their belts (*Glocke* means "bell"). These caps, reminiscent of stained-glass windows, have an electric light inside; several are on display at the **Monats-Schlößchen** at Hellbrunn (just outside Salzburg). In return for their New Year's wish, runners are rewarded with a special hole-less doughnut, the *Glöcklerkrapfen.* Although the satisfaction of legions of stained-glass-hat fetishists seems enough, the masked figures also get money and refreshments from the citizenry, which indicates a little about their origin—a long, long time ago, seasonal workers needed such handouts to survive. On the Sunday after November 25, about 30 bird-catcher clubs in the Salzkammergut region organize a **bird exhibition.** The birds squawk away the winter in people's living rooms and are then released. A **Christmas passion play** is performed every fourth year (next in 2002) at Bad Ischl. Introduced a few years ago to replace the town specific guest cards, the **Salzkammergut Card** (65AS; available at local tourist offices) gives 25% discounts on most local sites and attractions.

GMUNDEN

Gmunden, a pretty resort town on the **Traunsee,** has an illustrious guest-book and plenty of natural attractions. It is the birthplace of Austrian playwrite Thomas Bernhard and was the favorite watering-hole of many *Biedermeier* artists, as well as for certain Russian and German noblemen. The town is renowned for its ceramics, as well as for its sunny lakeside beaches and stately mountains.

🛈 **ORIENTATION AND PRACTICAL INFORMATION. Trains** run frequently to Gmunden from **Salzburg** (1½hr., every hr., 154AS) and **Linz** (45min., every hr., 114AS), both via **Attnang-Puchheim. Buses** connect Gmunden to the rest of the region, including **Grünau.** To reach the town center from the station, either turn left and follow Bahnhofstr. down the hill, or else hop on the tram in front of the station (16AS, day pass 22AS). From the tram's Franz-Josef Platz terminal, continue one block and turn left to reach the **tourist office,** Am Graben 2 (tel. 64305), which provides a list of *Privatzimmern* (210-300AS) and will call to find out if rooms are available (open Oct.-Apr. M-F 8am-noon and 2-6pm; May-June, Sept. M-F 8am-6pm, Sa 9am-noon; July-Aug M-F 8am-6pm, Sa-Su 9am-1pm and 5-7pm). A free accommodation phone is outside the office. Ebensee, 15km from Gmunden, has a **youth hostel** (tel. (06133) 6698). **Cruises** (tel. 65215) around the Traunsee on an old paddle steamer leave from the dock near Rathauspl. every 1½ hours. (daily May-Oct.; 20-85AS). The **postal code** is A-4810.

PHONE CODE	The **city code** for Gmunden is 07612.

📷 🏛 **SIGHTS AND MUSEUMS.** You can follow the lakeside, tree-lined Esplanade from the town center to the Habsburg **Villa Toscana,** where the St. Germain peace treaty was ratified in 1920, and to **Schloß Ort,** a picturesque Habsburger island castle that is now full of wine cellars. (Tel. 77815. Tours Th and Su 2:30pm; 40AS.) Imperial cousin Johannes Nepomuk Salvator bought the castle, married an actress, changed his name to Johannes Ort, then vanished in the Falklands.

Gmunden has been a ceramic producing town since the 15th century, as the **Standesamt** ceramics museum, further down the Esplanade, demonstrates (tel. 77103; open M-F 8am-noon, M and Th also 1-4pm, Sa 8-11am). Enjoy the ceramic chimes on the Renaissance town hall, Austria's only ceramic fountain in Rinnholzpl., and the showroom of **Gmunder Keramik,** on Keramikstr. off Bahnhofstr. (open M-F 9am-6pm, Sa 9am-1pm; call 786 to arrange a tour). The most diverse display of ceramics can be seen at the **Klo und So Museum für Historische Sanitärobjekte,** a collection of 19th- and 20th-century toilets. The eccentric exhibit includes the early 19th-century chameleon chair with a removable seat, *Biedermeier* wooden boxes, gilded *Jugendstil* toilets adorned with floral and faunal engravings, a *fin de siècle* circular bench draped in red robes and tassels, international specimens including short, blue-tiled Japanese urinals, a selection of potties, and ceramic flushers galore. The *pièce de résistance* is the Habsburg room where you can see Franz-Josef's bedroom john and Sisi's ornate bidet. There isn't info about the toilets in English, so you are left wondering how one used the pot resting on the elaborate 1m metal structure, or the box covered in knives. (Pepöckhaus, Traung. 4. Tel. 79 42 94. Open May-Oct. Tu-Sa 10am-noon and 2-5pm, Su 10am-noon. 20AS.) Admission to the Klo and So also includes entrance to the **Volkskunde-Ausstellung,** an exhibit of regional folklore in the same building (open May-Oct. Tu-Sa 10am-noon and 2-5pm, Su 10am-noon). Across the street, the **Kammerhofmuseum,** housed in the area's original salt mines administration building, focuses on salt mining, and local art and artists, including Brahms, who visited Gmunden often. On display are Brahms's *Bösendorfer,* slippers, and toothbrush, as well as photos donated by his close friend and Gmundenite, Dr. Miller zu Aichholz. (Open May-Oct. Tu-Sa 10am-noon and 2-5pm, Su 10am-noon. 20AS.)

UPPER AUSTRIA

Festwochen Gmunden, an outdoor concert series, takes place from mid-August to early September (tickets 60-440AS; info tel. 70630). From June to August, outdoor concerts are held on the Esplanade or on boats. Get info at the tourist office.

NEAR GMUNDEN: GRÜNAU IM ALMTAL

To get to Grünau, a bus runs frequently from Gmunden (info at the tourist office). A small regional train runs to Grünau from Wels (every 2hr.). Call ahead to the hostel, and one of the staff will pick you up at the station.

The mountain-locked town of Grünau im Almtal is not really on the way to or from anywhere, but it is an attractive destination in its own right. Sitting in the middle of the **Totes Gebirge** (Dead Mountains), Grünau is a tiny community with an incredible backyard ideal for hiking, skiing, boating, fishing, swimming, and relaxing. Ready to faciliate any and all of these activities, **The Treehouse,** Schindlbachstr. 525 (tel. (07616) 8499; fax 8599; email treehousehotel@hotmail.com; www.hostels.com/treehouse) is a backpacker's dream resort. This secluded 40-bed lodge seems more like a quality hotel than a hostel (minus a few hundred schillings). Each room has its own bathroom with private shower and goosedown blankets. Once you've settled in, take advantage of its many facilities: tennis court, movies, library, sauna, and basketball hoop (all free of charge, equipment provided), plus 2 bars for nighttime revelry. **Mountain bike** rental costs 50AS per day. The staff will organize adventure tours including **paragliding** (900AS), **canyoning** (650AS), **rafting** (550AS), **bungee jumping** (990AS, only on weekends), a flight over the mountain surroundings (300AS per person, 4 person min.), and **horseback riding** (100AS per hr.). For winter visitors, the **ski lift** is a 5-minute walk from the front door, and snow-gear (jackets, snowsuits, gloves, etc.) is provided free of charge. Guests receive a discount on lift tickets (200AS) and ski and snowboard rental (100AS, 150AS). The staff will also drop you off at a nearby mountain or lake and let you **hike** your way home with their (free) hiking map. If absolutely nothing strikes your fancy, you are welcome to hang around the lodge all day in your pajamas. (Doubles 220AS per person, triples 210AS, quads 190AS, 6-bed dorm 180AS. Breakfast buffet included. 3-course dinners 90AS. MC, Visa, and traveler's checks.)

BAD ISCHL

Bad Ischl (pop. 15,000) was a salt-mining town for centuries, until a certain Dr. Franz Wirer arrived in 1821 to study the curative properties of the heated brine baths in the area. Pleased with his findings, he began to prescribe brine bath vacations in Bad Ischl for his patients as early as 1822. Real fame descended on the resort only when the brine's healing powers kept the Habsburgs from sputtering into extinction. Archduke Francis Charles and Archduchess Sophia journeyed to Bad Ischl seeking a cure for their state of childlessness and soon managed to produce 3 sons, the so-called **Salt Princes.** When the first Salt Prince, Franz Joseph I, ascended the throne in 1848, he made Bad Ischl his annual summer residence for 40 years. His mother presented a luxury villa to Franz-Josef's bride, Sisi, as a wedding present. Noblemen, rich merchants, and well-known composers like Brahms, Bruckner, and Lehár followed the imperial couple to Bad Ischl, and the Dalai Lama came through town in June 1998.

🛈 **ORIENTATION AND PRACTICAL INFORMATION.** Though it is one of the only towns in the Salzkammergut not on a lake, Bad Ischl lies at the junction of the **Traun** and **Ischl** rivers, which form a horseshoe around the city. The Ischl runs from the Wolfgangsee to the Traun on the way to the Danube. Bad Ischl is within splashing distance of 8 Salzkammergut pools: the Hallstättersee, Gosausee, Wolfgangsee, Mondsee, Attersee, Traunsee, Grundlsee, and the Altausee. Only 1 **train** comes through the station, running between **Attnang-Puchheim** in the north (84AS) and **Hallstatt** (36AS) and **Bad Aussee** (80AS). Indirect trains go to **Vienna** (390AS), **Linz**

(147AS), and **Zell am See** (310AS). **Buses** connect Salzburg to Bad Ischl (1½hr., every hr. 6:40am-7:15pm, 100AS), stopping in Fuschl and St. Gilgen. **By car,** Bad Ischl lies on Rte. 158 and 145. From **Vienna,** take A-1 West to Rte. 145 at the town of Regau. From **Innsbruck** or **Munich,** take A-1 East past Salzburg and exit onto Rte. 158 near Thalgau. From **Salzburg** proper, the best way is to take Rte. 158 straight through St. Gilgen and Fuschl.

Adjacent to the **bus station** (tel. 23113), the **train station** (tel. 24 40 70) has **bike rental** (summer only; mountain bikes 150AS per day, 670AS per week; discount with train ticket) at the **luggage storage** window (open daily 8am-5:15pm; 30AS per piece per day; ring for service). **Lockers** (20-30AS) are around the corner. The **tourist office** (tel. 27 75 70 or 23 52 00; fax 277 57 77) is straight out of the train station and 2 minutes down the road, across from the large, pillared **Kaiser Therme** building at Bahnhofstr. 1. The office has extensive lists of *Pensionen* and *Privatzimmer.* (Open June-Sept. M-F 8am-6pm, Sa 9am-4pm, Su 9-11:30am; Oct.-May M-F 8am-6pm, Sa 9am-4pm, Su 9-11:30am.) The mustard-colored **post office** is two minutes farther down Bahnhofstr., on the corner of Auböckpl. (open June-Sept. M-F 8am-8pm, Sa 9am-noon; Oct.-May M-F 8am-7pm, Sa 9-11am; phone, fax, and **currency exchange** available). The **postal code** is A-4820.

PHONE CODE	The **city code** for Bad Ischl is 06132.

■■ **ACCOMMODATIONS AND FOOD.** Every guest who stays the night in Bad Ischl must register with his or her individual hotel or pension and pay a *Kurtax,* a tourist tax levied by the local government. (June to mid-Sept. 15-20AS per person per night depending on proximity to the city center; Oct.-May 12-13AS.) Bad Ischl's **Jugendgästehaus (HI),** Am Rechenstag 5 (tel. 265 77; fax 265 77 75), is minutes from the *Kaiser*'s summer residence. From the tourist office, walk left on Bahnhofstr., turn right on Kaiser-Franz-Josef-Str., and keep going until you see the *Jugendgästehaus* sign to the left across from the gas station. The hostel offers clean 1- to 5-bed rooms off long corridors. (Dorms 155AS plus *Kurtax.* Sheets, showers, and breakfast included. Reception 8am-1pm and 5-7pm. Reservations recommended. Quiet hour 10pm; keys available.) If the hostel is full, try **Haus Stadt Prag,** Eglmoosg. 9 (tel./fax 23616), which has spacious rooms with balconies. From the train station, go left on Bahnhofstr., right on Kaiser-Franz-Josef-Str., and left on Kreuzpl. Follow until it becomes Salzburgerstr., and bear left on Stiegeng. at the *Goldschmied* sign. Continue along Stiegeng. and up the steps—Haus Stadt Prag is the pink building on your right. (Singles 280AS, with bath 360AS; doubles 500AS, 660AS; 30AS extra with balcony. Breakfast included.)

Restaurants are tucked into every possible niche along Schulg. and the other streets of the pedestrian zone. Right across from the Stadtpfarrkirche, **Café Ramsauer,** Kaiser-Franz-Josefstr. 8 (tel. 22408) serves up delicious and reasonably priced café fare (open M-F 9am-8pm; Sa-Su 11am-6pm). Almost as famous as the *Kaiser* himself is the **Konditorei Zauner,** Pfarrg. 7 (tel. 23522). Established in 1832, this crowded eatery has an international reputation for heavenly sweets and *tortes.* Zauner also operates a riverside restaurant-café on the **Esplanade.** Seat yourself and nosh on extravagant desserts (up to 90AS) or gourmet sandwiches (26-42AS). The **Konsum grocery store** is conveniently located at Auböckpl. 12 (open M-Th 8am-6pm, F 8am-6:30pm, Sa 8am-12:30pm). Browse at the **open-air market** held all day every Friday on Salinenpl.

■■ **SIGHTS AND ACTIVITIES.** Other than the baths, Bad Ischl's main attraction is what the Habsburgs left behind. Tours leave the **Trinkhalle** 2 blocks left of the tourist office (Su 10am, summer only Th 4pm, 25AS; free with guest card).

VILLAS. In 1854, Austria's last empress, Elisabeth, received the **Kaiservilla** as a wedding present from her mother-in-law. Though his wife didn't care for the place,

Emperor Franz-Josef made this his summer getaway palace and crammed it with expensive hunter gadgets. Inside, a vast collection of mounted chamois horns looks like the world's most decadent collection of coat hooks. Amidst the animal remains are many interesting relics of Franz Josef's reign, including the desk where he signed the declaration of war against Serbia in 1914 that led to WWI. Entrance is allowed only through a guided tour in German, with English text available. *(Tel. 23241. Open May to mid-Oct. 9-11:45am and 1-4:45pm. 95AS, 90AS with guest card, students 50AS.)* Buy tickets for the tour when you enter the **Kaiserpark** (off Franz-Josef-Str.). Also within the Kaiserpark, you'll find the ivy-covered **Marmorschlößl** (tel. 24422), which houses the **Photo Museum.** Entrance to the Photo Museum requires a pair of fluffy slippers (provided at the front desk) to protect the exquisite wood floors. Habsburg family photos complement temporary exhibitions. *(Open Apr.-Oct. 9:30am-5pm. 15AS, 12AS with guest card, students 10AS.)*

The **Lehár Villa,** former home of beloved operetta composer Franz, is worth a quick visit. *(Open May-Sept. daily 9am-noon and 2-5pm. Obligatory tour 55AS, with guest card 45AS; students and children 25AS.)*

PARISH CHURCH AND ORGAN. In the center of town, the **Stadtpfarrkirche** (city parish church) houses the magnificent **Kaiserjubiläumsorgel** (Emperor's Jubilee Organ). Turn left out of the tourist office, then right onto Kaiser-Franz-Josefstr.; the church will be on your left. Played by the likes of organ virtuoso and composer Anton Bruckner, the organ is one of the best in the world. Compact discs of performances are available for 230AS.

SALT MINES. A tour through Bad Ischl's **Salzbergwerke** salt mines gives you the inside track on salt mining, from far beneath the surface. *(Tel. 239 48 31. Open July-Aug. 10am-4:45pm, May 1-June and Sept. 1-20 9am-3:45pm. 135AS, with guest card 120AS, children 65AS.)* The mines are outside the city in Perneck and are best reached by car via Grazerstr. to Perneckstr. City bus #8096 also travels to Perneck and leaves from the *Bahnhof* 2 to 5 times daily (16AS, day pass 25AS). The last bus from Perneck is at 4:15pm.

SALT BATHS. Whether or not the **brine baths** that Dr. Wirer talked up so well really have curative powers, Bad Ischl certainly has a relaxed atmosphere. The bath facilities are mostly in the **Kaiser Therme,** a resort across from the tourist office on Bahnhofstr. 1. Splash around in the heated salt baths with whirlpool or consider relaxing in the spacious **sauna.** Release pent-up stress through a **full-body massage** (278AS for 25min.). Mud baths, acupuncture, and other more exotic experiences generally require a doctor's prescription. *(Tel. 23324; email Verwaltung@Kaisertherme.co.at; www.salzkammergut.at/badischl/Kaisertherme. Open M-Sa 9am-9pm, Su 1:30-9pm, last entrance 8pm. 111AS for 3hr., children 57AS. Sauna open Tu-Su 1:30-9pm, Th women only, Tu men only. Combined ticket with pool 153AS for 3hr., children 81AS.)*

HIKING. Hiking paths are shown on a 93AS map available at the tourist office. A good place is around the summit of nearby **Mt. Katrin** (1544m). Get to the **Katrinseilbahn** (cable car; 100AS) by taking a city bus from the train station (last bus 5pm) or by walking for 15 minutes. **Bikers** can get a small trail map (93AS) as well as a trail map which details the entire region (98AS). In winter, Bad Ischl maintains an excellent network of **cross-country skiing** trails (pick up free maps at the tourist office).

🎭 **ENTERTAINMENT.** For the low-down around town, pick up the brochure *Bad Ischl Events* from the tourist office. A free outdoor **Kurkonzert** takes place every day except Tuesday at the *Kurpark* along Wienerstr. (summer only, 10am and 4pm). The exact program of pieces to be performed by the 20-piece *Kurorchestra* is posted weekly on kiosks, in the hotels, and at the *Kurhaus* itself. Every year in mid-August, the **Bad Ischler Stadtfest** brings a weekend of music—classical, pop, jazz, boogie-woogie, oom-pah-pah, etc. Just before the *Stadtfest* on August 15th, the Bad Ischlers celebrate Franz Josef's birthday with live music on the Esplanade. From July 11th until August 29th, the **Bad Ischl Operetten Festspiele** celebrates the musical talent of operetta composer **Franz Lehár,** who lived in Bad Ischl for 30 years and created *The Merry Widow, Gypsy Love,* and *The Land of Smiles.* Tickets are available from *Büro der Operettengemeinde Bad Ischl,* Wiesengerstr. 7, A-4820 Bad Ischl (tel. 23839; fax 238 39 39; open M-Sa 9am-noon and 2-5pm; 200-500AS). After June 30, purchase tickets from the Bad Ischl *Kurhaus* (tel. 23766; fax 23384; open M-F 9am-noon and 3-6pm). From April to October, a **flea market** comes to the Esplanade on the first Saturday of the month. Bad Ischl indulges in all sorts of Yuletide festivities, including a **Christkindlmarkt** (Christmas market), Advent caroling in the *Kurhaus,* tours of elaborate **Weihnachtskrippen** (nativity scenes) in the area, and horse-drawn sleigh rides *(Pferdeschliffen).*

HALLSTATT

Teetering on the banks of the **Hallstättersee** in a valley surrounded on all sides by the sheer rocky cliffs of the Dachstein mountains, Hallstatt is easily the most beautiful lakeside village in the Salzkammergut, if not all of Austria. It was declared a UNESCO World Cultural Heritage site in 1997. This tiny village of 1100 inhabitants seems to defy gravity, clinging to the face of a stony slope. Over 4 millennia ago, a highly advanced culture thrived in Hallstatt, but they didn't come for the view—Hallstatt was a world-famous settlement back when Rome was still a village, thanks to its "white gold." The salt-rich earth also helped preserve Hallstatt's archaeological treasures, which are so extensive that the pre-historic era in Celtic studies (800-400BC) is dubbed the "Hallstatt era." Hallstatt merits more than a daytrip; stay the night in a room overlooking the clear blue lake.

⊠ ORIENTATION AND PRACTICAL INFORMATION. Hallstatt is on the *Hallstättersee,* an entrancing oasis at the southern tip of the Salzkammergut. From Salzburg, taking the **bus** (130AS) is the cheapest way to get to Hallstatt, but it requires layovers in both Bad Ischl and Gosaumühle. The **bus stop** is at the edge of downtown on Seestr., fielding frequent buses to nearby **Obertraun** (10min., 26AS). Hallstatt's **train station** lies on the opposite bank of the lake from downtown and has no staffed office. All trains come from Attnang-Puchheim in the north or Stanach-Irnding in the south. Trains run to **Attnang-Puchheim** (134AS), **Bad Ischl** (36AS), and **Salzburg** via Attnang-Puchheim (210AS). After every train, there is a **ferry** across to town that waits for all train passengers (last ferry 6:45pm, 23AS). If you arrive later, stay on the train to the next stop (Obertraun) and take a taxi (170AS) or walk (5km) to downtown Hallstatt. After a brief, spectacular trip across the lake, the ferry terminates at Landungspl.; it leaves again half an hour before the train departs. If **driving** from Salzburg or the Salzkammergut towns, take Rte. 158 to Bad Ischl and then Rte. 145 toward Bad Aussee. After Bad Goisern, it's approximately 5km to the narrow road leading along the Hallstättersee into Hallstatt. Automobile access to Hallstatt is severely limited. Ample day **parking** lots are available by the tunnels leading into town (free for guests staying in town).

The **tourist office** *(Tourismusbüro),* in the Kultur- und Kongresshaus at Seestr. 169 (tel. 8208; fax 8352, email hallstatt-info@EUnet.at; www.tiscover.com/hallstatt), offers free maps and finds vacancies among the plentiful, cheap rooms (open July-Aug. M-F 8:30am-6pm, Sa 10am-6pm, Su 10am-2pm; Sept.-June M-F 9am-noon and 2-5pm). There is an **ATM** next to the post office. **Public bathrooms** are adjacent to the Heimatmuseum. The **post office** Seestr. 160 (tel. 8201), below the tourist office, offers good **currency exchange** rates (open M-Tu and Th-F 8am-noon and 2-6pm, Sa 8-11am; exchange open until 5pm). The **postal code** is A-4830.

PHONE CODE	The **city code** for Hallstatt is 06134.

⌐ ACCOMMODATIONS. *Privatzimmer* at just-above-hostel prices are prevalent in Hallstatt. **Gästehaus Zur Mühle,** Kirchenweg 36 (tel. 8318), is close to the city center with pleasant 3- to 18-bed dorms and lots of English-speaking backpackers.

From the tourist office, walk up the hill as if heading toward the Heimatmuseum, then swing right at the end of the *Platz*. The hostel is through the little tunnel on the left, by the cascading waterfall. (Dorms 110AS. Showers and lockers included with deposit of 200AS. Sheets 35AS. Breakfast 40AS. Lunch and dinner available at the restaurant downstairs. Reception 8am-2pm and 4-10pm.) **Frühstückspension Sarstein,** Gosaumühlstr. 83 (tel. 8217), offers the prettiest accommodations in town, vistas of the lake and village, and a beachside lawn for sunning and swimming. From the tourist office, head toward the ferry dock and continue along the road nearest the lake (7-8min.) past the Pfarrkirchen steps. (Dorms 210AS, with bath 300AS. 20AS surcharge for 1-night stays. Hall showers 10AS for 10min. Breakfast included.) Frau Sarstein's sister **Franziska Zimmerman** (tel. 8309) lives up the block toward town on the other side of the street at #69 and offers similar (but fewer) accommodations. (Dorms 200AS. Showers 10AS. Breakfast included. 20AS surcharge for 1-night stays. Call ahead.) **Frühstückspension Seethaler,** Dr.-F.-Mortonweg 22 (tel. 8421), sits on the hill near the tourist office. Head uphill, bear left, and follow the signs. Many rooms have balconies with amazing lake views. (Dorms 195-215AS, with bath 280AS, with kitchen 380AS.) **Camping Klausner-Höll,** Lahnstr. 6 (tel. 8322), is 3 blocks past the bus stop on Seestr., one street from the public beach. (45AS plus 10AS tax, children under 14 25AS plus 5AS; tents 40AS; cars 30AS. Breakfast 100AS. Showers included. **Laundry** 60AS. Open mid-Apr. to mid-Oct. Gate closed daily noon-2:30pm and 10pm-7am.)

⬛ FOOD. Many of the guesthouses in Hallstatt have restaurants downstairs. **Gästehaus zum Weißen Lamm** (tel. 8311), across from the Heimatmuseum, serves large, tasty portions (open daily 10am-noon and 5-10pm). Head downstairs to the "mountain man's cellar" for 2 daily *Menü*s (90 and 120AS) for lunch and dinner, including soup, entree, and dessert. **Gästehaus zur Mühle,** below the hostel, offers pizza (68-94AS) and pasta (72-88AS) along with a wide range of salads (from 34AS). Three kinds of *canneloni* (one vegetarian) are 80-88AS each. (Open daily 10am-2pm and 4-10pm.) For cheaper, quicker fare, try **Imbiß Karl Forstinger** (tel. 6135 or 8219) on Seestr. near the bus station (hot dogs and bratwurst 35AS; open daily May-Oct. 10am-6pm). There's a **Konsum** right by the main bus stop at the edge of town (open M-F 7:30am-12:30pm and 3-6:30pm, Sa 7:30am-12:30pm and 2-5pm).

⬛⬛ SIGHTS AND ENTERTAINMENT. Hallstatt packs some heavy punches for tourists, despite its lean frame. The tourist office sells a 30AS English cultural guide, but exploring the narrow, crooked streets is entertainment in itself.

CHURCH AND CHARNEL HOUSE. St. Michael's Chapel at the **Pfarrkirche** offers a fascinating, if macabre, anthropological perspective on the famous prehistoric burial scene in Hallstatt. Next to the chapel is the parish charnel house, filled with remains of villagers dating from the 16th-century onwards. The Celts buried their dead high in the mountains, but Christians wanted to be buried in the churchyard. Unfortunately, they soon ran out of space on their steep hillside, so after 10 or 20 years, the skull and femurs of the deceased were transferred to the charnel house to make room for more corpses. (They're buried vertically as it is.) Each neatly placed skull was decorated with a wreath of flowers (for females) or ivy (for males) and inscribed with the name of the deceased and the date of death. The skulls were then packed in pyramids resting on a shelf which is supported by their neatly stacked femurs, tibiae, and fibulae. Today, bones are removed and painted only by special request. *(Open May-Sept. daily 10am-5pm. In winter, call the Catholic church (tel. 8279) for an appointment. 10AS.)*

HISTORICAL MUSEUMS. In the mid-19th century, an immense, incredibly well-preserved Iron Age archaeological find was discovered in Hallstatt, revealing a plethora of artifacts, a pauper's grave, and the well-maintained crypts of the ruling class—all circa 1000-500BC. The **Prähistorisches Museum** (tel. 8208), across from the tourist office, exhibits some of these treasures, including coiled copper jewelry from the tombs and artifacts from the excavation site on Hallstatt's *Salzberg* (salt mountain) that give scientific proof of prehistoric salt-mining activity. Extensive salt-trading brought bronze ornaments from Northern Italy and amber from the east coast to this remote valley. *(Open May-Sept. daily 10am-6pm. 50AS, students 25AS, 40AS for groups of 10 or more.)* The price of admission also covers entrance to the tiny **Heimatmuseum** around the corner, which has somewhat dusty exhibits on the artifacts of daily living, such as clothes, kitchenware, and mining tools. It also maps the work of Dr. Franz Morton, who studied the evolution of local fauna. *(Open May-Sept. daily 10am-6pm. 50AS, students 25AS.)*

SALT MINES. The 2500-year-old **Salzbergwerke** are the oldest saltworks in the world, though these days tourists have replaced miners in the tunnels. The guided tours (1½hr., in English and German) include a zip down a wooden mining slide on a burlap sack which leads to an eerie lake deep inside the mountain. *(Tel. 84 00 46. Open June to mid-Sept. 9:30am-4:30pm; Apr.-May and mid-Sept. to Oct. 9:30am-3pm. 135AS, with guest card 120AS, students 65AS, children under 4 not allowed in for safety reasons.)* To reach the salt mines, clamber up the steep path near the Pfarrkirche to the top (1hr.) or take the **Salzbergbahn** at the southern edge of town; follow the black signs with the yellow eyes to the bottom of the train station. *(June to mid-Sept. 9am-6pm; Apr.-May and mid-Sept. to Oct. 9am-4:30pm. Last train runs 30min. before the last tour. 60AS, round-trip 97AS, children 60AS.)* If walking from the tourist office, head away from the ferry dock along the lake, and turn right at the large bus circle.

HIKING. Hallstatt offers some of the most spectacular day hikes in the Salzkammergut, many through forests where drops of water cling to the pine needles year-round thanks to a climate very close to that of a temperate rainforest. The tourist office offers a Dachstein hiking guide (70AS; in English), which details 38 hikes in the area, as well as a mountain bike trail map (35AS). Beyond the Salzbergwerk yawns the **Echental,** a valley carved out millennia ago by glaciers and now blazed with trails leading deep into the valley. Hardy (or foolhardy) hikers can attempt the **Gangsteig,** a slippery, nefarious, primitive stairway carved onto the side of the cliff that makes up the valley's right wall—for experienced hikers only. Those without the gumption or experience can visit the **Waldbachstub waterfall** or the **Glacier Gardens** in the valley. These beautiful hills, nooks, and crannies are the scars left in the glacier's wake. The melting glacier water ("glacier-milk") was filled with so much sand and silt and rushed past at such a high velocity that it had the same effect as a sand-blaster, permanently scouring the rocks. To reach the Echental, head toward the Salzbergwerke and continue on either Malerweg or Echenweg; about 20 minutes later, a sign posts the area's layout. Gangstieg is about an hour up on the right side, while the glacier gardens are about 40 minutes up on the left, before the mountain tunnel. Up above the town lies the 700-year old **Rudolfsturm** (Rudolph's tower). Perched on a mountain 855m above the village, the lonely tower guards the entrance to the Salzburg Valley. For **wild water canoeing,** contact Gasthof Seewint (tel. 8246).

BOATING AND SKIING. For a view of the mountains from below rather than above, try a scenic boat trip around the lake (*Schiffrundfarten;* tel. 82 28), departing from either ferry landing. *(May to late Sept. 10:30am-4:45pm. 50min. ride 80AS.)* **Boat rental** costs 120AS per hour for an electric boat, 95AS for a paddle boat, and 75AS for a row boat. Winter visitors can take advantage of Hallstatt's free **ski bus** (contact the tourist office for info), which runs to the Krippenstein and Dachstein-West Ski areas, leaving Hallstatt several times a day; the last bus goes back at 4:05pm. The tourist office can provide a map for area skiing.

NEAR HALLSTATT: OBERTRAUN AND THE DACHSTEIN CAVES

To reach Obertraun from Hallstatt, catch the bus (26AS) at the stop near the lake, 6min. from the tourist office away from the ferry dock, or from the Obertraun-Dachsteinhöhlen rail station to the Dachstein cable car station. Ride the cable car 1350m up to "Schönbergalm" for the Ice and Mammoth Caves. (Runs 9am-5pm. Round-trip 171AS, children 105AS.) The Koppenbrüller cave is a 15min. walk from the bus stop in Obertraun.

At the end of the lake in Obertraun, the prodigious **Dachstein Ice Caves** testify to the geological hyperactivity that forged the region's natural beauty. There are 3 sets of eerily-illuminated caves: the **Rieseneishöhle** (Giant Ice Caves); the **Mammuth-öhle** (Mammoth Caves), even larger than the giant ones; and the **Koppenbrüller-höhle,** a giant spring in a valley below the village of Obertraun. (Tel. (06134) 84 00 46. Open May to mid-Oct. daily 9am-5pm. Admission to either Giant Ice Cave or Mammoth Cave 90AS, children 45AS; combined "Gargantuan Experience" 150AS, 75AS.) The **tourist office** is located in the Gemeindeamt, Obertraun 180 (tel. 351; open M-F 8am-noon and 2-6pm; in summer also Sa 9am-noon). Obertraun's bright yellow **Jugendherberge (HI),** Winkl 26 (tel. 360), is a refuge for summer hikers and winter skiers, as well as dozens of school children on class trips. Rooms are clean and institutional. (Dorms 130AS, under 19 90AS. Breakfast included. Reception daily 8-9am and 5-7:30pm. 10pm curfew.)

ST. WOLFGANG

According to local legend, Bishop Wolfgang of Regensburg hurled his axe into the valley of the **Abersee** in AD976. Where the axe landed, he built a church, and to protect it, Wolfgang supposedly battled the devil on a rocky outcropping. The remains of their struggle are still visible just north of town. Once its founder had been canonized for his miraculous feats, the church on the Abersee (now the **Wolfgangsee**) became the object of mass pilgrimage. The **Wallfahrtskirche** (pilgrimage church) is now home to a famous Michael Pacher altar triptych. St. Wolfgang still draws thousands of devotees on foot and many more tourists by car and bus, but the town's main draw is no longer St. Wolfgang himself, but rather the hotel *Zum weißen Rössl,* which inspired one of Austria's most beloved comic opera and *Heimatsfilm,* **The White Horse Inn.** Visitors can swim in the lake, or hike and ski on the nearby **Schafberg.**

■ **ORIENTATION AND PRACTICAL INFORMATION.** St. Wolfgang sprawls lazily on the shore of the Wolfgangsee, across the water from St. Gilgen. St. Wolfgang has no train station, but **buses** run every hour to **Bad Ischl** (35min., 5:17am-8:10pm, 55AS) and **Salzburg** (1½ hr., last bus 8:10pm mid-July to mid-Sept., 6:20pm otherwise; 111AS; change at Strobl). A breezy option is the Wolfgangsee **ferry** (tel. 223 20), which runs to nearby **St. Gilgen** (40min., 52AS) and **Strobe** (20min., 38AS) and between St. Wolfgang's 2 ferry landings at St. Wolfgang Markt and the Schaf-bergbahnhof. (Ferry runs May-Oct. 8:15am-6:15pm. Day and week passes available. Children ½-price. Eurailpass valid.) To get to St. Wolfgang from **Vienna** by **car,** take A1 West to Mondsee and then head south through St. Lorenz and Scharfling and on to St. Wolfgang. From **Salzburg,** take Rte. 158 east through Hof, Fuschl, and St. Gilgen.

St. Wolfgang is itself a minor miracle of civic planning, existing almost entirely without street names. A tunnel cuts around the downtown area, with the **bus stop** just outside its western entrance. The **tourist office,** Pilgerstr. 28 (tel. 2239; fax 22 39 81; email info@stwolfgang.gv.at; www.salzkammergut.at/wolfgangsee), is a block or so away (open summer 8am-noon and 1-6pm; winter 8am-noon and 2-5pm). Look for a pea-green building on the left, labeled *Marktgemeindeamt.* The **Wolfgangsee Info** pamphlet has addresses and prices for a vast selection of summer and winter activities. An **information kiosk** is farther down the main stretch, by Hotel Peter. **ATMs** are adjacent to the tourist office and in the wall of the **Sparkasse** in Marktpl. **Public bathrooms** are located at the bus stop and behind the tourist office. Reliable **currency exchange** rates are available at the **post office** (tel. 2201), around the corner and down the block from the bus stop (open M-F 8am-noon and 2-6pm, Sa 8-11am; exchange open M-F 8am-5pm). The **postal code** is A-5360.

PHONE CODE	The **city code** for St. Wolfgang is 06138.

The journey **is** the reward....

-Tao saying

Council *Travel*

Stop by one of our 65 offices listed
on www.counciltravel.com
Or call: 1-800-2COUNCIL

■■ **ACCOMMODATIONS AND FOOD.** Almost 2000 tourists troop through St. Wolfgang every sunny summer day. The tourist office's brochure lists a canon of hotels, *Pensionen*, and private rooms. St. Wolfgang has no youth hostel, but **Haus am See,** Michael-Pacher-Str. 98 (tel. 2224), has 50 beds in a rambling old house right on the lake. From the tourist office, simply continue down the main road away from the post office (7min.) until you reach the east entrance of the tunnel; the *Haus* is just beyond, on the right. Look for a *Zimmer frei* banner. The bathrooms are not as gorgeous as the view, but the shore access more than compensates. Herr Brosch will even let guests borrow his paddleboat and rowboat. (Singles 170-280AS; doubles 360-550AS; 2-room quads 800-1000AS. Prices depend on balcony and view. Hall showers. Breakfast included. Parking available. Open May-Oct.) The cheapest housing in St. Wolfgang might be in the Haus Am See's renovated **boathouse,** where 10 beds in singles and doubles start at 150AS. The rooms are primitive, but the balcony is literally over the lake and the boathouse has a large, well-kept grass area for sunning or picnicking. Also check out **Gästehaus Raudaschl,** Deschbühel 41 (tel. 2561), on the way to the major hiking paths. From the tourist office, continue down the main road, and turn left at Hotel Peter. Climb up the small hill, and it's on the left (5min.). This smaller *Pension* offers a private balcony in each of 7 well-furnished rooms. (Singles 210AS, with shower 250AS; doubles 380-420AS. Breakfast included. Open May-Oct.) You can set up your tent at **Appesbach,** Au 99 (tel. 2206; tents 120AS; one-time charge of 120AS; 75AS per night, children 45AS). **Camping Berau,** Schwarzenbach 16 (tel. 2543) rents tents for 60AS (one-time charge of 128AS; 73AS per night, children 50AS).

Most of St. Wolfgang's restaurants and *Imbiße* price their wares very competitively. Try any of the snack shacks lining the main road, where almost nothing is above 55AS. *Konditoreien* also serve up a local specialty—**Schafbergkugeln** (about 23AS), named after the mountain. A variant of the *Mozartkugel*, the *Schafbergkugel* is a tennis-ball-sized hunk of milk chocolate filled with cream, spongecake, nuts, and marzipan. Pick one up at **Bäckerei Gandl,** Im Stöckl 84 (tel. 2294; open daily 7am-7pm). **Cafe Dilara,** Markt 34 (tel. 3157), up the street from the church, serves relatively inexpensive pizzas (from 71AS) and salads (45-85AS). **Hauer's Imbißstube** (tel. 2574), a self-service restaurant, lies near the kiosk on the main road and serves up Austrian standards for under 90AS (open daily 9am-6pm). Across from the tourist office, the **ADEG** market sells fruits of all kinds and standard groceries (open M-Tu and Th-F 7am-noon and 2-6pm, Sa 7am-1pm).

▣ ▣ **SIGHTS AND ENTERTAINMENT.** For St. Wolfgang's top attraction, turn right out of the tourist office and head straight down the road to the **Wallfahrtskirche** (pilgrimage church) in the center of town. **Michael Pacher's altarpiece** is the magnificent focal point of the church's interior. Completed by Pacher in 1480, the altarpiece has 2 pairs of altar wings—originally, the inner shrine was revealed only on Easter and Christmas. Fully closed, the altar displays scenes of a humble pilgrim's life. With the outer wings open, 8 scenes in the life of Christ are revealed. The final pair of wings displays the Coronation of Mary, with Christ blessing his mother. The **Schwanthaler Altar** is in the middle of the church behind wrought-iron gates. Installed in 1676, the high-Baroque altar was originally made to replace Pacher's "obsolete" one, but the sculptor Thomas Schwanthaler bravely persuaded the abbot to leave Pacher's masterpiece alone. Together the altars almost overwhelm the church—don't miss smaller treasures like Schwanthaler's **Rosenkranzaltar** (Rose Garland Altar) in the Maria Chapel.

St. Wolfgang's other major attraction is the **Schafbergbahn** (tel. 22320), a romantic steam engine that laboriously ascends to the summit of Schafberg (1732m). The railway was built in 1892, and in 1964 Hollywood found it charming enough to deserve a cameo in *The Sound of Music*, with the Von Trapp children waving from the windows. From the top, dozens of trails wind down the mountain, leading to such nearby towns as St. Gilgen, Ried, and Falkenstein. Train tickets for the 40-minute ride run as steep as the mountain. (Train runs May-Oct., 1 per hr.

7:15am-6:40pm. Round-trip tickets discounted at 7:15 and 8:10am. Ascent 150AS, children 75AS, half-way 115AS, round-trip 260AS; Eurailpass valid.) If you must pay full price, you might as well take advantage of the special deal offered by the **Berghotel Schafbergspitze** (tel. 22 32 18), a lovely mountain inn peeking over the Schafberg's steepest face. For 500AS per person, you get a round-trip ticket on the railway, a night's lodging, and breakfast. Reserve in advance.

Nature-lovers will be in their element here—the Wolfgangsee provides plenty of water-sport activities. If you like **swimming**, you can go off the deep end at **Strandbad Ried** (tel. 2587; 40AS, children 20AS). **Water-skiing** is available through Stadler (tel. (0663) 917 97 53; 120AS per round) on the Seepromenade. Daredevils can try the water-ski jump. Rent **boats** at the beach on Robert-Stolz-Str. across from the tennis courts or in town at the landing near Marktpl. (Motor boats 30min. 90AS, 1hr. 150AS. Pedal boats 90AS. Row boats 55AS. Open in summer daily 8am-7pm.) **Hiking** the mountains at the lake's edge is another possibility. All trails are marked clearly and described in detail in the English *Info* brochure, free at the tourist office. The tourist office also sponsors guides. Hiking maps cost 10AS (small) and 65AS (big). To pass a Friday evening in St. Wolfgang, catch a production of local composer Ralph Benatzky's romantic-comic operetta "White Horse Inn" (a.k.a. *Zum Weißen Rössl*), which became world famous in 1930 (May, June, and Sept. F 7:30pm; tickets 220-360AS available through the *Singspielbüro*, tel. 2239).

MONDSEE

The Salzkammergut's warmest lake, the **Mondsee** (Moon Lake), is named for its crescent shape. Water sports are raised to a pinnacle in this stunning locale, taking on almost spiritual connotations. The town of Mondsee (pop. 2000) lies at the northern tip of the lake, adding its own quiet charm to the scene. The same Bishop Wolfgang who founded St. Wolfgang spent time here, as did Julie Andrews while filming the wedding scene in *The Sound of Music*.

◪ ORIENTATION AND PRACTICAL INFORMATION. Mondsee has no train station but is accessible by **bus** from Salzburg's main train station (50min., 1 per hr. 6:40am-7:20pm, 70AS). Buses also run 3 times a day from Mondsee to **St. Gilgen** on the Wolfgangsee (20min., 29AS). To get to Mondsee by car, take Autobahn A-1, or, for a more scenic drive, take Rte. 158 from Salzburg to St. Gilgen and then Rte. 154 along the edges of the lake to downtown Mondsee.

The **tourist office** *(Tourismusverband)*, Dr.-Franz-Müllerstr. 3 (tel. 2270 or 4270; fax 4470; email mondseeland.tourismus§upperaustria.or.at), is a 5-minute walk from the bus station, halfway between the church and the lake. From the bus stop, head up the road past the post office, turn right on Rainerstr., and continue to the end. Turn right again, and the office is on the left. The English-speaking staff gladly gives out every brochure they have and finds accommodations. Their free sightseeing pamphlet suggests various self-guided tours: the shortest (1-2hr.) covers just the town highlights; the longest (6-7hr.) requires a car. (Open mid-June to Aug. M-F 8am-6pm, Sa-Su 9-11am; Sept.-June M-F 8am-noon and 1-5pm.) The **post office,** on Franz-Kreuzbergerstr. to the left and across the street from the bus station, is the most convenient place for **currency exchange** (open M-F 8am-noon and 2-6pm, in summer also open Sa 8-10am; exchange closes at 5pm). There are **ATMs** at the Volksbank by the tourist office and at the Raiffeisenbank on Rainerstr. **Public restrooms** are under the *Rathaus* in Marktpl. The **postal code** is A-5310.

PHONE CODE	The **city code** for Mondsee is 06232.

▛▟ ACCOMMODATIONS AND FOOD. Mondsee is brimming with *Pensionen, Privatzimmer,* and hotels. The **Jugendgästehaus (HI)**, Krankenhausstr. 9 (tel. 2418; fax 24 18 75), has doubles and quads with private showers, as well as one 10-bed dorm. From the bus station, walk up Kreuzbergerstr. toward the post office, turn right on Rainerstr., walk uphill, then go left on Steinbachstr. At the first intersection, go left 10m and then right up narrow Krankenhausstr. Follow the signs to the hostel; it's hidden off a driveway to the left and uphill. The main entrance is below the brown balcony. It's often filled with groups, so call ahead. (Dorms 140AS; doubles 340-440AS; quads 560-680AS. Breakfast included; lunch and dinner available in restaurant. Non-members pay extra. Reception 8am-1pm and 5-10pm. Curfew 10pm; key available.)

Pizzeria Nudelini, Marktpl. 5 (tel. 4193), upstairs in the blue building just down from the church, sells inexpensive, delicious Italian-style pizza (68AS for a large cheese) and provides a terrific salad bar (small 38AS, large 58AS; open Su-W noon-2pm and 5:30-11pm, F-Sa 5:30-11pm). For delicious coffee and cake (and at better prices than the cookie-cutter cafés in front of the church), head to **Café Übleis,** Badg. 6 (tel. 2433), right by the tourist office. They specialize in homemade *Mozartkugeln* and ice cream. (Open July-Aug. 9am-11pm; Sept.-June 9am-9pm.) **China Restaurant,** Rainerstr. 13 (tel. 4468), has a great lunch deal that includes soup and an entree for 62 to 69AS (open daily 11:30am-2:30pm and 6-11pm; MC, Visa). **SPAR Markt** is on Steinbachstr. just past the main square on the way up to the hostel (open M-F 7:30am-6:30pm, Sa 7:30am-1pm). A **farmer's market** comes to town each summer in Karlsgarten, near the church (open Sa 8-11:30am).

■■ **SIGHTS AND OUTDOOR ACTIVITIES.** Mondsee is the closest lake resort to Salzburg and one of the least touristed, despite occasional air-conditioned tour buses which rumble in and out the town to see the local **Pfarrkirche,** site of the wedding scene in *The Sound of Music*. The church connects to the authentic remains of a Benedictine monastery dating from AD 748 that now peek out of plaster reconstruction in the **Museum Mondsee.** The museum holds an assortment of churchy odds and ends, of interest mainly for dedicated historians of Mondsee. (Open May-Sept. Tu-Su 10am-6pm; first 2 weeks of Oct. Tu-Su 10am-5pm, last 2 weeks Sa-Su 10am-5pm. 30AS, seniors 25AS, students 15AS.) The open-air **Freilichtmuseum,** on Hilfbergstr. (behind the church and uphill to the right), features a giant, 500-year-old smokehouse, dairy, and farmhouse all in one. A ticket gives free rein to wander all around playing with myriad antique farm tools and utensils. (Open May-Sept. Tu-Su 10am-6pm; Oct.1-14 Tu-Su 10am-5pm; Apr. and Oct. 15-31 Sa-Su and holidays 9am-5pm. 30AS, seniors 25AS, students 15AS.)

In summer, the Mondsee waters buzz with activity. **Alpenseebad,** the public beach (tel. 2291), is great for swimming, but jumping in at undesignated areas along the shore is forbidden by the lake's wildlife conservation laws (open in fair weather May-Sept. daily 8:30am-7pm; 30AS, children 12AS; after 1:30pm 18AS, 6AS). To go out a a little farther, rent a **boat** from Peter Hemetsberger (tel. 2460) on the shore by the playground, down the street from the tourist office (rowboats 75-90AS per hr., paddleboats 100AS, electric boats 130-150AS). Hemetsberger also offers *Seerundfahrten*, boat rides around the lake (40min. ride 63AS, 60min. 90AS, 90min. 120AS; children ½-price). **Water-skiing,** with Wasserskizentrum (tel. (0664) 43 23 103), costs 110AS per circuit, and 2-person rafting costs 120AS per circuit. The Wasserskiclub puts on a **Wasserskischau** (read: clowns on skis) at Mondsee-Kaipromenade (June and Sept. Sa 7pm; July-Aug. Tu 7pm and F 9pm; 25AS).

Mondsee holds the **Musiktage,** an annual classical music festival in early September. Contact the tourist office well in advance for more information. Every year **Hugo von Hofmannsthal's** 1922 morality play, *Jedermann*, is performed (in German) at the open-air **Freilichtbühne** theater every Saturday from mid-July to August (tickets 120-160AS; advance tickets are available at the Salzburger Sparkasse in Marktpl. and at the tourist office).

LOWER AUSTRIA
(NIEDERÖSTERREICH)

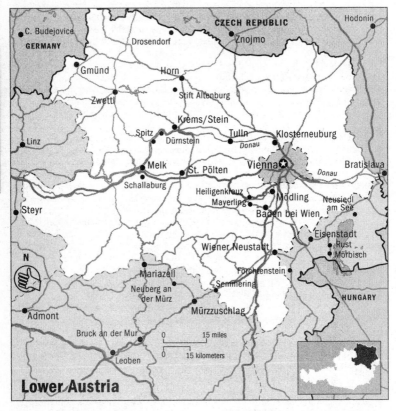

Lower Austria

Though it bears little resemblance to the prevailing stereotype of *Sound of Music* Austria, the province of Niederösterreich, with its rolling, forested hills carpeted with wildflowers, is the key to understanding Austrians' image of themselves. Niederösterreich accounts for a quarter of the nation's land mass—and 60% of its wine production. The region gets its name from its position on the lower end of the Danube, not from any southern orientation. Due to its proximity to Vienna and the variety of its attractions, Niederösterreich is perfect for daytrips. Rugged castle ruins that bear mute witness to Turkish invasions of yore lurk in the hills above medieval towns, ferry boats make languorous river cruises, while hikers and bikers enjoy the varied terrain. The food's nothing to sneeze at either: local specialties include *Wienerwald* cream strudel, a sinful mixture of flaky crust, curds, raisins, and lemon peel (it tastes *far* better than it sounds).

The **Wachau** region of Lower Austria, between the northwestern foothills of the Bohemian Forest and the southeast **Dunkelsteiner Wald,** is a magnificent river valley invoked nostalgically in many Austrian drinking songs. Savor celebrated

Wachau wines at the wine cellar of any local vintner. Off the tourist track, the **Waldviertel** region is a vast expanse of mountains and trees stretching between the Danube and the Czech Republic. Enjoy the forest, but beware—dangerous ticks here may carry a virus that results in *Gehirnentzündung* (inflammation of the brain), a disease similar to meningitis (see **Essentials: Health,** p. 22).

HIGHLIGHTS OF LOWER AUSTRIA

- After a relaxing cruise down the Danube, wander through medieval **Stein** (p. 284).
- Climb up to the ruins of Richard the Lionheart's prison, **Schloß Dürnstein** (p. 285).
- Marvel at **Melk's** big beautiful yellow Benedictine abbey built in 1089 (p. 285).
- Smell the roses, all 20,000 of them, in **Baden's** rosarium (p. 278).

ST. PÖLTEN

Like an aging opera star undergoing a makeover, St. Pölten (pop. 50,000) is attempting to cover up scars from WWII and pockmarks from her industrial past. In 1159, the Bishop von Passau granted a charter to St. Pölten, then called Aelium Cetium, making it the oldest city in Austria. It is, however, the youngest capital— St. Pölten didn't become the capital of Lower Austria until 1986. There are noticeable fault lines between St. Pölten's industrial heritage and its present bid for tourism, but you can find a little patch of consumerism in the shopping-oriented Baroque *Altstadt* and loads of small summer music festivals. Be sure to pick up an English copy of the amusing city brochure.

⊠ ORIENTATION AND PRACTICAL INFORMATION. The **train station,** on Bahnhofpl. near the pedestrian zone, sends direct trains to **Hütteldorf** and the **Vienna Westbahnhof** 2-3 times per hour (114AS). Right in front of the train station, the **bus depot** runs infrequent buses to **Melk** and **Krems.** A free schedule is available at the bus information booth.

Kremsergasse divides the town in half. As you leave the train station and cross Bahnhofpl., Kremserg. is diagonally to your left. Follow it until you hit Riemerpl., and turn right to reach St. Pölten's center, the **Rathausplatz.** The **tourist office** (tel. 35 33 54; fax 333 28 19), is in the Rathauspassage, the tunnel beneath the *Rathaus.* The staff provides information about St. Pölten, regional events, and the wonders of the surrounding countryside. They'll also give you a room list, lead you on a 1-hour **tour** of the inner city (call up to a week in advance), and rent a **cassette tour** in several languages for 20AS. (Open M-F 8am-6pm; April-Oct. M-F 8am-6pm, Sa 9:30am-5pm, Su and holidays 10am-5pm.) There is a a free reservations phone next door on the wall of the Reisebüro. The best place to **exchange money** is the **Bank Austria,** Rathausg. 2 (tel. 54919; fax 54575), across the street from the tourist office. You can **rent bikes** (tel. 323 38 74) at the train station (150AS, with train ticket 100AS; open daily 5:45am-10pm). **Lockers** are available 24 hours a day (30AS). The main **post office,** Bahnhofpl. 1a, is right by the station (open M-F 7am-8pm, Sa 8am-1pm). The **postal code** is A-3100.

PHONE CODE	The **city code** for St. Pölten is 02742.

⌖⌑ ACCOMMODATIONS AND FOOD. St. Pölten works well as a day trip, especially since the town lost its only youth hostel a few years ago. You might consider staying in the hostels in **Krems** (tel. (02732) 83452; see p. 281), **Melk** (tel. (02752) 2681; see p. 285), or **Vienna** (see p. 96). The tourist office maintains a list of *Privatzimmer,* most of which are outside the city limits.

St. Pölten's local specialties include oysters, fried black pudding, and savory Wachau wine. A comfortable Viennese café with newspapers and lingering guests, **Café Melange,** Kremserg. 11 (tel. 2393), on the second floor, draws a younger crowd (open M-F 7:30am-6:30pm, Sa 7:30am-5pm). **Café Punschkrapfel,** Domg. 8

(tel. 6383), is named for its specialty—a small, chocolate, pink-frosted rum cake. Other offerings include fruit frappes (34AS) and a salad buffet (35AS), which taste best in the popular outdoor seating area. (Open M-F 7am-7pm, Sa 7am-1pm, 7am-6pm on the first Sa. of the month.) Cheap and healthy fixings await at the **Julius Meinl** supermarket, Kremserg. 21 (open M-F 7:30am-6pm, Sa 7:30am-12:30pm).

■ 🖫 **SIGHTS AND ENTERTAINMENT.** St. Pölten's architecture suffered heavy damage during WWII, and since then, the city has tried very hard to compensate. As a result, much of the sightseeing in St. Pölten involves pink facades.

THE OLD TOWN. The 13th-century **Rathausplatz** at St. Pölten's core, built on the site of a 1st-century Roman settlement, bears witness to this overzealousness. The building at Rathauspl. 2 earned the name **Schubert Haus** due to Franz's frequent visits to the owners, Baron von Münk and family. A neo-Grecian Schubert (bare-chested, no less) conducts above the window at the portal's axis. Turn right out of the tourist office onto Rathausg., which becomes Riemerpl. and then Wienerstr., turn right on Ledererg., and follow it past Dr. Karl-Renner-Promenade to see the only *Jugendstil* (Art Nouveau) **synagogue** in Lower Austria. Architect Joseph Maria Olbrich designed several other *Jugendstil* buildings in St. Pölten's *Altstadt*.

Shopping has been St. Pölten's official pastime since the Romans rolled down **Wienerstraße.** After 1100, the street became the central axis of the bourgeois-trader settlement established by the Bishop of Passau. **Herrenplatz** has witnessed centuries of haggling at St. Pölten's daily market. A narrow alley just after Wienerstr. 31 leads to **Domplatz,** which retains much of its charm despite its new-found parking-lot status. The remains of the Roman settlement of Aelium were discovered here when some sewer installers tripped over Roman hypocausts (ancient floor heating systems). Stop by the **Dom (cathedral)** itself to see its salmon tones and gilded Baroque encrustations, added by Prandtauer when he transformed the original Roman basilica (open daily until 6pm; free). Budget shoppers should check out the **flea market** at *Einkaufszentrum Traisenpark* just outside town on Sundays, 8am-3pm.

HISTORICAL MUSEUM. St. Pölten maintains only one major museum, the encyclopedic **Stadtmuseum,** which houses a very thorough permanent collection describing St. Pölten from pre-Roman times to the present, containing artifacts ranging from transplanted church pews to 18th-century cloth samples. *(Prandtauerstr. 2, near the Rathaus. Tel. 333 26 43 or 2601. Open 9am-5pm. 20AS, students 10AS.)*

THEATERS. The town supports two theaters. **Die Bühne im Hof** has mostly modern theater and dance performances. *(Linzerstr. 18. Tel. 35 22 91; fax 52294. Prices range from 70 to 350AS, depending on what's showing. Students and seniors 50% off.)* The **Landeshauptstadt Theater** stages traditional opera and ballet. *(Rathauspl. 11. Tel. 352 02, ext. 19. Tickets run 160-290AS, but the box office sells a few 150AS standing room tickets on evenings of performances.)* Seasonal festivities include the **St. Pöltner Festwoche,** which brings all kinds of events to local theaters and museums at the end of May. From the end of September to early October, the **Sacred Music Festival** features free concerts in various churches. The **Donaufestival** from June to early July celebrates dance, theater, and music in the *Festspielhaus*. *(For information, call 2356; for tickets call 2122.)*

BADEN BEI WIEN

Baden is a favorite weekend spot for Viennese and globe-trotters alike to rest their weary bones, thanks to the healing effects of Baden's sulfur springs. Since the days of Roman rule, these naturally heated jets of water springing from the ground have been harnessed and transformed into therapeutic spas, attracting bathers from all corners of Europe. The Holy Roman Emperors used Baden as a summer retreat, and the honor became official in 1803 when Emperor Franz I moved the summer court here. The Emperor gave Baden an imperial reputation, and many celebrities have since relaxed at its baths, including Mozart, Schubert, Strauss, and Beethoven. Under imperial patronage in the 19th century, city notables generated magnificent specimens of architecture and art, turning Baden into a wonderland of pastel buildings. As a tribute to the Emperor's presence, the town created a **rosarium,** extending from the center of town to the **Wienerwald** (Vienna Woods; 90,000m²), with over 20,000 roses. With one step, you can leave behind the carefully tended roses and enter the enormous, trail-laced *Wienerwald*. With another, you can wine, dine, and gamble in the town's jumble of upscale restaurants, shops, and casinos, or unwind at a rejuvenating spa. Baden's prices are, however, the snakes slithering through this paradisiacal garden; resist temptation by making Baden a daytrip from Vienna, only 27km away.

◪ ORIENTATION AND PRACTICAL INFORMATION. The easiest way to get to Baden is by the **Badener Bahn,** a tram that runs from Vienna's Karlspl., beneath the Opera House, to Baden's Josefspl. (60min., every 15min. 5am-10:30pm, 57AS). **Trains** also travel frequently between Vienna's Südbahnhof (4:40am-11:15pm, 57AS) and Josefpl. (4:16am-11:43pm). By **car** from the west, take Autobahn West to "Alland-Baden-Mödling" (Bundesstr. 20). From Vienna, take Autobahn South (Süd) and exit at "Baden."

Baden's **tourist office,** Brusattipl. 3 (tel. 86800; fax 44147), is accessible from the Josefpl. station. Walk toward the fountain, keep right, and follow Erzherzog-Rainer-Ring to the second left (Brusattiplatz). The tourist office awaits at the end of the cul-de-sac. The staff speaks English and will provide English brochures on request. In the summer, they offer **free tours** of the *Altstadt* (1½hr., M at 2pm and Th at 10am,), the wine region (2hr., W at 3pm), including wine tastings (Th 4-7pm or by appointment), and guided **hiking** and **mountain-biking** tours (except in August). (Open May-Oct. M-Sa 9am-12:30pm and 2-6pm, Su 9am-12:30pm.) The train station offers **bike rental** (50AS) and **luggage storage** (20AS). For emergency help, call the **police** (tel. 400 ext. 26). You'll find clean and free **public toilets** at Brusattiplatz, the Rosarium, and the train station. The **postal code** is A-2500.

PHONE CODE	The **city code** for Baden is 02252.

▐▗ ACCOMMODATIONS AND FOOD. If you want to spend the night in Baden despite admonishments from your pocketbook, the tourist office can give you a list of lodgings with prices and descriptions. One good bet is **Pension Steinkellner,** Am Hang 1 (tel. 86226), which offers decent rooms at reasonable prices. It's quite a walk from the center of town, up Füsslauerstr. from Josefspl. and right at the fourth stoplight, but the proprietors will pick you up if you call ahead. (330AS per person for singles or doubles, including shower, linen, and breakfast.)

Food in Baden is plentiful but, unfortunately, not cheap. **Café Damals,** Rathausg. 3 (tel. 42686), in a cool, ivy-hung courtyard facing the Hauptpl., is a relaxing place to lunch and linger, but expect to pay upwards of 80AS for a filling lunch (open M-F 10am-midnight, Sa 10am-5pm). **Zum Vogelhändler,** Vöslauerstr. 48 (tel. 85225), is a pub where Baden youth gather to imbibe the local wine and snack on small, hot dishes. Their specialty, *Nockerl* (home-made noodles), is available in many varieties (including vegetarian) for 60-87AS. (Open 6pm-2am. Live music some nights.) If you're looking for a little history with your *Tafelspitz* (boiled beef), visit the **Gasthaus zum Reichsapfel,** Spielg. 2, the oldest guesthouse in Baden. Follow Antong. one block from Theaterpl.; the restaurant is on the corner. Gasthaus zum Reichsapfel has served hungry wayfarers since the 13th century. Those less interested in the history may still be entertained by the chess, checkers, and huge collection of *Hagar the Horrible* comic books and *Mad* magazines—in German, of course. (Open Su-M and W-Sa 11am-2pm and 5-11pm.) **Sektbar Schluckspecht,** Josefpl. 3, is where Baden "nightlife" happens. Go for snacks (38-120AS), drinks, and the saloon-like decor (open M-Th 10:30am-2am, F 10:30am-4am, Sa 9:30am-4am, Su 4pm-2am). For a meal on the run, **Billa,** Wasserg. 14, lies on the way from the train station to the *Fußgängerzone* (open M-Th 7:30am-6:30pm, F 7:30am-8pm, Sa 7am-5pm). You'll find a **farmer's market** at Grüner Markt on Brusattipl. (open M-F 8am-6pm, Sa 8am-1pm).

⊙ 🏛 SIGHTS AND MUSEUMS. The thermal baths were Baden's biggest attraction in the days of Mozart and Beethoven (and Augustus), and they are still the siren call for guests today. Although they smell like sulfur (i.e. like rotten eggs), they're warm, relaxing, and good for you.

THERMAL BATHS. The **Strandbad** lets you simmer in the hot sulfur thermal pool and cool off in normal chlorinated pools. Kids will get hysterical over the huge water slide and pool—hardly Roman, but definitely fun. *(Helenenstr. 19-21. Tel. 48670. Open M-F 8:30am-7:30pm, Sa-Su 8am-6:30pm. M-F 67AS, Sa-Su 79AS; after 1pm, 57AS and 67AS. Swimming pool only 25AS.)* From May until September 28, visit the smaller (but just as toasty) pool at Marchetstr. 13, behind the *Kurdirektion* (49AS). The *Kurdirektion* itself, Brusattipl. 4 (tel. 44531), is the center of all curative spa treatments, housing an indoor thermal pool mainly for patients but open to visitors (72AS). The spa has underwater massage therapy (295AS), sulfur mud baths (305AS), and regular or "sport" massages (310AS). A gigantic new spa complex called the Römertherme Baden, which just opened in November 1999, offers even more soothing luxuries. *(Brusattiplatz 4. Tel. 45030; www.roemertherme.at; open daily 10am-11pm.)*

PARK AND CASINO. North of Hauptpl. via Maria-Theresa-G. lies Baden's glory, the **Kurpark**. Set into the southeast edge of the *Wienerwald*, this carefully landscaped, shady garden is studded with statues of celebrated guests, including Mozart and Beethoven. The park became an important frolic zone in Europe when the Congress of Vienna met in the early 19th century. When European statesmen escorted the Imperial Court to Baden, throngs of townspeople would gather to watch the dignitaries strut through the park after Sunday Mass. The delightful **Theresiengarten** was laid out in 1792 and the flower clock in the middle of the *Kurpark* grass began ticking in 1929. If you're feeling lucky, visit the **Casino** in the middle of the park. *(Opens daily at 3pm. Must be 19 or older. Semi-formal dress required. Free entrance.)*

MUSEUMS. The **Emperor Franz-Josef Museum**, Hochstr. 51 (tel. 41100), sits atop the Badener Berg at the end of the park (follow signs through the *Sommerarena* along Zöllner and Suckfüllweg) and holds exhibitions of folk art, weapons, religious pieces, and photography. *(Open Apr.-Oct. Tu-Su 1-7pm; Nov.-Mar. Tu-Su 11am-5pm.)* A **Doll and Toy Museum**, Erzherzog-Rainer-Ring 23 (tel. 41020), displays over 300 dolls from different countries, including a 12mm Tyrolean doll from the early 1800s. Among the collection's other knick-knacks are teddy bears, Japanese dolls, and marionettes from Prague. *(Open Tu-F 4-6pm, Sa-Su and holidays 9-11am and 4-6pm.)*

THE OLD TOWN. Centered around Hauptpl., Baden's lovely *Fußgängerzone* features the elaborate **Dreifaltigkeitsäule** (Trinity Column), erected in 1718 to thank God for keeping the plague from Baden, as well as the **Rathaus** and Franz Josef I's summer home at #17. The **Beethovenhaus**, at Rathausg. 10, is where the composer spent his summers from 1804 to 1825, banging out part of *Missa Solemnis* and much of his *Ninth Symphony*. The museum features the composer's death mask and locks of hair. *(Open Tu-F 4-6pm, Sa-Su and holidays 9-11am and 4-6pm.)*

🎭 FESTIVALS. Baden also hosts a wide range of festivals, most notably the **Beethoven Festival** from mid-September to early October, which features performances by famous Austrian musicians and film screenings at the Stadttheater. For tickets, contact *Kulturamt der Stadtgemeinde Baden*, Hauptpl. 1, A-2500 Baden (tel. 868 00; fax 868 00 210). From late June to mid-September, the **Sommerarena** in the *Kurpark* stages magnificent, open-air performances of classic Viennese operettas, including works by Fall and Lehár. For tickets, call 48547, write to *Stadttheater Baden Kartenbüro*, Theaterpl. 7, A-2500 Baden, or stop by the box office in the Stadttheater on Kaiser-Franz-Ring-Str. (Open Tu-Sa 10am-1pm and 5-6:30pm, Su and holidays 10am-noon. 150-500AS, standing room 40AS.) Last-minute tickets, if there are any left, go on sale for half-price 30 minutes before the concert.

Throughout June, Baden blooms with the **Badener Rosentage**, a multi-week celebration of roses at the height of the season. Most activities, including children's theater and puppet shows, are free; they take place throughout the *Badener Rosarium*, where you can also rent boats and float on a shady pond. (Open 9am-7pm. 40AS for 30min., 70AS for 1hr.) World-class **horse racing** occurs near the Casino from June to September. Dial 88773 or 88697 for details. In September, Baden hosts **Grape Cure Week,** a Bacchanalian gathering of local wineries in Hauptpl. selling fresh grapes and grape juice. The theory behind it is that one should irrigate one's system, and the best way to do so is gobble grapes (1kg of grapes per day). Some take the medicinal philosophy to heart, but for most, it's an excuse to party. For details, stop by one of the *Buschenschenken.* (Stands open daily 8am-6pm. First 500 guests get free grape juice.)

THE DANUBE (DONAU)

The "Blue Danube" may largely be the invention of Johann Strauss's imagination, but this mighty, muddy-green river still merits a visit. The Danube was once Europe's most important trade conduit, and the *Nibelungenlied* sagas made famous by Wagner took place along its shores. Glide between its banks on a ferry or pedal furiously along its shores on a bike—either way, you'll experience the exhilarating, fluid beauty of Austria's most famous river.

The legendary **Erste Donau Dampfschiffahrts-Gesellschaft** (DDSG—creators of the longest known German word in existence, *Donaudampfschifffahrtgesellschaftkapitänswitwe,* which translates as "the widow of a captain working for the Danube Steamship Company") runs ships every day from May to late October along the Danube. The firm operates an office in **Vienna,** I, Friedrichstr. 7 (tel. 58 88 00; fax 588 80 440; email info@ddsg-blue-danube.at; www.ddsg-blue-danube.at). Elsewhere, tickets are available at most tourist offices. On Sundays during the summer, **ferries,** complete with didactic commentary, run from Schwedenplatz in Vienna to **Krems, Melk, Dürnstein, Tulln,** and the **Wachau valley.** During the week, ferries run between the towns of the Wachau valley (3 per day, 190AS, round-trip 260AS; bike transport is free but call ahead). **Hydrofoils** will take you to **Bratislava** (1¾hr., 240AS, round-trip 360AS) or **Budapest** (5-6hr., 780AS, round-trip 1100AS). Eurailpass and ISIC holders get a 20% discount on travel within Austria, and families may travel for half-price (minimum 1 parent and 1 child ages 6-15; under 6 travel free with a parent). Contact the DDSG or local tourist offices for special ship/bus and ship/train ticket combinations. Specialty tours include the *Nibelungen,* which sails through the areas described in the ancient saga, a summer solstice cruise *(Sonnendfahrt),* which steams by the Midsummer's Night bonfires in the Wachau valley, and a *Heurigen* ride with a live *Liederabend* trio. Other exciting options include a trip past Hundertwasser's most famous monuments on a boat designed by the Austrian eco-architect himself.

Bicyclists should take advantage of the **Lower Danube Cycle Track,** a velocipede's Valhalla. This riverside bike trail between Vienna and Passau links most Danube villages, and offers captivating views of crumbling castles, latticed vineyards, and medieval towns. Area tourist offices carry the route map and bike rental information—you can **rent bikes** at the Melk, Spitz, and Krems train stations. Between Krems and Melk along the Vienna-Grein bike route, numerous ruined castles testify to Austria's quite dignified historical pedigree. One of the most dramatic fortresses is the 13th-century **Burg Aggstein-Gastein,** formerly inhabited by Scheck von Wald, a robber-baron known to fearful sailors as **Schreckenwalder** (the terror of the woods). The lord was wont to impede the passage of ships with ropes stretched across the Danube and then demand tribute from his ensnared victims.

KREMS AND STEIN

Over the river and through the woods, in the Danube valley at the head of the Wachau region, the hybrid town of Krems/Stein is surrounded by lush, green hills filled with terraced vineyards. Historically, Krems and Stein shared a mayor to

LOWER AUSTRIA

THE WISE WOMEN OF KREMS

Lower Austria is packed not only with yellow remnants of the Habsburg days, but also a few *memento mori* from prehistoric times. Krems is one of Austria's top paleontology centers, and its researchers have recently unearthed the remains of a 32,000-year-old hunting community settled in the Danube bend near a place now named Galgenberg. Among the usual shards of bone and clay animal figurines, archaeologists excavated eight pieces of slate that, when fitted together, form a well-endowed female statuette. Fanny von Galgenberg, named for the famous dancer Fanny Elßler, is Austria's oldest known work of art and the world's only known female sculpture from the Aurignae Period. Barely three inches tall and half an inch thick, the figure is engraved with sketches and positioned in a pose that classifies her as part of the archetypal prehistoric Venus figures, like her much younger sister symbol of fertility, the "Venus of Willendorf," who was found between Krems and Melk. The Renaissance Simandl fountain in Krems's *Fußgängerzone* depicts a pleading man kneeling before his robust, stern wife. In Renaissance Krems, the women held such influence over their men that they closed down the Simandl brotherhood, a small town fraternity of carousing and late-night debauchery.

coordinate trade and military strategy on the critical Danube trading route, and through the years the two towns have grown into each other's territories. Much of the region's wealth came from the tolls on this riverbend's Danube traders—no wonder the Kremser Penny was the first coin minted by the Habsburgs.

The stuccoed walls of **Krems** have a frivolous pastel charm, channeling wanderers to a modern, shop-filled *Fußgängerzone* (when medieval Stein's your neighbor, Baroque *is* modern). Krems has a varied array of attractions, ranging from art exhibits to sports galas. **Stein,** the older half of the duo but now just a district of Krems, seems still to live in the first millennium—its crooked, narrow, cobblestone passages twist and wind back on themselves. In the valley around Krems/Stein, vineyards cultivate 120 different wines according to French wine legend **Hans Moser's** now-standard "raised vine" technique, which lifts the poor vines from whence they had lain, technologically impaired, for centuries. Head for **Kellergasse,** the high street in Stein that lies next to those hills of plenty, where *Heurigen* offer the fruit of these vines as well as great views of the **Stift Göttweig** (abbey) across the Danube.

7 ORIENTATION AND PRACTICAL INFORMATION. Most visitors arrive on bicycles, but the **train station** is a five-minute walk from Krems's *Fußgängerzone*. Stein is west of Krems, bracketed by Steiner Kellerg. and Steiner Landstr. To get to the *Fußgängerzone*, exit the front door of the *Bahnhof*, cross Ringstr., and follow Dinstlstr. The station has **lockers** for 30AS, **luggage storage,** and **bike rental** (tel. 825 36 44; 150AS per day, 120AS per half-day; with train ticket 100AS, 80AS). Regional trains connect Krems to **Vienna** (Spittelau station; 139AS) through Tulln. Travelers to other big cities must change trains in St. Pölten (76AS). In front of the station is a **bus depot.** Both buses and trains leave every 30 minutes for routes to Melk and St. Pölten. Krems lies along the popular **DDSG ferry** route from **Passau** through **Linz** and **Melk** to **Vienna** (for information, see p. 281). The ferry station is on the riverbank close to Stein and the ÖAMTC campground, near the intersection of Donaulände and Dr.-Karl-Dorreck-Str. To reach Krems from the landing, walk down Donaulände, which becomes Ringstr., then take a left onto Utzstr. To reach Stein, follow Dr.-Karl-Dorreck-Str. and then take a left onto Steiner Landstr.

The **tourist office** is housed in the Kloster Und at Undstr. 6 (tel. 82676; fax 70011; www.tiscover.com/krems). From the train station, take a left on Ringstr. and continue (15min.) to Martin-Schmidt-Str. Turn right and follow the street to the end; the office is across the street and to the right. The excellent staff has amassed tons of information on accommodations, sports, and entertainment, as well as the indispensable *Heurigen Kalendar*, which lists the opening times of regional wine taverns. Guided walking tours in several languages leave for Krems or Stein

(1½hr., 600AS per group or 20AS per person if more than 20 people show up). They also book hotel reservations. (Open Easter-Oct. M-F 9am-7pm, Sa-Su 10am-noon and 1-7pm. In winter M-F 9am-6pm.) **ATMs** dot the shopping streets, but the **post office** also offers **currency exchange** (tel. 82606) and is right off Ringstr. on Brandströmstr. (Open M-F 8am-noon and 2-6pm, Sa 8-11am.) You can **rent bikes** at the Donau Campground (half-day 40AS, full-day 60AS) and the train station (90AS per day, with ticket 40AS). **Public toilets** are at the tourist office and in the *Stadtpark*. The **postal code** is A-3500.

PHONE CODE	The **city code** for Krems/Stein is 02732.

◨◩ ACCOMMODATIONS AND FOOD. No matter where you stay, ask your hosts for a **guest card** that grants a number of discounts. The **Jugendherberge Radfahrer (HI),** Ringstr. 77 (tel. 83452; for advance bookings, call the central office in Vienna at 586 41 45 or fax at 586 41 453), is a clean, close-quartered hostel accommodating 52 in comfortable 4- and 6-bed rooms. (Members only. Dorms 180AS. 20AS surcharge on stays less than 3 nights. Tax, breakfast, bicycle storage, and sheets included. Lockers 10AS. Reception 7-9:30am and 5-8pm. Open Apr.-Oct. Call ahead.) Karl and Ingred Hietzgern's **Baroque Bürgerhaus,** Untere Landstr. 53 (tel./fax 76184 or 74036), stands in the *Altstadt* of Krems. From the train station, walk straight ahead, cross Ringstr., continue 2 blocks to Untere Landstr., and turn right. During the Middle Ages, the building was three small houses, which were joined with one facade in the Baroque period. The Hietzgerns have filled the house with *Jugendstil* furniture and hand-painted wood and will happily tell you about anything and everything Krems. (2- and 3-bed dorms with shower 310AS; for stays of 3 nights or more 285AS; open mid-June to mid-Sept.) Although slightly more expensive, Krems's oldest guesthouse, the centrally located **Hotel-Restaurant "Alte Post,"** Obere Landstr. 32 (tel. 82276; fax 84396), will host you comfortably amid its old doll collection, dark velvet couches, terry-cloth curtains, and garden café. Follow directions for Baroque Bürgerhaus, but turn left on Untere Landstr., which becomes Obere Landstr. (Singles 340AS, with shower 480AS; doubles 620-820AS. Breakfast included.) In addition, *Privatzimmer* abound on Steiner Landstr. For a more earthy experience, try **ÖAMTC Donau Camping,** Wiedeng. 7 (tel. 84455), situated on a grassy Danube riverbank near the highway. (50AS per person plus 10.50AS tax, children 35AS; tents 30-60AS (bring your own); cars 40AS. Reception 7:30-10am and 4:30-7pm. Showers included. Electrical hookup 25AS. Facilities for disabled guests. Open Easter to mid-Oct.)

The area around the pedestrian zone in Krems overflows with restaurants and street-side cafés. **Schwarze Kuchl,** Untere Landstr. 8 (tel. 83128), offers a salad buffet (small 38AS, large 55AS), assorted goulashes (39-78AS), and bread (open M-F 8:30am-7:30pm, Sa 8:30am-2pm). In the same building, you'll find the famous **Café-Konditorei Hagmann** (tel. 83167; www.hagmann.co.at/konditorei), known throughout Krems for its outstanding pastries and chocolates, which rival any in Vienna. Try the *Marillenstrudel* (28AS), but beware—you may find yourself returning for breakfast, lunch, and dinner. Grab a *Wachauer Kugel* (ball of chocolate and nougat) for the road. (Open M-F 7am-7pm, Sa 7am-5pm.) At **Haus Resch,** Steiner Kellerg. 40 (tel. 82636), you can sample the strong wines (18AS for a quarter liter) in the vineyard. To round off your decadence, share the cheese platter with a friend (48AS). **Haus Hamböck,** Steiner Kellerg. 31 (tel. 84568), has a charming leafy terrace with a view of the town's spires and a restaurant bedecked with old *Faß* (kegs), presses, and other vineyard tools. The proprietor gives free tours of the cellar, with a free tasting. (Wine 22AS a glass, snacks 30-50AS. Open daily 3pm or until people leave.) The cheapest eats in town are at the **Julius Meinl** supermarket, in front of the train station or on the corner of Gaheisstr. and Obere Landstr. (open M-F 7:30am-6:30pm, Sa 7:30am-5pm).

◫▥ SIGHTS AND MUSEUMS. Both Krems and Stein have a plethora of historical attractions, spanning nearly every architectural style to cross the Alps.

THE OLD TOWN. In Stein, fascinating old buildings line **Steiner Landstraße,** a well-preserved vestige of the Middle Ages. Krems's *Fußgängerzone*, the center of mercantile activity, runs down Obere and Untere Landstr. The entrance to the pedestrian area is marked by the Steiner Tor, one of four medieval city gates flanked by two Gothic towers. Inside the *Tor*, you'll find a refreshing mix of shops, sights, and eateries. Not heavily touristed, this section of town is a great place to meander past the city's architectural treasures. Market places line Obere Landstr., starting with **Dominikanerpl.,** home of the **Dominikanerkirche,** now the Weinstadt Museum. Farther down the pedestrian zone is **Pfarrkirche Platz,** home of the Renaissance **Rathaus** and the **Pfarrkirche** with its piecemeal Romanesque, Gothic, and Baroque architecture. Once there, walk up the hill to the **Piaristenkirche** to see life-sized depictions of Jesus' crucifixion. At the end of the pedestrian zone stands the **Simandlbrunnen,** a fountain depicting a husband kneeling in front of his stern wife.

CITY MUSEUM. Built in the Dominikanerkloster, the excellent **Weinstadt Museum** features a curious combination of paintings by the world-renowned Baroque artist Marten Johann Schmidt and, in the cloister cellars, archaeological treasures from the Paleolithic Era through the Middle Ages. The changing exhibits cover subjects ranging from local folklore to Apocalyptic art. *(Kornermarkt 14. Tel. 80567 or 80 15 72; fax 80 15 76. Open Mar.-Nov. M-Th 9am-6pm, Sa-Su 1-6pm. 40AS.)*

ART MUSEUM. To enhance Krems' cultural offerings, **Kunsthalle Krems** has recently opened a new facility on the corner of Steiner Landstr. and Dr.-Karl-Dorreck-Str. From the tourist office, turn right and walk down Undstr., under the overpass, at which point the street becomes Steiner Landstr. The enormous exhibition hall always has fascinating cultural and historical exhibits, often about postmodern or non-European art. *(Steiner Landstr. 8. Tel. 82669; fax 826 69 16. Open Tu-Su 10am-6pm. 40-90AS, discounts for students and seniors.)*

WINE CELLARS. Once you've covered the history, drink in the joys of the present state of the area. Above Krems and Stein, the lovely terraced vineyards, with the vines photosynthesizing in neat little rows, tempt travelers to seek a bottle of wine and a patch of grass in the sun. The **Heurigen** (wine cellars) are not to be missed. Plan carefully, however—the *Heurigen* can stay open only three weeks every two months from April to October. Better-safe-than-sorry types pick up a schedule from the tourist office; press-your-luck gamblers just stroll down Kellerg. in Stein and hope to happen upon on an open cellar. If you don't have time for *Heurigen*, stop by the city-owned **Weingut Stadt Krems,** on the edge of the pedestrian zone. Go to the end of Obere Landstr., through the gate, and to the right. This winery lacks an attached restaurant, but it does offer free tours of the cellar and bottling center. The free tastings that follow the tour usually seduce visitors into buying a bottle of wine, which runs 40-100AS. *(Stadtgraben 11. Tel. 80 14 40; fax 80 14 42. Open for tours M-F 8am-noon and 1-4pm, Sa 8am-noon.)* Those who can still walk straight should lunch down to the historic abbey cellar of **Kloster Und,** Undstr. 6 (tel. 73073; fax 832 23 78), by the tourist office. *(Open March-Dec. 24.)* The cellar has all of Austria's regional wines—for 180AS, you get a basket of bread, mineral water to cleanse the palate, and two hours to weave through the selection of more than 100 wines, from the noble Riesling of Wachau to the nutty Neuburger of Burgenland. For those with a smaller appetite or budget, you can try just 6 wines for 70AS. Bring a sweater—dry white wines complain if not kept at 10 to 11 degrees Celsius.

⚐ FESTIVALS. Krems is a happening festival town, celebrating everything from apricots to wine. Check with the tourist office for exhaustive info. Each year the **Donaufestival,** from mid-June to early July, brings open-air music and dancing, kicking off a summer of cultural activities that includes theater, circus, symposia, *Lieder*, folk music, even flamenco dancing. From July 15 to August 15, Krems hosts a **Musikfest,** featuring a number of organ, piano, and quartet concerts that take place in the Kunsthalle and various churches. Tickets are available at the tourist office and *Österreichticket* (tel. (01) 53601). From August 27 to September

5, Krems hosts the Lower Austria Wine Fest, which features wine tastings, culinary specialties, presentations, and folklore. DDSG offers a 40% reduction on ferry rates between Krems and Melk for the occasion. Throughout the year, many **churches** have sacred music and organ concerts, which resonate beautifully within Gothic vaults and are usually free.

NEAR KREMS: DÜRNSTEIN

Trains connect Dürnstein to Krems (every hr. 6am-8pm, 25AS) and Vienna's Franz Josef Bahnhof (every hr., 145AS). To reach town from the train station, descend the hill, turn right, and pass through the underground walkway (5min.). Boats dock at the DDSG ferry station on the Donaupromenade, a riverside road with beaches and bike paths. To reach town from the landing docks, turn right on Donaupromenade and left on Anzugg. which intersects with Hauptstr.

Located a bend or two down the Danube from Krems, among deep green vineyards, Dürnstein is a hilltop medieval village with a mythic charm that attracts tourists and locals alike. The main draw is hiking up to the ruined **castle** at the highest point of the town where **Richard the Lionheart,** captured on his way back from the Third Crusade in 1192, was imprisoned. Apparently the English king threw the Austrian flag to the ground upon his arrival in the Holy Land, starting a fierce quarrel with Leopold V, Duke of Austria. The Holy Roman Emperor was short of cash and ordered Richard held for ransom; Leopold was happy to help out for a cut of the booty. When Richard's ship was wrecked en route to England, he was forced to cross Austria disguised as a peasant. Leopold's men recognized him despite the costume and locked him up (giving **Robin Hood** time to flourish under evil Prince John). Meanwhile, Richard's faithful minstrel wandered through Austria, looking for his master by whistling his favorite tune. When the minstrel got to Dürnstein, Richard heard him whistling and whistled back. The minstrel went back to England and collected the 15,000 silver pounds for Richard's ransom, of which Leopold got a hefty share. With the money, Leopold built the town of Wiener Neustadt.

Although Richard's capture was the last big splash onto history pages for the Kuenninger dynasty, they continued to prosper on their home turf, building the **Augustiner Chorherrenstift,** an enormous Baroque abbey commissioned by the daughter of the penultimate heir of the family line in 1372 and dedicated to the Virgin Mary. Joseph II dissolved it at the same time he dismantled most of Austria's ecclesiastical institutions and introduced the re-useable coffin, but it has been well-maintained nevertheless. You'll get mesmerizing views from the grandiose blue and white church steeple. Beware the creepy skeletons that guard the elegant interior of the church from all sides. (Tel. (02711) 375; fax 432. Open Apr.-Oct. 9am-6pm. 25AS, with tour 40AS, tour for students 35AS.)

The **tourist office** (tel. (02711) 200) is located in a shack in a parking lot down the hill and to the right of the train station. The office and the local *Rathaus* (on Hauptstr.) provide lists of *Privatzimmern* (from 180AS) and open *Heurigen*. (Tourist office open M and W-F noon-7pm, Sa 11am-7pm.)

MELK

The enormous yellow mass of Melk's monastery floats over dark blue Danube waters and stucco houses of the village below in one of the most surreal vistas you'll find in Austria. Melk's eerie monastery was constructed atop the cliffs in AD 994 as a Babenberg residence, until Margrave Leopold II turned it over to Benedictine Abbot Sigibod, thus begetting the Benedictine monastery and, subsequently, the village of Melk. The monastery was a renowned ecclesiastical force in the medieval world, famed for its monumental library and learned monks (who incidentally merited several admiring references in Umberto Eco's novel *The Name of the Rose*). Today, the abbey still wields power as one of few ecclesiastical institutions that report directly to the Pope, with no bishop as middle-man. The area is famous for its gorgeous scenery; over 400,000 folks visit Melk each year as a daytrip from Vienna or a stop on the Passau-Vienna cycling route. Nevertheless, Melk remains a living monastery, home to 20 monks who toil away, praying, farming, and teaching Austrian youth at the highly scholastic monastery school. Below the abbey, the town is a charming jumble of Renaissance houses, narrow pedestrian zones, cobblestone streets, old towers, and remnants of the medieval city wall.

⚐ ORIENTATION AND PRACTICAL INFORMATION. Trains link Melk to Vienna's Westbahnhof (1½hr., 150AS) via St. Pölten. **Bike rental** (full-day 150AS, half-day 120AS; with rail ticket 100AS, 80AS), **currency exchange,** and **luggage storage** (30AS) are all available at the station. Just outside the station's main entrance is the **bus depot.** Bus #1451 chugs from Melk to Krems (80AS) and #1538 from Melk to St. Pölten (46AS). Melk lies on the **DDSG ferry** route between Vienna and Passau (from Vienna 530AS; from Krems 238AS; for more information, see p. 281).

Melk's **tourist office,** Babenbergstr. 1 (tel. 523 07 32 or 523 07 33; fax 523 07 37), on the corner of Babenbergstr. and Abbe-Stadler-G., has maps and pamphlets on the town's history and athletic activities in the Wachau region. From the train station, walk down Bahnhofstr. and then straight on Bahng. Turn right at Rathauspl. and cross, staying to the right until you hit Abbe-Stadler-G. The office has large **lockers** (10AS) and bike racks., and makes free room reservations (open July-Aug. daily 9am-7pm; Sept.-Oct. and Apr.-June M-F 9am-noon and 2-6pm, Sa 10am-2pm). The **post office** is at Bahnhofstr. 3 (open M-F 8am-noon and 2-6pm, Sa 8-10am). The **postal code** is A-3390.

PHONE CODE	The **city code** for Melk is 02752.

⌂ ACCOMMODATIONS. To really soak in the cozy atmosphere of Melk, stay in one of the many *Privatzimmer* throughout town or on a country farm. (List available from the tourist office. Prices range from 170-250AS per person. Amenities vary. Breakfast included.) If that doesn't strike your fancy, the recently renovated **Jugendherberge,** Abt-Karl-Str. 42 (tel. 52681; fax 54257), is about a 10-minute walk from the train station (turn right as you exit and follow the green signs). This clean hostel offers 104 beds with checkered sheets in quads with private showers and hall toilets. Beware of rampant school groups. (Dorms 174.50AS; under 19 140AS. Tax 10.50AS. Breakfast and bicycle storage included. Reception 8-10am and 5-9pm. Open Apr.-Oct.) **Camping Kolomaniau** (tel. 53291) overlooks the Danube next to the ferry landing. Follow Kremserstr. to the Danube, cross the bridge, and keep right along Rollfährestr. (35AS, children 20AS; tents 35AS; cars 25AS. Tax 10.50AS. Showers 15AS. Reception 8am-midnight.)

☐ FOOD. Restaurants abound on Rathauspl., but look farther afield for less tourist-oriented joints. A 5-minute walk away from the monastery through Hauptpl. brings you to **Pizzeria "Venezia,"** Linzerstr. 7 (tel. 51224), where you can choose from 16 lunch *Menü* options ranging from 55 to 85AS (open daily 11am-2:30pm and 5pm-midnight). For more regional cuisine, eat with the locals at **Finnis Beis'l,** Sterng. 13 (tel. 51549), known for its home cooking. From the tourist office, veer right off Hauptpl. onto Sterng. Rustic decor complements the light, but filling entrees (50-95AS; open Tu-Sa 4pm-midnight). Black lacquered wood and oh-so-chic decor greet you at **Il Palio,** Wienerstr. 3 (tel. 54732), home of fantastic ice-cream concoctions (open daily 9am-midnight). At night, the streets may seem empty, but **"Nostalgiebers 1" Alt Melk,** Wienerstr. 25 (tel. 4458), certainly won't be. Step into the intimate warmth of deep red velvet curtains, cream-colored walls, and old black-and-white photo portraits and enjoy a *cabernet sauvignon* (28AS) or a milkshake with the genial, mixed-age crowd. (Live music 1st and 3rd Th of each month. Open Su-Th 4pm-2am, F-Sa 4pm-4am.) During the day, **SPAR Markt,** Rathauspl. 9, has bread to spread, pears to share, apples to grapple, oranges to…well, um…never mind (open M and W-F 7am-6pm, Sa 7am-noon).

LOWER AUSTRIA

SIGHTS AND OUTDOOR ACTIVITIES. To visit Melk is to visit the **Benedik-tinerstift** (Benedictine abbey), which commands fantastic views of the city and the surrounding Danube countryside. Melk's offerings, however, extend beyond the monastery walls to Melk's lush surroundings, ideal for outdoor activities.

BENEDICTINE MONASTERY. The yellow **Benediktinerstift** lights up the entire countryside, inviting pilgrims to enter God's army. The only part open to the general public is the secular wing, where such notables as Emperor Karl VI, Pope Pius VI, and Napoleon took shelter in the imperial chambers. The wing is filled with informative exhibits (in German) and various Baroque optical tricks, including a portrait of Leopold II, whose eyes follow you about the room, and a flat ceiling that appears to be a dome when viewed from the center of the room. Habsburg portraits line cool marble halls: in an act of political deference, royal consort Franz I points to his wife, the reigning Maria Theresa. The stunning **abbey library** is brimming with sacred and secular texts painstakingly hand-copied by monks. The two highest shelves in the gallery are fake—in typical Baroque fashion, the monks sketched book spines onto the wood to make the collection appear even more formidable. The **church** itself, maintained by 20 monks, is a Baroque masterpiece. Maria Theresa donated the two skeletons that adorn the side altars—unknown refugees from the catacombs of Rome, lounging in full costume. The centerpiece of the monastery is the **Melker Kreuz** (Melk Cross)—gold, jewels, the works, all circa 1363 (see **Hidden Treasure**, p. 288). The monks keep up with the times, curating

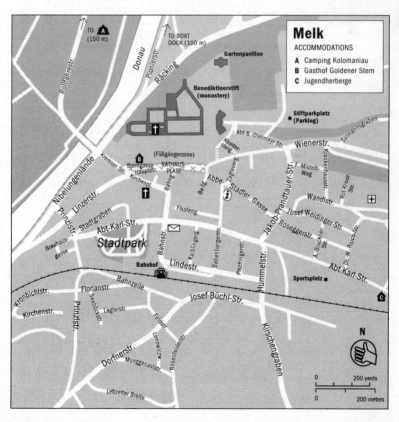

LOWER AUSTRIA

LOWER AUSTRIA

HIDDEN TREASURE The crown jewel of Melk's *Benediktinerstift* is unquestionably the *Melker Kreuz*, a bejeweled and gilded cross that contains a splinter believed to be a tiny fragment of the cross upon which Jesus was crucified. Crafted in 1363, the cross is two-faced: the "wealthy" side sparkles with diamonds, rubies, emeralds, and fresh water pearls from the Danube, while the "sacred" side depicts the crucified Christ and the four Evangelists at each of its rounded points. On two occasions, the cross has been stolen from the monastery, but each time has made its way back to the abbey by supernatural means (once by sailing itself back on a boat). Legend has it that anyone who opens the cross to look at the relic will be blinded by the holiness of the sight. For whatever reason, Melk's treasure is not on public display. Hidden in the bowels of the abbey, the cross may be loaned out for a sacred symposium at the turn of the century, but the abbey is still in negotiations with insurance companies.

temporary exhibits of contemporary art and even commissioning artist Peter Bischof to create new murals over weather-ruined frescoes in the interior of the main courtyard. *(Abbey open daily Apr. and Oct. 9am-5pm; May-Sept. 9am-6pm. Last entry 1hr. before closing. Guided tours Nov.-Mar. every hour in German, and every day at 3 pm or by arrangement in English. 65AS, students 30AS, tour 20AS extra. Call 231 22 32 for more information.)*

CASTLE. Five kilometers out of town is **Schloß Schallaburg,** one of the most magnificent Renaissance castles in central Europe. The castle's architecture is reason enough to visit: Romanesque, Gothic, Renaissance, and Mannerist influences converge in the terra-cotta arcades of the main courtyard. The floor is composed of a 1600-piece **mosaic** depicting mythological figures and gods. *(Tel. (02754) 6317. Open May-Sept. M-F 9am-5pm, Sa-Su 9am-6pm. 80AS, students 30AS. Call ahead for a tour.)* The castle doubles as the **International Exhibition Center of Lower Austria** (tel. 6317), which goes out of its way to bring foreign cultures to life. Buses leave Melk's train station daily at 10:30am and 3:10pm and leave the castle 15 minutes later. (10min., 30AS.) Or you can hike up to the complex; ask the tourist office for a map from Melk to the palace.

OUTDOOR ACTIVITIES. Hikers can enjoy the network of trails surrounding Melk that wind through tiny villages, farmland, and wooded groves. The tourist office provides a great map, which lists area sights and hiking paths, and handouts on the 10km Leo Böck trail, 6km Seniorenweg, and 15km Schallaburggrundweg. **Cyclists** might enjoy a tour along the Danube toward Willendorf on the former canal-towing path. The 30,000-year-old **Venus of Willendorf,** an 11cm voluptuous stone figure and one of the world's most famous fertility symbols, was discovered there in 1908. A copy is now on display in Vienna (the original is locked up). For a more sedate option, **ferries** travel to the other side of the Danube to **Arnsdorf,** where the local *jause* (an Austrian version of British high tea), here called *Hauerganse* (vintner's special), will load enough carbos to send you through the vineyards and apricot orchards back to Melk. The ferry returns past the **Heiratswald** (Marriage Woods). Romantic Melk awards a young sapling tree to couples who marry in Melk, which the happy couple plants and tends for the rest of their lives.

▣ FESTIVALS. The **Sommerspiele Melk** (Melk Summer Festival) comes to town in early July. An open-air stage in front of the monastery's pavilion provides the perfect setting for enjoying world-class theater (in German) on warm summer nights. Tickets (150-350AS) are available at the Melk city hall, theater ticket offices, travel agencies throughout Austria, and the box office next to the monastery after 7:15pm, before performances. (Performances mid-July to mid-Aug. Th-Sa 8:30pm. For more information, call 52307 or fax 523 07 27.)

LIECHTENSTEIN

A recent Liechtenstein tourist brochure unfortunately mislabeled the already tiny 160km² country as an even tinier 160m². As a matter of fact, this is approximately how much most tourists see of the world's only German-speaking monarchy, as most travelers usually pause only long enough to buy the obligatory postage stamp and hastily record the visit in a passport. Liechtenstein is tiny and heavily touristed, but it has some unique characteristics, primarily the fact that it has a ruling monarch, Prince Hans Adam II, son of Prince Franz Josef II, who was the first ruler to actually live in Liechtenstein since the present dynasty took control of the country in 1699. Before that, the family ruled Liechtenstein from their estates in the former Czechoslovakia. Liechtenstein's ties to Switzerland were established in 1923 with a customs and monetary union, replacing a similar agreement with the Austro-Hungarian empire that lasted from 1852 to 1919. Yet while Liechtenstein may not have an army or independent foreign representation, it sure has cash.

The tourist business, boosted by some shrewd business decisions made by the last prince, has brought tremendous wealth to the citizenry of Liechtenstein. Luxury cars are the transportation of choice for the farmers of upper Liechtenstein. The cliff-hanging roads they drive on are the gateways to those places in Liechtenstein that are truly worth visiting—the unspoiled mountains a world away from the tourist traps below. Lower Liechtenstein is perfect for biking, while Upper Liechtenstein offers hiking and skiing prospects that outweigh the capital's limited charms. The **Liechtenstein Alpine Association** offers free guided full- and half-day hikes every Thursday during the summer, and the Saturday newspaper publishes routes and contact numbers.

HIGHLIGHTS OF LIECHTENSTEIN

■ Sniff and swish wine from the **Prince's private vineyards** in Vaduz (p. 291).
■ Scan both the Swiss and Austrian Alps from the **Pfälzerhütte,** a short hike from Malbun (p. 292).
■ Relive your childhood stamp-collecting mania in the one-room **Briefmarkenmuseum** (Stamp Museum) in Vaduz (p. 291).

VADUZ AND LOWER LIECHTENSTEIN

The hamlet of Vaduz is Liechtenstein's capital and tourist center. It's not a budget-friendly place and you don't get much for your money. As the old saying goes, "There is no *there* there." Vaduz is a town of tourists traveling in packs, furiously scrambling to find *something* worthy of a photo opportunity. Often, they find nothing more than the mass-produced sculptures sold in front of tourist malls. Fortunately, Vaduz is surrounded by countryside that invites camping and biking.

🔽 ORIENTATION AND PRACTICAL INFORMATION.

Although trains from Austria and Switzerland pass through the country, Liechtenstein itself has no rail system. Instead, it has an efficient and cheap **postal bus** system that links all 11 villages (short trips 2.40SFr; SwissPass valid). A one-week bus ticket (10SFr, students 5SFr) covers all (and we mean *all*) of Liechtenstein as well as buses to Swiss and Austrian border towns. The pass quickly becomes worthwhile. The principality is a 20-minute bus ride from **Sargans** or **Buchs** in Switzerland and **Feldkirch** in Austria (3.60SFr).

Vaduz

ACCOMMODATIONS
A Hotel Post
B Jugendherberge (HI)

TO SCHAAN AND 🅰 (2 km)

0 ——— 100 yards
0 ——— 100 meters

Schloßstr.
Landstr.
Giessen Canal
Mareestr.
Fürst-Franz-Josef-Str.
Hinterg.
Mitteldorf
Egertastr.
Herreng.
Leftstr.
Am Schragen Weg
Aulestr.
Städtle
Bergstr.
Kirchstr.
Heiligkreuz

N

Ski Museum 🏛
Denner Superdiscount
Rathaus
Car Park
Staatliche Kunstsammlung
Schloß Vaduz
Briefmarken-museum
National Museum 🏛

Biking is a great way to get around the lower country, but can be both difficult and dangerous on mountain roads. For the **police,** call 117. In a **fire,** call 118. In a **medical emergency,** dial 144. The principality has used the Swiss franc as its currency since 1924 and has adopted the Swiss postal and telephone systems. The **postal code** is FL-9490.

Liechtenstein's **national tourist office,** Städtle 37 (tel. 392 11 11 or 232 14 43; fax 392 16 18; email touristinfo@lie-net.li), one block up the hill from the Vaduz postal bus stop, will stamp your passport with Liechtenstein's bi-colored seal (2SFr). It also locates rooms free of charge, makes hotel reservations (2SFr), and distributes free maps and advice on hiking, cycling, and skiing in the area. (Open June-Oct. M-F 8am-noon and 1:30-5:30pm, Sa 9am-noon and 1-4pm, Su 10am-noon and 1-4pm; Nov.-May M-F 8am-noon and 1:30-5:30pm. English spoken.) For **currency exchange** at acceptable rates, go to Switzerland. No kidding. **Rent bicycles** (20SFr per day) at **Mellinger AG,** Kirchstr. 10 (tel. 232 16 06) or at **Rad-Zenterttermann,** Feldkirchstr. 74 (tel. 233 35 36). It helps to call ahead. The tourist office sells bike maps for 2.50SFr. The main **post office** (tel. 232 21 55) is near the tourist office and has an amazing selection of…postage stamps (open M-F 7:45am-6pm, Sa 8-11am).

| **PHONE CODE** | Liechtenstein uses the Swiss **country code** (41) and international dialing prefix (00). The **city code** is 075 country-wide. |

⬛⬛ ACCOMMODATIONS AND FOOD. Budget housing options in Vaduz itself are few and far between, but neighboring **Schaan** is more inviting. The welcoming staff at budget-friendly **Hotel Post** (tel. 232 17 18), facing the back of the Schaan post office (easily accessible by bus #1 from Vaduz), makes up for somewhat shabby accommodations; the light bulbs have no covers and the floor is barely covered by the rug, but there are plenty of open places in which to relax, including the garden terrace outside the restaurant. (Singles 35SFr, with shower 45SFr; doubles 70SFr, with shower 90SFr. Breakfast included. Reception 6am-noon.) Liechtenstein's lone **Jugendherberge (HI members only),** Untere Rütig. 6 (tel. 232 50 22; fax 232 58 56), also in Schaan, is more aesthetically pleasing but less service-oriented. From Vaduz, take bus #1 (dir.: Schaan) to "Mühleholz," walk toward the intersection with the traffic lights, and turn left down Marianumstr. Walk four to five minutes and follow the signs to this spotless pink hostel, set on the edge of a farm. Be prepared for the bad American rock music piped through all the rooms from 7:30am until 10pm. (Dorms 26.30SFr; doubles 64.60SFr; family quads 113.20SFr. Showers and breakfast included. Dinner 12SFr. Laundry 8SFr. Reception M-Sa 7-9:30am and 5-10pm, Su 7-9:30am and 6-10pm. Lockout 9:30am-5pm. Curfew 10pm. Open Mar.-Nov. 15.)

Lower Liechtenstein's 2 peaceful **campgrounds** are easily accessible by postal bus. For **Camping Bendern** (tel. 373 12 11), take bus #50/51 (dir.: Schellenberg) to "Bendern" and walk past the village church (6SFr per person; tents 4SFr; showers 1SFr). **Camping Mittagspitze** (tel. 392 26 86), between Triesen and Balzers on the road to Sargans, offers gorgeous sites at the foot of the mountain near a cold Alpine brook. (8.50SFr; tent 5SFr. Shower and pool included. Reception 8-10am and 4-8pm. Open year-round.)

Eating out cheaply in Liechtenstein is extremely challenging. Groceries and a fantastic array of Swiss chocolate are available at **Migros**, Aulestr. 20, across from the tour bus parking lot (open M-F 8:30am-1pm and 1:30-6:30pm, Sa 8am-4pm). In the same shopping complex, **Azzuro Pizza** (tel. 232 48 18) serves take-out pizzas for 7-14SFr and 8SFr kebabs (open M-F 8am-8pm, Sa 8am-5pm, Su 10am-5pm).

⬛ SIGHTS. 12th-century **Schloß Vaduz,** the regal home of Hans Adam II, Prince of Liechtenstein, presides above the town. Although the interior of the ruler's residence is off-limits to the bourgeois masses, you can hike up to the castle for a closer look and a phenomenal view of the whole country. The trail begins down the street from the tourist office, heading away from the post office. (Numerous signs reading "Castle this way: No visit" are only meant to prevent commoners from knocking on the royal front door and inviting themselves inside. Only rich politicians, students with very good university final exams, and retirees are asked to visit the Prince…usually on New Year's Day.) Reproductions of the royal art collection almost inevitably end up on postage stamps in the one-room **Briefmarkenmuseum (Stamp Museum)** on the other side of the tourist office (open daily Apr.-Oct. 10am-noon and 1:30-5:30pm; Nov.-Mar. 10am-noon and 1:30-5pm; free). Groups of 10 or more can arrange to visit the **Hofkellerei des Regierenden Fürsten von Liechtenstein** (Wine Cellars of the Ruling Prince of Liechtenstein) and taste wines from the Prince's private vineyards (tel. 232 10 18; reservations required; 20SFr per person). Smaller groups (up to 3) can try knocking on the door of the wine cellars. If the cellar has an open bottle, they'll often let you try some.

UPPER LIECHTENSTEIN

Despite the country's diminutive size, different areas of Liechtenstein have distinct traits, which become more noticeable the higher up you get. The "upper" in Upper Liechtenstein refers to the region's elevation rather than a northern position. These heights are where the real character and beauty of Liechtenstein lie. The roads that snake their way up the mountainsides to tiny villages, such as **Triesenberg** and **Malbun,** allow for spectacular views of the Rhine Valley and the surrounding Alps. Buses make the short run to all these towns from Vaduz in under 40 minutes, and the trips are well worth the effort even if you're only spending one day in the country.

TRIESENBERG. The first town up the mountain (serviced by bus #10) is **Triesenberg**, a town founded in the 13th century by the Walsers, a group of Swiss immigrants forced to flee Valais due to overpopulation, religious intolerance, and natural disaster. The **Walser Heimatmuseum** chronicles the Walsers' religious customs, hut construction, cattle trade, and crafts (open Tu-F 1:30-5:30pm, Sa 1:30-5pm, Su 2-5pm; Sept.-May closed Su. 2SFr, children 1SFr). The ultra-friendly **tourist office** (tel. 262 19 26; fax 262 19 22) is in the same building as the museum and has the same hours. The most stunning **hike** for views of the Rhine Valley begins near Triesenberg. Take bus #30 (dir.: Gaflei, which leaves infrequently but on time) or drive to **Gaflei**. From the parking lot where the bus stops, head toward the gravel path across the street. Look for the trail on the left, and follow signs to "Silum" and then to "Ob. Tunnel, Steg." The level trail wanders through low Alpine forest and grazing meadows. At the end, walk through the damp old tunnel, then down the narrow road to Steg, where bus #10 runs back to Vaduz or Schaan every hour (whole hike 1½hr.).

MALBUN. On the other side of the mountain, secluded **Malbun** is undoubtedly the hippest place in the principality, harboring approachable people, affordable ski slopes, and plenty of hiking, not to mention a **tourist office** (tel. 263 65 77; open May-Oct. and Dec.-Apr. M-F 9am-noon and 1:30-5pm, Sa 9am-noon and 1-4pm). During the winter two chair lifts, four T-bars, and two ski schools service you and not too many other people. (Day pass 33SFr; 6-day pass 136SFr, off-season 129SFr.) Right in the middle of town, **Malbun A.G.** (tel. 263 97 70 or 262 19 15) offers 1-day classes (60SFr), 3-day classes (140SFr), and private snowboard lessons (1 day 210SFr). **Malbun Sport** (tel. 263 37 55) rents skis and snowboards. Cross-country skiing is available 2km from Malbun in Steg.

During the summer the #10 bus from Vaduz and Schaan (40min., 1 per hr. all year, 2.40SFr) is full of hikers heading to Malbun for its mountain **hiking**. The most acclaimed hike in town is a round-trip hike to **Pfälzerhütte**. The best starting point is from the top of the only chairlift open in the summer, the Sareiserjoch (round-trip 11.70SFr, one-way 7.50SFr; students 9.50SFr, 5.90SFr). This trip up the mountain is worthwhile just for the views of the Austrian and Swiss Alps, even if you're not into hiking. For the hike, signs for Pfälzerhütte (be sure to turn left off the main trail after 5 minutes) will lead you over Augustenberg (at 2359m the second highest peak in Liechtenstein). There are a number of ways back to Malbun. One good option is to head toward Gritsch and then Tälihöhi (whole hike 5hr.).

The best place to stay for hiking and skiing access is the superb chalet duo of ▓**Hotel Alpen and Hotel Galina** (tel. 263 11 81; fax 263 94 46). The young couple who runs these wooden-paneled hotels is an experienced source of information on outdoor activities in the area. (Reception in Hotel Alpen for both. Singles 40-65SFr, with shower 70-100SFr; doubles 80-130SFr, 140-200SFr. Breakfast and heated pool included. Open mid-May to Oct. and Dec. 15-Apr. 15.)

LIECHTENSTEIN

SWITZERLAND

US$1 = 1.516 SWISS FRANCS (SFR)	1SFR = US$0.659
CDN$1 = 1.023SFR	1SFR = CDN$0.977
UK£ = 2.428SFR	1SFR = UK£0.412
IR£1 = 2.034SFR	1SFR = IR£0.491
AUS$1 = 0.984SFR	1SFR = AUS$1.016
NZ$1 = 0.798SFR	1SFR = NZ$1.252
SAR1 = 0.248SFR	1SFR = SAR4.025
1AS = 0.116SFR	1SFR = 8.589AS
1DM = 0.819SFR	1SFR = DM1.220
1K⁻ = 0.044SFR	1SFR = 22.614K⁻
EURO€1 = 1.602SFR	1SFR = EURO€0.624

PHONE CODES	The **country code** for Switzerland is 41. For international calls from Switzerland, add the prefix 00.

The unparalleled natural beauty of Switzerland *(die Schweiz, la Suisse, la Svizzera, Confederatio Helvetica)* seduces hikers, skiers, bikers, paragliders, and scenery gazers from all over the globe to romp about its Alpine playground. Three-fifths of the country is dominated by mountains: the Jura cover the northwest region, bordering France, while the Alps stretch gracefully across the entire lower half of Switzerland, flirting with Italy in the southern Lepontine chain and colliding with Austria in the eastern Rhaetian Alps. The rest of Switzerland is blanketed with verdant meadows ripe for frolicking, pristine glacier lakes, and tiny hilltop hamlets as well as urban centers of culture and commerce.

The Swiss people share no common language or religion, yet have managed to coexist (more or less) peacefully for centuries. As a people, they defy classification—they value their history and traditions, but not to the point that visitors can expect to see alp-horn blowing, lederhosen-clad mountain men prancing about the slick *Bahnhofstrasse* of Zurich's shopping district. While the stereotypes of Switzerland as a "Big Money" banking and watch-making mecca are true to some extent (nearly 4% of the Swiss are employed in the banking industry), its energetic youth culture belies the staid reputation which plagues Switzerland.

Switzerland is adept at welcoming tourists with open arms. The Swiss have raised the hospitality industry to an art; service, food, and accommodations are consistently high quality even at the most modest *pensions*. Its efficient and comprehensive public transportation system makes Switzerland an ideal destination for the independent traveler. Although Switzerland is not known for being cheap, the thrifty traveler can always find a bargain. And in Switzerland, the best things—warm Swiss hospitality and sublime vistas—are priceless.

BUILDING THE SWISS CONFEDERATION:

Switzerland is a confederation made up of 23 cantons (states) and 3 sub-cantons. The confederation grew gradually from the three original Forest Cantons (Uri, Schwyz, and Unterwalden) who joined together in 1291. Today, the cantons, clockwise starting with Bern, the capital, are: Bern (incorporated 1353), Lucerne (1332), Obwalden and Nidwalden (1291, originally part of Unterwalden), Zug (1352), Uri (1291), Schwyz (1291), Zurich (1351), Schaffhausen (1501), Thurgau (1803), Appenzell (1501), St. Gallen (1803), Glarus (1352), Graubünden (1803), Ticino (1803), Valais (1815), Geneva (1815), Vaud (1803), Fribourg (1481), Neuchâtel (1815), Jura (1978), Solothurn (1481), Basel (1501), and Aargau (1803).

A BRIEF HISTORY OF SWITZERLAND

350,000 BC Paleolithic hunters drop a hand wedge near Basel, giving modern achaeologists proof of their existence.

30,000 BC Glaciers melt; Neolithic cultures establish themselves in the Rhone and Rhine Valleys.

3000-1800 BC Neolithic Swiss settlers build lake villages.

From 500 BC Celts occupy western Switzerland while Rhaetians settle the east. The Helvetii become a powerful Celtic tribe.

58 BC Caesar defeats Helvetii at Bibracte, beginning Roman rule.

AD 101-150 Celtics, Rhaetians, and Romans peacefully coexist.

260 Germanic tribes attack; Swiss militarize in defense.

ca. 500 Barbarians form permanent settlements: Burgundians control the western territories, while the Alemanni

PRE-HISTORY: FROM CAVE MEN TO CELTS

Before there was cheese, chocolate, and the Swatch watch, there was ice. For hundreds of millennia, Switzerland was blanketed with glaciers several thousand meters deep. While evidence of human habitation in the area dates back 350,000 years, only after the last glacial period 30,000 years ago did early Swiss stop chasing reindeer through mountain valleys and start establishing permanent settlements. Hunter-gatherer cave-dwelling Stone-Agers traded in their hard rock for heavy metal as Iron Age **Celts** built their houses on stilts near lakes, swamps, and rivers. By 750 BC, Switzerland had become an important center of Celtic culture. The artistic and warlike **Helvetii,** the most prominent Swiss-Celtic tribe, gained notoriety for their (largely unsuccessful) attempts to invade Roman Italy in 222 BC and again as allies of Carthage between 218 and 203 BC (when they assisted Hannibal and his elephants in their famous crossing of the Alps). Their attempts to advance into Gaul in 58 BC were halted by Julius Caesar, who first crushed, then colonized the Helvetians. Romanized between 47 BC and AD 15, they survived as a settled, peaceful, urban civilization for the next two centuries. Helvetian lands extended across the Alpine valleys of central Switzerland, while the east (present-day Graubünden) was populated by the **Rhaeti,** an Etruscan tribe. Rhaetian women, refusing to succumb to Roman conquest, were said to have hurled their own children at attackers in desperation. **Rhaeto-Romansh**, a combination of Roman Latin and the Rhaetian Tuscan dialect, is still spoken in former Rhaetian territories as testimony to their fierce devotion to their ancient culture.

Around AD 250, constant raids from Germanic tribes forced Switzerland to militarize, changing it from a peaceful farming province into an armed frontier. As Roman influence waned in the 5th century, the tribes began to form permanent settlements. **Burgundians** settled the west, merging peacefully with the Romanized Celts and absorbing their culture and language. The more aggressive **Alemanni** foisted their own culture on the Celts of central and northern Switzerland as well as on rival Germanic tribes. They eventually pushed the Burgundians west to the Sarine River, which remains the border between German and French Switzerland.

AGAINST THE EMPIRE: AN ALEMANNI LEGACY

The feisty Alemanni, with their aversion to conformity and centralized government, set the stage for centuries of Swiss individualism. The Alemanni did not establish a utopian society free of class stratification, but their use of a people's assembly and majority rule in making communal decisions was a step in the right direction. With this commitment to democratic village life, their descendents were understandably a bit peeved when Holy Roman Emperor Rudolf of Habsburg attempted to take three of their communities (Uri,

TELL-TALE As part of the Holy Roman Empire, the citizens of the Forest Cantons were willing to recognize the emperor as their overlord, but refused any other feudal obligations. When Emperor Rudolf dispatched deputies to do his dirty work (tax-collecting, fining, jailing), the freemen of the Forest Cantons were less than thrilled. Even then, no one liked paying taxes. Legend has it that a particularly haughty Habsburg henchman by the name of Gessler demanded that all freemen bow to his hat in homage. The rebellious descendents of the Alemanni had other ideas. According to the tale, a freeman named William Tell journeyed with his son to the town of Altdorf in canton Uri, where he encountered the knavish Gessler. Tell blatantly ignored Gessler's hallowed hat, which got Gessler's panties in a bunch. Gessler promptly had Tell arrested, and ordered Tell to shoot an arrow through an apple on his son's head. Tell, an expert Swiss marksman, hit the apple and spared his son, then was quick to tell Gessler the next arrow had his name on it. The legend, immortalized in Schiller's play in 1804, has come to symbolize the Swiss rough-and-ready mountaineer spirit that vanquishes tyranny in the name of freedom and independence. See Schiller's version of *Wilhelm Tell* during your summer jaunt in Interlaken.

Schwyz, and Unterwalden—the "Forest Cantons") under his direct control. Switzerland had been loosely united since 1032 as part of the **Holy Roman Empire,** but it was not until Rudolf's crusade in the late 13th century that the Swiss decided to rebel (see **Tell-Tale,** p. 295). In a secret pact, the three Forest Cantons signed their **Everlasting Alliance** in 1291—an agreement that obligated the cantons to defend each other from outside attack. The Swiss consider this moment to be the beginning of the Swiss Confederation (which celebrated its 700th anniversary in 1991). The Everlasting Alliance also marked the beginning of 350 years of struggle against the **Habsburg Empire.** In 1315, the Swiss and the Habsburgs duked it out at the Battle of Morgarten. The Swiss emerged victorious, forcing the Habsburgs to agree to a truce and grant the alliance official recognition.

Over the next several centuries, the three-canton core of Switzerland expanded despite conflict between the Everlasting Alliance and the Habsburg Emperors. One by one, Bern, Lucerne, Zurich, Glarus, and Zug jumped on the Confederation bandwagon, but a union of such fiercely independent and culturally distinct states made for an uneasy marriage. In the mid-15th century, social tensions between the town and country residents erupted in civil war. The **Swabian War** with the Habsburgs of 1499-1500 brought virtual independence from the Holy Roman Empire, but domestic struggles continued as cultural and religious differences between the cantons festered.

REFORMATION TO REVOLUTION

With no strong central government to settle quibbles between cantons of different faith, the Swiss were ill equipped to deal with the major religious reform that transformed Europe in

---

dominate central and northeastern Switzerland.

610 Irish monks found the monastery in St. Gallen.

1032 Switzerland is loosely united under the Holy Roman Empire.

1200 Construction of the St. Gotthard Pass opens trade routes through Alpine valleys.

1273 Rudolf of Habsburg becomes Holy Roman Emperor, taking control of the Forest Cantons.

1291 Rudolf of Habsburg dies. Uri, Schwyz, and Unterwalden sign Everlasting Alliance for mutual protection against enemies—the beginning of the Swiss Confederation.

1315 In the Battle of Morgarten, Swiss defeat the Habsburgs, then renew their alliance at the agreement of Brunnen.

1436 Cultural differences between cantons result in a civil war.

1460 The Austrians

SWITZERLAND

are driven out of Thurgau; Basel University is founded.

1499 The Swabian War leads to independence from Holy Roman Empire.

1519 Ulrich Zwingli leads religious reform in Zurich.

1536 John Calvin preaches Puritanism in Geneva.

1618-48 The Thirty Years War rages. The Peace of Westphalia gives Switzerland independence from the Austrian Empire, ending 350 years of struggle.

1762 Jean Jacques Rousseau (born in Geneva in 1712) publishes *The Social Contract*.

1789 The French Revolution begins.

1793 The Swiss Guardsmen defending Louis XVI are massacred in Paris.

1798 French troops occupy Vaud, Fribourg and Solothurn.

1798-1803 The French impose a central government: the Helvetic Republic. The Swiss have

the 16th century. The **Protestant Reformation** rocked Switzerland to its foundations. As Lutheranism swept Northern Europe, radical theologian **Ulrich Zwingli** of Zurich spearheaded his own brand of reform that advocated a less literal reinterpretation of the symbols and gestures of Catholicism. In 1523, the city government of Zurich sanctioned Zwingli's proposed *Theses* and strengthened Zwingli's hold over the local government, banning the differently minded Anabaptists and imposing harsh disciplines on its residents. Meanwhile, in Geneva, French-born lawyer and priest **John Calvin** preached a doctrine of predestination based on a rigid moral framework. He soon took a theocratic grip of Geneva and instituted puritanical reforms, turning Geneva into a shining example of the ideal of Protestant social control unsullied by the evils of pastry eating, dirty dancing, and sniffing in church. While Zurich and Geneva became strongholds of the Protestant movement, the rural Forest cantons remained loyal to the Catholic faith. They saw the Reformation as a product of wayward-thinking city dwellers. Religious differences combined with tensions between urban and rural cantons resulted in full-fledged battle, climaxing in Zwingli's death and the defeat of the Protestants at Kappel in 1531. The confederation finally interceded in the mid-16th century, granting Protestants freedoms but prohibiting them from imposing their faith on certain others.

Despite religious differences, the confederation remained neutral during the **Thirty Years War,** escaping the devastation wrought on the rest of Central Europe. The 1648 **Peace of Westphalia** granted the Swiss official neutrality and independence from the Austrian Habsburg Empire, ending 350 years of strife.

Free from the Austrians but not the French, Swiss independence was short lived. Caught up in Revolutionary fervor and perhaps inflamed at the Swiss Guard, who loyally defended King Louis XVI and the royal family until their death, French troops invaded Switzerland in 1798 and, by Napoleon's order, established the **Helvetic Republic.** Napoleon's republic restructured the relationship between the cantons and the federal government, giving more power to the central body. This had not been a popular idea since early spats with the Holy Roman Empire, and the Swiss were not about to simply watch the French install their puppet government, no matter

MUSCLE FOR HIRE The Swiss may be neutral, but no one could ever call them wimps. For five centuries Swiss soldiers hired themselves out as mercenaries, fighting battles for every major European power. Meddling in other countries' affairs had repercussions: the Swiss Guard's loyal defense of the unpopular Louis XVI during the French Revolution earned them a brutal massacre. When the Swiss revised their constitution in 1874, they outlawed the practice of providing mercenaries to foreign armies. The one exception to the rule is the Swiss papal guard, which has defended the Vatican (in original costume designed by Michelangelo) since 1505. Even these guys get a little trigger happy at times—in May of 1998, commander of the Swiss Guard Alois Estermann shot his wife and another guard, then killed himself in a moment of madness.

how noble-minded their other reforms might have been. In 1803 the Swiss overthrew Napoleon's regime, leading to brief anarchy. Napoleon's **Mediation Act** settled the whole nasty affair, and established Switzerland as a confederation of 19 cantons (by this time including Basel, Schauffhausen, and Appenzell, who had joined in the 1500s; and St. Gallen, Aargau, Graubünden, Thurgau, Ticino, and Vaud). After Napoleon's defeat at Waterloo, the Congress of Vienna added Geneva, Neuchatel, and the Valais to the Confederation and officially recognized Swiss neutrality

NEUTRALITY AND DIPLOMACY: 1815 TO THE 20TH CENTURY

Neutrality established, Switzerland could turn its attention to domestic issues. Industrial growth brought relative material prosperity, but the era was not exactly golden. The Mediation Act disappeared with Napoleon, and the **Federal Pact** of 1815 that replaced Napoleon's decrees once again established Switzerland as a confederation of sovereign states united only for common defense—united foreign policy was still impossible. Because of logistical barriers (each canton had its own laws, currency, postal service, weights, measures, and army) the inhabitants of one canton regarded the inhabitants of other cantons as foreigners. Furthermore, religious differences continued to create increased tension between cantons.

These religious differences led, in 1846, to the formation of a separatist defense league of Catholic cantons known as the **Sonderbund,** composed of Lucerne, Uri, Schwyz, Unterwalden, Zug, Fribourg, and Valais. In July 1847, the **Diet,** a parliamentary body representing the other cantons, declared the Sonderbund incompatible with the Federal Pact and demanded its dissolution. In keeping with the fashion of the time, a civil war broke out. It only lasted 25 days. The Protestant federalist forces were victorious, and the country wrote a new constitution modeled after that of the United States in 1848 (modified in 1874). Finally balancing the age-old conflict between federal and cantonal power, the constitution guaranteed republican and democratic cantonal constitutions and set up an executive body for the first time. The central government then established a free-trade zone and unified postal, currency, and railway systems accross all the cantons.

Once turmoil had given way to stability, Switzerland cultivated its reputation for resolving international conflicts (or at least getting its name on anything diplomatic). The **Geneva Convention of 1864** established international laws for conduct during war. Geneva also became the headquarters for the **International Red Cross.**

Not quite free of the tangle of alliances that characterized Europe's turn-of-the-century balance of power, Switzerland's neutrality was tested in both the **Franco-Prussian war** and **World War I** as French- and German-speaking Switzerland claimed different cultural loyalties.In 1920, Geneva welcomed the headquarters of the ill-fated **League of Nations,** solidifying Switzerland's reputation as the center for international diplomacy. At the onset of **World War II,** Switzerland mobilized 20% of the population for a defensive army. Luckily for the Swiss,

other ideas. Anarchy ensues.

1803 Napoleon's Mediation Act settles strife.

1815 The Congress of Vienna recognizes Swiss neutrality.

1831 The cantons create a constitution, establishing a weak central body.

1863-4 The first Geneva convention takes place; the Red Cross is established.

1874 The constitution is revised, giving more power to the central government.

1882 The Gotthardbahn (railway across the Alps) is opened.

1914 WWI begins; the Swiss stay out of it.

1920 Switzerland joins the League of Nations after their neutrality is assured.

1939 WWII begins— the Swiss remain neutral, though the threat of a Nazi invasion causes a mobilization of ground troops.

1939-1945 Switzer-

Hitler's plan to invade Switzerland was thwarted by Allied landings and distractions on the North African front. Both sides found it useful to have Switzerland (and its banks) as neutral territory. While some Jews, escaping Allied prisoners, and other refugees from Nazi Germany found safe haven in Switzerland, the Swiss government, not eager to incur the wrath of the monster that surrounded it, generally impeded passage through its territory and assumed the hiding-tortoise position. Aside from some accidental bombings in 1940, 1944, and 1945, Switzerland survived the war unscathed.

As the rest of Europe cleaned up the rubble of two world wars, Switzerland nurtured its already sturdy economy. Zurich emerged as a banking and insurance center, while Geneva invited international organizations, including the World Health Organization, the World Council of Churches, and the World Jewish Congress, to set up shop. Although Geneva became the headquarters for international diplomacy, Switzerland remained isolationist in its relations with the rest of Europe, declining membership to the United Nations, NATO, and the European Economic Community.

CONTEMPORARY POLITICS

Switzerland's policy of armed neutrality persists to the present: there is no standing army, but every adult male faces compulsory military service. The desire to keep an army of any sort seems to be fading, as illustrated by a 1989 referendum proposing to disband the army. Switzerland has become increasingly wealthy, liberal, successful, and service-oriented since WWII, and is still fiercely independent and wary of entanglements with the rest of Europe. After years of economic stagnation, Swiss citizens continue to disagree about the **European Union** (EU) issue—a recent vote rejecting the treaty on a **European Economic Area** (EEA) yielded a voter turnout of near 80%. The division between those who opt to resist change in order to retain *Sonderfall Schweiz* **(the Swiss Way)** and those who envision growth and involvement with the EU reveals a split along linguistic lines: all six Francophone cantons lean towards integration, while the German-speaking cantons and Italian-speaking Ticino resist economic interdependence. Presently, bilateral discussions are taking place between Switzerland and the EU, and within the next three years the Swiss will vote again on whether or not to join the EU.

While conservative in some respects (women were not allowed to vote in Switzerland until 1971), the Swiss are remarkably progressive in other areas. In 1999, two women were elected to the seven-member Bundesrat (executive authority), one of whom, **Ruth Dreifuss,** will serve a one-year term as president. Switzerland has one of the world's most stringent ecological policies to protect its fragile Alpine environment. The Swiss recycle industriously and produce about half as much waste per person per year as Americans do (but still more than many EU countries). The Swiss also have instituted a radical drug policy in which drug-addicts are not forced to abandon their habit, and heroin may even be prescribed to severe addicts. This controversial policy, aimed at reducing the crime and prostitution associated with drug use, has seen success in the reduction of both crime and hard drug use since 1991. In a recent vote, the Swiss decided to continue the program.

In the past few years, Swiss banks have come under intense scrutiny for their "blind account" policy, which allowed Holocaust victims and Nazi leaders alike to deposit money during WWII. Government investigations are currently reviewing Switzerland's actions in relation to Nazi assets, treatment of Jewish refugees, and unclaimed accounts. To appease international Jewish groups, the Swiss National Bank has contributed US$69 million to a Special Fund for Holocaust Victims.

Swiss government is based on a three-tiered system of communes, cantons, and confederation. Over 3000 communes (the smallest administrative unit of government) compose the 26 cantons. Each canton has its own constitution, legislature, executive office, and judiciary system. The cantons are in turn incorporated into the Confederation and its two-chamber legislature, the Federal Assembly. One chamber, the National Council, distributes its 200 seats based on population; the other, the Council of States, distributes equal seats to the cantons. Decisions of the Federal Assembly take effect only with a majority in both chambers.

The executive branch consists of a group of 7 members—the **Bundesrat (Federal Council)**—elected to 4-year terms by a joint meeting of both legislative chambers. No canton may have more than 1 representative in the Bundesrat at a time. The Bundesrat chooses a president from among its ranks. The president only holds office for 1 year, and the post is more symbolic than functional. **Referenda** and **initiatives** make political decisions a part of the daily life of the Swiss people.

CULTURE AND CUSTOMS

PEOPLE

The Swiss are quite conservative (though their rampant festival scene might convince you otherwise—see **Festival Fever**, p. 303). They are generally very law-abiding, hard-working, and proper. Be punctual and mind your manners: remember to say hello and goodbye to shopkeepers and proprietors of bars and cafés, and always shake hands when being introduced to a Swiss person. As a result of all this propriety, the Swiss have a high standard of living, a life expectancy of 78 years, and virtually no illiteracy. When the dust settled after the Protestant Reformation, Switzerland ended up almost evenly divided between Catholics (46%) and Protestants (44%), though Protestantism has been in slight decline since World War II. The Swiss have been quite tolerant of other religious groups, for example allowing the Mormons to build a temple in Zollikofen (near Bern) in the 1950s. Geneva, the "City of Peace," shelters various international religious organizations representing 130 faiths, such as the World Council of Churches, the Baha'i International Community, the Lutheran World Federation, the Quaker UN Office, the Christian Children's Fund, and the World Jewish Congress.

In general, Swiss are active people, encouraged to venture outdoors by the alluring mountain landscape. Skiing and hiking are national pastimes, with more than 40% of the population regularly wandering through the countryside. Watch for the Swiss at the Winter Olympic Games and you'll see their hobbies pay off. Other favorite pursuits include swimming, mountain-climbing, bicycling, and soccer.

LANGUAGE

When in Switzerland, try to speak as the Swiss do (whatever the language happens to be). Many people speak English, though it is not a compulsory subject in schools, but you're always better off trying one of Switzerland's three and a half official federal languages first: German, French, Italian, or Romansh (which is only partially an official federal language). Each language spans a particular geographic region: German is spoken by 64% of the population throughout the bulk of central and eastern Switzerland. In western Switzerland, French is the language of choice

A CRASH COURSE IN SWISS GERMAN

Though you'll most likely never need to speak Swiss German, it is a charming, folksy language that reflects the traditional character of Swiss culture. If you want to pick it up, start with basic practical terms that are nearly the same in all dialects, such as the days of the week: *Mäntig, Zyschtig, Mittwuche, Donschtig, Frytig, Samschtig, Sunntig,* or the months: *Jänner, Horner, März, April, Mei, Brachmonet, Höimonet, Ougschte, Herbstmonet, Wymonet, Wintermonet, Chrischtmonet.* Even if you haven't mastered these tongue-twisters, watch out when buying cereal—be sure to distinguish between *Müesli,* the famous granola, which literally means "little smashed-up things," and *Müsli,* the common misspelling, which means "little mice."

for 19% of the Swiss, while 8% speak Italian, primarily in the southern Ticino region. Romansh is spoken by less than 1% of the population, but it has historical and ethnic significance after having survived for hundreds of years in the isolated mountain valleys of Graubünden. If you don't speak any of these languages, at least greet people with *Grüezi* and ask s*prechen Sie Englisch, parlez vous anglais,* or *lei parla inglese* (depending on where you are, of course) before pouring out your heart. There is a bit of overlap between languages, and you'll hear people say *merci, ciao,* and *adiö* throughout Switzerland.

In contrast to Germany, where local dialects of German have been looked down on for centuries, German Switzerland celebrates its dialects, known collectively as Swiss German, or *Schwyzertüütsch.* Swiss German is as different from High German as Dutch or Danish, so don't expect to be able to understand it if you speak High German. Linguistically, Swiss German resembles Middle High German, which was spoken in Germany five hundred years ago. What can we say? The Swiss are conservative. Geographic isolation led to the development of highly differentiated dialects in each region with individual peculiarities of pronunciation, grammar, and vocabulary. *Wallisertütsch,* spoken in the southern Valais region, is one of the oldest Swiss German dialects and hence one of the least comprehensible, even to Swiss Germans. On the other hand, *Bärntütsch* and *Züritüütsch,* spoken around Bern and Zurich respectively, are more regular, though there is no official written standard of Swiss German. Though words like *chääschüechli* (cheesecake) and *chuchichäschtli* (kitchen cabinets) may sound harsh to Anglophone ears, most German Swiss prefer their dialect to High German. The Swiss identify with their language and will appreciate any effort you make to speak it, so take a deep breath and practice saying *Ufwiderluege* (goodbye)!

FOOD AND DRINK

Switzerland is not for the lactose intolerant. From rich and varied mountain **cheeses** (see **Say cheese!**, p. 301) to decadent milk chocolate, the Swiss are serious about their dairy products. They even have a dairy-based non-alcoholic beverage, *rivella,* which is recommended for pregnant women. Even the yogurt tastes better in Swizerland—and much of it is "bio" or organically processed. Best of all, these divine bovine goodies are always available for cheap at the local Migros or Co-op.

As far as **chocolate** goes, the Swiss have earned bragging rights for their expertise: with the invention of milk chocolate in 1875, Switzerland was poised to rule the world (it's just biding its time). Switzerland is home to some of the world's largest producers: **Lindt, Suchard,** and **Nestlé.** Visit the Lindt factory in Zurich or the Nestlé factory near Bulle to load up on free samples! **Toblerone,** manufactured in Bern, is an international favorite famous for the bits of nougat in creamy milk chocolate, packaged in a nifty triangular box. Chocolate comes in different percentages of concentration—the higher the percentage, the darker and more bitter the chocolate. The Swiss insist that chocolate is essential to any diet (*Let's Go* agrees). Don't be caught on a long hike or walk without your stash for that sugar-rush induced energy boost.

So you've had your fill of cheese and chocolate—what's the main course, you ask? It depends on what language your waiter is speaking. The flavor of regional cooking follows the contours of Switzerland's linguistic topography. The basic geography is simple and logical: Frenchified in the west, Italian in the south, and Swiss-German everywhere else. Each region is represented, however, in an array of "typical" Swiss dishes, which might include the Zurich speciality, *Geschnetzeltes* (strips of veal stewed in a thick cream sauce), *Luzerner Chugelipastete* (pâté in a pastry shell), *Papet Vaudois* (leeks with sausage from Vaud), *Churer Fleischtorte* (meat pie from Chur), and Bernese salmon. To match each local specialty, there is usually a bread specific to the region or town. Ask for it by name (e.g. when in St. Gallen, ask for *St. Galler-brot*) at the local market or bakery.

Switzerland's hearty peasant cooking will keep you warm through those frigid Alpine winters but will do a number on your cholesterol count. Nevertheless, you can spare the extra calories to indulge in these dishes. Bernese **Rösti,** a plateful of hash brown potatoes skilleted and occasionally flavored with bacon or cheese, is as prevalent in the German regions as **fondue** (from the French, *fondre*—to "melt") is in the French. Usually a blend of Emmentaler and Gruyère cheeses, white wine, *kirsch,* and spices, fondue is eaten by dunking small cubes of white bread into a *caquelon* (a one-handled pot) kept hot by a small flame. The mother of all cheese dips originated as a way to use up stale bread and cheese shavings. Valaisian **Raclette,** a favorite for small dinner parties, is made by cutting a large cheese in half and heating it until it melts; the melted cheese is then scraped onto a baked potato and garnished with meat or vegetables. Fondue and raclette, however, are traditionally wintertime treats. Ordering them in a restaurant on a hot day in July is a dead giveaway that you're a tourist, but these dishes are worth a few odd stares from the locals.

The world's chocolate experts would never neglect the lingering sweet-tooth. Indeed, the Swiss are adept at the art of **confectionery**. Among the most tempting cakes are the *Baseler Leckerli* (a kind of gingerbread), *Schaffhauser Zungen*, *Zuger Kirschtorte*, Engadin nutcakes, the *bagnolet crème* of the Jura (eaten with raspberries and anise seed biscuits), soda rolls, *rissoles* (pear tarts), the nougat and pralines of Geneva, and the *zabaglione* of Ticino. *Vermicelli* (not the Italian pasta but a dessert made of chestnut mousse) is popular all over Switzerland.

The Romans introduced **wine** to the region, but it was not until the 9th century that beer-drinking laity pried it away from the clergy—who used it, of course, for liturgical purposes. By the 19th century, production had grown so indiscriminately, and the results so middling, that consumers went back to drinking beer. But a wine statute in 1953 imposed rigorous quality controls, and since then Swiss wine has regained its reputation. Most wine is produced in the west and the Valais, about three-quarters of it white. The wine produced around Lake Zurich and in the Thurgau and Schaffhausen areas is predominantly *Blauburgunder*, with a small quantity of a *Riesling-Slyvaner* hybrid. Ticino specializes in reds made from the

SAY CHEESE! While the words "Swiss cheese" may conjure up images of lunch-boxed sandwiches filled with a hard, oily, holey cheese, Switzerland actually has innumerable varieties, each made from a particular type of milk. Cheese with holes is usually *Emmentaler,* from the eponymous valley near Bern, but nearly every canton and many towns have specialty cheeses. To name a few of the most well-known: *Gruyère* is a stronger and tastier version of *Emmentaler; Appenzeller* is a hard cheese with a sharp, fruity tang, sometimes made from sheep's milk instead of cow's milk; *tome* is a generic term for a soft, uncooked cheese similar to French *chèvre*. In the Italian regions, look for southern influences; cheese often resembles the *parmigiano* from Italy more than the hard mountain cheeses of the Alpine regions. Cheese in Switzerland is always superb in quality, as Swiss cheese standards are regulated by law. Their ultra-hygenic production methods result in virtually perfect cheese!

Merlot grape, and most restaurants offer a house wine as *nostrano* (one of ours). These wines are usually home-pressed blends, comparatively cheap, and delicious.

Each canton has its own local **beer,** a popular beverage in German-speaking Switzerland. Beer is relatively cheap, often less expensive than Coca-Cola. Order *ein helles* for a light beer, *ein dunkles* for a dark one (see **Frothy Facts,** p. 80).

THE ARTS

Yodeling, contrary to popular belief, is not the beginning or end of the Swiss art scene. A day spent viewing contemporary works by young Swiss artists at Zurich's cutting-edge Kunsthaus and a night spent prowling the city's underground music scene should dispel that misconception faster than you can say Heidi.

MODERN MUSIC

Switzerland is not known for its historical canon of established musical talent. The subversive artistic spirit of the late twentieth century, however, has generated a handful of musical groups that have their pulse on the sound of the next century. Most of them produce alternative music aimed at teenagers and twentysome-things, but their liberalism extends to all age groups, particularly in their swinging festivals that heat up the summer nights throughout Switzerland.

A sampling of currently popular bands might feature **Chitty Chitty Bang Bang**, a Franco-Swiss rock foursome which has self-produced two CDs and has performed in France, Russia, Germany, and throughout Switzerland. On another note, **Der Klang** has invented a French *chanson* style which has led them far from the well-trodden tracks of the genre. **Favez,** a Lausanne-based band, have recently replaced the faded rock finery of their past albums with a new acoustic sound, sombre and serious in tone. Popular not only in Switzerland but also in Germany and Japan, **Gotthard's** raw, bluesy vocals, solid hard-rock rhythms and plentiful solos recall the sound of Bon Jovi. A rock band with folk roots, Geneva's **Polar** has performed with the likes of Massive Attack and Fiona Apple. The hardcore band **Shovel,** describes its sound as somewhere between Helmet, Pearl Jam, and the Deftones.

The phrase "Swiss hip-hop" may incur some skepticism, but Switzerland does "represent" with a handful of French-Swiss groups, including Lausanne's **Legal, Rade,** and **Osez;** Geneva's **Fidel'Escro; CE-2P** from Vevey; and Neuchâtel's **La Sorcellerie.** Crossing over another unexpected genre is the jazz musician **Erik Truffaz,** who learned his trumpet skills from the famed Miles Davis. His sound combines jazz with rap and drum 'n bass influences.

20TH CENTURY PAINTING AND SCULPTURE

Even if you haven't heard of most Swiss musicians, chances are that you've run across the names of Swiss artists. There are a few early greats among them, such as **Urs Graf,** a swashbuckling, soldier-artist-poet skilled in court portraiture, and **Ferdinand Hodler,** an early Symbolist painter who used Swiss landscapes to convey metaphysical messages. In the 20th century, Switzerland has been a primary space for liberal experimentation. One of Switzerland's most famous artists is **Paul Klee,** a member of *der Blaue Reiter* (The Blue Rider) school led by **Kandinsky,** and of the Bauhaus faculty. His delicately colored watercolors and oil paintings helped shape the beginnings of abstraction, calling dominant modes of artistic expression into question.

During the World Wars, Switzerland's art scene was energized by an influx of talented refugees, a group of whom produced the **Dada** explosion in Zurich in 1916, including **Hans Arp, Richard Hülsenbeck, Janco, Tristan Tzara,** and **Hugo Ball.** Together they founded the "Cabaret Voltaire" and "Galerie Dada," short-lived centers of Dada activity. Marginal participants in the Zurich Dada scene later developed into artists in their own right. **Jean Tinguely** created kinetic, mechanized Dada fantasies that celebrated the beauty of motion.

SWITZERLAND

FESTIVAL FEVER Back in the 70s, a handful of Swiss hipsters put a new spin on the timeworn tradition of celebrating the harvest or honoring a religious holiday with a rip-roaring raucous festival. Taking the community-building spirit of the traditional festivals and adding some groovin' tunes gave birth to a new tradition: the "Open-Air" music festival. What started as a small movement has grown to encompass more than a dozen festivals in nearly every part of the Swiss countryside. Thousands of people flock from festival to festival all summer long, following the sounds of jazz, blues, folk, rock, pop, soul, funk, hip-hop, drum 'n bass, house, and techno. Best of all, as these concerts are aimed at a young crowd, tickets won't break your bank account. Here are a few highlights from summer 1999 (check websites for updated 2000 line-ups). Check out the University of Geneva's webpage at heiwww.unige.ch/switzerland/culture/events.htm or the Swiss search engine www.music.ch.

Bern, *Gurtenfestival.* This 3-day festival in mid-July attracts 15,000 visitors per day to the Gurten hill above Bern (5min. from town center). Features 2 stages, a half-pipe area, and a DJ area. The '99 lineup included Brit popsters Skunk Anansie, the French hip-hop group Alliance Ethnik, the quirky alt-rock Crash Test Dummies, and many more. (Tickets 59SFr, 89SFr, 129SFr for a 1-, 2-, or 3-day pass. Email info@gurtenfestival.ch; www.gurtenfestival.ch.)

Winterthur, *Winterthurer Musikfestwochen.* Celebrating its 25th anniversary in 2000, this 17-day festival in late August exhibits over 100 acts from multi-media genres. Indoor and outdoor events performed continuously over the 3-week period, with open-air festival the last weekend. Many events free. (Email info@musikfest-wochen.ch; www.winterthur.musikfestwochen.ch.)

Nyon (near Geneva), *Paléo Festival Nyon.* The millennium coincides with this festival's 25th birthday, so be prepared to party. Switzerland's largest open-air music festival wins the prize for diversity of acts, ranging from electric salsa, hip hop and reggae to trip hop, drum n' bass, and electronic vibes, as well as rock, pop, blues, and even traditional French *chanson.* Last year's line-up on the 5 stages ran the gamut from the USA's Fun Lovin' Criminals, Garbage, and Ben Harper to Great Britain's Heather Nova; the Italian Zucchero to French relic Charles Aznavour (and everything in-between). This 5-day festival in late July takes place on lush meadow land near the shores of Lake Geneva. A free campsite offers accommodations for thousands of festival-goers. (Tickets start at 25SFr per day. Email paleo@paleo.ch; www.paleo.ch.)

Leysin, *Leysin Alpes Festival.* Billed as "not your average festival," this 3-day fest in mid-August focuses on new up-and-coming groups from "the independent circuit." 2 huge tents showcase hip-hop, badass hardcore, intelligent techno, dub, and songwriting acts in comfort, come rain or shine. More intimate concerts in Leysin itself and a local arts-and-crafts fair aim to bring the village and the festival closer together. Wild exhibitions including bellydancing, impromptu cybercafes, extreme sports, and DJs in teepees should be a trip. (Tickets 45SFr per day or 100SFr for three days with advance purchase. Free camping. www.hugo.ch/festival/leysin/.)

St. Gallen, *Open-Air St. Gallen.* This weekend-long festival in late June combines crowd pleasing pop like Canada's Barenaked Ladies with less mainstream bands like the London underground's Asian Dub Foundation. (Tickets 144SFr for a 3-day pass. Email uandermatt@openairsg.ch; www.openairsg.ch)

Zurich, *Streetparade.* For one day in early August more than 400,000 house and techno fans congregate on the streets of Zurich and stay to party afterwards. No invitation necessary. (www.street-parade.ch.)

Bellinzona (in Canton Ticino), *Bellinzona Blues Festival.* Free piazza performances of blues bands brighten Bellinzona for 3 days in late June. Contact the Bellinzona tourist office for more information (tel. 825 21 31; fax 825 38 17).

Gampel (between Sion and Visp), *Open-Air Gampel* '99 featured Fine Young Cannibals, Culture Club, and Björn Again. Tel. (027) 932 50 13, email openair-gampel@rhone.ch, www.openairgampel.ch. Tickets available through Hello Yellow.

SWITZERLAND

Between and after the wars, Switzerland still attracted liberal artistic thinkers. The **Zurich School of Concrete Art,** which operated primarily between wars, combined elements of Surrealism with ideas from Russian Constructivism in an attempt to work with objects and environments to explore interactions between humans and space. **Max Bill**'s Mondrian-derived canvases, focusing on color relationships and the texture and form of the surface itself, are quintessential Concrete paintings. The school includes Paul Klee and **Meret Oppenheim,** a Surrealist famous for her *Fur Cup.* The philosophy guided sculptor **Alberto Giacometti** to play with spatial realities in his creations of the 1930s. Later, Giacometti rejected the premise of Surrealism in order to concentrate on a deep representationalism, creating small, exaggerated, slender figures like *Man Pointing.* After sitting out the Second World War in London and spending time in Prague, Austrian Expressionist painter **Oskar Kokoschka** moved to Switzerland in 1953, settling in Villeneuve. When Kokoschka died in 1980, his widow Olda found herself with an embarrassment of pictures and subsequently founded the Foundation Oskar Kokoschka in the Musée Jenisch in Vevey.

LITERATURE

EARLY EXAMPLES. Though Switzerland is not particularly renowned for its literary traditions, many famous and talented writers have called Switzerland home. Among them is **Jean-Jacques Rousseau**, best known for his *Social Contract* that inspired the French Revolution. He was born in Geneva in 1712 and always proudly recognized his Swiss background—despite the fact that he spent most of

EXILES AND EMIGRÉS
Ever since **Voltaire** came to Geneva in 1755 to do some heavy-duty philosophizing, Switzerland has been the promised land for intellectuals, artists, and soon-to-be-famous personalities. Some came seeking inspiration from Switzerland's raw physical beauty; others were on the lam from unfriendly governments. George Gordon, otherwise known as the opium-smoking Romantic **Lord Byron,** quit England in 1816 for Switzerland. Here he met **Percy Shelley,** and the two composed some of their greatest works. Byron wrote "Sonnet on Chillon" while brooding on Lake Geneva; Shelley crafted "Hymn to Beauty" and "Mont Blanc" in the vale of Chamonix. His wife **Mary Wollstonecraft Shelley** came across some ghost stories while in Switzerland, which, heightened by Switzerland's eternal mist and craggy Alps, inspired her masterpiece *Frankenstein.* Speaking of ghosts, such geniuses as **Gogol, Dostoyevsky, Hugo, Hemingway,** and **Fitzgerald** still haunt the Geneva countryside where they wrote when they were in more solid form. **James Joyce** fled to Zurich during World War I and stayed to scribble the greater part of his modernist work *Ulysses* between 1915 and 1919; World War II drove him to Zurich once again, where he died in 1941.

Other great minds flocked from Germany, Austria, and Italy. **Johann Wolfgang von Goethe** caught his first distant view of Italy from the top of St. Gotthard Pass in the Swiss Alps, the clouded path that would serve as an allegory for the rest of his life. **Friedrich Schiller** wrote about the massive church bell in Schaffhausen before penning *Wilhelm Tell.* While on holiday in the Engadin Valley, **Friedrich Nietzsche** went nuts, cooked up some historical and philosophical ramblings, and produced his mountaintop tome *Thus Spoke Zarathustra.* His complex personal relationship with **Richard Wagner** began here while Nietzsche held a professor's chair at Basel University. Wagner composed most of his major operas during his years in verdant Switzerland.

Thomas Mann also found refuge in Switzerland, using one of the Swiss Alps as the setting for his novel *The Magic Mountain.* Switzerland's recent acquisitions include writers and scientists from the former Eastern bloc, notably Russian author **Alexander Solzhenitsyn** and Czech novelist **Milan Kundera.**

his time outside the country and that the Swiss burned his books. A more conventional Swiss resident, **Jacob Burckhardt** promoted a new history of culture and art from his Basel home in the late 19th century. His works include *History of the Italian Renaissance* and *Cicerone: A Guide to the Enjoyment of Italian Art.*

ROMANTICISM. When Romanticism caught on in Swiss literature, **J.J. Bodmer** and **J.J. Breitinger**'s advocacy of literature in Swiss German brought them into conflict with many of their German contemporaries, who strove to standardize German through literature. The Swiss-born **Madame de Staël** (née Germaine Necker) was both an important writer in her own right and the driving force behind Romanticism's spread from Germany to France. As a result of her political intrigues and alleged rebuff of Napoleon's advances (she succeeded where Europe failed), de Staël was forced into a miserable exile in Coppet. Switzerland produced a few popular Romantic authors as well, most notably **Gottfried Keller**, who penned a classic 19th-century German *Bildungsroman*, entitled *Der Grüne Heinrich.* **Conrad Ferdinand Meyer** was another highly influential Swiss poet, whose writings, which feature strongly individualistic heroes, effectively unite characteristics of Romanticism and Realism.

20TH CENTURY. It is only in the 20th century that Swiss literature has come into its own with such greats as **Hermann Hesse**, who received he Nobel Prize for literature in 1946 for his collected oeuvre. Hesse's works, including *The Steppenwolf* and *Narcissus and Goldmund*, deal with the crisis of existence and the power of laughter. Another thinker concerned with the crisis of existence on a broad scale, **Carl Gustav Jung** set up a growing psychoanalytic practice in Zurich. He began as an acolyte of Freud but split off by 1915 when he wrote *Symbols of Transformation.* He invented the idea of the extroverted and introverted personalities, as well as the collective unconscious and its corollary, archetypes. Alongside Hesse and Jung, Switzerland has produced 2 widely respected modern playwrights and a formerly obscure novelist who wrote with such tiny handwriting that he fit entire works on café bills. Critics laud **Max Frisch** for his Brechtian style and thoughtful treatment of Nazi Germany; his most widely known works are the play *Andorra* and the novel *Homo Faber*, which was made into a film in the early 1990s. **Friedrich Dürrenmatt** has written a number of cutting, funny plays, most notably *The Visit of the Old Lady* and *The Physicists.* Both Dürrenmatt and Frisch are critical of but loyal to their home country. The novelist **Robert Walser** has been celebrated for his diffuse, existential works, though they were largely ignored until his death in 1956 by an audience expecting clearly defined morals and themes.

RECOMMENDED READING.
Why Switzerland? (1996). Jonathan Steinberg .
A Tramp Abroad (1879). Mark Twain.
Heidi (1902). Johanna Spyri.
Steppenwolf (1927). Hermann Hesse.

S W I T Z E R L A N D

BERNESE OBERLAND

If you made a list of things of which the Swiss are fiercely proud, the Bernese Oberland would be at the top of that list. When WWII threatened to engulf the country, the Swiss army resolved to defend this area, *le réduit*, to the last. Pristine and wild, the savage beauty of the Swiss Alps best lends itself to discovery through

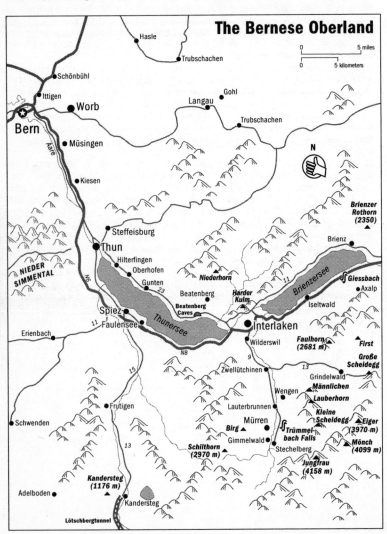

The Bernese Oberland

0   5 miles

0   5 kilometers

N

Hasle

Trubschachen

Schönbühl

Ittigen

Worb

Langau   Gohl

Bern

Müsingen   Trubschachen

Kiesen

Aare

Brienzer
Rothorn
(2350)

Steffeisburg

Brienz

Thun   Hilterfingen

Oberhofen   *Niederhorn*   11   *Brienzersee*   Giessbach

NIEDER
SIMMENTAL   Gunten   23   *Harder*   Axalp

N6   Beatenberg   *Kulm*

Beatenberg   Iseltwald

Caves

Spiez   *Thunersee*   Interlaken

Erlenbach   11   Faulensee   Wilderswil   *Faulhorn*   First
    N8   (2681 m)

Zwellütchinen   9   13   *Große
Scheidegg*

15   Grindelwald

Wengen   *Männlichen*
    Lauberhorn

Frutigen   Lauterbrunnen   *Kleine
    Scheidegg*   *Eiger*
Schwenden   *Mürren*   (3970 m)

Birg   *Trümmel-*
13   Gimmelwald   *bach Falls*   *Mönch*
    (4099 m)

Schilthorn   Stechelberg
(2970 m)

Jungfrau
(4158 m)

Kandersteg
(1176 m)

Adelboden   Kandersteg

Lötschbergtunnel

scenic hikes around the twin lakes, the **Thunersee** and **Brienzersee**. A young, international, and rowdy crowd migrates here every summer to get a fill of crisp Alpine air and clear, starry nights. Opportunities for paragliding, mountaineering, and whitewater rafting are virtually unparalleled. The metropolitan heartbeat of the region is exuberant, fun-loving Bern, the Swiss capital. Its wide, arcade-lined streets buzz with activity, while glowing green hills in the background hint at the splendor of the wilderness just a short train ride south.

The Bernese Oberland provides amazing and diverse hiking opportunities. Plan your trips wisely; expensive cable cars quickly drain a hiker's budget. Wherever possible *Let's Go* lists hikes you can do without mechanical assistance. Minimize transportation costs by using a town or village as a hub from which to explore the surrounding area. The 15-day **Berner Oberland Regional Pass** (200Fr; with Swisspass or half-fare card 160SFr; Eurailpass not valid) grants 5 days of unlimited regional travel and a 50% discount on the other 10 days. A 7-day variation is available for 160SFr, with 3 days of unlimited travel and 50% discount on the other 4 days. Both are available at train stations or any tourist office. Some cable cars give a 25% discount for Eurailpass and SwissPass .

HIGHLIGHTS OF BERNESE OBERLAND

■ Feed **Bern's** namesake bears in the **bear pits** (p. 313).
■ Indulge your Klee fetish in Bern's Kunstmuseum, home to the **world's largest collection of Klee** paintings (p. 313).
■ Fly high with the help of Interlaken's prime **paragliding** opportunities (p. 325).
■ Tackle glacier hiking on the **Eiger** from the village of Grindelwald (p. 328).
■ Experience authentic rural Switzerland in **Brienz's Swiss Open-Air Museum**, a showcase (sans kitsch) of traditional Swiss architecture and trades like iron-smithing and cheese-making (p. 319).

BERN

The Duke of Zähringen founded Bern in 1191, naming it for his mascot, the bear. The city has been Switzerland's capital since 1848, but don't expect fast tracks, power politics, or men in black—Bern prefers to focus on the lighter things in life. Some old wag once claimed that "Venice is built on water, Bern on wine." While the Bernese seem a bit too sober to merit the proverb, they do appreciate the grape, local Toblerone chocolate, and their sumptuous flower gardens. Situated in a bend of the winding Aare River, Bern's bridges span lush, green banks. Rebuilt in 1405 after a devastating fire, Bern's sandstone and mahogany buildings are dominated mainly by a fat *Bundeshaus* and the stately spire of the Gothic *Münster*.

GETTING TO BERN

The **Bern-Belp Airport** (tel. 960 21 11) is 20 minutes from central Bern and is served by Swissair (tel. 0848 800 700), Crossair (tel. 960 21 21), and Air Engadina (tel. 960 12 11). Direct flights go daily to Basel, Amsterdam, London, Lugano, Brussels, Munich, Paris, Rome, and Vienna. Fifty minutes before each flight, an airport bus that guarantees you'll make your flight runs from the train station (10min., 14SFr). Bern's main **train station,** in front of the tourist office, is a stressful tangle of essential services and extraneous shops. Check-in, information, buses, luggage watch, bike rental, and a pharmacy are upstairs; tickets, lockers, police, showers, toilets, and currency exchange are downstairs. If **driving** from Basel and the north, take A2 south to A1. From Lucerne or the east, take 10 west. From Geneva or Lausanne, take E62 east to E27/A12 north. From Thun or the southeast, take A6 north.

BERNESE OBERLAND

⑦ ORIENTATION AND PRACTICAL INFORMATION

Though it borders *Suisse Romande*, the French-speaking part of the country, Bern belongs to the German-speaking *Deutschschweiz*. Most of medieval Bern lies in front of the train station and along the Aare River. **Warning:** Like many cities, Bern has a nocturnal drug community that tends to congregate in the area around the Parliament park and terraces.

TRANSPORTATION

Trains: Bahnhofpl. For rail info, dial 157 22 22 (6am-10pm). The **rail information office** is open M-F 8am-7pm, Sa 8am-5pm. To: **Geneva** (2hr., every 30min. 5:45am-11:24pm, 50SFr); **Lucerne** (1½hr., every hr. 4:48am-11:16pm, 32SFr); **Interlaken** (50min., every hr. 6:20am-11:26pm, 25SFr); **Zurich** (1¼hr., every 30min. 5:52am-11:52pm, 48SFr); **Lausanne** (1¼hr., every 30min. 5:57am-11:24pm, 32SFr); **Basel** (1¼hr., every 30min. 4:48am-11:52pm, 37SFr); **Paris** (4½hr., 5 per day 6:45am-6:49pm, 92SFr); **Munich** (5½hr., 4 per day 6:10am-4:14pm, 123SFr); **Vienna** (10½hr., 3 per day 8:16am-9:16pm, 166SFr); **Salzburg** (7¼hr., 4 per day 8:16am-9:16pm, 135SFr); and **Milan** (3½hr., 14 per day 6:20am-11:26pm, 72SFr). Reduce all international fares by 25% for ages 26 and under.

Public Transportation: SVB (tel. 321 86 41; fax 321 86 86). A **visitor's card** from the ticket offices downstairs in the station or at the Jurahaus office, Bubenbergpl. 5 (tel. 321 86 31), entitles the holder to unlimited travel on all SVB routes and a 10% discount on city tours. 24hr. pass 6SFr; 48hr. 9SFr; 72hr. 12SFr. Automatic vendors dispense daypasses (7.50SFr) and one-way tickets (1-6 stops 1.50SFr; 7 or more stops 2.40SFr; Swisspass valid). Buses run 5:45am-11:45pm. **Nightbuses** leave the train station at 12:45, 2, and 3:15am on F-Sa nights, covering major bus and tram lines (5SFr). SVB offices in the train station distribute maps and timetables. Open M-W and F 6:30am-7:30pm, Th 6:30am-9pm, Sa 7:30am-6:30pm.

Taxis: Bären-Taxi (tel. 371 11 11) or **NovaTaxi** (tel. 301 11 11). Stands at Bahnhofpl., Bollwerk, and Casinopl.

Parking: Bahnhof (tel. 311 22 52), entrance at Schanzenbrücke or Stadtbachstr. **Parking Casino,** Kocherg. (tel. 311 77 76). **City West,** Belpstr. (tel. 381 93 04), costs 3.20SFr per hr., 28SFr for a day, 12SFr for 2nd and 3rd day.

Car Rental: Avis AG, Wabernstr. 41 (tel. 378 15 15). **Hertz AG,** Kochelstr. 1, Casinopl. (tel. 318 21 60). **Europcar,** Laupenstr. 22 (tel. 381 75 55).

Bike Rental: Blubike, Marktg. 27 (tel. 311 22 34), in the Intersport store, rents bikes for free. Just hand them a 20SFr deposit plus ID. Reserve ahead. Open M-W and F 8am-6:30pm, Th 8am-9pm, Sa 8am-4pm. Otherwise, try **Fly-Gepäck** (tel. (051) 220 23 74) at the station. 26SFr per day, 100SFr per week; mountain bikes 32SFr, 128SF; children's bikes 16SFr, 64SFr. Reservations recommended. Open 6:10am-11pm.

TOURIST AND FINANCIAL SERVICES

Tourist Office: Bern Tourismus (tel. 328 12 12; fax 312 12 33; email info@bernetourism.ch; www.bernetourism.ch), on the street level of the station. The office distributes maps and *Bern Aktuell,* a bimonthly guide to events in the city, and makes free room reservations. The 24hr. electronic board outside the office has a free phone line to hotels, computerized receipts, and directions in German, French, and English. **City tours** available by bus, on foot, or by raft. Tours daily in summer, 6-23SFr. Open June-Sept. daily 9am-8:30pm, Oct.-May M-Sa 9am-6:30pm, Su 10am-5pm. **Branch office** at the bear pits open June-Sept. daily 9am-5pm; Oct. and Mar.-May 10am-4pm.

Budget Travel: SSR, Rathausg. 64 (tel. 312 07 24). Take bus #12 to "Rathaus." Sells BIJ tickets, ISIC cards, Europass, etc. Open M-W and F 9:30am-6pm, Th 9:30am-8pm, Sa 10am-1pm. **Hang Loose,** Spitalg. 4 (tel. 312 34 24; fax 314 34 28; www.hangloose.ch) has BIJ and plane tickets and ISIC cards; matches SSR prices. Open M-F 9am-6pm, Th until 8pm, Sa 9am-noon.

Bern

ACCOMMODATIONS
A Pension Martahaus
B Hotel National
C Jugendherberge
D Hotel Landhaus

BERNESE OBERLAND

Laubegg-str.
Rosengarten
Aargauerstalden
Klösterlistutz
Bärengraben (bear pits)
Muristalden
Grosser Muristalden
Untertor-brücke
Nydegg-brücke
Nydeggstalden
Nydegg Kirche
Gerberng.
Kollerweg
Gerfenmätteliweg
Jungfraustr.
Dufourstr.
Schänzlistr.
Aare
N
Postgasshalde
Langmauerweg
Poste.
Gerechtigkeitsg.
Junkerng.
Schifflaube
Englische Anlagen (English Garden)
Marienstr.
Thunstr.
Museum of Communication
Altenbergstr.
1/4 mile
1/4 kilometer
Brunngasshalde
Rathausg.
Münster (cathedral)
Herreng.
Aarstr.
Kunsthalle
Helvetiastr.
HELVETIA-PLATZ
Historical Museum
Rabbental-str.
0
250 m
Kornhausstr.
Brunng.
Einstein Haus
Münsterg.
MÜNSTER PLATZ
Kirchenfeldbr.
Bernastr.
Kunstmuseum
Kram g.
Hotelg.
Casino-platz
Aare
Alpine Museum
TO NATURAL HISTORY MUSEUM (200 m)
Dalmazibrücke
Dalmaziquai
KORNHAUS-PLATZ
Schüttestr.
Nägelig.
Zeughausg.
Clock Tower
Theater-platz
Amthausg.
Kocherg.
Marzilibad
Aarst.
Marzilistr.
WAISENHAUS-PLATZ
Marktg.
BÄREN-PLATZ
BUNDES-PLATZ
Parliament
Terrasse
Bundesg.
Weiherg.
Münzrain
Funicular Train (Marzilibahn)
Marzilistr.
Brückenstr.
Speicherg.
Aarbergerg.
Neueng.
Spitalg.
Schauplatzg.
Heiliggeistkirche
Gurteng.
Christoffelg.
Bundes rain
Lorrainebrücke
Reitschule
Bollwerk
Kleine Schanze
Sulgeneckstr.
Neubrückstr.
Genferg.
BAHNHOF-PLATZ
i
Haupt-Bahnhof
Bundesg.
Synagogue
Gesellschaftsstr.
Sidlers
Universität
Hochschulstr.
FALKEN-PLATZ
Schanzenstr.
Bubenbergpl.
Hirschengraben
Effingerstr.
Monbijoustr.
Kapellenstr.
Schwarztorstr.
Längass-str.
Stadt Bach
Monbijoustr.

Embassies: Australia, (tel. 157 56 005). Visa and immigration information only. To get to the Canadian, U.K., and Irish embassies, take tram #3 (dir.: Saali) to "Thunpl." **Canada,** Kirchenfeldstr. 88 (tel. 357 32 00). Open M-F 8am-noon and 1-4:30pm. **Ireland,** Kirchenfeldstr. 68 (tel. 352 14 42). Open M-F 9:15am-noon and 2-4pm. **South Africa,** Alpenstr. 29 (tel. 350 13 13). Open 8am-12:30pm and 1:30-5:15pm. **U.K.,** Thunstr. 50 (tel. 352 50 21). Open M-F 8:30am-12:30pm and 1:45-5:15pm. **U.S.,** Jubiläumsstr. 93 (tel. 357 70 11). Take bus #19 (dir.: Elfenau) to "Ka-We-De." Open M-F 8:30am-5:30pm.

Currency Exchange: Downstairs in the station. No commission on traveler's checks. Credit card advances on DC, MC, and Visa. Western Union transfers. Open June to mid-Oct. dialy 6:15am-9:45pm; mid-Oct. to May 6:15am-8:45pm. **ATMs** at **Credit Suisse** and **Swiss Bank Corp.** Banks open M-W and F 8am-4:30pm, Th 8am-6pm.

LOCAL SERVICES

Luggage Storage: Downstairs in the train station. 24hr. Lockers 4-8SFr. **Luggage watch** at the Fly-Gepäck counter upstairs 5SFr. Open 6:10am-11pm.

Lost Property: Downstairs in the station. Open M-F 8am-noon and 2-6pm.

Bookstore: Stauffacher, Neueng. 25 (tel. 311 24 11). From Bubenbergpl., turn left on Genferg. to Neueng. 6 floors of books, including English and French. Open M-W and F 9am-6:30pm, Th 9am-9pm, Sa 8am-4pm.

Libraries: Municipal and University Library, Münsterg. 61 (tel. 320 32 11), stacks books for the central library of the University of Bern and the city's public library. Lending library open M-F 10am-6pm, Sa 10am-noon. Reading room open M-F 8am-9pm, Sa 8am-noon. **Swiss National Library,** Hallwylstr. 15 (tel. 332 89 11). Lending library and catalog room open M-Tu and Th-F 9am-6pm, W 9am-8pm, Sa 9am-2pm. Reading room open M-Tu and Th-F 8am-6pm, W 8am-8pm, Sa 9am-4pm.

Bi-Gay-Lesbian Organizations: Homosexuelle Arbeitsgruppe die Schweiz-HACH (Gay Association of Switzerland), c/o Anderland, Mühlenpl. 11, CH-3011. The headquarters of Switzerland's largest gay organization. **Homosexuelle Arbeitsgruppe Bern** (HAB), Mühlenpl. 11, Case Postale 312, CH-3000 Bern 13 (tel. 311 63 53). in Marzilibad, along the Aare. Hosts informal get-togethers W evenings, with coffee, drinks, and library access. **Schlub** (Gay Students Organization), c/o Studentinnenschaft, Lercheweg 32, CH-3000 Bern 9 (tel. 371 00 87).

Laundromat: Jet Wash, Dammweg 43 (tel. 372 50 45). Take bus #20 to "Lorraine." Wash 8kg for 5SFr, 5kg 4SFr; dryers 3SFr. Open M-Sa 7am-9pm, Su 9am-6pm.

Public Showers: At train station. Toilets 1-1.50SFr; showers 10SFr. Open 6am-midnight.

Information: General info tel. 111.

Pharmacy: In the station. Open 6:30am-10pm. **Bären Apotheke,** at the clock tower. Open M 1:45-6:30pm, Tu-W and F 7:45am-6:30pm, Th 7:45am-9pm, Sa 7:45am-4pm. AmEx, DC, MC, Visa. For the **24hr. pharmacy on duty,** dial 311 22 11.

EMERGENCIES AND COMMUNICATION

Emergencies: Police, tel. 117. **Ambulance,** tel. 144. **Doctor,** tel. 311 22 11. **Rape Crisis Hotline,** tel. 332 14 14.

Internet Café: Basement of JäggiBücher, Spitalg. on Bubenbergpl. 47-51 (tel. 320 20 20) in Loeb dept. store. 2 computers allow max. 20min. free, 2 more computers cost 5SFr per 30min. Open M-W and F 9am-6:30pm, Th 9am-9pm, Sa 8am-5pm. Second floor of **Stauffacher** bookstore (15SFr per hr.). **Medienhaus** Zeughausg. 14 (tel. 327 11 88), to the right off Waisenhauspl. Free. Open M-F 8am-6pm, Sa 9am-11pm.

Post Office: Schanzenpost 1, next to the train station. Address *Poste Restante* to Postlagernde Briefe, Schanzenpost 3000, Bern 1. Open M-F 7:30am-6:30pm, Sa 8-11am. Express counter M-F 6-7:30am and 6:30-10:30pm, Sa 7-8am and 11am-6pm, Su 3:30-10pm. **Postal Code:** CH-3000 to CH-3030.

PHONE CODE	The **city code** for Bern is 031.

ACCOMMODATIONS AND CAMPING

Bern's only bona fide hostel is usually reliable for a last-minute bed, but if it's full, cheap accommodations are rare. The tourist office has a list of **private rooms** available. Otherwise consider staying in Fribourg, 30 minutes from Bern by train.

Jugendherberge (HI), Weiherg. 4 (tel. 311 63 16; fax 312 52 40). From the station cross the tram lines and go down Christoffelg. Take the road through the gates to the left of the Park Café, and follow it down to Weiherg., following the hostel signs. Located on the banks of the Aare, the hostel has 186 beds. Communal hall showers. Spacious common areas feature a TV with CNN and life-sized chess on the patio. Dorms 20.25SFr; overflow mattresses on the floor 14SFr. Nonmembers add 5SFr. Breakfast 6SFr. Lunch or dinner 11SFr. **Laundry** 6SFr. 3-night max. stay. Reception June-Sept. daily 7-9:30am and 3pm-midnight; Oct.-May 7-9:30am and 5pm-midnight. Check-out 9am. Reservations by fax only. Curfew midnight. Closed 2 weeks in Jan. MC, Visa.

Landhaus Hotel, Altenbergstr. 4/6 (tel. 331 41 66; fax 332 69 04; email landhaus@spectravels.ch.) Take bus #12 (dir.: Schlosshalde) to "Bärengraben," and walk down to the Aare on the left. This renovated hotel is within walking distance of the bear pits and rose gardens. Dorms 30SFr; doubles with breakfast and bedding 110SFr, with shower 140SFr. Duvet for bedding 5SFr. Breakfast 7SFr. **Kitchen** access. Restaurant 6pm-midnight. **Laundry** 4-6SFr. **Internet access.**

Pension Marthahaus, Wyttenbachstr. 22a (tel. 332 41 35; fax 333 33 86; email martahaus@bluewin.ch). Take bus #20 to "Gewerbeschule," then the 1st right. Or walk from the station: turn left onto Bollwerk, cross Lorrainebrücke, bear right onto Victoriastr., then take the 1st left onto Wyttenbachstr. Motherly hostess maintains a comfortable *Pension* in a quiet suburb, offering fresh towels, fluffy blankets, TVs, and sparkly showers and sinks. Singles 60SFr, with shower 90SFr; doubles 95SFr, 120SFr; triples 120SFr, 150SFr. Prices drop 5-10SFr in winter. Breakfast included. **Laundry** 8SFr. Limited parking available. Reception 7:30am-9pm, and a porter accommodates latecomers. Reservations recommended. MC, Visa.

Hotel National, Hirschengraben 24 (tel. 381 19 88; fax 381 68 78). From the station, cross over the bus stops/tramlines to Bubenberg. on the right. Hirschengraben is the 2nd road downhill. Each room is furnished with antique furniture. Downstairs restaurant has a 15SFr *Menü*. Singles 60-75SFr, with shower 85-110SFr; doubles 100-120SFr, 120-150SFr; 3- to 5-person family room 170-260SFr. Breakfast included. Reception 7am-10:30pm, but the night porter opens the doors for latecomers. Reservations recommended in summer. AmEx, DC, MC, Visa.

Camping: Camping Eichholz, Strandweg 49 (tel. 961 26 02). Take tram #9 to "Wabern," backtrack 50m, and take the 1st right. This riverside location opposite the zoo is within earshot of snuffling wild boars, drooling bison, and bounding mountain goats. On-site restaurant. 6.90SFr, students 5.50SFr, children 3SFr; tents 5-8.50SFr; 2-bed rooms 15SFr. Showers 1SFr. Electricity 3SFr. **Laundry** 5SFr. Reserve ahead. Open May-Sept.

FOOD

Almost every locale ending in "-platz" overflows with cafés and restaurants, though the bigger ones tend to be pricier and more tourist-infested. Try one of Bern's hearty specialties: *Gschnätzlets* (fried veal, beef, or pork), *suurchabis* (a sauerkraut), or *Gschwellti* (steamed potatoes). The sweet-toothed will savor an airy meringue or home-grown **Toblerone chocolate.**

Manora, Bubenbergpl. 5A (tel. 311 37 55), over the tramlines from the station. As usual, this self-service chain tends to be overheated and crowded but serves big platefuls that are indisputably nutritious and cheap. Salad bar 4.20-8.90SFr; pasta 8-10SFr; veggie burger plate 9SFr. Open M-Sa 7am-10:30pm, Su 9am-10:30pm. .

Zähringerhof, Hallerstr. 19 (tel. 301 08 60). Take bus #12 (dir.: Längasse) to "Universität," continue up Schanzenstr., and turn right on Hallerstr. This neighborhood joint cooks up great Italian dishes, with pizza and pasta from 11SFr. Students and professors from the nearby university take advantage of the vine-enclosed terrace. Open 8:30-11:30am and 5pm-12:30pm.

Café des Pyrenées, Kornhauspl. 17 (tel. 311 30 63). Named after a novel by Swiss author Daniel Himmerberg, this expatriate-style bistro-café complete with a small sidewalk terrace is a haven for journalists, office-goers, and busy types. Inventive sandwiches (calamari 6.50SFr) and conservative spaghettis (9.50SFr). The spirits list is extravagant, with 6 types of Spanish brandy. Open M-F 9am-12:30am, Sa 8am-5pm.

Cave 49, Gerechtigkeitsg. 49 (tel. 312 55 92), is a spicy, dimly lit Mediterranean eatery. Enjoy *tortellini alla panno con parmesan* (14.50SFr) or a meaty paprika *chorizo* (6.50SFr). Beers from 2.70SFr. Open Tu-Su 10am-12:30am.

Pizza Camargue, Kramg. 42 (tel. 311 70 51). The brick and rippled-plaster dining room is an appropriately oven-like setting for a pizzeria. While serenaded by guitar, try some pizza (12-19SFr), pasta (11-20SFr), or lunch *Menüs* (11am-2pm; 14.80-16.80SFr) Open M 9am-11pm, Tu-Th 9am-1am, F-Sa 9am-2am, Su 11am-midnight.

Restaurant Marzilbrücke, Gassstr. 8 (tel. 311 27 80). Turn right from the hostel onto Aarstr. Escape the hostel dinner with a selection of curry dishes (23SFr) or a gourmet Italian pie (14.50-22.50SFr). The Australian bartender pours a wide selection of wines (4.20-7.50SFr) to the tunes of Peruvian pipes. Open M-Th 11:30am-11:30pm, F 11:30am-12:30am, Sa 4pm-12:30am, Su 10am-11:30pm. Pizzeria open 6-11pm.

MARKETS

Migros, Marktg. 40, Bubenbergpl. in the same building as Café Bubenberg. Open M-F 7:30am-7pm, Sa 7:30am-4pm.

Co-op, Spitalg. 1, Waisenhauspl. Open M-F 8am-7pm, Th 8am-9pm, Sa 8am-4pm. AmEx, DC, MC, Visa.

Reformhaus M. Siegrist, in the Marktg.-Passage (off Marktg.), is a popular health food market. Open M 2-6:30pm, Tu-F 8am-12:15pm and 1:30-6:30pm, Sa 7:45am-1pm.

Fruit and vegetable markets sell fresh produce daily on Bärenpl. (May-Oct. 8am-6pm) and every Tu and Sa on Bundepl. The off-the-wall **onion market** on the 4th M of Nov. is probably Bern's single best known festival.

📷 🏛 SIGHTS AND MUSEUMS

Bern is an easily walkable city. Most of the sights are laid out in a line starting at the Parliament. Several of Bern's museums sit in a compact ring around **Helvetiaplatz** across Kirchenfeldbrücke (accessible by tram #3 or #5).

THE OLD TOWN. Perhaps hearkening back to the flames that set Bern's houses ablaze in 1405, the solid medieval architecture of Bern's *Altstadt* glows red with Swiss flags and geraniums. Behind church spires and government domes, the lush hills along the Aare river create a cooling verdant backdrop. The massive **Bundeshaus** dominates the Aare. The politicians hide in the **Parlamentsgebäude.** *(Tel. 322 85 22. 45min. tour every hr. 9-11am and 2-4pm when Parliament is not in session. Free.)*

From the state house, Kockerg. and Herreng. lead to the 15th-century Protestant **Münster** (cathedral). The imagination of the late-Gothic period runs riot in the stern, Calvin-influenced portal sculpture of the Last Judgment, left intact during the Reformation, where the naked damned shuffle off unhappily to Hell on God's left. For a fantastic view of the Aare and beyond, climb the Münster's spire—it's among the tallest in all of Switzerland. *(Open Easter-Oct. Tu-Sa 10am-5pm, Su 11:30am-5pm; Nov.-Easter Tu-F 10am-noon and 2-4pm, Sa 10am-noon and 2-5pm, Su 11am-2pm. Tower closes 30min. before the church. 3SFr.)*

From the Bundeshaus, turn left off Kocherg. at Theaterpl. to reach the 13th-century **Zytglogge** (clock tower). At 4 minutes before the hour, figures on the tower creak to life with a couple of pallid rooster squawks; more entertaining are the fervent oohs and aahs of gathered tourists. *(Tours of the interior May-Oct. daily at 4:30pm. 6SFr.)* Walking through the city from the clock tower, on the edge of the *Altstadt*

BÄREN BRAIN Bern's citizens have got bears on the brain. The city's ursine mascot pervades even the most forsaken alleyways in the form of statuettes, fountains, flags, stained-glass windows, and matchbox covers. The *Bärengraben* are the pits just beyond the center of the city where live bears are kept like some sort of strange totem. Legend has it that Duke Berchtold V of Zähringen, founder of Bern, wanted to name the city after the first animal he caught when hunting on the site of the planned construction. The animal was a you-know-what, and Bern (etymologically derived from *Bären*) was born. The *Bärengraben* themselves weren't built until the Bernese victory at the Battle of Nouana in 1513, when they dragged home a live bear as part of the war booty. A hut was erected for the beast in what is now Bärenplatz (Bear Square) and his descendants have been Bern's collective pets ever since.

the slender fingerlike copper spire of the **Nydegg Kirche** rises from the intersection of Kramg. and Gerechtigkeitsg. The church stands on the remains of the Nydegg imperial fortress that was destroyed in the mid-13th century.

BEAR PITS. Across the Nydeggbrücke lie the **Bärengraben** (bear pits). The stone-lined pits date back to the 15th century, but they were recently renovated to provide the city's mascots with trees and rocks to clamber over, perhaps to make up in some way for the indignity of having to show off for gawking crowds and screaming kids. On Easter, newborn cubs are displayed in public for the first time. *(Open June-Sept. daily 8am-6pm; Oct.-May Th-M 8am-6pm. 3SFr to feed the bears.)* The tourist office at the pits also present **The Bern Show,** a slickly choreographed recap of Bernese history that melds into an overly-indulgent photo-montage. *(Every 20min. In German and English. Free.)* The path snaking up the hill to the left leads to the **Rosengarten;** sit among the blooms and admire one of the best views of Bern's *Altstadt.*

ART MUSEUM. Bern's **Kunstmuseum** sprawls over 3 floors and a couple of buildings, top-heavy with the world's largest Paul Klee collection: 2500 works, from his school exercise-books to his largest canvases, along with some works by his chums Kandinsky and Feininger, in room after room of Klee's geometrically dreamy art. A smattering of the century's big names are exhibited upstairs: Braque, Picasso, Giacometti, Ernst Kirchner, Pollock, and some Dada works by Hans Arp. The museum also has a chic café and screens art films. *(Hodlerstr. 8-12, near Lorrainebrücke. Tel. 311 09 44. Open Tu 10am-9pm, W-Su 10am-5pm. 6SFr, students and seniors 4SFr.)*

THE RIVER AARE. Several walkways lead steeply down from the Bundeshaus to the Aare; a cable car assists you on the way up (1SFr). The river itself is ideal for shady walks. On hotter days, locals dive lemming-style from the bridges to take a brisk ride on its swift currents (signs warn that only experienced swimmers should jump in). Along the banks, numerous sets of stone steps invite you to take the plunge. For a more languid afternoon of bathing and basking, the **Marzilibad public pool** lies on the river 3 minutes to the right of the hostel. *(Pool open May-Aug. M-Sa 8:30am-8pm, Sept. M-F 8:30am-7pm, Sa-Su 8:30am-6pm. Lockers and showers available.)*

GARDENS AND ZOO. The **Botanical Gardens** of the University of Bern, Altenbergrain, sprawl down the river at Lorrainebrücke. Exotic plants from Asia, Africa, and the Americas thrive next to native Alpine greenery. *(Take bus # 20 to "Gewerbeschule." Tel. 631 49 44. Park open Mar.-Sept. M-F 7am-6pm, Sa-Su 8am-5pm. Greenhouse open M-Sa 8am-5pm. Free.)* In a towering forest of cedar and pine, the 24-hour **Dählhölzli Städtischer Tierpark** (Zoo) gives you the chance to animal-watch at night, too. *(Tierparkweg 1. Walk south along the Aare or take bus #19 to "Tierpark". Tel. 357 15 15. Open daily in summer 8am-6:30pm; in winter 9am-5pm. 7SFr, students 5SFr. Parking available.)*

HISTORICAL MUSEUMS. The **Bernisches Historische Museum** is so big you won't know where to begin. Luckily, multilingual explanatory notes are available in many rooms of the museum's 7 jam-packed levels. Wide staircases lined with portraits of rotund Bernese citizens lead to evocative exhibits, from the Münster artifacts downstairs to the illuminated manuscripts in the Islamic collection. Nicolaus

BERNESE OBERLAND

FANCY FOUNTAINS As if bumpy cobblestone streets and happy-go-lucky pedestrians weren't bad enough, motorists in Bern also have to negotiate their way around the 16th-century fountains that squat squarely in the middle of many of the city's *Straßen*. These creations are painted with a symbol seen all over Switzerland—a figure atop a column—but the Bernese variety seem especially blinding. Most of the fountains, called *Brunnen*, are attributed to the artist Hans Gieng. Crafted from stone, the *Brunnen* have been restored repeatedly since the mid-1500s to maintain their gaudy color schemes (the city mascot, the bear, shows up in fire-engine red). Highlights include the *Simsonbrunnen* in Kramg., which depicts Samson wrestling a lion; the *Gerechtigkeitsbrunnen* on Gerechtigkeitsg., where the Justice stomps on the Pope, Emperor, Sultan, and Mayor; and the *Kindlifresserbrunnen* ("Child-Devourer Fountain") at Kornhauspl., tastefully translated as the "Ogre Fountain."

Manuel's witty, macabre *Dance of Death*, in which a jocular skeleton greets representatives of 24 professions, is one of the highlights. *(Helvetiapl. 5. Tel. 350 77 11. Open Tu-Su 10am-5pm. 5SFr, students 3SFr, free for those under 17 and school groups. Additional charge for special exhibitions. Free on Saturday.)*

In the **Swiss Alpine Museum,** intricate models of Switzerland's most popular mountains give a history of Swiss cartography. The 2nd-floor exhibit on mountain life may be more interesting—check out the devil masks used to protect against threats from the other world. *(Helvetiapl. 4. Tel. 351 04 34. Open mid-May to mid-Oct. M 2-5pm, Tu-Su 10am-5pm; mid-Oct. to mid-May M 2-5pm, Tu-Su 10am-noon and 2-5pm. 5SFr, students and seniors 3SFr.)*

At the bright, colorful **Museum of Natural History,** most people come to see Barry, the now-stuffed St. Bernard who saved over 40 people in his lifetime. Some of the other hyper-realistic dioramas, however, get a bit more intense—hyenas feed on zebra corpses, weasels carry stolen eggs from a henhouse away in their mouths, and more dynamic cousins of the *Bärengraben* bears dispute a recently downed moose. *(Bernastr. 15, off Helvetiapl. Tel. 350 71 11. Open M 2-5pm, Tu and Th-F 9am-5pm,W 9am-8pm, Sa-Su 10am-5pm. 5SFr, students 3SFr, free on Su.)*

MUSEUM OF COMMUNICATION. This museum looks into how we keep in touch, from tin cans to telnet. Its cheerful, kid-friendly multilingual exhibits and computer touch-screens manage to make mail entertaining. The museum houses the world's largest public display of postage stamps. *(Helvetiastr. 16, behind the history museum. Tel. 357 55 11. Open Tu-Su 10am-5pm. 5SFr, students 3SFr.)*

ALBERT EINSTEIN'S HOUSE. This small apartment where the theory of general relativity was conceived in 1905 is now filled with photos, a few of Einstein's letters, resonating brain waves, and not much else. The museum emphasizes that Albert loved Bern and Bern still loves Albert. *(Kramg. 49. Tel. 312 00 91. Open Feb.-Nov. Tu-F 10am-5pm, Sa 10am-4pm. 3SFr, students and children 2SFr.)*

🎵 ENTERTAINMENT AND NIGHTLIFE

Bern's cultural tastes run the gamut from classical music concerts to late-night café bands. Events are well-publicized on kiosks and bulletin boards. Publications like **Non-Stopp** (the "Going Out" section of the Bern newspaper) or **Gay Agenda** will be thrust into your hands on street corners or as you leave the train station.

PERFORMANCES AND FESTIVALS. Operas and ballets are performed at the **Stadttheater,** Kornhauspl. 20 (tel. 311 07 77; summer season runs July-August 17th; for ticket info, contact *Theaterkasse*, Kornhauspl. 18, CH-3000 Bern 7). The **Berner Altstadtsommer** features free dancing and music concerts, ranging from tango to jazz to funk to choral, in the squares of the *Altstadt*. Bern's **Symphony Orchestra** plays in the fall and winter at the *Konservatorium für Musik* at Kramg. 36 (tickets tel. 311 62 21). July's **Gurten Festival** (www.gurtenfestival.ch; see **Festival Fever,** p. 303) has attracted such luminaries as Bob Dylan, Elvis Costello, Björk, and Sinead O'Connor. Jazz-lovers arrive in early May for the **International Jazz Festival** (tickets at any Bankverein Swiss Bank branch). Other festivals include the Bernese Easter-egg market in late March and a notorious **onion market** (see p. 311) on the 4th Monday in November. The orange grove at *Stadgärtnerei Elfnau* (take tram #19 to "Elfnau") has free Sunday concerts in summer.

NIGHTLIFE. The fashionable folk linger in the *Altstadt's* bars and cafés at night. A seedier scene gathers under the gargoyles and graffiti of the Lorrainebrücke, behind and to the left of the station down Bollwerk.

Klötzlikeller Weine Stube, Gerechtigkeitsg. 62 (tel. 311 74 56). Bern's oldest wine cellar resonates with loud talk and slurred choruses of German drinking songs (wines 3.40-5.20SFr per glass). January and February bring the house specialty, *Treberwurst* (sausage cooked in wine liqueur). Open Tu-Th 4pm-12:30am, F-Sa 4pm-1:30am.

Art Café, Gurteng. 3 (tel. 311 42 64). A café by day and a smoky bar by night, the black and white decor sets a casually trendy tone. Occasional live acts and DJs. Beers from 3.50SFr. Open M-W 7-12:30am, Th-F 7-2:30am, Sa 8-2:30am, Su 6pm-12:30am.

Sous le Pont, (from Bollwerk, head left before Lorrainebrücke through the cement park), the den of alternative culture, is a fascinating stew of mismatched chairs and mesmerizing Eastern music. Pony-tailed waiters bring 3SFr beers to an un-naturally relaxed, predominantly male, clientele. Open M and Sa after 5pm, Tu-F 11pm-1am.

Reitschule, Bern Neubrückstr. 8 (tel 302 83 72), left off Bollwerk. A small room painted with bats and buddhas caters to a patchwork crowd of students and loafers. Beers from 3SFr; *Menüs* 5SFr. Open 8pm-whenever.

Dachstock, on the floor above, is an electronic music disco with talented DJs. Drinks 6-7SFr. Open M-Th 7am-12:30pm, F-Sa 7am-7pm and 8pm-2:30am, Su 6pm-12:30am.

Lirum Larum, Kramg. 19a (tel. 312 24 42). This whimsical bar, named after a nonsensical *Schwyzertüütsch* word, cultivates a topsy-turvy sense of style to a soundtrack of perky pop music. Beer from 3.50SFr. Open M-Th 6:30pm-12:30am, F-Sa 9pm-1:30am.

THE THUNERSEE

As the western member of the pair of lakes that frames Interlaken, the Thunersee's smaller size works to its advantage. The jade-green forests and distant snow-capped Jungfrau peaks seem immediately accessible from the sail-dotted waters of the lake. Its northwestern shores are strewn with castles, enchanting the surrounding towns and cloud-enshrouded peaks.

The Thunersee's three significant towns, **Thun, Spiez,** and **Interlaken,** all lie on the main Bern-Interlaken-Lucerne rail line. **Boats** putter to the smaller villages between the Thun and Interlaken West railway stations (June 26-Sept. 26, 2hr., every hr. 8:24am-8:10pm; special evening cruises available from June-Dec. Eurailpass, SwissPass, and Berner Oberland pass valid). A ferry day-pass good as far as **Brienz** (on the Brienzersee) costs 6.60SFr. **Berner Oberland passes** are also valid on ferries (7-day pass 165SFr, 15-day pass 205SFr). Point-to-point tickets may be cheaper depending on how much ground you wish to cover in one day. For current information, consult BLS shipping company (tel. 334 52 11; www.thunersee.ch).

THUN

Known as the "Gateway to the Bernese Oberland," Thun lies on the banks of the Aare river and the Thunersee. The city's name is derived from the Celtic "dunum," or hill settlement. The town's first settlements date back to 100BC. Graced by nearby castles of every imaginable size and most colors, the quiet, water-laced town confirms the words of Johannes Brahms: "Relaxing in Thun is delightful, and one day will not be enough."

BERNESE OBERLAND

■ **ORIENTATION AND PRACTICAL INFORMATION.** Thun's main street is the tree-lined boulevard Bälliz. The oldest squares and the castle (all hung with red-and-white flags) lie across the river from the train station on the Aare's north bank. Thun's **tourist office**, Seestr. 2 (tel. 222 23 40; fax 222 83 23), is outside and to the left of the station (open July-Aug. M-F 9am-7pm, Sa 9am-noon and 1-4pm; Sept.-June M-F 9am-noon and 1-6pm, Sa 9am-noon). **Trains** leave every hour for **Interlaken East** (14.60SFr) and **Interlaken West** (13.60SFr) and every half-hour for **Spiez** (6.20SFr) and **Bern** (12.60SFr). There is a rail **information desk** (tel. 222 95 86; open Mar. to mid-Oct. M-F 8am-7:40pm, Sa 8am-5pm; mid-Oct. to Feb. M-F 8am-6:30pm, Sa 8am-5pm). The **boat landing** (tel. 223 53 80) is to the right of the station. Boats depart for **Interlaken West** (16.60SFr), **Spiez** (8.40SFr), **Faulensee** (9.20SFr), **Hilterfingen** (4.60SFr), and **Oberhofen** (5.40SFr). The train station has **currency exchange** (open daily 5:50am-8:30pm), **bike rental** (26SFr per day; open M-Sa 7am-7:50pm, Su 8:20am-noon and 2-7:50pm), and **lockers** (3-5SFr). **Taxis** are usually waiting outside the train station, or dial 222 22 22. **Park** at the Parkhaus Aarestr. on Aarestr. (tel. 222 78 26; 1.50SFr per hr.). The **post office** is at Bälliz 60, opposite Mühlebrücke (open M-F 7:30am-6pm, Sa 7:30-11am). The **postal code** is CH-3600.

| PHONE CODE | The **city code** for Thun is 033. |

■ **ACCOMMODATIONS AND FOOD.** The tourist office has information on a few **bed and breakfasts** (starting at 45SFr). **Hotel Metzgern**, Untere Hauptg. 2 (tel. 222 21 41; fax 222 21 82), is on Rathauspl. From the station, turn left and follow the river on Aarestr., cross it at Allmend-Brücke and turn right. Sunny rooms are equipped with sinks. (Singles, doubles, and triples 55SFr per person the 1st night; 50SFr each additional night. Breakfast included. Reception Tu-Th 8am-11:30pm; F-Sa 8am-12:30am, Su 4-11:30pm. MC, Visa.) Campers should head to **Camping Bettlereiche** (tel. 336 40 67; fax 336 40 17). Take bus #1 to "Camping" or turn right from the station and walk 45 minutes. The campsite is crowded with schoolkids, but it's near the water and surrounded by hills. (Jul.-Aug. 15.60SFr; Apr.-June and Sept.-Oct. 12.10SFr. Showers included. Reception 8:30am-noon and 2-8:30pm. Visa, MC.)

Unlike hotel rooms, food in Thun is cheap. Affordable restaurants line Bahnhofstr., and both **Migros** and **Co-op** have markets and restaurants on Allmendstr. straddling the Kuhbrücke (both open M-W and F 8am-6:30pm, Th 8am-9pm, Sa 7am-4pm, Co-op also Su 7:30am-4pm). The **Brotbar**, Bälliz 11 (tel. 222 22 21), is equal parts corner bakery and swanky café. Cross the river at Allmend-Brücke and turn right on Bälliz. Try some *Brötli* (1.70SFr) or hearty potato bread (4.50SFr) while sipping exotic tea (3.80SFr). (Open M-W 7am-6:30pm, Th-Sa 7am-12:30am.) For delectable pastries and sandwiches in a comfy corner tea room, try **Confiserie Steinmann**, Bälliz 37 (tel. 222 20 47), between Brotbar and the post office. Enjoy tarts for 2.40SFr or a mouth-watering *Thuner Leckerli* made from honey, lemon rind, and nuts (6SFr for 5 pieces; open M-F 6am-7pm, Sa 7am-4:30pm, Su 8am-4:30pm). At the **open-air market** in the *Altstadt*, across the river from the train station, vendors hawk souvenirs, clothes, and fresh produce (open W and Sa 8am-9pm). A **food market** covers Bälliz all day on Wednesdays and Saturdays.

CASTLES. Schloß **Thun** is Thun's centerpiece, presiding over the town from the top of the *Altstadt*. From the station, bear left down Bahnhofstr. and go over two bridges, right on Obere Hauptg., left up the Risgässli steps, and left again at the top. The castle, topped by **Turm Zähringer**, houses a historical museum whose upper floors show off a collection of vicious weaponry. The tower was the site of a gruesome fratricide in 1322, when Eberhard of Kyburg unsportingly defenestrated his brother Hartmann. Downstairs in the *Rittersaal* (Knight's Hall) the castle hosts summer **classical music concerts** the last two weeks of June. (For concert tickets call 223 35 30 or contact the tourist office; tickets 40-60SFr. Castle tel. 223 20 01. Open June-Sept. 9am-6pm; Apr.-May and Oct. 10am-5pm. 5SFr, students 2SFr, children 1SFr.)

The very pink **Schloß Schadau,** in the Walter Hansen Schadaupark, was built in the style of the Loire castles. From the station, turn right and walk about 15 minutes. Once a museum, it is now a fabulous **restaurant.** Enjoy the view of the lake from the **Wocher Panorama.** (Seestr. 45. Tel. 223 14 32. Open Tu-Su May-Jul. and Sept.-Nov. 10am-5pm. 4SFr, students 3SFr, under 17 free.)

In neighboring Oberhofen, the 13th-century **Schloß Oberhofen** attracts visitors to its riotous gardens and museum of furniture from the 12th to 19th centuries. Medieval, Baroque, Renaissance, Louis XVI, and Napoleon III styles mingle freely. There's a lavishly languid Turkish smoking room upstairs and a pallet-furnished cell downstairs, with plenty of wall-mounted antlers in between. Take bus #21 to "Oberhofen Dorf," then head right to the lake, or hike up to the castle. (Tel. 243 12 35. Open mid-May to mid-Nov. daily 10am-noon and 2-5pm. 5SFr, students and seniors 3SFr. Garden open May-Oct. 9:30am-6pm.)

Bus #21 runs to Hilterfingen (10min. by foot), where **Schloß Hünegg** peers over the boat landing. The most elaborate of the *Thunersee* castles, its Victorian rooms are maintained in an appealing state of lived-in clutter (the cook has left out a bag of flour in the kitchen). The castle grounds, known as **Hünegg Park,** are the dim and leafy home of deer, rabbits, and lots of wild birds. (Tel. 243 19 82. Castle open mid-May to mid-Oct. M-Sa 2-5pm, Su 10am-noon and 2-5pm. 8SFr, students 7SFr.)

⚄ OUTDOOR ACTIVITIES. The popular local **hike** up **Heilingenschwendi,** the hillside above Thun on the lake's north shore, provides a view of the distant Jungfrau mountains. Past the casino and the village of Seematten, turn left, cross the river, and head up through the wooded ridge (1152m). Continue farther to the **Dreiländeregg** and **Niesenbänkli** for a panoramic view (3hr.). If you push on to the village of **Schwendi,** near the top, continue hiking a little farther to **Schloß Oberhofen** (see above), where you can catch bus #21 back to town. (Whole hike half-day.)

If the *Schlösser* stifle you, hit the water. The tourist office provides information on **sailing, wind-surfing, river-rafting,** and **boat rental.** Thun's outdoor **festivals** are wonderfully quirky: on the last Monday and Tuesday in September young cadets shoot it out in the *Altstadt* during the yearly **Ausschiesset.** A **William Tell Shoot** honors the cadet who takes the best aim at a model of Gessler (see **Tell Tale,** p. 295). The *Altstadt* rollicks with merry music during the **Festival of Barrel Organs and Ballad Singers** every July.

NEAR THUN: SPIEZ

Trains leave every 30min., connecting Spiez with Bern (30min., 17.20SFr), Thun (10min., 6.20SFr), and Interlaken West (20min., 8.60SFr). Boats float to Thun (11.20SFr) and Interlaken (8SFr).

Sleepy Spiez overlooks the *Thunersee.* Its most famous attraction is its castle, **Schloß Spiez,** a medieval fortress that has been added to throughout the centuries, bearing Romanesque, Gothic, and Renaissance flourishes. From the station, bear left on Bahnhofstr., turn right on Thunstr., and then left on Seestr., or just head towards it—it is visible from anywhere in town. You can stroll through the walled, lakeside gardens for free. Inside the fortress is a historical museum with enormous bear skins hanging above the mantelpiece and nearly Mediterranean views of the lake. (Tel. 654 15 06. Open July-Aug. M 2-6pm, Tu-Su 10am-6pm; Apr.-June and Sept.-Oct. M 2-5pm, Tu-Su 10am-5pm. 4SFr, students 3SFr.)

Spiez's **tourist office** (tel. 654 20 20; fax 654 21 92), left as you exit the train station, sells hiking maps and helps find inexpensive rooms for free (open July-Aug. M-F 8am-7pm, Sa 9am-noon and 2-4pm; May-June and Sept. M-F 8am-noon and 2-6pm, Sa 9am-noon and 2-4pm; Nov.-Apr. M-F 8am-noon and 2-5pm). The best place to stay is the **◪Swiss Adventure Hostel** (tel. (033) 733 73 73; fax 733 73 74), in the tiny town of Boltigen, 30 minutes from Spiez by train (dir.: Zweissimen). Housed in the old Hotel Bären, the Adventure Hostel has staked out its place as a restful, wholesome alternative to the partying adventure scene in Interlaken. The small adventure company that is run out of this hostel offers the same activities as the Interlaken companies, but here, after your canyoning trip, you get to eat dinner with your trip leader. The beautiful, inexpensive rooms were molded into the old hotel without affecting its charm. The hostel offers **Internet access** (14SFr per hr.), **mountain bike rental** (25SFr per day), a cellar **bar**, TV, and a restaurant with breakfast buffet (5SFr) and dinner buffet (15-20SFr) from an accomplished chef. If you do adventure activities through them, one night at the hostel is free. (4-10 bed dorms 18SFr per person, quad with shower 24SFr per person, double with shower 68SFr. 2 free shuttles run to and from Interlaken each day; call for times and availability. MC, Visa.)

The mountain piercing the sky above the city is the **Niesenberg** (2363m). Hikes on the mountain, while not for beginners, are accessible. Pick up hiking maps at tourist offices in Interlaken, Thun, or Spiez. Hiking all the way up or down the mountain is prohibited, but a **funicular** chugs to the top, and the **Lötschberg train** from Spiez (every hr., 7.20SFr round-trip) connects with the funicular at Mülenen. (May-Oct. 8am-5:30pm; 23SFr, 38SFr round-trip, 14SFr one-way to Schwandegg.) The funicular's builders pushed the frontiers of human achievement by building steps alongside the track, which became the **longest flight of steps in the world.** Unfortunately, only professional maintenance teams are allowed to use the steps (all 11,674 of them).

BRIENZ AND THE ROTHORN

Brienz is filled with anachronistic but authentic curiosities, including Switzerland's oldest cog steam railway, an enormous park full of preserved traditional Swiss dwellings, and wood-carvers galore (whatever you ever wanted in wood, you can get it here, even elephant and squirrel bookends). These institutions are maintained for the benefit of tourists, but Brienz somehow avoids being kitschy. The tempo of life here seems to be cued by the calm, clear waters of the bordering **Brienzersee,** which lies beneath sharp cliffs and dense forests.

◪ ORIENTATION AND PRACTICAL INFORMATION. Brienz makes an ideal daytrip from Interlaken by **train** (20min., 6:10am-9:53pm, 6.20SFr) or **boat** (1¼hr., every hr. 8:20am-5:32pm, 13.20SFr). Cruises on the Brienzersee depart from Interlaken's *Ostbahnhof* (June-Sept. every hr. 9:40am-6:05pm; Apr.-May and Oct. 3 per day, Eurail and Swisspass valid). The station, dock, and Rothorn cog railway terminus occupy the center of town, flanked on Hauptstr. by the post office, banks, and a supermarket. At the west end of town is Brienz-Dorf wharf; at the eastern end you'll find the hostel and campsites. Brienz's **tourist office,** Hauptstr. 143 (tel. 952 80 80; fax 952 80 88), across and left from the train station, is especially helpful for info on wood-carving cottages (open July-Aug. M-F 8am-6:30pm, Sa 9am-noon and 4-6pm; Sept.-June M-F 8am-noon and 2-6pm, Sa 8am-noon; May-June closed Sa). The train station **rents bicycles** (26SFr per day), **exchanges currency,** and has **lockers** (2SFr; all open 5:50am-11pm). The **post office** is next door (tel. 951 25 05; open M-F 7:45am-6pm, Sa 8:30-11am). The **postal code** is CH-3855.

PHONE CODE	The **city code** for Brienz is 033.

◪◪ ACCOMMODATIONS AND FOOD. For a place to sleep, cross the tracks at the station to the shore path, and walk left (15min.) to find the **Brienz Jugendherberge (HI),** Strandweg 10 (tel. 951 11 52; fax 951 22 60). The *Lager*-style bunks at this lakeside hostel are overpriced, but doorstep access to lake walks compensates. (Dorms 25.50SFr; doubles 61SFr. Breakfast included. Dinner 11.50SFr. **Kitchen** facilities. **Bicycles** 15SFr per day. Reception 7:30-10am and 5-10pm. Open Apr.-Oct.) Inquire at the tourist office about **private rooms. Hotel Sternen am See,** Hauptstr. 92 (tel. 951 35 45), left from the station on the main road, has a lakeside terrace. (Singles 50-60SFr; doubles 80SFr, with shower 140SFr; triples 120SFr, 160SFr; quads with shower 200SFr. Breakfast included. Reception 8am-8pm. MC, Visa.) Two campgrounds lie just past the hostel on the waterfront. The first one,

Camping Seegärtli (tel. 951 13 51), is more secluded and offers free lake-swimming and fresh bread at 8am (7SFr; tents 5-7SFr; cars 3SFr; reception 8am-8:30pm; open Apr.-Oct.). Continue straight on the same road to the larger **Camping Aaregg** (tel. 951 18 43; fax 951 43 24), which has an on-site restaurant. (9.20SFr; tents 13SFr. Bikes 20SFr per day. Reception 8am-noon and 2-9pm. Open Apr.-Oct.) **Restaurant Adler,** Hauptstr. 131 (tel. 951 41 00), has a terrace with a spectacular view of the *Brienzersee* and the Axalphorn (fondue special 18SFr, veggie dishes 13SFr, Spanish *paellas* 17-19SFr, Oberland specialties 14-16SFr; open June-Oct. 7:30am-11:30pm; Nov.-May Tu-Su 8am-11:30pm). **Steinbock Restaurant** (tel. 951 40 55), farther along Hauptstr., has outside tables and a warm wooden interior (Swiss-style macaroni with apple sauce 16SFr, veggie dishes 12-17SFr; open 8am-11pm; AmEx, DC, MC, Visa). A **Co-op** is on Hauptg. across from the station (open M-Th 7:45am-6:30pm, F 7:45am-8pm, Sa 7:45am-4pm; MC, Visa).

📷 **MUSEUMS.** ▨**The Swiss Open-Air Museum,** on Lauenenstr. in the nearby town of Ballenberg, is an amazing 80-hectare country park dedicated to the preservation of Swiss heritage. Authentic rural Swiss houses are clumped by geographical region into tiny villages, minus the people. Most of the houses in the park were simply transplanted from their endangered original locations, and many have live exhibitions of traditional trades, such as iron-smithing or cheese-making. (Tel. 951 11 23. Open mid-Apr. to Oct. 10am-5pm. 14SFr, with visitor's card 12.60SFr, students 12SFr.) The park is about an hour's walk from the Brienz train station, but a **bus** (every hr. 7:56am-7:02pm, round-trip 5.60SFr) connects the two.

If the museum doesn't satisfy your cultural-history cravings, Brienz has woodcarvers galore. The largest displays are at the cantonal wood-working schools in town. The **Schnitzlerschule** (Wood-Carving School; tel. 951 17 51) and the **Geigerschule** (Violin-Making School; tel. 951 18 61) both have display halls about their craft. To reach both, follow the main street away from the station and hostel (15min.), then turn right on Schneeg. Home to 10 students, the *Geigerschule* houses a collection of antique instruments and a showroom of gleaming, finished violins for 5000SFr each. (Both open Sept.-May M-F 8-11am and 2-5pm.; June-Aug. call for opening hours. Free.) Many local wood-carvers also let you watch them work; contact the tourist office for a list.

▨ **OUTDOOR ACTIVITIES.** The most accessible mountain in Brienz is the **Rothorn** (2350m) mainly because of the **Brienz Rothorn Bahn** (tel. 951 44 00), which huffs and puffs its way up the mountain (June-Oct., every hr., last ascent 4pm, last descent 4:55pm). At 107 years old, it is the oldest cog steam railway in Switzerland, and rather pricey (42SFr, round-trip 66SFr; with Bernese Oberland pass 20SFr, 32SFr; with Swisspass 31SFr, 48SFr). Get off at **Planalp,** half-way up the mountain, for medium-range hikes down. Follow the railway down, turning left below Planalp to head through Baalen and Schwanden (3½hr.). From the summit, head east toward the lake and turn right at the Eiseesaltel, continuing down to Hofstetten, Schwanden, and Brienz (4hr.). If you can't bring yourself to leave the summit, check into the **Berggasthaus** (tel. 951 12 21; fax 951 12 51; dorms 32SFr; singles 65SFr; doubles 130SFr; hall showers; breakfast included; reception 7:30am-10pm).

To reach Brienz's lower peak, the **Axalphorn** (2321m), you can take a bus from the station to **Axalp** (8:20am-4:40pm, 8.40SFr) and head up either the east or west ridge (800m, half-day). Bring a map (check the tourist office at Brienz) and some navigational skills, since both paths are indistinct in places.

Boat service gives easy access to the wild, romantic south shore of the lovely Brienzersee. Float 10 minutes from Brienz (5.60SFr) or 1 hour from Interlaken to **Giessbach Falls,** where you can climb along its 14 frothy cascades. The walk up the falls brings you to a palatial hotel (15min.), which is also accessible by cable car from the dock (4.50SFr, round-trip 6SFr). From the hotel, cross the bridge over the falls, but make sure to turn left along the stream to see all the waterfalls. At the top, a ridge walk leads to the right over the lake, and then down to the breezy lakeside village of Iseltwald, where you can catch the ferry back to Brienz.

BERNESE OBERLAND

LOCH MEIRINGEN? Meiringen's mythic Gorge of Aare, a narrow mountainside chasm so deep that light barely penetrates its recesses, is said to harbor the fearsome Tatzelwürmli, a scaly Nibelungian worm of monstrous proportions. Recently, a foreign photographer from Berlin named Balkin visited Meiringen and "accidentally" snapped photos of what he claimed was the Tatzelwürmli in its natural habitat. Resembling a very fat snake, the *Wurm* was brown with liver spots on its skin, and possessed a forked tongue. Balkin published his film in the *Berlin Illustrated Newspaper,* unleashing a torrent of speculation about the the snake-like inhabitant of Meiringen's rocky slopes. Although serious investigations have long since died out, the town still remembers its dragon by means of strange Tatzelwürmli candy, shaped like the beast down to the marzipan tongue, cream belly, and bloody strawberry-candy teeth. Ward off dragon scourges by eating the poor beast in sugary effigy.

NEAR BRIENZ: MEIRINGEN AND REICHENBACH FALLS

One train connects Meiringen to Brienz (10min., 4.40SFr) and Interlaken (30min., every hr. 5am-8:57pm, 10SFr), and another to Lucerne (every hr. 7:04am-7:25pm, 17.20SFr).

When the glaciers receded from the area around Meiringen they deposited soft limestone that was easily shaped and eroded by the runoff from melting ice. As a result, Meiringen is surrounded by a striking landscape comprised of glacial gorges, steep limestone cliffs, and thunderous waterfalls. The natural drama has served as fodder for many a fertile imagination. The legendary fork-tongued **Tatzelwürmli** is said to inhabit the nearby **Aareschlucht (Gorge of the Aare)**, and **Sherlock Holmes** and arch-nemesis Professor Moriarty plunged to their "death" together in the Reichenbach Falls above town.

A series of cave-passageways clinging to the side of the cliff takes you over the water running through the **Aareschlucht,** which is 200km deep and only one meter wide at points. Follow signs from Bahnhofstr. for the 10-minute walk. (Open Apr.-Nov. 9am-5pm. 6SFr, students 4SFr, with guest-card 5SFr.) On certain summer nights the gorge is illuminated by floodlights (July-Aug. W and F 9-11pm). In nearby **Rosenlaui** (postbus dir.: Schwarzwaldalp) there is another glacial gorge (open May-Oct. 9am-5pm; 6SFr, 4SFr students). It is a 45-minute round-trip walk through the gorge, but the reward is the Rosenlaui valley, with views up to the melting giant.

The town has done its best to capitalize on its famous literary connections. The tiny **Sherlock Holmes Museum** (tel. 971 42 21), inside the old Anglican church just past the tourist office, blurs fact and fiction, sometimes paying tribute to the exploits of Holmes and sometimes to his creator Sir Arthur Conan Doyle (open May-Sept. Tu-Su 1:30-6pm; Oct.-Apr. by appointment; 3.80SFr, with guest-card 2.80SFr). If that doesn't satisfy your Holmes fetish, you can trek up to the **Reichenbach Falls,** where Holmes plummeted to his fictional death. The highlight may be the ride up to the falls in the 100-year-old wooden open-air funicular. To reach the funicular walk down Bahnhofstr. and turn right on Alpbachstr. (Open mid-May to Sept. 8:15am-5:45pm; one-way 5SFr, round-trip 7SFr.)

During the last week in June and the first week in July, Meiringen hosts **Musikfestwochen,** a classical music festival (www2.mountain.ch/mufewo; tickets 30-50SFr, students 12-20SFr).

INTERLAKEN

In AD 1130, two literal-minded Augustinian monks named the land between the **Thunersee** and the **Brienzersee** "Interlaken," which means "between lakes." Interlaken lies between the pair of crystal-blue lakes at the foot of the largest mountains in Switzerland: the **Eiger, Mönch,** and **Jungfrau.** With easy access to these adventure playgrounds, Interlaken has earned its rightful place as one of Switzerland's prime tourist attractions. Swiss-German is drowned out by the chorus of English, but the tourism explosion has spurred the development of some of Swit-

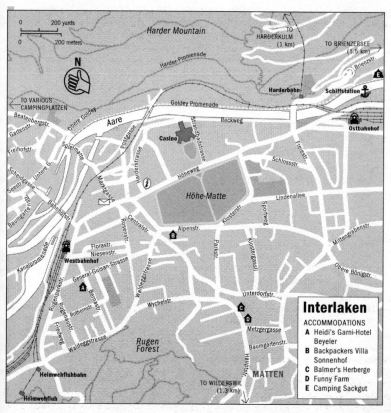

Interlaken

ACCOMMODATIONS

A Heidi's Garni-Hotel Beyeler
B Backpackers Villa Sonnenhof
C Balmer's Herberge
D Funny Farm
E Camping Sackgut

zerland's most varied and exciting accommodations. Beneath the enchanting sight of the Jungfrau rising 4158m above the gardens lining Höheweg, Interlaken spreads out around a large central green, the **Höhenmatte,** whose main function seems to be as a landing pad for the hundreds of paragliders that drift down from the skies each day. Interlaken, alongside Queensland, New Zealand, is one of the paragliding capitals of the world, thanks to the gentle and stable winds controlled by the mountains rearing up throughout the valley.

ORIENTATION AND PRACTICAL INFORMATION

Interlaken lies south on A6, west on A8, and north on Route 11, and the city has 2 train stations. The **Westbahnhof** stands in the center of town bordering the *Thunersee*, near most shops and hotels; trains to Bern, Basel, and other western towns stop here second, and cost slightly less from here. The **Ostbahnhof,** on the *Brienzersee*, is 10 minutes from the town center by foot or bus (3SFr), and is cheaper for connecting to eastern towns. Both stations have hotel prices posted and direct free phones for reservations. Beware of hostel hustlers at the station; take your time in deciding where to stay—it can make or break your vacation.

PHONE CODE	The **city code** for Interlaken is 033.

Trains: The **Westbahnhof** (tel. 826 47 50) and **Ostbahnhof** (tel. 828 73 19) have trains to: **Bern** (5:32am-9:28pm, 25SFr); **Basel** (5:32am-9:53pm, 56SFr); **Zurich** (5:32am-

10:03pm, 62SFr); **Geneva** (5:32am-9:29pm, 65SFr); **Lucerne** (5:32am-9:57pm, 27SFr); and **Lugano** (7:12am-5:17pm, 72SFr), among others. **Jungfraubahnen,** Harderstr. 14 (tel. 828 71 11; fax 828 72 64) runs all trains to the small towns before Jungfrau. Swisspass valid for Wengen, Grindelwald, and Mürren, 25% discount at higher stops. Eurailpass 25% discount on mountain trains. Trains to the **mountains** leave every 30min. from the Ostbahnhof to: **Wengen** (6:35am-11:32pm, 11.80SFr), **Grindelwald** (6:24am-11:32pm, 9.40SFr), **Mürren** (15.60SFr, change at Lauterbrunnen), **Lauterbrunnen** (6:35am-11:32pm, 6.20SFr), **Kleine Scheidegg** (35SFr), and the **Jungfraujoch** (158.20SFr round-trip; see **The Jungfraujoch,** p. 327).

Taxis: City Taxi (tel. 823 33 33). **Bödeli Taxi** (tel. 0800 801 802). **Interlaken Ost** (tel. 822 80 80).

Parking: Parking is 2SFr per hr. at the train stations, behind the casino, and on Centralstr.

Bike Rental: At either **train station,** 26SFr per day, mountain bikes 30SFr. Open 5am-10pm. **Zumbrunn Velo,** Postg. 4 (tel. 822 22 35), 1 block from the tourist office, towards the train station, has flourescent city bikes for 8SFr per day, mountain bikes 18SFr. Open Tu-Sa 8am-noon and 1:30-6:30pm. **Intersport Oberland,** Postg. 16 (tel. 822 06 61; fax 822 73 07) 20SFr per day, mountain bikes 30SFr, in-line skates 20SFr. Open M-F 8am-noon and 1:30-6:30pm, Sa 8am-noon and 1-4pm. Hotel Sonnenhof and Balmers have bike rental as well.

Tourist Office: Höheweg 37 (tel. 822 21 21), in the **Hotel Metropole.** From the Westbahnhof, turn left on Bahnhofpl. and right on Bahnhofstr., which becomes Höheweg. From the Ostbahnhof, turn right as you exit. Free maps and schedules, tickets to the Jungfraujoch. Open July-Aug. M-F 8am-noon and 1:30-6:30pm, Sa 8am-5pm, Su 5-7pm; Sept.-June M-F 8am-noon and 2-6pm, Sa 8am-noon.

Currency Exchange: Credit Suisse and **Swiss Bank** near the Westbahnhof have **ATMs,** as do both train stations. You'll get average rates on currency exchange at the **train station** (although you might do 1% better in town). No commission on traveler's checks. Credit card advances and Western Union transfers. Open daily 8am-noon and 2-6pm.

Bookstore: Buchhandlweg Haupt, Höheweg 11 (tel. 822 35 16). English-language books, German and French dictionaries, and travel books. Open M-F 8:30am-6:30pm, Sa 8:30am-4pm.

Library: Marktpl. 4 (tel. 822 02 12). German, French, and English books. Open July-Aug. M, W, F, and Su 4-6pm, Tu and Th 9-11am and 3-7pm. Sept.-June M-Tu and Th-F 4-6pm, W 9-11am and 3-7pm, Sa 10am-noon.

Laundromat: Self-Service Wash & Dry, Beatenbergstr. 5. Cross the bridge next to the Westbahnhof and take the 2nd right on Hauptstr. The manager will do your laundry for 12SFr per load; do it yourself for 10-11SFr. Open 24hr. **Spot On,** Hauptstr. 16, opposite Balmer's, demands 20SFr a load. Open 8am-8pm.

Snow and Weather Info: For the Jungfrau, call 855 10 22.

Late-Night Pharmacy: Call 111. **Grosse Apotheke,** Bahnhofstr. 5A (tel. 822 72 62), is open M-F 7:30am-6:30pm, Sa 7:30am-5pm. AmEx, MC, Visa.

Emergencies: Police, tel. 117. **Hospital,** tel. 826 26 26. **Doctor,** tel. 823 23 23.

Internet Access: The **Backpacker's Villa Sonnenhof** has 4 computers (12SFr per hr.). The American expatriate owner of **The Wave,** Rosenstr. 13 (tel. 823 40 32), provides late-night Internet access (16SFr per hr., 12SFr for students). Go right at the main circle between the station and the tourist office. Open M-Sa 11am-12:30am, Su 4pm-12:30am. **Balmer's** also has Internet on 2 computers for 20SFr per hour.

Post Office: Marktg. 1 (tel. 224 89 50). From the Westbahnhof, go left on Bahnhofpl. Open M-F 7:45am-noon and 1:30-6:15pm, Sa 8:30am-11am. **Postal Code:** CH-3800.

▌ ACCOMMODATIONS AND CAMPING

There are tons of beds in Interlaken, but if you want the same adventures with less of a crowd, trek out to the **Swiss Adventure Hostel** in Boltigen (see p. 317).

HOSTELS

▧ Backpackers Villa Sonnenhof, Alpenstr. 16 (tel. 826 71 71; fax 826 71 72; email backpackers@villa.ch; www.villa.ch) diagonally across the Höhenmatte from the tourist office. This central but secluded, remodeled villa (read: mansion) hints at its loftier beginnings 150 years ago. The spacious, airy rooms have beautiful wooden balconies with million-dollar views of the Jungfrau to the south and Harder Mann to the north. The friendly young couple that runs the hostel provide tons of services for the twentysome-thing crowd, including TV with CNN, **mountain bike rental** (30SFr per day), **laundry** (12SFr per load, full service), and **Internet access** (12SFr). 4- to 6-bed room 29SFr per person, triple 33SFr per person, doubles 74SFr, including **kitchen** use, towels, sheets, breakfast, recreation room, lockers, showers, and advice on outdoor activities. 3SFr extra for Jungfrau view, balcony, and in-suite bathroom. Call well in advance for reserva-tions. Reception 7:30-11am and 4-9pm. No curfew; no surcharge. AmEx, MC, Visa.

▧ Funny Farm, (tel. (079) 652 61 27), behind Hotel Hatterhof, down Hauptstr. from Balmer's in the nearby village of Matten. Take bus #5 to "Hotel Sonne" (2.20SFr) and then backtrack 1min., or walk diagonally across the Höhenmatte from the tourist office, then follow signs for Balmer's down Parkstr. More commune than youth hostel, this vast estate is con-stantly changing according to the interests of the guests. Currently, Funny Farm offers **tennis, basketball, volleyball,** an **archery range,** an enormous **swimming pool,** an **outdoor bar** and nightly bonfire, indoor **nightclub,** and **didgeridoo-making workshops.** Another ephemeral delight is the "Out on the Grass" open-air music festival which will be held in the new amphitheater in July/Aug. 2000. Dorms 25SFr. Breakfast included. **Internet access** 12SFr. No curfew or lockout.

Heidi's Garni-Hotel Beyeler, Bernastr. 37 (tel./fax 822 90 30). From the Westbahnhof, turn right, go left on Bernastr. (behind the Migros), and walk straight for about 3min. Eccentric fraternal twins Walter and Herbert preside over a rambling old house deco-rated with sleds, bells, old photographs, and carousel horses. Private rooms with bath have balconies, views, and Swiss furniture. Common room with TV and CNN. Dorm 20SFr, 2- to 4-bed room 25-30SFr per person, doubles 60-80SFr. Cheaper off-season. Sheets and shower included. Fully-furnished **apartments** with kitchen, balcony, phone, and TV (2-night min.) doubles 80-90SFr, quad 150SFr. **Bikes** 25SFr per day. MC, Visa.

Suzi's Bed and Breakfast, Gen. Guisanstr. 31 (tel. 822 25 45; email lotschberg@inter-lakentourism.ch), offers a private retreat from Interlaken's hyper-social hostel world in a quiet enclave behind Hotel Lotschberg. Suzi's husband Fritz can advise you on hikes. Guests receive a 20SFr discount on paragliding (150SFr regularly). Doubles Oct.-May 95SFr; June-Sept. 110SFr. Breakfast included. **Internet access** for guests 10SFr per hr. **Mountain bikes** 35SFr.

Balmer's Herberge, Hauptstr. 23-25 (tel. 822 19 61; fax 823 32 61), in the nearby vil-lage of Matten. Take bus #5 to "Hotel Sonne" (2.20SFr) and then backtrack 1min., or walk diagonally across the Höhenmatte from the tourist office and follow signs down Parkstr. from either station. From June to Aug., Balmer's runs a shuttle bus from both stations every hr. Sign in, drop off your pack, and return at 5pm when beds are assigned (no reserva-tions). Balmer's is Switzerland's oldest private hostel (around since 1945), but it is thoroughly American. Without the paper Swiss flags on the hamburgers and the Rugen-brau beer that flows freely, guests might forget they are in Switzerland. To enjoy the dorms or Balmer's **tent** (a huge white circus tent with no insulation a few blocks farther from town), you must value comradeship above comfort. Balmer's provides **mountain bike rental** (30SFr per day), nightly movies, TV with CNN and MTV, a book exchange, **Internet access** (20SFr per hr.), a **kitchen** (1SFr per 20min.), **laundry** (8SFr per load), a mini-department store (open 7:30am-9pm), and safety deposit boxes (2SFr for the entire stay). After 10pm, activity shifts underground to the new **Metro Bar** (beers 4.50SFr). Participate with caution—wake-up music starting at 7:30am drives half-con-scious guests out by 9:30am, and everyone must re-register and change beds each night. In winter, there are **free sleds** and a 20% discount on ski and snowboard rental. 8-bed dorms and tent 19SFr in summer, 24SFr in winter; 3- or 4-bed room 24SFr, 28SFr per person. Doubles 28SFr, 35SFr per person. If beds are full, crash on a mattress

(13SFr). Showers 1SFr per 5min. of hot water. Breakfast included. No one gets turned away, but it's best to show up early. Reception in summer 6:30am-noon and 4:30-11pm; in winter 6:30-9am and 4:30-11pm. AmEx, MC, Visa with 5% surcharge.

Jugendherberge Bönigen (HI), Aareweg 21 (tel. 822 43 53; fax 823 20 58), is a 20min. bus ride away from Interlaken. Take the hourly bus #1 or #3 (dir.: Bönigen) to "Lütschinenbrücke" (3 stops). Catering to a younger crowd, this hostel is far removed from the adventure scene in Interlaken. The *Brienzersee* laps at the back doorstep. Try to snag a 6-bed room instead of the 25-bed "Good Morning" dorm on the top floor. 6- and 25-bed dorms 26.40SFr; 4-bed dorms 30.40SFr; doubles 78SFr. Breakfast, showers, sheets, and **kitchen** use included. Lockers 20SFr deposit. Dinner 11.50SFr. **Laundry** 8SFr. **Bike rental** 15SFr. Reception 6-10am and 2pm-midnight. Reserve at least 2 days in advance June-Aug. Closed mid-Nov. to mid-Dec.

CAMPING

Camping Sackgut (tel. (079) 656 89 58) is closest to town, just across the river from the Ostbahnhof and near the *Brienzersee*. Head toward town, but turn across the 1st bridge and another right on the other side. 7.60SFr; tent 6.50-14.50SFr. Reception 9-11am and 4-7pm. Open May-Oct.

Camping Jungfraublick (tel. 822 44 14; fax 822 16 19). Take bus #5 from the Westbahnhof, and continue 5min. past Balmer's on Gsteigstr. This peaceful location has splendid mountain views. 12SFr; off-season 7SFr. Open May-Sept.

Camping Jungfrau (tel. 822 57 30), is nearly within the bounds of the city, near the *Thunersee*. Turn left from the station on Bahnhofstr., then left on Seidenfadenstr. and right on Steinlerstr. This campground has a **kitchen**, tennis, swimming, and TV. 5-7SFr per person; tent site 8-15SFr. For backpackers with tent, 10SFr per person for everything.

Lazy Rancho (tel. 822 87 16, fax 823 19 20). Go past Camping Jungfrau and left down Bockstorweg. This spacious, clean campground is equipped with a swimming pool, grocery store, **kitchen**, and **laundry** facilities. 7-9.50SFr per person; tent site 7-10SFr. Showers 0.50SFr. Open Mar.-Oct.

◗ FOOD

Interlaken has a wide range of restaurants, covering the pricey, the scuzzy, and lots of affordable restaurants in between. Generally, the Balmer's crowd eats at Balmer's (fondue, bratwurst, and burgers under 10SFr), the hostel crowd eats at the *Jugendherberge* (11.50SFr), and the Funny Farm folks eat in the renovated cable car, but don't be afraid to venture outside for a bite.

Café Restaurant Spatz, Spielmatte 49 (tel. 822 97 22). Head up the tiny street, left from the station, which leads up along the river, and turn left on Spielmatte. This riverside café serves up the cheapest fondue in town (16.50SFr); a platter of chicken, potatoes, and veggies (13.50SFr); and *Apfelstrüdel* with whipped cream (4.50SFr) on a terrace overlooking the river. Open daily 8:30am-10pm.

Confiserie Schuh (tel. 822 94 41), across from the tourist office, has been an Interlaken landmark since the 19th century. Chocolate boots (from 1.60SFr) and strawberry tarts (3.90SFr) sell like mad in the summer. Open Tu-Su 8am-10:30pm.

Mr. Hong's Chinese Take-Out, Marktg. 48 (tel. 823 55 44). For evenings too beautiful to eat inside, friendly Mr. Hong cooks up a variety of stir-fries to go. Chomp on mixed veggies (10SFr), sweet and sour chicken (13SFr), or shrimp fried rice (13SFr). Open Apr.-Oct. 11:45am-10pm; Nov.-Mar. 11:45am-9pm.

El Azteca (tel. 822 71 31), on the pedestrian Jungfraustr. towards the station from the tourist office, has a large menu of Mexican and Swiss dishes. The tantalizing options surpass any ordinary taco or burrito, but the best deals are the 4 daily *Menüs*, 2 Mexican (15SFr), 1 Swiss, and 1 vegetarian (13.50SFr). Open daily in summer 7am-12:30am; in winter daily except W 7am-2pm and 6pm-12:30am. AmEx, Visa, MC.

MOUNTAIN MANN One of the eeriest and most fascinating sights in the Bernese Oberland is the face in the Harder Mountain, called the Harder Mann. His features are the rocky cliffs and a few fortuitously placed trees. On a clear day he is easy to see, a pale triangular face resting against a pillow of trees on one side and a wedge of naked rock on the other. His black moustache has a certain despondent droop, and his deep-socketed eyes have a melancholic, hunted look. He is visible from almost anywhere in town, directly opposite the Jungfrau. The story goes that a strolling monk became possessed and chased a small girl off a cliff. As punishment, he was turned to stone. It might make sense if he hadn't been given the best view in Interlaken, doomed to look at the Jungfrau, Mönch, and Eiger peaks for all eternity, a view for which tourists pay dearly. For the children of Interlaken, there is a happier story: every year the Harder Mann comes down from the mountains to fight off winter. On January 2, they celebrate this fight with wooden Harder Mann masks and a large carnival. Hikers can hike this landmark, but they should not leave the marked paths. Every summer people die attempting to climb roped-off areas.

Matahari, General Guisanstr. 31 (tel. 823 80 01), off Bahnhofstr. behind the Migros. Thai parasols decorate this spicy haunt, which concocts Indonesian *Rijstafel* on a banana leaf for 20SFr. Fresh-from-the-wok, all-you-can-eat specialties 24SFr. Asian specialties (often veggie-happy) from 12SFr. *Menüs* 12SFr. Open W-Su 11am-2:30pm and 5:30pm-midnight. AmEx, DC, MC, Visa.

MARKETS

Migros, across from the Westbahnhof, also houses a restaurant with giant prancing cows on the ceiling. Open M-Th 7:30am-6:30pm, F 7:30am-9pm, Sa 7:30am-4pm. Restaurant also open Su 9am-5pm.

Co-op, Bahnhofstr. 35 (tel. 826 44 80), on the right after you cross the bridge to the left of the station. Market open M-Th 8am-6:30pm, F 8am-9pm, Sa 7:30am-5pm. Restaurant open M-Th 8am-6:30pm, F 8am-9:30pm, Sa 8am-4:30pm, Su 9am-5pm.

◪ OUTDOORS NEAR INTERLAKEN

ADVENTURE SPORTS

Interlaken's steep precipices, raging rivers, and wide-open spaces serve as prime spots for such adrenaline-stimulating activities as paragliding, whitewater rafting, bungee jumping, and canyoning (a sport where wet-suited, harnessed future stunt-doubles rappel and swim down a waterfall). Three companies provide guests with opportunities for these activities. The competition has driven prices down, and most companies charge the same for similar services. **Alpin Raft** (AR; tel. 823 41 00; fax 823 41 01), the original company, has the wildest, Australian guides. **Alpine Center** (AC; tel. 823 55 23; fax 823 07 19), the newest and smallest company, provides the most personal service. **Adventure World,** Kirchg. 18 (AW; tel. 826 77 11; fax 826 77 15), is the largest company; it's usually a little more expensive than the others. All prices include transportation to and from any hostel in Interlaken. All 3 companies offer **paragliding** (AR/AC 140SFr, AW 150SFr; AC offers longer flights as well); **canyoning** (AR/AC 125SFr, AW 130SFr); **river rafting** (AR/AC 85SFr, AW 90SFr); and **skydiving** (380SFr). Alpin Raft and Adventure World also offer **bungee jumping** (100-220SFr) and **hang gliding** (AR 155SFr, AW 170SFr). A number of horse and hiking tours, as well as rock-climbing lessons, are available upon request. Minutes from Interlaken on the Brienzersee, Alpin Raft's **sea-kayaking** provides a strenuous day in the sun and on the water (54-70SFr).

The independent **Swiss Alpine Guides** (tel. 822 60 00; fax 822 61 51) lead full-day ice-climbing clinics (June-Oct., 135SFr), as well as full-day glacier treks which journey to the icy world on the other side of the Jungfrau (daily in summer; 120SFr). Interlaken's winter activities include skiing, snowboarding, ice canyoning, snow rafting, and glacier skiing. Contact **Verkehrsverein Interlaken (tourist office),** Höheweg 37 (tel. 822 21 21; fax 822 52 21) or any of the adventure companies for information. There are 3 **skiing** areas in the Jungfrau region (for information, dial 828 71 11; www.jungfraubahn.ch; 1-day passes 52SFr, 2-day 105SFr).

> Interlaken's adventure sports industry is thrilling and usually death-defying, but accidents do happen. On July 27, 1999, 19 adventure-seeking tourists were killed by a sudden flash flood while canyoning on the Saxeten river. Be aware that you participate in all adventure sports at your own risk.

HIKES FROM INTERLAKEN

The towns closer to the mountains are where the serious hiking starts, but Interlaken has a few good hikes of its own. The most worthwhile hike climbs to the **Harder Kulm** (or Harder Mann, see **Mountain Mann** below). Only the Jungfrau can be seen from Interlaken itself, but from the top of this half-day hike, all 3 peaks are put in front of you for comparison. This view is a striking mountainscape, with the black, triangular face of the Eiger framed by the other two snowy behemoths. The easiest starting point is near the Ostbahnhof. From the Ostbahnhof, head toward town and take the first road bridge right across the river. On the other side, the path has yellow signs (destination: Harderkulm) that later give way to white-red-white *Bergweg* flashes on the rocks. From the top, signs lead back down to the Westbahnhof. To avoid the climb or the descent (or both), a funicular runs from the trailhead near the Ostbahnhof to the top (May-Oct.; 12.80SFr, 20SFr round-trip; 25% discount with Eurailpass and SwissPass; 2hr. up, 1½hr. down).

More horizontal trails lead along the lakes that flank the city. Turn left from the train station, then left before the bridge and follow the canal over to the nature reserve on the shore of the *Thunersee*. The trail winds up the Lombach river, then through pastures at the base of the Harder Kulm back towards town (2hr.).

NIGHTLIFE

Interlaken's nightlife heats up during high season but never quite gets red-hot. **Balmer's** (see p. 323) is like a freakin' frat, in part because the beer is cheap (4.50SFr; bar open 9pm-1am). Many revelers head to **Buddy's,** Höheweg 33, a small, crowded English pub where the beer is also cheap (3-5SFr) but the **email** ain't (6SFr for 15min.; bar open daily 10am-12:30am). The drunken herds then migrate to Interlaken's oldest disco, **Johnny's Dancing Club,** Höheweg 92, downstairs in the Hotel Carlton (drinks from 6SFr; open Tu-Su 9:30pm-3am). For smoky blues try **Brasserie,** Rosenstr. 17 (tel. 822 32 25), where live bands play Thursdays. The beer isn't bad, either (from 3SFr; open M-Sa 8:30am-12:30am, Su 3pm-12:30am).

If you want to experience the whole "Swiss" thing, there's the **Swiss Folklore Show** (tel. 827 61 00) at the casino for 16SFr (8:30pm M and W-Sa July-Aug., sporadically May-Oct.). At 6:30pm the theater serves fondue and ice cream for an additional 39.50SFr. The other apex of Interlaken's cultural life is the summer production of Friedrich Schiller's **Wilhelm Tell** (in German; English synopsis 2SFr). Lasses with flowing locks and 250 bushy-bearded local men wearing heavy rouge ham up the tale of the Swiss escape from under the Habsburg thumb. The showmanship is complete—20 horses gallop by in every scene, and a vaudeville-like stage around the corner from Balmer's allows the cast to make real bonfires. A cunning distraction leaves you pondering whether they actually shoot the apple off the boy's head. (Shows late June to mid-July Th 8pm; mid-July to early Sept. Th and Sa 8pm.) Tickets (22-34SFr) are available at Tellbüro, Bahnhofstr. 5A (tel. (036) 822 37 22; open May-Sept. M-F 8:30-11:30am and 2-5pm; Oct.-Apr. Tu 8-11am and 2-5pm), or at the theater on show nights. Children under 6 are not admitted.

NEAR INTERLAKEN: ST. BEATUS'S CAVES

To get to the caves, walk 15min. uphill from the Sundlauenen Schiffstation, a 30min. boat ride from Interlaken (every hr. 7:34am-6:34pm), or take bus #21 (8.20SFr round-trip from Interlaken). You can also walk from Interlaken (2hr.) or Beatenberg (1hr.).

Down below from Beatenberg village, the **Beatushöhlen** (St. Beatus's Caves) riddle the hillside. You can spelunk through 100m of glistening stalactites, waterfalls, and grottoes. At the entrance a wax St. Beatus (the Irish hermit and dragon-slayer) stares down some (also wax) cavemen; at the exit, a sarcastic little dragon bids you *"Auf Wiedersehen."* Even on hot summer days, the cave stays a cool 8 to 10° C. One-hour tours leave every half-hour from the entrance. Admission includes entry to the **Caving Museum** (tel. (033) 841 10 64), 5 minutes downhill. (Caves open Apr.-Oct. 10:30am-5pm. Museum Apr.-Oct. Tu-Su noon-5pm. 14SFr, students 12SFr, children 6SFr.) This tiny room chronicles the discovery and mapping of Swiss grottoes.

THE JUNGFRAU REGION

A few miles south of Interlaken, the hitherto middling mountains rear up and become hulking white monsters. Welcome to the Jungfrau, home to Europe's largest glacier and many of its steepest crags and highest waterfalls. The Jungfrau region's list of firsts reflects its irresistible appeal to sportsmen: the first Alpine mountaineering, the first skiing, and the first part of Switzerland opened to tourists. In summer, the Jungfrau region's hundreds of kilometers of hiking blast the senses with spectacular mountain views, wildflower meadows, roaring waterfalls, and pristine forests. The 3 most famous peaks in the Oberland are the **Jungfrau,** the **Eiger,** and the **Mönch.** In English, that's the Maiden, the Ogre, and the Monk. Natives say that the monk protects the maiden by standing between her and the ogre. Actually, the Jungfrau is 4158m high, so she'd probably kick the Eiger's puny little 3970m butt. On the other side of these giants, a vast glacial region stretches southward, where 6 major glaciers, including the **Grosser Aletschgletscher,** at 45km long the largest in Europe, converge at **Konkordiaplatz.**

From Interlaken, the valley splits at the foot of the Jungfrau. The eastern valley contains Grindelwald, with easy access to the glaciers. The other valley—the Lauterbrunnen—holds many smaller towns, including Wengen, Gimmelwald, Murren, and Lauterbrunnen. The 2 valleys are divided by an easily hikeable ridge, with the Mannlichen at the far end, and the Kleine Scheidegg at the closer end near the Jungfrau. Because of their proximity, hikes in different towns can frequently be combined—even if you're only staying in one town, look at hiking suggestions for other towns. If you plan on doing any serious **hiking**, be sure to get a copy of the *Lauterbrunnen/Jungfrau Region Wanderkarte* (15SFr at any tourist office), which gives an overview of all of the hikes.

THE JUNGFRAUJOCH

The most arresting ascent in the Jungrau region is up the **Jungfraujoch**, a head-spinning, breath-shortening, 3454m adventure on Europe's highest railway. Chiseled into solid rock, the track tunnels right through the Eiger and Mönch mountains. Its construction was one of the greatest engineering feats of all time, taking 16 years and a work force of 300 men. The line was to have gone even higher to the Jungfrau summit itself (4158m), but by 1912 the project was so over budget that the final 700m were left to hard-core mountaineers. Thanks to the rarefied air's lack of pollution, the top now shelters Europe's highest manned meteorology station and the **Sphinx Laboratory** for the study of cosmic radiation. Half a million visitors per year explore the **Ice Palace** (free), a super-smooth maze cut into the ice. Beware skidding children and blindness due to flash photography. Siberian huskies pull lazy mountaineers across the snow on sleds for 10SFr. Budget sportsmen opt for free "snow-hurtling," i.e. sledding down bunny-level slopes on garbage bags (bring your own bag). If the weather is perfect, try the 30-minute, snowy trek to the **Mönchsjoch** climbing hut. For more passive entertainment, gaze out at the frozen expanse of the **Jungfraufirm glacier** skidding down the backside of the mountain.

Trains start at Interlaken's Ostbahnhof and travel to Grindelwald and Lauterbrunnen, continuing to **Kleine Scheidegg** and finally to the peak itself. The entire trip costs an enormous sum, but the "Good Morning" ticket makes things significantly cheaper (available for departures between 6:24-7:30am, returning before noon). All tickets are round-trip, and there is no way down from the top except by train (Eurail 25% off, SwissPass 30% off). (From Interlaken Ost 169.40SFr, "Good Morning" ticket 130.40SFr; Lauterbrunnen 141.20SFr, 102.20SFr; Grindelwald 142SFr, 103SFr; Wengen 130SFr, 91SFr; Murren 160SFr, 121SFr.) Call 855 10 22 for a **weather forecast** or use the cable TV broadcast live from the Jungfraujoch and other high-altitude spots (in all tourist offices and big hotels). Bring winter clothing and food—it can be 10°C (50°F) on a July day, and in winter alcohol thermometers crack and car antifreeze freezes.

GRINDELWALD

Grindelwald crouches beneath the north face of the Eiger—the apex of any climber's career—within walking distance of the only glaciers in the Bernese Oberland accessible by foot. It is a cold-weather Shangri-La for hikers, climbers, and skiers, though the number of tourists might dissuade you. Although it only has 2 streets of any size, Grindelwald is the most developed part of the Oberland's valleys.

⚆ ORIENTATION AND PRACTICAL INFORMATION. The Berner-Oberlander-Bahn runs from **Interlaken's** Ostbahnhof (9SFr; sit in the rear half). Trains to **Kleine Scheidegg** (26SFr, 45SFr round-trip; Eurailpass and Swisspass 25% discount) and the **Jungfraujoch** (round-trip 142SFr, with "Good Morning" ticket 103SFr; Eurailpass and Swisspass 25% discount) start from the station. There is also a bus from Balmer's (round-trip 15SFr). The **tourist office** (tel. 854 12 12; fax 854 12 10), located in the Sport-Zentrum in the middle of town, to the right of the station, provides chairlift information and a list of free guided excursions (open July-Aug. M-F 8am-7pm, Sa 8am-5pm, Su 9-11am and 3-5pm; Sept.-June M-F 8am-noon and 2-6pm, Sa 8am-noon and 2-5pm). Do **laundry** at **Wash 4 Dry** (tel. 853 11 68) opposite Hotel Adler on Haupstr., where you'll pay 3SFr for washing and 1SFr for 10 minutes of drying. You'll find **Internet access** at **Ernst Schudel's,** opposite the tourist office (15SFr per hr.; open daily 9am-noon and 2-6:30pm). The **post office** is opposite the station (open M-F 8am-noon and 1:45-6pm, Sa 8-11am). The **postal code** is CH-3818.

PHONE CODE	The **city code** for Grindelwald is 036.

▐▐ ACCOMMODATIONS, CAMPING, AND FOOD. Although it is quite a hike from town, the **Jugendherberge (HI)** (tel. 853 10 09; fax 853 50 29), located in an enormous wooden chalet above town, is beautiful inside and out. Head left on the main street from the station (5-7min.), then cut uphill to the right (8min.) by the tiny brown sign, just before "Chalet Alpenblick," and turn left at the fork by the blue SJH sign. The dark, wood-paneled living rooms have fireplaces, and many rooms have balconies facing the Eiger. (Dorms in winter 28SFr, in summer 30.50SFr; doubles with toilet and shower 41.50SFr, 46SFr. Non-members add 5SFr. Breakfast, lockers, and sheets included. Dinner 11.50SFr. **Laundry** 5SFr. **Mountain bike rental** 15SFr per day. Reception M-Sa 6:30-9:30am and 3-11pm, Su 6:30-9:30am and 5-11pm. No lockout.)

The bright blue **Mountain Hostel** (tel. 853 39 00; fax 853 47 30), on the opposite side of the train station at the Grund station next to the river, is equally far from town, but also charming. Turn right out of the train station, then immediately right on small trails towards "Grund." Go downhill, bearing right at the Glacier Hotel, to the bottom of the valley. Or, take the train from Grindelwald to Grund (3.80SFr). Renovated in 1996, the hostel has gleaming 4- and 6-bed dorms and a plush reception area with TVs, table tennis, and billiards. (Dorms 32SFr; doubles 84SFr. Sleep sack 5SFr. Buffet breakfast. Outside cooking facilities 0.50SFr. **Laundry** 12SFr.)

The only hostel in the town itself is **Lehmann's Herberge** (tel. 853 31 41). Follow the main street past the tourist office and look on the right. Enjoy the comfort of Verena and Fritz Lehmann's home as well as their hearty breakfasts, homemade down to the butter and jelly. (Dorms and doubles 45SFr per person, after 1st night dorms 40SFr. Bath and breakfast included.) One hour from town but just a step from the Upper Glacier, **Hotel Wetterhorn** (tel. 853 12 18) has snug, quilted dorm-beds. (Dorms 38SFr, singles 65SFr, doubles 105SFr. Breakfast included.) The Grosse Scheidegg bus (5.40SFr) stops at the door. **Gletscherdorf** (tel. 853 14 29; fax 853 31 29) is the nearest of Grindelwald's **campgrounds.** From the station, take a right, then the first right downhill after the tourist office, then the third left. The small grounds have clean facilities and a phenomenal mountain view. (9SFr; tents 5-15SFr. Showers included. Reception M-Sa 8-10am and 5-8pm, Su 5-8pm.)

Frugal gourmets shop at the **Co-op** across from the tourist office (open M-F 8am-6:30pm, Sa 8am-4pm). A **Migros** is farther along the main street away from the station (open M-F 8am-noon and 1:30-6:30pm, Sa 8am-5pm). For huge plates of *Rösti*, omelettes, salads, and fresh-baked desserts, hit the **Tea Room Riggenburg** (tel. 853 10 59) on the main street past the tourist office away from the station. Drink a huge hot cocoa (3SFr) on the heated terrace as sparrows dive-bomb for crumbs. Main courses include toasts smothered in cheese and other toppings (11-17SFr), cakes (2SFr), and more extravagant frozen desserts (9-20SFr). (Open Tu-Sa 8am-10pm, Su 10am-9pm.) **Gepsi Bar** (tel. 853 21 21) is just past the tourist office on the left. Watch cows go crazy in this upbeat bar/restaurant where the kids yodel like berserkers. Swiss music night is Wednesday, and Gepsi Toast happens every happenin' Tuesday (for 3SFr). Entrees start at 12SFr, beer at 4SFr. Grindelwald plate goes for 18SFr. Bar open 5pm-1am. **Ye Olde Spotted Cat** is on Hauptstr. (tel. 853 12 34). Winston Churchill and Field Marshall Montgomery visited the place (see the wall). Scratch a few wooden cats' heads while sipping cheap beer. (Open summer 11am-12:30am; winter 3pm-2:30am.)

⚠ OUTDOOR ACTIVITIES NEAR GRINDELWALD. Only Zermatt could challenge Grindelwald's claim as Switzerland's premier **hiking** hotspot. The town has nearly everything: easy valley walks, high-altitude level walks, accessible glaciers, and peaks to challenge top climbers, while most hikes are possible without the aid of exorbitantly expensive trains and cable cars.

GLACIER HIKES. The unique aspect of Grindelwald hiking is its immediate access to two glaciers. Both are Alpine trails for those with good boots and a willingness to use their hands a bit. To reach the hike that leads up the side of the **Upper Glacier** *(Obere Grindelwaldgletscher)*, take the postal bus from Grindel-wald (dir.: Grosse Scheidegg) to "Oberslaubkule," and walk uphill to where signs point to "Glecksteinhütte" to the right. Access to the **Lower Glacier** *(Untere Grind-elwaldgletscher)* is closer to town. Walk up the main street away from the station until signs point downhill to "Pfingstegg." A funicular can take you up through the forest to the Pfingstegg hut (9.20SFr), or there are trails up. From Pfingstegg, signs lead up the glacial valley to "Stieregg," a hut that offers food to the weary. The trail is moderately steep, but conquerable in sneakers. The farther you go on this trail, the trickier and steeper it becomes (4 hr. round-trip without funicular).

TO THE FAULHORN VIA THE BACHALPSEE (1-7HR.). The best strenuous hike away from the glaciers leads up to **Faulhorn** (2681m) via the *Bachalpsee*. The easiest starting point is near the HI hostel. From the hostel, head uphill on the road (left at the Y) until signs lead upwards to Allflue. To Allflue and slightly beyond is not too exciting forest-hiking, though Allflue provides nice views down into town.

From Allflue, go uphill for more than an hour to Waldspitz. The final hike from Waldspitz to Bachsee and the Faulhorn is through beautiful highland meadows with waterfalls and streams meandering through (5hr.). On the way down, head to **Bussalp** (2hr.), where a bus goes back to Grindelwald. For those with a little less stamina and a bit more money, the **First Bahn** goes straight from town to a station only 1 hour away from the Bachsee, knocking 2 to 3 hours off the hike (28SFr, round-trip 45SFr. Open 8:30am-4:30pm). An easy, level 1-hour hike that offers great views of the glaciers running down to Grindelwald runs from the top of the First Bahn to Grosse Scheidegg, where you can catch a bus to Grindelwald.

TO THE MÄNNLICHEN (1HR.). On the other side of the valley is another easy (though more expensive) hike, reached by the **Männlichen Gondalbahn** (tel. 854 80 80), the longest cable car route in Europe (8am-4pm, 28SFr, round-trip 45SFr; 25% discount with Swisspass, 50% with Eurailpass). From the Männlichen station, a quick circular hike scales the **Männlichen** peak, which separates Grindelwald and the Lauterbrunnen Valley, before continuing as a flat, 1-hour hike to Kleine Scheidegg and its intimate views of the Eiger, Mönch, and Jungfrau. This hike is even easier (and free) as part of the day hike from **Wengen** (see p. 332).

MECHANICALLY-ASSISTED HIKES. Grindelwald's **First Mountain** provides idyllic scenery complete with marmots, icebergs, lakes, rare flowers, and excellent access to the Faulhorn and Schwarzhorn peaks. First Mountain provides tons of hiking, unlike the less accessible Jungfrau and Schilthorn. You can take the First Bahn there (tel. 833 50 50; in winter 8:30am-3:45pm, in summer 8:30am-4:30pm). The **Kleine Scheidegg railway** (tel. 828 71 11) costs 26SFr, round-trip 43SFr, and the tiny **Pfingstegg cable car** on the path to the Lower Glacier costs 9.20SFr, round-trip 14SFr (10:55am-5:45pm). Show your railpass at all trains and lifts. Past the tourist office from the station stands the **Bergführerbüro** (Mountain Guides Office) and **Ski School** (tel. 853 52 00; fax 853 12 22), which sells hiking maps and coordinates rugged activities like glacier walks, ice climbing, and mountaineering. (Open June-Oct. M-Sa 9am-noon and 3-6pm, Su 4-6pm. 1-day activities about 100-400SFr. Reserve ahead for multi-day expeditions.)

SCHYNIGE PLATTE DAY HIKE. A satisfying day hike in clear weather is the climb from **First** to **Schynige Platte** (2070m), which weaves past hidden high-alpine valleys and the lovely *Bachalpsee* (2265m) up to the Faulhorn peak (2680m). (Path generally closed Oct. to mid-June because of snow.) A compact version of the First-Schynige Platte hike involves taking the cable car to First, hiking up the Faulhorn (the path crosses large, slippery snowbanks), descending to Bussalp, and catching the bus back to Grindelwald. This version captures the long views and marmot glens of the longer walk but is cheaper and more manageable. You can even walk down from First or Grosse Scheidegg back to Grindelwald, a 2- or 3-hour downhill stroll through fields and pastures. A new hiking route follows the **Eiger Trail** (5hr. up and down) from the Eiger Glacier Station (70SFr from Grindelwald) to the Jungfraujoch for spectacular views of the North Wall, ice fields, rock formations, and waterfalls. (Guided tour every Tu and W June-Oct; tel. 853 52 00.)

LAUTERBRUNNEN

The "many springs" that give Lauterbrunnen its name are really 72 waterfalls that plummet down the sheer walls of the narrow, glacier-cut valley. The town of Lauterbrunnen, which lies in the middle of the valley of the same name, has as a neighbor Switzerland's highest waterfall, the **Staubbach Falls** (280m), which inspired Goethe's poem "Song of the Spirit over the Waterfall" (set to music by Franz Schubert). Mendelssohn composed some of his "Songs without Words" in Lauterbrunnen as well. Easily accessible by car and train from Interlaken, Lauterbrunnen is an ideal base for hiking and skiing throughout the Jungfrau region, as well as exploring the mountain villages of Wengen, Murren, and Gimmelwald.

⌖ ORIENTATION AND PRACTICAL INFORMATION. The Lauterbrunnen **tourist office** (tel. 855 19 55; fax 855 36 04) is 200m to the left of the train station on the main street (open M-F 8am-noon and 2-7pm; July-Aug. also Sa 9am-noon and 3-7pm and Su 9am-3pm). **Trains** connect every 30 minutes with **Interlaken Ost** (6.20SFr), **Wengen** (5.60SFr), **Kleine Scheidegg** (25.60SFr), **Jungfraujoch** (round-trip 140.80SFr, "Good Morning" ticket 101.80SFr), and **Mürren** (9.40SFr). The station has **lockers** (2SFr) and **currency exchange**. The **post office** is between the train station and the tourist office (open M-F 7:45-11:45am and 1:45-6pm, Sa 7:45-11am). The **postal code** is CH-3822.

PHONE CODE	The **city code** for Lauterbrunnen is 033.

▮⌂ ACCOMMODATIONS AND FOOD. To reach the **Valley Hostel** (tel. 855 20 08), head left off the main street, down a driveway, and past the Co-op on the right. This clean hostel has comfy beds (with fuzzy, cow-patterned sheets) and a view of the Staubbach Falls. (Dorms 20SFr; 1 double room 50SFr. Showers, sheets, and **kitchen** access included. **Laundry** 8SFr. You can request a fondue (in advance) for 15SFr. Reception 6:30am-10pm.) **Matratzenlager Stocki** (tel. 855 17 54) is an old farmhouse whose main room has been partitioned into a sleeping area with a long row of mattresses and a spice-stocked kitchen. Leave the train station's rear exit, descend the steps, cross the river, turn right, and walk 200m. The sign on the house to the right reads *"Massenlager."* (13SFr. Reception 10am-6pm. Open Jan.-Oct. Reserve ahead.)

For more comfort and privacy than the Matratzenlager can offer, go to ▧**Hotel Staubbach** (tel. 855 54 54; hotel@staubbach.ch; www.staubbach.ch), one of the oldest hotels in town, which was recently converted by Craig and Corinne Rochinn-Müller into an affordable bed and breakfast. From the station, follow the main street towards the waterfall (400m); the hotel is on the left. The comfortable rooms, most with private bath and shower, have unobstructed views of the Staubbach Falls. (Singles 50SFr, with shower 60SFr; doubles 80-100SFr; 3- to 6-bed rooms family suites 35-40SFr per person. 5SFr extra per person in high season for all rooms. Parking and hearty breakfast buffet included.) Below Hotel Staubbach, on the main street near the church, the **Chalet im Rohr** (tel./fax 855 21 82), looks like a picture-book chalet, complete with dark wood, intricate carvings, and bright hanging flowers (26SFr per person for singles, doubles, triples, and quads; **kitchen** facilities 0.50SFr; parking available).

Lauterbrunnen also has 2 souped-up campsites with cheap eats. **Camping Jungfrau** (tel. 856 20 10; fax 856 20 20), up the right fork of the main street from the station toward the Staubbach Falls, is an enormous compound that provides cheap beds, kitchens, showers, lounges, and a mini-department store. (8-10SFr; tents 6-15SFr; dorms 20-22SFr. Breakfast 7SFr. Restaurant *Menüs* 10-14.50SFr. **Laundry** 5SFr. Reception in summer 7am-9pm; winter 8am-noon and 2:30-6:30pm. AmEx, DC, MC, Visa.) **Camping Schützenbach** (tel. 855 12 68; fax 855 12 75) is on the way to Trümmelbach from the station (15min.; follow the signs). Take a left on the main road and a left over the river by the church. (6SFr; tents 11SFr; dorms 16-19SFr; doubles with sink 46-56SFr; 4-bed "tourist rooms" in barracks-like huts 18-20SFr per person. Shower 0.50SFr. **Kitchen** facilities 1SFr. **Laundry** 5SFr. Reception 7am-noon and 2-7pm. Fully equipped grocery store.) Near the post office, there's a small **Co-op** (open M-F 8am-noon and 2-6:30pm, Sa 8am-noon and 1:30-4pm.)

⚐ HIKING AROUND LAUTERBRUNNEN. Lauterbrunnen's greatest hikes are the few flat trails that lead up the valley, away from civilization. The main trail can be followed to a number of logical hiking destinations as long as you choose. To get on this trail, follow the right branch of the main road as it leaves town (towards Camping Jungfrau). The road slowly dwindles to a narrow path before becoming a dirt trail through the woods.

SONGS OF THE WATERFALL From its most famous visitor, J.W. Goethe, who immortalized the valley's Staubbach Falls in his "Gesang der Geisten über den Wassern," to lesser-known but fiercely loved painters, the Lauterbrunnen Valley has inspired poet and artist alike with its silvery cascades. The last verse of Goethe's poem, possibly the most famous lines in German verse, were set to music by Schubert when he visited the falls. Lord Byron was inspired to write *Manfred* here. Among the many other renowned people who have paid tribute to the Staubbach and Trümmelbach Falls are Caspar Wolf, Albrecht von Haller, Alexandre Calame, Conrad Escher von der Linter, Kaiser Wilhelm, and Napoleon I's wife, Marie Louise von Habsburg, while her husband plotted his comeback in Elba.

TRÜMMELBACH FALLS. The first, most-touristed segment of the trail leads to the **Trümmelbach Falls,** 10 glacier-bed chutes that gush up to 20,000L of water per second, generating mighty winds and a roaring din (40min.). The falls are the only drains of the glacial run-off of the Eiger, Mönch, and Jungfrau glaciers. Explore tunnels, footbridges, and an **underground funicular** (10SFr; with Jungfrau region visitor's card 9SFr; open July-Aug. 8:30am-6pm; Apr.-June and Sept.-Nov. 9am-5pm). The falls can also be reached by bus from Lauterbrunnen (every hr., 3.20SFr).

The trail leading to the Trümmelbach Falls is a veritable waterfall parade, passing, in succession, the Staubbach Falls, Spissbach Falls, Agertenbach Falls, and Mümenbach Falls. After the small trail leads off to the right towards the Trümmelbach Falls, the trail becomes noticeably less trafficked as it makes its way toward **Stechelberg,** passing even more waterfalls (1½hr. from Lauterbrunnen). Stechelberg, a tiny village with a small grocery store, is the last place to catch a bus back to Lauterbrunnen (4.40SFr) before the trail moves on. From Stechelberg, the trail begins to climb, entering the very end of the valley, which is accessible only by dirt road. To stay on the trail, enter Stechelberg and follow its one road to the end. From Stechelberg, the **Schilthorn Bahn cable car** runs to **Gimmelwald** (7.20SFr), **Mürren** (14SFr), **Birg** (33.20SFr), and the **Schilthorn** (48SFr). The first 2 are free with SwissPass, with Eurailpass 25% off all 4 destinations. Since Gimmelwald and Mürren are carless by law, leave your car at the parking lot near the cable car (day 5SFr, week 21SFr, month 30SFr) or back at Lauterbrunnen.

NATURE RESERVE. The next destination is the 2-building enclave **Trachsellavenen,** 50 minutes from Stechelberg. Trachsellavenen is the departure point for the trail leading into the nature reserve that fills the end of the valley. A 2½-hour mountainous hike brings you to the tiny *Oberhornsee*, which sleeps peacefully beneath the Tschingel glacier.

BICYCLING. Imboden Bike Adventures (tel. 855 21 14), on the main street of Lauterbrunnen, rents out mountain bikes at 20-30SFr per day. On the popular **Mürren Loop,** take your bike for no extra charge on the funicular to Grütschalp (6.60SFr), pedal along to Mürren and Gimmelwald, and free-wheel it down to Stechelberg and Lauterbrunnen. Imboden lets you leave the bike at Central Sport in Wengen opposite the tourist office or the sports center in Mürren for no extra charge. (Open Tu-Su 9am-noon and 2-9pm.)

WENGEN

Tiny Wengen occupies the only ledge on the cliff-curtained Lauterbrunnental. In rather untraditional Swiss style, Wengen residents did not try to tame the cliff with a road, so it is only accessible by train. The only transportation around town is provided by hotel golf carts and a few taxis, but Wengen retains a surprisingly modern feel in spite of the lack of cars. The village offers raw grandeur and tumultuous waterfalls along with gentle slopes for local hiking and skiing.

🔃 ORIENTATION AND PRACTICAL INFORMATION. Wengen is accessible by hourly **trains** from **Interlaken** (45min., 6:27am-11:27pm; 11.80SFr) and **Lauterbrunnen** (15min., 6:05am-11:05pm, 5.60SFr) towards **Kleine Scheidegg** (7:57am-7pm, 20SFr) and the **Jungfraujoch** (9am-6:10pm, 130SFr, morning ticket 91SFr). Leave cars in the Lauterbrunnen **parking garage** (9SFr per day). To reach the **tourist office** (tel. (033) 855 14 14; fax 855 30 60), turn right from the station, then immediately left. The office issues hiking details and finds you a tennis partner. (Open mid-June to mid-Sept and mid-Dec. to Easter M-F 8am-noon and 2-6pm, Sa 8:30-11:30am and 4-6pm, Su 4-6pm; mid-Oct. to mid-Dec. and Apr. to mid-June M-F 8am-noon and 2-6pm, Sa 8:30-11:30am.) At the **train station** you can **exchange currency,** and book hotel rooms. The **pharmacy** (tel. 855 12 46), left out of the station, is 2 minutes past the tourist office (open M-F 8am-noon and 2-6:30pm, Sa 8am-noon and 2-5pm). For the **hospital,** dial 826 26 26. The **post office** is next to the tourist office (open M-F 8am-noon and 1:45-6pm, Sa 8-11am). The **postal code** is CH-3823.

PHONE CODE	The **city code** for Wengen is 033.

🖪🖫 ACCOMMODATIONS AND FOOD. The funkiest place to eat, sleep, drink, and sit around is **Hot Chili Peppers** (tel. (033) 855 50 20), smack dab in the center of town. Turn left from the station and head past the tourist office. This Tex-Mex eatery-turned-hostel has spacious rooms above the restaurant/bar. (Dorms 24-26SFr; breakfast 8SFr. Private rooms 44SFr per person, including breakfast and **kitchen** access. Sheets 5SFr. Beers 3.50SFr; *sangria* 3.50SFr; *chili con carne* in a bread bowl 12SFr; house sandwich 9.50SFr; chips 'n' salsa 5SFr. Reception and restaurant 8am-2am.) If Chili Peppers is full, **Eddy's Hostel** (tel. (033) 855 16 34; fax 855 39 50) has 3-story bunks and 20 beds to a room. Make a sharp right from the station and walk along the tracks. Check in at Hotel Eden. (Dorms 26SFr. In winter 30SFr, including hall shower. 4SFr discount with *Let's Go.* Breakfast buffet 15SFr. Reception 7am-10pm.) **Eddy's Corner** has beer (4.50SFr a pint) and main courses like bratwurst and spaghetti (from 7.50SFr). Opposite the station is a **Co-op** supermarket (open M-F 8am-12:15pm and 1:30-6:30pm, Sa 8am-6pm).

🔃 OUTDOOR ACTIVITIES. Ski passes for the Wengen-Kleine-Scheidegg-Männlichen area start at 52SFr for 1 day, 95SFr for 2; for longer periods, purchase a Jungfrau regional pass (ages 6-16 50% discount, ages 16-20 20%). Ski rentals are 28SFr per day, 105SFr for 6 days. Boots are 15SFr, 52SFr. The **Swiss Ski School** (tel./fax (033) 855 20 22), by the Co-op 1 minute right of the station, is the cheaper of the town's 2 schools (open late-Dec. to early Apr. Su-F 8:30am-noon, 1-2:30pm, and 3:30-6pm, Sa 9-11am and 4:30-6:30pm). For **snow information** for the Jungfraujoch, dial 855 10 22. For a **weather report,** dial 157 45 06. As you watch golf carts schlepping lazy tourists around, you may find it hard to believe that Wengen attracts the athletically intense to its slopes and trails twice a year. Every January, Wengen hosts the (skiing) World Cup's longest and most dangerous downhill race, the **Laubehorn.** Hotels generally won't allow you to book rooms until about a week in advance so that they can guarantee all the racers and support crews a place to sleep. The downhill course starts 2315m above Kleine Scheidegg, curls around Wegenalp, and ends at Ziel (1287m) at the eastern end of the village, a drop of nearly 1200m in 2½ minutes. In early September, Wengen marks the 30km point of the **Jungfrau marathon.** Beginning in Interlaken, hundreds of runners huff and puff their way to Kleine Scheidegg, a tortuous 1424m ascent.

Wengen's elevation from the valley floor puts it close to the tree line and provides spectacular views. One 7-8 hour **hike** from Wengen traverses the ridge dividing the valleys before the Jungfrau, above the tree line almost the entire time, taking you past the top stations of all the 40-50SFr cable cars and trains. Few hikes offer as greatly varied and always spectacular a set of views as this one, which can be easily partitioned into shorter hikes. The hike begins with an ascent of **Männli-**

chen. Walk up the main street, away from the tourist office, and towards the end of town; follow signs upwards to "Männlichen" (red-and-white marked trail). In the beginning, be careful to always follow signs to Männlichen, up the mountain. Even below the tree line, the trail wanders upwards through a meadowed lane, cleared by the cows that will surely accompany you in the early part of the journey. As is true for the whole ascent of Männlichen, there are views of the glacier-laden side of the Jungfrau and the cliff-curtained Lauterbrunnen valley. Towards the top, be sure to turn left when another, unmarked trail merges in. The climb to the Männlichen saddle steeply zigzags upwards for about 3 hours. From the saddle, you can join tourists who took the cable car from Grindelwald for a 15-minute stroll up to the peak, a vertical promontory with a 360° view of the Bernese Oberland. Walk back down to the Männlichen cable car station and restaurant, then follow the signs to **Kleine Scheidegg.** This highly populated trail curves, without climbing, around the contour of the ridge, all the while looking down on the Grindelwald valley and up to the towering Eiger, Mönch, and Jungfrau. You can take the train from Kleine Scheidegg down to Wengen (20SFr) or Grindelwald (27SFr), or you can hike back to Wengen. Cross over the train tracks and follow the red-and-white trail, rather than the train tracks. This trail passes the Mönch and Jungfrau as close as is possible on foot, before swinging back towards Wengen (2½hr. downhill).

MÜRREN

The quiet, car-free streets of Mürren are lined primarily with hotels and guesthouses that sprouted up when Mürren invented slalom skiing. Most people only pass through Mürren on their way to the Schilthorn, the "Magic Mountain," climbed by Hans Castorp in the famous novel by Thomas Mann. However, the challenging hiking, spectacular views, and utter tranquility of this little ledge make it a worthwhile detour.

🔏 **ORIENTATION AND PRACTICAL INFORMATION.** Get to Mürren by cogwheel **train** from **Lauterbrunnen** (6:25am-8:30pm, 9.40SFr), or by **cable car** from **Stechelberg** (14.40SFr) or **Gimmelwald** (7.40SFr). Alternatively, **hike** from Gimmelwald (30min. uphill). From the station, the road leading into town forks in two; nearly everything, except the tourist office, is on the lower left fork. The cable car is at the opposite end of town from the train station, on the lower road. The **tourist office** (tel. 856 86 86; fax 856 86 96), in the sports center 5 minutes from the station, off the right fork, has information about *Privatzimmer*, hiking trails, and skiing prices (open July-Aug. M-F 9am-noon and 1-6:30pm, Sa 1-6:30pm, Su 1-5:30pm; Sept.-June M-F 9am-noon and 2-5pm). The Salomon Station next to the cable car rents mountain **bikes** (35SFr per day) and has **Internet access** (12SFr per hr.; open daily 8:30am-5pm). The **pharmacy** is on the left fork near the Co-op (open M-Sa 8am-noon and 2-6pm). For **medical assistance,** dial 855 17 10. For the **police,** dial 856 80 81. **Lockers** are at the train station (2SFr). The **post office** is on the station side of the main street (open M-F 8am-noon and 2:30-5:30pm, Sa 8-10:15am). The **postal code** is CH-3825.

PHONE CODE	The **city code** for Mürren is 033.

📞📷 **ACCOMMODATIONS AND FOOD.** Mürren has some good housing options, but head to Gimmelwald for more variety and lower prices (see p. 336). The most traditional Swiss lodgings in town happen to be run by an enthusiastic British woman at the **Chalet Fontana** (tel. 855 26 86). The 7 private rooms come with tea and coffee for the taking (Nov.-Sept. 35-45SFr per person, breakfast included; Oct. 30SFr per person, no breakfast; reservations recommended). More institutional, but still comfortable and airy, is the **Hotel Belmont** (tel. 855 35 35; fax 855 35 31), right next to the train station (4-bed dorms 39SFr; doubles 90SFr, with shower 130SFr; breakfast included; AmEx, MC, Visa).

Mürren has a **Co-op** (tel. 855 13 18) on the town's main walkway (open M-F 8am-noon and 1:45-6:30pm, Sa 8am-noon and 1:45-4pm), which comes in handy for picnics and trips to Gimmelwald. Eating out in Mürren is unexpectedly cheap. You can get *raclette* for as little as 11SFr at **Hotel Alpina**. Next door to the Co-op is ▓**Restaurant Stägerstübli** (tel. 855 13 16), a local gathering spot serving food lovingly prepared in the time-taught kitchen. The creamy, rich *raclette* (14SFr) melts in your mouth, as does the tender lamb (15-22SFr; open Su-M and W-Th 9am-11:30pm, F-Sa 9am-12:30am). **Singapore Snacks & Drinks** (tel. 856 01 10), off the left fork from the train station, serves steaming, spicy Asian food with cheap pan-fried noodles (*Wonton* noodles 11.50SFr, vegetable fried rice 12.50SFr).

▟ OUTDOOR ACTIVITIES NEAR MÜRREN.

UP THE SCHILTORN. The most talked about journey this side of the Lauterbrunnen Valley is the short (albeit expensive) cable car trip to the **Schilthorn** (2970m) made famous by the alpine exploits of James Bond in *In Her Majesty's Secret Service* (incidentally the worst James Bond ever; from Mürren 34SFr, round-trip 57SFr; morning ticket 43SFr round-trip). At its apex spins the immoderately priced **Piz Gloria Restaurant**. High-altitude restaurants charge snooty prices. A James Bond breakfast costs a shocking 22.50SFr, and it won't make you suave, either. Daily *Menüs* cost between 19SFr and 29SFr. Warm up (in summer or winter) with *Glühwein* (mulled wine; 7SFr), and take in the astounding 360° panorama from the Schilthorn station's deck. Bear in mind that there is very little to do at the top when it's cloudy.

GRÜTSCHALP TO MÜRREN HIKE (1-2HR.). You don't have to pay anything to appreciate the pastoral views below—**hikes** bring you to equally stunning vistas (get a friend to spin you around and it will be almost the same as Piz Gloria, albeit without fluorescent lighting). One trail, easily broken up into smaller segments, goes from the far end of Mürren (the **Grütschalp** cable car station) to far beyond the end of Gimmelwald, making its way through a dense network of worthwhile stops. Starting from Grütschalp (accessible by train from Mürren) a flat, 1-hour hike follows the train tracks to Mürren. A more mountainous, isolated route takes twice as long, and is twice as rewarding. Both trails start across the tracks from the station balcony. The easier trail is marked with a yellow sign to Mürren, while the mountainous hike is demarcated by the red-white-red "Mürren Höhenweg" sign. After an initial steep ascent the trail wanders through buttercup meadows that stretch before the rising peaks of the Eiger, Mönch, and Jungfrau. When the trail splits, head to "Allmenhubel," then down to Mürren (2hr.).

WATERFALL AND CHEESE HIKE TO GIMMELWALD (2½HR.). From the far side of Mürren the road leads to Gimmelwald (30min.), or you can take the detour waterfall and cheese route (2½hr.). Turn right before the cable car station, and then right again on the trail that branches off towards **Suppenalp.** On the climb to Suppenalp, be sure to stay essentially parallel to the cable car lines. From the high-altitude valley of Suppenalp, follow the trail under the cable car lines to Shiltalp, where there is an obligatory stop at the hut for fresh, cheap milk (sorry, no skim) and cheese (both made that day). Go halfway down the hill to Gimmelwald to turn right at the sign for Spielbodenalp. Walk down along the stream where signs point to **Sprutz,** a waterfall that the trail ducks behind. From Sprutz the trail descends to Gimmelwald.

STECHELBERG AND OBERSTEINBERG (1½-5HR.). If you still haven't had enough hiking, go downhill to Stechelberg, or around the ridge in the nature reserve around Obersteinberg. The descent to Stechelberg—down the hill by the Mountain Hostel, over the river, and through the woods—gives a great long view of the sheer rock slabs lining the Lauterbrunnen Valley. It's a grand approach to the **Trümmelbach Falls** (1½hr.), with a return facilitated by the cable car (see p. 332). Or, 5 minutes after the river crossing on the Stechelberg path, you can fork right and climb along the flank of the unsettled Lauterbrunnen valley head. The trail reaches the **Obersteinberg hut** (3hr.), where you can stay overnight, then continue on to the **Oberhornsee** (5hr.).

BALLOONING, SKIING, AND SNOWBOARDING. Mürren pioneered 2 graceful ways of enjoying the mountains. In 1910 the first Alpine balloon crossing was made from the village, a fact now celebrated annually in mid-August with an **international ballooning week** that fills the skies with big colorful bulbs. The other sport, **slalom skiing**, took off with even more panache. Mürren was the stage for the first major slalom (1922), the first ski school (1930), and the first World Championship for downhill slalom (1931). **Ski passes** for the Mürren-Schilthorn area are 50SFr for one day and 254SFr for a regional week pass; ages 6-16 receive a 50% reduction, ages 16-20 20%. The **ski school** (tel. 855 12 47) has classes for downhill, slalom, and snowboarding. Six half-days of group lessons cost 130SFr. The **Inferno Run** seeks volunteers every January (usually for 3 days from the 20th) for the Inferno downhill ski. The Inferno Triathlon takes place in August; the Mürren-Schilthorn stretch comes last.

NEAR MÜRREN: GIMMELWALD

Follow the lower road in Mürren downhill for 30min. to Gimmelwald, or take the cable car (6.80SFr) from either Mürren or Stechelberg (just up the valley from Lauterbrunnen).

Gimmelwald is little more than a farming town of slightly over 100 people that was stopped in its developing tracks over 50 years ago when it was generously, though perhaps overcautiously, labeled an avalanche zone. Yet somehow a number of wonderful lodgings have snuck their way into a few of the old farmhouses. The great lodgings here make for a lively social scene in high season. Be forewarned that Gimmelwald has no supermarket, so stock up in Mürren or Lauterbrunnen.

Accommodations in Gimmelwald allow you to sleep like a cow or a king—it's your choice. The unifying factors are a fair price and a caring host. All the beds are on one small trail that leads from the bottom of the town road to the top. At the bottom of the trail, next door to the cable car station, the **Mountain Hostel** (tel. 855 17 04), is run by a laid-back couple, Petra and Walter, who try to get to know their guests by name. The beds come with a communal **kitchen** and access to life's essentials—fresh bread (3SFr), milk (2SFr), and chocolate (2SFr). The close quarters do a good job of promoting the most active social scene in Gimmelwald. You can reserve a bed, but only after 9:30am on the day you plan to arrive. Come early, as beds fill fast. (Dorms 16SFr. Showers 1SFr for 3min. of hot water. Reception 8:30-11am and 5:30-10:30pm.) You can sign up for rooms when the reception is closed—drop your pack, take a hike, and be back for the 5:30pm check-in. At **Hotel Mittaghorn** (tel. 855 16 58), at the top of the trail, you can sample some *Glühwein* (mulled wine) or Heidi cocoa (spiked with peppermint *schnapps*) made by the owner, Walter. In his Edelweiss suspenders, Walter has been presiding over his place for a long time, cooking a 3-course dinner for his guests for only 15SFr. The attic/loft is filled with old, wooden beds that go for 25SFr a night. (Doubles 60-70SFr; triples 85SFr; quads 105SFr. Add 6SFr for a 1-night stay. Showers 1SFr for 5min. Order meals in advance. Open May-Nov.) Esther at **Esther's Bed and Breakfast** (tel. 855 54 88) is also kept busy with visitors; so many, in fact, that she hasn't been able to find time for breakfast, so for the time being it is only **Esther's Bed.** She does, however, offer a free **kitchen** and shower. (Singles 30SFr; doubles 70-85SFr; triples 90SFr; quads 140SFr.) Esther is also in charge of a barn where you can sleep (19SFr; breakfast included).

WESTERN BERNESE OBERLAND

KANDERSTEG

Kandersteg sits center stage on a natural amphitheater, against a vivid backdrop of jagged cliffs, enormous rock formations, and mountain peaks with glaciers spilling over the top. Short day-hikes lead to isolated glacial lakes, mountain passes with views of the entire Bernese Alps, and some of the largest glaciers in Europe. Slightly out of the way, Kandersteg seems to have been overshadowed by towns nearer the Jungfrau, but in terms of hiking, it outshines them all.

🎫 **ORIENTATION AND PRACTICAL INFORMATION. Trains** connect Kandersteg to **Spiez** (30min., every hr. 6:34am-10:40pm, 15.40SFr) and then **Interlaken** (1hr., 23SFr). One counter at the train station has **bike rentals** (26SFr per day), **currency exchange**, and **luggage storage** (5SFr; open daily 7:10am-7:35pm). Follow the road perpendicular and to the right of the train station about 100m until it meets the main road. Everything is accessible from this point. Turn left to reach the **tourist office** (tel. 675 80 80; fax 675 80 81), which has **Internet access** (10SFr per hr.) and hiking information (open July-Sep. M-F 8am-noon and 1:30-6:30pm, Sa 8:30am-noon and 1:30-4:30pm; Oct.-June M-F 8am-noon and 2-5pm). Available here as well as at most shops in Kandersteg is the **Kandersteg Wanderkarte** (hiking map; 15SFr), an invaluable resource for any hike. The **postal code** is 3718.

PHONE CODE	The **city code** for Kandersteg is 033.

🏠🍴 **ACCOMMODATIONS AND FOOD.** Kandersteg isn't particularly prepared for an influx of budget travelers. There are a few options in town, but the best idea might be to make your way up to the less trafficked locales of the many *Berg-gasthäuser* (mountain guesthouses). The closest thing to a hostel in town is the **Hotel National** (tel. 675 10 85; fax 675 22 85), which has a number of rooms filled with somewhat dilapidated old bunk beds. Turn right on the main road from the station and walk 5 to 10 minutes. (Dorms 22SFr, sleepsack 5SFr; doubles 84SFr. Breakfast 8SFr per person, but the money might be better spent at a bakery in town.) Also providing low-priced shelter is the **Rendez-vous** camping and restaurant complex, above town. Turn left from the station road, right on the trail just after the tourist office, then follow the camping signs at the top of the road. **Restaurant Rendez-vous** (tel. 675 13 54) has a room of *Lager* style beds (read: long rows of matresses; 12SFr, with breakfast 20SF), while **Camping Rendez-vous** (tel. 675 15 34), on the same spot at the base of the Oeschinensee chair lift, lets you sleep on the ground (7SFr, tent spot 6-12SFr; free showers).

📷**Hotel Schweizerhof** (tel. 675 19 19), on the riverfront in the center of town, is a gastronomic gem. The wooden-shingled pagoda draws you in, only to have the enormous menu of perfectly cooked dishes blow you away. Light summer dishes cost 14.50SFr, while the wide range of vegetarian dishes go for 13-15.50SFr. For heartier appetites, there are *Menüs* that include a salad and noodle dish (15.50-27SFr). To top it off, try the cheap dessert crêpes (5.50-9SFr; open daily 9am-10pm). For picnics, the **Co-op** stands at attention between the station and the town (open M-F 8am-noon and 1:30-6:30pm, Sa 8am-5pm).

🥾 **OUTDOOR ACTIVITIES.** Kandersteg has some of the most exciting and varied **hiking** in all of Switzerland. Some of the longest glaciers in Europe, most notably the **Kanderfirm,** run along the eastern side of town, and you can hike right to the foot of them. The astoundingly blue **Oeschinensee** is surrounded by steep cliffs that rise to glacial peaks. On the eastern end of the lake, a small mountain **guesthouse** welcomes those seeking to leave the world behind (accessible by chairlift 10SFr, or an easy 1½hr. walk).

HIKING AROUND THE OESCHINENSEE (20MIN.-1HR.20MIN.). The most easily accessible hiking in Kandersteg traverses the area around the Oeschinensee. The quickest hike leads from the top of the **Oeschinenseebahn** (13SFr, round-trip 18SFr; half-fare card valid), which leaves from Camping Rendez-vous. From the top, a 20-minute trail rolls to the edge of the blue lake bordered on all sides, except for where you stand, by sheer rock walls. If you would rather spend an hour more hiking and save the 13SFr, follow the trail that climbs from the end of the road to Camping Rendez-vous and up to the lake. The low pass which the trail crosses does a terrific job of separating the Oeschinensee from civilization below. Right on the shore of the lake stands the **Oeschinensee hut** (tel. 675 11 19; fax 675 16 66), which makes a perfect base for further exploration, but is also nice enough to warrant staying even if you want to go no further. The 25 *Lager*-style beds adjoin a living room and TV room, and come with a homemade breakfast every morning (35-40SFr, doubles 120-140SFr). Right next to the hut is a small dock with paddleboats and rowboats that allow you to disturb the perfect calm of the sheltered lake (paddleboats 22SFr per hr., rowboats 16SFr per hr.).

GLACIER HIKES (2-4HR.). A steep, rocky trail—to be attempted only with hefty boots—shoots upwards from the cabin for 3 hours to **Früdenhorn hut.** A less steep but longer trail enters the uninhabited glacier region between the Kandersteg valley and the Jungfrau region. A 4-hour trek brings you to **Blüemlisalp hut,** which cowers beneath the **Blüemlisalp glacier.** For those with insatiable glacial appetites, the hike to the **Kanderfirm glacier** might prove more satisfying. Take the morning bus to Selden (10SFr; reservations required at the tourist office) and continue out on the road until it turns into a trail which, after 2 hours, comes to the western edge of the icy tongue.

GSTAAD AND SAANEN

At the juncture of four alpine valleys, Gstaad and its earthier sister, Saanen, are at the heart of Swiss skiing country. The family resemblance is strong, in the dark wood structures with sloping roofs and massive surrounding mountains. Saanen inhabits the scenery with contented ease. Gstaad, however, trades in goats for glitz—its bevy of 5-star hotels and cardigan-draped tourists make it a glamorous anomaly amongst small towns and placid farmland.

■ **ORIENTATION AND PRACTICAL INFORMATION.** By **train**, Gstaad is accessible from **Montreux** (1½hr., every hr. 6:12am-9:30pm, 24SFr, round-trip 41SFr) or **Interlaken** (1¾hr., every hr. 7:44am-8:43pm, 32SFr, round-trip 55SFr). From Gstaad station you can reach Saanen by train (5min., every hr. 2.40SFr; from Montreux, it's the stop right before Gstaad) or post bus (8min., every hr., 3SFr). **Buses** also run to **Les Diablerets** (1hr., 8:27am-3:27pm, 11.80SFr). The train station in Gstaad has 3-5SFr **lockers**, **bike rental** (26SFr per day, 20SFr per half-day; mountain bikes 32SFr, 25SFr), **currency exchange,** and a **ski rack.** Gstaad has a very well-organized **tourist office** (tel. 748 81 81, for room reservations and package deals, tel. 748 81 84; fax 748 81 83; email gst@gstaad.ch; www.gstaad.ch), just past the railway bridge on the main road to the right of the station (open July-Aug. M-F 8:30am-6:30pm, Sa 9am-6pm, Su 10am-noon, 4-6pm; Sept.-June M-F 8:30am-noon and 1:30-6pm, Sa 9am-noon). Saanen's main street also has a tourist office (open M-F 8:30am-noon and 2-6pm, Sa 9am-noon and 2-6pm). Gstaad's **post office** is next to the train station (open M-F 7:45am-noon and 1:45-6pm, Sa 8-11am). In an **emergency,** dial 117. For **taxis,** dial 744 80 80. The **postal code** is CH-3780.

PHONE CODE	The **city code** for Gstaad is 033.

■■ **ACCOMMODATIONS AND FOOD.** Gstaad proper has few hotels with fewer than 3 stars, but the tourist office publishes a list of budget options, usually far from town. In town, private homes often post signs for rentable rooms, as well.

The **Jugendherberge** (tel. 744 13 43) in Saanen is definitely the most preferable alternative. From Saanen station, turn right on the main street and follow the "youth hostel" signs (10min.). This utterly rural hostel creaks like your favorite rocking chair but offers lots of amenities: billiards, **bike rental** (15SFr) and **repair,** a TV room, a playground, a library (with English books), and foosball, which you might have to wrest away from the legions of school groups who descend here on vacation. (Dorms 28-29SFr, doubles 39.40SFr, triples and quads also available. Prices drop 2.50SFr in low season. Children ages 2-6 half price, under 2 free. Breakfast and sheets included. Dinner 11.50SFr. Reception 7-10am and 5-10pm. Curfew 11pm, though you can obtain the access code if you'll be out late. Closed Nov. 1-Dec. 10. Phone ahead.) **Camping Bellerive** (tel. 744 63 30) lies just off the road between Gstaad and Saanen, about 15 minutes from either. (In summer 6.40SFr, children 3.20SFr. In winter 7.50SFr, 3.20SFr. Tent 5.30SFr. Tax 2.40SFr, children 1.20SFr. Check-in 9-10am and 6-7pm, but you can arrive at any time.) The **Saanen campsite** (tel. 744 61 91; fax 744 60 42) is on the edge of town. Cross the tracks behind the stations and head left along the river. (5SFr, 4.40SFr in low season; tent 6SFr; caravan 14SFr. Electricity 4SFr. Check-in 6-7pm, but you can arrive at any time. MC, Visa.)

Back in Gstaad, budget diners should take advantage of the **Co-op,** left on the main street from the train station (open M-Th 8am-12:30pm and 1:30-6:30pm, F 8am-12:30pm and 1:30-8pm, Sa 8am-4:30pm; restaurant open M-Th 8am-6:30pm, F 8am-8pm, Sa 8am-4pm, Su 9am-5pm). In front of the train station, the **Hotel Berner-hof café** (tel. 748 88 44) serves up a reasonably priced *menu du midi* (15-19SFr) and a healthy selection of vegetarian dishes (15-18SFr), along with views of the mountains (open Su-Th 6am-11:30pm, F-Sa until 12:30am). For your red-blooded protein fix, slide into soft leather chairs and have a burger and fries with a beer (14-18SFr) or ribs and a salad (16.50SFr) at **Richi's Pub** (tel. 744 57 87), just after the church on the main street to the right of the station (open noon-12:30am).

🔣 **OUTDOOR ACTIVITIES.** Gstaad and Saanen share a superlative sports scene. Two companies, Eurotrek (tel. (01) 462 02 03) in Gstaad and Swissraft (tel. 744 50 80) in Saanen, arrange adventure activities. Both companies do **white-water rafting** (Eurotrek: 98SFr for 3 hr., ages 12-16 70SFr; Swissraft: 99SFr for 3hr.). In July and August, Swissraft also goes **canyoning** (80SFr for 3hr.). You can try **ballooning** with CAST Balloonfahrten (tel. 744 62 59; 390-500SFr) or Hans Büker (tel. (026) 924 54 85; 485SFr for 1½-2hr.). To ride air currents up to 2500m, **paragliding** (tel. (079) 22 44 270; email parasport@spectraweb.ch; www.beo.ch/gstaad/paragliding) is another option (130SFr for a trial day, 190SFr for a tandem flight). To see the countryside with at least your horses' feet planted firmly on the ground, try **horse-trekking** (tel. 744 24 60; 22SFr per lesson) or riding in a **horse-drawn cart** (tel. 744 24 60; 30min. ride; 30SFr per person; 5 person min.). Rounding out your options are 150km of hard-core **mountain-bike trails;** the tourist office publishes a map and guide describing distances and difficulty. For the **indoor public pool** (tel. 744 44 16), turn right on the main road out of the station, right after the river, and right at the end of the road; it's in the sportszentrum to the left. (Open M 2-9pm, Tu and Th 10am-9pm, W and F 10am-10pm, Sa-Su 10am-7pm. 9SFr, with visitor's card 8SFr.) In July, the annual **Swiss Open Tennis Tournament** (tel. (01) 22 25 60 60; ticket information tel. 748 83 66; www.swissopen.ch) challenges the green lawns of Wimbledon with grueling clay-court action (July 8-16, 2000; single tickets 40-100SFr, passes 380-430SFr).

A challenging panoramic **hike** up the **Giferspitz horseshoe** conquers the mountains without skis. Turn right on the main road from Gstaad station, left on the main road just before the river, and take the second big road on the right over the river (with signs to "Bissen"; the turn is 1km from Gstaad). Follow the yellow *Wanderweg* signs for "Wasserngrat" up the hill to the top cable car station (1936m). The fit and adventurous continue up to the **Lauenehorn** (2477m) and, after a rocky scramble, farther to the **Giferspitz** (2541m), Gstaad's tallest peak. The path circles down

GSTAAR-STRUCK Celebrities were first drawn to Gstaad in the 1940s and '50s by the quality of its international boarding schools. Prince Ranier of Morocco spent his boyhood at the city's Le Rosey school; he later returned to show off the town to his wife, Grace Kelly—and to show her off to the town. Gstaad filled with affluent British and Americans, who established an informal literary and artistic clique. Audrey Hepburn made frequent visits, and Elizabeth Taylor relaxed here with her two-time husband Robert Burton (maybe dreams of Taylor's Swiss chateau convinced Burton to try again). Not far down the hill, American economist John Kenneth Galbraith spent peaceful and efficient winters on the third floor of a château. Bill Buckley, Galbraith's political archrival, did the same, and the two engaged in good-natured competition to fill Gstaad's bookstore with more of their respective books.

to Bissen again, but a bus eases the descent (1800m ascent; perfect weather only; allow 1 day). A shorter, more accessible hike starts with a cable car ascent to Wispile and a 2-3-hour hike to the **Lauenensee**, a lake and waterfall nature reserve.

In winter, Gstaad turns to **skiing**, with 250km of runs and 69 lifts. Expert skiers will find little to challenge them, but intermediate ones will be very happy. The **Top Card ski pass** (tel. 748 82 82; fax 748 82 60; email ski.gstaad@gstaad.ch; www.skigstaad.ch) is 48SFr a day for one sector; a 2-day pass for 90SFr covers all sectors; more limited passes are slightly cheaper. A week of skiing will run about 263SFr, depending on your age. For the dedicated, a **season ski pass** (890SFr) from the Gstaad region gives allows skiing in Oberengadin/St. Moritz, Kitzbühel/Tirol, Adelboden-Lenk, Alpes Vaudoises, Ordino-Arcalis, and Pal Arinsal (Andorra). Consult the tourist office for details on **heliskiing, snowboarding, curling,** and **skating.** There are 3 **snowboarding parks** in the region and a **glacier** for year-round skiing.

The musically-minded can partake of **Musiksommer,** an annual late-summer event created by virtual Gstaad resident and violinist Yehudi Menuhin (tel. 748 83 33; musiksommer@gstaad.ch). 1999 performers included cellist Mstislav Rostropovich and violinist Sarah Chang. (Tickets 25-125SFr.)

ZURICH
AND CENTRAL SWITZERLAND

Contrary to the mountain-minded stereotype, some parts of Switzerland are flat. Most of them lie in the central to northeastern part of the country, where the mountains of the Bernese Oberland dwindle down to manageable foothills around Lucerne, Schwyz, Zug, Aargau, and Zurich. With more hospitable terrain, Central Switzerland is considerably more populated than the mountainous cantons. The higher density of humans brings a greater mass of cultural artefacts—innovative museums, enchanting castles, and medieval *Altstädte* give this region its allure.

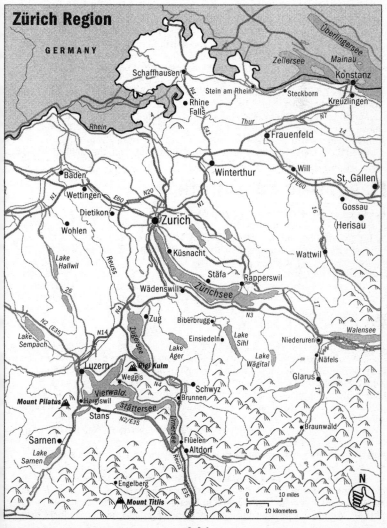

Zürich Region

GERMANY

Überlingersee

Zellersee Mainau

Schaffhausen

Konstanz

Stein am Rhein Steckborn

Kreuzlingen

Rhine
Falls

Rhein

Thur

Frauenfeld

Winterthur Will

St. Gallen

Baden

Wettingen

Dietikon

Zurich

Gossau

Wohlen

Herisau

Lake
Hallwil

Küsnacht

Wattwil

Stäfa Rapperswil

Wädenswil Zürichsee

Lake
Sempach

Zug Biberbrugg

Einsiedeln Lake
Sihl

Niederuren

Walensee

Lake
Ager

Lake
Wägital

Näfels

Luzern

Rigi Kulm

Weggis

Zugersee

Schwyz

Glarus

Mount Pilatus Hergiswil

Vierwald.
Stättersee

Brunnen

Stans

Braunwald

Sarnen

Flüelen
Altdorf

Lake
Sarnen

Engelberg

Mount Titlis

0   10 miles

0   10 kilometers

N

ZURICH (ZÜRICH)

Switzerland has one bank for every 1200 people, and half of those banks are in Zurich. The battalions of briefcase-toting, Armani-suited executives charging daily through the world's fourth-largest stock exchange and largest gold exchange pump enough money into the economy to keep the upper-crust boutiques and illustrious restaurants thriving. There is, however, more to Zurich than money. The city was once the focal point of the Reformation in German Switzerland, led by the anti-Catholic firebrand Ulrich Zwingli. In the 20th century, however, Zurich's Protestant asceticism succumbed to avant-garde artistic and philosophical radicalism. While James Joyce toiled away at *Ulysses*, the quintessential modernist novel, in one corner of the city, Russian exile Vladimir Lenin read Marx and dreamt of revolution in another. Meanwhile, brouhaha brewed next door as a group of raucous young artists calling themselves the Dadaists founded the seminal proto-performance art collective, the Cabaret Voltaire. A walk through Zurich's *Altstadt* and student quarter will immerse you in the energetic youth counter-culture that spawned these subversive thinkers, only footsteps away from the rabid capitalism of the famous Bahnhofstraße shopping district.

▐ GETTING TO ZURICH

Because PTT buses cannot go into Zurich proper, the easiest way into the city is by plane, train, or car. **Kloten Airport** (tel. 816 25 00) is Swissair's main hub (tel. 157 10 60 for general flight information) with daily connections to Frankfurt, Paris, London, and New York. **Trains** leave every 10 to 20 minutes from the airport for the *Hauptbahnhof* in the city center (5:36am-12:10am; 6SFr; Eurailpass and Swisspass valid), where trains from all over Europe arrive. **By car,** A1 connects Bern, Austria, and southern Switzerland to Zurich. From Basel, A2 connects directly to Zurich. From Geneva, take A1 to Lausanne, A9 to Vevey, and A12 to Zurich.

✦ ORIENTATION

Zurich sits in the middle of north-central Switzerland, close to the German border on some of the lowest land in Switzerland. Although the suburbs sprawl for miles, most of the activity within Zurich is confined to a relatively small, walkable area. The **Hauptbahnhof** sits at the top of Bahnhofstr., which overflows with bankers and well-coiffed shoppers by day and falls dead quiet when the shops and banks close at 6pm. The **Limmat River** splits the city down the middle on its way to the **Zürichsee.** Grand bridges, offering elegant views of the stately old buildings that line the river, bind the two sectors together. The university district on the hillside of the lively far bank pulses with crowded bars and hip restaurants, all loud and lively into the wee hours of the night, particularly on Niederdorfstr. By contrast, Zurich's Left Bank is rather conservative and very expensive. Sprawling along the Limmat, the *Altstadt* is a giant pedestrian zone. The **Sihl River** edges the other side of the city, connecting with the Limmat just north of the train station. The *Altstadt*'s **Limmatquai,** which becomes Uto-Quai and Seefeldquai across the bridge from the *Hauptbahnhof*, is a favorite strolling destination for many residents and tourists.

Schweizerisches Landesmuseum

Museumstr.

Simliquai

Neumühlequai

Stampfenbachstr.

Weinbergstr.

Sonneggstr.

Universität Str.

TO (1 km)

Walcher.

River Sihl

Kasernenstr.

Gessneraliee

Hauptbahnhof

Auf der Mauer

Leonhardstr.

Rämistr.

BAHNHOFPL.

BEATENPL.

Bahnhofbr.

Tannenstr.

Schützengasse

Lowenstr.

Schweizerg.

Beateng.

Universität Zürich

LOWENPL.

Usteristrasse

Mühlesteg

Limmatquai

Niederdorfstr.

Zähringerstr.

Künstlerg.

Bahnhofstr.

Bahnhofquai

Uraniastr.

Rud. Brunbr.

Mühleg

ZÄHRINGERPL. (PREDIGERPL.)

Seilergraben

Uranistr.

Oetenbachg.

Lindenhofpl.

Reinweg

Fortuna g.

Brunng.

St. Anna

Kuttelg.

Rindermarkt

Neumarkt

Pelikanstr.

Augstinerg.

Spiegelg.

Untere Zäune

Nüschelerstr.

WEINPL.

Rathusbrücke

Marktg.

Obere Zäune

PELIKAN-PL.

Bahnhofstr.

Rathaus

Münsterg.

St. Peter's

Limmatquai

American Express

Waag g.

MÜNSTERHOF

Kirchg.

Kunsthaus Zürich

Talacker

Bären g.

Talstr.

PARADEPL.

Poststr.

Münsterbr.

Grossmünster

Hirschengraben

Heimstr.

Fraumünster

Kappelerg.

Limmat

Oberdorfstr.

Bleicherweg

Talstr.

Börsenstr.

Stadthausquai

Fraumünster

Limmatqu.

Rämistr.

Claridenstr.

Dreikönigbr.

Stadelhoferstr.

Beethovenstr.

24hr. Pharmacy

BELLEVUEPL.

BURKLIPL.

Quaibr.

Utoquai

Ferry Terminal

Gotthardstr.

Stockerstr.

General Guisan quai

General Guisan quai

Zürichsee

TO (2 km)

N

0   200 yards

0   200 meters

Zurich

ACCOMMODATIONS

A Justinusheim
B Lydiaheim
C Martahaus
D Hotel Splendid & Hotel Schäfli
E Hotel Biber
F Zic-Zac Rock-Hotel
G Jugendherberge

CENTRAL SWITZERLAND

7 PRACTICAL INFORMATION

TRANSPORTATION

Trains: Bahnhofpl. To: **Winterthur** (25min., every 15min. 5:21am-12:23am, 10.60SFr); **Lugano** (3hr., every hr. 6:33am-10pm, 62SFr); **Lucerne** (1hr., every hr. 6am-12:15am, 22SFr); **Geneva** (3hr., every hr. 5:27am-10:03pm, 77SFr); **Basel** (1hr., 2-4 per hr. 4:46am-12:03am, 31SFr); **Bern** (1¼hr., 1-2 per hr. 4:46am-12:03am, 48SFr); **Paris** (8hr., every hr. 4:46am-11pm, 100SFr); **Munich** (4hr., 4 per day 7:33am-5:33pm, 91SFr); **Milan** (4½, every hr. 5:07am-10:07pm, 75SFr); **Vienna** (9hr., 3 per day 7:10am-10:33pm, 132SFr); and **Salzburg** (6hr., 3 per day 7:10am-10:33pm, 101SFr).

Public Transportation: Trams criss-cross the city, originating at the Hauptbahnhof. Long rides (more than 5 stops) cost 3.60SFr (press the blue button on automatic ticket machines), and short rides (less than 5) cost 2.10SFr (yellow button)—the city is small enough to avoid long rides for the most part. Buy a 24hr. *Tageskarte*, valid on trams, buses, and ferries, if you plan to ride several times (7.20SFr). Purchase a ticket before boarding and validate it by inserting it into the ticket machine. Policeman won't hesitate to fine you (50SFr and up) if you try to ride for free. *Tageskarten* are available at the tourist office, hotels, hostels, the automatic ticket machines, or the **Ticketeria** under the train station in Shop-Ville (open M-Sa 6:30am-7pm, Su 7:30am-7pm). The Ticketeria also offers 6-day cards (36SFr, under 25 27SFr). All public buses, trams, and trolleys run 5:30am-midnight. Nightbuses run from the center of the city to outlying areas F-Sa at 1,1:30, and 2am.

Ferries: Boats on the **Zürichsee** leave from Bürklipl. and range from a 1½hr. cruise between isolated villages (every 30min. 11am-6:30pm, 5.40SFr) to a "grand tour" (4-5hr., every hr. 9:30am-5:30pm, 20SFr). Ferries also leave from the top of the Bahnhofstr. harbor (daily every 30min. 10am-9pm, 3.60SFr). The Zürichsee authorities (tel. 487 13 33) offer themed tours—there's even a chance for a jump-suited night on the Zürichsee with the "Swiss Elvises" (July W 8pm, 22SFr). On the **Limmat River,** boats run daily Apr.-Oct. (1hr., 6.80SFr). Eurailpass valid on all boats; free with *Tageskarte*.

Taxis: Hail a cab or call **Taxi 2000 Zürich** (tel. 444 44 44), **Zürich Taxi** (tel. 222 22 22), or **Taxi for the disabled** (tel. 272 42 42). 6SFr plus 3SFr per km.

Car Rental: The best place to rent cars is at the tourist office, where they have special deals with the companies. With **Europcar,** at the tourist office (tel. 214 40 00), get a car with unlimited mileage for 109SFr per day, 77SFr for 3+ days. **Branches** at the airport (tel. 813 20 44; fax 813 49 00); Josefstr. 53 (tel. 271 56 56); and Lindenstr. 33 (tel. 383 17 47). **Hertz** (tel. 814 05 11), at the airport, Morgartenstr. 5 (tel. 242 84 84), and Hardturmstr. 319 (tel. 272 50 50) charges 98SFr per day. **Avis** (tel. 800 77 33), at the airport, is 202SFr per day.

Parking: Metropolitan Zurich has many public parking garages, but Zurich police advise parking in the suburbs and taking a tram or train from there for maximum safety and minimum traffic congestion. **Universität Irchel** (tel. 634 11 11), near the large park on Winterthurstr. 181, and **Engi-Märt**, Seestr. 25 (tel. 202 11 42), are suburban lots. City parking costs 2SFr for 1st hr., 2SFr each subsequent 30min.; "Blue-Zone" 24hr. parking 10SFr; 0.50SFr per hr. in the suburbs. In the city, try garages at major department stores: **Jelmoli**, Steinmühlepl. (tel. 220 49 34), **Migros Limmatplatz**, Limmatstr. 152 (tel. 277 21 11), and **Globus** (tel. 221 33 11) at Löwenstr. (open M-F 7am-7:30pm, Th 7am-10pm, Sa 7am-5pm; 1hr. 2SFr, 2hr. 5SFr).

Bike Rental: At the baggage counter (*Gepäckexpedition Fly-Gepäck*) in the station. 19SFr per day; mountain bike 25SFr; 6SFr surcharge if you leave it at another station. Open daily 6:45am-7:45pm. **Free bike loans** at Globus (tel. (079) 336 36 10); Enge (tel. (079) 336 36 12); Oerlikon (tel. 336 36 13); Altstetten (tel. 336 36 14); and Hauptbahnhof (tel. 323 48 58), at the very end of track 18. Passport and 20SFr deposit.

Hitchhiking: Hitchers to Basel, Geneva, Paris, or Bonn often take streetcar #4 to "Werdhölzli" or bus #33 to Pfingstweidstr. Those bound for Lucerne, Italy, and Austria usually take streetcar #9 or 14 to "Bahnhof Wiedikon" and walk down Schimmelstr. to

Silhölzli. For Munich, hitchers have been seen taking streetcar #14 or 7 to "Milchbuck" and walking to Schaffhauserstr. toward St. Gallen and St. Margarethen, or taking the S1/S8 train to Wiedikon and hitch at Seebahnstr.

TOURIST AND FINANCIAL SERVICES

Tourist Offices: Main office (tel. 214 40 00; fax 215 40 44; email information @zurichtourism.ch; www.zurichtourism.ch; hotel reservation service tel. 215 40 40), in the main station. *Über*-friendly and multilingual staff. Concert, movie, and bar information in German and English. Copies of *Zürich News*, which prints restaurant and hotel listings. Decipher the German *ZüriTip*, a free entertainment newspaper, for tips on nightlife and alternative culture. Walking tours (see below). Reservation desk finds rooms after 10:30am. Open Apr.-Oct. M-F 8:30am-8:30pm, Sa-Su 8:30am-6:30pm; Nov.-Mar. M-F 8:30am-7pm, Sa-Su 8:30am-6:30pm. For bikers and hikers, the **Touring Club des Schweiz** (TCS), Alfred-Escher-Str. 38 (tel. 286 86 66), has maps and travel info.

Tours: The tourist office leads frequent, expensive tours: the "Stroll through the Old Town" (2hr., 18SFr, May-Oct. M-F 2:30pm, Sa-Su 10am and 2:30pm); a trolley tour of major sites (2hr., Apr.-Oct. 10am, noon, and 2pm; Nov.-Mar. noon and 2pm; 29SFr); and the same tour plus a cable car and boat ride (2½hr., April-Oct. 9:30am, 39SFr).

Budget Travel: SSR, Ankerstr. 112 or Leonardstr. 10 (tel. 297 11 11). Open M 12:30-6pm, Tu-F 10am-6pm. **Branch** office at Bäckerstr. 40 (tel. 241 12 08). Student package tours, STA travel help, ISIC cards. Open M 12:30-6:30pm, Tu-F 10am-6:30pm, Sa 10am-1pm. **Globe-Trotter Travel Service AG,** Rennweg 35 (tel. 213 80 80; fax 213 80 88), specializes in overseas travel. Caters to individual travelers, particularly campers (no package tours), and arranges European transport and accommodations. Student discounts, STA tickets, and ISIC cards available. Open M-F 9am-6pm, Sa 9am-2pm.

Consulates: U.K., Minervastr. 117, 8032 Zürich (tel. 383 65 60), near Kreuzpl. Open M-F 9am-noon. **U.S. Consulary Office,** Dufourstr. 101 (tel. 422 25 66). Visas available only at the embassy in Bern. Open M-F 10am-1pm. **Australian, Canadian, Irish,** and **South African** citizens should contact their embassies in Bern. **New Zealand's** consulate is in Geneva.

Currency Exchange: At the main train station. Cash advances with DC, MC, and Visa, with photo ID. Open 6:30am-10:45pm. **Credit Suisse,** Bahnhofstr. 53, 2.50SFr commission. Open M-F 9am-6pm, Th 9am-7pm, Sa 9am-4pm. **Swiss Bank,** Bahnhofstr. 45 and 70, also charges 2.50SFr, and its ATMs take MC and Visa. Branches at Paradepl. and Bellevuepl. (open M-F 9am-5:30pm). **ATMs** are all over, but most only take MC.

American Express: Uraniastr. 14, CH-8023 (tel. 228 77 77). Mail held. Travel services. Checks cashed and exchanged, but limited banking services. ATM. Open M-F 8:30am-6pm, Sa 9am-1pm. **Traveler's check toll-free emergency line:** tel. (0800) 55 01 00.

LOCAL SERVICES

Luggage Storage: At the station. Lockers 4SFr and 8SFr per day. Luggage watch 5SFr at the *Gepäck* counter. Open 6am-10:50pm.

Bookstores: Just off Bahnhofstr. at Fusslistr. 4, **Orelli Fussli** (tel. 884 98 48; open M-F 9am-8pm, Sa 9am-4pm) is a budget bookstore stocked with travel guides. Near the lake, **Librairie Payot,** Bahnhofstr. 9, has a slightly better selection of English books, as well as many travel books. Open M noon-6:30pm, Tu-F 9am-6:30pm, Sa 9am-4pm. **Internet Press,** in the train station, has the best selection of English periodicals. **Travel Bookshop** and **Travel Maps,** Rindermarkt 20 (tel. 252 38 83) live up to their names. Open M 1-6:30pm, Tu-F 9am-6:30pm, Sa 9am-4pm.

Libraries: Zentralbibliothek, Predigerpl. (tel. 261 72 72). Open M-F 8am-8pm, Sa 8am-5pm. **Pestalozzi Library,** Zähringerstr. 17 (tel. 261 78 11), has foreign magazines and newspapers. Open June-Sept. M-F 10am-7pm, Sa 10am-2pm; Oct.-May M-F 10am-7pm, Sa 10am-4pm. Reading room open M-F 9am-8pm, Sa 9am-5pm.

Bi-Gay-Lesbian Organizations: Homosexuelle Arbeitsgruppe Zürich (HAZ), Sihlquai 67, P.O. Box 7088, CH-8023 (tel. 271 22 50), offers a library, meetings, and the free newsletter *InfoSchwül* (open Tu-F 7:30-11pm, Su noon-2pm and 6-11pm). **Frauenzentrum Zürich,** Matteng. 27 (tel. 272 85 03), provides information for lesbians. Ask the tourist office for **Zürich Gay Guide,** listing groups, discos, saunas, bars, and restaurants.

Laundromat: Selbstbedienung-Wäscherei (tel. 242 99 14), in the train station. Wash and dry 5kg for 10.20SFr. Open daily 6am-11pm.

Public Showers and Toilets: At the train station. Toilets 1.50SFr. Showers 10SFr. Open daily 6am-midnight.

24-Hour Pharmacy: Theaterstr. 14 (tel. 252 56 00), on Bellevuepl.

EMERGENCIES AND COMMUNICATIONS

Emergencies: Police: tel. 117. **Fire:** tel. 118. **Ambulance:** tel. 144; English spoken. **Medical Emergency:** tel. 261 61 00. **Rape Crisis Line:** tel. 291 46 46. **First Aid:** tel. 361 61 61.

Internet Access: The **ETH library,** Ramistr. 101, in the Hauptgebäude, has several free computers. Take tram #6, 9, or 10 to "ETH," enter the large main building and take the elevator to floor H. Open M-F 8:30am-9pm, Sa 9am-2pm. **Internet Café,** Uraniastr. 3 (tel. 210 33 11; email info@cafe.ch), in the Urania Parkhaus. 5SFr per 20min. Open M 10am-6pm, Tu-Th 10am-midnight, F-Sa 10am-2am, Su 10am-11pm. At **Cybergate,** at STARS (opposite the Bahnhofpl. tourist office), munch tacos with a cyberjunkie crowd. 5SFr for 20min., 15SFr for 1hr. Open daily 11:30am-11pm. Restaurant open 11am-midnight. AmEx, DC, MC, Visa.

Post Office: Main office, Sihlpost, Lagestr. 2, just behind the station. Open M-F 7:30am-8pm, Sa 8am-4pm. Address *Poste Restante* to: Sihlpost, Postlagernde Briefe, CH-8021 Zürich. **Branches** throughout the city. **Postal code:** CH-8021.

PHONE CODE	The **city code** for Zurich is 01.

▐ ACCOMMODATIONS AND CAMPING

The few budget accommodations in Zurich are easily accessible via Zurich's public transportation. Reserve at least a day in advance, especially during the summer.

Justinus Heim Zürich, Freudenbergstr. 146 (tel. 361 38 06; fax 362 29 82). Take tram #9 or 10 to "Seilbahn Rigiblick" (which passes James Joyce's old house) then take the hillside tram (by the Migros) uphill to the end. Quiet, cheap, private rooms with views of Zurich below. Singles 35SFr, with shower 60SFr; doubles 80SFr, 100SFr; triples 120SFr, with shower 140SFr; all rates reduced for multiple week stays. Breakfast and kitchen access included. Reception daily 8am-9pm.

Martahaus, Zähringerstr. 36 (tel. 251 45 50; fax 251 45 40). Left out of the station, cross Bahnhofbrücke, and take the 2nd (sharp) right after Limmatquai at the Seilgraben sign. The most comfortable budget accommodations in the *Altstadt*. Partitioned dorms have clean beds, lockers, night-lights, and towels. The dorm room has its own large balcony. Dorms 35SFr, singles 70SFr, doubles 98SFR, triples 120SFr. Breakfast included. Airport shuttle after 6:20am every hr. 20SFr. Reception 24hr. AmEx, DC, MC, Visa.

Jugendherberge Zürich (HI), Mutschellenstr. 114 (tel. 482 35 44; fax 480 17 27). Take tram #7 (dir.: Wollishofen) to "Morgantal" and walk 5min. back toward Zurich along Mutschellenstr. The enormous hostel stays open all day and night to welcome travelers, which may account for the long lines at breakfast, the cramped quarters, and the bathroom graffiti. Tune in to CNN or watch one of the free nightly movies. Dorms 31SFr., doubles with toilet and shower 90SFr. Non-members add 5SFr. Laundry 8SFr. All-you-can-eat dinner 11.50SFr. Showers, sheets, and breakfast included. Lockers available, but bring your own padlock. 24hr. reception. Check-out 6-10am. No lockout. MC, Visa.

Foyer Hottingen, Hottingenstr. 31 (tel. 256 19 19; fax 261 93 19). Take tram #3 (dir.: Kluspl.) to "Hottingerpl." In the summer, **women only** are allowed in the partitioned dorms of this impeccably clean and newly renovated house with modern facilities and multilingual staff. Dorms in 11-bed room 30SFr, in 4-bed room 40SFr; singles 65SFr; doubles 100SFr. Breakfast and **kitchen** access included. Reception 6am-midnight.

The City Backpacker-Hotel Biber, Niederdorfstr. 5 (tel. 251 90 15; fax 251 90 24). Cross Bahnhofbrücke in front of the station, then turn right on Niederdorfstr. Spiraling out from the narrow, creaky steps in the traditional *Altstadt* building are the well-used rooms of Biber, which boasts a party-happy rooftop deck and a prime location for bar-hopping. Pick up a free copy of *Swiss Backpacker News* to supplement your itinerary. In summer, 4- to 6-bed dorms 29SFr; singles 65SFr; doubles 88SFr. In winter, dorms 27SFr; doubles 88 SFr. **Kitchen** access and showers included. Lockers available. Sheets 3SFr. **Laundry** 9SFr. **Internet** 10SFr per hr. Reception 8am-noon and 3-10pm.

Zic-Zac Rock-Hotel, Marktg. 7 (tel. 261 21 81; fax 261 21 75; email rockhotel.ch@bluewin.ch). A night in "Pink Floyd" or "Led Zeppelin?" It's possible only at Zic-Zac, Switzerland's first and only rock 'n' roll hotel. Funky furniture, trendy lighting, and rock 'n' roll superstar names distinguish each room. All rooms have TV and phone. Singles 65SFr, with shower 85SFr; doubles 110SFr, 150SFr; studio 150SFr; triples 150SFr, 160SFr; quads with shower 240SFr. Breakfast 8.50SFr. Reception 24hr.

Hotel Splendid, Roseng. 5 (tel. 252 58 50; fax 262 61 40), is a small hotel atop a pop-ular piano bar. Newly renovated rooms are small and sparsely furnished. Convenient for Niederdorfstr. nightlife. Singles 56-70SFr; doubles 93-110SFr. Breakfast 10SFr. Show-ers included. Reception 5:30am-2am. Check-out 11am. AmEx, DC, MC, Visa.

Hotel Schäfli, Baderg. 6 (tel. 251 41 44; fax 251 34 76), is an old hotel above the Dou-ble U bar on Niederdorfstr. Singles 60SFr; doubles 102SFr. Showers included.

Lydiaheim, Leonardstr. 13 (tel. 252 41 27). Take tram #6 or 10 to "Haldenegg." Just below the university, this pension, offers quiet clean rooms watched over by guardian nuns. Singles 60SFr; doubles 100SFr. Breakfast and towels included.

Camping Seebucht, Seestr. 559 (tel. 482 16 12; fax 482 16 60). Take tram #11 to Bürklipl. where you catch bus #161 or 165 to "Stadtgrenze." Scenic lakeside location makes up for the trek. Market, terrace, and café on premises. Tents and caravans avail-able. 8.50SFr per person; 12SFr per tent. Showers 2SFr. Reception 7:30am-noon and 3-10pm. Open May to late Sept.

○ FOOD

Zurich's 1300+ restaurants cover every imaginable ethnic, dietary, and religious preference. The cheapest meals in Zurich are available at *Würstli* stands, which sell sausage and bread for 5SFr. For heartier appetites, Zurich prides itself on its *Geschnetzeltes mit Rösti*, slivered veal in cream sauce with hash-brown pota-toes. Check out the *Swiss Backpacker News* (available at the tourist office and Hotel Biber) for more info on budget meals in Zurich (see also p. 351).

RESTAURANTS

▨ **Bodega Española,** Münsterg. 15 (tel. 251 23 10). Catalan delights served by charis-matic waiters. The delicate but filling egg and potato tortilla dishes go for 15.50SFr, while the enormous salads are 9.50SFr. Open 10am-12:30am.

▨ **Hiltl,** Sihlstr. 28 (tel. 227 70 00). Trade carrot sticks with the vegetarian elite at this swank restaurant, where the lack of meat makes things surprisingly cheap. Highlights include the all-day salad buffet for 4.60SFr per 100g (15SFr for large salad), and the Indian buffet at night (same price). Open M-Sa 7am-11pm, Su 11am-11pm.

Johanniter, Niederdorfstr. 70 (tel. 251 46 00). Of all the Swiss restaurants on Nieder-dorfstr., Johanniter may be the favorite among locals, with the best food for the least money, all with elegant sidewalk seating. Hearty Swiss *Rösti* and noodle dishes run from 15-18SFr, with plenty to choose from. Open Su-Th 10am-2am, F-Sa 10am-4am.

Zeughauskeller, Bahnhofstr. 28a (tel. 211 26 90), near Paradepl. 17th-century knights stare hungrily down from the walls of this *Biergarten* which serves Swiss specialties like fondue, *Rösti* and sausage from multilingual menus. The cheapest specialties are their filling *Wurst* plates (15SFr). Open daily 11:30am-11pm.

Gran-Café, Limmatquai 66 (tel. 252 31 19). Separated from the rushing Limmat river only by the street, you can sit outside and enjoy some of the cheapest meals around

(*Menüs* start at 12.80SFr). Save room for the equally cheap sundaes (5-6SFr). Each day also has a *Menü* (11.80SFr), guaranteed in 7min. or it's free. Start your timers. Open M-F 6am-midnight, Sa-Su 7:30am-midnight.

Mensa der Universität Zürich, Rämistr. 71 (tel. 632 62 11). Take streetcar #6 to "ETH Zentrum" from Bahnhofpl. or take the red Polybahn uphill from Central Station. Hot dishes 7.50SFr with ISIC card, salad buffet 6SFr. Open July 15-Oct. 21 M-F 11am-2pm; Oct. 22-July 14 M-F and alternate Sa 11am-2:30pm and 5-7:30pm. Mensa B open M-F 6:30am-7:30pm. **Mensa Polyterrasse** is just down the street at Rämistr. 101. 8.50SFr with ISIC. Open M-Sa 11:15am-1:30pm and 5:30-7:15pm. Self-service cafeteria open Oct. 22-July 14 M-F and alternate Sa 11am-2:30pm, July 15-Oct. 21 M-F 7am-5:30pm. Closed during winter vacations.

Schalom Café Restaurant, Lavaterstr. 33 (tel. 201 14 76). Take tram #5, 6, or 7 to "Enge" on General Willis; turn right on Lavaterstr. Precautionary security will buzz you into this kosher ocean. More expensive, though they do have sandwiches from 8.50SFr, and *falafel* (9.50SFr). Open M-Th 11am-2:30pm and 6-10pm, F 11am-2:30pm.

CAFÉS

Sprüngli Confiserie Café, Paradepl. (tel. 224 47 11), is a Zurich landmark, founded by one of the original Lindt chocolate makers who sold his shares to his brother. A chocolate heaven, the *Confiserie-Konditorei* concocts exquisite confections and delicious sundaes (8.50-12SFr) with homemade ice cream and sherbet, served on the Bahnhofstr. patio. Lunch *Menüs* 19.50-24.50SFr. Confectionery open M-F 7:30am-8pm, Sa 8am-4pm. Café open M-F 7:30am-6:30pm, Sa 7:30am-5pm.

Zähringer Café, Zähringerpl. 11 (tel. 252 05 00), across the square from the library, above the *Altstadt*. Sip coffee, frappes, or other caffeinated beverages with a hip young crowd. Opens early on weekends so late-night revelers can top off the night with requisite grease (*Rösti* topped with a fried egg 13SFr). Open M 6pm-midnight, Tu-F 8am-midnight, Sa-Su 5am-midnight.

Café Odeon, Limmatquai 2, Bellevuepl. Frequented by an ebullient gay and straight crowd, Odeon provides a popular place to chit-chat and sip espresso. Open Su-Th 7am-2am, F-Sa 7am-4am.

Infinito Espresso Bar, Sihlstr. 20, is chic and angular with a broad coffee selection. Espresso from 3SFr, beers from 6SFr, sandwiches and snacks 4-9SFr. Open M and W-F 7am-9pm, Sa 8:30am-5:30pm.

MARKETS AND BAKERIES

Two bakery chains, **Kleiner** and **Buchmann,** are everywhere in Zurich, offering freshly baked bread, sweets (whole apricot pies around 9SFr), and *Kuchen* (*Bürli* rolls 0.50SFr, *Chäschüechli* 2SFr) for reasonable prices (open M-F 6:30am-6:30pm). The 24-hour vending machine in the Shop-Ville beneath the train station has pasta, juice, and other staples, but you may feel uncomfortable heading over there alone at night.

Farmer's Market, at Bürklipl. Fruit, flowers, and veggies. Tu and F 7am-noon.

Co-op Super Center, straddling the Limmat River next to the train station, is the Co-op to end all Co-ops. Open M-F 7am-8pm, Sa 7am-4pm. **Branches** at Albisstr. 54, next to the tram stop near the hostel (open M-F 8am-12:30pm and 1:30-6:30pm, Sa 7:30am-4pm); and at Bahnhof Enge (open M-F 7:30am-6:30pm, Sa 8am-4pm).

Migros, Mutschellenstr. 189, near the hostel (open M-F 8am-6:30pm, Sa 8am-4pm with adjoining café); under the train station in Shop-Ville (open M-F 7am-8pm, Sa-Su 8am-8pm); and at Bahnhof Enge (open M-F 6:30am-6:30pm, Sa 7:30am-12:15pm).

🔲 SIGHTS

THE OLD TOWN. It's virtually inconceivable to start your tour of Zurich anywhere except the stately **Bahnhofstraße,** which begins just outside the *Hauptbahnhof* and runs to the head of the Zürichsee. Shaded by the trees along this causeway of capitalism, shoppers peer into the windows of Cartier, Rolex, Chanel, and Armani. Renting just one square meter of the street would run you 250,000SFr; start saving up for that lemonade stand. To avoid the I'll-just-charge-it urge, take refuge in the antique, curiosity, and second-hand shops of the *Altstadt.* Halfway down Bahnhofstr. lies **Paradeplatz,** the town center, under which Zurich's banks reputedly keep their gold reserves. Across the river over Rathausbrücke, **Spiegelgasse** is Zurich's memory lane. Commemorative plaques honor the greats: Wladimir Illitsch Uljanow (aka "Lenin") at #14, German author Georg Büchner at #12, and "Cabaret Voltaire" (former haunt of Hans Arp, Tristan Tzara, and Hugo Ball) at #3 (which is now a funky bar called "Castel Dada"). At the Zürichsee end of Bahnhofstr., **Bürkliplatz** hosts a colorful Saturday **market** (May-Oct. 7:30am-3:30pm), with vendors hawking everything from vinyl records to elephantine cowbells to Swiss Smurfs. Across Quaibrücke from Bürkliplatz, locals stroll and rollerblade along the tree-lined Uto-Quai, throwing bread to the Zürichsee swans and their cygnets.

CATHEDRALS. Right off Paradepl., the 13th-century **Fraumünster** stands on the site of a church founded in the 9th-century by the daughters of the local sovereign. The simplicity of its Gothic lines are offset by the vivid stained-glass chancel windows (installed in 1970) and rose transept window (1978), designed by **Marc Chagall.** Despite his Jewish ancestry, Chagall agreed to design the windows for the Protestant church in the late 1960s. The merging of Old and New Testament stories in the 5 windows reveals Chagall's radical personal interpretation of the texts. The red window on the far left is the Prophet window, followed by the blue window depicting Jacob's Ladder. Jesus Christ stands in the top of the green central window, with the yellow Zion window to the right. The blue window on the far right symbolizes the Law, crowned by Moses and the 10 Commandments. A more subdued window called "the heavenly Paradise," designed by Augusto Giacometti in 1930, is hidden in the northern transept. Outside the church on Fraumünsterstr., a mural decorates the Gothic archway in the courtyard, picturing Felix and Regula, the decapitated patron saints of Zurich with their heads in their hands.

The **Grossmünster,** where Zwingli spearheaded the Reformation in German-speaking Switzerland, stonily faces off the *Fraumünster* across the river. The building is primarily Romanesque, with twin Neo-Gothic towers (added in 1786) that have become a symbol of Zurich. The choir is ablaze in color from the blood-red and cobalt-blue stained-glass windows, depicting the Christmas story, which were designed in 1933 by **Augusto Giacometti.** Below the windows, one of Zwingli's bibles lies in a protected case near the pulpit from which he preached. One of the Romanesque columns presents a legend concerning Charlemagne's horse. While pursuing a stag all the way from Aachen (in northern Germany), the horse is supposed to have stumbled over the graves of Felix and Regula, 3rd-century Christian martyrs, prompting the Holy Roman Emperor to found *Grossmünster.* Venture downstairs to the 12th-century crypt to see Charlemagne's statue and 2m-long sword. If you're feeling active, head up the many twisting stairs to the top of one of the towers for a panoramic view of Zurich. (*Church open Mar. 15-Oct. 9am-6pm; Nov.-Mar. 14 10am-5pm. Tower open Mar.-Oct. daily 1:30-5pm, Oct.-Mar. Sa-Su 1:30-4:30pm. 2SFr for entrance to the tower.*)

OTHER SIGHTS. Near the *Fraumünster,* **St. Peter's Church** has the largest clock face in Europe; the second hand extends nearly 4m. Down Thermeng. from St. Peter's, recently excavated Roman baths dating from the 1st century are visible beneath the iron stairway. Up the steps at the intersection of Strehlg., Rennweg, and Glockeng., the park **Lindenhof,** the original site of Turricum, is the namesake and birthplace of Zurich. A great refuge right in the midst of the city, the parks has a giant chess board and sweeping views of the river and the *Altstadt.*

UNIVERSITY AND ZOO. Above the town on the *Grossmünster* side of the river, the **University of Zurich** presides over the city. The school—the first in Europe to admit women—was home (briefly) to Einstein and the inventors of the electron microscope. From the university, trams #6, 9, and 10 run uphill to "Zoo" and the **graves** of authors **James Joyce** and **Elias Canetti** in the Fluntern Cemetery. The **Zürich Zoo,** beside the cemetery, exhibits over 2000 animal species. *(Zürichbergstr. 221. Tel. 252 71 00. Open Mar.-Oct. 8am-6pm; Nov.-Feb. 8am-5pm. 14SFr, students 7SFr.)*

PARKS AND GARDENS. Zurich's many parks provide needed respite from the cacophonous urbanity of Switzerland's largest city. Two botanical collections, on opposite sides of the city, have exciting collections. The University's **Botanical Garden,** which is nowhere near the university, has 3 glass domes housing savanna, sub-tropical, and tropical collections, with human-sized lilies standing outside. Even the horticulturally challenged will enjoy strolling outside through clumps of myrtle and lavender, lounging on the surrounding grassy hills, and watching lily-leaves bob up and down. (To get there, take tram #2 or 4 to "Höschg." Zollikerstr. 107. Tel. 385 44 11. Open Mar.-Sept. M-F 7am-7pm and Sa-Su 8am-6pm. Free.) Across the city, the **Stadtgärtnerei** attracts botanists and ornithologists alike to the moist **Palmhouse/Aviary,** which has artificial streams running through it. The Aviary houses 17 species of tropical birds, including 2 fantastically plumed green parrots and a mime bird, all of which are free to whiz around the building, past your shoulder and over your head. (Sackzeig 25-27. Take tram #3 to "Hubertus" and head down Gutstr. Tel. 492 14 23. Open 9-11:30am and 1:30-4:30pm. Free.) The lush, perfect-for-a-picnic **Rieterpark,** overlooking the city, creates a romantic backdrop for the **Museum Rietberg** (take tram #7 to "Museum Rietburg").

Uetliberg, the "top of Zurich," is the king of picnic spots, with a view of Zurich's urban sprawl on one side and the pristine countryside on the other. The flat walk from Uetliberg to Felsenegg is a peaceful escape from the city's hustle and bustle. From Zurich's *Hauptbahnhof,* take the train to "Uetliberg" (15min., every 30min., discount with *Tageskarte*), then follow the yellow signs to Felsenegg (1½hr.). A cable car runs from Felsenegg to Adliswil, where a train returns to Zurich (buy tickets at any train or cable car station or at most hotels; free with Eurailpass). When the weather heats up, visit the **bathing** parks along the Zürichsee. **Strandbad Mythenquai** lies along the western shore. (Take tram #7 to "Brunaustr." and follow the signs. Tel. 201 00 00. Open M-F 9am-8pm, Sa-Su 9am-7:30pm; 5SFr.)

🏛 MUSEUMS

Zurich has channeled much of its banking wealth into its universities and museums, fostering very smart people and outstanding collections. The larger institutions hold the core of the city's artistic and historical wealth, but many of the smaller museums are equally spectacular. The specialized schools of the university open the doors of their museum collections to the public.

ART MUSEUMS. Even if you abhor big cities, one compelling reason to come to Zurich is the incredible ▨**Kunsthaus Zürich,** on Rämistr., which covers Western art from the 15th century on with an undeniable bias in favor of the 20th century. The museum does a wonderful job of mixing in famous locals—the Giacomettis (all of them), Segantini, and Hodler, to name a few—with the international set, so that no element of the exhibition ever grows stale. The Alberto Giacometti loft is particularly well done in its juxtaposition of the spindly sculptures he became famous for with the not-so-spindly paintings he was doing at the same time. *(Take tram #3, 5, 8, or 9 to "Kunsthaus." Heimpl. 1. Tel. 251 67 65. Open Tu-Th 10am-9pm, F-Su 10am-5pm. 4SFr, students and disabled 3SFr. Su free. Added charge for special exhibits.)*

In self-confident contrast, ▊**Museum Rietberg** presents an exquisite collection of Asian, African, and other non-European art, housed in 2 mansions in the Rieter Park. **Park-Villa Rieter** features internationally acclaimed exhibits of Chinese, Japanese, and Indian drawings. **Villa Wesendonck** stores most of the permanent collection of sculptural art from the non-Western world, some of it 2 millennia old. "Oracles" will be the subject of a special exhibit from November 1999 to February 2000, and "Korea, the Old Kingdom" will be featured from March through July 2000. *(Take tram #7 to "Museum Rietberg." Gablerstr. 15. Tel. 202 45 28. Open Tu-Sa 1-5pm, Su 10am-5pm. Regular admission 5SFr, students 3SFr. Special exhibits and permanent collections 12SFr, students 6SFr.)* The **E.G. Bührle Collection** puts another unique spin on the history of art. In 20 years, E.G. Bührle amassed his sizable star-studded collection, funded by proceeds of his industrial career. It is fascinating to see one man's perception of art—traditional as it may be—and how his collection and tastes developed over the years. *(Take tram 2 or 4 (dir.: Tiefenbrunnen) to "Wildbachstr." From Seefeldstr. turn left on Münchaldenstr., walk uphill, and turn right on Zollikerstr. Zollikerstr. 172. Tel. 422 00 86. Open Tu and F 2-5pm, W 5-8pm. 9SFr, students 3SFr.)*

ARCHAEOLOGICAL MUSEUM. As impressive as the collection of Greek and Roman vases and busts filling the first floor lecture hall of the ▊**Museum of Classical Archaeology** is, it seems nothing more than a foil for the astonishing basement, which houses replicas of nearly every great statue in the ancient world from 800 BC on. *(Take tram #6, 9, or 19 to "ETH." Rämistr. 73. Tel. 257 28 20. Open Tu-F 1-6pm, Sa-Su 11am-5pm. Free.)*

DESIGN MUSEUM. The ▊**Museum für Gestaltung** consists of enormous spaces adjoined to the School of Design, where varying displays of student work, a collection of vintage advertisement posters, and temporary exhibits on steam shovel art, Buckminister Fuller, or giant corn, vie for attention, with the unifying objective to consider design as it relates to man. *(Take tram #4 or 13 to "Museum für Gestaltung." Ausstellungsstr. 60. Tel. 446 22 11. Open Tu and Th-F 10am-6pm, W 10am-9pm, Sa-Su 11am-6pm. Hall and gallery 10SFr, students 6SFr.)*

CHOCOLATE MUSEUM. Visitors to the **Lindt and Sprüngli Chocolate Factory** are welcomed with an open box of Lindt chocolate and a movie about chocolate machines. The chocolate spree ends as visitors leave with free boxes of—what else?—souvenir Lindt chocolate. *(Take the train S-1 or S-8 to "Kilchberg" from the Hauptbahnhof (5.40SFr) or bus #165 to "Kilchberg." From the stop, turn right out of the station, left down the first street, and an immediate right for a 3min. walk straight to the factory. Seestr. 204 (tel. 716 22 33). Open W-F 10am-noon and 1-4pm. All exhibits in German. Free.)*

COFFEE MUSEUM. The **Johann Jacobs Museum: Collection on the Cultural History of Coffee** commemorates that foundation of modern civilization and kernel of all that is good and right and wholesome in the world, a.k.a. the coffee bean. The museum houses black-box display cases into which visitors peer to see historical and modern coffee pots. The place is caffeinated down to the bean-patterned rug on the stairs. At the end of the exhibits, enjoy a cuppa joe in the villa's drawing room. *(Take tram #2 or 4 to "Feldeggstr." and walk 2min. down Feldeggstr. The museum is on the right at the end of the street. Seefeldquai 17 (tel. 388 61 51). Open F-Sa 2-5pm, Su 10-5pm. All exhibits in German; summaries in English. Free.)*

SWISS NATIONAL MUSEUM. The **Schweizerisches Landesmuseum** may be old news for field-tripping Swiss schoolkids, but it provides fascinating insights into Swiss history. Skip the rather generic first floor of medieval artifacts, but do inspect the castle rooms, which contain 16th-century astrological instruments, Ulrich Zwingli's weapons from the Battle of Kappel in which he died (1531), and a tiny bejeweled clock, with a golden skeleton morbidly pointing to the hour. *(Museumstr. 2. Tel. 218 65 11. Open Tu-Su 10:30am-5pm. Free. Special exhibits around 8SFr)*

OTHER MUSEUMS. Opposite the Zurich Ballet House, **Museum Bellerive** specializes in constantly changing "out-of-the-ordinary" exhibits. The displays may sound tame, but the museum takes them in unexpected directions—the recent "Made in

DA, DA, DA The silent walls of Spiegelg. 3 in Zurich's *Altstadt* witnessed one of the most rebellious movements in the history of art and theater. The infamous years between the World Wars offered no lull for the city's citizens, as a group of angry young artists spilled their creativity into the craziest forms of art. The result was *Dadaism*, an art which refused to be art, and a style whose guiding principle was confusion and paradoxical humor. Dada's aim was to provoke a rude awakening from standardized thought and bourgeois preconceptions. Dada is said to have taken its name either from the French word for "hobby-horse," which Hugo Ball selected by sticking a penknife into a German-French dictionary, or from the refrain of two Romanian founders of the movement, who used to mutter "Da, da" ("yes, yes" in Romanian). Distinguished painter/sculptor Alberto Giacometti, in a sojourn in Zurich, entered the fray—it is said that one day, he opened the door of Cabaret Voltaire, stepped out, shouted, "Viva Dada!" at the top of his lungs, and disappeared as promenadeurs on the Limmatquai stopped in their tracks. Lenin was also reputedly a fan of Cabaret Voltaire. Today's Cabaret Voltaire is preserved in the entrails of the disco/bar Castel Dada (see p. 352).

Japan" exhibited a room full of plastic Japanese meals. "Theater" is the theme of the November 1999 to February 2000 show; "Hair" is coming March to May 2000. *(Take tram #4 or 2 (dir.: Tiefenbrunnen) to "Höschg." and walk right on Höschg. to #3. Tel. 383 43 76. Open June 13 to Sept. 13 Tu and Th-Su 10am-6pm, W 10am-9pm. 6SFr, students 3SFr.)*

If you have extra time on your hands, no money, and an abiding interest in dead animals, head to the **Paleontology and Zoological Museum,** which provides a shiny new home for stuffed mammals from around the world. *(Take tram #6, 9, or 10 to "ETH." Karl-Schmid-Str. 4. Tel. 634 38 38. Open Tu-F 9am-5pm, Sa-Su 10am-4pm. Free.)*

♫ ENTERTAINMENT AND NIGHTLIFE

For information on after-dark goings-on, check **ZüriTip** or the posters that decorate the streets and cinemas at Bellevuepl. or Hirschenpl. **Niederdorfstr.** rocks as the epicenter of Zurich's nightlife. Due to the number of strip clubs, however, women may not want to walk alone in this area at night. On Friday and Saturday nights during the summer, Hirschenpl. on Niederhofstr. hosts sword-swallowers and other daredevil street performers from around the world. Other hot spots include Münsterg. and Limmatquai, both lined with cafés and bars that overflow with people well into the wee hours of the morning. Beer in Zurich is pricey (from 6SFr). A number of cheap bars have established themselves on Niederdorfstr. near Muhleg. The **Zürich Night Card,** available at the main tourist office, entitles the holder to discounts on Zurich's nightlife offerings, as well as free public transport for 3 consecutive evenings after 5pm (20SFr). If all else falls through, go to the cinema. Most movies are screened in English with German and French subtitles (marked E/d/f). Films generally cost 13SFr. After July 18, the **open-air cinema** at Zürichhorn (take tram #4 or 2 to "Fröhlichstr.") attracts huge crowds to its lakefront screenings. To ensure a seat, arrive at least an hour before the 9pm showing (15SFr) or reserve a seat at the open-air ticket counter at the Bellevue tram station.

Casa Bar, Münsterg. 30 (tel. 262 20 02), is a tiny, crowded pub with 1st-rate live jazz. Drink prices hasten poverty (beer from 9.50SFr). No cover. Open daily 7pm-2am.

Castel DADA, Münsterg. 26 (tel. 266 10 10), next to Casa Bar. On the former site of the "Cabaret Voltaire," this lively bar and disco keeps the inner chamber intact. Beers from 6.50SFr. Open Su-Th 6pm-2am, F-Sa 8pm-2am. Disco open until 4am.

Bar Odeon, Limmatquai 2 (tel. 251 55 20), Bellevuepl. Thornton Wilder and Vladimir Lenin used to get sloshed in this posh, artsy joint. Great street-side seating. Beers from 6SFr. Open 7am-2am, F-Sa 7am-4am.

Oepfelchammer, Rindermarkt 12 (351 23 36). This popular Swiss wine bar (3-5SFr per glass) has low ceilings and wooden crossbeams covered with initials and messages from 200 years of merry-making. Those who climb the rafters and drink a free glass of wine from the beams get to engrave their names on the furniture. It's harder than it looks. Open Tu-Sa 11am-midnight.

Luv, Dufourstr. 43 (tel. 262 40 07), entrance around the corner on Kreuzstr. Take tram #2 or 4 to "Kreuzstr." With its bizarre music (watch for Tuesday SciFi jazz night or Wednesday Laundry Day) and dance floor, Luv attracts all types, from spike-heeled to spike-headed. Beer starts at 6SFr. Tu and Su 5SFr, F-Sa 13SFr. Open Su-Th 8pm-2am, F-Sa 9pm-4am. Concerts at 9:30pm.

Cinecittà Bar Club, Stadthausquai 13 (tel. 211 57 52). Sleek, young, black-leather-clad Swiss clamor to enter this male-dominated bar on the banks of the Limmat. Theme nights include Pizza Disco, AmaZone, and Gay Happening on Su. F-Sa 8SFr; obligatory coat check. Open M 9pm-4am, Tu-Th 6-9pm, F-Sa 9pm-5am.

Emilio's Bagpiper Bar, Zähringerstr. 11 (tel. 252 05 00). A gay bar (the first in Zurich) serving good drinks, snacks, and occasional male strip shows. Extremely crowded on weekends. Beers 4.30SFr. Open daily 3pm-midnight.

NEAR ZURICH: EINSIEDELN

When the wandering monk St. Meinrad was looking for a good place to become a hermit, he avoided locales with direct train lines to Zurich. Trains leave Zurich for Wädenswil (on their way to Chur) every 20 minutes, connecting to Einsiedeln 15 minutes later (15.40SFr one-way, 30.80SFr round-trip).

Just an hour by train from Zwingli's Protestant pulpit in Zurich, the tiny town of Einsiedeln attracts pilgrims from all over Europe to its spectacular cathedral and legendary Black Madonna. To find the **Klosterkirche** (cathedral), turn right onto the small lane in front of the train station and left on Hauptstr. Consecrated in 1735, the cathedral's Milanese exterior with twin lemon-shaped domes dominate the surrounding hills. The Asam brothers dreamed up the interior; its ornate Baroque ceiling overflows with plump, blushing cherubs floating by an overwhelming pastel background of lavender, green, and gold. At 4pm each day (except Sunday) the monks sing *Vespers* and *Salve Regina*, and then recess to the Madonna Chapel to practice their Gregorian chant. Bring coins if you feel inspired to light a candle for meditation (1SFr). The 1m-high **Black Madonna,** resplendent in Royal Spanish attire against a glowing backdrop of golden clouds, is the cathedral's centerpiece. Years of smoky candlelight and underground storage during the French invasion have darkened the figure. An Austrian craftsman once restored her natural color, but locals, refusing to accept the change in hue, had her painted black again. The **monastery** that stretches back from the cathedral offers tours of its horse stables and renowned **library** every Saturday at 2pm. The gates are usually open, and the pastoral grounds, protected by the crumbling walls of the monastery, are worth a stroll any day. Behind the monastery, short trails lead into the hills where the monastery horses graze.

WINTERTHUR

Once the country home of eastern Switzerland's wealthy industrialists, Winterthur (VIN-ter-tur) today houses the fruits of their labor. Though Winterthur is overshadowed in all things commercial by its omnipotent neighbor, Zurich, the incredible array of museums in Winterthur—mostly endowed by those deceased wealthy industrialists—make it an excellent daytrip from Zurich (but not on Mondays, when the museums are closed).

⚐ ORIENTATION AND PRACTICAL INFORMATION. Trains run 4 times every hour to **Zurich** (21.20SFr round-trip) and connect there to Basel and Geneva; trains leave twice an hour for **St. Gallen** (35SFr round-trip). Almost all **buses** to the downtown area leave from just right of the station. **Parking** is available at **Parkhaus Theater am Stadtgarten** and **Parkhaus Winterthur,** both off Museumstr., and **Parkhaus SSB** at the station for 1SFr per hour. Winterthur's **tourist office** (tel. 267 67 00; fax

CENTRAL SWITZERLAND

267 68 58), to the right of the train station, overflows with pamphlets packed with excursion ideas and museum info and offers a free hotel reservation service (open M-F 8:30am-6:30pm, Sa 8:30am-4pm). On the left side of the station, you'll find **currency exchange** (open daily 6:10am-9pm), **bicycle rental** (26SFr per day; open M-Sa 7am-7pm, Su 8:10am-12:30pm and 12:50-7pm), and **luggage storage** (5SFr; same hours as bike rental). The **post office** is opposite the train station (open M-F 7:30am-6:30pm, Sa 7:30-11am). The **postal code** is CH-8401.

PHONE CODE	The **city code** for Winterthur is 052.

⚑⌂ ACCOMMODATIONS AND FOOD. For some nearly authentic 13th-century castle living, try **Jugendherberge Hegi (HI),** Hegifeldstr. 125 (tel. 242 38 40; fax 242 58 30), inside the **Schloß Hegi.** To reach the castle, take postal bus #680 to "Schlossacker." You can also take the train or bus # 1 to "Oberwinterthur Bahnhof." Exit the station, turn left and continue through the pedestrian underpass, turn left on Hegifeldstr., then walk 10 minutes to the castle, which lies just past the houses. Surrounded by meadows, hedges, and fruit trees and serenaded by clucking hens and turkeys, the hostel offers no-frills, medieval dwelling. (Dorms 16SFr, including sheets. Kitchen facilities. Reception 7-10am and 5-10pm. Checkout 7-10am. Lockout M and F 10am-5pm, Tu-Th and Sa-Su 10am-2pm. Curfew 11pm. Open Mar.-Oct.)

Most food options are located downtown, near Marktg., which is lined with food stands. The cheapest restaurant food in town is available at the **Migros Restaurant**, on the second floor of Neuweisen, a big mall-like structure (open M-F 8:15am-6:30pm, Sa 7:30am-4pm). Go through the tunnel under the train station and follow the signs. Another local fave, **Pizzeria Pulcinella** (tel. 212 98 62), is right off Marktg. on Metzg. (Pizza 13-19SFr inside or 11-15SFr takeout and Italian specialties for under 28SFr. Open M-F 11:15am-1:45pm and 5:45-11:30pm, Sa-Su 5:45-10:30pm.) Fruit and vegetable **markets** invade the streets of the *Altstadt* on Tuesdays and Fridays. The **Hegimart** supermarket is conveniently located opposite the Schloß Hegi hostel (open Su-F 8:15am-12:15pm and 2:30-6:30pm, Sa 8am-2pm).

☉⌂ SIGHTS AND MUSEUMS. Since museums are Winterthur's biggest draw, there are two things you should get as soon as you arrive. The first is a **Tageskarte** (7.20SFr), which will get you to the museums. The second is a **museum pass** (20SFr for 1 day) which will get you into the museums and save you money if you plan on visiting at least 3 of Winterthur's fifteen museums. A brochure covering all of them is available at the tourist office.

OSKAR REINHART COLLECTION. Winterthur's most generous art patron was Oskar Reinhart, as the 2 museums housing his collection demonstrate. The largest of these is the ▨**Museum Oskar Reinhart am Stadtgarten,** Stadthausstr. 6, in the center of town. Turn right out of the station, then go left on Stadthausstr. for 2 blocks. The museum specializes in the work of Swiss, German, and Austrian painters, particularly portraits. Glass steps lead to the beautifully remodeled fourth floor, which houses temporary exhibits. *(Tel. 267 51 72. Open W-Su 10am-5pm, Tu 10am-8pm. 8SFr, students 6SFr.)*

A smaller but more impressive collection is preserved just outside of town in the ▨**Sammlung Oskar Reinhart am Römerholz,** Haldenstr. 95. Take bus #10 to "Haldengut" (departs hourly from the station); turn left off the bus and head up Haldenstr. for 10 minutes. In addition to works by old masters such as Cranach, Holbein, Rubens, El Greco, and Goya, the museum showcases masterpieces by 19th-century French artists, including Cézanne, Manet, Daumier, van Gogh, and Renoir. *(Tel. 269 27 40. Open Tu-Su 10am-5pm. 8Sfr, students 6SFr.)*

ART MUSEUM. Winterthur's large **Kunstmuseum,** Museumstr. 52, houses some renowned Impressionist pieces, but its specialty is modernist art by the likes of Klee, Kandinsky, Mondrian, Léger, and Arp. Turn left from the station, right on Museumstr., and left on Lindstr. The collection is displayed in a fittingly modern setting in the newly-built addition. In the summer, temporary exhibits of contemporary art energize the museum. *(Tel. 267 51 62. Open W-F 10am-5pm, Tu 10am-8pm. Prices hover around 10SFr, students 6SFr.)* The city library and the **Museum of Natural Science** are in the same building. *(Tel. 267 51 66. Tu-Su 10am-7pm. Free.)*

PHOTOGRAPHY MUSEUM. Among Winterthur's smaller museums, you'll find the unique **Fotomuseum,** 44 Grüzenstr., housed in a former factory. Take bus #2 to "Schleife," walk down Palmstr,. across from the bus stop, for 2 blocks. The museum, which serves as the center of the counter-culture crowd in Winterthur, features exhibitions of photography, lectures, and discussions. *(Tel. 233 60 86. Open Tu-F noon-6pm, Sa-Su 11am-5pm. 8SFr, students 5SFr.)*

TECHNORAMA DER SCHWEIZ. The **Swiss Technology Museum,** Technoramastr. 1, is easily reached by taking bus #5 (dir.: Technorama) to the last stop. All displays in this enormous scientific playground are in German, but many of them are self-explanatory and some are beautiful enough to belong in Winterthur's art museums. Try your hand at textile production or water music, or test your hand-eye coordination in the jumbo-jet flight simulator. *(Tel. 243 05 05. Open Tu-Su and public holidays 10am-5pm. 15SFr, students 10SFr.)*

CHURCH. While wandering around the *Altstadt*, visit the **Stadtkirche** by walking up Untertorstr., just right of the station, for 6 blocks to Obere Kirchg. The church was built in 1180, renovated in the late Gothic style between 1501 and 1515, and now blazes with Alberto Giacometti's stained-glass windows and Paul Zehnder's 1925 murals of brightly colored Bible stories. *(Open daily 10am-4pm.)*

OTHER SIGHTS. If you're up for a jaunt into the country, check out **Castle Mörsburg,** former home of the 13th-century Kyburg dynasty, which now holds 17th- to 19th-century fine art and furniture. Take bus #1 to "Wallrüti," then follow the yellow signs for a 40-minute hike through forest, fields, and farms. The fortress is a favorite spot for weekend family hikes and school bike tours. *(Tel. 337 13 96. Open Mar.-Oct. Tu-Su 10am-noon and 1:30-5pm; Nov.-Feb. Su 10am-noon and 1:30-5pm. Free.)*

Schloß Hegi, Hegifeldstr. 125, overlooks the grassy meadows of Oberwinterthur (see directions to youth hostel). The original heirs to this 13th-century castle still maintain the creaky staircases, 800-year-old tower, cannon, and iridescent stained glass. *(Tel. 242 38 40. Open Mar.-Oct. Tu-Th and Sa 2-5pm, Su 10am-noon. Free.)*

CENTRAL SWITZERLAND

LUCERNE (LUZERN)

Lucerne just may be the fondue pot at the end of the *Regenbogen* (rainbow)—the Switzerland traveler's dream come true. Lucerne combines the museums, festivals, and nightlife of the cosmopolitan cities to the north with the outdoor opportunities of the natural splendor to the south. Lucerne's position in the heart of Switzerland makes it a daytrip departure point *par excellence*. Throw in one of the most engaging *Altstädte* in Switzerland, cruises on the placid **Vierwaldstättersee,** and hikes up the queenly peaks of Mt. Pilatus and Rigi Kulm, and you have enough to keep a visitor enthralled for days. What's more, Lucerne retains a welcoming small-town feel, so that by the end of your stay, you may feel like you've found your second home.

▮ ORIENTATION AND PRACTICAL INFORMATION

The **Reuss River** flows through the center of Lucerne, feeding into the Vierwaldstättersee (Lake Lucerne) near the Bahhofplatz. The train station, tourist office, and post office line up along Zentralstr. on the bank south of the Reuss, while the streets of the *Altstadt* twist through the northern bank. The city is connected by the ancient **Kapellbrücke,** which spans the Reuss between Bahnhofstr. on the south bank and Rathausquai on the north.

Trains: Bahnhofpl. (tel. 157 22 22). To: **Basel** (1¼hr., 2 per hr. 5:26am-11:10pm, 31SFr); **Bern** (1½hr., 1-2 per hr. 5:26am-11:16pm, 32SFr); **Geneva** (3hr., every hr. 5:55am-9:29pm, 70SFr); **Interlaken** (2hr., every hr. 6:30am-6:35pm, 26SFr); **Lausanne** (2½hr., every hr. 5:55am-10:05pm, 58SFr); **Lugano** (2¾hr., every hr. 7:17am-8:39pm, 55SFr); **Zurich** (1hr., every hr. 4:59am-11:10pm, 22SFr); and Zurich **airport** (1¼hr., every hr. 4:59am-10:10pm, 26SFr).

Public Transportation: VBL buses depart from in front of the station and provide extensive coverage. With a ho(s)tel stamp on a guest card you can buy a 3-day bus pass for 8SFr at the tourist office. 1 zone 1.70SFr, 2 zones (to the youth hostel) 2SFr, 3 zones 2.50SFr. *Tageskarte* 10SFr, 2-day pass 15SFr. SwissPass valid.

Taxis: Cabs congregate in front of the train station, at Schwanpl., at Pilatuspl., and in front of the Municipal Theater. Tel. 211 11 11, 310 10 10, or 250 50 50.

Car Rental: Epper, Horwerstr. 81 (tel. 310 14 33). Compact car 88SFr per day for up to 200km of driving; 0.25SFr per additional km; 20SFr insurance. **Europcar,** Luzernerstr. 17 (tel. 444 44 44) has small VWs for 118 SFr; 27SFr insurance. **Hertz,** Luzernerstr. 44 (tel. 420 02 77; fax 429 88 03), rents Renaults for 73SFr per day.

Parking: Lucerne has many expensive parking garages, including **Bahnhof-Parking,** Bahnhofpl. 2, under the train station, and **City Parking,** Zürichstr. 35 (tel. 410 11 51). Parking garages run 25-50SFr per day. Free guest parking at the **Transport Museum.**

Bike Rental: At the **train station,** 26SFr per day. Open 7am-7:45pm. Also at the **Backpackers** hostel, 7SFr per day.

Tourist Office: In the train station (tel. 410 71 71; fax 410 73 34). Free city guide (with unwieldy map), more detailed map (1SFr), and free hotel reservation service. **Guided walking tours** of major monuments (mid-Apr. to Oct. M-Sa at 9:45am and 2pm; Nov. 4-Apr. 13 W and Sa 9:45am; 15SFr including a drink). Ask about the **Visitor's Card,** which, in conjunction with a hotel or hostel stamp, gives discounts at museums, bars, car rental, and more. Open May-Oct. M-F 8:30am-7:30pm, Sa-Su 9am-7:30pm; Nov.-May M-F 8:30am-6pm, Sa 9am-6pm, Su 9am-1pm.

Budget Travel: SSR Reisen, Grabenstr. 8 (tel. 410 86 56). ISIC cards, student travel deals, and discount flights. Open M-W and F 10am-6pm, Th 10am-8pm.

Currency Exchange: At the station. Open M-F 7:30am-8:30pm, Sa-Su 7:30am-7:30pm. **Migros bank,** Seidenhofstr. 6, off Bahnhofstr. Open M-W and F 9am-5:15pm, Th 9am-6:30pm, Sa 8:15am-noon.

American Express: Schweizerhofquai 4, P.O. Box 2067, CH-6002 (tel. 410 00 77). Mail held and checks cashed for members. Travel services open M-F 8:30am-6pm, Sa 8:30am-noon. **Currency exchange** open M-F 8:30am-5pm, Sa 8:30am-noon.

Luggage Storage: Downstairs at the station. **Luggage watch** 5SFr per item. Open 6am-9pm. **Lockers** 3-8SFr.

Bookstores: Raebes, (tel. 229 60 20). Turn left from station on Zentralstr. and then walk down Frankenstr. Sophisticated selection of English literature, travel books, maps, and **free Internet access** for customers. Open M-F 8am-6:30pm, Sa 8am-4pm. For English magazines, check out the kiosk in the bottom of the train station.

Bi-Gay-Lesbian Organizations: Schwullesbisches Zentrum Uferlos, Geissenteinring 14. (tel. 360 30 14) hosts activities, bars, café nights, social events, and the smaller group **Why Not,** Postfach 2304, CH-6002 Luzern, which offers discussion groups for young gays at W 8 and 11:30pm. **Homosexuelle Arbeitsgruppen Luzern (HALU),** Postfach 3112, CH-6002 Luzern, PC-Konto 60-5227-2 (tel. 360 14 60), publishes a monthly calendar of events available at the tourist office.

Laundromat: Jet Wasch, Bruchstr. 28 (tel. 240 01 51). Wash and dry 16SFr; wash, dry, and fold 19SFr. English-speaking staff. Open May-Oct. M-F 8:30am-12:30pm and 2:30-6:30pm, Sa 9am-1pm; Oct.-Feb. M-F 8:30am-12:30pm, Sa 9am-1pm.

Emergency: Police, tel. 117. **Fire,** tel. 118. **Ambulance,** tel. 144. **Medical Emergency,** tel. 111. For the **24hr. pharmacy** on duty, dial 248 81 17.

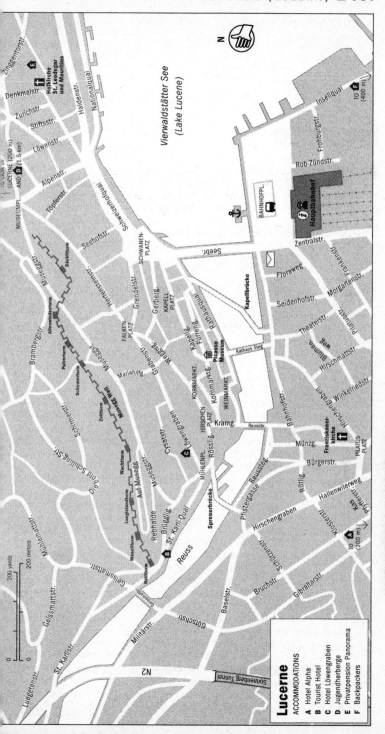

Lucerne

ACCOMMODATIONS

A Hotel Alpha
B Tourist Hotel
C Hotel Löwengraben
D Jugendherberge
E Privatpension Panorama
F Backpackers

Internet Access: C+A Clothing on Hertensteinstr. at the top of the Altstadt has 2 free, though very busy, terminals (M-W 9am-6:30pm, Th-F 9am-9pm, Sa 8:30am-4pm). **Parterre,** Mythenstr. 7 (tel. 210 40 93), off Neustadtstr. near Bundespl., is a cool local bar with a patio and 4 computers (15SFr per hr.).

Post Office: Main branch near the station on the corner of Bahnhofstr. and Bahnhofpl. Address *Poste Restante* to: Postlagernde Briefe, Hauptpost; CH-6000 Luzern 1. Open M-F 7:30am-6:30pm, Sa 8-11am. **Emergency post** at Luzern 2, behind the main station. **Postal Code:** CH-6000.

PHONE CODE	The **city code** for Lucerne is 041.

♠ ACCOMMODATIONS AND CAMPING

Relatively inexpensive beds are available only in limited numbers in Lucerne, so call ahead in order to ensure a roof over your head.

Backpackers, Alpenquai 42 (tel. 360 04 20; fax 360 04 42), 15min. from the station. Turn right from the station on Inselquai, and follow it through the small industrial area along the lake until it turns into Alpenquai; the hostel is on the right. Brand-new and lovingly decorated rooms with balconies and lake or mountain views, plus a comfy dining room with fresh flowers and hundreds of travel books and magazines. Lakeside location puts you next to the grassy lake park and just over a small bridge from a sandy beach. A bomb-shelter and "survival" kits (8SFr) of pasta, sauce, and wine await in case of Armageddon in the tiny but well-stocked and cheap store. 2-bed dorms 26.50SFr, 4-bed dorms 21.50SFr. **Kitchen** facilities. Sheets 2SFr. **Bike rental** 7SFr per day. **Laundry** 8SFr. Tickets sold for cable cars on all the local mountains. Reception 7:30-10am and 4-11pm. No lockout.

Hotel Löwengraben, Löwengraben 18 (tel. 417 12 12; fax 417 12 11). At the top of the *Altstadt*, near the city wall on the first paved street. Until September 1998 Hotel Löwengraben was a prison providing full services to the miscreants of Luzen. In only 7 months the building was converted into a hostel providing full services to the traveler. Downstairs from the cells are 3 small food counters (Japanese, Italian, and Swiss), a daytime bar with **Internet access** (15SFr per hr.), an outside patio, and a bar that hosts all-night dance parties (for guests only) every Sa during the summer. 8-bed dorm 19.99SFr, 4-bed dorm 27-31SFr, 3-bed dorm 31-35SFr, double with shower 90SFr. Sheets included.

Jugendherberge (HI), Sedelstr. 12 (tel. 420 88 00; fax 420 56 16). During the day, take bus #18 to "Jugendherberge." After 7:30pm, take bus #19 to "Rosenberg" and walk in the direction of the bus, but turn right at the fork. This white-concrete building has a beautiful valley view you'll have to share with up to 18 fellow travelers. Beds have fresh sheets and night lights. In high season (May-Oct) dorms 30.50SFr, in low season 28SFr; doubles 37.50SFr, 35SFr; doubles with shower 43.50SFr, 41SFr. Breakfast buffet, lockers, sheets, and shower included. Dinner 11.50SFr. **Laundry** 12SFr. Reception 7-10am and 2pm-midnight. Call ahead in summer. AmEx, DC, MC, Visa.

Tourist Hotel Luzern, St. Karliquai 12 (tel. 410 24 74; fax 410 84 14). From the station, walk on Bahnhofstr., along the river, cross over the river at Speurbrucke and then make a left onto St. Karliquai—the hotel is right in front of the old city wall. Cheap, clean rooms with views of the river and Mt. Pilatus in the distance. 11-bed dorm without breakfast 20SFr. 4-bed dorms 43SFr, students 39SFr; doubles 108SFr, 98SFr. In winter, rooms 10-15SFr less per person. Add 10SFr per person for private shower. Breakfast included. Free luggage storage. **Laundry** 10SFr. **Bike rental** 15SFr per day. **Internet access** 10SFr per hr. Reception 7am-10:30pm. AmEx, MC, Visa.

Privatpension Panorama, Kapuzinerweg 9 (tel. 420 67 01; fax 420 67 30; email panorama@swissonline.ch). Take bus #7 or 5 (dir.: Wesemlin) to "Kapuzinerweg" and go up the steps. For 5SFr, the owner will pick you up at the station. Clean, spacious rooms on a hill with unbeatable sunset views of Mt. Pilatus or the *Altstadt*. Singles 45SFr, doubles 70-90SFr, triples 120SFr, quads 140SFr. Apartment for 2 people 100-120SFr. Breakfast, **kitchen** facilities, and limited parking included. **Laundry** 5SF. Ring the bell or yell for reception. AmEx, MC, Visa.

Hotel Alpha (tel. 240 42 80; fax 240 91 31), at the corner of Pilatusstr. and Zähringerstr. From the station, walk 10min. left down Pilatusstr. This enormous *Pension* is in a residential area just outside the city. The airy rooms are spick-and-span. Singles 60SFr; doubles 92SFr, with shower 120SFr; triples with shower 123SFr; quads with shower 156SFr. Prices 2-3SFr cheaper in winter. Breakfast included. Reception daily 7am-9:30pm. AmEx, MC, Visa.

Camping: Camping Lido, Lidostr. 8 (tel. 370 21 46; fax 370 21 45), 30min. from the station on the Lido beach. Cross the Seebrücke and turn right along the quay, or take bus #2 (dir.: Würzenbach) to "Verkehrshaus." Mini-golf, tennis, and swimming nearby. 6.50SFr; tent 3SFr; car 5SFr. Showers 0.50SFr per 3min. Reception daily 8am-6pm. Open Mar. 15-Oct.

Camping Horw (tel. 340 35 58). Take bus #20 (dir.: Horw) to "Horw Rank." Quiet campsite by a lake. 11SFr per person; 5.80SFr per tent. Showers included.

⬛ FOOD

Markets along the river purvey inexpensive picnic goods on Saturday and Tuesday mornings, but the restaurants in supermarkets and department stores offer the cheapest sit-down meals in town. The restaurant upstairs in **Migros** on Hertensteinstr. has entire meals with a salad and drink starting at 7.50SFr (open M-W 8am-6:30pm, Th-F 8am-9pm, Sa 8am-4pm). Just up from Migros, Weggisgasse, and Rossligasse—together one long street—are lined with good places to catch a quick bite. **Hotel Drei Könige,** Bruchstr. 35 (tel. 240 88 33), serves heated kosher food for 45SFr per meal (open 11:30am-1:30pm and 6-9pm; call ahead).

Krone, Rösslig. 15 (tel. 419 44 90). A favorite for tourists as the best place for a quick, cheap meal. Great variety, with hamburgers, calamari, lasagna, and kebabs, all around 9SFr. *Menüs* 11SFr. Open 7am-7pm daily. AmEx, MC, Visa.

Heine Bakery, Falkenpl. (where Weggisg. meets Hertensteinstr.), is locally famous for the 20 different types of flaky-crusted, densely filling tarts cooked each day. Good for meals or desserts, all under 5SFr. Open M-W 7am-6:30pm, Th-F 7am-10pm, Sa 9am-6pm.

Pourquoi Pas, Nationalquai (in front of the Musikpavillon), along the far side of the lake from the station. This is the little crêpe stand that could—thanks to their quality product and loyal customers. Sugar crêpes only 4SFr; for 7.50SFr you can put anything you want on it. 10% discount for City Backpacker hostelers. Open M-F 11:45am-1:30pm, and 5-8pm, Sa-Su 1pm-whenever.

Kam Tong Chinese Take Away, Inselquai 8, turn right in front of the station and then right on Inselquai to reach this dim, red-papered eatery with cheap but tasty Asian fare. Most meals are from 10-15SFr. Soups 5SFr, vegetable fried rice 10SFr. Open M-W 9am-6:30pm, Th-F 9am-9pm, Sa 9am-4pm.

Opus, Bahnhofstr. 16 (tel. 226 4141). The cheapest restaurant along the expensive quays lining the river in the *Altstadt*. The extra francs are justified by the excellent food, service, and views. Veggie and pasta dishes (from 19SFr); small portions of all dishes available (15SFr). Open M-F 8:30am-12:30am, Sa 8am-12:30am, Su 10am-12:30am.

Ciao Pep, Murbacherstr. 4 (tel. 228 90 50). Turn left on Zentralstr. from the station, then right on Murbacherstr. Munch on panini sandwiches (8.50SFr), pizza (from 14SFr), or pasta (from 12SFr) in a garden setting. Open 7am-12:30am.

Cafeteria Emilio, Grendelstr. 10., in the *Altstadt* off Schwanenpl. Locals help themselves to the filling yogurt and *muesli* (7.20SFr), while tourists head for the mini-pizza and salad combo (9SFr) or the tortellini (10.80SFr). Open M, W, and F 6:30am-8pm, Th 6:30am-10pm, Sa 7am-6pm, Su 9am-6pm.

MARKETS

Migros, Hertensteinstr. 44. Open M-W 8:30am-6:30pm, Th-F 8:30am-9pm, Sa 8am-4pm. Restaurant has the same hours.

Reformhaus Müller, Wienmarkt 1. Sells tofu, lentils, and organic, whole-grain bread. Open M 1:30-6:30pm, Tu-F 8:15am-noon and 1:30-6:30pm, Sa 8am-4pm.

Co-op, Kasernepl. Open M-W and F 8am-6:30pm, Th 8am-9pm, Sa 8am-4pm.

👁 🏛 SIGHTS AND MUSEUMS

THE OLD CITY. The *Altstadt* is famous for its frescoed houses and oriel windows, especially those on the buildings on Hirschenpl. To quickly get into the medieval mood, enter the *Altstadt* through the **Kapellbrücke,** a 660-year-old wooden roofed bridge. It was accidentally set on fire by a barge in 1993, but horrified citizens restored it within a few months. Further down the river, the **Spreuerbrücke** gives an idea of what the Kapellbrücke looked like before the fire. Both bridges have painted triangle ceiling supports; those on the Spreuer allow you to confront your mortality in Kaspar Meglinger's eerie *Totentanz* (Dance of Death) paintings.

On the hills above the river, the **Museggmauer** and its towers are what remains of the ramparts of the medieval city. After all these years, they still define the city skyline, especially when illuminated at night. Walk up the trail on the far side of the wall to reach the stairs up to the towers and path along the wall. Three of the towers, the Schirmerturm, Männliturm, and Zeitturm, have stairs to the top. The **Zeitturm** (clock tower) provides a particularly pleasing panorama of the city. To find the tower, walk along St. Karliquai, turn right (uphill), and follow the brown castle signs. *(Open 8am-7pm.)*

LION MEMORIAL AND GLACIER GARDEN. The city mascot is the dying Lion of Lucerne (portrayed in the **Löwendenkmal** carved out of a cliff on Denkmalstr. by Danish sculptor Bertel Thorvaldsen), who casts his pained eyes over a reflecting pool. Mark Twain described the lion as "the saddest and most moving piece of rock in the world." The 9m monument honors the Swiss Guard who defended Marie Antoinette to the death at the Tuileries in 1798. From the station, cross Seebrücke to Schwanenplatz, follow Schweizerhofquai to right, and turn left on Denkmalstr. Next door to the lion, the **Glacier Garden** is a lunar landscape of smooth rocks curved and pot-holed into odd almost-sculptures all accompanied by mood music, just like they had in the last ice age. Admission includes the **Glacier Garden Museum,** next to the oriental *Spiegellabyrinth* (mirror maze)—be careful not to lose yourself (or your mind). *(Open Apr.-Oct.15 9am-6pm; Mar. and Oct. 16-Nov. 15 9am-5pm; Nov. 16-Feb. Tu-Su 10:30am-4:30pm. 8SFr, with visitors card 6.50SFr, students 6SFr.)*

PICASSO MUSEUM. 200 emotionally charged photographs of Picasso on display at the ☐**Picasso Museum** present a slice of the great artist's life. In the last few years of Picasso's life, close friend David Duncan captured him delicately sucking the last pieces of fish from a skeleton, trying his foot at ballet, and creating from every angle. By the 117th picture showing Picasso's mourning widow, you'll be mourning with her. *(Am Rhyn Haus, Furreng. 21. Tel. 410 35 33. Open Apr.-Oct. 10am-6pm; Nov.-Mar. 11am-1pm and 2-4pm. 6SFr, with guest card 5SFr, students 3SFr.)*

TRANSPORTATION MUSEUM. The ☐**Verkehrshaus der Schweiz** (Transport Museum) is the Disney World of transportation. If you can drive, fly, steer, float, or roll it, it's here. Climb into big-rigs and jet planes or go for a ride in virtual reality, but don't miss the museum's real highlight: the trains. Even the children's train that chugs around the floor is an authentic steam engine. The museum also has a planetarium and screens 7 IMAX shows per day. *(Lidostr. 5. Take bus #6, 8, or 24 to "Verkershaus," or walk along the lake for 15min. Tel. 370 44 44. Open Apr. 4-Oct. 9am-6pm; Nov.-Mar. 10am-5pm. 18SFr, students 16SFr. Imax 14SFr. Both 28SFr, students 24SFr; 33% discount with Eurailpass or guestcard.)*

WAGNER MUSEUM. The **Richard Wagner Museum,** Wagner's secluded lakeside home, now exhibits original letters, scores, and instruments. Wagner's years in Lucerne, often known as the "Tribschen years" (1866-1872), were marked by an enormous creative output, as well as private happiness—it was here that he wed Cosima von Bülow. *(Wagnerweg. 27. Take bus #6 or 8 to "Wartegg.," or turn right from the station and walk 25min. along the lake. Tel. 360 23 70. Open mid-Mar. to Nov. Tu-Su 10am-noon and 2-5pm. 5SFr, students and guest card holder 4SFr.)*

⚔ OUTDOOR ACTIVITIES

Clearly, the best way to get out on the **Vierwaldstättersee** (Lake Lucerne) is to take a **boat ride.** The cheapest option is to take one of the **ferries** that service the many tiny villages that dot the lake. Not only can you enjoy the magnificent scenery in a relaxing way, but you can also disembark at any one of the lakeside villages to explore further. Glass-blowing demonstrations lie in wait at **Hergiswil,** while a short but scenic hike lurks at **Bürgenstock,** ex-U.S. president Jimmy Carter's top choice in Swiss resorts. For an easy walk along the lake, alight at **Weggis.** The length of the journey determines the fare; consult the Lucerne tourist office for specifics on each town.

A more expensive and tourist-oriented option is to take a **lake cruise.** SGV boats (tel. 367 67 67) leave from the piers in front of the train and bus stations (SwissPass and Eurailpass valid). Try to catch one of their 5 steam ships whose internal workings are on display in the middle of the ship. The cruises are actually also passenger ferries that stop at all the lakeside towns, but the tourist office and boat company have put together a yellow pamphlet with possible trips that last from 1-6 hours with no change of boats (1hr. 11SFr, 2-3hr. 28SFr, 4hr. 38SFr, 6hr. 42SFr). These boats can also be used to get to the starting points for the ascents of Rigi, Pilatus, and Stanserhorn (see p. 362). Many of the evening trips are on the water for the sunset—find out the sunset time and check the schedule.

For more vigorous exertion, Lucerne's adventure provider **Outventure** (tel. 611 14 41) will meet you at the Lucerne tourist office to take you **paragliding** (160SFr), **canyoning** (95SFr), **bungee jumping** (99SFr), or **rafting** (98SFr).

🎵 NIGHTLIFE AND FESTIVALS

Due to noise regulations, the *Altstadt* falls silent after 7pm. Most of the action moves to Haldenstr. and the streets near the station. The closest bar to town on Haldenstr. is the **Hexenkessel,** Haldenstr. 21 (tel. 410 92 44 or 410 92 64), which goes for a mock-pagan look. Replete with broomsticks, it boils Lucerne's twenty-somethings in a 2-story cauldron of loud music and spinning DJs. Saturday night is "Heaven's Gate," while the odd Thursday brings live music. (Obligatory beer 7SFr; no cover. Open 9pm-2:30am.) Down the street lies the bright yellow **Kursaal,** Haldenstr. 6, with its ritzy casino offering poker, blackjack, and low-stakes gambling to the masses. Further down Haldenstr. beneath the Carlton Hotel, **Club 57** is the coolest of the local hangouts. During the week, 57 plays hip world music; on weekends, DJs spin.

Three blocks down Pilatusstr. from the station on Winklereidstr. 24, **Pravda** (tel. 210 22 44), is *the* dance club for Lucerners (open M-Th 10pm-2:30am, F-Sa 10pm-4am). **Cucaracha,** Pilatusstr. 15 (tel. 210 55 77), has a daily happy hour (5-7:30pm) and offers free Tex Mex snacks with your drink (Coronas 7.50SFr; open daily 5pm-midnight). **Uferlos Bar,** Geissensteinringstr. 14 (tel. 360 30 14 or 360 14 60), is a popular gay and lesbian hangout. **Schüur** is hidden beside the train tracks so guests can be as loud as they please, at the hippest concerts in town. Follow Zentralstr. alongside the train tracks and turn left onto Lagensandbr. The club is on the left side, on the other end of the bridge. Cheap(er) beers cost 4SFr (open W-Sa 7pm-4am).

Lucerne attracts big names for its summer **Blues Session** (July 21-29, 2000) and fall **Blues Festival** (Nov. 16-19, 2000). 1999 saw Bo Diddley and Buddy Guy visit the Vierwaldstättersee (contact the tourist office or visit www.bluesfestival.ch for more information). August 19 to September 19 of 2000 will see the return of the

International Festival of Music. The festival celebrates primarily classical music, but also features contemporary world music. For tickets or further info, contact: Internationale Musikfestwochen Luzern; Postfach/Hirschmattstr. 13; CH-6002 Luzern (tel. 210 35 62; fax 210 77 84; tickets 20-220SFr). There is a movie every night during July and August with **Open Air Kino Luzern,** at the outdoor theatre in the Seepark near Backpacker's Luzern (14SFr per seat)—most movies are in English, so check on any poster in town, or at the tourist office, to see what's playing. The **Nationalquai** is the scene for free summertime **Pavillon Musik** concerts, featuring brass and jazz bands playing Hollywood tunes, Gershwin, Duke Ellington, and even Andrew Lloyd Weber, every other night from June to August. Every summer, elite crews from all over the world row their boats to Lucerne for the **National and International Rowing Regattas** on the Rotsee by the hostel (10SFr entry fee). From July 8th to the 13th in 2000, the regattas will be the Swiss National Championships and Olympic Qualifiers. On Saturdays and Tuesdays from 8am to noon, catch the **flea market** (May-Oct.) along Burgerstr. and Reusssteg.

NEAR LUCERNE: MOUNT TITLIS

Take the train from Lucerne to Engelberg (1hr., 14.80SFr), and the cable car from Engelberg to Titlis (first ascent from Engelberg 8:30am, last ascent from Engelberg 3:40pm, last descent from Titlis 4:50pm; 73SFr, with Eurailpass and Engelberg guest card 58.40SFr, with Swisspass 54.80SFr). Guided tours are available from Lucerne (including round-trip rail and Titlis fares 85SFr, same discounts).

Near the small town of **Engelberg,** south of Lucerne, visitors can ride the world's first revolving cable car (tel. 639 50 50) to the crest of **Mount Titlis** (3020m), the highest outlook-point in central Switzerland. The panoramic ride gives magnificent views of the crevasses below and peaks above. The top is an active glacial outpost, with an observation deck and restaurant, a glacial grotto, free tube rides down an ice slide, and free guided **glacier hikes** from the top cable car station to the peak of the mountain (3hr., Tu 9am, reserve at the tourist office).

The little village of Engelberg itself is no great shakes, but if you want to stay you can stop over at the **Jugendherberge Berghaus (HI),** Dorfstr. 80 (tel. (041) 637 12 92), just a 10-minute walk out of town. Turn left off Bahnhofstr. onto Dorfstr., and keep walking. (Dorms 26SFr 1st night, then 23.50SFr; doubles 32SFr, 29.50SFr. Non-members add 5SFr. Dinner 11.50SFr. Laundry 3SFr. Breakfast and sheets included. Reception 8-11am and 5-10:30pm.) Engelberg's **tourist office,** Klosterstr. 3 (tel. 637 37 37; fax 637 41 56), is a left on Bahnhofstr. from the train station, a right onto Dorfstr., and another right onto Klosterstr. (open June 23-Oct. 19 M-Sa 8am-6:30pm, Su 4-7pm; Oct. 20-Dec. 15 M-F 8am-noon and 2-6:30pm, Sa 8am-6:30pm; Dec. 16-Apr. 13 M-Sa 8am-6:30pm, Su 8am-6pm; Apr. 14-June 21 M-F 8am-noon and 2-6:30pm, Sa 8am-6:30pm).

NEAR LUCERNE: MOUNT PILATUS AND THE RIGI KULM

The trip up the mountain is at least half the fun of this day trip—which, depending on your route, uses 4 different types of transportation. The most memorable trip takes the 1½hr. boat ride from Lucerne to Alpnachstad, ascends with the steepest cogwheel train in the world (48° gradient), descends by cable car to Krienz, and takes the bus back to Lucerne (entire trip 77.60SFr, with Eurail or Swisspass 40SFr). From June 16 to Sept 9, the Pilatus Railway (tel. (041) 329 11 11) offers ½-price fares after 4:30pm from Alpnachstad and Krienz on Th-Sa (29SFr for just the railway and cable car). It is slightly cheaper if you ride the cable car both ways. With a little more time and exercise you can cut down on the price by using your feet. Take the train or boat to Hegiswil and a 3hr. hike up the hillside to Fräkmüntegg, a half-way point on the cable car (22SFr, 25% discount for SwissPass and Eurail). While you miss the cog train, the hike offers constant views back to the lake and Lucerne.

Like a big gnarly apparition, **Mt. Pilatus** bumps and grinds its way 2132m to the top of Lucerne's southern sky. Standing at the top of this solitary geological mess provides phenomenal views of the Alps to the south. All of the irregularities allow for numerous quick jaunts to the various craggy promontories rising up around the station and restaurant at the top. Across the sea from Mt. Pilatus soars the **Rigi Kulm,** which has a view of the lake and its magnificent neighbor. Sunrise on the summit

TALL TALES Mt. Pilatus' imposing facade has haunted the minds of locals for millennia, and, in turn, has spawned numerous myths and legends. The most oft-told legend, and source of the mountain's name, said that the infamous Pontius Pilate was buried on the mountain. It was believed that each year on Good Friday, Pilate would emerge from the grave to wash his bloodied hands in the lake below. According to legend, any attempts to challenge Pilatus' dominion over the mountain brought storms of fury, so climbing the mountain was prohibited. In 1585, a priest and a few townsmen decided to test the story by going into the foothills and creating a ruckus. When there was no retribution, the spell was declared broken, and the cable car and cog railway were immediately built. Since then, there have been numerous Pilate-sightings; however, very few have been scientifically documented. Go at your own risk.

is a Lucerne must; sunsets get good reviews, too (see Mark Twain's 1879 travelogue *A Tramp Abroad*). Staying at **Massenlager Rigi Kulm** (tel. (041) 855 03 03) on the summit makes early morning viewing possible. Part of Hotel Rigi Kulm, this dormitory has 28 simple bunks (25SFr; reception open daily 8am-10pm). Trips to Rigi begin with a ferry ride to Vitznau and a cogwheel train ride on the mountain railway to the top. Rigi can also be conquered by foot. It takes 5 hours from Vitznau to the top, and 3 hours from Rigi Kaltbad, where the train can take you the rest of the way. Return down on the train, take the cable car from Rigi Kaltbad to Weggis, and return to Lucerne by boat (round-trip 84SFr, with Eurailpass and Swisspass 42SFr, with Half-fare Card 39SFr). In between the elevation of Rigi and Pilatus, but far lower in price, is the **Stanserhorn** (1900m), the poor man's Pilatus. Standing just southwest of Mt. Pilatus, the Stanserhorn has the same alpine view you get from Mt. Pilatus, but includes Mt. Pilatus in that view as well. The open-air train that connects halfway up with a cable car for the ascent and descent leaves from Stans, a quick train ride from Lucerne (ascent & descent 44SFr, with Swiss Pass and Eurailpass 22SFr).

NEAR LUCERNE: SCHWYZ

To get to Schwyz, take the 40min. train ride from Lucerne (12.60SFr). To get to the town, take a 5min. bus ride from the station (2.40SFr) to "Schwyz Postplatz."

One of the 3 original cantons, and the namesake of Switzerland, Schwyz is the home of Switzerland's founding documents. These documents, along with a few historical museums that have sprung up around it, make Schwyz a worthwhile daytrip for any history buff. In the center of town is the **Bundesbriefmuseum** (Museum of Swiss Federal Charter), down Bahnhofstr. from Postplatz. The centerpiece here is the original document from 1291 that shaped the 3 original cantons—Uri, Schwyz, and Unterwalden—into an Eternal Alliance (though at the time it was primarily a mutual defense pact against the Hapsburgs). The seal of Schwyz is missing, but other than that the document is in remarkably good condition, as are the numerous sealed documents around it—later treaties that brought more cantons into the pact and letters from foreign monarchs recognizing the union. (Open May-Oct. Tu-F 9-11:30am and 1:30-5pm, Sa-Su 9am-5pm; Nov.-Apr. Tu-F 9-11:30am and 1:30-5pm, Sa-Su 1:30-5pm. 4SFr, students 2.50SFr.) Next door, above the Postplatz, the **Forum der Schweizer Geschichte** (Forum of Swiss History; tel. 819 60 11) is a brand new museum with 3 floors chronicling Swiss living from the 13th to the 18th century with interactive exhibits (open Tu-Su 10am-5pm; 5SFr, students 3SFr). If you want to see how they were really living you can check out **Bethlehem House,** Switzerland's oldest wooden house, built in 1287. Bethlehem House shares the same grounds as the **Ital Reding house,** Schwyz's grandest house, which has an ornately carved interior and is adorned with local art (both open Tu-F 2-5pm, Sa-Su 10am-noon and 2-5pm; 4SFr admission for each, 2.50SFr for students).

There is no full-fledged tourist office in Schwyz, but there is a counter in the post office, which is not, however, in Postplatz. Turn left on Bahnhofstr. (not at the Bahnhof), where the bus lets you off, and then right on Schmiedg. to reach the **post office/tourist office** (open M-F 7:30am-noon and 1:30-6:30pm, Sa 8-11am).

CENTRAL SWITZERLAND

NORTHEASTERN SWITZERLAND

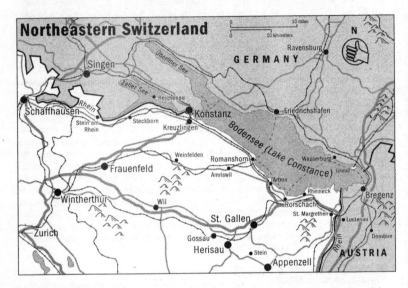

Northeastern Switzerland

Some of Switzerland's best preserved and least populated areas are found in Northeastern Switzerland, which encompasses the cantons of Schaffhausen, St. Gallen, Thurgau, Glarus, and Appenzell. Though it has few large cities, this region is geographically very diverse, stretching from magnificent waterfalls near Schaffhausen to the lofty mountains which surround Appenzell. As a result, Northeastern Switzerland is a veritable paradise for nature lovers and sports enthusiasts, who can sail on the **Bodensee** and bicycle around it, or ski, snowboard, and hike in the mountains of St. Gallen. The smaller towns throughout the region are also charming, such as Stein am Rhein's perfectly preserved medieval *Altstadt* (old town) and the traditional farmhouses in Appenzell village.

HIGHLIGHTS OF NORTHEASTERN SWITZERLAND

◾ St. Gallen's grandiose **Stiftsbibliothek** will knock the socks off even the most Baroque-savvy library lover (p. 374).

◾ Bask in the mist of one of Europe's largest waterfalls, the **Rheinfalls**, which Goethe mistook for the source of the ocean (p. 367).

◾ Avoid crowds and scale mountains around **Appenzell**. Visit the *Wildkirchli*, a 400-year-old chapel built into the cliff face (p. 377).

SCHAFFHAUSEN

During WWII, the United States inaugurated the bad habit of bombing the wrong places due to cartographers' gaffes by targeting Schaffhausen, making it one of the only Swiss cities to be harmed by the war. In spite of this, Schaffhausen retains an expansive and authentic medieval *Altstadt*, one of the most impressive in all of Switzerland. Gilded bay windows, handmade shopkeepers' signs, and fountains decorate the pedestrian streets and give you a glimpse into Switzerland's past.

Schaffhausen's **Munot Fortress**, built in the 1500s, stands tall and valiant above the city. Since no one ever attacked, it proved rather unnecessary, and the citizens apparently used the time spared from military operations to kick back—the local *Falkenbier* is reputedly the best in the canton, and a mug or two of the frothy ferment will put you in an excellent mood to enjoy the ambience and architecture.

⚐ ORIENTATION AND PRACTICAL INFORMATION. Schaffhausen is easily accessible by train, bus, and boat. If you're in the mood for exploration, you might consider a **Tageskarte** (27.50SFr), which allows one day of unlimited travel on Bodensee area railways, waterways, and roadways, including those belonging to Schaffhausen, Stein am Rhein, Constance, and St. Gallen. **Trains** arrive in Schaffhausen every hour from **Zurich** (6:15am-12:45am; 16.40SFr), **St. Gallen** (29SFr), **Winterthur** (10SFr), and **Kreuzlingen** (15.40SFr). Numerous **ferries** traverse the Bodensee, departing from Schaffhausen to **Stein am Rhein** (3 per day, 14.80SFr) and **Konstanz** (3 per day, 26SFr). **Parking** is available in the parking garage off Rheinstr., in the lots near the cathedral, off Moeratz, and behind the train station. The local **tourist office** (tel. 625 51 41; fax 625 51 43) looks out onto the lively Fronwagpl. at the head of Vordenstr., to the right. From the train station, head down Schwertstr., the narrow street to the right, and turn right at the fountain in the main square. The office gives city tours in German, French, or English. (Open Apr.-Sept. M-F 9am-5pm, Sa 10am-4pm, Su 10am-1pm; Oct.-Mar. M-F 9am-5pm, Sa 10am-2:15pm. Tours Apr.-Oct. M, W, and F 2:15pm; 1½hr. 10SFr, children 5SFr.) At the station, you can **exchange currency** (M-Sa 7am-7pm, Su 9am-5pm), **rent bikes** (26SFr per day with photo ID, 20SFr with SwissPass; 6SFr extra to return bike at another station), and **store luggage** (5SFr; open M-F 6am-8pm; Sa-Su 8am-8pm). The **postal code** is CH-8200.

| PHONE CODE | The **city code** for Schaffhausen is 052. |

⚐⚐ ACCOMMODATIONS AND FOOD. Schaffhausen's **Jugendherberge Belair (HI)**, Randenstr. 65 (tel. 625 88 00; fax 624 59 54; email schaffhausen@youthhostel. ch), is in the newer—i.e., early 19th-century—section of town. Take bus #6 (dir.: Neuhausen) to "Hallenbad" and the hostel is across the street from the bus stop. Once a villa, the building that now houses the huge hostel is surrounded by shady birch paths and pine-filled glades. Hermann Hesse was frequently a guest of the villa's former owner, and his novel *Rosshalde* is partially set in the house. (Dorms 23SFr, singles 29SFr, doubles 58SFr. Non-members 5SFr extra. Breakfast, sheets, and showers included. Reception 7-9am and 5:30-10pm. Check-out 9am. Curfew midnight; keys available.) A public **swimming pool** just down Randenstr. (2 min. to the left) completes the luxury. (Open M-F 8am-9pm, Sa 8am-8pm, Su 9am-8pm. Adults 5SFr, ages 16-18 4SFr, under 16 3SFr.) **Camping Rheinwiesen** (tel. 659 33 00) stands at the edge of the Rhine, 3km from Schaffhausen. Take the train (dir.: Kreuzlingen) to "Langewiesen," where you'll be able to see the campground on the waterfront. (6SFr; tents 15SFr.; Sept.-June 4SFr; 8SFr.)

The Fronwagpl. comes alive during the day with outdoor cafés, inexpensive food vendors, restaurants, and live entertainment ranging from mimes to fire-breathers. The owner of **Restaurant Tiergarten** (tel. 625 32 88), on Münsterplatz across from the Allerheiligen Monastery, adds atmospheric spice to the already tasty menu by serving a different national cuisine each year and decorating to extremes. Past influences include the Caribbean, Greece, Mexico, and Australia. Bratwurst and *Rösti* for 15SFr are among the permanent Swiss classics. (Open daily 9am-11pm.) If you're not in the mood to sit around, grab some take-out at **Chinatown**, 36 Vorstadt (tel. 624 46 77), a snappy restaurant ideal for those itching to picnic out in the sun (dishes 14.50SFr and under; open daily 11am-11pm).

Schaffhausen's modern **Migros** supermarket, Vorstadt 39, puts up a good medieval front, staking a spot in the Gothic alleys that define Schaffhausen (open M-F 8:15am-8pm, Sa 7:30am-4pm). Stock up on fresh produce at the **farmer's market** at *Johannkirche* (Tu and Sa 7-11am).

🔲 🎵 **SIGHTS AND ENTERTAINMENT.** Throughout the *Altstadt*, colorful frescoes, fountains, intricate clocks, and woodcarvings transport you into an age of knights, heraldry, and Teutonic bravery. While wandering through the twisted streets, keep your eyes trained upwards to see the decorated bay windows (designed as status symbols) and colorful murals on the medieval buildings. You can review your classical history in the ornate oriel windows on the guild house **Goldener Ochsen,** at the corner of Vorstadt and Löwengässchen, or just enjoy the colorful murals decorating the **Haus zum Ritter,** on Vordergasse, which have been called "the most significant Renaissance frescoes north of the Alps."

ALLERHEILIGEN MONASTERY. The medieval wonders continue on the outskirts of the *Altstadt*, in the labyrinthine **Kloster Allerheiligen** (All-Saints Monastery) complex. From the station, take Schwertstr. up to Vorderg., then turn right on Münsterg. The monastery, with its herb garden, enclosed courtyard, and Schiller bell (the inspiration for Schiller's famous poem, "Song of the Bell"), is a peaceful refuge from the bustling city. Within the cloister, you'll find the **Museum zum Allerheiligen,** which encompasses a **Natural History Museum** and the **Kunstverein Schaffhausen.** The museum offers an array of exhibits ranging from stuffed boars to modern art. Though many natural history and art displays are not particularly engaging or well-maintained, the museum has an incredible display of Roman artifacts, as well as memorabilia from the 11th-century abbey that stood on the same site, such as a late Gothic refectory and preserved chapels with faded stone tombs, that cannot be depreciated by method of presentation. The highlight is the onyx, a bedazzling hunk of gold jewels and a priceless cameo styled in the 1st century AD in Augustan Rome. If you mistakenly believed that Switzerland has always been neutral, check out the military display to see how the Swiss have forcefully corrected this misconception in centuries past. In another recess of the museum lie several thousand-year-old illuminated manuscripts. *(Tel. 633 07 77; fax 633 07 88. Open in summer Th-F 10am–noon and 2-5pm, Sa-Su 10am-5pm; otherwise Th-Su 2-5pm. Free.)*

Attached to the cloister is the **Münsterkirche,** a combination of medieval architecture and 20th-century furnishings, with simple wooden pews set against Cubist stained-glass windows. During the Reformation, Protestants stripped the 11th-century church of ornamentation, leaving the interior cool and white.

MODERN ART MUSEUM. Just across the street from the 11th-century cloister, modernity intrudes into Schaffhausen's medieval self-consciousness in the form of the **Hallen für Neue Kunst**, 23 Baumgartenstr. This old warehouse by the river has been converted into four floors of permanent gallery space for twelve avant-garde artists. Each floor is littered with massive, seemingly indecipherable shapes, colors, and even sounds; the unifying theme is the grand scale on which each piece is executed. *(Tel. 625 25 15. Open May-Oct. Sa 2-5pm, Su 11-5pm; 7SFr.)*

MUNOT FORTRESS. Presiding over all this grandeur, old and new, is the 16th-century **Festung Munot,** which offers the most convincing proof of Schaffhausen's medieval past. Reach the fortress by turning right at the head of Schwertstr., then left on Vorderg., continuing all the way up. After climbing the narrow steps leading through the vineyards that carpet the hill from the fortress, you'll enter the cavernous, dimly-lit interior, where skylights cast yellow circles onto the cold, stone floor, conjuring up visions of townsfolk huddling around fires to the thunder of catapults. An observation deck at the top of the tower's steep stone ramps looks out over the sinking wood-shingled roofs that stretch down to the river, the vineyards, and the moat (which has been transformed into an animal husbandry area).

The vineyards and moat are maintained by a family that lives in the bell tower, maintaining the agrarian foundation upon which this erstwhile feudal estate was built. *(Open daily May-Sept. 8am-8pm; Oct.-Apr. 9am-5pm. Free).*

NEAR SCHAFFHAUSEN: THE RHEINFALLS

The Rheinfalls are just a 15-minute ride from Schaffhausen, in Neuhausen am Rheinfall. Take trolleybus #1, 6, or 9 (dir.: Neuhausen) from the Schaffhausen train station to "Neuhausen Zentrum," then follow signs down the hill to the falls.

The **Rheinfalls** are one of Europe's largest waterfalls, though their scope isn't nearly as grand as that designation might lead you to expect. They are, however, majestic enough that Goethe believed them to be the source of the ocean. There are paths all around the falls, or you can take a boat for a closer look from the bottom of the falls. Contact **Werner Mändl** (tel. (052) 672 48 11) for more information or just look for the boats when you reach the falls. Boats depart every 10 minutes from both the Neuhausen side of the falls (by Schlößli Wörth) and Schloß Laufen. (May-Aug. 10am-6pm; prices from Neuhausen 5.50SFr, children 5-11 3SFr, from Schloß Laufen 6.50SFr, 3.50SFr.) **Rhein Travel**, Schlauchbootfahrten, 8455 Rüdlingen (tel. (01) 867 06 38), has information about **river rafting**. A bridge over the falls leads to **Schloß Laufen**, from where, for 1SFr, you can follow winding stairs down the steep face of the hill to the foot of the falls.

In the turrets of Schloß Laufen, **Jugendherberge Schloß Laufen am Rheinfalls (HI)** (tel. (052) 659 61 52; fax 659 60 39) shelters weary backpackers. Take the train: "Schloß Laufen am Rheinfalls," two stops from Schaffhausen, and then walk up the stairs to the castle and follow the signs for the hostel. From June to October, you can also get to Schloß Laufen by taking PTT bus S33, which leaves once an hour between 7am-6pm and drops you right at the door of the castle. Simple rooms recall the castle's 15th-century origins and offer splendid views of the Rhine. The hostel fills up quickly; reserve in advance. (Dorms 22SFr; triples 72SFr; quads 96SFr. 5SFr extra for non-members. Breakfast included for dorms. Kitchen facilities 2SFr. Reception 8-9:30am and 5-9pm.) The **Bannerstube** (tel. 659 67 67) in the castle serves a number of reasonably priced dishes, including delectable salads and the acclaimed *Füürtopf à discretion*, and has a fantastic view of the falls. (Soups 6-8SFr. Pasta from 14SFr. Children's menu available. Open daily Apr.-Oct. 11:30am-midnight, Oct.-Mar. closed M-Tu.)

STEIN AM RHEIN

In addition to cobblestone streets and old fountains, the tiny *Altstadt* of Stein am Rhein has more painted surface per cubic meter than any town would know what to do with. Density is what distinguishes Stein am Rhein from other Swiss hamlets, and the small size of the town bespeaks the medieval burghers' efforts to squeeze in as much as possible between the wide river and the immediately adjoining hillside. A port of call for the brightly colored ferries that cruise the lake, Stein am Rhein has nimbly converted its vantage point on the Rhine into an unobtrusive tourist industry. Unfortunately, Stein am Rhein has sacrificed some of its quiet and charm by allowing cars to course through the *Altstadt*.

⑦ ORIENTATION AND PRACTICAL INFORMATION. To reach the city from the station, head down Bahnhofstr., turn right on Wagenhauserstr., and left on Charreg., which will take you over a bridge and into the *Rathausplatz* in the center of the *Altstadt*. **Trains** connect Stein am Rhein to **Schaffhausen** (6.80SFr), **St. Gallen** (24SFr), **Winterthur** (11.80SFr), and **Konstanz** (9.40SFr). **Buses** connect the city to the string of small towns in the area and to Germany. **Boats** depart three times per day (once on Sunday) for **Schaffhausen** (1¼hr., 14.80SFr), **Konstanz** (2½hr., 17.80SFr), and other Bodensee towns. **Parking** is available on all streets skirting the Altstadt, and along Hemihoferstr., off Untertor (open 10am-6pm). Stein am Rhein's

YODELING FOREVER Yodeling is usually regarded as part of the picture-book image of Switzerland, alongside holey cheese and numbered bank accounts. For the 100,000+ people who gather every three years at the Federal Yodeling Festival, the traditional Alpine song with alternating high falsetto and low chest notes is more than a a cherished tradition; it is a matter of national pride at a time when neutral Switzerland feels increasingly isolated and unloved, its reputation tarnished by allegations of wartime collusion with the Nazis. "We Swiss have had to take a little bit of criticism in the last few years," Swiss Vice President Adolf Ogi said. "But no one has ever criticized us for our yodelers, alphorn blowers and flag swingers," he told a cheering crowd at the 1999 festival in Frauenfeld, a sedate state capital of 22,000 people in the gentle hills of northeast Switzerland.

The origins of yodeling are shrouded in antiquity, but its often piercing tones carry long distances and can help lone mountaineers locate each other. In its basic form, "natural yodeling," it has no words and is based on a melody, revolving around six syllables. It has been suggested that yodeling may have started as an imitation of the haunting, echoing sound of the alphorn, another traditional means of communication in the high Alps. The long and somewhat impractical tube-like wooden instrument, sometimes 13 feet long, underscores many of the yodeling groups here. Now played in trios, quartets and groups of 10 or more, it has enjoyed a revival after coming close to extinction at the beginning of this century. Similar instruments were documented as far back as Roman times. Yodeling, with its emphasis on melody rather than words, is part of the cement that holds together this nation of 7 million with its four different languages, advocates say. In 2002, the national festival will head to the western city of Fribourg, straddling the language divide between French and German speakers. The tradition lives on among Swiss who have moved away from their home, with participants from as far afield as Canada, New Zealand and South Africa.

tourist office, Oberstr. 9 (tel. 741 28 35; fax 741 51 46), lies on the other side of the *Rathaus* (open M-F 9-11am and 2-5pm.). The train station has **currency exchange** and **bike rental** (26SFr per day, half-day 20SFr; open M-F 6:15am-7:35pm, Sa 6:15am-6:35pm, Su 7:15am-7:35pm). There is an **Internet café** (which also serves cheap pizza) in **Kiosk Charregass,** Oberg. 12: turn right on Brodlaubeg. and right on Oberg. (open Tu-Su 10am-11pm; 7.50SFr for 1/2 hour). The **post office** is at the train station (open M-F 7:30am-noon and 2-6pm, Sa 8-11am). The **postal code** is CH-8260.

PHONE CODE	The **city code** for Stein am Rhein is 052.

■▢ ACCOMMODATIONS AND FOOD. The family-oriented **Jugendherberge (HI)** stands at Hemihoferstr. 87 (tel. 741 12 55; fax 741 51 40). From the train station, take the bus (dir.: Singen) to "Strandbad," cross the street by the pizzeria, and walk along the gravel path for about 2 minutes to the end. You'll see the flags in front of the hostel across the street. Though the hostel itself is somewhat drab, the staff is helpful and many rooms look out on the Rhine. (Dorms 23SFr; doubles 29SFr. Non-members add 5SFr. Breakfast, sheets, and showers included. Reception 7:30-9am and 5:30-10pm. Curfew 10:30pm; keys available. Open Mar.-Oct.)

Picnickers fill up their baskets at the **Co-op** at the corner of Rathauspl. and Schwarzhorng. (Open M-F 8:15am-12:15pm and 2-6:30pm, Sa 8am-4pm.) The many outdoor restaurants and cafés around the *Rathausplatz* provide great people-watching venues. The two young owners of **Restaurant Roten Ochsen,** Rathauspl. 9 (tel. 741 23 28), are dedicated to preserving the tradition connected with this wooden hall, which has served hungry wanderers for 500 years. Their pride in the establishment is reflected in every mouth-watering 10SFr *Wurst*. (Open Tu-Sa 10am-11:30pm, Su 10am-6pm.) **The Spaghetteria,** Schifflände 8 (tel. 741 22 36), sits directly on the Rhine and serves cheap and tasty Italian fare, with pasta dishes from 11SFr and beers at 4.80SFr for 0.5L. The restaurant houses the **world's longest piece of spaghetti** at 182.42m. (Open Mar. 15-Oct. Su-Th 9am-11pm, F-Sa 9am-midnight. Free beer with lunch if you show your Let's Go.) **Café "Zur Hoffnung"** is chock full of chocolate and luck-bringing Steiner Scherben (open Tu-Sa 8am-6pm, Su 9am-6pm.) For wonderfully smooth, cheap ice cream (1.40SFr per scoop), visit **Il Gelato,** next to the *Rathausplatz* at 12 Understadt (Mar.-Oct. daily 10am-9pm).

📷🚗 **SIGHTS AND ENTERTAINMENT.** Stein am Rhein first came into prominence in the 12th century with the establishment of the **Kloster St. George** (tel. 741 21 42). You can reach the Benedictine monastery by heading up Chirchhofplatz from the Rathausplatz. (Open Mar.-Oct. Tu-Su 10am-5pm. 3SFr, students 1.50SFr.) The rooms are wonderfully preserved in their 16th-century state, just as the 5-foot tall monks (judging by the doors) left them. Among the ornate wooden engravings, try to find St. George (who slew the dragon and after whom the cloister is named). As there are no lights, try to go when it is bright outside for the best view of the delicate paintings and engravings. To the right of the monastery, you can admire the exterior of the stately **Rathaus,** which is closed indefinitely.

On Untertor, the **Wohnmuseum Lindwurm,** Understadt 18 (tel. 741 25 12; fax 741 45 82), reconstructs domestic life as it was in the 19th century. This homespun museum is surprisingly large and covers aspects of both indoor and outdoor living (live chickens and all). (Open Mar.-Nov., W-M 10am-5pm; 5SFr, 3SFr students.) The museum also has information about Stein am Rhein's most dramatic event: the open-air play **"No e Wili,"** which is only performed every 10 years (next performance in 2005).

A 40-minute hike will take you straight up the mountain to a vantage point from the castle on **Hohenklingen.** To reach this trail, follow Brodlaubeg. out of town until you reach signs that point out the rest of the way. When the trail meets the road near the top, the castle is to the left, with meadows and panoramas to the right.

THE BODENSEE REGION

The third largest lake in Europe, the **Bodensee** (Lake Constance) forms a graceful border at the conjunction of Austria, Switzerland, and Germany. Ancient castles, manicured islands, and lots of tanning opportunities draw residents of all 3 countries (and then some) to the lake throughout the summer to at least partially relieve pent-up *Mittelmeerlust* (longing for the Mediterranean). The lake presents a good excuse for sneaking over into Germany, but don't forget your passport.

KONSTANZ (CONSTANCE)

Spanning the Rhine's exit from the Bodensee, the elegant university city of Konstanz has never been bombed. Though most of the city is in Germany (including the phone and currency systems), part of it extends into Switzerland, and the Allies were leery of accidentally striking neutral territory, though they took a few shots at Schaffhausen for some inexplicable reason. The Swiss half of the city is called Kreuzlingen, but everything worth seeing and doing is in Konstanz (except for the hostel). Its narrow streets wind around beautifully painted Baroque and Renaissance facades in the *Altstadt*, while gabled and turreted 19th-century houses gleam with a confident gentility along the river promenades.

🚩 **ORIENTATION AND PRACTICAL INFORMATION.** Trains connect Konstanz/Kreuzlingen to **Stein am Rhein** (30min., every hr., 9.40SFr) and **Schaffhausen** (1hr., every hr., 15.40SFr). The tourist office offers a 2-day city pass (DM34) that covers transportation on buses, the ferry, the Weiße Flotte ship line to Meersburg and Mainau, a city tour, and admission to Mainau (see p. 371). Buy individual tickets for the **Weiße Flotte** in the building behind the Konstanz train station (open March

N.E. SWITZERLAND

to mid-Oct. 7:40am-6:35pm). Follow the underground passage near the tourist office to the harbor; otherwise, buy your tickets on the ship. **Giess Personenschiffahrt** (tel. (07533) 2177; fax (07533) 986 66) runs private boats hourly from behind the train station to **Freizeitbad Jakob** and **Freibad Horn** and leads tours of the Bodensee. (45min., June-Aug. daily 10:50am-5:50pm; May and Sept. Su only. DM8, children DM4.) **Buses** in Konstanz cost DM2.40 per ride, DM10 for a 5-ride ticket, and DM7 for a 1-day ticket for 2 adults and 3 children. The **Gästekarte**, available at any place of accommodation in the city for a stay of 2 nights or more (including the youth hostel) costs DM1.50 per day and gives you public transit within Konstanz, free or discounted admission to some sights, and a free dunk in Jakobsbad. Rent **paddleboats and rowboats** at Am Gondelhafen (tel. 21881; open April-Oct. daily 10am-dusk; DM12-16 per hr.). Rent **bikes** from **Kultur-Rädle**, Blarerstr. 19 (tel. 27310; DM10 per ½-day, DM17 full day). For a cheap ride somewhere in Germany, try the **Mitfahrzentrale**, Münzgasse 22 (tel. 19440; fax 79259; open M 2-6pm, Tu-F 9:30am-12:30pm and 2-6pm, Sa 10am-2pm). For a **taxi**, dial 22222.

The **tourist office**, Bahnhofspl. 13 (tel. 13 30 30; fax 13 30 60; email info@tourist information.stadt.konstanz.de), in the arcade to the right of the train station, provides an excellent walking map (DM0.50) and lots of information about the area. The staff finds rooms for a DM5 fee in private homes (3-night minimum stay), or in hotels for shorter stays. (Open May-Oct. M-F 9am-8pm, Sa 9am-4pm, and Su 10am-1pm; Nov.-March 9:30am-12:30pm and 2-6pm.) City **tours** (DM10) depart from the office as well. (April-Oct. M-Sa at 10:30am and Su at 2:30pm). Clean your clothes at **Waschsalon und Mehr**, Hofhalde 3 (wash DM7, dry DM5 per 10min; open M-F 10am-7pm, Sa 10am-4pm). Check **email** at **Schulze & Schultze Internet Café**, Pfauengasse 2 (tel. 152 74), near the Schnetztor in the southwest corner of the Altstadt (DM7.50 per 30min.; open until 1am). The **post office**, 78462 Konstanz, Markstatte 4, is near the train station (open M-F 8:30am-6pm, Sa 8:30am-noon).

PHONE CODE	The **city code** for Konstanz is 07531,

▌ ACCOMMODATIONS. Finding lodging in popular Konstanz can induce some massive migraines. Call ahead to secure a place at the **Jugendherberge Kreuzlingen (HI)**, Promenadenstr. 7 (tel. from Germany (00 41 71) 688 26 63, from Switzerland (071) 688 26 63; fax 688 47 61). South of the border in Kreuzlingen, Switzerland, this lakeside hostel is actually closer to downtown than the Konstanz hostel, but it's still a long walk (20min.). From the station, turn left, cross the bridge over the tracks, turn right, and go through the parking lot to the checkpoint "Klein Venedig." Keep on Seestr. until the sharp right curve, where, instead of following the street, you'll continue straight ahead on the gravel path through the gate, past the billy goats, through the Seeburg castle parking lot, and right up the hill to the building with a flag on top. (23SFr per person. 2.50SFr cheaper March-April and Oct.-Nov. Breakfast and sheets included. Rents mountain **bikes** for 15SFr per day, kayaks for 12SFr per 2hr. Reception 8-9am and 5-9pm. Curfew 11pm. Open March-Nov. Generally booked with school groups mid-May through June.)

Your next best bet is **Jugendherberge "Otto-Moericke-Turm" (HI)**, Zur Allmannshöhe 18 (tel. 322 60; fax 311 63), which is considerably less luxurious, with cramped rooms in a former water tower next to a graveyard, though it has a terrific view. Take bus #4 from the train station to "Jugendherberge" (7th stop); backtrack and head straight up the hill. (DM30, over 26 DM35. Members only. Breakfast and dinner included. Sheets DM5.50. Reception April-Oct. 3-10pm; Nov.-March 5-10pm. Curfew 10pm. Lock-out 9:30am-noon. Call ahead.) **Jugendwohnheim Don Bosco**, Salesianerweg 5 (tel. 622 52; fax 606 88), is also cheap. From the station, take bus #1 to "Salzberg." Walk toward the intersection along Mainaustr. and keep on going. Or take bus #4, 9B, or 15 to the same stop, but cross Mainaustr. at the intersection and turn left. Walk 200m past the intersection, and follow the sign down the path to the right. Choose from 39 channels in the lively dayroom. (DM28 per person. Breakfast included. Sheets DM6.50. Curfew 10pm.) **Campingplatz Konstanz-Bruderhofer,** Fohrenbühlweg 50 (tel. 313 88 or 313 92), is even cheaper. Take bus #1 to "Staad." The campground is along the waterfront. Call ahead, as it also fills up fast. (DM6.50 per person; DM5.50-8.50 per tent.)

◪ **FOOD.** Compared to the rest of Switzerland, German Constance has refreshingly low prices. The **University Mensa** (cafeteria) dishes out Konstanz's cheapest food. Lunches, including dessert, cost DM8-9. (Open M-F 11:15am-1:30pm.) The cafeteria on floor K6 has lighter fare and doesn't require ID (DM2-5; open M-Th 7:45am-6:30pm, F 7:45am-5pm; Aug. M-F 11am-2pm). Take bus #9 from the train station to "Universität." The **Fachhochschule Mensa** also comes with a view. An ISIC is required for a changecard; ask the attendant. The hassle is worth it—meals cost DM4.40. (Open M-F 8:30am-4pm.) Stroll through the small streets surrounding the *Münster's* northern side: it is the oldest part of Konstanz, and now the center of its vibrant alternative scene, with health-food stores, left-wing graffiti, and student cafés. It's hard to get a seat in the very popular and dimly lit **Sedir,** Hofhaldestr. 11 (tel. 293 52). Choose from meat or vegetarian Turkish dishes (DM8-12; open M-F 11:30am-2pm and 6pm-1am, Sa noon-3pm and 6pm-1am, Su 6pm-1am; kitchen open until 1:45pm and 11:30pm). For groceries, head to **Tengelmann** at the corner of Münzgasse and Brotlaube (open M-F 8:30am-8pm, Sa 8am-4pm).

◨◪ **SIGHTS AND OUTDOOR ACTIVITIES.** Konstanz's **Münster** (cathedral), built over the course of 600 years, has a 76m Gothic spire and a display of ancient religious objects. Alas, the tower is subject to renovation until 2003. (Church open daily 10am-5pm. Free.) The **Rathaus** tells the tale of Konstanz's history with its elaborate frescoes. Wander down **Seestraße,** near the yacht harbor on the lake, or down **Rheinsteig** along the Rhine, to two picturesque waterside promenades. The tree-filled **Stadtgarten,** next to Konstanz's main harbor, provides an unbroken view of the Bodensee and of the statue of the voluptuous *Imperia* who guards the harbor. Across the Rhein from the Altstadt, near the "Sternenplatz" bus stop, is the **Archäologisches Landesmuseum,** Benediktinerpl. 5 (tel. 510 38 39; fax 68452), a 3-floor assemblage of all things ancient from Baden-Württemberg—jewels, spearheads, and re-assembled skeletons. (Open Tu-Su 10am-6pm. DM4, students DM3.) Get your fill of fossils, minerals, and ecological enlightenment at the **Bodensee-Naturmuseum,** Katzgasse 5-7. (Tel. 91 42 58; fax 258 64. Open May-Aug. 10am-8pm and Sept.-April 10am-6pm.)

Konstanz has several **public beaches;** all are free and open May to September. Take bus #5 **Strandbad Horn** (tel. 635 50), the largest and most crowded; it sports a section for nude sunbathing modestly enclosed by hedges. In inclement weather, head next door to **Freizeitbad Jakob,** Wilhelm-von-Scholz-Weg 2 (tel. 61163), a modern indoor-outdoor pool complex with thermal baths and sun lamps. Walk 30 minutes along the waterfront from the train station, or take bus #5 to "Freizeitbad Jakob." (Open daily 9am-9pm. DM8, students DM5.) **Strandbad Konstanz-Litzelstetten** and **Strandbad Konstanz-Wallhausen** can both be reached via bus #4. The twentysomething set frolics on the beach at the university. Take bus #4 to "Egg" and walk past the *Sporthalle* and playing fields, or take a 10-minute walk down through the fields from the Konstanz youth hostel.

DAYTRIPS FROM KONSTANZ

NEAR KONSTANZ: MAINAU

Mainau is a 15-minute bus ride from Konstanz. From the Konstanz train station, take bus #4 (dir.: "Bettingen") to "Mainau" (2 per hour). Or take a boat trip from behind the train station. (One-way DM5.40, round-trip DM9. Island open mid-March to Oct. 7am-8pm; Nov. to mid-March 9am-5pm. DM17, students DM9, seniors DM13.50, children DM5.50; after 6pm and Nov. to mid-March DM9, students and children free.)

The entire island of Mainau is a rich and magnificently manicured garden, the result of the horticultural prowess of generations of Baden princes and the Swedish royal family. A lush arboretum, exotic birds, and huge animals made of flowers surround the pink Baroque **palace** built by the Knights of the Teutonic Order, who lived here from the 13th to the 18th century. Now thousands of happy little tourists scamper across the foot bridge from Konstanz to pose with the blooming elephants and take in the unparalleled view of the Bodensee amid 30 different varieties of butterflies and a near-tropical setting. Amazingly, dozens of palm trees thrive here year-round thanks to the lake's moderating effect on the climate and the magic green thumbs of the island's massive gardening army. In summer, preserve your rapidly diminishing D-marks by waiting until after 6pm, when students get in for free and the island is tranquil and swathed in sunsets.

NEAR KONSTANZ: MEERSBURG

Meersburg is 30min. from Konstanz by boat (2 per hour, DM5.20). The town has no train station but the nearest one is in Überlingen, 30min. away by bus #7395 (DM5, every 30min.).

Overlooking the Bodensee, the massive medieval fortress of **Burg Meersburg** (tel. (07532) 80000) towers above the charming town of Meersburg. Begun in the 7th century, the **Altes Schloß**, Germany's oldest inhabited castle, now houses deer antlers, rusting armor, and a very deep dungeon (open March-Oct. daily 9am-6:30pm; Nov.-Feb. 10am-6pm. DM9, students DM7, children DM5.50). In the 18th century, a prince bishop found the Altes Schloß unworthy to house his regal self, so he commissioned the pink Baroque **Neues Schloß** (tel. (07532) 41 40 71). Elaborately frescoed, it now houses the town's art collection, the **Schloßmuseum,** and the **Dorniermuseum,** with models of Dornier airplanes (open Apr.-Oct. daily 10am-1pm and 2-6pm. DM5, students DM4). Meersburg's quirky, crowdy **Zeppelinmuseum,** Schloßpl. (tel 79 09), between the two castles, presents anything remotely connected with zeppelins, including two full-sized zeppelin flight attendant mannequins and a 30-minute film on the history of the flying cigars (open Apr.-Oct. daily 10am-6pm; DM5, students DM4.50). To catch a view of the Bodensee against an alpine backdrop, trek up past the Altstadt, cross the intersection at Stettenerstr., and turn left onto Droste-Hülshoff-Weg, just before the orange house. Follow the signs for "Alpenblick." Or stroll the leisurely **Uferpromenade** along the harbor.

The **tourist office,** Kirschstr. 4 (tel. (07532) 43 11 10; fax 43 11 20; www.meersburg. de), provides free city maps and a list of accommodations. Climb the stairs from the sea-level Unterstadtstr., past the castle and the half-timbered houses, and continue through the Marktplatz towards the church; it's on the right. (Open May-Sept. M-F 9am-6:30pm, Sa 10am-2pm; Oct.-April M-F 9am-noon and 2-5pm.) The office also offers city **tours** every Wednesday at 10:30am and Saturday at 2pm (summer only; DM5). To reserve **rooms,** consult the **Zimmervermittlung,** Untere Stadtstr. 13 (tel. 804 40; fax 804 48), at the bottom of the stairs (open M-F 8:30am-noon and 2-6pm, Sa 9am-12:30pm; DM2 fee). **Haus Mayer Bartsch,** Stettenerstr. 53 (tel./fax 60 50), has rooms with TV and balcony. From the Marktplatz, go up Obertorstr. through the gate, then head straight and bear right onto Stettenerstr. Keep on truckin'; it's on the left past the gas station. (Singles DM45, with bath DM60; doubles DM85, with bath DM135.) For tasty and honestly priced pizza and spaghetti (DM9-16.50, slices DM3) in this city of sky-high prices, **Da Nico,** Untere Stadtstr. 39 (tel. 64 48), provides a view of the lake and speedy pasta service. (Open daily 11am-11:30pm.)

ST. GALLEN

Though it lacks the medieval charm of Schaffhausen, St. Gallen's easy access to Zurich, Germany, Austria, the *Bodensee*, and small mountain villages makes it a popular stopover for people moving between these places. The relatively modern *Altstadt* livens up on weekend nights when students from St. Gallen University descend from their hill to party off stress. During the day, St. Gallen has a few cultural gems to share—most notably the venerable grandeur of the *Stiftsbibliothek*, a Baroque library named a World Heritage Treasure by UNESCO.

🛈 ORIENTATION AND PRACTICAL INFORMATION

Trains: To: **Zurich** (1hr., 5:09am-10:41pm, 29SFr); **Geneva** (4½hr., 5:09am-8:43pm, 95SFr); **Bern** (2½hr., 5:09am-10:43pm, 65SFr); **Appenzell** (30min., 5SFr); **Lugano** (4hr., 74SFr); and **Munich** (3hr., 63SFr, under 26 49SFr).

Buses: Single fare 2SFr, children 1SFr, *Tageskarte* (day pass) 7SFr, 6 rides 10SFr. Buy tickets at each stop; multi-fares and *Tageskarten* available at large kiosks or the **VBSG Transit Authority** across from the train station.

Taxis: Sprenger AG, Rohrschacherstr. 281 (tel. (0800) 55 10 30).

Car Rental: Herold Autovermietung AG, Molkenstr. 7 (tel. 228 64 28; fax 228 64 25). 77SFr per day, 195SFr for weekend (3 days). **Budget Rent-A-Car** or **Europacar/Interrent,** City Garage AG, St. Leonhardstr. 35 (tel. 222 11 14; fax 222 01 57). 132SFr per day, F-M package for 244SFr. 10% discount with student ID.

Parking: Neumarkt Parking Garage (tel. 222 11 14). Conveniently located near the Neumarkt Supermarket on St. Leonhardstr. 5am-9pm 2SFr per hr.; 9pm-5am 1SFr per hr. Open M-Sa 5am-12:30am. **Rathaus Parking Garage** (tel. 223 60 00). 7am-10pm 1.80SFr per hr.; 10pm-7am 0.50SFr per hr. Open 24hr. Or park in one of the city's **blue zones** M-F for 5.50SFr per day, free Sa-Su.

Tourist Office: Bahnhofpl. 1a (tel. 227 37 37; fax 227 37 67). From the train station, cross the bus stop and pass the fountain on the left; the tourist office is on the right. The staff makes hotel reservations within St. Gallen for free. Maps, brochures, and a **city tour** are also available. (Tour June 12-Sept. 28 M, W, and F 2pm. 15SFr, museum admissions and snack included.) Office open M-F 9am-noon and 1-6pm, Sa 9am-noon.

Currency Exchange: Union Bank of Switzerland (UBS), Bahnhofpl., is convenient and the staff can be very helpful. Open M-W and F 9am-4:30pm, Th 9am-6:30pm.

Luggage Storage: At the train station. Lockers 3-5SFr. Luggage watch 5SFr. Open M-F 7:30am-7:45pm, Sa-Su 7:30am-noon and 2-6:45pm.

Laundromat: Quick Wash, Rohrschacherstr. 59 (tel. 245 31 73). Take bus #1 to "Stadttheater." Soap 0.80-2.50SFr, wash 6-8SFr, dry 1.80-3.80SFr. Open M-Sa 8am-10pm.

Internet Access: Media Lounge, 10 Katerineng. (tel. 244 30 90). With your back to the bus stop at Marktpl., cross at far right into Katerineng. This hip lounge with pop music offers cheap access to your neglected email account. 2SFr minimum; after 10min. 1SFr for 5min., 12SFr for 1hr. Open M-F 9am-9pm, Sa 10am-5pm. For free access, you can trek up to the **St. Gallen University Library,** 50 Dufourstr. (in the middle of campus), where there are four computers in the lobby with Net access. Take bus #5 to "Universität." Open M-Th 8am-7:45pm, F 8am-6:45pm, Sa 10am-1:45pm.

Post Office: St. Leonhardstr. 7, across the street and to the right of the train station exit. Open M-F 7:30am-6:30pm, Sa 7:30-11am. **Postal Code:** CH-9000.

PHONE CODE	The **city code** for St. Gallen is 071.

🛏 ACCOMMODATIONS

Jugendherberge St. Gallen (HI), Jüchstr. 25 (tel. 245 47 77; fax 245 49 83; email stgallen@youthhostel.ch). Right of the train station, you'll find the small Appenzeller/ Trogener station with two tracks (#12 and 13). Take the orange train from track #12 (dir.: Trogener) to "Schülerhaus." From the stop, walk uphill on the right, turn left across the train tracks at the sign for the hostel, and walk downhill 2min. Perched on a hill overlooking St. Gallen, this friendly hostel is filled with bright murals and an international student crowd. Extra perks include a breakfast room, terrace, barbecue pit, grassy lawn, juke box, library, and board games. Fall asleep to the tuneful clanking of Swiss cowbells. Breakfast, shower, and sheets included. Parking available. Apr.-Nov. dorms 24SFr, singles 58SFR, doubles 66SFr. Non-members add 5SFr. Reception M-Sa 7-10am and 5-10:30pm, Su 6-10:30pm. Check-out 9am (9:30am in winter). Lockout 10am-5pm, but lounge is open. Closed Dec. 15-Mar. 7.

Hotel Elite, Metzgerg. 9-11 (street opposite bus station) (tel. 222 12 36; fax 222 21 77). This well-scrubbed hostel offers simple, neat rooms with chocolates on the pillows and is conveniently located near the Marktpl., the bus station, and the *Altstadt*. Singles 60SFr, with shower 70SFr; doubles (only with shower) 110SFr. Breakfast included.

Hotel Weisses Kreuz, Engelg. 9 (tel. 223 28 43; fax 223 28 43), up the street from the far left of the Marktpl. bus station, sits atop a lively bar run by a cheerful staff. Scuffed wooden stairs lead up through storage spaces to plain ooms and hall showers in need of some renovation, but beds are clean and the location is great for digging into night-life in the *Altstadt*. Singles 45SFr; doubles 80SFr, with shower 100SFr. Breakfast and hall showers included. Reception M-F 6:30am-2pm and 5pm-midnight, Sa 7:30am-1pm, Su 8am-noon and 6:30pm-midnight.

◗ FOOD

RESTAURANTS

Pizzeria Testarossa, Metzgerg. 20 (tel. 222 03 30), lies a short distance up the street directly across from the bus station. Secluded on a rooftop patio, choose from delicious vegetarian pizzas (from 13SFR), and numerous "make-your-own-pizza" options. Open Tu-F 10am-midnight, Sa-Su 10am-2pm and 5pm-midnight. AmEx, MC, Visa.

Restaurant Spitalkeller, Spitalg. 10 (tel. 222 50 91). From Marktpl., head down Marktg., left on Spitalg. This smoky, wooden-raftered joint with simple hand-engraved tables is a rustic oasis in the sea of urbanity which surrounds it. Try some hearty Alpine food suited for mountain folks, such as Appenzeller macaroni with sausage or Ticino *Rösti* (with tomatoes and cheese) 12.50SFr. Daily *Menü*s from 10SFr. Open Tu-Sa 8am-midnight.

Christina's, Weberg. 9 (tel. 223 88 08). Since the Swedish chef left here to make it big with the Muppets, the menu has been in transition, but is always *très chic*. Veggie dishes from 17SFr. Fish and meat dishes from 19SFr. Open Tu-Th 9:30am-11:30pm, F-Sa 9:30am-12:30am, Su 10am-11:30pm. AmEx, MC, Visa.

Restaurant Scheitlinsbüchel, Scheitlinsbüchelweg 10 (tel. 244 68 21), stands in a meadow on a hill overlooking the bustle of the city. Instead of turning left to the youth hostel from the main road, turn right into a small parking lot; as the small road enters the woods, turn left on the marked *Wanderweg;* when you reach the road again, go left to reach the farmhouse restaurant where traditional Swiss *Rösti* (from 14.50 SFr) is served on an open patio. (Open Tu-Su 9am-10pm). Running past the house are numer-ous trails that will take you up to an abbey and into the hills to commune with the cows.

MARKETS

Migros, St. Leonhardstr., 2 blocks up from the train station. Open M-W and F 8am-6:30pm, Th 8am-9pm, Sa 7:30am-5pm. Buffet restaurant in separate building behind the market open M-W and F 6:30am-6:30pm, Th 6:30am-9pm, Sa 6:30am-5pm.

Public market, on Marktpl. Fresh produce, bread, and meat daily 7am-7pm.

▣ 🏛 SIGHTS AND MUSEUMS

Aside from the aptly named Museumstraße where St. Gallen's four museums reside, St. Gallen's main attractions are centered around the magnificent *Stifts-bibliothek* (abbey library). From the far left of the station, walk up Bahnhofstr. to Marktpl., then left on Marktg. to the abbey.

STIFTSBIBLIOTHEK. Anyone who loves books will marvel at St. Gallen's main attraction, the Stiftsbibliothek. Even for the blasé, the first step into the sparkling room is astounding. To see all the perfectly preserved golden spines staring out from between the lavishly carved and polished exotic wood bookcases, awed visi-tors shuffle across the shiny parquet in huge gray slippers that the library provides to protect the floors. The library maintains a collection of 140,000 volumes and 2000 manuscripts, 500 of which date from before 1200 AD, including 3rd- and 5th-century snippets from Virgil and early bibles. Although the appearance of the resident death-blackened mummy might indicate otherwise, the *Stiftsbibliothek* is a living, lending library serving scholars from around the globe. Umberto Eco was seen sniffing around here to get inspiration for *The Name of the Rose*. *(Tel. 227 34 15. Open Apr.-Nov. M-Sa 9am-noon and 1:30-5pm, Su 10am-noon and 1:30-4pm; Dec.-Mar. M-Sa 9am-noon and 1:30-4pm. 7SFr, students 5SFr.)*

The **Kathedrale St. Gallen,** a part of the abbey founded in the 8th century and renovated in the mid-18th, has enormous windows that cast light on the golden gate spanning the interior of the church. *(Tel. 227 33 88. Open daily 7am-6pm except during Mass.)* The bright abbey courtyard is ideal for a picnic or sunbath. On the far side of the abbey from the library sits the **Evangelical Church of St. Lawrence,** founded in the 9th century. Its small interior (compared to the grand cathedral) showcases castle-like organ pipes, Easter egg wall patterns, and a geometric, blue ceiling. *(Open M-F 9:30-11:30am and 2-4pm.)*

ART MUSEUM. This four-room **Kunstmuseum** has a small but costly collection that juxtaposes modern and traditional art. Housed in the same building, the equally minute **Natural History Museum** rotates various exhibits of Mother Nature's creations, such as the wolf, arranged in thoughtful, interpretative installations. *(Museumstr. 32. Follow the Marktplatz away from the train station to reach Museumstr. Tel. 245 22 44. Both museums open Tu-Sa 10am-noon and 2-5pm, Su 10am-5pm. 6SFr, students 4SFr. One ticket grants admission to all four museums.)*

HISTORICAL MUSEUM. Divided into two parts, St. Gallen's enormous, slightly disorganized **Historisches Museum** investigates traditional Swiss culture and other native cultures of the world. The local half of the museum displays linen processing, ancient kitchens, a random barber shop, and spiky weapons a tad more formidable than the modern Swiss army knife. The **Ethnology Collection** (tel. 242 06 43) provides a tour of various native cultures, carefully avoiding over-interpretation and allowing authentic artifacts to speak for themselves. *(Museumstr. 50 Tel. 242 06 42. Open Tu-Sa 10am-noon and 2-5pm, Su 10am-5pm. 6SFr, students 2SFr.)*

OTHER SIGHTS. For a nice walk and view of the St. Gallen valley (and perhaps a glimpse of a few endangered species), visit the **Peter and Paul Wildpark,** on Rosenberg in Rotmonten. Take bus #5 (dir.: Rotmonten) to "Sonne" and then walk uphill the hill for about ten minutes. There is a well-tended trail leading through the park, ensuring that you don't miss the ibex, which the park has saved from near extinction. *(Tel. 222 67 92. Open 24hr. Free.)* For a tamer excursion, explore the campus of the **St. Gallen University.** Take bus #5 (dir.: Rotmonten) to "Universität." The huge park donated to the city of St. Gallen in 1963 provides a magnificent view of the city and the Bodensee.

♪ ENTERTAINMENT AND NIGHTLIFE

St. Gallen's *Altstadt* resonates with techno beats and the heavy clink of beer mugs. Cafés and bars in Marktpl. are popular but money-hungry. Head instead for the streets radiating out from Marktpl., which are speckled with cheaper, hole-in-the-wall bars and their tattooed, chained, and bejewelled clientele. Clubs tend to be clustered together, particularly around Goliathg. and Brühlg. Dance places aren't good places to drink, as beers are always expensive there.

Filou, Schwertg. (tel. 222 35 96). Follow Goliathg. from Marktpl. to the end, then curve around 200 feet to the right. This smoky bar pumps 80s rock and cheap beer for a twenty-something crowd. Beer guzzlers overflow into the camp-like picnic tables outside. Good luck finding space to dance on the weekend. Open M-Sa 5pm-midnight.

Birreria, Brühlg. 45 (tel. 223 25 33). Over 150 types of beer let you take a barley trip around the globe without moving your lazy gut. Take them away or drink them at the bar. Open M 11am-midnight, Tu-Th 9am-midnight, F-Sa 9am-1:30am.

Goliathstübli, Goliathg. 27 (tel. 222 35 96). This is a dark, local joint with red velvet walls, a crooked wooden bar, and a diverse crowd. Open M-Sa 10am-1am, Su 2:30pm-1am.

N.E. SWITZERLAND

Ozon, Goliathg. 28 (tel. 244 81 24). Non-stop chrome and mirrors lend the illusion of size to this compact club. If the flashing lights and smoke don't stun you, the prices will (beer from 9SFr). The music selection changes each night, with hip-hop and soul during the week and dance music from the 70s and 80s on the weekend. Cover usually 10SFr. Open Su and Tu-Th 10pm-2am, F-Sa 10pm-3am.

Trichsli Dancing, Brühlg. 18 (tel. 226 09 00). Dance-floor action is projected onto a field of screens. This club features local bands, karaoke, and other theme nights (foxtrot, anyone?). Things gets hopping late at night, so make this your last stop. Su-W no cover, Th-Sa 7-17SFr. Open July-Aug. Th-Tu 10pm-5:30am; Sept.-June 9pm to whenever.

On a more cultured note, the **Stadttheater,** Museumstr. 24 (tel. 242 06 66), housed in a fancy Art Nouveau building, hosts over 200 concerts and dramatic works by renowned artists and musicians year-round. There are several **movie theaters** at Marktpl., the largest being the **Scala Kinocenter and Bar** (tel. 228 08 60) on the Marktplatz, with 5 screens.

For real party animals, St. Gallen's celebration of music and general debauchery takes over the fields surrounding the town at the end of June. The **Open Air St. Gallen Music Festival** (tel. 222 21 21; www.openairsg.ch—see **Festival Fever,** p. 303; box office address: Open Air St. Gallen Festival Boutique, Bahnhofstr. 6, CH-9000, St. Gallen, Switzerland) features over 20 live bands. Past headliners have included Metallica, Garbage, Red Hot Chili Peppers, Cypress Hill, the legendary B.B. King, and the Godfather of Soul, James Brown. You must buy a ticket for all 3 days. Tickets run 144SFr, but housing is included if you bring a tent and camp out (showers and toilets available). Otherwise, stay in St. Gallen and take the free shuttle bus from the train station to the concert grounds.

APPENZELL

Though the smallest canton in Switzerland, Appenzell is world-reknowned for its *Appenzeller Käse* (cheese). The highly conservative Appenzeller people have maintained the traditional Swiss agrarian lifestyle—favorite pastimes in the region are still herding animals and hiking. The canton is dotted with tiny villages, but Appenzell town is the regional gathering place for democratic meetings and various agricultural shows. The twisting streets of Appenzell take you past the painted wooden barns and houses that comprise the small town. Outside of this modest population cluster, people are spread out all over the surrounding countryside, which makes Appenzell a region best explored on foot. Over the centuries, local herdsmen have developed an extensive and densely concentrated network of trails in the hills and mountains for shepherding their various flocks. These paths are still used for the same purpose; on the trails you will frequently pass herders dressed in traditional garb. The *Gasthäuser* (guesthouses) liberally sprinkled along the trails provide a night's rest and a luxurious respite from Alpine hikes.

The Appenzell region attracts Swiss folk from nearby cities looking to get back to their roots with a rustic weekend getaway. Thus far, the region has managed to avoid the onslaught of Americans and foreigners that has hit the more glamorous (and pricier) St. Moritz and Interlaken areas, keeping its authenticity intact.

🖬 **ORIENTATION AND PRACTICAL INFORMATION.** The rattling but prompt **Appenzellerbahn** chugs between Appenzell and **St. Gallen** twice an hour from 6am-midnight (1hr., 10SFr). From St. Gallen and **Herisau** (an easier connection to Zurich), there is a regular train to **Zurich** (1hr.). The same train continues on from Appenzell to its last stop in **Wasserauen,** a tiny hamlet that serves as a gateway to the Alpenteil valley (2.40SFr extra). 3- and 5-day cards are valid for regional train and cable cars (78SFr and 98SFr respectively, 25% reduction for SwissPass and Eurail), but these cards are only worthwhile if you will be riding the cable cars frequently. The Appenzell **tourist office,** Hauptg. 4 (tel. 788 96 41; fax 788 96 49; www.appenzellerland-ferien.ch), is next to the *Rathaus* (open June-Oct. M-F 9am-noon and 2-5pm, Sa 9am-noon and 2-4pm; Nov.-May M-F 9am-noon and 2-5pm, Sa 9am-noon and 2-4pm). From the train station, walk down Bahnhofstr., bearing right as the road curves and intersects Hauptg. The tourist office is to the left of the church. The office makes hotel reservations, books cable car excursions, sells detailed hiking maps, and gives specific dates for all of Appenzell's farm festivals. The tourist office arranges different activities every day: a free tour of the Appenzeller Alpenbitter factory, which is responsible for production of the region's unique and delicious alcoholic drink, departs from Weissbadstr. 27 on Wednesdays at 10am; there's a course in woodcarving on Thursdays at 2pm where, for 20SFr, you can make your own butter dish. The tourist office also has information about **Herr Fässler,** a friendly Swiss farmer and cheesemaker in Grosshütter who loves talking about cheese—for free! (Mid-June to mid-Sept.) For all tourist office-sponsored events, register the day before by 5pm. The **postal code** is CH-9050.

PHONE CODE	The **city code** for Appenzell is 071.

▞▞ ACCOMMODATIONS AND FOOD. The ever-present aroma of Appenzeller cheese lingers around **Gasthaus Hof** (tel. 787 22 10; fax 787 58 83), on Landsgemeindeplatz in the center of town, a bustling family-run restaurant that provides guest rooms in a separate house. (Dorms 28SFr; singles 65SFr, 95SFr with shower; doubles 110SFr, 130SFr with shower. Breakfast included. Check-in 11am. Restaurant open 8am-11pm.) Picturesque lodgings await at **Haus Lydia,** Eggerstrandenstr. 53 (tel. 787 42 33). A staff member will pick you up at the train station if you call ahead. Otherwise, walk 20 minutes from the station on Bahnhofstr. and turn right on Gringelstr., left on Weissbadstr., right on Gaiserstr., and right onto Eggerstrandenstr. Run by a friendly, English-speaking family, Haus Lydia provides large rooms with great pastoral views and a kitchen for guest use. When the weather's good, the sons of the owners provide musical entertainment. (Singles 35SFr, with shower 40SFr; doubles 60SFr, with shower 65SFr. Breakfast included. Reservations required.) Many hiking trails are dotted with **Gasthöfe** (guesthouses), splendid old farmhouses and restaurants for the road-weary. For more information on guesthouses in the mountains, see **Hiking near Appenzell,** p. 377.

You can get the energy you'll need for hiking at **Restaurant Traube,** Marktg. 7, near the Landsgemeindeplatz (tel. 787 24 19), which serves up Appenzeller specialties by candlelight. (Appenzeller specialties 13-18.50SFr; Appenzeller beers 3.50SFr. Open Mar.-Jan. Tu-Su 9am-midnight.) For groceries, try the **Co-op,** on Zielstr., which heads away from the train station (open M and Th 8am-12:15pm and 1:30-6:30pm, Tu-F 8am-12:15pm and 1:30-8pm, Sa 8am-4pm).

◪ SIGHTS. Since Appenzell's most breathtaking sights are all around it, there isn't much to the city except the **Rathaus,** which houses the museum, town hall, cantonal library, and tourist office. The Großratssaal, with its intricately carved wooden walls and 16th-century frescoes, is particularly remarkable. Tucked inside the *Rathaus* and the adjoining Haus Buherre Hanisefs, the **Museum Appenzell** chronicles local culture in 6 floors of displays in the wooden-raftered house. A video on lace-making, shown in English and German, is surprisingly captivating, and exposes the realities of idealized traditional Swiss life. (Hauptg. 4. Tel. 787 9631. Open Apr.-Oct. daily 10am-noon and 2-5pm; Nov.-Mar. Tu-Su 2-4pm. 5SFr, students 3SFr.) Next door, the stately **Pfarrkirche St. Mauritius** shows off its Rococo stained-glass windows and a magnificent golden chandelier. (Open daily 9am-7pm.)

⚑ HIKING NEAR APPENZELL. Deep in the heart of the Alpstein, Appenzell offers great hiking without the temperature extremes of Zermatt or the Ticino region. Ask at the tourist office for *Wandervorschläge: Appenzellerland,* which has a detailed map with all rest areas, or buy a more comprehensive topographical map at a bookstore. Hiking options range from easy walks through the green pastures to strenuous overnight treks. For the former, walk along the Sitter River to

Weissbad by turning left on Hauptg. out of the tourist office and following the signs (1hr.). For the latter, the best place to begin is tiny **Wasserauen,** the last stop on the Appenzeller Bahn (10min. from Appenzell). From there, you can enter the mountains in several ways.

> Though the rewards are great, hiking around Appenzell can be physically strenu-ous, as the trails wind steeply up and down these mountains. The upper regions of this area tend to stay snow covered late in the year and some parts are cov-ered year-round. Use caution: do not hike into snowy areas when there is low vis-ibility. See **Wilderness Safety,** p. 34 for more information.

EBENALP TO WILDKIRCHLI. The first option is the **Ebenalp Cable Car,** across the street from the small train station, which does the climbing for you (cable car runs daily from 7:30am-7pm; 22SFr round-trip, 17SFr one-way up, 13SFr down; students and SwissPass or Eurail holders 12SFr round-trip, 9SFr or 6.50SFr one-way). A quick (30min.) and popular hike leads down from the Ebenalp (top station) through caves to the **Wildkirchli,** a 400-year-old chapel built into the cliff face and manned until recently by a hermit priest. Just beyond Wildkirchli lies **Berggasthaus Äscher** (tel. 799 11 42). At 150 years old, Äscher is the oldest *Gasthaus* in the region. Tucked into the sheer cliff face, one interior wall is actually the rocky mountain slope. As is standard for most *Gasthäuser,* Äscher has a restaurant and 40 simple beds, consisting of mattresses laid side by side on the floor. (Dorms 25SFr. Breakfast included. No showers.)

WASSERAUEN TO SEEALPSEE. For a more strenuous entry into the mountains you can hike from Wasserauen to the alpine lake **Seealpsee** (1hr.). Turn left out of the train station and follow the road until it forks. The trail begins at the left fork (just past the Alpenrose). Yellow signs marked *Seealpsee* point out the trail as it rises steeply first through spruce forests lined with waterfalls, and then through high alpine meadows used for cattle grazing (evidenced by the inescapable clank-ing cow bells). At the top, the trail passes a few farm houses and ends at ■**Berg-gasthaus Seealpsee** (tel. 799 11 40, winter tel. 799 14 40; fax 799 18 20), the second of two guesthouses on the trail. The wonderful Dörig-Klossner family who have run the guesthouse for generations know every detail about the surrounding coun-try. Its pristine location near the peaceful waters of the Seealpsee make it a perfect base from which to ascend the surrounding peaks. It's a good place to stop in for advice or for a meal—try the homemade spinach *Spaetzli.* (Dorms 25SFr, doubles 90SFr. Breakfast included. Showers 2SFr.)

UP TO SÄNTIS. The climb to **Säntis** (2503m), the highest mountain in the region, is an overnight trip from Wasserauen via *Seealpsee.* From *Seealpsee* hike to **Meglis-alp** (1hr.), a cozy cluster of half a dozen farmhouses at the peak. Among the farm-houses is **Gasthof Meglisalp** (tel. 799 11 28), a great place to stay for a night with the cows and the people who tend them. (Dorms 26SFr, singles 47SFr, doubles 94SFr. Breakfast included). To get to Säntis from Meglisalp, head either to *Rotsteinpass* (more difficult) or *Wagenlücke* (easier), and then up to Säntis (both trips 3hrs.). Two guesthouses sit on top of Säntis. The older and more personal house is **Gast-haus Säntis** (tel. 799 11 60, winter tel. 799 14 11), which provides a good night's rest before you hike back down. (Dorms 35SFr, singles 54SFr. Breakfast included.) There are numerous routes from Säntis back to Wasserauen; the road-weary can take the cable car down from the town of **Schwägalp,** a neighboring town to Appen-zell (20-30SFr round-trip; 10-20SFr one-way).

GRAUBÜNDEN

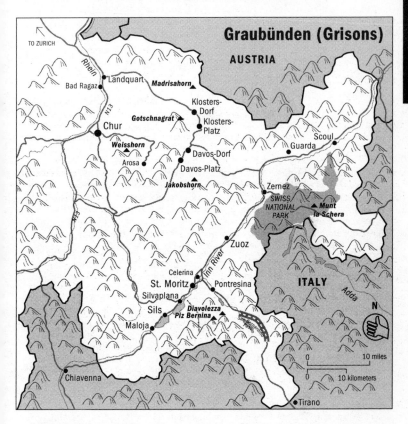

Graubünden (Grisons)

TO ZURICH

AUSTRIA

Rhein

Bad Ragaz

Landquart

Madrisahorn

Klosters-Dorf

Chur

Gotschnagrat

Klosters-Platz

Weisshorn

Scoul

Guarda

Arosa

Davos-Dorf

Davos-Platz

Jakobshorn

Zernez

SWISS NATIONAL PARK

Munt la Schera

Zuoz

Inn River

Celerina

St. Moritz

Pontresina

ITALY

Adda

Silvaplana

Sils

Diavolezza

Piz Bernina

N

Maloja

0   10 miles

0   10 kilometers

Chiavenna

Tirano

The largest, least populous, and most alpine of the Swiss cantons, Graubünden is made up of remote valleys and snow-clad peaks that are bound to bring out the wild-hearted, lusting-for-life yodeler in everyone. Deep, rugged gorges, forests of larch and fir, and eddying rivers imbue the region with a wildness seldom found in ultra-civilized Switzerland. The area is also a microcosm of Swiss cultural heterogeneity—from valley to valley the language slips from German to Romansh to Italian, with a wide range of dialects in between. Though only 1-2% of the country (and 26% percent of the canton) converses in the ancient Romansh tongue, the language is carefully preserved in schools and books—especially hymnals—and is recognized as an official language, on par with *Schwyzertüütsch* (Swiss-German), Italian, and French.

Graubünden has been known to the world since 1864 through the efforts of St. Moritz hotel pioneer Johannes Badrutt. The innkeeper made four British summer visitors an offer they couldn't refuse: if they came in winter and didn't like it, he would pay their travel costs. If they liked it, he'd let them stay as long as they wanted, *for free.* Alas, that was the last of cheap housing in St. Moritz and Davos—the two big resorts—and the little towns in their vicinity. There is, however, more to Graubünden than glamorous ski resorts, as travelers willing to go a little farther afield discover to their delight. Many communities in the canton, such as Zuoz, Scuol, and Guarda, are as unspoiled as the landscape, traditional villages whose beauty rivals that of the nearby mountains.

Unfortunately, travel is not cheap in Graubünden. It costs far more to go from Chur to St. Moritz than from Chur to Zurich. If you're planning on moving around much within Graubünden, invest in the **Graubünden Regional Pass,** which allows 5 days of unlimited travel in a 15-day period and a 50% discount on other days (140SFr, children under 16 70SFr), or 3 days of unlimited travel in a 7-day period and a 50% discount on the other days (105SFr, children 52.50SFr). The Regional Pass primarily works on the **Rhätische Bahn** (**Viafer Retica** in Romansh), Graubünden's own train company. If you plan on using cable cars, the **Regional Pass Plus** is a good idea (15 days 190SFr, under 16 95SFr; 7 days 135SFr, under 16 67.50SFr; 30% discount with Half-fare Card). These passes are issued in Switzerland only from May to October. **SwissPasses** are valid as well. Visitors should plan excursions carefully in this part of the country, especially in ski season (Dec.-Apr.), when reservations are absolutely required. Beware—virtually everything shuts down in May and June.

HIGHLIGHTS OF GRAUBÜNDEN

■ Ascend Munt la Schera's panoramic pedestal in the **Swiss National Park** (p. 390).

■ Delve into the psychological underworld of Expressionist Ernst Kirchner at his eponymous museum in **Davos** (p. 386).

■ Ski and snowboard for cheap in secluded and spectacular **Arosa** (p. 384).

■ Windsurf **Silvaplana's** shimmering lake under high-pressure Alpine winds (p. 399).

CHUR

Chur is the capital of Graubünden and, at 5000 years old, probably Switzerland's oldest settlement. Its museums and hip restaurants give Chur—a town in the most rural and wild canton—an unexpected cultural and artsy edge. People hang out in Chur; the many sidewalk restaurants and benches tend to be full most of the day. Most of this activity occurs in the newer parts of the city near the train station. Peaceful walking in the quiet *Altstadt*, whose centerpiece is a cavernous 12th-century cathedral, is another favorite leisure activity in Chur. The city is an important transportation hub for southern Alpine Switzerland and the Ticino region.

⊡ ORIENTATION AND PRACTICAL INFORMATION. Trains connect Chur to the rest of Switzerland: **Zurich** (1½hr., every hr. 4:54am-11:10pm, 38SFr); **Basel** (2½hr., every hr. 4:54am-9:51pm, 62SFr); **Disentis** (for the **Furka-Oberalp line;** 1¼hr., every hr. 5:47am-10:10pm, 26SFr); **Arosa** (1hr., every hr. 5:28am-11pm, 11.80SFr); **St. Gallen** (1½hr., every hr. 4:54am-10:22pm, 34SFr); and **St. Moritz** (2hr., every hr. 5:10am-10:52pm, 41SFr). Postal buses run to **Bellinzona** (2½hr., 5 per day, 84SFr). The train station has **currency exchange, luggage storage** (5SFr), and **bike rental** (20SFr at baggage check; open 5:40am-9:15pm). **Lockers** (2SFr) are outside.

To get to Chur's **tourist office** (*Kurverein*), Grabenstr. 5 (tel. 252 18 18; fax 252 90 76), from the train station, walk to the left and up Bahnhofstr.; at the first large intersection (Postpl.), turn left on Grabenstr. The office finds rooms for free (open M 1:30-6pm, Tu-F 8:30am-noon and 1:30-6pm, Sa 9am-noon). Graubünden's **regional tourist office,** Alexanderstr. 24 (tel. 254 24 24; fax 254 24 00), located in Chur, stocks brochures for every city in the canton. From the station, go down Bahnhofstr. and turn left on Alexanderstr. (open M-F 8am-noon and 1:30-5:30pm).

F. Schuler, Gäuggelistr. 11 (tel. 252 11 60) has a small selection of **English books** (open M 1-6:30pm, Tu-Th 8:30am-6:30pm, F 8:30am-9pm, Sa 8:30am-4pm). **Internet access** is a 10-minute walk from town at **Rampa Conputers Internet Cafe,** Tittwiesenstr. 60 (tel. 284 89 28). Walk through the tunnel under the train station, turn right, make a hard left onto Daleurstr., then a quick left onto Tittwiesenstr. (Open M-F 8am-noon and 1:30-6:30pm. 5SFr for 20min., 12SFr for 1hr.) Do your **laundry** at **Mal-**

tesen's Wash Self-Service, Malteserg. 1. Wash and dry is 9SFr (open M-Sa 9am-midnight, Su noon-midnight). In an **emergency,** dial 117. **Raetus Apotheke (pharmacy)** (tel. 250 15 15) is at Bahnhofstr. 14 (open M-Th 7:30am-6:30pm, F 7:30am-9pm, Sa 7:30am-5pm). The **post office** is just left of the train station (M-F 7:30am-12pm and 1:30-6:30pm, Sa 8-11am). Chur's **postal code** is CH-7000. All directions given for Chur are from Postpl., two blocks up Bahnhofstr.

PHONE CODE	The **city code** for Chur is 081.

ACCOMMODATIONS AND FOOD. No luxurious budget accommodations await in Chur; the lack of a youth hostel is sorely felt. One good option is staying in nearby **Bad Ragaz,** p. 382, but if you need to be in Chur, try high-altitude **Hotel Rosenhügel,** Malixerstr. 32 (tel./fax 252 23 88), which has scuffed-up rooms with pipes running through them but an affable staff. From Postpl. turn right on Grabenstr. and follow as it becomes Engadinestr. and crosses the bridge. Across the bridge climb Malixerstr. on your right. (15min. Singles 50SFr; doubles 90SFr, with shower 100SFr. Breakfast and parking included. Reception 8am-midnight. AmEx, DC, MC, Visa.) **Hotel Schweizerhaus,** Kasernenstr. 10 (tel. 252 10 96; fax 252 27 31) is over the same bridge on Weischdörfli. Once you have passed every nudie-bar in Chur, the street becomes Kasernenstr. Iron-spring cots in miniature rooms cost 30SFr per person. (Breakfast 5SFr. Reception open 7am-noon.) **Camp Auchur,** Felsensustr. 61 is a grassy campsite on the Rhine. Take bus #2 to "Obere Au" past the sports complex; it's on the left, on the gravel path. (6SFr, tents 6-12SFr. Electricity 3.30SFr. Showers 0.50SFr. Equipped with kiosks and restaurant.)

Chur has a number of trendy eating establishments. The best budget option is the **Shoarma Grill,** Untereg. 5 (tel. 252 73 22). Turn right on Grabenstr. from Postpl., then left through the arches to reach Unterg. (Kebabs 8SFr. Falafel with veggies 7SFr. Beer from 3.50SFr. Open Tu-F 11:45am-2pm and 5pm-midnight, Sa 11:45am-midnight, Su 2-10pm.) **Restaurante Controverse,** Steinbruchstr. 2 (tel. 252 99 44), reached by turning left on Grabenstr., which turns into Steinbruchstr., tries very hard to live up to its name with an Art Nouveau decor combined with Louis XIV drapes, black coffee tables, neon lights, and lip-smacking good food. Spaghetti is 10-20SFr, oriental noodles 10.50SFr, and wines 4-8SFr. (Open M-Sa 11am-2pm and 5pm-midnight, Su 6-11pm.) Follow Poststr. from Postpl., and turn left at St. Martin's Church to reach **Restaurant Falken,** St. Martinspl. 9, which uses organic ingredients (veggie *Menüs* 15SFr; open M-Sa 9am-midnight). For a late-night drink, try the **Street Café,** Grabenstr. 47 (tel. 253 79 14), where classical statues peer down from the mirrored, red-draped walls that provide intimate drinking enclaves within the larger hopping bar; beers start at 3.50SFr. The **Street Castle** upstairs is a *Ritterstil* (knight-style) chamber where wine flows from the decanter and cask (from 4SFr; cover F-Sa in winter; open 9am-midnight). Six floors of shopping, including a market with fresh, inexpensive, and tasty breads and sandwiches on the first floor, await at the **Manor** on Bahnhofstr. (open M-Th 8:30am-6:30pm, F until 9pm, Sa until 5pm).

SIGHTS AND MUSEUMS. Chur's sights are all within walking distance of the town's center. The highlight, a 12th-century Romanesque **Dom** (cathedral) at the top of the old town, displays 8 altarpieces in addition to the **Hochaltar,** a flamboyant 15th-century masterpiece of gold and wood. The musty, dark interior adds ambience but decreases the visibility of these objects, even on the sunniest day. The crypts, where the Capuchin martyr St. Fidelis is buried, also house the **Dom-Museum,** replete with relics. (Tel. 252 92 50. Open Tu-Sa 10am-noon and 2-4pm.) Downhill, the **Martinskirche** counters the cathedral's grandiose flair with understated simplicity: the church's sole decorations are 3 stained-glass windows by Augusto Giacometti. The eerie panels depict the birth of an oddly beefy Christ. Clad in blood-red instead of her usual blue, Mary stares with wide eyes beside her thoroughly befuddled husband.

Chur's **Bündner Kunstmuseum,** Bahnhofstr. 35 (tel. 257 28 68), at the corner of Bahnhofstr. and Grabenstr., blazes with the art of the 3 Giacomettis: Giovanni, Alberto, and Augusto. Works by Swiss artists Angelika Kauffman and Ferdinand Hodler occupy the ground floor. (Open Tu-W and F-Su 10am-noon and 2-5pm, Th 10am-noon and 2-8pm. 10SFr, students 7SFr.) The **Retic Museum,** Quaderstr. 15 (tel. 257 28 88), houses a collection of tapestries, coins, and archaeological trivia that document the origin of "Rhaetia" and its development into the current Swiss canton of Graubünden (open Tu-Su 10am-noon and 2-5pm. 5SFr, students 2SFr, seniors and groups 3SFr).

NEAR CHUR: BAD RAGAZ

Bad Ragaz is accessible by train from St. Gallen (1¼hr., 27SFr) and Chur (15min., 7.40SFr).

A massage at Bad Ragaz's thermal baths may relax your weary muscles, but it will certainly put stress on your wallet. Luckily, a stroll down the wide, tree-lined streets that meander from Bad Ragaz's traffic-free *Bahnhofplatz* may be (almost) as soothing. Bad Ragaz is famous as the home of Heidi, and has thus dubbed itself "Heidiland." Short hikes from the top of mountains serviced by expensive cable cars allow you to explore the area immortalized by Johanna Spyri's beloved tale. To reach Bad Ragaz's **tourist office** *(Kurverein)*, Maienfelderstr. 5 (tel. 302 10 61), turn left on Maienfeldstr. from Bahnhofstr. (open M-F 9am-6pm, Sa 9am-noon and 1-4pm). **Currency exchange, luggage storage** (10SFr per article), and **bike rental** (26SFr per day) are available inside the train station. For an affordable breath of class and genuine comfort, stay at **Hotel Bergadler,** Bahnhofstr. 29 (tel. (081) 302 18 13), whose owner has made sure that nothing in her house is mass-produced, from the crocheted table covers to the kitschy paintings adorning the walls to the great breakfast served to guests. (Singles 40SFr, with shower 60SFr; doubles 80SFr, 120SFr. Reception open 9am-noon. Closed Jan.-Feb. V, MC, AE.)

A 1-day pass to the **Tamina Therma** (thermal baths) grants you access to the town spa's 3 pools (tel. (081) 303 27 47; open M-Su 7:30am-9pm; 18SFr). You'll have to pay extra, however, to get into the solarium, waterfalls, watery lounges and grottoes. The **cable car** from Bad Ragaz to Paradiel will take you to the starting point of a 30-minute **hike** to **Heidi's house.** (Tel. (081) 302 36 38. Daily 8:30am-noon and 1:30-5pm. 24SFr.)

AROSA

The secluded town of Arosa—reached only by a spectacularly scenic 1-hour train ride from Chur—climbs the hillside opposite a panoramic snow-covered mountainscape. If you find yourself in any building without a view, you're in the wrong place. Thanks to the "discovery" of the area's stimulating climate in 1888, Arosa has matured from a simple farming village to a full-service tourist depot, with great skiing in winter and hiking in summer. The majority of tourists are down-to-earth German-speaking folk, however, which allows Arosa to avoid the glitz that clings to mountain resorts over the mountain in the Engadine Valley. Its countless peaks, including the 2653m Weisshorn, have been transformed by 15 ski lifts into a skiing paradise that rivals any in Graubünden. The company that owns these lifts has recently established large, well-equipped dormitories that rent cheap, comfortable rooms complete with ski passes, making the area perfect for young budget-conscious skiers and snowboarders. Fortunately for the avid summer hiker, developed ski trails dominate only one side of the valley. On the other side, hiking trails stretch infinitely to isolated valleys.

■ **ORIENTATION AND PRACTICAL INFORMATION.** Arosa is accessible by **train** only by way of a scenic route from **Chur** (1hr., every hr., 11.80SFr). A **free shuttle bus** (every 30min. in summer, every 7min. in winter) transports visitors between the hottest spots in town, including the ski lifts. It also covers the 10-minute walk from the train station to the tourist office (get off at "Casino"). To walk from the train station, turn right, then right again on Poststr. The pink **tourist office** (*Kurverein;* www.arosa.ch) arranges hiking trips and ski lessons and makes free hotel reservations (open Dec. 7-Apr. 13 M-F 9am-6pm, Sa 9am-5:30pm, Su 4-6:30pm; Apr. 14-Dec. 6 M-F 8am-noon and 2-6pm, Sa 9am-1pm; June 29-Aug. 17 also open Sa 2-4pm). **Parking** is free in summer at the **Parking Garage Obersee,** 2SFr per hour in winter. Beware—a strict traffic ban has been imposed from midnight to 6am every night. The **train station** provides **currency exchange** (M-Sa 5:30am-9pm, Su 6:30am-9pm), **lockers** (2SFr), and **bike rental** (26SFr, mountain bikes 30SFr). In an **emergency,** dial 117. The **post office** is in Arosa's main square, to the right of the train station (open M-F 7:45am-noon and 1:45-6:30pm, Sa 8-11am). The **postal code** is CH-7050.

PHONE CODE	The **city code** for Arosa is 081.

⌐ **ACCOMMODATIONS.** Most lodgings in Arosa are near the tourist office. Arriving in town without reservations is a bad idea; reserve well in advance for prime ski-season. Two large dorm-houses owned by ski-development company Arosa Bergbahnen rule the budget accommodations scene in Arosa (tel. 378 84 23 for both). Rooms come with an affordable ski lift ticket package. The centerpiece of their development is ▩**Haus Florentium**. The enormous former convent buried in the woods at the top of the town has been converted to a 150-bed party house complete with large lounging rooms, balconies, and an old chapel-cum-disco. To reach the Haus follow the cobblestone path down the hill from the tourist office, turn right at the road at the top, left at the gravel path for Pension Suveran, then right at the path in front of the pension. (Dec.-Apr. 1-night stay, 2-day ski pass 140SFr; 6-night stay, 7-day ski pass 430SFr, under 19 387SFr. July-Aug., no packages, 36SFr per night, under 19 30SFr. Breakfast included.) The smaller **Haus Bellaval,** right above the train station, offers basic dorms and not much else. (Open all year. In winter (with lift pass only) 1-night stay, 2-day ski pass 132SFr, under 19 118SFr; 6-night stay, 7-day pass 382 SFr, under 19 339SFr. In summer (with lift pass for two operating hiking lifts) 1-night stay, 2-day pass 53SFr, under 19 40SFr.)

In summer, lifts are not necessary for hiking access, so the better choice (and closer to more hiking trails) is the **Jugendherberge (HI),** Seewaldstr. (tel./fax 377 13 97), which has a friendly, multilingual staff. Go past the tourist office and bear left down the hill (you'll see a sign). Each dorm has a balcony overlooking either the *Untersee* or the rugged Engadine slopes. Be sure to stock up on 0.50SFr coins for the shower. (Dorms 26SFr; doubles 96SFr. Sheets and hearty breakfast included. Bag lunch 7.50SFr; dinner 12SFr. Reception 7-10am and 5-10pm. No lockout. Curfew 10pm; key available. Open mid-June to mid-Oct. and mid-Dec. to mid-Apr.) For more luxurious, private living, **Pension Suveran** (tel. 377 19 69; fax 377 19 75) is the quiet, homey, wood-paneled chalet you came to Switzerland to find. Follow directions to Haus Florentium. (In summer, singles 47SFr, doubles 84SFr. In winter, 58SFr, 106SFr. Add 10SFr in winter for stays of less than 3 nights. Breakfast included. Closed in Nov.) **Camping Arosa** (tel. 377 17 45; fax 377 30 05), downhill from the hostel, is open year-round in a valley with a brook and offers showers (0.50SFr) and cooking facilities (7.30-8.30SFr, children 4-4.50SFr; tents 4.50SFr; check-in 5-5:30pm).

LUGE MUCH? Before the advent of spandex uni-suits and titanium, flying down mountains was a very simple affair. As early as 1883, the natives of Arosa found their sleds missing and the hills outside the town sprinkled with recovering English invalids. These dashing chaps officially brought the sport of tobogganing to Switzerland in 1883 when they started the Davos Tobogganing Club and inaugurated the famed Cresta Run. Among the many innovations tested on the Arosa hills were iron runners and the head-first plunge technique. A quote from *The Bystander* in 1905 perhaps summed it up best: "Tobogganing itself is absurd. It glories in being absurd."

🍴 **FOOD.** The best budget eatery in Arosa is **Orelli's Restaurant,** Poststr. (tel. 377 12 08), down the hill from the tourist office. Hikers young and old chomp happily in this family restaurant decorated with Mickey Mouse and stained glass. Thriftmeisters can eat soup and 4 slices of bread for only 4.50SFr while gazing at the panoramic view. A special vegetarian *Menü* (9.50-14SFr), salad buffet (7-14SFr), and warm entrees (7.50-16SFr) round out your options. (Open 7:30am-9pm. Closed May and Nov. MC, Visa.) **Café/Restaurant Oasis** (tel. 377 22 20), diagonally across the street from Orelli's, has an outdoor deck just over Poststr., suitable for people-watching and mountain-gazing. Entrees include spaghetti *bolognese* for 11SFr, or chicken *cordon bleu* with fries for 15SFr. (Open 8:30am-11pm.) You'll want to save a few francs for dessert at **Café-Confiserie Kaiser** (tel. 377 34 54), on Poststr. around the bend from Orelli's. This cozy café concocts killer confections (meringues 7SFr). The *Menüs* aren't too bad either (spaghetti 11SFr, *Spätzle-Gemüse gratin* 14SFr). Get groceries at the **Co-op,** before the tourist office on Poststr. (open M-F 8am-12:30pm and 2-6:30pm, Sa 8am-4pm), or **Denner Superdiscount** in the main square (open M-W and F 8:30am-12:15pm and 2:30-6:30pm, Sa 8:30am-12:15pm and 1:15-5pm).

🎿 **OUTDOOR ACTIVITIES AND ENTERTAINMENT.** If you're not staying in a dorm with a package ski deal, you can buy separate passes for the 15 **ski lifts and cableways** that hoist skiers to the 70km network of slopes in the Arosa-Tschuggen ski area. Ticket offices in Arosa love making passes (all-day passes, morning passes, afternoon passes, 1½-day passes, "choose-your-day" passes, etc. 50SFr per day; 256SFr for 1 week; 385SFr for 2. AmEx, DC, MC, Visa). The smaller Tschuggen-sector day pass is 30SFr. Children under 15 ski for half-price; ages 16-19 and seniors get a 15% discount.

When the snow melts, spring uncovers baby rabbits and over 200km of flower-covered **hiking** paths. An **Alpine guide** leads 7- and 9-hour hikes at beginning, intermediate, and advanced levels for only 10SFr. (Late June to mid-Oct. Tu-Th. Contact the tourist office for details.) For a mellow hike below the treeline, start at the hill right of the Co-op and trek along the ridge overlooking the Obersee to the small town of Maran, where you can catch a bus back to Arosa (1hr.) Though not necessary for access to good hiking, two cable cars operate in summer. The **Weisserhornbahn cable car,** above the train station, whisks travelers to the top of the Weisserhorn (every 20min. 24SFr, round-trip 30SFr; 30% off with SwissPass). From the 2653m summit, you can gaze upon all of the Engadine, all the way to San Bernardino. At the other end of town (accessible by bus) is the **Hörnli-Express.** A 1½-hour hike follows the ridge between lifts; longer hikes wind into the valleys opposite the town.

For the more sedentary, the **fish** of the *Obersee* and local rivers bit friskily. Permits are available from the tourist office (day 25SFr, week 65SFr, 2 weeks 100SFr, month 125SFr). The Untersee's **free beach** welcomes swimmers and sunbathers. The **International Jazz Festival** in late July grants free admission to various local venues. The festival features New Orleans jazz played by American, Swiss, Australian, and English bands. Previous performers include Tuba Fats and Jambalaya. The **Humorfestival** revs up in mid-December with artists from all over the world putting up comedy shows, pantomimes, and skits (tickets 30SFr; available at the tourist office). Listen to country music and buy discounted spring ski passes at the **Ski and Country Festival** in mid-March

DAVOS

Davos sprawls along the valley floor under 7 mountains laced densely with the wires of chair-lifts and cable cars. Because of its sprawling nature, Davos is not a particularly easy place to get around without a car. Settled in 1289 by the Wallisers, Davos emerged as a health resort in the 19th century and quickly became a finely tuned ski center that challenges St. Moritz as the ski and spa capital of Graubünden. The influx of tourists in recent decades has given Davos the impersonal feel of a large tourist center, but the thrill of carving your turns down the famed run from Weissfluhgipfel to Kublis (with a 2000m vertical drop) may just make up for that.

⊠ ORIENTATION AND PRACTICAL INFORMATION. Davos is easily accessible by **train** from **Chur** via **Landquart** (1½hr., every hr. 4:59am-9:06pm, 26SFr) or **Klosters** (7.40SFr) on the Rhätische Bahn lines. The town is divided into two areas, **Davos-Dorf** and **Davos-Platz,** each with its own train station and linked by the long **Prome-nade.** Davos-Platz is the site of the tourist office, main post office, and most other places of interest to budget travelers. Davos-Dorf is closer to the quiet *Davoser-see.* **Buses** (2SFr, with SwissPass 1SFr) run between the 2 train stations and stop near major hotels and the hostel on the *Davosersee.* For travelers with cars, **park-ing lots** line the Promenade and Talstr. but be aware that the Promenade traffic is one-way heading west (parking generally 1SFr per hr.; free at *Kongresszentrum*). Rent **bikes** at the Davos-Dorf station (26SFr per day).

The high-tech **main tourist office** *(Kurverein)*, Promenade 67 (tel. 415 21 21; fax 415 21 00; email davos@davos.ch; www.davos.ch), in Davos-Platz, plans skiing and hiking packages and helps find rooms, though not for most budget accommoda-tions. Walk up the hill to the right of the Davos-Platz train station and then right along the Promenade for 5 minutes. The tourist office is on the left. A smaller **branch office** is across from the Davos-Dorf train station. (Both offices open M-F 8:30am-6pm, Sa 8:30am-5pm; phone lines open 8am-7pm daily.) The train stations **exchange currency, store luggage** (5SFr; Davos-Platz open M-Sa 4:50am-9pm, Su 5:50am-9pm; Davos-Dorf open daily 6am-8pm), and rent **lockers** (2SFr). There is **Internet access** at **Rampa,** Promenade 123 (12SFr per hr.; open M-F 8am-noon and 1:30-6:30pm, Sa 8am-4pm; AmEx, MC, Visa). Dial 111 for **emergency** or a **late-night pharmacy.** The main **post office** is in Davos-Platz at Promenade 43 (open M-F 7:45am-6pm, Sa 8:30am-11pm). The **postal code** is CH-7270.

PHONE CODE	The **city code** for Davos is 081.

⊠⊡ ACCOMMODATIONS AND FOOD. Wherever you stay, ask for the Davos **visitor's card,** which grants unlimited travel on the city's buses and reduced tickets for plays, concerts, ice rinks, swimming pools, and golf courses. The folks at **Jacob-shorn ski mountain** have made their youth-oriented mountain accessible to budget travelers by opening 3 dorm houses for winter thrill-seekers that are sold as a package with their ski passes (passes good only for Jacobshorn mountain; tel. for all 3 dorms 414 90 20, fax 414 91 09; all 3 open Nov.-May; all credit cards accepted). All 3 houses have essentially the same furnishings: plain white rooms and down quilts to keep you warm. House #1, the **Snowboarder's Palace,** Oberestr. 45-47, located right above the Davos-Platz tourist office, is closest to town, and has the most authentic ski-lodge appearance, complete with wooden balconies (1-night, 2-day ski pass 150-160SFr; 6-night, 7-day ski pass 480-540SFr; breakfast included). Closer to the main ski lift is house #2, the bland **Guest House Bolgenhof,** Brämabüel-str., right beneath the Davos-Platz train station (1-night, 2-day ski-pass 160SFr; 6-night, 7-day ski-pass 540SFr; breakfast included). The most hopping house is house #3, the **Bolgenschanze,** Skistr. 1, conveniently located over the bar where much of the aprés-ski debauchery occurs (1-night, 2-day ski-pass 160SFr; 6-night, 7-day ski pass 600SFr; breakfast and dinner included; must be over 18).

For more reclusive types, and in the summer when the big dorms are closed, the **Hotel Montana,** Bahnhofstr. Dorf 2 (413 34 08) is a great buy, and very accessible from the Davos-Dorf station. The hotel has clean, carpeted rooms for 1 to 4 people with TV and shower or bath. (In summer, 25SFr per person; in winter, 60SFr. Reception at bar downstairs. Open daily 11am-midnight.) **Camping Färich** (tel. 416 10 43) in Davos-Dorf is a 4-star facility relatively close to the ski lifts and attrac-tions of the town. Take bus #1 (dir.: Pischa) to "Stilli." (4.50SFr per person, chil-dren half-price; tents 6SFr. Open May 18-Sept. 29.)

Haven't had your *Rösti* fix for the day yet? Visit **Röstizzeria,** Promenade 128 (tel. 416 33 23), and satisfy your craving for as little as 14.50SFr in a dining room deco-rated with carved wood and Japanese fans. There's also pizza from 11SFr. (Open 6-11pm; AmEx, MC, Visa.) The bright, flowery, locally beloved **Café-Konditorei**

Weber, Promenade 148 (tel. 410 11 22), in Davos-Dorf, is a good stop for a hot drink on a cold day (open daily 6:30am-7pm). Grab a Bud and a bar stool—American style—at **Café Carlos,** Promenade 58 (tel. 413 17 22), in a mall opposite the tourist office in Davos-Platz. The restaurant offers American standards (burgers and sandwiches), and everything is under 20SFr. (Open 8am-midnight. AmEx, MC, Visa.) A **Migros** is located on the Promenade in both Davos-Dorf (open M-F 8:30am-12:30pm and 1:30-6:30pm, Sa 8am-4pm) and Davos-Platz (open M-F 8:30am-6:30pm, Sa 8am-4pm). An enormous brand-new **Co-op** is across from the train station. (Open M-F 8am-6:30pm, Sa 8am-5pm; restaurant open M-Th 8am-6:30pm, F 8am-8pm, Sa 8am-5pm, Su 10am-6:30pm.)

🔘 **SIGHTS AND ACTIVITIES.** To get in shape for Davos' outdoor activities, you can exercise your eyes at the Davos **Kirchner Museum** (tel. 413 22 02), the frosted glass structure opposite the Hotel Belvedere on the Promenade, between Dorf and Platz. The museum houses an extensive collection of Ernst Ludwig Kirchner's artwork. This avatar of 20th-century German Expressionism lived in Davos for nearly 20 years before his death, and is buried in the Davos cemetery. The museum's talented curators are kept on the move with an ever-changing exhibition that places Kirchner's work alongside the work of related artists. (Open daily Dec. 25-Easter 10am-noon and 2-6pm; off season daily 2-6pm. 8SFr, students 5SFr.)

Davos proudly presents Europe's largest natural **ice rink** (tel. 415 36 00; 22,000m^2), with space for figure skating, ice dancing, hockey, speed skating, and curling (open only in winter; admission 5SFr; skate rental 5.50SFr). In the summer, enjoy the public indoor/outdoor **swimming pools** with **sauna** and solarium. (6.50SFr, students 4.50SFr.) At the **Davosersee,** you can swim, sail, and windsurf.

🏔 **OUTDOOR ACTIVITIES.** Davos has outdoor attractions for all seasons and travelers at just about every level of physical fitness, ranging from intense skiing to spectacular hikes to peaceful funicular rides and garden rambles.

SKIING

Davos provides direct access to 3 mountains—the Parsenn, Jakobshorn, and Schatzalp—and 5 **skiing areas,** covering every degree of difficulty. **Parsenn,** with its long runs and fearsome vertical drops, is the mountain around which Davos built its reputation. Unfortunately, Parsenn's fame has brought the hordes of tourists which can create long lines up to 2 hours long for the main lift. Passes to Parsenn also allow access to 3 other mountains (day pass 54SFr). **Jacobshorn** has found a

---

BUNA SAIRA! Switzerland's oft-forgotten fourth national language, Romansh, is spoken only in the province of Graubünden, where it is an official cantonal language along with German and Italian. Up until about 1850, it was the most spoken language in the canton. By 1880, Romansh speakers dropped to 39.8% of the population, a percentage that kept dropping, then leveled out as the primary language for 23.6% of the residents in Graubünden. In some villages like S-chanf, Romansh speakers are in the majority, and even in large towns like Chur they form a quarter of the population. All Romansh speakers (except toddlers) are fully bilingual. Romansh is taught in the schools, and its speakers support five Romansh newspapers and 13 to 14 hours of TV broadcast time in Romansh. The language is supported by the Swiss government, but its survival is threatened by the fact that its speakers are divided by at least four major dialects that arose from the mountain isolation of many high-altitude villages. Romansh didn't become a written language until the 16th-century, when people began publishing tracts on preserving Romansh identity. Now, Romansh has a small literature of its own and translations of everything from the Bible to Asterix comics. Maybe when you're traveling through Switzerland, you'll overhear someone calling out, "Bun di!" (hello), "grazia" (thank you), or even "Tge bel che ti es!" (how beautiful you are!).

niche with the younger crowd, especially since the opening of a snowboarding "fun-park" with 2 half pipes. To accommodate younger skiers on tight budgets, combination ski pass and lodging deals (see p. 385) are available (day pass alone 50SFr). The smallest mountain is **Schatzalp** (day pass 26SFr). The **regional ski pass** covers all 7 mountains in the Davos-Klosters area, including unlimited travel on most transport facilities, and doesn't cost much more than individual mountain tickets (2 days 116SFr, 1 week 268SFr). Comprehensive information and maps are available at the tourist office. In addition to downhill runs, Davos boasts 75km of **cross-country trails** throughout the valley, including a flood-lit trail at night and a trail on which dogs are allowed. **The Swiss Ski School of Davos,** Promenade 157 (tel. 416 24 54; fax 416 59 51), offers lessons, starting at 30SFr for a half-day downhill lesson and at 55SFr for a half-day snowboard lesson.

HIKING

Davos doesn't wilt when the snow melts; instead, Davos's snowless slopes display a web of over 450km of hiking trails. One main ski lift on each mountain is open in summer, and many of the area's trails depend on these lifts to bring hikers out of the densely inhabited valley. The last Saturday in July brings the **Swiss Alpine Marathon,** a grueling 72km mountain race.

PANORAMAWEG (2HR.). The Panoramaweg, a relatively flat trail that follows the contours of the broad nude hills above town, offers views of the valley and the southern Swiss Alps. The hike begins from either the top of the Gotschnabahn (from Klosters) or from the "Panoramaweg" stop on the Parsennbahn, and traverses the distance in between. There is another cable car in the middle that allows you to shorten the trip (36SFr, SwissPass and Half-fare Card 50% reduction).

DAVOS-PLATZ TO MONSTEIN (5HR.). A more isolated hike into an adjoining valley requires no cable car. Take bus #8 from Davos-Platz to Sertig-Dörfli where the hike begins. From Sertig-Dörfli follow signs to "Fenezfurgga," which will take you up 600m past waterfalls and through a valley that divides the 3063m Hoch Duncan and the 3006m Alpihorn. A wall of cold stone does a good job helping you feel isolated from the resort world beyond. The trek ends in Monstein, where buses connect to Glaris and then Davos.

ALPINE GARDEN. A hike (or funicular ride) up to the Schatzalp reveals the Alpine Garden with 800 different species of plants. (Open mid-May to Sept. 9am-5pm. 3SFr. Guided tours in German M 2pm—other languages by arrangement.)

NEAR DAVOS: KLOSTERS

Klosters-Platz and Klosters-Dorf are connected to Chur through Landquart (1hr., every hr. 5:21am-9:29pm, 19SFr) and St. Moritz (2hr., every hr. 5:38am-9:27pm, 34SFr). Local buses run between Dorf and Platz and the major ski lifts (1-6 stops 1SFr, 7-10 2SFr, more than 10 3SFr; free with guest card).

Across the Gotschna and Parsenn mountains lies Davos's sister ski resort, Klosters. Though Klosters is but 10 minutes from Davos by train, it is a world removed in atmosphere. While Davos makes an extra effort to be cosmopolitan, Klosters retains much of its rural alpine charm, from the friendly locals to the traditional Engadine-style chalets with their asymmetric roofs. If you don't want the bustle of Davos, peaceful Klosters offers access to the same outdoor activities; most ski packages include mountains from both towns, and Klosters' main ski lift takes you to a pass where you can ski down to either town.

◪ ORIENTATION AND PRACTICAL INFORMATION. Like Davos, Klosters is divided into **Klosters-Platz** and **Klosters-Dorf,** connected by a 5-minute bus ride or a 3-minute train ride; most activity occurs in Platz. There are tourist offices in both Platz and Dorf, but the **main tourist office** *(Kurverein)* is in Klosters-Platz (tel. (081) 410 20 20; fax 410 20 10; email info@klosters.ch; www.klosters.ch). From the train station turn right, turn right again at the Co-op, and cross the street to the building with the "i." The friendly staff can help locate lodgings, suggest hikes, and **exchange currency.** They offer the **Klosters guest card** (also available at hotels), valid for bargain tickets to events and reduced admission to local facilities. (Open May-Nov. M-F 8:30am-noon and 2:30-6pm, Sa 8:30am-noon and 2:30-5pm; Dec.-April M-F 8:30am-noon and 2:30-6pm, Sa 8:30am-noon and 2-6pm, Su 9-11:30am and 3:30-6:30pm.) The Klosters-Platz **train station** provides **currency exchange** (open 6am-8:30pm), **lockers** (2SFr), and **luggage storage** (open 6am-8:30pm; 3SFr) and **rents scooters** (18SFr per day, 12 SFr per half-day). Rent **bikes** all over town (info tel. 410 20 20), including **Madrisa Sport** (tel. 422 28 65) on Haus Bahnhofpl. (38SFr per day; 130SFr for 6 days). The **Helios Apotheke (pharmacy),** is opposite the main tourist office (open M-F 7:45am-noon and 2-6:30pm; Sa 7:45-noon and 2-4pm; dial 111 for late-night help). The **post office** is right from the station (open M-F 7:30am-noon and 1:45-6:15pm; Sa 8:30-11am).

⌂ ACCOMMODATIONS AND FOOD. Jugendherberge Soldanella (HI), Talstr. 73 (tel. (081) 422 13 16; fax 422 52 09), is run by a friendly and knowledgeable family. Head right from the Klosters-Platz train station, bear left at the rotary, turn right on Talstr., and hike 10 minutes uphill. This massive, renovated chalet with wood paneling, a comfortable reading room, and a flagstone terrace treats guests to a view of the Madrisa and distant glaciers. (Dorms 25.50SFr; doubles 32.50 per person, with sink 36.50SFr. Family rooms 36.50SFr per person. Tourist tax 1.90SFr per day in summer, 2.20SFr in winter; half-price for children. Sheets and breakfast included. Dinner 11.50SFr. Reception 7-9:30am and 5-10pm. No lockout or curfew. Closed Easter-early July and mid-Oct. to mid-Dec. AmEx, MC, DC, Visa.) At **Schweizerhaus** (tel. (081) 422 14 81) near the Klosters-Dorf train station, you'll find newly remodeled, well-lit rooms close to the smaller Madrisa ski mountain. The young owner is a good source of information for outings. (Dorms 40SFr, in winter 50SFr. Breakfast, sheets, and TV included. Closed May and Nov.) Some great deals await in *Privatzimmer (*private rooms) from 15SFr (list at tourist office). **Gasthaus Casanna,** Landstr. 171 (tel. 422 12 29; fax 422 62 78), is a locally favored joint offering traditional Swiss dishes (around 12.50SFr), such as delicious homemade *Spaetzli* with mushrooms (open M-F 7:30am-midnight; closed Nov.). **Hitz bakery** serves sugary treats and fresh bread (open in summer M-F 7am-6pm, Sa-Su 7am-5pm; in winter daily 7am-6:30pm). The **Co-op** has cheap groceries, and the restaurant upstairs serves *spaghetti Napoli* for 8SFr (open M-F 8am-12:30pm and 2-6:30pm, Sa 8am-4pm; restaurant open M-Sa 9am-8pm, Su 10am-8pm).

⚑ OUTDOOR ACTIVITIES. Klosters is first and foremost a ski town, though much of its activity revolves around Davos. **Ski passes** for the Klosters-Davos region run 116SFr for 2 days and 268SFr for 1 week (includes public transportation). Klosters does have 2 ski mountains of its own. The **Madrisabahn** leaves from Klosters-Dorf (1-day pass 43SFr, 6-day pass 198SFr). The **Grotschnabahn** ticket also gives access to Parsenn and Strela in Davos and Madrisa in Klosters (1-day pass 54SFr). The **ski school** in Klosters, located in the tourist office, offers ski and snowboard lessons for children and adults (group lessons from 50-60SFr per day; call 410 20 28 the day before to book private lessons).

In the summer, the tourist office has an extensive list of **hiking** suggestions, with exact directions, elevation levels, anticipated times, and a trail map. Got vertigo? Stay close to the luscious green valley floor and make a large loop, going from the Klosters Protestant church up-valley on Monbielstr. to Monbiel. Loop again around toward the left and follow the signs to Pt. 487 and Monbieler Wald. The trail ends at the Alpenrösli restaurant, where you can grab Talstr. back to the hostel. The **Klosters Adventure Program** offers guided hikes and mountain tours, canyoning, horseback riding, river rafting, glacier walks, canoeing, mountain-bike tours, paragliding, and more every weekday mid-June to mid-October (guided day-hike 30SFr, river rafting 80SFr).

LOWER ENGADINE VALLEY

The Engadine Valley takes its name from the Romansch name *(En)* for the Inn River that flows through the valley and on through Innsbruck, Austria. One transportation line runs from Maloja, at one end of the valley, to Scuol on the other side, connecting all towns by train or short bus rides. The region is divided into the Upper and Lower Engadine, divided by the border town of Brail, just west of Zernez and the Swiss National Park.

The Lower Engadine valley represents Graubünden at its purest. Skiing never quite caught on here, and, unaltered by the swift torrent of change brought by the ski industry, the people maintain a strong connection to their land and culture. The Lower Engadine is a stronghold of the **Romansh language,** and nearly every sign is printed in this Latinate relic. The region may not be a skier's paradise, but **hikers** revel in the untouched Alpine ecosystem of the **Swiss National Park** just south of the valley. Regional travel is easy with the **Lower Engadine Regional Pass** that covers all trains and post buses in the area (3 days of 7 45SFr, with half-fare card 35Fr; 7 days of 14 65SFr, 50SFr).

TRANSPORT HUB: ZERNEZ

Zernez is a gateway to the **Swiss National Park,** and home to the headquarters of the park, the **National Parkhouse. Trains** depart from Zernez for **Scuol** (30min., every hr. 6:53am-9:13pm, 11.80SFr) and **Samedan** (30min., every hr. 6:31am-9:04pm, 12.60SFr) with connections to the rest of Switzerland, including **St. Moritz** (45min., 16.40SFr). The train station has **luggage storage** (5SFr) and **currency exchange** (open M-Sa 6:20-7am and 8am-7:30pm, Su 8:10am-12:40pm and 2:10-5:40pm).

From the train station, the road to the left that curves through town leads to the **tourist office** *(Kurverein*; tel. (081) 856 13 00; fax 856 11 55; open in summer M-F 8:30am-noon and 2-6:30pm, Sa 9-11am and 2-4pm; in winter M-F 8:30am-noon and 2-5:30pm, Sa 9-11am and 2-4pm). The same road continues to the **National Parkhouse** (tel. (081) 856 13 00); turn right at the T. Like the park, the parkhouse is only open in summer. It provides information about trail safety and has an extensive selection of maps. (Open daily in summer 8:30am-6pm.) The parkhouse also houses a small **museum,** primarily for children, about the park (same hours, 4SFr). For **bike rentals** (35SFr per day) and any emergency outdoor gear (it's expensive, so only buy what you need), visit **Sport Sarsura,** right before the tourist office (open M-F 8am-noon and 2-6:30pm, Sa 8am-noon and 2-5pm). The **Co-op** is across the street (same hours as sports store).

Hotel Post (tel. 851 55 00, fax 851 55 99), left from the main intersection, is a classy hotel that offers less classy rooms in a back building. The dorms are minimal but clean; rooms overlook a parking lot. (Dorms 18SFr, sleepsack 5SFr, breakfast 12SFr. Reception open daily 9am-10pm. Closed Nov.-Dec. Visa, MC.) There is camping at **Camping Cul** (tel. 856 14 62), across the train tracks from town, on the river (6.50SFr, tents 4SFr, open May-Oct. 15). For some of the best pizza in Graubünden head to **Grotia Pizzeria Mirta,** at the main intersection (pizza 13-17SFr; open Tu-Su 8am-10pm; closed May and Nov.; Visa).

THE SWISS NATIONAL PARK

The Swiss National Park offers hikes with views that rival the best hiking areas elsewhere in Switzerland, with one crucial difference: the park's isolation from man-made constructs (including the ubiquitous cowbell) allows hikers to experience the undiluted wildness of the natural terrain. The park became the first national park in the Alps when it was established in 1914. While its size (only 169km²) pales in comparison to American or Canadian national parks, efforts to protect the ecological balance in the park are far more vigorous than in its North American counterparts. In an effort to minimize disturbance, the park has fewer trails than other mountainous areas in Switzerland, but the lower density of trails in no way limits possibilities for incredible hiking. In fact, the successful conservation movement creates the rare opportunity to hike among marmots, ibexes, eagles, bearded vultures, and other creatures seen nowhere else.

⚐ PRACTICAL INFORMATION. Transportation in the park is not complicated. One road goes from Zernez through the middle of the park. **Post buses** leave from **Zernez** and stop at numbered parking places along the road within the park, where the trails start. A road from **Scuol** skirts the western edge of the park, and has the same bus setup. Many landmarks and landforms have Romansh names. The word for "mountain" is *piz*, *val* is "valley," *ova* is "stream," *pra* is "meadow," and *chamana* means "mountain hut."

⚐ ACCOMMODATIONS. Almost all hikes leave from one of the parking places clustered around **Hotel Il Fuorn** (tel. 856 12 26, fax 856 18 01). If it's a convenient location you want, Il Fuorn is perfect. Unfortunately, the sagging foam matresses in the dorm beds provided in the shack across the road from the main hotel would give even the weariest hiker trouble sleeping. For a little more comfort, the hotel beds are a wise splurge. The food, while not bad, is ridiculously overpriced—when the next building is 10km away, you're at their mercy. (Dorms 17SFr, breakfast 12SFr. Singles 60SFr, breakfast included. Open May-Oct.) There are **mountain huts** at the end of some hikes (ask at Parkhouse).

⚐ HIKING. There are few level trails in the park. Most trails in the park involve a lot of climbing, often into areas still covered in snow. Be sure to check in at the **Parkhouse** in Zernez to see which trails are navigable. Their advice is not tempered by paranoia of liability, so when they say a trail is too dangerous, they mean it. The trails that require no mountaineering gear are marked with white-red-white blazes. The Swiss are practically mountain goats so even some of the non-mountaineering routes can be tricky.

FROM SCUOL AND BACK (5HR.). Take the bus (dir.: Scharl) to "Val Minger" (9.4SFr; with Eurail, SwissPass 4SFr), which takes you over cliff-hanging roads with views into valleys consumed by avalanches. From the bus stop, cross the bridge and turn left on the trail, which begins with a slow and steady climb up rocky stream beds. The excitement lies behind you with views of **Piz Pradatsch.**

When the trail moves above the tree line it enters a half-pipe shaped valley with meadows closely cropped by ibex and red deer. At the end of the valley the solitary, majestic **Piz Plavna Dadaint** serves as a beacon to pull you through the valley to the **Sur il Foss pass.** The view here is unique for its intimacy—all the towering mountains are little more than a narrow valley away. From Sur il Foss you can head around the head of the valley to the **Val dal Botsch pass,** which then leads to Il Fuorn in the center of the park. This route is only safe in later summer when the snow has melted, and even then should only be attempted with hiking poles and very sturdy boots. The saner route leads right, toward "Tarasp Fontana." The initial descent can be tricky, depending on recent rock slides, so don't hesitate to use your hands here. The trail passes into a wide rocky plain, bordered by cliffs that create a visual tunnel, training all eyes forward to the mountain range over Scuol, and backward to Piz Nair and the peaks in front of it. The trail heads through the woods to **Tarasp,** where a bus returns to Scuol (every hr. 7:45am-6:30pm).

TO MUNT LA SCHERA (5HR.). Take the bus from Zernez to Il Fuorn (Parking 6) and head back down the road to Parking 5. Follow the trail originating there to Alp Buffolora and Munt la Schera. Some trails have viewpoints; this entire trail *is* a viewpoint. The inauspicious beginnings, a gradual 1-hour ascent through the woods, bring you above the tree line where the trail curves around the side of the mountain, with each turn exposing another view of some of Switzerland and Italy's mightiest mountains and lushest valleys. Follow the sign up to **Munt la Schera** to take it all in at once. Take a few deep breaths before heading for the summit. While standing on the flat top of Munt la Schera you may feel you are resting on a pedestal overlooking the entire world. From the top, Munt la Schera appears to be encircled by a moat, which in turn is completely surrounded by hulking mountains, leaning in to see the view that you have. From the top follow signs to "Buffolora." If the view from Munt la Schera doesn't have you singing yet, the ridge you walk, hemmed by endless meadows, will undoubtedly put you in a mood to do your Julie Andrews routine. The trail quickly descends Munt la Schera, then leisurely winds down to **Buffolora** where buses return to Il Fuorn and Zernez.

TO THE BEARDED VULTURE NEST (3HR.). This hike is particularly well-known because it passes the nesting site of bearded vultures, rare birds with a 3m wingspan. Take the bus from Zernez along the main road through the park to Parking 8 for a shorter hike that gets you into the body of the park. From Parking 8 follow signs to "Stablechod." The first 2 rest stops are open fields where marmots run wild, whistling all the while. The trail climbs steeply to the **Margunet saddle,** with dramatic views of narrow valleys on either side. The saddle is the best place to spot bearded vultures. From the saddle follow signs down to **Il Fuorn.** The trail traverses a valley destroyed by an avalanche in the winter of 1999.

NEAR THE SWISS NATIONAL PARK: SCUOL

The Scuol train station sits at the end of the line. Trains depart Scuol every hour (5:55am-10:34pm) for Zernez (11.80SFr), Samedan (24SFr; for connections to the rest of Switzerland), and St. Moritz (26SFr), among other destinations.

Scuol, the biggest town in the Lower Engadine, is also the closest thing to a resort in the area, thanks to its spas. The development here, however, has been done in tactful moderation and does not approach the level of commercialization found in ski capitals of the Upper Engadine. All goods and services are centralized on the main street ("Stradun"), along with a few beautifully grand hotels. Spreading between the Inn River below the town and the rugged peaks above is the *Altstadt*, complete with narrow cobblestone streets.

⌷ ORIENTATION AND PRACTICAL INFORMATION. The train station **rents scooters** for 18SFr per day, **changes currency,** and **stores luggage** for 5SFr (open daily 5:30am-8:30pm). From the train station, walk to the left and turn right at the first street, bear right at the intersection, then turn left on Stradun. One of the first buildings you will reach is the **tourist office** *(Kurverein;* tel. (081) 861 22 22, fax 861 22 23, www.scuol.ch; open M-F 8am-noon and 2-6:30pm, Sa 10am-noon and 2-6pm, Su 4-6pm). Get **Internet access** at the **Glatscharia,** where you can check email while savoring a bowl of gourmet ice cream (12SFr per hr., open Tu-Su 1:30-8pm). Farther down on the left is **Sport Heinrich Scuol** (tel. 864 19 56), where you can buy last minute hiking gear before you hit the mountains (and high-altitude prices) (open in summer M-F 8am-noon and 2-6:30pm, Sa until 5pm; in winter M-F 8am-noon and 1:30-6:30pm, Sa until 6pm). On the right is the **Apotheke Engadinaisa** (tel. 864 13 05) for all your **pharmaceutical** needs (open M-F 8am-noon and 2-6:30pm, Sa 8am-noon and 2-4pm). In an **emergency** dial 864 93 70.

⌷⌷⌷ ACCOMMODATIONS, FOOD, AND ENTERTAINMENT. There are no institutionalized budget lodgings in Scuol, but there are 20 or so houses scattered throughout the *Altstadt* that offer **private rooms** for under 30SFr, including breakfast. The tourist office compiles a list of rooms; call ahead for availability. **Gurlaina Camping** (tel. (081) 854 15 01) lies on the opposite bank of the Inn River (6SFr, tent 12SFr; prices subject to change). The cheapest non-pizzeria eatery in town is **Hotel Lischama** (tel. (081) 864 11 71), which is just enough off the beaten track to avoid most tourists. To get there, backtrack from the tourist office, and bear left at the fork. They offer a whole page of *Rösti* specialties from 11.50SFr, as well as pizzas and pastas. (Open daily 8am-midnight.)

The spa **Engadin Bad Scuol** (tel. 861 20 00) is in the center of town, with an entrance on the main street. The newly renovated complex includes saunas, salt baths, cold and hot water grottoes, and their specialty, the combined Roman-Irish bath—a great way to end a hard day's hike through the wind-chilled Alps (23SFr per day; open M-Sa 8am-10pm, Su 9am-10pm.)

NEAR THE SWISS NATIONAL PARK: GUARDA

To reach Guarda take the train from Zernez (6.80SFr) or Scuol (6.20SFr). Both connect to a postal bus which climbs to Guarda (every 2hr. 8:41am-6:44pm, 2.40SFr).

Across the river from the undisturbed nature of the Swiss National Park dwells the undisturbed late-medieval village of Guarda, high above the main thoroughfare of the Lower Engadine. The hill that separates Guarda from its train station isolates the town from any signs of modern times. The townfolk are super-friendly here—the enormous partitioned doors on all the houses often have the top half open as a welcome to neighbors and anyone else who may wander by. Follow the one main road to the top of the town for the **tourist office** (*Kurverein;* tel. 862 23 42, fax 862 21 66; open in summer M-F 10-11am and 3:30-5:30pm, in winter M-F 4-5:30pm). A **market** also awaits near the bottom of town (M-F 8am-noon and 2-6pm, Sa 8am-noon and 2-4pm).

Two of the sweetest women in the world are in charge of the 15 or so relatively cheap **private rooms** in Guarda. Frau Franziscus, in *Chasa* **(House) 46,** offers spacious single rooms with a desk, a big comfortable bed, and a sweet-smelling bathroom, right on the town square (32SFr per person, breakfast 8SFr; open June-Dec.). If Chasa 46 is full, consider the equally luxurious, but slightly more expensive **Pension Val Tuoi** (tel. 862 24 70, fax 862 24 07), with private bathrooms (singles 44SFr, with 2 or more persons 37SFr; breakfast included; open daily 7:30am-10pm June-Dec.). The only cheap place to eat in town is **Hotel Piz Buin,** cooking up homemade dishes for under 15SFr (open daily 9am-11pm from late June-Mar. Visa, MC).

ZUOZ

Though technically in the Upper Engadine, Zuoz's adherence to architectural and linguistic (Romansh) traditions, as well as the friendly attitude of the citizens, mark it as a Lower Engadine town. Its position on the border of both regions makes it a good central point from which to explore the Engadine Valley. Burnt to the ground by residents in 1499 to keep it from the Austrians, Zuoz was rebuilt in the early 16th century and remains essentially unchanged today. Ibexes, pinwheels, and flowers float on the whitewashed walls of village houses, and a big carved bear defends the fountains from bloodthirsty Imperial Habsburg troops. Zuoz takes pride in its unique holidays and traditional festivals. On March 1, the **Chalandamarz** engulfs all of Engadine as young boys wander from house to house, ring huge bells, and sing songs to drive off evil spirits and welcome the spring. Originally a pagan fertility rite, the more peculiar **San Gian's Day** commemorates John the Baptist on July 24, when village boys spritz girls with water from Zuoz's many fountains. The Swiss maidens then flee to their houses and pour buckets of water over the boys' heads. Perhaps there's some Italian blood in this region yet.

⏅ ORIENTATION AND PRACTICAL INFORMATION. Zuoz is a short train ride from **St. Moritz** (30min., every hr. 6:53am-9:26pm, 8.60SFr), **Zernez** (20min., every hr. 6:30am-9:10pm, 8.60SFr), and **Samedan** (20min., same train as St. Moritz, 5.60SFr). The train station provides **luggage storage** (5SFr), **bike rental** (26SFr), and **currency exchange** (open M-Sa 6:40am-6:30pm, Su 8:30-11:45am and 1:15-6:30pm). The **tourist office** (*Kurverein;* tel. 854 15 10; fax 854 33 34; email zuoz@compunet.ch; www.zuoz.ch) on Via Maestra provides keys for the church and tower and suggests **hikes.** From the station walk up La Passarella, directly opposite the station. At the top of the pedestrian walkway, turn right on the main street, and the tourist office will be past the main square on your right. (Open July-Aug. and Dec.-Apr. M-F 9am-noon and 3-6pm, Sa 9-11am; May-June and Oct.-

Nov. M-F 9am-noon and 3-5pm.) **Internet access** is available at 1computer in **Klari-nos Restaurant** (15SFr per hr., M-Sa 8:30am-7:30pm). For a late-night **pharmacy,** dial 111. The **post office** is in the train station (open M-F 8am-noon and 2-5:30pm, Sa 8-11am). **The postal code** is CH-7524.

PHONE CODE	The **city code** for Zuoz is 081.

■┌ **ACCOMMODATIONS AND FOOD.** The cheapest lodgings are in the center of town at **Ferienlager Sonder** (tel. 854 07 73). Head down Via Maestra from the tourist office and turn left on tiny Chanels at the sign for "Ferienlager" for simple rooms in a 16th-century building. (Dorms 20SFr. **Kitchen** use 10SFr; sleep sack 5SFr.) At the 400-year-old **Chesa Walther** (tel. 854 13 64) opposite the tourist office, zebra, cougar, and other critter skins adorn the ivy-tangled walls, competing for space with gold-fringed mirrors and antique Graubünden stoves (dorms 35SFr; partial **kitchen** facilities 5SFr). The **Crusch Alva,** in the main square, was the bishop's resting place as he made his grand tours through Graubünden in the 16th century. They have since added a menu for plebeians with a selection of worldly offerings including American burgers, Mexican tortillas, Chinese egg rolls, and Graubünden *Capons* and *Spaetzli.* (Most meals 15-18SFr. Open daily 8am-mid-night. Visa, MC). Raw materials for a meal await at the **Co-op** opposite the station (open M-F 8am-12:15pm and 2-6:30pm, Sa 8am-5pm) or at **Volg** supermarket next to the tourist office (open M-F 8am-noon and 2-6:30pm, Sa 8am-noon and 2-4pm).

◐ ⚔ **SIGHTS AND OUTDOOR ACTIVITIES.** The small **Church San Luzius** on Via Maestra has sweet-smelling pine pews and hymnals in Romansch. Next door is the **prison tower**—preserved as the last wrongdoer left it—filled with blood-curdling, gut-wrenching implements of torture and chilling dungeon cells you can climb into (ask the tourist office for the key).

Zuoz woos **bikers** with 37km of marked trails. For **hikers,** the National Park is right next door, but Zuoz offers a few distinctive hikes of its own. In remembrance of the great artist, the **Via Segantini** leads to views as beautiful as the artist's paint-ings of glacier-laden mountains such as the 4049m **Piz Bernina.** The path begins just past the Hotel Engiadina, on Via Maestra. Turn right on Chröntschet, then cross the driveway to private houses, which will take you to the gravel path labeled "Via Segantini." The trail requires minimal effort and goes from Zuoz to La Punt (2hr.) and Bever (4hr.), where you can catch a train back to Zuoz.

For a more rugged afternoon, follow the **Ova d'Arpiglia** to a crashing 35m water-fall. To find the trail, turn left from the train station and go through the underpass toward the river. Cross the river on the smaller bridge, turn right after the bike rental, and follow the dirt road heading into the woods. At the first sign head to "Arpiglia," at the second "Mont Seja," and at the third "Sagl d'Arpiglia" which leads along the stream bank and a larch-lined path to the waterfall. The path then climbs steeply to a green meadow to the right of the falls that burgeons with purple wild-flowers, known locally as the **"Stairway to Heaven."** Signs point the way from this perfect picnic haven back to Zuoz (round-trip 1½hr.).

UPPER ENGADINE VALLEY

The Engadine Valley is known to the outside world primarily for the **skiing** in the Upper Engadine, where 350km of ski trails and 60 ski lifts lace the valley and thou-sands of ski bunnies gather each year. Unlike Zermatt and Grindelwald, where Japanese and American tourists abound, the Upper Engadine attracts mostly Ger-man and Swiss visitors to its trails. Connoisseurs rate the downhill skiing in the Upper Engadine just behind the Jungfrau and Matterhorn regions. The trails lead you away from the valley's resort facade and into the Swiss wilderness. With all these mountains there is, of course, great **hiking** too. The most unique hiking skirts the melting glaciers flowing down from Piz Bernina (at 4049m the highest in the region) and its neighbors. For hikes that don't involve expensive cable cars, Sils and Maloja are good starting points.

Ski rental is standard throughout the region (downhill 35-45SFr per day, cross-country 25SFr). Novices should head for **Zuoz** or **Corviglia (St. Moritz),** experts for **Diavolezza (Pontresina), Corvatsch (Silvaplana), Piz Nair (St. Moritz),** or **Piz Lagalb (Pontresina)** (tel. (081) 830 00 00; www.skiengadin.ch). One-day passes are available for each town (St. Moritz and Celerina are together, as are Sils and Silvaplana). Multiple-day passes are available only for the entire Engadine region—they're not much more expensive and they cover most trains and buses as well (2-day pass 106SFr, 5-day pass 264SFr, 10-day pass 444SFr). Anyone hoping to catch a glimpse of Hollywood should head for **St. Moritz.** Cross-country fanatics should glide to **Pontresina,** where hundreds train for the cruel and unusual **Engadine Ski Marathon,** stretching from Maloja to Zuoz. The race takes place every year on the second Sunday in March (call (081) 842 65 73 or fax 842 65 25 for application/registration; entry fee 70SFr). **Ski schools** in just about every village offer private lessons.

PONTRESINA

Unlike nearly every other town in the Engadine, Pontresina does not lie on the Inn River. Instead, Pontresina has staked its place—away from the bustle of the rest of the Upper Engadine—in one of the highest wind-sheltered valleys of the region, at the confluence of two major rivers that come tearing down from the mountains above. Its enclosure on 3 sides by mountains (only one of which is used for skiing) makes it a favorite among mountaineering types. Every morning, the famous Diavolezza glacier tour draws hordes of hikers. In winter, Pontresina becomes the cross-country skiing capital of the Upper Engadine, with the youth hostel standing as the capitol building at the intersection of the trails. The youth hostl is a tourist magnet in the summer as well, providing the cheapest and most accessible lodings in the region.

⚐ ORIENTATION AND PRACTICAL INFORMATION. Trains run to **St. Moritz** (10min., every 30min. 7am-7:40pm, 4.40SFr) and **Chur** through **Samedan** (2hr., every hr. 7am-8:58pm, 41SFr). **Postal buses** connect Pontresina to the villages of the Upper Engadine Valley all the way to **Maloja.** The train station provides **currency exchange, luggage storage** (5SFr), and **bike rental** (26SFr) all at 1 counter (open daily 6:40am-7pm) as well as **lockers** (2SFr). To get to the town center from the train station, turn right on Via de la Staziun and follow as it winds over 2 rivers, then uphill to the center of town (10min.). The **tourist office** (*Kurverein;* tel. 838 83 00; fax 838 83 10; email pontresina@compunet.ch; www.pontresina.com) occupies the modern "Rondo" building where the Via de la Staziun meets the town. The office plans free excursions (see p. 395), gives hiking advice, and finds hotel vacancies. (Open M-F 8:30am-noon and 2-6pm, Sa 8:30am-noon and 3-6pm. From July-Aug. and Dec.-Mar. also open Su 4-6pm.) The **postal code** is CH-7504.

PHONE CODE	The **city code** for Pontresina is 081.

⚑ ACCOMMODATIONS. The **Jugendherberge Tolais (HI)** (tel. 842 72 23; fax 842 70 31), in the modern, salmon-pink building directly across from the train station, is convenient for early-morning ski ventures and connections throughout the Engadine Valley. The hostel has a restaurant, with great deals for hostelers, table tennis, swings, a soccer field, and knowledgeable service. (Christmas-Easter and July-Oct. dorms 30SFr; other times 27.50SFr. Doubles 110SFr, 105SFr. Breakfast, lockers, and sheets included. Buffet dinner at 6:30pm 11SFr, mandatory in high season. **Laundry** 8.50SFr. Reception 7:30-9:30am and 4-10pm. No lockout. Quiet time from 10pm. AmEx, MC, Visa. Closed April-May.) In the heart of town, **Pension Valtellina** (tel. 842 64 06) is owned by a gentle Italian grandmother who furnishes her cozy rooms with pink bathrooms and warm down blankets. (Singles 54-58SFr; doubles 96-98SFr. Breakfast included. Closed June and early Dec.) The tourist office also has an extensive list of **private rooms** starting at 25SFr per person. **Camping Plauns** (tel. 842 62 85) offers all the amenities a tent-dweller could hope for, from showers to clotheslines. From the trail head just above the train station, walk 3km towards the Bernina Pass to Morteratsch; you can also take the train (dir.: Tirano) to "Morteratsch" (4.40SFr). (7.50SFr; tents 9SFr. Open June to mid-Oct. and mid-Dec. to mid-Apr.)

◻ **FOOD.** The **Puntschella Cafe-Restaurant** (tel. 838 80 30), is the birthplace of the *Engadiner Torte* (a local delicacy made from candied almonds, raisins, layers of cream and nut puree, and crunchy crust; 4.50SFr). The bakery is filled with glazed fruit delicacies, and the restaurant offers local specialties (salad and entree 15SFr). Eat on the back terrace while gazing at Piz Bernina. To reach Puntschella, follow Via Maestra uphill from the tourist office and turn right on Via de Sunovas. (Open in summer 7am-10pm, in winter 7am-9pm. AmEx, Visa, MC.) Down the hill from the tourist office on Via Maestra (5min. walk) you'll find the **Pizzeria Sport Pavillion** (tel. 842 63 49), looking out on tennis courts and Piz Bernina (pizzas 13-18SFr, from 10-11pm all pizzas 10SFr; pasta under 20SFr). The **Co-op** resides at the corner of Via Maestra and Via da Mulin (open M-F 8am-12:15pm and 2-6:30pm, Sa 8am-5pm).

▣ **SIGHTS.** In a well-preserved 17th-century farmhouse, the **Museum Alpin**, Chesa Delnon (tel. 842 72 73), up the street from the tourist office on the left, presents life in the Engadine as it used to be: void of wimpy polypropylene and high-tech hikers and full of bearded, pipe-smoking, wool-clad mountaineering men with picks and ropes. Sixty varieties of recorded bird calls arranged by species twitter forth at the touch of a button in the aviary room, also home to 133 stuffed representatives of Engadine fowl. The brilliantly lit mineral collection displays the hidden beauty you've been hiking over. (Open June-Oct. M-Sa 4-6pm; 5SFr, children 1SFr). At the highest point of the village, the bare exterior of the **church of Santa Maria** conceals a number of well-preserved frescoes, including the **Mary Magdalene cycle** from AD 1495. (Open June-Oct. 3:30-5:30pm.)

▨ **OUTDOOR ACTIVITIES.** In winter Pontresina is a center for **cross-country skiing.** The youth hostel is the *Langlaufzentrum* (cross-country center), and all trails are free for guests. In summer there are a number of **hikes** between the **Muottas Maragl cable car** (one-way 16SFr; base accessible by postal bus to St. Moritz) and the **Piz Languard** and the cable car below it. The level "Hohenweg" rambles above the valley between the cable cars (4hr.). A more demanding route leads from the Muottas Muragl to the **Alp Segantini**, where the famous painter spent his last years (1¼hr.). The trail then climbs to Piz Languard, which offers oft-photographed views up the snaking Morteratsch glacier to the 4049m **Piz Bernina** (3hr.). To reach the Piz Languard more quickly, take the **Alp Languard chairlift** from town (one-way 14SFr, round-trip 20SFr; SwissPass discount). From the top of the lift follow signs to the steep 2½-hour hike to the peak and restaurant.

For more intimate contact with the **glaciers**, there are a number of options. The sedentary traveler can take the train (dir.: Tirano) to "Diavolezza" (6.20SFr) and then the cable car to the top of the **Diavolezza glacier** (one-way 19SFr, round-trip 26SFr; with SwissPass and Half-fare card 12SFr, 18.20SFr), which sits just above the valley between Piz Palu and Bernina. Bring sunglasses; the snow makes the view from the top nearly blinding to the naked eye. It is possible to hike into the glacial bowl and then down the Morteratsch glacier. The **Mountain Climbing School of Pontresina** (tel. 838 83 33) leads the 4-hour hike. (22SFr. Hikes daily at noon; meet at the top of the Diavolezza cable car between 10-11:30am.) The other option is to meet the glaciers up close and personal. Take the train from Pontresina (dir.: Tirano) to "Morteratsch" (4.40SFr) and walk as far up to and alongside the Morteratsch glacier as you desire. From the train stop it is 30 minutes to the glacier, and 3 hours to the highest hut on the glacier. Signs mark the glacier's recession since the turn of the century along the gushing river created by the melting waters.

Guests of Pontresina—that's you—are entitled to a number of **free sports, tours,** and **excursions,** including free trout **fishing** in Lej Nair and Lej Pitschen, free botanical excursions, and free excursions to experience an unforgettable **sunrise** on Piz Lagalb (contact the tourist office for details). If you're tired of physical exertion, **horse-drawn carriage** and winter **sleigh rides** promise a good time. Dial 842 60 57 for booking, or go to the carriage depot above the train station. (Carriages hold 2-4 people. For the 1hr. trip between Pontresina and Rosegtal, one-way 85SFr, round-trip 130SFr.)

ST. MORITZ

In St. Moritz are the hangers-on of the rich...the jewel thieves, the professional backgammon players and general layabouts, as well as the high-class ladies of doubtful virtue (if such a thing still exists)...

—Peter Viertel

Chic, elegant, and exclusive, St. Moritz (1856m) is one of the most famous ski resorts in the world. Renowned as a playground for the rich and famous, this "Resort at the Top of the World" will convert almost anyone into a (window-)shopper, tempted by Armani, Calvin Klein, and Prada. St. Moritz hosted the Olympic Games in 1928 and 1948, catapulting itself into the international spotlight. Today, the town offers every winter sport imaginable from world-class skiing and bobsledding to golf, polo, greyhound racing, cricket on the frozen lake, and *Skikjöring*—a sport similar to water skiing in which the water is replaced by snow and the motorboat is replaced by a galloping horse.

◪ **ORIENTATION AND PRACTICAL INFORMATION.** Trains run every hour to **Chur** (2hr., 41SFr), **Zuoz** (30min., 8.60SFr), **Celerina** (5min., 2.40SFr), and **Pontresina** (15min., 4.40SFr). Yellow **postal buses** (*not* the local blue buses) cover almost all the same routes as the trains. They also provide the only public access to the southwest tip of the Upper Engadine Valley, since St. Moritz is the railway terminus. Buses run twice every hour to **Silvaplana** (15min., 3.60SFr), **Sils** (20min., 6.20SFr), and **Maloja** (40min., 9SFr), departing from the left of the train station. Two trains leave St. Moritz whose journey is more important than the destination. From the Engadine Valley to the Matterhorn, the legendary **Glacier Express** covers the 270km to **Zermatt** in a leisurely 8 hours (departing at 9, 9:30, and 10am, 147SFr, SwissPass valid), affording ample time to take in the magnificent Alpine landscapes while crossing 291 bridges and going through 91 tunnels. If you can't sit still for that long, the **Bernina Express** makes the excursion to **Tirano, Italy** (2½hr., every hr., 29SFr, SwissPass valid). It's the only Swiss train that crosses the Alps without entering a single tunnel. The **train station** provides **currency exchange** and Western Union services, **luggage storage** (5SFr), and **bike rental** (26SFr per day), all at the same counter (open 5:30am-10:10pm), and **lockers** (2SFr). Bikes can also be rented at the youth hostel for 15SFr per day.

The resort's **tourist office** (*Kurverein*), Via Maistra 12 (tel. 837 33 33; fax 837 33 77; email kvv@stmoritz.ch; www.stmoritz.ch), is in the center of town. From the train station, cross the street, climb Truoch Serlas, and take Via Serlas to the left past the post office. As you pass the Badrutt's Palace Hotel on your left, turn right up the Réduit Passage. Emerge from the shopping arcade onto Via Maistra; the tourist office is on the right. The office provides free hotel reservations (tel. 837 33 99; fax 837 33 66), skiing info, and advice on hiking in the smaller towns of the Engadine Valley. (Open July to mid-Sept. and mid-Dec. to mid-Apr. M-Sa 9am-6pm; May-June and Nov. M-F 8am-noon and 2-6pm, Sa 9am-noon.) In an **emergency**, dial

111. The **post office** (open M-F 7:45am-noon and 1:45-6:15pm, Sa 8-11am) is located on Via Serlas on the way to the tourist office and has a 24-hour **ATM**. **Internet access** is available in Champfer, the next town west of St. Moritz, at **Hotel Europa** (17SFr per hr.; accessible by postbus dir.: Sils). The **Galerie Apotheke (pharmacy),** is located next to the Giardino Cafe on Via del Bagn (open M-F 8am-noon and 2-6:30pm, Sa 8am-noon and 2-5pm). The **postal code** is CH-7500.

PHONE CODE	The **city code** for St. Moritz is 081.

⌐ ACCOMMODATIONS. With a cappuccino maker in the main lobby, the **Jugendherberge Stille (HI)**, Via Surpunt 60 (tel. 833 39 69; fax 833 80 46), provides welcome luxury after the trek up there. Follow the signs around the lake to the left of the station (30min.), or take the postal bus (dir.: Maloja) to "Hotel Sonne" (2.40SFr) and go left on Via Surpunt for 10 minutes. Bigger and better than your average hostel with wall-to-wall carpeting, small dorms (max. 4 per room), private showers, a pool table (2SFr), and cheap **mountain bike rental** (15SFr). (Dorms in high season (July-Aug. and Dec. 18-Apr. 29) 43SFr, low season 40.50SFr; doubles 111SFr, 106SFr; with shower 134SFr, 126SFr. Non-members add 5SFr. Sheets, showers, lockers, breakfast, and dinner included—show up before 7:15pm for dinner. Reception 7-10am and 4-10pm. No lockout. Curfew midnight; keys available. Quiet hours from 10pm. AmEx, MC, Visa.) For more privacy, head next door to the **Sporthotel Stille** (tel. 833 69 48; fax 833 07 08), which provides simple, bare rooms. (In summer, singles 65SFr, doubles 110SFr; breakfast included. In winter, singles 97SFr, doubles 164SFr; breakfast and dinner included.) For **camping,** you have two options: catch the postal bus (dir.: Sils-Maloja) and push the *halt an* button to request a special stop at "Olympiaschanze," 1 stop after "St. Moritz Bad Signal" (4.50-6.50SFr, children half-price; tent 5-6SFr; open May 19-Sept. 27); or take a different bus to Silvaplana (10min., every 30min. 7am-9pm, 3.60SFr) and sleep on the beach at **Camping Silvaplana** (tel. 828 84 92; 7.60SFr; tent 5-7SFr; open mid-May to mid-Oct.).

◌ FOOD. If you know where to look, you can eat like a king in St. Moritz without paying 5-star prices. A good place to start is **Restaurant Hauser,** on Sonnepl. Walk 1 block down the street that runs straight from the tourist office to take advantage of the diverse, relatively inexpensive menu (Bratwurst and fries 14.50SFr, tofu pad thai 16.50SFr), and a terrace for glitterati gazing. (Open M-Sa 7:30am-8:30pm Su 9am-8:30pm.) The red-checked **Restaurant Engadinia**, P. da Scoula (tel. 833 32 65), is best known for fondue (26.50SFr per person) and raclette (28.50SFr per person; open M-Sa 8:30am-11pm). Groceries are available at the **Co-op Center,** one square up from the tourist office or at Via dal Bagn 20, the main road between Dorf and Bad, en route to the youth hostel (open M-F 8am-12:15pm and 2-6:30pm, Sa 8am-12:15pm and 2-5pm). If you're here in late January, sample the culinary delights of the annual week-long **St. Moritz Gourmet Festival.**

▥ MUSEUMS. Follow Via Maistra from the tourist office to Sonnepl., then bear right on Via Somplaz to the **Segantini Museum,** Via Somplaz 30 (tel. 833 44 54), dedicated to the Italian Expressionist painter who spent the last years of his life in nearby Maloja. His work strikes a delicate balance between depicting a fairy-tale Switzerland and the harsh realities of farming life. Save the airy *Kuppelsaal*, containing the Alpine trilogy "Birth," "Nature," and "Death," for last. (Open June-Oct. and Dec.-May Tu-Su 10am-noon and 3-6pm. 10SFr, students 7SFr.) The **Engadiner Museum,** Via dal Bagn 39 (tel. 833 43 33; fax 833 50 07), between Bad and Dorf, gives tourists a sneak-peek at the intricately carved wood interior of those unassuming white houses. The house, built in 1905, features tiny gnomish doorways, beautiful and unpronounceable *Chuchichästlis* (cupboards), and a macabre 17th-century 4-poster sick-bed with a skeleton on the ceiling alongside an inscription that translates as, "As you are, I would like to be" (i.e., still alive). (Open June-Oct. M-F 9:30am-noon and 2-5pm, Su 10am-noon; Dec.-Apr. M-F 10am-noon and 2-5pm, Su 10am-noon. 5SFr, students 4SFr, children 2.50SFr.)

⚞ OUTDOOR ACTIVITIES. You've probably heard about St. Moritz's **skiing**—need we say more? (Call 830 00 99 for ski packages; day passes 52-55SFr. See p. 393.) Each year the **bobsled** run from the '28 and '48 Olympics is rebuilt by 14 skilled laborers with 5000m³ of snow and 4000L of water for the **St. Moritz Tobogganing Club** (tel. 833 46 09). They let you share the fun, but at a rather steep price (200SFr gets you 1 run, 1 drink, and 1 photo; call ahead as slots fill up quickly).

Believe it or not, more guests visit St. Moritz in the summer than in the winter to take advantage of the **hiking**. For a relaxing hike, follow the trail from St. Moritz to **Pontresina** (1½hr.). Go under the train station to "See" exit, and cross the bridge on the other side to find the trailhead. Follow the signs to "Pontresina" from there. The wide gravel trail winds through preserved forest and past the marsh surrounding Staz lake on a level path. For a more demanding excursion (3hr.), ride from St. Moritz up to **Piz Nair** (3075m; 14SFr, round-trip 21SFr; under 17 7SFr, 10.50SFr). After admiring the rooftop view of the Engadine, the most rewarding choice is the steep hike down to **Suvretta Lake** (2580m). Picnics at the isolated lake, in the shadow of majestic **Piz Julier** (3380m), are a must. Follow the Ova da Suvretta back down to the Signalbahn or St. Moritz. Other summer activities in St. Moritz include **windsurfing** (tel. 833 44 49; 2hr. rental 30-40SFr, private lessons 50SFr per hr., 10 lessons 240SFr), **river rafting** (75-99SFr per half-day), and **horseback riding** (tel. 833 57 33; 45SFr per hr., 80SFr for 2hr.).

DAYTRIPS FROM ST. MORITZ

NEAR ST. MORITZ: CELERINA

Celerina is accessible from St. Moritz by train (2.4SFr, 2 per hr. 6:54am-10:57pm) or postbus (3SFr), which leave from the front of the Cresta Palace on Via Maistra.

Celerina—a satellite of St. Moritz—offers access to the same hiking and skiing (lift passes for the towns are interchangeable). They are close enough that the bobsled run in the 1928 and 1948 Olympics started in St. Moritz and finished in Celerina, so sleeping in Celerina and playing in St. Moritz is certainly a viable option.

With its geometric design and empty, polished hallways, the **Inn Lodge** (tel. (081) 834 47 95) blends into the industrial sector in which it's located. Walk down the main street to the right of the train station and follow it all the way down, past the circle, to turn right just before the road meets the highway. (Dorms in summer 25SFr, in winter 40SFr. Sheets and breakfast included.) In the center of town (turn left at the circle down the main street from the train station), the **Alten Brauerei** (tel. (081) 832 18 74) offers slightly overpriced dorms and *Lager* (camp) lodgings above a newly renovated bar and **restaurant** (sandwiches 5-7SFr, pasta 11-14SFr, regional dishes 14-21SFr; kitchen open 11:30am-2pm and 6-9pm). The dorms have sinks and big windows, while the *Lager* is communal living at its best with 60 people in one room. (In summer *Lager* 30SFr, dorms 50SFr, single 70SFr; in winter dorms 55SFr, single 80SFr. Breakfast included.) Across from the tourist office is a **Volg** supermarket (open M-F 8am-noon and 2-6:30pm, Sa 8am-noon and 2-4pm). If Volg isn't going to cut it, head for the elegant pueblo-style interior of **Restaurant La Court** (tel. (081) 837 01 01), in Hotel Chesa Rosatsch on the river. Eat under the restaurant's huge skylight or outside by the river. (Salad buffet 7.70SFr, lasagna 13.50SFr, *Capuns* (ham and potato wrapped in leaves) 18SFr. Open noon-10pm.)

GRAUBÜNDEN

NEAR ST. MORITZ: SILVAPLANA

Silvaplana is a 1hr. hike or 10min. bus ride from St. Moritz (every 30min. 7am-9pm, 3.60SFr).

At the foot of the Julier mountain pass in the magnificent Upper Engadine lake country, Silvaplana seems to be the meeting place for young thrill-seekers not interested in the flashiness of St. Moritz. Silvaplana's main attraction is the *See* (lake), which is usually covered with the brightly-colored sails of windsurfers. The **tourist office** *(Kurverein)*, 1 block up from the bus stop at the corner of Via Maistra and Via dal Farrer, can help plan hikes, arrange windsurfing lessons, or reserve a room (tel. (081) 838 60 00; fax 838 60 90; email silvaplana@bluewin.ch; www.silvaplana.ch; open M-F 8:30am-6pm).

All the water activities are based around the campground at the far end of town. The **windsurfing** in Silvaplana is world-famous. Every August, Silvaplana hosts the international **freestyle championships** and the **Surf Marathon,** as well as the **Swiss National and European Windsurfing Championships** (Aug. 15-22). Rent **sailboards** next to the campground. (Tel. (081) 828 92 29. 1hr. 20-25SFr, with wet-suit 25-30SFr; 2hr. 30-40SFr, 40-50SFr; 1 day 50-60SFr, 70-80SFr. Group lessons start at 50SFr per hr. Longer lessons advised for novices: 9hr. 240SFr, 18hr. 380SFr. Open June 15-Sept. 15 daily 9am-7pm.) Silvaplana's hyperactive breezes frolic with kites, the fancy loop-de-looping variety, christened at the town's annual **kite festival** (Oct. 9-10 in 2000). The folks in Silvaplana invented **kite sailing,** a sport where the sail on your windsurfer is replaced by a parachute, which allows for jumps 10m in the air (a variation is done on waterskis). Kite sailing can be arranged at the store opposite the tourist office (tel. (081) 828 97 67; www.kitesailing.ch; in winter 3hr. lesson and rental 50SFr, in summer 100SFr).

For **hiking,** Silvaplana's best offerings involve the **Corvatsh cable car,** which provides access to the glaciers surrounding Piz Bernina. The cable car makes 2 stops: the top station has the most breathtaking views, while the middle station allows for an incredible hike. The Swiss train-gods have created a special **Wanderbillet** so you can do both: go all the way to the top for the views, then come halfway down to do the hike (*Wanderbillet* 27SFr, all the way up and down 32SFr). For the hike, walk from the middle station to the hut at Fourcla Surlej and from there down to Pontresina (5hr.). For flatlandlubbers, Silvaplana's **Sportszentrum Mulets** (tel. 828 93 62) offers tennis (18SFr per hr.), volleyball (2hr. 20SFr), ping-pong (4SFr per hr.) and soccer (2hr. 60SFr). In winter, soccer gives way to ice-skating, hockey, and that esoteric and bizarre European pastime, curling.

NEAR ST. MORITZ: SILS

Take a postal bus from St. Moritz (every 30min. 7:25am-8:25pm, 6SFr).

More than a century ago, **Friedrich Nietzsche** praised Sils as "the loveliest corner of the Earth," adding, "It is good to live here, in this bracing cold air, where in a wonderful way nature is simultaneously both wildly 'festive' and mysterious—in fact, I like Sils-Maria more than any other place." Sils proves that a lot of rich people have read Nietzsche since then, as it has become the understated resort getaway for the wealthy in-crowd who want privacy more than St. Moritz glamour. Fortunately, all this cash has helped preserve, rather than exploit, the tranquil terrain.

Sils has a number of wonderfully rejuvenating **hikes.** A soothing 20-minute hike leads to the tip of the tiny forested peninsula just west of town called **Chaste.** Follow the main road toward the lake and at the meadow turn left at the sign for "Chaste." At the tip, you'll discover a stone engraved with one of Nietzsche's sermons. Another easy hike leads from the same spot and goes around the roadless south shore of the lake to the medieval village of **Isola,** set on a small peninsula (45min.). For a slightly more vertical climb, hike up **Val Fex.** The trail begins opposite the tourist office and winds its way beneath glaciers and 1000m peaks en route to the tiny hamlets of **Platta** (30min.), **Crasta** (50min.), and **Curtins** (1½hr.). If you're tired of walking, let horse-drawn omnibuses do the work for you (Crosta one-way 60SFr, round-trip 100SFr; Curtins one-way 80SFr, round-trip 140SFr; bus holds 1-4 people). Sils offers **skiing** from the **Furtschellas cable car,** in conjunction with Silvaplana's slope (day pass 47-55SFr).

After a morning hike, stop by the **Nietzsche House** (halfway between the post office and the tourist office along Sils' main road), where the philosopher spent his summers and from 1883 to 1888 (before his final mental breakdown). Exhibitions include his workroom (preserved in its original Spartan decor), Nietzsche-inspired modern art, and two death masks: the genuine one and another his sister Elisabeth Foerster-Nietzsche had sculpted because she thought the real one was not "impressive" enough. (Open Tu-Su 3-6pm. 4SFr, students 2SFr.) If Sils enchants you as it did Nietzsche, the **tourist office** (tel. 838 50 50; fax 838 50 59; email info@sils.ch), down the street to the left from the bus stop, can provide hiking and skiing maps and call hotels for vacancies (open M-F 8:30am-6pm, Sa 9am-noon and 4-6pm; Dec.-Easter also Su 4-6pm).

ITALIAN SWITZERLAND

(TICINO, TESSIN)

Ever since Switzerland won the Italian-speaking canton of Ticino (Tessin, in German and French) from Italy in 1512, the region has been renowned for its mix of Swiss efficiency and Italian *dolce vita*—no wonder the rest of Switzerland vacations here. The charred-wood chalets of Graubünden and the Bernese Oberland are replaced by jasmine-laced villas painted the bright colors of Italian *gelato*. Come here for lush, almost Mediterranean vegetation, emerald-green lakes, and shaded castles. Pastel church facades lead to ancient sanctuaries where faith, not tourism, is still the main draw. The **Ticino Card,** available at major tourist offices, provides 3 days of free or half-price travel on local boats, cable cars, and other regional transportation (June 15-Oct. 15; 55SFr, family card 75SFr).

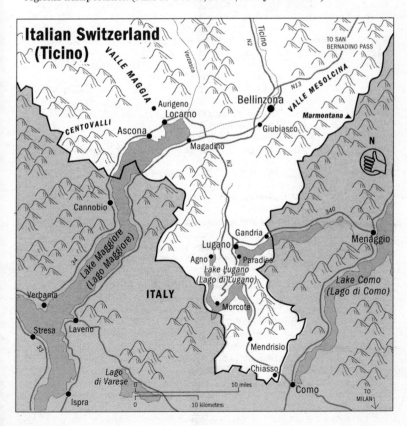

HIGHLIGHTS OF TICINO
■ Sail across Lake Lugano to the romantic ports of **Morcote** and **Gandria** (p. 418).
■ Bask in the tropical sun or pay tribute to a failed Utopia in **Ascona** (p. 410).
■ Groove to bass-heavy beats at the **Bellinzona Blues Fest** (p. 403).
■ Couldn't crash Cannes? Try the International Film Festival in **Locarno** (p. 409).

BELLINZONA

Three medieval castles preside over Bellinzona, reminding visitors of days of yore when Bellinzona was a strategic Milanese fort for guarding trade routes through the San Bernadino and St. Gotthard passes. Bellinzona is still an important crossroads for tourists on their way to the lake resorts of southern Ticino. Those who linger, however, discover an exciting blend—unique to this Ticinese capital city—of sleek modernity and enchanting remnants of the past. The villas and vineyards in the surrounding hills cast a pastoral calm over the city, disrupted only once a year by the bass-heavy beats of the **Bellinzona Blues Fest.**

7 ORIENTATION AND PRACTICAL INFORMATION. Bellinzona is easily accessible by **train** (rail info tel. 157 22 22). Make connections in Bellinzona to **Basel** (4hr., every 30min. 6:06am-11:35pm, 74SFr); **Lugano** (30min., 2 per hr. 5:07am-12:36pm, 10.80SFr); **Locarno** (20min., 2 per hr. 5:38am-12:38am, 6.80SFr); **Lucerne** (2¼hr., 6:06am-9:07pm, 52SFr); **Zurich** (2½hr., every 30min. 6:26am-9:07pm, 56SFr); **Milan** (2hr., every hr. 5:07am-1:20am, 54SFr); and **Rome** (7hr., every hr. 5:07am-12:36am, 148SFr). To Milan and Rome, under 27 receive 25% off. Trains to and from **Geneva** require a change in **Domodossola,** Italy (5½hr., 10 per day, 95SFr) or **Olten** (6hr., about 2 per hr. 6:06am-6:26pm, 102SFr). Post **buses** leave from the station for **Chur** (3 hr., every hr. 6:05am-5:07pm, 52SFr), **San Bernardino** (1¼hr., every hr. 6:05am-9:07pm on weekdays, until 11:07pm on weekends, 30SFr),and elsewhere in eastern Switzerland. **By car,** arrive from the north on N2/E35 or N13/E43; from Lugano or the south, on N2/E35 north; from Locarno or the west, on Rte. 13 east. The train station has **currency exchange, luggage storage** (5SFr at baggage check), **lockers** (3-5SFr), and **bike rental** (at baggage check; 26SFr per day, 21SFr for half-day; mountain bikes 32SFr, 25SFr; open 8am-9pm). Public **parking** is available at the train station or in the Colletivo at P. del Sole, off Viale Stazione to the right down Largo Elvetica (1SFr per 45min.; open 7:30am-10pm). Bellinzona's **tourist office,** 2 Via Camminata (tel. 825 21 31; fax 825 38 17), adjacent to the city hall, makes free hotel reservations. From the train station, walk left 10 minutes along Viale Stazione, past P. Collegiata, and along Via Nosetto, bearing to the left around the city hall. (Open M-F 8am-6:30pm, Sa 9am-noon.) The **post office** on Viale Stazione is a block left from the station (open M-F 6:30am-6:30pm, Sa 8-11am). The **postal code** is CH-6500.

PHONE CODE	The **city code** for Bellinzona is 091.

7 ACCOMMODATIONS AND FOOD. Housing options in Bellinzona are bland and not cheap, but otherwise fine. To reach **Hotel Moderno Garni,** 17b Viale Stazione (tel./fax 825 13 76), turn left from the station, right on Via Claudio Pelladini, and take an immediate right again on Via Cancelliere Molo. All rooms have new carpeting and a sink; half also have balconies. (Singles 55SFr; doubles 90SFr, 120SFr with shower; triples 120SFr, 150SFr; quads 160SFr, 200SFr. Breakfast included. Reception in the hotel café M-F 6am-10:30pm, Sa 7am-10:30pm. MC, Visa.) If the Moderno Garni is full, **Hotel San Giovanni,** 7 Via San Giovanni (tel./fax 825 19 19), has tidy rooms with private showers. From the station, turn left on Viale Stazione and right down Scalinata Dionigi Resinelli; continue straight for 100m. (Singles 50SFr, 60SFr with shower; doubles 90SFr, 100SFr. Breakfast included. Parking available. Reception M-Sa 6:15am-midnight, Su 7am-noon. MC,

Visa.) Take postal bus #2 to "Arbedo Posta Vecchia" to **Camping Bosco de Molinazzo** (tel. 829 11 18; fax 829 23 55). **Laundry, swimming pool,** and **bike rental** are also available. (4.50-6SFr, children half-price; tent 5.50SFr. Open Apr. 2-Oct. 17.)

Those who are nobles in spirit but peasants in pocket head to **Ristorante Inova,** Viale Stazione 5, in the Innovazione. The self-serve king offers the usual wide selection. (Entrees 10-13SFr, salads 4.20-9.90SFr. Open M-W, F 8:30am-6:30pm, Th 8:30am-9pm, Sa 8am-5pm.) Otherwise, fill up on cappuccino (3SFr), *panini* (5SFr), choco-bugs (2.50SFr), and huge pizza slices (7SFr) at **Peverelli Panetteria Tea Room Pasticceria** in P. Collegiata off Viale Stazione (open M-F 7am-7pm, Sa 7am-6pm). **Migros** is in P. del Sole, across from the Castelgrande entrance (open M-F 8am-6:30pm, Sa 7:30am-5pm). **Bio Casa,** on the way to the tourist office, stocks organic fruits and veggies, tofu burgers, and vitamins (open M-F 8:30am-6:30pm, Sa 8am-5pm; MC, Visa). The huge **outdoor market** along Viale Stazione lays out everything from typical fruits and breads to incense and rugs (open Sa 8am-noon).

■ **SIGHTS.** Available at the castles and the tourist office, a **"3 Castelli" ticket** (8SFr, students 4SFr) grants entry to all 3 castles.

CASTLES. Rising 50m above the P. del Sole on a huge hunk of rock, the oft-renovated **Castelgrande** occupies a site inhabited since the neolithic period (5500-5000 BC) and fortified from the 4th century on. Construction on the current fortress began in the 13th century with major enlargements in 1473-86. The *bianca* (white) and *nera* (black) towers, rising 27 and 28m high, date from the 13th and 14th centuries. The town transformed the castle from 1984-91 in an effort to make it more hospitable to tourists, adding an elevator, an expensive courtyard restaurant, and a concrete and TV-laden **museum** containing scores of wall fragments and old coins. The overall effect is more of a convention center than a historical monument. The Castelgrande is accessible by the free elevator near P. del Sole or by the winding paths up the hill from P. Collegieta and P. Nosetto. *(Open Tu-Su 10am-6pm. 4SFr, students 2SFr.)*

Another 90m above Castelgrande, on the opposite hill, the smaller but more satisfyingly dank **Castello di Montebello** offers visitors working drawbridges, ramparts, dungeons, and views as far as Lake Maggiore on a clear day. The tower and former residential quarters now house an **archaeological and civic museum** containing vases, jewelry, and ceramics, as well as the usual ancient bric-a-brac of ceremonial and military arms. The castle can be reached on foot from Piazza Collegiata up the slippery mossy steps of Sallita alla Motta or by bus from Viale Stazione. *(Open Tu-Su 10am-6pm. Museum 2SFr, students 1SFr.)* Worth a look but not the walk, the **Castello di Sasso Corbaro** (230m above city level), the smallest of Bellinzona's 3 castles, surveys the Ticinese mountains. The Duke of Milan had the place slapped together in 6 months after the battle of Giornico—it now hosts temporary art exhibits.

CHURCHES. Tucked away among villas and hotels, a number of notable churches grace Bellinzona. On the P. Collegiata at the end of the Viale Stazione, the **Chiesa Collegiata dei SS Pietro e Stefano** shows off an early Renaissance facade flanked by trumpeting heralds. The interior features numerous paintings and frescoes (attributed to Simone Peterzano), overhung by a gilded canopy.

A fire charred the interior of the 15th-century **Chiesa Santa Maria della Grazie** (now being restored), but the nearby **Chiesa di San Biagio** flaunts a gigantic 16th-century painting of St. Christopher and a flock of saints on its columned interior. From the train station, walk 15 minutes to the left or take bus #4 to "Cimiterio"; cross under the railroad tracks, turn left up the stairs, turn left again, and follow the tracks 50m. Across from the Chiesa di San Biagio is the **Villa dei Cedri,** which houses the **Civica Galleria d'Arte** (tel. 821 85 20) collections. Focusing on the "figurative" art of Switzerland and Italy at the turn of the century, realism and symbolism intermingle in the exhibits. Though the thickly-applied oils of Cavalli and black-and-white etchings of Monico are intriguing, lesser fans of the period may feel as though they're wandering through an over-priced private gallery. The small surrounding park is peaceful and shaded. *(Grounds open Apr. 1-Sept. 30 8am-8pm, Oct. 1-Mar. 31 9am-5pm. Museum open Tu-Sa 10am-noon and 2-5pm, Su 10am-5pm. 8SFr, free for children and students with I.D.)*

🔊🎵 OUTDOOR ACTIVITIES AND ENTERTAINMENT. The **Ticino River** is perfect for idle strollers out for balmy breezes and mountain scenery. For a 45-minute **hike** with grand views of Sasso Corbaro and the valley, take a short post bus ride to Monti di Ravecchia. The trail begins at the hospital parking lot and follows an ancient mule path, leading to now-deserted Prada, an ancient trading post possibly dating to pre-Roman times.

The annual **Blues Festival** draws crowds to Switzerland in late June (tentatively scheduled for June 29-July 1, 2000). Previous performers include Luther Allison and Joe Louis Walker. The 1st night is free and the other 2 are 10SFr each. Opera lovers with a bit of extra cash will relish the blockbuster productions of the Bellinzona **Open Air Opera** in late July and early August. Major works such as "Carmen" and "Aida" are mong recent presentations. Prices range from 50-130SFr; contact the tourist office or **Ticket Corner** (tel. 0848 800 800; www.ticketcorner.ch).

Near Bellinzona, **Alcatraz** (tel. 859 31 34), the biggest dance club in Ticino, draws partiers from the nearby countryside. Take the train to nearby Riazzino, but hurry, Cinderella—the club closes at 3am, but the last train runs at midnight. Taxis are available but rates are exorbitant.

LOCARNO

On the shores of **Lago Maggiore,** Locarno basks in near-Mediterranean breezes and bright Italian sun. Locarno was chosen to host the 1925 interwar peace conference, supposedly because the mistress of one of the representatives insisted that the conference be held on *Lago Maggiore*. Perhaps the *bella donna* needed some work on her tan. This relatively unspoiled resort town has a tropical feeling, perhaps because it gets over 2200 hours of sunlight per year—the most in all of Switzerland. During its world-famous **film festival** each August, Locarno swells with people enjoying balmy evenings of *al fresco* dining beneath palm trees. All this worldly languor coexists in relative peace with the piety of the worshippers in the churches of the **Città Vecchia** (old city). At the foot of the Ticinese hills, Locarno is an excellent starting point for mountain hikes along the **Verzasca** and **Maggia valleys,** or for regional skiing.

🔢 ORIENTATION AND PRACTICAL INFORMATION

By car, Locarno is accessible from motorway N2, which extends from Basel to Chiasso (exit: Bellinzona-Süd). **Piazza Grande,** home of the International Film Festival, is Locarno's anchor, with the town's cultural and commercial life centering around its arcades. Just above P. Grande, the *Città Vecchia* is home to 16th- and 17th-century architecture, as well as luxurious, yet economical accommodations. **Via Ramogna** connects the Piazza to the train station. **Via Rusca** extends from the other side of the Piazza to the Castello Visconteo. South of the Piazza lies the residential district, containing many vacation homes.

Trains: P. Stazione (tel. 743 65 64). To: **Bellinzona** (20min., every 30min. 5:30am-1:09am, 6.80SFr), connecting every hour north to **Lucerne** (3hr., every 30min. 6:06am-10:17pm, 56SFr) and **Zurich** (2¾hr., every hr. 6:26am-9:07pm, 60SFr), and south to **Lugano** (45min., every 30min. 5:07am-12:36am, 28SFr) and **Milan** (2½hr., several per day 6:30am-8:30pm, 63SFr). For **Zermatt** (4hr., 88SFr), **Montreux** (4¾hr., 74SFr), or **Geneva** (5¾hr., 91SFr), change trains in **Domodossola,** Italy (1¾hr., 2 per hr. 6:05am-7:20pm, 41SFr).

Buses: Buses depart from the train station or from the lakeside of Piazza Grande to nearby towns such as **Ascona** (#31) and Minusio. Buses also run regularly through the **San Bernardino Pass** to Eastern Switzerland.

Ferries: Navigazione Lago Maggiore, 1 Largo Zorzi (tel. 751 18 65), conducts tours of the entire lake, all the way into Italy. A full day on the Swiss side of the lake costs 10SFr. Sail to Ascona (1hr., 10 per day, day pass 11SFr) or the Island of Brissago (1¼hr., 10

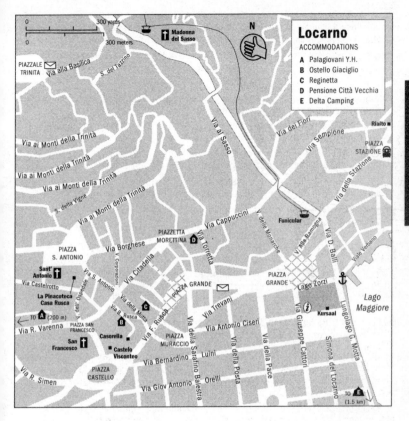

ITALIAN SWITZERLAND

per day, day pass 20SFr; ages 6-16 receive 50% discounts). A "holiday" card for all of the *Lago Maggiore* and 50% off on the *Lago di Lugano* is 33SFr for 1 day, 54SFr for 3, and 72SFr for 7.

Car Rental: Hertz SA, Garage Starnini SA, Via Simpione 12, Muralto (tel. 743 50 50).

Taxi: Chauffered comfort is only a phone call away at tel. 743 11 33.

Parking: Metered public parking found on Via della Posta and major streets (1SFr per ½hr.). At the same rates, the 24hr. parking garage, **Autosilo Largo SA** (tel. 751 96 13), beneath the *Kursaal*, is accessible from Via Cattori (open 8am-10pm).

Bike Rental: At the train station. Citybikes 27SFr per day, mountain bikes 37SFr per day. Open 10am-9pm. 6SFr fee for returning a bike to another station. At the youth hostel, 20 mountain bikes available for 15SFr per day, 10SFr per half-day.

Tourist Office: Largo Zorzi (tel. 751 03 33; fax 751 90 70, email locarno@ticino.com; www.lagomaggiore.com), on P. Grande. From the main exit of the train station, walk diagonally to the right, cross Via della Stazione, and continue through the pedestrian walkway (Via alla Ramogna). As you come out, cross Largo Zorzi to your left; the tourist office is in the same building as the *Kursaal* (casino). Hotel reservations cost 5SFr. Pick up a free map of Locarno and browse the many brochures. The office also organizes **bus excursions** around *Lago Maggiore* and beyond. City tours in English leave the tourist office mid-Mar. to mid-Oct. M at 9:45am, 5SFr. Open July 19-Aug. 15 M-F 9am-7pm, Sa 10am-5pm, Su 10am-4pm; mid-Mar.-July 19 and Aug. 15-mid-Oct. closed at 4pm on Sa; rest of the year, closed Sa-Su.

Currency Exchange: Try any one of the banks lining P. Grande, or at the train station. Station open 6:30am-8:30pm; banks open M-F 9am-4:30pm. Western Union at station open M-Sa 8am-6pm. **ATMs** (which accept MC and Visa) at the station and post office.

Luggage Storage: At the train station, 5SFr. Open 10am-9pm. **Lockers** 3-5SFr.

Bookstore: Fantasia Cartoleria Libreria, 32 P. Grande, next to the Co-op. English books, travel books, and maps; open M-F 8am-6:30pm, Sa 8:30am-5pm.

Emergencies: Police, tel. 117. **Fire,** tel. 118. **Road info,** tel. 163. **Weather,** tel. 162. **Medical Assistance,** tel. 111. **Ambulance,** tel. 144.

Pharmacy: Farmacia Celesia, P. Grande (tel. 751 16 19). The **24hr. pharmacy** changes every week; call (079) 214 6084.

Internet Access: Computer World, ViaS. Gottardo 1 (tel. 743 61 43; email info @compuworld.ch). From the front of the station, cross the street and head uphill—look for the yellow Rialto. 1SFr per 5min. Open M-F 9am-noon and 2-6:30pm, Sa until 5pm.

Post Office: P. Grande. Open M-F 8am-6:30pm, Sa 8:30am-5pm. **Postal Code:** CH-6600.

PHONE CODE	The **city code** for Locarno is 091.

ACCOMMODATIONS

A display board outside the train station allows free phone calls to most of the city's hotels and pensions. Reserve everywhere a week in advance during high-season; during the film festival, book a year ahead.

Pensione Città Vecchia, 13 Via Toretta (tel./fax 751 45 54; email cittavecchia @datacomm.ch). From P. Grande, turn right on Via Toretta (*not* vigola Toretta; look for a brown sign with the *alberghi* on it) and continue to the top. With the best prices in town and a location to match, the *pensione* is usually full. The co-ed rooms and bathrooms are simple but clean. The talkative owner makes recommendations about what's doin' in Locarno. Dorms 22-24SFr; singles 33-35SFr; doubles 60-73SFr. Small breakfast and sheets (included for singles and doubles) 4.50SFr each. Phones open 8am-9pm; check-in 1-6pm; reservations 1-9pm; call ahead if arriving after 6pm. Open Mar.-Oct.

Palagiovani Youth Hostel (HI), 18 Via Varenna (tel. 756 15 00; fax 756 15 01). From station, turn left, follow Via alla Romogna to P. Grande, and turn right on Via della Motta. Take the left fork (Via B. Rusca) past P.S. Francesco, then take Via Varenna to hostel (HI signs point the way from Via Varenna on). High hedges and floral bushes conceal a thoroughly renovated convent with its own pop music radio station (Radio Ticino, 90.7FM and 100.5FM). 2- to 6- bed rooms, most with balconies, sinks, lockers. Several rooms have **kitchenettes** at no extra charge. Dorms 31SFr, with shower and bathroom 38SFr; doubles 33SFr, 443SFr (subtract 2.50SFr in low season). Sheets and breakfast included. Lunch and dinner 11.50SFr each. **Laundry** 6SFr. Towels 1.50SFr. Mountain **bikes** 15SFr per day, 10SFr for ½day. Reception in summer 8-10am and 3-11:30pm; in winter 8-10am and 4-11:30pm .

Ostello Giaciglio, 7 Via Rusca (tel. 751 30 64; fax 752 38 37). Walk to the end of the P. Grande, turn right onto Via della Motta, and take the left fork in the road onto Via Rusca. Black-and-white-checked dorms off marble-floored hallways cost 30SFr per person. **Kitchen** facilities available, along with a sauna (20SFr) and **tanning salon** (5SFr). Rowdy high-school groups tend to take over during July-Aug. AmEx, MC, Visa.

Reginetta, 8 Via della Motta (tel./fax 752 35 53; email reginetta.locarno@bluewin.ch; www.reginetta.ch). Walk along the arcades to the end of P. Grande, and make a right onto Via della Motta. This recently restored hostel has pine furniture, soft carpet, and an airy breakfast room. Cull good advice on local sights and events from the friendly owner or the bulletin board. 42SFr per person, with breakfast 49SFr. **Bike rental** 25SFr per hour. Showers included. Reception 8am-9pm. Open Mar.-Oct. AmEx, MC, Visa.

Delta Camping, 7 Via Respini (tel. 751 60 81; fax 751 22 43; www.campingdelta.com). A 30min. walk along the lakeside to the right from the tourist office (turn left at the info map) brings you to campstyles of the rich and famous. A reservation fee of 100SFr, which is not deducted from the bill, is required July-Aug. Adjacent to a golf course and rocky beach; a restaurant, supermarket, and **bike rental** are on site. Mar.-May and Oct. 10SFr, kids 5SFr, plots 20-30SFr; June and Sept. 11SFr, 5SFr, 25-30SFr; July-Aug. 17SFr, 5SFr, 30-40SFr. Reception 8am-10pm.

Tenero: The nearby town of Tenero has 7 lakeside camping sites; only a few are cheaper than Delta Camping. **Verbano-Lido** (tel. 745 10 20; fax 745 16 22) charges fixed prices for 2 people starting at 36SFr in high season, 23SFr in low season; **Lago Maggiore** (tel. 745 18 48; fax 745 43 18), 34SFr and 26SFr; or **Tamaro** (tel. 745 21 61; fax 745 66 36), 41SFr and 22SFr. Reservation fees 40-70SFr. All sites are packed with amenities. A full list is available at the tourist office. A free boat connects Tenero to Locarno (June-Sept., 5 per day 8:40am-5:45pm), and a bus service schlepps campers from the dock or the train station (July-Aug.; free).

🍴 FOOD

Though most of Locarno's restaurants are pricey, many offer *panini*, pasta and pizza in the 10-20SFr range, leaving ample funds for that nectar of the gods, *gelato*.

Campagna da Ernesto, Via Castelvotto 16 (tel. 751 99 47), right behind the Chiesa San Antonio, has a terrace shaded by grapes and flowering trees. Pizzas 11-19SFr, pasta of the day 13SFr, minestrone 7SFr. Open 7am-midnight. MC, AmEx, Visa.

Inova, 1 Via della Stazione (tel. 743 76 76), left as you exit the station. This huge, self-serve restaurant brings affordable, balanced meals to your fingertips: breakfast 5.20SFr, salad bar 4.90-9.90SFr, pasta buffet 8.50SFr, meaty menus 11.90-14.90SFr. Open M-Sa 7:30am-10pm, Su 8am-10pm.

Ristorante Debarcadero, (tel. 752 05 55) on Largo Zorzi by the ferry dock. At one of the very few spots on the lake that's affordable and not attached to a hotel, join a young crowd here for pizza (from 9.50SFr), frappés (7SFr), and beer (tap 3.60SFr, bottled 5-6SFr), accompanied by Top 40 selections surging from the stereo. Open 8am-midnight.

Gelatina Primavera, 4 Via dell'Ospedale (tel. 751 77 36), across from the Chiesa San Francesco. Grab a store-made ice cream cone (2.30-5.50SFr) and cool off. Sandwiches from 5.50SFr and brick oven pizza from 11SFr. Open 8am-midnight.

Contrada, 26 P. Grande (tel. 751 48 15), is one of the older, more traditional establishments among the legions that line the P. Grande. The covered terrace is ideal for people-watching. Pizzas and pasta (10.50-19SFr). The *Mövenpick* ice cream is creamier and richer than your typical *gelato*. Open 8am-midnight. AmEx, MC, Visa.

MARKETS

Supermarkets: Aperto, at the station (open 6am-10pm); **Co-op,** 28 P. Grande (open M-F 8am-7:30pm; Sa 8am-5pm); **Migros,** P. Grande (open M-Sa 9am-7pm).

Farmers' Markets (all in nearby Italian towns accessible by ferry): **Cannobio** (Su; ferries at 9:15 and 10:30am, 1hr., round-trip 21SFr); **Luino** (W; ferries at 9, 10, 11am, and 1:10pm, 1½hr., 23SFr); and **Intra** (Sa; ferries at 9:15 and 10:30am, 2½hr., 27SFr). Bring your passport.

👁 🏛 SIGHTS AND MUSEUMS

MONASTERY. For centuries, visitors have journeyed to Locarno solely to see the church of **Madonna del Sasso** (Madonna of the Rock) founded over 500 years ago when a Franciscan monk had a vision telling him to build a church high above the city. Its orange-yellow hue renders it immediately recognizable from anywhere in town. The church is accessible by a **funicular** that leaves every 15 minutes from a small station just left of the McDonald's (6SFr round trip, 4.50SFr with Swiss-Pass). The true budget traveler will make the 20-minute trek up the smooth stones of the Via al Sasso (off the Via Cappuccini in the *Città Vecchia*), accompanied by capricious lizards scuttling across the path. On the way up, visitors pass by a sequence of life-size wooden niche statues depicting scenes from Christ's passion, including a *Pietà*, a Pentecost, and a 1650 Last Supper. The **sanctuary** itself envelopes the visitor with gilded carvings, frescoes, and statuary. Don't miss the panoramic view out of the city from the ramparts.

The museum next door, in the oldest part of the complex, houses a collection of ancient reliquaries and pilgrims souvenirs, but its highlight is definitely the 2nd floor collection of disaster paintings—near drownings, fires, attempted murders, battles, carriage and train accidents, and lightning strikes—all commissioned by survivors of the events thanking the Madonna for answering their prayers and intervening to save their lives. Miniature "ex-voto" body parts commemorate physical healings. *(Grounds open daily 7am-9pm. Museum open Apr.-Oct. M-F 2-5pm, Su 10am-noon and 2-5pm. 2.50SFr, students 1.50SFr. English guidebooks at the entrance are free.)*

CHURCHES. The **Chiesa San Francesco,** the church that houses the monastic order that founded the Madonna del Sasso, rests in more modest surroundings within the city. From P. Grande, turn right on Via B. Rusca and left on Via S. Francesca. Founded by the Franciscans shortly after the death of St. Francis of Assisi in the 13th century, the church displays a melange of all-but-faded frescoes beneath a sagging roof. Built from stones scavenged from a demolished castle, its exterior contains incongruous inscriptions from the material's original incarnation. Similarly, a vanished cemetery once surrounded the building, of which the only remnant is a curious skull-and-crossbones from the Orelli family monument, now used as an entrance stone in the courtyard in front of the church.

Uphill 2 blocks on the Via dell'Ospedale, the cavernous **Chiesa San Antonio** presides over the outskirts of the *Città Vecchia*. Built between 1668 and 1674, its pastel interior is still fairly well-preserved. Circular patches of sunlight illuminate a large fresco depicting Christ being taken off the cross. The cultural museum in the **Pinacoteca Communale,** across the way, is housed in a renovated palace. The museum hosts changing exhibitions of lesser-known but quality artists. *(Tel. 756 31 85. Open Tu-Su 10am-6pm. 7SFr, students 5SFr, under 17 1SFr.)*

CASTLE AND ARCHAEOLOGICAL MUSEUM. Down the Via F. Rusca from the P. Grande, the **Castello Visconteo** gazes on Locarno. After learning about the history of Locarno, wander through dungeons and up towers where soldiers poured boiling oil on attackers in the truly pacific spirit of the Middle Ages. The medieval castle, constructed between the 13th and 15th centuries, houses the **Museo Civico e Archeologico** which exhibits Roman glassware, pottery, and coins. *(Tel. 756 31 80. Open Apr.-Oct. Tu-Su 10am-5pm. 5SFr, students 3SFr.)*

◪ OUTDOOR ACTIVITIES

ON THE LAKE. The deep blue water of the Lago Maggiore is a delight to the eyes, but if you want more immediate contact with the lake, a **ferry** ride to points on both the Swiss and Italian shores is an excellent idea (see p. 404). The tropical **Isole di Brissage** is especially popular for its **botanical gardens** (tel. 791 43 61/62), which were cultivated by a baroness blessed with a love of botany and plenty of funds, who bought the island in 1885. Exotic plants from Asia, the Americas, Australia, and Africa intermingle with delicate stands of bamboo and conceal splendidly colored exotic birds. (Free guided tour daily at 2:30pm. Admission 6SFr. English guide 2SFr. Open 9am-6pm.) To power your own way around the lake, you can **rent** your own boat from **Marca Brusa,** along the water towards Delta Camping (pedal boats 14-18SFr for 1hr., 8-12SFr for 30min.; motor boats 40SFr, 25SFr). To cool off, don your swimsuit and head to the **Bagno Spiaggia Lido** (tel. 751 44 08), near Camping Delta for a dip in a pool or the lake itself (6SFr, students 4SFr; open 9am-7pm).

Or, seek out a stretch of the **Fiume Maggia,** the rock-strewn artery that feeds into the lake, for free bathing pleasure.

HIKING THE VAL VERZASCA (3½HR.). To escape the city, head out on post bus #630.55 to **Sonogno** (1hr. 10min., 16.40SFr, 32SFr round-trip, SwissPass valid) and hike amid the extraordinary peaks at the end of **Val Verzasca** (Verzasca valley). From the bus stop, take the 1st left and follow the yellow signs to **Lavertezzo.** The trail is marked by yellow signs with direction and town names, as well as by painted white-red-white blazes. Pass through cool, shady glens and rocky river-beds as you follow the Verzasca river through the valley. Close to Lavertezzo, the river eases its rapid pace, making swimming possible, but pick your swimming hole carefully, as undercurrents can be strong and it's colder than you think. Climb the **Ponte dei Salti,** a vaulted stone bridge built at the end of the Middle Ages, and gaze into the clear green ponds. You can finish at any point on the hike by meeting the postal bus that stops along the valley.

ADVENTURE SPORTS. The Verzasca valley has sent scores of visitors into dizzy-ing adrenaline rushes with its world-famous **bungee jump** off the Verzasca dam. The 220m jump, conquered with such panache by James Bond in *Goldeneye*, costs 244SFr the 1st time (with training, drink, and diploma) and 195SFr for subsequent leaps. You can even jump at night. Contact **Trekking Team** (tel. (01) 950 33 88; email info@trekking.ch; www.trekking.ch). They also offer **canyoning,** cave exploration, and a 70m bungee jump (125SFr first time, then 100SFr) in **Centovalli.**

🎵 NIGHTLIFE AND FESTIVALS

As the sun sets and the temperature drops, diners linger under the arcades of the P. Grande. High-rollers lay down their chips at the gold-tinged **Kursaal** (casino) next to the tourist office. (Open Su-Th. noon-2am, F-Sa noon-4am. Must be over 19. Proper attire required: no shorts or T-shirts.) The **Katjaboat** (tel. (079) 686 39 90), a little yellow vessel that departs in front of the Hotel Rosa, down the Via Ver-bano from the ferry dock, offers a light-hearted serving of romantic cheesiness. For only the price of a drink (minimum 5SFr, beer 6SFr, wine 10SFr), the young-at-heart enjoy a 20-minute mini-tour of the lake to wonderfully sappy piped-in music. (Boat runs 10am-1am, though its schedule tends to be as free-spirited as its atmo-sphere.) Catch recent American and Italian movies for 10SFr at the **Cinema Rex** on Via Bossi next to the Co-op, just off P. Grande, or nurse a long drink at one of the numerous cafés along P. Grande. The **Record Rock Café,** Via Trevani 3 (tel. 751 4433, turn left on Via Vittore Pedratta from P. Grande), a Hard Rock clone, pumps out American and English rock from the 1950s to today (open July-Aug. Tu-Su 5pm-1am; Sept.-June Tu-Su 4pm-1am; cover 10SFr). Despite the sign over the bar that reads "All you need is love," you'll still need 6SFr for beer and 9SFr for a cock-tail. Live bands play from September to June.

For 11 days every August, everything in Locarno halts for the **International Film Festival,** one of the 6 most important movie premiere events in the world. Unlike Cannes, no invitations are required. Over 150,000 big screen enthusiasts descend upon the resort for the spectacle—book your room 6 months to a year ahead to stand a chance. The famous centerpiece of the festival is a giant 26m by 14m out-door screen set up in Piazza Grande for big name premieres by the likes of Jean Luc Goddard, Woody Allen, Spike Lee, and Bernardo Bertolucci. Smaller screens throughout the city highlight young filmmakers and groundbreaking experimenta-tion. (Festival information: International Film Festival, Via della Posta 6, CH-6601 Locarno; tel. 756 21 21; email info@pardo.ch; www.pardo.ch.) In the 2nd half of July, Locarno teams up with Ascona to host **Ticino Musica,** a festival of classical music focused on young musicians and students, featuring concerts, operas, and master classes at several venues. Tickets are available at either tourist office or at the door of any event. (Tel. 980 09 70; www.ticinomusica.com.)

NEAR LOCARNO: AURIGENO

From the train station in Locarno, take bus #10 (dir.: Valle Maggia) to "Ronchini" (25min., every hr. 5:30am-11:35pm, 6.80SFr). Cross the street and turn right from the bus stop, then follow the hostel signs into the forest (15min.).

Hidden among chestnut trees, waterfalls, and dozens of lakes in Ticino's largest valley, Valle Maggia, is the village of Aurigeno. The primary reason to visit Aurigeno is to take a "vacation from your vacation" at ◪**Baracca Backpacker** (tel. (079) 207 15 54; fax 207 15 54), a tiny hostel with lots to offer. It has only 10 beds, but unlimited access to the peaceful outdoors, and a home-like atmosphere. Beo the bird noisily greets each new arrival, and the youthful couple who run the hostel provide fresh herbs for cooking, and a wood-working shop for tinkering. While you're escaping from civilization, use the **kitchen, rent a bike** (12-13SFr per day), or explore the **hiking, climbing,** and **swimming** possibilities in the area. (Dorms 22SFr. Sheets 3-5SFr. Reception 9-11am and 5-10pm. Open April-Oct.)

ASCONA

In his memoirs of Ascona, *The First Step into Wonderland*, Jacob Flach effuses, "Here lies a piece of the Mediterranean Sea embedded in rough mountains, a sun-bathed, blooming cape of the Côte d'Azure, a mile of the Riviera beach sprinkled with azaleas and carnations, and a good dose of the blue sky!" While they may not be as eloquent as Flach, the German-speaking Swiss who spend their summer vacations in this supremely romantic resort village on the shores of Lake Maggiore definitely share his love for it. In addition to enjoying Ascona's tropical sunshine and sparkling water, history buffs can trace the steps of the leftist thinkers and bohemian artists who tried to establish Utopia on the mountain above, known as **Monte Verità,** around the turn of the century.

🔢 **ORIENTATION AND PRACTICAL INFORMATION.** Reach Ascona by **bus** #31 from Locarno (15min., every 15min. 6:23am-midnight, 2.40SFr), or by **ferry** (1hr., 10 per day, day pass 11SFr). The **tourist office** (tel. 791 00 90; fax 792 10 08; email ascona@etlm.ch; www.ascona.ch), in the Casa Serodine, behind the Chiesa SS Pietro e Paolo, **exchanges currency** at standard rates (open Mar. 20-Oct. 20 M-F 9am-6pm, Sa 10am-4pm; Oct. 21-Mar. 19 M-F 9am-noon and 1:30-4pm). **Guided tours** of Ascona leave from the office (March-Nov., Tu 10am, 30min., 5SFr). For **parking,** try the **Autosilo** at the corner of Via Papio and Via Buonamno. **Rent bikes** at **Cicli Sport Shop,** Via Circonvallazione 14 (tel. 791 76 27). (15-20SFr per day. Open M, W, F 10am-12:30pm and 1:30-4:30pm, Tu 10am-12:30pm, Sa 9am-noon.) The **post office,** at the corner just uphill from the bus stop at the intersection of Via Papio, Via Borge, and Via Locarno, has a **24-hour ATM** (open M-F 7:30am-noon and 1:45-6pm, Sa 8-11am). The **postal code** is CH-6612.

PHONE CODE	The **city code** for Ascona is 091.

🍴🛏 **ACCOMMODATIONS AND FOOD.** Though it has only 4500 inhabitants, Ascona (with help from its neighboring twin, Losone) maintains over 3000 hotel beds. Unfortunately, very few fall into a budget price range, so you may want to stay in Locarno. Otherwise, try the rooms above the **Ristorante Verbano** (tel. 791 12 74), Via Borgo near the modern art museum, left from the post office (45SFr per person, breakfast included). The simple rooms overlooking the lake at **Casa Moscia,** Via Moscia 89 (tel. 791 12 68; fax 791 59 32), are fairly affordable but about 3km outside of town; take bus #21 to "Moscia" from the post office (singles and doubles 36-60SFr per person; hall showers only). A free hotel reservation board hangs at the bus stop—another option is to ask the tourist office for a list of **camere private** (private rooms; 35-70SFr per person).

Grab a bite to eat at **Otello** on Via Papio 8 (tel. 791 33 07), just downhill from the bus stop. Their specialty is crêpes (from 6.50SFr), but they also have cheap Italian food. Occasionally, you can hear New Orleans jazz from the bandstand on the terrace in back. (Open 7:30am-midnight; hot food 11:30am-11:30pm. MC, Visa.) **Ristorante La Torre,** Piazzo Motta 61 (tel. 791 54 55), offers prime views of the lake as well as pizza and pasta (starting at 11.80SFr) and salads (from 6.70SFr; open Mar.-Oct. and Dec. 27-Jan.6 9am-midnight; closed Nov. 3-Dec. 22; rest of the year, closed M-Tu). You can't miss the **Co-op**'s orange sign down Via Papio from the bus stop, or **Migros** farther down the same street (both open M-F 8am-7:30pm). A **market** spills onto the P.G. Motta along the lake every Tuesday from 10am-5pm.

■ ▥ **SIGHTS AND MUSEUMS.** The post bus stop at the corner of Via Borgo and Via Papio, at the edge of the old city, leaves you within walking distance of all the sights and the waterfront (8min., 6 per day 10am-6:15pm, 1SFr).

THE OLD CITY. At the edge of the *Città Vecchia*, 1 block downhill from the bus stop on Via delle Cappelle, the *pesca*-hued 15th-century courtyard of the **Collegio Pontifico Papio** is framed by banana trees and adorned with the coat of arms of many a departed collegiate administrator. Presiding over the still-operating Superior private school (est. 1399), the adjacent church of **Santa Maria della Misericordia** spruces up its dim interior with 15th-century frescoes by Seregnesi and Antonio da Tradate and a brand-new organ. From the bus stop, turning right on the Via Collegio before the Pontifico Papio takes you into the heart of the *Città Vecchia*, with its narrow, banner-hung streets and wrought-iron balconies. Turn right again at the end of the street to find the **Chiesa SS Pietro e Paolo,** whose slender, stone clock tower marks Ascona along the lake. The basilica and 3 enclosed naves date from the 16th century, while the frescoes inside are a century older.

MUSEUMS. Across the street from Chiesa SS Pietro e Paolo, the rich stucco of the **Casa Serodine** is all that remains of what was once a Renaissance artist colony. Today, private galleries line the winding streets, promoting such artists as Niki de St. Phalle, Marc Chagall, and Georges Braque. Down Via Borgo just before the waterfront, the **Museo Comunale d'Arte Moderna** has an extensive permanent collection that includes works by Klee, Utrillo, Amiet, and Jawlensky, as well as temperas by Russian Marianne Werefkin that evoke Edvard Munch in their swirling lines. *(34 Via Borgo. Tel. 791 67 57 or 780 51 00. Open Mar.-Dec. Tu-Sa 10am-noon and 3-6pm, Su 4-6pm. 5SFr, students and seniors 3SFr.)*

The **Museo Casa Anatta** immortalizes the dashed dreams of Utopia in documents and photographs (unfortunately without English labeling). Walk up the hilly

---

PARADISE LOST Around the turn of the last century, a distinctly left-of-center collection of anarchists, agrarians, artists, philosophers, vegetarians, and writers sought Utopia on the banks of the *Lago Maggiore*. Political refugees, including Russian anarchist Michail Bakunin, sought refuge in Ascona in the late 1800s. In 1889, the Locarnese philosopher Alfredo Pioda proposed the establishment of a lay convent for international intellectuals to be named "fraternitas," on La Monescia, the hill behind Ascona. Though his vision never came to fruition, thinkers seeking connections between humankind, nature, the world, and the universe came to La Monescia anyway. The hill was renamed "Monte Verità" ("mount of truth") by Henri Oeden-Koven and Uda Hoffman, a pair of free spirits who founded a vegetarian and naturalistic community there in 1900. Meanwhile, Ascona's reputation as a cultural center for the elite continued to grow, drawing the likes of D.H. Lawrence, James Joyce, Hermann Hesse, and Karl Jung (and, in the 20s and 30s, members of the German avant-garde and Dadaists like Klee, Arp, and Segal). The **Museo Casa Anatta** (anatta means "soul" in Sanskrit) preserves the Utopian ideals that flourished during Monte Verità's heyday.

Strada della Collina from the bus stop. *(Tel. 791 03 27. Open Apr.-June and Sept.-Oct. Tu-Su 2:30-6pm; July-Aug. Tu-Su 3-7pm. 6SFr, students 4SFr.)*

WATERFRONT SIGHTS. Heading down Via Borgo from the bus stop brings you to the shores of the lake, where countless terrace restaurants are the place to see and be seen. To the left along the water from Via Borgo, at the end of Piazza G. Motta, the sole remaining tower of the 13th-century **Castello dei Ghiriglion,** 26 P.G. Motto, has been reborn as a hotel and expensive restaurant. Further along the waterfront, just past the Eden Roc hotel, the **Museo Epper** hosts temporary exhibitions of 20th-century art. *(14 Via Albarelle. Tel. 791 19 42. Open Apr.- June and Sept.-Oct. Tu-F 10am-noon and 3-6pm, Su 3-6pm; July-Aug. Tu-F 10am-noon and 8-10pm, Sa-Su 8-10pm. Free.)*

⚑ OUTDOOR ACTIVITIES. As in Locarno, you can tour the *Lago Maggiore* by **renting a boat.** Zandonella, along the water near the Via Borgo, is one good place to start (pedal boats 10SFr for 30min., 16SFr for 1hr.; motor boats 25SFr, 40SFr). In late June and early July, Ascona sets up the bandstands and claps its hands to the beat of the **New Orleans Music Festival** (in 2000, June 30-July 9). Musicians play jazz, gospel, soul, blues, and even zydeco on the waterfront and in local cafés. If you're around in August, consider stopping by for the **International Horse Jumping Competition,** or the **International Music Weeks** of classical music (late Aug. to mid-Oct.). Locarno's discotheque crowd flocks to Ascona's subterranean dance club, **Cincilla,** Via Moscia 6, located with several other bars and clubs beneath mysterious arcades beside *Lago Maggiore* to the right of Via Borgo. (Open W-Th and Su 10pm-5am. Must be 18.)

LUGANO

Lugano, Switzerland's third-largest banking center, rests in the crevassed valley between San Salvatore and Monte Brè. Warmed by a Mediterranean climate, Lugano's shady streets are lined with tiles, climbing vines, and blood-red wildflowers. Lugano draws plenty of visitors with its seamless blend of religious beauty, artistic flair, and natural spectacle. Younger Swiss vacationers flock to either of the 2 extraordinary youth hostels in town, both built from luxury villas, with swimming pools and magnificent gardens. By day, crowds throng the markets and piazzas, while bars, cafés, and the annual **Jazz Festival** keep the streets full at night.

▐ GETTING TO LUGANO

The small **Lugano-Agno Airport** services Crossair flights from Basel, Bern, Geneva, London, Nice, Rome, and Zurich. Trains connect the Lugano train station to the airport (every 20min., 4.40SFr). A **shuttle** (tel. (079) 221 4243) runs from the station (every hr. 7:40am-8pm) to the airport (8SFr), town center (10SFr), or other locations upon request (13SFr). From **Geneva** in the west, **trains** run to Lugano through **Domodossola, Italy** (change trains in Locarno). From **Chur** and **St. Moritz** in the east, postal buses go to **Bellinzona** (3hr., every hr. 6:05am-5:07pm, 52SFr), where you can catch a train to Lugano (30min., 2 per hr. 5:07am-12:36am, 10.80SFr). The only direct connections are from **Zurich** and **Bern** in the north. To reach Lugano by **car,** take Rte. N2/E35 (or just follow the signs).

▐ ORIENTATION AND PRACTICAL INFORMATION

Lugano's large pedestrian zone is bounded on one side by the ridge where the train station sits, Corso Pestalozzi, and the Fiume Cassarate canal on the other. A 15-minute walk from the station, the arcaded **Piazza della Riforma** is the town's center. Northwest of this, the **Piazza Cioccaro** is serviced by a **cable car** that runs from the waterfront to the station (0.90SFr, SwissPass valid, 5:20am-11:50pm).

Trains: P. della Stazione (tel. 157 22 22). To: **Locarno** (via Bellinzona, 1hr., every 30min. 5:37am-12:04am, 16.40SFr); **Basel** (4hr., every hr. 5:37am-11:07pm, 81SFr); **Bern** (through Lucerne, 4½hr., every hr. 5:37am-7:12pm, 77SFr); **Geneva** (through Domodossola, 6¾hr., 105SFr); **Zurich** (3hr., every hr. 5:57am-8:39pm, 62SFr); and **Milan** (1½hr., every hr. 5:38am-9:48pm, 14SFr).

Public Transportation: Buses run from the neighboring town to the center of Lugano and also traverse the city. Schedules and automatic ticket machines at each stop. 1.20-1.90SFr per ride, 24hr. "Carta Giorno" (day pass) 5SFr. SwissPass valid.

Taxis: Associazone Concessionari Taxi, tel. 922 88 33 or 922 02 22.

Car Rental: Avis, 8 Via C. Maraini (tel. 913 41 51). **Hertz,** 13 Via San Gottardo (tel. 923 46 75). **Europcar,** 24 Via M. Boglia, Garage Cassarate (tel. 971 01 07).

Parking: Autosilo Balestra, off Via Pioda, on Via S. Balestra, charges 1SFr for 1hr., 4SFr for 3, 25SFr for 12. Overnight parking 6SFr. Open 24hr. **Autosilo Central Park** on river

Lugano

ACCOMMODATIONS

A Ostello della Gioventù
B Pension Selva
C Casa della Giovane
D Hotel Montarina
E Hotel Garni Zurigo
F Hotel Pestalozzi

towards Paradiso costs 6SFr for 3hr., and 12SFr for 12hr. City parking meters 1SFr per hr., 2SFr for 1½hr.

Bike Rental: At the baggage check in the station. Mountain bikes 32SFr per day, 25SFr per half-day; city bikes 26SFr, 21SFr. 6SFr to return at another station. Open 8am-6pm.

Tourist Office: (tel. 913 32 32; fax 922 76 53; email ltoinfo@lto.ch) in the Palazzo Civico, Riva Albertolli, at the corner of P. Rezzonico. From the station, cross the footbridge labeled "Centro," and proceed down Via Cattedrale straight through P. Cioccaro as it turns into Via Pessina. Turn left on Via dei Pesci, a left on Riva Via Vela, which becomes Riva Giocondo Albertolli. The office is just past the fountain on the left, across the street from the ferry launch. Pick up free maps or make hotel reservations (4SFr). The tourist office also offers a free **guided city walk** Apr.-Oct. at 9am on Mondays, starting at Chiesa degli Angioli. Open Apr.-Oct. M-F 9am-6:30pm, Sa 9am-12:30pm and 1:30-5pm, Su 10am-2pm; Nov.-Mar. M-F 9am-12:30pm and 1:30-5pm.

Consulates: U.K., 22 Via Sarengo; CH-6903 Lugano, P.O. Box 184. Tel. 950 06 66. Open M-F 10am-noon.

Currency Exchange: In the train station. Open M-Sa 7:10am-7:45pm, Su 8am-7:45pm.

Luggage Storage: Lockers at the train station. Open 24hr. 3-5SFr.

Lost Property: Check the *Fundbureau* of the Polizei Communale, on the P. Riforma, on the other side of the same building as the tourist office. Tel. 800 71 10. Open M-Sa 10am-4pm.

Bookstore: Melisa, 4 Via Vegezzi, across from post office (tel. 923 83 41), stocks English-language books downstairs. Open M-F 8am-12:30pm and 1:30-6:30pm, Sa 8am-12:30pm and 1:30-5pm. AmEx, MC, Visa.

Library: Biblioteca Cantonale, 6 Viale Cattaner (tel. 911 53 50). From the tourist office turn left and walk along waterfront; library is in the Parco Civico, just before Fiume Cassarante canal. Open M-F 9am-7pm, Sa 9am-noon and 2-5pm; July-Aug. closed on Sa.

Medical Services: tel. 111. **First Aid,** tel. 805 61 11.

Emergencies: Police, tel. 117. **Ambulance,** tel. 144. **Fire,** tel. 118.

Internet Access: City Disc (tel. 924 14 00; www.citydisc.ch), 1 block up Via P. Peri from P. Dante. 4SFr for 20min., 10SFr per hr. Open M-W, F 9am-6:30pm, Th 9am-9pm, Sa 8am-5pm. Or, at the **library** next to Biblio-Café Tra, 3 Via Vanoni (tel. 923 27 07; email tra@vtx.ch). 8SFr per hr. Open M-W, F 9am-6:30pm, Th 9am-8:30pm, Sa 5-6:30pm.

Post Office: Via della Posta, 2 blocks up from the lake near Via al Forte. Open M-F 7:30am-6:15pm, Sa 8-11am. Travelers' checks cashed. Telephones, telegraphs, and faxes at the Via Magatti entrance to the PTT building. **Postal Code:** CH-6900.

PHONE CODE	The **city code** for Lugano is 091.

■ ACCOMMODATIONS

Lugano's lakesides are lined with luxury hotels and restaurants, but excellent bargains can be found in the center of town and on the oustskirts.

Hotel Montarina, 1 Via Montarina (tel. 966 72 72; fax 966 12 13), just behind the train station. Walk 200m to the right from the station, cross the tracks, and walk 1min. uphill. Converted from a luxury villa, this newly renovated independent hostel attracts young families and students with its **swimming pool,** well-groomed grounds, volleyball, ping-pong, chandeliered reading room, and terrace with a view. The dorms get rowdy in summer, when vacationing youth party hard. Dorms 20SFr; singles 50-65SFr; doubles 80SFr, 120SFr with bath. **Laundry** (4SFr, soap 1.50SFr). Good cheap coffee (1SFr). Buffet breakfast 12SFr. Sheets 4SFr. Reception 8am-10pm. Open Mar.-Nov.

Ostello della Gioventù (HI), Lugano-Savosa, 13 Via Cantonale (tel. 966 27 28; fax 968 23 63). Note: there are 2 streets called Via Cantonale, one in downtown Lugano and one in Savosa, where the hostel is. Take bus #5 (leaves from left of the station; go down the 2nd ramp, cross the street, and go uphill 100m) to "Crocifisso" (6th stop), then backtrack a bit and turn left up Via Cantonale. Also a former luxury villa, this sprawling hostel has secluded gardens and a **pool** with a waterslide, and a decidedly elegant atmosphere. Dorms 17SFr; singles 32SFr, with kitchenette 42SFr; doubles 46SFr, 60SFr. Price drops after 3 nights. Apartments available for families (7-day min. stay; 80-120SFr per day). Breakfast 7SFr. 1SFr for **kitchen** use (after 7pm only). Sheets 2SFr. Reception 7am-12:30pm and 3-10pm. Curfew 10pm; keys available on request. Reserve ahead. Open mid-Mar. to Oct.

Casa della Giovane, 34 corso Elvezia (tel. 911 66 46; fax 911 66 40), across the street from Basilica Sacro Cuore. Take bus #9 (leaves opposite train station) to "Corso Elvezia." This modern peach and blue building has bright, immaculate rooms for **women only.** The beautiful rooftop terrace with views of lake and mountains allows some serious tanning. 4-bed dorms 20SFr. Singles 50SFr, doubles 60SFr (breakfast included). Breakfast 4.50SFr. Lunch or dinner 12SFr. **Laundry** 5SFr. Reception 7am-11pm. Under age 18, curfew 9:30pm; ages 18 and up M-Th 11:15pm, F-Su 2am. Reserve ahead.

Hotel Pestalozzi, 9 P. Indipendenza (tel. 921 46 46; fax 922 20 45), on the main *piazza* away from the waterfront, 2 blocks up from the casino. Live it up for a night in this upscale hotel. Flowers spill over onto halls leading to attractive wood-floored rooms, all with sink, some with balcony. Singles 60SFr, with toilet 74SFr, shower 92SFr, bath 96SFr; doubles 100SFr, 128SFr, 144SFr, 154SFr; triples 140-230SFr. Breakfast included. Lunch or dinner 13-18SFr. Reception 6am-11pm. Reserve ahead. Visa, MC.

Pensione Selva, 36 Via Tesserete (tel. 923 60 17; fax 923 60 09). Take bus #9 (leaves opposite the station) to "Sassa," then walk along Via Gottardo for 250m and turn right on Via Tesserete. A path overhung with grapes leads to the cozy *pensione* with an outdoor **pool** and terrace. Singles 55SFr, with shower 78SFr; doubles 102SFr, 136SFr. Reception 8am-midnight. Closed in Nov.

Hotel Garni Zurigo, 13 corso Pestalozzi (tel. 923 43 43; fax 923 92 68), down the street from the AmEx office. All rooms have radio, TV, and telephone; velvet chairs in the reception add some swank. Singles 60SFr, with shower 85-95SFr; doubles with bath 130-140SFr; triples with shower 160SFr. Breakfast and parking included. 24hr. reception. Closed in Dec. AmEx, MC, Visa.

Camping: There are 5 campsites, all in **Agno.** Check with the tourist office for a complete list. For **La Palma** (tel. 605 25 61; fax 604 54 38) or **Eurocampo** (tel. 605 21 14; fax 605 31 87), take the FerroVia-Lugano-Ponte-Tresa (FLP) train to Agno (4.40SFr). From the station, turn left, then left again on Via Molinazzo. La Palma 7SFr, Eurocampo 7.50SFr; tents 6-10SFr. All sites have showers. Open Apr.-Oct.

◖ FOOD

Lugano's many outdoor restaurants and cafés pay homage to the canton's Italian heritage, serving up plates of *penne* and *gnocchi* and freshly spun pizzas. Lugano's specialty is (very visibly) sausage. For some quick *al fresco* shopping and eating, **Via Pessina** off P. Riforma livens up at midday with outdoor sandwich and fruit shops. **Salumeria,** 12 Via Pessina, is one of the better ones—you can buy some of the sausage, too.

La Tinèra, 2 Via dei Gorini (tel. 923 52 19), behind Credit Suisse in P. della Riforma. Tucked away in an alley off a cobblestone road, this low-lit underground restaurant has great daily specials (13-18SFr). Try the sausage with *risotto* (12SFr). Open M-Sa 11am-3pm and 5:30-10pm. AmEx, MC, Visa.

Ristorante Inova, on the 3rd floor of Placette Department Store in Piazza Dante. Budget eaters can't beat these self-serve victuals no matter what town they're in. Salad bar (4.20-9.90SFr), pasta bar (7.50-9SFr per plate), and other warm entrees-of-the-day (10-13SFr). Open M-Sa 7:30am-10pm, Su 10am-10pm.

Ristorante Cantinone, P. Cioccaro, behind P. Dante (tel. 923 10 68). This popular establishment has the weighty reputation for dishing out the best pizza in town under its pink-

and-white striped umbrellas. Try the Tuscan pizza with apples and nuts (15SFr). Pizza and pasta 10-17.50SFr. Salads 7-16SFr. Open 9am-midnight. AmEx, MC, Visa.

Ristorante Sayonara, 10 Via Soave (tel. 922 01 70; fax 922 07 56), in P. Cioccaro across from Cantinone (look for turquoise umbrellas). A huge lunchtime crowd comes for homemade pasta (14-18.50SFr; half-portions 9.50-13SFr) and pizza (from 11SFr). Open 8am-midnight. AmEx, MC, Visa.

Vanini, P. della Riforma (tel. 923 82 84). As pink as a scoop of *fragola* (strawberry) gelato, the homemade icy delights here are the best in town. 2.50SFr for 1 scoop—or splurge on a decadent dessert, like the Coupe Gandria, a masterpiece in strawberry and vanilla masterpiece adorned with bananas and cherries (9.60SFr). Open 8am-1am.

Pestalozzi, 9 P. Indipendenza (tel. 921 46 46), in the hotel. This non-alcoholic restaurant offers well balanced, veggie-friendly menus (9.50-16SFr) including tofu burgers. *Lasagne bolognese* and mixed salad 9.50SFr. Open 11am-9:30pm. MC, Visa.

MARKETS

Migros, 15 Via Pretoria, 2 blocks left of post office down Via Pretorio in the center of town, offers fresh pasta and delicious *ciabatta* (a crusty Italian bread). The food court on the ground floor saves the near-penniless with huge slices of various pizzas (from 2.50SFr) and sandwiches (from 2.30SFr). Open M-F 8am-6:30pm, Sa 7:30am-5pm.

Reformhaus Centro Dietetico Müller in the Quartiere Maghetti (next to Chiesa San Rocco). All things organic. Open M-F 8am-6:30pm, Sa 8am-5pm.

Aperto, in the station. True to its (Italian) name, "open" daily 6am-10pm.

Public Market, P. della Riforma. Sells seafood and produce of the region and yummy veggie sandwiches (4SFr). Open Tu and F 8am-noon.

👁 🏛 SIGHTS AND MUSEUMS

CHURCHES. The frescoes of the 16th-century **Cattedrale San Lorenzo,** just below the train station, gleam with colors that are still vivid, despite their advanced age. Two blocks to the left of the P. della Riforma, in the Piazza Maghetti, the small but densely decorated 14th-century **Chiesa San Rocco** houses an ornate Madonna altarpiece and gruesome Discopli frescoes of apostles being flayed alive and shot through with arrows. The national monument **Basilica Sacro Cuore,** on corso Elevezia across from the Casa della Giovane, is more sparing in its ornamentation, but the painted angels seem to fly right off the walls. Frescoes ringing the altar feature hikers walking alongside the disciples. The most spectacular fresco is Bernardio Luini's gargantuan **Crucifixion,** in the **Chiesa Santa Maria degli Angiuli,** to the right of the tourist office on the waterfront. Packed with dozens of figures in perpetual motion, angels flock to the main focal point, the crucified Christ.

ART MUSEUMS. Aside from the churches, Lugano's best known cultural attractions are its art museums—past and present (see **Art for Art's Sake?,** p. 416). The largest museum in town is the **Museo Cantonale d'Arte,** which has a permanent col-

---

ART FOR ART'S SAKE? The **Thyssen-Bornemisza Gallery** once housed one of the most outstanding private collections in Europe, until the owner (a fantastically rich old Baron) and his young Spanish wife (a former beauty queen) started looking around for a new home for all of those Rembrandts, Dürers, Van Goghs, and Kandinskys. In the international bidding war that ensued, the collection moved into the hands of the Spanish government for a while to up the ante. Spain became attached to the paintings, so the Baron talked them into building a museum and paying him a cool US$350 million for the stash. Spain wins, Switzerland loses, end of story. The gallery in Lugano, still maintained by the very piqued Swiss, is open to the public with the leftovers. Learn a lesson in Swiss tact by asking the guides—with the best look of open innocence you can muster—where all of the paintings have gone.

lection of 19th- and 20th-century art, including works by Swiss artists Vela, Ciseri, Franzoni, and Klee, and temporary modern art exhibits as well. *(10 Via Canova, across from the Chiesa San Rocco. Tel. 910 47 80. Open Tu 2-5pm, W-Su 10am-5pm. Special exhibits 12SFr, students 7SFr; permanent collection 7SFr, students 5SFr.)*

An elegant lakeside villa houses the intriguing **Museo delle Culture Extraeuropee,** on the footpath to Gandria in the Villa Heleneum. The masks, statues, and shields from distant lands stand out against the villa's marble floors and wall paintings. *(324 Via Cortivo. Tel. 971 73 53. Open Mar. 5-Oct. 31 W-Su 10am-5pm. 5SFr, students 3SFr.)* The **Museo d'Arte Moderna,** Villa Malpensata, to the right of the tourist office, has a decent collection of European and American 20th-century art, as well as annual retrospectives and special exhibitions. *(5 riva Caccia. Tel. 944 43 70. Open only for special exhibitions.)* The **Thyssen-Bornemisza Gallery,** in Villa Favorita, Castagnola, used to be a world-class museum, but nearly all of the paintings worth seeing were auctioned off to the Spanish government. Today, the gallery is open out of sheer stubbornness, with lackluster modern art on display. *(Take bus #1 (dir.: Castagnola) to "Villa Favorita" or catch a ferry to Castagnola. Open Apr.- Oct. F-Su 10am-5pm. 10SFr, students 6SFr.)*

▓ OUTDOOR ACTIVITIES

PARKS AND GARDENS. Lugano's waterfront parks are ideal places for introspection or play. The **Belvedere,** on quai riva Caccia, is an enormous sculpture garden with emphasis on modernist metalwork. The garden stretches along the lakeside promenade to the right of the tourist office towards Paradiso. In the other direction, the less whimsical but more serene **Parco Civico** is brightened by flowerbeds along the water and trees that reach down with willowy, long arms to touch the lake. A great place to watch Ticinese walking their dogs; backpackers have been known to (illegally) crash here. (Open Mar. 1-Oct. 31 6:30am-11:30pm; Nov. 1-Feb. 28 7am-9pm.)

BOATING. To enjoy the lake, try a **ferry ride**. The dock for the **Societa navigazione del Lago di Lugano** (tel. 923 17 79; email lake.lugano@bluewin.ch) is to the left of the tourist office. Various tours of the lagoon-like Lake Lugano offer glimpses of the tiny, unspoiled towns along the shore, including **Gandria** (10SFr, round-trip 16.60SFr), **Morcote** (14.40SFr, 23.80SFr), and **Paradiso** (2.40SFr, 4SFr). A "grand tour" of the lake is 28.60SFr; 50SFr gets you 7 days of unlimited lake travel. Conduct your own tours by **renting a boat**. Various points on the lake rent pedal boats (7SFr for 30min.). **Rent a Boat Saladin** (tel. 923 57 33), to the right of the tourist office, provides motor boats at 40SFr for an hour (no license required; open 8am-9pm). Instead of more *gelato*, cool off at the **Bagno Pubblica** on riva Caccia towards Paradiso (tel. 994 20 35; lake swimming 4SFr, children 2SFr; open May 16-June 30 and Aug. 14-Sept. 13 9:30am-6:30pm; July 1-Aug. 15 9:30am-8pm).

HIKING. Though the tops of the Ticinese mountains are cluttered with tourists, the unhampered views stretch into Italy. The tourist office and hostel both have topographical maps and trail guides (the tourist office sells them; the hostel lends them). **Monte Brè** (933m) and **Monte San Salvatore** (912m), are especially tempting hikes. Monte Brè's **funicular** is down the river to the left of the tourist office (13SFr, round-trip 19SFr; ages 6-16 6.50SFr, 9.50SFr). The San Salvatore funicular is 20 minutes from the tourist office, down the river to the right in Paradiso (12SFr, round-trip 18SFr; ages 6-16 6SFr, 9SFr). With a 13th-century church teetering on craggy cliffs that extend to the water, San Salvatore is easily the more striking of the pair. Hike down from the peak through chestnut forests to **Morcote**, on the shore, where you can catch a ferry back to Lugano (14.40SFr, SwissPass valid). The walk from the summit takes about 3½ hours. More daring hikers should ask at Hotel Montarina for info on hiking **Monte Boglio**.

ADVENTURE SPORTS. Travelers feeling the uncontrollable urge to throw themselves off cliffs should seek relief with the **ASBEST Adventure Company,** Via Basilea

28, CH-6903 Lugano (tel. 966 11 14; www.tourism.ticino.ch/text/asbest.html), based in the Hotel Continental, next to Hotel Montarina. In the winter, **snowshoe** and **ski** (full-day 85SFr) or **tandem paraglide** over icy crags (150SFr). **Canyoning** (from 70SFr) and **river-diving** (85SFr) are nice in Ticino because the water isn't as cold as the numbing mountain Alpine glacier streams. Or choose between **rock-climbing** (85SFr), **mountain biking** (25SF), and the insane **Rap-jump,** a kind of slow-motion spinning bungee jump (85SFr). AmEx, MC, Visa.

♫ NIGHTLIFE AND FESTIVALS

The arcades of the town *piazze* fill at night with people taking a *passaggio*, or a stroll around the city center in their best duds to see and be seen. The outdoor cafés of P. della Riforma are especially lively. Poker and slot machines will swallow your cash at **Casino Kursaal di Lugano** (tel. 923 51 017), to the left of the tourist office (slot machines open noon-4am, gaming tables open M-Sa 9pm-3am, Su 4-7pm; disco open 11pm-4am; min. age 20). On the way to the casino, stop in at the **Pave Pub,** riva Albertolli 1 (tel. 922 07 70), a self-proclaimed *museo di birra* (beer museum), offering 50 different beers with a great lakeside view of the fountains (beers start at 4-5SFr; open 11am-1am). Expect a serious change of pace at the **Biblio-Café Tra,** 3 Via Vanoni (tel. 923 23 05). From P. Dante, head down the Via Pretorio and turn left on Via A. Vanoni. This laid-back café evokes a bit of leftist Spain with bossa nova and battered wood tables. Locals and subversives consume 3.40SFr beers. (Open M-Th 9am-midnight, F 9am-1am, Sa 5pm-1am.) The Latin American **Mango Club,** 8 P. Dante (tel. 922 94 38), mixes live salsa and techno for a sweaty good time (open from 11pm until last person leaves).

Festivals liven up the lakefront in Lugano even more. From the end of June to early August, **Cinema al Lago** shows international films on the beach. A huge screen is installed at water level on the lake, with 1000 seats available for viewers (7SFr, under 17 5SFr). During the first 2 weekends in July, Lugano's **Jazz Festival** heats up at no charge. Previous performers include Miles Davis and Bobby McFerrin. The looser **Blues to Bop Festival** celebrates R&B, blues, and gospel at the end of August, hosting international singers as well as local amateurs. The festive season wraps up with the **Wine Harvest Festival** in late September and early October, drowning those faded summer memories.

DAYTRIPS FROM LUGANO

NEAR LUGANO: MORCOTE

Take a post bus from Lugano (board at P. Rezzonico or Via S. Balestra; 30min., 2 per hr. 6:35am-7:22pm, 7.40SFr, round-trip 14.80SFr). A ferry ride takes 50min. (8 per day 8am-6:30pm, 14.40SFr, round-trip 23.80SFr).

One of the swankiest small towns along Lake Lugano, Morcote basks in the luxury of summer villas, private art galleries, and fine dining. The town has its roots in fishing; as visitors browse the upscale shops, however, only the faint rocking of boats moored on the shore recalls that modest past—tourism has turned out to be a bigger fish. The town extends on either side from Piazza Grande. Behind the Piazza, narrow cobbled *strecia* climb up **Mount Arbostoro.** Sightseers willing to tackle a few hundred bumpy steps are rewarded with placid views as far as Italy and as near as the **Chiesa di Maria del Sasso,** parts of which were built in the 13th century. To get to the church from P. Grande, head left and turn up the Strecia di Mort, following the signs uphill. The sanctuary is fittingly ornate, with chandeliers dripping colored glass and rich crimson drapery shrouding the shrine to the Madonna. Intricate frescoes depict saints and popes; Adam and Eve frolic over the organ. To the right of P. Grande, the **Parco Scherrer** delights in more worldly pleasures. Curvy stone paths wind through the **botanical gardens,** encountering carefree statues. (Open Mar. 15-June 31 and Oct. 1-31 10am-5pm; July-Aug. until 6pm. Admission 7SFr, students 5SFr, under 17 1SFr.)

Several restaurants offering Italian and Ticinese specialties line P. Grande. The **Antico Caffe dei Barcaioli** (tel. 996 31 85), right in front of the ferry landing, is ideally located and affordable. Lakeside tables allow for plenty of people-watching as you munch on pizza (10-12SFr), veggie *focaccia* (7SFr), or homemade *tiramisù*, served by a friendly staff (7.50SFr; open 10am-midnight).

NEAR LUGANO: GANDRIA

A sandy walk from Lugano along the lakeshore (1hr.) leads to Gandria. Boats also travel from Lugano (every hr. 8:30am-9:15pm, 10SFr, round-trip 16.60SFr, SwissPass valid).

A grizzled fishing village that once attracted pirates to its shores, Gandria now attracts visitors of the map-and-walking-stick variety with its quiet sense of historical adventure. Narrow passageways and precipitous staircases hewn from stone evoke an era when marauders, not tourists, walked this town. Naughty pirates went to **Chiesa Parrochiale San Vigilio** for confession, lured by the gold crown over the altar. From the boat landing, walk up the stairs, turn left, stroll about 100m, turn right at the "Commestibili" sign, and climb the stairs to the church.

A short boat ride from Gandria's town center to **Cantine di Gandria** (boat stop "Museo delle Dogane," round-trip 7SFr) leads to the **Swiss Customs Museum.** The museum glorifies beret-wearing Swiss border guards with an array of contraband ranging from cocaine-filled condoms and passport forgeries to fake Levi's jeans. The 140-year-old building that houses the museum served as a barracks for frontier guards until just after WWII, when men complained that their isolation from women was preventing them from finding wives. (Tel. 910 48 11. Open 1:30-5:30pm. Free. Exhibits in Italian and German, with some introductory notes in English and French.) For a place to rest after an exhausting day of lounging by the lake, stroll over to **Hotel Miralago** (tel. (091) 971 43 61; fax 971 41 13), at the boat landing. The hotel offers very pink tropical rooms with floral everything and a leafy lakeside breakfast terrace. Five rooms hold 2-4 people each. (39SFr per person. Breakfast included. Reception 10:30am-midnight. Open Mar.-Nov.)

NEAR LUGANO: COMO, ITALY

Trains from Lugano bridge the 25km to Stazione San Giovanni (tel. (0147) 88 80 88) in Como several times each day (23-43min., 1-2 per hr., 12SFr).

Though an unworldly magnificence lingers over the northern reaches of Europe's deepest lake (410m), the peaceful Lake Como is not a figment of your imagination. Bougainvillea and lavish villas adorn Lake Como's craggy backdrop, warmed by the heat of the sun and cooled by lakeside breezes. Situated on the southwest tip of the lake, Como is a major silk manufacturer for the Italian fashion industry, but it has fortunately managed to preserve the languorous atmosphere that makes it an enjoyable daytrip. Classical Roman scholars Pliny the Elder and Pliny the Younger were among the first to recognize Como's charms, building villas throughout the countryside. After dinner, the entire city migrates to the waterfront for a *passeggiata* among the wisteria of 18th-century villas. From the station, head down the stairs, walk straight ahead, and cross through the little park to reach the main square, **Piazza Cavour,** which opens onto the waterfront, while **Lungo Lario Trento** winds its way around the mouth of the lake. To get to the commercial center from P. Cavour, follow Via Plinio to Piazza Duomo, where it becomes Via Vittorio Emanuele II. The **tourist office,** P. Cavour 16 (tel. 031 26 20 91), in the largest lakeside *piazza* near the ferry dock, has maps and extensive info in English (open M-Sa 9am-12:30pm and 2:30-6:30pm, Su 9am-1pm). You can **exchange currency** at the tourist office, train station, or post office.

■ **SIGHTS.** Near P. Cavour, Como's **Duomo,** begun in the 14th century, but not completed until the 18th, is famous for its harmonious combination of Gothic and Renaissance elements. The life-like sculptures animating the church's exterior are the Rodari brothers' work. Statues of Pliny the Elder and Pliny the Younger guard the door, which may seem incongruous in light of the fact that Pliny the Younger ordered the assassination of 2 early Christian nuns. (Open daily 7am-noon and 3-7pm.) Como's sturdy town hall leans up against the *duomo*, with thick pillars, colonnaded windows, and multicolored marble balconies. Two blocks from the *duomo*, **Chiesa di San Fedele** bears a resemblance to Ravenna's Byzantine churches. This is not surprising since the Lombards built the oldest parts of the church (notably the altar and the blind arcade) during the same period. Nearby, Giuseppe Terragni's **Casa del Fascio** stands as a stern reminder of Italy's ignominious past. It was built in 1939 to house the Fascist government, and has become an icon of Modernist Italian architecture, quite a contrast to the heavy masonry of typical Fascist architecture.

△ OUTDOOR ACTIVITIES. To take advantage of the scenic surroundings, ride the *funicolare* from P. de Gasperi 4 (tel. 031 30 36 08), at the far end of Lungo Lario Trieste, up to **Brunate** for access to pleasant hikes and expansive views. (Cars depart in summer every 15min.; in winter every 30min. Last return in summer Su-W 10:30pm, Th-Sa midnight; in winter daily 10:30pm. Adults one-way L4100, round-trip L7200, if purchased through the hostel L5000. Children one-way L2700, round-trip L4500.) Three rough-and-ready *baite* (guest houses) along the trail provide room and board in private or dorm-style rooms for about L30,000. In the off-season, check with the tourist office for hours.

Across the lake from the *funicolare*, the **Tempio Voltiano** (tel. (031) 57 47 05) is dedicated to the inventor of the battery, Alessandro Volta. (Open in summer Tu-Su 10am-noon and 3-6pm; in winter 10am-noon and 2-4pm. Admission L4000, groups and children under 6 L2500.) The villas lining the lake include the **Villa "La Rotonda"** and the **Villa Olmo** in the park of the same name (gardens open daily Apr.-Sept. 8am-11pm; Oct.-Mar. 9am-7pm). On the outskirts of town, 20 minutes down Vio Borgovico from the San Giovanni station, **Lido Villa Olmo,** Via Bellinzona 2 (tel. 031 57 08 71), provides a large lawn area for sunbathing, and a sandy stretch of beach. Tops are not required, but bathing caps are. (Admission L8000, L5000 if you buy tickets at the youth hostel. Open daily 10am-6pm.)

VALAIS (WALLIS)

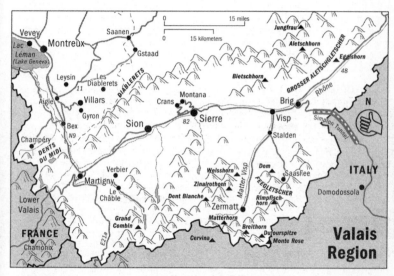

The territory bounded by Canton Valais occupies the deep, wide glacier cleft shaved by the Rhône river. In the west, Martigny and Sion are Francophone; upriver in Brig, Swiss-German dominates. In eastern Valais rise the southern slopes of the Bernese Oberland peaks; in the west along the Italian border, the Valais Alps and the Matterhorn rear their mighty heads. Though the high mountain resorts can be over-touristed, the inherent drama of the region's spectacular peaks and hulking glaciers still inspire strings of superlatives or awe-struck silence.

HIGHLIGHTS OF VALAIS

■ Strap on your crampons and grapple the glacier in **Zermatt** (p. 428).
■ Edge toward the extreme—attempt tandem flight in **Verbier** (p. 438)
■ Travel back to days of old when knights were bold and serfs were oppressed at the ruined castles of **Sion** (p. 421).

SION

Perfect for those travelers with short attention spans, Sion is an amalgam of most things Swiss. There's a little something for every taste—a 2-hour stroll takes you down wide, commercial streets and cobbled alleys, past looming mountains and the Rhône river, through silent châteaux and fertile vineyards. Though the city's third bid for the Winter Olympics was just turned down, Sion keeps chugging, its somewhat unremarkable urban landscape sharpened by 3 crumbling castles and the atmosphere enhanced by several notable music festivals.

🛈 ORIENTATION AND PRACTICAL INFORMATION. Trains pass every 30 minutes in each direction along the Rhône Valley, going west (4:55am-11:07pm) to **Martigny** (15min., 8.60SFr), **Aigle** (35min., 17.20SFr), **Montreux** (50min., 23SFr), and **Lausanne** (1¼hr., 30SFr); and east (6:04am-12:52am) to **Sierre** (10min., 5.60SFr) and **Brig** (30-45min., 17.20SFr), where you connect to **Zermatt** (55.20SFr) and **Saas Fee**

(29.20SFr). The **train station** (tel. 329 22 22; open 6am-8:45pm) provides **currency exchange** (open 6am-8:30pm), **lockers** (3-5SFr), **luggage storage** (5SFr for 24hr.; open 6am-8:45pm), **bike rental** (citybikes 20SFr per half-day, 26SFr per day; mountain 25SFr, 32SFr), and a **rail information** office (open M-F 8:30am-noon and 1:30-6:30pm, Sa 8am-12:30pm and 1:45-5pm). Just outside, Switzerland's largest **post bus station** congests the square with a blur of yellow buses, going near and far.

To get to the **tourist office,** pl. de la Planta (tel. 322 85 93; fax 322 18 82; email info@siontourism.ch; www.siontourism.ch), from the train station, walk directly up av. de la Gare, and turn right on rue de Lausanne (open July 15-Aug. 15 M-F 8:30am-6pm, Sa 10am-4pm; Aug. 16-July 14 M-F 8:30am-noon and 2-5:30pm, Sa 9am-noon). The office provides free room reservations, a ticket corner (tel. 322 85 93) for tickets to any event from Sion to Geneva, and 2-hour **guided tours** (July-Aug. Tu and Th 4pm, additional group tours on request; 8SFr, children and students 5SFr). For a **taxi,** dial 322 32 32. For the **police,** dial 117. In a **fire,** dial 118. For an **ambulance,** dial 144. **Pharmacie Berger** (tel. 22 42 35), on av. du Midi just off av. de la Gare, is one of several drugstores (open M 1:30-6:30pm, Tu-F 8am-noon and 1:30-6:30pm, Sa 9am-noon and 1:30-5pm) and will provide **emergency after-hour services** (10SFr fee). **Internet access** is available at **Quanna**, in the train station (tel. 321 10 60; open M-Th 11am-11pm, F 11am-midnight, Sa 10am-midnight, Su 5-11pm; 6SFr per 30min., 10SFr per hr.). The **post office,** pl. de la Gare, is left of the train station (open M-F 7:30am-6:15pm, Sa 8:15-11am). The **postal code** is CH-1950.

PHONE CODE	The **city code** for Sion is 027.

⌐ ACCOMMODATIONS. Built in 1991, the **Auberge de Jeunesse (HI),** av. de l'Industrie 2 (tel. 323 74 70; fax 323 74 38), maintains clean bathrooms, skinny semicircular balconies, and lockers in every room. From the station, walk left and down the stairs to rue de la Blancherie; continue left underneath the train tracks. Although it's big, the hostel can often be fully booked by marauding school groups in July and August. The next closest HI hostel is in Montreux (ack!), so call ahead. (4-bed dorms 26.80SFr; 2-bed dorms 33.80SFr, 30.30SFr. Breakfast included. Dinner 11.50SFr if you reserve it. **Kitchen** facilities 2SFr. Reception 7:30-9:30am and 5-10pm, until 9pm from Dec.-Apr. Curfew 10:30pm; keys on request. Lockout 9:30am-5pm. MC, Visa, AmEx.) Staying anywhere else will give your wallet a painful sting. The cheapest hotel rooms are at the smartly renovated **Hôtel Elite,** av. du Midi 6 (tel. 322 03 27; fax 322 23 61), on the edge of the *vieille ville* and surrounded by stores and cafés. From the station, head up av. de la Gare and turn right. Enjoy pristine rooms with TV, phone, private (if tiny) bathroom, and mountain views. (Singles 70SFr; doubles 120SFr. Prices 5SFr less after 2 nights. Breakfast included. Reception 6:30am-midnight. AmEx, MC, Visa.) Enterprising (or desperate) travelers seeking a cheap bed can try some of the villages outside Sion. The tourist office's booklet *Sion* gives details. (In **Pont-de-la-Morge** singles run 35-40SFr, doubles 68-80SFr; in **Saint-Léonard** 50-70SFr, 70-90SFr. Post buses run to both towns.) **Camping Les Lles,** rte d'Aproz (tel. 346 43 47; fax 346 68 47), is a 5-star riverside site. Take a very short ride on post bus #2 to Aproz. (7.80SFr, tents 9SFr; in low-season 6.20SFr, tents 6.50SFr. Open Jan.-Oct.)

⌐ FOOD. The streets of the *vieille ville* are lined with cafés and restaurants. Unlike most of them, the **Café des Châteaux,** rue des Châteaux 3 (tel. 372 13 96) is unpretentious, family-friendly, and affordable. From the tourist office, continue on rue de Lausanne, left on rue du Grant-Pont, and right on rue des Châteaux. (Salads 5-17SFr, fondue 19-22SFr, *escargots* 13SFr. Open M and W-Sa 8am-midnight, Su 10am-midnight.) Hang out with locals at the **Restaurant la Bergère,** av. de la Gare 30 (tel. 322 14 81), which specializes in pizza and pasta (14-17SFr) and sandwiches (2.50-5SFr; open M-F 6am-1am, Sa 10:30am-1am, Su 4pm-1am; AmEx, DC, MC, Visa). **Manora,** at the corner of av. du Midi and rue de la Dent-Blanche, on the ground floor of the Placette department store and supermarket, leads the pack of the self-serve restaurants (*Menüs* 10-14SFr, salad bar 4.20-9.90SFr; open M-Th 8am-7pm, F 8am-7:30pm, Sa 8am-6pm, Su 8am-4pm). Picnics await immediate assembly at **Co-op City,** pl. du Midi, right off av. de la Gare along av. du Midi (open M 1-6:30pm, Tu-Th 8:30am-6:30pm, F 8:30am-7:30pm, Sa 8am-5pm), or **Migros** supermarket and restaurant (main courses 8-15SFr) in the Centre Commercial Metropole on av. de France, 1 block left from the station (open M 1:30-6:30pm, Tu-Th 8:15am-6:30pm, F 8:15am-7:30pm, Sa 8am-5pm). A **produce market** occupies the pl. de la Planta every Friday from 8:30am to 6pm.

☎ 🏛 SIGHTS AND MUSEUMS. It's a knotty problem: how does one keep the peace between a bossy bishop, a grumpy chapter, and a fractious town? Sion's solution was to build the bishop's house, the towering **Château de Tourbillon,** on one hill; the chapter's seat, the **Château de Valère,** on another; and the municipal powerhouse, the **Château de la Majorie et du Vidomnat,** downtown. (A laser beam darts around this power triangle Th-Su nightfall-1am.) The first 2 castles stare each other down from across the hilltops, each providing a panorama of the valley, the Rhône, the Alps, and the city itself. To reach the third château, proceed from the station up av. de la Gare, turn right on rue de Lausanne, left on rue du Grand-Pont, then right up the narrow rue des Châteaux just past the orange town hall.

MUSEUM OF FINE ARTS. To the left is the Château de la Majorie et du Vidomnat, home to the **Musée des Beaux-Arts.** Fans of Valaisian art will enjoy the numerous scenes of rural life and portraits of wrinkly elders; even the uninitiated will enjoy the experimental 8-piece metal sculpture suspended from the ceiling of the stark Jesuit chapel (open only during temporary exhibits)—from the right viewpoint, it resolves into a seamless crystal circle. *(Pl. de la Majorie 15-19. Tel. 606 46 70. Open Tu-Su 10am-noon and 2-6pm. 5SFr, students 2.50SFr.)*

HISTORICAL MUSEUMS. The Château de Valère also houses the **Cantonal Museum of History and Ethnology,** which is incredibly informative to French speakers. *(Tel. 606 47 10. Open Tu-Su 10am-noon and 2-6pm. 5SFr, students 2.50SFr.)* Up the hill to the right from the Château de la Majorie, the world's oldest working organ (c.1390-1430) still pipes among the faded murals of the intriguing **Basilisque du Château de Valère.** Its annual festival of ancient organ music takes place every Saturday at 4pm in July and August (20SFr, students 10SFr).

The more challenging hill on the left projects higher with the fire-ravaged ruins of the **Château de Tourbillon.** Once the summer residence of the bishop, it is now the seasonal nest of mice and the odd sparrow. Although little remains to provoke the imagination but a crumbling shell, the payoff for the grueling hike is definitely the view. *(Open mid-Mar. to mid-Nov. Tu-Su 10am-6pm. Free.)*

Sion's most amusing museum is the **Natural History Museum,** right past pl. de la Planta and the tourist office. There are stuffed armadillos, 3 sets of Siamese goats (2 stuffed, 1 skeleton), a plastic glacier, and the contorted body of a mountain deer pulled from a glacier in 1920 after centuries on ice. *(42 av. de la Gare. Tel. 606 47 30. Open Tu-Su 2-6pm. 3SFr, students 1.5SFr, children under 6 free.)*

🎭 ENTERTAINMENT. The *vieille ville* hosts several annual music festivals. The open-air **Jazz Festival** takes over the streets at 11pm on Friday the last weekend of June (10-25SFr, festival passes 150SFr; tickets available at tourist office or at the gate). Summer evenings bring **free concerts** of classical music through the **Academie de Musique** (tel. 322 66 52). From July to September there are also major orchestral events during the **Tibor Varga Festival** (tel. 323 43 17; email festivargasion @vtx.ch; www.nouvelliste.ch/varga/tvarga.html; tickets 20-80SFr, available through the tourist office ticket corner).

Sion's other favorite pastime is wine-tasting. Most cafés have white-washed terraces where patrons sip *Valais Fendant* or *Johannisberg-Tavillon*, the leading labels in town. Consult the tourist office for organized **wine-tasting excursions** and a list of local cellars. A long-distance path through the vineyards, *le chemin du* *vignoble*, passes close to Sion and through tasting territory. Always ring before you arrive at a *cave*, and try to rustle up a group if you want the proprietor to be more welcoming. One *centre de dégustation* is **Les Celliers de Champsec**, av. Grand-Champsec 30 (tel. 203 56 83), just across the river (open M 2-6:30pm, Tu-F 10am-noon and 2-6:30pm, Sa 10am-noon and 2-5pm).

ZERMATT AND THE MATTERHORN

A trick of the valley blocks out the great Alpine summits ringing Zermatt, allowing the Matterhorn (4478m) to rise alone above the town. Instantly recognizable and stamped on everything from scarves to pencils by Zermatt's merchants of kitsch, the peak still causes you to catch your breath whenever you look up. At dawn it blazes bright orange; some days—some weeks—it is swathed in clouds, completely hidden from view. Zermatt itself is mostly a missable tourist trap. The main road, Bahnhofstraße, is populated in equal measure by ruddy hiker/skier types and their more sedate shopping bag-laden counterparts. You can escape it all with a short hike or cable car ride to lonely Alpine meadows and splintered icefalls—feasts for the eye are the real reason to visit.

ⓘ ORIENTATION AND PRACTICAL INFORMATION

To preserve the Alpine air from exhaust fumes, Zermatt has outlawed cars and buses; locals in toylike electric buggies alternately dodge and target pedestrians. The town of **Täsch**, one stop before Zermatt, has **parking garages** for 10SFr per day; the large, outdoor lot by the rail station is 5-6.50Fr per day (and has a reservation board for hotels in Zermatt). Zermatt is only accessible by the **BVZ (Brig-Visp-Zermatt) rail** line (SwissPass valid). Many of the town's hotels and restaurants line Bahnhofstr., which runs in front of the station.

PHONE CODE	The **city code** for Zermatt is 027.

Trains: Bahnhofpl. (tel. 966 47 11). Jump on the BVZ at **Brig** (1½hr., 38SFr, round-trip 63SFr); **Visp** (if coming from Lausanne or Sion; 35SFr, round-trip 60SFr); **Stalden-Saas** (if coming from Saas Fee; 1hr., 31SFr, round-trip 53SFr); or **Täsch** (every 20min., 7.20SFr). Trains leave Zermatt for **Brig** (every hr. 6am-9:10pm) and **Täsch** until 11:10pm. The station has a free direct phone line to Zermatt's hotels, as well as **lockers** (2-5SFr, open 5:45am-8pm) and **hotel taxis,** waiting to round up guests after each train arrives.

Tourist Office: Bahnhofpl. (tel. 967 01 81; fax 967 01 85; email zermatt@wallis.ch; www.zermatt.ch), in the station complex. Free booklets *Prato Borni* and *Zermatt* tell you all you need to know. Hiking trail map (*Wanderkarte*) 27.90SFr. Open mid-June to mid-Oct. M-F 8:30am-6pm, Sa 8:30am-7pm, Su 9:30am-noon and 4-7pm; mid-Oct. to mid-June M-Sa 8:30am-noon and 1:30-7pm.

Currency Exchange: Zermatt Tours, next to the tourist office. No commission. Open July 1-Sept. 30 and Dec. 15-Apr. 15 M-Sa 8:30am-noon and 2-6pm, Su 9am-noon and 3-6pm; Oct. 1-Dec. 14 and Apr. 16-June 30 M-F 8:30am-noon and 2-6pm, Sa 8:30am-noon and 2:30-6pm. **Banks** are generally open M-F 9am-noon and 2:30-6pm.

Bike and Ski Rental: Roc Sport (tel. 967 39 27) on Kirchstr. Go left at the church. Mountain bikes 35SFr per day. 10% discount on bikes and skis for youth hostelers. Open M-Sa 8am-noon and 2:30-7pm, Su 8am-noon and 3:30-6:30pm. Its outlet, **Julen Sport** (tel. 967 43 40) on Hoffmattstr., has skis but no bikes. Open M-Sa 8:30am-noon, 2-7pm. AmEx, DC, MC, Visa. Otherwise, try **Slalom Sport** (tel. 966 23 66) on Kirchstr. Open M-Sa 8am-noon and 2-7pm, Su 8am-noon and 4-6:30pm. Or **Bayard Sports** (tel. 966 49 60) directly across from the station. Open M-Sa 8am-12:30pm and 2-7pm; Su 8am-noon, 2-7pm.

Snow and Alpine Center: Bahnhofstr., right from the station past the post office, houses the **Bergführerbüro** (Guide's Office; tel. 966 24 60) and **Ski School Office** (*Skischulbüro;* tel. 967 24 66; email skischule.zermatt@spectraweb.ch). Posts detailed weather forecasts every morning for the next 4 days, sells ski passes, and coordinates guided private and group climbing expeditions. In summer, groups go daily up the **Breithorn** (120SFr), **Pollux** (230SFr), and **Castor** (240SFr). Prices do not include equipment, hut accommodations, or lifts to the departure points. Hiking the Matterhorn is expensive and requires technical experience and at least a week's prior training. If you do decide to hike, get insured or be prepared to risk a 4-figure helicopter rescue bill from Air Zermatt. Open July-Sept. M-F 8:30am-noon and 4-7pm, Sa 4-7pm, Su 10am-noon and 4-7pm. Ski/snowboard lessons 80SFr for 1hr., 210SFr for 3 hr. Center open M-Sa 8am-noon and 3-7pm, Su 10am-noon and 4-7pm.

English-Language Library: In the English Church on the hill behind the post office. Small collection of battered novels loaned on the honor system. Be honorable!

Weather Conditions: Dial 162 or check the window of the *Bergführerbüro*. **Winter Avalanche Information,** tel. 187.

Emergencies: Police, tel. 117. **Fire,** tel. 118. **Ambulance,** tel. 67 12 12. **24hr. Alpine Rescue,** tel. 1414.

Pharmacy: Pharmacie Internationale Zermatt (tel. 966 27 27), Bahnhofstr. to right of station. High season hours M-Sa 8am-noon and 2-7pm; Su 10am-noon. Emergency service for 10SFr surcharge (tel. 966 27 27).

Internet Access: Get your email fix at **Matterhorn Hostel** for 10SFr per hr. **Hotel Post** (tel. 967 19 32), Bahnhofstr. to the right of the station, charges 2SFr for 15 min., 1.50SFr each additional 15 min.

Post Office: Bahnhofstr., in Arcade Mont-Cervin 5min. to the right of the station. Open M-F 8am-noon and 1:30-6pm, Sat 8:30-11am. **24hr. ATM.** Postal Code: CH-3920.

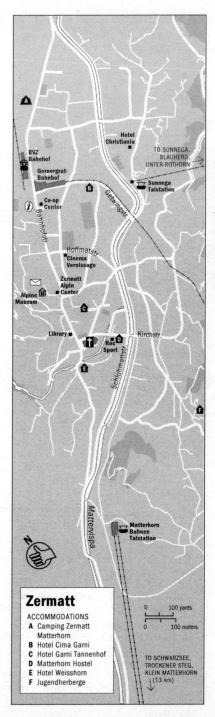

Zermatt

ACCOMMODATIONS
A Camping Zermatt Matterhorn
B Hotel Cima Garni
C Hotel Garni Tannenhof
D Matterhorn Hostel
E Hotel Weisshorn
F Jugendherberge

0   100 yards
0   100 meters

TO SCHWARZSEE, TROCKENER STEG, KLEIN MATTERHORN ↓ (13 km)

VALAIS

█ ACCOMMODATIONS

Climbers, hikers, and snowboarders buoy up the demand for budget beds in Zermatt. Finding a dorm bed on the spot can be a squeeze July through August, Christmas and New Year's, and mid-February through mid-March. Many hotels in winter and all chalets in summer only accept bookings for a week at a time. In desperation, some campers are tempted to park their bods illegally in the wide-open spaces above town—this practice can incur fines between 50 and 100SFr.

The Matterhorn Hostel (tel./fax 968 19 15; email matterhorn.hostel@smile.ch), is a 12min. walk from the station. Turn right on Bahnhofstr., left at the church, and take the first right after the river onto Schluhmattstr. Hostel is 150-200m up the street. This young independent hostel, decorated with graffiti art, attracts similarly youthful outdoor adventurers. Metal bunks 24-29SFr in summer, 29SFr in winter. Breakfast 6SFr. Dinner 12SFr *Menü* or à la carte (10-20SFr) in summer. **Internet access** 10SFr per hr. Coin-operated **laundry** 2-8SFr for wash and dry. Downstairs bar serves beer for 3SFr. TV room, games, no curfew. Reception 7:30-11am and 4-10pm. AmEx, MC, Visa.

Hotel Bahnhof (tel. 967 24 06; fax 967 72 16; email Hotel_Bahnhof@hotmail.com), on Bahnhofstr. 1min. from the station—turn left. Recently renovated rooms offer hotel housing at hostel rates with no hike from the station. Dorms 30SFr; 4-bed rooms with private showers 40SFr; singles 52SFr, with shower 56SFr; doubles 82-88SFr. **Laundry** 3SFr. No breakfast, but one of the few places with a **kitchen** and large dining room. Lockers for all. Open mid-Dec. to mid-Oct. Reception 8:30am-around 8pm.

Jugendherberge (HI), Winkelmatten (tel. 967 23 20; fax 967 53 06), is a 15min. hike from the station, the last part up a steep hill. Turn right along Bahnhofstr. and left at the church. Cross the river, take the second street to the right (at the Jugendherberge sign), and select the left fork in front of Hotel Rhodania. Fully loaded, if predictably institutional hostel, where you get all the goodies...for a higher price. Unobstructed views of the Matterhorn from bedroom windows, friendly staff, giant outdoor chess set, ping-pong, and foosball await. Dorms 41.50SFr in high season, 39SFr in low; one double 103SFr, 98SFr. Breakfast, sleepsack, showers, and **dinner** (kosher and vegetarian available) included. **Laundry** 8SFr per load. Closed May and late Oct. to mid-Dec. Reception 7-9:30am and 4-11pm in summer, 6:30-9:30am and 4-11pm in winter. AmEx, DC, MC, Visa.

Hotel Garni Tannenhof (tel. 967 31 88; fax 967 51 73). From the station, turn right on Bahnhofstr., walk 300m, turn left at Bayard Sports and then take the first right. The most affordable and plush of the tourist-magnet budget hotels, it features thick rugs, huge leather chairs, and a solicitous staff, not to mention the excellent breakfast. Every room comes with a radio and telephone. Singles 45-50SFr; with private shower 58-80SFr; doubles 90-100SFr, 110-120SFr; triples 105-120SFr. Reception 7am-7pm. Reserve at least 1 month in advance in winter, 2-3 weeks in summer. Closed Oct. 20-Dec. 5. AmEx, DC, Visa.

Hotel Weisshorn, Bahnhofstr. (tel. 967 11 12; fax 967 38 39). From the train station, turn right along Bahnhofstr. The hotel is 30m past the church. Low, paneled ceilings, winding staircases, and cushy beds draw guests to this hotel. Rates vary depending on season. Singles 46-54SFr, with private shower, TV, and phone 65-75SFr; doubles 84-100SFr, 112-132SFr; triples 114-138SFr. Breakfast included. Reception 7am-10pm. Reservations necessary in winter high season, up to two months in advance. MC, Visa.

Hotel Cima Garni (tel. 967 23 37; fax 967 55 39), 250m from the station, straight down Getwingstr., to the left of Swiss Souvenirs. This bed and breakfast blends a standard Swiss exterior (red shutters on brown building) with an interior of subdued grays and very shiny pine paneling—you can almost smell the polish. Clean, bright rooms sport Matterhorn paintings and varying color schemes. Singles and doubles 50-60SFr per person in summer, 70-90SFr in winter. Breakfast included. Visa.

Camping Alphubel (tel. 967 36 35), in Täsch. What with Zermatt being car-free and all, caravaners and motorists can park their vehicles and stay here. From the station, cross the parking lot and turn right in front of the tourist offices past the river, then right across the railroad tracks. 5.50SFr, ages 6-16 2.50SFr; tent 7SFr, 5SFr; car 5.50SFr; caravan 6SFr. Showers. Open May to mid-Oct.

Camping Matterhorn Zermatt, Bahnhofstr. (tel./fax 967 39 21), is 5min. to the left of the train station. Though the mountains are pretty, the spotty, grass-covered area looks onto train tracks. Showers included. July 15-Aug.15 9SFr, children 6SFr; otherwise, 8.50SFr, 5SFr. Reception May-Sept. 8:30-10am and 5:15-7pm.

Mountain Huts: The tourist office has a list of private huts in the Zermatt area. For 23SFr a night, they offer a good deal for serious climbers, but others will find them too high for a proper night's sleep. **Schönbiel** (tel. 967 13 54; 2694m), **Rothorn** (tel. 967 20 43; 3177m), the crowded **Gandegg** (tel. (079) 607 88 68; 3029m), **Hörnli** (tel. 967 22 64; 3260m), and **Monte Rosa** (tel. 967 21 15; 2795m; crampons and guide advised) are all open July-Sept. and accessible to walkers if there's no snow. All are about a full day's hike from Zermatt.

FOOD AND NIGHTLIFE

Rather than charging the usual inflated Alpine prices, a large number of the cafés along Bahnhofstr. leave both your wallet and your stomach pretty full. Several supermarkets provide picnic supplies for day hikes.

RESTAURANTS AND BARS

Walliser Kanne (tel. 966 46 10), Bahnhofstr., next to the post office. A great place to people-watch, this popular establishment offers good Swiss fare including *Käsespatzle* (homemade pasta with cheese, 16.50SFr), *Käseschnitte mit Schinken and Tomate* (toasted cheese with ham and tomato, 16SFr), and fresh strawberries in whipped cream (9SFr), as well as the usual pizza and pasta (15-19SFr). Open 11:30am-2pm and 6-10pm. AmEx, DC, MC, Visa.

Café-Konditorei Hörnli, (tel. 967 44 57), Bahnhofstr. across from Hoffmattstr, is a relaxed, quiet little place, lit by tiny futuristic lamps suspended at asymmetric heights where locals go on lunch breaks. Breakfast 9SFr, salads 8.50SFr, sweet crêpes 4-7.50SFr. The bakery downstairs has a mouth-watering selection of everything nice. Café open 7:30am-7pm, bakery open M-Sa 7:30am-noon and 2-6:30pm.

Pöstli "Brown Cow" Pub (tel. 967 19 32), Bahnhofstr. past the post office in the Hotel de la Post. The lively thirty-something clientele appreciates the whimsical cow-pattern decor (even painted on the metal ceiling fans) and back-to-basics greasy-spoon food. Potato skins 9.50SFr, or sadistically chomp on a burger, 11-15SFr. Heineken 3.40SFr. Open 8am-midnight.

The North Wall Bar (tel. 967 28 63). Head over the river on Kirchstr. and take the second right en route to the youth hostel. No frills, 100%-English-speaking climbers' haunt where skiing and mountaineering videos play every evening alongside the less dynamic (but still potentially dangerous) dart games. This is the place to scrounge a job in Zermatt. The kitchen will serve you anything you like, as long as it's "the hottest pizza in the Alps" (10SFr, plus 1SFr for fancy topping like mussels, corn, broccoli, or egg). At 4.50SFr for 0.5L, the beer is probably the cheapest in town. Open mid-June to Sept. and mid-Dec. to Apr. 6:30pm-12:30am, pizza served until 10pm.

The Pipe Surfer's Cantina, (tel. 213 38 07; www.webyourworld.com). Go right on Bahnhofstr. from the station, then left at the church onto Kirchstr. Overlooking the cemetery, this après-snowboarding bar has an Australian/Mexican twist for those tired of crowded Swiss-specialty restaurants. Every night is a special night—on Mondays, Fosters are 4SFr all night long, and Thursday is "surf night." Frozen margaritas 6SFr, beer 3.50SFr.

Food on the weekends (variety of salads 14SFr). Free shot with coupon from Jugendherberge. Open M-F noon-1:30am, Sa-Su 3pm-1:30am.

Café du Pont (tel. 967 43 43), 7min. from the station on Bahnhofstr., next to Hotel Weisshorn. Zermatt's oldest restaurant shows its age just a bit, but it makes up for it in atmosphere. Browse through the large multilingual menus, burnt into slabs of wood hanging from the wall, then decide between stick-to-your-ribs Swiss dishes like *raclette* (7.50SFr), *Rösti* (11-15SFr), and *fondue du Pont* (22SFr). Sandwiches 6.50SFr. Open June-Oct. and Dec.-Apr. daily 9am-11pm; food served until 10pm.

Swiss Rock Café, Bahnhofstr. near the post office (tel. 966 87 39). This sleek piano-bar serves never-ending bratwurst with baked potatoes (17SFr), chicken skewers with herb butter (21SFr), and beer at 5.20SFr for 0.5L. 2-for-1 drinks 6-7pm. Live music 9pm daily. Open 10am-midnight. Closed mid-Oct. to Nov.

Grampi's Pub (tel. 967 77 88), Bahnhofstr. across from Pöstli Pub. This centrally located bar thumps with pop dance music by night. Draft beer 3.80SFr for 0.25L; bottled beer 4.50-7SFr; long drinks 11-13SFr. DJ 8:30pm-3am. Open 8:45am-3am (downstairs bar until 4am, restaurant 5pm-1am).

MARKETS

Co-op Center, across from the station. Open M-Sa 8:15am-12:15pm and 1:45-6:30pm, Su 4-6:30pm.

Migros, Hoffmattstr., down from Bahnhofstr. between the station and the church. Open M-Sa 8:30am-12:15pm and 2-6:30pm, Su 4-6:30pm.

⛰ OUTDOOR ACTIVITIES

SKIING

Seventy-three lifts, 14,200m of combined elevation, and 245km of prepared runs make Zermatt one of the world's best-equipped ski centers. Serious skiers will find real challenges here, as well as **Europe's longest run**—the 13km trail from Klein Matterhorn to Zermatt. Where it really outshines its rivals, however, is in its ski-mountaineering potential. The town also has more **summer ski trails** than any other Alpine ski resort—36 sq. km of year-round runs between 2900 and 3900m. In the summer, the **ski school** (tel. 967 24 66) offers group classes for skiing and snowboarding (either activity: 1 day 40SFr, 5 days 200SFr). **Ski and boot rental** is standard throughout the area—57SFr for 1 day, 207SFr for 6—but youth hostelers get an additional 10% discount at **Roc Sport** (see p. 424). Finding a reliable sports store is not a problem (most shops open daily 8am-noon and 2-7pm). Zermatt's **ski passes** operate on a regional system. You can buy passes for any combination of days and regions (Matterhorn complex, Gornergrat complex, and Sunnegga complex). For example, the Matterhorn region costs 58SFr for 1 day, 246SFr for 6 days; all 3 regions combined cost 60SFr, 306SFr. The Klein Matterhorn/Trockener Steg sub-region is now combined with Italy's **Mt. Cervinia** (1 day 58SFr, 6 days 260SFr).

HIKING

Outstanding walks into the world of glaciers and high mountains spread from Zermatt in every direction. Although these paths are well-made and well-marked, a proper non-panoramic map is essential for safety and adds to your appreciation of the mountains. Lifts and railways to the south and east are also valuable hiking tools; they can save you difficult climbs and precious energy. SwissPasses will win you a 25% discount on many of these lifts, but Eurailpasses are generally not valid. Prudent walkers should come prepared (see **Essentials: Health** p. 22). Zermatt is particularly prone to sudden electrical storms, and you may need to dive for cover. The *Bergführerbüro* posts a conservative illustrated weather forecast in its window on Bahnhofstr. To rent hiking boots, try **Matterhorn Sport,** Bahnhofstr. (tel. 967 29 56), which also rents out climbing equipment; **Glacier Sport,** Bahnhofstr.

(tel. 968 13 00) across from Walliser Kanne; or **Burgena Sport,** Bahnhofstr. (tel 967 27 94) next to Grampi's pub. (1-day rentals are 14SFr; 7 days 52SFr; 14 days 80SFr. All stores open daily 8am-noon and 2-7pm.)

TO THE WEST AND NORTHWEST. West of Zermatt, the mountains are savage, spiky pinnacles. The **Zinalrothorn** (4221m), **Obergabelhorn** (4063m), and **Dent Blanche** (4357m) are some of the toughest climbs around. An easier walk to **Zmutt** (1936m, 1hr.) and the **Schönbielhütte** (2694m, 4hr.), leads along the base of these magnificent peaks and offers the most dramatic encounter with the Matterhorn's north face. The path is wide, clear, and well-marked, and the views get exponentially better as you ascend. From Zermatt, follow Bahnhofstr. past the church, then follow the sign to the right. Climb the steady slope through Arolla pines to the weathered chalets of the hamlet of Zmutt. The path levels out as it continues through the meadows above a small reservoir, granting views of the Hörnli ridge and the Matterhorn. As you go on, the Matterhorn's north wall, which drops 200m with an average gradient well over 45°, comes into breathtaking view. The hike becomes more difficult as it ascends past lakes and waterfalls at the outlet of the rock-strewn **Zmuttgletscher** and follows the lateral ridge to the **Schönbielhütte,** an ideal spot for lunchtime carbo-loading of pasta or *Rösti* at the restaurant while you examine the icefalls rising from 3 sides. On the return journey, the valley frames the **Rimpfischhorn** (4199m) and **Strahlhorn** (4190m). The full-day hike is 25km, covering 1050m of gentle elevation.

TO THE SOUTHWEST. No visit to Zermatt is emotionally complete without struggling up to the **Hörnlihütte,** the base camp for the normal route up the Matterhorn and a good platform for watching brightly colored dots claw their way upward along the ridge. The 1600m ascent is for the fit and well-booted only (a good walking stick or ski pole is also recommended); a cable car to the **Schwarzsee** (2552m) saves you 900m of elevation (20SFr; round-trip 31.50SFr). Leave Zermatt along the left bank of the Matter Vispa, as for the Zmutt/Schönbielhütte hike. After a few minutes of climbing, 2km or so from Zermatt, a wide track marked *"Zum See, Schwarzsee und Hörnlihütte"* heads down left across the river. Follow the 3-hour path as it zigzags steeply up to the tiny lake, the Schwarzsee, and admire the monstrous Gorner gorges on the left. A group of climbers caught in a snowstorm built the chapel on the lake in an act of piety when their prayers were answered and the clouds miraculously lifted. The path becomes rockier and wilder as it joins the true northeast ridge of the Matterhorn, climbing gently at first but ending in a merciless, exposed *arête* (sharp ridge) by the buildings at Hörnli (*Schwarzsee* to Hörnli takes about 2hr.). Be aware that casual hikers *cannot* continue above the hut. More than 500 people have died in the kilometers above this point, as a sobering walk around Zermatt's cemeteries will prove. A guide, perfect physical condition, a 4am start, and extensive rock-climbing experience (at least PD+) are essential for proceeding. To descend a different way, bear right at the *Schwarzsee* to the Furgg cable car terminus and follow the path down to the back. The path traverses a steep cliff but is stable underfoot and has even closer views of the gorges carved by the **Gornergletscher.**

TO THE SOUTH. South from Zermatt the Matterhorn changes its clothes again, this time parading the pyramidal west face. This direction is the way to wilderness—steep icefalls peel off the **Breithorn** (4164m), and below the icefalls are the glacier-scoured, sun-bleached boulder fields. The highest **cable car** in Europe alights on the **Klein Matterhorn,** 6km from the Matterhorn (operates high-season 7am-6pm; 45.50SFr, round-trip 73SFr). A track leads out from the tunnel below the viewing platform to **Gobba di Rollin** (3899m), following the T-bar all the way, but the hike requires good weather, caution, and a tortoise pace due to the altitude. From the Trockner Steg cable-car station (2939m), however, you can walk back to Zermatt: leave the complex on the Monte Rosa side away from the Matterhorn and follow the path to the left along the gully in front of you (2½hr.).

TO THE SOUTHEAST AND EAST. Southeast from Zermatt are the **Monte Rosa** (4634m) and the **Liskamm** (4527m), the second and third highest mountains in Switzerland, respectively. Leonardo da Vinci, incidentally, thought the Monte Rosa was the highest mountain on Earth. Among its unlikely conquerors have been Pope Pius XI, who pioneered a new route to the Grenzsattel in 1889, and a youthful Winston Churchill, who climbed the monster in 1894. From the southeast, framed by woods and reflected in lakes, the Matterhorn takes on its most-familiar angle, reproduced on everything from tea towels to cookie tins. A rack railway winds up to the best viewpoint, the **Gornergrat** (3090m; 38SFr, round-trip 63SFr) by way of **Riffelalp** (2211m; 17.20SFr, round-trip 32SFr). Other stops include **Riffelberg** (2582m; 27SFr, round-trip 46SF) and **Rotenboden** (2815m; 34SFr, round-trip 58SFr).

The Gornergrat swarms with as many as 5,000 visitors per day at the height of the season. The train departs opposite Zermatt's main station (7am-7pm). The train's main path from Zermatt follows the right bank of the river upstream, stopping at all the stations. The round-trip hike to Gornergrat demands a great deal of stamina; grabbing a lift for part of the ascent will preserve your strength for clambering around the top or taking a more interesting path down. From the top, tracks lead down to the wide, flat **Gornergletscher** and along the ridge toward the **Stockhorn** (3532m). A cable car also runs to this point (12SFr each way). From Rotenboden you can divert to the Monte Rosa hut (2½hr.), following the glacier. Each destination provides a closer encounter with the ice but loses a fraction of the panorama that makes the Gornergrat so special. You can also descend after the Riffelalp station by following the contour around to the *Grüensee*, facing the snout of the **Findelngletscher,** then crossing the river and returning to Zermatt by way of the **Moosjesee** and the **Leisee,** 2 small pools that provide a beautiful foreground to the Matterhorn. The *Leisee* is also accessible by the first stop on the **Sunnegga-Rothorn** rail line (Zermatt to Sunnegga 13.20SFr one-way, 18.40SFr round-trip). The small village of **Findeln** is only half an hour away, and the slightly farther town of **Ried** boasts the best apple cake in the area (1hr.).

TO THE NORTHEAST AND NORTHWEST. Compared to the well-trodden highways south of Zermatt, the slopes to the north are much better-known during ski season. Rockier and steeper, these difficult paths lead to proper summits rather than scenic huts or viewpoints. A **northeast hike** starts from the Zermatt station. Head down to the river beside the Gornergratbahn, cross it, turn left, then hop on the Sunnegga-Rothorn railway and lift as far as **Blauherd** (2560m; 24SFr, round-trip 32.40SFr). A wide path gently circles the **Unterrothorn**'s right flank to a mountain pass at 2981m. Take the series of zigzags on the right (some offering fixed handrails) up to the **Oberrothorn** (3415m), a satisfying rocky fang. A **northwest hike** begins midway between the church and post office, opposite Hotel de la Poste on Bahnhofstr. The path initially climbs steeply toward **Alterhaupt** (1961m) and **Trift** (2337m), then levels off. The little-known glacier cirque beneath the icefalls of the **Obergabelhorn** and **Zinalrothorn** provides a turn-around point, but supermen and women will bear right up the **Metterhorn** (3406m), accessible to agile walkers and a popular endurance-training hike for those about to try the Matterhorn. The guides office organizes a more accessible excursion north to the Gornerschlucht canyon, the **Gorge Adventure**. Always above rushing water, even first-time mountaineers can traverse narrow bridges and rock faces with the aid of a guide and safety cables (95SFr per person).

ADVENTURE SPORTS AND SWIMMING

If the skiing or hiking doesn't look good, there are still other outdoor activities to try. For **paragliding**, AirTaxi (tel. 967 67 44) offers tandem flights. **Zermatt Mule Trekking** (tel. (079) 285 66 38; www.rhone.ch/zermatt-mule-trekking), between the train station and Täsch, offers guided rides. (2-3hr. to Zmutt, Findeln, or Ried, 35SFr per hr. Longer trips 160SFr per day. Open 8am-noon and 2-6pm.)

Zermatt is at least 3 hours from any worthwhile indoor attraction; when it rains you will wish you were anywhere else. The posher hotels have **swimming pools,** with Hotel Christiania (tel. 967 19 07) offering the biggest. Follow the right bank of the river to the left past the Rothorn/Sunnegga cable railway station. (10SFr, children 6SFr. Open M, W, and F-Su 8-10:30am and 1:30-7:30pm, Th 8-10:30am and 1:30-9pm.) For an additional 10SFr, you can work up a sweat in the sauna. Other hotels offer massages for those weary hiking muscles.

🎵 🏛 ENTERTAINMENT, FESTIVALS, AND MUSEUMS

The **Cinema Vernissage** (tel. 967 66 36), next to Julen Sports on Hoffmattstr., has 2 or 3 screenings nightly Monday to Saturday of nearly new releases, usually in English. In the latter half of July, films are shown at the **open air cinema** (10-15SFr; café open M-Sa 5pm-midnight; AmEx, DC, MC, Visa). Another rainy day refuge is the **Alpines Museum** near the post office. Here, the courage of those adventurers who first conquered regional peaks with (by modern standards) absurd equipment is proven by paraphernalia of their not-so-fortunate comrades: broken ropes, mangled shoes, and bashed-in lanterns found with corpses sometimes months after tragic falls. Special attention is given to the first ascent of the Matterhorn, over half of whose expedition were killed on July 14, 1865, on their way back down. A haunting photograph is all that remains of one such victim, Lord Alfred Douglas (love of Oscar Wilde's life), whose mortal remains were never found. Recovered remains of victims of the Matterhorn are buried in the cemetery, next to the church with picks and ropes defiantly carved into their graves. (Tel. 967 41 00. Open June-Sept. 10am-noon and 4-6pm; Dec.-May M-F and Su 4:30-6:30pm. Closed Nov.-Oct. 5SFr, children 1SFr. Guide in English 1SFr.)

Elaborating on Zermatt's favorite topic, early July brings the **Mountain Film Festival,** during which films about, well, the mountains, receive their due in open air. August brings the **Alpine Folklore Parade,** when locals take a break from their mountain chores mid-month and dust off their alphorns and traditional dress. The Roman Catholic church sporadically hosts **classical music concerts** (25SFr) throughout the month, and at the end of August, runners in the **Matterhornlauf** climb 1001m from Zermatt to the *Schwarzsee* at the foot of the Matterhorn.

TRANSPORT HUB: BRIG

A junction town at the base of the Simplon, Furka, and Grimsel passes, Brig has traditionally been a place to change your horses and trade your wares. Even now, the town is more of a place to go through than to. Nevertheless, Brig burgeons with old-fashioned hotels, pleasant, slate-grey streets, and narrow houses. Along the Rhône valley, **trains** run to **Sierre** (30min., every 30min. 4:20am-11:17pm, 12.60SFr), **Sion** (40min., every 30min. 4:20am-11:17pm, 17.20SFr), **Lausanne** (1½-2hr., every 30min. 4:20am-10:12pm, 45SFr), and **Geneva** (2¾hr., every 30min. 4:20am-10:12pm, 60SFr). Through the Lötschberg tunnel, trains head to **Bern** (1¾hr., every hr. 4:45am-10:04pm, 50SFr) and **Interlaken** (1½hr., every hr. 4:45am-10:04pm, 42SFr). The Simplon tunnel trains lead to **Domodossola** in Italy (30min., every hr., 12.60SFr) and **Locarno** (2½hr., every hr., 50SFr, change at Domodossola). Bus lines spread through the surrounding hillsides from Bahnhofpl. The most important one departs for **Saas Fee** (1¼hr., every hr. 6:15am-8:15pm, 17.20SFr) outside the station exit.

The helpful **rail information office** (tel. (027) 922 24 44) helps bewildered travelers sort all of this out and offers **Internet access** (open M-F 8am-6:30pm, Sa 8am-4:30pm; 6SFr per 30min., 11SFr per hr.). If you feel the need to explore, get information from the **tourist office** (tel. (027) 921 60 30; fax 921 60 31; email info@brig-tourismus.ch; www.brig-tourismus.ch), up the yellow stairs on the first floor of the train station (open M-F 8:30am-noon and 1:30-6pm, Sa 8:30am-noon and, in summer, 2-5:30pm). The station has **currency exchange** (tel. (0512) 25 82 30; open M-Sa 6:15am-7:30pm, Su 7:50-11:45am and 2-6pm), **lockers** (3-5SFr), **luggage storage** (5SFr; open 8am-noon and 1-5:20pm), and a free phone line to hotels.

SAAS FEE

Nicknamed "the pearl of the Alps," Saas Fee (1800m) occupies one of Switzerland's most dramatic sites. In a hanging valley above the Saastal, the city snuggles among 13 grand 4000m peaks, including the **Dom** (4545m). The glacial ice of the **Feegletscher** comes so low that you can visit the primordial giant on a 30-minute evening stroll. To protect all this alpine glory, the entire resort town is closed to cars, giving electrically powered mini-vans and trucks free run of the rambling streets. The town is not nearly as tourist-choked as Zermatt. A similar abundance of red knee-highs and sleek neon suits, however, proves that Saas Fee's main draw is also the outdoor scene. Town officials prohibit disturbing "the fairy-like charm of Saas Fee" after 10pm (noisemakers fined 200SFr). The raucous silence of the encroaching glacier will have to do.

7 ORIENTATION AND PRACTICAL INFORMATION. A **post bus** runs (every hr. 5:35am-7:35pm) to **Brig** (1¼hr., 17.20SFr, round-trip 32SFr); **Visp** (50min., 14.60SFr, 29.20SFr), which connects to Lausanne, Sion, and the rest of Valais; **Stalden Saas** (40min., 11.80SFr, 23.60SFr), which connects to Zermatt for another 30SFr; and **Saas Grund** (10min., 3SFr, 6SFr). Reserve a seat on all buses starting at Saas Fee at least 2 hours before departure. Dial 957 19 45 or drop by the bus station (open 7:30am-12:35pm and 1:15-6.35pm). Drivers can **park** at the lower end of the village with a guest card from their hotel (1 day 13SFr, in summer 11SFr; with guest card after 2nd day 9SFr, 7.50SFr).

The **tourist office** (tel. 958 18 58; direct reservations 958 18 68; fax 958 18 60; email to@saas-fee.ch; www.saas-fee.ch), opposite the bus station, dispenses seasonal information, hiking advice, guides, and reasonably useful town maps. (Open July to mid-Sept. and mid-Dec. to mid-Apr. M-F 8:30am-noon and 2-6:30pm, Sa 8am-7pm; Su 9am-noon and 3-6pm; mid-Sept. to mid-Dec. and mid-Apr. to June M-Sa 8:30am-noon and 2-6pm; Su 10am-noon and 4-6pm). In an after-hours emergency, call the **pharmacist** at 957 44 17 or (079) 417 67 18. During business hours, visit Vallesia Apotheke (tel. 957 26 18), farther up the main street to your right outside the tourist office (open M-Sa 8:30am-noon and 2-6:30pm). In an **emergency**, dial 117. **Internet access** is available at Hotel Dom (tel. 957 51 01; email Hotel.Dom@saas-fee.ch; www.saas-fee.ch/dom) on the main street (10SFr per ½-hr., 18SFr per hr.). The bus depot has small **lockers** (2SFr) and houses the **post office** with public **fax** and **24-hour ATM** (open M-F 8:15am-noon and 2-6pm, Sa 8:15-11am). For a **weather report**, dial 162 or 157 61 52. The **postal code** is CH-3906.

PHONE CODE	The **city code** for Saas Fee is 027.

ACCOMMODATIONS. While spine-tingling mountain exploits are Saas Fee's main draw, beware—this resort is not for the financially faint of heart. The town's unofficial mascot, the merry marmot, may not be quite so chipper when he receives his hotel bill. To complicate housing further, from early May to mid-June lifts, restaurants and hotels shut down for maintenance, renovations, and vacations for townspeople—keep this fact in mind when planning your visit.

Travelers willing to sacrifice comfort can find bargains in hotel basements. The cheapest is **Hotel Garni Imseng** (tel. 958 12 58, fax 958 12 55). From the station, head down the main street, left of the tourist office, then turn left and pass the church. Next to the 3-star hotel's bakery, 7 rows of bunks are stacked 3 high like filing cabinets, with no space between rows. The whole thing looks suspiciously like a boiler room, but at least you'll wake to the smell of fresh bread and you just might have the 21 beds to yourself. (20SFr. Sheets 5SFr. Breakfast 15SFr.) Across the street and behind Hotel Feehof Garni, the subterranean dorm at the **Hotel Berghof** (tel. 957 24 84; fax 957 46 72) bears a striking resemblance to the one at Garni Imseng, though a bit more spacious. Store your bags in the new, unforgettably pink lockers. (Dorms 25SFr, 35SFr with breakfast. Bring your own sheets.

The MCI WorldCom Card.

The easy way to call when traveling worldwide.

The MCI WorldCom Card gives you…

- Access to the US and other countries worldwide.
- Customer Service 24 hours a day
- Operators who speak your language
- Great MCI WorldCom rates and no sign-up fees

For more information or to apply for a Card call:

1-800-955-0925

Outside the U.S., call MCI WorldCom collect (reverse charge) at:

1-712-943-6839

COUNTRY	WORLDPHONE TOLL-FREE ACCESS #
Argentina (CC)	
To call using Telefonica ■	0800-222-6249
To call using Telecom ■	0800-555-1002
Australia (CC) ♦	
To call using AAPT ■	1-800-730-014
To call using OPTUS ■	1-800-551-111
To call using TELSTRA ■	1-800-881-100
Austria (CC) ♦	0800-200-235
Bahamas	1-800-888-8000
Belgium (CC) ♦	0800-10012
Bermuda ÷	1-800-888-8000
Bolivia (CC) ♦	0-800-2222
Brazil (CC)	000-8012
British Virgin Islands ÷	1-800-888-8000
Canada (CC)	1-800-888-8000
Cayman Islands	1-800-888-8000
Chile (CC)	
To call using CTC ■	800-207-300
To call using ENTEL ■	800-360-180
China ÷	108-12
For a Mandarin-speaking Operator	108-17
Colombia (CC) ♦	980-9-16-0001
Collect Access in Spanish	980-9-16-1111
Costa Rica ♦	0800-012-2222
Czech Republic (CC) ♦	00-42-000112
Denmark (CC) ♦	8001-0022
Dominican Republic	
Collect Access	1-800-888-8000
Collect Access in Spanish	1121
Ecuador (CC) ÷	999-170
El Salvador	800-1767

COUNTRY	WORLDPHONE TOLL-FREE ACCESS #
Finland (CC) ♦	08001-102-80
France (CC) ♦	0800-99-0019
French Guiana (CC)	0-800-99-0019
Guatemala (CC) ♦	99-99-189
Germany (CC)	0-800-888-8000
Greece (CC) ♦	00-800-1211
Guam (CC)	1-800-888-8000
Haiti ÷	193
Collect Access in French/Creole	190
Honduras ÷	8000-122
Hong Kong (CC)	800-96-1121
Hungary (CC) ♦	00▼800-01411
India (CC) ÷	000-127
Collect Access	000-126
Ireland (CC)	1-800-55-1001
Israel (CC)	
BEZEQ International	1-800-940-2727
BARAK	1-800-930-2727
Italy (CC) ♦	172-1022
Jamaica ÷	Collect Access 1-800-888-8000
(From Special Hotels only)	873
(From public phones)	#2
Japan (CC) ♦	To call using KDD ■ 00539-121▶
To call using IDC ■	0066-55-121
To call using JT ■	0044-11-121
Korea (CC)	To call using KT ■ 00729-14
To call using DACOM ■	00309-12
To call using ONSE	00369-14
Phone Booths÷	Press red button, 03, then ★
Military Bases	550-2255
Lebanon	Collect Access 600-MCI (600-624)

COUNTRY	WORLDPHONE TOLL-FREE ACCESS #
Luxembourg (CC)	0800-0112
Malaysia (CC) ♦	1-800-80-0012
To call using Time Telekom ■	1-800-18-0012
Mexico (CC) Avantel	01-800-021-8000
Telmex ▲	001-800-674-7000
Collect Access in Spanish	01-800-021-1000
Monaco (CC) ♦	800-90-019
Netherlands (CC) ♦	0800-022-9122
New Zealand (CC)	000-912
Nicaragua (CC)	Collect Access in Spanish 166
(Outside of Managua, dial 02 first)	
Norway (CC) ♦	800-19912
Panama	108
Military Bases	2810-108
Philippines (CC) ♦	To call using PLDT ■ 105-14
To call using PHILCOM	1026-14
To call using Bayantel	1237-14
To call using ETPI	1066-14
Poland (CC) ÷	00-800-111-21-22
Portugal (CC) ÷	800-800-123
Puerto Rico (CC)	1-800-888-8000
Romania (CC) ÷	01-800-1800
Russia (CC) ♦ ÷	
To call using ROSTELCOM ■	747-3322
(For Russian speaking operator)	747-3320
To call using SOVINTEL ■	960-2222
Saudi Arabia (CC) ÷	1-800-11
Singapore	8000-112-112
Slovak Republic	(CC) 0042-I-00112
South Africa (CC)	0800-99-0011
Spain (CC)	900-99-0014

Worldwide Calling Made Easy

The MCI WorldCom Card, designed specifically to keep you in touch with the people that matter the most to you.

www.wcom.com/worldphone

Please cut out and save this reference guide for convenient U.S. and worldwide calling with the MCI WorldCom Card.

And, it's simple to call home or to other countires.

1. Dial the WorldPhone toll-free access number of the country you're calling from (listed inside).

2. Follow the easy voice instructions or hold for a WorldPhone operator. Enter or give the operator your MCI WorldCom Card number or call collect.

3. Enter or give the WorldPhone operator your home number.

4. Share your adventures with your family!

COUNTRY		WORLDPHONE TOLL-FREE ACCESS #
St. Lucia ✛		1-800-888-8000
Sweden (CC) ◆		020-795-922
Switzerland (CC) ◆		0800-89-0222
Taiwan (CC) ◆		0080-13-4567
Thailand ★		001-999-1-2001
Turkey (CC) ◆		00-8001-1177
United Kingdom	(CC) To call using BT ■	0800-89-0222
	To call using CWC ■	0500-89-0222
United States (CC)		1-800-888-8000
U.S. Virgin Islands (CC)		1-800-888-8000
Vatican City (CC)		172-1022
Venezuela (CC) ✛ ◆		800-1114-0
Vietnam ●		1201-1022

(CC)	Country-to-country calling available to/from most international locations.
✛	Limited availability.
▼	Wait for second dial tone.
▲	When calling from public phones, use phones marked LADATEL.
■	International communications carrier.
★	Not available from public pay phones.
◆	Public phones may require deposit of coin or phone card for dial tone.
●	Local service fee in U.S. currency required to complete call.
►	Regulation does not permit Intra-Japan calls.
✧	Available from most major cities

MCI WorldCom Worldphone Access Numbe

MCI WORLDCOM

Closed in May.) One of the town's better values is **Pension Garni Mascotte** and its two sister chalets, **Alba** and **Albana** (tel. 957 27 24; fax 957 12 16). Head down the road opposite the station, just left of the tourist office. At the main street, turn right and continue up the hill for 200m; Mascotte is on the left. (Alba dorms 27-30SFr. Albana 5-bed dorms 28-33SF; 4-bed dorms 30-35SFr; 2-bed dorms 38-48SFr. Albana's rooms have shower and toilet. Smarter rooms in Mascotte 45-55SFr. Breakfast included. Add 10SFr for half-pension. **Laundry** facilities, ski storage, and TV lounge. Open mid-Dec. to Apr. and July-Sept.) Across the street from Garni Imseng, **Hotel Garni Feehof** (tel. 957 23 08; fax 957 23 09) doubles the price but lifts quality of life exponentially. Warm, wooden, and wonderful, nearly all the creaky pine rooms have balconies and deliciously soft beds. (Singles 39-57SFr in summer, 45-66SFr in winter, with breakfast and shower. In winter, reserve 2 weeks in advance.) If you're not burdened by luggage of the unwieldy, matched variety, a spunky alternative to staying in Saas Fee proper is a night in a **mountain hut.** The **Mischabelhütte** (3329m; tel. 957 11 17; 26SFr), **Hoh-saas** (3098m; tel. 957 17 13; 22SFr), and **Weissmieshütte** (2726m; tel. 957 25 54; 30SFr) above Saas Grund are all accessible from July to September. All 3 huts serve breakfast and dinner to compensate for the trek up. The Saas Fee tourist office and Bergführerbüro have further details.

⬛ FOOD. In Saas Fee, where there's a hotel, there's a restaurant. **Spaghetteria da Rasso** (tel. 957 15 26), 2 minutes to the left of the pharmacy under the Hotel Britania, has 14 variations on spaghetti (13-20SFr; half-portions also available), plus pizza (15-19SFr, minis 10.50-12.50SFr), salads (6-9SFr), and garlic bread (3.50SFr). The shady terrace, wooden gnomes, and occasional accordionists attract quite a crowd. (Open June-Sept. 10am-11:30pm; Oct.-Dec. F-Sa 10am-11:30pm; winter Tu-Su 10am-11:30pm; AmEx, MC, Visa.) Though it's certainly not difficult to find Swiss specialties around town, the **Restaurant Chämi-Stuba** (tel. 957 17 47), on the main street near the church, is a large, family-owned establishment, candle-lit and quiet. (Bratwurst with onion sauce and *Rösti* 15SFr, a rather alcoholic Valaisian fondue 22SFr, and a credible version of *Apfelstrudel mit Vanillesauce* 5SFr. Open 9am-midnight.)

Hungry shoppers can choose between 3 **supermarkets** in small Saas Fee, and all 3 have the same hours (M-Sa 8:30am-12:15pm and 2:15-6:30pm). Near the tourist office and Pension Mascotte is the Supermarkt, right next to the pharmacy on the main street. A small Konsum Center stands next to the ski school across from the Alpine guide picture board. The pick of the lot, though, is the super-duper new Migros, just down the hill from the church.

⬛ OUTDOOR ACTIVITIES. Once properly nourished, visitors turn their attention to the mountains. Two **cable cars** to **Felskinn** (3000m) and a discreet **underground funicular,** the "Metro Alpin," to **Mittelallanin** (3500m) enable summer **skiers** to enjoy 20km of runs and a stupendous Alpine view (round-trip to Mittelallanin, 7:30am-3:45pm, 58SFr; to Felskinn, 7:15am-4:15pm, 30SFr). In winter, an immense network of lifts opens to the delight of impatient skiers (day ski passes 58SFr, children 35SFr; 6 days 270SFr, 162SFr; 13 days 480SFr, 288SFr). For those as-of-yet disinclined toward inclines, the **Ski School** (tel. 957 23 48), across the street from the church, offers group skiing or snowboarding lessons. (Skiing 45SFr for 3 hr., 168SFr for 1 week; snowboarding 45SFr for 2 hr., 1 week 153SFr. Slight reductions available in late Jan. Open M-Sa 9:30-11:30am and 3-6pm.) In Saas Fee, if it doesn't sell stuffed marmots, it **rents skis.** Stores in the **Swiss Rent-A-Sport System** (look for the black and red logo) offer 2 to 3 grades of equipment (skis 28-50SFr per day, 6 days 105-180SFr; snowboards 28-38SFr, 80-105SFr; boots 15-19SFr, 52-77SFr). The *über*-organized can call ahead of time and have equipment set aside for their arrival; call or fax the main Swiss Rent-A-Sport outlet in town, **Anthamatten Sport Mode** (tel. 958 19 18; fax 957 19 76; across from the Spaghetteria).

VALAIS

In summer, Saas Fee is among the best places to enjoy **Alpinism.** The **Alpine Guide's office** (tel. 957 44 64), in the same building as the ski school, has a selection of climbs to 4000m summits for both amateurs and experts (open M-Sa 9:30am-noon and 3-6pm). Day tours run anywhere from 130 to 395SFr per person.

Hikers have 280km of marked trails from which to choose, but the whole mountain-town thing tends to create rather steep paths. A lovely half-day walk begins with a cable-car ride to **Plattjen** (2570m). For picture-perfect views of the Dom and Lezspitze, a path leads to the right and zigzags left after 5 minutes. From the top it descends for 15 minutes, then heads left around the cirque, spiralling slowly down below the **Feegletscher.** The view opens up to the other high peaks as you drop down to the **Gletschersee** (1910m) at the glacier snout. The path then gently follows the left bank of the outlet stream back to Saas Fee. For a hard, steep trek, hike up to the **Mischabelhütte** (3329m), which has the single best panorama of the Saas Fee cirque accessible to walkers. From the pharmacy on the main street, turn right after the church and take the right fork 100m farther on. Check for snow cover before you leave, however—the last part of the hike is rocky and highly unpleasant with any hint of ice (1550m ascent, full-day, June-Sept. only).

Casual strollers can head out of town along the main street and through the athletic facilities, turning right at the fork towards the stream. An easy path leads up to a water mill powered by rushing rapids and the Café Gletscher Grotto. A **Saas Valley Hiking Pass** (149SFr, family rate 299SFr) provides access for 1 week to all cable cars and post buses in the valley and entrance to the ice pavilion at **Mittelallanin,** the **Bielen Recreation Center,** and other museums. The pass is available at the tourist office or any cable car station. Most lifts close from May to early June and from mid-October to mid-December, when bad weather renders many hikes impassable.

On rainy days, you can amuse yourself at the **Bielen Recreation Center** (tel. 957 24 75), next to the bus station. The complex has an expensive but excellent **swimming pool** and **jacuzzi.** (Open June 1-9pm, July-Oct. 10am-9pm. 12SFr, with guest card 10SFr; children 7SFr, 6SFr.) The guide's office organizes an outing to a nearby gorge every Monday and Friday that is accessible all year long, even in bad weather. Similar to the Gorge Adventure in Zermatt, kids as young as 10 can scuttle along water-carved rock faces, aided by safety equipment (65SFr).

MARTIGNY

Strategically located at the foot of the Grand St. Bernard Pass, French-speaking Martigny (pop. 15,000) was established by Roman Emperor Claudius during the first century AD to control trade routes between Switzerland and Italy, making it the oldest town in Valais. A medieval castle towers over the suburban town, its slack posture mirroring the valley's trees, beaten into tilted poses by the winds. Rather than resting on its Roman laurels or wallowing in its medieval splendor, however, Martigny is definitely living this century. Thanks in large part to the **Fondation Gianadda,** Martigny is a major center for modern art and classical music. For the more adventurous, Martigny provides access to **Mont Blanc** (4807m), the highest mountain in the Alps, which straddles the French and Italian borders.

◪ **ORIENTATION AND PRACTICAL INFORMATION.** Frequent **trains** run west to **Lausanne** (50min., every 30min. 5:10am-11:27pm, 23SFr); **Montreux** (30min., every 30min. 5:10am-11:27pm, 14.60SFr); and **Aigle** (17min., every 30min. 5:10am-11:27pm, 9.40SFr); and east to **Sion** (15min., 3 per hr. 6:08am-12:36am, 8.60SFr). Two private lines leave for **Orsières,** where you can change for **Aosta** in Italy via the **St. Bernard Pass** (2hr., 6 per day 8:10am-5:38pm, 31.40SFr); and for **Châtelard** where you can change for **Chamonix** in France, a starting point for the 10- to 14-day Mont Blanc circuit (1¾hr., every hr. 6:41am-7:52pm, 30SFr). **Buses** run to Champex and the Col de la Forclaz pass, starting points on the Swiss side of the mountain. The train station (tel. 752 22 22; open M-Sa 5:45am-8:45pm, Su 6:15am-8:45pm) provides **currency exchange, lockers** (3-5SFr), **luggage storage** (5SFr), **bike rental** (26SFr per day; mountain bike 32SFr per day), and a **rail information** office (open M-F 9am-noon and 1:30-6pm, Sa 9am-noon and 1:30-5pm).

Martigny's **tourist office,** pl. Centrale 9 (tel. 721 22 20; fax 721 22 24), is straight down av. de la Gare at the far corner of pl. Centrale (open July-Aug. M-F 9am-6pm, Sa 9am-noon and 2-6pm, Su 10am-noon and 4-6pm; Sept.-June M-F 9am-noon and 1:30-6pm, Sa 9am-noon). Get **Internet access** at Le Coin Internet at the Casino (tel. 722 13 93; www.cybercasino.ch), halfway between the station and pl. Centrale on rue de la Gare (20SFr per hr.; open M-Sa 6:30am-midnight, Su 6:30am-11pm). The **hospital** (tel. 721 97 21) has a switchboard that connects you to the late-night doctor and **pharmacy.** Pharmacie Centrale (emergency tel. 722 55 56) is part of Migros supercenter at pl. du Manoir 5. For an **ambulance,** dial 721 95 50. For the **police,** dial 117. The **post office,** av. de la Gare 32 (tel. 722 26 72), between the station and the tourist office, has a public **fax** and a **24-hour ATM** (open M-F 7:30am-noon and 1:30-6:30pm, Sa 7:30-11am). The **postal code** is CH-1920.

PHONE CODE	The **city code** for Martigny is 027.

ŕ ACCOMMODATIONS. Since travelers in Martigny are mainly business types, budget pickings are slim. Commuting from the recently built Auberge de Jeunesse in **Sion** (see p. 422) is an excellent and more affordable idea, especially if you have a railpass. Otherwise, try **Le Ranch El Capio** (tel. 723 27 83), on Autoroute N9 (Sion-Simplon), or a 30-minute walk from the train station: turn left and walk to Rue Simplar, left again until the Aoste-Chamonin Autoroute overpass, left up the highway, then right toward Sion, and continue straight on until you see signs to the left. The ranch rents horses (23SFr per hr., 50SFr per ½-day), and has 4- to 6-bed rooms for 13SFr per person and singles for 20SFr. Breakfast is 6SFr. Giddy-up, Herr Kuhboy. Closer to the train station, the **Hôtel du Stand,** av. du Grand-St.-Bernard 41 (tel. 722 15 06; fax 722 95 06), lies straight past the tourist office near the Fondation Gianadda. The wood-paneled rooms come with a full bathroom. The restaurant downstairs has a *plat du jour* for 16SFr and 3-course *Menüs* for 22-30SFr. (Singles 65SFr; doubles 94SFr; triples 120SFr. Breakfast and parking included. Reception 7am-midnight. Sauna 5SFr. Reserve ahead July-Sept. MC, Visa.) **Camping Les Neuvilles,** rue du Levant 68 (tel. 722 45 44), packs its shaded plot with motor homes. From the station, head straight on av. de la Gare, take the second left on av. des Neuvilles, and turn right onto rue du Levant. Amenities include playgrounds, a store, **laundry** machines, a **sauna,** a solarium, and miniature golf. (6SFr, tents 7.50SFr, 4-person bungalow 85SFr; Sept.-June 5SFr, 60SFr, 60SFr. Dorm beds 20.60SFr. Shower included. Reception July-Aug. 8am-noon and 1:30-10pm.)

ŗ FOOD. Cafés crowd Martigny's tree-lined pl. Centrale, some with *Menüs* in the 15-25SFr range. For even cheaper fare, **Lords' Sandwiches,** av. du Grand-St.-Bernard 15 (tel. 723 35 98), serves 36 kinds of sandwiches (3.80-11.70SFr), including a bacon burger with fries, and the Zeus, an overstuffed roast beef sandwich (open M 7am-10:30pm, Tu-F 7am-midnight, Sa 8:30am-midnight, Su 3-10:30pm). **Le Rustique,** av. de la Gare 44 (tel. 722 88 33), lives up to its name with a dark wood interior with nature scenes painted on stucco. Enjoy savory crêpes (9.50-13.50SFr) or sweet ones (4.50-9.50SFr), and wash them down with a 3.50SFr mug of cider. (Open 11:30am-10:30pm.) For straightforward Italian food, locals recommend **Pizzeria au Grotto,** rue du Rhône 3 (tel. 722 02 46), off rue Marc-Morand to the left of pl. Centrale. The Grotto has pizzas (11-17SFr) and pasta entrees (12-20SFr; kitchen open M-Th, Su 11:30am-2pm and 6-10pm, F-Sa 11:30am-2pm and 6-11pm; MC, Visa).

The immense **Migros** supermarket at pl. du Manoir 5, just off pl. Centrale, has 18 different boutiques, a restaurant, and moving sidewalks (open M-Th 8:15am-6:30pm; F 8:15am-8pm; Sa 8am-5pm). Down rue de la Poste from the post office, a **Co-op** offers similar services (open M-Th 8:15am-6:30pm; F 8:15am-8pm; Sa 8am-5pm). Stroll down av. de la Gare on Thursday mornings to buy edible and wearable goods at the **public market** (open 7:30am-noon).

VALAIS

BATTLE ROYAL The fighting cows of Valais have been, since medieval times, the privilege of the rich, the spectacle of the poor, and the lifelong devotion of breeders. After all, the first Swiss-domesticated cows (little neolithic specimens) were found in Valais, near Martigny. Since then, the highest reverence has been accorded to the *Hérens* strain, valued for its fine milk and meat, and particularly mountain-adapted nature. Such vigor is not only a matter of physique—*Hérens* females have an aggressive streak that reveals itself in their violent, profound eyes, hot blood, and savage aspect. For hundreds of years breeders have raised cows in hopes of achieving success at the annual cow fights *(Combats de Reines)*. These fights did not occur officially in Martigny until 1923, when they began to be institutionalized as more than just an odd folk tradition. When facing off, the combatants (called "*lutteuses*," or "wrestlers") exhibit a veritable repertoire of well-documented moves and behaviors, from preliminary head movements and *escarpier* (pawing the ground), to head-on and lateral attacks. After a mighty struggle, whichever animal is not lying on the ground receives an extra-special bell and some salt from her owner, along with the distinction of being *la reine*, the queen, of the herd. All in a day's work.

SIGHTS AND MUSEUMS. Martigny's most engaging attraction is the **Fondation Pierre Gianadda.** Head down the rue Hôtel-de-Ville behind the tourist office and follow the signs. The permanent collection includes works by Cézanne, Van Gogh, Ensor, Van Dongen, and Picasso, while the central atrium hosts blockbuster international traveling exhibitions—on the plate for 2000 are Kandinsky from January to June, and Van Gogh from June to November. The exhibits tend to overshadow the rest of the foundation, including the mildly interesting **Gallo-Roman Museum,** which showcases classical works like the Octoduran bronzes discovered in Martigny and a 3-horned bronze bull's head. Downstairs, the more entertaining **Automobile Museum** exhibits more than 50 vintage cars—Bugattis, gleaming early Peugots, and a Rolls Royce Silver Ghost—built between 1897 and 1939, most in working condition. The garden surrounding the Fondation is populated with excellent modern sculptures, including some by Brancusi, Miró, and Rodin. More archaeological finds hide among the hedges (Rue du Forum 59. Tel. 722 39 78; www.gianadda.ch. Open 9am-7pm. 12SFr, students 5SFr, family ticket 25SFr. Tickets include admission to the Gallo-Roman and Automobile Museums, the temporary exhibitions, and the Sculpture Gardens. Free guided tours W at 8pm or by prior arrangement. Wheelchair accessible.) The foundation hosts classical music concerts, many in conjunction with the **Festival Tibor Varga** and the **Montreux-Vevey Classical Music Festival** (see p. 468).

The tourist office leads 1½-hour **guided tours** of Martigny, including the Fondation (July-Aug. 10am, 2pm; by appointment the rest of the year; 12SFr, students 5SFr, family ticket 25SFr). If you want to explore on your own, the ever-helpful office distributes a brochure that will guide you on a walking tour of Martigny's Roman ruins *(promenade archéologique)*. Past the railroad tracks, remnants of a Roman road point toward Britannia and, through the pass, Roma. Nearby, the grassy 4th-century **Amphithéâtre Romain** is the spectacular setting for the final contest of the Valais **cow fighting** season. Pamplona, this is not. 50m away from the Fondation, signs lead to the remains of a temple to the **sun god Mithra** dating from the 3rd century AD (now under some apartment building). **Le Château de la Bâtiaz,** the ruins of a 13th-century castle that once belonged to the bishops of Sion, overlooks Martigny from the hill. From the station, head along av. de la Gare, and turn right at pl. Centrale along rue Marc-Morand. Climb the massive stone tower extending over an outcropping of bare rock for a bird's-eye perspective of the flat Rhône floodplain. (Open mid-July to mid-Aug. 10am-6pm. Free.)

ENTERTAINMENT AND FESTIVALS. Martigny hosts the **Foire du Valais,** the regional trade fair of Valais, in the blue and yellow CERM convention center in early October (5-10SFr). Local businesses and farmers offer their wares, from shoes to marble sculptures. The final Sunday brings all-day **cow fighting,** the knock-'em-all-down finale of which decides the reigning queen of all Valaisian cows. The event is a must-see if you are in southern Switzerland. The **Foire du Lard** (Bacon Fair) has overtaken the pl. Centrale every first Monday in December since the Middle Ages. Traditionally, Valais mountain folk descended on Martigny to stock up on pork products for the winter, but now the festival has expanded to a large open-air market—although the theme is still "pig."

Martigny also sponsors film, theater, and music festivals throughout the year, notably the **International Folklore Festival** every two years. The city is also an important venue for the annual **Tibor Varga Classical Music Season,** which brings big-league European orchestras and performers like Alfred Brendel and Vladmir Ashkenazy to town every July and August. Tickets are available through the Fondation Gianadda (20-80SFr), or TicketCorner (tel. (0848) 80 08 00; www.nouvelliste.ch/varga/tvarga.htm).

VERBIER

Although it may seem to be a typical mountain town, Verbier is sleek and modern compared to the artificially rustic decor of many other ski towns. Cobblestones are nowhere to be found along the winding streets, and the countless multi-star hotels and sports stores are streamlined, shiny derivations of the classic chalet design. The slopes are the big story in Verbier; its entire transportation system seems designed to churn Rayban-wearing ski and snowboard enthusiasts from one cable car to another. Other indoor and outdoor sports thrive as well, casting an athletic glow over the town and pushing the envelope of the edgy and the extreme. Verbier's ongoing expansion up the mountain only accentuates the sense of a town on the move.

■ **ORIENTATION AND PRACTICAL INFORMATION.** Getting to Verbier is a 2-step process—from Martigny to Le Châble, then from Le Châble to Verbier. Martigny lies on the high-speed train line that connects the Lake Geneva cities (Montreux, Lausanne) to Sion and Brig. The **St. Bernard Express** runs trains to **Le Châble** (30min., every hr. 7:12am-7pm, 9.40SFr, Eurailpass and SwissPass valid). You can take the **post bus** (25min., every hr. 6:55am-8pm, 5SFr) or the **cable car** (10min., runs nonstop June 26-Aug. 29 7:45-11:45am and 1-5:45pm, 7SFr, round-trip 10SF) to Verbier, depending on when you arrive in Le Châble. The **last bus** from Verbier to Le Châble leaves at 7pm. In the winter, a bus goes **directly** from Martigny to Verbier, but reservations are crucial, as there is only 1 bus on Friday evenings, and 3 on Saturdays. **Téléverbier** offers **free bus** service throughout the town. The station at Le Châble offers **currency exchange,** or try the **24-hour ATM** at the Banque Cantonale du Valais, on pl. Centrale across from and to the right of the tourist office.

The **tourist office** (tel. 775 38 88; fax 775 38 89; email verbiertourism@verbier.ch; www.verbier.ch), pl. Centrale, publishes the amazingly informative booklet *Le Guide* in 4 languages. From the cable car, head down rue de Médran. (Open M-F 8:30am-noon and 2-6:30pm, Sa 9am-noon and 4-6pm, Su 9am-noon. Extended winter hours.) **Bike rental** is available at Ski Service, on the rue de Médran off pl. Centrale (25SFr for half-day, 35SFr for 1 day). For a **taxi,** dial 771 77 71 or 775 25 11. In an emergency, call the **police** at 117 or the **hospital** at 771 66 77. The **pharmacy** is to the right of the tourist office (tel. 771 66 22, emergency tel. 771 23 30, open M-Sa 8:30am-12:15pm and 2:30-6:30pm, Su 10am-12:15pm and 5-6:30pm; MC, Visa, AmEx, DC). Check your **email** at Harold's, on the pl. Centrale near the rue de Médran (tel. 771 62 43; open 11am-1:30am, 5SFr per 15min.). The **post office** is just off pl. Centrale on rue de la Poste (open M-F 8am-noon and 2-6pm, Sa 8-11am) and also serves as the post bus station. The **postal code** is CH-1936.

| PHONE CODE | The **city code** for Verbier is 027. |

VALAIS

▐▔ ACCOMMODATIONS. Verbier is cursed with the double whammy of being somewhat removed from normal transit routes and lacking a hostel. There are mountain huts and vacation chalets available through prior arrangement (contact the tourist office), but budget hotels are the best option for individual travelers. In town, the **Hotel Rosablanche,** rue de la Barmette off rue de Médran near pl. Centrale (tel. 771 55 55; fax 771 70 55), has spartan rooms and a miniature golf course. (Singles and doubles 40SFr per person, 50SFr with shower. Breakfast included. Reception 8am-11:30pm. Visa, AmEx.) Hotels are somewhat cheaper in Le Châble, so making the short commute isn't a bad idea. For the truly motivated, **Auberge de la Jeunesse (HI)** (tel. 776 23 56; fax 776 13 12) is a bus ride away from Le Châble in **Bruson** (10min., every hr. 7:10am-6:15pm). Though it doesn't offer meals, the 40 beds are only 10SFr (15SFr in high season). In winter there's a **campsite** (tel. 776 20 51) outside Le Châble.

◖▌ FOOD. Though Verbier is well on its way to major ski resort status, many of its restaurants are laid-back and budget-friendly; the influx of young, adventurous internationals keeps the nightlife jumping and accessible to Anglophones. Restaurants, bars, and clubs pack the pl. Centrale and the roads radiating from it. ◕**Le Crock Bar** (tel. 771 69 34), up rue des Creux from pl. Centrale, draws hip locals and sportsters alike with the easy funk of its multi-colored tile exterior, terra-cotta bar, and long leather couches. Frequent concerts (rock, funk, jazz) accompany creative *panini* sandwiches (7.50SFr; open 10am-2pm). **Le Monde des Crêpes,** down rue de la Poste from pl. Centrale, puts an alternative twist on the traditional crêperie (salty crêpes 5.90-9.70SFr, dessert crêpes 5.40-11.80SFr, cider 2.70SFr; open M-Th 9-11:30am, F-Sa 9:30-11:30am, 2:30-6pm).

For excellent Italian specialties, hike up the rue des Creux from pl. Centrale to the **Pizzeria Al Capone** (tel. 771 67 74). Shorten the walk by taking the Téléverbier bus to "Brunnet." Diners get an eyeful of snow-capped peaks and neon paragliders. (Pizzas 13-16.50SFr, gnocchi 16-17SFr, *plats du jour* 20-22SFr. Open daily 9am-midnight.) **Le Caveau** (tel. 771 22 26), to the right of the tourist office, serves up plenty of Swiss and local specialties through its wine-cask entrance. The subtly-lit interior, like much else in Verbier, is traditional with a touch of modern wackiness (what is that tropical wooden bird doing there anyway?). Try the hot goat cheese over a salad (15SFr), or the *assiette du jour* (about 20SFr; open noon-2pm, 6:30-10pm). To go the picnic route, try **Migros,** down rue de Verbier from pl. Centrale (open M-Sa 8:30am-12:15pm and 2:30-6:30pm), or the **Co-op,** down rue de la Poste (open M-Sa 8:30am-12:15pm and 2:30-6:30pm, Su 9:30am-noon and 5-7pm).

◪▟ OUTDOOR ACTIVITIES AND ENTERTAINMENT. Regional **ski** runs total 400km; Verbier's best runs are on the **Mont Fort glacier** (3329m), which offers skiing and snowboarding all year long. A behemoth of a cable car, the **Téléjumbo** (reach it by bus), can carry 150 passengers at a time to the glacier via Col des Gentianes (also the site of a snowboard half-pipe). From the Médran station, another cable car runs through Les Ruinettes to **Attelas** (2193m), and further to **Mont Gelë** (3023m). Ski pass prices and cable car schedules are complicated, based on the length and area of validity—make sure to pick up the pertinent info at the tourist or Téléverbier offices. (1-day pass for the 4-valley region and Mont Fort 56SFr; for the Verbier slopes only, 50SFr. 3-day passes 145SFr; 139SFr plus a 10SFr deposit for passes of 3 or more days. Photo ID required. Non-skier day pass 36SFr, 20SFr. Ages 17-20 15% reduction, seniors and ages 7-16 40% reduction.) Rental shops in Verbier abound; **Ski Service** (tel. 771 67 70), down rue de Médran between pl. Centrale and the cable station, operates through the Rent-A-Sport system. (Skis 28-50SFr per day, snowboards 38-50SFr, shoes 15-19SFr. Open 10am-12:30pm and 3-6:30pm. MC, Visa, AmEx.) The tourist office makes recommendations to would-be skiers based on skill level; they do the same for the 400km of summer **hiking trails** in the area.

For those looking for a little extra adventure, the **Bureau des Guides** (tel. 775 33 64) offers multi-day, guided excursions, hikes, and courses on everything from canyoning to ice climbing (lodging included). There are plenty of opportunities to join the flock of **paragliders** who dot the skies above Verbier. **Max Biplace** (tel. 771 55 55 or (079) 219 36 55) offers tandem flights—book them at La Fantastique (tel. 771 41 41); the **Centre Parapeute,** near the Centre Polysportif (tel. 771 68 18), offers tandem paragliding (150SFr) and hanggliding (250SFr). The multi-level **Centre Polysportif** (tel. 771 66 01), downhill from pl. Centrale on rue de la Poste, has a **swimming pool** (7SFr, children 5SFr), **ice-skating** (6SFr, 4SFr), **squash** (12-14SFr per 30min.), and **tennis** (23SFr per hour; open 10am-9pm; outdoor pool closes at 7pm).

Every summer Verbier draws an impressive array of performers to its **classical musical festival** (in 2000, July 25-Aug. 6). Recent attendees include James Levine, Evgeny Kissin, Sir Neville Marriner, and the Emerson Quartet. Tickets range from 30-115SFr and are available from the ticket corner next to the Médran cable car station (tel. 771 82 82; www.verbierfestival.com), though free events are posted each day of the festival (ticket corner open 10am-noon and 2-6pm).

LAKE GENEVA REGION (LAC LÉMAN)

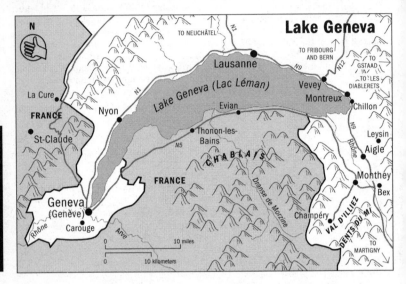

All around Lac Léman, hills dotted by villas or festooned with the terraced garlands of ripening grapes seem tame and settled—until the haze clears and the rough-hewn mountain peaks behind the hills become visible. In that moment, the lake discards its cultivated prettiness and urbanity for the energizing promise of unpopulated wilderness and wide lonely expanses. Many travelers suffer financial anxiety when they consider venturing into the prosperous Lake Geneva region, since high-altitude prices are the general rule in Geneva, Lausanne, and Montreux, but courageous adventurers discover that the towns along the lake abound with at least three of Switzerland's cheapest commodities: peace and quiet is just a short stroll along the tree-lined quay or up into the vine-laced hills, chocolate is available for a pittance nearly everywhere, and the unforgettable views are, as always, free.

HIGHLIGHTS OF LAKE GENEVA

- Explore **Geneva's** effervescent nightlife in the *vieille ville* and Carouge, as well as its outstanding museums (see p. 453).
- Follow in the footsteps of T.S. Eliot, Dickens, and Henry James down **Lausanne's** beautiful lakeside streets (see p. 457).
- Join the crowds at **Montreux's** famous jazz festival, or just come to see the Château de Chillon and the city's flower-lined quays (see p. 468).

GENEVA (GENÈVE, GENF)

"I detest Geneva," muttered Napoleon Bonaparte shortly before "liberating" the city in 1798, "they know English too well." They still do. Geneva is very much a cosmopolitan city: only one-third of the population are genuine *Genevois;* the other two-thirds are foreign-born internationals or transplants from other cantons. The large concentration of international banks and multinational organizations preserves the intricate mixture of the city's voices—quite a contrast to Switzerland's other, mostly homogeneous towns. Indeed, many say that all Geneva holds in common with the rest of Switzerland is its neutral foreign policy and the state religion, banking.

The French Emperor had to contend with more than linguistic contempt. He knew all too well that Geneva's citizens had a long and belligerent tradition of doing battle to protect their political and religious independence. Medieval Geneva fended off constant attacks, protecting its strategic site on the outflow to Lac Léman. In 1536, however, Geneva openly welcomed the Protestant Reformation. The townspeople voted to convert *en masse* and invited an unknown 25-year-old, John Calvin, to their cathedral. His fiery sermons from Geneva's pulpit between 1536 and 1564 brought in waves of persecuted French and Italian refugees to the "Rome of Protestants." Geneva then waged a hard-won battle for freedom from the Catholic House of Savoy, whose Duke sought to crush both Protestantism and Genevan democracy (see **Soup's On,** p. 452).

Unfortunately, Calvin then adopted the manner of the Catholic rule, renamed it the Protestant rule, and proceeded to burn his detractors. The Reformists' ardent zeal continued for at least another century and a half, exemplified by the burning of Rousseau's books in a square just blocks from the house in which he was born. But Geneva's cosmopolitanism eventually won out, and the city became a gathering place for aesthetes and free thinkers. Voltaire lived and worked in the Geneva area for 23 years, and his compatriot Madame de Staël later held her salons in nearby Coppet. In the early 19th century, mountain-loving romantics Shelley and Byron found inspiration in the city's surroundings. Mary Wollstonecraft Shelley created *Frankenstein*'s monster here, and George Eliot set up house in Geneva, the city of her hero, Jean-Jacques Rousseau. One of Geneva's most famous political refugees was Lenin, who sat around from 1903 to 1905 and again in 1908 before being quietly shipped back to Moscow in a sealed train by Western leaders hoping to disrupt the turn-of-the-century Russian government.

Today's Geneva memorializes both extremes of its varied history; street names alternate between rigid reformers and free-thinking artists and intellectuals. The *Genevois* that populate the wide quays and narrow *melles*, though, buzz with the fashionable vibrancy of an utterly cutting-edge, globalized metropolis. There are more McDonalds here than you'll find in the rest of Switzerland; thankfully, there are more "traditional Swiss" restaurants in cubby-hole locations than McDonalds.

Neon-topped temples to international commerce intermingle with the serious business of world affairs. Under the inspiration of native Henri Dunant, the **International Committee of the Red Cross** established itself in Geneva in 1864, and nations from around the world signed the peace-keeping First Geneva Convention in the same year. In 1919, Geneva's selection as the site for the League of Nations confirmed the city's reputation as a center for both international organizations and arbitrations. Geneva still retains the European office of the **United Nations** and dozens of other international bodies ranging from the Center for European Nuclear Research to the World Council of Churches.

▆ GETTING TO GENEVA

Geneva's **Cointrin Airport** is a **Swissair** hub, with direct flights to New York, Paris, London, Amsterdam, and Rome. To reach the city from the arrivals hall, go up a level and head outside to catch bus #10 to town (15min., every 6min., 2.20SFr). The ticket dispenser requires exact change—large bills can be broken at the changemat behind the escalator. For a shorter trip to Gare Cornavin, take the train (6min., every 10 min., 4.80SFr). Geneva has two rail stations. **Gare Cornavin** is the primary station and departure point for all major Swiss and foreign cities. The second station, the tiny Gare des Eaux-Vives on the eastern edge of the city, connects to France's regional rail lines. By **car,** Geneva is more accessible from France than from the rest of Switzerland. To drive to Geneva from the west, take A40 which continues on to Lausanne and Montreux. From the south take N201 north. From the north, take A40 from France and within Switzerland. From the east, take A40 west. N1 is the best way to reach Geneva from Lausanne or Montreux. Don't go crazy looking for the route numbers—they're not all that visible. You'll be better off just following the signs for Geneva posted on all of the auto routes. Hugely popular **ferries** (CGN; tel. 741 52 31) connect Geneva to Lausanne and Montreux, departing from quai du Mont-Blanc. A round-trip ticket (47-57SFr, ages 16-25 half-off, seniors 20% discount) includes the option of returning to Geneva by train, so sight-seeing itineraries need not depend on the infrequent boat services.

◪ ORIENTATION

Geneva began as a fortified city on a hill, and the historic *vieille ville*'s labyrinthine cobbled streets and quiet squares around John Calvin's *Cathédrale de St-Pierre* still occupy the heart of the urban landscape. Across the Rhône River to the north, billionaires' banks and five-star hotels gradually give way to lakeside promenades where couples stroll along a backdrop of swaying boats and hillside towns. Farther north, another hill holds the United Nations, Red Cross, and World Trade Organization, as well as rolling green parkland. Across the river to the south lies the village of Carouge, home to a concentration of student bars and clubs (take tram #12 to "pl. du Marché").

Be sure to carry your passport with you at all times; the French border is never more than a few minutes away and regional buses frequently cross it, as does the local tram at Moillesulaz (#12 or 16). City buses provide swift service, with major hubs at the Gare Cornavin, Rd.-Pt. de Plainpalais, and pl. Bel Air (near the *ponts de l'Ile*); trips that stay within zone 10 (most of the city) officially cost 2.20SFr, but ticket purchasing is largely on the honor system and some devious backpackers try to get away with riding for free. Be warned, however: those caught without a ticket face a 60SFr fine, and playing confused anglophone will probably not work well. Much of this small city (pop. 180,000) can easily be walked in good weather.

◪ PRACTICAL INFORMATION

TRANSPORTATION

Flights: Cointrin Airport (tel. 717 71 11, flight information tel. 799 31 11; fax 798 43 77) is a hub for **Swissair** (tel. (0848) 80 07 00). Several direct flights per day to New York, Paris, London, Amsterdam, and Rome. **Air France** (tel. 827 87 87) has 7 per day to Paris, and **British Airways** (tel. (0848) 80 10 10) has 7 per day to London.

Trains: Gare Cornavin, pl. Cornavin. To: **Lausanne** (40min., every 10-20min., 20SFr); **Bern** (2hr., every hr., 40SFr); **Zurich** (3½hr., every hr., 77SFr); **Basel** (3hr., every hr., 72SFr); **Montreux** (1hr., 2 per hr., 29SFr); **Interlaken** (3hr., every hr., 65SFr); **Paris** (3hr.40min., 8 per day, 196SFr, under 26 166SFr); **Milan** (4hr., 6 per day, 164SFr, under 26 132SFr); and **Vienna** (10-12hr., 2 per day, 361SFr). To book a seat on long-distance or international trains, join the throng at reservation and information (open M-F 8:30am-7pm, Sa 9am-5:30pm). Train schedules at www.sbb.ch. **Gare des Eaux-Vives** (tel. 736 16 20), on av. de la Gare des Eaux-Vives. Tram #12, "Amandoliers SNCF" connects to France's regional rail lines through **Annecy** (1½hr., every hr., 14.50SFr) or **Chamonix** (2½hr., 4 per day, 20.40SFr). The ticket machine at the station does not return change. Open 6:30am-8:30pm.

Public Transportation: Geneva has an efficient bus and tram network. **Transport Publics Genevois** (tel. 308 34 34), next to the tourist office in Gare Cornavin, provides a free map of local bus routes called *Le Réseau.* Open 6:15am-8pm. 2.20SFr buys 1hr. of unlimited travel on any bus; 3 stops or fewer 1.50SFr. Full-day passes 5SFr for 1 zone, 8.50SFr for 4. SwissPass valid on all buses; Eurailpass not valid. Buses run roughly 5:30am-midnight. A new Noctambus takes tardy travelers to the suburbs. Buy multi-fare

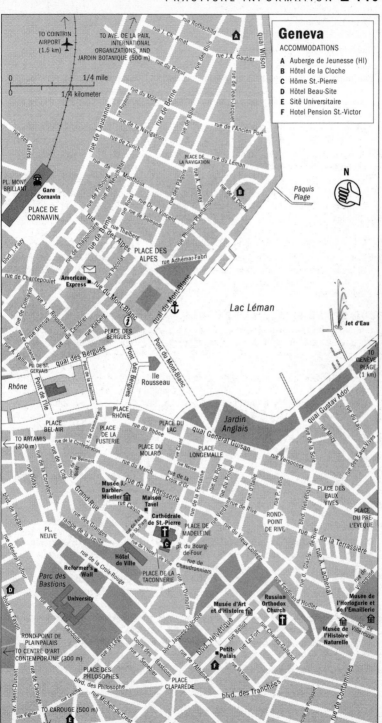

Geneva

ACCOMMODATIONS

A Auberge de Jeunesse (HI)
B Hôtel de la Cloche
C Hôme St.-Pierre
D Hôtel Beau-Site
E Sitê Universitaire
F Hotel Pension St.-Victor

LAKE GENEVA

and day tickets at the train station, others at automatic vendors at every stop. Stamp multi-use tickets before boarding or risk 60SFr fines.

Taxis: Taxi-Phone (tel. 331 41 33). 6.30SFr plus 2.70SFr per km. Taxi from airport to city 25-30SFr., max. 4 passengers (15-20min.).

Car Rental: Avis, rue de Lausanne 44 (tel. 731 90 00). **Europcar,** rue de Lausanne 37 (tel. 732 52 52; fax 738 17 80). **Budget,** rue de Zurich 36 (tel. 900 24 00), is the cheapest: rentals start at 86SFr per day. All have offices at Cointrin, but check for airport surcharges (around 11%).

Parking: On-street 1SFr per hr. The garage (tel. 736 66 30) under Cornavin station (enter at pl. Cornavin) is 2SFr for 1hr., 6SFr for 2. **Garage Les Alpes,** rue Thalberg, is 2SFr per hr. weekdays, 1SFr per hr. nights and weekends. Digital boards on highways list several car-parks and the number of vacant spaces.

Bike Rental: Geneva is pedal-happy with well-marked bike paths and special traffic lights for spoked traffic. For routes, get *Itineraires cyclables* or *Tours de ville avec les vélos de location* from the tourist office. Behind the station, **Genève Roule,** pl. Montbrillant 17 (tel./fax 740 13 43), has 28 free bikes available (sponsored by the Red Cross). A 50SFr deposit is required; hefty fine if bike is lost or stolen. Slightly nicer neon bikes start at 5SFr per day. Open 7:30am-9:30pm.

Hitchhiking: *Let's Go* does not recommend hitchhiking. Hitchers say, however, that Switzerland is one of the safer countries in Europe in which to hail a ride. Those headed to Germany or northern Switzerland take bus #4/44 to "Jardin Botanique." Those headed to France take bus #4/44 to "Palettes," then line D to "St. Julien."

TOURIST AND FINANCIAL SERVICES

Tourist Offices: At information offices (marked by a blue lower-case "i" sign), the free must-haves are the city map and *Info Jeunes/Young People.* The **main office,** rue du Mont-Blanc 3 (tel. 909 70 00; fax 909 70 11; email info@geneve-tourisme.ch; www.geneve-tourisme.ch), lies 5min. away from Cornavin towards the pont du Mont-Blanc. By 2000 it may move to the Central Post office building. English-speaking staff books hotel rooms (5SFr fee), offers **walking tours,** and provides information on anything from local events to vegetarian and kosher restaurants. The office maintains a free direct phone line to Geneva hotels in Gare Cornavin. Open June 15-Aug 31 M-F 8am-6pm, Sa-Su 8am-5pm; Sept. 1-June 14, M-Sa 9am-6pm. During the summer, head for the magic bus, Geneva's **Centre d'Accueil et de Renseignements** (CAR; tel. 731 46 47), parked by the Metro Shopping entrance to Cornavin Station. The office answers all sorts of questions and posts a daily updated list of musical and theatrical performances. Open June 15-Sept. 15 9am-11pm. As a last resort, the **Anglo-phone** (tel. 157 50 14), a 24hr. hotline (in English), answers questions for 2.13SFr per min.

Budget Travel: SSR, rue Vignier 3 (tel. 329 97 34 or 329 97 33; www.ssr.ch), off av. Henri-Dunant near Plaine de Plainpalais by the Forget-Me-Not hotel, offers youth and student fares. Open M-F 9:15am-6pm, Sa 9am-noon. AmEx, MC, Visa.

Consulates: Australia, chemin des Fins 2 (tel. 799 91 00; fax 799 91 78). **Canada,** rue du Pré-de-Bichette 1 (tel. 919 92 00; fax 919 92 77). **New Zealand,** chemin des Fins 2 (tel. 929 03 50; fax 929 03 77). **South Africa,** rue de Rhône 65 (tel. 849 54 54; fax 849 54 32). **U.K.,** rue de Vermont 37 (tel. 918 24 00; fax 918 23 33). **U.S.,** World Trade Center Bldg. #2 (tel. 798 16 05; recorded information 798 16 15). Call each office to schedule appointments.

Currency Exchange: ATMs, which offer the best rates, dot Geneva. For traditional service, **Gare Cornavin** has good rates and no commission on traveler's checks, advances cash on credit cards (min. 200SFr), and arranges Western Union transfers. Open Nov. 1-Mar. 31 6:45am-8pm, Apr. 1-Oct. 31 6:45am-9:30pm. Western Union open 7am-7pm.

American Express: rue du Mont-Blanc 7, P.O. Box 1032, CH-1211 Geneva 01 (tel. 731 76 00; fax 732 72 11). Mail held 2-3 months; arrangements can be made for over a year. All banking services; reasonable exchange rates. Hotel and train (30SFr) reservations and tickets for city tours and excursions. Open in summer M-F 8:30am-6pm, Sa 9am-noon; in winter M-F 8:30am-5:30pm, Sa 9am-noon.

LOCAL SERVICES

Luggage Storage: Gare Cornavin. 3-10SFr per day. Open 4:30am-12:45am.

Lost Property: rue des Glacis de Rive 7 (tel. 787 60 00). Open M-F 7:30am-4pm.

English-Language Bookstores: ELM (English Language and Media) Video and Books, rue Versonnex 5 (tel. 736 09 45; fax 786 14 29), has a quality range of new books in English and a book-ordering service. Open M-F 9am-6:30pm, Sa 10am-5pm. AmEx, DC, MC, Visa. The adjoining video store (tel. 736 02 22) rents videos in English (from 5.50SFr), but you must be a member. Open M-F 9am-8pm, Sa 10am-7pm. **Librairie des Amateurs,** Grand Rue 15 (tel. 732 80 97), in the *vieille ville*. Classy secondhand dealer. Open M 2-6:30pm, Tu-F 11am-6:30pm, Sa 2pm-5pm. **Book Worm,** rue Sismondi 5 (tel./fax 731 87 65; debrandt@mail.excite.com), near the train station off rue de Berne. 3 long-haired chihuahuas keep watch over this genteel store (run by an American couple) of used books and classic English-language videos (4-5SFr for 2 days). Tea room serves tea with a biscuit (2SFr), lunch (F-Su 12:30-2:30pm, 14.50SFr), and desserts (6SFr). Open Tu-Sa 10am-8pm, Su 12-6pm. AmEx, MC, Visa. **Payot Libraire,** rue de Chantepoulet 5 (tel. 731 89 50), is Geneva's largest chain of bookstores. Open M 1-6:30pm, Tu, W, F 9am-6:30pm, Th 9am-8pm, Sa 9am-5pm. AmEx, DC, MC, Visa.

Library: American Library, rue de Monthoux 3 (tel. 732 80 97), at Emmanuel Church. 20,000 titles. 1-month membership (25SFr) allows you to borrow books (6 max.) for 2 weeks and offers a small but eclectic collection of books on tape (2SFr). Open Tu and F 12:30-5pm, W 2-7pm, Th 2-5pm, Sa 10am-4pm, Su 11am-12:30pm.

Bi-Gay-Lesbian Organizations: Dialogai, rue de la Navigation 11-13 (tel. 906 40 40; www.hivnet.ch/dialogai). From Gare Cornavin, turn left and walk 5min. down rue de Lausanne; turn right onto rue de la Navigation. Resource group with programs from support groups to outdoor activities. Publishes *Dialogai,* a guide to French-speaking Switzerland's gay scene. Mostly male, but women are welcome. Phone-line and center open M-Th 2-7pm. **360°,** 25 rue de Lausanne (tel. 740 00 71), publishes a magazine, *360°,* and maintains a more socially and politically oriented office at 2 pl. Grenus (tel. 087 887 93 60) with walk-in hours on Su from 4pm-9pm. Open 10am-7pm. **Gay International Group** (GIG; tel. (087) 880 30 02; taped message 789 18 62) is for international gay visitors or semi-permanents in Geneva, including Anglophones. Communal meals every 6 weeks. **Centre Femmes Natalie Barney** (women only), 19 Chemin Chateau Bloch (tel. 797 27 14), offers similar services to Dialogai, but is smaller and lesbian-oriented. 24hr. answering machine; live phone answering W 6-8pm.

Travelers with Disabilities: CCIPH (Centre de Coordination et d'Information pour Personnes Handicapées), 28 Bld. du Pont d'Arve (tel. 809 53 98). The tourist office also provides a free comprehensive guide to the city for the disabled, called *Guide à l'Usage des Personnes Handicapées,* which includes oversized maps.

Laundromat: En 5 Sec SA, rue Cornavin 5 (tel. 732 32 57), just 2min. from Gare Cornavin. Open Su-F 7:30am-6:45pm, Sa 8am-12:30pm. **Salon Lavoir St. Gervais,** rue Vallin 9 (tel. 731 26 46), off pl. St. Gervais. Wash 5SFr, dry 1SFr per 12min., detergent 1SFr. Open M-Sa 7:30am-9pm, Su 10am-9pm.

Public Showers: Point d'Eau, rue Chandieu 4 (tel. 773 42 240). Take bus #8 to "Canonnière" and turn right onto rue de Vermont; it's on the left. Free hot showers and personal hygiene center for the ripe backpacker. Open Sa-Tu 10am-2pm, W-F 3-7pm.

EMERGENCIES AND COMMUNICATIONS

Emergencies: Police, rue Pecolat 5 (tel. 117), next to post office. **Fire,** tel. 118. **Ambulance,** tel. 144.

Rape Crisis Hotline: Viol-Secours (tel. 345 20 20). Open M 2-6pm, Tu 1-6pm, W 4-8pm, Th 9am-1pm, F 2-5pm.

Late-Night Pharmacy: Every night a changing set of 4 pharmacies stays open late (9 or 11pm). Consult *Genève Agenda* for addresses and phone numbers or call 144 or 111 (7pm-8am). The pharmacy at the train station has the longest regular hours.

Medical Assistance: Hôpital Cantonal, rue Micheli-du-Crest 24 (tel. 372 33 11). Bus #1 or 5 or tram #12. Door #2 is for emergency care, Door #3 for consultations. Walk-in clinics dot the city; call the **Association des Médecins** (tel. 320 84 20) for further information.

Internet Cafés: Café Video ROM, Pl. de Cornavin (tel. 901 16 21). Surf for 5SFr per hr. Open M-Th 11am-8:30pm, F-Sa 11am-10pm, Su 1-8:30pm. **Point 6,** rue de Vieux-Billard 7a (tel. 800 26 00) rents spots at the screen for 7SFr per hr. Open 10am-midnight. **Funet Internet Café,** rue de Lausanne 44 (tel. 738 50 00; fax 738 50 21). Turn left on rue de Lausanne from Gare Cornavin and walk 5min. to find 7 PCs loaded with the latest netware. 15min. for 5SFr; 30min. 7SFr; 1hr. 12SFr. Open M, Tu, F 9am-10pm, W-Th 9am-8:30pm, Sa noon-10pm, Su noon-7:30pm. MC, Visa. **Internet Café,** rue de Monthoux (tel. 900 12 91), across from the American Library. Open 11am-midnight. Internet access also available in increasing numbers of hostels as well as in the artists' colony (see **Artamis—Geneva's Guerrilla Artist Colony,** p. 450).

Post Office: Poste Centrale, rue de Mont-Blanc 18, a block from Gare Cornavin in the stately Hôtel des Postes. Open M-F 7:30am-6pm, Sa 8-11am. Address *Poste Restante* to CH-1211, Genève 1 Mont-Blanc. **Postal Code:** CH-1211.

PHONE CODE	The **city code** for Geneva is 022.

■ ACCOMMODATIONS AND CAMPING

Geneva is one of the most cosmopolitan cities in the world, and its 5-star hotel system is geared more toward the international banker or diplomat than the friendly budget traveler. Luckily, the seasonal influx of university students and interns has created a second network of decently-priced hostels, pensions, and university dorms moonlighting as summer hotels. The indispensable *Info Jeunes* lists about 50 options; we list the highlights below. The tourist office publishes *Budget Hotels*, stretching definitions a bit to include rooms at 120SFr per person. Even for the shortest stays, reservations are a must. For longer stays, check *Tribune de Genève*'s weekly supplement of apartment classifieds or the tourist office's board. Employees of international organizations can contact the **Centre d'Accueil pour les Internationals de Genève,** rue de Varembé 9-11 (tel. 327 17 77).

Auberge de Jeunesse (HI), rue Rothschild 28-30 (tel. 732 62 60; fax 738 39 87). Walk 15min. left from the station down rue de Lausanne, then right on rue Rothschild. Take bus #1 (dir.: Wilson) to the end of the line. Don't expect atmosphere; do expect a comfortable last-minute bunk and a ton of people to meet. Check-in lines can be long. Get your hands on an arrival slip and fill it out before you get to the window to avoid losing your place and extending an already tedious wait. Amenities include a sizable lobby, restaurant (dinner 11.50SFr, with dessert and drink 14SFr), **kitchen** facilities, TV room with CNN, library, and snack bar. Dorms 23SFr; doubles 60SFr, with shower 70SFr; quads 99SFr. Breakfast, hall showers, sheets, and lockers included. **Laundry** 6SFr. Special facilities for disabled guests. 5-night max. stay. Reception in summer 6:30-10am and 4pm-midnight; in winter 6:30-10am and 5pm-midnight. Lockout in summer 10am-4pm, in winter 10am-5pm. Curfew midnight. MC, Visa.

Cité Universitaire, av. Miremont 46 (tel. 839 22 11; fax 839 22 23). Take bus #3 (dir.: Crêts-de-Champel) to the last stop. Find the bus at pl. de 22 Cantons on the far right as you exit the train station; buses stop in front of "Le Popeye" restaurant. This institutional college housing in a modern tower block has TV rooms, newspapers, restaurant, disco (all-night dancing Th and Sa, free to residents), ping-pong (paddles at the reception), tennis courts, **Internet access** (7 computers), small grocery shop, and discount plane tickets. 4 dorms (July-Sept. only) 17SFr, including lockers; singles 38SFr; doubles

55SFr; studios with kitchenette and bathroom 68SFr. Hall showers included. Reception M-F 8am-noon and 2-10pm, Sa 8am-noon and 6-10pm, Su 9am-11am and 6-10pm. Lockout 10am-6pm and curfew 11pm, both for dorms only. AmEx, MC, Visa.

Hôme St-Pierre, cours St-Pierre 4 (tel. 310 37 07; fax 310 17 27). Take bus #5 to "pl. Neuve" or walk 15min. from the train station: cross the Rhône at pont du Mont-Blanc, then go up rampe de la Treille and take the 3rd right. Mere seconds from the west entrance of the cathedral, this 150-year-old "home" has comfortable beds, a large **kitchen,** and a dining room. Enjoy the music of the *vieille ville* (including a church bell serenade every 15min.), spectacular rooftop views, and a convivial atmosphere. **Women only.** Dorms 22SFr; singles 36-45SFr; doubles 50-60SFr. Breakfast (M-Sa) 5SFr. Showers and lockers included. Laundry 7SFr. Reception M-Sa 9am-noon and 4-8pm, Su 9am-noon. No lockout or curfew. Popular, so reserve ahead. AmEx, MC, Visa.

Hôtel de la Cloche, rue de la Cloche 6 (tel. 732 94 81; fax 738 16 12), off quai du Mont-Blanc across from the Noga Hilton. A converted mansion, each room has chandeliers, antique mirrors, balconies, and TVs. Singles 50SFr; doubles 80SFr; triples 95SFr; quad 130SFr. Prices go down 5-10SFr in winter. showers included. Breakfast 5SFr. Reception 8am-midnight. Reserve 2-3 weeks in advance in summer. AmEx, MC, Visa.

Centre St-Boniface, av. du Mail 14 (tel. 322 26 00; fax 322 26 01). Take bus #1, tram #13, or 4/44 (dir.: Voirets) to "Cirque," then continue down av. du Mail. To walk from the station (20min.), head right on blvd. Fazy, across pont de La Coulouvrenière and along av. du Mail. This Jesuit-run center only has singles (40SFr). Some have shower and balcony. Access to kitchen, TV room, and dining room included. No breakfast, but residents get 10% off at the restaurant next door, La Pleine-Lune, with a card from the reception. Reception M-F 9am-noon and 4-7pm. Reservations preferred.

Hôtel Beau-Site, pl. du Cirque 3 (tel. 328 10 08; fax 329 23 64). Take bus #1 or 4/44 to "Cirque," or walk from the station: turn right on blvd. Fazy, cross the Rhône at pont de la Coulouvrenière, and follow blvd. Georges-Favon to pl. du Cirque (20min.) Paneled rooms with quilt-covered beds and semi-antique furniture—some even have marble fireplaces to accompany the ornamental plaster moldings. Singles 57SFr, with shower 68SFr, with bath 80SFr; doubles 79SFr, 80SFr, 108SFr; triples 98SFr, 105SFr, 120SFr; quads 106SFR, 112SFr. All rooms with sink and radio. 6 sinkless rooms available for 45SFr each. Call ahead for availability. 10% student discount. Breakfast included; free coffee and tea in lobby 10am-10pm. Reception 7am-11pm; call if you'll be arriving later. AmEx, MC, Visa.

Hotel Pension St-Victor, rue François-le-Fort 1 (tel. 346 17 18; fax 346 10 46; email stvictor@iprolink.ch; www.saint-victor.ch). Take bus #3 or 5 to "pl. Claparède" or bus #17 to "Petit Palais." An elegant building with a view of the Russian Church's gilded domes, this pension offers large, clean rooms with healthy plants and dark wood furniture. Homemade jam and eggs fresh from the owner's farm for breakfast. **Internet access** 1SFr per 3min. Singles from 68SFr; doubles 98SFr; triples 130SFr. Reception M-Sa 7:30am-7:30pm, Su 7:30am-6pm. Reservations imperative. MC, Visa.

Camping Pointe-à-la-Bise, Chemin de la Bise, (tel. 752 12 96). Take bus #9 to "Rive" then bus E (north) to "Bise" (about 7km). 6SFr per person. No tents provided, but beds are 18SFr each. Reception 8am-noon and 4-8pm. Open Apr.-Oct.

Camping d'Hermance, rue du Nord 44 (tel. 751 14 83). Take bus E north, 14km out of town. 1 person 10SFr, 2 17SFr. Open all day. Consult *Info Jeunes* (at the tourist office) for additional locations.

☉ FOOD

It's true that you can find anything from sushi to *paella* in Geneva, but you'll generally need a banker's salary to foot the bill. For a picnic, shop at the ubiquitous supermarkets. Many supermarkets also have cafeterias with some of the best deals available, and *Info Jeunes* lists many university cafeterias that won't tax your wallet. Carry a water bottle to avoid the exorbitant cost of micro-sized drinks.

Boulangeries and *pâtisseries* offer unparalleled opportunities for gourmet food at budget prices—6SFr goes a long way when you combine a fresh loaf of bread with an avocado and tomatoes from Migros or Co-op. *Pâtisseries* and pasta/pizza parlors permeate **place du Bourg-de-Four,** below Cathédrale de St-Pierre, as do some of the best cafés. There's also **Carouge** (take tram #12 to "pl. du Marché"), a suburb that's easy on your budget and loaded with relaxed ambience.

Restaurant Manora, rue de Cornavin 4 (tel. 909 44 10), 3min. from the station on the right in the Placette department store. This huge self-serve restaurant with a fresh, varied, high-quality selection offers salads (from 4.20SFr), fruit tarts (3.20SFr), entrees cooked on the spot (from 11SFr), and maybe the only free water in all of Geneva. Wheelchair accessible. Open M-Sa 7am-9pm, Su 9am-9pm.

Le Rozzel, Grand-Rue 18 (tel. 312 42 72). Take bus #5 to pl. Neuve, then walk up the hill past the cathedral on rue Jean-Calvin to Grand-Rue. This Breton-style *crêperie* with outdoor seating on the most elegant street in the *vieille ville* serves large dinner crêpes (7-17SFr), dessert crêpes (5-12SFr), and cider (4.50SFr). Open M-F 8am-10pm, Sa 10am-10pm. AmEx, MC, Visa.

Chez Costa, pl. de Rondeau 1 (tel. 300 13 66), in Carouge. Walk 1min. downhill from tram #12 or #1 to "Carouge," or meander down rue Ancienne from the "Ancienne" stop. Red plush upholstery and dark wood create a tranquil interior, but the shaded outdoor patio is the real treat. Breakfast 3-3.50SFr, steak 16-20Fr, *plat du jour* 12SFr.

La Crise, rue de Chantepoulet 13 (tel. 738 02 64). From the station, turn right on rue de Cornavin and left on rue de Chantepoulet. Watch the owner, Mme. LeParc, cook your food in this veggie-friendly restaurant. Healthy portions, slender prices: quiche and veggies 8.50SFr; soup 3.50SFr; beer or wine 3SFr. Open M-F 6am-8pm, Sa 6am-3pm.

Auberge de Saviese, rue des Pâquis 20 (tel. 732 83 30; fax 784 36 23). Take bus #1 to "Monthoux." From Gare Cornavin, turn left onto rue de Lausanne, then right on rue de Zurich, until you hit rue des Pâquis. Share coffee (1.90SFr) with locals breakfasting behind newspapers (9-11am). In addition to a *plat du jour* at lunchtime, the regular menu features an excellent *fondue au cognac* (19SFr), *raclette* with all the trimmings (29SFr), pasta (15-19.50SFr), and salads (12-20SFr). Open M-F 9am-11pm, Sa-Su 6-11pm. AmEx, DC, MC, Visa.

Tea Room Biscotte, Rd-Pt. Plainpalais (tel. 329 36 21). Take bus #3 or tram #12 to "Plainpalais," where a university crowd enjoys quiche and salad (9SFr) in an airy, cheerful atmosphere. Open M-F 6am-6:45pm, Sa 6am-5pm.

Les 5 Saveurs, rue du Prieuré 22 (tel. 731 78 70). Just off rue de Lausanne, 2 blocks from the *Auberge de Jeunesse.* Take the #4 bus to "Prieuré." Tropical plants, cheesy posters, and Filipino flags make this an honest-to-goodness *barrio* on the streets of Geneva. Try the fresh, imported mangoes, unusual ice creams, and Filipino candies. Buffet 16.50SFr. Open 11:30am-12:30am.

Les Armures, rue du Puits-St-Pierre 1 (tel. 310 34 42; fax 818 71 13), 30 seconds from the main entrance to the cathedral. One small step up in price, one giant leap up in atmosphere. Wear clean socks. A plaque announces that President Clinton ate here, and for a small splurge you can too. Good-sized fondue 22-25SFr; pizza 13-16SFr. Open noon-3pm, 6pm-midnight. AmEx, MC, Visa.

Sunset, rue St-Léger (tel. 320 15 13), off pl. des Philosophes. Is it the angel fish or the well-stocked bar that brings vegetarian students from the nearby university to this restaurant in droves? Polls suggest the angel fish. Tropical murals and a fishtank try to evoke a resort atmosphere (and almost succeed). *Pita au champignons* (pita with mushrooms, 16SFr), inventive salads (15-18SFr), and gnocchi (16SFr). Open M-F 7:30am-6pm. AmEx, MC, Visa.

MARKETS

Co-op, Migros, Grand Passage, and **Orient Express** branches speckle the city. On Sundays, the few options include Gare Cornavin's **Aperto** (open daily 6am-10pm) and scattered neighborhood groceries and bakeries.

Co-op (tel. 319 60 48), on the corner of rue du Commerce and rue du Rhône, in the Centre Rhône Fusterie. The restaurant on floor one has *Menüs* from 9.50SFr and salads for 2.30SFr per 100g, plus a sizeable wine gallery. Open M 9am-6:45pm, Tu, W, and F 8:30am-6:45pm, Th 8:30am-8pm, Sa 8:30am-5pm. MC, Visa.

Migros, av. de Lausanne 18-20 (tel. 738 68 88), left from Gare Cornavin on the mezzanine level of Centre Commercial Les Cygnes. Also has reasonably priced (5-10SFr) cafeteria with salad bar. Open M,W,F 8am-7pm, Th 8am-8pm, Sa 8am-6pm.

Les Halles du Molard, 48 rue de Rhône, on the pl. du Molard, offers an array of gourmet delights, including fresh produce, a *fromagerie*, and still-swimming seafood. Open M-W and F 7:30am-6:45pm, Th 7:30am-8pm, Sa 8am-5:45pm.

Marché des Eaux-Vives, bd. Helvétique, between cours de Rive and rue du Rhône. Huge dairy, vegetable, and flower market. Open W and Sa 8am-1pm.

Public Market, rue de Coutance, leading down to the river just above the Pont de l'Ile. Fresh fruits and cheese. Open M-Sa 8am-6pm. Another produce market is located on Rd-Pt. de Plainpalais Tuesday and Friday mornings.

🔭 SIGHTS

For centuries Geneva was tightly constrained by a belt of fortified walls and trenches. By the mid-19th century when they were finally removed, the city's most interesting historical sites were already established in a dense, easily walkable space. The tourist office offers 2-hour **walking tours** during the summer. *(June 14-Oct. 2 M-F 10am. Sa throughout the year. 12SFr, students and seniors 8SFr, children 6SFr.)* Qualified guides lead tours on all things *Genevois:* the Reformation, internationalism, the Red Cross, the *vieille ville*, and the city's museums. Recordings of the tours are available in winter, and a portable cassette player will walk you through 2000 years of Geneva's history for 10SFr plus a 50SFr deposit.

CATHEDRAL. The *vieille ville*'s **Cathédrale de St-Pierre,** the belly button of the Protestant world, is as austerely pure as on the day that Calvin stripped the place of its popish baubles. From its altar, Calvin preached to full houses from 1536 to 1564; today you can gawk at (but not sit in) his chair. The brightly painted **Maccabean Chapel,** restored in flamboyant style, gives an idea of how the cathedral walls might have looked pre-Reformation. The 157-step **north tower** provides a commanding view of the old town's winding streets and flower-bedecked homes. *(Open June-Sept. M-Sa 9am-7pm, Su 11:30am-7pm; Oct.-May Tu-Su 10am-noon and 2-5pm. Closed Su mornings for services. Tower closes 30min. earlier and costs 3SFr July-Aug. Bell-ringing Sa afternoon and free organ recital Sa 6pm.)* The ruins of a Roman sanctuary, a 4th-century basilica, and a 6th-century church rest in an **archaeological site** below the cathedral. *(Open June- Sept. Tu-Su 11am–5pm; Oct.-May Tu-Sa 2-5pm. 5SFr, students 3SFr.)*

OLD CITY. Surrounding the cathedral are medieval townhouses and burger-scaled mansions that make up Geneva's *vieille ville*. One minute from the west end sits **Maison Tavel,** Geneva's oldest civilian medieval building, a posh fortified urban palace. The 14th-century structure now houses a historical municipal **museum** (see p. 451). The **Old Arsenal** a few steps away houses 5 cannons and a mural depicting the arrival of Huguenot refugees and Julius Caesar. Across the street is the **Hôtel de Ville** (town hall), whose components date from the 15th through 17th centuries. It was here that world leaders met on August 22, 1864 to sign the **Geneva Convention** governing conduct during war.

The **Grand-Rue,** which begins at the *Hôtel de Ville*, is crammed with medieval workshops and 18th-century mansions, often featuring hastily added third or fourth floors, the makeshift result of the real estate boom following the influx of French Huguenots after Louis XIV repealed the Edict of Nantes. Plaques commemorating famous residents abound, including one at #40 marking the birthplace of philosopher **Jean-Jacques Rousseau.** Antique shops and art galleries line the Grand-Rue, and nighttime brings live jazz to the restaurants and cafés.

LAKE GENEVA

ARTAMIS: GUERRILLA ARTIST COLONY What do you do when you're a young artist in Geneva and have no place to work? If there's 300 others like you, you shut down the tourist industry until the city gives you a place of your own. That's what happened in the summer of 1996 when a group of artists staged a sit-in demonstration at place du Bourg-de-Four just below the Cathédrale de St-Pierre. They ripped up pavement, built bonfires, and confused the hell out of tourists for six days until the city capitulated and granted them a no-rent lease for an abandoned industrial park on the left bank, now called Artamis (tel. 320 39 30; www.artamis.org). You'll find it at 12 rue de Strand, on the #2 and 10 bus lines ("Palladium"). Rising from the wreckage of an old factory, this ten-building complex displays high-quality graffiti and houses a mix of thriving art workshops, theaters, and fund-raising facilities as well as some of the best deals in town. There's an **Internet café** (5SFr per hr.), a movie theater (2SFr), and bars. Electronic music enthusiasts should stop by the Database building, a recording studio where many of the top house and jungle DJs in the area come to experiment and exchange ideas. Some of their efforts are put on Internet stream radio at www.basic.ch. All facilities and the main phone line (with information on performances and events) are open 4pm to 2am.

Heading away from the *vieille ville* on rue de Chaudronniers brings you to the glittering domes of the **Russian Orthodox Church,** rue Toepffer, next to the Musée d'Art et d'Histoire. Step inside for the hauntingly lovely ikons, stained glass, and heavy incense-weighted air. Photography, short skirts, and shorts are not allowed.

WATERFRONT. Descending from the cathedral toward the lake is akin to being yanked forward 600 years. The streets widen, buses scuttle back and forth, and every corner sports a chic boutique or watch shop. On the waterfront, the **Jet d'Eau,** down quai Gustave-Ador, spews a spectacular plume of water 140m into the air. The sight is a self-consciously invented tourist spectacle. It was inspired by a faulty piping jet, which used to be located downstream on the Rhône, that inadvertently gurgled water each evening when craftsmen turned off hydraulic pressure taps that pressurized their workshops. At any given time from March to October, the world's highest fountain keeps about 7 tons of water aloft.

The floral clock in the nearby **Jardin Anglais** pays homage to Geneva's watch industry with over 6,500 plants and has the world's largest second hand (2.5m). The clock is probably Geneva's most overrated attraction and was once the city's most hazardous. Almost a meter had to be cut away from the clock because tourists, intent on taking the perfect photo, continually backed into unfortunate encounters with oncoming traffic.

The rose-lined quays lead to two fun-parks. On the north shore, **Pâquis Plage,** at quai du Mont-Blanc, is popular with the *Genevois. (2SFr; open 9am-8:30pm.)* Farther from the city center on the south shore, **Genève Plage** offers a giant waterslide, an Olympic-sized pool, volleyball and basketball tournaments, and topless sunbathing for 5SFr. The source of these waters, the Rhône, was consecrated by the pope during a particularly bad outbreak of the bubonic plague as a "burial" ground for plague victims. As you frolic in the lake, be reverent or revolted accordingly.

Ferry tours leave from quai du Mont-Blanc and offer an easier-on-the-feet way to see Geneva. **Swiss Boat** (tel. 732 47 47) and **Mouettes Genevoises** (tel. 732 29 44) provide winter cruises narrated in English (35min. 8SFr, children 5SFr; 1hr. 12SFr, 7SFr; 2hr. 20SFr; 15SFr). **CGN** (tel. 741 52 31 or 741 52 35) has been sending cruises to lakeside towns, including Lausanne, Montreux, and the stupendous Château de Chillon, for the past 125 years (round-trip 32-50SFr, Eurailpass and SwissPass valid). The tourist office's brochure *Les Heures Bleues* provides more details.

PARKS AND GARDENS. Geneva is a city bedecked with sumptuous gardens. Strategically scattered throughout the city, you'll be sure to find one by wandering a few blocks in any direction. Below the cathedral on the Rue de la Croix-Rouge, the

Parc des Bastions' leisurely loveliness stretches from the Place Neuve to the Place des Philosophes. On one flank, **Le Mur des Réformateurs** (Reformers' Wall) displays a sprawling collection of bas-relief narrative panels, an array of multilingual inscriptions, and the towering figures of the Reformers themselves. As the largest "Elite Four" (Knox, Beze, Calvin, and Farel) jostle each other sternly for "leader of the Protestant pack" bragging rights, Cromwell and Rhode Island's Roger Williams trail behind. The imposing campus of **Geneva University** sits opposite the wall, with unreformed couples and sunbathers in between.

Strolling north along the river quays brings you to the lush **Parc Mon-Repos** (off av. de France) and **La Perle du Lac** (off av. de la Paix), where panting joggers and playful kids stream along curvy paths painted with an impossibly varied palette of floral hues. At the **Jardin Botanique,** opposite the World Trade Organization, basilica-shaped greenhouses grow a collection of rare plants whose aromas waft across rue de Lausanne. (Open Apr.-Sept. 8am-7:30pm; Oct.-Mar. 9:30am-5pm. Free.) Venturing a little farther (and farther uphill) brings you to **Parc de l'Ariana,** where you can stroll the impressive grounds surrounding the United Nations building and the Ariana pottery museum (see p. 453).

On the opposite (south) side of the lake, past the Jet d'Eau on quai Gustave-Ador you'll find **Parc la Grange,** which features a garden of 40,000 roses, at their peak bloom in June. Next to la Grange, **Parc des Eaux-Vives** is the perfect spot for a picnic or an impromptu frisbee game.

INTERNATIONAL HILL. Spectacular views of Lac Léman with Mont-Blanc in the background can be found in the series of garden-parks up the hill behind the train station. The **Museum of the History of Science** (see p. 453) lives in one and the **World Trade Organization** (WTO) lies in another farther north. For even better vistas, climb higher to Geneva's international city, where embassies and multilateral organizations abound. The best of these (from a tourist's point of view, of course) is the **International Red Cross,** which contains its own museum (see p. 451). In the Red Cross's shadow stands the European headquarters of the **United Nations,** housed in the building that used to shelter the now defunct League of Nations. The guided tour of the UN is quite dull, despite some art (typical title: "Peace: There is Room for All") donated by all the countries of the world and an opportunity to sign "The Golden Book of Peace." *(Open July-Aug. 9am-6pm; Apr.-June and Sept.-Oct. 10am-noon and 2-4pm; Nov.-Mar. M-F 10am-noon and 2-4pm. 8.50SFr, seniors and students 6.50SFr, children 4SFr, children under 6 free. For information, contact the Visitors' Service (tel. 907 45 60; fax 907 00 32), which also conducts 1hr. tours in any of 15 languages when a sizable group requests them.)* The constant traffic of international diplomats (often in handsome non-Western dress) provides more excitement than anything the tour guides have to say. There's also a not-so-subtle display of Cold War one-upmanship: the armillary sphere depicting the heavens and donated by the U.S. stands next to a monument dedicated to the "conquest of space" donated by the former USSR.

🏛 MUSEUMS

Geneva is home to many exceptional museums, usually housed in splendid surroundings, whether architectural or natural. Fortunately, a good number of them are free; unfortunately, the most interesting aren't.

RED CROSS MUSEUM. Check your ironic detachment at the door of the 🖾 **International Red Cross and Red Crescent Museum,** lest it be ripped forcibly from you during this powerful tour of *Let's Go*'s pick as best museum in Geneva. Built into a hillside and towering over the nearby UN on several levels, the Red Cross tour employs images, not rhetoric, to drive home its emotional narrative of historic humanitarianism. The stark, unadorned glass and steel building houses a maze of provocative graphics and audiovisual displays. Dostoyevsky's keynote words: "Each of us is responsible to all others for everything," resonate much more after a visit here. 7 million POW records, including de Gaulle's, from WWI, reside here. Displays in English, French, and German. *(Take bus #8, F, V or Z to "Appia" or "Ariana." Av. de la Paix 17. Tel. 748 95 11; fax 748 95 28. Open Su-M and W-Sa 10am-5pm. 10SFr, students and seniors 5SFr, under 12 free. Self-guided audio tours 5SFr.)*

ART MUSEUMS. If you visit just one art museum in Geneva, the ▨ **Petit-Palais** should be it. This beautiful mansion contains paintings, sculptures, and drawings by Picasso, Renoir, Gauguin, Cézanne, and Chagall. The inventive basement *salles* present themed exhibitions: the influence of primitive art on modern aesthetes, the nude female form, and radiant meditations on nature. *(Take bus #17 to "Petit Palais" or #1, 3, or 5 to "Claparède." Terrasse St-Victor 2, off bd. Helvétique. Tel. 346 14 33. Open M-F 10am-6pm, Sa-Su 10am-5pm. 10SFr, students and seniors 5SFr. Visa.)*

For a more historically comprehensive overview, visit the **Musée d'Art et d'Histoire,** where you'll find a high quality collection of art and artifacts ranging from neolithic tools and an open Egyptian sarcophagus with an unwrapped mummy to Renaissance and contemporary art. The spacious central courtyard juxtaposes a traditional fountain with modern metal sculpture and excavated stone panels. *(Take bus #3, 5, 6, or 8 to "Athenée," or bus #17 to "St. Antoine." rue Charles-Galland 2 (tel. 418 26 00). Open Tu-Su 10am-5pm. Museum free; temporary exhibit rates vary.)*

Where, oh where, has the avant-garde art of the 1970s and 80s gone? The **Centre d'Art Contemporaire,** is a good place to look. The museum displays a huge diversity of works, from Minimalist paintings to bulbous sculptures and landscape photographs. On Tuesdays at 6:30 (except July-Aug.), you can absorb the wisdom of experts at a free lecture. *(Take bus #3: "Cirque," walk down the Ave. de Mail, and turn right on Rue des Vieux-Grenadiers. Rue des Vieux-Grenadiers 10. Tel. 320 61 22. Open W-Su noon-8pm, T noon-9pm; 4SFr, students 2SFr.)*

HISTORICAL MUSEUMS. You can ponder the nature of humanity as you browse the varied collection at the **Musée d'Ethnographie,** which includes Japanese Samurai armor, Australian aboriginal paintings, and a shrunken Bolivian mummy. *(Take bus #1 or 4 to "Bains." Head down rue de Bains past the automobile museum and turn left onto bd. Carl-Vogt. Bd. Carl-Vogt 65-67. Tel. 418 45 50; email jerome.ducor@ville-ge.ch; www.ville-ge.ch/musinfo/ethg/index.htm. Open Tu-Su 10am-5pm. Permanent exhibits free. Temporary exhibits 5SFr, students 3SFr, children free.)*

Once your sociological appetite has been whetted, seek out the **Musée Barbier-Mueller** and its 3 floors of what the ethnocentric once called primitive art, encompassing time periods as distant as early European and regions as far-flung as southern Africa. Photographs of the objects in their original settings put the frequently changing exhibitions in context. *(From the Grand Rue in the vieille ville, turn onto rue de la Pélisserie and left on rue Jean-Calvin. Rue Jean-Calvin 10. Tel. 312 02 70; email musee@barbier.mueller.ch. Open 11am-5pm. 5SFr, children 3SFr.)*

Pack rats will find a museum after their own hearts at **Maison Tavel,** next to the Hôtel de Ville. This house stores everything that the city couldn't bear to throw away, including the 1799 guillotine from pl. Neuve, a collection of medieval front doors, and a vast zinc and copper model of 1850 Geneva that took 18 years to build. Guidebooks in 6 languages available at the entrance. *(Rue du Puits-St-Pierre 6. Tel. 310 29 00. Open Tu-Su 10am-5pm. Free.)*

SOUP'S ON Before it became part of the Swiss Confederation, Geneva warded off almost-constant attack from the French House of Savoy. After sporadically battling for over 200 years, the city finally triumphed due to Swiss practicality. On the night of December 11, 1602, Savoyard soldiers attempted to scale the city walls. A lone housewife saw the attack and proceeded to dump a pot of boiling soup on the soldiers' heads, buying enough time to sound the city's alarm. Each year, the **Festival of the Escalade** (climbing) celebrates this event, as costumed citizens reenact the battle and children eat chocolate *marmites* (pots) filled with marzipan vegetables.

SCIENTIFIC MUSEUMS. At the other end of the academic spectrum, the **Musée d'Histoire des Sciences,** housed in an elegant *palazzo* facing the lake, showcases esoteric scientific gear. Downstairs starts sensibly enough with sundials, astrolabes, globes, and a telescope or two, but upstairs gets odder and bloodier with amputation saws, a wax model of a syphilis patient's erupting facial sores, skull drills, and the gruesomely crude tools of early gynecology and obstetrics. Exhibits in French. *(Take bus #4/44 to "Sécheron." Villa Bartholoni, rue de Lausanne 128, in the park at La Perle de Lac. Tel. 731 69 85. Open W-M 1-5pm. Free.)*

The more natural side of the sciences is on display at the **Musée d'Histoire Naturelle,** which is filled with crowded animal exhibits—more a tribute to taxidermy than a re-creation of natural habitats—that seem designed for grade-school field trips. *(Take bus #6 (dir.: Malagnou) to "Museum." Rte. de Malagnou 1. Tel. 418 63 00. Open Tu-Su 9:30am-5pm. Free.)*

MUSEUM OF WATCHES AND ENAMELING. Got the time? Visit **Musée de l'Horlogerie et L'Émaillerie,** where ear competes with eye for the visitor's attention and pleasure. Stroll to the rhythms of hundreds of still-functioning antique horologic masterpieces, a complex beat punctuated every few minutes by chimes, bells, cuckoos, or clockwork musical interludes. Fingernail-sized wonders, free-standing giants, and 80s swatches compete to be the first to ring before the hour and confuse wrist-watched tourists. *(Take bus #1, 6, or 8 to "Museum." Rue de Malagnou 15. Tel. 418 64 70. Open W-M 10am-5pm. Museum free; temporary exhibits 5SFr, students 3SFr.)*

SWISS GUARD MUSEUM. Military history buffs will enjoy a rare treat at **Château de Penthes** (Museum of the Swiss Abroad), an ivy-cloaked chateau that features a small collection focused on the world-famous, flamboyantly dressed Swiss Guard. Stroll the surrounding parks—Lac Léman will never look quite so languid from anywhere else. *(Take bus V or Z to "Penthes." Chemin de l'Impératrice 18. Tel. 734 90 21. Open Tu-Su 10am-noon and 2-6pm. Guides in French, English, and German. Grounds open 9am-7pm. 5SFr, students and children 1.50SFr.)*

CERAMICS AND CAR MUSEUMS. The mind-numbingly complete collection of ceramics at **Musée Ariana** calls to mind all the knick-knacks collecting dust on your grandmother's shelves. The collection resides in a late 19th-century monumental medley of colored marble that combines neo-Baroque and neo-Classical elements in cheerful tackiness. *(Take bus #8 or 18 to "Appia" or U-2 to "Ariana." Av. de la Paix 10. Tel. 418 54 50; email ariana@ville-ge.ch; www.mah.ville-ge.ch. Open Su-M and W-Sa 10am-5pm. Free.)* To recall memories of your grandfather's garage, visit the **Jean Tua Car and Cycle Museum,** with its collection of 70 cars as well as motorcycles and bicycles, most dating back to before 1939. *(Take bus #1 to "Bains," by rue des Grenadiers. Rue des Bains 28-30. Tel. 321 36 37. Open W-Su 2-6pm. Admission 8SFr, students 6SFr, children 4SFr.)*

VOLTAIRE MUSEUM. Finally, Voltaire devotees can find their niche at the **Institut et Musée Voltaire,** an 18th-century mansion (Voltaire's home from 1755-1760) stuffed with Voltaire memorabilia. The museum's collection consists mainly of printed matter, manuscripts, and iconographical documents. Particularly diverting are Huber's cartoons of the *philosophe*, Frederick of Prussia's sycophantic letters, and Voltaire's cantankerous replies to Rousseau. Some paintings and sculptures, including works by Houdon. *(Take bus #6 or 26 to "Prairie" or #7, 11, or 27 (dir.: Lignon) to "Délices." Rue des Délices 25. Tel. 344 71 33. Open M-F 2-5pm. Free.)*

🎵 ENTERTAINMENT AND NIGHTLIFE

There is enough to do in Geneva to keep even the most sophisticated traveler happy. *Genève Agenda*, available at the tourist office, is your guide to fun, with event listings ranging from major festivals to movies (be warned—a movie runs about 15.50SFr).

SHOPPING

Budget travelers should think about limiting their shopping in Geneva to the windows, especially on the upscale rue Basses and rue du Rhône. The *vieille ville* contains scads of galleries and antique shops to explore. Those looking for Swiss souvenirs like Swiss Army knives and watches should head to the department stores. **La Placette** in pl. Cornavin is particularly good for the cheap and chintzy (open M-F 7:30am-5pm, Th 7:30am-8pm, Sa 8am-5pm). Exquisite Swiss chocolate is sold in any supermarket, but the specialty store *par excellence* is **Chocolats Micheli,** rue Micheli-du-Crest 1 (tel. 329 90 06), which produces confectionery works of art (open Tu-F 7am-7pm, Sa 8am-5pm). Bargain hunters head to Plainpalais to browse at the huge **flea market** (open W and Sa 8am-5pm) and **food market** (T and F). Smaller markets grace pl. de la Madeleine (M-Sa 8am-7pm) and pl. de la Fusterie (Th all day). A **book market** fills the Esplanade de la Madeleine (M-Sa 8am-7pm). More ephemeral wares bloom at the **flower market,** usually hidden amid the sprawling outdoor cafés in pl. du Molard (M-Sa).

FESTIVALS

Summer days bring festivals, free open-air concerts, and **free organ music** in Cathédrale de St-Pierre. In July and August, the **Cinelac** turns Genève Plage into an open-air cinema that screens mostly American films. Check the listings in *Genève Agenda* for indoor cinemas (films marked "v.o." are in their original language with French and sometimes German subtitles while "st. ang." means that the film has English subtitles). There's also the biggest celebration of **American Independence Day** outside the U.S. on July 4 and the **Fêtes de Genève** in early August filled with international music and artistic celebration culminating in a spectacular fireworks display. **La Bâtie Festival,** a performing arts festival traditionally held late August to early September, draws Swiss music-lovers for a 2-week orgy of cabaret, theater, and concerts by experimental rock and folk acts. Many events are free; students pay half-price for the others (regular prices 10-32SFr). For information, call 738 55 77 or email batie@world.com.ch. **Free jazz concerts** take place in July and August at the *Théâtre de Verdure* in Parc de la Grange. Most parks offer free concerts; check at the tourist office for information. The best party in Geneva is **L'Escalade,** commemorating the dramatic repulsion of invading Savoyard troops (see **Soup's On,** p. 452). The revelry lasts a full weekend and takes place in early December.

CAFÉS, BARS, AND NIGHTCLUBS

Summer nightlife centers around the cafés on the lakeside quays, where the city drinks, converses, flirts, and spies. Two popular areas brimming with nocturnal revelry are **Place du Bourg-de-Four,** below Cathédrale de St-Pierre, and the village of **Carouge** (take tram #12 to "pl. du Marché"). Carouge gained a reputation for fun all the way back in Calvin's day, when those who wished to defy their leader's ban on cafés gathered outside the city limits to drink the night into oblivion.

🎨 **Au Chat Noir,** rue Vautier 13, Carouge (tel. 343 49 98). Take tram #12 to "pl. du Marché," off the far left end of the square. The upside-down car hanging from the ceiling is a puzzle, but the sensuously curved old bar and dark red curtains set the mood in this popular venue for jazz, funk, rock, salsa, and sax-moaning blues. Live concerts every night (showtime 9:30pm, 15SFr cover.) Beers 5SFr, sangria 10-12SFr. Open M-Th 6pm-4am, F 6pm-5am, Sa 9pm-5am, Su 9pm-4am.

La Clémence, pl. du Bourg-de-Four 20 (tel. 312 24 98). Generations of students have eaten at this famous, chic bar, named after the big bell atop the Cathédrale de St-Pierre. Tables overflow into the square come nightfall, and a crew of teen-idol waiters tends to a chatty, artsy clientele. Come for breakfast (croissant 1.20SFr, coffee 2.70SFr) or beer (4-8SFr). Open M-Th 7am-12:30am, F-Sa 7am-1:30am.

Abag Brasil, 10 rue des Vieux Grenadiers, near the *Centre d'Art Contemporaine.* With all the rowdiness of a post-*futbol* match bash, world rock and a funky neighborhood draw a mixture of black-turtlenecked dreadlocked free spirits. Open Th-Sa 11pm until late.

Flanagan's, rue du Cheval-Blanc 4 (tel. 310 13 14), off Grand Rue in the *vieille ville*. Friendly bartenders pull a good beer in this Irish cellar bar. Chat merrily in the mother tongue amid dusty, liquor-inspired memorabilia. Pint o' Guinness 8SFr; 6SFr during happy hour, 5-8pm daily. Live music Th-Sa 10am-2am. Open 4pm-2am.

Sunset Café, rue de la Navigation (tel. 906 40 47), next to Dialogai. A single strand of red lights traverses this sophisticated little café. Fresh flowers brighten the red walls and curtains, and salsa music accompanies your gourmet nibblings (gazpacho 6SFr, carpaccio with apples and salad 10SFr). Gay-friendly. Open W-Su 5pm-midnight.

Demi-Lune Café, rue Etienne Dumot 3 (tel. 312 12 90), just up the street from pl. du Bourg-de-Four. Munch *tapas*-style food (6-7SFr) or hamburgers (9-11SFr) or just get sloshed (beer 3.50SFr) while listening to John Coltrane in this low-key, funky little café-bar in the *vieille ville*. Open 11am-11:30pm.

Petit Palais, tour de Boël 6 (tel. 311 00 33), is a fantastic discotheque-cabaret for the adventurous. From the pl. du Molard, turn right onto rue de Marché and head up and around to the left of the Confederation Center. Ring and the bouncer will slide back a panel, revealing live DJ techno, psychedelic lighting, transparent stairs with a waterfall beneath them, and a cage of dancers of both sexes who strip in the wee hours. Open 11am till morning; free "erotic show" Su-Th 11:30pm-2:30am.

Post Café, rue de Berne 7 (tel. 732 96 63; www.postcafe.ch), left off rue de Mont-Blanc. Billing itself as an "international meeting point," this popular joint attracts a range of Anglophones from older International School kids to young businessmen and twenty-something expat Americans. Guinness 8SFr, sandwiches (3.80SFr), and friendly atmosphere amid arcade games and TV-broadcasted soccer matches. Happy hour 5-8pm. Open M-F 7am-2am, Sa 10am-2am, Su 4pm-2am. AmEx, MC, Visa.

NEAR GENEVA: ANNECY, FRANCE

A mixture of SNCF buses and trains (tel. 08 36 35 35 35), as well as Voyages Frossard buses (tel. 0450 457 390) cover the 30km between Annecy and Geneva (1hr., 7 per day, 52F).

Just 30km into France, Annecy's narrow cobblestone streets, winding canals, turreted castle, and overstuffed flower boxes make it appear more like a fiberglass fairy-tale fabrication than a modern city with 120,000 inhabitants. This capital of Haute Savoie consistently claimed the title in the National Flower City contest until its continued success forced it to withdraw permanently from the competition. Annecy has ceded its floral crown, but visitors still can't resist the magic of the lake and mountains. Most activity centers around Lac Annecy, southeast of the train station. A canal runs east to west through the old town, leaving the elevated château on one side and the main shopping area, closer to the *centre ville*, on the other. To reach the tourist office from the station, take the underground passage to rue Vaugelas, turn left, and walk straight for 4 blocks. The tourist office is straight ahead in the Bonlieu shopping mall, 1 rue Jean Jaurès (tel. 04 50 45 00 33 or 04 50 45 56 66; fax 04 50 51 87 20), on pl. de la Libération. Ask for the helpful *Guide Pratique d'Annecy* or, for hikes, the *Sentiers Forestiers* (20F) or the free *Randonnées Pedestres*. (2hr. tours (32F) in summer M-Sa 10am and 3pm. Open daily July-Aug. 9am-6:30pm; Sept.-June M-Sa 9am-noon and 1:45-6:30pm, Su 3-6pm.)

🖼 🏃 **SIGHTS AND OUTDOOR ACTIVITIES.** A stroll through the *vieille ville* may cost you several rolls of film and a hundred sighs. The **Palais de l'Isle** (tel. 04 50 33 83 62) is a 12th-century fortress which was originally the home of the de l'Isle family. The tiny, turreted building forming a skinny island in the middle of the canal was converted into a prison in the 1400s and is now a museum devoted to Annecy's history—it's far more impressive from the outside. The passages of **quai Perrière, rue de l'Isle,** and **rue Ste-Claire** to the south of the fortress are Annecy at its most charming. Cross the street from the tourist office to walk through the **Champ de Mars,** a long field dotted with *boules* players, sunbathers, and picnickers stretching out to the lake. At the mouth of the Canal du Vassé, which runs along the Champ de Mars, is the **Pont des Amours** (Bridge of Love), one of few that merits

its cheesy name. The **Jardin de l'Europe,** a web of paths surrounding manicured hedges, fountains, and statues, juts out into the water beyond the bridge.

Another 12th-century château towers over Annecy, a short but steep climb from the *vieille ville*. Once a stronghold of the counts of Geneva, the castle and its imposing parapets now house unexciting archaeological and artistic exhibits. The 15th-century wooden statuary is worth a look. Temporary shows are often well-mounted, and the **Observatoire Régional des Lacs Alpins,** in the rear of the castle, has displays on lake ecosystems as well as a cool aquarium. If the exhibits don't impress you, the view will. (Tel. 04 50 33 87 30. Open June-Aug. daily 10am-6pm; Sept.-May W-M 10am-noon and 2-6pm. Château 30F, students 10F. Grounds free.)

After a stroll through the bustling streets, you may opt for a swim in the cold, crystalline lake. **Plage des Marquisats,** south of the city down rue des Marquisats, is free but crowded. The **Club de Voile Française** rents **kayaks** from the Plage des Marquisats (35F per hr.). Or escape on a pedal boat from **Bateaux Dupraz** on quai Napoleon; some boats have a slide to aid your descent into the water. (Tel. 04 50 51 52 15. 35-52F per 30min., 60-88F per hr.; tours of the lake 52-55F. V, MC.) It costs 18F to swim at the glamorous **Parc Public de l'Impérial,** an aquatic wonderland with waterslides, sailing, tennis, swim lessons, and a casino. (20min. up av. d'Albigny. Tel. 04 50 23 11 82. Open May-Sept. daily 10am-7:30pm.) For steeper challenges, a dozen breathtaking hikes climb the **Semnoz,** a limestone mountain south of the city. The **Office National des Forêts** distributes a color map, *Sentiers Forestiers*, with several routes (20F at the tourist office or hostel). One of the best begins at the Basilique, right near the youth hostel. If you're staying in town, take bus #91 (summer only) to "Tillier." Then, from the Basilique, continue along the road until you reach a small parking lot. From there, follow the signs for la Forêt du Crêt du Maure. A two-hour hike with beautiful views of the lake, the city, and the mountains follows the Ste-Catherine and GR96 trails in a meandering circle around the Semnoz forest. Long-haulers may consider a bigger portion of the GR96, which circles the lake on a trail marked with yellow and red lines. There's an exquisite, 16km scenic *piste cyclable* (bike route) that hugs the lake shore from Sevrier to Doussard. After that, you can complete the entire loop (32km) on the main road, but be careful for increased traffic. The **Bureau des Guides,** 17 fbg. Ste-Claire (tel. 04 50 45 60 61), covers all mountaineering activities, including hikes, rock-climbing, ice-climbing, and canyoning excursions. (Open daily 5:30-6:30pm. Hikes 80F per half-day, 120F per day. Sign up night before.) For info on sports in the area, call **Annecy Sport Information,** 7 fbg. Ste-Claire (tel. 04 50 33 88 31; M-F 3-7pm). The *Guide Pratique* has info on outdoor recreation.

⛯🏮 FOOD AND ENTERTAINMENT. Whether you choose a restaurant on the canal or a lakeside picnic, the surroundings will be as enjoyable as the food. At **Quoi de n'Oeuf,** 19 fbg. Ste-Claire (tel. 04 50 45 75 42), eggheads jump at the 50F all-you-can-eat *tartiflette*, salad, and dessert (open M-Sa noon-2pm and 7-10pm; V, MC). Fill your picnic basket with the soft local *reblochon* cheese at the morning **markets** on pl. Ste-Claire (Tu, F, and Su) and on **bd. Taine** (Sa). Grocery stores line av. de Parmelan, and a **Prisunic supermarket** fills the better part of pl. de Notre-Dame (open M-Sa 8:30am-7:30pm). At night, relax at the bars lining the canal in the *vieille ville*. Students stream into **Le River's Café,** 2 rue de la Gare (tel. 04 50 45 48 11), which overflows with cheap drinks, billiards, and funky painted patio furniture. **Redz,** 14 rue Perrière (tel. 04 50 45 17 13), caters to an older and more moneyed crowd, but really packs 'em in after 11pm. **Café Curtis,** 35 rue Ste-Claire (tel. 04 50 51 74 75), maintains an easy-going atmosphere in its crowded blond-wood bar with 10F wine and 13F Kronenbourg. Performing arts and cinema go up at the **Théâtre d'Annecy** (tel. 04 50 33 44 11) in the Bonlieu Mall across from the tourist office (about 95F, students 40F). *Fête* fetishists can pick up schedules at the Comité des Fêtes kiosk across from the tourist office. A small **jazz festival** heats up the middle two weekends of July (60-100F). The grandpappy of them all is the **Fête du Lac,** the first Saturday in August, with fireworks and water shows (35-270F).

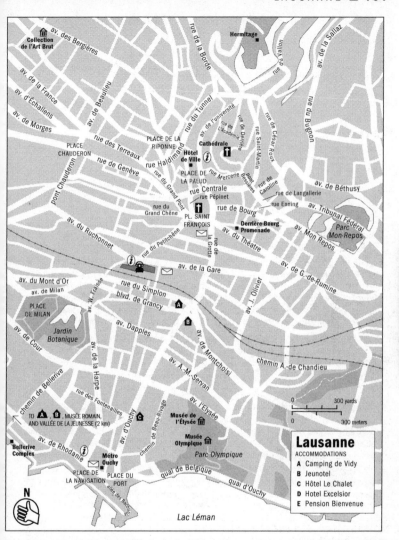

Each year the floats on the lake take on wacky themes such as "Monsters and Legends," "Adventures in the Far West," and "Beyond the Planet Earth."

LAUSANNE

Two thousand years ago, Romans came to the little town of Lausanne on the shores of Lac Léman and found it so enticing that they stayed until the collapse of their empire. Hundreds of years ago, the city inspired a different sort of *roman* with the arrival of Dickens and Thackeray. T.S. Eliot managed to create the apotheosis of high Modernist pessimism here, writing *The Wasteland* near the placid Ouchy shoreline and the medieval labyrinth of the *vieille ville*. Today, Lausanne's unique museums, distinctive neighborhoods, varied festivals, and magnificent parks make it well worth a stay.

⑦ ORIENTATION AND PRACTICAL INFORMATION

Lausanne was built on 3 steep hills that connect via vaulted bridge roads over valleys below, which makes two-dimensional maps confusing. The train station is half-way between the *vieille ville* and the lakefront. The **Métro Ouchy** and buses #1, 3, and 5 serve the station. Most buses are routed to pl. St. François, in the center of the city. Though the town is compact, the steep hills make public transportation a welcome relief. Particularly useful is Lausanne's small underground metro, which runs from the lakefront into the heart of downtown.

TRANSPORTATION

Trains: pl. de la Gare 9 (tel. 157 22 22; 1.19SFr per min.) To: **Montreux** (20min., every 30min. 5:45am-11:57pm, 9.40SFr); **Geneva** (50min., every 30min. 4:20am-12:46am, 20SFr); **Basel** (2½hr., 2 per hr. 5:21am-9:10pm, 62SFr); **Zurich** (2½hr., 3 per hr. 5:21am-10:25pm, 67SFr); and **Paris** (4hr., 4 per day, 7:36am-5:52pm, 93SFr).

Public Transportation: The 5-stop **Métro Ouchy** runs from the *vieille ville* to the Ouchy waterfront. The **Métro Ouest** runs from the center of town west to the University of Lausanne and the Federal Institute of Technology M-Sa 5am-midnight, Su 6am-midnight. Buses cross the city and run roughly 6am-midnight (check bus stops for specific lines). Exact change needed. 3-stop ticket 1.30SFr; 1hr. pass 2.20SFr; 24hr. pass 6.50SFr. Métro free with SwissPass or Museum Passport, but not with Eurailpass.

Ferries: CGN, av. de Rhodanie 17 (tel. 0848 81 18 48). To: **Montreux** (1½hr., 6 per day, last ferry 6:05pm, one-way 19SFr, round-trip 32SFr); **Geneva** (3½hr., 4 per day, last ferry 5:15pm, one-way 31SFr, round-trip 48SFr); **Evian** (last ferry 12:15am, one-way 14SFr, round-trip 24SFr). Ages 16-25 50% off, senior discount 20%. Purchase tickets at dock. Eurail and SwissPass valid. Open M-F 7:30am-noon, 2-5:30pm.

Taxis: Available at rue Madeleine 1, pl. St. François, Place de la Navigation, and in front of the station. Or, call the **taxibus** (tel. (0800) 080 03 12) or **taxiphone** (tel. (0800) 80 18 02). For 24hr. service call (0800) 81 08 10.

Car Rental: Avis, av. de la Gare 50 (tel. 340 72 00; fax 340 72 09). **Hertz,** pl. du Tunnel 17 (tel. 312 53 11). **Europcar,** av. Rochonnet 2 (tel. 323 91 52).

Parking: Parking Simplon-Gare, rue du Simplon 2 (tel. 617 67 44), behind the station, (entrance on Blvd. de Grancy), costs 0.60SFr per 40min. (less for extended usage), 20SFr overnight. Open M-F 8am-7pm, Sa 8am-5pm. On city streets, white zones indicate unlimited parking, red zones allow 15hr. parking, blue zones 1½hr. To park on the street, pick up a parking disc from the tourist office. Set the present time and the maximum stay time, and leave the disc displayed on the dashboard.

Bike Rental: (tel. (0512) 24 21 62), at the baggage check in the station. Rentals 26SFr per day, 20SFr per half-day. Return bikes at another station for an additional 6SFr. Open 6:40am-7:30pm.

TOURIST AND FINANCIAL SERVICES

Tourist Office: Main office (tel. 617 73 73; email information@lausanne-tourisme.ch; www.lausanne.tourisme.ch) in the main hall of the train station. Open 9am-9pm. **Branch office** across from Place de la Navigation (bus #2: Ouchy). Pick up the *Plan Officiel* (a map and public transportation guide) and *Welcome to Lausanne* (booklet listing cheap hotels and private rooms) for free. The staff sells **Lausanne Passes** (see Lausanne Pass p. 461) and makes hotel reservations for 4-6SFr. Wheelchair accessible. Open Apr.-Sept. 9am-9pm, Oct.-March 9am-6pm.

Budget Travel: SSR Voyages, blvd. de Grancy 20 (tel. 617 56 27; fax 616 50 77; www.ssr.ch/ssr), 2 streets downhill from the station past the overpass; turn right. Books student tickets and organizes group travel. Open M-F 9:15am-6pm, Sa 9am-noon.

Currency Exchange: At the station (tel. 312 38 24). Good rates. No commission on traveler's checks. Western Union transfers 7am-7pm. Cash advances with AmEx, DC, MC, Visa. Open 6:20am-7:30pm.

American Express: av. Mon Répos 14 (tel. 310 19 00; fax 310 19 19), across from parking garage. Cashes traveler's checks, sells airline tickets, and holds mail for 2 months. Travel services open M-F 8:30am-5:30pm; financial office open 2-5:30pm.

Luggage Storage: At the train station. Lockers 3SFr and 5SFr per day. Open 24hr.

Lost Property: pl. Chauderon 7 on the lower level (tel. 315 33 86). Open M-F 8am-12:15pm and 1:45-6pm, Sa 8am-noon.

LOCAL SERVICES, EMERGENCIES, AND COMMUNICATION

Bookstore: Payot Libraire, pl. Pépinet 4 (tel. 341 31 31; fax 341 33 45). Large Anglophone section with contemporary and classic fiction, some nonfiction, and plenty of *Let's Go.* Open M 1-6:30pm, Tu-F 8:30am-6:30pm, Sa 8:30am-5pm.

Library: Cantonal and University Palais de Rumine, pl. de la Riponne 6 (tel. 316 78 80; www.unil.ch/BCU). Open for borrowing M-F 10am-6pm, Sa 9am-noon. Reading room open M-F 8am-10pm, Sa 8am-5pm. Borrowing card free with ID.

Laundromat: Quick Wash, bd. de Grancy 44, 2 streets downhill behind the train station; turn right. Wash and dry around 12SFr. Open M and W-Su 9am-8:30pm, Tu noon-8:30pm.

PHONE CODE	The **city code** for Lausanne is 021.

Emergency: Police, tel. 117. **Fire,** tel. 118. **Ambulance,** tel. 144. **Crisis Line,** tel. 143.

24-Hour Pharmacy: Dial 111 to find out which pharmacy is open all night; they rotate weekly. **24hr. medical service,** at the hospital (tel. 314 11 11).

Internet Access: E.S.F., pl. St-François 12 (tel. 320 41 60; fax 320 41 61). 5SFr. per 30min. Open Tu-F 10am-6:30pm, Sa 10am-5pm.

Post Office: Centre Postal, av. de la Gare 43bis (tel. 344 35 13), on the right as you exit the station. Address *Poste Restante* to: 1000 Lausanne 1 Cases. Open M-F 5am-10pm, Sa 5am-11am. Express mail M-F 6:30-7:30am, noon-1:30pm, and 6:30-10pm, Sa 6:30-8am 11am-2pm, and 5-10pm. **Postal Code:** CH-1001. To dispatch your postcard from the site where in 1783-1793 Edward Gibbon wrote his *Decline and Fall of the Roman Empire,* visit **Poste St. Françoise,** 15 pl. St-François (tel. 344 38 31). Open M-F 7:30am-6:30pm, Sa 8-11am. **Postal Code:** CH-1002.

▉ ACCOMMODATIONS AND CAMPING

As the home of the world's oldest hotel school, Lausanne has a well-deserved reputation for service-industry excellence. The city offers a huge range of accommodations, from *fin de siècle* palaces to lakeside tent plots. It's a good idea to pick up the tourist office's list of cheap hotels, private boarding houses, and family *pensions* since innumerable festivals, conferences, and congresses can make housing scarce. The owners of these establishments generally prefer stays of at least three nights and often as long as a month. Since Lausanne is a university town, many hoteliers and private citizens cater to those on a student budget. Travelers looking for apartments to rent can turn to the local paper *24 Heures,* which carries regular listings, or to the notice boards of big department stores.

Jeunotel (HI), Chemin du Bois-de-vaux 36 (tel. 626 02 22; fax 626 02 26). Take bus #2 (dir.: Bourdonnette) to "Bois-de-Vaux." Cross the street and follow the signs. This large and gleaming hostel with the cleanliness of a hospital ward is down a long concrete driveway on your right just past the *Musée Romain de Lausanne-Vidy.* Courtyards with ping pong tables, techno blaring from the bar, and a mostly young backpacker crowd enliven its concrete sterility. Dorms 24-31SFr; singles 42SFr, with shower 57SFr; doubles 86SFr, with shower 104SFr; triples and quads 34SFr per person. Monthly rates available. Wheelchair accessible. Reservations wise in the summer. MC, Visa.

Pension Bienvenue, rue du Simplon 2 (tel. 616 29 80), 5min. from the train station. Turn right along av. de la Gare, right on av. d'Ouchy, right after the bridge. **Women only.** This 25-room *pension* offers communal TV rooms, **laundry, kitchen,** a piano, and free breakfast. Hall showers and bathrooms only. Singles 40SFr; doubles 70SFr (additional 3% tax). Special rates for extended stays. Reception 8-11:30am and 5-9pm.

Hotel "Le Chalet," av. d'Ouchy 49 (tel. 616 52 06). Take Métro Ouchy to "Jordils" or bus #2 (dir.: Bourdonnette) to "Jordils." Built in 1877, this chalet has been run by the same charmingly eccentric matron since 1940. Each room has a sink and balcony. Mixing with guests are occasional *literati* hoping to commune with the spirit of longtime guest August Strindberg in the evergreen garden. Singles 49-62 SFr; doubles 88SFr; 1 'family room' triple 99 SFr. Hall showers. Breakfast 9SFr. Reception 8am-9pm.

Hotel Excelsior, chemin du Closelet 6 (tel. 616 84 51; fax 616 84 58), 5min. from the train station. Turn right along av. de la Gare, right on av. d'Ouchy, and left after the bridge on Closelet. In the middle of a renovation, Excelsior's spacious rooms balance the cramped, run-down hallways and shared bathrooms. Singles 60SFr, 98SFr with shower; doubles 100SFr, 140SFr. Reception 8am-10pm every day. AmEx, MC, Visa.

Camping de Vidy, chemin du Camping 3 (tel. 622 50 00; fax 622 50 01; www.campinglausannevidy.ch). Take bus #2 (dir.: Bourdonnette) to "Bois-de-Vaux." Cross the street and go down chemin du Bois-de-Vaux past Jeunotel and under the overpass. The office is straight ahead across rte. de Vidy. Restaurant (8am-midnight), supermarket, playground, and swimming **pool** (2SFr). Reception 8am-12:30pm and 5-8pm. 6.50SFr, students 6SFr; tents 7-11SFr; 1- to 2-person bungalow 54SFr; 3- to 4-person bungalow 86SFr. Tax 1.20SFr per tent, 1.40SFr per vehicle. Showers included. Electricity 3SFr. Wheelchair accessible.

◖ FOOD

No visit to Lausanne is complete without a taste of Lac Léman's famous perch or *papet vaudois* (a local delicacy made of leeks, potatoes, cabbage and sausage). Restaurants, cafés, and bars cluster around pl. St.-François and the *vieille ville;* while *boulangeries* sell cheap sandwiches on every street. Surprisingly fresh fare and crusty bread await at Metro stations. Numerous groceries, frequent markets, and an abundance of parks make for affordable and pleasant picnics.

Crêperie d'Ouchy, pl. du Port 7 (tel. 616 26 07), to the left of the Place de la Navigation (take bus #2 to Ouchy). Locals linger in the relaxed atmosphere here to savor conversation and the lake view from the outdoor patio. Crepes 4.50-18SFr. Try the seasonal specialty garnishes, like fresh fruit and ice cream in the summer. Open spring 11am-11pm; summer 9am-midnight; fall 11am-11pm; winter noon-8pm. Wheelchair accessible.

Manora, pl. St-François 17 (tel. 320 92 93), beneath Zürich Bank sign. Proffering "the longest buffet in Lausanne." Open 7am-10:30pm. Hot food 11am-10pm. Buffet 10:45am-10:30pm.

Au Couscous, rue Enning 2 (tel. 321 38 40). From pl. St.-François, head away from the Zurich Bank sign and turn left up the hill, then right on rue de Bourg; it's at the end. Inside, a North African theme prevails with red tablecloths, a mosaic-tiled floor, and sequined pillows. Extensive, veggie-friendly menu (14-24SFr). Couscous is the real specialty (21-30.50SFr), but the informative menu contains other Tunisian specialties. Open M-F 11:30am-2pm, and Su-Th 6:30pm-midnight, F-Sa 6:30pm-1am.

Crêperie "La Chandeleur," rue Mercerie 9 (tel. 312 84 19). From the pl. St.-François head down the rue Pépinet to the pl. de la Palud; rue Mercier is off the far right side. Enjoy custom-made crepes, whether traditional (with butter, sugar, or honey 4-8SFr), sugar-deprived (with ice cream 7-10SFr), or gourmet (*flambées* with choice of liqueur 8-11SFr). Open Tu-Th 11am-10pm, F-Sa 11am-11:30pm. DC, MC, Visa.

Le Barbare, Escaliers du Marché 27 (tel. 312 21 32), at the top of steps off the far right side of the pl. de la Palud. Stop by for lunch or a mid-afternoon treat after climbing the Cathedral Tower. Sandwiches 4.50SFr, omelettes 7-9SFr. Try the *Chocolate Maison Viennois avec Chantilly,* a rich chocolate drink. Open M-Sa 8:30am-midnight.

MARKETS

Migros, 2 av. de Rhodanie (tel. 613 26 60), 30 seconds to the right of Metro Ouchy or bus #2 stop "Pl. du Navigation," as well as at several other locations throughout the city. M-Sa 9am-7pm, Su 8am-9:45pm during spring and summer.

Co-op, blvd. de Grancy (tel. 616 40 66). From the train station, head downhill past the overpass; turn right on blvd. de Grancy. Open M-F 8am-7pm, Sa 8am-5pm.

Produce markets, at the pl. de la Palud and the rue de Bourg behind the pl. St.-François. W and Sa mornings.

👁 🏛 SIGHTS AND MUSEUMS

A Lausanne tourist brochure makes the odd statement, "In Lausanne, people are consuming culture as others swallow vitamins." Perhaps something was lost in the translation, but nevertheless, 650,000 visitors flock to Lausanne's lovely *vieille ville* and excellent museums each year. From the psychotic art of the **Collection de l'Art Brut** to the photographic archives of the **Elysée** (which recently featured works by both David Hockney and Richard Gere) to the stunning video collections of the **Olympic Museum,** the city's exhibits are all about quirkiness. For multi-day visits, the **Lausanne Pass** is a great deal, entitling visitors to museum discounts and free public transportation in and around Lausanne (15SFr for 3 days).

THE OLD CITY AND CATHEDRAL. The medieval town center is known as the *vieille ville,* but the true old city is on the waterfront where digs have unearthed 2000-year-old remains of the *Vicus de Lousonna.* You can stroll through it and see the foundations of a temple, the remains of a basilica, a forum, a few villas, and the traces of a complete Gallo-Roman colony. (Take bus #2 to "Bois-de-Vaux" and follow signs.) Vidy gradually decayed as Rome waned, and the town's inhabitants moved up to the more easily defended hills of the *cité.* The population grew and built up the town, making it the largest in Switzerland by the time the Gothic **cathédrale** was consecrated in 1275 under Holy Roman Emperor Rudolph and Pope Gregory X. Take bus #16 to "Cathédrale" or climb series of medieval covered stairs to the hilltop, where the cathedral's huge wooden doors open up into the hushed, vaulted space illuminated by flashes of stained glass. Climb the 200-step **tower** for a spectacular view of the city, lake, and mountains beyond. Lausanne is one of the last towns in Switzerland to retain a night watchman who cries the hour from 10pm to 2am. *(Cathedral open July to mid-Sept. 7am-7pm; mid-Sept. to June 7am-5pm. Free guided tours July-Sept. at 10:30, 11:15am, 3, and 3:45pm. Tower open 8:30-11:30am and 1:30-5:30pm. 2SFr, children 1SFr.)*

Below the cathedral, the Renaissance **Hôtel de Ville** (city hall), with its bronze dragon roof, serves as a meeting point for guided **tours** of the town. *(Tours M-Sa 10am and 3pm. 10SFr, students free, English available.)* Also below the cathedral is the pl. de la Riponne, presided over by the majestic **Palais de la Rumine,** which houses the Cantonal and University Library, as well as several small archaeological and zoological museums. *(Palais de la Rumine open M-F 7am-10pm, Sa 7am-5pm, Sun 10am-5pm.)*

ART MUSEUMS. The ▓ **Collection de l'Art Brut** is an utterly original gallery filled with disturbing and beautiful sculptures, drawings, and paintings by artists on the fringe—institutionalized schizophrenics, poor and uneducated peasants, and convicted criminals. Nearly as fascinating as the works are the biographies of their tortured creators, displayed in English and French and often accompanied by intense photographed portraits. From a prison cell wall painstakingly carved with a broken spoon to intricate junk and sea-shell masks, this collection of obsessions started by radical primitivist Jean Dubuffet ranks as Lausanne's most satisfying collection. *(Take bus #2 or 3 to "Jomini." Av. Bergières 11. Tel. 647 54 35. Open Tu-Su 11am-1pm and 2-6pm. 6SFr, students and seniors 4SFr, under 15 free.)*

On a more conventional note, the **Musée de l'Elysée** houses an engaging series of diverse exhibits and photographic archives, ranging from 1820 prints to contemporary artistic endeavors in film. The basement's resonant tile and hushed atmosphere make the images even more haunting. *(Take bus #2 to "Croix d'Ouchy" and go downhill, then left on av. de l'Elysée. Av. de l'Elysée 18. Tel. 617 48 21; email dgirardin@ping-net.ch; www.elysee.ch. Open Tu-W and F-Su 10am-6pm, Th 10am-9pm. Archives open Th by appointment. 5SFr, students 2.50SFr.)* North of the *vieille ville*, the **Hermitage** is a magnificent house given over to temporary exhibitions that vary from single artists and special themes to individual public and private collections. Call ahead for a schedule, since the museum closes between shows. *(Bus #16 to "Hermitage" stops infrequently out front. Rte. du Signal 2. Tel. 320 50 01. Open Tu-W and F-Su 10am-6pm, Th 10am-9pm. 13SFr, students 5SFr, seniors 10SFr, under 19 free. AmEx, MC, Visa.)*

OLYMPIC MUSEUM. The **Musée Olympique** is a high-tech temple to modern Olympians with a smaller exhibit dedicated to the ancient games. An extensive video collection that allows visitors to relive any requested highlight since the games were first filmed. The bilingual English/French displays of medals, mementos, and equipment arranged around the central spiral ramp swarm with kids. Wheelchair accessible via av. de l'Elysée. *(Take bus #2 or Métro: "Ouchy." Quai d'Ouchy 1. Tel. 621 65 11; www.museum.olympic.org. Open May-Sept. M-W and F-Su 9am-6pm, Th 9am-8pm; Oct.-Apr. Tu-W and F-Su 9am-6pm, Th 9am-8pm. 14SFr, students and seniors 9SFr, ages 10-18 7SFr, families 34SFr max. MC, Visa. The idyllic grounds are a better deal for free.)*

HISTORICAL MUSEUM. History buffs will enjoy poking around the **Musée Romain de Lausanne-Vidy,** next door to Jeunotel, the excavation site of a Roman house whose wall murals still display bright colors. Wade knee-deep through local school children to examine 2 floors of carvings, tools, pots, and coins from the Vicus de Lousonna archaeological site down the street; interactive computer stations answer questions like "What was the Forum?" *(Take bus #1 and 4 to "Maladière," or #2 to "Bois-de-Vaux." Signs point the way. Chemin du Bois-de-Vaux 24. Tel. 652 10 84. Open Tu-W and F-Su 11am-6pm, Th 11am-8pm. Wheelchair accessible. 4SFr, students free.)*

WATERFRONT. A sign along the waterfront declares Ouchy to be "a free and independent community," and indeed its slower tempo, indulgent hotels, and eco-modern sculptures strikingly set it apart from the *vieille ville*. Ouchy's main promenades, the **quai de Belgique** and **place de la Navigation,** are both excellent spots to exercise those calf-muscles. The local word is that Lausanne's women have the best-looking legs in Switzerland, the hard-won prize of a life spent hiking the city's hills. You can see more of Ouchy's inhabitants at the **Bellerive Complex** (take bus #2 to "Bellerive"), a beach park where locals set their children loose on spotless, activity-filled lawns while both genders go topless and take in some sun. *(Open mid-May to Aug. daily from 9:30am until dark or rain. 4.50SFr, students and seniors 3SFr, under 17 2SFr. 0.50SFr discount after 5pm.)*

PARKS AND GARDENS. The Bellerive Beach is just one of Lausanne's many natural oases. At the **Vallée de la Jeunesse** rose garden, an unassuming path of wildflowers bends to reveal a spectacular display of 1000 bushes arranged in a terraced semi-circle around a fountain to the tune of thousands of birds. More exotic birds trill from the aviaries of the downtown **Parc du Mon-Repos.** Centering around a small chateau where Voltaire wrote from 1755 to 1757 and where the original Olympic museum was housed, the park includes venerable trees, an orange grove, and a small stone temple. The region's propensity to bloom is channeled at the **Derrière-Bourg Promenade,** where flowers depict events from the canton's history. Those more inclined to stroll can explore gorgeous shore-line trails between Ouchy and **Lutry,** a medieval village 4km away; tired feet can ride back to the *quai* on bus #9.

The **Botanical Garden of Lausanne** is in one section of pl. de Milan-Montriond Park, just up the hill from the bus #1 stop "Beauregard." A wandering path takes you past rose bushes, herbs, and signs describing the local fauna, but the observation spot atop a hill next to the gardens steals the show with its unobstructed panorama of the lake. A sign names each peak visible across the water and the date on which they were first conquered by climbers. The surrounding neighborhood is charming and peacefully untouristed. *(Av. de Cour 14bis. Tel. 616 24 09. Park open Mar., Apr., Oct. 10am-12pm, 1:30-5:30pm; May-Sept. 10am-12pm, 1:30-6:30pm.)*

🎵 🎭 ENTERTAINMENT AND NIGHTLIFE

For every exhibit in Lausanne's museums, there are several performances already in progress on stage and screen: the **Béjart Ballet, Lausanne Chamber Orchestra, Cinémathèque Suisse, Municipal Theatre, Opera House,** and **Theatre of Vidy** reflect Lausanne's thriving cultural life. The tourist office publishes *Momento*, a monthly update and schedule of the most significant events, and posters on the streets and in *tabacs* should clue you in on everything else. For information, reservations, and tickets, call *Billetel* (tel. 310 16 50). The **Festival de la Cité** (July 7-15, 2000) brings the *vieille ville* to life with free theater and dance events. Swiss craftwork fills the **Marché des Artisans** in pl. de la Palud from 10am to 7pm on the first Friday of every month from March to December. A **Lunapark** (attraction park) sets up rides and carnival games at Bellerive annually May 15-June 15. As for nightlife, you can't heave a brick in the pl. St.-François without putting it through the window of a cabaret or hitting the bouncer of a night-club. (He will hit back.) *Lausannois* party-goers inhabit the bars until 1am (2am on weekends) and dance at the clubs till 4 in the morning. The seriously hard-core then head over to the bar in the train station, which opens at 5am.

The Mad, rte. de Genève 23 (tel. 312 29 19, info 312 11 22). Go left as you exit the Lausanne-Flon Metro stop, then walk 3min. down rte. de Genève. On a street lined with clubs, The Mad sticks out—that might have something to do with the large pink condom that graces its exterior, a 5-floor warehouse discotheque splashed with bright colors and the slogan "Mad But Not Mad" crawling up it. Pulse-pounding, platform-stomping, fog-spewing, weird-clothes-wearing dance parties surround a 3rd-floor chill-out room with ambient music and relaxing lighting. World-class DJs spin trance W, house Th, and progressive stuff F-Sa. Gay night Su. Beer 7.50SFr, mixed drinks 14SFr. Open Tu-Su 11pm-5am. Cover 20SFr F-Sa before midnight, 25SFr after midnight.

Dolce Vita, rue César Roux 30 (tel. 311 40 19). From pont Bessières, head up rue Caroline past the large crossroads. This funky room with frequent live shows of rap, indie, world music, and blistering acid jazz also hosts a rock festival every April. Beer 4-5SFr. Happy hours W-Th and Su 10pm-midnight (beer 2SFr). Open Su and W 10pm-2am, F-Sa 10pm-4am; in summer also Th 10pm-3am. Weekend cover 5-25SFr.

Bleu Lézard, rue Enning 10/Lausanne 1003 (tel. 321 38 30). From pl. St-François turn left to rue de Bourg, then head right past Au Couscous. Yuppie types crowd this bistro, but somehow it's not too pretentious. Decor by local artists. Beer 3.20SFr, mixed drinks 3.30SFr-9SFr. Vegetarian dishes 15SFr-30SFr. Open M-Th 6pm-1am, F-Sa 8pm-2am, Su 9pm-1am. Hot food M-Sa 11:30am-2pm and 6:30-10:30pm, Su 10am-5pm and 6:30-10:30pm.

Au Lapin Vert, ruelle du Lapin Vert (tel. 312 13 17), off rue de l'Académie behind the cathedral. This upscale version of the hole-in-the-wall pub blasts English rock at mellow students and young professionals. Beer 3.50SF, mixed drinks 9-10SFr. Open Su-Th 8pm-2am, F-Sa 8pm-3am.

D! Club, ruelle de Grand Pont, is Lausanne's other hot discotheque. Go left out of the Lausanne-Flon Metro stop, walk under Rue de Grand Point bridge, and turn left; it's at the far end of the parking lot under a support wall. 10SFr cover. Open Th 11:30pm-4am, F-Sa 11:30pm-5am, Su 10pm-2am.

Ouchy White Horse Pub, av d'Ouchy 66 (tel. 616 75 75). The equestrian theme clashes works strangely with the bright plaster molding and neon-filled jars. Beer on tap 5-7SFr per pint. *Tapas* 4.80-9.20SFr. Hamburger, fries, and coke 13SFr. Open 7am-1:30am. Kitchen closes 12:30am. AmEx, DC, MC, Visa.

MONTREUX

Locals describe their home as somewhat staid, and for half the year, they're right. With the blossoms of May, however, strains of *le jazz* float over the city and ticket counter telephones start ringing. The **Montreux Jazz Festival** in early July draws thousands to the most swingin' party of the year, and between its luxurious old-fashioned hotels and palm trees, the city becomes Switzerland's best approximation of a seaside resort. A bevy of luminaries have passed through Montreux—Miles Davis was here, as were Freddie Mercury and Igor Stravinsky. Once the big shebang has come and gone, Montreux hosts smaller music festivals throughout the year. Writers of earlier generations (most famously Lord Byron) were inspired by Montreux's magnificent **Château de Chillon,** a disturbingly evocative medieval fortress that glowers over the eastern shore of Lake Geneva.

🚆 ORIENTATION AND PRACTICAL INFORMATION

Montreux and its surroundings rise rapidly from the eastern shores of Lake Geneva to the edge of the Alps at Les-Roches-de-Naye Jardin. Luckily for those backpackers who are running out of steam, the train station is within easy walking distance of most city sights. Hiking up rue du Marché will bring you to the *vieille ville*, of interest for the views as much as for the architecture.

> **Trains:** (tel. 963 45 15) on av. des Alpes. To: **Geneva** (1hr., every 30min. 5:39am–11:39pm, 29SFr); **Lausanne** (20min., every 5-25min. 5:31am-12:09pm, 9.40SFr); **Bern** (1½hr., every hr. 5:39am-10:39pm, 40SFr). Direct trains also go to **Martigny, Aigle, Sion,** and **Brig** and (literally) through the mountains to **Gstaad.**

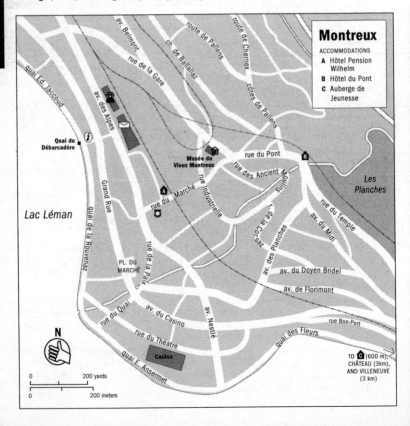

Public Transportation: Buy tickets at the back of the bus. A map divides the area into several zones; your fare will depend on the number of zones you cross to reach your destination. 1 zone 2SFr, juniors 1.50SFr; 2 zones 2.60SFr, 1.80SFr; 3 zones 3.30SFr, 2.30SFr; 4 zones 4SFr, 2.80SFr. SwissPass valid. Day-pass 7.50SFr, 5SFr; available at tourist office. Special late-night buses run during the Jazz Festival.

Boats: CGN, quai du Débarcadère (tel. 963 46 55), next to the tourist office. To: **Lausanne** (1½hr., 7 per day, 19SFr); **Geneva** (5hr., 3 per day, 36SFr); **Vevey** (25min., 6 per day, 8SFr); shorter rides to **Villeneuve** and **Château de Chillon.** Buy tickets at the quay, tourist office, or on board. Eurailpass and SwissPass valid. Reduced rates for ages 16-25.

Tourist Office: pl. du Débarcadère (tel. 962 84 84 or 963 81 13; fax 963 78 95; email tourism@montreux.ch; www.montreux.ch). Descend the stairs opposite the station and head left on Grand Rue; the office is on the right. The harried staff shares the office with desks for festival tickets and bus and train information. Free hotel reservation service within Montreux. Neither the free photocopied map nor the 1SFr map has all of Montreux's street names, so grab the excellent **free map** from **Union de Banques Suisses,** av. de Casino 41. Tourist office open June-Aug. 9am-7pm; Sept.-Oct. M-Sa 9am-noon and 1:30-6pm, Su 9am-noon; Nov.-Apr. M-F 9am-noon and 1:30-6pm, Sa 9am-noon.

Bike Rental: At the baggage check in the train station. 26SFr per day, 20SFr per half-day; mountain bikes 32SFr, 25SFr. 6SFr charge to return bikes to other stations (including Martigny, Aigle, and Sion) by prior arrangement. Open Nov.-May 5:50am-8:30pm, June-Oct. 5:50am-9:30pm. AmEx, MC, Visa.

Luggage Storage: At the station. Lockers 3-5SFr, open 5:50am-8:45pm. Luggage watch 5SFr per bag. Open Nov.-May daily 5:50am-8:30pm, June-Oct. 5:50am-9:30pm.

Budget Travel: SSR Voyages, av. des Alpes 25 (tel. 961 23 00; fax 961 23 06). Open M-F 9:15am-12:30pm and 1:30-6pm, Sa 9:30am-12:30pm.

Currency Exchange: Good rates and no commission at the station. Western Union transfers and credit card advances. Open 5:50am-9pm. Banks in Montreux are generally open M-F 8:30am-12:30pm and 1:30-4:30pm.

Bookstore: Payot Libraire, av. du Casino 42 (tel. 963 06 07). Open M 10:30am-12:30pm and 1:30-6:30pm, Tu-F 8:30am-12:30pm and 1:30-6:30pm, Sa 9am-5pm. AmEx, DC, MC, Visa.

Laundromat: Salon-Lavoir, rue Industrielle 30. Open M-F 7am-6pm, Sa 7am-5pm. 5SFr per load.

Jazz Hotline: tel. 983 82 82. Open May through the end of the festival.

Late-Night Pharmacy: tel. 962 77 00.

Emergencies: Police, tel. 117. **Fire,** tel. 118. **Ambulance,** tel. 144. **Hospital,** tel. 966 66 66.

Internet Access: Internet Palace, Grand Rue 100 (tel. 962 10 93; email internet. palace@montreux-palace.com; www.montreux-palace.com), next to the Montreux Palace. 20SFr per hr., students 15SFr; 30min. 11SFr, 7.50SFr. Open T-Th and Su noon-8pm, F and Sa noon-11pm.

Post Office: Av. des Alpes 70. Left as you exit the station. Address *Poste Restante* to: CH-1820 Montreux 1. Open M-F 7:30am-6pm, Sa 8-11am. **Postal Code:** CH-1820.

PHONE CODE   The **city code** for Montreux is 021.

ACCOMMODATIONS AND CAMPING

Cheap rooms are scarce in Montreux and almost non-existent during the jazz festival. Hotels and hostels are often fully booked before May. Revelers frequently stash their bags in the train station lockers and crash on the lakefront, but the police will move lakeside sleepers out at 7am. Ask at the tourist office for the lists of *Pensions et Petits Hôtels* or studio apartments available during the festival. If

LAKE GENEVA

you still can't find a room, try the hostel in Vevey. Otherwise, take bus #1 to "Ville-neuve," 5km away, where there are a handful of budget hotels, or consider commuting from Lausanne or Martigny.

Auberge de Jeunesse Montreux (HI), passage de l'Auberge 8 (tel. 963 49 34; fax 963 27 29). Take bus #1 on Grand Rue (dir.: Villeneuve) to "Territet." Head up the street, take the 1st right (rue du Bocherex), and go down the stairs (passage de l'Auberge). Or, walk 20min. along the lake past the Montreux Tennis Club. This thoroughly modern, social hostel is 5 seconds from the lakefront (and also, unfortunately, from noisy train tracks). 112 beds in 4-, 6-, or 8-bed dorms. Dorms 29SFr, doubles 38SFr, with shower 42SFr. Prices drop 2SFr in low season. Non-members add 5SFr per night. Breakfast and linens included. Dinner 11SFr. Lockers 2SFr deposit. **Laundry** 8SFr, including detergent. TV room. Free (non-affiliated) parking nearby. Reception Apr.-Sept. 7-10am and 4-11pm; Oct.-Mar. 7:30-9:30am and 5-10pm. Lockout 10am-4pm. Check-out 9:30am in winter, 10am in summer. Curfew midnight; keys available with a passport deposit. Wheelchair accessible. AmEx, DC, MC, Visa.

Hôtel Pension Wilhelm, rue du Marché 13-15 (tel. 963 14 31; fax 963 32 85). From the station, walk left 3min. up av. des Alpes and left on rue du Marché, uphill past the police station. Four generations of Wilhelms have operated this 60-bed hotel for over 100 years. All rooms have sinks. Doubles 50SFr, with shower and toilet 120SFr; single occupancy in off season 65SFr. Breakfast included. Reception M 7am-3pm, Tu-Su 7am-midnight. Closed Oct.-Feb., though it is possible to stay in winter if you call ahead.

Hôtel du Pont, rue du Pont 12 (tel./fax 963 22 49), at the top of the *vieille ville.* From the station, turn left 800m from the station on av. des Alpes (3min.) then right up rue du Marché. Continue uphill until it becomes rue du Pont; the hotel is on the left. Large rooms with bathrooms and TVs. Singles, doubles, and triples 60SFr per person. Breakfast included. Dinner 14.80SFr. Reception M 7am-3pm, Tu-F 7am-midnight, Sa-Su 8:30am-midnight. AmEx, MC, Visa.

Camping: Les Horizons Bleus (tel. 960 15 47). Take bus #1 to "Villeneuve." From the bus stop, follow the lake to the left (5min.) to this lakeside site. 7SFr per person, ages 6-16 4SFr; 6-12SFr per tent; tax 0.50SFr. Showers included. Electricity 3.50SFr. Discount in winter. Reception 9am-12:30pm and 4-9pm.

▢ FOOD

Montreux is very pricey; for lakeside dining, pack a picnic. The tourist office publishes a catalog listing establishments by cuisine, but it omits price ranges.

RESTAURANTS

Babette's, Grand Rue 60 (tel. 963 77 96), downstairs from the station to the left. This casual restaurant serves crêpes of all types for lunch (10-13.50SFr) and dessert (6-8.50SFr). Sandwiches to go at the outside counter 5-13SFr. Open 5am-7pm.

The White Horse, 28 Grand Rue (tel. 963 15 92). A sign on the door declares this an "authentic" English pub. Not bloody likely, but the food is good and the atmosphere friendly, from the francophone staff to the fuzzy white dog who snores at customers' feet. Sandwiches 7-9SFr; salads 6-8SFr; pizza 9.50SFr; beer 4-8.50SFr per pint. Pinball, darts, foosball, and arcade games in back. Open M-Sa 10am-1am, Su 3pm-midnight.

La Locanda, av. du Casino 44 (tel. 963 29 33), is a small restaurant with a cozy decor. Large pizzas 15-20SFr; salads 15SFr, *Menüs* with pasta, steak or fish 16.50SFr. Open M-Sa 11:30am-2:30pm and 6pm-midnight. AmEx, MC, Visa.

Restaurant Le Palais "Hoggar," quai E. Ansermet 14 (tel. 963 12 71), next to the Hostellerie du Lac. Blue-tiled walls complement the lakeside mountain view. Chicken curry 21.50SFr. 20 ice cream flavors. Open Feb.-Dec. daily 11am-10:30pm. AmEx, DC, Visa.

Caveau des Vignerons, rue Industrielle 30bis (tel. 963 25 70), at the top of rue du Marché, serves Swiss dishes in a candlelit cave. Cook your own meat at the table (with salad and potatoes 30SFr). Cheese fondue 20SFr; perch 15SFr. Open M-F 8:30am-midnight, Sa 3pm-midnight. Closed 3wks. in summer. AmEx, MC, Visa.

MARKETS

Marché de Montreux, place du Marché. Covered outdoor market of fresh fruits, vegetables, meats, cheeses, breads, and pastries along both quai de la Rouvenaz and quai Jaccoud. Every Friday 7am-3pm. Also look for the **flea market** at this site.

Migros, av. du Casino 49. Restaurant next door. Open M 9am-7pm, Tu-Th 8am-7pm, F 8am-9pm, Sa 7:30am-5pm. Restaurant opens 30min. earlier M-F.

Co-op, Grand Rue 80. Open M-F 8am-12:15pm and 2-6:30pm, Sa 8am-5pm.

👁 🏛 SIGHTS AND MUSEUMS

The Montreux-Vevey **museum passport** (15SFr), available at the tourist office, covers entry to 10 museums.

THE OLD TOWN. From the museum, the *vieille ville* is just a few minutes up the rue du Pont. A refreshing world away from the craziness of the waterfront, the rue de Temple offers pure views and a quiet walk to the stone **Église de Montreux.**

MONTREUX HISTORY MUSEUM. The **Musée du Vieux-Montreux,** on the outskirts of the *vieille ville*, chronicles Montreux's history from Roman times through its "colonization" by the resort industry in the late 19th century. *(Rue de la Gare 40. Tel. 963 13 53. Open Apr.-Oct. 10am-noon and 2-5pm. 6SFr, students and seniors 4SFr, under 17 free.)*

CHÂTEAU DE CHILLON. The gloomy **Château de Chillon** is not only the main sightseeing draw in Montreux; it is also one of Switzerland's most visited attractions. Built on an island, Chillon is a 13th-century fortress with all the comforts of home: prison cells, a torture chamber, an armory, and booby-traps to fend off attackers who get past the moat. The eerie chateau inspired narratives by Rousseau, Victor Hugo, and Alexandre Dumas, as well as Lord Byron's *The Prisoner of Chillon*, which tells the tale of François de Bonivard, a priest who was manacled to one of the castle's dungeon pillar for 4 years in the 16th centur. His crime was preaching Reformation doctrine. When Protestant soldiers from Bern took over Montruex in 1536, they booted out the Catholic Duke of Savoy and freed poor Bonivard. The souvenir shop sells copies of the poem (see p. 467), and you can see where Byron scratched his name into a dungeon pillar. A brochure leads you through a tour of 28 chilly and chilling rooms, including courtyards, dungeons, the Great Hall, and the Duke of Savoy's furnished living quarters. *(Take the CGN ferry (11SFr, ages 16-25 5.50SFr) or bus #1 to "Chillon" (2.60SFr, juniors 1.80SFr). Tel. 963 39 12; www.chillon.ch. Open Apr.-Sept. 9am-6pm; Mar. and Oct. 9:30am-5pm; Nov.-Feb. 10am-4pm; 7SFr, students 5.50SFr, ages 6-16 3.50SFr.)*

PRISON IS A HOLY PLACE

Eternal Spirit of the chainless Mind
Brightest in dungeons, Liberty! thou art;
For there thy habitation is the heart—
The heart which love of thee alone can bind;

And when thy sons to fetters are consigned—
To fetters, and the damp vault's dayless gloom,
Their country conquers with their martyrdom
And Freedom's fare finds whys on every wind.
Chillon! Thy prison is a holy place
And thy sad floor an altar—for't was trod,
Until his very steps have left a trace
Worn, as if thy cold pavement were a sod,
By Bonivard! —May none those marks efface!
For they appeal from tyranny to God.

—Lord Byron, excerpt from "The Prisoner of Chillon"

LAKE GENEVA

♫ MUSIC FESTIVALS

The **Montreux Jazz Festival,** world-famous for exceptional musical talent and one of the biggest parties in Europe, pushes everything aside for 15 days starting the first Friday in July. You can peek at the program for 2000 as early as April 15; headliners in 1999 included B.B. King, Herbie Hancock, David Sanborn, REM, and (expanding the definition of jazz to impossible limits) Alanis Morissette. Demand has sent ticket prices into the stratosphere: individual tickets range from 59-99SFr. Standing room tickets range from 39-69SFr. Write to the tourist office well in advance for information and tickets. The **jazz hotline** in Montreux, run by the **Jazz Boutique** ticket sellers at Grand Rue 100, is active from mid-March through the summer (tel. 963 82 82; Su-F 10am-12:30pm and 2-6:30pm, Sa 10am-5pm). The **postal address** for ticket orders is Grand Rue 100, CP1325, CH-1820 Montreux. You can also get tickets from **Union de Banque Suisse** "ticket corners" in major Swiss cities, or at www.montreuxjazz.com. Most events sell out before July, some as early as January. If you can find a room but no tickets, come anyway for the **Jazz Off,** 500 hours of free, open-air concerts by new bands and established musicians. The 1999 festival also added a free, open-to-the-public solo jazz piano competition.

From late August to early October, the **International Classical Music Festival** takes over with operas, symphonies, and classical recitals performed by musicians from as far away as Moscow and Memphis. Tickets to concerts in Montreux and neighboring Vevey, Martigny, St. Maurice, and Chillon range from 10-140SFr. Contact the Office of the Classical Music Festival, to the left of the Casino, at rue du Théâtre 5, 1st Floor, Case Postale 162, CH-1820 Montreux 2. (Tel. 966 80 25; fax 961 10 12; email courrier@montreux-festival.com; www.montreux-festival.com. Office open M-F 10am-1pm and 2-7pm, Sa 10am-1pm.)

♬ NIGHTLIFE

Montreux caters to all tastes and personalities, from carefree campers to 5-star fops. Don't worry about finding the "place to be" in this town—if you're by the water, especially in early July, you're there.

Casino de Montreux, rue du Théâtre 9 (tel. 962 83 83). From av. du Casino, turn on rue Igor Stravinsky toward the lake. The casino draws mobs of quarter-jingling tourists to its flashy slot machines. The charm of the original 1881 casino (which helped launch the

THE PASSING OF A GIANT On July 8, 1991, at the Montreux Jazz Festival, the great jazz trumpeter Miles Davis played his last live performance. An historic concert, Davis played in the style that launched his early career. Davis was a bona fide jazz hero, pioneering the "fusion" of jazz and rock and the invention, with Gil Evans, of "cool" jazz. In their revolutionary collaboration, Davis and Evans broke away from the frenetic scale structure of be-bop improvisation. Davis's smooth, modal improvisations, heard on such albums as *Kind of Blue* and over the rich orchestral settings of the Gil Evans Orchestra on *Sketches of Spain,* influenced a whole generation of artists, including John Coltrane and Bill Evans. Although other artists expanded and developed modal jazz, Davis moved on and never looked back, abandoning some of his most-loved works for over 20 years until Quincy Jones stepped in. Jones had long wanted to do a concert with Davis and revive Davis' early material. When Davis finally agreed, the two performed together at Montreux with the Gil Evans Orchestra (then under the direction of Evans's son, Miles) and the Charles Grundtz Concert Jazz Orchestra, playing songs that hadn't been performed live for a generation. Jones has said that he had never seen Davis as pleased and as connected with the audience in any other concert. Several weeks later, Davis fell ill, and died of pneumonia on September 28, 1991.

careers of Igor Stravinsky and composer Ernest Ansemet) is largely gone, but it's still worth stopping by to cap off a day of languid indolence for slots and video poker (M-F 3pm-4am, Sa-Su noon-4am), and *boule,* a roulette variant (8pm-2am). Dance club downstairs (M-Sa 10pm-4am).

Duke's Jazz Bar, Grand Rue 97 (tel. 962 50 70), 50m down Grand Rue toward Vevey past the Auditorium Stravinsky. Enter through the posh Royal Plaza Inter-Continental Hotel. As a venue for the Montreux Jazz Festival, this high-class establishment bursts at the seams for 2½ weeks in July. After performing, artists often stay to hang out. Celebrate with 295SFr champagne or stick to the impressive 6-7.50SFr range of beers. Open Su-Th 6pm-1am, F-Sa 6pm-2am (though the party never ends during the festival).

Rock Café, rue de l'Auberge 5 (tel. 963 88 88), up the stairs from the youth hostel. Its name and guitar-art may aspire to imitate the Hard Rock, but this neighborhood bar can't escape its more down-to-earth, "grungy" style. Loud music, young crowd, billiard room, video games, darts, and pinball. Beer 6SFr per pint; choose among bottles from 8 countries. Open Su-Th 5pm-midnight, F-Sa 5pm-2am. AmEx, DC, Visa.

VEVEY

Vevey experienced its heyday as a resort town back in the 19th century, when hordes of upper-class English made it a virtual colony of the Queen's empire. The upside to its decline in the 20th century is that Vevey has avoided the 5-star stratification of nearby Montreux. Charlie Chaplin fled here from McCarthyism in 1953 and Jean-Jacques Rousseau, Victor Hugo, Fyodor Dostoevsky, Henry James, le Corbusier, and Graham Greene have all worked within its borders. Vevey remains handsome and well-preserved, its friendly residents creating a serene sense of community along the shore of Lake Geneva.

🛈 ORIENTATION AND PRACTICAL INFORMATION. There are 3 ways to reach Vevey from Montreux: take **bus** #1 to "Montreux" (20min., every 10min., 3SFr); ride the **train** (5min., every 30min., 3SFr); or cruise over on a **boat** (20min., 5 per day, 8SFr, reduced fare for ages 16-25). The **tourist office** is at Grand-Place 29 (tel. 922 20 20; fax 922 20 24; email veveytourism@vevey.ch; www.veveytourism.ch). To get there from the station, cross pl. de la Gare, go past av. de la Gare, and turn left on av. Paul Cérésole. At the end of the road, cut across the parking lot toward the columned arcade; the office is inside. (Open June 15-Sept. 15 M-Sa 8:30am-6pm; Sept. 16-June 14 M-F 8:30am-noon and 1:30-6pm, Sa 8:30am-noon.) **Lockers** (3-5SFr) and **bike rental** (city bike 26SFr per day and 20SFr per half-day; mountain bike 32SFr, 25SFr; open 7:30am-7:30pm) are available at the station. In an **emergency,** dial 117. The **post office** is across pl. de la Gare (open M-F 7:30am-6pm, Sa 8-11am) and has a 24hr. **ATM.** The **postal code** is CH-1800.

PHONE CODE	The **city code** for Vevey is 021.

🍴🛏 ACCOMMODATIONS AND FOOD. Overlooking Grand-Place just off the waterfront is the **⚑Riviera Lodge,** pl. du Marché 5 (tel. 923 80 40; fax 923 80 41). Sixty bright, shiny rooms (renovated in 1997) offer attractively modern, lavish facilities. The entrance foyer has lockers and an activities/dining room. On the 5th floor, the reception desk manned by a friendly, multilingual staff shares space with a terrace, a spotless **kitchen, laundry facilities** (7SFr), and several common rooms. (4-, 6-, or 8-bed dorms 20SFr; doubles 70SFr. Breakfast 7SFr. Sheets 5SFr. Reception 8am-8pm. Call if arriving later.) Many family homes also house travelers; one possibility is **Pension Bürgle,** rue Louis Meyer 16 (tel./fax 921 40 23), just off Grand-Place. The rooms are large; many have balconies and TVs. (40SFr per person. Payment for 1st night required for reservations. Breakfast included. Dinner 12SFr. Reception 7am-11pm.)

For cheap, fresh food, check out the **produce** (and **flea) market** at the Grand-Place (pl. du Marché; Tu and Sa mornings 8:30am-noon). The rest of the week, do-it-yourself fare can be had at **Migros** (open M 9am-6:30pm, Tu-W 8am-6:30pm, Th

8am-8pm, F 8am-6:30pm, Sa 7:30am-5pm; restaurant opens 30min. earlier M-F) and **Co-op** (same hours), across av. Paul Cérésole off Grand-Place. Café-restaurants with *Menüs* for 12-15SFr line Grand-Place, but food is cheaper away from the lakefront. Next to the train station entrance stands an **Aperto convenience store** (open 6am-9:30pm). Cross the square from the station to the post office and follow the underpass (passage St. Antoine) across the tracks for a more interesting experience. At the top of the stairs, in Vevey's industrial area, signs hang for **Les Temps Modernes,** rue des Deux Gares 6 (tel. 922 34 39). A factory-turned-café, record store, and dance studio, it has become a cultural junction for local artists. Live jazz and contemporary rock (Th-Sa) jolt the central stage area. (Salads 5-14SFr. *Plats du jour* 13-16SFr. Beers 5SFr; 1SFr more during performances. Open M-W 11am-midnight, Th 11am-1am, F 11am-2am, Sa 5pm-2am.)

📷 **MUSEUMS.** Though not as thrilling as Montreux's *Château de Chillon*, Vevey's museums are distinctive and well put-together. For an excellent deal, pick up a **Montreux-Vevey Museum Passport** (15SFr), which grants free entrance to 10 museums. Many of these museums can be reached on a stroll by the lake towards the neighboring town of Tour-de-Peilz.

ART MUSEUM. The **Musée Jenisch** displays an above-average assemblage of works by such Swiss artists as Arp, Baselitz, Klee, and a room of spontaneous, spry watercolors and pastels by adopted citizen Oskar Kokoschka—he lived in nearby Villeneuve for the last 25 years of his life. *(Av. de la Gare 2. Tel. 921 29 50. Open Tu-Su Mar.-Oct. 11am-5:30pm; Nov.-Feb. 2-5:30pm. 10SFr, students 5SFr. Special exhibit rates vary. Tours 12SFr.)*

SWISS CAMERA MUSEUM. Near the tourist office, signs point to the **Swiss Camera Museum,** where 3 floors are filled with historic photographic equipment from daguerreotypes to early spy cameras. The upper floors take you all the way to the advent of cinema. Though there are several hands-on exhibits, the more technical explanations can be hard to handle without a good knowledge of French. *(Ruelle des Anciens-Fossés 6. Tel. 925 21 40; fax 921 64 58. Open Tu-Su Apr.-Oct. 11am-5:30pm; Nov.-Mar. 2-5:30pm. 5SFr, students 4SFr, children free. Tours 3SFr.)*

FOOD MUSEUM. An unlikely, but interesting collection, the **Alimentarium/Food Museum,** on the corner of rue du Léman and quai Perdonnet, tells the story of food from its production in the sun to its processing in the human body. Food processing machinery, Nestlé commercials, and human-sized hamster wheels are some of the highlights of this child-friendly museum. *(Tel. 924 41 11. Open Tu-Su Apr.-Oct. 10am-5pm; Nov.-Mar. 10am-noon and 2-5pm. 6SFr, students and seniors 4SFr, school groups free.)*

GAME MUSEUM. At the end of the quai, in the 13th-century Savoy Château de la Tour-de-Peilz, the **Swiss Museum of Games** is a shrine to the twin ideals of skill and chance with its display of ancient chess pieces, cardboard Cold War games, and Nintendo. Multilingual exhibits wax philosophical on the sociology of games and the implications of virtual reality, but it's more fun to just play with the toys. *(Tel. 944 40 50; fax 944 10 79. Open Tu-Su 2-6pm. 6SFr, students 3SFr, under 17 free. Tours 4SFr.)*

🎭 **FESTIVALS AND ENTERTAINMENT.** Vevey's big production number is the **Fête des Vignerons** (Festival of the Wine-growers), a 2-week long Bacchanalian gala featuring parades, open-air performances, and a carnival that's heavy on both mythology and free-flowing wine. That's the good news. The bad news is that the next one won't be until 2024. You've got plenty of time to make reservations or read up on Vevey's most venerated tradition (www.fetedesvignerons.ch.) On years when the *Fête des Vignerons* is not being held, the **Folklore Market** (in pl. du Marché; open mid-July to Aug.) allows you to sample all the local wine you can hold for only the price of the first glass. Year-round, the **Winetrain** winds its way through 8km of villages and vineyards in Lavaux (every hr. from Vevey station; round-trip up to 10SFr, children 5SFr, SwissPass and Eurailpass valid.) The tourist office has a list of tasting venues, a map with directions to Chexbres and Puidox (the two wine centers), and a guide to six hiking tours of the region.

In July and August, an **open-air cinema** at pl. Scanaven brings classical and current flicks to Vevey (13SFr). The summertime **International Comedy Film Festival,** dedicated to former resident Charlie Chaplin, features official competitions during the day and more accessible screenings at night (13SFr). Classical music lovers get their due at the end of August with the **International Classical Music Festival,** hosted jointly by Vevey and Montreux every year. The music festival attracts several renowned international orchestras as well as noted soloists for a series of concerts and master classes. Venues lie in both cities; the **Theatre of Vevey,** rue de Théâtre 4 (tel. 923 53 96), provides information and handles reservations and ticket sales for Vevey.

TRANSPORT HUB: AIGLE

Most travelers who zip through the rail hub of Aigle barely notice it out of their train window, but this tiny town with an impressive 12th-century château is well-known to locals for its excellent white wines and indulgent, vine-laced beauty. Cradled at the meeting point of several mountain valleys, Aigle is an important transport junction for many of the Alpine resort towns hidden deep in the Vaud Alps (*Alpes Vaudoises*), on the high-speed train line connecting the Lake Geneva cities (Geneva, Lausanne, Montreux) to Martigny and Sion. The quickest connections are to **Montreux** (10min., 2 per hr. 6:17am-12:29am, 5SFr) and **Lausanne** (30min., 2 per hr. 5:45am-11:57pm, 13.60SFr). A **cog railway** from Aigle services **Les Diablerets** (50min., 6:27am-9:28pm, 10SFr) and **Leysin** (30min., every hr. 6:04am-10:38pm; SwissPass valid). A **bus** connects Aigle and **Villars** (30min., every hr., 8SFr), where another cog railway (dir.: Bex) runs to **Gryon** (15min., 3SFr, Eurail-pass and SwissPass valid; see p. 475).

LES DIABLERETS

One of the few Swiss towns that can claim 2 high seasons, Les Diablerets' pan-piping little devils frolic year-long among creaky chalets and glacial slopes. There may be only five lifts open on Diablerets' glacier in July and August, but the snow is 100% guaranteed. Come winter, the town stresses substance over the snootier stylings of local rivals Gstaad, Crans-Montana, and Verbier. The results: a younger, more sports-driven crowd. Snowboarders will appreciate the respect they receive, and hikers can putter about peacefully on the varied terrain.

◨ ORIENTATION AND PRACTICAL INFORMATION. Three public transport services connect Les Diablerets to the rest of Switzerland: the **train** down to **Aigle** (50min., every hr. 6:27am-9:28pm, 10SFr); the **post bus** over the mountains to **Gstaad** (via the Col du Pillon, in summer 5 per day 9:39am-5pm, 11.80SFr); and the **BVB bus** to the mountain town of **Villars** (via Col de la Croix, 35min., 3 per day 10am-5:05pm, 10.80SFr). In summer, local buses are the only way to reach the Diablerets glacier **cable cars.** The first bus leaves at 9:39am and the last returns at 4:50pm, so plan accordingly or get ready for a 45-minute walk.

The **tourist office,** rue de la Gare (tel. 492 33 58; fax 492 23 48; email diablerets@bluewin.ch; www.alpes.ch/diablerets), in a chalet down the road to the right of the station, publishes a devilishly impressive range of literature. It keeps a list of activities and events like the **Adventure Sports Weekend** (25 sports over 2 days, June 21-22), the giant **Rösti Festival** at Isenau (mid-July to mid-Aug.), the **Crossing-roads Country Music Festival** (early Aug.), and the **International Alpine Film Festival** in late September. (Tourist office open July 3-Aug. 29 and mid-Dec. to Apr. 8:30am-6pm; June 1-July 2 and low season M-Sa 8:30am-12:30pm and 2-6pm, Su 9am-12:30pm.) For **taxis,** dial (079) 205 05 55. The **pharmacy** (tel. 492 32 83) is just before the bend in rue de la Gare, right of the station (open M-F 8am-12:30pm and 3-6:30pm, Sa 8am-12:30pm and 3-6pm, Su 10am-noon and 5-6pm). In **emergencies,** dial 492 32 83. For an **ambulance,** dial 494 50 30. For the **police,** dial 492 24 88. Turn right out of the train station for the **post office** (open M-F 8am-noon and 2:30-6pm, Sa 7:45-10:45am.) The **postal code** is CH-1865.

PHONE CODE	The **city code** for Les Diablerets is 024.

▐ ACCOMMODATIONS. The cheapest accommodations are on the outskirts of town. **Les Diablotins,** rte du Pillon (tel. 492 36 33; fax 492 23 55), is a big modern block popular with young snowboarding groups. From the station, turn right, bend left around the hairpin turn at the pharmacy, and turn right along rte du Pillon at the top of the hill. Avoid the ensuing 20-minute uphill walk by calling from the station; the hostel will send a minibus. 2- to 4-bed rooms are in good shape (all have private sinks and most have balconies) in spite of the thousands of schoolkids that trmp through the halls and shared showers each year. This large establishment has shared showers, 4 dining halls, several lounges, and a bar and disco—all segregated by age and noise-tolerance levels. (Jan. 3-Jan. 21 and Apr.-Christmas 32SFr, youth under 18 27SFr; Christmas-New Year's and Feb. 5-Mar. 11 44SFr, youth 37SFr; Jan. 21-Feb. 5 and Mar. 11-Apr. 24 40SFr, youth 34SFr. Price drops 3-4SFr after 4 nights. Breakfast included. Dinner 16SFr. Reception 8am-noon and 2-6pm. Reserve ahead in winter. AmEx, DC, MC, Visa.) For a more outdoorsy experience, take the Aigle train one stop to "Vers l'Église," go left past the post office and church, and cross the railroad tracks and the river to get to **Camping La Murée** (tel. 492 21 99), a quiet site in a tiny valley town. (6.50SFr in the summer, 7SFr in winter; tents 12.50-39SFr. Showers included. Reception 6-7pm.)

◖ FOOD. Right from the station along rue de la Gare, **Pam Super Discount** stocks the cheapest groceries (open M-F 7:30am-noon and 2-6:30pm, Sa 7:30am-noon and 2-6pm). The **Co-op** is on rue de la Gare, left of the station (open M-F 8am-12:15pm and 2:15-6:30pm, Sa 8am-6pm). At **Le Muguet** (tel. 492 26 42), opposite the tourist office, try a dessert crepe (5-10SFr) with *chocolat viennois* (3.80SFr), or a dish of *chantilly crême* (1.50SFr). Cross the channel for their sandwiches (7SFr) and the all-important pot of tea. (Open 6:30am-7pm; food served until 6pm. Visa.) Just around the bend by the pharmacy, **Pizzeria Locanda Livia** (tel. 492 32 80) serves 22 kinds of pizza (13-19.50SFr, 4SFr less for miniature version), including a 4-cheese pizza with gruyère called *rêve de souris* (mouse's dream). (Open Th-Tu after 11:30am and after 6:30pm. MC, Visa.)

◪ OUTDOOR ACTIVITIES. Les Diablerets' year-round **skiing** just got better with the 1999 addition of a new **cable car,** which goes from the Col du Pillon above the village to Cabane, then to the glacier at Scex-Rouge. Diablerets day passes, combined Diablerets/Villars passes, Alpes Vaudoises transportation and lift passes, and other **ski passes** are for sale at the tourist office. Through the **Swiss Village Club,** many hotels offer special deals that include stay-and-ski passes, a fondue evening, tobogganing, curling, skating, and babysitting services. The tourist office can offer suggestions, but you must book directly with the hotel. **Jacky Sports** (tel. 492 32 18; www.swissrentasport.ch), near the tourist office, rents **ski equipment** (skis 28-50SFr per day, snowboards 28-38SFr, boots 15-19SFr; special rates for multi-day rentals; open 9am-noon, 2-6pm; in high season M-F 8:30am-noon and 2-6:30pm, Sa-Su 8:30am-6:30pm; AmEx, DC, MC, Visa). The **ski school** (tel. 492 20 02), in the tourist office, offers lessons (6 days 125SFr, children 117SFr).

Jacky Sports also rents **mountain bikes** (35SFr per day, 5 days 110SFr). One full-day circuit, also possible on foot, leaves from the tourist office. Head around the hairpin turn at the junction with Col du Pillon road. Climb upwards to La Ville and its long view of the Diablerets glacier spilling high above the village. Turn right along the valley wall to Métraille and La Crua, and begin a long descent to the crag-cradled Lac Retaud and Col du Pillon before free-wheeling back to Les Diablerets. (Attempt only in good weather.) For a good hike that can be done in several segments to suit ability, head deeper into the mountains by turning right across the river at the pharmacy, then right again so that you are facing the **Sommet des Diablerets** (3209m) and the glacier. The valley sides close in as you continue the level riverside walk, which deposits you on the stage of a rugged 200m-high amphitheater at **Creux de Champ** (1hr., 160m ascent). The path starts to climb steeply up the sides to the **Refuge de Pierredar** at 2278m (3hr. above Les Diablerets, 1110m ascent). The agile can then push on up to **Scex Rouge** (2971m), the cable car terminus on the glacier, which affords an unforgettable alpine view (full day hike, high summer and perfect weather only; guide recommended). For a more relaxing trek, take the guided tour of mountainside medicinal plants given Thursdays by a local apothecary (meet at 8:30am at tourist office; 26SFr; children with parents free).

For those daredevils who find hiking and biking banal, Les Diablerets's adventure sports awaken the death wish within. **Mountain Evasion** (tel./fax 492 12 32) is anything but; they organize **canyoning** (80-160SFr), **ice canyoning** (65SFr), **glacier bivouacs** (120SFr), **rappelling** (85SFr), and guided **hiking** and **mountain biking** (50-120SFr), not to mention **luging** (16SFr, 36SFr with fondue). (Winter office in the Maison du Tourisme, summer office in a little wooden shack along the river. At the pharmacy turn right across the river, then left onto the Chemin de Vernex. Open 5:30am-6:30pm. MC.) Left from the train station and past the post office along rue de la Gare, **Centre ParAdventure** (tel. 492 23 82; email cevic@bluewin.ch) offers **paragliding** (60-150SFr), **canyoning** (80SFr), and the fat-wheeled **mudbike** (open 9-9:30am and 5:30-6:30pm). Snowboarders may be happy to know that the **New Devil School of Snowboarding** (tel. (079) 412 62 40) has entered its bid for the town's corniest name pun (2hr. lesson 20SFr, under 18 16SFr; 3-day rental 85-117SFr).

LEYSIN

In this laid-back town where people show up to work in sweats and flannels, the locals aren't so local. Leysin is full of ex-roaming backpackers who came, saw, and stayed on to bolster the outdoor industry, find Swiss spouses, and teach at the clutch of American and Japanese colleges and international schools in the area. The town offers long views of the mountain-girded Rhône Valley and the distant shores of Lac Léman. In the surrounding mountains, sports enthusiasts can ski, snowboard, climb, mountain bike, paraglide, and hike.

7 **ORIENTATION AND PRACTICAL INFORMATION.** The only way to reach Leysin by public transport is the **cog railway** from Aigle. The railway leisurely chugs passengers to the top of the steep climb (30min., every hr. 6:04am-10:38pm; Swiss-Pass valid). There are 4 stops: Leysin-Village (7.80SFr), Versmont, Feydey (9SFr), and Grand-Hôtel (9.60SFr). The **tourist office** (tel. 494 29 21 or 494 22 44; fax 494 16 16; email tourism@leysin.ch; www.leysin.ch), located in the Centre Sportif just up the road to the left from pl. du Marché, provides **hiking maps** (open M-F 8am-9pm, Sa-Su 9am-9pm). There is a **24-hour ATM** at the **Banque Cantonal Vaudous** just below Hefti Sports. For a **taxi**, dial 493 22 93 or 494 25 55. There is a free hourly **shuttle** to help you up and down the hillside, including a stop at the hostel (runs June 26-Sept. 20 and Dec.15-Apr.15). **Rent bikes** at the station at usual rates, or from **Hefti Sports** (mountain bikes 25SFr per half-day). **Pharmacie Leysin** (tel. 493 45 00) sells medicines next to the Hefti Sports on pl. du Marché (open M-F 8:30-noon and 2-6:30pm; Sa 9am-12:30pm and 2-5pm, Su 11am-noon, 6-6:30pm). For an **ambulance,** dial 144. For the **police,** dial 493 45 41. In an **emergency,** dial 117. In a **fire,** dial 118. There are 2 **post offices,** one next to the Feydey station (tel. 494 14 06) and one down the hill in Leysin-Village on rue du Village (tel. 494 12 05). A set of stairs descends from Feydey to the town center. (Feydey post office open M-F 7:30am-noon and 2-6pm, Sa until 11pm; Leysin post office open M-F 8-11am and 2:30-6pm, Sa 8:30-11am.) The Feydey office is also the departure point of the **bus** to Le Sépay. The **postal code** is CH-1854.

PHONE CODE	The **city code** for Leysin is 024.

LAKE GENEVA

⌐ ACCOMMODATIONS. Just 50m from skiing and biking trails, the ⚐**Hiking Sheep Guesthouse,** Villa La Joux (tel./fax 494 35 35; email hikingsheep@leysin.net; www.leysin.net/hikingsheep) has shining wooden bunks, a convivial dining room, breathtaking balconies, and pristine **kitchen** facilities. Take the cog rail to "Grand Hôtel" and turn left on the gravel road, or catch the shuttle in high season. Friendly owner Gérard goes the extra mile for his guests, supplying satellite TV, log fires, BBQs, cooking lessons, game and meditation rooms, **Internet access, laundry** (10SFr), afternoon hiking tours, and life advice. (June 15-Dec. 15 dorms 26SFr, doubles 33SFr; Dec. 16-June 14 dorms 30SFr, doubles 35SFr; for children subtract about 1SFr. Buffet breakfast 8SFr, English breakfast 10SFr. Sheets included. Check-out 10:30am. MC, Visa.) In town, the **Hotel Bel Air** (tel. 494 13 39; fax 494 13 69) has simple rooms and tranquil views (singles 35-40SFr; doubles 90SFr, with shower 110SFr; breakfast included; Visa, AmEx). The **Hotel de la Paix** (tel./fax 494 13 75), on av. Rollier, is opposite the "Versmont" train stop. Narrow hallways connect old-fashioned rooms with fading prints of *belle epoque* Leysin. (Singles 45-63SFr, with shower 60-73SFr. Doubles with shower 104-124SFr. Breakfast included. Lunch or dinner 25SFr, both 37SFr. Reception 8am-8pm. AmEx, MC, Visa.) **Camping Semiramis** (tel. 494 18 29; fax 494 20 29) is a large grassy field at the foot of a hill near an evergreen forest. From Leysin-Village station, walk left on rue de Village, then right on rue du Suchet past the post office. (5.80SFr in summer, 6.20SFr in winter, children 3SFr, 5SFr; tents 3-4SFr. Showers included. AmEx, DC, MC, Visa.)

▓ FOOD. A **Co-op** supermarket is just off the big bend in rue Favez, below pl. du Marché and the Centre Sportif (open M-F 8am-noon and 2-6:30pm, Sa 8am-6pm, Su 8:30am-1pm). **L'Horizon** (tel. 494 15 05) is a local fave. A level 15-minute walk from the hostel past cow pastures gets you an excellent fondue (18-19SFr). Try the local valley delicacy, *Williamine*, a pear schnapps. (Open 10:30am until the last customer leaves; closed Su night and M.) **La Prafandaz,** a longer walk from the hostel past more cows (signs point the way), is a slightly off-the-wall chalet decorated with a ticking-udder cow clock and ample evidence of the owner's love of mushrooms—he makes his own sauce from hand-picked specimens. The house specialty, *les rosettes,* consists of meat, vegetables, or salmon rolled into home-made pasta, grilled, and smothered in a rich, bubbling sauce for 18SFr. (Open after 10:30am, flexible closing.) A stroll to the Feydey district and **La Grotta** (tel. 494 15 32) promises hearty Italian food (pizzas 10-18SFr, pastas 12-20SFr), and the added attraction of the owner's Swatch collection—a dazzling expo of all the editions since 1983, including special music alarm, beeper, and ski-pass versions. (Open Tu-Su 8:30am-midnight.) Slightly cheaper food awaits at **La Nonna Restaurant Pizzeria** (tel. 494 21 94), above the Centre Sportif. The giant cactus and fishing nets suggest a bit of an identity crisis. (*Menüs* 15-20SFr, pasta 14-22SFr, 19 exotic pizzas (many vegetarian) 15.60-19.70SFr. Open M-F 7:30am-11:30pm, Sa 8am-11:30pm.)

▚ OUTDOOR ACTIVITIES. A **Leysin Holiday Card** (distributed after 1 night at any hotel or hostel) grants a 10-50% discount at any of Leysin's sports centers, cable cars, and ski lifts. For guided **hiking** and **adventure sports** contact the **guides office** (tel. 494 18 46; email eal@leysin.net; www.leysin.net). The most unusual **hike** is **La Via Ferrata** (the "iron path"), a series of metal safety cables, steps, and rungs that ascends **La Tour d'Aï** (Leysin's highest peak at 2331m), accommodating all levels of hikers. The 2½-hour hike from the village winds past a cheese farm full of bovine beauties into steep wildflower fields; (small) signs point out the Via Ferrata. The necessary gear is available from **Hefti Sports** (16SFr; tel. 494 16 77), 2 minutes from the Centre Sportif on pl. du Marché (open M-F 9am-noon and 2-6pm, Sa 9am-noon and 2-5pm). Hefti Sports also rents **ski equipment** (skis 28-50SFr per day, boots 15-19SFr, snowboards 28-38SFr). 1-day **ski passes** average 40SFr, children 25SFr; weekly passes are available. At the end of January, the pros appear for the **European Snowboarding Championships** held in Leysin every year (Jan. 17-23, 2000).

There are two sports centers in the village. **Centre Sportif,** in the Place Large (tel. 494 29 21; email o.t.leysin@pingnet.ch; www.leysin.ch), has squash and tennis courts, a climbing wall, and **pools** and Turkish bath (open 10am-8pm; pools have slightly shorter hours). Downhill near the campsite, the **Crettex-Jaquet Centre des Sports** (tel. 494 24 42) offers **ice skating** (6.50SFr, students 4.50SFr; skate rental 4SFr, 3SFr). For **paragliding,** call **École Parapante** (tel. 494 26 02 or (079) 638 26 02).

GRYON

The tiny town of Gryon has experienced a population boom in recent years—from 800 to 1,000. Rather than risk a greater unemployment rate as a result of this 25% increase, the proud locals have an ordinance which allows only one child from each family to stay in the town. The kids have a tendency to come back though, drawn to Gryon's virtually untouched, tranquil setting in the mountains, within reach of the Dents du Midi and the Les Diablerets glacier. The neighboring town of **Villars** (45min. on foot uphill) is bigger, busier, packed with hotels, and at the foot of 120km of **ski runs.** Gryon offers peace, relaxation, and a history older than Switzerland (dating back to 1189). There are only two ways to reach Gryon: by **cog railway** from **Bex** (30min., every hr., 5.60SFr, Eurailpass and SwissPass valid), which lies on the main rail line connecting the Lake Geneva cities (Geneva, Lausanne, Montreux) to Aigle, Martigny, and Sion, or by **foot** from **Villars** (one stop further on the cog rail; 45min. walk from the hostel). **Buses** connect Villars through Col de la Croix to **Les Diablerets** (35min., 3 per day 10am-5:05pm, 10.80SFr) and another to **Aigle** (30min., every hr., 8SFr). The **tourist office** (tel. (024) 498 14 22; fax (024) 498 26 22) is uphill on the route de Villars, about 10 minutes from the hostel (open M-Sa 8am-noon and 2-6pm, Su 9am-noon, 4-6pm).

Gryon's main draw for world-weary travelers is its hostel, the ◪**Swiss Alp Retreat,** housed in the **Chalet Martin** (tel./fax (024) 498 33 21; email chaletmartin @yahoo.com; www.gryon.com). From the station, walk past the post office and Co-op and the hostel will be on your left. This backpacker's nirvana is a teeming pocket of Australian and Swiss enthusiasm high in the Alps. Owners Bertrand and Robyn (and a super-friendly young staff) maintain a cooperative style of management that's a little different—expect communal kitchen facilities, co-ed dorms, and no formal reception. New arrivals are immediately sucked into the bohemian, Anglophone-with-any-accent backpacker crowd. Happy to "take a vacation from their vacation," world travelers passing through Gryon have been known to stay...and stay. In the 7 years it took for the hostel to grow from 4 beds to 87, 10 couples who met at the Chalet Martin have gotten married. It must be the spring water. The hostel's amenities include discounted **ski rentals, Internet access** (10SFr per hour), **video rental** (2SFr) from a small but entertaining collection, and **laundry** (3-5SFr). The main chalet has recently been renovated to feature homey common rooms and funky wood-framed showers. Chalet Martin's real attraction, however, is its prime location for taking advantage of the surrounding outdoors. The hostel has daily sign-ups for **cheese farm tours, paragliding, thermal baths** (in Villars), and various excursions (like a ski trip to Zermatt). They also lend out maps to hikers. (Dorms in summer 17SFr for the first night, then 15SFr; in winter prices about 3SFr more. Overflow mattresses possible. No meals, but large kitchen facilities available. Call ahead. Check-in 9am-9pm.)

LAKE NEUCHÂTEL REGION

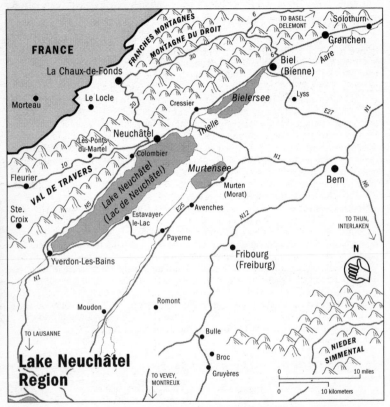

FRANCE

La Chaux-de-Fonds

Morteau

Le Locle

Cressier

Bielersee

Lyss

FRANCHES MONTAGNES

MONTAGNE DU DROIT

TO BASEL, DELEMONT

Solothurn

Grenchen

Biel (Bienne)

Aare

Les Ponts du-Martel

Neuchâtel

Colombier

Thielle

Fleurier

VAL DE TRAVERS

Lake Neuchâtel (Lac de Neuchâtel)

Murtensee

Murten (Morat)

Bern

Ste. Croix

Estavayer-le-Lac

Avenches

Payerne

TO THUN, INTERLAKEN

Yverdon-Les-Bains

Fribourg (Freiburg)

N

Lake Neuchâtel Region

TO LAUSANNE

Moudon

Romont

Bulle

Broc

Gruyères

TO VEVEY, MONTREUX

NIEDER SIMMENTAL

0   10 miles

0   10 kilometers

The aqua hues of Lake Neuchâtel and the verdant Jura mountains imbue the Lake Neuchâtel region with an intimate charm. In connection with the upcoming National Exhibition (Expo '01, a celebration of all things Swiss), however, the Three-Lake Region of **Lake Neuchâtel, Bielersee**, and **Murtensee** is attempting to establish itself as the new tourist hotspot in Switzerland. Their hope is that winter-time thrill-seekers will flock to Lake Neuchâtel with the same enthusiasm as nature-lovers who enjoy its mild climate the rest of the year.

HIGHLIGHTS OF LAKE NEUCHÂTEL REGION

■ Experience **Neuchâtel's** lively café culture, relax on a lakeside promenade, and catch a bird's-eye view from the *Tour des Prisons* (p. 478).

■ Stroll through the lush vineyards of **Cressier** and sample the new wine (p. 479).

■ Cycle or hike along the **Jura** mountains to explore hidden hamlets (p. 477).

■ Unwind at the Musée International d'Horlogerie in **La Chaux-de-Fonds** (p. 482).

NEUCHÂTEL

Alexandre Dumas described Neuchâtel as appearing to be carved out of butter. Although he was no doubt referring to the unique yellow stone that characterizes the city's architecture, Dumas's comment could easily be mistaken for a reference to the calorie-laden treats in local *pâtisseries*. *Neuchâteloise* cuisine prides itself on its distinctive quality, especially in fondue, sausages, and fresh fish from the lake and nearby rivers. The town's vitality stems from its medieval beauty, thriving café scene, and extraordinary placement on Lake Neuchâtel.

◪ ORIENTATION AND PRACTICAL INFORMATION. Neuchâtel sits atop a tube-shaped lake near the French border and the rugged Jura mountains. The city centers on pl. Pury, a major square and the hub of every bus line. **Trains** connect Neuchâtel to **Basel** (1¾hr., every hr. 6am-10pm, 35SFr); **Bern** (45min., every hr. 5:09am-12:15am, 17.20SFr); **Interlaken** (2hr., every hr. 5:38am-10:14pm, 41SFr); **Geneva** (1½hr., every hr. 5:55am-11pm, 41SFr); and **Fribourg** (1hr. via Ins, every hr. 5:09am-10:15pm, 19SFr). A series of stairs leads down to the shore from the station, and bus #6 goes to pl. Pury, the central **bus stop. Ferries** provide service to **Murten** (1¾hr., 4 per day, 15.40SFr) and **Biel** (2¼hr., 3 per day, 23SFr), departing from the Port de la Ville, just behind the post office, free with Eurail or SwissPass.

From pl. Pury, face the lake and walk 2 blocks to the left to find the **tourist office**, Hôtel des Postes. City maps are free, and the deluge of brochures will fit the needs of everyone. A useful regional **biking** guide is 5.50SFr. Also available is *La Route du Vignoble Neuchâteloise*, a list of all local vineyards. (Tel. 889 68 90; fax 889 62 96; email neuchatel@tourisme.ch; www.etatne.ch; open June-Sept. M-F 9am-7pm, Sa 9am-noon, Su 4-7pm; Oct.-May M-F 9am-noon and 1:30-5:30pm, Sa 9am-noon.) The **post office** is in the same building (open M-F 7:30am-6:30pm, Sa 8-11am). The train station houses a tourist office geared toward rail travel, and **bike rental** is available at the baggage check (26SFr per day). For the **police**, dial 722 22 22; for the **hospital**, tel. 722 91 11. The **postal code** is CH-2001.

PHONE CODE	The **city code** for Neuchâtel is 032.

⌂ ACCOMMODATIONS. Even if the ▨**Oasis Neuchâtel**, rue de Suchiez 35 (tel. 731 31 90; fax 730 37 09), weren't the only hostel in town, it would still be the best place to stay. From the station, take bus #6 to "pl. Pury," then bus #1 (dir.: Cormondrèche) to "Vauseyon." Head uphill immediately to your right and follow the rue du Suchiez up and to the right. The hostel is on the left, marked by yellow happy faces. Perched on a hilltop, this exotically decorated, quirky house offers 38 beds, table tennis, darts, a BBQ, and an eco-friendly, multilingual atmosphere. (4- to 6-bed dorms 23SFr; doubles 56SFr; 2- to 4-person garden teepee in summer 20SFr per person. Breakfast, shower, and sheets included. Free on your birthday! Reception 8-10am and 5-9pm. No curfew. Reservations recommended July-Aug.) If Oasis is full, check the *Hôtel Restaurant* guide for cheap options in nearby towns. The closest **campground** is in Columbier: **Camping Colombier** (tel. 841 24 46), on the lakefront, has earned a 4-star rating. (25SFr; no tents provided. July-Aug. 15 add 2SFr. Open Mar.-Oct.)

◻ FOOD. Neuchâtel may live off tourists in July and August, but the rest of the year it's a university town, which means good, cheap food. **Crêperie Chez Bach et Buck,** av. du Premier-Mars 22 (tel. 725 63 53), 5min. down the street from the tourist office, counters its laid-back atmosphere with an intensely detailed list of choices. Enjoy sugar crepes with fruit or ice cream for 2.70-6.80SFr, or salty crepes with meat or cheese for 2.50-9.80SFr. (Open M-Th 11:30am-2pm, F-Sa 11:30am-2pm and 5:30-11:30pm, Su 6-10pm.) At **A.R. Knecht Boulangerie, Pâtisserie,** pl. des Halles 6 (tel. 725 13 21), on the left facing away from the lake, locals munch croissants stuffed with spiced ham (1.70SFr), lacy fruit tarts (3.10SFr), and the house specialty *pain noix* (3.10SFr). (Open Tu-Sa 6am-6:30pm.) Further up the pl. des Halles, the unassuming bistro **Appareils de Chauffage et de Cuisine** (tel. 721 43 96) serves up a well-endowed *plat du jour* consisting of meat or fish, vegetables, and a starch to the strains of subdued, cool jazz (open M-Th 7am-1am, F-Sa 7am-2am, Su 7pm-1am). This café is a source of income for the **Centre d'Art Neuchâtel** next door (CAN; tel. 724 01 60; www.can.ch/can), an experimental art center. In the town center, **Migros,** rue de l'Hôpital 12, has groceries (open M 1:15-6:30pm, Tu-W 8am-6:30pm, Th 8am-8pm, F 7:30am-6:30pm, Sa 7:30am-5pm). A **Co-op** hangs out downhill and across the main road from the hostel, and there's an **Aperto** in the station (tel. 721 20 41; open 6am-10pm).

■ **SIGHTS.** Neuchâtel is like the Rubik's cube: physically small but culturally huge. You can traverse the town in minutes, unless it happens to be the last weekend in September when the 3-day **wine festival** is going on, in which case it may take hours to wade through throngs of drunks enjoying parades, jazz concerts, and wine feasts. A Swiss museum passport, available at many museums, costs 30SFr and grants you free admission to most museums.

THE OLD TOWN. The heart of town is the *vieille ville*, which is dominated by a cobble-stone marketplace (pl. des Halles), 1 block to the right of pl. Puny, home of the thrice-weekly market *(T, Th, and Sa 6:30am-noon).* Get an overview of the entire city with a **guided tour.** *(During the summer only; check at the tourist office for specific times and departure locations. 8SFr, under 13 3SFr.)*

CHURCHES, CASTLES, AND DUNGEONS. From the pl. des Halles, turn left onto the rue de Chateau (marked by the red-faced clock, the **Tour de Piesse**) and climb the stairs on your right to reach both the **Collégiale** (a church) and the **chateau** which gives the town its name. Begun in the 12th century, construction of the church took so long to complete that architectural styles changed from Romanesque to Gothic. The golden stars and blue skies of the vaulted ceiling arch harmoniously over stained-glass windows and faded wall murals reinstalled after all the iconoclastic Reformation fervor died down. The gaudy **Cenotaph**, a sculptural composition of the Counts of Neuchâtel from 1372 on, was covered during the Reformation to prevent destruction and is covered again today for restoration scheduled for completion by mid-2000. *(Church open Oct.-Mar. 9am-6:30pm, April-Sept. 9am-8pm; free concerts the last Friday; free.)* Next door, the 12th-century chateau served as the seat of the Count of Neuchâtel during the Middle Ages. Look for splotches of red on the old outside walls, remnants of a disastrous fire in 1415 that literally baked the yellow stone. Today the bureaucrats of the cantonal government sit behind the striped shutters and flower boxes. The interior can be seen only on free but dull guided tours (in English) which meet in the courtyard. *(Tours Apr.-Sept. M-F every hr. on the hr. 10am-noon and 2-4pm, Sa 10-11am and 2-4pm, Su 2-4pm.)* A small cloister garden connects the chateau to the **Tour des Prisons** on rue Jehanne-de-Hochberg. The 125-step ascent allows you to examine the tiny wooden cells used until 1848 and enjoy a magnificent view from the top. *(Open Apr.-Sept. 8am-6pm. 0.50SFr.)*

ART AND HISTORY MUSEUM. To begin a tour of Neuchâtel's cultural offerings, start at the **Musée d'Art et d'Histoire,** which houses an eclectic collection of paintings, coins, weapons, and textiles that tells the history of Neuchâtel. The uncanny 18th-century automatons created by Jacquet-Droz are the museum's pride and joy; 2 barefoot boys in velvet coats scribble away while a lady plays the harpsichord. Performances are on the first Sunday of each month at 2, 3, and 4pm. Upstairs, the Art Nouveau decorations of the cupola include oil paintings (one of which portrays Neuchâtel as the "Intellectual Life"), stained glass, and sculpted angels that literally fly out of the walls. *(From pl. des Halles, walk toward the lake and turn left onto esplanade Léopold-Robert 1. Tel. 717 79 20; fax 717 79 29. Open Tu-Su 10am-5pm. 7SFr, students 4SFr, under 17 and Th free.)*

NATURAL HISTORY MUSEUM. The **Musée d'Histoire Naturelle** sits atop the rue des Terreaux, to the left off rue de l'Hôpital. This spunkier version of the standard natural history museum displays examples of Switzerland's animals, stuffed and mounted in surprisingly entertaining dioramas of their natural environment. *(Turn right from the pl. des Halles onto the Croix du Marché, which becomes rue de l'Hôpital. Open Tu-Su 10am-5pm. 6SFr, students 3SFr, free W.)*

Further along rue de l'Hôpital, elegant gates and 2 alluring sphinxes invite a stroll into place du Peyrou. The crunchy gravel walks of the formal garden lead to the Hôtel du Peyrou, the home of Jean-Jacques Rousseau's friend and publisher, Pierre-Alexandre du Peyrou. Behind the mansion, the small **Archaeological Museum** is the home base for a passionate, expanding local investigation into the region's remote past. The museum houses some of the results of these continuing activities: pottery shards give way to increasingly recognizable artifacts, including an entire 7th-century grave and handsome marble busts from the Roman era. *(Av. du Peyrou 7. Tel. 889 69 10; fax 889 62 68. Open Tu-Su 2-5pm. Free.)*

OTHER SIGHTS. Neuchâtel's other attractions cater to the sense of taste. Visitors can sample chocolates at the **Wodey-Suchard chocolate factory,** rue du Seyon 5, directly behind the pl. Pury. *(Open M 11am-6:30pm, Tu-F 6:30am-6:30pm, Sa 6:30am-5pm).* Venture out to nearby Cressier (see p. 479) for **wine tasting** in leafy vineyards. Hard-core cheese enthusiasts can pilgrimage out to the **Fromagerie Les Martel (cheese factory)** in neighboring Les Ponts-de-Martel for a tour and demonstration. *(40min. bus ride from train station. Tel. 937 16 66. Open 8am-noon, 5-7pm. Free.)*

⚡ ENTERTAINMENT. The university crowd makes the nightlife in Neuchâtel predictably lively; the city is famous among regional club-goers for its techno DJs. Opposite Crêperie Bach et Buck, the **Casino de la Rotonde,** Foubourg du Lac 14 (tel. 724 48 48), has 2 dance clubs specializing in jungle (beers 3-5SFr; admission from 10SFr; open F-Su 10pm-4am.) Just behind the casino stands the **Bar Au 21,** Foubourg de Lac 23 (tel. 725 81 98). Nurture beers (2.50-4.50SFr) or long drinks (6-8SFr) under Pink Floyd posters or play pinball and foosball with a clientele generally younger than the club's name suggests. (Open M-Th 7pm-midnight; F 7pm-1am, Sa 5pm-1am, Su 5pm-midnight.)

The popular **Shakespeare Pub,** rue des Terreaux 7, across from the Musée d'Histoire, caters to a somewhat older, blue-collar crowd. Medieval timbers and stone walls loom over a 3-story pit lit by a combo of disco lights and British street lamps. (Open Tu-Su 8:30pm-4am. Men pay 13SFr to get in with one drink voucher on weekends.) Dance music tends toward Prince. (Beer 4-5SFr., long drinks 8.50-13.50SFr. Prices go up after 1am.) Consume beer (7SFr), burgers (7-8SFr), and/or pizza (7-12SFr) all night long at the **Garbo** bar-discoteque, rue de Chavannes 5 and 7 (tel. 724 31 81; www.garbo.ch), 1 block to the left of the Shakespeare Pub. Walk in past the mylar-wrapped walls and foam space rocks for karaoke (Tu-Th) and blistering techno (F-Sa. Open 10pm-6am.)

NEAR NEUCHÂTEL: CRESSIER

Trains make the 10min. trip from Neuchâtel to Cressier (every hr. 5:39-11:22pm, 3.60SFr).

Just minutes away from Neuchâtel by train but a world away in lifestyle, the sleepy medieval wine-making hamlet of Cressier presents a perfect opportunity for a day trip. Built around a tiny chateau that today houses the local government, the medieval village packs no less than 7 **caves** (wine cellars) where friendly local vintners are glad to offer tours of their facilities and answer questions about grapes. The finale, of course, is *la dégustation*, sampling wines poured by the hands that make them. Simply ask the vintner: *"Deguster du vin, s'il vous plaît?"* Choose from *chasselas*, *pinot noir*, or *l'oeil-de-perdrix*, or leave it to the expert *("Votre choix")*, to receive a glass of Cressier wine, straight from the vineyard's barrels.

Many *caves* line the one and only main street. Of note is the particularly traditional and congenial *cave* of **Jean-Paul Ruedin,** rte. de Troub 4 (tel. (032) 757 11 51), just around the corner from the train station. Jean-Paul is the 14th Ruedin son to operate the family vineyards since Jacques Ruedin first planted the grapes in 1614.

Recently honored for their sparkling *Chasselas* and strong, pure *Pinot Noir*, the Ruedin *cave* exudes a laid-back, philosophical attitude towards their craft; as the door declares, "*Aimer le vin c'est aimer la vie*" ("To love wine is to love life". Open Tu-F 8am-noon and 1:30-5:30pm, Sa 9-11:30am.) For an especially varied vineyard visit, attend a *dégustation extraordinaire* hosted by the **Maison Vallier,** 1 rue Vallier (behind and to the left of the chateau), Friday evenings from 5-7:30pm, where various vintners present their wares (Apr.-Oct.).

Though sampling is encouraged, it is considered impolite not to buy afterwards. The cheapest bottles start around 9SFr, to which 4SFr can add a fresh baguette, cheese, and chocolate from the **Co-op** next to the church on rue Gustave Jeanneret (open M-Tu and Th-F 7:45am-12:15pm and 2-6:30pm, W 7:45am-12:15pm, Sa 7:45am-12:15pm and 1:30-6pm). Take your bounty with you on a 10min. stroll up into the vineyards for panoramic views of the valley by following the yellow *tourisme pédestre* signs off rue de Chateau. A little extra effort brings you to the tiny town of **Combe**, where the tinkling of cowbells accompanies the lake view.

For a splurge, you can enjoy farm fresh regional delicacies at **La Croix Blanche,** rue de Neuchâtel 12 (tel. (032) 757 11 66), across from Jean Ruedin, including local trout (15SFr) and fondue (18.50SFr). Upstairs, the restaurant's hotel offers spacious singles for 70SFr or doubles for 90SFr, shower, TV, and breakfast included. Hotel guests also get special lunch and dinner of regional delicacies and "surprises of the owner" for 15SFr. Reception hours vary; arrangements can be made at the café. (Open M-Tu, Th-Su 7-11:30am and 7pm-midnight. AmEx, MC, Visa.) A few doors down, the **Hôtel de la Couronne,** rue de Neuchâtel 2 (tel. (038) 47 14 58; fax (038) 47 32 01) serves a range of fresh fishies (22-24SFr). Upstairs, the attic rooms feature half-timbered walls. (Singles 60SFr; doubles 90SFr. Shower included. Reception at the bar. Restaurant open Tu-Th 8am-2pm and 4-11:30pm, F 8am-2pm and 4pm-12:30am, Su 9am-4pm.)

NEAR NEUCHÂTEL: YVERDON-LES-BAINS

Trains run from Yverdon direct to Neuchâtel (25min., every hr., 11.80SFr), Geneva (50min., every hr., 29SFr); Lausanne (30min., every hr., 12.60SFr); and Basel (2hr., every hr., 48SFr). The train station is located at ave. de la Gare 1 (tel. 425 21 15; open 6am-10pm).

What's in a name? In the case of Yverdon-les-Bains, it's the essence of the town's existence, the **thermal baths** for which it is named. When Roman settlers discovered the source of the hot springs some 1500 years ago, they began cultivating the curative powers of the mineral-rich waters to ease all manner of ailments. Today the **Centre Thermal,** off ave. des Bains (tel. (024) 423 0232), and its glitzy adjoining hotel entice visitors with 4 pools and therapeutic treatments ranging from electotherapy to massage. Although the clientele is weighted toward an older crowd, the center also offers recreational activities for sprightlier guests. A word to the wise—plug your nose, since the healing powers of the springs come at the price of their sulfurous stench. To get there from the train station, head left down the ave. de la Gare to the ave. Haldimand then follow the signs, or take bus #2 or #3 to "Praire" and continue down the ave. des Bains. (Open M-F 8am-10pm; Sa-Su 9am-8pm. Admission to the baths 13SFr, ages 3-16 8SFr, other facilities charge separately.) Even the **tourist office,** on pl. Pestalozzi in the *centre ville*, a 3-minute walk straight ahead from the station (tel. (024) 423 62 90; fax (024) 426 11 22; email tourisme.info@yverdon-les-bains.ch, www.yverdon-les-bains.ch/tourisme), calls itself the office of "thermalisme" (open Apr.-Oct. M-F 8:30am-noon and 1:30-6pm; Nov.-Mar. M-F 8:30am-noon and 1:30-5:30pm; June-Sept. also Sa 9am-noon; July-Aug. M-F 8:30am-6pm).

■ **ACCOMMODATIONS AND FOOD.** The **Auberge de Jeunesse,** rue de Parc 14 (tel. 425 12 33; fax 426 00 96), is a 60-bed establishment reminiscent of summer camp, as many of the bunks are crammed into 2 mobile homes outside the main building. (Dorms 20.50SFr per night. Breakfast and shower included. Reception daily 7-9:30am and 5-10:30pm.) From the station, cross the river to the right and head down the riverside path for 10 minutes. The **Hôtel du Lac,** rue des Cygnes 25 (tel. 425 23 07; fax 426 66 36), features clean, if rather unadorned, rooms. (Singles 40SFr, doubles 70SFr, triples 90SFr. Hall showers. Reception M-F 7:30am-11pm, Sa 8:30am-2pm. AmEx, MC, Visa.)**Boulangeries** and cafés cluster in the colorful streets radiating from the centre ville; most feature regional specialties (like perch or **papet vaudois,** made of sausage and vegetables), but the best carnivorous fare awaits at the **Restaurant des Sports,** rue de Milieu 7 (tel. 425 27 63), past the church (various types of entre côte around 31SFr). Unfortunately, the most affordable accommodations are outside the centre ville, well after the medieval facades have melted into 20th-century suburbia.

⚠ OUTDOOR ACTIVITIES. Though Yverdon sits on the southwestern shore of Lake Neuchâtel, the only good way to get close to the water is to picnic on the narrow strip of beach, approximately 15 feet wide, enjoy the velodrome-like effect of the surrounding hills. Head down the pecheurs behind and to the left of the station and turn right on ave. des Iris. Nearby is a forested area containing 47 **standing stones,** a sort of neolithic mini-Stonehenge dating back to 4,000 BC. Yverdon's aesthetic appeal in concentrated in the centre ville, a smallish square flanked by the Savoy château to the left and the 18th-century Baroque church on the right. The château was built in 1260 by the Dukes of Savoy to protect Yverdon on the east, a role fulfilled in part by the lake on the north and the river Thiele on the west (though you'd never know it from its rather anemic size today). The square, 4-towered edifice houses a museum (tel. (024) 425 93 10) containing prehistoric artifacts as well as items from Yverdon's days as the Roman camp of **Eburondunum** (where is gets its name). (Museum open Oct.-May Tu-Su 2-5pm; June-Sept. Tu-Su 10am-noon and 2-5pm. 6SFr, students 5SFr.) The tourist office resides in the Hôtel de Ville next to the château, an 18th-century structure that is now a venue for temporary free exhibits.

LA CHAUX-DE-FONDS

Sprawling, lakeless, and largely devoid of medieval charm, La Chaux-de-Fonds seems an unlikely attraction amid the more scenic *villes* in the mountains of French Switzerland. But the city, birthplace of the architect Le Corbusier and auto magnate Louis Chevrolet, magnetizes visitors by means of time and technology. A major historic watchmaking center, the town showcases a museum exploring "man and time," the best horological gallery in Switzerland. Dubbed Europe's highest city thanks to its 1000m altitude, La Chaux-de-Fonds is a comfortable home base for skiers and mountain bikers wanting to explore mountain trails. The city's surging night scene has locals from Neuchâtel eagerly making the 40-minute train trek (every hr., 10SFr) on weekends to dance and drink the night away.

▊ ORIENTATION AND PRACTICAL INFORMATION. The **tourist office,** Pl. le Corbusier 1 (tel. 919 68 95; fax 919 62 97; email montagnes@ne.ch; www.ne.ch), occupies the ground floor of Espacité, a giant silver and red building. From the station, walk straight 1 block, then turn on av. Léopold-Robert. Ride the elevator (free) to the 14th floor for a panoramic view of the area after picking up a 2SFr city map and free info on activities. (Open Sept.-June 9am-12:15pm and 1:30-5:30pm, Sa 9am-12:15pm and 1:30-5pm; July-Aug. M-F 9am-6:30pm, Sa 9am-12:15pm and 1:30-5pm.) **Skiers** can take a regional train to **Tête de Ran** (1422m), in **Les Hauts-Geneveys** (tel. 853 11 51), for downhill or cross-country (lift tickets 15SFr per day), or a bus to **La-Vue-des-Alpes** (tel. 853 30 18), which offers night-skiing and ski lessons. (Buses run 3-4 times per day W and Sa-Su 9:15am-5:15pm. Reservations necessary at tel. 926 12 75.) In summer, bikers and hikers enjoy well-marked trails (**rent bikes** at the station, but ask the tourist office for trail maps and bike rental information.)

| PHONE CODE | The **city code** in La Chaux-de-Fonds is 032. |

■□ ACCOMMODATIONS AND FOOD. The dim but spotless and roomy **Auberge de Jeunesse (HI),** rue du Doubs 34 (tel. 968 43 15; fax 968 25 18), sits at the corner of rue du Stand behind a wrought-iron gate; take bus #4 (dir. L'Hôpital) to "Stavay-Mollondin," walk a block, then turn right on rue du Stand. The 98 beds are rarely full. (Dorms 24SFr, doubles 31SFr. 4-6 bed "family" rooms 24SFr per person, with sink 26SFr. Subtract 2.50SFr in off-season. Non-members add 5SFr. Breakfast and sheets included. Hall showers only. **Laundry** 6SFr (no dryers). Dinner 11.50SFr. Reception 7:30-9am and 5-10pm in winter, 7:30-9:30am and 5-10:30pm in summer. Wheelchair accessible. AmEx, DC, MC, Visa.)

Cheap food is most easily obtained in megastores like the **Co-op Super Centre** on rue du Modulor, left off av. Léopold-Robert before the tourist office (open M 1:30-6:30pm, Tu, W, F 8am-6:30pm, Th 8am-8pm, Sa 8am-5pm) or the *plats du jour* (6-10SFr) at the **Migros** restaurant two blocks right of the station on the 4th floor of the Metropole Center (M 1-6:30pm, Tu, W, F 11am-6:30pm, Th 11am-8pm, Sa 11am-5pm). **Le P'tit Paris,** rue du Progrès 4 (tel. (039) 28 65 33), is a student-crowded café with vaulted ceilings and live jazz and blues in the musty **Paris Cave** in back. Continue down the road from the tourist office, turn left on rue du Stand, then right on rue du Progrès. Indulge in a shrimp cocktail for 8SFr or beer 2.60SFr. (Concerts 10-15SFr. Open M-Th 8am-midnight, F 8am-2am, Sa 9am-2am, Su 4pm-midnight.)

▣ ◨ SIGHTS AND ENTERTAINMENT. The fascinating **Musée International d'Horlogerie,** in the Parc des Musées, chronicles humanity's quest to measure the great continuum, from Stonehenge to the atomic clock. Here, the vast and the minuscule unite. Dardi's astrarium and Ducommun's planetarium illustrate the rigidly timed dance of the planets in the Ptolemian and Copernican systems. Sleek cylindrical and spherical display cases rise eerily from the floors and hang from the ceiling like space-age stalagmites and stalactites, accompanied by exhibits in English, German, and French. Dominating one corner of the park outside, the **carillon,** an artistic conglomeration of steel pipes and colored slats, measures time to the hundredth of a second and emits acoustically precise musical ditties in sync with carefully orchestrated panel movements every 15 minutes. (From the station, turn right on the rue des Musées and follow it to the right of the Metropole Center. Rue des Musées 29. Tel. 967 68 61; fax 967 68 89. Open June-Sept. Tu-Su 10am-5pm; Oct.-May 10am-noon and 2-5pm. 8SFr, students 4SFr; free Su 10am-noon.)

Next door, the **Musée des Beaux-Arts** looks like a cross between a pseudo-Roman bath and a parking garage. The sparse collections of not-so-great 19th- and 20th-century Swiss derivatives of French schools aren't really worth the effort. But there are 2 pockets of dense excellence: a room full of Le Corbusier paintings wild with color and chaos that contrast startlingly with the functional and minimalist straight lines of his architectural style, and another filled with recently bequeathed paintings, including works by Delacroix, Van Gogh, Gauguin, Renoir, and Courbet. (Rue des Musées 33. Tel. 913 04 44; fax 913 61 93. Open Tu and Th-Su 10am-noon and 2-5pm. W 10am-noon and 2-8pm. 6SFr, 8SFr for temporary exhibits, students 3SFr, 4SFr. W free.)

MAN AND MACHINE Born Charles Edouard Jeanneret-Gris in 1887, **Le Corbusier,** architect, city planner, and painter, is a monumental presence in 20th-century art. This son of a La-Chaux-de-Fonds watchmaker rebelled against the inertia of 19th-century nationalism and historicism, seeking pure, precise forms motivated by function rather than cultural reference. He therefore designed in glass and reinforced concrete, a revolutionary choice of material that countless others repeated throughout the 20th century. He was also infatuated with iconic machines of modernity, like the automobile and the airplane, and believed that houses and cities should be designed and organized like machines in their economy of structure and efficient use. As he said in *Toward a New Architecture,* "the house is a machine for living."

For a literal taste of history, investigate the **Musée Paysan et Artisanal** (Museum of Farming and Crafts), Crêters 148 (tel. 926 71 89). This authentic 16th-century farmhouse reconstructs the home, workshop, sausages, and general lifestyle of the medieval peasant family. It illustrates how the confinement of long Jura winters gave rise to the region's watchmaking obsession. Take Bus #3 (dir.: Les Foulets) to "Polyexpo." (Open May-Oct. T-Th, Sa 2-5pm, F 2-7pm, Su 10am-noon; Nov.-Apr. W, Sa-Su 2-5pm. 3SFr, students 2SFr.)

If you're feeling restless at night, take a 20-minute stroll under the stars from the hostel to the very edge of town to the **Bikini Test,** La Joux-Perret 3 (tel. 968 06 66). From the hostel, walk downhill 7 blocks to rue de la Serre, then turn left and go around the Place des Lilas. The street becomes rue du College. Head for the music. Converted from a late medieval barn, the discoteque sports murals of monsters and musicians cavorting on a lunar landscape. Inside, robot gargoyles glare down on the 2nd story loft as the DJ mixes salsa with techno. Kids dance and drink away (beer 3-5SFr) while smoke drifts by. Downstairs, the chill-out room shows shark movies and Monty Python clips. For a closer nightspot, try the popular **Dublins,** 32a rue Docteur Coutery (tel. 914 11 18). Walk 3 blocks left from the hostel, then left and downhill. On weekends, rowdy 20-somethings turn out for 2.50SFr beers, spilling out into the cobblestones beyond the pub doors.

BIEL (BIENNE)

In 1765, Rousseau spent what he called the happiest moments of his life in Biel. However, little of the fortified town remained unchanged through the tumultuous years that followed the philosopher's sojourn. In 1798 Biel was overrun by Napoleon's armies, laying the foundation for the city's present bilingualism (60% speak French, 40% German). Industrial parks for Rolex and Omega now overpower the vestiges of the *Altstadt* Rousseau loved, but Biel's proximity to Lac Bienne (Bielersee) and surrounding hills, has made it a popular stop for nature-lovers.

🔁 **ORIENTATION AND PRACTICAL INFORMATION. Trains** run to Biel from **Solothurn** (20min., every hr. 5:42am-12:15pm, 8.60SFr); **Bern** (30min., every 30min. 5:35am-12:01am, 11.80SFr); and **Neuchâtel** (20min., every 30min. 5:39am-midnight, 10SFr). The Biel **tourist office** (tel. 322 75 75; fax 323 77 57) is just outside the train station at Bahnhofpl. (Open M-F 8am-12:30pm and 1:30-6pm; May-Oct. Sa 9am-3pm as well.) The train station **exchanges currency** (M-F 6am-8pm, Sa-Su 6am-7pm), **rents bikes** (20SFr, half-day 16SFr; mountain bike 26SFr, 21SFr), rents **lockers** (3-6SFr; open 5am-12:30am), and **stores luggage** (5SFr per day; open 7am-9pm). You can call a **taxi** at tel. 32 21 11 11. For the **police,** dial 344 51 11; for the **hospital,** tel. 324 24 24. The **post office** (tel. 321 18 40) is just left of the train station.

PHONE CODE	The **city code** for Biel is 032.

🍴 **ACCOMMODATIONS AND FOOD.** Since few budget accommodations grace Biel, consider making it a daytrip from Solothurn, Neuchâtel, or Bern. If you do decide to stay, **The Hostel,** Solothurnerstr. 137 (tel. 341 29 65; email hostelbiel @access.ch), is the quintessential backpacker's lodge. Take bus 3N or 3S to "Renferstr.," walk back to the corner and turn right. A tie-dyed sign marks the hostel on the left, which has 45 sheeted beds, no lockout, no curfew, free breakfast, and **kitchen** access. (Dorm singles 23SFr, doubles 60SFr. Reception 8am-10pm.)

For picnic supplies, there is always **Migros,** Freierstr. 3, 1 block straight ahead from the station (open M-W, F 7:30am-6:30pm, Th 7:30am-9pm, Sa 7:30am-4pm), the **Co-op,** Rechbergerstr. 1, left from the station at Bahnhofpl. and right on Rechenbergstr. (open M-F 8am-12:30pm and 2-6:30pm, Sa 7:30am-4pm), or the **Aperto** in the station (open 6am-10pm). In front of Migros, numerous cafés and restaurants in the *Zentralplatz (Place Centrale)* satisfy those post-hike munchies. The

Atomic Café, Bahnhofpl. 13, across and left of the station, decorated with corrugated steel bars, offers a regional wine from Twann (3.50SFr) and **Internet access.** (3SFr per 30 min. Open M-F 7am-12:30am, Sa 10am-12:30am, Su 10am-8pm.)

🄰 **HIKING.** The 2 best **hikes** from Biel pass through magnificent gorges: the walk to **Twannbachschlucht** leads to mountaintop fields ripe for picnics, while the trek to **Taubenloch** threads through a rugged canyon and its canopy forest.

TWANNBACHSCHLUCHT (3HR.). To get to Twannbachschlucht, take bus #11 from the train station to "Magglingen/FuniMacolin," then take the rail car from Biel to Magglingen (every 15min; 4.20SFr, SwissPass and Swiss Card valid.) From this vantage point, 3 different paths lead to **Twannberg,** the starting point of the Twannbachschlucht hike. The trail follows a ridge above Lake Biel and passes through dense forest and flower-filled meadows, ending in the picture-book town of Twann at the bottom of the gorge. Return to Biel by **train** (5min., every hr., 3.60SFr) or lake **ferry** (6.20SFr, Eurailpass not valid), or move on to Neuchâtel.

TAUBENLOCH (40MIN.). Taubenloch is a less ambitious hike, though its more dynamic terrain makes it perhaps more rewarding. Buses #1, 2, and 3 run to "Taubenloch" where you can enter the canyon through the Zum Wilden Mann restaurant's garden (2SFr suggested donation). Legend has it that a beautiful maiden nicknamed "Die Taube" ("The Dove") threw herself to her death here to escape an enamored tyrant. The trail hugs the edges of 30m drops of sheer rock walls carved eons ago by the rushing rapids below. Waterfalls plunge past mossy cliffs, illuminated by the sunlit green canopy above. Many hikers turn back at the water treatment plant, but hungrier souls who press on just a few minutes will find the **Eau de Berge du Taubenloch restaurant** at Frinvillier 2535 (tel./fax 358 11 32). Fill up on a delicious three-course *Menü* for under 14SFr while the owner's baby goats and friendly dog romp around your feet. (Open Tu-Sa 9am-11pm, Su 9am-7pm.) The well-marked walk back from Frinvillier to Biel takes about 1 hour. Vineyards line the lake, ripe for a walking tour or bike ride (1-4hr., map at tourist office).

🄴 **ENTERTAINMENT.** A **boat tour** of the lake provides a leisurely introduction to the city. To reach the harbor and beach from the train station, turn left at Bahnhofpl., follow the road around to the left, and look for the brown-and-white signs for *Schiffländle* and *Débarcadère*. Boat tours range from 12.40SFr (Biel-Twann, 30min.) to 46SFr (Biel-Murten, 3hr. and Biel-Solothurn, 2½hr.) round-trip. In early July, an **open-air cinema** called "Yellow Movie Nights" runs recent releases in **Schloßpark Nidau**. Tickets (15SFr) can be purchased at the tourist office or through Hello Yellow (tel. 157 18 18; www.post.ch).

DEATH, A MAIDEN, AND A LINDEN TREE

Once upon a time (June 22, 1476) in a land far, far away (Fribourg), there lived an old man named Nicholas who declared that he would give his daughter Beatrice's hand in marriage to the man who proved himself most valiant on the battlefield. As the knights went off to fight Charles the Bold in Murten, Beatrice waved a linden branch at Rudolphe, her childhood love. Determined to win her hand, Rudolphe proved himself the bravest knight on the battlefield—at the cost of a mortal wound. Undaunted, he ran back to Fribourg, waving a linden branch and shouting "Victory!" When he finally reached Beatrice's balcony in pl. Hôtel de Ville, he collapsed. Beatrice ran to her love, who could say only "Homeland! Love! To Heaven!" before dying in her arms. The town planted the linden branch as a relic of the victory in the square. In 1984, a traffic accident uprooted the tree, but the town salvaged a shoot and replanted it in the original spot, where it flourishes today. In memory of the battle and of Rudolphe's plight, runners from Murten and Fribourg race between the two cities every October.

FRIBOURG (FREIBURG)

Modern Fribourg stretches in front of the train station with a mix of stores and concrete apartment buildings, while its *vieille ville*, established on the banks of the Sarine by the Zähringen dynasty in 1157, stretches down the wooded hills of the gorge to the river. The contrast is stark, and is only one of the dichotomies that compose Fribourg's multi-faceted personality. Young Swiss are drawn to Fribourg by both the university and the siren call of lakes and mountains. The town has a penchant for modern art, open-air shopping, and fine dining, but its most distinctive attractions are quiet remnants of medieval religious fervor. Fribourg was an isolated bastion of Catholicism during the Reformation; even the local brew, Cardinal beer, celebrates a 19th-century bishop. Meanwhile, Fribourg bridges the Swiss linguistic divide: 30% of the population firmly count themselves *Freiburger*, the remaining 70% *Fribourgeois*.

⛊ ORIENTATION AND PRACTICAL INFORMATION. Fribourg sits on the main rail line between Zurich and Geneva. **Trains** leave for **Bern** (25min., every 30min. 5:15am-12:15am, 11.80SFr); **Lausanne** (50min., every 30min. 6:20am-11:47pm, 23SFr); **Basel** (1¾hr., every 30min. 6:14am-11:16pm, 48SFr); **Neuchâtel** (1hr., every hr. 5:46am-9:46pm, 19SFr); and **Interlaken** (1½hr., every hr. 5:15-9:50pm, 35SFr). For a **taxi,** dial (079) 219 46 10. **GFM buses** for **Bulle** and the Schwarzsee (13.60SFr each) leave from the station. Fribourg's **tourist office,** av. de la Gare 1 (tel. 321 31 75; fax 322 35 27; email info@FribourgTourism.ch; www.FribourgTourism.ch), 100m to the right of the station door, makes hotel reservations for a 5SFr fee (open M-F 9am-12:30pm and 1:30-6pm, Sa 9am-12:30pm and 1:30-4pm; closed Sa afternoons Oct.-May). **Exchange currency** at the train station (open 6am-8:30pm) or at one of the many banks lining rue du Romont. **Lockers** (3-5SFr), **luggage watch** (open 7am-7:55pm; 5SFr per item), and **bike rental** (20SFr per day, ID deposit) are available at the station. Dial 117 for the **police** and 112 for general **emergencies.** **Internet access** is available at the **Scottish Bar,** rte. de Jura 67 (tel. 466 82 02; scottish.mcnet.ch). Take bus #3 to "Vuille," or turn left onto rue de l'Hôpital from pl. Georges Python and walk about 15 minutes (open M-Sa 8am-midnight; 10SFr per hr.). The **Café des Grand Places,** on the Grand Places to the right off Av. de la Gare, offers access for 10.20SFr per hour. The **post office,** av. de Tivoli, is the skyscraper left of the station (open M-F 7:30am-6:15pm, Sa 8-11am). The **postal code** is CH-1700.

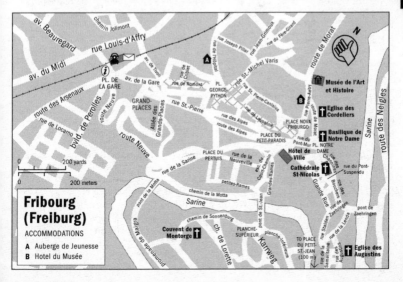

Fribourg (Freiburg)

ACCOMMODATIONS
A Auberge de Jeunesse
B Hotel du Musée

| PHONE CODE | The **city code** for Fribourg is 026. |

ACCOMMODATIONS AND FOOD. Fribourg's peaceful **Auberge de Jeunesse** stands at rue de l'Hôpital 2 (tel. 323 19 16; fax 323 19 40). Head left out the train station and walk past the overpass, across av. de Tivoli, past the post office, onto the narrow rue du Criblet, left at the playground, and up the path to the hostel. The hostel is a converted hospital, with long, quiet corridors. (Dorms 25.45SFr. Non-members add 5SFr. Breakfast, sheets, and showers included. Lunch and dinner 11.50SFr. Lockers, **laundry, kitchen,** and ping-pong tables available. Reception 7:30-9:30am and 5-10pm. Open Feb.-Nov. Reservations recommended.) **Hotel du Musée,** rue Pierre Aeby 11 (tel./fax 322 32 09), is above a Chinese restaurant (turn left off pl. Nova-Friburgo). Large, well-furnished rooms have plush carpets. (Singles 40-45SFr, with shower 50-55SFr; doubles 80-90SFr, 90-100SFr. Breakfast 5SFr. Open M-Th 10am-2:30pm and 5pm-11:30pm, F-Sa 10am-2:30pm and 5pm-midnight. AmEx, MC, Visa. Reserve 2-3 days ahead.) From the station, campers can catch a GFM bus to "Marly," where **Camping La Follaz** (tel. 436 24 95) has lakeside plots and showers (reception 9am-10pm; 5SFr, tents 8.20SFr; open Apr. to mid-Oct.).

Small cafés selling quasi-Italian or German Swiss dishes populate almost every main street in the *vieille ville,* as well as rue de Romont. For great, cheap food and a laid-back student atmosphere, head to ■**Café Populaire,** rue St. Michel 3 (tel. 322 62 97), off pl. Georges Python. Outside, twenty-somethings lounge over coffee and beer (3.50-6SFr) while inside a short-order chef at the **Mr. James** counter serves up huge juicy burgers for 5-8SFr. Patrons at the long wooden tables can enjoy the vegetarian or meat *plat du jour* (11SFr) or partake of the only bagels available this side of Zurich. (Open M-Th 7am-11:30pm, F-Sa 7am-1:30am; Mr. James opens at 9am.) **Bindella Ristorante Bar,** rue de Lausanne 38 (tel. 322 49 05), cooks inventive, high-quality pasta (from 11.50SFr) and pizza dishes in a low-lit interior. Come hear free live jazz on the last Thursday of every month at 8:30pm. (Open M-Sa 9am-11:30pm.) An airier Mediterranean design brightens the **Restaurant des Marechaux,** rue des Chanoines 9 (tel. 322 33 33), behind and to the right of the cathedral. Feast on Greek *spanakopita* with *tzatziki* (9SFr) or various *souvlaki* (19-25SFr) in this veggie-friendly establishment, overlooking the gorge (open 5pm-midnight). **Perriard Boulangerie,** rue de Lausanne 61 (tel. 322 34 89), will satisfy your sweet-tooth with a variety of pastries and confectionery delights (*noisettines* 2SFr, breads 1-3SFr; open Tu-F 7:30am-7pm, Sa 7:30am-6pm, Su 8am-6pm). A **produce market** stands in pl. Georges Python between rue de Romont and rue de Lausanne (T, W 7am-noon) or in pl. Hôtel de Ville (Sa 7am-noon). The virtually inseparable supermarket twins, **Co-op** and **Migros,** share the same street (6a and 2 rue St.-Pierre) and the same hours (open M-W, F 8am-7pm, Th 8am-9pm, Sa 8am-4pm). There is a **supermarket** in the basement of La Placette Shopping Mall (the 1st building on rue de Romont) and a **Manora** self-service restaurant on the 6th floor with meat, fruit, salad, and dessert kiosks that produce a fine meal for 8-15SFr (open M-W, F 8am-7pm, Th 8am-9pm, Sa 8am-4pm).

SIGHTS AND MUSEUMS. Fribourg's beautiful churches, monasteries, and convents naturally lend themselves to a walking tour.

THE OLD TOWN. From the station, head down rue de Romont, past pl. Georges Python, and along rue de Lausanne and its pink-bannered open-air shopping galleries. Rue de Lausanne empties into pl. Nova-Friburgo, a busy intersection with a fine view of the **Hôtel de Ville** and its fanciful clock tower. Pantaloon-clad Renaissance automatons regularly chime in the hours. A fountain of St. George dominates the courtyard below, and gives unexpected showers to visitors and the commemorative **Morat Linden Tree** in heavy winds. A descendant of a 500-year-old linden in Murten (Morat), it was planted in 1984 to commemorate the trouncing of Charles le Téméraire by Murten and its *Fribourgeois* allies in 1476 (see **Death, a Maiden, and a Linden Tree,** p. 484).

ART AND HISTORY MUSEUM. Off pl. Nova-Friburgo to the left, rue Pierre Aeby leads to the **Musée d'Art et d'Histoire.** Skip the run-of-the-mill 18th-century portraiture—the haunting historical artifacts are the meat of the collection. Look for the Hans Gieng wood carvings and the gleefully macabre, bejeweled skeleton of St. Felix (1755). *(Rue de Morat 12. Tel. 305 51 40. Open Tu-W and F-Su 10am-5pm, Th 10am-5pm and 8-10pm. Free; special exhibits 6-10SFr, student discount.)*

MONASTERY AND CHURCHES. From the museum, backtrack on rte. de Morat to the **Église des Cordeliers,** part of a Franciscan monastery. The unassuming facade masks a colorful interior, featuring vividly animated paintings framed by pastel marble, where an elaborate altar lies in star-studded darkness. *(Open Apr.-Sept. 7:30am-7pm; Oct.-Mar. 7:30am-6pm.)* Farther down the road is the **Basilique de Notre-Dame,** whose dim, incense-laden atmosphere contrasts sharply with the bright, ornate Église des Cordeliers. Across pl. Notre-Dame rises the bell tower of the **Cathédrale St.-Nicolas,** the focal point of Fribourg. It took over 200 years to erect the Gothic columns, now smoke-blackened, that shoot upwards into pointed arches and elegant stained-glass windows. View the town from the 76m, 368-step **tower.** *(Cathedral open M-F 6:15am-7pm, Sa 7:45am-7pm, Su 9am-9:30pm. Free. Tower open June-Aug. M-Sa 10am-noon and 2-5:15pm. 3SFr, students 2SFr.)* Head behind and to the right of the cathedral on rue des Chanoines, right on rue de Zähringen, left on rue Stalden, and left on rue de la Lendeto reach the rue des Augustins and its highlight, the 13th-century **Église des Augustins.** Although only order members can enter all the way, visitors can examine the monastery's huge, eagle-topped altarpiece. Two tiny chapels sit high on the hill above town. The postage-stamp sized **Chapelle de St. Jost** is closed to the public, but the **Chapelle de Lorette,** housing an illuminated statue of the Virgin Mary, welcomes visitors. *(Open Mar.1-Oct. 31 T, Th, Sa-Su.)*

🎵 **FESTIVALS AND NIGHTLIFE.** Fribourg's university, music conservatory, art groups, and civic institutions host several festivals throughout the year, including a **Carnival** (a Mardi Gras type party in the *vieille ville* in Feb.), an **International Film Festival** (March 12-19, 2000), an **International Guitar Festival** (early April), an **International Jazz Festival** (mid-July), and the **Belluard Bollwerk International** festival of modern dance performances (late June to early July). **Open-air cinema** runs from mid-July to mid-August (get advance tickets from the tourist office).

For night owls, 🎵**Café Belvedere,** Grand Rue 36 (tel. 323 44 07), at the top of Stalden, resembles a 3-dimensional M.C. Escher drawing, with comfortably worn couches perfect for intimate conversation. Plenty of alterna-intellectuals lounge on terraces overlooking the gorge, sampling the wine or beer of the month (3.50-5SFr) while listening to the pleasantly dippy music. *Menüs* feature salads, pasta, and various fowl for 11.50-13.50SFr. (Open M-Tu 11:30am-11:30pm, W-Th 11:30am-12:30am, F 11:30am-3am, Sa 10:30am-3am, Su noon-midnight.) The **Café des Grand Places,** 12 Grand Places (tel. 322 26 58), plays live funk, blues, salsa, industrial hard-core, and karaoke, depending on the night. The restaurant upstairs serves inexpensive ethnic specialties, like 6SFr *samosas* and an 18SFr enchilada platter. (Open Tu-F 11am-11:30pm, Sa-Su 6pm-3am. Music starts at 9pm. AmEx, MC, Visa.)

NEAR FRIBOURG: GRUYÈRES

GFM buses connect Fribourg and Gruyères (via Bulle) every hour (40min., last departure 9:35pm, 16.40SFr). Trains pass through Gruyères every hour as well (last departure 8:17pm).

Tiny Gruyères carries a weighty reputation for its cheese. Unfortunately, the whole town is painfully conscious of it. The local tourist industry goes to absurd extremes (strategically placed milk cows, locals in dubiously medieval garb chirping the virtues of their wares, and suspiciously artificial-smelling smoke permeating a castle whose hearths have been bare and unlit for years), but the towering beauty of the surrounding mountains overcomes the kitsch. A château filled with contemporary art and the milky calm of working cheese dairies make this eccentric town well worth a daytrip. The **Fromagerie de Gruyères,** cheese factory *par*

GOT MILK? Before most kids hear of watch-making or political neutrality, they know about Swiss cheese. But the 84,000 tons of cheese Switzerland produces annually don't consist of only the familiar, hole-ridden variety. While most of it (56,500 tons) is the recognizable Emmental, 22,000 tons is Gruyère, a creamier cousin. The region has been making cheese since the 12th century, though today's dairy artisans operate in modern facilities amid expansive cow pastures. Two varieties of cows contribute their milk to the effort: *tachettée rouge* (red) and *noir* (black). Each animal produces around 30 kilos of milk each day, which is transported to the *fromagerie* (cheese factory). Workers process 3 million kilos a year by pouring it into large vats, where it is centrifuged, matured with bacteria, congealed with natural enzymes into a yogurt-like consistency, and heated to get rid of excess liquid (which is saved to feed pigs). Each cheese round is then pressed into shape for 18 hours until it reaches 800 kilos per cm^2, before it is stamped for quality and authenticity.

---

excellence, is near the train station. Though currently under construction, it will be ready in April 2000 to dazzle visitors once again with multilingual presentations, cheese-making demonstrations, and a slide show detailing how "the best milk cows get to know the finest bulls in the world." The truly lactose-devoted can take a GFM bus to "Moléson-sur-Gruyères" to the **Fromagerie d'Alpage** (tel. (026) 921 10 44). An anachronistic phenomenon, this 17th-century factory makes cheese the old-fashioned way, over a huge cauldron on the fireplace (free demonstrations daily at 3pm mid-May to mid-Oct.). With the obligatory cheese-history lesson under your belt, you can lay siege to the steep hill. Steep. The **tourist office** (tel. (026) 921 10 30; fax 921 38 50) lies at the top of the stairs leading to the *vieille ville* from the **parking lot** (office open mid-May to Oct. M-Su 9am-noon and 1:30-5:30pm; Oct. to mid-May M-F 10am-noon and 1:30-5:30pm).

With the Dent-de-Broc mountains looming in the background, one beautiful vista follows another as the geranium-lined main street leads to the **Château de Gruyères** (tel. (026) 921 21 02). Between the 11th and 16th century, 19 counts lived lawlessly within its walls; the last Gruyère was exiled in 1554. Only the dungeons remain of the original feudal castle; the living quarters burned to the ground in 1493 and were rebuilt as the first Renaissance castle in the Northern Alps. They now house the **International Center of Fantastic Art,** a museum that roams freely between the erotic, the demonic, and the grotesque. (Open June-Sept. 9am-7pm, Mar.-May and Oct. 9am-noon and 1-5pm; Nov.-Feb. M-F 9:30am-noon and 1:30-4pm, Sa 10:30am-noon and 1:30-5pm. 5SFr, students 2SFr, essential English guide 0.50SFr.) Historical tapestries and **Franz Lizst's** pianoforte (yup, he lived here too) are displayed upstairs. Both the château and *vieille ville* are reliably flooded with more tourists than locals and cows combined. The gravel path around the castle and a short walk downhill to the right of the main street provide some relief from souvenir shops and bring those magnificent mountains a little closer. When hunger strikes, a meal of Gruyère's cheese fondue can prove a budget buster (18-40SFr), but the region's other specialty, *la double-crème de la Gruyère avec fraises* (strawberries in clotted cream), is deliciously affordable (10-13SFr).

NEAR FRIBOURG: MURTEN (MORAT)

Murten is accessible from Fribourg (26min., every hr. 5:41am-12:27am, 10SFr); Neuchâtel (30min. via Ins, every hr. 5:12am-10:13pm, 10.80SFr); and Bern (45min. via Lyss, every hr. 5:47am-10:27pm, 11.80SFr). LNM ferries run from Neuchâtel (90min., 5 per day 9:25am-6pm, 15.40SFr), and offer lake cruises (13.20SFr; tel. (032) 725 40 12).

The lakeside town of Murten maintains an amicable bilingualism, despite the predominance of German over the 12% French-speaking minority (who call the town "Morat"). Only at the end of the town's main street do the 2 languages literally go their separate ways: the road splits into Französischkirchg. on the left and Deutschkirchg. on the right. Murten/Morat, surrounded by its medieval *Ringmauer/ramparts*, overlooks the pale blue **Murtensee/Lac de Morat.** This high-altitude town has a bloody history: Charles the Bold, Duke of Burgundy, was defeated in 1476 by an army of the old Swiss Confederacy in what came to be known as the Battle of Murten; Napoleon defeated a similar contingency in 1798, laying the foundation for Murten's French-speaking community.

Largely free from the crass commercialism that infects other nearby villages, Murten makes for a leisurely daytrip. The train station (tel. 670 26 46), in the same tiny square as the post office, **changes currency** and **rents bikes** (26-32SFr per day). Turn right from the station to find a **Co-op** grocery store halfway up Bahnhofstr. with a cafeteria upstairs (entrees 9.90-10.90SFr; open M-Th 8am-7pm, F 8am-8pm, Sa 7:30am-4pm). At the end of Hauptg., the **tourist office** is on the left (Kirchg. 6; tel. 670 51 12; fax 670 49 83; open M-F 9am-noon and 1:30-6pm, Sa 10am-2pm).

As Bahnhofstr. curves uphill, it leads to the swaying lindens that mark the entrance to the **Schloß (château),** with its imposing square tower. Now the home of several administrative offices, the château also hosts occasional dramatic productions. The main street, Hauptstr. (to the right of the château), catches the eye with numerous flags blazoned with the cantonal symbol, the lion, hung from its arcades. Turn right off Hauptg. to Deutschkirchg. to climb up to the **ramparts** for views of the red-clay-tiled roofs below and the lake beyond. On the other side of the ivy-covered walls is the **Stadtgraben**—gardens rife with roses, pink honeysuckle, and multicolored lupins.

The *Stadtgraben* path descends the ramparts and ends at the linden tree park. Follow Lausannestr. in the opposite direction and obey the signs to reach the town's old mill, now the **Murten Historisches Museum.** The water wheel still churns outside; inside you'll find a collection ranging from neolithic remains to bottles of Murten's famously strong and famously psychedelic *absinthe* (see **Poison Vert,** below). (Tel. 670 31 00. Open May-Oct. Tu-Su 10am-noon and 2-5pm; Oct.-Dec. and Mar.-Apr. Tu-Su 2-5pm; Jan.-Feb. Sa-Su 2-5pm. 4SFr, students 2SFr.)

LAKE NEUCHÂTEL

NORTHWESTERN SWITZERLAND

Covering the cantons of Basel (-Stadt and -Land), Solothurn, and Aargau, northwest Switzerland is gently beautiful. Its subtle charms include a rich Humanist tradition, excellent museums, and charming old town centers. It's a difficult region to avoid, since Basel is a major transportation hub for travel to and from Germany and France. Despite their proximity to France and French-speaking Switzerland, the cantons of northwestern Switzerland are German-speaking. Most towns have French variants of their names, but don't let that confuse you.

HIGHLIGHTS OF NORTHWEST SWITZERLAND

- After a whirlwind museum orgy in the afternoon, bar-hop in the **Basel** *Altstadt* until the wee morning hours (p. 497).
- Forget *Mardi Gras*—catch *Fasnacht* fever in **Basel** (p. 490).
- Stomp Ninja-style through Roman sewers in **Augusta Raurica** (p. 498).
- Guzzle *mai-tais* in "Honolulu" during **Solothurn's** topsy-turvy carnival. (p. 500).

BASEL (BÂLE)

Situated on the Rhine near France and Germany, Switzerland's third largest city is home to a large medieval quarter as well as one of the oldest universities in Switzerland—a school whose graduates include Erasmus of Rotterdam, Bernoulli, and Nietzsche. The kids keep Basel young, and the biggest party of them all, Basel's *Fasnacht*, rivals the French *Mardi Gras;* residents have a mad carnival before the onset of Lent. The murmur of the Rhine wending its way to Germany accompanies riverside walks. On the left bank, the *Münster* presides over the *Altstadt* in a towering conglomeration of red sandstone, stained glass, and sprouting spires. Farther along the river, the elegant St. Alban district houses 30 carefully assembled museums in its hilly streets. Basel takes great pride in its cultural heritage; as you wander the streets you'll encounter art from Roman times to the 20th century, serenaded by music students on every street corner.

▐ GETTING TO BASEL

The **Euroairport** (tel. 325 31 11; fax 325 25 77) serves continental Europe; most trans-continental flights are routed through Zurich, though there is a flight direct to **New York** (daily except W, 11:55am). There are several daily flights to Geneva and Zurich. Shuttle buses run passengers between the airport and the SBB train station (every 20-30min. 5am-midnight). The city has 3 **train stations:** the French SNCF station is next door to the Swiss SBB station in Centralbahnpl., and trains from Germany arrive at the DB station (Badische Bahnhof). City trams to the town center depart from the SBB (M-F every 5min., Sa-Su every 15min.). **Buses** to Swiss, French, and German cities depart from their respective train stations. Basel stands at the crossroads of Switzerland, France, and Germany. If **driving** from France, take A35, E25, or E60; from Germany, E35 or A5. From within Switzerland, take Rte. 2 north.

ⓘ ORIENTATION AND PRACTICAL INFORMATION

Basel sits in the northwest corner of Switzerland, so close to France that the *Tour de France* often traverses the city. Groß-Basel (Greater Basel), where most sights are located, lies on the left bank of the Rhine; Klein-Basel (Lesser Basel) occupies the right bank. Pick up a city map (0.50SFr) and other useful publications at either of the 2 tourist offices. To reach **Marktplatz** on foot from the SBB and SNCF stations, cross the Centralbahnpl., go left on Elisabethenanlage, right down Elisabethenstr., and left on Freie Str. (20min.) From the DB station, follow Rosentalstr. (which becomes Clarastr. and then Greifeng.) over the Mittlere Rheinbrücke and around to the left on Eiseng. (15min.).

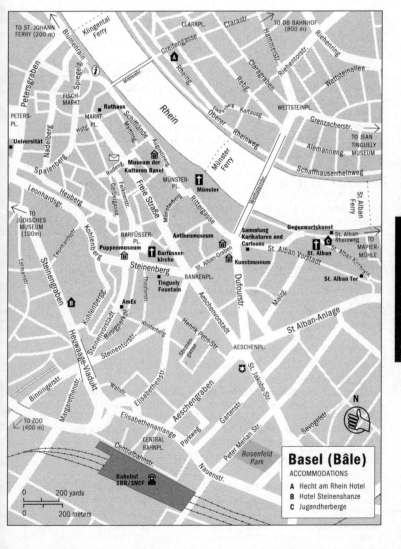

Basel (Bâle)

ACCOMMODATIONS

A Hecht am Rhein Hotel
B Hotel Steinenshanze
C Jugendherberge

N.W. SWITZERLAND

Trains: SNCF station (tel. 157 22 22), on Centralbahnpl. **SBB station** (tel. 157 22 22; 1.19SFr per min.), on Centralbahnpl. **DB station** (tel. 690 11 11), across the Rhine down Greifeng. To: **Zurich** (1hr., every 15-30min. 4:45am-midnight, 31SFr); **Geneva** (3hr., every hr. 4:41am-9:53pm, 72SFr); **Lausanne** (2½hr., every hr. 6:22am-9:22pm, 62SFr); **Bern** (1¼hr., every hr. 4:41am-midnight, 37SFr); **Salzburg** (via Zurich, 7hr., 5 per day, 5:51am-9:01pm, 228SFr); **Vienna** (via Zurich, 10-12hr., 5 per day, 5:51am-9:01pm, 290SFr); **Paris** (5-6hr., 10 per day, 5:53am-12:28am, 138SFr); **Munich** (via Stuttgart, 5¼hr., every hr. 7:05am-8:13pm, 204SFr); **Milan** (via Lucerne or Bern, 4½-6hr., every hr. 5:54am-10:13pm, 159SFr). Make international connections at the French (SNCF) or German (DB) stations. 25% discount on international trips for travelers age 16-25.

Ferries: 4 cable **ferries** cross the Rhine: the **Vogel Gryff** at Klingental; the **Leu** below the Münster terrace; the **Wild Maa** at St. Alban; and the **Ueli** at St. Johann. In summer, boats run 9am-7pm; in winter 11am-5pm. Rhine **cruises** depart from the *Schiffstation* (tel. 639 95 00) next to the tourist office (4 per day May-Oct. 13; station open M-F 9am-12:15pm and 1-7pm, Sa 11am-4pm, Su 8am-3pm). Enjoy "Samba Night" or one of the other special Rhine cruises (varying times and prices; check at the station). Round-trip to Rheinfelden 53SFr, to Waldhaus 27SFr. Tickets available 30min. before departure.

Public Transportation: Trams and buses run daily 6am-midnight. Most sights are within zone #10. 1-zone tickets 2.80SFr, day ticket 7.80SFr; ages 6-16 half-price. Automatic vendors at all stops sell tram tickets. Maps at tourist office or train station.

Taxis: In front of the train station, or call **MiniCab 33er,** tel. 271 11 11, **Taxi AG,** tel. 633 33 33, or **Taxi Central,** tel. 271 22 22.

Parking: Jelmoli, Rebg. 20; **Aeschen,** Aeschengraben 7; **Bahnhof SBB,** Güterstr. 2.50SFr per hr.

Bike Rental: At train stations. 26SFr per day, 16SFr per ½-day; mountain bikes 32SFr, 25SFr. Open M-Sa 7am-9pm.

Tourist Office: Basel Tourismus, Schifflände 5 (tel. 268 68 68; fax 268 68 70; email office@baseltourismus.ch, www.baseltourismus.ch). From the SBB station, take tram #1 to "Schifflände." The office is on the river, near the Mittlere Rheinbrücke. Lists of hotels, restaurants, museums, cultural events, and tours and excursions in Basel and the surrounding area. Open M-F 8:30am-6pm. A **bus tour** of the city leaves from the SBB station (May-Oct. at 10am, 20SFr). The **branch office** (tel. 271 36 84; fax 272 93 42; email hotel@messebasel.ch) at the SBB station also makes hotel reservations (10SFr). Open M-F 8:30am-7pm, Sa 8:30am-12:30pm and 1:30-6pm, Su 10am-2pm.

Currency Exchange: At any bank or the SBB station bureau (open 6am-9pm).

American Express: Reise Müller, Steinenvorstadt 33, CH-4002 (tel. 281 33 80). Take tram #1 to "Barfüsserpl."; the office is 1 block from the square. Checks cashed, mail held. Open M-F 9am-6:30pm, Sa 10am-4pm.

Luggage Storage: At all stations. Lockers 3-5SFr, 24hr. access. Storage 5SFr per day, open 6:30am-10pm.

Bookstores: Buchhandlung Bider und Tanner, Bankenpl., Aeschenvorstadt 2 (tel. 206 99 99; fax 206 99 90), is Basel's travel bookshop. Open M-W and F 8:15am-6:30pm, Th 8:15am-8pm, Sa 8:15am-5pm. **Jäggi Bücher,** Freie Str. 32 (tel. 261 52 00; fax 261 52 05), carries English-language paperbacks. Open M-F 9am-6:30pm, Sa 9am-5pm.

Emergencies: Police, tel. 117. **Medical,** tel. 144. **Hospital,** tel. 265 25 25.

Hotlines: Helping Hand, tel. 143. **Assistance For Young Women Travelling Alone,** tel. 271 37 23. Open M-F 8am-7:30pm, Sa 8am-1pm.

Bi-Gay-Lesbian Organizations: Arcados (gay center), Rheing. 69 (tel. 681 31 32; fax 681 66 56), at Clarapl. has oodles of information on bars, restaurants and hangouts. Open Tu-F 12-7pm, Sa 11am-4pm.

Internet Access: Internet Center, Steinenvorstadt 79 on Heuwaage (tel. 699 18 48; email centerbasel@datacomm.ch, www.datacomm.ch). From Barfüsserpl. follow Steinenvorstadt to the end. From train station, head left and follow signs for zoo and

Heuwaage. 5SFr per hr., 3SFr per 30min. Open M-W 9am-10pm, Th and Sa 9am-midnight, Su 4-10pm. Another branch is across the Rhine at Rebgasse 17 (email centerrebgasse@datacomm.ch). Open M-F 9am-7pm, Th 9am-8pm, Sa 10am-5pm.

Post Office: Rüdeng 1. Take tram #1 or 8 to "Marktpl." and walk 1 block back away from the river. Open M-F 7:30am-6:30pm, Sa 8am-noon. **Emergency Post:** To your right as you exit the station. Open M-F 6-7:30am and 6:30-10pm, Sa 6-8am and 11am-8pm, Su 9am-noon and 3-10pm. Only accepts packages, EMS, and priority mail. **Poste Restante address:** *Postlagernde Briefe*, Rüdengasse, CH-4001 Basel 1. **Postal Codes:** CH-4000 to CH-4051.

PHONE CODE	The **city code** for Basel is 061.

ACCOMMODATIONS AND CAMPING

Basel is an exciting town with an animated *Altstadt*, superb museums, and a raucous nightlife—don't miss it because you didn't call ahead. There is but one overpacked hostel and very few hotels remotely approaching budget status. Stop reading this sentence and make a reservation. Now. Trust us.

Jugendherberge (HI), St. Alban-Kirchrain 10 (tel. 272 05 72; fax 272 08 33). Take tram #2 to "Kunstmuseum" and turn right on St.-Alban-Vorstadt, then left at the church. Or walk 10-15min. from the SBB station down Aeschengraben to St. Alban Anlage. At the tower, follow the signs down the hill. Near a calm stretch of the river, this curious old building is a mecca for skyscraper-weary travelers. The efficient institutional setup has lockers for every bunk, wheelchair access, TV, phones, and a day-pass for public transportation. Dorms 28.60SFr; 2- or 3-bed rooms 39.60-49.60SFr, single occupancy 69.60-79.60SFr. Reduce by 2.50SFr Jan. 1-Feb. 19 and Nov.-Dec. Breakfast, showers, and sheets included. Dinner and lunch 11.50SFr. **Laundry** 7SFr. Reception 7-10am and 2pm-midnight. Check-out 7-10am. Reservations recommended. MC, Visa.

Hotel-Pension Steinenschanze, Steinengraben 69 (tel. 272 53 53; fax 272 45 73). From the SBB station, turn left on Centralbahnstr. and follow signs for Heuwaage (5min.) Under the large bridge, go up the ramp to Steinengraben and turn left. 3-star advantages abound: rooms with phone, radio, TV, private bathrooms, and balconies over the hotel garden or the street. Breakfast included. Singles 110-130SFr, under 25 with ISIC 60SFr; doubles with shower 160-190SFr, 100SFr. 3-night max. stay for students. Daytime luggage storage. 24hr. reception. AmEx, DC, MC, Visa.

Hecht am Rhein, Rheing. 8 (tel. 691 22 20; fax 681 07 88). Cross the Mittlere Rheinbrücke and turn right onto Rheing. Lone women may not feel comfortable in the neighborhood. Single 70SFr, with river view 80SFr; doubles with sink and telephone 120SFr, 130SFr. Breakfast and hall showers included. AmEx, DC, MC, Visa.

Camping: Camp Waldhort, Heideweg 16 (tel. 711 64 29), in Reinach. Take tram #11 to "Landhof." Backtrack 200m toward Basel, cross the main street, and follow the signs. Beautiful location far from Basel but in a residential area. Reception 7am-12:30pm and 2-10pm. 7SFr; tents 10SFr. Open Mar.-Oct.

FOOD

With all the students about, relatively cheap eateries are numerous. Barfüsserpl., Marktpl., and the streets connecting them are especially full of restaurants.

Zum Schnabel, Trillengässlein 2 (tel. 261 49 09). From Marktpl., walk one block on Hutg. (by EPA) to Spalenberg., then turn left onto Schnabelg. In this corner terrace, Italian-speaking servers present well-prepared German dishes. 12.80SFr buys bratwurst with caramelized onions, *Rösti*, and a salad. Pasta 12.80-19.80SFr. Open M-Th 8am-midnight, Sa-Su 8am-1am. AmEx, DC, MC, Visa.

Café XL, Steinenvorstadt 27 (tel. 281 10 88), between Barfüsserpl. and Heuwaage, has a creative variety of crepes (try "Boris Becker" with Nutella filling, 6.30SFr, or "Crêpe Bombay" with chicken curry, 9.50SFr) and salads. Fruit *Punsches* tempt the eye and wallet (hot green punch, mandarin with Curacao blue 8.50SFr). Open M-Th 9am-midnight, F-Sa 9am-2am, Su noon-11pm.

Hirscheneck, Lindenberg 23 (tel. 692 73 33). Cross Wettsteinbrücke and take the first left onto Kartansgasse. An unabashedly left-of-center restaurant-bar where dreadlocks, piercings, and the hammer and sickle prevail. Features at least 2 vegetarian and organically grown dishes every day. *Menü* 11.50-16.50SFr. Open M-Sa 2pm-midnight, Su 10am-midnight. Kitchen open M-Sa 6:30-10:30pm, Su 10am-4pm.

Café Barfi, Leonhardsberg 4 (tel. 261 70 38), to the right of Gerberg. from Marktpl. The turbaned proprietor serves up mostly Italian dishes with some surprises, like *samosas* (5.50SFr). Outdoor diners enjoy accordion serenades. Daily *Menü* 16.50-17.50SFr. Open M-Sa 10am-11pm. MC, Visa.

Topas Kosher Restaurant, Leimenstr. 24 (tel. 206 95 00), next to the Basel Synagogue and down the street from the Marcel Hess (the self-proclaimed "kosher sausage king") deli. *Menüs* from 14SFr. Open Su-Th 11:30am-2pm and 6:30-9pm, F 11:30am-2pm. Friday dinner and Saturday lunch by reservation only.

MARKETS

Migros, Steinenvorstadt, Clarapl. 17. Open M-W and F 8am-6:30pm, Th 8am-9pm, Sa 7:30am-5pm. At Bahnhof SBB. Open M-F 6am-10pm, Sa-Su 7:30am-10pm.

Co-op, on Centralbahnpl. across from the Schifflände station: "Steinenvorstadt." Open M-F 6am-10pm, Sa-Su 7:30am-10pm.

Public market, on Marktpl. Fresh fruits, vegetables, and baked goods every weekday morning. Open until 6:30pm on M, W, and F; Tu, Th, and Sa until 1:30pm.

◉⚠ SIGHTS AND HIKING

Basel's easy-to-use pedestrian tourist signs will help you negotiate your way around the city's curving, interlacing streets. Marktpl., which sits near the river at the culminating point of Freie Str. and other major shopping avenues, is the center of the *Altstadt* (old town).

THE OLD TOWN. The very red **Rathaus,** erected in the early 1500s to celebrate Basel's entry into the Confederation, brightens Marktpl. with its blinding facade adorned with gold and green statues. In an attempt to gain influence in state affairs, Basel's then-powerful guilds locked the government inside the *Rathaus* in 1691. While the politicians starved inside, guild members partied outdoors, feasting on ale and sweets in an uprising later dubbed the "Cookie Rebellion." *(Guided tours Tu 3-4pm; meet in the courtyard. 10SFr, children 5SFr.)* Behind the Marktpl., tread softly on the **Mittlere Rheinbrücke,** which is 775 years old. Built in 1225, the bridge connects Groß-Basel to Klein-Basel. A block away from Marktpl. in the heart of the *Altstadt*, a colorful Gothic fountain livens up the **Fischmarkt.** Leading off of Fischmarkt, the tiny **Elftausendjungfern-Gässlein** (Lane of 11,000 Virgins) is famous for St. Ursula's pilgrimage of girls to the Holy Land during the Children's Crusade. The medieval practice of gaining indulgences by walking this lane is now defunct, but people still stagger through after overindulging at nearby bars.

CATHEDRAL. Behind Marktpl. along the Rhein, the **Münster,** Basel's medieval treasure, stands on the site of an ancient Celtic settlement and a Roman fort. The red sandstone facade features hundreds of figures in various acts of piety ranging from trumpet-playing to dragon-slaying. Behind the altar, gilt Latin inscriptions memorialize the life of Erasmus, the renowned scholar and staunch Catholic who remained loyal to his faith even after his beloved Basel joined the Reformation in 1529. When he died, the city set aside dogma to give him a proper Catholic burial in its Protestant cathedral. Bernoulli, the mathematician who discovered the math

LIZARD LUNACY In 1529, Basel's residents enthusiastically joined the Reformation and threw out the bishop, but they kept his *crozier* (staff) as the town's emblem. The staff shares this honor with the basilisk (Basel-isk), a creature part bat, part dragon, and part rooster, which spawned what may have been the world's first and only public trial and execution of a chicken. In 1474, a hen allegedly laid an egg on a dung heap under a full moon, an action sure to hatch the horrible creature. The bird was tried, found guilty, and beheaded, and the egg was ceremonially burnt.

behind the spiral and laws concerning flight, also rests in the cloister. The **tower** provides the city's best view of the Rhine, Klein-Basel, and Black Forest tower. *(Open in summer M-F 10am-5pm, Sa 10am-4pm; in winter M-Sa 11am-4pm, Su 2-4pm. Free. Tower closes 30min. before the church. 3SFr. Due to recent suicides, you can't go up alone.)*

UNIVERSITY QUARTER. Head down one of the tiny alleys off Fischmarkt to reach Petersgraben, which leads to the Peterspl. and the University quarter. The **University of Basel,** founded in 1406, is Switzerland's oldest university. Its library houses rare volumes from Erasmus, Luther, and Zwingli. The grounds are ideal for picnicking, napping, or reading Kant. Bargain-hunters flock here every Saturday morning for the **flea market,** which starts at 9am and goes until early afternoon. Around the corner from the university library, the 700-year-old **Spalentor** (gate tower), one of the original city wall's 3 remaining towers and one of the most impressive gates in Switzerland, marks the edge of the *Altstadt.*

ST. ALBAN DISTRICT. A stroll down the Rhein from the *Münster* or down Freie Str. from Marktpl. brings you to the **St. Alban district,** home of many established Basel families, where a refined, pastel-and-eggshell theme dominates the architecture. St.-Alban-Vorstadt leads up to **St. Alban-Tor,** another of the old city gates.

TINGUELY FOUNTAIN. For a contrasting aesthetic, walk from Marktpl. toward Barfüsserpl. onto Theaterpl., where the spectacular **Jean Tinguely Fountain,** also known as the **Fasnachtsbrunnen,** captures a moment of modern chaos as iron sculptures parodying human foibles spew water.

ZOO. The **Zoologischer Garten,** one of the best zoos in Europe, is a 10-minute walk down Steinenvorstadt from Barfüsserpl.; follow signs along the wooden path, or take tram #1 or 8 to "Zoo Bachletten." The zoo is famous for successfully breeding several endangered species, and the gardens are as much of an attraction as the animals. Restaurants, picnic areas, and ice cream vendors abound. *(Binningerstr. 40. Tel. 295 35 35, fax 281 00 05, www.zoobasel.ch. Open daily May-Aug. 8am-6:30pm; Sept.-Oct. and Mar.-Apr. 8am-6pm; Nov.-Feb. 8am-5:30pm. 12SFr, students 10SFr.)*

HIKING. 1200km of yellow *Wanderweg* marked trails crisscross the countryside around Basel. Take Bus #70 to "Reigoldswil" to take the **Gondelbahn** to the Jura mountain peak "Wasserfallen" (937m) and hike through the woods nearby. (Wasserfallen-Waldenburg 2½-3hr.; Wasserfallen-Jägerwegli 1½-2hr.).

▥ MUSEUMS

Basel's 30 museums may seem overwhelming, but they warrant more than a casual glance. The **Kunstmuseum** is deservedly the most famous, but many esoteric galleries are also fascinating. Subjects range from medieval medicine to mechanized mannequins. Pick up the comprehensive museum guide at the tourist office, or visit Basel's website, www.unibas.ch/museum. A **Swiss Museum Pass,** valid for one month (all over Switzerland at participating museums) costs 30SFr.

ART MUSEUMS. Basel is home to several world-class art museums. The ◪**Fondation Beyeler,** one of Europe's finest private art collections, radiates excellence in the quality of its pieces. African statues are placed alongside exotic works by

POISON VERT Though the Swiss drinking age is only 16, and beer is cheaper than Coca-Cola, there is one guilty pleasure the Swiss no longer enjoy. *Absinthe*, a potent anise-flavored liquor, has been banned in the country since 1912. Absinthe is the product of 5 herbs (Wermmtkraut, Melisse, Fenchelsamen, Anis, and Stem-Anis) which are combined with alcohol, fermented, and heated. A French doctor first brought the elixir to Switzerland for medicinal use; when he died, the recipe he left with his housekeeper gained popularity as an *aperitif*, reaching its prime in the late 19th century. The liquor, dubbed *le poison vert* ("the green poison"), was a bit too potent, perhaps—it was blamed for hallucinations, epileptic incidents, and poisonings. In the infamous 1905 Commugny murders, an allegedly absinthe-induced stupor drove a man to kill his wife and children. Soon after, absinthe was banned for consumption in Switzerland and France. A weaker derivative, *Ricard*, is served in restaurants; for the real deal, head to England.

Rousseau and Matisse, and an outdoor lily-pond is a window-pane away from being a Monet masterpiece. *(Baselstr. 101, Riehen. Take tram #6 to "Riehendorf" then walk straight for 5min. Tel. 645 97 00. Open 10am-6pm, W 10am-8pm. 12SFr, students 9SFr.)*

Equally impressive on a larger scale is Basel's ■**Kunstmuseum** (Museum of Fine Arts). In 1661, the culturally-minded city started the first independent public gallery in Switzerland. A formidable slab and marble structure, the *Kunstmuseum* houses extensive, outstanding compilations of old and new masters. The Picasso collection was acquired when a resoundingly affirmative electoral referendum persuaded the city government to grant the museum money to buy two. Touched by such enthusiasm, the artist himself donated 4 more. *(St. Alban-Graben 16. Accessible by tram #2. Tel. 206 62 62; fax 206 62 52. Tu-Su 10am-5pm. Combined ticket with Museum für Gegenwartskunst 7SFr, students 5SFr. Special exhibition rates. Free first Su of every month.)*

Most of Basel's really modern art is found at the ■**Museum für Gegenwartskunst** (Museum of Contemporary Art), between the youth hostel and the Rhine. Browse the thoughtfully arranged collections, including important pieces by Calder, Johns, Warhol, Lichtenstein, and Pollock, and video art by Gary Hill, Bill Viola, and Matthew Barney. *(St. Alban-Rheinweg 60. Tel. 272 81 83; fax 272 80 62. Open Tu-Su 11am-5pm. Combined ticket with Kunstmuseum 7SFr, students 5SFr. Special exhibition rates. Free first Su of every month.)*

The upper 2 floors of the **Antikenmuseum** (Museum of Ancient Art) are crammed with boring vases, but the Egyptian and Etruscan busts, glassware, and sarcophagi on the lower floors are worth your while. *(St. Alban-Graben 5. Tel. 271 22 02; fax 272 18 61. Open Tu-Su 10am-5pm. 5SFr, students 3SFr. Free first Su of every month.)*

PAPER MILL. A quick float down the river past the hostel brings you to the **Papiermühle,** a restored medieval mill with a noisy water wheel which continues to mash rags so that visitors can make their own paper. Try writing with a quill or typesetting a souvenir. The main exhibit is a fun, well-presented love-letter to the written (or printed) word, from the Rosetta Stone to the Gutenberg press. *(St. Alban-Tal 37. Tel. 272 96 52; fax 272 09 93. Open Tu-Su 2-5pm. 9SFr, students 6SFr. Family ticket 22SFr.)*

MUSEUM JEAN TINGUELY. Everything rattles and shakes in this intriguing homage to the Swiss sculptor's vision of metal and movement. The alarming "le Ballet des Pauvres" is a fury of twisting skeletal figures. *(Grenzacherstr. 210. Take tram #2 or 15 to "Wettsteinpl." and bus #31 to "Museum Tinguely." Tel 681 93 20; fax 681 93 21. Open W-Su 11am-7pm. 7SFr, students 5SFr.)*

ETHNOLOGY AND NATURAL HISTORY MUSEUMS. A mansion topped by Neoclassical friezes houses the **Museum der Kulturen Basel,** and its excellent collection of non-Western art. In the same building, the **Naturhistorisches Museum** has engaging exhibits of woolly mammoths and inventive displays of model animals against their own skeletal mirror images. *(Augusting. 2. Tel. 266 55 00; fax 266 56 05. Both muse-*

ums open Tu-Su 10am-5pm. 6SFr, under 13 4SFr. Special rates for temporary exhibitions. Free first Su of every month.)

CARTOON AND CARICATURE COLLECTION. The German sketches in the **Sammlung Karikaturen and Cartoons** possess a universally expressive wit, plus inclusions from the 20th-century funnies like *Peanuts* and *Calvin and Hobbes.* (St. Alban-Vorstadt 28. Tel. 271 13 36; fax 274 03 36. Open W and Sa 2-5:30pm, Su 10am-5:30pm. 6SFr, students 3SFr.)

HISTORICAL MUSEUM. The **Barfüsserkirche** collection includes stained glass windows emblazoned with cantonal coats-of-arms, stunning iconography, and the oldest *crozier* city banner. The interior is an old church with pink stone columns and huge windows veiled in transparent linen. Downstairs, re-created rooms showcase medieval and Renaissance furnishings. *(Steinenberg 4, on Barfüsserpl.. Tel. 271 05 05; fax 271 05 42. Open M and W-Su 10am-5pm. 5SFr, students 3SFr, free on the 1st of the month.)*

OTHER MUSEUMS. The **Jüdisches Museum der Schweiz (Jewish Museum of Switzerland)** contains small, well-organized exhibits on the law, the Jewish year, and Jewish life. *(Kornhausg. 8. Take bus #37 to "Lyss." Tel. 261 95 14. Open M and W 2-5pm, Su 11am-5pm. Free.)* The **Puppenmuseum (Toy Museum) Basel** holds 4 floors of toys, densely packed into dark display cases. *(Steinenvorstadt 1. Tel. 225 95 95; fax 225 95 96. Open M-W and F-Su 11am-5pm, Th 11am-8pm. 7SFr, students 5SFr, under 16 free.)*

♫ ENTERTAINMENT AND NIGHTLIFE

CARNIVAL. In a year-round party town, Basel's carnival, or **Fasnacht**, still manages to distinguish itself as fun fun fun. The festivities commence the Monday before Lent with the *Morgestraich*, a not-to-be-missed 4am parade over 600 years in the running, and end precisely 72 hours later (March 13-15 in 2000). Fife and drum music plays to revelers in brilliant masks that lampoon the year's local scandals. The goal is to scare away winter (it rarely succeeds). The tourist office provides lists in English of Basel's other cultural offerings, including concerts, plays, ballets, gallery exhibits, fairs, and other happenings.

BARS AND NIGHTCLUBS. A university town through and through, Basel's nightlife reflects the influence of student patrons. Start bar-hopping at **Barfüsserplatz,** where students sit at outdoor tables and drink wine on the steps of the Barfüsserkirche. The two most popular local beers are **Warwick** and **Cardinal.** When the bars close, kids in black often head for after-hours clubs. Most places have a 21 and older policy, but the crowds get younger on weekends.

Atlantis, Klosterburg 13. From Bankenpl., it's off Elisabethenstr. to the right. Big. Hot. Smoky. Loud. Raucous. This multi-level, sophisticated bar sways to reggae, jazz, and funk. Bands play every night the Italian soccer team does not. Concerts 10-23SFr. Open M-Th 11am-2am, F 11am-4am, Sa 5pm-4am (kitchen open 11am-2pm and 6pm-2am).

Brauerei Fischerstube, Rheing. 45 (tel. 692 66 35). Cross Mittlere Rheinbrücke and take the 1st right. This old-school *Biergarten* is adjacent to Basel's only brewery, crafting 4 of the best beers in town. The delectably sharp *Hell Spezial* goes well with the homemade pretzels. *Bier* 2.50SFr-5.90SFr. Open M-Th 10am-midnight, F-Sa 10am-1am, Su 5pm-midnight. MC, Visa.

Caveau Mövenpick Wine Pub, Grünpfahlg. 4 (tel. 261 22 12), across Gerberg. from the post office, has a fine regional wine selection, particularly Alsatian. 4.90-10SFr. Open M-Sa 11am-midnight.

Babalabar, Gerberg. 74 (tel. 261 48 49), to the left off Gerberg. from Barfüsserpl., is a dark, modern dance club for the beautiful people. Go for techno nights or samba rhythms from the Latin-crazy DJ. Cover Su-Th 5SFr, F-Sa 10SFr. Open in summer M 9pm-2am, Tu-Su 10pm-morning.

Fifty-fifty, Leonardsburg 1 (tel. 261 33 22), next to Babalabar. 50s Americana on the walls; wine, beer, and "energy drinks" for under 5SFr. Beers 3.80SFr; after 10:30pm, 5SFr. "Gourmet" burgers 14-19SFr, buffalo wings with blue cheese dip (30 pieces) 35SFr. Open W-Th 6:30pm-1:30am, F-Sa 6:30pm-3:30am. Strict 21+ policy.

Dupf, Rebg. 43 (tel. 692 00 11). Cross Weitsteinbr. and turn left onto Rebg. This chic, well-coiffed gay and lesbian bar welcomes a mixed crowd. Beers from 3.80SFr. It sponsors a "Travestaile" (a very popular song) in November. Open daily 5pm-whenever.

Elle et Lui, Rebg. 39 (tel. 691 54 79). Dupf's younger, bohemian next-door neighbor, Elle et Lui caters to gay and lesbian clientele of all ages and tastes. Open 4pm-morning, summer 6pm-morning.

Pickwick Pub, Steinenvorstadt 13 (tel. 281 86 87), near Barfüsserpl. This English-style pub, draped in football memorabilia, hosts a salt-of-the-earth crowd of students and adults alike. Bartenders are happy to go the extra mile. Beers from 3.80SFr. Open Su-W 11am-midnight, Th 11am-1am, F-Sa 11am-3am.

Willi's Café, Gerbgässlein 2 (tel. 261 98 30) has the cheapest beer in town. From Barfüsserpl., turn left off Gerber. at Fricker's department store, then head right. Off-duty businessmen chug amidst American paraphernalia and lots of chrome. Beers from 3.50SFr. Live DJ F-Sa. Open Tu-Sa 4:30pm-midnight.

NEAR BASEL: AUGUSTA RAURICA

To get to the ruins from Basel, take the hourly regional train (dir.: Laufenberg) 3 stops to "Kaiseraugst" (15min., 4.80SFr). A ferry (tel. 639 95 00) runs from Schifflände, by the Basel tourist office, to Kaiseraugst (2hr., 4 per day, May 1-Oct. 17, 19.20SFr, round-trip 35SFr, ages 6-16 ½-price).

The twin towns of **Kaiseraugst** and **Augst** will take you farther back than medieval Basel. Founded in 43 BC, **Augusta Raurica,** the oldest Roman colony on the Rhine, grew into an opulent trading center by the 2nd century. After destruction at the hands of the Alemanni in the late 3rd century, the Romans built an adjacent fortress. Ongoing excavations continue to uncover temples, baths, and workshops. Most of the attractions are in Augst, clustered around the small **Roman Museum** (tel. 816 22 22; fax 816 22 61), a 10-minute walk from the station. Plenty of signs point the way. Though its exhibit on Roman gastronomy (featuring a continuous video of 2 people eating) has a mesmerizing juvenile appeal, more entertaining is a ramble through the fields to the **Roman Farm Animal Park,** where bullying pigs and selfish donkeys butt heads. (Sites and museum open Mar.-Oct. M 1-5pm, Tu-Su 10am-5pm; Nov.-Feb. Tu-Su 10am-noon and 1:30-5pm. Museum 5SFr, students 3SFr; parks free.) You can also stomp through sewers Ninja-style in the cold, dark, damp **Roman cellars** and **sewers** dating from 43 BC.

SOLOTHURN

Sandwiched snugly between the Jura Mountains and the Aare River, Solothurn compactly captures the best of Switzerland in its enchanting *Altstadt.* The city's charm rubs off on its inhabitants—the friendliness of shopkeepers and restauranteurs is palpable. Annual film, classical music, and literature festivals attest to the town's love affair with culture; citizens of Solothurn unleash their rambunctious side during their rowdy Winter Carnival. Rounding out the Solothurn experience, the Jura mountains offer endless biking and hiking prospects.

⊠ ORIENTATION AND PRACTICAL INFORMATION. Trains leave Solothurn for **Basel** (1hr., every hr. 5:39am-11:14pm, 25SFr), **Neuchâtel** (45min., every hr. 5:42am-11:13pm, 18SFr), and **Bern** (40min., every 30min. 5:18am-11:20pm, 13SFr). For hiking tips, a map, or free room reservations, head to the **tourist office,** Hauptg. 69 (tel. 626 46 46; fax 626 46 47; email info@stadt-solothurn.ch; www.stadt-solothurn.ch).

From the train station, walk through the underpass toward the *Zentrum* and follow Hauptbahnhofstr. across Kreuzackerbrücke up Kroneng. The office is left of the cathedral. (Open M-F 8:30am-noon and 1:30-6pm, Sa 9am-noon.) **Exchange currency** or **rent bikes** (26SFr per day, mountain bike 32SFr per day) at the **train station** (both open 5am-8:50pm). For **taxis,** dial 622 66 66 or dial 622 22 22. **Lockers** (3-5SFr, 24hr.) and **luggage storage** (5SFr; 5am-8:30pm) are at the station, as is an Aperto **supermarket** (open 6am-10pm). For the **police,** dial 117; in case of **fire,** dial 118; for the **hospital,** dial 627 31 21. For the **post office,** go past the hostel on Postpl., turn left off Kreuzackerbrücke, and onto Landhausquai (tel. 625 29 29; open M-F 7:30am-6pm, Sa 8-11am). The **postal code** is CH-4500.

PHONE CODE	The **city code** for Solothurn is 032.

◾▦ ACCOMMODATIONS AND FOOD. Overlooking the Aare river on the edge of the *Altstadt*, the **Jugendherberge "Am Land" (HI),** Landhausquai 23 (tel. 623 17 06; fax 623 16 39), is a slick, high-tech vision of glass and steel incongruously framed by the exterior of a 1642 schoolhouse. From the train station, walk over Kreuzackerbrücke and take the first left onto Landhausquai. Picture windows overlooking the river and chrome track lighting keep the place well lit day and night. Amenities include a pool table, roof terrace, music room, and conference room. (Dorms 26.50SFr, with sink 29SFr. Doubles 47SFr. Triples with shower 37SFr per person. Breakfast and sheets included. Non-members add 5SFr. Lunch and dinner 11.50SFr. Reception 7:30-10am and 4:30-10:30pm.) The **Hotel Kreuz,** Kreuzg. 4 (tel. 622 20 20; fax 621 52 32), offers more privacy but less sparkly newness. Go left off Kreuzackerbrücke before the hostel. (Spartan singles 48-58SFr; doubles 82-87SFr. Prices drop for multiple nights. Breakfast and hall showers included. Reception M-Th 9am-11:30pm, F 9am-12:30am, Sa-Su 2-11:30pm.)

In the *Altstadt*, sounds of chatter and clinking silverware from the numerous affordable cafés and restaurants waft through the air. The **Taverna Amphorea,** Hauptg. 51 (tel. 623 67 63), down the street from the tourist office towards Marktpl., exudes a Mediterranean sense of relaxation while dishing up large portions of vegetarian-friendly Greek and Middle Eastern specialties for under 20SFr (open Tu and Th 11am-11:30pm, W 9am-11:30pm, F 11am-12:30am, Sa 9am-12:30am). From Marktpl., turn left on Hauptg., then left on Stalden to find the **Sandwich House,** Stalden 9 (tel./fax 623 33 78), which puts a techno twist on the friendly neighborhood deli. Survey an astounding array of edible things to put between two halves of a fresh roll, made to order for 4.50-16SFr. (Open M-W and F 8:30am-6:30pm, Th 8:30am-9pm, Sa 11am-5pm, Su 1:30-5:30pm.) The **Café Bar Landhaus,** (tel. 621 62 11; fax 621 52 32) on Landhausquai next to Hotel Kreuz, is trendy in a friendly, laid-back way. Well-balanced *Menüs* 14-18SFr, vegetarian options aplenty. Beer 3.80-6SFr. (Open M 6:30am-2pm, Tu-Th 6:30am-2pm and 5pm-2am, F 6:30am-2pm and 5pm-3am, Sa 8am-3pm, Su 10am-6pm.) Stock up on foodstuffs at the **Manora** grocery store/restaurant on Gurzelng. to the left off Marktpl. (open M-W and F 9am-6:30pm, Th 9am-9pm, Sa 8am-5pm), or try the **farmer's market** at Marktpl. (W and Sa 8am-noon). **Co-op** and **Migros** are outside old city walls behind the post office (both open M-W and F 8am-6:30pm, Th 8am-9pm, Sa 7:30am-5pm).

▣ ▥ SIGHTS AND MUSEUMS. Solothurn's well-preserved Baroque architecture is enough to justify a visit to the city, but several interesting museums augment the visual menu, as does the **Red Tower** on the Marktpl., which sports several clock faces and a macabre little skeleton.

CATHEDRAL. Built in 1762-73 by a Ticino architect, the cheerful Italianate architecture of the **Kathedrale St. Ursen** (Cathedral of St. Ursus) greets visitors with bubbling fountains as they cross the Kreuzackerbrücke. The cathedral, frothily adorned with ornate golden sunbursts, is dedicated to St. Ursus, the patron saint of Solothurn who lost his head here during Roman times for refusing to worship Roman gods. Its **tower** provides the *Altstadt's* best view. *(Church open 8am-noon and 2-7pm. Oct.-Easter closes at 6pm. Tower 2.50SFr.)*

SCIENCE MUSEUM. The **Naturmuseum** presents entertaining hands-on exhibits on everything scientific. Examine a butterfly wing at high magnification and experiment with the human muscular system—and don't forget to bring the kids. *(Klosterpl. 2, within the town walls to your right as you cross Kreuzackerbrücke. Tel. 622 70 21. Open Tu-W and F-Sa 2-5pm, Th 2-9pm, Su 10am-noon and 2-5pm. Free.)*

MILITARY MUSEUM. For anyone who played with little toy soldiers, the **Museum Altes Zeughaus** blows them up to their full size. Housed in an arsenal that dates back to 1609, the museum holds row after row of gory instruments of death, from medieval daggers and suits of armor to WWII artillery. *(Zeughauspl. 1, to the left of the cathedral. Tel. 623 35 28. Open May-Oct. Tu-Su 10am-noon and 2-5pm; Nov.-Apr. Tu-F 2-5pm, Sa-Su 10am-noon and 2-5pm. 6SFr, students 4SFr.)*

ART MUSEUM. On the fringes of town, the staid **Kunstmuseum** houses an extensive collection of post-1850 Swiss works and lesser-known Impressionist and Romantic paintings. The temporary exhibits (recently, elegantly stoic Indonesian statues) tend to be more stimulating than the permanent collection. *(Werkhofstr. 30. Tel. 622 23 07. Open M-W and F-Sa 10am-noon and 2-5pm, Th 10am-noon and 2-9pm, Su 10am-5pm. Free, but it is worth a donation to see the Jean Tinguely collection box in action.)*

CASTLE. Schloß Waldegg is surrounded by wheat fields and tree-lined walks that contrast nicely with the ruler-perfect formal French gardens. The panorama of the Jura mountains outside the castle is more enjoyable than the museum inside, which can't decide whether to preserve the neoclassical decor or present it to visitors. *(Take bus #4 to "St. Niklaus" and walk 10min. up Riedholzstr. Open Apr. 15-Oct. 31 Tu-Th, Sa 2-7pm, Su 10am-noon and 2-5pm; Nov.-Apr. 14 Sa-Su 10am-noon and 2-5pm. Wheelchair accessible. Parking available. 6SFr, students 4SFr.)*

⚑ OUTDOOR ACTIVITIES. The Jura mountains over Solothurn encourage fans of Mother Nature to get up close and personal. Marked **hiking** and **biking** trails lead through the Jura to nearby Altreu (2hr.), where the oldest and best-known stork colony in Switzerland rests and poops. The trek to the **Weissenstein Alpine Center** is more challenging and rewarding. (Hike 2hr. Trail head at the corner of Wengisteinstr. and Verenawegstr.; follow the yellow signs to Weissenstein.) Take the chairlift (13SFr, students 6.50SFr) down from Weissenstein and hop on a train (4.40SFr) in Oberdorf to return. **Boat tours** leave Solothurn for Biel and from there to Murten or Neuchâtel. (2½hr., 26SFr, round-trip 45SFr. Free with SwissPass.) In the winter, **cross-country skiing** dominates the athletic scene. Weissenstein (1280m) has 7km of trails and chairlifts for downhill skiing on 2 small slopes best suited to beginners.

🎵 ENTERTAINMENT AND NIGHTLIFE. Various **festivals** enliven Solothurn several times a year. In 2000, the **Swiss Film Festival** will bring celluloid lovers to the city January 18-23. On March 2 in 2000, the **Chesslete**—festivities intended to drive away winter—marks the beginning of the week-long topsy-turvy Carnival. The festivities include fantastical masks, raucous *Guggenmusik*, and re-naming the town "Honolulu," since that tropical city is exactly on the other side of the world from Solothurn. Swiss writers gather to read, drink, and sit on panels during the annual **literature festival** (June 2-4 in 2000). When the jazz festival winds down in nearby Montreux, in Solothurn fans of classical music and opera find their party just beginning with the arrival of the **Classic: Open Air Fest** (July 7-22 in 2000.)

Nightlife in Solothurn does not exist outside of the Thursday-Saturday window. Hipsters can find each other on weekends for live rock and funk at the **Creep Club**, Dammstr. 59 (tel. 621 20 60; www.solnet.ch/creep). Continue down the river past the post office and turn right on Dammstr. For dance music there's **Kofmehl Fabrik**, Gibelinstr. (tel. 623 50 60), on the outskirts of town. From Creep Club, go to the end of Dammstr., turn left on Segelzstr., and right on Gibelinstr. Amidst fields and cows, this former metal factory is decked out in trippy graffiti. Kofmehl holds occasional movie nights. **Löwen,** Löweng. 15 (tel. 622 50 55), a block behind the hostel, serves up good beer, cheap Italian food (pasta and pizza for under 16SFr), and a mix of world music (funk, jazz, reggae) to a mixed local crowd (open M 11am-2pm and 6-11:30pm, W-F 11am-2pm and 6pm-12:30am, Sa 6pm-12:30am, Su 6pm-11:30pm). A few doors down from Taverna Amphorea in the old town, **The Cinema Palace,** Hauptg. 57 (tel. 622 25 15), shows recently released, subtitled American films (13-15SFr).

APPENDIX

HOLIDAYS AND FESTIVALS

The *International Herald-Tribune* lists national holidays in each daily edition. If you plan your itinerary around these dates, you can encounter the festivals that entice you and circumvent the crowds visiting the ones that don't. This information is also valuable when determining when to arrive where—many services shut down on holidays and could leave you strapped for food and money in the event of an ill-timed arrival. Note also that in Austria, the first Saturday of every month is *Langer Samstag* (long Saturday); most stores stay open until 5pm. In small towns, stores are often closed from noon Saturday until 8am Monday—important to remember when stocking up on food for weekends. Check the individual town listings and the index for information on the festivals below.

AUSTRIA

DATE	FESTIVAL	REGION
January 6	Epiphany	National
January	Hahnenkamm World Cup Ski Races	Kitzbühel
February 1-16	Fasching (Carnival)	Regional
April 21-24	Easter	National
May 1	Labor Day	National
Mid-May to Mid-June	Wiener Festwochen	Vienna
June 1	Ascension Day	National
June 12	Whit Monday	National
June 22	Corpus Christi Day	National
June 6-7	Procession of Samson	Tamsweg
End of July	Salzburg Festival	Salzburg
Late July to Mid-August	Music Festival	Bregenz
Late July to Late August	Salzburg Music Festival	Salzburg
August 1	Folklore fair	Villach
August 3-4	Fröhlichgasse	Graz
August 14	Eve of the First Feast of the Assumption	Wörther See
August 15	Feast of the Assumption	National
October 26	Flag Day	National
November 1	All Saints' Day	National
November 11	St. Martin's Day	Regional
November 29	Kathreinsonntag	Regional
December 8	Feast of the Immaculate Conception	National

SWITZERLAND

DATE	FESTIVAL	REGION
March 1-3	Fasnacht (Carnival)	Basel
April 21-24	Easter	National
April 22-29	European Watch, Clock, and Jewelry Fair	Basel
May	International Jazz Festival	Bern
May 1	Labor Day	Regional
June 1	Ascension	National

June 12	Whit Monday	National
June	International June Festival: classical music, theater, art	Zurich
June 22	Corpus Christi	National
June 15-20	International 20th-century Art Festival	Basel
July 2-17	International Jazz Festival	Montreux
August 1	Swiss National Day	National
August 24-27	Folklore Festival	Fribourg
September 12-13	Knabenschiessen	Zurich
October 22-November 6	Autumn Fair	Basel
November 21	Traditional Onion Market	Bern
December 11-12	Escalade (Historic Festival)	Geneva

MEASUREMENTS

Austria and Switzerland use the metric system. Conversions are provided below for our American readers. Unconventional local units for measuring wine or beer are explained in the text when necessary. Note that gallons in the U.S. are not identical to those across the Atlantic; one U.S. gallon equals 0.83 Imperial gallons.

MEASUREMENT CONVERSIONS

1 inch (in.) = 25.4 millimeters (mm)	1 millimeter (mm) = 0.039 in.
1 foot (ft.) = 0.30 m	1 meter (m) = 3.28 ft.
1 yard (yd.) = 0.914m	1 meter (m) = 1.09 yd.
1 mile = 1.61km	1 kilometer (km) = 0.62 mi.
1 ounce (oz.) = 28.35g	1 gram (g) = 0.035 oz.
1 pound (lb.) = 0.454kg	1 kilogram (kg) = 2.202 lb.
1 fluid ounce (fl. oz.) = 29.57ml	1 milliliter (ml) = 0.034 fl. oz.
1 gallon (gal.) = 3.785L	1 liter (L) = 0.264 gal.
1 acre (ac.) = 0.405ha	1 hectare (ha) = 2.47 ac.
1 square mile (sq. mi.) = 2.59km^2	1 square kilometer (km^2) = 0.386 sq. mi.

DISTANCE (IN KM)

To convert from kilometers to miles, multiply the distance by 0.625. From miles to kilometers, muliply by 1.6. Distances may vary depending on the type of transportation used and the route traveled. In certain cases, traveling through a neighboring country such as Germany or Italy can be the fastest route.

	Basel	Bern	Geneva	Graz	Innsbruck	Interlaken	Linz	Locarno	Lugano	Salzburg	Vienna	Zermatt
Bern	71											
Geneva	187	129										
Graz	597	610	718									
Innsbruck	290	303	418	307								
Interlaken	98	43	230	581	278							
Linz	509	536	658	158	245	517						
Locarno	180	135	204	520	235	92	478					
Lugano	201	158	219	512	233	114	476	21				
Salzburg	410	433	554	200	137	412	108	370	369			
Vienna	658	684	801	138	383	661	151	615	608	249		
Zermatt	169	105	126	602	311	72	555	82	95	447	694	
Zurich	76	98	224	525	216	92	443	135	153	102	591	159

APPENDIX

CITY PHONE CODES

CITY TELEPHONE CODES			
Basel	061	Linz	0732
Bern	031	Lucerne	041
Bregenz	05574	Interlaken	036
Geneva	022	Innsbruck	0512
Graz	0316	Lugano	091
Linz	0732	Salzburg	0662
Innsbruck	0512	Vienna	01
Lausanne	021	Zermatt	027
Liechtenstein	075	Zurich	01

LANGUAGE

Confronted with Switzerland's four official languages and the countless dialects of German spoken throughout Austria and Switzerland, many travelers feel somewhat intimidated by the thought of communicating. German in particular is perceived as a difficult language by many English speakers, perhaps because of the three genders, four cases, and five ways of saying "the." Yet all of these rules make German a crossword puzzle just waiting to be figured out. The fact of the matter is that a little language training goes a long way. Once you know the basic question words and a few verbs, you can ask nearly any question. Each of the following phrasebooks is designed to help you master your most urgent communicative needs in each of the major languages spoken in Austria and Switzerland. Each phrasebook is preceded by a pronunciation guide. Don't be afraid to attempt to use the phrases listed; with a little practice, they'll roll off your tongue.

The first, perhaps most helpful phrase a traveler should learn is "Sprechen Sie Englisch?," "Parlez-vous anglais?," or "Lei parla inglese?" (for use in the appropriate regions). Even if the person you ask doesn't speak English, he/she will appreciate your attempt to speak their language. Fortunately, most younger Austrian and Swiss urbanites speak at least a smattering of English—usually much more— thanks to the establishment of English as a requirement for high school diplomas. Outside of cities and among older residents, however, the English proficiency becomes less reliable and you may have to rely on phrasebooks or an impromptu translation by the local tourist office.

If you're unsure in a foreign vocabulary, it's best to err on the side of formality. For example, it never hurts to use phrases like *Herr* (Mr.) or *Frau* (Mrs.), the Italian terms *Signore* and *Signora*, or the French equivalents *Monsieur* and *Madame* (Mrs.). *Fräulein*, on the other hand, is a loaded word and should be avoided by shakier German speakers, since it sometimes carries class connotations. When in doubt, use the formal pronoun (*Sie* in German, *Vous* in French, *Lei* in Italian) with the plural form of the verb. People will let you know when it's time to switch to more familiar language.

GERMAN PRONUNCIATION

Once you learn a few rules of German pronunciation, you should be able to sound out even the longest compound noun. Consonants are the same as in English, with the exception of C (pronounced K); J (pronounced Y); K (always pronounced, even before N); P (nearly always pronounced, even before F); QU (pronounced KV); S (pronounced Z at the beginning of a word); V (pronounced F); W (pronounced V); Z (pronounced TS). The ß, or *ess-tsett*, is simply a double S. Pronounce SCH as SH. In Austria, R is rolled in the front of the mouth, while CH is pronounced in Switzerland with the hoarse, throat-clearing sound that people often erroneously associate with German. Vowels are as follows: A as in "father";

E as the A in "hay" or the indistinct vowel sound in "uh"; I as the ee in "cheese"; O as in "oh"; U as in "fondue"; Y as the oo in "boot"; AU as in "sauerkraut"; EU as the oi in "boil." With EI and IE, pronounce the last letter as a long English vowel—*heisse* is HY-ssuh; *viele* is FEEL-uh.

GERMAN PHRASEBOOK

USEFUL PHRASES

ENGLISH	GERMAN
Hello.	Hallo
Excuse me/sorry	Entschuldigung.
Thank you (very much).	Danke (schön).
Could you please help me?	Können Sie mir bitte helfen?
Good morning.	Guten Morgen
Good afternoon. (in Switzerland)	Guten Tag/Grüss Gott Gruezi/Gruessach.
Good evening.	Guten Abend.
Good-bye.	Tschüß! (informal); Auf Wiedersehen! (formal)
Good night.	Gute Nacht
What?	Was?
When(what time)?	Wann?
Why?	Warum?
Where is...?	Wo ist?
My name is...	Ich heisse...
What is your name?	Wie heissen Sie?
Where are you from?	Wo kommen Sie her?
I'm from ...	Ich komme aus...
How are you?	Wie geht's?
I'm fine.	Es geht mir gut.
I'm not feeling well.	Mir ist schlecht.
I have a headache.	Ich habe Kopfweh.
I need a doctor.	Ich brauche einen Arzt.
Leave me alone.	Lass mich in Ruhe.
I'll call the police.	Ich rufe die Polizei.
Help!	Hilfe!

ENGLISH	GERMAN
Do you speak English?	Sprechen Sie Englisch?
I can't speak German.	Ich kann kein Deutsch.
I don't understand.	Ich verstehe nicht.
Please speak slowly.	Sprechen Sie bitte langsam.
Please repeat.	Bitte wiederholen Sie.
Pardon? What was that?	Wie, bitte?
Yes/No	Ja/nein
Maybe	Vielleicht
I would like...	Ich möchte...
I'm looking for...	Ich suche...
I need...	Ich brauche...
How much does that cost?	Wieviel kostet das?
OK.	In Ordnung.
I don't know.	Ich weiss nicht
Wo ist die Toilette?	Where is the toilet?
Is...available?	Ist... erhältlich? (things) Ist...frei? (rooms)
Please	Bitte
How do you say that in German?	Wie sagt man das auf Deutsch?
What does this mean?	Was bedeutet das?
No thanks	Nein, danke
I don't smoke.	Ich rauche nicht.
Where is the phone?	Wo ist das Telefon?
I am a student (male/female).	Ich bin Student/Studentin.
Are there student discounts?	Gibt es Studentenermässigungen?
No problem	Kein Problem

DIRECTIONS AND TRANSPORTATION

ENGLISH	GERMAN
(to the) right	rechts
(to the) left	links
straight ahead	geradeaus
here	hier
there	da
far	fern
near	nah
Where is this train going?	Wo fährt dieser Zug hin?
When does the train leave?	Wann fährt der Zug ab?

ENGLISH	GERMAN
Where is...?	Wo ist...?
the train station?	der Bahnhof?
the tourist office?	das Touristbüro?
the post office?	die Post?
the old town?	die Altstadt?
the hostel?	die Jugendherberge?
the campground?	der Campingplatz?
a grocery store?	ein Supermarkt?
the bus stop?	die Haltestelle?

When is the next one?	Wann ist der nächste?		I want to go to...	Ich möchte zum/nach...
Hält der Zug/der Bus...?	Does the train/bus stop..?		I would like a ticket to...	Ich möchte eine Fahr-karte nach...
Please stop.	Bitte halten Sie.		one-way	einfache Fahrt
Which bus goes to...	Welcher Bus fährt nach...?		round-trip	hin- und zurück
North/South	Nord/Süd		East/West	Ost/West

TIMES AND HOURS

ENGLISH	GERMAN		ENGLISH	GERMAN
At what time...?	Um wieviel Uhr...?		open	geöffnet
What's the date?	Der wievielte ist heute?		closed	geschlossen
What time is it?	Wie spät ist es?		morning	der Morgen
It is 5 o'clock.	Es ist 5 Uhr.		evening	der Abend
It's early.	Es ist früh.		afternoon	der Nachmittag
It's late.	Es ist spät.		night	die Nacht
opening hours	die Öffnungszeiten		break time, rest day	die Ruhepause, der Ruhetag
daily	täglich		Monday	Montag
weekly	wochentlich		Tuesday	Dienstag
monthly	monatlich		Wednesday	Mittwoch
annually	jährlich		Thursday	Donnerstag
today	heute		Friday	Freitag
tomorrow	morgen		Saturday	Samstag
yesterday	gestern		Sunday	Sonntag
now	jetzt		immediately	sofort
January	Januar		February	Februar
March	März		April	April
May	Mai		June	Juni
July	Juli		August	August
September	September		October	October
November	November		December	Dezember

FOOD AND RESTAURANTS

ENGLISH	GERMAN		ENGLISH	GERMAN
breakfast	das Frühstück		Check, please.	Die Rechnung, bitte.
lunch	das Mittagessen		Service included.	Bedienung inklusiv.
dinner/supper	das Abendessen		I would like to order...	Ich hätte gern...
to snack	naschen		Do you have vegetarian food?	Haben Sie vege-tarisches Essen?
snack food	Knabberzeug		I'm a vegetarian.	Ich bin Vegetarier/Vege-tarierin.
It tastes good.	Es schmeckt mir gut.		I'm a vegan.	Ich bin Veganer/in.
It tastes awful.	Es schmeckt widerlich.		I am diabetic.	Ich bin Diabetiker
bread	das Brot		rice	der Reis
meat	das Fleisch		water	das Wasser
vegetables	die Gemüse		tap water	das Leitungswasser
cheese	der Käse		roll	das Brötchen
wine	der Wein		beer	das Bier
sausage	die Wurst		pork	das Schweinfleisch
chicken	das Huhn		beef	das Rindfleisch
potatoes	die Kartoffeln		french fries	die Pommes-frites
sauce	die Soße		No mayonnaise, please	ohne Mayonnaise, bitte.
tea	das Tee		with ketchup/catsup	mit Ketschup

hot chocolate	heisse Schokolade
coffee	das Kaffee
I'm thirsty.	Ich habe Durst.

jelly	die Marmelade
jelly doughnut	ein Berliner
I'm hungry.	Ich habe Hunger.

MISCELLANEOUS WORDS

ENGLISH	GERMAN
happy	glücklich
sad	traurig
young	jung
old	alt
hot	heiß
cold	kalt
because	weil
a strike	ein Streik
hospital	das Krankenhaus
pharmacy	die Apotheke
sick	krank
Non-smoking	Nichtraucher
Do you have a room (single, double) free...	Haben Sie ein Zimmer (Einzelzimmer, Doppelzimmer) frei...
for tonight?	für heute abend?
for tomorrow?	für morgen?
with bathroom/ shower?	mit W.C./ Dusche?
with breakfast?	mit Frühstuck?
toilet	die Toilette/das WC
key	der Schlüssel
cheap sale	Sonderangebot
Whereof one cannot speak, thereof one must be silent.	Worüber man nicht sprechen kann, darüber muß man schweigen.
bagpipes	der Dudelsack

ENGLISH	GERMAN
bad	schlecht
good	gut
small	klein
big	groß
empty	leer
full	voll
dangerous	gefährlich
safe	ungefährlich
Caution!	Achtung!/Vorsicht!
Danger!	Gefahr!
Fire!	Feuer!
Smoking	Raucher
Where can I buy something to eat?	Wo kann ich etwas zy essen kaufen?
telephone number	die Telefonnummer
to exchange	wechseln
money	Geld
travelers check	Reisecheck
reservation	die Reservierung, Die Vorbestellung
supplement	der Zuschlag, Aufschlag
seat reservation	Platzkarte
Quick! Throw me the ladder.	Schnell, wirf mir den Leiter zu.
chimney sweep	der Schornsteinfeger

FRENCH PRONUNCIATION

French pronunciation is more difficult than German, as many of the letters in a word are silent. Do not pronounce any final consonants except L, F, or C; an E on the end of the word, however, means that you should pronounce the final consonant sound, e.g., *muet* is mew-AY but *muette* is mew-ET. This rule also applies to plural nouns—don't pronounce the final S. J is like the S in "pleasure." R is rolled in the front of the mouth even more than in Austria. C sounds like a K before A, O, and U; like an S before E and I. A ç always sounds like an S. Vowels are short and precise: A as the O in "mom"; E as in "help" (é becomes the a in "hay"); I as the ee in "creep"; O as in "oh." UI sounds like the word "whee." U is a short, clipped oo sound; hold your lips as if you were about to say "ooh," but say ee instead. OU is a straight OO sound. With few exceptions, all syllables receive equal emphasis.

FRENCH PHRASEBOOK

USEFUL PHRASES

ENGLISH	FRENCH
Hello.	Bonjour.

ENGLISH	FRENCH
Do you speak English?	Parlez-vous anglais?

Excuse me.	Excusez-moi.	I don't speak French.	Je ne parle pas français.
I'm sorry.	Je suis désolé.	I don't understand.	Je ne comprends pas.
Thank you (very much).	Merci (beaucoup).	Please speak slowly.	S'il vous plaît, parlez moins vite.
Could you please help me?	Est-ce que vous pouvez m'aider?	Please repeat.	Répétez, s'il vous plaît.
Good evening.	Bonsoir.	Excuse me?	Pardon?
Good-bye.	Au revoir.	Yes/No	Oui/Non
When?	Quand?	No problem.	Ce n'est pas grave.
Who?	Qui?	What's this called in French?	Comment ça se dit en français?
Why?	Pourquoi?	What is it?	Qu'est-ce que c'est?
When?	Quand?	How much does this cost?	Ça coûte combien?
Where is ...?	Où est...?	OK.	D'accord.
My name is...	Je m'appelle...	I would like...	Je voudrais...
What is your name?	Comment vous appellez-vous?	I am looking for...	Je cherche...
Where are you from?	Vous venez-d'où?	the bathroom	les toilettes
I am from...	Je viens de...	I don't know.	Je ne sais pas.
How are you?	Comment ça va?	Please	S'il vous plaît
I am ill/I am hurt.	J'ai mal/Je suis blessé.	What does this mean?	Qu'est-ce que c'est ça?
I have a headache.	J'ai mal à la tête.	No thanks.	Non, merci.
I need a doctor.	J'ai besoin d'un médecin.	No problem.	Ce n'est pas grave.
Leave me alone.	Laissez-moi tranquille.	I am a student.	Je suis étudiant(e).
I'll call the police.	J'appelle la police.	Are there student discounts?	Est-cu qu'il y a des tarifs réduits pour les étudiants?
Help!/Please help me.	Au secours!/Aidez-moi, s'il vous plaît.	I don't smoke.	Je ne fume pas.
Stop/Enough!	Arrête! (sing.) Arrêtez! (plur.)	See you tomorrow.	A demain.

DIRECTIONS AND TRANSPORTATION

ENGLISH	FRENCH	ENGLISH	FRENCH
(to the) right	à droite	Where can I find...?	Où est-ce que je peux trouver...?
(to the) left	à gauche	the ATM?	le guichet automatique
straight ahead	tout droite	the restaurant?	le restaurant?
here	ici	the police?	la police
there	là-bas	the train station?	la gare?
near	près de	the post office?	la poste?
far	loin	the old town?	la vieille ville?
beyond	au-delà de	the tourist office?	le bureau de tourisme?
east/west	est/ouest	the hostel?	l'auberge de jeunesse?
north/south	nord/sud	a grocery store?	le supermarché?
Where is this train going?	Quelle est la destination de la train?	the bus stop?	l'arrêt d'autobus?
Which bus goes to...?	Quel bus va à...?	one-way ticket	un billet aller-simple
Please stop.	Arretez, s'il vous plaît.	round-trip	aller-retour

TIMES AND HOURS

ISH	FRENCH	ENGLISH	FRENCH
at time?	À quelle heure?	open	ouvert
time is it?	Quelle heure est-il?	closed	fermé

It is 5 o'clock.	Il est 5 heure.
It's early.	Il est tôt.
It's late.	Il est tard.
daily	chacque jour
weekly	chacque semaine
annually	chacque anneé
today	aujourd'hui
tomorrow	demain
yesterday	hier
now	maintenant
immediately	tout-de-suite
always	toujours
except	sauf
until	jusqu'à
January	janvier
March	mars
May	mai
July	juillet
September	septembre
November	novembre

opening hours	les heures d'ouverture
morning	le matin
afternoon	l'après-midi
evening	le soir
night	la nuit
rest day	fermeture
Monday	lundi
Tuesday	mardi
Wednesday	mercredi
Thursday	jeudi
Friday	vendredi
Saturday	samedi
Sunday	dimanche
holidays	jours fériés (j.f.)
February	février
April	avril
June	juin
August	août
October	octobre
December	décembre

FOOD AND RESTAURANTS

ENGLISH	FRENCH
restaurant	un restaurant
lounge, café	le café
pastry shop	la pâtisserie
meal	le repas
included	compris
breakfast	le petit déjeuner
lunch	le déjeuner
dinner	le dîner
supper	le souper
water	l'eau
wine	le vin
wine hall	la cave
I'm diabetic.	Je suis diabétique.
I'm a vegetarian.	Je suis végétarien(ne)
I'm hungry.	J'ai faim.
I'm thirsty.	J'ai soif.
Waiter!	Monsieur!
Waitress!	Madame!
a reservation	une réservation
Sorry, we're full.	Non, c'est complet.

ENGLISH	FRENCH
The bill, please.	L'addition, s'il vous plaît.
meat	la viande
bacon	le bacon/le lard
beans	les haricots
beer	la bière
bread	le pain
cheese	le fromage
chicken	le poulet
beef	le b œuf
egg	un œuf
coffee	le café
tea	le thé
hot chocolate	le chocolat chaud
french fries	les pommes frites
dessert	le dessert
milk	le lait
mushrooms	les champignons
onions	les oignons
pasta	les pâtes
a roll	un petit pain

MISCELLANEOUS WORDS

ENGLISH	FRENCH
cold	froid
hot	chaud
stamps	le timbre
telephone	le téléphone
telephone number	le numero de téléphone
one-way street	rue à sens unique

ENGLISH	FRENCH
a room	une chambre
single room	une chambre simple
with	avec
a shower	une douche
exchange money	échanger de l'argent
money	l'argent

APPENDIX

dead-end street	une impasse/ cul de sac		do not enter	passage interdit
You're cute.	Tu es mignon.		What are you studying?	Qu'est-ce que vous étudiez?
I'm a math major.	J'étudie les maths.		How fascinating.	Comme c'est intéressant.

ITALIAN PRONUNCIATION

Italian pronunciation isn't too complicated. There are 7 vowel sounds in standard Italian: A as in "father," I as the ee in "cheese," U as the oo in "droop," E either as ay in "bay" or eh in "set," and o both as oh in "bone" and o as in "off." Save for a few quirks, Italian consonants are easy. H is always silent, R is always rolled. C and G: are hard before a, o, or u, as in *cat* and *goose*, but they soften into ch and j sounds, respectively, when followed by i or e, as in English *cheese* and *jeep* or Italian *ciao* (chow), "goodbye," and *gelato* (jeh-LAH-toh), "ice cream." CH and GH are pronounced like k and g before i and e, as in *chianti* (ky-AHN-tee), the Tuscan wine, and *spaghetti* (spah-GEHT-tee), the pasta. Pronounce gn like the ni in *onion*, so that *bagno* ("bath") is "BAHN-yoh." Gli is like the lli in *million*, so *sbagliato* ("wrong") is said "zbal-YAH-toh." When followed by a, o, or u, SC is pronounced as sk. *Scusi* ("excuse me") yields "SKOO-zee." When followed by an e or i, sc is pronounced sh as in *sciopero* (SHOH-pair-oh), "strike."

ITALIAN PHRASEBOOK

USEFUL PHRASES

ENGLISH	ITALIAN		ENGLISH	ITALIAN
Hello (informal)	Ciao		Do you speak English?	Lei parla inglese?
Excuse me.	Scusi/permesso		I don't speak Italian.	Non parlo italiano
I'm sorry.	Mi dispiace		I don't understand.	Non capisco
Could you help me?	Potrebbe aiutarmi?		Please speak slowly.	Parla più lentamente.
Good day/Hello	Buongiorno		Could you repeat that?	Potrebbe ripetere?
Good evening	Buona sera		Pardon?	Come?
Good night	Buona notte		Is there someone who speaks English?	C'è qualcuno che parla inglese?
Goodbye (formal)	Arrivederci/ ArrivederLa		Yes/ No/ Maybe	Sì/ No/ Forse
Please	Per favore/Per piacere		I don't know.	Non lo so.
Thank you	Grazie		OK	D'accordo.
You're welcome	Prego		What does this mean?	Cosa vuol dire questo?
My name is...	Mi chiamo...		I understand	Ho capito.
How are you?	Come sta (formal)/stai?		What do you call this in Italian?	Come si chiama questo in italiano?
I am well.	Sto bene		How do you say...?	Come si dice...?
I have a headache.	Ho un mal di testa.		I am a student (male/ female).	Sono studente/studentessa.
I need a doctor.	Ho bisogno di un medico.		I would like...	Vorrei...
Leave me alone!	Lasciami in pace!		a student discount	sconto studentesco
I'll call the police.	Telefono alla polizia!		what/when/who?	Cosa/quando/chi?
Help!	Aiuto!		where/which/why?	Dovè/quale/perchè?

DIRECTIONS AND TRANSPORTATION

ENGLISH	ITALIAN		ENGLISH	ITALIAN
turn left/right	Gira a sinistra/destra		Where is...?	Dov'è...?
ght ahead	sempre diritto		How do you get to...?	Come si arriva a...?
	qui/qua		Do you stop at...?	Ferma a...?

far	li/là
near/far	vicino/lontano
What time does the train for... leave?	A che ora parte il treno per...?
Where does the bus for... leave?	Da dove parte l'autobus per...?
the next train	l'ultimo treno
north/south	nord/sud
east/west	ovest/este

the beach?	la spiaggia?
the center of town?	il centro?
the post office?	l'ufficio postale?
the train station?	la stazione?
the tourist office?	l'ufficio turistico?
one-way	solo andata
round-trip	andata e ritorno

TIMES AND HOURS

ENGLISH	ITALIAN
At what time...?	A che ora...?
What time is it?	Che ore sono?
It's noon.	È mezzogiorno.
now	adesso/ora
tomorrow	domani
today	oggi
yesterday	ieri
right away	subito
soon	fra poco/presto
this/that	questo/quello
who	chi
where	dove
which	quale
when	quando
what	che/cosa/che cosa
why/because	perchè
after(wards)	dopo
daily	quotidiano
weekly	settimanale
monthly	mensile
January	gennato
March	marzo
May	maggio
July	luglio
September	settembre
November	novembre

ENGLISH	ITALIAN
open	aperto
closed	chiuso
morning	mattina
afternoon	pomeriggio
evening	sera
night	notte
rest day	riposo
already	già
before	prima
Monday	lunedi
Tuesday	martedi
Wednesday	mercoledi
Thursday	giovedi
Friday	venerdi
Saturday	sabato
Sunday	domenica
holidays	giorno di festa
weekdays	i giorni feriali
early	in anticipo/presto
late	in ritardo/tardi
February	febbraio
April	aprile
June	guigno
August	agosto
October	ottobre
December	dicembre

FOOD AND RESTAURANTS

ENGLISH	ITALIAN
breakfast	la (prima) colazione
lunch	il pranzo
dinner	la cena
dessert	il dolce
waiter/waitress	il/la cameriere/a
the bill	il conto
may I have my check?	Mi dà il conto per favore
cover charge	il coperto
service charge/tip	servizio
included	compressa
bakery	panetteria/pasticceria

ENGLISH	ITALIAN
in tomato sauce	al pomodoro
in spicy tomato sauce	all'arrabbiata
with onions and bacon	all'amatriciana
in a meat sauce	alla bolognese
in a cream sauce with eggs, ham, and cheese	alla carbonara
with ham	con prosciuttio
with four cheeses	quatro formaggi
with artichokes	ai carciofi
with mushrooms	ai funghi
green beans	fagiolini
salad	insalata

restaurant	il ristorante
tea	il tè
hot chocolate	una cioccolata
mineral water	l'acqua

tomatoes with mozarella cheese and basil	insalta caprese
beer	una birra
coffee (espresso)	un caffè
coffee with milk	un caffe latte

MISCELLANEOUS WORDS

ENGLISH	ITALIAN
grocery store	alimentarii, drogheria
ticket	biglietto
no entry	divieto di accesso
smokers	fumatori
schedule	orario
Mr.	Signor
Mrs.	Signora
Miss	Signorina
child	il bambino
May I buy you a drink?	Posso offrirle qualcosa da bere?

ENGLISH	ITALIAN
Italian ice cream	gelato
cold	freddo
hot	caldo
good	buono
bad	cattivo
beautiful	bello/bella
often	spesso
always	sempre
never	mai
Would you buy me a drink?	Può offrirmi qualcosa da bere?

NUMBERS

NUMBER	GERMAN	FRENCH	ITALIAN
0	null	zéro	uno
1	eins	un	due
2	zwei or zwoh	deux	tre
3	drei	trois	quattro
4	vier	quatre	cinque
5	fünf	cinq	sei
6	sechs	six	sette
7	sieben	sept	otto
8	acht	huit	nove
9	neun	neuf	dieci
10	zehn	dix	undici
11	elf	onze	dodici
12	zwölf	douze	tredici
13	dreizehn	treize	quattordici
14	vierzehn	quatorze	quindici
15	fünfzehn	quinze	seidici
17	siebzehn	dix-sept	diciasette
18	achtzehn	dix-huit	diciotto
19	neunzehn	dix-neuf	dicianove
20	zwanzig	vingt	venti
21	einund-zwanzig	vingt et un	ventuno
30	dreißig	trente	trenta
40	vierzig	quarante	quaranta
50	fünfzig	cinquante	cinquanta
60	sechzig	soixante	sessanta
70	siebzig	soixante-dix	settanta
80	achtzig	quatre-vingt	ottanta
90	neunzig	quatre-vingt-dix	novanta
100	(ein)hundert	cent	cento
101	hunderteins	cent-et-un	centouno
1000	(ein)tausend	mille	mille

INDEX

D

E

ABOUT LET'S GO

FORTY YEARS OF WISDOM

As a new millennium arrives, *Let's Go: Europe*, now in its 40th edition and translated into seven languages, reigns as the world's bestselling international travel guide. For four decades, travelers criss-crossing the Continent have relied on *Let's Go* for inside information on the hippest backstreet cafes, the most pristine secluded beaches, and the best routes from border to border. In the last 20 years, our rugged researchers have stretched the frontiers of backpacking and expanded our coverage into Asia, Africa, Australia, and the Americas. We're celebrating our 40th birthday with the release of *Let's Go: China*, blazing the traveler's trail from the Forbidden City to the Tibetan frontier; *Let's Go: Perú & Ecuador*, spanning the lands of the ancient Inca Empire; *Let's Go: Middle East*, with coverage from Istanbul to the Persian Gulf; and the maiden edition of *Let's Go: Israel*.

It all started in 1960 when a handful of well-traveled students at Harvard University handed out a 20-page mimeographed pamphlet offering a collection of their tips on budget travel to passengers on student charter flights to Europe. The following year, in response to the instant popularity of the first volume, students traveling to Europe researched the first full-fledged edition of *Let's Go: Europe*, a pocket-sized book featuring honest, practical advice, witty writing, and a decidedly youthful slant on the world. Throughout the 60s and 70s, our guides reflected the times. In 1969 we taught travelers how to get from Paris to Prague on "no dollars a day" by singing in the street. In the 80s and 90s, we looked beyond Europe and North America and set off to all corners of the earth. Meanwhile, we focused in on the world's most exciting urban areas to produce in-depth, fold-out map guides. Our new guides bring the total number of titles to 48, each infused with the spirit of adventure and voice of opinion that travelers around the world have come to count on. But some things never change: our guides are still researched, written, and produced entirely by students who know first-hand how to see the world on the cheap.

HOW WE DO IT

Each guide is completely revised and thoroughly updated every year by a well-traveled set of over 250 students. Every spring, we recruit over 180 researchers and 70 editors to overhaul every book. After several months of training, researcher-writers hit the road for seven weeks of exploration, from Anchorage to Adelaide, Estonia to El Salvador, Iceland to Indonesia. Hired for their rare combination of budget travel sense, writing ability, stamina, and courage, these adventurous travelers know that train strikes, stolen luggage, food poisoning, and marriage proposals are all part of a day's work. Back at our offices, editors work from spring to fall, massaging copy written on Himalayan bus rides into witty, informative prose. A student staff of typesetters, cartographers, publicists, and managers keeps our lively team together. In September, the collected efforts of the summer are delivered to our printer, which turns them into books in record time, so that you have the most up-to-date information available for your vacation. Even as you read this, work on next year's editions is well underway.

WHY WE DO IT

We don't think of budget travel as the last recourse of the destitute; we believe that it's the only way to travel. Living cheaply and simply brings you closer to the people and places you've been saving up to visit. Our books will ease your anxieties and answer your questions about the basics—so you can get off the beaten track and explore. Once you learn the ropes, we encourage you to put *Let's Go* down now and then to strike out on your own. You know as well as we that the best discoveries are often those you make yourself. When you find something worth sharing, please drop us a line. We're Let's Go Publications, 67 Mount Auburn St., Cambridge, MA 02138, USA (email: feedback@letsgo.com). For more info, visit our website, http://www.letsgo.com.

Next time, make your *own* hotel arrangements.

Yahoo! Travel

READER QUESTIONNAIRE

Name: _____

Address: _____

City: _____ **State:** _____ **Country:** _____

ZIP/Postal Code: _____ **E-mail:** _____ **How old are you?** ____

And you're...?   in high school   in college   in graduate school

     employed   retired   between jobs

Which book(s) have you used? _____

Where have you gone with Let's Go? _____

Have you traveled extensively before?   yes   no

Had you used Let's Go before?   yes   no   **Would you use it again?**   yes   no

How did you hear about Let's Go? friend   store clerk   television

     review   bookstore display

     ad/promotion   internet   other: _____

Why did you choose Let's Go?   reputation   budget focus   annual updating

     wit & incision   price   other: _____

Which guides have you used?   Fodor's   Footprint Handbooks   Frommer's $-a-day

     Lonely Planet   Moon Guides   Rick Steve's

     Rough Guides   UpClose   other: _____

Which guide do you prefer? Why? _____

Please rank the following in your Let's Go guide: (1=needs improvement, 5=perfect)

packaging/cover	1 2 3 4 5	food	1 2 3 4 5	maps	1 2 3 4 5
cultural introduction	1 2 3 4 5	sights	1 2 3 4 5	directions	1 2 3 4 5
"Essentials"	1 2 3 4 5	entertainment	1 2 3 4 5	writing style	1 2 3 4 5
practical info	1 2 3 4 5	gay/lesbian info	1 2 3 4 5	budget resources	1 2 3 4 5
accommodations	1 2 3 4 5	up-to-date info	1 2 3 4 5	other: _____	1 2 3 4 5

How long was your trip?   one week   two wks.   three wks.   a month   2+ months

Why did you go?   sightseeing   adventure travel   study abroad   other: _____

What was your average daily budget, not including flights? _____

Do you buy a separate map when you visit a foreign city?   yes   no

Have you used a Let's Go Map Guide?   yes   no   **If you have, which one?** _____

Would you recommend them to others?   yes   no

Have you visited Let's Go's website?   yes   no

What would you like to see included on Let's Go's website? _____

What percentage of your trip planning did you do on the web? _____

What kind of Let's Go guide would you like to see? recreation (e.g., skiing)   phrasebook

     spring break   adventure/trekking   first-time travel info   Europe altas

Which of the following destinations would you like to see Let's Go cover?

     Argentina   Brazil   Canada   Caribbean   Chile   Costa Rica   Cuba

     Morocco   Nepal   Russia   Scandinavia   Southwest USA   other: _____

Where did you buy your guidebook?   independent bookstore   college bookstore

     travel store   Internet   chain bookstore   gift   other: _____

Please fill this out and return it to **Let's Go, St. Martin's Press,** 175 Fifth Ave., New York, NY 10010-7848. All respondents will receive a free subscription to **The Yellowjacket**, the Let's Go Newsletter. You can find a more extensive version of this survey on the web at http://www.letsgo.com.